To Francis Wal[...]
student, whose
work I hope to see
flourish.

N.Y.C.
8/14/68

Baily W. Diffie

Latin-American Civilization
Colonial Period

LATIN-AMERICAN CIVILIZATION

Colonial Period

by

BAILEY W. DIFFIE

with the assistance of
Justine Whitfield Diffie

1967

OCTAGON BOOKS, INC.

New York

"Look how singular a thing the work of a primitive race, the thought of a civilized."

WOODROW WILSON

BIBLIOGRAPHICAL INTRODUCTION
TO OCTAGON EDITION

ALMOST a quarter of a century has passed since this book was first published. The original text is now reissued with a bibliographical introduction. Some will ask, with good reason, why there should not be a complete revision. To this the reply is that a revision would alter the form of a book which has become a sort of landmark. However its readers may have classified it, good or bad, most have conceded it one thing—it is different from all other works in English covering the entire colonial period. To rewrite it would destroy some of its chief characteristics. A new book is indeed needed, but a revision of this one is not.

Even those points which some find objectionable, or wrong, have become a part of the essence of the work. So the decision was made to reissue it as it has stood since the day of publication, correcting only a few obvious misprints, and to include with it some of the principal new and old works which have a bearing on the various chapters. The bibliography and comments follow the original organization as closely as seems feasible, but there is not exact coordination. Some of the chapters have been combined to avoid repetition of the same books and articles. With the new material, the reader will be able to make his own revisions—in his mind, in his classroom, or in print.

The number of students of Latin American culture has increased since the first publication of this book. Hundreds of colleges now have thousands of students annually enrolled in a dozen different aspects of the history, economics, politics, literature, archaeology, anthropology, and ethnology of the area. The United States has produced more works—and good works—since World War II than in all our previous history. France, England, Germany, and even such areas remote from Latin America as Sweden and Japan, have produced many scholars—small in number in comparison with the United States, but high in quality. Spaniards have rewritten the history with a fresh vigor and a viewpoint—some would say a bias—which owes much to developments in that nation since 1936. Portuguese scholars of first rank have published much in recent years, especially on their lost empire, which they see with nostalgia—to use their own word, *saudades*. In Latin America itself there has been a notable broadening of interest in and a great increase of official support of the scholar.

The result of all this effort is a mountain of books and articles that defies even the most indefatigable student. Several thousand new books and articles in dozens of learned journals on a bewildering number of topics appear annually. Some of these have been read by the author of this book and it is hoped that their listing here, with comments on a few, will assist the student in bringing himself approximately up to date.

To cite all important works is impossible. The reader may fail to find his favorite book or article, that is his own.

ACKNOWLEDGEMENTS

Good books are the product of the combined efforts of many; the mistakes can be laid at the door of one—the author.

Few authors can be more beholden to their students than I. If I should attempt to name a few, an injustice would be done to many. I feel deep gratitude toward the students who have taught me the little I know and absolve them from blame for what I have not learned. To all those at my own City College, at the Graduate Center of The City University of New York, at Columbia University, at New York University, and at The University of Texas, I give thanks.

New York City   Bailey W. Diffie
September, 1966

ABBREVIATIONS

AH — *Agricultural History*
AA — *American Anthropologist*
AER — *American Economic Review*
TAm — *The Americas*
ACHN — *Anais do IV Congresso de História Nacional*
AEMS — *Anuario de Estudios Americanos, Sevilla*
AHDE — *Anuario de Historia del Derecho Español,*
AHM — *Anuario de Historia Mexicana*
AIIHR — *Anuario del Instituto de Investigaciones Históricas,* Rosario, Argentina
ANCU — *Archivo Nacional de Cuba*
BNA — Biblioteca Nacional, *Annaes,* Rio de Janeiro
BBAcSc — *Boletim Bibliográfico da Academia das Sciências de Lisboa,* 1910
BBAM — *Boletín Bibliográfico de Antropología,* México
BHAB — *Boletín de Historia e Antigüedades,* Bogotá
BACH — *Boletín de la Academia Chilena de la Historia*
BHC — *Boletín Histórico,* Caracas
BANHC — *Boletín de la Academia Nacional de Historia,* Caracas
BAHQ — *Boletín de la Academia Nacional de la Historia,* Quito
BANM — *Boletín del Archivo General de la Nación,* México
BHi — *Bulletin Hispanique,* Bordeaux, 1899-
BIHRL — *Bulletin of the Institute of Historical Research,* London
CHR — *Catholic Historical Review*
MP — *Congresso do Mundo Português,* Lisbon, 1940, 19 vols., *Publicações*
CIHD — *Congresso Internacional de História dos Descobrimentos,* Lisbon, 1960
CAM — *Cuadernos Americanos,* México
CHM — *Cuadernos de Historia Mundial*
CH — *Current History*
EHR — *Economic History Review*
FA — *Foreign Affairs*
GR — *Geographic Review*
HAHR — *Hispanic American Historical Review*
HBA — *Historia,* Buenos Aires
HM — *Historia Mexicana*
HT — *History Today*
IIC — *Instituto Indigenista de Colombia*

IAEA — *Inter-American Economic Affairs*
RIB — *Inter-American Review of Bibliography*
ICLBS — *International Colloquium on Luso-Brazilian Studies*
JAH — *Journal of African History*
JEH — *Journal of Economic History*
JIAS — *Journal of Inter-American Studies*
JNH — *Journal of Negro History*
JPE — *Journal of Political Economy*
JWH — *Journal of World History*
LL — *Letras,* Universidad Nacional de San Marcos, Lima
MBEB — *Manual bibliográfico de Estudos brasileiros,* Rio de Janeiro, 1949, ed. by Rubens Borba de Moraes and William Berrien
MA — *Mid-America*
MPA — Museu Paulista, *Annaes*
PAIGH — *Pan American Institute of Geography and History,* Mexico
PAPS — *Proceedings of the American Philosophical Society*
PAJHS — *Publication of the American Jewish Historical Society*
RPPL — *UNESCO, Repertorio de publicaciones periódicas actuales latinoamericanas, 1958*
RANP — *Revista del Archivo Nacional del Peru*
RBCS — *Revista Brasileira de Ciências Sociais*
RCHG — *Revista Chilena de Historia y Geografía*
RHSP — *Revista de História,* São Paulo
RHAM — *Revista de Historia de America*
RIBo — *Revista de las Indias,* Bogotá
RIS — *Revista de Indias,* Spain
RIHDBA — *Revista del Instituto Histórico del Derecho,* Buenos Aires
REHM — *Revista de la Junta de Estudios Históricos de Mendoza*
RUY — *Revista de la Universidad de Yucatán*
RMIAC — *Revista del Museo e Instituto Arqueológico,* Cuzco
RO — *Revista de Occidente,* Madrid
RIAGP — *Revista do Instituto Archeológico e Geográfico Pernambucano*
RIHGB — *Revista do Instituto Histórico e Geográfico Brasileiro*
RIHGSP — *Revista do Instituto Histórico e Geográfico de São Paulo*
RIHGRGS — *Revista do Instituto Histórico e Geográfico do Rio Grande do Sul*
RH — *Revue Hispanique*
RHST — *Royal Historical Society,* Transactions
SAQ — *South Atlantic Quarterly*

GUIDES TO STUDY*

BIBLIOGRAPHIES, REVIEWS, GUIDES AND CATALOGUES

Spain and Portugal

Benito Sánchez Alonso, *Fuentes de la historia española e hispanoamericana*, 3 vols., Madrid, 1952

R. Foulché-Delbosc and L. Barrau-Dihigo, *Manuel de l'Hispanisant*, 2 vols., New York, 1951

Indice histórico español, quarterly, Barcelona, 1953—

Fortunato de Almeida, *História de Portugal*, 6 vols., 1922-29

Dorris V. Welsh, *A Catalog of the William B. Greenlee Collection*, Chicago, 1953

Spanish America

R. A. Humphreys, *Latin American History: A Guide to the Literature in English*, Oxford, 1958

Handbook of Latin American Studies, Harvard, 1936-51; Florida, 1951-

Hispanic American Historical Review, Baltimore, 1918-22; Duke, 1926-

Ruth L. Butler, *Guide to the Hispanic American Historical Review, 1918-1945*, Duke, 1950

Charles Gibson and E. V. Niemeyer, *Guide to the Hispanic American Historical Review, 1946-1955*, Duke, 1958

Review of Inter-American Bibliography, Pan American Union, 1951-

The Americas. A Quarterly Review of Inter-American Cultural History, Washington, 1944-

Americas, 1949-

Bulletin of Hispanic Studies, Liverpool, 1923-

Bulletin Hispanique, Bordeaux, 1899-

Revista de Historia de América, México, 1938-

Historia, Buenos Aires, 1955-

Revista de História, São Paulo, 1950-

Revista chilena de historia y geografía, Santiago, 1911-

Anuario español e hispano-americano del libro y de las artes gráficas, Madrid, 1947-

Anuario de Estudios Americanos, Indices, 1944-1963, Sevilla, 1964

Bibliografía española, Madrid, 1958

Bibliografía americanista española, 1935-1963, Seville, 1964

---

*The reference forms adopted here are the simplest and briefest in order to include the maximum number of works.

Boletín bibliográfico de antropología americana, México, 1937

José Antonio Calderón Quijano and Luis Navarro García, *Guía de los documentos sobre la historia de América y España moderna en la Biblioteca Nacional de Paris, Museo Británico y Public Record Office de Londres,* Sevilla, 1962

Howard F. Cline, "The *Relaciones Geográficas* of the Spanish Indies, 1577-1586," *HAHR,* 44 (Aug. 1964)

Donald B. Cooper, "A Selective List of the Colonial Manuscripts in the Archives of the Department of Health, Mexico City," *HAHR,* 42 (Aug. 1962)

Stoyan Gavrilovic, "Hispanic American History Research Opportunities in Yugoslav Archives," *HAHR,* 42 (Feb. 1962)

Gabriel Giraldo Jaramillo, *Bibliografía de bibliografías colombianas,* Bogotá, 1954

Lino Gómez Canedo, *Los archivos de la historia de América colonial,* México, 1961

R. R. Hill, *The National Archives of Latin America,* Harvard, 1945

John P. Harrison, *Guide to Material on Latin America in the National Archives,* Washington, 1961

Hispanic Society of America, *Catalogue of the Library,* G. K. Hall, 10 vols., Boston, 1962

James Ferguson King, "The Negro in Continental Spanish America, Bibliography," *HAHR,* 24 (Aug. 1944)

Seymour B. Liebman, "The Abecedario and a Check-List of Mexican Inquisition Documents at the H. Huntington Library," *HAHR,* 44 (Nov. 1964)

Juan A. Ortega y Medina, *Historiografía soviética iberoamericanista, 1945-1960,* México, 1961

José M. Pérez Cabrera, *Historiografía de Cuba,* México, 1962

Raul Porras Barrenechea, *Fuentes históricas peruanas,* Lima, 1954

Catts Pressoir, Ernst Trouillot et Henock Trouillot, *Historiographie d'Haiti,* México, 1953

Roberto Ramos, *Bibliografía de la historia de México,* 1956

Donald Robertson, *Mexican Manuscript Painting of the Early Colonial Period,* Yale, 1959

Francisco Vindel, *Mapas de América en los libros españoles de los siglos XVI al XVIII,* Madrid, 1955

Charles C. Griffin, "Aspectos económico-sociales de la época de la emancipación, una bibliografía, 1949-1959," *Actas y ponencias, el movimiento emancipador,* Caracas, 1961

Interpretations of Spain

Américo Castro, *España en su historia,* Buenos Aires, 1948; English tr., *The Structure of Spanish History,* Princeton, 1948

Ramón Menéndez Pidal, *The Spaniards in Their History,* tr. by Walter Sharkie, London, 1951

Claudio Sánchez Albornoz, *España, un enigma histórico,* 2 vols., Buenos Aires, 1956

Histories of Spain and Latin America

Pedro Aguado Bleye, *Manual de Historia de España,* 3 vols., Madrid, 1958

Rafael Altamira, *Manual de historia de España,* 2d ed., Buenos Aires, 1946; Muna Lee, tr., *A History of Spain,* Van Nostrand, 1949

Antonio Ballesteros y Berreta, *Historia de España,* 12 vols., 1919-36

Antonio Ballesteros y Beretta, *Historia de América y de los pueblos americanos*, 23 vols., Barcelona, 1936-

Karl Brandi, *The Emperor Charles V*, tr. by C. V. Wedgwood, New York, 1939

R. T. Davies, *The Golden Century of Spain, 1501-1621*, St. Martins, 1954

J. H. Elliott, *Imperial Spain, 1469-1716*, St. Martins, 1964

John Lynch, *Spain Under the Hapsburgs*, Oxford, 1964

Charles E. Chapman, *A History of Spain*, Free Press, 1963

William C. Atkinson, *A History of Spain and Portugal*, Penguin, 1960

John A. Crow, *Spain*, Harper, 1963

Emilio González López, *Historia de la civilización española*, Las Americas, 1959

Ricardo Levene, ed., *Historia de América*, 14 vols., Buenos Aires, 1948-

Harold Livermore, *A History of Spain*, Farrar, 1959

Ramón Menéndez Pidal, ed., *Historia de España*, 10 vols., 1936-

Jean H. Mariéjol, *The Spain of Ferdinand and Isabella*, tr. by B. Keen, Rutgers, 1961

J. Vicens Vives, ed., *Historia social y económica de España y América*, 4 vols., Barcelona, 1957-59

Portugal

Fortunato de Almeida, *História de Portugal*, 6 vols., Coimbra, 1922-29

Fortunato de Almeida, *História da igreja em Portugal*, 4 vols., Coimbra, 1910-22

Congresso do mundo português: Publicações, 19 vols., Lisbon, 1940

Henrique da Gama Barros, *História da administração pública em Portugal nos séculos XII-XV*, 2d ed., 12 vols., Lisbon, 1945-60

Alexandre Herculano, *História de Portugal*, 8th ed., 8 vols. [1908-14?]

H. W. Livermore, *A History of Portugal*, Cambridge, England, 1947

C. E. Nowell, *History of Portugal*, Van Nostrand, 1952

Damião Peres, ed., *História de Portugal*, 8 vols., Barcelos, 1928-38

Elaine Sanceau, *The Perfect Prince, Dom João II*, Oporto, 1959

Interpretations of Spain in America

Florentino Pérez Embid and Francisco Morales Padrón, *Acción de España en América*, Barcelona, 1958

Julián M. Rubio, *Los grandes ideales de España imperial en el siglo XVI*, Valladolid, 1938

Carlos Sanz, "El nuevo mundo, etapa de la historia universal," *AEMS*, 1961

José Tudela, ed., *El legado de España a América*, Madrid, 1954

Luis Alberto Sánchez, "A New Interpretation of the History of America," *IIAHR*, 23 (Aug. 1943)

Silvio Zavala, *New Viewpoints on the Spanish Colonization of America*, Pennsylvania, 1943

Silvio Zavala, *The Political Philosophy of the Conquest of America*, México, 1953

PRINCIPAL TEXTS, GENERAL HISTORIES AND
INTERPRETATIONS OF LATIN AMERICA

H. M. Bailey and A. P. Nasatir, *Latin America*, Prentice Hall, 1960

John Francis Bannon and Peter Masten Dunne, *Latin America*, Bruce, 1947

John A. Crow, *The Epic of Latin America*, Doubleday, 1948

Donald Marquand Dozer, *Latin America*, McGraw-Hill, 1963

Francisco Antonio Encina, *Historia de Chile desde la prehistoria hasta 1891*, 20 vols., Santiago, 1946-

Charles Gibson, *Spain in America*, Harper and Row, 1966.

Charles C. Griffin, "Francisco Encina and Revisionism in Chilean History," *HAHR*, 37 (Feb. 1957)

John E. Fagg, *Latin America*, McMillan, 1963

Hubert Herring, *A History of Latin America*, 2d ed., Random House, 1964

Vera Brown Holmes, *A History of the Americas*, 2 vols., 1950, 1964

Samuel Guy Inman and Carlos E. Castañeda, *A History of Latin America for Schools*, New York, 1944

Preston E. James, *Latin America, A Geography*, Odyssey, 1959

Benjamin Keen, ed., *Readings in Latin American Civilization*, Houghton Mifflin, 1955

Salvador de Madariaga, *The Fall of the Spanish American Empire*, Collier, 1963

Salvador de Madariaga, *The Rise of the Spanish American Empire*, Collier, 1963

Francisco Morales Padrón, *Historia de América*, 2 vols., Madrid, 1962

Dana Gardner Munro, *The Latin American Republics*, Appleton-Century Crofts, 1960

Henry B. Parkes, *A History of Mexico*, Houghton Mifflin, 1960

Mariano Picón-Salas, *A Cultural History of Spanish America*, California, 1962

J. Fred Rippy, *Latin America*, Michigan, 1961

Lesley Byrd Simpson, *Many Mexicos*, California, 1961

Alfred Barnaby Thomas, *Latin America*, McMillan, 1956

Mary W. Williams, Ruhl J. Bartlett, and Russell E. Miller, *The People and Politics of Latin America*, Ginn, 1955

A. C. Wilgus, *Readings in Latin American Civilization*, Barnes and Noble, 1946

D. E. Worcester and W. G. Schaeffer, *Growth and Culture of Latin America*, Oxford, 1956

Woodrow Borah, et al., "Colonial Institutions and Contemporary Latin America," *HAHR*, 43 (Aug. 1963)

Lewis Hanke, ed., *Do the Americas Have a Common History? A Critique of the Bolton Theory*, Knopf, 1964

Stanley J. Stein, "The Tasks Ahead for Latin American Historians," *HAHR*, 41 (Aug. 1961)

Booksellers Catalogues

A. Palau y Dulcet, *Manual del Librero Hispano-Americano*, 2d ed., 1964

R. R. Bowker, *Libros en venta en Hispanoamérica y España*, ed. by Mary C. Turner, New York, 1964

Strechert-Hafner, *Latin American Cooperative Acquisition Project*, 31 East 10th St., N.Y. 10003

Chapter 2

THE INDIANS CONQUER AMERICA

IN recent years the historian's reading glass, the archaeologist's spade, and the anthropologist's eye have helped us take a closer look at Indian culture. Conclusions about the pre-conquest Americans are on no firmer ground than they were, but our information is much greater. In fact, the division of scholars into *Indianistas* and *Hispanistas* is now perhaps more sharply defined than, shall we say, in Prescott's time. A renewed Hispanism under the name of *Hispanidad,* a sentimental version of pan-Hispanism, has opposed a sentimental Indianism, a sentimental Africanism, and now opposes a sentimental Mestizonism.

What we know of the pre-conquest American is outlined in works by Pedro Armillas, Juan Comas, and several others; John Collier writes more from the heart than from the head.

The always fascinating question of the origin of the Indian has a reverse twist in the works of Thor Hyerdahl who seeks to show that some Pacific island cultures could have originated in America. Kenneth Mac-Gowen and Joseph A. Hester, Jr., hold that "we know that man was here before the chill of the last Ice Age settled on the land," which would give the Indians much more time than the standard guess of 15,000 years. That such may be the case is indicated by Richard S. MacNeish who believes that corn may have originated some 14,000 years ago in the Tehuacán Valley south of Mexico City. See also other useful works listed below.

For both Maya and Aztec civilizations there are new or revised editions of older works. Alfonso Caso stresses the religious zeal of the Aztecs, making human sacrifice seem a positively humanitarian custom. Howard Cline shows the difficulties of Indianist studies. New translations of Motolinía and Sahagún, the latter from the Aztec for the first time, are available. Victor W. von Hagen, industrious worker, has a reverence for all things Indian; he remarks about human sacrifice: "It is of course pure calumny to say that anthropophagy was involved—if it occured at all, it was ceremonial cannibalism." Sounder works are by Fredrick A. Petersen, J. Eric Thompson, George C. Valliant, and Eric Wolf.

Inca studies are less passionate, perhaps because a social revolution has not placed the Indians and Mestizos on top as in Mexico. There are, however, a variety of views represented in a new edition of José de Acosta's work, in Louis Baudin's study of a "Socialist" empire, in other works by Brundage, and Bushnell, and in a new translation of Garcilaso by H. V.

Livermore. Other important works can only be listed. J. Alden Mason's is excellent and generally sympathetic to his subjects. Among other new studies, see those of Ake Wedin, who demonstrates that chronology prior to the coming of the Spaniards in 1532 is without reliable foundation; he takes exception especially to Rowe's conclusions.

Pedro Armillas, *The Native Period in the History of the New World,* México, 1962

Juan Comas, *Bibliografía selectiva de las culturas indígenas,* México, 1953

Julian H. Steward, ed., *The Handbook of South American Indians,* 6 vols., Washington, 1946-50

John Collier, *The Indians of the Americas,* Norton, 1947

Thor Hyerdahl, *Kon-Tiki,* Rand McNally, 1960

Kenneth Macgowen and Joseph A. Hester, Jr., *Early Man in the New World,* Doubleday, 1962

Richard S. MacNeish, "The Origins of New World Civilization," *Scientific American* (Nov. 1964)

Edmund Stephen Urbanski, "Where is the Cradle of Indo-American Civilization?," *América indígena,* México, 1962

Robert Wauchope, *Lost Tribes and Sunken Continents,* Chicago, 1962

Hannah M. Wormington, *Origins,* México, 1953

Harold E. Driver, ed., *The Americas on the Eve of Discovery,* Indiana, 1963

Jack D. Forbes, ed., *The Indian in America's Past,* Nevada

Sylvanus G. Morley, *The Ancient Maya,* 3d ed., Stanford, 1956

R. L. Roys, *The Indian Background of Colonial Yucatán,* Washington, 1943

Herbert J. Spinden, *Ancient Civilizations of Mexico and Central America,* 3d ed., New York, 1958

Herbert J. Spinden, *Maya Art and Civilization,* Indian Hills, Colorado, 1957

J. E. S. Thompson, *The Rise and Fall of Maya Civilization,* Oklahoma, 1954

Alfonso Caso, *The Aztecs,* tr. by Lowell Durham, Oklahoma, 1958

Howard F. Cline, "Problems of Mexican Ethno-History," *HAHR,* 37 (1957)

Toribio de Motolinía, *Motolinía's History of the Indians of New Spain,* tr. by Francis Steck, Washington, 1951

Bernardino de Sahagún, *General History of the Things of New Spain,* Santa Fé, 1960

Victor W. Von Hagen, *The Aztec,* New York, 1958

Frederick A. Peterson, *Ancient Mexico,* Putnam's, 1959

George C. Vaillant, *The Aztecs,* Penguin, 1960

Eric Wolf, *Sons of the Shaking Earth,* Chicago, 1959

Howard F. Cline, *William Hickling Prescott,* Duke, 1959

Francisco Mateos, *Obras del P. José de Acosta de la Compañía de Jesús,* Madrid, 1954

Louis Baudin, *A Socialist Empire, the Incas,* Van Nostrand, 1961

Edward Hayams, *The Last of the Incas,* Simon and Schuster, 1963

Alain Gheerbrant, *The Incas, the Royal Commentaries of the Inca Garcilaso de la Vega,* Orion, 1961

Garcilaso de la Vega, *Royal Commentaries of the Incas,* tr. by H. V. Livermore, Austin, 1966

J. A. Mason, *The Ancient Civilizations of Peru,* Penguin, 1957

Harold Osborne, *Indians of the Andes,* London, 1952

Victor W. Von Hagen, ed., *The Incas of Pedro Cieza de León,* Oklahoma, 1959

Ake Wedin, *La cronología de la historia incaica,* Madrid, 1963

John H. Rowe, "Absolute Chronology of the Andean Area," *American Antiquity,* (X 1945)

Julian H. Steward and Louis C. Faron, *Native Peoples of South America,* McGraw-Hill, 1959

Chapter 3

ENTER THE EUROPEANS

THE EUROPEAN BACKGROUND

Recent research has progressively indicated the need to understand America's European and other non-American origins.

So much that is today American came from the Iberian Peninsula, and so much that was Iberian came from Rome, that our studies must begin far back. But so much that was Roman was altered by medieval developments that these too must be considered.

The basic histories of Spain and Portugal, already cited, can be the beginning of study. Other works on Rome, on the Moslems, and on the Jews are required reading. Havinghurst has examined the Pirenne thesis that the Moslems rather than the Barbarians disrupted the Roman civilization. Lybyer, in an old but neglected study, absolved the Turks of the accusation that they cut East-West connections and forced Atlantic expansion.

PORTUGAL

On Portuguese development see particularly the 19 volume publications of the *Congresso do Mundo Português* which carries a variety of articles on all phases of the civilization and exploration of Portugal; the publications of other congresses herein cited should also be noted. My own *Prelude to Empire* attempts to demonstrate that Portugal's history up to the time of Henry the Navigator prepared the basis for overseas expansion.

On Henry himself there is nothing essentially new, though a somewhat vain contention has arisen that he was never Grandmaster of the Order of

Christ because he signed himself merely as *Regedor e governador*. He was often referred to as *mestre,* however, and Fortunato de Almeida in his monumental history of the church in Portugal calls him Grandmaster. Elaine Sanceau's work is the best, though not the very latest.

The *Sesmaria,* so important in Portugal and Brazil, is discussed by Virginia Rau and others, as is the market or fair. Prester John, a figure of mystery, has been studied by Beckingham and Huntingford, and Slessarev. The Infante Dom Pedro, a real but slightly-known figure of great influence in Portugal, is now better known thanks to Francis Rogers. There are various works on the Jews and the Inquisition after 1536 in Portugal. And a recent and significant work by Dias on the rise of capitalism is not to be neglected.

SPAIN

Some of the main influences in medieval Spain may be found in Xitzhak Baer's work on the Jews, in Gonzalez Palencia on Christians and Moslems, and in Cagigas on "Ethnic-religious Minorities." Lévi-Provençal and Sánchez Albornoz stand out among medieval specialists.

Two excellent studies, of the types needed to show the European background, are the articles by Bishko and Ruth Pike. See also the articles by Charles Verlinden on Italian influences and on slavery.

THE GREAT DISCOVERIES

Columbus and the question of pre-Columbian discoveries is too fascinating to lie dormant. Many new studies have been made, often partisan in tone, and none definitive. Columbus made the effective discovery of America. With the exception of the Vikings, no other discovery is certain.

The Viking discoveries were rediscovered in the fall of 1965 with the publication of a map, the first, showing Vineland as described in the Sagas. We may accept a Viking discovery of Greenland and other western lands, though the map itself would not necessarily prove this. Medieval cartographers, ill-informed, decorated their maps with known and vaguely reported lands, always adding on and never subtracting, the result being a cluttered ocean of islands often seen in different locations. The part of the newly discovered map to the south is much like the Dulcert map of 1339, the Pizzigani map of 1367, the André Bianco map of 1436, and the Soligo map dated prior to 1460. All show non-existent lands of such similar imaginary shape as to indicate a common misinformation in the 14th and 15th centuries. The Bianco map and the new map are world maps, in-

accurate about Africa and Asia in similar ways. It may be observed that
Bjarni Herjolfsson reached America before Leif Ericson—but Leif's name
is easier to remember.

The contributions to Atlantic discovery by the English, French, Italians,
Catalans, Balearians, and Moslems, are subject to much controversy in
which personal passion and national pride are sometimes substituted for
missing evidence. The standard histories will all have something indefinitive
to say about this. The contrasting views of the Portuguese and Spaniards
may be seen in two fine works by Damião Peres and Florentino Pérez
Embid.

The Portuguese have paid great attention to Jaime Cortesão's theory
about the alleged "Politics of Silence" followed by the crown in order to
hide Portuguese pre-Columbian discoveries. Discoveries were kept secret,
he holds, though many were made. Thus, Columbus discovered only what
the Portuguese knew long before. Cortesão's views should be compared
with Ballesteros. Armando Cortesão has published a nautical chart which
he dates as 1424 and which, he holds, proves early Portuguese discovery
of Brazil. If we accept the "Politics of Silence," we must explain how such
discoveries were kept secret from the foreign chart makers whose works
are the only slight proof of new discoveries. Recent works by Skelton,
Davies and True seem to show that secrecy was not possible and that the
English and others knew of Portuguese and indeed other explorations.

The extensive writing about Columbus has yet to uncover ideas that
are both new and acceptable, but the works here cited by Morison, Ballesteros, Keene, Vigneras, Madariaga, Mateos and Weckman, Williamson,
Nowell and others have kept up the search for new information.

Vespucci, also, is the subject of constant effort to unravel mysteries.
The main point at issue is whether he made four voyages as related in
Mundus Novus and *Lettera di Amerigo Vespucci delle isole nuovamente
trovati in quatro suoi viaggi* (known also as *Lettera al Soderini*), published
respectively in 1504(?) and 1506(?), or only two voyages as indicated in
three letters to Lorenzo di Pier Francesco de Medici, not found until long
after Vespucci's death. The four-voyage thesis is upheld by Levillier and
Arciniegas, while Magnaghi, Pohl, and Marcondes de Souza, believing the
Mundus Novus and the *Lettera* to be unauthorized and inaccurate com-
pilations of Vespucci's letters, admit only two voyages (which would be
those of 1499-1500 and 1500-1501).

On the theory of empire we have good studies by J. H. Parry, English,
and Juan Beneyto Pérez, a Spaniard, who contrasts Spanish and Portuguese
concepts.

THE CONQUESTS IN AMERICA

On the conquest of Mexico we have a new edition by Irving Leonard of Bernal Diaz's history as translated by Maudslay, as well as a study of Bernal Diaz by Cerwin. Lesley Byrd Simpson has translated Gómara's biography of Cortés. Barrios Berumen continues a pro-Cortés work, as does Madariaga, but Henry Wagner is a bit less of the hero worshipper.

The pro-Aztec view is represented by Salvador Toscano and León-Portilla, whose work attempts to see the conquest through the Aztec picture writing, albeit already influenced by the post-conquest mixed culture. We may also note works by Gardner on the conquest of Mexico, and interesting works on the horse in the conquest by Cunninghame-Graham (new edition), Tinker, Howard, and Johnson.

Chamberlain on Yucatan and Honduras, Rodríguez on Central America, Romoli on Balboa, and Varner on Garcilaso's Florida are all good. Note that Simpson points out that Cortés, equipped with steel tools, took six months to hack his way to Central America over terrain supposedly heavily populated, barely escaping starvation. The northward expansion in Mexico will be noted in connection with Chapter 17.

The conquest of New Granada has been the subject of works by Arciniegas, Nogales Hidalgo, and Góngora. The works of Juan Friede are outstanding.

A number of valuable contributions to the history of the conquest of Peru are listed, with special attention to be given to the articles by George Kubler; there is also a useful article by Nowell on the White King.

Nowell has also given us an edition of Magellan's voyage in keeping with his usual high standard, and the biography of Magellan by Parr brings much new archival material.

Finally, for an over-all survey of the various views of the Spanish conquest see the work by Arnoldsson Sverker.

THE EUROPEAN BACKGROUND

Richard E. Sullivan, *Heirs of the Roman Empire,* Cornell, 1964

Alfred F. Havinghurst, *The Pirenne Thesis,* Praeger, 1958

A. H. Lybyer, "The Influence of the Rise of the Ottoman Turks upon the Routes of of Oriental Trade," *AHA Annual Report,* 2 vols., Washington, 1914

Portugal

B. W. Diffie, *Prelude to Empire, Portugal Overseas before Henry the Navigator,* Nebraska, 1960

Ernle Bradford, *A Wind from the North, the Life of Henry the Navigator,* Harcourt Brace, 1960

Gilbert Renault, *The Caravels of Christ,* Putnam's Sons, 1959

Elaine Sanceau, *Henry the Navigator,* Norton, 1947

Virginia Rau, *Subsídios para o estudo das feiras medievais portuguesas,* Lisbon, 1943

Virginia Rau, *Sesmarias medievais portuguesas,* Lisbon, 1946

Vicente Antonio Esteves de Carvalho, *Observaçoes históricas e críticas sobre nossa legislaçao agrária,* Lisbon, 1815

Vicente José Ferreira Cardoso da Costa, *Memória sobre a origem e progressos da emphyteuse e sua influência sobre a agricultura em Portugal,* Lisbon, 1802

Damião Peres, "A actividade agrícola em Portugal nos séculos XII a XIV," *MP,* II

Luiz Augusto Rebello da Silva, *Memória sobre a população e a agricultura de Portugal desde a fundação da Monarchia até 1865,* Lisbon, 1868

Eduardo Friere de Oliveira, *Elementos para a história do município de Lisboa,* 19 vols., Lisbon, 1882-1911

C. F. Beckingham and G. W. B. Huntingford, *The Prester John of the Indies,* 2 vols., Cambridge, England, 1961

Vsevolod Slessarev, *Prester John,* Minnesota, 1959

Francis M. Rogers, *The Travels of the Infante Dom Pedro of Portugal,* Harvard, 1961

J. Mendes dos Remédios, *Os Judeos em Portugal,* 2 vols., 1928

Antonio Baião, *Episódios dramáticos da inquisição portuguêsa,* 3 vols., 1919

Antonio Baião, *A inquisição em Portugal e no Brasil,* 1906

Alexandre Herculano, *História da origem e estabelecimento da inquisição em Portugal,* tr. by J. C. Branner, Stanford, 1926

Manuel Nunes Dias, *O capitalismo monárquico português (1415-1549),* 2 vols., Coimbra, 1963-

Spain

Xitzhak Baer, *A History of the Jews in Christian Spain,* Philadelphia, 1961

Angel González Palencia, *Moros y cristianos,* Madrid, 1945

Isidro de las Cagigas, *Minorías étnico-religiosas de la Edad Media española,* 2 vols., Madrid, 1947-48

E. Lévi-Provençal, *Historia de la España musulmana,* 2 vols., Madrid, 1950-53

R. Dozy, *Histoire des Musulmans d'Espagne,* 4 vols., Leyden, 1932

Claudio Sánchez Albornoz, see works listed in *Homenaje* by M. del Carmen Carlé and N. Guglielme, Buenos Aires, 1957

Charles J. Bishko, "The Peninsular Background of Latin American Cattle Ranching," *HAHR,* 32 (Nov. 1952)

Charles J. Bishko, "The Iberian Background of Latin American History," *HAHR,* 36 (Feb. 1956)

Ruth Pike, "The Genoese in Sevilla and the Opening of the New World," *JEH,* 1962

Charles Verlinden, "Italian Influence in Iberian Colonization," *HAHR,* 33 (1953)

Charles Verlinden, *L'esclavage dans l'Europe médiévale, péninsule ibérique,* Bruges, 1955

The Great Discoveries

C. M. Boland, *They All Discovered America,* Affiliated Publishers, 1961

R. A. Skelton, *The Vinland Map and the Tartar Relation,* Yale, 1965

Damião Peres, *Descobrimentos portugueses,* Porto, 1943

Farley Mowat, *Westviking, the Ancient Norse in Greenland and North America,* Atlantic-Little Brown, 1965

Eric Oxenstierna, *The Norsemen,* Greenwich, Connecticut, 1964

Actas, Congresso internacional de história dos descobrimentos, Lisbon, 1961

Mundo Português, II, III

Paul Hermann, *The Great Age of Discovery,* Collier

Charles-André Julien, *Les voyages de découvertes et les premiers establissements,* Paris, 1948

I. A. Langnas, *A Dictionary of the Discoveries,* New York, 1959

J. H. Parry, *Europe and a Wider World, 1415-1715,* London, 1949

J. H. Parry and P. M. Sherlock, *A Short History of the West Indies,* London, 1956

Boise Penrose, *Travel and Discovery in the Renaissance, 1420-1620,* Atheneum, 1962

Frederick J. Pohl, *Atlantic Crossings before Columbus,* Norton, 1961

Charles Verlinden, "Le problème de l'expansion commerciale portugaise au Moyen Age," *Biblos,* 23 (1947)

Charles Verlinden, "Deux aspects de l'expansion commerciale du Portugal au Moyen Age," *Revista Portuguesa de História,* IV (1947)

James Duffy, *Shipwreck and Empire,* Harvard, 1955

João de Barros and Diogo de Couto, *Da Ásia,* 24 vols., 1778-

Fernão Lopes de Castanheda, *História do descobrimento e conquista da Índia pelos portugueses,* 3d ed., 4 vols., 1924-33

A. da Silva Rego, *Portuguese Colonization in the XVI Century,* Witwatersrand University Press, 1959

Florentino Pérez Embid, *Los descubrimientos en el Atlántico y la rivalidad castel-lano-portuguesa hasta el tratado de Tordesillas,* Sevilla, 1948

Jaime Cortesão, "Do sigilo nacional sobre os descobrimentos," *Lusitânia,* I (1924)

Jaime Cortesão, "Teoria geral dos descobrimentos portugueses," *MP,* III

Jaime Cortesão, *A política de sigilo nos descobrimentos,* Lisbon, 1960

Antonio Ballesteros y Beretta, *Génesis del descubrimiento,* Barcelona, 1947

Armando Cortesão, "Cartographic Indications of Otherwise Unknown Early Portuguese Voyages," *CIHD,* II

Armando Cortesão, *The Nautical Chart of 1424 and the Early Discovery and Cartographical Representation of America,* Coimbra, 1954

António Baião, Hernani Cidade and Manuel Múrias, *Historia da expansão portuguesa no mundo,* 3 vols., Lisbon, 1937-40

Alberto Iria, *Descobrimentos portugueses, O Algarve e os descobrimentos,* Lisbon, 1956

João Martins da Silva Marques, *Descobrimentos portugueses,* Lisbon, 1944

Charles de la Roncière, *La découverte de l'Afrique au Moyen Age,* 3 vols., Cairo, 1924-27

C. Ley, ed., *Portuguese Voyages, 1493-1663,* Dent, 1947

Vitorino Magalhães Godinho, "Les grandes découvertes," *Bulletin des Etudes Portugaises,* Coimbra, 1953

Arthur Davies, "João Fernandes and the Cabot voyages," *CIHD,* II

R. A. Skelton, "The Cartographic Record of the Discovery of North America," *CIHD*, II

R. A. Skelton, "English Knowledge of the Portuguese Discoveries in the XV Century," *CIHD*, II

José Alberto Aboal Amaro, *El piloto desconocido, un andaluz descubrió América en 1484?*, Montevideo, 1957

R. Majó Framis, *Vidas de los navegantes, conquistadores y colonizadores españoles de los siglos XVI, XVII, XVIII*, Madrid, 1946

C. E. Nowell, "The Columbus Question," *AHR*, 44 (July 1939)

William J. Wilson, "The Historicity of the 1494 Discovery of South America," *HAHR*, 22 (Feb. 1942)

Charles E. Nowell, "Reservations Regarding the Historicity of the 1494 Discovery of South America," *HAHR*, 22 (Feb. 1942)

Antonio Ballesteros y Beretta, *Cristóbal Colón y el descubrimiento de América*, Barcelona, 1945

Benjamin Keen, ed., *Life of the Admiral Christopher Columbus by his Son Ferdinand*, New Brunswick, 1958

The Journal of Christopher Columbus, tr. by Cecil Jane, Potter, 1960

Salvador de Madariaga, *Colón*, London, 1949

Enrique Bayerri y Bertomeu, *Colón, tal cual fué*, Tortosa, 1961

Samuel E. Morison, *Christopher Columbus, Mariner*, Little, Brown, 1955

Arthur Davies, "The Loss of the Santa María Christmas Day, 1494," *AHR* (1953)

F. Mateos, "Bulas portuguesas y españolas sobre descubrimientos geográficos," *Missionalia hispánica*, 1962

Luis Weckman, *Las Bulas alejandrinas de 1493 y la teoría política del papado medieval*, México, 1949

Samuel E. Morison and Mauricio Obregón, *The Caribbean as Columbus Saw It*, Atlantic-Little, Brown, 1964

Bradley Smith, *Columbus in the New World*, Doubleday, 1962

J. A. Williamson, ed., *The Cabot Voyages and Bristol Discovery under Henry VII*, Hakluyt Society

L. A. Vigneras, "New Light on the 1497 Cabot Voyage to America," *HAHR*, 36 (Nov. 1956), in which is included

Johan Day, "Al muy magnífico y virtuoso Señor el Señor Almirante Mayor," *HAHR*, 36 (Nov. 1956)

Alberto Magnaghi, *Amerigo Vespucci—studio critico*, 2 vols., Roma, 1924

F. J. Pohl, *Amerigo Vespucci*, Columbia, 1944; new edition, Octagon Books, 1966

Germán Arciniegas, *Amerigo and the New World*, Knopf, 1955

José Aboal Amaro, *Amerigho Vespucci, ensayo de bibliografía crítica*, Madrid, 1962

Roberto Levillier, "Mundus Novus, Origen de la fama de Vespucio," *RIB*, IX; and *America la bien llamada*, 2 vols., Buenos Aires, 1948

T. O. Marcondes de Souza, *Amerigo Vespucci e suas viagens*, São Paulo, 1954

Edward Rosen, "Copernicus and the Discovery of America," *HAHR*, 23 (May 1943)

Bartolomé de las Casas, *Historia de las Indias*, 3 vols., México, 1951

Marcel Bataillon, "Una nueva edición de la Historia de las Casas," *HAHR*, 38 (Nov. 1958)

Juan Pérez de Tudela Bueso, ed., *Obras escogidas de Fray Bartolomé de las Casas,* Madrid, 1958

Revista de Indias, ten articles, Spain, 1957-58

Gonzalo Fernández de Oviedo, *Natural History of the West Indies,* Chapel Hill, 1959

Daymond Turner, "Gonzalo Fernández de Oviedo's Historia General y Natural," *JIAS* (Apr. 1964)

J. H. Parry, *The Spanish Theory of Empire in the XVI Century,* Cambridge, England, 1940

Juan Beneyto Pérez, "Tésis portuguesas y españolas sobre reino e imperio," *MP,* II

The Conquests in America

Bernal Díaz del Castillo, *Historia verdadera de la conquista de la Nueva España,* México, 1961

Bernal Díaz del Castillo, *Discovery and Conquest of Mexico,* tr. by A. P. Maudslay, ed. by Irving A. Leonard

Herbert Cerwin, *Bernal Díaz, Historian of the Conquest,* Norman, 1963

Francisco López de Gómara, *Cortés, The Life of the Conqueror by his Secretary,* tr. by L. B. Simpson, Berkeley, 1964

Hernando Cortés, *Five Letters, 1519-1526,* tr. by J. Bayard Morris, Norton, 1962

Harry M. Rosen, *Conquest, Dispatches of Cortés from the New World,* Grosset and Dunlap, 1962

Ernesto Barrios Berumen, *La conquista española,* México, 1954

Maurice Collis, *Cortés and Montezuma,* Harcourt Brace, 1955

Fernando Benítz, *La ruta de Hernán Cortés,* México, 1956

Salvador de Madariaga, *Hernán Cortés,* Regnery, 1955

H. R. Wagner, *The Rise of Fernando Cortés,* Los Angeles, 1944

Salvador Toscano, *Cuauhtémoc,* México, 1953

Miguel León-Portilla, *The Broken Spears, the Aztec Account of the Conquest,* Beacon Press, 1962

C. Harvey Gardner, *The Constant Captain Gonzalo de Sandoval,* Carbondale, Illinois, 1961

C. Harvey Gardner, *Naval Power in the Conquest of Mexico,* Austin, 1956

R. B. Cunningham-Graham, *The Horses of the Conquest,* Norman, 1949

Edward L. Tinker, "The Horsemen of the Americas," *HAHR,* 42 (May 1962)

Robert West Howard, *The Horse in America,* Chicago, 1964

John J. Johnson, "The Introduction of the Horse into the Western Hemisphere," *HAHR,* 23 (Nov. 1943)

R. S. Chamberlain, *The Conquest and Colonization of Yucatán, 1517-1550,* Washington, 1948

R. S. Chamberlain, *The Conquest and Colonization of Honduras, 1502-1550,* Washington, 1953

Mario Rodríguez, *Central America,* Speculum, 1965

Kathleen Romoli, *Balboa of Darien,* New York, 1953

Garcilaso de la Vega, *The Florida of the Inca, A History of the Adelantado Hernando de Soto,* ed. by J. J. and J. G. Varner, Austin, 1951

Germán Arciniegas, "Germans in the Conquest of America, a XVI Century Venture," *HAHR*, 24 (Feb. 1944)

Germán Arciniegas, *The Knight of El Dorado*, New York, 1953

Juan Friede, ed., *Documentos inéditos para la historia de Colombia*, 4 vols., Bogotá, 1955-56

Juan Friede, *Vida y viajes de Nicolás Féderman*, Bogotá, 1961

Juan Rodríguez Freile, *The Conquest of New Granada*, London, 1961

Octavio Nogales Hidalgo, "Ensayo de investigación biográfica sobre el adelantado Sebastián Benalcazar," *BANQ* (Jan. 1962)

Mario Góngora, *Los grupos de conquistadores en Tierra Firme, 1509-1530*, Santiago, 1962

C. E. Nowell, "Aleixo García and the White King," *HAHR*, 26 (1946)

R. C. Murphy, "The Earliest Spanish Advances Southward from Panama along the West Coast of South America," *HAHR*, 21 (1941)

Pedro de Cieza de León, *The Incas*, tr. by Harriet de Onís, Norman, 1959

M. J. Quintana, *Vida de Francisco Pizarro*, Madrid, 1959

George Kubler, "A Peruvian Chief of State: Manco Inca (1515-1545)," *HAHR*, 24 (1944)

George Kubler, "The Behavior of Atahualpa, 1531-1533," *HAHR*, 25 (1945)

Rolando Mellafe and Sergio Villalobos, *Diego de Almagro*, 2 vols., Santiago, 1954

Sergio Villalobos, "Almagro y los Incas," *RCHG*, 1962

José A. de Ramón Folch, *Descubrimiento de Chile y compañeros de Almagro*, Santiago, 1953

Ida S. W. Vernon, *Pedro de Valdivia, Conquistador of Chile*, Austin, 1946

Stephen Clissold, *Conquistador: The Life of Don Pedro Sarmiento de Gamboa*, London, 1954

Charles McKew Parr, *So Noble a Captain: The Life and Times of Ferdinand Magellan*, New York, 1953

C. E. Nowell, *Magellan's Voyage around the World*, Northwestern, 1962

Sverker Arnoldsson, *La conquista española de América según el juicio de la posteridad*, Madrid, 1960

Chapter 4

LAND AND LABOR

THE original thesis propounded by this book emphasized the importance of land use and land ownership. The turmoil over land control in recent times suggests there is no reason to alter this thesis; numerous publications show its overwhelming importance throughout pre- and post-conquest history.

Studies of the *repartimiento* and *encomienda* in Spain and America make them better understood. See the works by Chamberlain, Góngora,

Kirkpatrick, and Simpson. Simpson now lays less stress on the *encomienda* in the 17th and 18th centuries, saying: ". . . although it was not definitely abolished until the 18th century, by the end of the 16th it had ceased to exercise any vital function in .colonial life." This could be true if we view it as a para-feudal institution, but less certainly true if we consider its influence in establishing the conqueror's hold on the Indians. Chamberlain, in examining the post-conquest Maya situation, holds that the difference was "not so much one of the principles as of degree"—the Spanish work load was heavier. See Chamberlain's excellent study of the literature about the *encomienda*. For a study of the land system viewed as collectivistic see Alfonso Caso. For those not yet acquainted with the *encomienda* system, it may be observed that it never gave legal title to land but often facilitated control by the Spaniards.

The encroachment of large holdings on smaller ones was a dominating theme of the colonial period. Whetten remarks: "For nearly four hundred years, with but minor reverses, the hacienda gradually gained ascendancy and slowly but steadily devoured the village lands and even the villages themselves." Chevalier agrees with this position essentially but holds that haciendas arose from lands first granted in usufruct only. Keen's translation of Zorita makes available one of the most violent anti-Spanish documents. Charles Gibson has made fundamental studies of Indian-Spanish relations: his works are indispensable. His conclusion: the *Leyenda Negra* is essentially true. He dwells, however, more on what the Spaniard did to the Indians than what they contributed to them.

Landholding in Venezuela, Colombia, Peru, and other areas may be studied in the works of Arcila, Friede, Romero, and others cited. Romero's views emphasize what he calls the social transformation after conquest when "private property of the Roman type, inviolable, hereditary and selfish, replaced the right to work and the altruistic customs." Rowe's analysis of Spanish-Indian relations conforms to the usual view—usurpations of the Indian's land and the abuse of the Indians themselves.

The classic history of Spain's "conflict of conscience" with Las Casas representing one side and Juan Ginés de Sepúlveda the opposite has produced an abundance of new studies. Lewis Hanke has emerged as the most important scholar in this field; his works constitute a veritable intellectual history of 16th-century Spain. His many works are cited, the latest being a review of the whole literature in answering Ramón Menéndez Pidal's vitriolic attack on Las Casas. Edmundo O'Gorman, a Mexican scholar, contends that both sides spoke for justice to the Indians—only their methods differed. Numerous other studies are listed.

Those fond of comparing the Anglo-American with the Spanish-American experience are referred to Alden T. Vaughan's *New England Frontier* which defends the New Englanders against Mark Twain's quip that they "first fell upon their knees and then upon the aborigines."

T. Lynn Smith, *Agrarian Reform in Latin America*, Knopf, 1965

Diego Luis Molinari, *El nacimiento del Nuevo Mundo, 1492-1534*, Buenos Aires, 1941

Armando Melón and Ruiz de Gordejuela, *Los primeros tiempos de la colonización*, Barcelona, 1952

José M. Ots Capdequi, *El régimen de la tierra en la América Española durante el período colonial*, Ciudad Trujillo, 1946

Robert S. Chamberlain, "Castillian backgrounds of the repartimiento-encomienda," *Contributions to American Anthropology and History*, Washington, 1939

Mario Góngora, *El estado en el derecho indiano, época de la fundación*, Santiago, 1951

Ursula Lamb, *Fray Nicolás de Ovando*, Madrid, 1956

Ursula Lamb, "Christóbal de Tapia vs. Nicolás de Ovando, A Residencia Fragment," *HAHR*, 33 (Aug. 1953)

F. A. Kirkpatrick, "The Landless Encomienda," *HAHR*, 19 (1939), 22 (1942)

L. B. Simpson, *The Encomienda in New Spain*, Berkeley, 1950

R. S. Chamberlain, *The Pre-Conquest Tribute and Service System of the Maya*, Coral Gables, 1951

R. S. Chamberlain, "Simpson's *The Encomienda in New Spain* and Recent Encomienda Studies," *HAHR*, 34 (May 1954)

Alfonso Caso, "Land Tenure among the Ancient Mexicans, *AA* (Aug. 1963)

Nathan Whetten, *Rural Mexico*, Chicago, 1948

François Chevalier, *Land and Society in Colonial Mexico*, tr. by Alvin Eustis, Berkeley, 1963

Alonso de Zorita, *Life and Labor in Ancient Mexico*, tr. by Benjamin Keen, Rutgers, 1965

Charles Gibson, *Tlaxcala in the XVI Century*, New Haven, 1952

Charles Gibson, "The Transformation of the Indian Community in New Spain," *Cahiers d'Histoire Mondiale*, II, Paris, 1955

Charles Gibson, *The Aztecs under Spanish Rule*, Stanford, 1964

Eduardo Arcila Farías, *El régimen de la encomienda en Venezuela*, Sevilla, 1957

Francisco González de Cossío, *Historia de la tenencia y explotación del campo*, 2 vols., México, 1957

Juan Friede, *El indio en la lucha por la tierra*, Bogotá, 1944

Juan Friede, *Los indios del alto Magdalena, 1609-1931*, Bogotá, 1943

Oscar Malea Olguín, "Prosiguen las informaciones sobre encomiendas," *RANP*, 1960-61

Ramón José de Armando, "La encomienda de don Juan de Cuevas, *BACH*, 1960

K. V. Fox, "Pedro Muñiz, Dean of Lima and the Indian Labor Question," *HAHR*, 42 (Feb. 1962)

Javier Prado, *Estado social del Perú durante la dominación española*, Lima, 1941

Emilio Romero, *Historia económica del Perú,* Buenos Aires, 1949

John H. Rowe, "The Incas under Spanish Colonial Institutions," *HAHR,* 37 (May 1957)

Thomas R. Ford, *Man and Land in Peru,* Florida, 1955

Jean Borde and Mario Góngora, *Evolución de la propiedad rural,* Santiago, 1956

M. Gamio, "Static and Dynamic Values in the Indigenous Past," *HAHR,* 23 (Aug. 1943)

Lewis Hanke, "The Requerimiento and Its Interpreters," *RHAM,* I (1938)

Lewis Hanke, "Free Speech in XVI Century Spanish America," *HAHR,* 26 (May 1946)

Lewis Hanke, *Bartolomé de las Casas,* The Hague, 1951

Lewis Hanke, *Bartolomé de las Casas, Bookman, Scholar and Propagandist,* Pennsylvania, 1952

Lewis Hanke, *Bartolomé de las Casas, Historian,* Florida, 1952

Lewis Hanke, *Aristotle and the American Indian,* Chicago, 1959

Lewis Hanke, "The Dawn of Conscience in America," *PAPS,* 1963

Ramón Menéndez Pidal, *El Padre Las Casas,* Madrid, 1963

Lewis Hanke, "More Heat and Some Light on the Spanish Struggle for Justice in the Conquest of America," *HAHR,* 44 (Aug. 1964)

Edmundo O'Gorman, "Critique of Lewis Hanke on the Spanish Struggle for Justice," *HAHR,* 29 (Nov. 1949)

Fernando de Medina Díez, "Una polémica que dura cuatro siglos," *JIAS,* 1964

Sverker Arnoldsson, *La leyenda negra,* Göteborg, 1960

Manuel Giménez Fernández, *Bartolomé de las Casas,* Sevilla, 1953

Manuel Giménez Fernández, *Política de Carlos I en Indias,* 2 vols., Sevilla, 1960

J. M. Van der Kroef, "Francisco de Vitoria and the Nature of Colonial Policy," *CHR,* 35 (July 1949)

José A. Llaguno, *La personalidad jurídica del indio y el III Concilio Provincial Mexicano,* México, 1963

Pierre Chaunu, "Las Casas et la première crise structurelle de la colonisation espagnole," *Revue Historique,* 1963

Manuel López Amabalis, "Sobre la ilegitimidad de la conquista, *RUY,* 1962

Bartolomé de las Casas, *Los tesoros del Perú,* Madrid, 1958

Alden T. Vaughan, *New England Frontier,* Little, Brown, 1965

Chapter 5

FARM AND RANCH

A COMPANION thesis to the importance of land ownership is that farming and the introduction and use of domestic animals were the essence of colonization—military operations being a necessary prelude. This is in agreement with Parker's observation that "almost every inhabitant of colonial Central America was in one way or another a farmer."

The difficulties in developing the tropics are noted by the studies of Gourou and McNeil. The problem posed by lateritic soils has in fact only recently been recognized by scientists and has yet to be discovered by the sentimental defenders of the "fertile tropics." The minerals versus agriculture conflict may be noted among the authors cited here, Vives remarking, for example, that the "more intelligent colonists" dedicated themselves to agriculture. The rise at an early date, with vicissitudes, of the sugar industry and the importance of live stock are emphasized by Ratekin, Ely, Bishko, Dusenberry, and Simpson.

Franklin D. Parker, *The Central American Republics,* Oxford, 1964

Pierre Gourou, *The Tropical World,* London, 1961

Mary McNeil, "Lateritic Soils," *Scientific American,* 1964

Jaime Vicens Vives, *Historia social y económica de España y América,* Barcelona, 1957-

M. Ratekin, "Early Sugar Industry in Española," *HAHR,* 34 (Feb. 1954)

Roland T. Ely, *Cuando reinaba su majestad el azúcar,* Buenos Aires, 1963

Ramiro Guerra y Sánchez, *Sugar and Society in the Caribbean,* Yale, 1964

C. J. Bishko, "The Peninsular Background of Latin American Cattle Ranching," *HAHR,* 32 (Nov. 1952)

William M. Dusenberry, *The Mexican Mesta,* Urbana, Illinois, 1963

Nathan L. Whetten, *Guatemala, the Land and the People,* Yale, 1961

Russell H. Fitzgibbon and F. C. Wooten, *Latin America, Past and Present,* Heath, 1946

Lesley Byrd Simpson, *Exploitation of Land in Central Mexico in the XVI Century,* Berkeley, 1952

Carl Ortwin Sauer, *Land and Life,* Berkeley, 1963

Chapters 6, 18

MINING IN AMERICA

IN addition to the studies made by Humboldt in the late colonial period and the modern studies by Haring and Hamilton, all cited before, a number of others have appeared. Haring's *Spanish Empire in America,* and studies by Vives, Bargallo, Hanke, Wagner, West, and Muro are all valuable. West's work shows the nature of a mining community. Nesmith and Meek study coinage, the latter showing the shortage of small coins and the use of goods for bartering.

Motten's work discusses mining techniques as well as their influence on intellectual life; Whitaker shows the attempts to find better methods. Howe discusses the mining guild. Moreyra y Paz-Soldan discusses ownership arising from royal grants. Gwendolin Cobb remarks: "The flesh of swine and llamas was the Potosi Indians' most common meat. Despite the prohibition of killing llamas and alpacas, the Indians of Potosi slaughtered forty thousand every year for their own needs." She adds that in the market "1000% profit was not unusual."

Among the works cited we may note Carmagnani's sophisticated analysis, and Raymond de Roover's and Joseph A. Schumpeter's work on the influence of precious metals in world economic development.

Adolf M. Abich, "The Hundredth Anniversary of the Death of Alexander Von Humboldt," *HAHR*, 38 (Aug. 1958)

Val Gendron, *The Dragon Tree, A Life of Von Humboldt*, Longmans, Green and Co., 1961

Rayfred L. Stevans-Middleton, *La obra de A. Von Humboldt en* México, 1956

Angel Rubio, "Alejandro de Humboldt," *RIB*, 12

Juan Bautista Lavalle, "Humboldt en Hispanoamérica," *RIB*, 12

Helmut de Terra, "A. Von Humboldt's Contributions to Science," *RIB*, 12

Helmut de Terra, *Humboldt*, Knopf, 1955

Arthur P. Whitaker, "Clarence H. Haring," *HAHR*, 41 (Aug. 1961)

Modesto Bargallo, *La minería y la metalurgía en la América española, época colonial*, México, 1955

H. R. Wagner, "Early Silver Mining in New Spain," *RHAM*, 14 (1942)

Luis Muro, "Bartolomé de Medina, introductor del beneficio de patio en Nueva España," *HM*, 1964

Robert C. West, *The Mining Community in Northern New Spain*, Berkeley, 1949

R. S. Nesmith, *The Coinage of the First Mint of the Americas at Mexico City, 1536-1572*, New York, 1955

W. T. Meek, *The Exchange Media of Colonial Mexico*, Knip's Crown, 1948

Clement G. Motten, *Mexican Silver and the Enlightenment*, Philadelphia, 1950

Arthur P. Whitaker, "The Elhuyar Mining Missions and the Enlightenment," *HAHR*, 31 (Nov. 1951)

Walter Howe, *The Mining Guild of New Spain*, Harvard, 1949

Lewis Hanke, *The Imperial City of Potosí*, The Hague, 1956

Lewis Hanke, *Bartolomé Arzans de Orsua y Vela's History of Potosí*, Brown, 1966

Bartolomé Arzáns de Orsúa y Vela, *Historia de la Villa Imperial de Potosí*, 3 vols., eds. Lewis Hanke and Gunnar Mendoza, Providence, R.I., Brown University Press, 1965.

Manuel Moreyra y Paz-Soldán, *En torno a dos valiosos documentos sobre Potosí*, Lima, 1953

Gwendolin B. Cobb, "Supply and Transportation for the Potosí Mines," *HAHR*, 29 (Feb. 1949)

Robert C. West, *Colonial Placer Mining in Colombia,* Baton Rouge, La., 1952

Juan Friede, *Documentos sobre la fundación de la Casa de Moneda en Santa Fé,* Bogotá, 1963

Marcello Carmagnani, *El salariado minero en Chile colonial,* Santiago, 1963

O. Bermúdez, *Historia del salitre,* Santiago, 1963

Raymond de Roover, "New Interpretations of the History of Banking," *JWH,* II (1954)

Joseph A. Schumpeter, *History of Economic Analysis,* Oxford, 1954

Chapters 7, 19

MANUFACTURING AND DOMESTIC TRADE

ADDITIONAL information on pre-conquest trade and manufacturing will be found in the citations in Chapter 2.

The much-heralded Inca road system (trails is a better word) has been examined by Gerbi and Von Hagen, whose difficulties in tracing the roads in modern times are similar to those of Almagro in dealing with the expedition to Chile.

For the post-conquest period several works have revealed much more about the system of *gremios* and other controls. See those of Lee, Smith, Rodríguez, Dusenberry, Moorhead, and Guthrie—all related to New Spain. The conditions of Guatemala are studied by Smith, Beeson, and Floyd. Price movements and price controls may be seen from studies by Longhurst and Romano. Manuel Carrera Stampa, who has analyzed the weights and measures as well as the guilds, holds that Spanish techniques displaced Indian systems and that the changes constituted an industrial revolution.

Antonello Gerbi, *Caminos del Perú,* Lima, 1944

Victor W. Von Hagen, *Highway of the Sun,* Duell, Sloan and Pearce, 1955

Alfredo Benavides, "Los caminos de la zona norte de Chile al iniciarse la conquista española," *BACH,* 1959

Jan Bazaut, "Evolución de la industria textil problana, 1554-1845," *HM,* 1964

M. Carrera Stampa, "The Evolution of Weights and Measures in New Spain," *HAHR,* 29 (1949)

M. Carrera Stampa, *Los gremios mexicanos,* México, 1954

R. L. Lee, "Grain Legislation in Colonial Mexico," *HAHR,* 27 (1947)

R. S. Smith, "Sales Taxes in New Spain," *HAHR,* 28 (1948)

R. S. Smith, "The Institution of the Consulado in New Spain," *HAHR,* 24 (Feb. 1944)

R. S. Smith, "The Consulado in Santa Fé de Bogotá," *HAHR,* 45 (1965)

Mario E. Rodríguez, *El tribunal del consulado de Lima,* Madrid, 1960

W. H. Dusenberry, "The Regulation of Meat Supply in Sixteenth Century Mexico City," *HAHR*, 28 (Feb. 1948)

Max L. Moorhead, "The Private Contract System of Presidio Supply in Northern New Spain," *HAHR*, 41 (Feb. 1961)

Chester L. Guthrie, "Colonial Economy, Trade, Industry, Labor in Seventeenth Century Mexico," *RHAM*, VII (1939)

R. S. Smith, "Indigo Production and Trade in Colonial Guatemala," *HAHR*, 39 (May 1959)

Kenneth H. Beeson, "Indigo Production in the Eighteenth Century," *HAHR*, 44 (May 1964)

Troy S. Floyd, "The Guatemalan Merchants, the Government and the Provincianos, 1750-1800," *HAHR*, 41 (Feb. 1961)

John E. Longhurst, "Early Price Lists in Lima and Petition for Redress," *HAHR*, 31 (Feb. 1951)

Ruggiero Romano, "Movimiento de los precios, siglo XVIII," *Desarrollo Económico*, 1963

Chapters 8, 20

INTERNATIONAL TRADE

AND TRADE REFORM

THE standard works on Spanish trade policy by Haring, Hamilton, Vives, and others have been cited. Other important works are by Pujol, Elliot, and Carande, the latter's showing the fundamental nature of Charles V's economic situation. Ruth Pike's discussion of Sevilla in the 16th century is on a high scholarly level.

Clarence H. Haring's review of his own works and those of others, especially those of the Chaunus, offer the best summary of the literature to date. The Chaunus' compilation of statistics and study of Spanish policy is an archive in itself.

Juan Cortés has attempted to measure Spain's economic attitudes by examining the literature. Interesting.

Suggestions for establishing comparative rules for the study of European overseas expansion are made by Mauro and Easterbrook. Spain's foreign rivals are studied by Crouse, Lussagnet, Andrews, Unwin, Quinn, and others; piracy, by Gerhard and Carse.

A work not to be missed is Mattingly's *Armada,* which brilliantly discusses the international situation in 1588. Lewis is more interested in the battle itself.

The Dutch in the West Indies have been the subject of a revealing study by Engle Sluiter, and on a wider scale, by Boxer and Davies.

Of the numerous studies of Spain's attackers and rivals in the 17th and 18th centuries, a few are listed. The studies reveal much of the contraband, trade, and war which beset Spain.

Inter-colonial trade is the subject of works by Woodrow W. Borah (Pacific Coast) and Arcila Farias (Mexico-Venezuela). The Manila trade has received the attention of Schurz and Alessio Robles.

The trade of the Plata region, so much of it contraband, is the subject of studies by Mario Rodríguez, who shows early economic rivalries, and by Lewin, Molina, and Kroeber.

Spain's efforts in the 18th century to adjust to a rapidly changing world conditions were largely successful, but she was still unable to catch up with the rest of Europe. Hamilton has studied the efforts to organize an efficient bank; two excellent books by Herr and Sarrailh show reform movements. The thorough study by Shafer of the Economic Societies should dispel any notions that the economic enlightenment had not reached Spain's world in the 18th century. See also the article by Smith on Adam Smith's *Wealth of Nations in the New World.*

Jaime Carrera Pujol, *Historia de la economía española,* 5 vols., Barcelona, 1943-47

J. H. Elliott, *Imperial Spain, 1469-1716,* St. Martin's, 1963

Ramón Carande, *Carlos V y sus banqueros,* Madrid, 1943

Earl J. Hamilton, "The Role of Monopoly in the Overseas Expansion and Colonial Trade of Europe before 1800," *AER,* 1948

Earl J. Hamilton, *War and Prices in Spain, 1651-1800,* Cambridge, Mass., 1947

Ruth Pike, "Seville in the XVI Century," *HAHR,* 41 (Feb. 1961)

C. H. Haring, "Trade and Navigation between Spain and the Indies, a Re-View, 1918-1948," *HAHR,* 40 (Feb. 1960)

Pierre Chaunu, *Séville et l'Atlantique,* 12 vols., 1955-

Juan B. Cortés, S. J., "The Achievement Motive in the Spanish Economy between the XIII and XVIII Centuries," *Economic Development and Cultural Change,* 1961

F. Mauro, "Towards an 'Intercontinental Model': European Overseas Expansion," *EHR,* 1961

W. T. Easterbrook, "Long-Period Comparative Study: Some Historical Cases," *JEH,* 1957

Francisco Morales Padrón, *El comercio canario-americano,* Seville, 1955

N. M. Crouse, *French Pioneers in the West Indies, 1624-1664,* Columbia, 1940

N. M. Crouse, *The French Struggle for the West Indies, 1665-1713,* Columbia, 1943

Suzanne Lussagnet, ed., *Les français en Amérique pendant la deuxième moitié du XVI siècle,* Paris, 1953

Kenneth R. Andrews, ed., *English Privateering Voyages to the West Indies,* Glasgow, 1959

Rayner Unwin, *The Defeat of John Hawkins, A Biography of His Third Slaving Voyage,* Macmillan, 1960

David Beers Quinn, ed., *The Roanoke Voyages, 1534-1590,* Hakluyt, 1955

I. A. Wright, *Further English Voyages to Spanish America, 1583-1594,* Hakluyt, nos. 62 (1929), 71 (1932), 99 (1951)

D. B. Quinn, "Some Spanish Reactions to Elizabethan Colonial Enterprises," *RHST,* 1951

Frank Aydelotte, "Elizabethan Seamen in Mexico and Ports of the Spanish Main," *AHR,* 1942

G. Connell-Smith, "English Merchants Trading to the New World in the Early XVI Century," *BIHRL,* London, 23 (1950)

G. P. Insh, *The Darien Scheme,* London, 1947

Peter Gerhard, *Pirates on the West Coast of New Spain,* Glendale, 1960

R. Carse, *Age of Piracy,* Rinehart, 1957

Garrett Mattingly, *The Armada,* Houghton Mifflin, 1960

Michael Lewis, *The Spanish Armada,* Mcmillan, 1960

Engel Sluiter, "Dutch-Spanish Rivalry in the Caribbean," *HAHR,* 28 (May 1948)

Engle Sluiter, "Dutch Maritime Power and the Colonial Status Quo," *PHR,* 1942

David W. Davies, *A Primer of Dutch XVII Century Overseas Trade,* The Hague, 1961

C. R. Boxer, *The Dutch in Brazil,* Oxford, 1957

R. A. Humphreys, *The Diplomatic History of British Honduras,* London, 1961

J. Marino Incháustegui, *La gran expedición inglesa contra las Antillas Mayores,* México, 1953

A. P. Thornton, *West India Policy under the Restoration,* Oxford, 1956

R. T. Davies, *Spain in Decline, 1621-1700,* St. Martin's, 1957

Sir Alan Burns, *History of the British West Indies,* London, 1954

A. P. Thornton, "Spanish Slave Ships in the English West Indies," *HAHR,* 35 (Aug. 1955)

Vera Lee Brown, "South Sea Company and Contraband Trade," *AHR,* 21

George H. Nelson, "Contraband Trade under the Asiento, 1730-1739," *AHR,* 41

Enrique Marco Dorta, *Cartagena de Indias,* Cartagena, 1960

Charles E. Nowell, "The Defense of Cartagena," *HAHR,* 42 (Nov. 1962)

Richard Pares, *War and Trade in the West Indies,* Oxford, 1936

Ernest G. Hildner, Jr., "The Role of the South Sea Company in the Diplomacy Leading to the War of Jenkin's Ear," *HAHR,* 18 (Aug. 1938)

Richard Pares, *Colonial Blockade and Neutral Rights,* Oxford, 1938

Allan Christelow, "Great Britain and the Trades from Cadiz to Lisbon to Spanish America and Brazil," *HAHR,* 27 (Feb. 1947)

Allan Christelow, "Contraband Trade between Jamaica and the Spanish Main," *HAHR,* 22 (May 1942)

R. A. Humphreys, "Richard Oswald's Plan for an English and Russian Attack on Spanish America, 1781-1782," *HAHR,* 18 (Feb. 1938)

Allan Christelow, "French Interest in the Spanish Empire, Duc de Choiseul, 1759-1771," *HAHR,* 21 (Nov. 1941)

Manuel Luengo Muñoz, "Génesis de las expediciones militares al Darien en 1785-1786," *AEMS,* 1961

Robert S. Smith, "Shipping in the Port of Veracruz," *HAHR,* 23 (Feb. 1943)

Sergio R. Villalobos, "El comercio extranjero a fines de la dominación española," *JIAS,* 1962

José Martínez Cardós, "Un informe de Campillo sobre la propuesta de una compañía holandesa," *RIM,* 1961

Regine Pernoud, "Diario inédito de un viaje de Chile y del Perú," *BACH,* 1960

Woodrow W. Borah, *Early Colonial Trade and Navigation between Mexico and Peru,* Berkeley, 1954

Eduardo Arcila Farías, *Comercio entre Venezuela y México en los siglos XVII-XVIII,* México 1951

Vito Alessio Robles, *Acapulco en la historia y en la leyenda,* México, 1932

William L. Schurz, *The Manila Galleon,* Dutton, 1959

María Lourdes Díaz-Trechuelo Spinola, *La Real Compañía de Filipinas,* Seville, 1965

Mario Rodríguez, "The Genesis of Economic Attitudes in Rio de la Plata," *HAHR,* 36 (May 1956)

Boleslao Lewin, "Un documento acerca del comercio interlope en el Rosario del siglo XVIII, *AIIHR,* 1957

Raul A. Molina, "La defensa del comercio del Rio de la Plata por el Lic. D. Antonio de León Pinelo," *HBA,* 1962

Clifton B. Kroeber, *The Growth of the Shipping Industry in Rio de la Plata, 1794-1860,* Wisconsin, 1957

Earl J. Hamilton, "Plans for a National Bank in Spain, 1701-1783," *JPE,* 1949

Richard Herr, *The Eighteenth Century Revolutions in Spain,* Princeton, 1958

Jean Sarrailh, *L'Espagne éclairée de la seconde moitié du XVIIIe siècle,* Paris, 1954

Jean Sarrailh, "La España de Carlos III," *CAM,* 1963

Robert J. Shafer, *The Economic Societies in the Spanish World,* Syracuse, 1958

Robert S. Smith, "The *Wealth of Nations* in Spain and Hispanic America," JPE, 1957

Chapter 9

INDIAN CLASSES, CUSTOMS AND POPULATION

MOST of the fundamental works useful here have been cited in connection with Chapters 2 and 4. A few additional works by Konetzke, Bagú, and others are listed.

The important question of the population in 1492 has become one of the most researched subjects. Its significance lies in the use of population as a "measuring rod" of Spanish civilization in America. The relationship to the *Leyenda Negra* is direct: the larger the population in 1492 and the more people killed as a result of the conquest, the blacker Spain's record, i.e., the less of "legend," the more of "black."

Studies by Rodolfo Barón Castro and Ángel Rosenblat show conventional results: a population for all America of some 13 to 15 million, with Mexico between 4 and 5 and Peru-Bolvia just under 3. Steward gives about 10 million for South America; Brainerd gives about 5 million for Yucatan and other Maya regions.

Mexico's population has recently been estimated at startlingly higher figures, matching or surpassing those of Las Casas and others in early conquest times. The new estimates are mainly the work of Borah, Cook and Simpson, with Kubler also an important contributor. They all accept the belief that there was a great decrease after the conquest, perhaps amounting to 90% in the first century.

Kubler pointed out some years ago the difficulties of making a correct estimate and concluded that all the uncertainties made an accurate count next to impossible.

Borah, Cook, and Simpson nevertheless rely on some of the sources Kubler doubted. In studies made as individuals or in collaboration, a few years back, they placed the population of central Mexico at some 10-11 million in 1519, which they believed dwindled to under two million by 1607 and to fewer still by 1650.

Their studies are distinguished from others not only by their higher estimates, but also by their more refined methodology. They use pre-conquest tribute records gathered precisely from those sources Kubler rejected, as well as post-conquest census figures. Though they suggest that their estimates are hypothesis, they write in a manner which indicates they believe themselves firmly right and challenge doubters.

Their methods required them to estimate the number of Indians free from tribute, the population not under tribute, the slaves free of tribute, the number of artisans who paid in unusual types of tribute, *Mayeques* bound to the soil and otherwise tribute free, the number who paid half tribute, the frequency of tribute payments, the rate of assessment, and the size of the family. All these calculations are based on their reading of Aztec picture writing as well as on Spanish census records, which were made long after the beginning of the conquest.

To facilitate their calculations they reduced everything to a common denominator, the *manta* or standard piece of cloth. This in turn required them to estimate the Spanish price of the *manta* and reduce it to the 1519 equivalent. Also, the Indian units for measuring grain and beans were converted to Spanish fanegas. By calculating the estimated yield of crops in 1519 and the estimated acreage under crop, their latest figures show 25,000,000 for Central Mexico in 1519.

Their studies thus show 125 to the square mile for the whole region considered, or 2000 to 3000 for the Valley of Mexico, 12,000 for the cities, and a total of 235,000 for ancient Mexico City. We may note that the ancient city, before the lake was partially drained by the Spaniards, contained about three to four square miles of land surface. This would mean some 60,000 to the square mile in comparison with New York City's approximately 27,000 or Manhattan's 75,000. Both are areas where high-rise buildings prevail.

Though these figures could be correct they are not necessarily so. Modern statisticians are hardly likely to accept the basis on which the statistics rest. The amount of land needed to support such a population does not allow for the rotation of fields necessary to keep lateritic soils in fertility. Some of the population estimates they give would allow a population three times the present-day number in the same area.

Other aspects of their studies need to be noted. They lay great stress, as does Gibson, on erosion of the soils because of the Spanish plow and the domestic animals. This would seem to require a belief that a dwindling population causes more soil erosion than a high one, i.e., that soil erosion increased as population decreased. Could this be true? Also, cows, horses, hogs, sheep, and chickens produced a rich fetrilizer unknown before the conquest. Would this not increase food?

This question need not be considered closed. Young scholars might find a fertile field to cultivate here. We may note one more thing. A mid-17th century study quoted by Guthrie gives Mexico City a half million or more people. This would be a third to a half of all Mexico in 1650 as estimated by the scholars quoted above.

Angel Rosenblat has subjected the works of Borah, Cook and Simpson to an exhaustive analysis in a paper delivered before the 37th Congress of Americanists, rejecting their method and their results, and reaffirming his estimates made in 1954.

The estimate of the population of the Inca Empire has not been the subject of such intense research. Rowe, already cited, has tended to pare some previous high figures, though allowing more than double the number accepted by this book. Kubler has studied the later colonial period.

Any new estimates will have to be made with caution. Ake Wedin, in a work published in 1965, demonstrates that no certain reliance can be placed on the alleged decimal division of the population into civil or military groups. Thus, to rely on such a system to calculate the number of people can lead to considerable error.

Richard Konetzke, *Colección de documentos,* 3 vols., Madrid, 1958-62

Sergio Bagú, *Estructura social de la colonia,* Buenos Aires, 1952

Guillermo S. Fernández de Recas, *Cacicazgos y nobiliario indígena de la Nueva España,* México, 1961

Rodolfo Barón Castro, "El Desarrollo de la población hispanoamericana," *CHM,* II (1959)

Ángel Rosenblat, *La población indígena y el mestizaje en América,* 2 vols., Buenos Aires, 1954

Julian Steward, *Native Peoples of South America,* McGraw Hill, 1959

George E. Brainerd, *The Maya Civilization,* McBride, 1954

Franz Termer, "The Density of Population in the Maya Empires," *Proceedings, International Congress of Americanists,* I (New York, 1949)

Sherburne F. Cook and Lesley Byrd Simpson, *The Population of Central Mexico in the XVI Century,* Berkeley, 1948

Woodrow Borah and S. F. Cook, *The Population of Central Mexico in 1548,* Berkeley, 1960

Sherburne F. Cook, *Soil Erosion and Population in Central Mexico,* Berkeley, 1949

Woodrow Borah, *New Spain's Century of Depression,* Berkeley, 1951

L. B. Simpson, *Exploitation of Land in Central Mexico in the XVI Century,* Berkeley, 1952

Woodrow Borah, "Francisco de Urdiñola's Census of the Spanish Settlements in Nueva Viscaya, 1604," *HAHR,* 35 (Aug. 1955)

Sherburne F. Cook and Woodrow Borah, "The Rate of population Change in Central Mexico, 1550-1570," *HAHR,* 37 (Nov. 1957)

Sherburne F. Cook and Woodrow Borah, *The Indian Population of Central Mexico, 1531-1610,* Berkeley, 1960

Woodrow Borah and Sherburne F. Cook. *The Aboriginal Population of Central Mexico on the Eve of the Spanish Conquest,* Berkeley, 1963

George Kubler, "Population Movements in Mexico, 1520-1600," *HAHR,* 22 (1942)

Chester L. Guthrie, *RHAM,* VII (1939)

José Miranda, "La población indígena de la Nueva España en el siglo XVII," *HM,* 1963

Delfina E. López Sarrelangue, "La población indígena en el siglo XVIII," *HM,* 1963

John H. Rowe, "The Incas under Spanish Colonial Institutions," *HAHR,* 37 (May 1957)

George Kubler, *Indian Caste of Peru, 1795-1940,* Washington, 1952

Ake Wedin, *El sistema decimal en el imperio incaico,* Madrid, 1965

Edward H. Spicer, *Cycles of Conquest, the Imapct of Spain, Mexico and the United States on the Indians of the Southwest, 1533-1960,* Tucson, 1962

Chapters 10, 21, 22

PEOPLE AND WORK:
THE CLASS STRUCTURE

THE QUEST of Spain for an Indian policy and the conditions of Indians under Spanish rule have been treated in Chapters 2 and 9 and in the works of Rowe, Gibson, Simpson, and others.

One of the major problems in addition to labor policy was disease, discussed by Cooke for the Aztecs, Dobyns for the Andes, and more generally by Ashburn. For other problems such as vagabondage, see Martin; for coca chewing, Gagliano; for pulque, Gonsalves de Lima, who perpetuates the modern myth that before the conquest pulque was solely a ceremonial drink.

The Negro in the New World is now the subject of many works, but not of a definitive treatment. A fairly recent starting point may be seen in Tannenbaum's *Slave and Citizen;* Elkins work on the United States should also be considered. The reissue of Work's bibliography makes available once again the single most important book of its kind. James F. King has published a selective bibliography. In addition to works by Rippy, Browning, Wyndham, Román Beltrám, and Roberto MacLean y Estenós, we especially cite Zelinski, who shows the pattern of Negro settlement. For the Negro in Mexico see Aguirre Beltrán and for South America, Romero; for Puerto Rico see Díaz Soler and for Colombia, James F. King and Alonso de Sandoval. Still others are Nuñez Ponte on Venezuela, Irene Diggs on Rio de la Plata, Fernández Saldaña on Uruguay, and Bravo Hayley on Chile. For a good work on Indian-Negro relations see Silvio Zavala.

The Mestizo has received the particular attention of Magnus Mörner in recent years. He has written, and inspired others to write, numerous works. The meaning of the term and the complexity of the study have been revealed more and more by his efforts. See the published proceedings of the Congress held under his auspicies in Stockholm in 1960 and of another Congress held at Columbia University in December, 1965, to be published by Cornell University.

The special issue of the *Revista de Indias* herein cited broadens the word to take in not only mixtures of people but of plants and animals as well—a concept which is more properly acculturation, as there are no mixtures of corn and wheat or burros and llamas so far as this writer knows. Other studies cited below make contributions to the subject.

Social change and class mobility are treated in many of the works just cited. Lyle McAlister has made basic studies on this with regard to Mexico, revealing more mobility in the 18th century than previously suspected.

Sherburne F. Cook, "The Incidence and Significance of Disease among the Aztecs," *HAHR*, 26 (Aug. 1946)

P. M. Ashburn, *The Ranks of Death, A Medical History of the Conquest of America*, New York, 1947

Norman F. Martin, *Los vagamundos en la Nueva España*, México, 1957

Alvaro Jara, "Una investigación sobre los problemas del trabajo en Chile durante el período colonial," *HAHR*, 39 (May 1959)

Alicia Bazan Alarcón, "El Real Tribunal de la Acordada," *HM*, 1964

Joseph A. Gagliano, "The Coca Debate in Colonial Peru," *TAm*, 1963

Gonsalves de Lima, *El Maguey y el Pulque*, 1956

Frank Tannenbaum, *Slave and Citizen, The Negro in the Americas*, New York, 1946

Stanley Elkins, *Slavery, A Problem in American Institutional and Intellectual Life*, Chicago, 1959

M. N. Work, *A Bibliography of the Negro in Africa and America*, New York, 1928 (reprinted by Octagon Books, 1965)

James F. King, "The Negro in Continental Spanish America, A Selected Bibliography," *HAHR*, 24 (Aug. 1944)

James F. King, "Evolution of the Free Slave Trade Principle in Spanish Colonial Administration," *HAHR*, 22 (1942)

James F. King, "Negro History in Continental Spanish America," *JNH*, 29 (1944)

James B. Browning, "Negro Companions of the Spanish Explorers," *Howard University Studies in History*, 11 (1930)

J. Fred Rippy, "The Negro and Spanish Pioneers in the New World," *JNH*, VI (1921)

N. A. Wyndham, *The Atlantic and Slavery*, Oxford, 1935

Román Beltrán, "Africa en América," *CAM*, 1944

Roberto MacLean Estenós, *Negros en el Nuevo Mundo*, Lima, 1948

Wilbur Zelinski, "The Historical Geography of the Negro Population of Latin America," *JNH*, 1949

Gonzalo Aguirre Beltrán, "The Slave Trade in Mexico," *HAHR*, 24 (Aug. 1944)

Gonzalo Aguirre Beltrán, *La población negra de México, 1519-1810*, México, 1946

Fernando Romero, "The Slave Trade and the Negro in South America," *HAHR*, 24 (Aug. 1944)

Luis M. Díaz Soler, "Historia de la esclavitud negra en Puerto Rico," *RO*, 1953

James F. King, *Negro Slavery in New Granada*, Berkeley, 1945

Alonso de Sandoval, *De instauranda aethiopum salute, El mundo de la esclavitud negra en América*, Bogotá, 1956

J. M. Nuñez Ponte, *Ensayo histórico acerca de la esclavitud y su abolición en Venezuela*, Caracas, 1954

Irene Diggs, "The Negro in the Viceroyalty of the Río de la Plata," *JNH*, 1951

Irene Diggs, "Color in Colonial Spanish America," *JNH*, 1951

J. M. Fernández Saldaña, "Los negros en el Uruguay," *La Prensa,* Buenos Aires (Aug. 1938)

Domingo Amunátegui Solar, "La trata de negros en Chile," *RCHG,* 44 (1922)

Julio P. Bravo Hayley, "Abolición de la esclavitud en Chile," *El Mercurio,* 1939

Silvio Zavala, "Relaciones históricas entre indios y negros," *RIBo,* 1946

James F. King, "The Colored Castes and American Representation in the Cortes of Cadiz," *HAHR,* 33 (Feb. 1953)

Magnus Mörner, ed., *El mestizaje en la historia de Ibero-America,* México, 1961

Claudio Estevan Fabregat, "El mestizaje en Iberoamérica," *RIM,* 1964

Revista de Indias, 24 (1964)

Magnus Mörner and Charles Gibson, "Diego Muñoz Camargo and the Segregation Policy of the Spanish Crown," *HAHR* (Mar. 1962)

Rodolfo Kusch, *La seducción de la barbarie, análisis herético de un continente mestizo,* Buenos Aires, 1953

Thomas B. Hinton, *A Survey of Indian Assimilation in Eastern Sonora,* Arizona, 1959

L. N. McAlister, "Social Structure and Social Change in New Spain," *HAHR,* 43 (Aug. 1963)

L. N. McAlister, *The "Fuero Militar" in New Spain, 1764-1800,* Florida, 1957

Ernesto Lemoine Villicaña, "Un notable escrito póstumo del obispo de Michoacán," *BANM,* 1964

Chapters 11, 23, 24, 25

LATIN AMERICAN CULTURE

THE BASIC works useful here have been cited in Chapters 2, 9, and 10.

A very large body of research concerned with both Indian and Spanish culture has accumulated during the last generation. The dichotomy of values is as sharp as ever, as is seen in quotes from two eminent Mexican scholars. From José Vasconcellos: "Spain destroyed nothing, because nothing worthy of conservation existed when she arrived in these lands, unless the poisonous spiritual weed of the cannibalism of the Caribs, the human sacrifice of the Aztecs, or the brutalizing despotism of the Incas, is considered sacred." Manual Gamio, on the other hand, wants to revive the ancient mythology, "that inexhaustible source of powerful inspirations," from which the Indians "will feel the esthetic capacity of their forefathers rise anew in their minds, will produce a grandiose work of art, and will find the spiritual satisfaction which accompanies that sublime task."

From the numerous publications cited below the reader can find his own way among the opposing views. One of the principal efforts of the Indianist school has been to reconstruct the "literature" of the unlettered. By drawing from the post-conquest chronicles—some by Mestizos—and by interpreting the folklore more or less freely, modern scholars have produced a large number of books and articles. We are thus getting a double interpretation of Indian thought, first from a Garcilaso, Sahagún, Mendieta, or Torquemada, and second from the modern who reads into it what he wishes to find. This is illustrated by Caso, León-Portilla, and Sejourné, who all hold that the Aztecs and their kinsmen developed a philosophy comparable to that of Europe.

The archaeologists have literally uncovered more substantial evidence of the glories of the Indian past. The long list of works that could be cited is merely suggested by a few samples here. One small but useful and ingenious work is Sanchez's *Arithmetic in Maya*. The explorations and excavations continue and only by following the archaeological reviews can the reader keep up to date.

The Spanish background and the imported Spanish culture have been extensively studied by numerous scholars in all countries, United States scholar taking the lead in several fields. Descriptions of the New World at the time of discovery both by contemporaries of discovery and by moderns and general histories of culture by such men as Picón-Salas and Henríque Ureña facilitate the acquisition of a general knowledge.

A more fundamental study can be made from the work of Menéndez Pelayo on Spanish culture or from the histories of the literature of the various countries. For those interested in special subjects, there are available works on music, painting, sculpture, architecture, textiles, pottery, gold and silver smithy, and other arts.

The schools of study reflect the Indianist or Hispanist leanings of the authors. But we do have from Kubler, Baer, Baird, Sanford, Keleman, Schuster, and others a new knowledge and often a greater appreciation of colonial architecture and other colonial arts.

The study of education, literature, law, science, philosophy, and all other intellectual activities has benefitted from studies by Barth, Larroyo, Javier Malagón, and numerous others who research these subjects for their own professions or countries.

University education has been studied by Mendoza, Ildefonso Leal, Addy, Lanning, and many others. Lanning has particularly enriched the field with his works on universities in general and on San Carlos in particular. He is a proponent of the idea that the Enlightenment in the universities than has been generally believed.

The question of what the colonies were allowed by law to read, and what they actually did read, has intrigued Irving Leonard and others. Leonard, in his *Books of the Brave,* among other works, and other scholars, including Bernstein, Castanian, Spell, Schons, and Burrus, have published book lists showing a wide range of books theoretically prohibited. Arrom and Leonard have also increased our knowledge of the colonial theatre.

Related to this we may cite new knowledge about scientific developments and expeditions from works by Moll, Leonard, and Steele, the latter whose *Flowers for the King* is a very interesting and enlightening work.

J. Alden Mason, *The Ancient Civilizations of Peru,* Penguin, 1957

José Vasconcelos, *México,* 4th ed., México, 1938

Manuel Gamio, "Static and Dynamic Values in the Indigenous Past of America," *HAHR,* 23 (Aug. 1943)

Luis Nicolau D'Olwer, *Cronistas de las culturas precolombinas,* México, 1963

Betty J. Meggers and Clifford Evans, eds., *Aboriginal Cultural Development,* Smithsonian, 1963

G. H. S. Bushnell, *Ancient Arts of the Americas,* Prager, 1965

H. D. Disselhoff and S. Linné, *The Art of Ancient America,* Crown, 1960

George Kubler, *The Art and Architecture of Ancient America,* Penguin, 1962

Samuel K. Lothrop, et al., *Essays in Pre-Columbian Art and Archaeology,* Harvard, 1961

G. H. S. Bushnell and Adrian Digby, *Ancient American Pottery,* Putnam, 1956

Henry Lehmann, *Pre-Columbian Ceramics,* tr. by Galway Kinnell, Viking, 1962

Andre Emmerich, *Gold and Silver in Pre-Columbian Art,* University of Washington

H. Ubbelohde-Doering, *The Art of Ancient Peru,* London, 1952

Raymond H. Thompson, ed., *Migrations in New World Culture History,* Arizona, 1958

Francisco Monterde, *Literaturas indígenas de América,* Collier, 1962

Laorette Sejourné, *Pensamiento y religión del México antiguo,* México 1957

Alfonso Caso, *El Pueblo del Sol,* México, 1953

M. León-Portilla, *Las literaturas pre-colombinas de México,* Collier, 1962

A. Barrera and S. Redón, tr., *El libro de los libros de Chilam Balam,* México, 1948

M. León-Portilla, *Aztec Thought and Culture,* tr. by J. E. Davis, Oklahoma, 1963

Angel María Garibay, *Historia de la literatura nahuatl,* 2 vols., México, 1953-54

Cottie A. Burland, ed., *The Selden Roll,* Berlin, 1955

Ignacio Bernal, *México before Cortez,* tr. by W. Barnstone, Dolphin

Miguel Covarrubias, *El águila, el jaguar y la serpiente,* México, 1961

Raul Flores Guerrero, *Historia del arte mexicano,* Hermes, 1962

Fernandez Justino, *Arte mexicano,* México, 1961

John Lloyd Stephens, *Incidents of Travel in Yucatan,* Oklahoma, 1962

Robert Wauchope, *Ten Years of Middle American Archaeology,* Tulane, 1961

Robert Wauchope, *Exploration and Excavation in the American Tropics,* Chicago, 1965

Sylvanus G. Morley, *The Ancient Maya,* Stanford, 1956

J. Eric Thompson, *The Rise and Fall of Maya Civilization,* Oklahoma, 1954

Charles Gallenkamp, *Maya,* New York, 1959

xliv   *Bibliographical Introduction*

Paul Rivet, *Maya Cities,* London, 1960

Alfred M. Tozzer, *Chichén Itzá and Its Cenote of Sacrifice,* 2 vols., Cambridge, Mass., 1957

Eduardo Noguera, *Arqueología de Mesoamérica,* Collier, 1962

Philip Drucker, et al., *Excavations at La Venta, Tabasco,* Washington, 1959

Doris Stone, *The Archaeology of Central and Southern Honduras,* Cambridge, Mass., 1957

Karl Ruppert, J. Eric Thompson, Tatiana Proskouriakoff, *Bonampak, Chiapas, Mexico,* Washington, 1955

Walter Krickeberg, *Las antiguas culturas mexicanas,* México, 1961

Los Mayas del sur y sus relaciones con las Nahuas meridionales, Sociedad mexicana de antropología, México, 1961

Ernesto C. Aguilar, *Los Mayas en la historia de la cultura,* Universidad de San Carlos, Guatemala, 1961

Tatiana Proskouriakoff, *An Album of Maya Architecture,* Washington, 1956

Tatiana Proskouriakoff, *A Study of Classic Maya Sculpture,* Washington, 1950

Alfred Kidder II and Carlos Samoyoa Chinchilla, *The Art of the Ancient Maya,* New York, 1959

Irmgard G. Kimball, *Mayan Terracottas,* Praeger, 1963

J. Eric Thompson, *A Catalog of Maya Hieroglyphs,* Oklahoma, 1962

J. Eric Thompson, *Maya Hieroglyphic Writing,* Oklahoma, 1960

George I. Sánchez, *Arithmetic in Maya,* Austin, 1961

Estudios antropológicos publicados en homenaje al doctor Manuel Gamio, México, 1956

Emilio Estrada, *Las culturas pre-clásicas del Ecuador,* Guayaquil, 1958

Wendell C. Bennett and Junius B. Bird, *Andean Culture History,* New York, 1949

Wendell C. Bennett, *Ancient Arts of the Andes,* New York, 1954

Hiram Bingham, *Lost City of the Incas,* Atheneum, N.Y., 1948

Estuardo Nuñez, "Literatura sobre Machu Picchu," *JIAS,* 1963

R. Cuneo Vidal, "Las cuatro etapas o épocas históricas en la civilización peruana," *RMIAC,* 1963

Hermann Leicht, *Pre-Inca Art and Culture,* Orion, 1960

Miguel Mujica Gallo, *The Gold of Peru,* Recklinghausen, 1959

Enzo Carli, *Pre-Conquest Goldsmiths' Work of Colombia,* London, 1959

José Pérez de Barradas, *Orfebrería prehispánica de Colombia,* 2 vols., Madrid, 1958

John V. Murra, "Cloth and Its functions in the Inca states," *AA,* 1962

Raoul D'Harcourt, *Textiles of Ancient Peru,* Seattle, 1963

John Bakeless, *Eyes of Discovery,* Dover, 1950

Peter Schrag and Van R. Halsey, *European Mind and the Discovery of a New World,* Heath

George M. Foster, *Culture and Conquest,* New York, 1960

Mariano Picón-Salas, *A Cultural History of Spanish America,* tr. by I. Leonard, Berkeley, 1963

Pedro Henríquez Ureña, *A Concise History of Latin American Culture,* tr. by G. Chase, Praeger

Eleanor L. Turnbull, ed., *Ten Centuries of Spanish Poetry*, Baltimore, 1955

Marcelino Menéndez y Pelayo, *Obras* (several editions)

Valentine de Pedro, *América en las letras españolas del siglo de oro*, Buenos Aires, 1954

Otis H. Green, *Spain and the Western Tradition*, 2 vols., Wisconsin, 1963

Carlos González Peña, *History of Mexican Literature*, tr. by G. B. Nance and F. J. Dunston, Dallas, 1943

Francisco Lange, "Los estudios musicales de la América Latina," *HLAS*, 1937

Robert Stevenson, *Spanish Music in the Age of Columbus*, The Hague, 1960

Robert Stevenson, "Music in Quito," *HAHR*, 43 (May 1963)

Robert Stevenson, "Colonial Music in Colombia," *TAm*, 1962

Robert Stevenson, *The Music of Peru*, Washington, 1960

Lota M. Spell, "Music in the Cathedral of Mexico in the XVI Century," *HAHR*, 26 (Aug. 1946)

François Cali, *The Spanish Arts of Latin America*, Viking, 1961

Diego Angulo Iñiguez, *Historia del arte hispanoamericano*, Barcelona, 1956

Manuel Romero de Terreros, *Los principales pintores de la Nueva España*, Buenos Aires, 1937

Kurt Baer, *Architecture of the California Missions*, Berkeley, 1958

Kurt Baer, *Painting and Sculpture at Mission Santa Barbara*, Washington, 1955

Joseph Armstrong Baird, Jr., *The Churches of Mexico*, Berkeley, 1962

George Kubler, *Mexican Architecture of the XVI Century*, 2 vols., Yale, 1948

George Kubler and Martín Soria, *Art and Architecture in Spain and Portugal and Their American Dominions*, Penguin, 1959

Millard Meiss, et al., *Latin American Art, Baroque Period*, Princeton, 1963

Pál Kelemen, *Baroque and Rococo in Latin America*, New York, 1951

Trent Elwood Sanford, *The Story of Architecture in Mexico*, New York, 1947

Alfred B. Schuster, *The Art of Two Worlds*, Praeger, 1959

E. W. Weismann, *Mexico in Sculpture*, Harvard, 1950

Manuel Toussaint, *La catedral y las iglesias de Puebla*, México, 1954

Emilio Harth-Terré and Alberto Márquez Abanto, "Las bellas artes en el virreinato del Perú," *RANP*, 1960, 1961

Fr. José María Vargas, "Las artes en Quito en el siglo XVI," *BANHQ*, 1962

Felipe Cossío del Pomar, *Arte del Perú colonial*, México, 1958

Enrique Marco Dorta, *La arquitectura barroca en el Perú*, Madrid, 1957

H. E. Wethey, *Colonial Architecture and Sculpture in Peru*, Harvard, 1949

José de Mesa and Teresa Gisbert, *Holguín y la pintura altoperuana del virreinato*, La Paz, 1956

Martin S. Soria, *La pintura del siglo XVI en Sudamérica*, Buenos Aires, 1956

Jean Charlot, *Mexican Art and the Academy of San Carlos*, Austin, 1962

P. J. Barth, *Franciscan Education and the Social Order in Spanish North America*, Chicago, 1945

Francisco Larroyo, "La educación," *México y la Cultura*, México, 1961

Alfonso Reyes, "Las letras patrias," *México y la Cultura*, 1961

Francisco Rosado Canton, *Historia de la instrucción pública en Yucatán,* México, 1943

Elí de Gortari, *La ciencia en la historia de México,* 1963

Javier Malagón, "Four Centuries of the Faculty of Law in Mexico," *HAHR,* 32 (Aug. 1952)

Ricardo Archila, *Historia de la medicina en Venezuela,* Caracas, 1961

César Angeles Caballero, "La erudición en el virreinato del Perú," *RANP,* 1961

Vicente T. Mendoza, *Vida y costumbres de la Universidad de México,* México, 1951

Ildefonso Leal, "La Universidad de Caracas," *RHC,* 1962

George M. Addy, "The Reforms of 1771, Salamanca Enlightenment," *HAHR,* 41 (Aug. 1961)

John Tate Lanning, *Academic Culture in the Spanish Colonies,* New York, 1940

John Tate Lanning, *The University in the Kingdom of Guatemala,* Ithaca, 1955

John Tate Lanning, *The Eighteenth Century Enlightenment in the University of San Carlos de Guatemala,* Ithaca, 1956

Irving A. Leonard, *Books of the Brave,* Harvard, 1949

Irving A. Leonard, "On the Lima Book Trade, 1591," *HAHR,* 33 (Nov. 1953)

Irving A. Leonard, *Baroque Times in Old Mexico,* Michigan, 1959

Harry Bernstein, "A Provincial Library in Colonial Mexico," *HAHR,* 26 (May 1946)

Donald G. Castanien, "The Mexican Inquisition Censors a Private Library," *HAHR,* 34 (Aug. 1954)

Dorothy Schons, *Book Censorship in New Spain,* Austin, 1949

José J. Arrom, *El teatro de hispanoamerica,* Havana, 1956

Juan Uribe-Echevarría, *Cervantes en las letras hispanoamericanas,* Santiago, 1949

José Toribio Medina, *Historia de la imprenta,* 2 vols., Santiago, 1892

Ghislan Gouraige, *Histoire de Littérature Haitiènne,* Port-au-Prince, 1960

Ernest J. Burrus, "Two Lost Mexican Books of the Sixteenth Century," *HAHR,* 37 (Aug. 1957)

Agustín Millares Carlo, ed., *Obras completas de Juan Ruiz de Alarcón,* I, México, 1957

Alfonso Méndez Plancarte, ed., *Obras completas de Sor Juana Inés de la Cruz,* III, México, 1955

Pedro Lira Urquieta, "El México de Sor Juana Inés de la Cruz," *Finis Terrae,* 1962

Xavier Tavera Alfaro, *El nacionalismo en la prensa mexicana del siglo XVIII,* México, 1963

Luis Martínez Delgado and Sergio Elías Ortiz, *El periodismo en la Nueva Granada, 1810-1811,* Bogotá, 1961

José María Vergara y Vergara, *Historia de la literatura en Nueva Granada,* 3 vols., Bogotá, 1958

Juan D. García Bacca, *Antología del pensamiento filosófico en Colombia,* Bogotá, 1955

Alexander A. M. Stols, *Historia de la imprenta en el Ecuador,* Quito, 1953

Jorge Carrera Andrade, *Galería de místicos y de insurgentes,* Quito, 1959

D. W. McPheeters, "The Distinguished Peruvian Scholar Cosme Bueno," *HAHR,* 35 (Nov. 1955)

Carlos E. Paz-Soldán, *Himnos a Hipólito Unánue,* Lima, 1955

Ricardo Donoso, *Un letrado del siglo XVIII*, Buenos Aires, 1963

Guillermo Furlong, *Historia y bibliografía de las primeras imprentas rioplatenses*, Buenos Aires, 1953

Guillermo Furlong, *Escritores coloniales rioplatenses*, 3 vols., Buenos Aires, 1952-53

Enrique de Gandia, *Historia de las ideas políticas en la Argentina*, Buenos Aires, 1960

Hector José Tanzi, "Breve historia de la imprenta en el Río de la Plata," *HBA*, 1961

Eugene M. Wait, "Mariano Moreno," *HAHR*, 45 (Aug. 1965)

Julio Jiménez Rueda, *Historia de la cultura en México*, México, 1950

Aristides A. Moll, *Aesculapius in Latin America*, Philadelphia, 1944

Flora de la real expedición botánica del Nuevo Reino de Granada, Madrid, 1954

R. A. Steele, *Flowers for the King*, Duke, 1964

Hipólito Ruiz, *Travels of Ruiz, Pavón, and Dombey in Peru and Chile*, tr. by B. E. Dahlgren, Chicago, 1940

Jorge Juan and Antoni de Ulloa, *A Voyage to South America*, tr. by John Adams, Michigan, 1964

Lesley B. Simpson, ed., *Journal of José Longinos Martínez*, San Francisco, 1961

Chapters 12, 13, 26

RELIGION AND THE CHURCH

THE NEW studies of religion are numerous in keeping with the overwhelming importance of the subject in both pre- and post-conquest America.

Mexican scholars, among them Caso, Sejourné, Flores Guerrero, and others cited in Chapters 9 and 10, have found in the Aztec gods a pantheon worthy of a place alongside the Greek gods and even the Christian saints. Whether correct or not, this attitude at least emphasizes the rigid control in the hands of the Indian priests.

The entry of Christianity brought about the well-known conflict of the religions with the general triumph of Catholicism but with vestiges of pre-conquest paganism, which anti-clericals delight to mention. The tendency has been, nevertheless, to give credit to the missionaries for their good works and to minimize the blame for their failures and erring members. This is in part due to the entry of many Catholic scholars into the field and to the more sympathetic treatment given by secular historians.

We may mention that Ricard can be consulted along with Braden, as used extensively in this book; there are studies by Borges, Barth, Phelan, Tibesar, Millé, Bayle, Jacobson, Bannon, Dunne, and many others listed below. A recent convenient work is Mörner's on the Jesuits. Poole's study of the right to make war on the Indians is an interesting examination of a vital subject.

Church structure and organization and the relation of church and state have been extensively studied by Gómez Hoyos, Gabriel Pérez, Frederick Pike, Padden, Shiels, and others. Shiels has a decided pro-clerical position; Parkes may be called anti-clerical. Pike, though Catholic like Shiels, is somewhere between the positions of Parkes and Shiels.

The Inquisition, also, has been the subject of new studies. Pinta Llorente rehabilitates the Inquisition to some extent; Toscano Moreno defends Torquemada. The Jews are subject of studies by Liebman and Wiznitzer. Richard Greenleaf demonstrates the oversimplification of the usual statement that the Indians were free from Inquisition trials. Boleslao Lewin, alarmed at the *Leyenda Dorada* building up around the Inquisition, tries to restore the traditional anti-Inquisition position. Tambs considers criticism of the Inquisition anachronistic; the studies of Liebman and Wiznitzer indicate that those who would absolve the Inquisition with light penance are somewhat tolerant of evil. These authors also have revealed— if they be right—that Jews in America were far more numerous than previously suspected.

Guillermo Raul Flores, *Historia general del arte mexicano,* México, 1962

Jacques Soustelle, *The Daily Life of the Aztecs,* Macmillan, 1961

Robert Ricard, *La conquista espiritual de México,* México, 1947

Lesley Byrd Simpson, *Many Mexicos,* Berkeley, 1952

Pedro Borges, *Métodos misionales,* Madrid, 1960

J. L. Phelan, *The Millennial Kingdom of the Franciscans in the New World,* Berkeley, 1956

P. J. Barth, *Franciscan Education and the Social Order in Spanish North America,* Chicago, 1945

Antonine Tibesar, *Franciscan Beginnings in Colonial Peru,* Washington, 1953

Andrés Millé, *Crónica de la orden franciscana,* Buenos Aires, 1961

C. Bayle, *El clero secular,* Madrid, 1950

Leon A. Ybot, *La iglesia y los eclesiáticos españoles,* Barcelona, 1954

J. U. Jacobson, *Educational Foundations of the Jesuits in XVI Century New Spain,* Berkeley, 1938

Peter Masten Dunne, *Pioneer Jesuits in Northern Mexico,* Berkeley, 1944

W. E. Shiels, *Gonzalo de Tapia,* New York, 1934

C. M. Lewis and A. J. Loomie, *The Spanish Jesuit Mission in Virginia,* North Carolina, 1953

Francisco J. Alegre, *Historia de la provincia de la compañia de Jesús de Nueva España,* Rome, 1956

Francisco Zambrano, *Diccionario bio-bibliográfico de la Compañía de Jesús en México,* México, 1961

José Gil Fortoul, "La obra de los misioneros," *BANHC,* 1961

Isidro Felix Espinosa, *Crónica de los colegios de propaganda fide de la Nueva España,* Washington, D.C., 1964

John McAndrew, *The Open Air Churches of XVI Century Mexico,* Harvard, 1965

S. Poole, "War by Fire and Blood, the Church and the Chichimecas," *TAm,* 1965

Fintan B. Warren, *Vasco de Quiroga and his Pueblo-Hospitals of Santa Fe,* Washington, 1963

Alberto Lee López, "Clero indígena en el arzobispado de Santafé en el siglo XVI," *BHAB*

F. Mateos, *Historia general de la Compañía de Jesús,* Madrid, 1944

Josefina Plá, "Las misiones jesuíticas Guaraníes," *CAM,* 1963

Magnus Mörner, *The Political and Economic Activities of the Jesuits in the La Plata Region,* tr. by A. Read, Stockholm, 1953

Magnus Mörner, *The Expulsion of the Jesuits from Latin America,* Knopf, 1965

Guillermo Kratz, *El tratado hispano-português de 1750,* Rome, 1954

Esteban Fontana, "La expulsión de los jesuitas de Mendoza," *RCHG,* 1962

Miguel Batllori, *El Abate Viscardo,* Caracas, 1953

Martin P. Harney, *The Jesuits in History,* Loyola, 1941

Ruben Ugarte Vargas, "Fray Martín de Porras, siglo XVII," *RANP,* 1961

Rafael Gómez Hoyos, *La iglesia de América en las Leyes de Indias,* Madrid, 1961

Angel Gabriel Pérez, *El patronato español en el Virreyno del Perú,* Belgium, 1937

Pedro Borges, "La Santa Sede y América en el siglo XVI," *AEAM,* 1961

Frederick Pike, ed., *Conflict between Church and State in Latin America,* Knopf, 1964

R. C. Padden, "The Ordenanza del Patronazgo, 1574," *TAm,* 1956

Juan I. Larrea, *La iglesia y el estado en el Ecuador,* Seville, 1954

Eduardo Luque Angel, *El derecho de asilo,* Bogotá, 1950

Monseñor José Vicente Castro Silva, "Del gobierno eclesiástico de Santafé de Bogotá," *BHAB,* 1963

Cristina Campo Lacasa, "Notas generales sobre la historia eclesiástica de Puerto Rico," *AEMS,* 1961

W: Eugene Shiels, *King and Church,* Chicago, 1961

Henry B. Parkes, *A History of Mexico,* Boston, 1960

Studies Presented at the Conference on the History of Religion in the New World During Colonial Times, Washington, 1958

Miguel de la Pinta Llorente, *La inquisición española,* Madrid, 1958

Cecil Roth, *Spanish Inquisition,* Norton, 1964

Alejandro Toscano Moreno, "Vindicación de Torquemada," *HM,* 1963

Seymour B. Liebman, "The Abecedario and a Check List of Mexican Inquisition Documents at the Henry E. Huntington Library," *HAHR,* 44 (Nov. 1964)

Seymour B. Liebman, *A Guide to Jewish References in the Mexican Colonial Era,* Philadelphia, 1964

Josephine Y. McClaskey, *Inquisition Papers of Mexico,* Washington, 1947

Yolanda Mariel de Ibañez, *La Inquisición en México, siglo XVI,* México, 1956

Ruben Villaseñor Bordes, *La Inquisición en la Nueva Galicia, siglo XVI,* Guadalajara, México, 1959

Seymour B. Liebman, "Hernando Alonso, the First Jew on the North-American Continent," *JIAS,* 1963

Seymour B. Liebman, "The Jews of Colonial Mexico," *HAHR,* 43 (Feb. 1963)

Seymour B. Liebman, "Research Problems in Mexican Jewish History, *American Jewish Historical Quarterly,* 1964

Arnold Wiznitzer, "Crypto-Jews in Mexico during the XVI Century," *American Jewish Historical Quarterly,* 1962

Arnold Wiznitzer, "Crypto-Jews in Mexico during the XVII Century," *American Jewish Historical Quarterly,* 1962

Richard E. Greenleaf, "The Inquisition and the Indians of New Spain," *TAm,* 1965

Boleslao Lewin, *La Inquisición en hispanoamérica,* Buenos Aires, 1962

Lewis A. Tambs, "The Inquisition in XVIII Century Mexico," *TAm,* 1965

Luis Merino, *Estudio crítico sobre las "Noticias secretas de América,"* Madrid, 1956

Ricardo Donoso, "Noticias Secretas," *RHAM,* 1957

Asunción Lavrin, "Eclesiastical Reform of Nunneries in New Spain," *TAm,* 1965

Jaime Suriá, "La primeria cofradía de Caracas," *BHC,* 1963

Francis J. Weber, "The Pious Fund of the Californias," *HAHR,* 43 (Feb. 1963)

Ricardo Lancaster-Jones, "Bienes del convento augustino de Guadalajara," *HM,* 1964

George M. Foster, "Cofradía y compadrazgo en España e Hispanoamérica," *Guatemala Indígena,* 1961

Oscar Olguín Malca, "La casa de ejercicios y hospital de mujeres de Icá," *RANP,* 1961

Chapters 14, 15, 27

COLONIAL LATIN AMERICAN GOVERNMENT

THE STUDIES cited for Chapter 3 can be used here.

On the theoretical position of the Spanish Empire see Menéndez Pidal, García Gallo, Vance, and Gómez Duran. The contact of Spaniards and Indians is best portrayed in the works of Charles Gibson on the Aztecs and Tlaxcalans. The sentimentalists will be pleased with Von Hagen on the Aztecs and Incas. For all matters relating to the administration and military of the Incas, Ake Wedin's small work is indispensable.

The history of Spain pertinent to its colonial government may be read in Parry, Maravall, Lynch, and Elliott. Frankel's examination of the *Siete Partidas,* Basadre's history of law, Zavala's and Ots y Capdequi's study of juridical institutions, and Altamira's and Malagón's works cover the legal aspects. There are numerous special studies such as those by Chamberlain and Lohman Villena on the Corregidor, Parry on the Audiencia, and Rubio Mañé, Haddick, Bobb, and others on the viceroyalty. Other studies deal with the cabildo, the sale of public office, visitadores, and the Indian cabildo.

Although this book does not deal with the Wars of Independence, a few works are mentioned which are useful to the student of the colonial period.

Humphrey's study of historiography of the wars is the place to start. Charles Griffin shows social and economic backgrounds; Madariaga sees the Spaniards with eyes that are pro-Hispanist but not pro-Hispanidad; his views on Bolivar should be compared with those of Masur. Guillén examines the conscience of Spain vis à vis the revolutionary colonies. Some of the chief biographies, studies of social conditions, and special events of the wars are listed, though the interested reader will want to rely more on Humphrey.

Ramón Menéndez Pidal, *El imperio hispánico y los cinco reinos,* Madrid, 1950

Alfonso García Gallo, *Los orígenes de la administración territorial de las Indias,* Madrid, 1944

John Thomas Vance, *The Background of Hispanic-American Law,* New York, 1942

José Gómez Durán, *El régimen jurídico-financiero colonial,* Madrid, 1946

Charles Gibson, *Tlaxcala in the XVI Century,* New Haven, 1952

Charles Gibson, *The Aztecs under Spanish Rule,* Stanford, 1964

Fray Diego Durán, *The Aztecs,* tr. by Dorris Hayden and Fernando Horcasitas, Orion, 1964

Victor Von Hagen, *Aztec, Man and Tribe,* New American Library, 1958

Charles Gibson, *The Inca Concept of Sovereignty and the Spanish Administration in Peru,* Texas, 1948

John Howland Rowe, "The Incas under Spanish Colonial Institutions," *HAHR,* 37 (May 1957)

Sally Falk Moore, *Power and Prosperity in Inca Peru,* Columbia, 1958

Burr C. Brundage, *Empire of the Inca,* Oklahoma, 1963

Ake Wedin, *El sistema decimal en el imperio incaico,* Madrid, 1965

J. H. Parry, *The Spanish Theory of Empire in the XVI Century,* Cambridge, England, 1940

J. H. Elliott, *Imperial Spain, 1469-1716,* St. Martin's, 1964

José Antonio Maravall, *Carlos V y el pensamiento político del renacimiento,* Madrid, 1960

John Lynch, *Spain under the Hapsburgs,* I, Oxford, 1964

Sir Charles Petrie, *Philip II of Spain,* Norton, 1963

Guenter Lewy, *Constitutionalism and Statecraft during the Golden Age of Spain,* Geneva, 1960

R. S. Chamberlain, "The Corregidor in Castile in the XVI Century," *HAHR,* 23 (1943)

Mauricio Guzmán, ."El faccionalismo, supervivencia medieval en América Latina," *JIAS,* 1963

Víctor Frankl, "Hernán Cortés y la tradición de las Siete Partidas," *RHAM,* 1962

Jorge Basadre, *Los fundamentos de la historia del derecho,* Lima, 1956

Silvio A. Zavala, *Las instituciones jurídicas en la conquista de América,* Madrid, 1935

José María Ots Capdequí, *Instituciones,* Barcelona, 1958

José María Ots Capdequí, *El siglo XVIII español en América,* México, 1945

Rafael Altamira, *Manual de investigación de la historia del derecho indiano,* México, 1949

Javier Malagón Barceló, *La literatura jurídica española del siglo de oro en la Nueva España,* México, 1960

Clarence H. Haring, *The Spanish Empire in America,* Harcourt Brace, 1963

José Gil Fortoul, *Obras Completas,* 6 vols., 1954-56

Guillermo Lohmann Villena, *El corregidor de indios en el Perú bajo los Austrias,* Madrid, 1957

J. H. Parry, *The Audiencia of New Galicia in the XVI Century,* Cambridge, England, 1948

J. Ignacio Rubio Mañé, *Introducción al estudio de los virreyes de Nueva España,* 2 vols., México, 1955, 1959

Cayetano Alcazar Molina, *Los virreinatos en el siglo XVIII,* Barcelona, 1945

Bernard E. Bobb, *The Viceregency of Antonio María Bucareli in New Spain, 1771-1779,* Texas, 1962

Jack Allen Haddick, *The Administration of Viceroy José de Iturrigaray,* Texas, 1954

Manuel Moreyra y Paz Soldán and Guillermo Céspedes del Castillo, eds., *Virreinato peruano, documentos,* 3 vols., 1954-

Guillermo Lohmann Villena, *El Conde de Lemos, Virrey del Perú,* Madrid, 1946

José Luis Musquiz de Miguel, *El Conde de Chinchón, Virrey del Perú,* Madrid, 1945

Vicente Rodríguez Casado and José Antonio Calderón Quijano, eds., *José Fernando de Abascal y Sousa, Memoria de Gobierno,* 2 vols., Madrid, 1944

Vicente Rodríguez Casado and Guillermo Lohmann Villena, eds., *Joaquín de la Pezuela, Memoria de Gobierno,* Sevilla, 1947

Jesús M. Covarrubias Pozo, "Tercer libro del cabildo de elección de alcaldes y regidores indios del Cuzco," *RMIA,* 1963

Daniel Valcárcel, "La familia Lavalle y el cabildo de Lima, 1790-1800," *RANP,* 1960

John Preston Moore, *The Cabildo in Peru under the Hapsburgs,* Duke, 1954

Julio Alemparte Robles, *El cabildo en Chile colonial,* Santiago, 1940

Flavio A. García, "Los cabildos abiertos del Uruguay," *RCHG,* 1960

Frederick B. Pike, "The Cabildo and Colonial Loyalty to Hapsburg Rulers," *JIAS,* 1960

Charles Gibson, "Rotation of Alcaldes in the Indian Cabildo," *HAHR,* 33 (May 1953)

J. H. Parry, *The Sale of Public Offices in the Spanish Indies under the Hapsburgs,* Berkeley, 1953

Edberto O. Acevedo, "El juicio de Residencia al corregidor Villalobos," *REHM,* 1962

Carlos Molina Argüello, *El gobernador de Nicaragua en el siglo XVI,* Seville, 1949

John J. TePaske, *The Governorship of Spanish Florida, 1700-1763,* Duke, 1964

Helen H. Tanner, *Zéspedes in East Florida,* Miami, 1963

Sergio Martínez Baeza, "Tribulaciones de un funcionario del siglo XVIII," *RCHG*, 1962

Emilio Robledo, *Bosquejo biográfico del Sr. Oidor Juan Antonio Mon y Velarde*, 2 vols., Bogotá, 1954

Ricardo Zorraquín Beçú, *La organización política argentina en el período hispánico*, Buenos Aires, 1959

Guillermo Céspedes del Castillo, *Lima y Buenos Aires*, Sevilla, 1947

John Lynch, *Spanish Colonial Administration, 1782-1810*, London, 1958

John Lynch, "Intendants and Cabildos in the Viceroyalty of La Plata," *HAHR*, 35 (Aug. 1955)

R. A. Humphreys, "The Historiography of the Spanish American Revolutions," *HAHR*, 36 (1956)

Causas y caracteres de la independencia hispanoamericana, Madrid, 1953

Charles C. Griffin, "Economic and Social Aspects of the Era of Spanish American Independence," *HAHR*, 29 (1949)

Charles C. Griffin, *Los temas sociales y económicos en la época de la Independencia*, Caracas, 1962

Charles C. Griffin, *The United States and the Disruption of the Spanish Empire*, New York, 1937

Salvador de Madariaga, *The Rise of the Spanish American Empire*, London, 1947

Salvador de Madariaga, *The Fall of the Spanish American Empire*, London, 1947

Lyle McAlister, "The Reorganization of the Army in New Spain, 1763-1767," *HAHR*, 33 (Feb. 1953)

Lyle McAlister, *The "Fuero Militar" in New Spain, 1765-1800*, Florida, 1957

Carlos M. de Bustamante, *Cuadro histórico de la revolución mexicana*, México, 1961

Lillian E. Fisher, *Champion of Reform, Manuel Abad y Quiepo*, New York, 1955

W. H. Timmons, "José María Morelos, agrarian reformer?" *HAHR*, 45 (May 1965)

Eduardo Arcila Farías, *Economía colonial de Venezuela*, México, 1946

Francisco A. Encina, *Bolívar y la independencia*, Santiago, 1957

Robert L. Gilmore, "The Imperial Crisis, Nueva Granada, in 1809," *HAHR*, 40 (Feb. 1960)

H. R. Plata, *La antigua provincia del Socorro y la Independencia*, Bogotá, 1963

Angel César Rivas, Enrique Bernardo Nuñez, and Mario Briceño Irragorri, *La colonia y la independencia*, Caracas, 1949

R. Caillet-Bois and J. R. L. Fortin, "La invasión inglesa de 1806, vista por un oficial de la marina francesa," *RCHG*, 1960

R. A. Humphreys, *Liberation in South America, 1806-1827, the Career of James Paroissien*, London, 1952

Tulio Halperín Donghi, *Tradición política española*, Buenos Aires, 1961

Boleslao Lewin, et al., *De la colonia a la emancipación, 1810-1960*, Rosario, Argentina, 1960

Carlos Ponce Sangines and Raul Alfonso García, eds., *Documentos para la historia de la revolución de 1809*, 3 vols., 1953-54

Marcello Carmagnani, "La oposición a los tributos en la segunda mitad del siglo XVIII," *RCHG*, 1960

George Kubler, *The Indian Caste of Peru, 1795-1940*, Washington, 1952

Boleslao Lewin, *La rebelión de Tupac Amaru,* Buenos Aires, 1957

Daniel Valcarcel, *Rebeliones indígenas,* Lima, 1946

Daniel Valcarcel, *La rebelión de Tupac Amaru,* México, 1947

"Para la historia del 10 de agosto de 1809," *BANQ,* 1963

Alfredo Ponce Ribadeneira, *Quito, 1809-1812,* Madrid, 1960

Julio F. Guillén, *Independencia de América y su reflejo en la conciencia española,* Madrid, 1944

W. S. Robertson, *The Life of Miranda,* 2 vols., North Carolina, 1929

H. G. Warren, "The Early Revolutionary Career of Juan Mariano Picornell," *HAHR,* 22 (1942)

John Rydjord, *Foreign Interest in the Independence of New Spain,* Duke, 1935

A. P. Whitaker, "The Commerce of Louisiana and the Floridas at the end of the XVIII Century," *HAHR,* VIII (1928)

R. F. Nichols, "Trade Relations and the Establishment of the United States Consulates in Spanish America, 1779-1809," *HAHR,* 13 (1933)

Harry Bernstein, *Origins of Inter-American Interest, 1700-1812,* Pennsylvania, 1945

Frances Armytage, *The Free Port System in the British West Indies, 1766-1822,* London, 1953

R. A. Humphreys, "Economic Aspects of the Fall of the Spanish American Empire," *RHA,* 1950

John Rydjord, "The French Revolution and Mexico," *HAHR,* 9 (1929)

W. S. Robertson, *Rise of the Spanish-American Republics as Told in the Lives of Their Liberators,* New York, 1918

W. R. Manning, ed., *Diplomatic Correspondence of the United States concerning the Independence of the Latin-American Nations,* 3 vols., New York, 1925

Sir Charles Webster, *Britain and the Independence of Latin America,* 2 vols. Oxford, 1938

Gerhard Masur, *Simón Bolívar,* Washington, 1933

Bartolomé Mitre, *Historia de San Martín,* 1907

Salvador de Madariaga, *Bolívar,* London, 1952

Gerhard Masur, "The Conference of Guayaquil," *HAHR,* 31 (1951)

Vicente Lecuna, "Bolívar and San Martín at Guayaquil," *HAHR,* 31 (1951)

Vicente Lecuna and H. A. Bierck, eds., *Selected Writings of Bolívar,* 2 vols., New York, 1951

F. L. Hoffman, "The Financing of San Martín's Expeditions," *HAHR,* 32 (1952)

V. A. Belaunde, *Bolívar and the Political Thought of the Spanish American Revolution,* Johns Hopkins, 1938

C. Parra-Pérez, *Bolívar, A Contribution to the Study of his Political Ideas,* Pittsburg, 1935

J. F. King, "The Colored Castes and American Representation in the Cortes of Cádiz," *HAHR,* 33 (1953)

H. F. Peterson, "Mariano Moreno: the Making of an Insurgent," *HAHR,* 14 (1934)

Benjamin Keen, *David Curtis DeForest and the Revolution of Buenos Aires,* Yale, 1947

T. B. Davis, *Carlos de Alvear, Man of Revolution,* Duke, 1955

P. A. Martin, "Artigas, the Founder of Uruguayan Nationality," *HAHR,* 19 (1939)

J. Street, "Lord Strangford and Río de la Plata, 1808-1815," *HAHR,* 33 (1953)

Chapter 16

AGRICULTURE AND EXPANSION
IN SOUTH AMERICA

THE FURTHER development of the colonies after the 16th century, the settlement of new areas, the growth of agriculture, and the raising of livestock can all be seen in numerous new publications.

The works listed below are grouped roughly under the headings: (1) Ecuador (2) Peru and Bolivia (3) Chile (4) Río de la Plata (Paraguay and La Plata in general) (5) Venezuela and Colombia.

Ecuador

R. Andrade, *Historia del Ecuador,* 7 vols., Guayaquil, 1937

González Suárez, *Historia general de la República del Ecuador,* 7 vols, Quito, 1890-1903

A. Pareja Díaz Canseco, *Historia del Ecuador,* 2 vols., Quito, 1958

Jorge Pérez Concha, *Ensayo histórico-crítico de las relaciones diplomáticas del Ecuador,* 2 vols., Quito, 1958

O. E. Reyes, *Historia de la República,* Quito, 1931

Homero Viteri Lafronte, "Gonzalo Díaz de Pinedo, fundador, escribano, alcalde y gobernador de Quito," *BAHQ,* 1962

Peru and Bolivia

Jorge Basadre, *Historia de la República del Perú,* 5th ed., 7 vols., Lima, 1961-62

Fray Diego de Córdova Salinas, *Crónica franciscana del Perú,* Washington, 1957

Thomas E. Ford, *Man and Land in Peru,* Florida, 1955

Boleslao Lewin, *Descripción del virreinato del Perú, Crónica inédita de comienzos del siglo XVII,* Rosario, Argentina, 1958

Héctor Martínez, "Evolución de la propiedad territorial en el Perú," *JIAS,* 1963

J. Edgardo Rivera Martínez, "El Perú en la literatura de viaje europea de los siglos XVI XVII, XVIII," *Letras,* Lima, 1960

G. Pons Muzzo, *Historia del Perú,* 5 vols., Lima, 1950

R. Vargas Ugarte, *Historia del Perú,* 3 vols., 1949-56

C. Wiesse, *Historia del Perú,* 4 vols., Lima, 1930-35

P. Díaz Machicao, *Historia de Bolivia,* 3 vols., La Paz, 1955

E. Finot, *Nueva historia de Bolivia, Interpretación sociológica,* Buenos Aires, 1946

Chile

Oscar Bermúdez, *Historia del salitre desde sus orígenes hasta la Guerra del Pacífico,* Santiago, 1963

Jean Borde and Mario Góngora, *Evolución de la propiedad rural en el Valle del Puangue,* 2 vols., Santiago, 1956

Leopoldo Castedo, *Resumen de la historia de Chile de Francisco A. Encina,* 3 vols., Santiago, 1954-55

F. A. Encina, *Historia de Chile desde la prehistoria hasta 1891,* 20 vols., Santiago, 1941-1952

Censo de 1813 levantada por Don Juan Egaña, Santiago, 1953

Juan Luis Espejo, *La provincia del Cuyo del Reino de Chile,* 2 vols., Santiago, 1954

J. Eyzaguirre, *Fisonomía histórica de Chile,* México, 1948

V. F. Frías, *Historia de Chile,* 4 vols., Santiago, 1947-49

L. Galdames, *Historia de Chile,* Santiago, 1952

Mario Góngora, "Notas sobre la encomienda chilena tardía," *BACH,* 1959

Alvaro Jara, *Guerre et société au Chile, Essai de sociologie coloniale,* Paris, 1961

Alvaro Jara, "Fuentes para la historia del trabajo en el reino de Chile," *BACH,* 1959

Ricardo Marín Molina, *Condiciones económico-sociales del campesino chileno,* Santiago, 1947

Pedro S. Martínez, "Reconocimiento de nuevas rutas entre el Virreinato del Plata y Chile," *AHM,* 1961

Pedro S. Martínez, "Las communicaciones entre el Virreinato del Rio de la Plata y Chile," *BACH,* 1963

José Armando de Ramón, "Gestación del descubrimiento de Chile central," *BACH,* 1959

Agnes Stapff, "La renta del tabaco en el Chile," *AEMS,* 1961

José Toribio Medina, *Colección de documentos inéditos para la historia de Chile,* 5 vols., new ed., Santiago de Chile, 1956-61

Río de la Plata

Efraím Cardozo, *El Paraguay colonial,* Buenos Aires, 1959

J. C. Chaves, *Compendio de historia paraguaya,* Buenos Aires, 1958

J. Prieto, *Paraguay, la provincia gigante de las Indias,* Buenos Aires, 1951

Rubin Bareiro Saguier, "Guaraní, Proud Mark of the Paraguayan," *TAm,* 1964

E. R. Service, *Spanish-Guaraní Relations in Early Colonial Paraguay,* Michigan, 1954

E. R. Service, "The Encomienda in Paraguay," *HAHR,* 31 (May 1951)

Harris Gaylord Warren, *Paraguay,* Oklahoma, 1949

Marcel Bataillon, *Introducción a Concolorcorvo,* San Marcos, 1960

Ricardo Caillet-Bois, ed., *Documentos para la historia argentina, 1913-1955*

Enrique de Gandía, *Buenos Aires colonial,* 2 vols., Buenos Aires, 1957

Horacio C. E. Giberti, *Historia económica de la ganadería argentina,* 2d. ed., Buenos Aires, 1961

Luis Roque Gondra, *Historia económica de la República Argentina,* Buenos Aires, 1943

Alberto Gerchunoff, *The Jewish Gauchos of the Pampas,* New York, 1955

Yvette Billod, tr., *Itinéraire de Buenos Aires a Lima,* Paris, 1961

Gustavo Gabriel Levene, *La Argentina se hizo así,* Buenos Aires, 1960

Gustavo Gabriel Levene, *Historia ilustrada de la Argentina,* Buenos Aires, 1963

V. F. López, *Historia de la República Argentina,* Buenos Aires, 1952

Ricardo Rodríguez Molas, "El gaucho rioplatense," *JIAS,* 1963

Ralph A. Molina, "Una historia inédita 'de los primeros ochenta años de Buenos Aires," *RHAM*, 1961

R. A. Molina, "La expulsión de los portugueses de Santa Fé," *HBA*, 1963

Edmundo M. Narancio, "Los cabildos abiertos en Montevideo," *RIHDBA*, 1963

E. Palacio, *Historia de la Argentina*, Buenos Aires, 1954

Mario Rodríguez, "The Genesis of Economic Attitudes in the Rio de la Plata," *HAHR*, 36 (May 1956)

Pedro Santos Martínez, "Régimen jurídico y económico de las aguas en Mendoza," *RIHDBA*, 1961

Pedro Santos Martínez, "Mendoza de la provincia de Cuyo durante el virreinato," *AEMS*, 1961

James R. Scobie, *Argentina, A City and a Nation*, New York, 1964

V. D. Sierra, *Historia de la Argentina*, 3 vols., Buenos Aires, 1956-57

Alfred J. Tapson, "Indian Warfare on the Pampa during the Colonial Period," *HAHR*, 42 (Feb. 1962)

Carl C. Taylor, *Rural Life in Argentina*, Baton Rouge, 1948

E. Vera y González, *Historia de la República Argentina*, Buenos Aires, 1944

Enrique Williams Alzaga, *La pampa en la novela argentina*, Buenos Aires, 1955

M. Schurmann Pacheco and M. L. Coolighan Sanguinetti, *Historia del Uruguay*, 2d. ed., Montevideo, 1957

Venezuela and Colombia

Eduardo Arcila Farías, *Economía colonial de Venezuela*, México, 1946

Alfredo Boulton, et al., "¿Fué Caracas fundada en 1566?" *BHC*, 1963

Juan Friede, "Fray Pedro de Aguado con ocasión del 450 aniversario de su nacimiento," *HAHR*, 44 (1964)

Enrique Ortega Ricaurte and Ana Rueda Briceño, *Historia documental del Chocó*, Bogotá, 1954

De G. Morón, *Los orígenes históricos de Vevezuela, 1500-1550*, Caracas, 1963

José M. Pérez de Ayala, *Baltasar Jaime Martínez Compañon, Prelado español de Colombia y el Perú*, Bogotá, 1955

J. M. Siso Martínez, *Historia de Venezuela*, México, 1954

Uribe C. Andrés, *Brown Gold, The Amazing Story of Coffee*, New York, 1954

Fray P. Aguado, *Recopilación historial*, ed. by Juan Friede, 4 vols., Bogotá, 1957

Orlando Fals Borda, "Odyssey of a XVI-Century Document, Fray Pedro de Aguado's *Recopilación Historial*," *HAHR*, 35 (May 1955)

Academia colombiana de historia, *Curso superior de historia de Colombia*, 6 vols., 1950-51

Chapter 17

AGRICULTURE AND EXPANSION IN NORTH AMERICA

THE TERRITORIES grouped in New Spain, around the Gulf of Mexico and in Mexico itself, and in the Caribbean have been the subject of new studies and interpretations. Historians of the West and Southwest United States have written numerous fundamental works. Missionary activities have been viewed as frontier movements and missionaries as pioneers. Their contribution to colonial life is in general appreciated more than in the past, as noted in Chapters 12-13. The land and its importance, the live stock industry, and mining—all are better understood in light of the new works.

The readings listed below have been grouped in general under the headings: (1) Central America (2) Mexico: General Works (3) Mexico: Specialized Works (4) Mississippi and Florida (5) the Cattle Industry (6) the Caribbean.

Central America

Ernesto Alvarado García, *Historia de Centroamérica,* Tegucigalpa, 1949
J. Milla, *Historia de la América Central,* Guatemala, 1937
F. D. Parker, *The Central American Republics,* London, 1964
R. H. Valle, *Centroamérica en la historia,* México, 1951
R. Fernández Guardia, *Cartilla histórica de Costa Rica,* San José, 1946
C. Monje Alfaro, *Historia de Costa Rica,* San José, 1947
G. Sandner, *La colonización de Costa Rica,* San José, 1962-64
Amy E. Jensen, *Guatemala, A Historical Survey,* New York, 1955
Troy S. Floyd, "The Guatemalan Merchants, the Government and the Provincianos," *HAHR,* 41 (Feb. 1961)
R. E. Durón, *Bosquejo histórico de Honduras,* San Pablo de Sula, 1927
A. R. Vallejo, *Compendio de historia social y política de Honduras,* Tegucigalpa, 1926
P. Gavida, *Historia moderna de El Salvador,* 1958

Mexico: General Works

José Bravo Ugarte, *Compendio de historia de México,* México, 1955
Vicente Riva Palacio, *Resumen integral de México,* 2 vols., México, 1951
J. L. Schlarman, *México, tierra de volcanes,* México, 1953
A. Toro, *Compendio de historia de México,* 3 vols., México, 1933
Bravo Ugarte, *Historia de México,* 3 vols., México, 1941-44, 1959
Silvio Zavala, *Aproximación de la historia de México,* México, 1953

Mexico: Specialized Works

J. F. Bannon, *Bolton and the Spanish Borderlands,* Oklahoma, 1964
J. F. Bannon, *The Mission Frontier in Sonora,* New York, 1955
H. E. Bolton, *Coronado on the Turquoise Trail,* New Mexico, 1949
Woodrow Borah, *New Spain's Century of Depression,* Berkeley, 1951
Woodrow Borah, "Un gobierno provincial de frontera en San Luis Potosí," *HM'* 1964
H. J. Bruman, "Early Coconut Culture in Western Mexico," *HAHR,* 25 (1945)
E. J. Burrus, "Francesco Maria Piccolo, Pioneer of Lower California," *HAHR,* 35 (Feb. 1955)

Carlos E. Castañeda, *Our Catholic Heritage in Texas,* 6 vols., Texas, 1938-50

Robert G. Cleland, *From Wilderness to Empire, A History of California,* Knopf, 1959

H. J. Cline, "Civil Congregations of the Indians in New Spain," *HAHR,* 29 (1949)

Eleanor B. Adams and Fray Angélico Chávez, *The Missions of New Mexico, 1776,* New Mexico, 1955

W. Donahue, "The Missionary Activities of Fray Antonio Margil de Jesús in Texas, 1716-1722," *TAm,* 1955

R. A. Donkin, "The Contribution of the Franciscan Missions to the Settlement of Alta California," *RHAM,* 1961

Omer Engelbert, *The Last of the Conquistadores, Junipero Serra,* Harcourt Brace, 1956

Rosa Feijóo, "El tumulto de 1624," *HM,* 1964

Jack D. Forbes, *Apache, Navaho, and Spaniard,* Oklahoma, 1960

José L. Franco, ed., *Documentos para la historia de México,* Havana, 1961

Luis Navarro García, "La Gobernación y Comandancia General de las provincias internas del norte de Nueva España," *RIHDBA,* 1963

Maynard J. Geiger, *Palou's Life of Fray Junípero Serra,* Washington, 1955

Maynard J. Geiger, *The Life and Times of Fray Junípero Serra, O. F. M.,* Washington, 1959

G. P. Hammond, "Oñate's Effort to Gain Political Autonomy for New Mexico," *HAHR,* 32 (1952)

G. P. Hammond and Agapito Rey, eds., *Don Juan de Oñate,* 2 vols., New Mexico, 1953

G. P. Hammond and Agapito Rey, eds., *Narratives of the Coronado Expedition,* New Mexico, 1940

Maurice G. Holmes, *From New Spain by Sea to the Californias,* Glendale, 1963

Nicolás de Lafora, *Description of the Frontier of New Spain,* tr. by Lawrence Kinnaird, Berkeley, 1958

Ernesto Lemoine Villicaña, "Proyecto para colonización y evangelización de Tamaulipas en 1616," *BANM,* 1961

Peveril Meigs, ed., *The Dominican Mission Frontier of Lower California,* Berkeley, 1935

José Miranda, "Fisonomía del noreste de México en la época colonial," *CAM,* 1962

J. S. Cummins, ed., *The Travels and Controversies of Friar Domingo de Navarrete, 1618-1686,* Hakluyt, 1965

Ignaz Pfefferkorn, *A Description of Sonora,* tr. by Theodore F. Treutlein, 2 vols., New Mexico, 1949

Philip Wayne Powell, *Soldiers, Indians and Silver,* Berkeley, 1952

Carl Sauer, *Colima of New Spain in the XVI Century,* Berkeley, 1948

France V. Scholes, *Church and State in New Mexico, 1610-1650,* New Mexico, 1937

France V. Scholes, *Troublous Times in New Mexico, 1650-1670,* New Mexico, 1942

Michael F. Thurman, "The Establishment of the Department of San Blas and Its Initial Naval Fleet," *HAHR,* 43 (Feb. 1963)

Cabeza de Vaca, *Adventures in the Unknown Interior of America,* tr. by Cyclone Covey, Collier, 1961

María del Carmen Velásquez, *Colotlán, Doble frontera contra los bárbaros,* México, 1961

Ernesto Lemoine Villicaña, "Documentos para la historia de la ciudad de Valladolid, hoy Morelia," *BANM,* 1962

Ernesto Lemoine Villicaña, "La relación de la Guacana, Michoacán de Baltasar Dorantes Carranza, 1605," *BANM,* 1962

Fintan Warren, "Jesuit Historians of Sinaloa-Sonora," *TAm,* 1962

Robert S. Weddle, *The San Sabá Mission,* Texas, 1964

G. P. Winship, *The Coronado Expedition, 1540-1542, Washington,* 1896

F. B. Warren, "The Construction of Santa Fé de México," *TAm,* 1964

Mississippi and Florida

J. A. Robertson, tr., The Gentleman of Elvas' *"True Relation of the Hardships Suffered by Governor Fernando de Soto of Florida,"* 2 vols., Florida, 1932-33

Charles W. Arnade, *Florida on Trial,* Florida, 1959

Jack D. L. Holmes, "Some Economic Problems of Spanish Governors of Louisiana," *HAHR,* 42 (Nov. 1962)

Henry Folmer, *Franco-Spanish Rivalry in North America, 1524-1763,* Glendale, 1953

Lawrence Kinnaird, ed., *Spain in the Mississippi Valley,* 2 vols., Washington, 1949

Gonzalo Solís de Merás, *Pedro Menéndez de Avilés,* tr. by J. T. Connor, Florida, 1964

Charmion Shelby, "The Effect of the Spanish Reoccupation of Eastern Texas upon French Policy in Louisiana," *HAHR,* 24 (Nov. 1944)

C. M. Lewis and A. J. Loomie, *Spanish Jesuit Missions in Virginia, 1571-1572,* North Carolina

H. H. Tanner, *Zéspedes in East Florida,* Florida, 1963

John J. Tepaske, *The Governorship of Spanish Florida, 1700-1763,* North Carolina, 1964

The Cattle Industry

Charles Arnade, "Cattle Raising in Spanish Florida," *AH,* 1961

Donald Brand, "The Early History of the Range Cattle Industry in Northern Mexico," *AH,* 1961

François Chevalier, *Land and Society in Colonial Mexico,* Berkeley, 1963

William H. Dusenberry, *The Mexican Mesta,* Illinois, 1963

Odie B. Faulk, "Ranching in Spanish Texas," *HAHR,* 45 (May 1965)

Richard J. Morissey, "The Northward Expansion of Cattle Ranching in New Spain, 1550-1600," *AH,* 1951

Manuel Romero de Terreros, *Antiguas haciendas de México,* México, 1956

Nathan L. Whetten, *Rural Mexico,* Chicago, 1948

The Caribbean

G. Castellano, *Panorama histórico,* Havana, 1934

Ramiro Guerra y Sánchez, *Sugar and Society in the Caribbean,* Yale, 1964

R. Guerra y Sánchez, *Manual de historia de Cuba,* Havana, 1938

P. J. Guiteras, *Historia de la isla de Cuba,* 3 vols., Havana, 1927-28

F. Portuondo, *Curso de historia de Cuba,* Havana, 1945

F. Portuondo, *Historia de la nación cubana,* 10 vols., Havana, 1952

R. Marrero Aristy, *La República Dominicana,* 2 vols., Ciudad Trujillo, 1955

G. A. Mejía, *Historia de Santo Domingo,* 7 vols., Ciudad Trujillo, 1948-54

A. del Monte y Tejada, *Historia de Santo Domingo,* 3 vols., Ciudad Trujillo, 1952-53

D. Bellegarde, *Histoire du peuple haitien,* Puerto Principe, 1953

R. Pattee, *Haiti,* Madrid, 1956

BOOK III

COLONIAL BRAZIL

Bibliographical Reviews

Anais das bibliotecas e arquivos de Portugal, Coimbra, 1915

Bibliografia Brasileira, Rio de Janeiro, 1940

Bibliografia de História do Brasil, Rio de Janeiro, 1949

Boletim Bibliográfico, São Paulo, 1943

Boletim Bibliográfico Brasileiro, Rio de Janeiro, 1952

Boletim de Bibliografia, Biblioteca Nactional de Lisboa, 1935

Boletim Internacional de Bibliografia Luso-Brasileira, Fundação Gulbenkian, Lisboa, 1960

Brasilia, Coimbra, 1942

Luso-Brazilian Review, University of Wisconsin, 1964

Revista de História, São Paulo, 1950

Revista do Instituto Arqueológico Histórico e Geográfico Pernambucano, Recife, 1863

Revista do Livro, Rio de Janeiro, 1956

Revista Portuguesa de História, Coimbra, 1941

Studia, Revista Semestral, Lisboa, 1958

Bibliographies

Antonio Anselmo, *Bibliografia das bibliografias portuguezas,* Lisbon, 1923

William C. Atkinson, *British Contributions to Portuguese and Brazilian Studies,* London, 1945

Herbert Baldus, *Bibliografia crítica da etnologia brasileira,* São Paulo, 1954

Diogo Barbosa Machado, *Biblioteca Lusitánia,* 4 vols., 2d ed., Lisbon, 1930-36

Joaquim Bensaude, *Luciano Pereira da Silva e a sua obra,* Coimbra, 1927

Manuel Bernardes Branco, *Portugal e os estrangeiros,* 5 vols., 1879, 1893-95

Manoel dos Santos, *Bibliografia geral,* 2 vols., Lisbon, 1914-25

George C. A. Boehrer, "Brazilian Historical Bibliography, *RIB,* 2ª XI, no. 2

Rubens Borba de Moraes, *Bibliographia Brasiliana,* 2 vols., Rio de Janeiro, 1958-59

Brazil: *Official Standard Names*, U. S. Office of Geography, Washington, 1963

E. Bradford Burns, "A Working Bibliography for the Study of Brazilian History," *TAm*, 1965

    Excellent. See works in Burns not listed in my bibliography.

Alice P. Canabrava, *Manual de Estudos Brasileiros*, Rio de Janeiro, 1949

José do Canto, *Colleção Camoneana*, Lisbon, 1895

Carr L. Donald, "The New Series on Brazilian Municípios," *HAHR*, 38 (Nov. 1958)

E. de Castro Rebello, *Capistrano de Abreu e a Síntese Histórica*, Rio de Janeiro, 1956

Catálogo das Edições da Agência Geral do Ultramar, Lisbon

Catálogo dos Manuscritos Ultramarinos da Biblioteca Pública Municipal do Porto, Lisbon, 1938

Gilbert Chase, *A Guide to Latin American Music*, Washington, 1945

Proceedings of the International Colloquium on Luso-Brazilian Studies, Vanderbilt, 1953

III Colóquio Internacional de Estudos Luso-Brasileiros, Lisbon, 1959

Congresso Internacional de História dos Descobrimentos, Lisbon, 1961

Armando Cortesão, *Cartografia e Cartógrafos portugueses*, 2 vols., Lisbon, 1935

Bernardo Costa Coutinho, *Bibliographie franco-portugaise*, Porto, 1939

Exposição do Livro Brasileiro Contemporâneo, Lisbon, 1957

Luisa Fonseca, "O Maranhão," *MP*, XI

Martinho da Fonseca, *Elementos Bibliográficos para a História das Guerras chamadas da Restauração*, Coimbra, 1927

Martinho da Fonseca, *Lista de alguns catálogos de bibliothecas públicas e particulares*, Lisbon, 1913

Frederick W. Ganzert, "Varnhagen and his História Geral do Brasil," *HAHR*, 17 (May 1937)

Grande Enciclopédia Portuguêsa e Brasileira, Lisbon, 1935

William B. Greenlee, "A Descriptive Bibliography of the History of Portugal," *HAHR*, 20 (Aug. 1940)

Guia das bibliotecas brasileiras, Rio de Janeiro, 1955

Ruth E. Holmes, *Bibliographical and Historical Description of the Rarest Books in the Oliveira Lima Collection at the Catholic University of America*, Washington, 1927

H. L. Johnson, "The Brazilian Mirror: Some Brazilian Writings in English Translation," *TAm*, 21 (1965)

C. K. Jones, "Hispanic American Bibliographies," *HAHR*, VI (Feb. 1926)

Américo Jacobina Lacombe, *Brasil: Período Nacional*, México, 1956

Henrique de Campos Ferreira Lima, "Documentos manuscritos no Arquivo Histórico Militar," *MP*, XI

José Carlos de Macedo Soares, "Fontes da história da igreja católica no Brasil," *RIHGB*, 1953

Alexander Marchant, *Boundaries of the Latin American Republics*, Washington, 1944

José Antônio Gonçalves de Melo, *Estudos Pernambucanos*, Recife, 1960

Francisco Morais, *Catálogo dos manuscritos da Biblioteca Geral da Universidade de Coimbra relativos ao Brasil*, Coimbra, 1941

Richard M. Morse, "Some Themes of Brazilian History," *SAQ*, 1962

Alvaro Magalhães, ed., *Dicionário enciclopédico brasileiro ilustrado*, 2 vols., São Paulo, 1957

Memórias da Academia Real das Sciências de Lisboa, 20 vols., Lisbon, 1797-1939

Memórias de Litteratura Portugueza, 8 vols., Lisbon, 1792-1856

"Material Relating to Brazil in the National Archives, Washington," *HAHR*, 22 (1942)

José Oliam, *Historiografia Mineira*, Belo Horizonte, 1959

Manoel de Oliveira Lima, "Portuguese Manuscripts in the Ibero-American Library at the Catholic University," *HAHR*, VIII (May 1928)

P. Lee Phillips, *A List of Books, Magazine Articles, and Maps Relating to Brazil, 1800-1900*, Washington, 1901

George Raeders, *Bibliographie Franco-Brésilienne, 1551-1957*, Rio de Janeiro 1960,

Virginia Rau and Maria Fernanda Gomes da Silva, *Os manuscritos do Arquivo da Casa de Cadaval Respeitantes ao Brasil*, 2 vols., Coimbra, 1958

António Simões dos Reis, *Bibliografia das bibliografias brasileiras*, Rio de Janeiro, 1942

Revista do Livro, 5 vols., Rio de Janeiro, 1956

José Honório Rodrigues, *Brasil: Período Colonial*, México, 1953

José Honório Rodrigues, *A Pesquisa Histórica no Brasil*, Rio de Janeiro, 1952

José Honório Rodrigues, "Affonso Taunay e o revisionismo histórico," *RHAM*, 1961

José Honório Rodrigues, *Historiografía del Brasil, Siglo XVI*, México, 1957

José Honório Rodrigues, *Historiografía del Brasil, Siglo XVII*, México, 1963

José Honório Rodrigues, *Historiografia e bibliografia do dominio holandês no Brasil*, Rio, 1949

José Honório Rodrigues, *Teoria da História do Brasil*, 2 vols., São Paulo, 1957

José Honório Rodrigues, ed., *Correspondência Capistrano de Abreu*, 3 vols., 1954-56

José Honório Rodrigues, "Octávio Tarquinio de Sousa," *HAHR*, 40 (Aug 1960)

José Honório Rodrigues, "Affonso d'Escragnolle Taunay," *HAHR*, 38 (Aug 1958)

José Honório Rodrigues, *As fontes da história do Brasil na Europa*, Rio de Janeiro, 1950

José Carlos Rodrigues, *Biblioteca Brasilense*, Rio de Janeiro, 1907

James Alexander Robertson, "The Oliveira Lima Collection," *HAHR*, III (Feb. 1920)

Antônio Simões dos Reis, *Bibliografia das bibliografias brasileiras*, Rio de Janeiro, 1942

Robert C. Smith and E. Wilder, *Guide to the Art of Latin America*, Washington, 1943

Nelson Werneck Sodré, *O que se deve ler para conhecer o Brasil*, Rio de Janeiro, 1960

Stanley Stein, "The Historiography of Brazil, 1808-1889," *HAHR*, 1960

Visconde de Taunày, *Escriptores Coloniaes*, São Paulo, 1925

Hélio Vianna, *Capistrano de Abreu, Ensaio biobibliográfico*, Rio de Janeiro, 1955

Hélio Vianna, "Atuais tendências da historiografia brasileira," *RIB*, 2ª XII, 1963

Chapter 28

BRAZIL IN FORMATION

THE STUDY of Brazil has been facilitated by the publication of a number of new histories and the reissue of several older works. Some of the principal studies are listed below.

While Brazilian history offers no controversial subjects as heated as the Las Casas debates, the questions of a pre-Cabral discovery, of accident or intention in his discovery, taken with the Vespucci mystery, provide interesting material. Though all have been added as a part of the discussion of discovery in Chapter 3, a few other points may be mentioned. Jaime Cortesão, always the leader among pre-Cabral advocates, also has something to say on Cabral. Fontoura da Costa, Duarte Leite, Greenlee, Marcondes de Souza, and Nowell discuss the discovery, Nowell tending to accept pre-Cabral claims.

The improbability of the success of a policy of secrecy is demonstrated in the articles by Skelton and others cited in Chapter 3.

The first years of the colony are covered by Almeida Prado, some of whose works are cited within the book and some here, and by Greenlee. Marchant's discussion of the feudal and capitalistic elements found in the original Captaincies is a good summary of the literature. Other studies of the early period and the history of the early Jesuits are found in works by Nowell, Butler, Espinosa, Jacobson, Dominian, and others.

Jaime Cortesão and Pedro Calmón, *Brasil,* Barcelona, 1956

Pedro Calmón, *História do Brasil,* 7 vols., Rio de Janeiro, 1959

Celso Furtado, *The Economic Growth of Brazil,* Berkeley, 1963

Alexandre Herculano, *História de Portugal,* 8 vols., [1908-14?]

Américo Jacobina Lacombe, *Brazil,* Rio de Janeiro, 1954

Caio Prado Júnior, *História econômica do Brasil,* São Paulo, 1962

Sérgio Buarque de Holanda, *História Geral da civilização brasileira,* 4 vols., São Paulo, 1960-62

Robert C. Simonsen, *História econômica do Brasil,* 4th ed., São Paulo, 1962

João Ribeiro, *História do Brasil,* São Paulo, 1960

Luiz Augusto Rebello da Silva, *História de Portugal, XVII e XVIII,* 5 vols., Lisbon, 1940-41

Nelson Werneck Sodré, *Formação histórica do Brasil,* Rio de Janeiro, 1962

Nelson Werneck Sodré, *Raízes históricas do nacionalismo brasileiro,* Rio de Janeiro, 1960

Francisco Adolfo de Varnhagen, *História geral do Brasil,* 5 vols., São Paulo, 1927-36

Hélio Vianna, *Estudos de história colonial,* São Paulo, 1948

Hélio Vianna, *História diplomática do Brasil,* Rio de Janeiro, 1958

Hélio Vianna, *História do Brasil,* 2 vols., 2d ed., São Paulo, 1963

Sérgio Buarque de Holanda, *Raíces del Brazil,* México, 1955

Sérgio Buarque de Holanda, *Visão do Paraíso,* Rio de Janeiro, 1959

Jaime Cortesão, *Cabral,* Rio de Janeiro, 1944

Guido Po, "Contributo delle Marinerie italiane alle organizzazione della Marina portoghese," *MP,* III

Guido Po, "Partecipazione della marina genovese alla cooperazione data del Portogallo per la difesa Spagna cristiana contro i mussulmani," *MP,* III

A. Fontoura da Costa, *La Découverte du Brésil en 1500,* Lisbon, 1938

Duarte Leite, *Descobridores do Brasil,* São Paulo, 1946

W. B. Greenlee, ed., *The Voyage of Pedro Alvares Cabral to Brazil and India,* Hakluyt, 1938

Thomaz Oscar Marcondes de Souza, *A expedição de 1501-1502 e Amerigo Vespucci,* São Paulo, 1950

Charles E. Nowell, "The Discovery of Brazil," *HAHR,* 16 (Aug. 1936)

André L'Hoist, "L'origine du nom Brésil," *MP,* III

R. A. Skelton, "English Knowledge of the Portuguese Discoveries in the XV Century," *CIHD,* 1961

Alexander Marchant, "Colonial Brazil as a Way Station for the Portuguese India Fleets," *GR,* 1941

J. F. de Almeida Prado, *A Bahia e as Capitanias do Centro do Brasil,* São Paulo, 1948

W. B. Greenlee, "The First Half-Century of Brazilian History," *MA,* 1943

Henry H. Hart, *Luis de Camoens and the Epic of the Lusíadas,* Oklahoma, 1962

Alexander Marchant, "Feudal and Capitalistic Elements in the Portuguese Settlement of Brazil," *HAHR,* 22 (Aug. 1942)

Archivo do Estado de São Paulo, *Documentos interessantes para a história e os costumes de São Paulo,* 43 vols., São Paulo, 1899-1953

Julio de Mesquita Filho, ed., *Ensaios Paulistas, O Estado de São Paulo,* São Paulo, 1958

Aureliano Leite, *Subsídios para a história da civilização paulista,* São Paulo, 1954

Richard M. Morse, *From Community to Metropolis, São Paulo,* Florida, 1958

Affonso E. Taunay, *História da cidade de São Paulo,* São Paulo, 1954

Vitorino Nemesio, *O Campo de São Paulo,* Lisbon, 1954

Washington Luis Pereira de Souza, *Capitania de São Vicente,* São Paulo, 1956

J. P. Leite Cordeiro, *Braz Cubas e a Capitania de São Vicente,* São Paulo, 1951

C. E. Nowell, "The French in the XVI Century Brazil, *TAm,* 1949

Ruth L. Butler, "Thomé de Sousa, First Governor-General of Brazil," *MA,* 1942

J. M. Espinosa, "José de Anchieta," *MA,* 1943

J. M. Espinosa, "Gouveia, Jesuit Lawgiver," *MA,* 1942

J. M. Espinosa, "Fernão Cardim, Jesuit Humanist," *MA,* 1942

J. M. Espinosa, "Luiz da Grã, Mission Builder and Educator," *MA,* 1942

J. V. Jacobsen, "Jesuit Founders in Portugal and Brazil," *MA,* 1942

J. V. Jacobsen, "Nóbrega of Brazil," *MA,* 1942

Serafim Leite, *Breve itinerário para uma biografia de . . . Nóbrega,* Rio de Janeiro, 1955
Helen G. Dominian, *Apostle of Brazil,* 1958
Carlos Studart Filho, "Resistência dos indígenas a conquista," *RIC,* 1961

Chapter 29

FOREIGN RIVALRY AND PORTUGUESE EXPANSION

FOR ALMOST a cenutry and a half after discovery it was not clear whether Brazil would remain Portuguese or fall to others; and it was not known how far Brazil would extend beyond the Line of Demarcation. The efforts of the English, French, and finally the Dutch to take parts—or all—of Brazil were almost continuous.

The Governors-General after 1549 were busy with the foreign problem, as Ruth Butler shows. Pegano's brief study of Brazil in Spanish-occupation times is a subject demanding much more attention; our principal sources of information are still the general histories with insufficient discussions.

The Dutch occupation has been given much attention by the industrious Charles R. Boxer. His writings make the political and religious implications of the period much clearer than before and reveal the worldwide scope of Portugal's problems. Father Vieira has also been studied by Boxer, as well as by Batailllon and Azevedo. José Honório Rodrigues's bibliography of the Dutch period is, of course, an indispensable reference.

The multiple directions of Brazil's inland expansion have been extensively studied. There is a new edition of Carvajal's account of Orellana's discovery. Luciano de Castro and Ferreira Reis have studied the Amazon and Maranhão, the latter also the subject of works by Carlos Studart. Kiemen has revealed more of the Amazon and of Portugal's Indian policies.

From Bahia and São Paulo the *bandeiras* moved inland. Richard Morse has just published a translation of some of the accounts of this movement. Vianna Moog compares the *Bandeirantes* with the pioneers. Read Hernani Cidade for a Portuguese view. The monumental work of Taunay is the most important single printed source of information; he later added to it several other studies. Manoel Cardozo and Holanda have excellent studies, which are less romantic perhaps than Taunay's.

Spanish-Portuguese rivalry in the regions drained by the Plata has been studied by Canabrava, Hanke, Hutchins, and Lafuente Machain, among others. The Spanish viewpoint is found in Ricardo Levene's monumental history. Of the numerous other works listed, we can call attention only to those of Mörner, Arthur Ferreira, Carlos Teschauer, Dauril Alden, Mario Rodríguez, and Jaime Cortesão. On the origins of large landholdings in the south of Brazil see Dante de Laytano. Buarque de Holanda gives his attention to what he calls *Monções,* the westward movements which depended on the rivers and the rains in order to penetrate the interior.

R. L. Butler, "Duarte da Costa, Second Governor-General of Brazil," *MA,* 1943

R. L. Butler, "Mem de Sá, Third Governor-General of Brazil, 1557-1572," *MA,* 1944

Joseph de Anchieta, S. J., *De gestis mendi de saa, dos feitos de Mem de Sá,* Rio de Janeiro, 1958

Sebastião Pegano, "O Brasil e suas relações com a Corôa da Espanha ao tempo dos Felipes (1580-1640)," *RIHGSP,* 1961

C. R. Boxer, *The Dutch in Brazil, 1624-1654,* Oxford, 1957

C. R. Boxer, *Salvador de Sá and the Struggle for Brazil and Angola, 1602-1686,* London, 1952

C. R. Boxer, "Salvador Correia de Sá e Benavides and the Reconquest of Angola in in 1648," *HAHR,* 28 (1948)

C. R. Boxer, "English Shipping in the Brazil Trade, 1640-1665," *Mariner's Mirror,* 1951

C. R. Boxer, "As primerias frotas da Companhia do Brasil, 1648-1652," *ACHN,* 1950

C. R. Boxer and C. de Azevedo, *Fort Jesus and the Portuguese in Mombasa, 1593-1729,* Hollis and Carter, 1960

C. R. Boxer, *A Great-Luso-Brazilian Figure, Padre Antonio Vieira, 1608-1697,* London, 1957

C. R. Boxer, "Padre Antonio Vieira, S. J., and the Institution of the Brazil Company in 1649," *HAHR,* 29 (1949)

Marcel Bataillon, "Le Brésil dans un vision d'Asie selon le P. Antonio Vieira," *RIB,* 2ᵃ XII

J. Lucio de Azevedo, *História de António Vieira,* Lisbon, 1931

D. W. Davies, *A Primer of Dutch Seventeenth Century Overseas Trade,* The Hague, 1961

A da Silva Rêgo, *A dupla restuuração de Angola, 1641-1648,* Lisbon, 1948

José Honório Rodrigues, *Historiografia e bibliografia do domínio holandês no Brasil,* Rio de Janeiro, 1949

H. C. Heaton, ed., *The Discovery of the Amazon according to the Account of Friar Gaspar de Carvajal,* tr. by B. T. Lee, New York, 1934

Fray Gaspar de Carvajal, *Relación del nuevo descubrimiento del famoso río grande de las Amazonas,* México, 1955

Mathias C. Kiemen, *The Indian Policy of Portugal in the Amazon Region, 1614-1693,* Washington, 1954

Mathias C. Kiemen, "The Indian Policy of Portugal in America with Special Reference to the Old State of Maranhão, 1500-1755," *TAm,* 1948-49

Luciano de Castro, *A Questão do Amazonas nos tratados de París e de Madrid,* Oporto, 1945

Artur Cesar Ferreira Reis, *O processo histórico da economia maranhense,* Rio de Janeiro, 1944

Artur Cesar Ferreira Reis, *História do Amazonas,* Manaus, 1931

Carlos Studart, *O antigo estado de Maranhão e suas Capitanias feudais,* Fortaleza, 1960

Joaquim Alves, *História das Sêcas, séculos XVII a XIX,* Fortaleza, 1953

Mário Martins Meireles, *História do Maranhão,* Rio de Janeiro, 1960

Carlos Eugênio Pôrto, *Roteiro do Piauí,* Rio de Janeiro, 1955

Leonardo Mota, "Datas e fatos para a história do Ceará," *RIC,* 1961

Richard Morse, *The Bandeirantes,* Borzoi, 1965

Vianna Moog, *Bandeirantes and Pioneers,* New York, 1964

Hernani Cidade, *O bandeirismo paulista na expansão territorial do Brasil,* Lisbon, 1954

Affonso Taunay, *História geral das bandeiras paulistas,* 11 vols., São Paulo, 1924-50

Affonso Taunay, *História das bandeiras paulistas,* 3 vols., São Paulo, 1954

Visconde de Taunay, *A grande vida de Fernão Dias Paes,* São Paulo, 1931

M. S. Cardozo, "The Last Adventure of Fernão Dias de Pais, 1674-1681," *HAHR,* 26 (1946)

Sérgio Buarque de Holanda, *Caminhos e fronteiras,* Rio de Janeiro, 1957

Alice Canabrava, *O comércio português no Rio da Prata, 1580-1640,* São Paulo, 1944

Lewis Hanke, "The Portuguese in Spanish America with Special Reference to the Villa Imperial de Potosí," *RHAM,* 1961

John A. Hutchins, "Portugal's Interest in the Control of the Coast of Southern Brazil and the Mouth of the Rio de la Plata," *ICLBS,* III, Lisbon, 1957

R. de Lafuente Machain, *Los portugueses en Buenos Aires,* Buenos Aires, 1931

Olinto Sanmartin, *Bandeiras no sul do Brasil,* Pôrto Alegre, 1949

Arthur Ferreira, *História Geral do Rio Grande do Sul, 1502-1957,* Rio de Janeiro, 1958

Magnus Mörner, *The Political and Economic Activities of the Jesuits in the La Plata Region, The Hapsburg Era,* Stockholm, 1953

Carlos Teschauer, *História do Rio Grande do Sul dos dois primeiros séculos,* 3 vols., Pôrto Alegre, 1920, 1922

J. Costa Rêgo Monteiro, *A colônia do Sacramento, 1680-1777,* 2 vols., Pôrto Alegre, 1937

Mario Rodríguez, "Dom Pedro of Braganza and Colônia do Sacramento, 1680-1705," *HAHR,* 38 (May 1958)

J. C. Rêgo Monteiro, *Dominação espanhola no Rio Grande do Sul, 1763-1777,* Rio de Janeiro, 1937

Dauril Alden, "The Undeclared War of 1773-1777, Climax of Luso-Spanish Platine Rivalry," *HAHR,* 41 (Feb. 1961)

Luís Ferrand de Almeida, *A diplomacia portuguesa,* Coimbra, 1957

Jaime Cortesão, *Alexandre de Gusmão e o Tratado de Madrid,* 3 vols., Rio de Janeiro, 1950-52

Octavio Gil Munilla, *El Río de la Plata en la política internacional,* Sevilla, 1949

Dante Laytano, *História da propriedade das primeiras fazendas do Rio Grande do Sul,* Pôrto Alegre, 1945 (and other articles in *RIHGRGS,* 1935, 1938, 1939, etc.)

Sérgio Buarque de Holanda, *Monções,* Rio de Janeiro, 1945

Chapter 30
MANUFACTURING, MINING AND TRADE

THE ECONOMIC history of Brazil is still largely unstudied. Many of the known facts of its history have the sound of improvisation and invention. The connection of Brazil with Portugal and of both with the world economy is not thoroughly understood. Some progress is being made and a few important works have appeared.

The discovery of gold and later of diamonds in quantity was the most dramatic event in Brazil's economic history. This has found a historian in Charles Boxer. His work, *The Golden Age,* with boundaries encompassing a broader period than his title suggests, broaches the fundamental economic, social, and political consequences of the rivers of gold and diamonds flowing out of Minas Gerais first and western lands later. There are also other studies by Manoel Cardozo, Augusto de Lima, and Oliveira Torres.

On the largely unresearched history of colonial industries something can be gotten from Rogers on iron and steel and from Alden on an 18th century entrepreneur. Myriam Ellis's study of salt as a monopoly helps one to understand the colonial economic concept held by Portugal and others. See Mauro's excellent monographs, as well as those of Godinho and Freitas. Celso Furtado's insistence that manufacturing was almost nil follows the usual interpretation that the Treaty of Methuen of 1703 killed industry in Portugal and Brazil. See also Hermenegildo de Sousa on Methuen.

For the Marquis of Pombal see Carneiro de Mendonça and Azevedo. Wanderley Pinho's study of an *engenho* and Taunay's study of coffee give us histories of two important crops—coffee only becoming important late in the colonial period. For a better understanding of land, see the works on the *sesmaria* by the Marquês de Aguiar, Ruy Cirne Lima, and Lima Pereira.

Charles R. Boxer, *The Golden Age of Brazil, 1695-1750,* Berkeley, 1962

M. S. Cardozo, "The Brazilian Gold Rush," *TAm,* 1946

M. S. Cardozo, "The Guerra dos Emboabas," *HAHR,* 22 (1942)

M. S. Cardozo, "The Collection of the Fifths in Brazil," *HAHR,* 20 (Aug. 1940)

Augusto de Lima Junior, *A capitania de Minas Gerais,* 2d ed., Rio de Janeiro, 1943

Augusto de Lima Junior, *Vila Rica do Ouro Preto,* Belo Horizonte, 1957

Augusto de Lima Junior, *História dos diamantes nas Minas Gerais,* Lisbon, 1945

João Camillo de Oliveira Tôrres, *História de Minas Gerais,* 5 vols., Belo Horizonte, 1961

Pedro Batalha Reis, *Cartilha de Numismática Portuguesa,* Lisbon, 1952

Severino Sombra, "História monetária do Brasil colonial," *RHSP*, 1959-

Myriam Ellis, "Contribuição ao estudo do abastecimento das zonas mineradoras," *RHSP*, 1958

Mafalda P. Zemella, *O abastecimento da capitania das Minas Gerais no sémulo XVIII*, São Paulo, 1951

Eduardo Brazão, *As expedições de Duclerc e Duguay-Trouin ao Rio de Janeiro, 1710-1711*, Lisbon, 1940

G. A. Tasso Fragoso, *Os franceses no Rio de Janeiro*, Rio de Janeiro, 1950

Edward J. Rogers, "The Iron and Steel Industry in Colonial and Imperial Brazil," *TAm*, 1962

Dauril Alden, "Manoel Luís Vieira," *HAHR*, 39 (Nov. 1959)

Dauril Alden, "Yankee Sperm Whalers in Brazilian Waters," *TAm*, 1964

Myriam Ellis, *Aspectos da pesca da Baleia no Brasil colonial*, São Paulo, 1959

Myriam Ellis, *O monopólio do sal no Estado do Brasil*, São Paulo, 1955

Frederic Mauro, *Le Brésil au XVIIe siècle*, Coimbra, 1963

Frederic Mauro, *Le Portugal et L'Atlantique au XVIIe siècle*, Paris, 1960

Vitorino Magalhães Godinho, "Le Portugal, les flottes, 1670-1770," *RH*, 1953

Carlos Hermenegildo de Sousa, *O Tratado de Methuen na economia nacional*, Aveiro, 1938

Gustavo de Freitas, *A Companhia Geral do comércio do Brasil, 1649-1720*, São Paulo, 1951

Marcos Carneiro de Mendonça, *O Marques de Pombal e O Brasil*, São Paulo, 1960

Marcos Carneiro de Mendonça, *A Amazonia na era pombalina*, 2 vols., São Paulo, 1963

João Lúcio de Azevedo, *O Marquês de Pombal e a sua época*, Lisbon, 1931

Documentos para a história do açucar, 2 vols., Rio de Janeiro, 1954, 1956

Wanderley Pinho, *História de un Engenho do Recôncavo*, Rio de Janeiro, 1946

Marquês de Aguiar, "Fragmentos de uma Memória sôbre as sesmarias da Bahia," *RIHGB*, III

Ruy Cirne Lima, *Pequena história territorial do Brasil, sesmarias e terras devolutas*, Pôrto Alegre, 1954

J. Otaviano de Lima Pereira, "Origem da propriedade no Brasil e o Município de São Paulo, *Política*, I

Affonso Taunay, *Pequena história do café no Brasil*, Rio de Janeiro, 1945

C. L. Chandler, "List of the United States Vessels in Brazil, 1792-1805," *HAHR*, 26 (1946)

Chapter 31

SOCIETY AND CULTURE

BRAZILIAN preoccupation with racial composition continues. On the Negro we have Goulart, Ramos, and Taunay. Zelinsky's work on the geography of slavery has been mentioned. Carneiro studies Palmares; Rodrigues seeks to tie Brazil and Africa together—with political implications. Raymond S. Sayers has made a valuable study of the Negro in literature; Richard Morse examines the changing status of the Negro.

The Portuguese element in Brazil, though basic, has not attracted as much research as the Negro. Brazilians pay little attention to their Lusitanian ancestry. However, Mendes Correia, a Portuguese scholar, devotes some attention to it. Silva Lopes examines the Brazilian nobility.

A number of studies of race relations have appeared, the most realistic being by Charles Boxer. His conclusions are somewhat at variance with Portuguese claims but not out of line with recent Brazilian studies such as those by Diégues Junior and Florestan Fernândes. The largely white immigration into Rio Grande do Sul is the subject of Ornellas's work. From Dauril Alden we get the first serious attempt at population statistics. Azevedo, Rodrigues, and Wiznitzer study Jewish elements.

Our main information on intellectual developments still comes from the general histories, but there are special studies. On late colonial times see the works of Costa, which very recently translated. The fundamental work explaining the Enlightenment in the 18th century is Father Luís António Verney's *Verdadeiro Methodo de Estudar*. He serves as a sort of intellectual beacon in the Pombal period; he, or at least his spirit, inspired the reform of the university in 1772. Consult also other works by Ferreira, Pina, Lessa, and Frieiro. E. Bradfor Burns has made excellent studies on what might be called "Books of the Brazilian Brave"—though he does not use that title; he also has an article on Azeredo Coutinho.

An introduction to Brazilian art may be found in Goodwin's *Brazil Builds*. Other studies by Bury, Campiglia, Arroyo, and Smith are all good. The essentially Portuguese origins of Brazilian art may be seen from these studies as well as in the architecture of the churches and public buildings of colonial Brazil; private dwellings also reflect the Portuguese influence.

Maurício Goulart, *Escravidão Africana no Brasil*, São Paulo, 1949

Arthur Ramos, *The Negro in Brazil*, tr. by R. Pattee, Washington, 1951

Affonso de Escragnolle Taunay, *Subsídios para a história do tráfico africano no Brasil*, São Paulo, 1941

Wilbur Zelinsky, "The Historical Geography of the Negro Population of Latin America," *JNH*, 1949

Edison Carneiro, *O Quilombo dos Palmares*, São Paulo, 1947

Edison Carneiro, *Ladinos e crioulos*, Rio de Janeiro, 1964

Carlos B. Ott, *Formação e evolução étnica da Cidade do Salvador*, 2 vols., Salvador, 1955-57

Lycurgo Santos Filho, *Uma comunidade rural do Brasil antigo*, São Paulo, 1956

José Honório Rodrigues, "The Influence of Africa on Brazil and of Brazil on Africa," *JAH*, 1962

José Honório Rodrigues, *Brasil e Africa*, Rio de Janeiro, 1961

Richard Morse, "As metamorfoses do negro," *AA*, 1964

Raymond S. Sayers, *The Negro in Brazilian Literature*, New York, 1956

A. A. Mendes Correia, "O elemento português na demografia do Brasil," *MP*, XI

Carlos da Silva Lopes, "Ensaio sôbre a Nobreza Portuguêsa," *Revista do Instituto Heráldico Genealógico*, São Paulo, IX

Registro de estrangeiros nas capitanias, 1777-1879, Rio de Janeiro, 1963

Manuel Diégues Júnior, *Etnías e culturas no Brasil*, Rio de Janeiro, 1956

L. A. Costa Pinto, "As classes sociais no Brasil, *RBCS*, 1963

Florestan Fernandes, *Mudanças sociais no Brasil*, São Paulo, 1960

Charles R. Boxer, *Race Relations in the Portuguese Colonial Empire*, Oxford, 1963

Manoelito de Ornellas, *Gaúchos e beduínos*, Rio de Janeiro, 1956

Dauril Alden, "The Population of Brazil in the Late XVIII Century," *HAHR*, 43 (May 1963)

J. Lúcio de Azevedo, *História dos Christãos Novos Portugueses*, Lisbon, 1921

João Lúcio de Azevedo, *Novas epanáforas*, Lisbon, 1932

José Honório Rodrigues, "Os Judeus no Brasil," *O Jornal*, 1952

Arnold Wiznitzer, *Jews in Colonial Brasil*, Columbia, 1960

Arnold Wiznitzer, *The Records of the Earliest Jewish Community in the New World*, New York, 1954

Fernando de Azevedo, *A cultura brasileira*, Rio de Janeiro, 1943

Moreira de Azevedo, "Instrução pública nos tempos coloniais do Brasil," *RIHGB*, 55

Hélio Viana, "Educação no Brasil colonial," *EHC*, São Paulo, 1948

João Cruz Costa, *Esbozo de una historia de las ideas en el Brasil*, México, 1957

João Cruz Costa, *A History of Ideas in Brazil*, Berkeley, 1964

Mario Brandão and M. Lopes d'Almeida, *Universidade de Coimbra*, Coimbra, 1937

Estudos de História Colonial, São Paulo, 1948 (articles by various people)

Francisco Morais, *Estudantes da Univerdidade de Coimbra nascidos no Brasil*, Coimbra, 1959

Luís António Verney, *Verdadeiro Methodo de Estudar*, 2 vols., 1746; A. Salgado Júnior, ed., 5 vols., Lisbon, 1949-52.
    Indispensable to understand the background of Enlightenment.

Alcides Bezerra, "A filosofia na fase colonial," *PAN*, Rio de Janeiro, 1935

J. Bethencourt Ferreira, "Contribuiçãa de estudo sôbre a 'Viagem filosófica' do Dr. Alexandre Rodríguez Ferreira," *MP*, 11

Luiz de Pina, "Materiais para a história das ciências no Brasil," *MP*, 11

Claudio Ribeiro de Lessa, "As bibliotecas brasileiras dos tempos coloniais," *RIHGB*, 1947

Eduardo Frieiro, *O Diabo na Livraria do Cônego*, Belo Horizonte, 1945

Bradford E. Burns, "The Enlightenment in Two Colonial Brazilian Libraries," *JHI*, 1964

Bradford E. Burns, "The Role of Azevedo Coutinho in the Enlightenment of Brazil," *HAHR*, 44 (May 1964)

Carlos Rizzini, *O Livro, o Jornal e a Tipografia no Brasil,* 1946

Philip L. Goodwin, *Brazil Builds, Architecture New and Old,* New York, 1943

John Bury, "Jesuit Architecture in Brazil," *The Month,* 1950

G. Oscar Campiglia, *Igrejas do Brasil,* São Paulo, 1957

Leonardo Arroyo, *Igrejas de São Paulo,* Rio de Janeiro, 1954

Robert C. Smith, *As Artes na Bahia,* Salvador, 1954

Carlos Molina Massey, *Los holandeses y la cultura artistica de Baia, Anães do Arquivo Público de Bahia,* 26, Bahia, 1938

Gastão Cruls, *Aparência do Rio de Janeiro,* 2 vols., Rio de Janeiro, 1952

Chapter 32

THE CHURCH IN BRAZIL

THE CHURCH was so closely woven into the fabric of Brazilian history that we have cited its actions in all the previous chapters. Although Gilberto Freyre may be right in asserting that "there was never in colonial Brazil a really powerful church or a strong clergy," little if anything remained outside its influence.

On general church history we have the works of Barbosa and Dornas Filho; Röwer is the chief historian of the Franciscans. The Jesuits have, however, dominated the writing of history as much as they dominated the colonies. The late Father Serafim Leite with his 10-volume history of the Jesuits in Brazil and numerous other works is the outstanding historian. Father Luís G. Jaeger is editing a large work on southern Brazil. Based though they are on vast documentary sources, these works on the missionaries by clerics give what is perhaps an over-favorable view, with all of the virtues and few of the failings of the churchmen noted. To be consulted also are works on Vieira. Brazão brings us the concordats affecting Brazil. Non-Catholic religions are studied by José Carlos Rodrigues.

Gilberto Freyre, *New World in the Tropics,* Knopf, 1959

Manuel Barbosa, *A Igreja no Brasil,* Rio de Janeiro, 1945

João Dornas Filho, *O Padroado e a Igreja Brasileira,* São Paulo, 1938

Basílio Röwer, *A Ordem Franciscana no Brasil,* Rio de Janeiro, 1947

Monsenhor José de Sousa Azevedo Pizarro e Araujo, *Memórias Históricas,* 9 vols., Rio de Janeiro, 1820-22, 1945-48 (index 1951)

Cândido Mendes de Almeida, *Direito Civil Eclesiástico Brasileiro,* 2 vols., 1866-73

Serafim Leite, *História da Companhia de Jesús no Brasil,* 10 vols., Rio de Janeiro, 1938-50

Serafim Leite, ed., *Cartas do Brasil do P. Nóbrega,* Coimbra, 1955

Miguel Battlori, *Biografía de Serafim Leite, S.J.*, Rome, 1962

Luis G. Jaeger, *Jesuitas no sul do Brasil*, 6 vols., Porto Alegre, 1952-56

António Vieira, *Sermoens*, 14 vols., Lisbon, 1679-1710

António Vieira, *Obras Escolhidas*, 12 vols., ed. by António Sérgio and Hernâni Cidade, Lisbon, 1951-54

Eduardo Brazão, *Colecção de Concordatas*, Lisbon, 1941

José Carlos Rodrigues, *Religiões Acatólicas no Brasil*, Rio de Janeiro, 1904

Chapter 33

COLONIAL BRAZILIAN GOVERNMENT

TWO HISTORIOGRAPHICAL guides, by Rodrigues and Lacombe, cover the essentials of government. Vianna's administrative and economic history serves as a good introduction to the entire period. In Fortunato de Almeida's history of Portugal the focus is on Portugal, but it contains an excellent outline with abundant bibliography. Marcelo Caetano, another Portuguese, should be consulted. There are various editions of the laws. For 17th century Brazil, the *Livro primeiro do governo* and Diogo de Campos Moreno's work are contemporary documents.

The place of the municipal government, *Senado da Câmara,* in the political structure and its influence varied considerably according to circumstances. Historians opinions are equally varied in assessing its place. See Richard Morse on general characteristics of Latin American municipal government. Amorim, Zenha, and Ribeiro all describe its main functions. The ideal for a Brazilian municipality was to obtain a charter modeled on that of Portugal, preferably on the city of Porto. The latest and most useful study is by Charles Boxer who compares the government of Bahia in Brazil with three other municipal governments in other parts of the Portuguese empire.

Among the other important institutions was the office of *Capitão Mor,* which was more talked about than studied. See the works of José de Mirales and Nilo Val.

During the 18th century there were indications of colonial dissatisfaction which were to lead to eventual independence. Mario Melo studies the *Guerra dos Mascates;* Ernesto Ennes, the efforts to make Manuel king of Brazil. The most famous of the movements was the *Inconfidencia Mineira* of 1789. There are studies by Marchant, Ennes, Lúcio José dos Santos, and Pereira dos Reis. The proceedings have also been published. Other conspiracies, such as those in Rio in 1794 and Bahia in 1798, may also be noted. See also Mendonça's work on the *Intendente Câmara*.

Other works listed below which cover the period of independence are those of Oliveira Lima, Varnhagen, Sergio Correia, and Tarquino de Sousa. These bring us a bit beyond the original closing date of this book, 1808, and into the beginning of an independent Brazil.

Américo Jacobina Lacombe, *Brasil, período nacional*, México, 1956

Hélio Vianna, *História administrativa e econômica do Brasil*, São Paulo, 1951

Fortunato de Almeida, *História de Portugal*, 6 vols.

Marcelo Caetano, *Tradições, princípios e métodos da colonização portuguêsa*, Lisbon, 1951

J. J. de Andrade e Silva, *Coleção cronológica da legislação portuguêsa*, Lisbon, 1856

João Pedro Ribeiro, *Collecção chronológica das leis posteriores as leis filipinas*, 6 vols., Lisbon, 1805-20

Antonio Lopes da Costa Almeida, *Repertório remissivo da legislação de marinha e do ultramar*, Lisbon, 1856

Livro primeiro do governo do Brasil, 1607-1633, Rio de Janeiro, 1958

Diogo de Campos Moreno, *Livro que dá Razão do Estado do Brasil, 1612*, ed. by H. Vianna, Recife, 1955

Richard M. Morse, "Some Characteristics of Latin American Urban History," *AHR*, 1962

Deolindo Amorim, "Da Evolução do Município no Brasil," *IV Congresso de História Nacional*, IX

Edmundo Zenha, *O Município no Brasil*, São Paulo, 1948

Maria da Conceição Martins Ribeiro, "Os oficiais da Câmara de São Paulo no século XVI," *Revista de Administração*, 1949

M. de Magalhães Basto, *Porto e Brasil*, Porto, 1946

Privilégios dos cidadãos do Porto, Porto, 1878 (and other editions)

Affonso Ruy, *História da Câmara municipal do Salvador*, Salvador, 1953

Charles R. Boxer, *Portuguese Society in the Tropics, the Municipal Councils*, Wisconsin, 1965

José de Mirales, "História Militar do Brasil," *ABN*, 22

Nilo Val, "Formação do Exército Brasileiro e sua evolução no século XIX," *1° Congresso internacional de História da América*, VII

Mário Melo, "A guerra dos mascates como afirmação nacionalista," *RIAGP*, 36

Ernesto Ennes, "Uma conspiração malograda em Minas Gerais para aclamar o Rei do Brasil," *MP*, 11

Alexander Marchant, "Tiradentes in the Conspiracy of Minas," *HAHR*, 21 (May 1941)

Ernesto Ennes, "A Inconfidência Mineira," *TAm*, 1950

Lúcio José dos Santos, *A Inconfidência Mineira*, São Paulo, 1927

P. Pereira dos Reis, *O colonialismo português*, São Paulo, 1964

M. S. Cardozo, "Another Document on the 'Inconfidência Mineira'," *HAHR*, 32 (1952)

Autos da Devassa da Inconfidência Miniera, 7 vols., Rio de Janeiro, 1936-38

Joaquim Norberto de Sousa e Silva, *História da Conjuração Mineira,* 2d ed., Rio de Janeiro, 1948

"A Devassa Ordenada pelo Vice-Rei, 1794," *ABN,* 61

Afonso Rui, *A primeira revolução social brasileira, 1798,* 2d ed., São Paulo, 1951

Marcos Carneiro de Mendonça, *O Intendente Câmara, 1764-1835,* Rio de Janeiro, 1933 (in which appears, "Sistema que mais convem . . . para a conservação dos seus vastos dominios . . .")

Manuel S. Cardozo, "A French Document on Rio de Janeiro, 1748," *HAHR,* 21 (Aug. 1941

José de Sousa Azevedo Pizarro e Araujo, *Memórias históricas do Rio de Janeiro,* 9 vols., Rio de Janeiro, 1820-22, 1945-48, 1951

Luiz Edmundo da Costa, *Rio de Janeiro in the Time of the Viceroys,* tr. by D. H. Momsen, Rio de Janeiro, 1936

J. C. Fernandes Pinheiro, "Os últimos Vice-Reis no Brasil," *RIHGB,* 28

Rocha Martins, *O Último Vice-Rei do Brasil,* Lisbon, N.D.

Manuel de Oliveira Lima, *Dom João VI no Brasil,* 2 vols., Rio de Janeiro, 1908

Francisco Adolpho de Varnhagen, *História da independência do Brasil,* São Paulo, 1957

Sergio Correia Costa, "A diplomacia europeia e a sucessão de D. João VI," *MP,* 11

Octávio Tarquino de Sousa, *A Vida de D. Pedro I,* 3 vols., São Paulo, 1954

PREFACE

A BOOK is never the product of one person alone. Many people are needed to furnish ideas from which a book springs, and the author is glad to acknowledge the help which so many have cheerfully given to the preparation of this book. First are my own students at the College of the City of New York. From their prodding and questions came the inspiration to attempt a book that would give a partial answer to the many questions that arise about Latin America. For whatever success I may have achieved, I am most indebted to them. If there is one principle to which the historian must adhere above all others it is the principle of free inquiry and honest thought. The historian who, because he belongs to a party, faction, or religion, inhibits his inquiry and curbs his conclusions, is not a historian: he is a propagandist for ideas which cannot bear up under the light of truth. I am fortunate in having been able to teach students whose keen minds and penetrating criticism spare no sacred cows. I repeat that it is to them that I owe my first debt.

So many others have assisted me that I find it difficult to name them all. My colleagues, Drs. Oscar Janowsky, Michael Kraus, Joseph E. Wisan, Louis Snyder, Francis Williamson, A. C. Wilgus, Sidney Pomerantz, and John Cox, have all made valuable suggestions. From numerous libraries in Paris, London, Madrid, Rio de Janeiro, Santiago de Chile, and other cities I bring pleasant memories, as well as the realization that a well-trained and educated library staff is the *sine qua non* of modern scholarship. My particular gratitude is extended to The Huntington Library of San Marino, California, for providing an unfailingly courteous and efficient corps of librarians, in a near-perfect environment for the scholar. My debt to the New York Public Library is even greater, and I can hope for nothing better than that I may in a peaceful future spend many more pleasant hours in further study there. To the library staff of my own school, The City College, I am still more particularly indebted. For thirteen years the City College librarians have rendered me constant and unwavering service. If I were to name all who have helped me I should have to list our entire staff, without omitting one.

Among those who have read parts of this work in manuscript are Professors Walter C. Langsam of Union College, Roland D.

Hussey of the University of California in Los Angeles, and Irving A. Leonard of the University of Michigan. Their expert attention has eliminated many errors. Mr. Alcibiades Claudio, one of my students, deserves particular thanks for the help he has rendered me. To my former student and present colleague, Dr. Harry Bernstein, I also owe a vote of thanks. In addition to the chapters he has helped me prepare and which bear his name, he has aided me constantly and patiently in every stage of the work. Dr. Howard Stock of the High School of Music and Arts of New York has for many years honored me with his friendship and scholarly counsel. His profound knowledge of the philosophers guided me along the difficult path which must be followed by those who study the culture of Latin America. Dr. Max Lieberman of New Utrecht High School has frequently given me the benefit of his knowledge of the Latin literatures and of the libraries of Europe. With his keen critical judgment and his original point of view, my good friend, Dr. Tomás Blanco, of San Juan, Puerto Rico, has often opened to me new lines of thought.

For invaluable assistance in proofreading I am deeply indebted to Miss Inez Pollak and Mrs. Muna Lee de Muñoz Marín.

The maps adapted from A. Curtis Wilgus' *Latin America in Maps* are used with the gracious permission of the author and the publishers (Barnes and Noble, New York, 1943).

Of the many who deserve my thanks, none come before my friends Edith and Joe Wisan. Their constant aid and encouragement through the years have opened the door to many opportunities which would otherwise have remained closed to me. I wish also to emphasize the debt I owe to Mrs. Frances Merrill, whose long editorial experience was placed at my service. Finally, I wish to acknowledge the help of those who have made my study and travel possible: Dr. C. W. Richards of Ardmore, Oklahoma, who helped me while I was an undergraduate; my parents and brothers, who assisted me beyond their means; the Rotary Club of Fort Worth, Texas, which enabled me to go to Spain to study from 1927 to 1929; the American Fund for Public Service, in 1929-30; and the Rockefeller Foundation, which granted me a Fellowship that enabled me to complete my research during 1940-41.

BAILEY W. DIFFIE

New York City
August, 1945

CONTENTS

Page

Book One: The Foundations of Latin America   I

   1. Introducing Latin America   3

   2. The Indians Conquer America   12

   3. Enter the Europeans   28

   4. Land and Labor   57

   5. Farm and Ranch   83

   6. Mining in America   104

   7. Manufacturing and Domestic Trade   120

   8. International Trade   142

   9. Indian Classes, Customs, and Population   165

   10. People and Work in the Sixteenth Century   190

   11. The Foundation of Latin-American Culture   211

   12. Religion and the Church   233

   13. Religion and the Church (continued)   248

   14. Foundations of Latin-American Government   270

   15. Foundations of Latin-American Government (con-
       tinued)   293

Book Two: The Evolution of Colonial Latin America to
       1810   313

   16. Expansion and Agricultural Development to 1810 ...   315

   17. Expansion and Agricultural Development (continued)   340

   18. Mining: Development and Influence in the Later Col-
       onial Period   366

   19. Evolution of Manufacturing and Trade   386

   20. Trade Policy and Reform to 1810   417

   21. Social Evolution to 1810: Populations   441

22. Social Evolution to 1810: Class Structure 460

23. Development of Education and Diffusion of Culture 492

24. Cultural Contributions of the Spanish Colonies 514

25. New Currents and Growth of the Scientific Spirit ... 542

26. Development of the Church to 1810 567

27. Government in Evolution 600

Book Three: Colonial Brazil 631

28. Brazil in Formation 633

29. Foreign Rivalry and Portuguese Expansion 652

30. Mining, Manufacturing, and Trade 674

31. Society and Culture 693

32. The Church in Brazil 718

33. Colonial Brazilian Government 739

Kings of Spain 754

Kings of Portugal 754

Brief Bibliography 755

Index 765

ILLUSTRATIONS

	Facing page
Portrait of Atahualpa	12
Volcano of Ixtacihuatl	12*a*
Don Pedro de Alvarado, Conqueror of Guatemala	36
Hernando Cortés, Conqueror of Mexico	37
Francisco Pizarro, Conqueror of Peru	50
Adelantado Sebastián Belacázar	50*a*
Balboa, Discoverer of the Pacific	60
Christopher Columbus	61
Maguey Plant	88
Mummy, Chancay region of Peru	180
Grave with burial urns, Chancay, Peru	180
Ceremonial vases, ancient Peru	208
Tiger devouring man, ancient Peruvian pottery	208
Monkey with baby on back, ancient Peruvian pottery	208
Aztec Calendar Stone	209
Details of Stone Work, Machu Picchu	209
Inca city of Machu Picchu, near Cuzco	209
Maya Architecture, Chichén Itza, Yucatán	224
Cross of Palenque, Chiapas	224
Mexico — Post-Conquest Scene	225
Curaca Costume	225
Aztec Sacrificial Stone	240

lxxxii

Facing page

Sacrificial Knife with stone blade, pre-Spanish 241

Juan Zumárraga, title page 260

Street in Cuzco 272

Court of government palace, Mexico 304

Maté cup 334

Colonial Aqueduct 334

Guachos 335

Hacienda de la Capilla, Puebla 335

De la obra "Descripción del Obsipado de Trujillo del Peru" 396

Colonial silver work, 18th century 397

Gilded bed, Peru 397

Carved wooden box, Ecuador 397

Sor Juana Ines de la Cruz, self-portrait 490

Portrait of Doña Juana María Romero 491

Portrait of D. Manuel Tolsa, by Rafael Ximeno 522

Door in Yepostlán 522

Sugar Mill in Brazil 658

Joao Fernandes Vieira 659

Travel in Brazil, by Wagener, Dutch, 17th Century 666

Portrait of Negro Servant in Brazil 694

Seventeenth-Century Ship 726

Santa Ifigenia Church, Minas Gerais, 1785 727

Santa Ifigenia, Minas Gerais, 1785 727

Quipu, the Inca counting device 742

Church in Cholula, Mexico 743

MAPS AND CHARTS

	Page
Latin America and the United States	4a
Indian Distribution in Latin America *ca.* 1500	12a
Growth of the Inca Empire	18a
Political Divisions of Spain and Portugal *ca.* 1200	28a
Trade Routes in Iberian Peninsula *ca.* 1300	28b
Portuguese Explorations	30a
Some Early Settlements in Spanish Colonies in North America	48a
Sixteenth-Century Spanish Missions and Settlements in Florida	50a
Spread of Spanish and Portuguese Conquests	50b
Voyages of Pizarro, 1524-1532	52a
Some Early Settlements in Spanish Colonies in Northern South America	56a
Mean Annual Temperatures, North and South America	84a
Average Annual Rainfall, South America	86a
Average Annual Rainfall, Central American Region	86b
Regions of Vegetation, South America	88a
Wind Currents Affecting Latin America	88b
Ancient Mexico City, detail map	178a
Ancient Mexico City and Environs	180a
Cuzco, Ancient and Modern	182a
Some Early Settlements in Spanish Colonies in Southern South America	320a
Spanish Missions in California, 18th Century	340a
Ports of Spanish America Authorized to Receive Spanish Ships, 1778	422a

lxxxiv

Newspapers of Colonial Latin America 554*a*

Theatres of Colonial Spanish America 554*b*

Jesuit and Other Missions Along the Uruguay, Paraná,
    Paraguay Rivers 580*a*

Jesuit Missions in Spanish North America, 1566-1767 . .   584*a*

Political Organization of Latin America in 1784 . . . . . .   624*a*

Intendancies in 18th-Century Mexico 626*a*

Distribution of Captaincies in Brazil 642*a*

Some Settlements in Brazil 646*a*

Livestock Regions of Brazil 664*a*

Brazil, Showing Roads, Water Routes, and Mineral De-
    posits 678*a*

Exports of Gold and Sugar from Brazil, 1520-1840 . . . . . .   690*a*

ABBREVIATIONS

Anais BNRio   *Anais da Biblioteca Nacional de Rio de Janeiro,* Rio de Janeiro, 1876—

Biblioteca JHN   *Biblioteca de la Junta de Historia y Numismática,* Buenos Aires, 1903—

BANHist   *Boletín de la Academia Nacional de la Historia,* Buenos Aires, 1924—

C. D. I. Ultramar Colección de documentos inéditos...de las antiguas posesiones españolas de Ultramar, Madrid, 1885-1932.

C. D. I. España   *Colección de documentos inéditos para la historia de España,* Madrid, 1842-1895.

C. D. México   Joaquín García Icazbalceta, ed., *Colección de documentos para la historia de México,* México, 1858-1866.

C. L. D. Peru   Horacio H. Urteaga and Carlos A. Romero, eds., *Colección de libros y documentos referentes a la historia del Perú,* Lima, 1916—

D. I. I.   *Colección de documentos inéditos relativos al descubrimiento, conquista, y organización...de Indias,* Madrid, 1864-1884.

Documentos historia de Argentina   *Documentos para la historia de Argentina,* Buenos Aires, 1913-1936.

García and Pereyra, *Documentos historia México,*   Genaro García y Carlos Pereyra, eds., *Documentos inéditos o muy raros para la historia de México,* México, 1905-1911.

Gobernación espiritual y temporal Gobernación espiritual y temporal de las Indias, in *C. D. I. Ultramar.*

H. A. H. R.   *The Hispanic American Historical Review,* 1918—

HCP Carlos Malheiro Dias, ed., *História da colonização portuguesa do Brasil,* 3 vols., Porto. Portugal, 1921-1926.

Leyes de Indias   *Recopilación de leyes de los reinos de las Indias,* 5th ed., Madrid, 1841.

Matienzo and Torres, *Doc. Hist. Río Plata* José Nicolás Matienzo and Luis M. Torres, eds., *Documentos para la historia del Virreinato del Río de la Plata,* 3 vols., Buenos Aires, 1912-1913.

Memorias de Virreyes, Perú Manuel Anastasio Fuentes, ed., *Colección de memorias de los Virreyes que han gobernado el Perú,* 6 vols., Lima, 1859-1860.

Nueva C. D. México Joaquín García Icazbalceta, ed., *Nueva colección de documentos para la historia de México,* 5 vols., México, 1886-1892.

Papeles varios *Papeles varios sobre administración, aduanas, aranceles...,* 6 vols., Madrid, 1730-1823.

Revista IHGB *Revista do Instituto Histórico e Geográphico Brasileiro,* Rio de Janeiro, 1838—

Latin-American Civilization

Colonial Period

Book I

The Foundations of
Latin America

Introducing Latin America

LATIN AMERICA IS THE PRODUCT of a fusion—Indian, European, and Negro. The interaction of the transplanted cultures of Western Europe and Africa with that of the native Indian determined the subsequent evolution of America. The objectives of the present work are to trace the processes by which this evolution was accomplished, or is being accomplished, since the complete synthesis is not achieved, and to show how the three cultures, sometimes remarkably similar and sometimes divergent, were mingled to form colonial Latin-American culture. This task has suggested a plan of approach differing in some respects from that of many excellent studies already published.

The colonial period is divided into two parts. The first, extending into the latter half of the 16th century, embraces the meeting of Indian, European, and Negro cultures and their partial fusion; the second comprises the evolution down to the Latin-American Wars of Independence. The point of departure is the European conquest; the method is to interweave the material relating to each culture in order to demonstrate how the amalgamation was brought about.

Several points should be noted about the present work. Since geography has no separate treatment, the pertinent features of Latin-American geography are discussed as they affect the Conquest, colonization, agriculture, general economy, or government of the Spanish and Portuguese colonies. The culture of the Indians is not discussed as a separate topic, but in relation to the economy, society, and government of the colonial period. The European background of Latin-American history, justly considered as of great importance and ably treated as a separate unit by many authors, is here, however, interrelated with each appropriate colonial factor which it influenced; i.e., instead of treating the

3

European background in a single chapter, this work explains influential elements in Latin-American history which derived from Europe in their relation to the Conquest, the economic development, the arts and fine arts, social structure, religion, and government. In Book I, beginning with Chapter IV, each succeeding topic has three parts, namely: the Indian elements, the European or Negro influences, and the fusion into the colonial synthesis.

Since the scope of this work is the whole of colonial Latin-American history, the aims are twofold: to present as complete a story as possible of all the influences that have gone into the making of Latin America, and to trace their effect up to 1810. Two methods are used to achieve these objectives: the inclusion of relevant information now found in the best secondary works; and the insertion of numerous quotations from the chief chronicles. Up to the present the amount of source material available in English to those seeking to know more of Latin America has been limited. Many of the chronicles have not been translated into English; those which have are frequently out of print and too expensive for the average library, or the translations are inaccurate. The readers of the following pages will be introduced to a portion of the sources from which any authoritative history of Latin America must be written, and thus may judge history for themselves through reading the words of men who were contemporaries of the events they recorded.

Since this plan of approach has led the author to a number of conclusions which differ in greater or lesser degree from those of many previous writers on the subject, some of the main points where the present interpretation diverges from customary views of colonial Latin-American history and institutions are briefly summarized here. The author makes no claim that all these points are original with him. While some are the result of his own interpretations of the sources for the colonial period, others are taken from recent studies by modern scholars and have already been accepted by many authorities. Some involve merely a difference of emphasis, rather than any disagreement on established facts.

Latin-American history has a theme that is not unique, but common to much history, in the sharp struggle for existence. In Latin America, however, this struggle centers specifically around the possession of land—in the pre-Conquest period as well as in the colonial period and later—and for that reason, land and its fruits furnish the best single key to the interpretation of Latin America. For thousands of years before the Europeans began settling America, the Indians were engaged in fratricidal struggles for the rela-

PHYSICAL MAP

Scale of Miles
0   500   1000

Latin America and the United States

4a

tively small amount of land capable of sustaining life with the methods of exploitation known to them. Out of this conflict had grown well-developed political and military systems designed to take and hold territories against other groups of peoples. Within each group, there were usually a privileged few who held the best of the land, but only, as a rule, by exercising a despotism in which there was little benevolence.

When the Europeans entered the American scene they brought systems of political control and land tenure that were essentially the same as those of the Indians. The Conquest of America was naturally a struggle of Europeans against Indians, but it had a more significant side, the use of one Indian group against another in a fashion that is popularly known today as "Fifth Column" activity. Oppressed or conquered peoples were found everywhere to help Cortés, Pizarro, or other conquerors take over the land.

But the military conflict was only one phase of the Conquest. Equally important was the establishment of a sound economy and the seizure of the Indian's land (and the Indian himself) by the European settlers. The first stage of this process took place in the Caribbean area, where there was a twenty-year period of settlement and adjustment before the occupation of the mainland could be successful. Most important among the problems solved by the new settlers was the transplanting of European plants and animals, greatly enriching the agricultural life of America. Without this the Conquest would perhaps have failed. To complete the Conquest, the European settlers had to have control of the land and of labor to work it. Both the European land-control system (the great estates, or latifundia) and labor system (serf and peasant labor) were similar to the systems known to the sedentary Indian tribes. Conquest saw the Europeans supplant the Indians as owners of most of the land (though not all by any means) and the fusion of the European and Indian land-control system into one—the latifundia system. It is particularly important to note that the pre-Conquest Indians were far from having equality of ownership or anything that approached a "communist" system of land holding.

While the Indians in several parts of America had made great progress in developing plants, fertilization of soils, and terracing of lands, their food-producing capacity was less than that of the invading Europeans, and their agricultural techniques less advanced. They had not invented the plow, nor had they domestic animals of importance (except the llama in the Andes). Indian agricultural economy was not an economy of abundance but of scarcity, and even of actual want. Nothing about pre-Conquest America is so true and so tragic as the chronic lack of enough food; and even that which they had was very unevenly divided between the Indian nobles and plebeians. Hunger has been Latin America's basic economic and social ill for many centuries.

When the Europeans came they brought a considerable amelioration of this widespread ill, although not enough even down to the present day. The Spaniards and Portuguese (as well as the English) came mainly as farmers, artisans, and tradesmen. They came to settle, to find new homes, and build new towns. And most of them engaged in such activity.

Thousands of Spaniards (but by no means the majority) went into mining. For this they have been condemned for centuries by foreigners (and sometimes by themselves) as nothing but a "gold-rush rabble"; the search for gold has too often been pictured as the chief economic ailment of colonial Latin America. Mining in reality was not a handicap to the Spanish colonies, but the ignition spark which started up their economic life. Without the discovery of gold and silver in quantities (mainly silver, by the way), the rate of conquest and settlement would have been much slower. While stress is usually placed on the enormous "loot" of Indian gold seized by the Spaniards, the truth is that the Indians had accumulated very little precious metal. The amount of booty was infinitesimal in comparison with the amounts mined by the Spaniards from deposits which the Indians had never discovered, and by technical processes of which the Indians had no knowledge. Furthermore, precious metals gave impetus to agriculture, manufacturing, and trade, rather than supplanted them. Finally, it was the precious metal produced by the Spaniards (and later by the Portuguese) which did so much to stimulate the economic revolutions of Europe that created our immense modern productive power. In some strange way, the production of gold and silver by the Spaniards has been made a peculiarly heinous crime, while the buccaneers who robbed them have been elevated into the ranks of heroes.

When the Spaniards (and other Europeans) reached America they introduced handicraft techniques far superior to all but the best of those practiced by the Indians. This is not to say that the Indians did not do some excellent work; they did. But the productive capacity after the Conquest was greater than before. Active and widespread trade was also a European contribution for, while it is customary to dwell on the restrictions laid on trade by the

Spaniards, the fact is usually overlooked that there was little trade to restrict before they came. Trade, both domestic (among the various parts of America itself) and foreign (with Europe and Asia), was a product of European occupation. The Spaniards restricted trade, of course, but there were also restrictions on the limited, localized commerce that existed before the Conquest. Spain's regulations have frequently been presented as peculiarly oppressive and exclusively Spanish, although in reality Spain's commercial policies were very similar to those common to all Europe at the time of the Conquest when the economy was being transformed from the medieval city-controlled guild systems to nationwide mercantilism. Before the Conquest the Indians had no really seaworthy merchant vessels and no merchandise-worthy overland roads (the Inca roads not excepted); after the Conquest seagoing vessels were built in America, and the roads, though very bad, were better adjusted to commercial transportation than before.

The measures of trade control adopted by the Spaniards were monopolistic in character, it is true, but they were not necessarily evil on that account. We are today adopting more and more practices that savor of monopoly, calling them "planned economy" and finding them good. As for manufactures, Spain's restrictions were rather slight in most cases, while in many ways Spain encouraged colonial industry.

For those who have looked on the Indians as plaster saints, some of the following pages will be a surprise. In the past it has often been the fashion to exalt the "Noble Redman" beyond credibility and to consider the invader as having wrought nothing but destruction. Granted that this extreme point of view has fallen of its own weight, there are still many misconceptions regarding the native civilizations. The Indians were organized into class societies (with a few possible exceptions among the more rudimentary societies) and the poor were ground under the heel of the rich. This system was sanctioned by the Indian laws and customs, and based on the inequalities of land ownership. The poor lived in miserable huts, did all the labor, and enjoyed none of the amenities of life, except indulgence in those forms of escape from misery and relief from oppression that characterize many other peoples in Europe and Asia. Drunkenness was widespread, and sexual mores fitted easily into a Puritan's description of sin.

The prevalence of drinking, incest, adultery, promiscuity, and homosexuality among the pre-Conquest Indians is emphasized here, even though such practices are by no means unknown to other peoples, only because too many writers have elaborated on the "corruption" of the Indians by the Europeans.

The greatest misconceptions about the pre-Conquest situation in America have arisen from the estimates of population. Some authors writing during the seventeenth and eighteenth centuries placed the population of all America at one hundred, and even three hundred millions of people. Many modern authorities have refuted such claims, while clinging to a belief that certain regions were heavily populated, particularly the Inca Empire and the Aztec Confederation. Calculations offered here, in chapter 9, based on pre-Conquest America's food-producing capacity, demonstrate that such large populations could not have existed. The Inca Empire, for example, probably had two or three millions of people instead of the eight, ten, or more millions frequently assigned to it. It is true that the Spanish Conquest was responsible for the destruction of much native life and property, but the enormous masses of people it supposedly annihilated were never there.

In the estimation of the Indian culture, it is fair to say that there were few respects in which it was equal to European importations, and many in which it was distinctly far behind. The cultural life of America (whether Spanish, Portuguese, or Anglo-American) is centuries advanced over what it would have been had America not been discovered by Europeans—judging by the cultural progress of the thousand years preceding the Conquest. In all those respects by which we usually measure the culture of a people, their daily life, their language and literature, their architecture (domestic and public), their craftsmanship, their painting and sculpture, their music, the Indians had but little to teach and much to learn from the Europeans.

To designate one culture as superior to another may not accord with certain anthropological doctrine. Modern schools of sociology, anthropology, and archeology have devised such terms as "adjustment to environment" and "well adapted to the conditions of life," deploring the use of terms that express the idea of "superior" and "inferior" civilizations. Yet they have not been able to avoid using those terms or their equivalents. Reference to recent works shows an abundance of such characterizations as "really high cultures," "matters of sexual morality," "less highly developed socially," "whose culture is almost as crude, if not cruder," "much simpler culture," "we can assume that there were nowhere in South America any higher civilizations," "all the higher cultures of the New World," "weaving was rather highly developed," "wonderful culture," "highest art products." The works of these and other writers abound in expressions that carry the idea of superior or inferior.

Furthermore, archeologists and anthropologists who specialize in native American cultures seldom hesitate to make a comparison in which the Indian civilizations are rated as equal or superior to those of Rome, Greece, or Egypt. It is only when the Indians come off second best that such comparisons become "unscientific." Actually, degrees of civilization exist and we all recognize them. To carry the "well adapted to the conditions of life" theme to the point where an Indian tepee becomes as high an architectural development as the Taj Mahal is to deny all concepts of progress. There is, however, no science of art appreciation. Every man has his own standard of esthetic values; in this book, European contributions to American culture are evaluated considerably above those of the Indians.

Where religion and the Church are concerned in Latin America, several points are made that carry more emphasis, or may be different from some other views on the subject. The essentially religious character of Spanish civilization can hardly be overstressed. When the Spaniards arrived, they found the bulk of the Indians equally zealous, and the quite similar religious practices were largely fused into one. Both the Spanish Church and the native religions played an important political role and so did the blended religion of the colonial period. Because of the pre-eminent place it occupied, the Church is entitled to claim a large share of the credit for the type of civilization developed in Latin America, and it cannot escape censure where censure is due. After the Conquest and Christianization of Latin America, the Church was very naturally a foreign institution, that is, it was the Spanish Roman Catholic Church. In its controlling personnel or management the church was not American at any time during the colonial period, nor has it yet become so entirely. Thus was produced a state within a state, a situation which is the root of some of the most important characteristics of Latin America.

Government was a fusion based on Indian and Spanish concepts that were very like—the authoritarian theory of rulers endowed by divine right to rule over other men. The Incas had a thoroughgoing despotism of this kind, and the Aztecs and some others were not far behind. Only a misconception of the meaning of democracy could lead anyone to speak of the Indian governments as democratic. Spain had merely to apply her own similar ideas to a situation which lent itself to her purposes. Governments at that time were less absolute, however, than many of the totalitarian governments were in 1943, and much autonomous local government (also despotic in character) was known to both Indians and colonials.

The Spanish and Portuguese conquests were continuing operations throughout the colonial period—almost constant expansion was the rule. The history of Latin America is often written, however, as if the Spaniards and Portuguese came in, conquered the natives, sat down, and promptly started to decline; and then, when the retrograde process was complete, the colonies revolted and became nations. Such a concept ignores what may possibly be the only lesson (or law) of history, that of growth and change. Both the Spaniards and Portuguese were pushing out and occupying new territories up to the time when the North Americans were winning their independence from the British; the Latin-American institutions also changed with the centuries. Mining expanded and led to the settlement of new territories and towns. Agriculture developed and found new markets in Europe; commerce, contraband and legal—but *American* commerce, in any case—prospered and excited the acquisitive instincts of almost every European nation; and government also evolved to meet the changing times, independence itself being a step in that evolution.

In this work a special effort has been made to present a clear picture of the cultural evolution of Latin America (chapters 23, 24, 25 and 31. It has been customary for centuries to picture Spain as keeping her colonies in absolute ignorance. Recently the absurdity of such an interpretation has been exposed by many able scholars. Now the pendulum has swung so far back that we may read the equally absurd statement that there were "no restrictions," and that culture in the colonies was "limitless and free." It should not be forgotten that Spain was governed by a divine-right concept of politics, and that her religion was considered the only true religion, and the Church its only true interpreter. Such a divine-right, religious culture differed essentially from our own democratic, secular society, and close supervision of the thoughts of Spanish subjects was deemed as natural then as freedom is to us. But, and here is an important fact to remember: at no time could the State and Church keep thought entirely in the desired channels, and even within the limits permitted there was considerable room for intellectual exercise.

The treatment Brazil receives here probably differs less from the orthodox than does that of the Spanish colonies. The early period of occupation of Brazil, 1500 to 1530, however, is not treated as one of Portuguese neglect (which is customary) but as one of preparation. The importance of economic matters and Brazil's connections with European markets is stressed. The establishment of the Captaincies in 1532-34 is regarded as a mixed capitalistic and feudalistic system. Particular attention is given the factors involved in the Portuguese penetration of the interior, mainly the increase and migration of livestock, and the hunt for slaves and precious metals. The benefits, rather than the disadvantages, of the Dutch invasion, 1630 to 1654, are emphasized. The agricultural decline usually blamed on the discovery of gold in 1694 is shown to have taken place half a century earlier, and to have had other causes, while the period of greatest mining activity, 1700 to 1760, coincided with general economic development. The Jesuits are praised here where praise is due, but evidence of certain short-comings of Jesuits and other churchmen is not overlooked. The cultural life of Brazil is presented as the product of a rural civilization, and as creating little that was original until the late eighteenth century.

The salient interpretations of this book have been set forth, but full exposition and sustaining proof can only be developed, of course, as the story unfolds.

The Indians Conquer America

IN SEARCH OF LAND AND WATER

THE DOMINATING THEME in the history of pre-Columbian America was the struggle for land and subsistence, a struggle in which men fought to overcome the obstacles of nature, to protect what they already had secured, and to take from their fellowmen. The story is not always a pretty one but it has its noble as well as ignoble moments. It is the story of the effort to rise from bare existence to higher living standards, and it is full of triumphs and laudable accomplishments.

Several thousand years ago, intermittent invasions of America began from Asia by way of the Bering Strait. Slowly the newcomers moved southward, [1] when nature or other men forced them to do so. These first men were still in the food-gathering stages of culture and they brought few of the primary elements of material civilization. The spear-thrower, perhaps the bow, the fire-drill, basket-making, and stone chipping represented their achievements. They knew nothing of agriculture and, except for a type of dog, nothing of domestic animals. They knew nothing of the wheel,

---

[1] J. Eric Thompson, *Mexico before Cortés* (New York, 1933); Philip Ainsworth Means, *Ancient Civilizations of the Andes* (New York: Scribners, 1931); Herbert J. Spinden, *Ancient Civilizations of Mexico and Central America* (New York: American Museum of Natural History, 1928); George C. Vaillant, *Aztecs of Mexico* (New York: Doubleday, Doran Company, 1941).

Many theories have been proposed in explanation of the presence of man in America. These include migrations from the lost continents of Mu and Atlantis, and hardly more probable, descent from the lost tribes of Israel, the Welsh, the Spanish bishops fleeing from the Moslems, the Homeric Greeks, or mariners coming from the East Indian Islands. Lewis Hanke in *The First Social Experiments in America* (Cambridge: Harvard University Press, 1935), pp. 3-7, offers a bibliography for this subject. It is entirely possible that small groups came from the Pacific islands or from Africa, but the bulk of evidence points to an Asiatic origin. Juan de Torquemada, in *Los veinte i un libros rituales i monarchia indiana* (2d ed.; 3 vols., Madrid, 1723), first published in Madrid in 1613, in Book I, chapters XI-XII, discusses the Indian idea of their own origin.

ATHABALIBA
ultimus Rex Peruanorum

Courtesy of the Pan American Union

PORTRAIT OF ATAHUALPA

VOLCANO OF IXTACIHUATL.

Courtesy of the Mexican Tourist Bureau

INDIAN DISTRIBUTION
IN
LATIN AMERICA
ABOUT 1500

Approximate areas inhabited by
Indians in higher stages of culture.

Approximate areas inhabited by
Indians in intermediate stages.

Approximate areas inhabited by
Indians in low stages of development.

Scale of Miles
0   500   1000   1500

Adopted from *History of the Latin-American Nations* by W. S. Robertson

12*a*

plow, pottery, weaving, or metal working. Migrations from Asia must have ceased before the Asiatics had domesticated animals and learned to cultivate rice, wheat, and other products of the Old World, or else the American Indians would have had these things. Later, the men of America were destined to develop their own plants. [2]

Except by inference, we know little of the migrations of men in America, but we do know that when Europeans lifted the curtain and revealed the American drama, warfare and conflict were the normal order from the Arctic Circle to Tierra del Fuego. Men were killing one another over hunting grounds, water-holes, river valleys, lake sites, flint beds, salt deposits, arable lands, and water for irrigation. Thus most of the area of America was inhabited by men living on a bare subsistence level, retarded by nature or by stronger men who prevented them from moving to better lands. But such a stage of civilization could support only a limited population. The majority of the people of the New World were concentrated in the more advanced, food-producing regions of Mexico, Central America, and the Andes.

The peoples inhabiting America in 1492 were divided into hundreds of language and sublanguage groups. For purposes of simplification, the following main groupings in Latin America may be distinguished:

1. The Nahua-speaking peoples: from Central Mexico to Nicaragua.

2. The Maya: Yucatán and Guatemala.

3. The Chibchas: Central America, western Colombia, and northwestern Ecuador.

4. The Quechuas: the Andean mountains from southern Ecuador to northern Chile.

5. The Aymarás: Highlands of Bolivia.

6. The Araucanian-Patagonians: southern Chile and the plains of southern Argentina.

7. The Guaraní and Tupí Indians: the forested portions of the northern La Plata basin, and Brazil.

8. The Caribs and Arawaks: Venezuela, part of the Guianas, Brazil, and the West Indies.

THE INCESSANT STRUGGLE: THE MEXICANS CONQUER MEXICO

In few places in America was there stability. The ownership of hunting grounds was frequently in dispute, and agricultural land-

---

[2] Vaillant, *Aztecs*, pp. 1-27.

rights were ill defined. Rival claimants were at war much of the time. While these rivalries were expressed in terms of tribe, their roots were often in the struggle for land rather than in "race" or "blood." The real conquest of America by the Indians centered in material resources. In Mexico, for example, the land wars were fought among people of the same language and customs.

It is not known who the earliest settlers of Mexico were, but the Nahua-speaking peoples dominated from about the eighth century, at which time the Toltec culture had developed. Toltec means "skilled workers," and many of the prehistoric monuments of Mexico indicate that their builders were worthy of their name. [3]

By about the twelfth century other invaders, of more limited culture but greater virility, pushed their way in. These were the *Chichimecas,* another of the Nahua-speaking peoples, of whom the Aztecs (Mexicans) were one branch. [4]

The latter had reached the central valley of Mexico where they settled about 1325 A.D. on islands in the lakes. There they lived by permission of the city of Azcapotzalco, to which for a time they paid tribute. But once settled, the Mexicans started on a path of conquest which gave them control of what is today central Mexico and carried them at times as far south as Guatemala. [5]

A sixteenth-century chronicler, Diego Muñoz Camargo, tersely describes the situation as follows: [6]

"Seditious ambition was presently introduced, and as . . . the empire of the Mexicans was expanding, they were not content with what was their own but rose in arms against the

[3] Torquemada, *Monarchia indiana,* Bk. I, chap. XIV; Herbert Ingram Priestley, *The Mexican Nation, a History* (New York: The Macmillan Company, 1930), pp. 15-33; William H. Prescott, *History of the Conquest of Mexico* (3 vols., New York: Harpers, 1843, and numerous other editions), I, Bk. I, chaps. I, II; Vaillant, *Aztecs,* pp. 1-86.

[4] The terms *Aztec* and *Mexican* are synonymous. On the origin of the Mexicans see *Origen de los mexicanos (Nueva colección de documentos para la historia de México,* [hereafter *Nueva C. D. México*], ed. García Icazbalceta, 5 vols., Mexico, 1886-1892), III, 281-308; Torquemada, *Monarchia indiana,* Bk. I, chaps. XV-XXVIII.

[5] Vaillant, *Aztecs,* pp. 214-19, stresses localism among the Indians and says that the subjected peoples retained much autonomy while paying tribute to the Aztecs. Torquemada, *Monarchia indiana,* Bk. II, has an excellent discussion of the coming of the Mexicans, their trials and sufferings, their wars for land, their subjection as tribute payers at first, and their triumph as tribute collectors later. See also Francesco Saverio Clavigero, *The History of Mexico,* tr. Charles Cullen (2 vols., London, 1787), Bks. II-V, for the expansion of the Mexican Empire, and Dissertations I-II, for origin of man in America, the principal epochs in Mexican pre-Cortés history, and a chronology of Mexican kings. Such accounts should not be considered accurate in detail, but they do show the general picture.

[6] The Spanish custom is to use two family names. The middle name is that of the father and the last the mother's. However, there are exceptions to this custom, and sometimes the father's name is used alone. More rarely, the mother's name is adopted and used as the surname.

people . . . [of the surrounding territory] without any justice
whatever . . . [and] since everything was turning out so successfully, they continued gaining and conquering territories and
provinces, making themselves the absolute lords, for with the
great armies they gathered together they terrorized the entire
land. Some provinces surrendered peaceably and other were conquered by force of arms . . . [and] there was neither province
nor kingdom which could confront them and which they could
not overcome and conquer." [7]

Presently an alliance was formed among Tenochtitlán, Téxcoco,
and Tlacopán, three cities located on the lakes of Mexico's central
valley, and their aggressive career continued until cut short by the
coming of the Europeans.

A predatory empire cannot be built up without the trappings of
militarism, and long before 1492 the Aztecs developed a philosophy
and technique of war, involving patriotism, nationalism, localism,
group loyalty, and religion, to lend idealism to their struggle for
existence. Bearing arms was the most honored occupation; the war
god, Huitzilopochtli, the most respected deity. War was a crusade;
salvation was certain for the soldier who died face to face with the
foe; and human blood alone could placate Huitzilopochtli to whom,
the chroniclers allege, twenty thousand people were sacrificed in
1487 alone. [8]

When Montezuma II (1466-1520) ascended the throne (1502),
the tribute-paying subjects of the Aztec realm felt the heavy weight
of the increased splendor of the court. Montezuma exacted gold,
silver, copper, cotton, salt, feathers, resins, maize, wax, honey,
pumpkin seed, and other products proportionate in amount to the
lands held by each tributary. Those who could, brought fish, sea
shells, cacao, henequen, rare fruits, and wild animals such as
jaguars, mountain lions, eagles, wolves, monkeys, and parrots. [9]

---

[7] Diego Muñoz Camargo, *Historia de Tlaxcala* (México, 1892), pp. 106-109.
Muñoz Camargo was himself a Tlaxcalan *mestizo* (mixed-blood), and thus he is
something of a national historian. His account needs some correction and must be
checked by archeological findings and by other sixteenth century chroniclers, but it
has the virtue of presenting the story of the Tlaxcalans, Aztecs, and other Indian
groups and their never ending quarrels in their true light—as struggles for possession of land. Muñoz Camargo could see behind tribal names and kinship relations to the powerful forces which motivated first the Indians (before the discovery)
and later the Europeans.

[8] Diego Barros Arana, *Compendio de historia de América* (2nd ed., 2 vols.,
Santiago de Chile, 1865), I, 48-50. See also Vaillant, *Aztecs,* pp. 103-07; 200-06;
211-23; 240-41. Twenty thousand, the number given by the sources, is perhaps an
exaggeration. Prescott, *Mexico,* I, Bk. I, chap. III.

[9] Muñoz Camargo, *Tlaxcala,* p. 139.

BROTHER'S BLOOD AND CLASS WAR

The story of the Tlaxcalans who lived to the east of the Aztecs but still on the central plateau, epitomizes the struggle for existence. [10] Like the Aztecs, they were a branch of the Nahua-speaking peoples and had come into the region at about the same time, but they had managed to maintain themselves in partial independence of the Aztec confederation. When they arrived, they had found the greater part of the country already inhabited by their relatives, the Aztecs, and the Tlaxcalans settled for a time around the central lakes where they were well received by earlier comers who recognized them as "kinsmen and relatives, . . . and who, seeing that such great numbers of people had no land in which to settle, supplied them and marked off a site where they could establish themselves until a place could be found for them to remain."

Kinship ties were, however, not strong enough for this hospitality to endure after it became apparent that the Tlaxcalans "occupied a great deal of land," and were "troublesome neighbors" who desired to expand. The Aztecs and their allies decided to get rid of them. Thus, driven from behind by stronger foes and always seeking the land and water that would give them life, they moved eastward, where they discovered unoccupied lands that were suitable for habitation. [11]

But no "promised land" was sufficient to settle the eternal struggle for territory and economic advantages. The Tlaxcalans fought with the Aztecs, who "managed by astuteness and cunning" to conquer everything around the Tlaxcalans down to the coast, and to cut them off from trade. At the time the Spaniards entered Mexico this conflict was still in progress, the Aztecs holding the Tlaxcalans virtually blockaded and "lacking every human need, since they had no cotton with which to make clothes, nor gold, nor silver with which to adorn themselves, nor cacao to drink, nor salt to eat." "All these things they lacked, and many others during the more than sixty years that the siege lasted." [12]

Not only was it necessary for the Tlaxcalans to win their territory by force of arms and defend it against the Mexicans, but they engaged in bloody internal wars over its ownership. Once settled, some of the Indians "began taking possession of all the land and making themselves very powerful landlords. And so . . . the

---

[10] Prescott, *Mexico*, I, Bk. III, chap. II. The origins of the wars between the Mexicans and Tlaxcalans are described in Torquemada, *Monarchia indiana*, Bk. II, chaps. LXX-LXXV.

[11] Muñoz Camargo, *Tlaxcala*, pp. 23-53.

[12] *Ibid*, pp. 107-108.

greater part of the plebeians . . . raising the cry of liberty . . . attacked the chief captains . . . in order to free themselves and to be the owners of what they had won and settled." In the "brutal and bloody civil war" which followed, "brother was against brother, fathers against sons, and sons against fathers." [13]

THE INCESSANT STRUGGLE EVERYWHERE

As we survey the American scene we may find this theme— the struggle for land—repeated a thousand times. An early chronicler, Pedro de Cieza de León, speaks of one of the tribes in Panama as invaders who "fought so fiercely with the natives of the land that they killed them all cruelly, and robbed them of their lands and became owners of their fields and inheritances." [14] References to Indians of present-day Colombia who "were forced at last to leave their native land," or who successfully captured a region "killing all the natives," are numerous. [15]

In the Caribbean islands the same situation existed. The sixteenth-century historian, López de Gómara, mentions that in Española [Hispaniola (Santo Domingo and Haiti)], "They [Indians] did not make war frequently, except over boundaries, or fishing grounds," [16] a statement which would apply equally well to Cuba, Puerto Rico, and the other islands.

THE INCAS BUILD AN EMPIRE

Nothing illustrates the fundamental economic struggle better than the history of the peoples who were united under the Incas. "In Peru, the Indians talk of nothing else except how some came from one part and others from another, and how through wars and conflicts some made themselves owners of the lands of the others; and indeed it seems true! . . . It can be clearly seen that the Incas made themselves lords of this kingdom by force and craftiness, since they say that Manco Capac, who founded Cuzco, had few scruples (tuvo poco principio) . . . from which it can be gathered that war and tyranny were as customary among these

---

[13] *Ibid.,* pp. 55-57.

[14] Pedro de Cieza de León, *La crónica del Perú, primera parte* (Sevilla, 1553, and numerous other editions). Citations here from *Biblioteca de autores españoles* (71 vols., Madrid, 1846-1880), vol. XXVI, chap. VI. See also Pedro Pizarro, *Relation of the Discovery and Conquest of the Kingdoms of Peru,* ed. and tr. Philip Ainsworth Means (2 vols., New York: The Cortes Society, 1921). The original manuscript is in the Huntington Library (No. 167) and differs in some respects from the Navarrete text Means used in making his translation. Pedro Pizarro questions the authenticity of Cieza and suggests that he might have taken bribes to praise certain men.

[15] Cieza, *ibid.,* chap. XXIV.

[16] Francisco López de Gómara, *La historia de las Indias* (Zaragoza, 1552-53). fol. XVII, recto.

Indians as in other parts of the world, since we read that tyrants established themselves as rulers of extensive dominions and kingdoms." [17]

Before and during the early days of the rise of the Incas, the territories of Peru were divided under governments that ranged from the rudimentary kinship type to more complicated territorial confederacies. The simpler units were headed by a *sinchi,* meaning "strong man," or war chief, who held office during times of stress, but descended to the level of other citizens in times of peace. The more complicated structures were ruled by a permanent chieftain known as the *curaca.* Both classes of states perennially were in a condition of war, because of an intense desire to possess fields for agriculture and llama herds. [18]

The sharp struggle for land might seem strange in an area as large as South America unless we remember that this continent has a relatively small amount of soil capable of sustaining even semi-civilized life under the methods of production that were available to the Indians. More than half the continent is jungle. Before the Spaniards came, the great plains of Brazil, Uruguay, and Argentina supported no domesticated animals and little other life. The Andean area, locale of the Inca Empire, suffers from two geographical defects that rendered most of it uninhabitable. The Pacific coastline is a desert from north Peru to north-central Chile. Only the narrow valleys watered by the freshets from the Andes, and comprising not more than three per cent of the coastline, are productive. The desert region extends over mountains into western Argentina, making a vast area too arid to be cultivated without irrigation. Furthermore, the western slopes of the Andes are deserts of giant rocky boulders, absolutely barren of plant life except in a few sheltered valleys. Since life was, and is, possible in the Andes only in such limited areas, men have always fought desperately to hold on to their valley lands.

The traditions preserved among the Indians show us a land bathed in blood. The chiefs "did not occupy themselves with anything but making war on their neighbors to despoil them of their possessions." [19] When peace came it "lasted but a short time in Peru, because the inhabitants, who had now grown numerous, be-

---

[17] Cieza, *Crónica,* chap. CXVI.

[18] Philip Ainsworth Means, *Ancient Civilizations,* pp. 284-85.

[19] Miguel Cabello Balboa, *Historia del Perú bajo la dominación de los Incas (Colección de libros y documentos referentes a la historia del Perú* [hereafter *C.L.D. Perú*], 2nd ser., eds. Horacio H. Urteaga and Carlos A. Romero; Lima, 1920), II, 3. This work was written from 1576 to 1586.

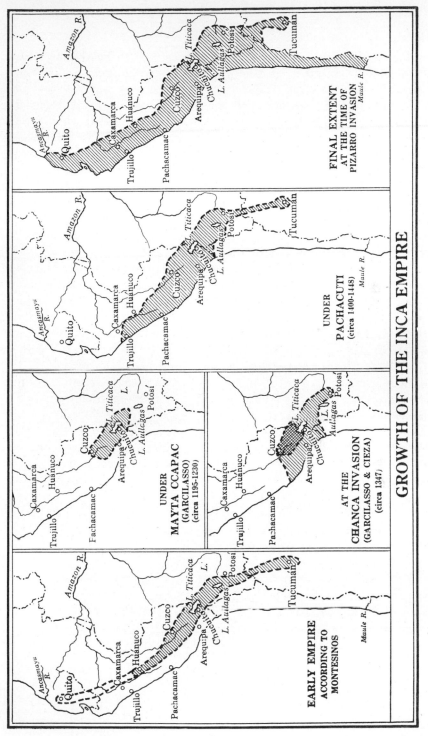

EARLY EMPIRE
ACCORDING TO
MONTESINOS

UNDER
MAYTA CCAPAC
(GARCILASSO)
(circa 1195-1230)

AT THE
CHANCA INVASION
(GARCILASSO & CIEZA)
(circa 1347)

UNDER
PACHACUTI
(circa 1400-1448)

FINAL EXTENT
AT THE TIME OF
PIZARRO INVASION

GROWTH OF THE INCA EMPIRE

18a

gan to quarrel among themselves over the waters and the pastures." [20]

INCA AGGRESSION BECOMES A PROFESSION

The interminable struggle for land as the indispensable prerequisite of life can be seen still more clearly in the rise of the Incas
where vast areas, rather than individual plots or provinces, were
at stake. The Incas were one of the numerous groups contending
for mastery in the Andean area. Perhaps as early as the eleventh
century (and probably not until the thirteenth) they settled at
Cuzco. In many respects their rise was similar to that of their
neighbors. Governed at first by a temporary chieftain, or *sinchi*,
they developed a class of permanent and hereditary rulers. Their
earliest historical ruler was the Inca Sinchi Roca. Gradually they
extended their rule, by threat of force where this was sufficient and
by use of force where imperative.

Conquest became the duty of each succeeding ruler, and tradition held nothing but contempt for the Inca who failed to extend
the empire. The heirs to the throne were trained for war and at
the age of eighteen given military investiture. The youth of the
nobility were put through a rigorous military and physical training, and if they passed the ordeals set for them, they were inducted
into the military ranks with great ceremony. War was the means by
which the Inca ruling caste increased its prerogatives. Military
service was obligatory for all, and the masses served in rotation.

The Inca system of conquest worked well. The olive branch was
extended in the mailed fist. Peace could be had from the Incas at
the price of submission and the payment of tribute; war meant
ultimate submission, plus devastation. Professing that they had a
civilizing mission, the Incas left a history of almost constant war
and conquest. [21] They imposed their language, religion, and economic supremacy upon the conquered. [22]

[20] Fernando de Montesinos, *Memorias antiguas historiales y politicas del Perú*,
written *ca.* 1642, *C.L.D. Perú*, VI, 5.

[21] William Robertson, *The History of America* (2 vols., London, 1777), Bk. VII,
gives a good picture of war technique and psychology. Robertson's work was well
received at the time it was published and continues to be of primary importance.
Translated into many languages, it has gone through numerous editions. Charles
III refused Robertson permission to study the Spanish Archives, and an attempt
was made to stop the circulation of the Spanish translation of his *History*. It
reached Latin America nevertheless, and enabled eighteenth-century *Americanos*
to see their land through the eyes of a foreign observer who has since been acknowledged as relatively impartial by Spanish historians.

[22] Cieza, *Crónica*, chap. XLI; Pedro de Cieza de León, *Segunda parte de la
Crónica del Perú que trata del señorío de los Incas Yupanquis y de sus grandes
hechos y gobernación*, ed. Marcos Jiménez de la Espada (Madrid, 1880), chap.
XXIV.

To maintain control over their large territories, they instituted the system of *mitimaes* or *mitmaccuna*. The *mitimaes* were people removed from one area to another. They fell into three classes: trustworthy subjects transferred to recently acquired territory; newly conquered peoples moved to within the old boundaries; and the military forces encamped throughout the empire. The mitimaes "were held in great honor by the Incas, and privileged, and considered second only to the *Orejones* [the Inca nobles] the noblest of the provinces." [23]

The Inca Garcilaso de la Vega, whose mother was a member of the Inca royal family and whose father was a Spanish conquistador, states that "they transplanted them [the mitimaes] also for another reason, and this was that when they had conquered some bellicose province . . . they removed a part of the people of the said province, and often they removed them all . . . to another of the conquered provinces, where, seeing themselves surrounded on all sides by loyal and peaceable vassals, they might also be loyal, bending the neck to the yoke that they could not now throw off." [24] The sons of the subject nobility were forced to live in Cuzco, where they might be trained in the language and government of the Incas and serve as hostages, guaranteeing the Incas against revolt. [25] The mitimaes were in fact the chief cog in the Inca's system of domination. Among their duties was that of aiding the stewards "to collect the tributes of the surrounding provinces." The capital of the Incas, Cuzco, "was more than six hundred leagues from Quito and still further from Chile," and "as all this long and narrow strip of land was inhabited by barbarian people, some of them very warlike," it was necessary for the Incas to maintain military garrisons. Thousands of people were transplanted for this purpose, so that "if the natives revolted, they . . . were punished and reduced to the service of the Incas." [26]

They had other duties also. "There were among them spies who were always listening to what the natives said [and] by this means everything was secure, for the mitimaes feared the natives and the natives the mitimaes, and all obeyed and served meekly. And if

---

[23] Cieza, *Señorío,* chap. XXII.

[24] Garcilaso de la Vega, el Inca, *Los comentarios reales de los Incas, primera parte* (2 vols., Lisbon, 1609), Bk. VII, chap. I; and *Segunda parte,* also known as the *Historia general del Perú* (Córdoba, 1617), and issued in several other editions and translations since. The edition used here is that published in Lima, 1918-1920, by H. H. Urteaga, all citations having been compared with the original where the meaning seemed obscure.

[25] Means, *Ancient Civilizations,* pp. 345-47; Bernabé Cobo, *Historia del Nuevo Mundo,* written in 1653 (Seville, 1890-1893), Bk. XII, chap. XXIII.

[26] Cieza, *Crónica,* chap. XLI.

among one or the other there were insurrections or plots or meetings, their perpetrators were severely castigated, because some of
the Incas were vindictive and punished without moderation and
with great cruelty."

The pay the mitimaes received also seemed desirable. They were
"given clothing of wool and feathers, or bracelets of gold and of
silver," as well as "women from among the many who were kept
in the name of the Inca, in each province, and as most of these were
beautiful, they valued them highly." [27]

The military system had as its object, of course, the complete
domination of the empire and its resources for the benefit of the
Inca and the Inca nobility. Garcilaso reminds us of this in his discussion of the mitimaes, where he says that "the Incas, moreover,
did this for their own good and in order to have maize for their
armies." [28] The supplies of arms, clothing, and food for the army
were kept in storehouses distributed along the roads throughout
the empire, and a garrison of soldiers was maintained at each
depot to protect the stores. Special agricultural lands were set aside
by the Inca to maintain the army. "The second part of the lands
and fields (tierras y heredades)," the sixteenth-century historian
José de Acosta says, "were for the Inca; from this part he maintained himself, his household (servicio) and soldiers, and therefore
this was the largest part of the tributes as may be seen from the
warehouses or public granaries (casas de pósito), which are longer
and wider than the warehouses of the [priests]." [29]

DESPOTISM WITHOUT BENEVOLENCE

With the machinery of war here outlined the Incas had extended
their power from northern Ecuador to Chile. [30] To the eastward
the boundaries reached only to the watershed of the Andes, except
in a few places where there were coca plantations on the eastern

---

[27] Cieza, Señorio, chap. XXII.
[28] Garcilaso, Comentarios, Bk. VII, chap. I.
[29] José de Acosta, Historia natural y moral de las Indias (Sevilla, 1590, and
other editions; the one used here being that of Madrid, 1894, 2 vols.) Bk. VI, chap.
XV, pp. 186-87.
[30] The conquest of the northern part of the empire was of recent date, and it
seems clear that the hold of the Incas had never been completely acknowledged by
the natives. That the empire extended to the Maule river in Chile is subject to
some doubt (although maintained by Garcilaso, Comentarios, Bk. VII, chaps.
XVIII-XX), because of other evidence by Garcilaso, Segunda parte, Bk. II, chaps.
XX-XXII, where he relates Almagro's expedition of discovery and conquest into
Chile in 1535.

Almagro spent several months on a trip which in theory he could have made
in a few days over supposedly fine roads, and he lost ten thousand of his fifteen
thousand Indians from starvation and cold, although it was summer in the southern
hemisphere. The Incas had doubtless made conquests in Chile, but the territory was
undeveloped and their hold on it insecure.

side of the mountains. If we are to understand the growth of the Inca empire, we must give some attention to how the military machine was employed, for its development and use were an essential part of the Inca expansion.

It is customary to stress the benevolence of the Incas, with the system of transplanting populations offered as proof, and neighboring Indians pictured as eager to surrender to the Inca. One example cited is that of the Chancas, who were defeated by the Incas and incorporated into the Empire. But in spite of the assertedly benign character of the Inca system, the conquered Chancas showed little appreciation for their rulers' kindness and soon "fled from the Inca's sway" to the east of the Andes.[31]

Much of the writing about the Incas has been inspired by Prescott, but his successors have paid too great attention to his rather romantic accounts of the Incas and too little to the specific instances of despotism he cites. Prescott was fully aware of the real character of Inca rule. He knew it to be a military despotism, based on the domination and exploitation of the land resources and people in the Andean area. "Not an insurrectionary movement could occur," he says, "not an invasion on the remotest frontier, before the tidings were conveyed to the capital, and the imperial armies were on their march across the magnificent roads of the country to suppress it. So admirable was the machinery contrived by the American despots for maintaining tranquility throughout their dominions!" To which he adds: "Notwithstanding the pacific professions of the Incas, and the pacific tendency, indeed, of their domestic institutions, they were constantly at war . . . Religion furnished a plausible pretext for incessant aggression, and disguised the lust of conquest in the Incas, probably, from their own eyes, as well as from those of their subjects."[32]

CIVIL WAR IN THE INCA DOMAIN

The empire was not thoroughly subjected despite the elaborate military system. Huayna Capac (1484 to 1528), last of the emperors of a united realm, who came to the throne after overcoming

---

[31] Means, *Ancient Civilizations*, pp. 245, 252.

[32] William Hickling Prescott, *History of the Conquest of Peru* (2 vols., New York, 1847, and numerous other editions), Bk. I, chap. II. Prescott has been considered the classic historian for the age of Ferdinand and Isabella, Charles V, Philip II, and the conquests of Peru and Mexico. Numerous works have been written since his appeared almost a century ago, but we can hardly say that any of the later books have superseded Prescott. Certainly they have not in literary charm. His romanticism is frequently a result of a literary excellence which blinds the reader to the harshness of what Prescott is describing. The aspects of Peru's history in which he has been superseded are more properly archeological than historical.

rival claimants, was faced with revolt at the time of his accession. [33]
Once in possession of the throne, he was forced to send an army
to reconquer peoples, among them the Huancavillcas, who had
submitted to his father and then revolted. Garcilaso tells the story
of this revolt, and remarks that if the rebels had been punished
as their treason deserved "not one of the whole of the nations would
have remained alive of any sex or age. But, the Inca Huayna
Capac, with his accustomed clemency . . . pardoned all the common people; and he also pardoned those who had been the authors
and executors of the treachery, who deserved death with all their
kinsmen; except as a reminder and punishment for their crime, he
beheaded only the tenth part of them." [34]

There were other uprisings and civil wars. Puná, an island conquered by Huayna Capac early in his reign, revolted together with
the adjacent mainland. Huayna Capac "ordered hanged all the
principal authors and counsellors of the rebellion and the most
important captains and soldiers." [35] A few years later, while
Huayna Capac was engaged in further wars of conquest, "news was
brought to him that the great province of the Chachapuyas . . .
had rebelled, feeling themselves secure because of their cragged
territory and the numerous and very bellicose people they had." [36]
Toward the end of his reign the Caranques, conquered earlier, revolted. Huayna Capac selected two thousand of the chief Indians
and "ordered [his followers] to behead all." [37]

The idea of extending the empire persisted, nevertheless, and
Huayna Capac added large areas to the Inca domain. Just at the
end of his reign, a temporary lull in the wars enabled Cieza to write
that "the empire of the Incas was so peaceful at the death of
Huayna Capac that in all its vast extent there was no one who
dared lift his head to revolt or refuse to obey, as much on account
of their fear of Huayna Capac as because of the mitimaes, who
were always at hand, and the military authority vested in them." [38]

But Huayna Capac had been dead only a short time when civil
war broke out between the two sons he had designated to share the
throne. Huáscar was accounted the legitimate heir, and received
the capital at Cuzco and the larger part of the empire. Atahualpa,
son of a princess of Quito and regarded as illegitimate, received

[33] Means, *Ancient Civilizations*, pp. 272-74.
[34] Garcilaso, *Comentarios*, Bk. IX, chap. III.
[35] *Ibid.*, Bk. IX, chap. VI.
[36] *Ibid.*, Bk. IX, chap. VII.
[37] *Ibid.*, Bk. IX, chap. XI; Cieza, *Crónica*, chap. XXXVII, says twenty thousand.
[38] Cieza, *Señorío*, chap. LXIX.

the northern part with its capital at Quito. The usual interpretation
given to this division is that Huayna Capac wished to leave something to his favorite son. It seems more likely that stronger reasons
than this prevailed. The northern part of the empire was newly
won, as yet far from pacified, and Atahualpa's appointment represented a concession to "home rule." Garcilaso states that Atahualpa
was named to "appease and tranquillize those newly gained maritime and mediterranean [mountain] provinces which . . `. had
never become tranquil under the dominion and government of the
Incas." [39] Atahualpa's uprising was little more than a continuation
of past civil wars.

The war that broke out between the brothers was carried on in
the best Inca tradition. Atahualpa captured Huáscar, and then began an attempt to exterminate Huáscar's family.

> "Atahualpa took a cruel advantage of his victory, because, with
> misrepresentation and pretense that he wished to restore Huás-
> car to his throne, he commanded that all the Incas of the whole
> of the realm be called, including the governors and other civil
> officials, as well as the marshals *(maeses de campo),* captains, and
> soldiers, to gather in Cuzco in order, he said, to conclude an
> agreement with them concerning certain charters and statutes
> that should henceforth be observed between the two monarchs,
> so that they might live in peace and brotherhood. . . . When he
> had gathered them all together, Atahualpa ordered that all
> should be killed in various ways, in order to insure himself
> against their organizing an uprising." [40]

Not content with killing off the royal family, Atahualpa and his
men executed almost all the captains and nobles they had imprisoned. Still unsatisfied, Atahualpa "sent an order that the greatest possible number of women and children of the royal blood should
be brought together, . . . and that they should be killed by degrees . . . with various and cruel punishments so that they might
be a long time dying." [41]

Nor did this end the bloodletting. Atahualpa ordered put to the
sword the servants of the royal household, punishing even the door-

[39] Garcilaso, *Comentarios,* Bk. IX, chap. XII.
[40] *Ibid.,* Bk. IX', *chap.* XXXV.
[41] *Ibid.,* Bk. IX, chap. XXXVII. The account of these massacres might be considered exaggerated if given by Garcilaso alone, but others agree with him and
add further details of cruelty. Cabello Balboa, chap. XXI, describes the disem-
boweling of pregnant women, and Sarmiento de Gamboa in his *Historia Índica,*
published by Richard Pietschmann as *Geschichte des inkareiches* (Berlin, 1906),
par. 66, p. 122, gives the same story. See vol. III, chap. XXXVII, p. 100, note 15,
of the Urteaga and Romero edition of Garcilaso.

keepers, stewards, cooks, gardeners, and woodcutters. He not only exterminated the individuals who served the royal household, but destroyed the towns that supplied them, beheading their inhabitants—men, women, and children—and burning and razing the houses and royal edifices. Garcilaso says "none of the towns that were within five, six, or seven leagues of Cuzco failed to suffer individual persecution from that cruelty and tyranny, in addition to the general persecution that the whole realm suffered, for throughout there was bloodletting, burning of towns, robbery, violence, rape, and other evils, such as are customary when military license is unrestrained *(según la liberated militar los suele hacer cuando toma la licencia de si mesma)*." Throughout the empire, Atahualpa ordered the war to be prosecuted with "fire and sword," and took an especially "bloody revenge" on the Cañaris, who had refused to join him in rebellion. The city of Tumipampa was "devastated." [42] According to Cieza, Atahualpa's general made a gold-embossed drinking cup from the skull of Atoco, Huáscar's general, who was murdered after his capture, and the majority of the prisoners taken by Atahualpa were killed on his orders. [43]

Although Spanish invasion coincided with the bloody civil war, much of the destruction of life and property in Indian America must be attributed to the intestine conflicts. Cieza de León, who never spared his own countrymen, condemning their every act of cruelty and destruction, remarks that because of the wars between Huáscar and Atahualpa, the people had "diminished greatly." [44]

When Pizarro reached Túmbez (which he had formerly seen in a state of peace) in 1532, he was "astonished on entering the town, to find it not only deserted, but, with the exception of a few buildings, entirely demolished. Four or five of the most substantial private dwellings, the great temple, and the fortress—and these damaged and wholly despoiled of their great interior decorations—alone survived to mark the site of the city, and attest its former splendor." The chieftains of the district "explained the dilapidated condition of the town by the long wars carried on with the fierce tribes of Puná, who had at length succeeded in getting possession of the place, and driving the inhabitants into the neighboring woods and mountains. The Inca, to whose cause they were attached, was too much occupied with his own feuds to protect them against their enemies." [45]

---

[42] *Ibid.*, Bk. IX, chap. XXXIX.
[43] Cieza, *Señorío*, chap. LXXII.
[44] *Crónica*, chap. LXXVII.
[45] Prescott, *Peru*, Bk. III, chap. III.

MEN FIGHT FOR LAND AND WATER

Everywhere the same story was repeated. In Chile, the endless struggle over land and waterways, which taken together meant food, clothing, and shelter, was in progress at the time the Spaniards arrived. Among the plains Indians of Argentina and Uruguay, the forest dwellers of Paraguay, and over the vast areas of Brazil, the struggle for existence was as certain as life and death. Variations on the theme naturally occurred: if the land was fertile, and the population was heavy, men fought over small plots; but the struggle was no less bitter on the vast plains where the population was sparse. In the region of the Caribbean, the islands were disputed between the sedentary Arawaks and the warlike Caribs, the latest claimants.

When Columbus entered America, he brought nothing new in essence to add to this incessant conflict. He brought only new men with the old desire, land. America was rocked from end to end with the ceaseless struggle. The Indians would have been too weak in any case to resist the stronger arms of the Europeans, but the disunion that existed everywhere facilitated the European task of conquest.

The story of America had begun with the first migratory tribes entering the New World, probably from Asia, in search of sustenance. Land and water were their goal, and they were driven on by nature's niggardliness or the pressure of other tribes. Vast as were the unpeopled reaches of the new continent, these Indians warred with one another for the possession of the fertile, game-bearing areas.

More advanced agricultural civilizations evolved in the food-producing regions of Mexico, Central America, and the Andes, where the cultivation of the land could support a denser population. Since the soil suitable for agriculture under the methods known to the Indians was limited, these civilizations were built in constant struggle for the possession of the land. Two Indian empires, that of the Aztecs in Mexico and that of the Incas in Peru, were in existence when the Spaniards entered America. These empires expanded through aggression, and inevitably their conquests were marked by exploitation of the conquered. Subject peoples rebelled, and the revolts were cruelly put down. Civil strife raged within the empires. In Mexico, Cortés found the Aztecs and their neighbors warring over the land. In Peru, the devastating civil war between the rival claimants to the Inca power had been going on for years when Pizarro came.

Throughout what is now Latin America, in Colombia and in the Caribbean islands, on the plains of Argentina and in Brazil, Indians slew Indians for land—the means of existence and the source of wealth. The Inca rulers fought for an empire; their subjects fought for small plots; but in substance the fight was the same. Land-hunger dominated pre-Colombian history; land-hunger continued to dominate after the conquest. The Europeans joined the civil wars, and the Indians continued to carry on their conquest of America, but this time for the benefit of the Europeans. Henceforth, America is a product of the fusion of the Indians with the invading Europeans.

Enter the Europeans

EUROPEAN PREPARATION FOR COLONIZATION

WHAT WOULD HAVE BEEN the evolution of an Indian America uninfluenced by Europeans nobody can say. Columbus's discovery projected the Europeans into the scene and profoundly influenced American destiny.

Europeans could hardly have colonized America had it not been for the political and economic growth that characterized Europe during the centuries prior to 1500. With the disintegration of the Roman Empire, Western Europe was broken up into political units much smaller (except for the brief interlude of Charlemagne) than modern Spain, France, or Germany. Hundreds of political entities, having neither horizontal nor vertical ties, were formed from the extensive *latifundia* (villas, great estates) of fifth century Rome. Feudalism gave these small political entities cohesion from the tenth century on, and eventually the national states of France, Portugal, and Spain evolved.

The later political development of medieval Europe was in large part a product of commercial expansion. A decline of trade activity, acting as both cause and effect, had accompanied the collapse of the Roman Empire. The world-wide economy of Rome was replaced in Western Europe by trade areas circumscribed by the bounds of the medieval manor or feudal estate. The radius of activity might be as little as ten or twenty miles. Trade flowed inward toward the center of this circumscribed area, and was concerned with foods and other bare necessities. An occasional itinerant merchant was the only exception to this rule.

Several influences slowly produced a revival of commerce. The Norsemen established trading colonies from Persia to Vineland (America) during the eighth to eleventh centuries; the trade of the Mohammedans flowed in through Sicily and Spain at the same

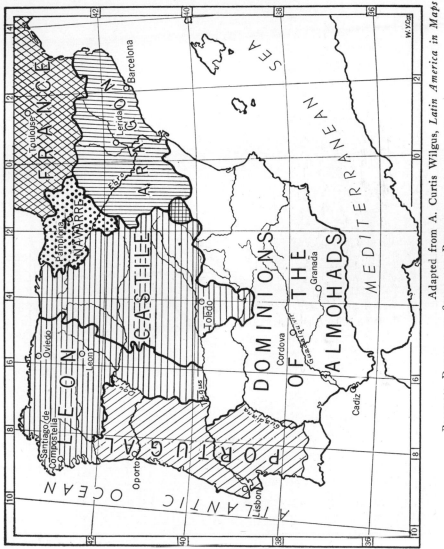

POLITICAL DIVISIONS OF SPAIN AND PORTUGAL ABOUT 1200 A.D.

Adapted from A. Curtis Wilgus, *Latin America in Maps*

28*a*

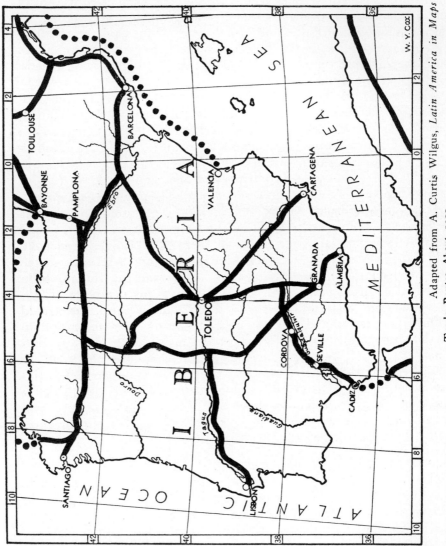

Adapted from A. Curtis Wilgus, *Latin America in Maps*

Trade Routes About 1300

W. Y. Cox

time; the Byzantine Empire multiplied its contacts with Western Europe. The two centuries of the Crusades increased trade enormously, and flourishing Italian towns dominated the Mediterranean and traded overland with German and Flemish towns, which in turn dominated the Baltic and North Seas. Europe came to know of the merchandise of the East again, as it had in Roman times. Such merchandise came in small quantities, for high prices, to few people, but the demand grew.

Further knowledge of the East came from travelers, missionaries and merchants. The Spanish Rabbi, Benjamín de Tudela, traveled as far east as Persia, and perhaps to India (1160-1173); John de Plano Carpini (1246) and William de Ruisbroek [Rubruquis] (1253-1254) penetrated Central Asia; the brothers Nicolo and Matteo Polo made two trips to China and the East (1260-1269 and 1271-1296) and were accompanied on the second trip by the son of Nicolo, Marco Polo, whose account of the trip has become a classic. Benedetto Vivaldi and Percivale Stancone formed a partnership to trade with India in 1313; Odorico de Pordenone (1314-1330) traveled to China, Central Asia and Malaysia; there was a Catholic bishop in Peking until 1368, and the Italian, John de Monte Corvino, occupied the bishopric to his death (b. 1247-d. 1328); the Spanish Franciscan, Pascual de Vitorio, penetrated Chinese Turkestan and died there (1338-1339). An accurate map of the Caspian Sea was made by Dulcert in Mallorca in 1339; and about 1340 Francisco Balducci Pegolotti described the road to China via the Black Sea and across Central Asia. Juan de Marignoli went to China overland and returned by sea (1339-1353); Giosafat Barbaro explored much of Russia (1436-1452); and many men of lesser fame, but probably of no less importance, attest the knowledge Europe had gained of the East.[1]

POLITICAL AND ECONOMIC GROWTH OF PORTUGAL

The Italian cities had prospered with the knowledge and trade they had gained, and it was only natural that Spain, Portugal, and others should desire to do the same. This was difficult owing to the high prices, high duties, excessive profits, and superior arms of the more established cities. One result was that Portugal, particularly, sought a way to circumvent the Italian monopoly. Her activities are best personified in the work of Prince Henry the Navigator, although he represents the organized efforts of a long-developing aspiration rather than the beginning of a new epoch.

---

[1] Gonzalo de Reparaz (Hijo), *La época de los grandes descubrimientos españoles y portugueses* (Barcelona: Editorial Labor, 1931), pp. 71-86.

During the reign of Alfonso IV (1325-1357), the Portuguese already had started their explorations into the Atlantic, and in the fourteenth century, Italians, Spanish, and Portuguese made other voyages. Lisbon and Porto were important centers of trade, serving as intermediary points on the sea route between the Mediterranean and the North Sea. Lisbon is described, during the reign of Fernando I (1367-1383), as being a "great city with a numerous and varied population," among whom were colonies of Genoese, Lombards, Aragonese, Moroccans, Milanese, Corsicans, and Biscayans, all enjoying numerous privileges and exemptions. To these may be added a growing Portuguese bourgeoisie, strong enough in 1384-1385 to depose the ruling house, which had the backing of the landed aristocracy, and seat another (in the person of João I) of their own choice. João I married the granddaughter of Edward III of England, forming an alliance that was destined to last many centuries and have important consequences. In 1415, the Portuguese and foreign bourgeoisie of Lisbon and Porto were instrumental in persuading João I to capture the Moorish city of Ceuta in order to establish trade there. All this prefaced Prince Henry's contribution.

Prince Henry established himself at Sagres in the southwestern tip of Portugal, and, surrounded by navigators, cosmographers, and every type of scientist and artisan needful to his purpose, pursued his triple religious, political, and commercial aims. He desired to make contact with a Christian king in Africa, called by the Europeans Prester John, for the religious and political benefits of an alliance against the Moors. He also sought to explore the coastline of Africa in order to establish trade and reach India. To his explorer, Antonio Gonçálvez, sent out to Africa, he gave instructions that he "not only wished to have knowledge of that territory, but also of the Indies, and the land of Prester John, if this were possible."[2]

The islands of Porto Santo and Madeira were occupied in 1418-1419 and the Azores in 1427-1432 with colonization following at once. Cape Bojador, hitherto the farthest point reached, was passed by Gil Eannes in 1434; Nuño Tristán reached Cape Blanco in 1441; Dionís Díaz reached Cape Verde in 1445. The Cape Verde Islands were occupied in 1457, and the equatorial islands of Santo Tomé and Príncipe in 1471. Bartholomew Díaz passed the Cape of Good Hope in 1487 (or 1488).

---

[2] Antonio Sergio de Sousa, *Historia de Portugal* (Barcelona: Editorial Labor, 1929), pp. 58-59.

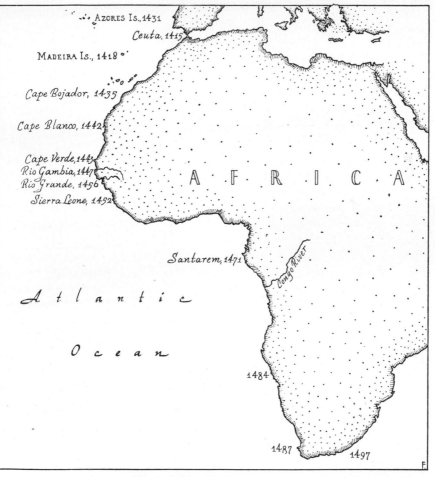

Azores Is., 1431
Ceuta, 1415
Madeira Is., 1418
Cape Bojador, 1435
Cape Blanco, 1442
Cape Verde, 1445
Rio Gambia, 1447
Rio Grande, 1456
Sierra Leone, 1452

AFRICA

Santarem, 1471

Congo River

Atlantic

Ocean

1484

1487   1497

F.

Adapted from A. Curtis Wilgus, *Latin America in Maps*
Portuguese Explorations

30a

The commercial aspects of these successes are evident in the organization of the Company of Lagos in 1444, designed to exploit African commerce and fishing. This company was instrumental in bringing to Portugal trade in slaves, gold, ivory, feathers, oils, and other products. A warehouse was established in Lagos with the title *Casa da Guiné*, and moved to Lisbon in 1481-1482 with the title of *Casa da Guiné e Mina*. It was subsequently called the *Casa da India*. All goods coming from overseas, including the slaves who were later sold in the *Casa dos Escravos*, had to be brought to this warehouse for registry and sale. Merchandise moved on to Flanders or to Mediterranean ports from these establishments.

As early as the thirteenth century, the commercial interests of Portugal in Flanders were so important that the merchants of Lisbon established a branch of their *Bolsa de comercio* there, and in 1383, Portuguese had their own house in Bruges. In 1445, this was moved to Antwerp and a factory house built.

The economic consequences of the discoveries were considerable, both to Europe and to the discovered lands. Prince Henry transplanted sugar cane in the Madeiras, and brought sugar-making experts from Sicily. Growing and refining soon developed. A monopoly was established in 1452, in accordance with the economic ideas of the times, and given to one Diego de Teive. The Prince received one-third of the sugar, and after Lisbon was provided with its annual consumption of 120,000 arrobas (1500 tons, the arroba=25lbs.), the balance was sent to Flanders, Genoa, Venice, and Aigues-Mortes. Vineyards were also planted and wine eventually surpassed sugar as the chief crop. The Azores supplied wheat, wine, cattle, and sugar. The Cape Verde Islands were populated with Negroes from Guinea, and cotton was cultivated. Santo Tomé and Príncipe became the center of a sugar industry, having more than eighty sugar mills by the middle of the sixteenth century; Santo Tomé alone produced more than 150,000 arrobas (1875 tons) annually. Portugal's commercial development was far advanced when Vasco da Gama reached India in 1498.

One other point should be noted. The bourgeoisie had placed their own king on the throne in 1385, had received every encouragement, and had every success. But the landed nobility were strong and demanded to be rewarded. They were given lands in Portugal and in the conquered territories as their part of the Portuguese expansion. Thus, Portugal had laid the groundwork for both trade and colonization.

Portugal was not the only country whose activities pointed toward further discovery. Italians made some expeditions into the Atlantic, and Spaniards made others. Spain occupied and colonized the Canaries early in the fifteenth century and developed a sugar industry there. Spain also interested herself in the East and in Prester John, Aragon sending a representative to Ethiopia in the fifteenth century. The Scandinavians had maintained contact with their Atlantic island, Iceland, and in 1472 Christian I of Denmark co-operated with Alfonso V of Portugal in sending Didrik Pining to Greenland (and perhaps Newfoundland). Two Portuguese, Alvaro Martins Homem and João Vaz Corte-Real, accompanied him. Bristol, England, carried on trade with Iceland at this time and perhaps knew of Pining's voyage. John Cabot lived in Bristol and had made voyages into the Atlantic, as had other Bristol merchants, without announced result, before Columbus discovered America.[3]

SPAIN'S ECONOMIC, POLITICAL, AND RELIGIOUS DEVELOPMENT

Spain had been laying the groundwork of her own colonial system during the same centuries. Numerous institutions destined to influence America were developed between 711 and 1492. This period, in which Christian Spain slowly expanded at the expense of Moorish Spain, has been named the Reconquest. It was not strictly a religious or racial crusade. The Cid, the national hero, fought on both sides; alliances of Christians with Moors to fight other Christians also allied with Moors were common; the noble Christian families not infrequently intermarried with noble Moors; and finally, the masses lived on the land continuously, whether their masters were Christians or Moors.

Economic factors played an important role in the conflict. When the Mohammedans drove the Visigothic Christians into the northwestern part of the peninsula, the invading nobility seized the lands of the defeated nobility. The mass of the people remained

---

[3] Sergio de Sousa, *op. cit.*, pp. 15-74; Gonzalo de Reparaz, *op. cit.*, pp. 55-133.

No attempt has been made here to study exhaustively all the early voyages. The emphasis is naturally on Portuguese and Spanish activity.

See Edward Potts Cheyney, *European Background of American History, 1300-1600* (New York and London, 1904), pp. 3-146; Edward Gaylord Bourne, *Spain in America, 1450-1580* (New York and London, 1904) pp. 3-19. In Ricardo Levene ed., *Historia de la nación Argentina* (10 vols. to date, Buenos Aires, 1936), II, 103-122, Hector R. Rattio has a chapter in which he accepts numerous pre-Columbian discoveries of America and concludes that Columbus was not really a discoverer in the strict sense of the word. All of Volume II of this work is devoted to the background of discovery and the discovery. The entire work written by the foremost living authorities of many nations, is one of the best collective histories yet published.

as they were. Those who, in the last days of Roman rule, were known as *coloni,* and in the Middle Ages as serfs, continued to cultivate the soil; the invasion merely exchanged Christian for Mohammedan nobles as masters. The Christian nobles, not the masses, lost their lands. The scene was exactly reversed during the Christian Reconquest. The Christian nobles, not the masses, sought to recover the peninsula from the Mohammedans. Land was the crux of the struggle. It might be a small plot, or it might be a kingdom, but land was the objective. Religion and "race" were secondary and tertiary, not primary issues. The average man was not molested in his religion.

"When cities and territories were captured by a Christian advance, it was the usual thing for the conquered Moors to remain there in the enjoyment of their own religion, laws, and property, and under the rule of their own local magistrates. They were generally and rightly regarded as a most valuable portion of the population from a financial and industrial point of view; they bore priceless aid to the Christians in restoring some measure of prosperity to the devastated lands. Down to the middle of the thirteenth century it is scarcely too much to say that they were not only gladly tolerated but highly esteemed. Many of the early Castilian monarchs deliberately strove to render the lot of the Moors who resided on their domains more agreeable than that which would have been their fate had they remained in the territories of the infidel. Any attempt to persecute them was vigorously resisted; they were protected, and often actively favored." [4]

Religion, nevertheless, played an essential part in the Reconquest. The clergy shared in the rewards, receiving land in return for supplying an ideology to what was essentially an economic struggle, just as they were doing in other parts of Europe. The clergy could convincingly argue that war against the Moors was a crusade of the true faith against the infidel, and they had powerful religious sanctions to use against those who refused to participate. The Christian sovereigns were willing to let the Church share in the resulting booty, since they feared its power less than that of the nobility. Religion thus had a role similar to that now assigned to national patriotism. [5]

Crown and Church were not the only beneficiaries of the Recon-

---

[4] Roger B. Merriman, *Rise of the Spanish Empire in the Old World and in the New* (4 vols., New York: the Macmillan Company, 1918-1934), I, 87-88.
[5] *Ibid.,* I, 58-59.

quest: the nobility, the knights, the townsmen, and even the serfs, who wished to gain freedom, participated.[6] Reconquest became the activity of all. The Moorish nobles were driven slowly back, and the civil wars between the Christians over the spoils were as cruel as those against the infidel. When the Reconquest was completed in 1492, thousands found themselves without occupation, and with unsatisfied ambitions. Some turned to despoiling the Moors and Jews, others eventually welcomed America as a possible answer to their desire for wealth and position.

The religious nationalism developed during the Reconquest was the spirit that animated the conquest of America. The tolerance that permitted the Moors and the Jews to preserve property and religion first weakened in the long-continued struggle between the Moorish rulers and the Christians, and then was transformed into violent intolerance during the ten-year war (1482-1492) for the conquest of Granada.[7]

In the drive for national unity, a difference of faith or language was intolerable. But the land motive was undoubtedly strong here also. When it was no longer possible to conquer Moorish territory, the attack was turned against the Moors and Jews within the Christian territory. The spoliation of the two peoples (many of whom had become converts to Christianity) was condoned on religious grounds. Hence the expulsion of the Moors and Jews in 1492 and later; hence the establishment of the religio-political instrument, the Inquisition (1478); hence the importance of religion in the conquest of America. Religion was in Spain, as elsewhere, as much a political matter as a personal one, as much a matter of state as of conscience, as much patriotism as spiritual passion.[8]

The Protestant Revolution furnished still another impulse to religious zeal. Charles V (1516-1556) was fighting the Moors in the Mediterranean and North Africa, the Turks in Central Europe, and the Lutherans in Germany. Before the end of the century, the Dutch Protestants and the English were added. It was only natural that religious differences were of paramount political importance. The Spaniards could hardly have avoided carrying their religio-political ideas to America where there were several million non-Christian Indians.

---

[6] Rafael Altamira, *Historia de España* (4th ed., 4 vols., Barcelona, 1928-29), I, 412-29; II, 5-28, 88-98 and *passim*.

[7] On Spanish toleration, see Ulick Ralph Burke, *A History of Spain* (2 vols., London and New York, 1895), II, 87-95.

[8] See Modesto Lafuente, *Historia general de España* (30 vols., Madrid, 1850-1867, and numerous editions), vol. VIII and *passim*, and C. S. Braden, *Religious Aspects of the Conquest of Mexico* (Durham, N. C.: Duke University Press, 1930), chap. I.

In brief, the elements entering into the conquest of America were: a drive for land and trade; a military caste seeking an outlet for its energies; a spirit of national unity and expansion, engendered by the Reconquest; a militant church, seeking souls for conversion and material wealth; and a fervent patriotism, expressing itself in terms of a fanatical religion.

COLONIZING THE CARIBBEAN

When Columbus sailed from Spain on August 3, 1492, he left behind an unfinished struggle for land and for religious and national unity. When he landed in America in October, he found a civil war in progress. Two groups were fighting for domination in the Caribbean, the Arawaks and the Caribs.[9] In his Journal, Columbus recorded his own reactions to the Indian struggles and the participation of the Spaniards.[10] The Arawaks Columbus saw as "a people who would better be freed and converted to our Holy Faith by love than by force." "They do not carry arms," he reported, "nor know what they are. . . . They have no iron: their spears are sticks without iron. . . . I saw some who had indications of wounds on their bodies, and I asked them by signs if it was that, and they showed me that other people came there from other islands near by and wished to capture them and they defended themselves." [11]

Some of the Indians manifested great fear of their enemies, stating that the "cannibals ate them" and were "very well armed." The reported cannibals lived on an island called *Bohio*, which may have been Española. Columbus promised that "the Sovereigns of

---

[9] There is not sufficient space to discuss the questions of Columbus's life. As far as the history of America is concerned, it makes no difference whether he was an Italian or of some other origin, or whether he had previous knowledge of America. Such matters are interesting and important, but not essential for the purposes of this book. For the life of Columbus see John Boyd Thacher, *Christopher Columbus* (3 vols., New York, G. P. Putnam's Sons, 1903-1904); Salvador Madariaga, *Christopher Columbus* (New York: The Macmillan Company, 1940); Samuel Eliot Morison, *Admiral of the Ocean Sea: A Life of Christopher Columbus* (2 vols., Boston: Little, Brown and Co., 1942).

[10] The holograph Journal of Columbus no longer exists, or at least its location is not known. The Journal was in the possession of Bartolomé de las Casas when he wrote his *Historia de las Indias* (5 vols., Madrid, *Colección de documentos inéditos para la historia de España*, LXII-LXVI, 1875-1876), about the middle of the sixteenth century. He abbreviated, apparently, leaving out much, paraphrased some parts and quoted others directly. Passages not in the Las Casas Version of the Journal are found in the *Historia*. The Journal as left by Las Casas was printed by Martín Fernández de Navarrete, *Colección de los viages y descubrimientos, que hicieron por mar los españoles desde fines del siglo XV* (5 vols., Madrid, 1825-1837), from which Thacher translated the version found in volume I of his history of Columbus.

[11] *Journal*, Oct. 11. The date appears in the *Journal* as October 11, although the discovery was not made until the next day. Columbus forgot to put a new date for the 12th, writing the events of the 12th under the date of the 11th.

Castile would order the Caribs destroyed." [12] Considerable evidence bears out Columbus' testimony that cannibalism was practiced in the new lands. "This barbarous and indomitable race," remarked one report written by a companion of Columbus, "feeds on human flesh. . . ." "The Cannibals themselves do not deny this, but openly affirm that they eat men." [13]

From the first, Columbus assumed that the newly-discovered lands belonged to his sovereign and that he was to settle, found towns, and Christianize the Indians. When he sailed for Spain in January 1493, he left a small settlement, La Navidad, on Española.[14]

Presumption of ownership was not based on discovery alone. Spain and Portugal had divided the Atlantic between them by the Treaty of Alcáçovas in 1479, which confirmed Spain in the possession of the Canaries, and gave Portugal the Azores, Madeiras, and other islands from the Canaries to Guinea. This treaty conformed to the medieval concept of exclusive rights, Venice, for example, having asserted and maintained the right to keep the Adriatic closed. It was also in conformity with the medieval custom of resorting to the Pope as arbiter.

When Columbus returned, the previous Atlantic agreement of Spain and Portugal was upset, since the newly-discovered lands were outside the bounds named in the Treaty of Alcáçovas. Ferdinand and Isabella appealed to Pope Alexander VI and a series of Papal Bulls divided the territories discovered, and to be discovered, between Spain and Portugal, Spain receiving everything west of a line of demarcation one hundred leagues west of the Azores and Cape Verde Islands. Portugal was angered by the Pope's action, and by threatening war, forced Spain to consent to revision of the papal grant. The Treaty of Tordesillas between Spain and Portugal (1494) placed the demarcation line 370 leagues west of the Cape Verde Islands. The division was vague but, backed by papal grants, both nations set out to make their claims effective.[15]

On the first voyage, Columbus had expressed a desire to bring

---

[12] *Journal,* November 23 and 26, December 26.

[13] The Syllacio-Coma Letter, published in Thacher, *Columbus,* II, 248-250. See other testimony in Thacher's *Columbus,* and also Girolamo Benzoni, whose *La Historia del Mondo Nuovo* was published in Venice in 1565 and issued as the *History of the New World,* ed. and tr. Admiral W. H. Smyth (London: The Hakluyt Society, No. 21, 1857).

[14] This colony had between 38 and 41 men (the number is disputed), and settlement at this time was caused by the wreck of one of Columbus' ships.

[15] See John Tate Lanning, "Colonial International Relations," in A. Curtis Wilgus, ed., *Colonial Hispanic America* (Washington, D. C.: The George Washington University Press, 1935), chaps. XII, XIII, and XIV.

Courtesy of the Pan American Union

DON PEDRO DE ALVARADO, CONQUEROR OF GUATEMALA

Courtesy of the Pan American Union

HERNANDO CORTÉS, CONQUEROR OF MEXICO

back to America "herds of cattle and other things" and he had left with the La Navidad colony "all the merchandise which the Sovereigns had ordered purchased for trading, of which there was a large quantity," as well as "seeds for sowing." Preparations for a second voyage by Columbus were soon under way. The terms in which it is described indicate the mixed religious, political, and economic motives of the age.[16]

"The King and the Queen who desired nothing other than to augment the Christian religion: and to reduce many simple nations to the divine worship . . . hoped in the beginning to derive the greatest advantage from these islands; having more regard for the augmentation of the faith than for any other utility. Therefore, their Most Serene Majesties caused to be prepared 17 ships . . . with 1,200 men with their implements, among which were smiths, hired artisans of all the mechanical arts, with some horsemen. Columbus prepared horses, hogs, cows, and many other animals with their males; vegetables, corn, barley, and other similar things, not only for living purposes but also for sowing; vines and many other plants from trees, which are not native there; because they did not find in all that island trees with which we have acquaintance: only pines and very high palms of marvellous hardness . . . . The said Admiral also prepared to carry with him all the implements of whatever art: as well as all those things which were required for a town which he had established in the new country." [17]

Columbus found La Navidad destroyed, and the inhabitants killed off either by disease or the Indians. He established another town, Isabel, which was moved in 1496 to Santo Domingo, the first permanent settlement of Europeans in the New World.

HUNGRY AMERICA: THE AGRICULTURAL BASE OF THE CONQUEST

The agricultural life of the colony began at once. The Spaniards found the soil around Isabel "so fertile that . . . within a period of sixteen days watermelons, cucumbers, pumpkins, and other similar things were formed: in XXXVI days they were gathered, better than ever were eaten." [18] There was a great deal to encourage the new settler who had come to the New World in search of economic and social advancement. The noble and the peasant, each in his respective sphere, hoped to find a better position than

---

[16] *Journal*, December 31 and January 2.
[17] The *Libretto*, quoted in Thacher, *Columbus*, II, 489. The number is sometimes given as 1,500 men.
[18] The *Libretto*, quoted in Thacher, *Columbus*, II, 496.

that he had left in Spain. And it was not outside the realm of possibility that the conquest of America, like the Reconquest of Spain, would offer opportunities to break through the bonds that held men within the lower social classes.

But some reports were cautious. Many things would be needed from Spain, it was pointed out, before the colony could be successful. A memorandum sent back to the Crown called for "provisions to which they [the colonists] are accustomed in Spain." It was urged that "this provision must continue until a supply is accumulated here from what shall be sowed and planted . . . . We are very sure, as the result makes it apparent to us, that in this country, wheat as well as the vine will grow very well: but the fruit must be waited for . . ." [19]

Not everything could go smoothly in a new colony. One of the fundamental problems of settling America soon appeared—the difficulty of operating from a base of supplies three thousand miles distant and six months away in time. The fertile soil produced marvelous vegetables, but the early settlers were accustomed to "wine and biscuit" and "salted meat." A still further demand was made for fresh meat and sheep, "more females than males," "and some little yearling calves, male and female," and asses and mares for labor and breeding as there were none of these animals in the New World.[19]

Thus food remained a primary problem, in spite of the abundance of green vegetables. Almost everywhere in the first years of the Conquest the settlers faced the fear of starvation. Food presented a more difficult problem than that of military conquest. It is for this reason that the occupation of the mainland was delayed many years until a secure supply from the Caribbean islands could be depended on. Spain was too far away. Later on, with the conquest of Mexico and Peru, food was more available, but America was not a land of abundance for the first settlers. Early descriptions of plenty were accompanied by pleas for food; Spain had to send to America many of the plants and practically all the animals used, and these had to have time to become acclimatized and mature before the penetration of the mainland could begin.[20]

[19] The *De Torres Memorandum*, Thacher, *Columbus*, II, 300.

[20] There are two views that can be taken about the relation of food to the Conquest. Some students hold that the Spaniards could not have conquered America without the food supplied by the Indians. They cite the failure to occupy Buenos Aires early in the sixteenth century because the Indians had no food to give them, and of the necessity of settling first at Asunción where there were agricultural Indians. On the other hand, the occupation of Buenos Aires came after the sources of food imported from Europe, particularly cattle, had multiplied on the Argentine

Agriculture in the Caribbean

Agricultural development in the Caribbean Islands was rapid. The typical island inhabitant was a Spanish farmer. "The classical conquistador, the almost mythical type of conquistador," as Carlos Pereyra remarks, "did not exist in the islands. He came from them, as he came from the peninsula, but he was very little the warrior in the islands and in the peninsula. Farmer and rancher, he enriched himself with the profits of the herd and the flock, he worked the sugar cane plantation and the sugar mill, and washed gold in the rivers. When he had a sufficiency or a large fortune—the greater part resulting from agriculture and cattle-raising activity— he left Española, or Cuba, or Jamaica, or Puerto Rico, or the Peninsula, to conquer continental empires or to fail tragically on some desert coast or in some marshy forest." [21]

The planting and reaping of crops was less spectacular than the heroic feats of arms of the almost superhuman conquistadores, but no less important. The agriculture and live stock of the Caribbean islands furnished the indispensable necessities to the conquistadores who went out from them or who came directly from Spain.

"It is said," Pereyra remarks, "that horses were one of the principal factors in the conquest of America. It is true, ... But if the horse was of real significance in the Conquest, the hog was of greater importance and contributed to a degree that defies exaggeration. The conquest of Mexico, Peru, and New Granada was the work of the Antillean planters who furnished the *empresarios* of the expeditions. What other reason is there for the failure of the first foundations of Buenos Aires except the lack of an agricultural and livestock base?" [22]

Oviedo, historian of the first half-century of Spanish conquest, describes the foundations of Caribbean agriculture and stock raising. He tells how the horses brought from Spain to Española multiplied so rapidly that they were soon exported to the other islands occupied by the Spaniards and to the colonies on the mainland;

plains. Certainly the Indians did not feed the Spaniards during the first twenty years of Caribbean colonization; and the plateau of Mexico north of the Central Valley was occupied only by nomadic food gatherers until Spanish livestock and farming made life on a sedentary basis possible. Cf. Tomás Blanco, *Prontuario histórico de Puerto Rico* (Madrid, 1935), pp. 24-25.

[21] Carlos Pereyra, *La obra de España en América* (Cartagena-Madrid, 1920), p. 120. Pereyra, whose other works will be cited as occasion arises, represents the school of historians which gives evidence to rectify the concept, coming largely from English, French, and American historians, that the occupation of America was a plundering and treasure-seeking adventure. The thesis upheld is that America was primarily agricultural during the colonial period, and that treasure seeking was not plunder but legitimate mining activity.

[22] Pereyra, *Obra*, pp. 120-121.

"and all the others found in the Indies have sprung from those of this island." The imported cattle also thrived to such an extent that "many have been killed . . . the meat of large numbers of them being wasted, in order to sell the hides and send them to Spain . . . . There are men in the city and in the island who have ten thousand head and much greater numbers of livestock." He enumerates also sheep, burros, and goats brought from Spain, and mules bred in the colony from Spanish burros and mares. "The countryside," he says, "is full of wild animals, cattle as well as wild dogs . . . which have taken to the woods." [23] This by no means ends Oviedo's list. He mentions, among the other things transferred to America, hens and roosters, which were "in great numbers in all parts of the Indies," and domestic pigeons and ducks.

These details emphasize a point of singular importance in early colonial history. The productive capacity of the Spaniards far outstripped that of the Indians of the Caribbean, and was likewise considerably ahead of that of the Indians of the mainland. Without the food provided by European plants and livestock, and the income received from marketing hides and other animal products, the Spaniards would have had much greater difficulty in maintaining themselves in the New World, not to speak of carrying through the fabulous task of conquest. This is all the more obvious when we realize that the Conquest was not the work of disorganized and impoverished adventurers alone, but also of rich and powerful cattle-raisers and sugar-plantation owners whose wealth made possible the long series of expeditions. Sporadic expeditions might have been made without them, but not the numerous and well-equipped ones which conquered New Spain, Central and South America.

From the time of Governor Ovando, (1502-1509), the Island of Española had "from ten to twelve thousand Spaniards." [24] many of whom were rich, or who soon became so with the profits derived from stock raising and farming. These men financed the expeditions of conquest, some of them going to the mainland themselves, and it was natural for them to expect a profit from their investments. Conquest was a business, as well as an adventure. The conquistadores may be compared with the modern army that goes out

[23] Gonzalo Hernández [or Fernández] de Oviedo y Valdés, quoted in Pereyra, op. cit., pp. 121-122. Oviedo came to America early in the sixteenth century and published Historia general y natural de las Indias in Sevilla in 1535. A portion of the second part of his history, Book XX, was published in Valladolid in 1552. The complete work was first published in 4 volumes in Madrid, 1851-1855. See Book XII, chap. IX.
[24] Pereyra, Obra, p. 124.

to add colonial possessions, and the *empresarios* who supplied them with the business man who steps in immediately to develop the colony with his capital. The relation of empresario and conquistador in the sixteenth century will be clearer if we note the early entrance of capitalistic enterprise into American economic life. The sugar industry is the best illustration.

Sugar cane, introduced into America with the second voyage of Columbus, rapidly became the most important agricultural product of Española and the other islands, from the standpoint of exportability and profit on investment. Soon after cane growing was begun, mills for sugar manufacture were installed. They called for large capital outlays both in equipment and in Negro slaves. Nevertheless, sugar grew into a leading and profitable industry in Española, Puerto Rico, and Jamaica. When Cortés conquered Mexico, he carried cane growing and the sugar mill with him. [25]

Furthermore, the settlers of the islands now represented all the types of colonists to be found later. Numbers of nobles from Spain, artisans, farmers, merchants, lawyers, officials, and Negro slaves were well established as the basis of Caribbean population. At a very early date, men brought their wives and daughters, and marriageable girls came with proper chaperons to seek husbands. Women from Spain were beginning to play a part in conquest and colonization within a decade after the establishment of a colony on Española.

The development of the agricultural life of the Caribbean islands paralleled the epoch of the great conquests. The two things cannot be separated since the former did much to make possible the latter. After the founding of Santo Domingo in 1496, Columbus discovered the north coast of South America (1498-1500), and Central America (1502-1504). Vicente Yáñez Pinzón (1499) and Diego de Lepe (1500) explored portions of the coastline from the eastern tip of Brazil northwestward. Within twenty years after discovery, most of the islands had settlements. Ponce de León began the conquest of Puerto Rico in 1508; Jamaica was occupied in 1509, and Cuba in 1511. Cuba had seven settlements. when Havana was settled in 1515; Española had seventeen chartered towns by 1513.

CONQUEST AND COLONIZATION OF THE MAINLAND: MEXICO

In the meantime settlements had begun on the mainland, supplied with food and other resources from the Islands. Alonso de

[25] Pereyra, *Obra,* p. 127.

Ojeda was granted a territory extending along the north coast of South America (in Colombia) as far west as Darién, and Nicuesa was granted territory then called Veragua, extending from Darién northwestward to Honduras. Both men made settlements in 1509, but starvation and hostile Indians attacked them, the leaders were deposed, and the survivors were gathered into a settlement called Santa María de la Antigua del Darién in Veragua, where, in 1511, Vasco Núñez de Balboa became provisional governor. From here he set out in 1513 and discovered the Pacific Ocean in September. Balboa was made "Adelantado of the South Sea" for this discovery, but political influence gave the governorship to Pedrarias Dávila in 1514 and the territory was renamed Castilla del Oro. Pedrarias and Balboa were never on good terms. In 1517 (or 1519), Pedrarias sent Francisco Pizarro to arrest Balboa as he was preparing to sail in search of Peru, and Balboa was beheaded.

Meanwhile, Yucatán was discovered in 1517 by Francisco Hernández de Córdova, during a slave-hunting expedition. Diego Velásquez, governor of Cuba, then commissioned Juan de Grijalva (1518) to follow up Córdova with a voyage for discovery and trade. Grijalva explored the coastline as far as what later became Vera Cruz. Velásquez decided on still another expedition and chose as its leader Hernando Cortés, a prominent planter of Cuba and the alcalde [mayor] of Santiago, who had been in America since 1504, and whose wealth aided materially in equipping the ships, buying horses, arming soldiers, and furnishing them with the necessary supplies of clothing and food.

Cortés sailed in November 1518 with six to seven hundred men, about eighteen horses, and a few light cannon, in eleven ships. The original scheme of Christianization, trade, and treasure broadened into conquest when he learned of the magnitude of the Aztec and surrounding dominions. He founded the city of Vera Cruz, and was elected Captain General and Chief Justice of the new town council *(cabildo)* which he set up there on the Spanish pattern. This gave him the official standing and the legal authority to colonize which he had previously lacked. Victory became the alternative to annihilation when he destroyed his fleet and marched inland toward the capital of Montezuma.

Cortés' conquest of Mexico with such a small force has been considered almost miraculous, but there were several factors operating in his favor. The first was the settlement of the Caribbean islands and the creation of a base for food, equipment, and soldiers. Secondly, Mexico was not so much conquered by the Spaniards as it was conquered by the Indians *for* the Spaniards. The latter simply made the most of the essential disunity prevailing among the Indians. It is well known that Cortés was aided by the Tlaxcalans, a tribe living east of Mexico City, and other tribes served the Spanish cause no less valuably. Montezuma's was a land of intertribal hatreds, which Cortés was able to utilize in persuading one Indian group to help him conquer the next. The Indians, who might have joined against the Europeans were, on the contrary, frequently ready to ally themselves with the newcomers in order to avenge old wrongs. In such a situation, diplomacy was as important as force; Cortés found civil war everywhere when he entered Mexico, and he was quick to take advantage of it.

Soon after landing in Mexico, Cortés found out that Montezuma had numerous enemies, "which he was delighted to hear."[26] He promptly initiated the technique that was to be useful throughout the conquest. The chief of Cempoala, an Indian town near Vera Cruz, sent presents to the Spaniards and in response "Cortés replied through Doña Marina and Aguilar, his interpreters, that he would pay for the gift in good works, and that if the Cacique [chief] would tell him what he wanted to be done that he would do it for them, for we were the vassals of a great prince, the Emperor Don Carlos, who ruled over many kingdoms and countries, and had sent us to redress grievances and punish evil doers, and to put an end to human sacrifices. And he explained to them many things touching our holy religion." This is the Spanish side of the story. It was repeated endlessly.

The Indian side of the story was just as familiar. When the Cacique heard this, he complained bitterly of Montezuma, "saying that he had recently been brought under his yoke; that all his golden jewels had been carried off, and he and his people were so grievously oppressed, that they dared do nothing without Montezuma's orders." This Cacique and other chiefs enumerated their many causes of complaint against Montezuma, telling of his great power. "Besides relating the way that they had been brought into subjection, they told us that every year many of their sons and daughters were demanded of them for sacrifice, and others for service in the houses and plantations of their conquerors; and they made other complaints which were so numerous that I do not remember them all; but they said Montezuma's tax-gatherers carried off their wives and daughters if they were handsome and ravished them,

---

[26] Bernal Díaz del Castillo, *A True History of the Conquest of New Spain*, ed. and tr. Alfred Percival Maudslay (5 vols., London: The Hakluyt Society, 1908-1916), I, 152.

and this they did throughout the land where the Totonac language was spoken, which contained over thirty towns." [27]

It was not difficult to capitalize on such enmity. Cortés, posing as the friend of the Cempoalan Indians, arrested Montezuma's tax-gatherers and drove out his garrisons. He moved inland to the town of Cingapacinga. Here he discovered that his Cempoalan allies were the enemies not merely of Montezuma but of Cinga-pacinga as well. The Indians of this latter town appealed to Cortés for protection against the Cempoalans, whose hostility was due to old disputes over land and boundaries. Cortés now curbed the Cempoalans who "had already begun to loot the farms," and thus gained new friends. He at once preached to them on the Catholic religion, and when the people of the neighboring towns had been assembled, they all gave their allegiance to the Spanish king.[28]

Still farther inland, after various skirmishes with the Indians, who were also converted into allies, the Spaniards reached the Tlaxcalan territory in the Central Valley. The Tlaxcalans, after some early opposition, became faithful friends. They explained to Cortés that their poverty was due to Montezuma, who prevented them from seeking even such necessities as salt, and that their ancestors' wealth had been extorted by the Aztecs. Cortés learned from them also that as all the provinces which had been subjected by Montezuma were ill disposed toward the Mexicans, and "as their inhabitants were carried off by force to the wars, they did not fight with good will." [29] This goes far to explain why Cortés conquered Mexico. He at no time faced a united enemy; nor did Pizarro, nor most of the other conquerors.

Cannibalism, which was again encountered here, might on first sight seem outside the theme of conquest, but it is pertinent. The struggle for existence was, we have seen, paramount in Indian America, and land, with whatever means of living it afforded, was of supreme importance. But any means of getting food was licit where an abundance was not to be had. Almost everywhere, except in the Inca Empire where a considerable quantity of meat was available, cannibalism was customary. The following quotation could be repeated a hundred times from as many authors: ". . . in this town of Tlaxcala we found wooden houses furnished with gratings, full of Indian men and women imprisoned in them, being fed up until they were fat enough to be sacrificed and eaten. These prisons we broke open and destroyed, and set free the prisoners

---

[27] Bernal Díaz, *Conquest of New Spain*, I, 165-168.
[28] *Ibid.*, I, 182-184.   [29] *Ibid.*, I, 284.

who were in them. . . . From now on, in all the towns that we entered the first thing our Captain ordered us to do was to break open these prisons and set free the prisoners." [30] The existence of cannibalism convinced the Spaniards of the righteousness of their cause. God had sent them to wipe out such atrocities, they believed. Their sincerity can scarcely be doubted, since they frequently risked offending allies on whose friendship their existence depended.

The Conquest seems to have been a case, however, of the various Indian groups hating, not the Spaniards less, but the Aztecs more. Cortés suggested to one of the Indian chieftains that he should make peace with Montezuma, but received the reply that peace was impossible since the Aztecs could not be trusted.

At Cholula, a town not far from Montezuma's capital, Cortés fought a battle that was in effect a massacre of the Indians. The victory was probably less important than the factionalism it revealed. After the battle "certain Caciques and priests of Cholula who belonged to other districts of the town, and said they were not concerned in the treason against us (for it is a large city and they have parties and factions among themselves), asked Cortés and all of us to pardon the provocation of the treachery that had been plotted against us, for the traitors had already paid with their lives." [31]

The Spanish massacres of the Indians at Cholula and elsewhere were brutal, but cruel slaughter characterized the Indian wars of other Europeans in their conquest of America. The history of America and Europe in war, and even in peace, is cluttered with acts of brutality as revolting as those of the Spaniards. Prisoners were usually considered so much excess baggage, and seldom held. They were murdered; and the Indians sometimes ate them.

It should be recalled that the conquest of America was going on simultaneously with the wars among the Christian factions in Europe. This was the epoch of the Religious Wars of France in the last half of the sixteenth century, when the country was devastated and thousands of peasants starved to death. On Saint Bartholomew's night alone (August 24, 1572), ten to twenty thousand Protestants were massacred in France. This was the epoch, too, of the Thirty Years War in Germany (1618-1648), which resulted in the disappearance of about two-thirds of the population and the destruction of five-sixths of the villages. The conquest of America wasted life and property, but the ravages do not compare with the toll taken by the wars in Europe.

---

[30] *Ibid.*, I, 288-289.   [31] *Ibid.*, II, 16.

After Cholula, the Cempoalan allies received permission to return home, since they feared Montezuma's revenge. Their return gave Cortés a strong force of friendly Indians to fortify his rear. A short time later, he entered Tenochtitlán, the Aztec capital.

The Spaniards found the dissensions within the ranks of the Aztecs themselves as sharp as those between the Aztecs and subject peoples. There was a standing dispute among the Aztec nobles as to who should occupy the throne, and Montezuma had several rivals. Cacamatzin, the Cacique of Téxcoco, sought the aid of the Cacique of Matalcingo against the Spaniards, but the latter refused help unless he could be assured of the kingship of Mexico. Cacamatzin, however, was determined to be king himself. Cortés, who had made Montezuma a prisoner, used this rivalry to foment further quarrels among the Indians. He suggested to Montezuma that he replace Cacamatzin with one of his own brothers; the two were already on bad terms.

On the advice of Cortés, Montezuma summoned Cacamatzin to Tenochtitlán, but received an insolent refusal. Things were going as Cortés wished. Montezuma then sent his followers to arrange the capture of Cacamatzin, and he was taken prisoner, together with the nobles who conspired with him against Montezuma.[32]

In the meantime there was an episode that characterizes the whole conquest. Cortés had originally been authorized by Diego Velásquez, governor of Cuba, to make the Mexican expedition but had rendered himself independent by setting up the Cabildo in Vera Cruz. Velásquez then received a grant from the Crown, and sent an expedition of thirteen hundred men to Mexico under the leadership of Pánfilo de Narváez with orders to imprison Cortés. Cortés received notice of this in May, 1520, and leaving Pedro de Alvarado to hold Tenochtitlán, hastened to the coast where he defeated Narváez and persuaded the men to join his own forces.

Cortés now was forced to hurry back to Tenochtitlán where the Indians had risen against the Spaniards. Heavy fighting lasted for several days, during which Montezuma was killed in some manner never satisfactorily explained, and the Spaniards attempted a retreat from the city. About half of the Spanish force was wiped out on the night of June 30, 1520, thus giving rise to the name it has since borne, *La Noche Triste*.

During the ensuing year, Cortés took refuge among the friendly Tlaxcalans, reorganized his army, obtained fresh recruits and supplies from the Islands, and made extensive explorations in Central

[32] *Ibid.*, II, 116-122.

Mexico. His preparations finished, he attacked the city of Tenoch-titlán on May 26, 1521, and besieged it until August, when it fell. Cuauhtémoc, who had succeeded to the headship of the Aztec confederation, was imprisoned. The city was renamed Mexico City, and its reconstruction begun in Spanish style.

The conquest of Mexico did not end with the capture of the capital. The city stands in the center of a valley more than seven thousand feet above sea level and surrounded by mountains rising to the perpetual snow line. The plateau north of the Central Valley extending northwest to New Mexico was inhabited mainly by nomadic Indians. Michoacán, toward the Pacific Ocean, was not subject to the Aztecs. The provinces south of the Central Valley were heavily populated agricultural areas, lying at lower levels and tapering down to the Tehuántepec isthmus. Over these vast territories, occupying a much larger area than the domain of the Aztecs, the Spaniards had yet to extend their authority. Cortés began this work at once, sending successive expeditions into the surrounding regions.

He fell heir to the position of leadership formerly held by the head of the Aztec chieftains, and the subservience and respect due a victor were his. Many of the Indian chiefs, both those who had been subject to Montezuma and those who had not, acknowledged his supremacy. He became a super-arbiter of Indian conflicts. "So great was the authority and position and command to which Cortés had attained, that they brought before him the disputes between Indians from distant lands, especially questions of chieftainship and overlordship . . . They came to Cortés concerning question as to whom the chieftaincy belonged, and who should be lord and should apportion lands or vassals or other property, as though he [Cortés] were the absolute master of the land, so that with his hand and authority he should raise the right claimant to be chieftain." [33]

Such petitions gave the Spaniards the opportunity needed to consolidate their power. Wherever possible, companies of Spanish soldiers were sent with Indian allies to subject various other Indian tribes. Pedro de Alvarado, Cristóbal de Olid, and Gonzalo de Sandoval were sent out frequently on expeditions of exploration and conquest, always taking advantage of the rivalries of Indian groups to facilitate their task. Thus the conquistador, Gonzalo de Sandoval, who had been sent out to the south and east of Mexico

[33] *Ibid.*, II, 289-90.

City to subdue the Zapotecs, was saved from defeat by using one faction of the Indians against another.[34]

CONQUEST OF CENTRAL AMERICA

The conquest of the Tehuántepec isthmus and Central America resulted in part from the participation of the Spaniards in Indian wars. Among the peoples who sent messengers to congratulate Cortés on his victory, and to offer themselves as vassals, were the inhabitants of Tehuántepec. The Zapotec messengers brought Cortés a present of gold and told him of other pueblos in their province, their inveterate enemies, situated on the south coast. It was asserted that the people were rich in gold, jewels and mines; and the Zapotecs begged Cortés for horsemen, musketeers, and crossbowmen to conquer this territory. Cortés was not slow to respond [35] and at once sent out Pedro de Alvarado, who reached Guatemala in 1524. Throughout his long march from Mexico City Alvarado was aided by Indian towns which solicited his help against neighboring communities; and the conquest of Guatemala was facilitated by the enmity among the Indian tribes.

Alvarado's expedition was only one of several into Central America which became the center of bitter and unscrupulous rivalry among competing conquerors. After Pedrarias had founded the town of Panama, he set out to extend his territories. The first voyage, however, was that of Gil González Dávila, assisted by Andrés Niño. Niño sailed along the Pacific coast of Central America and Gil González marched overland as far as Nicaragua, making peace with the powerful chieftain of this name, accumulating precious metals, and converting the Indians. When he returned to Panama in 1523, he found Pedrarias firmly opposed to him, and he was forced to return to Española. Pedrarias then sent out Francisco Hernández de Córdoba, who founded Granada and León in Nicaragua (1523), as well as other towns.

The story of the conquest of Central America from this point is too complicated for simplification; but it is worth following because it illustrates the fact that the Spaniards fought each other for land and wealth quite as bitterly as they fought the Indians. Besides Alvarado's expedition to Central America, Cortés sent another under command of Cristóbal de Olid. Olid captured Gil González, who had again entered Central America in 1524. Olid then rebelled against Cortés, who was forced to send a kinsman,

---

[34] *Ibid.,* IV, 230-31.
[35] *Ibid.,* IV, 241-242.

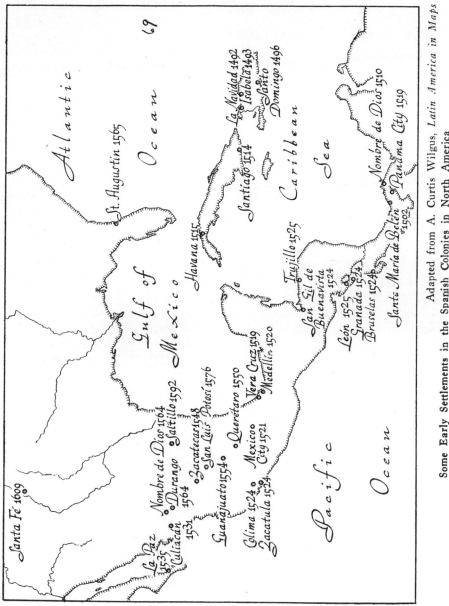

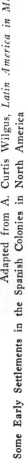

Santa Fé 1609

La Paz 1535
Culiacán 1531

Nombre de Dios 1564
Durango 1564
Saltillo 1592

Zacatecas 1548
San Luis Potosí 1576

Guanajuato 1554

Colima 1524
Zacatula 1524

Mexico City 1521
Querétaro 1550
Vera Cruz 1519
Medellín 1520

Havana 1515

Santiago 1514

La Navidad 1492
Isabela 1493
Santo Domingo 1496

St. Augustin 1565

Atlantic Ocean

Gulf of Mexico

Caribbean Sea

Pacific Ocean

Trujillo 1525

San Gil de Buenavista 1524
León 1525
Granada 1524
Bruselas 1524
Santa María de Belén 1502

Nombre de Dios 1510
Panama City 1519

69

Adapted from A. Curtis Wilgus, *Latin America in Maps*

Some Early Settlements in the Spanish Colonies in North America

48a

Francisco de las Casas, in pursuit of Olid; but Las Casas managed so badly that he fell prisoner to Olid, who now held two prisoners of importance. Las Casas and Gil González succeeded in killing Olid, however, whereupon Las Casas imprisoned Gil González and sent him to Mexico, whence he was dispatched to Spain to die in prison. To add to this complicated and unlovely tale, Hernández de Córdoba rebelled against Pedrarias and was captured and executed. Pedrarias then lost the governorship of Panama (1526), but was named governor of Nicaragua, dying in 1531 at the age of ninety.

Cortés himself had entered the picture at the time of the rebellion of Olid. Sending Las Casas by sea, he started an overland trek that brought him to Central America in 1525. The history of this expedition, as told by Cortés himself in his Fifth Letter and by Bernal Díaz, is the familiar one of Cortesian diplomacy and Indian factionalism.[36]

Far to the south in Chiapas, Cortés made some willing captives who reported that they had been held as slaves for more than twelve years by the Chiapanecs to work their plantations. They offered to aid Cortés in return for their freedom, an offer that was naturally accepted. During this journey, the Spaniards found other evidence of the ravages of inter-Indian warfare, such as the recently burned town of Tepetitan, and a new village being fortified against enemies who had destroyed two previous settlements. It is clear from reading Cortés' Fifth Letter and Bernal Díaz, as well as many other similar accounts of the Indian wars, that much of the destruction was, in fact, the work of Indians.

THE CONQUEST OF SOUTH AMERICA: VENEZUELA AND COLOMBIA

It seems no accident that the successful occupation of the north coast of South America waited until about the same epoch as the conquest of Mexico and Central America, and that the advance south into Peru was delayed until the Pacific Coast settlements in Panama and Central America were well established. The prerequisite of successful conquest, a base of supply, was furnished first by the Caribbean islands, and later by Panama and Central America.

A mere listing of explorations and colonization in the first quarter of the sixteenth century gives some idea of the activity in various

---

[36] For accounts of the conquest of Central America see C. E. Chapman, *Colonial Hispanic America* (New York: The Macmillan Company, 1933), p. 42; M. W. Williams, *The People and Politics of Latin America* (Boston: Ginn and Company, 1938), p. 119; Carlos Pereyra, *Historia de la América Española*, (8 vols., Madrid, N. D.), V, 115-124; Chester Lloyd Jones, *Guatemala Past and Present* (Minneapolis, 1940), pp. 3-12.

regions, and of the chronological relationship of the expeditions. Between 1510 and 1520, the first permanent settlements in Panama were made, Cuba was settled (1511), Ponce de León discovered Florida (1513), the Conquest of Mexico began, Juan Díaz de Solís found the Río de la Plata (1516), much of the coastline of the Gulf of Mexico was discovered by Alonzo de Pineda (1519), and Balboa planned an expedition to Peru. In the 1520's the conquest of Mexico and Central America was well advanced; the first permanent settlement was made in Venezuela at Cumaná; the coastline northward to perhaps Maryland was discovered by Lucas Vásquez de Ayllón; Florida and the southeast of the United States were explored by Pánfilo de Narváez (1528); an unsuccessful attempt to settle along the Río de la Plata was made by Sebastián Cabot (1526); Ferdinand Magellan's expedition sailed around the world (1519-1522); Santa Marta was settled in Colombia (1525); the Welsers received a grant in Venezuela (1528); and Francisco Pizarro and Diego de Almagro made their first two expeditions in search of Peru (1524 and 1526).

Not all these expeditions were colonizing successes, and the reasons for failure to settle were frequently found in the lack of an adequate food supply. This factor played a large part in the expeditions of Ayllón, Narváez, and Cabot, and was no less important in others.

After the settlement of Cumaná in 1520, Santa Ana de Coro, also in Venezuela, was established in 1527. The next important Venezuelan enterprise was that of the Welsers, the German banking and merchant firm. They had been granted a portion of Venezuela by Charles V, in accord with his policy of opening up his realms to all his subjects and partly in payment of his debts to them. The Welsers carried on a trade in pearls, but the slave traffic was the main business, and perhaps the chief opportunity for profit in an area that did not yet produce much that was exportable to Europe. They also sent several expeditions into the interior, one of which, led by Nikolaus Federmann, we shall consider later. Charles V canceled the Welser Concession and re-established Spanish rule in 1556. Caracas, the present capital, was founded in 1567.

Colombia's first permanent settlement was made at Santa Marta, by Rodrigo Bastidas in 1525. Since his expedition was promoted by the Crown with the same serious colonizing intentions that marked most of the enterprises from the time of Columbus's second voyage, Bastidas was required to take along fifty citizens, of whom a number were to be married men with their wives. García de Lerma was

FRANCISCO PIZARRO, CONQUEROR OF PERU

Courtesy of the Pan American Union

ADELANTADO SEBASTIÁN BELALCÁZAR, THE FIRST OF THE CONQUISTADORES TO
GO IN SEARCH OF THE GILDED KING

Adapted from A. Curtis Wilgus, *Latin America in Maps*
Sixteenth-Century Spanish Missions and Settlements in Florida

50a

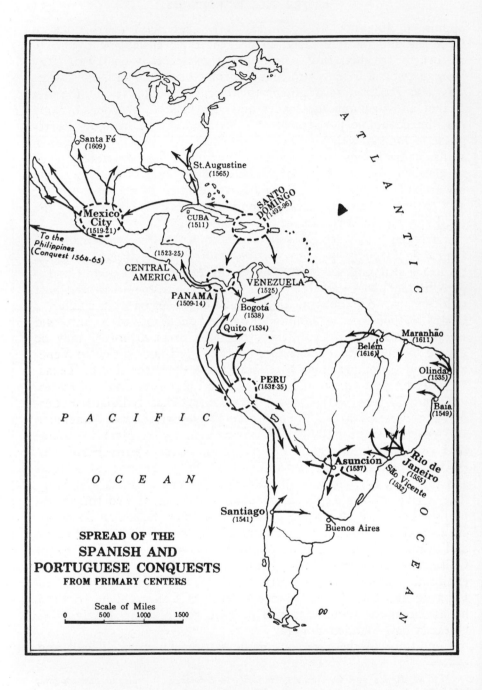

Santa Fé
(1609)

St.Augustine
(1565)

SANTO
DOMINGO
(1492-96)

Mexico
City
(1519-21)

CUBA
(1511)

To the
Philippines
(Conquest 1564-65)

(1523-25)

CENTRAL
AMERICA

PANAMA
(1509-14)

VENEZUELA
(1525)

Bogotá
(1538)

Quito (1534)

PERU
(1532-35)

Maranhão
(1611)

Belém
(1616)

Olinda
(1535)

Baía
(1549)

Asunción
(1537)

Rio de
Janeiro
(1555)

São Vicente
(1532)

Santiago
(1541)

Buenos Aires

A T L A N T I C

P A C I F I C

O C E A N

O C E A N

SPREAD OF THE
**SPANISH AND
PORTUGUESE CONQUESTS**
FROM PRIMARY CENTERS

Scale of Miles
0   500   1000   1500

appointed governor in 1528. He left Spain with instructions to treat the Indians humanely, to prevent their enslavement, and to restore to freedom and their homes those already enslaved. Fray Tomás Ortiz was sent with him as protector of the Indians. Lerma was also required to augment the European population of Santa Marta and promote the trades and agriculture. In order to carry out the economic portions of his instructions, he brought Portuguese colonists well supplied with seeds of cereals and garden stuffs, and cuttings for fruit trees. Various types of artisans, such as masons, blacksmiths, and carpenters also came as settlers. [37] On his arrival, Lerma found Santa Marta plagued by the ever-present and chronic complaint, lack of food. His work was to remedy the food shortage and reanimate the colony.

Cartagena, the second settlement in Colombia, was made by Pedro de Heredia in 1533 and became the base of exploring expeditions sent into the interior. Heredia himself went inland as far as Malambo, and gathered a treasure valued at a million and half gold ducats. "Six thousand ducats fell to the lot of each soldier, a larger fortune than was obtained by the conquerors of Mexico and Peru." [38] Some idea of the task faced by these explorers may be gained by noting that the area to be explored and settled in Venezuela and Colombia alone was about three times the size of Texas, or fourteen times the combined area of all the New England states.

Colombia was settled from three directions. Nikolaus Federmann, representing the Welsers, moved westward from Venezuela and reached the highlands of Colombia in 1538. Here he found that two expeditions had preceded him. After Pedro Fernández de Lugo conducted an expedition that failed because of a food shortage (1535), Gonzalo Jiménez de Quesada ascended the Magdalena river and in 1538, just before the arrival of Federmann, established the city of Bogotá. A short time later Sebastián de Belalcázar arrived. Belalcázar was one of the companions of Pizarro and Almagro, and had been appointed governor of Quito. From Quito he struck out for himself and, during the 1535-1538 period, explored southern and western Colombia, founded the cities of Popayán and Cali (1536) and explored the Cauca valley. In 1538 he ascended the mountains and reached the plateau shortly after Quesada had founded Bogotá.

Conditions in these regions made settlement more difficult and

---

[37] J. M. Henao and G. Arrubla, *Historia de Colombia*, (2 vols. in one, Bogotá, 1929), pp. 67-70.

[38] Henao and Arrubla, *Colombia*, p. 72.

less complete than in Mexico and Peru. In one thing, however, the story will have a familiar sound: the aid given the Europeans by the Indians served in a large measure to make colonization possible. Internal warfare among the Indians, and co-operation with the Europeans to secure allies against their ancient enemies, simplified the conquest. One of the chief achievements of the Spaniards in America was to give it greater unity than it had at the time of the Conquest. Whereas Latin America is today divided into only twenty nations speaking but three major languages, the Europeans found it divided into hundreds of contending tribes speaking hundreds of languages and dialects.

Another striking feature of the Conquest was that the more unified portions of America, politically speaking at least, were more readily subjugated. Mexico and Peru, unified to a greater extend than any other major regions, were conquered with comparative ease. Once the seat of the central government was captured, the principal battle was won. The case of the less centralized regions was far different. Here every separate group had to be conquered independently, and the task was for that reason much harder; it involved almost endless campaigns against uncivilized tribes in all but impenetrable regions. The Spaniards were impressed with this disparity in the speed of conquest, and Cieza offers an explanation that seems valid.

"Many are astonished," he says, "that these Indians [in Colombia], their settlements being frequently in regions easily conquered, have turned out so unconquerable and obstinate, while those of Peru, their valleys being so high up among snow-covered mountains and ranges with many crags and rivers, with a greater number of people than here, and vast uninhabited areas, serve faithfully and have been, and are so obedient. To which I answer that all the Indians subject to the district of Popayán are, and always have been unsubdued *(behetrías)*; they have never had rulers who made themselves respected. They are weak and lazy, and above anything else, they hate to work and to be held down . . . And when the Spaniards bear down on them, they burn the houses in which they live, which are made of wood and straw, and moving a league or two, or as far as they like, in three or four days they build another house, and in three or four more they plant . . . maize, and within four months gather it. And if they are pursued to that place also, they go farther . . . . Those of Peru work well and are tractable because they are more intelligent, and because all were conquered by the Inca

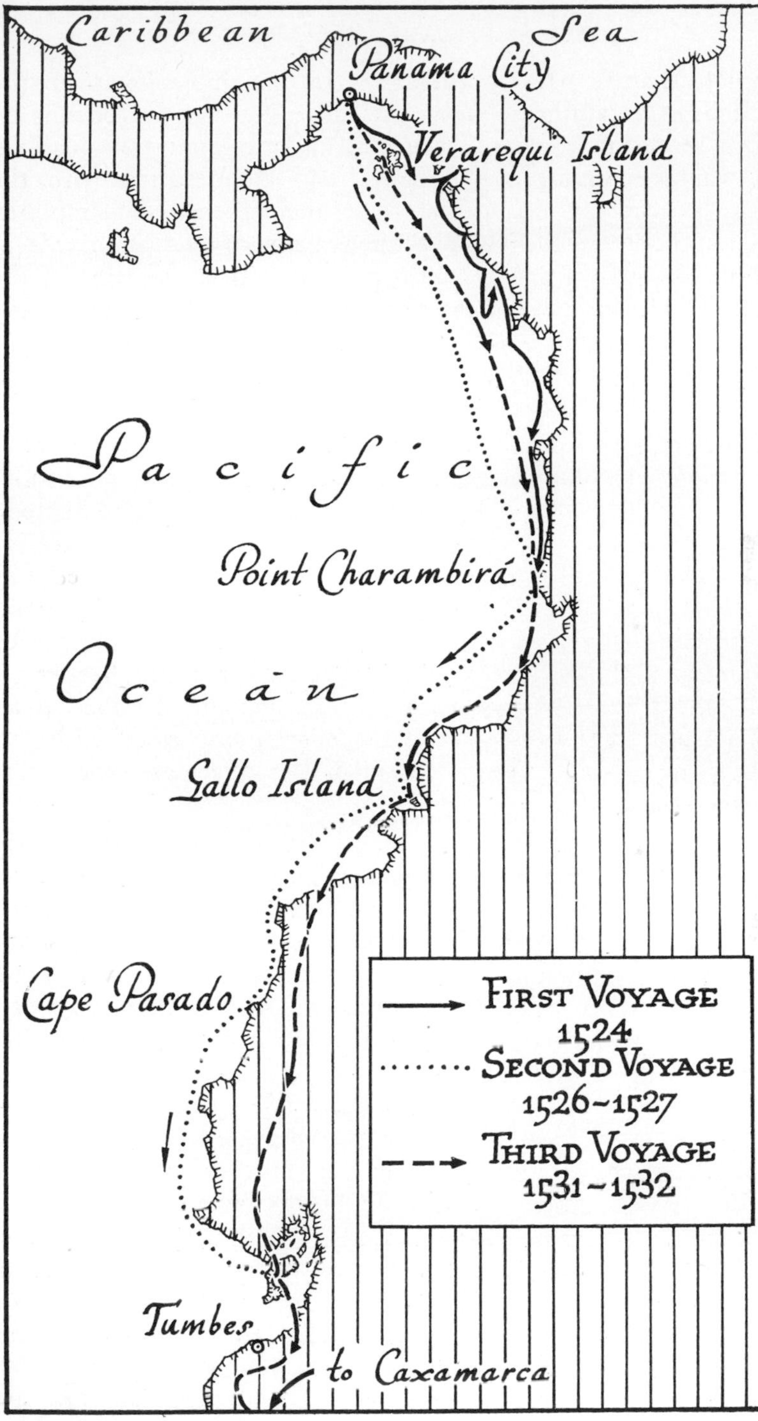

Caribbean Sea

Panama City

Verarequi Island

Pacific

Point Charambirá

Ocean

Gallo Island

Cape Pasado

	FIRST VOYAGE 1524
....	SECOND VOYAGE 1526~1527
	THIRD VOYAGE 1531~1532

Tumbes

to Caxamarca

Adapted from A. Curtis Wilgus, *Latin America in Maps*
Voyages of Pizarro, 1524-1532

kings to whom they paid tribute, always serving them, and they were born to this condition; . . ." [39]

In other respects, the state of affairs among the Indians of Colombia facilitated conquest as well as impeded it. Lack of integration among the Indians might, and did, in some places force starvation upon the Spaniards, but the same weakness of the Indians prevented them from offering organized resistance. Their own wars were of too long standing to permit even temporary union for the purpose of opposing invasion. "They all made constant and cruel war on each other," Cieza remarked, "and they differ from each other in languages in many regions, to such an extent that in every ward and on every hill there is a different language." [40] The law of conquest prevailed in Colombia up to the European entry, and in fact for many years thereafter.

THE CONQUEST OF PERU

In the meantime the conquest of Peru was in progress. While Balboa was engaged in the settlement of Panama, he heard of the land to the south, and was on the point of sailing for it when he was arrested and executed at the order of Pedrarias. In 1522, soon after Cortés had captured Mexico City, Pascual de Andagoya sailed down the coast as far as Peru and brought back stories of the Inca Empire. Shortly afterwards Pedrarias granted rights of exploration to Francisco Pizarro, Diego de Almagro and Hernando de Luque. Pizarro made two preliminary expeditions, in 1524 and 1526, before going to Spain where he signed a contract with the Crown for the conquest of Peru. Back in Panama, he set out in January, 1531, with 180 men and 27 horses. He landed in Guayaquil, and waited for the reinforcements coming under Hernando de Soto, who was later to explore what is now the south of the United States. This small band of men could not have conquered the Inca Empire with its 380,000 square miles of territory save for the state of disunity that prevailed within the empire.

The Inca Empire, as we have already seen, had been built up by a caste of predatory conquerors who were still extending their boundaries at the appearance of the Spaniards, but who were faced with rather frequent revolts within their realm. The bitter civil war between Huáscar and Atahualpa for the Inca throne was in progress when Pizarro came into Peru. "The war of the two brothers, kings Atahualpa and Huáscar," says Garcilaso, "was the

---

[39] Cieza, *Crónica*, chap. XIII.
[40] *Ibid.*, chap. XVIII.

total destruction of that Empire which facilitated the entry into the country of the Spaniards . . . for otherwise the country is naturally so rough and craggy, and has such bad [mountain] passes that a few men were enough to defend it." [41] Pizarro thus found the Inca Empire falling apart and he had only to ally himself with one of the factions to become master of the whole. The civil war was several years old when he arrived, much of the Empire already in ruins, and the greater part of the Inca nobility, administrative and military officials, dead or prisoners of Atahualpa. Immediate and organized opposition was possible only from Atahualpa; Pizarro seized him, posing as a friend of the deposed Huáscar. After Huáscar's death, he pretended to defend the legitimate line, the representatives of which remained in his power thinking that he intended to restore them to the throne. When organized opposition broke out in 1535, the Spaniards had already received very considerable reinforcements. They also had an abundance of Indian helpers who served as soldiers and held themselves to be "more subject than slave," gave "respect, obedience, and service, and faithfulness until death," and served as "spy, eavesdropper and sentinel" for the Spaniards. [42] The outcome of the struggle between Indians and Spaniards was not long in doubt; the Spaniards soon were masters of the country.

It was not long before the conquest resolved itself into a struggle between Spaniards. They had come to America to rise in the social scale and to better their respective economic positions. The Conquest, after the relatively ephemeral phase of the initial defeat of the Indians, became a contest among ever-increasing numbers of Europeans all seeking the same things. Turbulence and bloodshed were a natural outcome; but this was merely a prelude to the orderly process of economic development that began in the midst of the civil wars. One of the oldest of errors concerning the Conquest is to assume that it was nothing but war and destruction. In the very epoch in which the civil wars were fiercest, the economic development of America was proceeding rapidly and the foundations of future progress were being laid.

The story of the Conquest does not end here, of course. Chile was destined to be explored by Diego Almagro and conquered by Pedro de Valdivia, who began a task that was to be completed centuries later, but its story can best be told in conjunction with the development of Chile. The Río de la Plata region received settlers

---

[41] Garcilaso, *Comentarios*, Bk. I, chap. I.
[42] *Ibid.*, Bk. I, chap. XLI.

from four directions: from Peru, Chile, Spain, and Brazil. Here, too, the story is left to be told with the history of the region, as is that of the north of New Spain. The military aspects of these settlements were by no means unimportant, but a food supply was more so; food was what made conquest possible, and it was not available until the transplanted European plants and animals were more abundant.

The Essence of Conquest

The essence of the Conquest is to be found in the seizure of the land by the Spaniards and the introduction of plants and animals. The beginning of this process has been mentioned. The *real* conquest was the economic and social penetration; and with the task of depicting the first violent phases of the Conquest completed, we can turn to the details. It is important to know how the individual Spaniards got the land, began commerce, and promoted agriculture. For every Cortés who conquered an empire, there were thousands of Spaniards who received only a small piece of land; for every Pizarro and Heredia who seized the accumulated gold and silver, there were thousands of Spaniards who worked in the newly discovered mines. And in addition there were thousands of merchants and manufacturers who built up a great trade between America and Europe, and within America.

Manuel Colmeiro, the eminent Spanish economist, has accurately summarized the achievements we are now ready to study.

"The necessity of penetrating unknown seas quickened the progress of navigation; commerce changed its course and escaped from the narrow confines of the Mediterranean; the empires of Mexico and Peru with their extraordinary cultures and multitude of savage tribes and nations emerged from obscurity; new lands and fruits, useful animals, and workable materials were discovered; extensive markets were opened up, populous cities were erected; the Indians were oppressed and Negro slaves were introduced; greed fastened itself on the mines abundant in gold and silver; infinite numbers of Europeans crossed to America, some with lucrative employment, others desirous of growing rich with the booty of war, or peacefully by the cultivation of the fields, the grinding of sugar, or by commerce; the crops of the Old World were broadcast there, its trees and its plants were carried over, and its live stock disseminated and multiplied; missionaries came, preached and converted to the faith of Christ a part of the natives who, little by little, took on our language, conventions, and customs. In short, the colonial system was born." [43]

* * * * * * * *

The appearance of the Europeans in America had projected into a new scene an economic and political evolution under way in Europe for centuries. Following the discovery of new trade routes, Spain and Portugal had risen as nations and entered the competition for trade and territory. Portuguese expansion reached into Africa and eventually into America. The Reconquest of Spain from the Moors, a drive for national unification that was both economic and religious, widened out into the New World. In the Caribbean, Columbus claimed for Spain the land already disputed by the Indians.

Only when the island colonies had profitable plantations, and could serve as bases for supplies, was it possible to win the mainland. Aided by Indian dissensions, Cortés then conquered Mexico, allying himself with subjected tribes against the Aztecs, and playing one faction against another. In Central America, too, the conquerors used Indians against Indians, and against other Spaniards who competed for the new territories. The conquest of Venezuela and Colombia was more difficult, there being no centralized empire to fall with comparative ease once the capital was taken, and the uncivilized Indians, previously unsubdued, yielding less readily than the peoples long subject to Aztec or Inca rule. The conquest of Peru, which had waited on settlements in Central America, repeated the old tale of "divide and rule": Pizarro made the most of the bloody civil war in progress when he came.

The Conquest began in a setting of inter-Indian wars, and the conquerors joined the struggle, contributing their share of carnage and waste. But war and war's ravages were only a minor phase of the Conquest. Fundamentally, the Conquest was the seizure of the land by the Spaniards, and its economic and agricultural development. It is this phase of the Spanish penetration of America that we must now develop.

---

[43] Manuel Colmeiro, *Historia de la economía política en España* (2 vols., Madrid, 1863), II, 375-76.

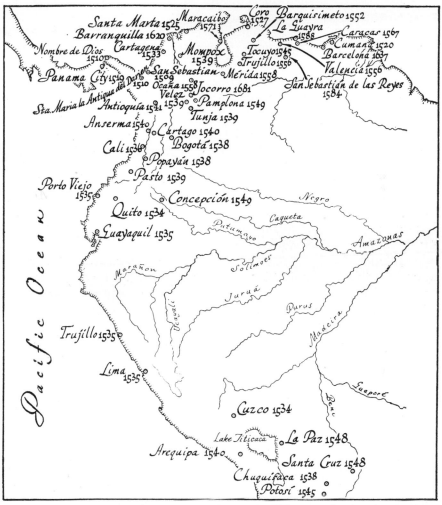

Santa Marta 1525
Barranquilla 1620
Nombre de Dios 1510
Panama City 1519
Sta. Maria la Antigua del Darién 1510
Cartagena 1533
San Sebastian 1509
Ocaña 1558 Socorro 1681
Velez
Antioquía 1541 1539 Pamplona 1549
Anserma 1540
Cali 1536
Cartago 1540
Bogotá 1538
Popayán 1538
Pasto 1539
Porto Viejo 1535
Concepción 1549
Quito 1534
Guayaquil 1535
Maracaibo 1571
Mompox 1539
Tocuyo 1545
Trujillo 1556
Mérida 1558
Coro 1527
La Guayra 1588
Barquisimeto 1552
Caracas 1567
Cumaná 1520
Barcelona 1637
Valencia 1556
San Sebastián de las Reyes 1584
Tunja 1539
Negro
Caqueta
Putumayo
Amazonas
Marañon
Solimoes
Juruá
Ucayali
Purus
Madeira
Guaporé
Beni
Trujillo 1535
Lima 1535
Cuzco 1534
Lake Titicaca
La Paz 1548
Arequipa 1540
Santa Cruz 1548
Chuquisaca 1538
Potosí 1545

Pacific Ocean

Adapted from A. Curtis Wilgus, *Latin America in Maps*
Some Early Settlements in the Spanish Colonies in Northern South America

Land and Labor

FUSION OF THE SPANISH AND INDIAN LAND SYSTEMS

SO FAR TWO MAIN THEMES have been followed: the Indian conquest and settlement of America, and the Spanish occupation. We shall now see how the individual Spaniard came into possession of the land, its people, and its products. The means employed naturally varied with the degree of land utilization developed by the Indians. In the West Indian Islands, the technique of acquisition was at first unformed; but as New Spain and Peru were conquered, there came into being a definite procedure based on the land systems of the Indians and the Spaniards. The fusion of the two produced the landholding system that prevailed throughout the colonial period.

THE SPANISH ASSUME OWNERSHIP OF AMERICA

The Spanish settlers assumed rights of ownership from the moment of discovery, and announced their intention of remaining permanently in America. [1] Columbus had hardly landed when he declared that there could be acquired from the Indians "great domains and riches and all their village for Spain." The new claimants signalized their ownership by the use of the Christian cross as their banner. The cross was planted, Columbus stated to Ferdinand and Isabella, "as a sign that Your Highnesses hold the land for your own and principally as a sign of Jesus Christ, our Lord, and in honor of Christianity." He also ordered the Indians well treated because "Your Highnesses will make them all Christians as they will all belong to you, for I regard them as yours . . . [and] this island and all the others are as much [yours] as Castile . . ."

---

[1] Antonio de Herrera, *Historia general de los hechos de los castellanos en las Islas y Tierra-Firme del Mar Océano* (2nd ed., 8 vols. in 3, Madrid, 1725-30), Decade I, Bk. I, chaps. XVII-XX. The first edition of this work dates from 1613; James J. Carney, "Early Spanish Imperialism," *H.A.H.R.*, XIX (May, 1939), 138-46.

The people were unarmed, he added, "and so they are suitable to be governed and made to work, to sow, and do anything else that shall be necessary." [2] He took no less precaution to impress on the Indians that the Spanish occupation was permanent, announcing that he had come with the purpose of "subjecting these islands to the authority of the powerful Spanish Sovereigns." [3]

Inducements to colonists were offered from the time of the third voyage of Columbus. He was authorized to make new settlements, and immigrants were granted wheat and barley for seed, and as many as twenty yoke of cows, mares, and other animals, all as loans. [4]

SPANISH ORIGINS OF THE COLONIAL LAND SYSTEM: ENCOMIENDAS AND REPARTIMIENTOS

To assume ownership of the land, lives, rights, properties, and possessions of the newly-discovered peoples was in keeping with the European custom of the time. In Spain and Portugal the entire Reconquest had followed this pattern. Christian warriors gradually won back the Peninsula from the Mohammedans, and by 1492 Spain and Portugal were divided into large estates, *latifundios,* the owners of which were the economic and political masters of the inhabitants.

"Progressively as the Christian reconquest was effected, the greater part of the land was divided, as is known, among the military orders, the nobles who were the leaders, and the clergy. The fertile Andalusian and Extremaduran lands were eagerly coveted by the Castilians. The Church, the military orders, and our entire nobility managed to grab a good part of this precious booty . . . To the common people who composed the majority of that army very little land was given." [5]

---

[2] *Journal,* November 16, and December 12 and 15.

[3] *Syllacio-Coma Letter,* cited in Thacher, *Columbus,* II, 256.

[4] *The Book of Privileges,* Document VI, probable date April 23, 1497, cited in Thacher, *Columbus,* II, 542.

[5] Pascual Carrión, *Los latifundios en España* (Madrid, 1932), p. 291. The record of what happened to the conquered Moors is not entirely clear and the practices do not seem to have been uniform. It is possible that the customs of the Middle Ages were less drastic than those of the late fifteenth century. "The very same day of the entry of the triumphant Christian army into the historical city [Sevilla] . . . THREE HUNDRED THOUSAND MOHAMMEDANS left it forever exiled, impoverished, with their eyes bathed in tears and turning at every step to look back." See Joaquín Guichot, *Historia de Andalucía,* IV, chap. V, cited in Carrión, p. 292. Another work, the title of which is significant, *Acerca del repartimiento de la propriedad rústica y urbana de los Moros de Sevilla que hicieron los Reyes Don Fernando III y Don Alfonso X,* gives still another picture of the Reconquest. "I learn," says the author, "from the LIBRO DE REPARTIMENTO, that among the Infantes, prelates, rico-hombres, knights, soldiers, officials, and other

When James the Conqueror captured Majorca, he divided the land "into allotments between the King and his nobles," and the "Moors who had offered to surrender in Majorca were made slaves, and distributed among the various estates into which the island had been divided." [6] The same system was employed in the conquest of the Canary Islands, where the chief officials of the conquering armies were given repartimientos. A few of the natives were allowed "to retain small and generally undesirable portions of land," while "others remained as tenants on the territories that had been handed over to the invaders." [7]

During the Reconquest, from the twelfth century onward, the great military orders of Calatrava, Santiago, Alcántara, and Montesa were rewarded not only with repartimientos of land, but also with important concessions granting rights of tax collecting, and "among the largest of these incomes were the rents of pasture lands granted to the orders as *encomiendas* or fiefs. These great estates comprised one hundred and five of the most frequented southern and western *dehesas* or pasturage districts" of Spain, and besides there were other taxes "which were collected not only from permanent residents in the *encomiendas,* but also from visiting migratory flocks." [8]

The *repartimiento* at this early date was a distribution among the conquerors of the lands of the conquered, frequently including the conquered themselves. The *encomienda,* as spoken of here, was a right to collect certain taxes from the people of a specified district. As late as the seventeenth century there were examples of legal actions brought in Spain against *encomenderos,* among them a successful one to prevent excessive taxation by an encomendero of the Order of Calatrava.

TRANSFER OF THE REPARTIMIENTO AND ENCOMIENDA TO AMERICA

It was only natural that the repartimiento and encomienda, given their long historical development in Spain, should migrate to America with the first settlers. Count Pedro Rodríguez de Campomanes,

---

persons who assisted in the conquest of Sevilla, the sovereigns Fernando III and Alfonso X made a *repartimiento* or *distribution* of the rural and urban property of the Moors defeated in the war, in which it seems that the victors despoiled the wretched vanquished in a vandalistic manner, not leaving them even a tiny place as a refuge, nor a hand-breadth of land on which to establish themselves." Cited in Carrión, *Latifundios,* pp. 292-93.

[6] Merriman, *Spanish Empire,* I, 315.

[7] *Ibid.,* II, 187-88.

[8] Julius Klein, *The Mesta: A Study in Spanish Economic History, 1273-1836* (Cambridge: Harvard University Press, 1920), pp. 239-40.

the Spanish statesman of the eighteenth century, pointed out the similarities of rights and privileges granted in twelfth-century Spain to the repartimientos given to the *conquistadores* of America. [9]

The Crown authorized Columbus to distribute to the settlers "the lands, hills, and waters by him considered proper for sowing corn and other seeds, planting orchards, cotton trees, flax, vines, trees, sugar canes, building houses, mills, and machines for the said sugar and other buildings profitable and necessary for their livelihood . . . according to their rank, their service to the Sovereigns, and the condition and quality of their person and estates." [The grantee was given the right to] "hold and possess . . . occupy, plant, and cultivate with power to sell, give, grant, exchange, alienate, mortgage, retain, and do therewith and therein whatever he may please and think fit as with his own property, for life, by a just and legal title." [10]

Acting with the authority thus conveyed, Columbus "distributed plots" of land as soon as he reached Española on his second voyage. This is the first example of individual land grants made by the Spaniards in America. [11]

Land without laborers to work it was useless, however, and the distribution of the Indians appeared at the same time as the direct land grants made by Columbus.

"The Admiral before he went to Castile, in 1496, about March, or the Adelantado [brother of Columbus] after the departure of the Admiral, imposed, in addition to the tributes that the chieftains and their people paid, or perhaps as the principal tribute paid (because I could not verify this point), the obligation on certain chieftains and [Indian] lords of taking charge of the cultivation of the lands of the Spanish Christian towns, and of working for them with all their people to furnish maintenance and give other personal services. This was the origin of the pestilence of the repartimiento and encomienda which has devastated and destroyed the whole of these Indies." [12]

Another version of this is worth citing. Herrera states:

---

[9] Klein, *Mesta*, p. 134; See also Antonio Ballesteros, *Historia de España y su influencia en la historia universal* (Barcelona: Casa Editorial Salvat, 1919), III, 255, 349.
[10] *The Book of Privileges,* Document XXII, July 22, 1497, cited in Thacher, *Columbus*, II, 547.
[11] Las Casas, *Historia*, Bk. I, chap. LXXXVIII.
[12] Las Casas, *Historia*, Bk. I, chap. CLI.

BALBOA, DISCOVERER OF THE PACIFIC

CHRISTOPHER COLUMBUS—A PAINTING IN THE NAVAL MUSEUM AT MADRID

"The Admiral distributed among them and gave them farms
. . . and this was the origin of the repartimientos or encomiendas throughout the Indies, because the Admiral gave them
through *cédulas* [writs] reading: *through such and such a cacique
so many thousand plants . . . are given and that cacique and his
people must work for whoever received those lands.*" [13]

The terms repartimiento and encomienda, at first used indis- ✱
criminately, as in the quotations above, to signify a distribution of
land or Indians, soon acquired new meanings which should be kept
in mind. During the first years of the Conquest, a repartimiento,
where used to indicate an allotment of Indians, was synonymous
with encomienda, and the conquistadores employed the two terms
interchangeably. In time, however, repartimientos became temporary allotments of Indians assigned to do a given task, while
encomiendas were grants made for the lifetime of the holder,
eventually becoming hereditary. Even after this distinction became
common, however, encomiendas were often called repartimientos
by the conquistadores. [14] Since the encomienda was the primary
basis of the Spaniards' control over Indian labor, without which the
cultivation of the land would have been all but impossible, it is
important to see its development. A discussion of the repartimiento
as a system of temporary allotments of Indians will be reserved
until later, along with other methods, such as slavery, employed by
the Spaniards to utilize Indian labor.

The encomienda was destined to endure practically to the end
of the colonial period, and to mold firmly certain aspects of economic life. [15] Columbus petitioned Queen Isabella in 1498 for permission to use Indian labor until the colony got a start, but he was
merely seeking to legalize a step already taken. In 1499, certain
caciques and their people were forced to work the lands which had
been assigned to the colonists. The embryonic system as yet had no
legal standing, however, for in 1501, Fray Nicolás de Ovando,

[13] Herrera, *Hechos castellanos,* Decade I, Bk. III, chap. XVI; and also Decade
I, Bk. V, chap. VI; Bk. VI, chap. XVII; Bk. X, chap. XII; Decade II, Bk. I,
chap. XI.

[14] Later the term repartimiento was used to designate the distribution of goods
to the Indians by the *corregidores* and *alcaldes mayores.* Infra pp. 620-21.

[15] Lesley Byrd Simpson, *The Encomienda in New Spain: Forced Native Labor
in the Spanish Colonies, 1492-1550* (Berkeley: University of California Press, 1929).
Simpson is the standard authority on the encomienda, and is especially valuable for
a study of its legal aspects. See also *Gobernación espiritual y temporal de las Indias,*
Bk. III, *(Colección de documentos inéditos . . . de las antiguas posesiones españolas
de ultramar* [hereafter *C.D.I. Ultramar*], 25 vols., Madrid, 1885-1932), vols. XXI,
XXII. See also F. A. Kirkpatrick, "Repartimiento-Encomienda," *H.A.H.R.,* XIX
(August, 1939), 372-79; Silvio R. Zavala, *La encomienda indiana* (Madrid, 1935).

newly appointed governor of the Indies, was instructed to treat the Indians as "good subjects and vassals of the Crown," and to permit them "to go in entire freedom about the island." [16]

Up to this time, the Crown policy was still seeking a way to treat the Indians as free vassals, but the situation soon changed. In 1503, Isabella stated that, inasmuch as it had been previously decreed that the Indian inhabitants and residents of the island of Española were "free and not subject," but that

> "as now we are informed that because of the excessive liberty enjoyed by the said Indians they avoid contact and community with the Spaniards to such an extent that they will not even work for wages, but wander about idle, and cannot be had by the Christians to convert to the Holy Catholic Faith . . . I command you, our said Governor, that beginning from the day you receive my letter you will compel and force the said Indians to associate with the Christians of the island and to work on their buildings, and to gather and mine the gold and other metals, and to till the fields and produce food for the Christian inhabitants and dwellers of the said island; and you are to have each one paid on the day he works the wage and maintenance which you think he should have . . . and you are to order each cacique to take charge of a certain number of the said Indians so that you may make them work wherever necessary, and so that on feast days and such days as you think proper they may be gathered together to hear and be taught in matters of the Faith . . . and do not consent or allow that any person do them any harm or oppress them . . . ." [17]

Thus did the encomienda, which had existed in fact almost from the day of the Spanish entry in Española, gain legal recognition. Many attempts were to be made to abolish it, but it was so well suited to the environment that it lasted for three centuries. The Indian chiefs of Española were distributed among the conquistadores, just as the land had been, and the system was extended to other territories *pari passu* with their conquest.

When Vicente Yáñez Pinzón was granted a contract to conquer Puerto Rico in April 1505, it provided for the distribution of the land and Indians among the conquistadores. [18] In the course of the

---

[16] Instructions of Ferdinand and Isabella to Fray Nicolás de Ovando, September 16, 1501, cited in Simpson, *Encomienda*, pp. 27-28.

[17] *Cédula* of Isabella to Ovando, December 20, 1503, cited in Simpson, *Encomienda*, pp. 30-31.

[18] *Asiento* of Ferdinand with Vicente Yáñez Pinzón, April 24, 1505, cited in Simpson, *Encomienda*, p. 34.

same year, Ferdinand approved the distribution of the Indians made by Ovando in Española. Furthermore, lands and Indians had been granted to many people at the Court of Spain. Ovando protested against this, pleading that there were not enough Indians for the people in Española; but the custom continued and the King was one of the chief encomenderos.[19] When Jamaica and Cuba were conquered, the distribution of the lands and Indians was immediately effected, and at about the same time the King issued various *cédulas* granting encomiendas at the pleasure of the Crown. There was also another aspect to the matter. "Most of the discoverers ventured forth at their own risk and expense," [20] expected a reward, and the Crown paid them with land and Indians.

Important efforts to modify the system were made in the early period, owing in part to the campaign waged by Bartolomé de las Casas and in part to the many complaints that came back from the New World.[21] The first attempt at reform was the promulgation of a new code, known as the Laws of Burgos, 1512. When this proved to be short of perfect, the New World was placed temporarily in the hands of three Jeronimite Friars, 1516 to 1520. But Charles V (1516-56), influenced by the humanitarians and fearful of creating a feudal class with excessive powers, decided that the encomienda must be abolished, and announced that "the Indians are free and should be given entire liberty, and we, in good conscience, cannot and should not give them in encomienda to anyone as hitherto has been done." [22] Charles reached this decision as Cortés was beginning the conquest of Mexico.

ESTABLISHMENT OF SPANISH LAND CONTROL IN MEXICO

To secure the proper credentials for colonization, Cortés not only founded Vera Cruz and attained official status through its *cabildo;* he also sent a letter to the Emperor and a messenger to the Audiencia (high court with judicial and administrative powers) of Española. From the Audiencia, Cortés received "authority to conquer the whole of New Spain and to brand slaves according to

---

[19] Simpson, *Encomienda,* pp. 37-56.

[20] Colmeiro, *Economía política,* II, 380-83.

[21] For documents on Las Casas see *Colección de documentos inéditos relativos al descubrimiento, conquista, y organización . . . de Indias* [hereafter *D.I.I.*] (42 vols., Madrid, 1842-95), VII, 5-352.

[22] Cited in Simpson, *Encomienda,* p. 77. The Laws of Burgos and the rule of the Jeronimite Friars are discussed in Simpson, *Encomienda,* pp. 48-79, and in his *Studies in the Administration of the Indians in New Spain: I. The Laws of Burgos of 1512* (Ibero-Americana: 7, Berkeley: University of California Press, 1934), pp. 1-27. The paleographic text of the Laws of Burgos is given in Roland D. Hussey, "Text of the Laws of Burgos (1512-1513) Concerning the Treatment of the Indians," *H.A.H.R.,* XII (August, 1932), 301-26.

the instructions that were sent, and to divide and make allotments of the Indians as was customary in the Islands of Española, Cuba and Jamaica." [23] He proceeded to do so, writing to the Emperor:

". . . in face of the importunities of your Majesty's officers and men which I could not in any way escape, it was almost necessary for me to deposit the chiefs and natives of these parts with the Spaniards, which I have done with proper consideration for their rank and the services they have rendered your Majesty. Thus, until something further is ordered, or this disposition is confirmed, the said chiefs and natives will serve the Spaniards with whom they have been deposited, and they will give them what they need for their support . . . . The best and most important provinces and cities have been reserved for your Majesty." [24]

The answer to this came as promptly as the means of communication permitted. On June 26, 1523, Charles wrote to Cortés recapitulating all the reasons for not granting encomiendas and added "Therefore you are not to make any repartimiento or encomienda in that land, or consent to any assignment of the Indians, but you are to allow them to live in liberty, as our vassals of Castile live, and if before the arrival of this letter you have given any Indians in encomienda to any Christians, you will . . . remove them . . . and you will allow them to live in entire liberty . . . ." The land, however, was to be divided among the settlers, who were to acquire title after five years of occupancy.[25]

All this was much easier said than done. Cortés' companions expected to be rewarded; they wanted land and Indians. Bernal Díaz reveals a feeling that was universal. "The Government of New Spain had no sooner been conferred on Cortés than it occurred to me and others of the original conquistadores," he says, "that it would have to be Cortés' duty to bear in mind all the hardships that ensued from the day that he set out from the Island of Cuba onwards, and remember who were the persons who supported him."[26] In the face of such expectations it mattered but little what Cortés and the Crown thought of the continuance of the encomienda. Circumstances determined matters for them.

[23] Bernal Díaz, *Conquest of New Spain*, IV, 218-19.
[24] Third Letter of Cortés to Charles V, May 15, 1522, cited in Simpson, *Encomienda*, pp. 81-82; and in a slightly different translation in *Hernando Cortés, Five Letters,* ed. and tr. J. Bayard Morris (New York: Robert M. McBride, 1929), pp. 240-41.
[25] Instructions of Charles V to Cortés, June 26, 1523, cited in Simpson, *Encomienda*, pp. 82-84.
[26] Bernal Diaz, *Conquest of New Spain*, IV, 338.

Distribution of encomiendas and land continued simultaneously with the conquest of Mexico. One of the explanations of the rapid spread of Spanish authority to outlying territory is to be found in the attractiveness of acquiring an encomienda, and with it, riches and high social position. The companions of Cortés pushed out energetically in all directions, in spite of dangers. Frequently the encomendero was compelled to subdue his Indians by force of arms, and "at the beginning, most of the provinces of New Spain rose in revolt when we demanded tribute from them, and even murdered their encomenderos." [27]

Encomiendas were nevertheless valuable property, and the competition for them was not hindered by too many of the rules of human decency. There can be small wonder that the rancors between the conquistadores were frequently deepseated enough to cause civil strife. In Mexico, Cortés was expected to "take count of Tom, Dick, and Harry and others who deserved it . . . and who were poor because the luck of [possessing] good Indians had not fallen to their share, for there was property to dispose of," but most of the Indians and land went to a few, leaving many others propertyless and in such a condition that they "wandered on . . . like a lame mule, dejected . . . and not enough to live on." [28]

Nor did the grant of an encomienda mean a guarantee of ownership. There were frequent occasions when one encomendero was deprived of his Indians in order that another might have them. Grants made by Cortés were annulled by the Audiencia which succeeded him, and these grants were in turn annulled by a second Audiencia. The story of how the encomiendas and land grants were distributed, annulled, and redistributed could be carried on endlessly. The instances given here are but an illustration of what happened throughout Mexico and Central America. [29]

FUSION OF AZTEC AND SPANISH LAND SYSTEMS

In Mexico the Spaniards came into contact with a land-control system that differed radically from that of the West Indian islands. Whereas the West Indies lacked a highly developed agriculture or conventionalized land control, the farming system in Mexico approached the maximal in hoe culture. The scarcity of good land on the central plateau enhanced its value, and the sharp struggle for

---

[27] Bernal Díaz, *Conquest of New Spain*, IV, 289-290.
[28] Bernal Díaz, *Conquest of New Spain*, IV, 340-41.
[29] Francisco A. de Icaza, *Conquistadores y pobladores de Nueva España. Diccionario autobiográfico sacado de los textos originales* (2 vols., Madrid, 1923), shows in the language of each of the early settlers his economic status and claims, whether or not he had Indians.

its possession, in progress for centuries, had led to its control by well defined codes and regulations. The tribute and land system evolved by the Aztecs and some of their predecessors permitted the landed nobility, the priests, and the military to skim off the cream of Mexican agricultural production. The Spanish problem was merely to seize mastery of an established system. This we have seen them doing.

In another characteristic the Mexican encomienda and land grant differed widely from the island system. The encomienda in the islands was made on the basis of a cacique and his followers (kinship units), while territorial considerations were relatively unimportant. In contrast to this, the assignments of Indians in Mexico were made on the basis of towns and villages (place units). This enabled the encomendero, in some cases, to become a landowner without having a formal grant. He replaced the Indian chieftain and collected the tributes which the Indian subjects were accustomed to pay. The original purpose of the grants of Indians, to furnish a living for the Spaniards, was altered and the encomendero came to consider himself the owner of the land as well as of the tribute from the land. This ownership was frequently confirmed by a later title.[30]

The size of the allotments varied greatly. Cortés received 22 towns with their surrounding territories, and 23,000 vassals (interpreted by Cortés to mean 115,000 people) in Morelos, Oaxaca, Puebla, Mexico (state), and Vera Cruz, then as now five of the richest and most populous sections of Mexico. The area of his territories was not less than 25,000 square miles (about five times the area of Connecticut). His rights included the lands and their occupants, woods, pastures, running and still water, with full criminal and civil jurisdiction over them, amounting to the rights of the monarch. This feudal grant, for such it was, illustrates the tendency in the New World to award lands on the model worked out in the Reconquest of Spain. Columbus had been given very ample powers, Pedrarias de Avila was sent to Panama with the title of *Adelantado* and considerable authority, and in this case Cortés obtained feudal powers and a title of nobility. Pizarro was

---

[30] This discussion of the relation of land ownership to the encomienda, and of the various methods by which the Spaniards acquired land, is based on George McCutchen McBride, *The Land Systems of Mexico* (New York: American Geographical Society, 1923), except where other citations are given. See also Prescott, *Mexico,* Bk. I, chap. V; and *Merced a Hernán Cortés de tierras inmediatas a México (Colección de documentos para la historia de México* [hereafter *C. D. México*], ed. García Icazbalceta, 2 vols., Mexico, 1866), II, 28-29.

shortly after to receive similar honors and powers.[31] Other large grants were made. The Duke of Atrisco received the fertile farming district of Tula with 300 families; Pedro de Alvarado, Xochimilco with its 30,000 people; and Juan Jaramilla, the entire province of Xilotepeque with 130,000 people. Juan de Villaseñor y Cervantes was given a large part of Guanajuato, his estate containing about 10,000 square miles. Most of the encomiendas, however, were smaller.

Titles were of two kinds: direct grants of land and encomiendas of Indians. The first encomiendas were temporary, and in addition to the attempts to suppress them already mentioned, another royal order to this effect was issued in 1530. The order could not be carried out, however, and in 1536 the Crown extended the encomiendas for a lifetime, with the right of inheritance for one generation.

But the encomienda as a feudal political institution was the antithesis of the Crown's policy of concentrating power in its own hands. The great encomenderos (particularly Cortés and Pizarro) were manifestly dangerous to the Spanish sovereigns. Desiring to curb this feudal tendency, and also to remedy many abuses of the encomiendas, the Crown decreed the New Laws in 1542, abolishing the encomienda. Revolt broke out in Peru as soon as the laws were applied; and in Mexico a revolt was avoided only by the discretion of the Viceroy in not enforcing the laws. The Crown was compelled to recognize the encomiendas anew. The right of inheritance was extended by stages to a third, fourth, and fifth generation. *De facto* the encomiendas had become hereditary property rights over human beings, and the land upon which they lived.

Encomiendas and large land estates were not available to everyone. Most of those who received land had to be content with small areas, without Indians. Small allotments were termed *peonías* (foot-soldier grants), and *caballerías* (horseman's grants), both types having been common during the Reconquest of Spain from the Moors. The size and quality of the *peonías* and *caballerías* were laid down in a *cédula* of 1513; and while the exact sizes varied with time and place, the peonía was theoretically enough to maintain a family, and might be a hundred acres more or less. The

---

[31] Lucas Alamán, *Historia de Méjico* (5 vols., Méjico: J. M. Lara, 1849-52), I, 38. Cortés held other valuable properties in mines; and in 1535 he created a *mayorazgo* (entailed estate) which was still in possession of his heirs, virtually intact and undivided, at the beginning of the nineteenth century, embracing at that time 5 *estancias*, 15 *villas*, 89 *haciendas*, 119 *ranchos* and 157 *pueblos* with some 150,000 inhabitants.

caballería was about five times as large and might run to more than a thousand acres, although the variations were great.

INDIAN ORIGINS OF THE MEXICAN LAND OWNERSHIP SYSTEM

The *cacicazgo*, or estate of an Indian chief, furnished another medium through which the Spaniards acquired land and position. In many cases *cacicazgos* were seized by force. In others the transfer was legal in form, marriage with the widow of a chief being the favorite method. The similarities of the Indian land system and the European feudal system aided greatly in this form of transfer. The feudalism of Europe is too well understood to warrant a description here, but the origins of the Indian system merit attention.

The landholding nobility among the Indians arose when

"towns and villages . . . were founded . . . [by] chieftains, captains, marshals, and other officials and commanders in the militia . . . [who established] very fine entailed estates . . . [and] the descendants of these families are esteemed as noblemen, because, even if they are poverty-stricken they do not work at any servile trade or low or menial tasks. Never will they consent to carry anything, or to dig with a hoe or plow, asserting that they are nobles and do not have to do these low and abject things, but only to serve in wars . . . and since they are gentlemen, to die like men, fighting . . . . [Any warrior who founded an] entailed estate . . . with all the lands that fell to his lot in the repartimiento, with wood lots, springs, rivers, or lakes, took the principal parts for the chief family . . . and then, from what remained, divided with the soldiers, friends and relatives . . . and all these were required to recognize the chief family, and to rally around and support it, to defend it and serve as palace guards, acknowledging allegiance with gifts of fowls, and game, flowers and boughs for the maintenance of the *casa de mayorazgo* [family estate]. And he who held this position was obligated to protect and cherish them as friends and kinsmen." [32]

The lands of such estates were distributed to *terrazgueros*, or "vassals, who as such paid tribute and vassalage from the products which they grew and gathered." Thus were created the estates which the Spaniards found on conquering Mexico and other parts of America.

Most of these estates fell to the conquistadores. Many Indian nobles were dispossessed, others killed in the wars, and their wives

---

[32] Muñoz Camargo, *Tlaxcala*, pp. 103-105. This is a description of the process among the Tlaxcalans, but it is applicable throughout America.

and daughters given to the conquistadores in marriage. The results to the Indian nobility were disastrous, since they were too proud to work. Alonso de Zurita, about 1560, mentioned that "the *señores,* both high and low, subordinates and chiefs, are so poor that they have nothing to eat, and they have been dispossessed of their fiefs *(señorios),* lands, renters, and serfs *(mayeques)* . . ." [33]

Thus far we have been talking of lands held by the Indian nobility, and which passed into the hands of a corresponding class of Spaniards. But the masses of the Indians were tenants and serfs, and their fate after the Conquest is one of the keys to the subsequent history of Mexico, and all Latin America.

Among the Aztecs the population was divided into *calpulli* (clans), which were both kinship and landowning units. *Calpulli* lands were held by the village in common, and if there was more than one calpulli in a village, each held its own specified portion. The common lands of the village, supplying wood, hunting, and other needs, were held without specific allotments and managed also by the calpulli. There were no common pastures, as in Europe, because no domestic animals existed to use them. Water rights were regulated by the village, and Indian custom passed into colonial law.

Arable lands were divided among the *maceguales* (family heads), who were equivalent to free landholders or peasant proprietors, each cultivating his own field. The family head received a definite allotment, known in the colonial period as *heredades* because they were inherited by successive generations. Individual allotments varied greatly in accordance with the quality of the soil, but were probably about five to eight acres. Each plot was marked off from the others, but just as the boundaries between villages were uncertain, so were the boundaries of the assigned lands, and quarrels over land were (and still are) frequent.

Other fields were set aside for the care of the local chieftain, official visitors, and the priesthood, and to furnish tribute and supplies for warfare. The calpulli was charged with seeing that such lands were cultivated, and the produce stored in the public granaries for the use of the various classes enumerated. The most important lands designated for tribute were those of the kings, known as "lands of the chief," consisting of about 163 acres, or in some cases twice as much, of the best land. Next came the *tecpan* or lands of

---

[33] Alonso de Zurita, *Breve y sumaria relación de los señores y maneras y diferencias que había de ellos en la Nueva España (Nueva C. D. México,* III, 71-227), p. 168.

the local chief, perhaps equivalent in size and quality to that of the kings. The *tecpantlaca,* a special class of workers, cultivated the fields and stored the produce, and were exempted from almost all other tribute. Public, as well as private, lands were inalienable, although they were sometimes rented out and the produce consigned to the public granary. The amount of land devoted to a king or chieftain was some twenty to eighty times that of a free land owner, or *macegual.*

Large estates worked by *mayeques* (serfs) had grown up by the time of the Conquest. The mayeques could neither move from, nor be removed from such estates, which were inalienable. The lord of the land gave them protection in return for produce and services, and they were exempt from the tribute paid by the maceguales, and from work on the public lands. Their position resembles closely that of the European serf. They were numerous enough to be recognized as a separate class by Spanish law after the Conquest. The Spaniards quickly applied the name of *tierras y vasallos patrimoniales* to express the similarity of these estates to the manors of Spain. By the time of the Spanish conquest of Mexico, some three thousand chieftains and others held such estates. Zurita says that "All these overlords, both supreme and subordinate, and many other individuals held private patrimonial estates, and with them their *mayeques* or *tlalmaites.*" Sometimes the lands of the chief went to his son, whether the son succeeded in office or not, and they might be divided among heirs; but they could not pass to the free peasants (maceguales).[34]

The estates for the upkeep of officials were owned by the public, nominally, but most of the offices were hereditary and the lands in effect family property. Some of the "individuals" spoken of as having lands may have had a thousand, or even four thousand acres of land.

The Aztec Confederacy was superimposed on the local systems. Tenochtitlán, Téxcoco, and Tlacopan, the three cities of the confederation, all held feudal overlordships over subjugated territory. Subordinate chieftains governed defined territories, similar in structure to those which the Spaniards called *señoríos* to indicate the broad political and economic powers of the rulers. Téxcoco held about thirty such señoríos, and Tenochtitlán held a number that supplied it with the food and made its existence possible, the city having no agricultural lands of its own. In speaking of these, Cortés remarked: "The city contains many large and fine houses,

---

[34] Zurita, *Breve y sumaria relación,* in *Nueva C. D. México,* III, 155-169.

and for this reason. All the nobles of the land owing allegiance to Muteczuma have their houses in the city and reside there for a certain portion of the year; and in addition there are a large number of rich citizens who likewise have very fine houses." [35]

THE COLONIAL LANDHOLDING TOWN

The founding of new towns by the Spaniards, and the blending of Spanish and Indian elements in the Indian villages were among the chief post-Conquest developments. The Spaniards began erecting new towns immediately. Some of these were rebuilt Indian cities, such as Téxcoco and Tenochtitlán,[36] others entirely new. Cortés divided the rebuilt city of Tenochtitlán into two parts. The central section was designated the *traza* and was reserved for the Spaniards; it was separated from the outer (Indian) section by four large canals. Cortés also divided the city among his followers, taking for himself, with other things, the two palaces of Montezuma.[37]

Other towns were built in regions where there had been no towns before. Some were founded as military outposts, some grew up as centers of the new and greatly augmented trade, and some began as religious centers. Some were Indian towns transferred to more favorable commercial routes (Puebla near the old Indian town of Cholula; Oaxaca near Zaachila); some were in former wastelands, converted into splendid pastures with the introduction of domestic animals (Toluca); some were seaports for which the Indians had previously had little use (Vera Cruz, Tampico, Acapulco); some were mining cities (Zacatecas, Pachuca, Guanajuato, San Luis Potosí, and many others); and some were new agricultural centers in rich valleys where the cultivation of wheat, sugar, and other European crops enabled a larger population to live (Cuernavaca, Orizaba, Morelos). Numerous other towns sprang up where previously only nomadic Indians had roamed.

In all these, the Spaniards became the chief property holders, the landholding town being one of the most important elements of Spanish civilization. This, like many other Spanish institutions, can be traced far back in history. The accent was distinctly on community activity, for while many of the residents owned their individual farms, much of the town's land was held in common. The typical Spanish town owned the following common lands: the

---

[35] Second Letter in *Hernando Cortés, Five Letters*, p. 92.
[36] Cortés describes the rebuilding of Tenochtitlán (Mexico City) in his third and fourth letters.
[37] Vicente Riva Palacio, ed., *México a través de los siglos* (5 vols., México, 1887-1889), II, 466-67.

propios, managed by the municipal officials for revenue production; an *ejido,* used for threshing grain, slaughter yards, playgrounds, and other purposes; *pastos comunes* or *dehesas,* pastures for the livestock of the villagers; and *montes,* or wood lots, which furnished fuel and lumber. Where irrigation was employed, the water rights were frequently owned and used in common. Each town had its *cabildo* (council), composed of *regidores* (councilmen), who elected the mayor *(alcalde),* or mayors, and other officials, and managed the town's affairs.

Only slight modifications occurred when the system was introduced into Latin America. A survey of the proposed town site was made, the lots marked off, and a distribution made among the settlers. The *empresario,* or promoter of the town, received the largest portion (perhaps a fourth), while the remainder was divided among the other settlers. For each town lot, an agricultural portion was also distributed, varying considerably in size according to the fertility of the land. Individual portions were limited to five *peonias* or three *caballerias* (five hundred to fifteen hundred acres), but were sometimes much smaller and sometimes larger. The Crown retained the ultimate title, the usufruct being in perpetuity and hereditary, except that the land might revert to the Crown if not properly used. Each town held the common lands enumerated above, administered by the municipal council, and set aside before individual allotments were made. Some lands were not assigned to any use or owner and were called *baldios,* the Crown holding title. Once the system was well established, each Indian settler would receive one lot, each European two, three, or four, the priest five, and the military commander three.

Indian towns not given in encomienda were directly subject to the King of Spain. New towns arose from the settlement of nomadic Indians, a movement begun as early as the first viceroy, Antonio de Mendoza (1535-1550), but greatly accelerated later when the Indians were gathered into *congregas* or towns on the Spanish model. This phase of Spanish policy will be taken up in a later chapter.[38] The laws provided that each Indian town, whether pre-

[38] Arthur Scott Aiton, *Antonio de Mendoza, First Viceroy of New Spain* (Durham, North Carolina: Duke University Press, 1927), p. 91. Aiton's work is the standard biography of the first viceroy. It covers the formative period and should be consulted for matters concerning the establishing of Spanish rule in America and the many political, social and religious problems of the early colonial epoch. The settlement of the Indians into towns has been studied in an excellent work by Lesley Byrd Simpson, *Studies in the Administration of the Indians in New Spain. II The Civil Congregation* (Ibero-Americana: 7, Berkeley: University of California Press, 1934), pp. 29-129. Also Lesley Byrd Simpson, *Many Mexicos* (New York: G. P. Putnam's Sons, 1941), pp. 88-102, for a good description of the Spanish and Indian towns.

Conquest or post-Conquest, should have ample lands. The town site *(fundo legal)* was to measure at least six hundred varas (vara= 2.78 ft.) in each direction from the church. Beyond this, a minimum of one square league (perhaps six to nine square miles) was to be set aside for an *ejido*. The ejido included common lands of every class and the individual allotments, and resembled the town lands of the pre-Conquest village, except for the addition of pastures. A town council administered the ejido and paid the taxes and other assessments due the King.

THE CHURCH AS A LANDHOLDER

The largest landholder in colonial Latin America was the Church. Both the Spanish Church and the Indian priesthoods had held large estates. Although the Spanish Crown had made efforts to curb the Church holdings, perhaps half of the land of Spain belonged to the Church at the beginning of the sixteenth century. The Crown, in order to avoid a similar situation in the New World, forbade the transfer of land to any "church, monastery or any other ecclesiastical person," [39] and provided that no site for a monastery or religious institution of any kind should be allotted without specific authority of the King or Viceroy. Nevertheless, the Church soon accumulated property. It received land in the islands; and Cortés gave it grants in Mexico. Custom dictated that property owners bequeath or donate some of their holdings to religious institutions. The Church soon became the chief money-lender and indirectly reaped the profits from lands it did not own. In practically every town and city, and around military posts, the clerical allotments were important. Many clerics received encomiendas, albeit illegally, and many missionary enterprises brought it new estates. Since church properties were held in mortmain its wealth steadily increased at the expense of the laymen.

LEGAL DEVICES FOR PROTECTING AND ACQUIRING LAND

Various legal devices enabled those who acquired land to keep it. The most important of these was the *mayorazgo*, an entailed estate, European in legal origin (although it has been noted that many Indian estates were similar to mayorazgos). It was inalienable and indivisible. It served to accumulate wealth in a few hands, with the concomitant result that the masses were prevented from acquiring any land except what they held in the village common holdings. There was some change in the ownership of land with time, but the tendency was for large estates to absorb small ones,

---

[39] McBride, *Land Systems of Mexico*, p. 51.

as well as the village lands, thus accentuating the inequality of land distribution.

Another legal device, the *composición,* aided the Spaniards in their acquisition of the New World. Land titles were very uncertain in the early period, since boundaries were indefinite; some estates were so large as to defy measurement, and others could not be surveyed because of natural obstacles. As a result of conflicting claims the same land would sometimes be claimed by the Crown, the Indians, and individual Spaniards. Disputes arose "which were at times decided by resort to arms . . . each one being interested in the extension of his own conquest," and it became necessary to establish some sort of order. The Crown tried to have surveys made and proper titles issued. The first of these titles, *composiciones,* were issued in 1571, and others followed in 1601, 1643, 1674, 1716, 1754, and at other dates. Detailed examination of titles proved to be impracticable, however, and in lieu of an accurate survey, the Crown granted composiciones to all holders within a given district in return for a contribution to the national treasury. A composición of this type declared that there no longer existed any unclaimed lands *(baldíos)* in the designated territory, thus establishing the titles of all holders. The effect was to deprive many Indians of their lands, since they were not acquainted with Spanish legal procedure. The Indians remained on the lands in most cases, but their rights were gone and their legal and economic situation insecure.

LAND DISTRIBUTION IN CENTRAL AND SOUTH AMERICA

The systems evolved in the islands and Mexico were applied further south. Pedrarias, Gil González Dávila, Pedro de Alvarado, and Cortés himself, all made grants of lands and encomiendas of Indians in Central America.[40] Fernández de Lugo, an *empresario* with a patent of conquest for Colombia, and son of the merchant and encomendero who had governed the Canary Islands, brought his father's methods to the New World. Jiménez de Quesada, Vadillo, and other conquistadores [41] of Colombia naturally applied the methods which by now were established. Many of the Indians of Central America and Colombia, like those of Mexico, resisted, and the lot of an encomendero in this region was not always easy. Pedro de Cieza de León in speaking of Arma in Colombia re-

---

[40] Pedro de Alvarado, *An Account of the Conquest of Guatemala in 1524,* ed. and tr. Sedley J. Mackie (New York: The Cortés Society, 1924).

[41] Germán Arciniegas, *The Knight of el Dorado* (New York: The Viking Press, 1942).

marked that "the Indians are so savage and cannibalistic that many of them have eaten the men who held them in encomienda." [42]

THE INCA LAND SYSTEM: THE AYLLU LANDS

It is in the Inca Empire, however, that we find the most interesting example of the blending of the Spanish and Indian land systems. Land was the fundamental form of wealth in the Andean region, and much that is significant in Inca civilization consequently derived from the prevailing mode of landholding.[43] There was in fact very little land suitable for agriculture, since mountains and deserts comprised most of the area as Viceroy Toledo (1569-82) noted in relating the efforts he had made to protect the lands of the Indians. "Among the most loved and valued things that the Indians have in that kingdom are the lands, because although it is very extensive, it has little soil fit for cultivation." [44]

Land ownership among the Andean Indians was of five different types: (1) the Ayllu lands, (2) the public lands of the Incas, (3) the lands of the Sun (religion), (4) the private lands of the Incas, (5) and the lands of the curacas, the local nobilities.[45]

The ayllu, a kinship unit similar to the Mexican calpulli, was the landholding unit of the common people. All the lands of its members were held by it, and were usually of three kinds: pasture, arable, and house plots. José de Acosta, who resided for many years in America, says:

"The third part of the land was given by the Inca to the community. It has not been determined how much this part was, whether more or less than that of the Inca and the Huacas [religion], but it is certain that care was taken that it should be

---

[42] Cieza, Crónica, chap. XIX.

[43] Means, Ancient Civilizations, pp. 288-302, has an interesting discussion of the importance of land as the chief form of wealth.

[44] Memorial de D. Francisco de Toledo, virrey del Perú, a Felipe II, sobre el estado en que dejó aquel virreinato, 1582 (Colección de documentos inéditos para la historia de España [hereafter C.D.I. España] 113 vols., +2 vols. Index; Madrid, 1842-95; 1930-31; XXVI, 122-59), pp. 148-49.

[45] The usual division is into the three parts, consisting of the lands of the Incas, the Sun, and the people. Means gives this division in Ancient Civilizations, p. 289. Barros Arana, América, I, 71-72, says four parts arriving at this by including the lands of the curacas. Professor Louis Baudin of the University of Dijon studied the system and came to the conclusion disclosed in the title of his work L'Empire socialiste des Inka (Paris: Institut d'Ethnologie, 1928). He denies with vigor that the land system was communistic, however, asserting that it did not "deserve such an epithet," thus making a distinction between communism and socialism that many will not accept. Furthermore, Baudin's concept of socialism admits a ruling class which he calls the "elite," and he explains that "a chasm separated the elite from the masses." The present account differs from all these and is based on sources contemporary with the early days of the Spanish occupation. See also Prescott, Peru, Bk. I, chaps. II, IV, and V.

enough to sustain the people. Of this third part, no individual owned anything for himself, nor did the Indians ever own anything individually, except by special favor of the Inca, and that part could not be alienated, nor even divided among the heirs. These community lands were distributed annually, and to each one was assigned the part necessary for the nourishment of himself and his wife and children, and thus some years it was more, and others less, according to the size of the family, for which purpose there were previously-determined measurements." [46]

More specific information as to the portion of the Indian masses is given by Inca Garcilaso de la Vega:

"Each Indian received a *tupu,* which is a fanega of land [about 1.59 acres], to plant in corn, but it is equal to one and a half Spanish fanegas [about 2.4 acres] . . . A tupu of land was enough to feed a married plebeian without children. As soon as he had children, he was given another tupu for each boy, and a half tupu for each girl. When the son married the father gave him the fanega of land that he had received for his food, because when the son was put out of the house the father could not retain the land. The daughters did not withdraw their share when they married, because it had not been given as a dowry but for food . . . the fathers kept the land if it was needed, and if not, they returned it to the [village] council, because nobody could either buy or sell land. The lands that were distributed for growing other crops that were not irrigated were given out just like those planted in corn." [47]

[46] Acosta, *Historia de las Indias,* Bk. VI, chap. XV.

[47] Garcilaso, *Comentarios,* Bk. V, chap. III. The size of a tupu has never been satisfactorily determined. Sir Clements R. Markham says, and this is accepted by Means, that a tupu measured sixty steps by fifty. See Means, *Ancient Civilizations,* p. 289. This would make it about two-thirds of an acre. But since the *fanega de tierra* of Spain is usually given as 1.59 acres, the tupu would be 2.4 acres according to Garcilaso. George McCutchen McBride, *The Agrarian Indian Communities of Highland Bolivia* (New York, 1921), p. 6, points out also that a tupu could be broken into sections, and hence the fifty by sixty-step fields noted by Markham might be only sections of the total tupu. Such factors as quality of land, location, and water would make absolute regularity impossible. The tupu was destined to support two adults, for which 2.4 acres would seem to be the minimum. The modern Maya Indians consume about 8⅔ bushels of corn per person a year. A couple would have needed some 17 bushels a year, making a family average about 40. The ears of corn found in Inca tombs are only three or four inches long, whereas modern ears average around ten inches for a yield of 20 bushels an acre. The Inca short ears might indicate a production under 5 bushels an acre, although close planting would offset small ears to some extent. Furthermore, if an adult couple needed only 2.4 acres in corn, why would they need, say, 9.6 acres for themselves and three infant sons? And again, if 2.4 acres was a fair work portion (with their other duties) for a couple, how could they work double, triple, or quadruple the amount? There seem to be a number of inexplicable contradictions.

THE LANDS OF THE INCAS, SUN, AND CURACAS

The amount of land allotted to the "plebeian" *(plebeyo)* was very small in comparison with the portions of the Incas and the Sun. Acosta says that "the Inca in laying out the towns that he conquered divided all the lands into three parts," the first part being dedicated to religion, with the produce consumed in sacrifices or used to support the ministers and priests. "The second part of the lands and fields was for the Inca. From this he maintained himself, his retinue . . . and his soldiers, and this was the greater part of the tribute as the depositories or public granaries demonstrate, these being longer and wider" than those belonging to the clergy. The third portion belonged to the communities. "The Inca made the same distribution of the live stock" [llamas] so that "one part was dedicated to their religion, another part to the King, and another was for the Indian themselves." "The herds of the Inca and the Huacas were numerous and large," whereas those of the community were "few and trifling." Acosta, however, fails to mention the portion held by the Curacas, or to distinguish between the Incas' public and private lands.[48]

More detail is found in Garcilaso's explanation of the landholding system. When the Inca conquered a new territory, he "gave orders for the augmentation of the arable lands, by which is understood those that grow maize" because "for the greater part, all of that country is poor in bread-producing lands; and for this reason they sought to augment it to the maximum extent that was possible." A considerable portion was terraced, and then divided into three portions, "one for the Sun, another for the King, and the other for the natives." Care was taken that the natives should have sufficient for their nourishment, and if more was needed, it was taken from the Sun and Inca, who, according to Garcilaso, occupied only those lands that "would have remained uninhabited *(desiertas)* without an owner." But Garcilaso also makes it clear that the Sun and the Inca got the best lands. "The terraces for the greater part," he says, "were adjudged to the Sun and the Inca, because he had directed their construction." Unirrigated lands were distributed in the same manner.

The subordinate nobility, however, received still other lands. "To the nobles such as the *curacas,* lords of vassals, they gave lands in proportion to the family they had of wives, children, con-

---

Notice also that Garcilaso does not indicate annual distribution of lands as Acosta does, but says that a father kept a son's portion until the son's marriage.

[48] Acosta, *Historia de las Indias,* Bk. VI, chap. XV.

cubines, and male and female servants." Such estates were hereditary and Garcilaso mentions that "among the curacas, lords of vassals, there were various customs in the inheritance of estates." The largest and best of these private, hereditary estates went to the Incas themselves. "To the Incas, who were those of the royal blood, they gave, in the same way, wherever they might live, the best of the land *(de lo mejor de la tierra)*, and this does nòt include the common share which they all held in the lands *(hacienda)* of the King and Sun, as children of the latter and brothers of the former." [49]

Thus there were five classifications of landholdings. The Incas held private, hereditary estates taken from "the best of the land." They also held a "common share" in the lands of the Inca (the public lands of the ruling class) and of the Sun. The curacas likewise held private hereditary estates. The common people (through their community organization, the ayllu) received a share in the remaining lands. Likewise, the livestock was so divided that the Incas had the great herds.

THE TRIBUTE SYSTEM OF THE INCAS

The Incas held more than land, however; they owned the right to the labor of the common Indians. This tribute and labor system is important, since in Peru as in Mexico, it supplied the basis for Spanish control and ownership after the Conquest. Acosta speaks of the "innumerable multitude of vassals, all working and striving to do whatever pleased their King," who received "the best of everything from each province . . . over and above the general tribute which all paid." He adds: "But the greatest wealth of those barbarian kings was that all their vassals were their slaves, whose labor they possessed to their full satisfaction." [50] On this point, Garcilaso is in substantial agreement. He says that in addition to the principal tribute, "which was the sowing of the land, and the gathering and caring for the crops of the Sun and the Inca," the Indians worked at "the making of clothing and shoes for use in wartime and for the poor." "The poorest grade" was for the "common people," another "finer" grade was for the "nobility," and still another "very fine" grade was for those of the "royal blood." "All these were made by the vassals and not by the Incas, who made not even their own clothing."

There was also an infinite amount of tribute work such as "the building of forts and royal buildings, constructing bridges, roads,

[49] Garcilaso, *Comentarios*, Bk. V, Chaps. I-III.
[50] Acosta, *Historia de las Indias*, Bk. VI, chap. XV.

terraces, and irrigation canals, and other works of common benefit
at which the Indians were kept constantly busy." The full enumeration includes every imaginable type of work of either a public or
private nature, including "anything else whatever for the common
welfare, or for their curacas, or in the service of the King," and
"all of this the law required them to do gratis, because it was for
the public welfare of each realm or province, and for all the Empire."

Garcilaso insists that "there was such a multitude of Indians,
and to each one fell such a small part of all these things, that they
did not suffer from the labor because they served in turn and together *(por rueda en común)*, with great care taken not to work
one harder than the others." On the other hand, he says that while
women and children were not required to work, they did so in order
to help "their fathers and husbands or their masters *(amos)*" finish
up the assigned tasks more quickly, those having large families being
"held to be rich men," while those who had not, were considered
poor, and that "of those who did not have [large families], many
fell ill from the long time they worked at their tasks before com-
pleting their tribute." [51]

THE COLONIAL LAND SYSTEM IN PERU

Into the situation just described came the Spaniards with their
own concepts of land-holding and serf distribution. In 1532 Pizarro
founded the town of San Miguel (moved later to Piura) in Peru.
He laid out streets, fort, church, town hall, dwellings, and an irrigation system, set up a municipal administration, distributed the
Indians in encomienda and made land grants. When Cajamarca
was occupied later, the Indians were distributed and land grants
made; and everywhere the procedure was similar. Passing along
the coast of Peru in 1548, Cieza de León saw a succession of
"farms and estates" established by the Spaniards, and he speaks
of the "mountain Indians [who] come down from their provinces
to work for the Spaniards who hold them in encomienda." [52]

Francisco Pizarro took for himself a choice encomienda at Atabillos reckoned at twenty thousand vassals, or one hundred thousand people. [53] Many large grants were made to Pizarro's companions. Cuzco was partitioned as soon as occupied. The temples,
palaces, and convents of the Indians were given to a select few of

---

[51] Garcilaso, *Comentarios,* Bk. V, chaps. VI-VII, X, XV-XVI.

[52] Cieza, *Crónica,* chap. LXIX.

[53] Means, *Fall of the Inca Empire* (New York: Charles Scribner's Sons, 1932),
p. 66.

the Spaniards, "lords of vassals who held repartimientos of Indians." There were, however, "a great many Spaniards who had no Indians." [54]

When Lima was founded in 1535 the lots were divided and the settlers given encomiendas. "And the year [1550] I left that kingdom," says Cieza de León, "there were many citizens (vecinos) among those who had encomiendas of Indians so prosperous and rich that their estates were worth a hundred and fifty thousand ducats, and eighty, and sixty, and fifty, and some more and some less. In a word, I left the greater part of them rich and prosperous, and frequently ships sail from the port of this city carrying eight hundred thousand ducats each, and some more than a million." Not all were so favored, however, and while some of the grants were "too large," "many of the conquistadores had no encomiendas of Indians." [55] Other encomiendas in Peru, as in Mexico, were gained through marriage of "many rich [Indian] widows to men who served the King." Garcilaso remarks that such marriages were made "throughout the whole Empire to give repartimientos of Indians to the candidates and pay them with the property of another, although there were also a great number of malcontents among them, some because they derived small incomes, and others because of the ugliness of the wives." [56]

The discontent that arose over the distribution was one of the most important causes of the civil wars in Peru from 1537 to 1554. Cieza, who had received and lost an encomienda, expressed a complaint common among the conquistadores. "Many of my companions," he says, "discoverers and conquistadores, who left Cartagena with me are without Indians, and people have them who got them by bribery (por dineros), and by having supported those in power, which certainly is no small evil." [57]

Encomiendas and land grants changed hands often in the first years of conquest. When Almagro and his followers returned from Chile, where they had spent much and gained little, they laid claim to Cuzco under the terms of Almagro's grant from the King, captured the city from Pizarro, and redistributed the grants already made by Pizarro. After Almagro was executed in 1538, still another redistribution was made.

Viceroy Blasco Núñez de Vela arrived in 1544, bringing with him the New Laws abolishing the encomiendas. The conquistadores

---

[54] Garcilaso, *Comentarios*, Bk. VII, chap. IX; Bk. IV, chap. II.
[55] Cieza, *Crónica*, chaps. LXXI, LXXVIII, LXXIX, LXXXVI, XCVI, CVII.
[56] Garcilaso, *Comentarios*, Part II, Bk. VI, chaps. II-III.
[57] Cieza, *Crónica*, chap. XVII.

rose under the leadership of Gonzalo Pizarro, executed the Viceroy, and rewarded themselves with the spoils taken from the henchmen of the King. A new representative of the Crown, Pedro de la Gasca, was sent out with orders modifying the New Laws, and was able to capture and execute Gonzalo Pizarro in 1548. He made still another distribution of encomiendas, taking from some and giving to others. To those who received nothing, he wrote that it was "because there was less cloth for distribution than he would have wished."

His division pleased few, and a new incipient rebellion had to be quelled. Some complained because La Gasca "gave them nothing, others because [they received] little, and others because he had made grants to those who had ill served the King." Some who had served Gonzalo Pizarro were rewarded with excellent grants where they expected death, while others who had served the King well got nothing. Some of the disappointed were sent off on other expeditions, because the Viceroy wanted to "throw out of the kingdom some of the many unemployed soldiers that were about." [58] Hernández Girón took advantage of the presence of the unemployed soldiers to rebel in 1553-54, and after the rebellion there were the usual redistributions, followed by still others when the Viceroy Hurtado de Mendoza (1556-1560) arrived. Many of the grants made by Hurtado de Mendoza were later canceled, and those who had been disinherited by him were rewarded by the Crown. [59]

After 1554 the cycle of civil wars ended in Peru and the King's justice was established, but the root of the evil was not removed. [60] Thousands remained without land or encomiendas; a few held the majority of both. A distinct landless class existed who lived poorly. Garcilaso points out that many "lived among the Indians because they had no money with which to buy clothes, the clothing from Spain being very expensive, and among the Indians they got along in any way they could." [61] In 1550, the soldiers of Cuzco mutinied because they had nothing to live on. [62] At this date Indian property had by no means ceased to exist, but the Indian landholding class had become distinctly subordinate to the conquerors.

[58] Garcilaso, *Comentarios*, Part II, Bk. VI, chaps. II-IV.
[59] Means, *Fall*, pp. 97-102.
[60] Juan Matienzo, *Gobierno del Perú*, written about 1570 and published in Buenos Aires, 1910. Matienzo gives a very good picture of Peru at this time. On the land situation see pp. 37-45, 50-63, 96-111. See also *Documentos referentes al virreinato del Perú, 1559-1570 (Nueva colección de documentos inéditos para la historia de España y de sus Indias*, 6 vols., Madrid, 1892-96), vol. VI.
[61] Garcilaso, *Comentarios*, Part II, Bk. VI, chap. XXIV.
[62] Herrera, *Hechos castellanos*, Decade VIII, Bk. VI, chap. VIII-X.

The Spaniards had founded a society based distinctly on class—after both Spanish and Indian models. A few people, protected in their privileges by entail and primogeniture laws, owned the bulk of the land and the labor of Latin America; the masses, prevented by law from acquiring property, owned little. Out of a total population of one hundred and sixty thousand Europeans in Spanish America in 1574, there were only about four thousand encomenderos. [63]

* * * * * * *

By this date (1574) it may be said that the Spaniards had laid the basis for the economic system that was to guarantee their possession of the New World. They required land and labor to work it if they were to profit from their colonies. While the means they employed to get them varied with the degree of land utilization and the labor systems already developed by the Indians, the conquerors took for granted the sovereignty of Spain over the territories and peoples they discovered, and almost at once introduced the Spanish system of repartimiento and encomienda—grants of land and labor to individuals. Although the Crown, in order to remedy the abuses and to prevent the rise of strong feudal lords in America, tried to abolish the encomienda, it suited too well the needs of the colonists, the demands of the conquerors that their risks and services be rewarded, and the basic Indian economy.

The conquerors had only to take over the Aztec landholding system, through which the nobility, the priesthood, and military controlled the majority of good land and received tribute in labor. The Inca land and tribute system also furnished a basis for the Spanish encomienda. Colonial landholding towns were founded on Spanish models, the more readily since the Aztec type of land-holding village was in many ways similar. The Church too, like the Indian priesthoods before it, grew into one of the chief land-holders, despite the efforts of the Spanish sovereigns to curb its expansion in the New World. The result was that large, hereditary estates, their masters owning both the land and labor, eventually received legal recognition, and became an established feature of Latin-American economy.

[63] López de Velasco, *Geografía y descripción universal de las Indias,* prepared in 1576 and published first in 1894, cited in Wilgus, ed., *Colonial Hispanic America,* pp. 161-65.

Farm and Ranch

AGRICULTURE BEFORE THE CONQUEST

ALTHOUGH AGRICULTURE WAS THE BASIC occupation of the great majority of the people of America, just as the system of land holding was the basic form of wealth, the greatest portion of America's territory was not fundamentally agricultural at the time of the Conquest. The hunter-fisher areas, practically devoid of cultivation of the soil, together with nomadic-agricultural areas in which game and fish were supplemented by limited land cultivation, comprised a great part of North America, north Mexico, some of Central America, and large parts of Venezuela, Colombia, Brazil, Uruguay, Argentina, Chile, Bolivia, Peru, Ecuador and the Caribbean. The areas where a relatively advanced agriculture was the basis of life were limited principally to the Mexican highlands from the Central Valley southward, the highlands of Central America, and the valleys of the Andes and sections of the Pacific Coast.

Many species of plants were produced in pre-Conquest America because of the great variety of climates and soils. The first Europeans to reach the New World were astonished at the number and quantity of new plants, and enumerated literally hundreds. The Jesuit historian, José de Acosta, lists dozens and concludes by saying "and a hundred other plants the names of which I do not remember." [1] The most important were maize, cotton, potatoes, yams, cactus, tomatoes, cassava (manioc), beans, vanilla, nuts of many kinds, melons, cacao, and maguey (agave). Among the

---

[1] Acosta, *Historia de las Indias,* Bk. IV, chaps. XVII-XXX, gives a full account of the plants of the New World; cf. Prescott, *Mexico,* Bk. I, chap. V; Prescott, *Peru,* Bk. I, chaps. IV-V; *Relación verdadera de algunas cosas de las muchas, que sucedieron al Padre Fray Alonso Ponce en Nueva España (C.D.I. España,* Vols. LVII-LVIII), LVII, 80-105, 295-97; Torquemada, *Monarchia indiana,* Bk. XIV, chaps. XLII-XLIII; Clavigero, *Mexico,* Bk. I, and Dissertation I, Section III; Dissertations III-IV.

medicines were cinchona (quinine), coca, ipecac, sarsaparilla, cascara, and tobacco.

Maize was the basic food crop, and was grown almost everywhere that water and climatic conditions made it possible. The highlands of Mexico and Central America, as well as the Andean valleys have been designated maize cultures from the prevalence of this grain. Cotton was the most essential plant for clothing, although in the Andes wool from llamas and other closely related animals was known. The more highly civilized Indians grew cotton, and spun and wove it for clothing.

INDIAN AGRICULTURE IN MEXICO AND CENTRAL AMERICA

The highlands of Mexico and Central America were the centers of an advanced agricultural development when the Spaniards came. Enough has been said to establish the fact that this area was characterized by a sedentary, farming civilization. Parts of Yucatán, too, had once been under intense cultivation, and some of it still was, albeit a decline had set in well before the arrival of the Spaniards. Agriculture in a more or less developed state existed in other regions of Mexico and Central America, but geographical conditions, which will presently be described, placed greater limitations on agriculture than is generally known.

Maize, beans, and maguey were the most important crops, although many others were also grown. Maize, which could be grown with irrigation, or in many areas where the rainfall was sufficient without being excessive (as it was in several regions of the tropical lowlands), was literally the staff of life to the Indians. Its yield made possible a concentration of people, but at the same time forced them to mold themselves to the inescapable natural factors which govern its growth: fertile land, water, intensive cultivation. It will not grow in poor, dry lands, nor will it mature where the rainfall is extremely heavy. Demanding a fertile soil, it forces the farmer to fertilize or clear new fields constantly. Indian Mexico had little to use for fertilizer, and new fields were at a premium, the demand far exceeding the supply and causing the conflicts over land previously described. [2]

Beans supplemented maize as a food, and in part made up for the lack of fertilizers. Being a leguminous plant, the bean, of which several types were known to pre-Cortesian Mexico and Central America, supplied much of the nitrogen which corn took from the ground. As a food, the bean probably ranked second to maize,

[2] Simpson, *Many Mexicos*, pp. 11-19.

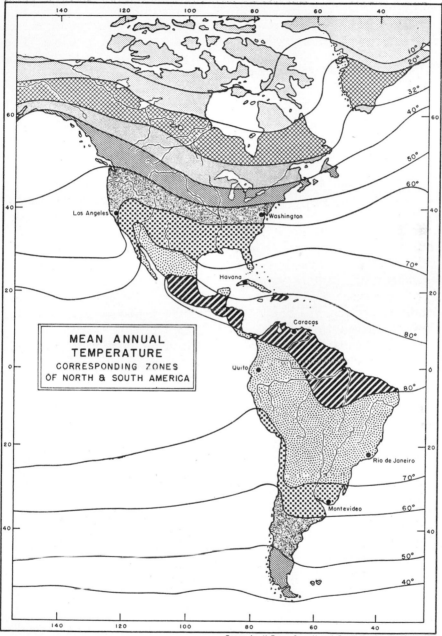

MEAN ANNUAL
TEMPERATURE
CORRESPONDING ZONES
OF NORTH & SOUTH AMERICA

Los Angeles

Washington

Havana

Caracas

Quito

Rio de Janeiro

Montevideo

Drawn by H. Roger Garrett and Frank Vereka; Washington, DC

84a

The maguey, however, deserves special mention. It occupied a unique place in Mexican life since from it alone could be drawn a round measure for each of man's essential needs: food, clothing, and shelter. In the words of wonder written by a sixteenth century historian:

"The tree of marvels is the maguey . . . it furnishes water, wine, oil, vinegar, honey, syrup, thread, needles and a hundred other things. It is a plant *(árbol)* which the Indians of New Spain hold in high esteem, and they ordinarily have one or a few of them around their homes to contribute to their livelihood, and it is also grown and cultivated in the fields. It has wide and thick leaves, at the end of which there is a sharp, stout point which is useful as a catch or fastener, like pins, or for sewing, and this is the needle. They make a sort of fiber or string from the leaf. The trunk, which is very thick, is cut when it is tender so as to make a large concave hole into which the sap from the roots rises, and this is a liquid that is drunk like water [*pulque*], and is refreshing and sweet. This same liquid boiled becomes wine and, when left to stand, sours and becomes vinegar, and when cooked still more . . . . it is like honey, and half-cooked it serves as syrup . . . . The wood of this plant is spongy and is useful to conserve fire. . . ."[3]

From the juice of the corn stalk a type of sugar was made; and chocolate was known as a drink and food of great nutritive value. The cactus plant was used as a food, and for the construction of fences and houses. The manioc plant furnished bread in many parts of the tropics.

THE INFLUENCE OF GEOGRAPHY

In few parts of the world, has geography offered so many aids and so many hindrances as in Latin America. The bulk of Latin America lies within the tropical or semitropical zones, but a large part is lifted above the heat by the mountains that run from northern Mexico, through Central America, to the southernmost part of Chile.

Because of this elevation, there are many valleys lying wholly within the heat belt that produce temperate-zone plants, while within a few miles tropical plants may be grown. For example, Mexico's Central Valley, Toluca Valley, Puebla, Pátzcuaro, Morelia, and Hidalgo, all six to eight thousand feet above sea level and surrounded by snow-covered mountains that cool them, produce

---

[3] Acosta, *Historia de las Indias,* Bk. IV, chap. XXIII.

the same temperate-climate products found in the northern part of the United States, Canada, and Europe. [4]

Within a radius of some three hundred miles of Mexico City may be grown most of the tropical and temperate-zone plants of the world. The inhabitants of these regions designate them as *tierras calientes* and *tierras frías,* and while the temperature differences may not always be noticeable to man, the change from "hot lands" to "cold lands" is disclosed by the exactness with which the tropical plants are divided from the temperate vegetation.

Balancing the temperate valleys are the tropical lowlands, many of which bear a great variety of excellent products; but other regions are rendered almost useless to man by an excess of water in some cases and a total lack in others. In some parts, agriculture is possible only with irrigation, by which "they made up for the lack of rain, which ordinarily is scarce along the coast, and in some places is completely lacking. This lowland has enormous uninhabitable stretches, sometimes because of the sand dunes, which are frightful, consisting of entire mountains of sand, sometimes because of the swamps, since, as the water comes down from the heights and finds no outlet, it frequently spreads out and makes marshes and flood lands . . . . In reality the greater part of the seacoast is like this in the Indies, especially the Pacific coast." [5]

The Pacific and Andean regions of South America have the same sharp contrasts as Mexico and Central America. Beginning in northern Peru and continuing almost to central Chile, the coastline is desert, absolute in some places and partial in others, except where mountain streams penetrate the sands and render the soil fertile. The mountains themselves form an immense wasteland. This Andean region was well depicted by Cieza de León:

"In order to make things more understandable, I shall explain that this land of Peru consists of three uninhabited cordilleras or ranges where men could not live in any circumstances. One of these cordilleras is the slopes of the Andes, covered with enormously dense thickets and consisting of such unhealthy lands that until you reach the other side of the mountain there are not now, and never were, any people. The other is the ridge which runs the length of this cordillera or mountain of the Andes, excessively cold, its summits being great peaks of snow which never ceases to fall. Nor could people live in this long and narrow stretch of mountains, in any circumstances whatever, because of

[4] Riva Palacio, *México,* II, 460-62.
[5] Acosta, *Historia de las Indias,* Bk. III, chap. XIX.

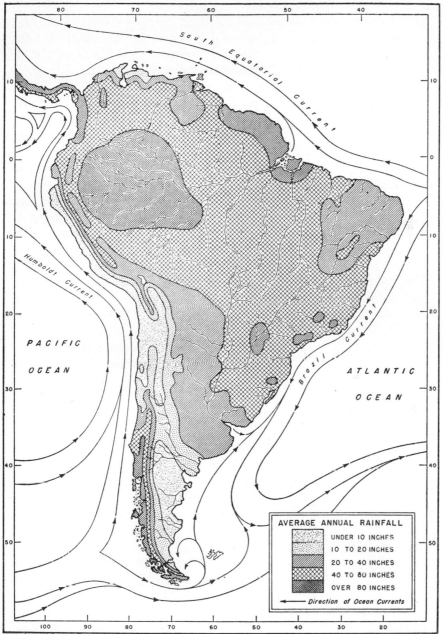

AVERAGE ANNUAL RAINFALL

UNDER 10 INCHES
10 TO 20 INCHES
20 TO 40 INCHES
40 TO 80 INCHES
OVER 80 INCHES
← Direction of Ocean Currents

Drawn by H. Roger Garrett and Frank Vereka, Washington, D.C.

86a

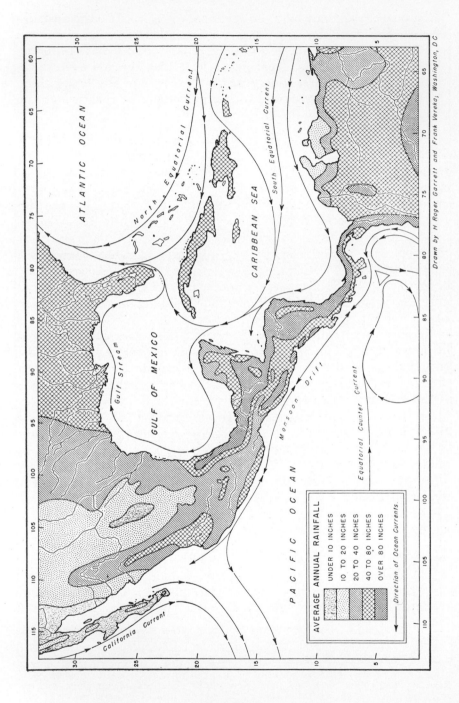

AVERAGE ANNUAL RAINFALL

UNDER 10 INCHES
10 TO 20 INCHES
20 TO 40 INCHES
40 TO 80 INCHES
OVER 80 INCHES

Direction of Ocean Currents.

ATLANTIC OCEAN

North Equatorial Current

CARIBBEAN SEA

South Equatorial Current

Gulf Stream

GULF OF MEXICO

Monsoon Drift

PACIFIC OCEAN

Equatorial Counter Current

California Current

Drawn by H Roger Garrett and Frank Vereka, Washington, D C

86b

the quantity of snow and the great cold . . . . The third cordillera I find to be the sand dunes that extend from Túmbez beyond Tarapacá, in which there is nothing whatever to see except mountains of sand and the tremendous heat that spreads over them, there being no water, nor grass, nor trees, nor any living thing except birds, which because of the advantage of their wings can go wherever they wish." [6]

The Andes run much higher than the mountains of Mexico. Throughout their length of some 3500 miles (with a width varying from 100 to 400 miles), there are few places where they can be crossed at an elevation of less than 12,000 feet. Some of the most important centers of population, Bogotá, Quito, Cuzco, and La Paz, lie from 9,000 to 12,500 feet high. Perpetually snow-capped mountains above these valleys help to lower the temperature. In the tropics, at altitudes from 4,000 to 9,000 feet, the temperature is cool, above that, cold. Temperate and cold-climate crops may be grown at such altitudes. The Pacific coastline, which would normally be intensely hot, is cooled by the Humboldt current which runs northward from the Antarctic.

Because of the mountains and deserts, this enormous region has little arable land, and but little more suitable for pasturage. The river valleys of the coast contain not more than three per cent of the land between the mountains and the sea, but they are the only arable sections. They furnished in ancient times, as they do today, the greater portion of the agricultural produce of the country. [7] All the agriculture and life of the coastline depend on the slender rivers that trace narrow green threads across the nearly endless sands. And this was as true of the Inca civilization as it is today. Then as now, the problem was to retain the mountain water for irrigation during the dry season. Much the same problem faced, and still faces, the valleys in the mountains. Here at altitudes ranging up to fourteen thousand feet, agriculture is pursued.

ANDEAN INDIAN FARMING: IRRIGATION, TERRACES, AND
      FERTILIZERS

In these difficult regions where nature placed many obstacles and rendered little aid to agriculture, the Indians could boast of

---

[6] Cieza, *Crónica*, chap. XXXVI; cf Herrera, *Hechos castellanos*, Decade V, Bk. I, chap. V.

[7] Today the whole cultivated area of Peru is about four million acres, of which these valleys are about one-sixth. This one-sixth of the area produces, however, almost half of the entire agricultural produce in value. George R. Johnson, and Raye R. Platt, *Peru from the Air* (New York: American Geographical Society, 1930), pp. 2-3.

notable achievements in the solution of agricultural problems. Irrigation, fertilization, and artificial construction of the soil were all known and used by the Indians at the time of the Spanish invasion.

In describing the agrarian life of the Inca Empire, Inca Garcilaso de la Vega attributes to the Incas many things that we know to be the work of preceding civilizations, but he gives an accurate picture of conditions in the last days before the Spanish conquest. When an Inca conquered new territories he ordered the increase of the arable areas, "by which is understood those that grow maize," because "it should be known that for the greater part all that country is poor in food-producing lands." The amount of arable soil was augmented by irrigation, and the hillsides were utilized by constructing terraces of rock, behind which the earth was filled up to the level of the terrace wall. They were irrigated by canals from the mountain streams, some of which were brought "fifteen or twenty leagues . . . to irrigate a very few *fanegas* . . . of maize lands so that they might not be wasted." [8]

The poorer lands were restored to fertility by allowing them to lie fallow, but the more valuable cornlands were kept constantly in production.

"In addition to the corn lands which were irrigated, they distributed others that were not irrigated, in which were planted without irrigation other seeds and vegetables that are of great importance, such as the potato, . . . and because they were unproductive for lack of irrigation they did not plant them more than one or two years and then distributed others, and still others, so that the first might rest, and this way they always kept their poor lands in good condition so that they would always produce in abundance. The corn lands were planted every year, for since they improved them with water and manure like a garden, they made them produce always." [9]

Fertilizer of several types was used. Throughout the mountain country "they used human manure around the maize because they say it is the best," but in regions where the llamas were numerous they used animal manure, because "they say it is more useful than any other." However,

"Along the sea coast from below Arequipa to Tarapacá, which is more than two hundred leagues of coast line, they use

[8] Garcilaso, *Comentarios,* Bk. V, chap. I.
[9] Garcilaso, *Comentarios,* Bk. V, chaps. I-II.

MAGUEY PLANT, MEXICO

CARIBBEAN SEA

PANAMA

CARACAS

CAYENNE

QUITO

PACIFIC

OCEAN

RIO DE JANERIO

ATLANTIC

OCEAN

SANTIAGO

MONTEVIDEO

REGIONS OF VEGETATION

FOREST

WOODLAND AND GRASSLAND

PRAIRIES AND PLAINS

SEMI—DESERT

DESERT

MOUNTAIN FLORA

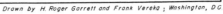

Drawn by H. Roger Garrett and Frank Vereka ; Washington, D.C.

88a

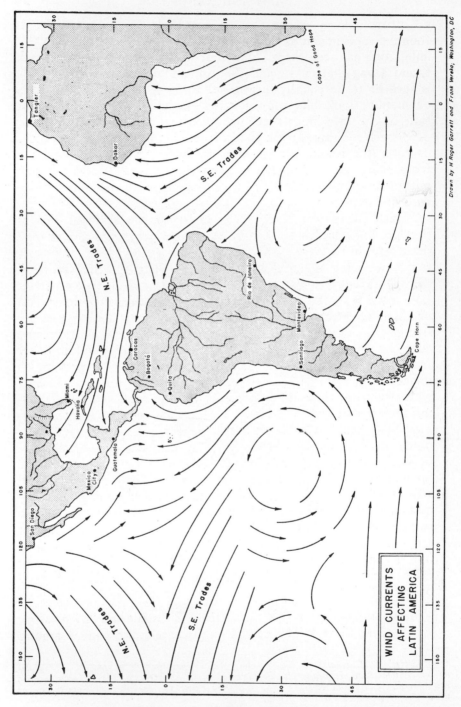

WIND CURRENTS
AFFECTING
LATIN AMERICA

N.E. Trades

S.E. Trades

N.E. Trades

S.E. Trades

Cape of Good Hope

Cape Horn

Tangier

Dakar

Miami

Havana

Caracas

Bogotá

Quito

Guatemala

Mexico City

San Diego

Rio de Janeiro

Montevideo

Santiago

Drawn by H. Roger Garratt and Frank Ireko, Washington, DC

no other manure except that of sea birds [*guano*], which are found . . . in bands so enormous that they are unbelievable unless one has seen them. They nest in some unpopulated islands found along that coast, and the amount of manure they deposit is such as to be equally incredible. From a distance the mounds of manure look like snow-covered mountain tops. During the time of the Inca kings there was such vigilance in the protection of these birds that, at the time of nesting, no one was permitted to enter the islands, under pain of death, to prevent the birds from being scared and driven from their nests. Nor was it permitted to kill them at any time, either on or off the islands, likewise under pain of death.

"Each island was reserved by order of the Inca for this or that province, and if the island was large it was given to two or three provinces . . . and the resident *(vecino)* of one town could not take manure from another district under pain of death, because this was theft; nor from his own district could he take more than the quantity assigned to him in proportion to his own lands, which was enough, and waste was punished as resisting the authorities. . . ." "Along other parts of the same coast . . . they fertilize with the heads of sardines and no other fertilizer. The natives of these regions . . . live with much difficulty since they have neither irrigation nor rain . . . . For which reasons, the natives, seeking moisture sufficient for planting maize, build their towns as close to the ocean as possible, remove the top sands that are on the surface of the earth, dig down, in some places a man's height and in others two, or more or less, until they reach the sea level; and for this reason the Spaniards called these places *ollas* (pots). Some are large and some small . . . . They plant with thick sticks, jabbing regularly measured off holes in which they bury the heads of sardines with two or three grains of maize . . . . Thus all of them everywhere planted what was necessary for the maintenance of their own homes, and so there was no need of selling food stuffs, nor to raise their prices, nor did they know the meaning of high prices." [10]

Where land was irrigated, the water was distributed "by measure . . . so that there might not be any quarrels and rancor among

---

[10] Garcilaso, *Comentarios*, Bk. V. chap. III. The Spanish phrase ". . . *y así no tenían necesidad de vender los bastimentos ni de encarecerlos, ni sabían que cosa era carestía*" can mean perhaps "nor did they know the meaning of need," but as used here it seems to refer to prices.

the Indians over its division." Each owner was granted a set number of hours for irrigation according to his needs, and none was given preference, "neither the richest, nor the noblest, nor the favorite or kinsman of the curaca, nor the curaca himself, nor the minister or governor of the king." A rigorous punishment was meted out to those who failed to irrigate their fields. [11]

The irrigation system of the • Andes was one of the most remarkable features of the Indian culture. The canals in the mountain valleys at times had a "trough of more than twelve feet" and ran "more than a hundred and fifty leagues" from the springs that furnished the source of the water. The chief handicap to the irrigation system was that "they did not know how to build . . . bridge arches with which to make short cuts across the gulleys and ravines. If a deep gulley cut across the way, they went up to its source in order to get around it, winding about all the mountains that were in the way." The sides of the irrigation canals were lined with large stone slabs to protect them. Both farm and pasture lands were so irrigated. [12]

Along the coast, the valleys were likewise irrigated where water was available from the mountain streams. They were described by Cieza as he saw them at the time of the Conquest.

"And as the rivers flow down from the mountains across these plains *(llanos)* and some of the valleys are wide and all are cultivated, or were cultivated when they were more heavily populated, they dug *(sacaban)* irrigation canals far and wide *(en cabos y por partes)*, and it is a wonderful thing to relate because they run them both high and low, along the slopes of the hill tops and the skirts of the mountains that extend into the valleys, and many of them cross the valleys themselves, some in this direction and some in that, so that it is a great pleasure to travel in those valleys because it seems as if one were walking in gardens and forests, delightful and cool. The Indians had, and still have great skill in drawing off the water and running it through these canals, and it has sometimes happened to me that when I stopped beside a canal and before I had finished putting up my tent, the canal would be dry because they had directed the water into another part. Because, except at the season when the rivers dry up, it is in the power of these Indians to direct the water wherever they wish." [13]

---

[11] Garcilaso, *Comentarios*, Bk. V, chap. IV.
[12] Garcilaso, *Comentarios*, Bk. V, chap. XXIV.
[13] Cieza, *Crónica*, chap. LXVI.

Still another feature of the agricultural system was the method of storing the crops, once they were gathered. The good order prevailing is illustrated by the granaries (*pósitos*) and the method of calculating the existing stores. The granaries of the Sun and the Inca were located in the chief centers of production and at frequent intervals. "The crops of the Sun and of the Inca were stored separately, each to itself, although in the same public granary (*pósito*)." Within the granaries the system was so regulated as to enable a quick and accurate count of the supplies, the grain being stored in hampers according to a definite plan. The description most frequently cited is Garcilaso's:

"The hampers were called *Pirua*. They were made of mud, mixed by treading, with an abundance of straw. During the time of their kings, the Incas, they were made with very great neatness. They were of a height more or less corresponding to the height of the walls of the warehouse (*aposento*) in which they were placed. They were narrow, square and of a piece (*enterizos*), so that they must have been made in molds of various sizes. They made them according to exact measurements (*por cuenta y medida*) some larger than others, of thirty, fifty, a hundred and of two hundred fanegas more or less, to suit their needs. Each size of hamper was in its own warehouse, because they had been made to measure. They were ranged against all four walls and along the center of the warehouse. Being in rows, there were passages between them so that they could be filled and emptied at will. The Indians never moved them from where they were placed. In order to empty the hamper, along the front of it they made a number of tiny windows . . . opening at regular intervals so as to judge from them the number of fanegas that had been taken out and how much remained without measuring. Thus, from the size of the hampers they knew easily the amount of maize in every warehouse and every storage center (*depósito*), and from the windows they could judge what they had taken out and what remained in each hamper. I saw some of these hampers that dated from the time of the Incas, and they were among the most excellent because they were in the house of the chosen virgins, the wives of the Sun, and they were made for the service of those women." [14]

After viewing an agricultural system as remarkable as that of the Aztecs and Incas, the modern student is likely to condemn the

[14] Garcilaso, *Comentarios*, Bk. V, chap. V.

Spaniards for having destroyed the Indian systems. Early chroniclers have done so, and modern historians have accused the
Spaniards of neglecting agriculture for mining. [15] But while we may
justly admire the excellent work of the Indians, and deplore the
destruction wrought by the Europeans, the contributions made by
the Spaniards deserve attention for the sake of historical accuracy. [16]

FARM AND RANCH IN THE CARIBBEAN

Every section of America naturally had its own special products,
and a study of each of these gives a better idea of America's agricultural development. The Caribbean, because of its prior discovery, was the first region to be developed. Columbus, it will be
recalled, was the founder of European agriculture in America, beginning the importation of plants and domestic animals on his
second voyage. Among the animals he brought, were "calves, goats
and sheep," as well as "eight sows," and "from these eight sows
have come all the hogs in the whole of the Indies to this day . . .
which are infinite." He also brought chickens and numerous types
of seeds. [17]

By the time Cortés went on his expedition to Mexico, the agriculture in the Caribbean islands was far advanced. This period is
often pictured as one in which the Spaniards were intent only on
conquest as a means of getting gold. But if that had been the case,
Francisco de Garay, the governor of Jamaica, could scarcely have
"got together one hundred and thirty-six horses and eight hundred
and forty soldiers" to participate in the conquest of Mexico, and
have "fitted them out well with all that was necessary, which was
cassava bread and salt pork and sun-dried beef, for there was already a sufficiency of cattle, and as he was a rich man, and it all
came from his own crops he did not feel the expense, and there was
a superabundance of men and horses . . ." [18]

Jamaican agriculture was especially prosperous in cotton.

"Cotton was the first profitable enterprise *(granjería)* of the
Spaniards in that island, because they forced the natives, especially the women, to make large pieces of cotton cloth, and
shirts, and hammocks used as beds, and these were brought to
this island and to Cuba and to Tierra-Firme, as soon as the

[15] Barros Arana, *América*, II, 61-62; Riva Palacio, *México*, II, 487-88.
[16] On the contributions of the Spaniards see Oviedo, *Historia*, Bks. VIII-XV;
Las Casas, *Historia*, Bk. I, Chap. LXXXIII; Navarrete, *Colección de viages*, I, 20-389.
[17] Las Casas, *Historia*, Bk. I, chap. LXXXIII.
[18] Bernal Díaz, *Conquest of New Spain*, IV, 247-48.

Spaniards went to these places, and sold there; and from those places they brought wine and flour of Castile, and oil and vinegar, and clothing of linen and wool, and other things that came from Castile, and which they needed; and from this island they carried cattle and mares, which have multiplied greatly there." [19]

Agriculture early proved to be the most profitable and stable occupation. The miners soon spent their earnings because of the high prices of food and clothing, and although the merchants made money they were also prone to spend it quickly. On the other hand "the profits of those times [were to be made] in nothing more nor less than raising pigs and cultivating cassava and other edible root plants, such as garlic and sweet potatoes." [20] There were other unmistakable signs of the early prosperity of the Caribbean islands. As early as 1518 one of the Oidores of Española wrote:

"Herds of cattle are found which were lost when they numbered thirty or forty, already branded, and at the end of three or four years appeared in the woods numbering three or four hundred. The same thing is true of the pigs, sheep and horses and other animals. An experiment has been made in the planting of wheat, and it grows very well and will yield two or three crops a year . . . . The woods are full of cotton, and I have now ordered the construction of mills to clean it . . . . There are also fields of sugar cane which are really marvelous, the cane as thick as a man's wrist and as tall as two men of medium stature. Permission has also been granted for the construction of sugar mills, which will come to be something of great wealth." [21]

The wheat proved a disappointment since it went to stalk and formed little grain, but other crops grew well. Sugar manufacture followed shortly after the planting of the cane in 1493. According to Oviedo, Gonzalo de Velosa "at his own expense of very large and excessive outlays . . . and much personal labor, brought sugar-making experts to this island, constructed a horse-powered sugar mill *(trapiche de caballos)*, and was the first to promote the making of sugar in this island." And he adds that the sugar industry in the island was one of the most profitable businesses anywhere in the world, despite having been introduced so recently. [22]

The owner of an unencumbered and well equipped sugar mill had a rich inheritance. Among the mills of the larger and efficient

[19] Las Casas, *Historia*, Bk. II, chap. LVI.
[20] Las Casas, *Historia*, Bk. II, chap. VI.
[21] *Carta del licenciado Zuazo*, D.I.I., I, 292-98.
[22] Oviedo, *Historia*, Bk. IV, chap. VIII.

type, there were some that cost more than ten to twelve thousand gold ducats before they were ready to start making sugar.[23] Oviedo says that an investment of fifteen thousand would not be exaggerated for the necessary Negroes (80 to 120),[24] the herd of cattle for the mill (1000 to 3000 head), the buildings, the experts, the carts for hauling, and the labor for preparing food and cultivating the cane. One mill was valued at fifty thousand ducats and brought in some six thousand ducats annually. In 1520, Española had at least twenty-eight sugar mills run with water power, and possibly others run by animal power. [25]

Sugar, along with hides, was a chief export, "and the ships that come from Spain continually return there with cargoes of very good sugar, and the skimmings and molasses that are wasted or given away in this island would enrich another large province. And the most marvelous thing . . . is that those who have come here within the last thirty-eight years, did not find one of these sugar mills in these Indies." [26]

At the same time, the animals in the Caribbean islands had increased beyond computation. "The cattle of the island of Española and of other islands of that region have multiplied . . . until they roam by the thousands, ownerless, through the woods and fields." Thousands were killed for the hides alone, the carcass being left where it fell, "there being no one to consume it, nor to want it because of the surplus that exists." Thousands of hides went to Spain with every fleet. Horses, mules, burros, goats, and sheep soon reproduced in every part of America after their first introduction to the Caribbean. [27]

FARM AND RANCH IN MEXICO

Not much time was wasted by the Spaniards in taking advantage of the fertile parts of Mexico, and of the good foundation laid by the Indians. Chickens and domestic fowls introduced from Spain helped to make food more abundant in America. Cortés fixed a price of a peso and a half for a hen, but in 1595 the price was only one *real,* or approximately one-twelfth of the price of Cortés' time." [28]

---

[23] While it is difficult to translate the values of that age into our money, it is safe to say that there were as few men who could invest ten thousand ducats as there are today who can invest a million dollars.

[24] Negroes were brought to America as early as 1502, when Ovando arrived.

[25] Peter Martyr, *De orbe novo* (New York, 1912), p. 52, cited by Roland D. Hussey, in Wilgus, *Colonial Hispanic America,* p. 322.

[26] Oviedo, *Historia,* Bk. IV, chap. VIII.

[27] Acosta, *Historia de las Indias,* Bk. IV, chaps. XXXII-XXXIV.

[28] Riva Palacio, *México,* II, 492.

Cortés himself planted wheat in Mexico. Andrés de Tapia, a companion, remarks that "some rice was brought him from the port; with it came three wheat grains. He ordered a Moor to plant them: one came up . . . . Now there is so much abundance of this wheat that in the year '39 I saw good, or rather excellent, wheat at less than a real the fanega . . . . The Marquis brought every type of livestock used in Spain for business, and [other] animals, and silkworms, and the viceroy D. Antonio [Mendoza] has helped greatly in this." [29] The first flour mills were near Mexico City and in time more were established in other cities, as the demand increased.

By 1552, the sugar production was so great as to permit export to Spain and Peru. López de Gómara wrote at this date:

"Besides gold and silver there has also been brought, of the very rich merchandise, much sugar and cochineal. Feathers and cotton, and many other things, are of some value. Few vessels go there that do not return laden. The same is not yet true of Peru . . . . Thus New Spain has been as profitable to Castile as Peru, although Peru is the more famous . . . . From there horses, sugar, meat and twenty other things are carried to Peru." [30]

SIGNIFICANCE OF DOMESTIC ANIMALS

Domestic animals were a Spanish contribution to America of an importance that cannot be exaggerated. When we recall that nowhere in America, except in a portion of the Andes, were there serviceable domestic animals, we can properly assess the benefits of their introduction. In an area double the size of the United States there were no domestic animals of much value for food or transportation. There were, however, immense tracts well suited to stock-raising. Abundant and excellent grasses of various kinds grew in Mexico and other parts of America, but these were of no use to the Indians before the Conquest. They were, in fact, a great handicap. The Indians could not cultivate the grasslands because they were unable to conquer them with their primitive hoe-culture, or because the rainfall was not sufficient. The Spaniards introduced domestic animals into these areas and bred them, soon producing millions. A list of the fertile valleys of Mexico unused by the Indians but converted into regions of abundance by the Spaniards

---

[29] *Relación hecha por el señor Andrés de Tapia, sobre la conquista de México,* (C. D. México, ed. García Icazbalceta, II, 554-94), pp. 592-93.

[30] Francisco López de Gómara, *Conquista de México* (Zaragoza, 1552-53), fol. CXXXVIII, verso.

is astounding, since some of these areas are today among the most productive.

Soon after the Conquest, cattle were so numerous in Mexico that they were causing wars between the peaceable agricultural Indians and the cattle raisers. This forced a resettlement, and the cattle raisers were sent north where their herds covered an area so large that it had "neither beginning nor ending," and "if one has not seen them with his own eyes he cannot enumerate nor appreciate" their great numbers.[31]

OTHER MEXICAN PRODUCTS

Sixteenth-century New Spain had another product that had been introduced from Europe in silk, and mulberry trees had been brought over for its culture. Silk-making in the colonies will be discussed in a later chapter on manufactures.

Maguey was one of the plants that lent itself most readily to commercial exploitation. Attention has been called to the numerous uses to which it was susceptible. The drink *pulque,* made from maguey, was extremely popular and soon there sprang up numerous *pulquerías* in the towns, villages and cities. Complaints against the drunkenness of the Indians, a custom that pre-dated the Conquest, were frequent and laws were passed to prevent the use of pulque, but to no avail. Even excommunication was tried, but this too failed. Pulque continued to be in demand, and the growth of the maguey plant was one of the most lucrative types of farming.[32]

Maize, which was the principal food of American origin, continued to be the leader after the Conquest. The Indian population did not change to wheat, and many of the Spaniards away from the cities ate maize rather than wheat. The cultivation of the crop continued much as it had for centuries past, each Indian village producing its own, frequently without adopting plow culture. Beans also supplied one of the staple foods.

Only a small proportion of New Spain was cultivated in the sixteenth century, as is true even today. Several things account for this. First and most important, hardly more than a tenth of the country is good agricultural land. The proportion was even less under Indian methods of cultivation, but increased some with the introduction of European farming techniques, plants and domestic animals. Enormous areas north of the Central Valley are too dry for farming without irrigation, and the geography of Mexico

[31] Muñoz Camargo, *Tlaxcala,* pp. 261-62.
[32] Riva Palacio, *México,* II, 489-90.

renders irrigation difficult and limited. The rivers instead of flowing along the great inland plateau, rush directly to the sea and their waters are lost for irrigation purposes. Most of the vast northern region is used mainly for grazing. On the other hand, large areas of the Gulf Coast and southern Mexico are super-humid, while other areas in this southern region are, strange as it seems, too dry. Even in regions where the rainfall is sufficient but not excessive, the terrain is often too rough for cultivation, with great mountain masses resembling a gigantic crumpled paper. Where the land is arable, the average yield of corn (and other crops) is low in modern times, and there is little reason to suppose that it was greater under the Aztecs or the sixteenth-century Spaniards. Agricultural production increased under the European methods introduced by the Spaniards, but not sufficiently for a high standard of living.

A second reason for the limited amount of land cultivated was, paradoxically enough, that small areas of certain regions would support numerous people on a low subsistence level. This was particularly true of the humid tropics. Here certain crops that flourished had value only for their immediate use as foods, and no surplus was produced. A surplus would only have been wasted since, although some crops found a market within the country or in Europe (sugar, cochineal, chocolate), others had little monetary value. One of the best examples of this was the banana. [33] After its introduction, the banana immediately became a main food in the lowlands and some of the valleys. A small patch of banana plants would support a large family throughout the year. Since a surplus would go to waste, and there was no market because almost everybody could produce his own, bananas were seldom a commercial product; nevertheless they furnished the principal food for many thousands of people.

A third factor that caused much land to lie uncultivated was the difficulty of transporting products to the cities. The cost soon ate up any possible profit, and thus as the distance from the city market grew, the proportion of cultivated land decreased. A fourth factor was the shortage of labor needed to cultivate all Mexico intensively. With no power-driven machinery, the task was, and is today, beyond the abilities of many more millions of people than Mexico has ever had. One other factor that certainly contributed greatly

[33] The strange paradox of Mexico's productive capacity (or incapacity) is well treated in Eyler N. Simpson, *The Ejido: Mexico's Way Out* (Chapel Hill: University of North Carolina Press, 1937), pp. 131-61. Simpson's conclusions are revealed in some of his sub-topics: "Relatively Small Amount of 'Good' Crop Land; Small Amount of Potential Crop Land; Low Yields."

to prevent better cultivation was the concentration of the land in
a few hands. A small minority had vast areas which they did not
need to cultivate intensively in order to live well; millions had
only enough for a bare subsistence, or perhaps hardly that.

FARM AND RANCH IN SOUTH AMERICA

What was true of the Caribbean islands and Mexico was also
true of the territories to the south, since Spanish conquest and
Spanish agriculture went side by side. The occupation of Panama
began as early as 1509, and from that time down to 1554 came the
conquests of Venezuela, Colombia, Ecuador, Peru, Bolivia and
Chile. The military expeditions with their consequent destruction
and loss of much of the best of the Indian cultures, and the almost
continuous wars between the Spaniards and Indians (and simultaneously among the factions of the Spaniards) would seem to have
left little time for peaceful occupations. But this was far from
being the case. Destruction was accompanied by rebuilding; warriors made war so that they might turn to the arts of peace.

THE FARM FOLLOWS THE CONQUEST: PANAMA AND COLOMBIA

As conquistador, farmer, and encomendero, participating in the
conquests of Colombia, Ecuador and Peru, Cieza de León wrote a
systematic chronicle of every place he visited, taking each valley
and settlement in turn and describing the life there both before
and after the Conquest. Since he wrote in harsh terms of the destruction of the Indians and their civilization, it is with some assurance that we may accept his word when it reflects credit on the
Spaniards.

In Panama, he noted farms and ranches with herds of cattle,
and groves of oranges, citrons, and figs, all imported from Spain.
He saw flourishing Spanish orchards ten or fifteen [34] years after the
founding of Bogotá. That the grasslands around Cali were unused, he attributed to the fact that "the Christians are too few in
number to occupy such extensive plains." More than once, his testimony bears witness to a condition obtaining in much of America:
a great part of the land remained unproductive until the Spanish
occupation. Between Cali and Popayán (Colombia), he found
many beautiful Spanish estates, where livestock, corn, barley, and
wheat were raised. Popayán had a flour mill, and corn bread was
no longer eaten "because of the abundance of wheat." [35]

---

[34] Cieza, *Crónica*, chap. II.
[35] Cieza, *Crónica*, *chaps. XXIV, XXVI,* 'XXX XXXIV.

ECUADOR AND PERU

In the economy of Ecuador, neither gold nor silver were paramount; agriculture and stock-raising held the first place. Besides the growing of wheat and barley, the areas in maize increased, and the potato, quínoa, and many other plants grew where cereals were not suited to the soil and the climate. Here again, livestock multiplied, goats in the lowlands and sheep on the mountains. The Spanish burro was adopted by the Indians. The hog and domestic fowl reached the remote villages.[36] Hogs were already "raised in greater numbers and of better quality than in most other parts of the Indies," and the hams and bacon were "as good as those of the Sierra Morena" in Spain, within a generation after the conquest of Ecuador.

In northern Peru, Trujillo had Spanish estates, all irrigated and planted in a great variety of "fruits of Spain." Around Lima were irrigated orchards and gardens, with native and imported fruits and vegetables, vineyards, livestock, and dovecotes.[37] Still farther south in the valleys of Ica and Nazca, despite the loss of many irrigation ditches in the wars of conquest, Cieza observed "large quantities of sugar cane from which a great deal of sugar is made, and other fruits which are carried for sale to the various cities of the kingdom."

The reports about the mountain valleys indicate the early progress of agriculture there. The land around Caxamarca was found to be "extremely fertile" and the wheat "as good as that of Sicily." There, as in Huánuco and other Andean valleys, livestock, maize, vegetables and fruits also abounded. [38] Cieza foresaw a great future for Peruvian agriculture:

"Some parts of the realm, such as the coast plains and the river valleys and the more temperate parts of the mountains, arc very fertile because wheat grows so beautifully and produces a very great yield, as do maize and barley. Vineyards are not few in number . . . and there are great hopes of making good wines. Oranges, pomegranates and other fruits, there are all these brought from Spain, as well as the native ones. Vegetables of all kinds are found, and, in sum, Peru is a great kingdom, and with time will be greater, because great cities will be established wherever conditions are suitable for their establishment. And after our generation, it will be possible to export from Peru

[36] Pereyra, *América española,* VI, 192.
[37] Cieza, *Crónica,* chaps. XLII, LXIX, LXXI.
[38] Cieza, *Crónica,* chaps. LXXV, LXXVII, LXXX.

to other regions wheat, wine, meats, wool, and even silks, because there are the most suitable conditions in the world for planting mulberry trees. There is only one thing that we can think of that has not been brought to the Indies, that is the olive tree, which after bread and wine is of the greatest importance." [39]

IMPORTANCE AND PROGRESS OF AGRICULTURE

Cieza's optimistic prophecy was largely confirmed within a generation. The Jesuit historian, Acosta, writing in 1590, gives a comprehensive list of the European plants already at home in the New World.

"The Indies have been better repaid in the matter of plants than in anything else, because those that have been brought to Spain are few in number and grow badly; those that have gone from Spain are numerous, and grow well . . . . In sum, almost everything good that is produced in Spain is found there, and in some places better and in others not so good; wheat, barley, garden stuff, greens and vegetables of all sorts . . . . Of the trees, those that have more generally grown there, and in more abundance, are the orange, lime, citron tree, and fruits of this family. In some places there are already woods and groves of oranges . . . . I have never been in any part of them where oranges did not grow . . . . *Duraznos* and their companions *melocotones* and *priscos* [types of peaches] and apricots have all grown well . . . . Apples and pears grow, but only moderately well; plums very scarcely, figs in abundance, especially in Peru: quince everywhere . . . . There are very good melons in some places, such as those of Tierra-Firme and some parts of Peru." [40]

The vineyards, producing "wine, vinegar, grapes, raisins, verjuice and syrup," were well developed by Acosta's time. Wine was the most important of the vineyard's products, although grapes did not grow well in the Caribbean and Tierra Firme, and wine could not be produced in Mexico (except around Parras, Coahuila and Santo Tomás, Baja California, developed after the sixteenth century), because the rains came in the wrong season. These areas imported wines from Spain. The situation was different in Peru and Chile, where "they make wine of a very good quality, and daily it increases in quantity as well as in excellence, for the manner of making it is improving, and it is a great source of wealth in those lands. The vineyards of Peru are usually in the hot valleys

[39] Cieza, *Crónica*, chap. CXIII.
[40] Acosta, *Historia de las Indias*, Bk. IV, chap. XXXI.

where they have ditches for irrigation, because there is no rain-fall along the coast plains, and in the mountains the rainfall does not come at the right time . . . . The vineyards have increased to such an extent that for this reason the tithes of the Church are today five or six times what they were twenty years ago." The wine from the coast was carried to Cuzco, Potosí and other interior cities and sold at about half of the price of the wines brought from Spain. Grapes were available in many places where wine was not made.

Sugar production had become even more prosperous than earlier, since cane grew not only in the Caribbean, but in numerous regions, including Peru, New Spain and Colombia. The consumption per capita was very great in the Indies, and the business of exporting it to Spain profitable. The owner of a sugar mill was accounted rich in Acosta's time, as he had been fifty years earlier. Some of the mills produced incomes that are impressive. "They assured me," says Acosta, "that the mill at Nasca [Peru] produced a profit of thirty thousand pesos or more yearly. The one at Chicama near Trujillo was also a paying business, and those of New Spain are not less so because it is absolutely fantastic the amount of sugar and preserves consumed in the Indies . . . Sugar is the most profitable business of those [Caribbean] islands, thanks to man's growing appetite for sweets." [41]

Olives were grown in Peru and other places, but only for eating. The oil was shipped from Spain. So numerous were the livestock that men with "sixty to a hundred thousand head of sheep" were considered to have "only moderate" fortunes, whereas the same number in Spain would have constituted "enormous wealth." [42]

The growth of mining, together with the depopulation of the Caribbean islands after the discovery of Mexico and Peru, and the fact that the Crown resorted to laws prohibiting emigration from the islands to the mainland, readily give rise to an assumption that the Spaniards had little interest in agriculture, and came to the New World for gold alone. Difficulties of the poorer colonists in finding a livelihood in America might tend to support such a conclusion. Before the middle of the sixteenth century, Fernández de Oviedo condemned those who, "thinking to flee from poverty and find food," found themselves "enmeshed in greater poverty, homeless, and perhaps dying uncoffined." [43]

But other factors in the agricultural development, quite aside

[41] Acosta, *Historia de las Indias,* Bk. IV, chap. XXXII.
[42] Acosta, *Historia de las Indias,* Bk. IV, chap. XXXIII.
[43] Oviedo, *Historia,* Bk. V, chap. X.

from mining, played their part in restricting chances for wealth from farms and ranches. By 1520, the West Indies had ceased in most respects to be a land of opportunity for the masses of the Spaniards there. The land grants had been extensive, and most of the population had remained without land and now had no hope of receiving any; livestock were either wild or owned by the proprietors of the landed estates; most of the people had no encomiendas; farming for export was confined to a few of the wealthy who, to use but one example, were the only people able to build a sugar mill, or arrange for other profitable commerce.

The majority of the people, deprived of opportunity by a regime of economic privilege, welcomed a chance to better themselves in Mexico or Peru. Many of them were content to start farming when they got land on the mainland, but many more, still pursued by economic furies that sanctioned a system whereby a few received larger grants, thus making it physically impossible for the majority to be granted anything, were condemned to live landless, or die fighting for land they never received. The economic growth of the West Indies was certainly not ruined by emigration, because the period of its trade and export to Spain begins contemporaneously with the conquests of Mexico and Peru, and these events, as we have seen, offered a market for agriculture produce of the Islands where none had existed before.

THE KING AND AGRICULTURE

The Crown encouraged agriculture from the first days of the discovery, supplying Columbus on his second voyage with every necessity for permanent settlement and agriculture, including the power to grant lands. Cortés asked for and received plants, animals, and general assistance. Antonio de Mendoza, first viceroy of Mexico (1535-1550), promoted the development of the silkworm, previously introduced, and in 1538, the Crown instructed him to bring agricultural experts to America.[44]

Skilled workmen were sent from the Canaries to the West Indies to develop the sugar industry. A temporary prohibition against production of wine on Española in 1503 was removed, and in 1519 the Casa de Contratación was ordered to send with every ship vines for planting. In 1520, sugar-making machinery was exempted from payment of import duty; and in 1529, it was prohibited in Española to seize sugar mills for debt. In 1531, the royal revenue from

---

[44] Riva Palacio, *México*, II, 491-94.

the entire island of Cuba was used to import Negro slaves to be sold to the planters on time payments.[45]

* * * * * * *

Before the Conquest, agriculture had furnished the livelihood for the majority of America's population, although relatively advanced methods of land cultivation were restricted chiefly to portions of Mexico, Central America, and the valleys of the Andes. While maize was the staple food crop, wide variations of climate and soil produced many species of native plants which the agricultural Indians put to good use. The farming systems of the Aztecs and Incas were ingenious in overcoming natural obstacles and scarcity of good soil, and in Peru, irrigation, terracing, and fertilization were all employed.

True as it is that the conquest by the Spaniards destroyed much of value in the native systems, Spanish contributions rapidly expanded American agriculture. The introduction of cattle and the plow made it possible to exploit land useless under the hoe-culture of the Indians. The Spaniards adopted many native plants, but they also brought in and naturalized the fruits, vegetables, and domestic animals of Europe. Colonial agriculture was encouraged and favored by the government of Spain, and plantations, orchards, gardens, vineyards and herds were flourishing from the first years of Spanish settlement. Though the land and the wealth were in the hands of a few, before 1600, the agricultural future of Latin America was assured.

---

[45] Clarence Henry Haring, *Trade and Navigation between Spain and the Indies in the Time of the Hapsburgs* (Cambridge: Harvard University Press, 1918), pp. 123-26.

Mining in America

Precious Metals in the Hands of the Indians

MINING WAS THE ELECTRIC SPARK that set off economic activity in America. The precious metals ignited an economic engine that, after the introduction of the European elements we have been discussing, had everything necessary for operation.

Knowledge of the precious metals was not confined to the post-Conquest period. A considerable amount of gold and silver had been accumulated by the Indians through river washings and mining. The total was not large, but it was amassed in a few places and in a few hands, and appeared to be much more than it actually was. When we say that the total was not large, however, we are making a comparison with the later amounts mined by the Spanish. At the time of discovery, the precious metals already in the possession of the Indians seemed fabulous to the discoverers.

Columbus came into contact with gold soon after he first reached the New World. He heard reports of an island where, the Indians told him "by signs", "the people on it gather gold with candles at night in the sand and afterwards with a hammer . . . make bars of it." This led Columbus to write that "without doubt there is a very great quantity of gold in this land, as these Indians I am bringing say, not without cause, that there are places in these islands where they dig the gold and wear it at the neck and in the ears and on the arms and on the legs and there are very heavy bracelets, and also there are precious stones and pearls and an infinite quantity of spices." [1] The two chief points on which the Spanish consistently dwelt, their religious mission and their quest of gold, must have impressed one of the Indians with Columbus, for on December 15 Columbus reports that this Indian explained to the others that the Spaniards "came from Heaven and that they were going in search of gold."

---

[1] *Journal,* November 12.

Small amounts, and large rumors of gold, continued to reach Columbus. On December 18 he noted that he had found little but had "learned from an old man that there were many islands in that vicinity at a distance of a hundred leagues and more, . . . in which a great quantity of gold is found and in the others there is so much that . . . there was an island . . . all gold, and there is such a quantity in the others that they gather it and sift it as with sieves, and melt it and make 'bars' and work it in a thousand ways: they show the manner in which this is done, by signs."

This is the first mention of placer mining, by means of which important quantities of gold were later produced in America.[2]

Bernal Díaz refers frequently to mines in various parts of Mexico. Iron was not used by the Indians and seems not to have been worked by them in any part of America. After the Conquest, the Indians of Mexico called iron "white copper," according to Muñoz Camargo, since they were acquainted with copper but not iron.[3]

Precious metals before the Conquest had small value, except as tribute or ornaments; only to a limited degree were they used as commodities exchanged in the markets like other produce. Most of the supply was the property of the chieftains and kings, who by one means or another had concentrated it in the temples and palaces in the form of ornaments, statuary, and household and table services of gold and silver. In Peru,

"The gold and silver and the precious stones which the Inca kings had in such great quantity, as is well known, were not an obligatory tribute that the Indians were required to give, because they were not considered as one of the things necessary for war or peace, and all this was not considered as either treasury or riches . . . They were valued only for their beauty and splendor, for ornaments and use in the royal palaces and temple of the Sun and Houses of the Virgins. . . ."[4]

The quantities of silver and gold in America had a tremendous effect on the imaginations of the Spaniards, as they have had on men ever since. Early descriptions show the wonder of the discoverers:

". . . And it is known from reliable histories that the Incas of Peru were not content with having only large and small vases

---

[2] For early mining in America see John Samuel Fox, *The Beginnings of Spanish Mining in America: The West Indies and Castilla del Oro* (Berkeley: University of California, Unpublished Doctoral Thesis, 1940.)

[3] Muñoz Camargo, *Tlaxcala*, pp. 210-11.

[4] Garcilaso, *Comentarios*, Bk. V, chap. VII.

of gold . . . but they also had chairs, and biers or litters of solid gold, and in their temples they placed various statues of solid gold. In Mexico also there was a great deal, although not so much. . . . The use of silver for shoeing horses because of the lack of iron [soon after the Conquest], and the paying of three hundred *escudos* of gold for one jug or pitcher of wine, along with other such excesses, would seem fictitious tales, but in fact more fantastic things than this took place." [5]

MINING AND PLUNDER

The small bits of gold the Indians had taken from the streams before the Spaniards came had not greatly affected the supply. From 1494, important finds of gold were made on the south side of Española, and Bartolomé Columbus transferred the principal settlement from north to south, founding what came to be the present city of Santo Domingo, the first of many prosperous cities that were to have their sites and livelihood determined by the mineral deposits of America.

From 1492 to about 1515, Española produced most of the treasure of the New World. Between 1515 and 1530, Puerto Rico exported almost as much and Cuba about half as much. After 1531, the precious metal output of the mainlands far exceeded that of the islands.[6] The produce of gold in the Antilles between 1501 and 1519 was about eight million *pesos*.[7]

---

[5] Acosta, *Historia de las Indias,* Bk. IV, chap. IV.

[6] Earl J. Hamilton, *American Treasure and the Price Revolution in Spain, 1501-1650.* (Cambridge: Harvard University Press, 1934), p. 43. Hamilton's work is the most recent study of mineral production. His figures are based on original sources showing the imports into Spain, not total American production. They are, therefore, lower in general than many previous estimates which are based on what was produced. Much American treasure never touched Spain or was not registered there, going out to other countries.

[7] Roland D. Hussey, "Colonial Economic Life" in Wilgus, *Colonial Hispanic America,* p. 321.

The following table shows the value of Spanish coins in the sixteenth century:

Coin	Value in Gold Marks	Maravedís	Grams Gold	Fineness
Castellano	1/50	480 to 490	4.5534	23 3/4 carats
Ducat	1/65 1/3	375	3.485	23 3/4
Real	1/67 silver	34	....	67/72
Mark (gold)	....	....	230.0675	....
Mark (silver)	....	2.278	....	....
Peso de Minas	1/50	450	4.18	22
Peso Fuerte	....	272 (8 reales)	25.563 (silver)	....
Peso de Oro de Tupuzque		272	....	....
Peso de Oro Corriente		300	....	....
Peso de Oro con 3 quilatos añadido		360	....	....
Peso de Oro de ley Perfecta		450	....	....
Peso de Oro de Minas		450	....	....

With the conquests of Mexico and Peru the principal production of precious metals shifted to these countries, and silver, which had not been found in the West Indies in quantities, outstripped gold in volume. The amount of treasure taken from the Indians in Mexico and Peru by Cortés and Pizarro has been overestimated. The treasure Montezuma offered to Cortés amounted to about 162,000 pesos,[8] as compared with the more than eight millions the Spaniards had already produced in the Islands. In 1552, Gómara remarked:

"It was very little silver and gold that Cortés and his companions found and saw in the conquest of New Spain, in comparison with what has since been taken from the mines, all of which, or very little less, has been brought to Spain. And though the mines have not been so rich, nor the sums brought so large, as those of Peru, they have been constant, and have doubled with time."[9]

The Inca treasures were greater than those of the Aztecs but not so large as sometimes supposed. The ransom of Atahualpa came to about 40,860 marks of silver and 971,125 pesos of gold, not including the King's fifth.[10]

A Mark of silver was 5 *pesos de oro* or 450 maravedís.

C. H. Haring, "American Gold and Silver Production in the First Half of the Sixteenth Century," *The Quarterly Journal of Economics*, (May, 1915), XXIX, 435, 478.

A Peso of 450 Maravedís was 42.29 grams of silver.

Hamilton, *American Treasure*, p. 32.

[8] Alexander de Humboldt, *Political Essay on the Kingdom of New Spain*, (4 vols., London, 1811), III, 111. The second French edition, *Essai politique sur le royaume de la Nouvelle-Espagne* (5 vols., Paris, 1811), III, 301. Both editions are cited here, the translation as *New Spain*, and the original French as *Nouvelle Espagne*, and while the translation is in general accurate, a few alterations in its text have been made when quoted. The works of Humboldt are perhaps the most important single source of information about Latin America during the eighteenth century, and on some matters before that time. Humboldt was one of the great intellectual figures of his day, his contributions to science being among the most important of the nineteenth century. It is singularly fortunate that a man of such calibre should have devoted so many years to study of America. He traveled over areas as distant as Peru and Pennsylvania from 1799-1804, and made exhaustive studies of agriculture, mining, trade, manufacturing, labor, ethnology, geography, astronomy, and, with his companion, Aimé Bonpland, botany and natural history generally. In addition to being a keen observer, Humboldt had access to many official records, some not today available, that lend his work a prestige not enjoyed by any other. In most respects his data have not been superseded to the present time.

[9] López de Gómara, *Conquista de México*, p. 138 verso.

[10] Prescott, *Peru*, Bk. III, chap. VII, estimated the value of Atahualpa's ransom at fifteen million dollars; Merriman, *Spanish Empire*, III, 565, reduces this by more than two-thirds; Means says the gold alone would have been worth some $2,650,000, and Shay estimated the purchasing power of the ransom at around fifty million dollars in modern times, Means, *Fall*, p. 41. Garcilaso de la Vega estimated the total of Atahualpa's ransom at 4,605,670 ducats. In the Act of Partition signed by Pedro Sancho, the four-fifths belonging to the men, and not including the King's fifth, came to 40,860 marks of silver and 971,125 *pesos* of gold. The mark was

When Cuzco was captured some 580,200 *pesos de oro* and 215,000 marks of silver were found, making a total of 255,860 marks of silver and 1,551,325 pesos of gold, not counting the one-fifth that went to the King from Atahualpa's ransom.[11]

Humboldt's calculations showed that "the conquests of Mexico and Peru did not throw into the hands of the Spaniards more than 80,000 marks of gold." He estimated all the "spoils,", as distinct from the mined treasure, at 186,000 marks of gold, equivalent to twenty-five million pesos.[12] If we make the most liberal interpretation possible, and count all imports into Spain between 1521 and 1545, a period of twenty-five years, as "plunder" (obviously this was not the case), the total is exceeded by the production of the new mines worked by the Spaniards in the ten-year period following 1545. True, the Spaniards did not get all the gold and silver that was in the possession of the Indians, but centuries of search have not uncovered the fabulous treasures the Indians were reported to have hidden, and belief in their existence is hardly reasonable. Within a few years after the discovery, the Spaniards undoubtedly mined more precious metals than the Indians had accumulated in many centuries (Table I).

TABLE I

Total Imports into Spain of Treasure in Pesos
(450 Maravedis) by Five-Year Periods
Except the first three year period

Period	Total
1503-1505	371,055.3
1506-1510	816,236.5
1511-1515	1,195,553.5
1516-1520	993,196.5
1521-1525	134,170.0
1526-1530	1,038,437.0
1531-1535	1,650,231.0
1536-1540	3,937,892.0
1541-1545	4,954,005.0
1546-1550	5,508,711.0
1551-1555	9,865,531.0 [13]

eight ounces of silver. Garcilaso, *Comentarios,* Part II, Bk. I, chap. XXXVIII. The various contemporary accounts vary slightly.

[11] Pedro Sancho, *Relación para Su Majestad,* cited in Garcilaso, *Comentarios,* Part II, Bk. I, chap. XXXVIII, notes 45 and 46; cf. *Relación del oro, plata y piedras preciosas que se fundieron, marcaron e quintaron en la fundición del Cuzco . . . 1535, D.I.I.,* XI, 503-582.

[12] Humboldt, *New Spain,* III, pp. 428-34; [*Nouvelle Espagne,* IV, pp. 252-58].

[13] Hamilton, *American Treasure,* p. 34.

EFFECTS OF MINING ON OTHER INDUSTRIES

The legend of the vast wealth plundered from the Indians helped to create the belief that the effect of precious minerals on America was particularly malevolent. To this idea, the graphic descriptions of the "gold rush" days have contributed. In their eagerness to impress their readers with the riches of America, the sixteenth-century chroniclers vied with each other in their descriptions of the mines, and left the impression that nothing but precious metal had any value to the Spaniards.

The Spaniards have been frequently presented by English, French, American, and other historians as gold-grabbing vandals who overran and sacked marvelous, indigenous civilizations. The desire for precious metals was presented as peculiarly Spanish and unquestionably heinous. The same historians have often glossed over the plundering of the treasure-laden Spanish ships by British and French buccaneers, stressing their daring rather than their piracy. While the benefits accruing to world commerce through the introduction of vast quantities of precious metals were recognized, Philip II of Spain was regarded as an ignoble miser for encouraging their production, and Queen Elizabeth admired for her cleverness in robbing him. Similarly, Americans have looked upon the rush of the Spaniards to gold mines as the rush of pigs to the trough; but the "forty-niners" were nation builders. "The bones of a hundred thousand Americans strewn from St. Louis to California" were symbols of Anglo-Saxon courage and initiative.

Such reactions to Spanish mining activities were the natural results of national commercial rivalries and religious prejudices. Latin Americans who took the same view were often seeking to disassociate themselves from the Spanish heritage, quite in the same way that the people of the United States nourished an anti-British tradition for more than a century, as a further declaration of independence from the yoke cast off.

Mining, as a matter of fact, played a progressive role. Where mines were discovered, the population grew, employment was available, farming flourished, trade boomed, cities sprang up, and urban civilization came into existence; a middle class was created; the buying power of the people increased; the products of Europe and Asia flowed in as the precious metal to pay for them flowed out; and world economic development was stimulated. A market was created for other American products; public revenues made possible magnificent public buildings, and in general America was able to grow.

MINING LAWS

Charles V and Philip II gradually applied the mining laws of Spain, with some modifications, to the New World.[14] In the regulations, the procedure governing discovery and staking claims was defined, and the conditions under which mines could be worked and owned were fixed. The Indians, as vassals of the Crown, were granted the same rights as the Spaniards to discover and work mines. Prior to the establishment of Spanish colonial government, no set rules were observed, naturally, and every discoverer of a mine proceeded immediately to work it. Afterwards the legally constituted authorities were given power to grant title to mining properties, and to collect the Crown's royalties. Offering rewards for finding mines was a common practice, and many prospectors made good sums from commissions received for discovery. Such rewards were usually offered by an *Adelantado* or a conquistador who had received a *capitulación* (contract) for discovery and settlement, and in 1530, Charles V decreed that two-thirds of the reward should be paid by the royal treasury and one-third by the operators of the mines. The viceroys were enjoined to give encouragement to the discovery and working of mines.

Among the privileges granted mining was that no attachment or foreclosure of the slaves, tools, and supplies used in working the mine could be ordered, nor could the operation of the mine be stopped by a creditor. A miner could be imprisoned only in the *real de minas* (mining town) where he lived. Tools for mining were provided from the royal revenues at moderate prices. If called to give witness before the Audiencia, miners were to be heard first and with dispatch. The maize and other tribute in kind paid to the Crown were sold to miners at low rates.

Royalties collected by the Crown varied greatly. In the early days as much as two-thirds was demanded as a severance tax, but this soon fell to one-third. With the development of mining the usual royalty was one-fifth, or the *quinto*. In accordance with Spanish law, a heritage of Roman Law, the Crown owned all the products of the subsoil and could therefore grant or withhold its use at will. Some mines were worked by the Crown.

IMPROVEMENT OF MINING TECHNIQUE: THE PATIO PROCESS

Mining received a great impetus in 1556 with the introduction by Bartolomé de Medina of the *patio* process for separating silver

---

[14] See *Ordenanzas de Minas de Guamanga*, 1562, and *Ordenanzas de Toledo*, 1571, *D. I. I.*, VIII, 449-484; *Gobernación espiritual y temporal*, Bk. IV, Titles X-XIV, in *C. D. I. Ultramar*, XXII.

from other substances with quicksilver.[15] The new technique proved much more efficient than the smelting methods and was immediately adopted. By 1562, Zacatecas had perhaps thirty-five plants in operation. The quality of the ore determined the process and smelting was still used in many mines. Juan Capellán improved the Medina system and Pedro Fernández de Velasco adapted it to the Peruvian metals in 1573. Two Peruvian miners, the brothers Juan Andrés and Carlos Corzo y Lleca, invented an improvement known as the *agua de hierro* process about the same time that Gabriel de Castro discovered the same method.

Quicksilver, or mercury, which had been mined in Spain and other parts of Europe for many centuries, now became a product of immense importance.[16] Upon its supply and distribution depended the amount of silver production, and in 1559 the Crown established a monopoly. Neither in Peru nor Mexico, either for small or large quantities, was there any legal commerce in mercury except through royal officials. In 1563, Enrique Garcés and Amador de Cabrera discovered the mercury mines at Huancavelica (Peru), described as "a mountain of extremely hard rock, soaked in quicksilver." [17] The Crown took this mine over, compensating the owners with 250,000 ducats.

The relation between the supply of mercury and the prosperity of the mines was direct and vital. Whenever the mercury supply failed for any reason, the mines would have to cease refining, great stocks of ore would pile up and large sums of capital be tied up for long periods until eventually unemployment resulted, the purchasing power of the people declined, and both agriculture and commerce were thrown into a depression. The supply might fail when war in Europe prevented shipments, or when pirates delayed or captured the ships, or, as in 1590 to 1594, when an epidemic in Spain prevented the fleet from sailing.

THE COLONIAL MINING INDUSTRY: MEXICO

When the Spanish occupied Mexico City, they set out industriously to seek the mines, which they supposed to be numerous, judg-

---

[15] The year is sometimes given as 1557. The whole origin of the system has been disputed. Some authors say Medina learned the process from a German miner; others that Medina adapted the process already used in Germany for gold. Who invented the process and when is of less importance than its effect on production. Pereyra, *Obra de España*, pp. 231-38; Hussey in Wilgus, *Colonial Hispanic America,* p. 321.

[16] The importance of quicksilver in American mining has been admirably treated by Arthur Preston Whitaker, *The Huancavelica Mercury Mine* (Cambridge: Harvard University Press, 1941), pp. 9-21 and *passim*.

[17] Pereyra, *Obra,* p. 235, note 2.

ing from the apparent abundance of gold and silver in the court of Montezuma. But such mines were very few, the abundance of gold and silver being the result of its accumulation in a few places and in a few hands throughout several centuries.

Finding only a few mines previously worked by the Indians, the Spaniards endeavored to discover new ones. A part of every step of the Conquest, and a concomitant of the occupation of territory, was the search for mines. The finding of even a small amount of gold or silver would lead to the settlement of a few Spaniards, perhaps only four or five, and around these would gather the Indians and their families. The result would be a new village or town, many of which became permanent settlements and exist today. Others disappeared.

Michoacán, to the west of Mexico City, was the site of the first important mine, discovered by the Spanish in 1525. Work had just begun when the mine vanished, probably because of one of the earthquakes frequent in Mexico. The tide of migration was attracted toward Michoacán, however, and it rapidly developed into one of the prosperous areas of the country. Other mines were worked around the valley of Toluca, and numerous *reales de minas,* or mining towns, sprang up in the mountains of Oaxaca, Tasco, Zultepec, and Pachuca.

The discovery of the mines of Zacatecas, in 1548, and Guanajuato, in 1558, opened the great mining epoch of Mexico. The region in which these mines were found lies north of the Central Valley of Mexico. Before the mines were exploited, there was no agriculture, no industry, no commerce, and the population consisted of a few primitive, nomadic tribes. Valleys abounding in excellent grasses had gone practically unused for centuries because there were no domestic animals to graze upon them. Excellent farm lands had remained unfruitful because Indian economy did not require their products. Important cities like Zacatecas and Guanajuato sprang up at once and dozens of smaller towns grew up, either around mines or in fertile valleys that now could be utilized because there was a market for their crops. Farms producing numerous tropical and temperate-zone fruits, vegetables, and grains, both native American and European, supplanted the unused grasslands. Thousands of cattle, horses, asses, sheep, and goats multiplied to fill the empty spaces.

Along the route from Mexico City to Zacatecas, or to Guanajuato, or any one of the numerous mining sites, arose small towns designed to protect the route to the mines and to furnish agricultural produce and meat to travelers. These were not mining sites, but agricultural centers taking their life from the traffic of the mine. Northward from Zacatecas as far as the Conchos River, settlements arose as the century progressed.

The mineral production of Mexico continued to expand steadily throughout the sixteenth century, with the fluctuations to be expected over such a long period. All studies reveal an increasing rate of production, however much authorities may disagree on the total amount produced.

By dividing the sixteenth century into quarter-century periods, we find that during the first period (1525-1550), Mexico sent to Spain approximately one and a half millions of pesos of precious metals; that in the second period (1551-1575), the sum was almost 10,000,000 pesos or about seven times as much as during the first period; and that in the last quarter of the century the production was in excess of 25,000,000 pesos, or seventeen times the amount sent from Mexico to Spain from the Conquest down to 1550. So great was the production after 1560 that in no subsequent five-year period did the remittances fail to exceed the total for the first 29-years, and the average annual production for 1596-1601 was equal to the total for the first 29 years under discussion (Table II).[17b]

TABLE II

Remittance of Bullion from New Spain, 1522-1601

	Pesos
1522-1550	1,538,598
1551-1575	9,878,386
1576-1601	25,708,223

GOLD AND SILVER: PERU

Mining in Peru followed roughly the pattern laid down in Mexico. Diligent search was made for the source of the gold and silver in the possession of the Indians, but only small lodes and

[17b] Haring, *Trade and Navigation*, Appendix V.

placer deposits were found. As in the case of Mexico, it is practically certain that the Indians of the Andes had never mined gold
or silver on a large scale, and the apparently fabulous sums they
possessed had been amassed over centuries.

Silver in quantities was discovered in 1545 when the Potosí
mines were opened. The discovery of Potosí was the most important event in American mining history up to that time, coming
as it did before the principal Mexican mines were opened. Potosí
became the most famous mining site in the world and its name
synonymous with incalculable riches.

Production rose steadily, with some fluctuations, throughout the
sixteenth century. Prior to 1560 Potosí produced about 56,000,000
pesos, which combined with the produce of other parts of Peru,
gave a total for the viceroyalty (including Chile) of about 84,-
350,000 pesos between 1533 and 1560 (Table III).

TABLE III

*Summary of Gold and Silver Production in the Years 1533 to 1560
in Mexico, Peru and Chile, Upper Peru, New Granada
and West Indies and Tierra Firme*

	Soetbeer	Lexis	Haring
Mexico:			
Gold	4,723,550	13,700,000	5,692,570
Silver	12,520,200	16,900,000	23,713,650
Peru and Chile:			
Gold	18,014,000	21,908,000 ⎫	
Silver	43,800,000	12,353,000 ⎭	28,350,000
Upper Peru:			
Gold	6,330,000	1,978,000 ⎫	
Silver	120,110,000	102,000,000 ⎭	56,000,000
New Granada:			
Gold	18,990,000	18,990,000	6,081,000
West Indies and Tierra Firme:			
Gold	10,880,000	18,990,000	19,000,000
Totals:			
Gold	58,937,550	75,566,000	
Silver	176,430,200	131,253,000	
Grand Totals:	235,367,750	206,819,000	138,837,000 [18]

More significant for an idea of the rate of production are the
statistics on Potosí from 1556, when the record of the *quinto* paid

---

[18] Haring, *"American Gold and Silver,"* p. 468, as amended by Dr. Haring.

to the Crown begins, to the end of the century. The average annual production for 1585-1600 was about three and one-half times the rate from 1556-1570 (Table IV).[19]

TABLE IV

Amount of Silver Registered in *Pesos de minas* from Potosí, 1556 to 1600

Year	Registered		Royalties	
	Total	Average	Total	Average
1556-1560	6,141,241	1,228,248.2	1,277,376	255,475.2
1561-1565	6,535,875	1,307,175.0	1,359,460	271,892.0
1566-1570	5,965,189	1,193,037.8	1,240,966	248,193.2
1571-1575	4,295,520	859,104.0	893,467	178,693.4
1576-1580	11,984,033	2,396,806.6	2,500,090	500,018.0
1581-1585	19,565.071	3,913,014.2	4,083,118	816,623.6
1586-1590	20,863,143	4,172,628.6	4,400,442	880,088.4
1591-1595	22,433,967	4,486,793.4	4,756,000	951,200.0
1596-1600	19,736,858	3,947,371.6	4,182,212	836,442.4

Adapted from Haring, *Trade and Navigation*, Appendix VI.
The peso de minas contained 450 maravedís instead of the 272 contained in the peso fuerte.

Potosí is high on the Bolivian plateau, and its discovery attracted the Spaniards (and Indians) to a region where few people had lived before. The results were far reaching. Agriculture and commerce developed to supply the demands of the mining city. As one eye witness records: "Many Spaniards became rich and went to Spain, prosperous just from taking *chuño* [made from Irish potatoes] to sell to the mines of Potosí." [20] "The estates and farms have a very great value at this time as a result of the riches that have been discovered in Potosí." [21]

The market became the most famous in Peru, inspiring one of the conquistadores to write:

"Throughout this kingdom of Peru it is known to us who have traveled over it that there were great *tianguez,* which are markets, where the natives traded their products, among which the largest and richest in former times was that of the city of

[19] The production of silver in the Cerro de Potosí during the 1545-1555 period has been one of the most controversial subjects in the history of America. The records for the period are not very clear, and all authors have had to do a great deal of reconstruction. For a discussion of the subject see: Bailey W. Diffie, "Estimates of Potosí Mineral Production, 1545-55," *H.A.H.R.*, XX (1940), 275-282.

QUINTO DE POTOSI

1545-48	830,565	pesos de minas (169,119 marcos)	
1548-52	1,136,000	" " "	
1552-57	1,566,000	" " "	
1558-60	708,945	" " "	
Totals	4,241,510	" " "	
	or		
	7,017,200	" of 8 reals	

Haring, "American Gold and Silver," p. 457.
[20] Cieza, *Crónica*, chap. XCIX.
[21] *Ibid.,* chap. CVII.

Cuzco . . . . But neither this market or *tianguez,* nor any other
in the kingdom equalled the superb one of Potosí; because so extensive was the trade just among the Indians, without the
Christians entering into it, that there was sold daily during the
time of the prosperity of the mines, twenty-five and thirty thousand pesos gold, and on the best days, forty thousand, a wonderful thing and I do not believe that any market *(feria)* in the
world would equal the trade of this one . . ." ". . . and
this fair or market was open from morning till dark, and as
silver was mined every day and these Indians are fond of eating
and drinking, especially those who trade with the Spaniards,
everything that was brought for sale was consumed, so that provisions and things necessary for their use were brought from
everywhere. And so, many Spaniards grew rich in Potosí just
from having two or three Indian women who traded for them
in this market . . ." [22]

New mining settlements throughout the world are traditional
centers of lawlessness, greed, murder, and highway robbery. Potosí
has been pictured as the archtype of such a mining town, but Acosta
indicates that there has been much exaggeration. In 1590 he remarked:

"The bars of silver are carried by road seventy leagues to
Arica, and formerly to Arequipa a hundred and fifty. And it is
a thing that I often was astounded to see that these pack-trains
of llamas carried a thousand or two .thousand bars, and much
more, worth three hundred thousand ducats, without any other
guard or defense except a few Indians to guide the llamas and
load them, and at most one Spaniard; and every night they slept
in the open field without any more precaution than I have mentioned. And although the road is so long and the guard so small,
none of the silver whatever was ever missing, such is the great
security with which one travels in Peru." [23]

GOLD AND SILVER: COLOMBIA AND CHILE

Colombia was the chief *gold* producer during the colonial period,
and yet is has received slight attention, or none at all, from many
historians of Spain's mining activity. The expedition of Pedro de
Heredia brought in 1,500,000 ducats gold in 1533, a greater sum
than either Cortés or Pizarro, but Heredia has lacked a Prescott
to publicize his adventures. Various estimates have been made of

---

[22] Cieza, *Crónica,* Ch. CX.
[23] Acosta, *Historia de las Indias,* Bk. IV, chap. XLI.

early production, modern figures accepting approximately 6,081,000 *pesos* from 1538, the year Bogotá was founded, to 1560.[24] The production of gold alone has been reckoned by modern estimates at some 4,115,295 ounces up to the end of the sixteenth century.[25] In succeeding years the yield was very much greater and we shall refer to it later.

The production of Chile in the sixteenth century does not compare in quantity with that of other regions, but mining had its place, and we shall later examine its importance in relation to other economic factors in Chile.

Gold and Silver: Total Production

Estimates of total mineral production of precious metals in America up to 1600 vary. The really important factor, however, is the progression of production. The first period, from 1492 to 1500, produced only a small amount of gold and silver from the West Indies. The second period, down to 1545, embraces the Conquest of Mexico, Central America, and a large part of South America, but no single large mine had been discovered prior to 1545. After 1545, with the discoveries of Potosí in Bolivia, and of Zacatecas, Guanajuato and San Luis Potosí in Mexico, the annual production rose rapidly. [26]

The weight of the precious metals is a more accurate indication of quantities than amounts stated in money values, since currency values have varied frequently in all countries ever since man has used money for exchange. The weight of gold sent to Spain in the last half of the sixteenth century was approximately double that of the first half, and the silver imports in weight were some twenty-seven times as great in the second half of the century as in the first half (Table V).

---

[24] Soetbeer estimates gold and silver for the same period at 18,990,000 *pesos,* and Restrepo, at 12,600,000. Harding, "American Gold and Silver," p. 464.

[25] H. F. Bain and Thomas T. Read, *Ores and Industry in South America* (New York: Harper and Brothers 1934), p. 49.

[26] Humboldt, *New Spain,* III, 433-34 [*Nouvelle Espagne,* IV, 259]. Soetbeer's statistics also illustrate the progression:

Gold and Silver production of America

Period	Annual Average in Pesos
1493-1500	485,000
1521-1544	2,966,000
1545-1560	12,945,000
1561-1580	12,003,000
1581-1600	17,284,000

Grand total for 100 years: 865,000,000 pesos fuertes.

These figures are higher than Humboldt's and both are probably too high. Haring, "American Gold and Silver," p. 458.

TABLE V

Total Decennial Imports Into Spain of Fine Gold and Silver— in Grams

Period	Silver	Gold
1503-1510	....	4,965,180
1511-1520	....	9,153,120
1521-1530	148,739	4,889,050
1531-1540	86,193,876	14,466,360
1541-1550	177,573,164	24,957,130
1551-1560	303,121,174	42,620,080
1561-1570	942,858,792	11,530,940
1571-1580	1,118,591,954	9,429,140
1581-1590	2,103,027,689	12,101,650
1591-1600	2,707,626,528	19,451,420 [27]

OTHER METALS: COPPER

So far our discussion of mining has been concerned with precious metals, since the mining of other metals in the colonies was far overshadowed by gold and silver. This does not mean that the Spaniards took no interest in the industrial metals. If they apparently neglected the copper mines known to the Indians, it was not for preoccupation with gold and silver, but for more prosaic economic reasons.

The Indians of Mexico and the Andes, and possibly of other parts of America, knew and worked copper. Tin and the working of bronze were also known.[28] They did not use iron, and their copper and bronze implements were still supplementary to stone. Copper and bronze for most purposes are inferior to iron as tool metals, and with the introduction of iron by the Spaniards, the less useful metals gradually lost ground to the better. Only in the modern electrical age have copper and tin assumed great importance again.

Copper continued to be mined after the Conquest in Chile, Cuba, Haiti and Venezuela; and in Mexico copper and possibly tin were worked.[29] Little of the copper was shipped to Spain. The American metal was more difficult to smelt, and could not compete in price with European copper because of the long haul to Europe. Hungarian copper could be sold in Spain at four pesos less per hun-

---

[27] Hamilton, *American Treasure*, p. 42.

[28] Haring, *Trade and Navigation*, p. 155; Humboldt, *New Spain*, III, 112-18 [*Nouvelle Espagne*, III, 298-308].

[29] Riva Palacio, *México*, II, 487.

dredweight than Chilean copper. In these circumstances, there is small wonder that America did not send copper abroad.

For the making of bells, cannon, and many other copper and brass objects, the mining of copper, zinc, and lead was carried on. The quantities are not easily estimated, and their effect on the life of the community cannot be determined exactly, but we may certainly conclude that America would have done without most of the things manufactured from these metals if imports from Europe had been necessary. Chile is estimated to have produced some 83,000 tons of copper during the colonial period, certainly not a very large quantity when measured by the enormous tonnages used today. But if we keep in mind that the industrial age had not arrived, the amount becomes more important.[30]

* * * * * * * *

The rapid expansion of Spanish mining in America contributed much to the growth of colonial economy. In comparison with the gold and silver the Spaniards took from the mines of Mexico and the Andes, the treasure found in the hands of the Indians by the conquerors, fabulous as they thought it, was small, and represented the hoard of years rather than extensive Indian mining. The Spaniards' search for the mines from which it came was encouraged and regulated by the Crown.

The great period of productivity began with the discovery of the Potosí silver mines in Bolivia in 1545, and the Zacatecas and Guanajuato mines in Mexico, and was stimulated by improved processes for extracting the metal from the ore. The quantities of precious metals sent to Spain increased steadily throughout the sixteenth century and later. While silver and gold dominated Spanish mining, copper, which the Indians had used for tools continued to be mined. As its export to Spain was not economically profitable, copper was used chiefly in American manufactures, for which only limited amounts were required.

The prosperity of the mines gave impetus to both commerce and agriculture and opened new territories for development. Population was attracted to the mining towns, which became thriving trade centers, while around them the soil was profitably cultivated and herds of cattle grazed on what had previously been wastelands. The wealth of the Spanish colonies was as much to be found in the agriculture and trade furthered by mining as in the gold and silver taken from the mines.

[30] Bain and Read, *Ores and Industry*, pp. 210-11.

7

Manufacturing and Domestic Trade

INDIAN HANDCRAFT

MANUFACTURING IN COLONIAL AMERICA was in the handcraft stage, necessarily so since the age of power-driven machinery was some centuries away. It was built on the handcraft cultures of Indian America plus the imported European crafts.

Indian America offered a wide variety in craft development. Columbus found some of the Indians of the Islands without knowledge of arms, while the Caribs apparently had an efficient type of weapon. Although the tropical climate did not make a great deal of clothing necessary, cotton was known and manufactured.[1] Caribbean houses were constructed of "thick reeds interlaced." Iron and steel are mentioned as metals of which they were "destitute." Altogether, the Indians of the Caribbean seemed to the men of Columbus and other early settlers to have only a rudimentary and primitive development in arts and crafts.[2]

HANDCRAFT IN MEXICO

When the Spaniards reached the mainland they were much more impressed by the crafts of the Aztecs and Mayas than they had been by those of the Caribbean Indians. Even here, to Spanish eyes, the objects used by masses were comparatively few and simply made. Among the Mayas the beds were woven straw mats and the chairs low stools. Clothing for men was confined to a breechclout of cotton for the common people, with the addition of sandals of leather or agave fiber, and a cotton throw over the shoulders for the rich. Women wore more ample clothing than men. Jewelry

---

[1] *Journal,* Dec. 26.
[2] Thacher, *Columbus,* I, 249-50; I. A. Wright, *The Early History of Cuba 1492-1586* (New York: The Macmillan Company, 1916), pp. 8-14.

was made of gold, silver, or semiprecious stones, and likewise, for the wealthy, beautiful articles made of feathers where available. Dishes and cooking vessels were pottery, with wooden and gourd auxiliaries. Many of the weapons, knives, and other such objects were chipped or polished stone, but the metal work in gold, silver, and copper was judged good by the Spaniards. One of the chief deficiencies for the development of manufacturing was the absence of the wheel. None of the Indians had any knowledge of the wheel for making pottery or other purposes.

The Aztecs on the whole had about the same handcrafts as the Mayas. [3] Cotton was manufactured and, except that the higher altitudes required more clothing, dress was much the same. Their pottery was, like the Maya pottery, beautifully colored but not extremely durable. The Spaniards were impressed by the contrast between the Indians of the Caribbean and the Aztecs, however, and wrote glowing reports of their crafts, such as the account Bernal Díaz gives of the crafts as he saw them practiced in Tenochtitlán:

"Let us go on to speak of the skilled workmen he (Montezuma) employed in every craft that was practiced among them. We will begin with the lapidaries and workers in gold and silver and all the hollow work, which even the great goldsmiths in Spain were forced to admire, and of these there were a great number of the best in a town named Atzcapotzalco, a league from Mexico. Then for working precious stones and *chalchihuites*, which are like emeralds, there were other great artists . . . great craftsmen in feather work, and painters and sculptors who were most refined . . . . The Indian women who did the weaving made an immense quantity of fine fabrics with wonderful feather work designs. . . ."

He also speaks of the "stonecutters, masons, and carpenters," and says that "as a consequence of so many crafts being practiced among them, a large number of skilled Indians were employed." [4] Paper was made from the agave plant, while skins of animals, and cotton cloth were also used for manuscripts. Sugar was manufactured from the juice of the corn stalk.

HANDCRAFT IN THE ANDES

In South America, particularly in the Andes, the development of industry had the same advantages of skilled labor enjoyed in Mexico. The Inca realm boasted expert workmen in pottery,

---

[3] Clavigero, *México,* Dissertation VI.
[4] Bernal Díaz, *Conquest of New Spain,* II, 67-69.

building, stone-cutting, metal and other crafts. Iron was not worked, as it was not in any part of America, but copper, tin, gold and silver were; and a variety of woodwork was done. The Andean Indians were expert weavers, and the dyes used in their cloth were excellent. Both men and women wove; which sex did the weaving depended on the quality of the cloth, and the region. Cotton and wool (from llamas) were both worked, the first mainly along the coast and the second principally in the mountains. Manufacture of household articles was universal, consisting of pottery dishes and cooking vessels, clay or stone stoves, wooden spoons, and gourds, along with other small articles. Wool and cotton were distributed to the households for manufacture, but clothing, shoes, and other things for the soldiers and nobility were made in special places by workmen (or women) dedicated to the task. [5]

In general, the masses of the Indians were self-sufficient in supplying their ordinary domestic needs:

"Another excellence, characteristic of the Indians of Peru, is the instruction of everyone from boyhood onward in all of the trades which a man needs for livelihood. Since among them there were no specialized tradesmen, as among us there are tailors, shoemakers and weavers, they learned to make everything necessary for themselves and their houses, and each provided for himself. All of them knew how to weave and make their clothes, and thus, when the Inca gave them wool he considered them dressed. All of them knew how to work and cultivate the land, without hiring other workmen. They all made their own houses, and the women were the ones who knew most about everything, serving their husbands with much solicitude, without being reared in luxury. Other trades, which are not necessary for the common and ordinary things of life, had their own special workmen, such as silversmiths, painters, potters, boatmen, auditors, and musicians; and in the trades of weaving, stone-cutting, or building, there were masters for fine work who were employed by the Lords. But the common people, as has been said, attended each one to what had to be done in his own house, without one paying another for this, and today the same thing is true, so that no one needs the service of another for his own house and self in the matter of shoes, clothing, building, sowing, and harvesting, and the making of the tools and instruments necessary for these things." [6]

---

[5] Means, *Ancient Civilizations*, pp. 311-12; Prescott, *Peru*, Bk. I, chaps. II, V.
[6] Acosta, *Historia de las Indias*, Bk. VI, chap. XVI.

INTRODUCTION OF EUROPEAN HANDCRAFT

These arts continued to be practiced after the Conquest, and in all probability far more things were manufactured in America than were imported. During the colonial period, most of the articles used were made in America, old crafts being retained and new ones adopted from the Europeans. Imports were restricted from the outset by the high prices of European-made products, and prices constantly rose, largely due to the precious metals coming from America. Las Casas speaks of "forty millions of revenue" and says that "more could be done with it than in these times with much more than a hundred millions." This is an indication that in fifty years prices had increased considerably. [7] Columbus was delayed in starting his third voyage because the merchants and farmers of Spain desired to profit from the American trade, and so raised their prices. [8] In consequence the Crown ordered all merchants and others to sell to Columbus at regular prices, and decreed a fine of ten thousand maravedís for every violation. [9] Legislation was powerless, however, and it has been stated that there is no example in the leading countries of Western Europe in the nineteenth and twentieth centuries of a price rise comparable to that in Spain during the first century of the Price Revolution. [10]

This was merely one of the conditions that stimulated early manufacturing in America of the articles for daily and practical use. America of the colonial period was forced to manufacture or do without most of the necessities of life. This seems to have been foreseen and provided for from the first. The Crown sent salaried skilled workmen with Columbus, and although the paying of their salaries was soon dropped, encouragement and aid continued to be given to skilled immigrants.

The policy of the Spanish government was to favor colonial manufactures, a policy based partly on the knowledge that the mother country could not supply her possessions with all they needed, and partly on the economic theory that exports from Spain were responsible for high prices, generally regarded as a great economic evil. In 1548, the Cortes of Valladolid petitioned the Crown to restrict certain exports to America, and added that it was for the best interest of Spanish consumers that the American colonies manufacture for themselves. In 1549, the government forbade

---

[7] Thacher, *Columbus*, I, 670; the best authority on the rise of prices is Hamilton, *American Treasure*, pp. 186-210, and *passim*.
[8] Thacher, *Columbus*, II, 548-49.
[9] Thacher, *Columbus*, II, 543.
[10] Hamilton, *American Treasure*, p. 210.

the manufacture of some types of finer cloths in Spain. Such policies naturally stimulated American manufactures in this period. [11]

In the matter of supplying its own requirements, America was not badly equipped. Of the basic needs of all people, food, shelter, and clothing, America furnished itself with all but a few luxuries in food, all its own shelter, and the bulk of its clothing. The exceptions fell mainly in the luxury class, and were within the purchasing power of only a few.

COLONIAL MANUFACTURING: NEW SPAIN

In New Spain where the crafts were already highly developed before the Conquest, the Indians soon learned the European skills. "Most of the Indian natives of these lands have successfully learned all the trades that there are among us in Castille, and have their shops of the trades, and artisans, and gain a living by it. . . . Not to waste more words, they carry on all trades very perfectly and even know how to weave tapestry cloths." [12]

Textiles were widely manufactured in Mexico and other parts of America soon after the Conquest. The silk industry began early. Although the instructions given in 1501 to Ovando, who was going out as governor of Española, envisaged the transplanting of silk-raising to America, and projects were presented by Las Casas and Lucas Vázquez de Ayllón for producing silk in the Caribbean and the southeastern part of the United States, there is no record of successful silk raising until Mexico was discovered.

Even here it is not clear who introduced silk worms and when. Hernando Cortés laid claims to having begun their culture as early as 1523 or 1524, and it is a matter of record that he had prosperous silk-growing activities on his estates at the time of his death in 1547. But Diego Delgadillo and others also claimed priority in the introduction of silk culture. [13] Among these was Marín Cortés, who alleged: "I was the first to grow mulberry trees in this land, and I have grown and prepared silk, and I have found dyes of bright red cochineal (carmesí) and other suitable and useful colors for silk." [14]

Bishop Zumarraga encouraged silk-raising, as did Viceroy An-

---

[11] Haring, *Trade and Navigation*, pp. 126-34.

[12] Bernal Díaz, *Conquest of New Spain*, V, 267-70; Prescott, *Mexico*, Bk. I. chap. V.

[13] For a history of silk culture in New Spain, see Woodrow Borah, *Silk-raising in Colonial Mexico (Ibero-Americana:* 20, Berkeley: University of California Press, 1943), pp. 1-14.

[14] Cited in Pereyra, *Obra*, p. 186. Pereyra gives the name as Martín Cortés and says he was neither of the sons of Cortés. Haring, *Trade and Navigation*, p. 126, calls him the son of Cortés. Borah, *Silk-raising in Colonial Mexico*, p. 10, shows that the name was Marín and that he was not a relative of Cortés.

tonio de Mendoza, although there is evidence that by about 1530 or 1531, before Mendoza arrived, silk culture was at least in the stage of experimentation. During the decade 1530-1540, it began to take on the proportions of a "wild-cat boom." [15] The industry grew so rapidly, in fact, that Mendoza and some of his successors were constrained to put a check on it lest it lead to abuse of the Indian laborers, and shift workers from other useful occupations. In the period between 1540 and 1555, it spread rapidly to many of the regions both north and south of Mexico City, and experiments were made in dozens of places. Contemporary evidence shows that it was a prosperous business in this epoch.

Father Motolinía wrote in 1541: "Although it is not very long since this industry (granjería) was begun in New Spain, it is said that more than fifteen thousand pounds of silk will be gathered this year, and it is of such an excellent quality that the master silk workmen who handle it say that the tonotzi is better than the joyante de Granada; and the joyante of New Spain is a silk of consummately fine quality. . . ." He adds, "It should be noted that silk is produced throughout every season of the year, not excepting a single month," because of the "great mildness" of the climate of Mexico. [16] Motolinía predicted that within a few years "more silk would be produced in New Spain than in all Christendom."

The industry was so flourishing that the silk makers organized and formed the syndicate of the Arte Mayor de Seda. Mexico in 1543 already had more than forty manufactories of velvets, and had issued regulations to guarantee the quality of the cloth. The city of Puebla received authorization to manufacture silks in 1548, without restrictions of any kind. For a generation after 1555, the silk raising of New Spain supplied the yarns for the growing silk guilds established in Mexico City and Puebla. Many artisans had been brought from Spain to weave the silk, and by 1572 the silks of New Spain were considered, except for the dyes, as good as those of Spain. [17] An indication of the industry's importance is a work by Gonzalo de Las Casas on the Arte para criar seda en la Nueva España, which was published in Granada in 1581, and reprinted in 1620.

In its epoch of prosperity, silk seems to have been a large-scale enterprise. Whereas in Spain silk raising was in the hands of small

---

[15] Borah, Silk-raising in Colonial Mexico, p. 14.

[16] Motolinía, Historia de los Indios de Nueva España, Espístola Proemial, in García Icazbalceta, C. D. México, I, 8-9. This work contains an excellent treatise on Motolinía and early Spanish Mexico by José Ramírez, cf. Vol. I, pp. XLV-CLIII.

[17] Borah, Silk-raising in Colonial Mexico, pp. 32-52.

farmers, in New Spain the growers were large operators who used the Indian workers (through one system or another) to gain their profits. The manufacturing was similarly limited to a few, the guilds not being open to Negroes or Indians, and their privileges being closely protected.

After its boom period from the fifteen-thirties, and its period of stabilization from about 1555 to 1580, the silk-raising industry entered a decline from which it never recovered. This has been attributed to many causes. The most logical seem to be: trade with the Philippine Islands after 1564-65 (and especially after 1579), which introduced cheaper silks from China; abuses of the Indians, which caused them to abandon silk-raising; lack of an adequate supply of the right type of labor; and restrictions placed for the benefit of the Spanish merchants (especially after 1597). Where some 20,000 pounds of raw silk, or more, had been produced in one year before the decline began, the crop of 1605 was down to 1500 pounds. [18]

The decline of silk-raising did not mean, however, an immediate falling off in manufactures. In fact, the cheaper silk from the Orient went into the looms of New Spain in competition with the native crop, and stimulated silk-weaving. By 1592, the major source of raw silk was from the Orient. [19] With the Oriental yarns, the New-Spanish manufacturers fabricated various types of cloth which found a ready market. More than 14,000 workers were employed in the factories of Mexico City, Puebla, and Oaxaca before the end of the sixteenth century. But weaving also suffered when restrictions were placed on the Mexico-Peru trade toward the century's close, and when, during the seventeenth century, contraband and other competitive factors intervened. [20] Also, among the silks from the East, were many types of finished products which competed with New-Spanish manufactures. Some silk was still raised during the seventeenth and eighteenth centuries, but it was not of great importance. Efforts were made to revive silk culture during the late eighteenth century, especially by Viceroy Revilla Gigedo, II, but without appreciable success.

New Spain had ample quantities of wool, and produced enough woolen cloth to supply her own needs and export to Peru. The hats made were cheaper and better than those of Spain and were likewise exported to Peru, according to the reports of Henry Hawks, an Englishman who lived in New Spain for five years. Mexico also

[18] Borah, *Silk-raising in Colonial Mexico,* pp. 85-101.
[19] *Ibid.,* p. 85.   [20] *Ibid.,* pp. 89-90.

developed furniture making, iron foundries, goldsmithing, saddlery, cabinet working, and porcelain, glass, and tile manufacturing at Puebla and other places.

COLONIAL HANDCRAFT: SOUTH AMERICA

In the Andes and other parts of South America, the colonial manufactures, based on both Indian and Spanish techniques, supplied the bulk of the needs of the people. Textiles were among the most important. After the Conquest, wool from sheep and goats displaced that of the llamas to a certain extent, but home manufactures continued to supply the masses.

North Peru manufactured lampwicks and matches for firelocks, and ship-rigging. As early as 1544, an *obraje,* or manufactory of cotton and woolen textiles, was established in Peru, and many others followed. Cotton was woven in New Granada from 1547 onward. In general, the quality of the textiles was inferior to those imported. "Whether because the wool is less fine, or because the *obrajes* do not work it well, clothing brought from Spain had a great advantage over that made in the Indies." [21] Lima manufactured cannon by the end of the sixteenth century.

Ecuador developed an industry for tanning hides and making leather goods, while *obrajes* turned out flannels, coarse frieze, blankets, and sackcloth for export as well as for domestic use. Cotton cloth was also woven. At La Tacunga and Ambato there were manufactories of ship-rigging for the vessels that made port in Ecuador and for the ships that were built in Guayaquil. [22]

In Chile, furniture making was developed, and at Arequipa in Peru the founding of bells became an important industry. All types of food were processed throughout America. Wheat flour, butter, lard, cheese, dried fruits, cigars, snuff, tobacco, and preserved fruits were commercial products. Gunpowder and soap were made universally. Leather was tanned and made into saddles, shoes, trunks, and cases, as well as numerous other articles. Pottery, baskets, and many types of woodwork flourished, and imported techniques were blended with native ones.

THE RISE OF SHIPBUILDING

Shipbuilding sprang up as one of the important industries almost with the first voyages. Columbus pointed out on his first expedition that he saw pines "so large and wonderful that he could not exaggerate their height and straightness, like spindles, both thick

---

[21] Acosta quoted by Hussey, in Wilgus, *Colonial Hispanic America,* p. 323.
[22] Pereyra, *América española,* VI, 192.

ones and slender ones." From these he expected that "ships could
be made and a great quantity of timber and masts for the largest
vessels of Spain." [23]

Balboa and others after him constructed vessels on the Pacific
coast. By 1533 more than thirty vessels were in service, all built
on the Pacific side, and one reached three hundred tons. The Bishop
of Nicaragua reported in 1545 that "ships are constantly under
construction," and other reports throughout the century indicate
that shipbuilding was an important industry. Havana was the center of the industry in the Caribbean but vessels were also built in
Mexico, Santo Domingo, Puerto Rico, Jamaica, Venezuela, and
Ecuador. [24]

TRADE BEFORE COLUMBUS: THE CARIBBEAN

Trade in pre-Conquest America, as everywhere in every period,
depended on the availability of articles for commerce, the need and
demand for them, and the roads and waterways between the centers of supply and demand. How much trade America enjoyed before the Conquest, especially in terms of trade statistics, cannot be
ascertained. The best we can do is indicate a few of the articles,
routes, and methods of Indian trade.

Columbus met a merchant in the Caribbean traveling in a long
log boat about eight feet broad and propelled by twenty-five
rowers. The boat carried an awning under which the merchant
and his merchandise were placed. This is usually cited to indicate
the existence of commerce among the Indians, but it also demonstrates that whatever seagoing commerce the Caribbean bore was
confined to log canoes. The experience of Columbus on the island
of Jamaica, where he was forced to spend several months because
he could not get transportation, and the descriptions of the suffering
of the men (Indians and Spaniards) who finally got to Española in
an Indian canoe, reinforces the evidence that the Indians had no
craft capable of carrying on widespread commerce, however useful
their boats were in coastwise travel and plying between the islands.

Bernal Díaz mentions, however, that in exploring the coast near
the region of Tabasco in Mexico, they saw houses and "thought
there must be a town close by, and as it was such a safe port we
considered that it would be a good place for a settlement, but we
found out that it was altogether uninhabited, and that the oratories
were merely those belonging to traders and hunters who put into

---

[23] *Journal*, Nov. 25.
[24] Haring, *Trade and Navigation*, pp. 266-68.

the port when passing in their canoes." [25] This would seem to indicate a regular, even if limited, commerce.

MEXICO

In the interior of Mexico, however, the activity of the markets
and the variety of wares aroused the admiration of the conquerors.
The account of Bernal Díaz is unrestrained in its enthusiasm.

"When we arrived at the great market place, called Tlaltelolco,
we were astounded at the number of people and the quantity of
merchandise that it contained, . . . gold, silver, and precious
stones, feathers, mantles, and embroidered goods . . . Indian
slaves both men and women. . . . Next there were other traders
who sold great pieces of cloth and cotton, and articles of twisted
thread, and there *cacahuateros* who sold cacao. In this way one
could see every sort of merchandise that is to be found in the
whole of New Spain, placed in arrangement in the same manner
as they do in my own country, . . . where each line of booths
has its particular kind of merchandise. . . . There were those
who sold cloths of henequin and ropes, and the *cotaras* (sandals)
with which they are shod, which are made from the same plant,
and sweet cooked roots, and other tubers. . . . In another part
there were skins of tigers and lions, of otters and jackals, deer
and other animals, and badgers and mountain cats . . . beans
and sage and other vegetables and herbs . . . fowls, cocks with
wattles, rabbits, hares, deer, mallards, young dogs . . . fruit-
erers and the women who sold cooked food, dough and tripe in
their own part of the market; then every sort of pottery . . .
honey and honey paste and other dainties like nut paste, and
those who sold lumber, boards, cradles, beams, blocks, and
benches, each article by itself, . . . they also sold many canoes
full of human excrement, and these were kept in the creeks near
the markets, and this they use to make salt for tanning skins. . . .
Paper . . . and reeds scented with liquid amber, and full of
tobacco, and yellow ointments . . . and much cochineal is sold
under the arcades which are in that great market place. . . .
There are also buildings where three magistrates sit in judgment,
and there are executive officers like *Alguacils* who inspect the
merchandise. I am forgetting those who sell salt, and those who
make the stone knives . . . and the fisherwomen, and others who
sell some small cakes made from a sort of ooze which they get
out of the great lake, which curdles, and from this they make

[25] Bernal Díaz, *Conquest of New Spain,* I, 45.

bread having a flavor something like cheese. There are for sale
axes of brass and copper and tin, and gourds, and gaily painted
jars made of wood. . . . There were many more merchants,
who, as I was told, brought gold for sale in grains, just as it is
taken from the mines. The gold is placed in thin quills of the
geese of the country, white quills, so that the gold can be seen
through, and according to the length and thickness of the quills
they arrange their accounts with one another, how much so many
mantles or so many gourds full of cacao were worth, or how
many slaves, or whatever other thing they were exchanging." [26]

"After having examined and considered all that we had seen
we turned to look at the great market place and the crowds of
people that were in it, some buying and others selling, so that the
murmur and hum of their voices and words that they used could
be heard more than a league off." [27]

In a letter written to the Emperor in October 1520, Cortés said
that the market place was "twice as large as that of Salamanca." [28]

As the expeditions of Cortés moved fanwise out from Mexico
City they encountered other signs of trade, but also found conditions which hampered its activity. The Indians of Chiapas "had
many warriors stationed at bad passes to rob the Indian merchants
who traded between one province and the other, and because of the
fear of them trade between one province and another was sometimes
stopped." [29]

Trade among the Aztecs and their confederates was an integral
part of the imperial system. Economic, governmental and military
functions were highly unified. The merchants had formed a guild
having its headquarters in Tlaltelolco (one of the components of
Mexico City) and vested with the exclusive privilege of carrying
on trade outside the central valley, and of furnishing foreign goods
to the inhabitants of the valley. The merchandising profession was
divided into three classes: the resident merchants of the valley;
the itinerant merchant who ventured into the neighboring and enemy
countries; and the slave traders. The guild had its own law courts,
its own religious organization and temple. The guild also had its
own army and with the authority of the chief of the confederation
(Montezuma), made war on the neighboring peoples who resisted
the entrance of its traders. The Aztecs had ennobled the mer-

[26] Bernal Díaz, *Conquest of New Spain*, II, 70-73.
[27] Bernal Díaz, *Conquest of New Spain*, II, 75.
[28] Second letter in Morris, *Hernando Cortés, Five Letters*.
[29] Bernal Díaz, *Conquest of New Spain*, IV, 293.

chandising profession and many of the members of the guilds were also members of the landed nobility.

Itinerant merchants carried on their trade by forming into groups—it is said there were sometimes five hundred or a thousand to a group—and moving on the prospective trade area with trains of goods carried by the servitors and slaves. They went in a body until they reached the frontier, where they divided into small units, disguised themselves, prepared their weapons for immediate battle, and ventured into the foreign territory. Those who survived this clandestine trade reunited again at the frontier to make the return journey. They also acted as spies and were the vanguard of Aztec conquest, reporting on the riches and resources of the areas into which they went. [30] Trade carried on under such handicaps, however, must have been on a small scale.

TRADE IN INDIAN SLAVES

Slave trading was an important part of the life of pre-Conquest America. War furnished the bulk of the slaves, but after capture they became one of the chief articles of trade. The Chiapanecs, for example, "had even brought other pueblos by force and made them settle and remain near to Chiapas, and held them as slaves and made them cultivate their fields." [31] This was enslavement of whole villages, not merely of a few of its people. "The Indians and Caciques commonly held a number of Indian men and women as slaves, and sold them and traded with them as one trades with any merchandise, and Indian merchants went from place to place and from market to market, selling them and bartering them for gold and cloths and cacao, and brought batches of fifteen to twenty or more for sale, tied together with collars and ropes [in a] much worse [way] than the Portuguese bring the Negroes from Guinea." [32]

This trade passed easily into Spanish hands after the Conquest. The Spaniards sent representatives to Spain to explain the situation to the Emperor, and these "took certain Mexican Indians as witnesses" to assist them in petitioning the Emperor "to do us the favor to grant us permission to pay them as tribute, and to buy them by barter in the same way that the Indians bought and sold them, and His Majesty was pleased to grant it, and ordered honest and competent persons to be appointed to take charge of the iron with which the branding was done." [33]

[30] Barros Arana, *América*, I, 53-54.
[31] Bernal Díaz, *Conquest of New Spain*, IV, 293.
[32] Bernal Díaz, *Conquest of New Spain*, V, 306-07.
[33] Bernal Díaz, *Conquest of New Spain*, V, 307. This was about 1522.

Trade among the Indians immediately became freer after the Conquest. Not only was the stoppage of trade because of wars between tribes less frequent, but some of the Indians whose trade activities had been curbed by the Aztecs could now traffic with ease. One of the motives that impelled the Tlaxcalan Indians to support the Spaniards was that the conquerors liberated them from Montezuma's economic blockade. The same was true of other parts of Mexico and Central America where the trade routes were now traversed by merchants, without the necessity of disguise and with a great variety of European and American goods. The routes to the mines and the newly opened up farming districts were busy arteries trafficking in gold and silver and the goods they would buy.

Much trade was carried on by barter, and continued to be so in many parts of America long after the Conquest.

"It is not found that the Indians used gold, nor silver, nor metal for money, nor for pricing things, they used it for ornament, as has been said. . . . For trading and buying they had no money, they merely exchanged some things for others. . . . There were some things held in greater value which were current as a price medium in place of money, and down to the present time this custom endures among the Indians. For example in the provinces of Mexico they use cacao, which is a small bean, in place of money, and with it they buy what they want. In Peru, coca, which is a leaf that the Indians value highly, serves for the same purpose; . . . and in Santa Cruz de la Sierra cotton cloth . . . . After the Spaniards came, the Indians also used gold and silver for buying, and at first there was no money, except that prices were stated in so much weight of silver. . . ." [34]

TRADE IN THE ANDES

In the Andean region we find the same lack of a monetary economy, and instead, a barter system in which one object was exchanged for another. [35] Determining the amount of commerce carried on under this system is difficult. Moreover the various accounts of the Inca economy reveal elements seemingly hard to reconcile. If the Incaic system was entirely monopolistic, the trade rested exclusively in the hands of the imperial officers. If not entirely monopolistic, in what goods, how largely, and under what conditions did private enterprise exist? To what extent could the ordinary *puric* (peasant landholder) market his own corn, potatoes,

---

[34] Acosta, *Historia de las Indias*, Bk. IV, chap. III.
[35] See Means, *Ancient Civilizations*, pp. 287-88, for a discussion of the concept of value among the Incas.

cotton, pepper, and oca? If the family was a self-sufficing unit, where arose the need or opportunity for trade?

And yet the trade did exist. Markets seem to have been a part of every town, and some of them are described as very large. One possible conclusion is that since the masses raised sufficient food for their own households, trade in foodstuffs was confined to the delicacies used by the nobles. To accept this conclusion, however, we must be prepared to accept the corollary that most people ate only one or two of the standard foods, since maize was not produced in the higher altitudes and some of the other products were not grown in the coast valleys.

Coca and tobacco were two products that might have contributed heavily to commerce. But coca, an imperial monopoly, and tobacco were used for medicinal purposes only. Household furnishings might have been commercial commodities, but the ordinary houses were nothing but mud shacks almost devoid of furniture. Under such circumstances, the most plausible explanation for trade is that a household produced more than it needed for its own wants and for paying tribute, and this surplus was marketed in exchange for other products which it had not produced. [36]

Since descriptions of the fairs and markets of the Indians by chroniclers who saw them are too numerous to leave any doubt about their existence, it is evident that the individual households were not entirely self-sufficient, but depended, at least in part, on local markets where they bartered their surplus for needed produce. It cannot be determined with any assurance just how heavy the trade was, or who controlled it. Considering the small buying power of the masses, and the restriction on travel in the empire, we may well doubt that there was anything beyond a limited barter trade. [37]

INCA TRADE: THE ROAD SYSTEM

Commerce necessitates means of communication, and some estimate of the business activity of the Inca Empire may be derived from a study of the roads.

Few things created by man have ever excited such extravagant praise as the Inca roads. Humboldt, who saw them as they were around 1800, compared them with the roads of the Romans; and the early chroniclers who saw them at the time of the Conquest vie with each other in revealing their grandeur.

Cuzco was the hub from which roads ran out to all the provinces.

[36] Means, *Ancient Civilizations,* pp. 309-11, 313-14.
[37] Means, *Ancient Civilizations,* pp. 309-325, discusses Inca markets.

There were two main roads traversing the Empire from Quito in Ecuador to central Chile, one following the coastline and the other the mountains. Various lateral roads connected the two.

Cieza marveled at the ability of the Incas to build roads "more than eleven hundred leagues long" and "constructed across mountains so rough and frightful that in some places, looking down, one was blinded; and some of the mountains were so steep and rocky that it was necessary to dig into the living rock of the mountainsides to make the road wide and smooth." In other places there were "ascents so high and rough that steps were built from the bottom to the top" to make possible the climb from the valleys to the mountains. "Let those who may read this book and who may have been in Peru consider the road that runs from Lima to Xauxa through the cragged sierras of Huarochiri and the snow-covered mountains of Pariacaca, and those who hear them will judge whether what they saw is not even more remarkable than what I write; and besides this let them remember the cliff that drops down to the Apurimac river." [38]

Another chronicler tells of the "breaking and smoothing down the stones where necessary and filling up and leveling off the ravines with stone and mortar, so that sometimes the work was built up from a depth of fifteen or twenty heights of a man *(estados)* And they say that this road was so level when finished that a cart could travel over it." The same author describes the coast road as being "almost forty feet wide, with very thick mud walls" through the valleys which "usually measure a league" across, and explains that "after emerging from the valleys they continue the same road across the sand dunes, driving up palings and stakes in a straight row so that travelers might not lose the road nor wander this way and that." [39]

The impression gained from reading the accounts of those who traveled over the roads during the Conquest however, is that many of them were rough and the mountain passes extremely difficult. [40]

Bridges of aloe-fiber rope were built to span the chasms in the mountains, and ferries were used where necessary across the rivers on the coast. In some places a single rope was swung across a chasm and the passage was effected by means of a basket pulled across by

    [38] Cieza, *Señorío*, chap. XV.

    [39] Augustín de Zárate cited in Garcilaso, *Comentarios*, Bk. IX, chap. XIII.

    [40] See a brief but interesting work, probably the first published on Peru, *La conquista del Perú*, of anonymous authorship Sevilla, April, 1534, edited with excellent critical notes by Alexander Pogo *(Proceedings of the American Academy of Arts and Sciences*, LX [July, 1930]), No. 8.

smaller ropes. At least one pontoon bridge was known, that across the Desaguadero river flowing out of Lake Titicaca. [41]

Such roads would have of course made possible a large foot traffic, and their mere existence would indicate a considerable need for them.

But the road system was not without its defects for commerce, and here and there we get a hint of some of these. Humboldt thought that thousands of men would be needed for fifty years to build the road he describes, but Cieza de León pictures the ease with which roads were built, and says that the whole road from Cuzco to Quito, five hundred leagues (fifteen hundred miles) as he describes it, was built so that Huayna Capac, the father of Huáscar and Atahualpa might have a smooth road for his conquest of Quito, and the whole of the storage houses, palaces, and other structures were transferred and rebuilt in a short time. [42] This would imply that the road was not too substantially made, and the engineering feats not too difficult.

The chronicles are full of admiration for work done on the slopes and steps, but they also suggest why these roads were partly useless after the Conquest. In travel by foot it is possible for men to climb steps; horses and carriages cannot, especially carts loaded with merchandise. The suspension bridges were equally unfitted for horse and carriage traffic. The roads of the Incas, far from comparing with those of the Romans, were mere footpaths, and could serve as trade arteries only for the relatively small amount of merchandise men could carry on their backs. The very passages where Cieza shows the most admiration for the Sierra route reveal its main defect—the failure to solve the problem of bridging chasms and constructing graded, winding roads up mountain sides. [43]

The coast roads of the Incas, except in small stretches through the river valleys, were actually not roads at all. The valleys covered less than three per cent of the coastline. Outside of these there was no road, only posts set up to outline a trail and prevent the traveler from getting lost. For any commercial traffic save what could be borne by human porters, the road was useless, as the desert sands made carriage and wagon transport impossible. [44]

---

[41] Means, *Ancient Civilizations,* pp. 329-31.

[42] Cieza, *Señorío,* chaps. XV, LXIII.

[43] Cieza, *Señorío,* chap. LXIII.

[44] The view here presented of the Inca road system is not entirely in accord with other accounts. The reader will want to examine further evidence. See especially, Alberto Regal, *Los caminos del Inca* (Lima, 1936); and Emilio Romero, *Historia económica y financiera del Perú* (Lima, 1937), pp. 64-86.

TRADE: WATER ROUTES

Given the impracticability of land travel for extensive commerce, the sea route was the only link between the various parts of the western coast. Most roads were confined to the valleys, and ran directly down to the sea to connect with coastwise vessels. The seacraft of the Indians were rafts made of light woods, upon which were erected deck houses, and their capacity and maneuverability in the water were both limited. [45] These were replaced by Spanish ships capable of seagoing and coastwise trade, functions beyond the native craft. Communication and trade tended to depend on the sea and almost every river mouth became a port of more or less importance, sending and receiving the exports and imports to and from the interior. The old Indian communication system gradually fell into decay as the new medium of commerce improved. The outlook of the Pacific coast was shifted from inland to seaward.

Mexico, Central America, and the northern coast of South America were without good roads. Cortés found no broad highways, but on the contrary struggled over difficult ground. His account of his trip into Central America abounds in descriptions of the difficult terrain traversed without the aid of roads. [46] The Mayas had broad roads at one time, but with their decline in the fifteenth century Mexico and Central America were left without anything to excite the admiration of the conquerors. In this case, the Indians admired the work done by the Spaniards. During the Central American campaign Cortés built a bridge of "such huge and thick timbers, that after it was made the Indians of Acala marvelled to see the timbers so placed. It took four days in the making." [47]

LACK OF PACK ANIMALS BEFORE THE CONQUEST

Commerce in America before the Conquest was greatly affected by the absence of pack animals, most of America having none whatever. Only the Andes were endowed with the llama, a pack animal capable of carrying a light load. In other regions goods were carried by men who served as beasts of burden. Even where the llama existed men still acted as pack animals at times. Humboldt comments on the lack of animals in New Spain: "Undoubtedly the want of domestic animals was less felt before the Conquest, when every family cultivated but a small extent of ground, and when a great part of the inhabitants lived almost exclusively on vegetables.

---

[45] Means, *Fall*, p. 20; and *Ancient Civilizations*, pp. 341-42.
[46] Fifth letter in *Hernando Cortés, Five Letters.*
[47] Bernal Díaz, *Conquest of New Spain*, V, 21.

However the want of these animals compelled a numerous class of the inhabitants, the Tlamama [Tamemes], to labour as beasts of burden, and to pass their lives on the highways. They were loaded with large leathern chests (in Mexican, *petlacalli,* in Spanish, *petacas)* which contained goods to the weight of 30 or 40 kilogrammes." [48]

PACK ANIMALS AFTER CONQUEST

With the progress of Spanish settlement animals gradually took the place of men in most parts of America. The horse was the favorite animal for riding, of course, but mules, burros, and oxen were better for drawing carts. [49] The shift from man to animals in transport, however, was not immediate. In some parts the terrain was so rough that even after the Conquest merchandise was perforce carried on the backs of men. To transport from Buenaventura "to the city of Cali the merchandise that is unloaded in this port, from which the entire province is supplied, the only means is the use of the mountain Indians whose customary work is carrying [things] on their backs, since it is impossible to carry them any other way. Because, if it were wished to make roads for pack trains (*recuas*), it would be so difficult that I believe it would not be possible to conduct loaded animals, owing to the tremendous roughness of the sierras, and although there is another road via the Cauca river where cattle and horses enter, they run great danger and many of them are killed, and they arrive in such a condition that they are not worth anything for many days." [50]

Slowly animals supplanted men, but time was needed for developing a sufficient number of pack animals, for the Indians to learn to use them, and for law and custom to stop, or restrict, the use of men as beasts of burden. The abuse of Indian carriers continued throughout the sixteenth, and into the seventeenth century. [51] More will be found on this point in the later discussion of Indian labor.

COMMERCIAL EXPANSION AFTER THE CONQUEST

Transportation difficulties could not deter the merchants, however, and in the midst of the Conquest, Cieza reported: "There

[48] Humboldt, *New Spain,* III, 47 [*Nouvelle Espagne,* III, 223-224].
[49] Riva Palacio, *México,* II, 491-92.
[50] Cieza, *Crónica,* chap. XXIX.
[51] Lesley Byrd Simpson, *The Repartimiento System,* in *Studies in the Administration of the Indian in New Spain),* pp. 15-16, 67-81; Thomas Gage, *A New Survey of the West Indies,* (New York, 1929), pp. 233-34.

is never any lack of traveling Spaniards who go from place to place occupying themselves in merchandising and business." [52] Trade prospered to such an extent that as early as 1547 the president of the Audencia of Lima, La Gasca, was able to borrow 300,000 pesos from eighty merchants of the city. [53] America's internal commerce grew in spite of all the obstacles that nature placed in its way. In the Caribbean, the trade void that had existed before Columbus was quickly filled, and ocean-going ships took the place of dugout canoes. [54]

On the Pacific, owing to the difficulty of traversing the coastal desert with heavy cargo, of cutting a path through jungle forests, or of crossing the Andean mountains with their innumerable canyons, the commercial lanes formed up and down the coast and in lateral roads leading into the mountains. Even in the twentieth century, an engineering skill which no previous age has known is faced with almost insurmountable tasks when called upon to build road or railroad in the Andes. Hence the importance of the Pacific Ocean as a medium of transport for all of the countries of western South America.

In Mexico and Central America the problem of transport was different. Whereas the Andes form a backbone that extends along the west side of South America, leaving a vast continent of jungle to the eastward, the highlands of Mexico and Central America are in the center of the country. These contain the best lands, the most temperate climate, and, before and since the Conquest, the mass of the population. The mountain barriers leading into the interior valleys had to be surmounted before contact could be made with the fertile and wealth-producing regions.

The Indians had not solved this problem of transport, and Spanish post-Conquest commerce was also impeded by the lack of communications. But economic necessity found a partial solution in cart roads and pack-animal trails. Not that good roads were built. Roads, if we think in terms of the Roman pavements or our modern highways, were almost unknown anywhere in the world in the sixteenth century. But a comparison of pre- and post-Conquest communications makes it obvious that the imperfect transportation system of the colonial period came nearer to a solution of one of the fundamental economic and social problems of America.

Commerce in Mexico centered in the Central Valley and flowed

[52] Cieza, *Crónica*, chap. XXVII.
[53] Means, *Fall*, pp. 94-95.
[54] Wright, *Cuba*, pp. 66, 190-212.

eastward to the port of Vera Cruz, south to Acapulco, and fanwise to supply the various inland centers. From Mexico City north to Zacatecas, Guadalajara, Guanajuato, San Luis Potosí, and the province of Pánuco, trade passed constantly, protected from the attacks of the Chichimecas (the "uncivilized" Indians) by a series of military posts. Roads were rough and difficult, streams were forded, ferried, or crossed on rattan bridges. As the number of Spanish towns and garrisons increased, and the Indians were forced to accept peace, traffic became more secure; but colonial Mexico (like the United States in a certain epoch) was troubled from time to time with highwaymen who impeded commerce. The cities formed a mutual protective society (known as the Santa Hermandad and modeled after a similar Spanish organization), established a system of courts presided over by the *jueces de acordada,* and thereby secured safety for their merchandise.

Internal commerce was free from tax until 1574. After that date certain taxes were levied, and we can judge of the commerce of America from the extensive list of taxed articles.

Trade Regulations and Monopolies

Much of the commerce of New Spain and America was carried on under government supervision. But the regulatory system, long a part of the European economics, under which trade was controlled by the guild, was in the sixteenth century evolving on a national basis into mercantilism. Commerce was carried on either under the close supervision of the government or *by* the government through its agents. Spain did not originate this form of economy, but Spain had more to develop and protect than its neighbors of the sixteenth century and so employed it extensively.

Some products were government monopolies. Among these were mercury, important for mining; salt, prime need of man and beast, and a favorite source of tax revenue; pepper; corrosive sublimate; gunpowder; and playing cards. These monopolies were not forced on trade by an arbitrary government; the merchants and manufacturers solicited their establishment and vied for concessions. In Peru an attempt to monopolize wheat and flour was defeated only by Royal decree.

The fair or market, the customary medium for exchanging goods in Europe until the industrial age, was used in colonial Mexico and Peru. During the sixteenth century (as well as later), Spanish law recognized and regulated the market, fixing certain market days in each city, town, and village. Sometimes these were held every week and sometimes less often. The larger towns had daily markets. Custom in many cases had fixed the market day and the law merely recognized the day when the local people with surplus goods either of agricultural or industrial origin, gathered to exchange their produce with one another or with itinerant merchants who made regular rounds of the markets.

The economic life of the market was not limited to retail sales. Wholesale buyers resorted to local markets to buy wheat, maize, beans, barley, cattle, sheep, horses, hides, and many hand-made articles in demand in the cities. Textiles were to be found of all kinds, from the best to the cheapest, according to the buying capacity of the people. In the larger cities, the itinerant merchants gathered to supply themselves with goods to be traded in village markets. The markets of the capital cities and other important towns were similar in nature to the international fair so well known in Europe, and operated under royal license.

The medium of exchange in the larger markets was usually money, but as the size of the market decreased the percentage of barter increased. Many Indian standards of value were employed. Where the barter system continued after the Conquest many people went to the markets carrying products which they intended to exchange, or brought maize to use as currency, while the cacao bean served as a medium of exchange recognized in Spanish legislation.

INTERCOLONIAL TRADE

Intercolonial commerce between the islands of the Caribbean and Mexico and northern South America, between Mexico and Central America, and between Mexico and Colombia and Peru began early after the Conquest and gathered momentum during the sixteenth century. This was a type of trade that either had not existed before the Conquest or had existed on such a small scale as to be negligible. The colonies were not long, however, in building up an active commerce. Ships from Acapulco made the Pacific ports of Central America. The South American ports of Buenaventura, Guayaquil, Callao and others drew their reason for existence from the trade that plied along the coast. Other ships left Vera Cruz and carried cargoes to the ports of Central America, Colombia, and Venezuela.

Among the numerous articles of the intercolonial trade were piece goods, woolens, and silks, which the merchants of Mexico furnished Peru and for which they received in payment gold and silver coins. Some of the merchandise came from the East, but much of it from Oaxaca and Puebla where there was a flourishing manufacture of silks, velvet, damask, mantillas, turbans, taffetas, and other luxury objects for which there was a demand among the wealthy of Peru. Pitch, tar, and tobacco were other products. So great was the trade, that considerable portions of the money coined in Peru came into New Spain and the Peruvian pesos were nick-named *peruleros* by the Mexicans. Chile, Argentine, Uruguay, and Paraguay also participated in this intercolonial trade before the end of the sixteenth century. "Foreign" commerce, of course, had not existed before the Conquest, but its importance grew to be such that it must be treated extensively in the following chapters.

* * * * * * * *

On their arrival in America, the Spaniards had found native handcrafts ranging from the most primitive in the Caribbean to a great variety of skills among the Aztecs and Incas. The Conquest brought in European handcrafts, but the importations of European products was limited, and confined chiefly to luxuries. Colonial America continued to manufacture most of the articles in common use, retaining many of the native crafts and introducing European industries and techniques. Encouraged by the policy of the government in Spain, the manufactures of New Spain and Peru prospered in the sixteenth century, an outstanding example being the silk industry of Mexico. Shipbuilding was a leading colonial enterprise from the start.

Indian trade before the Conquest likewise varied from the trifling canoe-borne barter of the Islands to the thriving and well-ordered markets of the Aztecs which so astounded the conquerors. But Indian trade was regional for lack of communications (even the celebrated Inca roads could serve as commercial routes only for what merchandise men could carry), good ships, and beasts of burden. The Spaniards supplied domestic animals and sea-worthy vessels. Colonial commerce flourished increasingly—within the colonies, in local markets and overland by cart roads and pack trails, and between the colonies, by sea to growing ports.

International Trade

THE BEGINNING OF FOREIGN TRADE:

A MERICAN TRADE WITH EUROPE began with the first voyage of
Columbus; and it is evident from Columbus's Journal that
trade was one of his primary objectives. Gold, as the most valuable
commodity, was never forgotten, but other products were mentioned no less frequently and with no less enthusiasm. "If I find
where there is a quantity of gold or spices," Columbus remarked,
"it will detain me until I obtain as much as possible of them."
Soon after this, Columbus received reports of islands he believed
were the East Indies, especially of Cuba, which he heard was "very
large and would yield much trade, and that there were upon it
gold and spices and large vessels and merchants."

After reaching Cuba, he still received news from the Indians
that "large ships belonging to the Great Khan came there." Reports of mastic, a resin highly prized as a medicine, caused Columbus to send out scouts who brought in samples; and on November
5 he noted finding a good harbor where a fort could be built, and
that "the merchants would be secure there from any other nation
whatever." When he was on the point of departure for Spain on
January 15, 1493, he wrote that there was "a great deal of cotton
there, very fine and long, and there is a great deal of mastic and
gold and copper . . . and pepper . . . Fifty caravels can be loaded
with it each year on that island of Española." [1] Time was to prove
his estimates far too optimistic. Slaves and brazil wood were two of
the products that appealed to Columbus as offering chance for
trade.

"From here may be sent, in the name of the Holy Trinity,
all the slaves that can be sold, as well as brazil wood . . ."

". . . provided there is no lack of ships to come for them, of

---

[1] *Journal*, October 10, 22, 28 and January 15.

which, I believe, with the help of Our Lord, there will be no lack, once the merchants become interested in this voyage." [2]

On the second voyage Columbus suggested that the "flocks and other supplies and things to settle the country and make use of the land" could "be paid for in slaves from among these cannibals, a very proud and comely people, well proportioned and of good intelligence, who having been freed from that inhumanity . . . will be better than any other slaves." [3]

In June, 1497, he received permission to export to the Indies, free of duty, as much as ten thousand bushels of wheat and about nine hundred bushels of barley on as many voyages as he cared to make during the ensuing five months. [4]

Other events of Columbus's third voyage likewise demonstrate that a large trade was already beginning. When he reached Santo Domingo in 1502, he found a fleet of about twenty-eight to thirty-one vessels loaded with cargo and ready to sail for Spain. Of this fleet all but three or four were destroyed by a hurricane. [5]

Regular commerce, encouraged by the Spanish sovereigns, developed between the Caribbean islands and Spain; and the opening up of Mexico created a Mexico-Caribbean trade as well as a Mexico-Spain trade. While Cortés was still in the process of conquering Mexico, "a large ship . . . arrived from Spain and the Canary Islands, laden with a great variety of merchandise, muskets, powder, crossbows and crossbow cords, and three horses, and other arms," and Cortés bought "all the arms and powder and everything else that she carried." [6]

That produce of value, besides jewels and precious metals, was being sent back from America is indicated by the fact that the French pirate, Jean Florin, who in 1523 captured the ships Cortés had sent with the Aztec treasures, at about the same time "robbed another ship that came from the Island of Santo Domingo and took over twenty thousand pesos de oro and a great quantity of pearls and sugar and hides." [7] How many more vessels came in these early years is not known, but ships landed at the river Espíritu Santo, Pánuco, Medellín and San Juan de Ulúa, in Mexico.

Early commerce was concerned with the products most essential to life: wheat, flour, olive oil, wine, and other foods, clothing, live-

[2] Bartolomé de Las Casas, *Historia de las Indias* Bk. I, chap. CLI
[3] *De Torres Memorandum,* cited in Thacher, *Columbus,* II, 302.
[4] Thacher, *Columbus,* II, 546.
[5] Thacher, *Columbus,* II, 578-79.
[6] Bernal Díaz, *Conquest of New Spain,* II, 304.
[7] Bernal Díaz, *Conquest of New Spain,* IV, 224.

stock, and arms. Horses and other animals were usually bought by merchants from farmers in the Caribbean, who also did a good business in cassava (manioc) and other farm products. Prices were extremely high at first, horses selling for as much as 4,000 pesos, a cape for 100 pesos, and a quire of paper worth 3 *reales* in Spain, for 10 pesos in New Spain. With the rapid development of wheat farming and the building of flour mills, wheat and flour were not imported, but wine and olive oil continued to be important elements of import trade. By the end of the century, thirty or forty ships were required to supply the annual demand of New Spain. [8] Linen and silk from Spain, woolens, porcelain, brick, roof-tiles, ship-rigging, paper, iron kitchen utensils, tiles, vinegar, liquor and soap were among the imports.

These products were paid for with precious metals, sugar, and hides from Mexico, Central America, and the Caribbean; tobacco from Venezuela, Guiana, and other regions; *cacao* from Tabasco and Venezuela; and cochineal, *palo de tinto* (logwood used for dyes), and indigo from Tabasco, Yucatán, Campeche, Laguna de Términos, Jicalango, and Oaxaca.

TRADE FROM PANAMA SOUTH

Trade with the southern continent flowed in through Cartagena in Colombia, or Nombre de Dios in Panama until 1584, and afterwards through Portobelo in Panama. [9] Panama City on the Pacific was the receiving point for merchandise going to and from Peru. Cieza de León who saw Panama prior to 1532, before Peru had been opened, and again after 1545, when the mines of Potosí were in operation, describes Panama City about 1550:

"The greater part of this city is settled as I have already explained by numerous and very honorable merchants from everywhere; they carry on trade in it and in Nombre de Dios, the commerce being so great that it can almost be compared with Venice, because it frequently happens that ships from the South Sea come to this city to discharge, laden with gold and silver; and the number of ships arriving at Nombre de Dios from the Atlantic is very great, from which a great part of the merchandise comes in ships into this realm via the Chagres river, and from this river which is five leagues from Panama, the goods

---

[8] Letter of Viceroy Marqués de Montes Claros to the King, *D.I.I.*, VI, 298-314.

[9] Allyn C. Loosley, "The Puerto Bello Fairs," *H.A.H.R.*, XIII (August, 1933), 314-35, rendered Puerto Bello, or Puerto Belo, on various maps. Herrera writes "Portovelo," cf. *Hechos castellanos*, Decade I, Bk. V, chap. VII.

are brought by numerous and very large pack trains that the merchants maintain for this purpose." [10]

Transportation across the isthmus was always a problem because of jungles, mountains, and swamps; and once across, contrary winds and currents made the trip to Peru long and difficult. One of the principal routes used was the Chagres River, and at Venta de la Cruz (Venta de Cruces), the city of Panama was permitted to build a warehouse in 1536. Storage rooms, rented to the merchants in the time of Philip II for a half peso a day, yielded the Crown as much as 10,000 pesos a year. [11] Numerous efforts were made to improve the road. In 1535, the Crown granted permission to two merchants to export from Peru to Spain an unlimited amount of wool for ten years, in return for their aid in maintaining the isthmian route. From Panama, merchandise was taken by sea to Buenaventura, Guayaquil, and Callao. Lima was the administrative and economic center of South America, and goods went from there to the interior of Peru, Bolivia, Chile, and the Plata.

Peru and Chile received the same goods, on the whole, as Mexico; but the export position of the Pacific coast colonies was less fortunate. Peru's colonial exports were largely precious metals. Silver and gold were almost the only products of sufficient value for weight to export with profit. The long route up the Pacific coast and across the isthmus was too expensive to enable Peru to compete with Mexico and the Caribbean in wool, hides, sugar, and other such articles. But Peru's loss was Mexico's gain. Besides metals, Peru had a market for only a few articles over which she had a monopoly, such as the wool of the llama, vicuña and guanaco.

The progression of trade during the sixteenth century is revealed by the receipts of the *Casa de Contratación*. During the period to 1530, the receipts were about 20,000,000 maravedís per annum on the average. During the next thirty years, the average was approximately 220,000,000 maravedís per annum or about eleven times greater, and during the third thirty-year period terminating with 1590, the receipts climbed to an average approximately twenty-five times greater. [12] Thus, American trade "boomed" during the sixteenth century, despite the many obstacles, natural and man-made.

---

[10] Cieza, *Crónica*, chap. II.
[11] Haring, *Trade and Navigation*, pp. 180-83.
[12] Haring, *Trade and Navigation*, Appendix IV.

EARLY SPANISH TRADE POLICY: EUROPEAN CONCEPT OF TRADE
   CONTROL [13]

American trade development was affected during the colonial
period by several factors, the first of which was, naturally, economic
and political subordination to Europe. Although the laws passed
by European governments were seldom scrupulously observed, they
nevertheless do reflect American trade development. Second was
the rivalry of European nations for American trade, Spain and
Portugal attempting to maintain, and France, England, and Holland trying to weaken the monopoly; and third was a constant
struggle between Portugal and Spain over certain parts of America.
There were three fairly distinct periods in this trade development:
(1) the preliminary policy of Spain, (2) the encroachment of other
nations, and (3) the evolution of a system of control designed to
maintain the monopoly of Spain.

Spain's colonial policy was quickly improvised in the first years
after the Conquest. This was natural and inescapable. Nobody
knew, or could know, much about America. The desire to find the
East Indies, and the belief that they had been found, dominated the
ideas of the merchants and the Crown. The realization that this
was not so, followed by the rapid unfolding of new lands apparently
unlimited in extent, required Spain to modify her policy in a series
of hasty, and sometimes contradictory, decisions. Spain was forced
to decide, first, how to deal with her own nationals, and then to
adjust her treatment of foreign nations. Thus the colonial mercantile policy of Spain was not determined within a vacuum, but
in the violent crosscurrents of human, economic, and national
passions.

Spain followed the economic policies prevailing in Europe in the
fifteenth and sixteenth centuries. It was an age when strict trade
regulation was the rule not merely by nations, but by cities. Imports, exports, and currency movements were closely restricted.
Export of bullion was prohibited by Henry VII of England, for
example, and this had been the policy of most of Europe for centuries. Venice monopolized the Adriatic and the eastern Mediterranean; Genoa contested the western Mediterranean with Aragon and Catalonia; Milan posted her soldiers at important points
throughout north Italy to force foreign merchants to go to Milan
to trade, where they were compelled to remain until they had spent

their money for Milanese products; and the Merchant Adventurers of London controlled the North Sea and expanded into the Baltic to invade the trade area of the Hanseatic League.

Within all of these areas the ever more important merchant class was carefully protected by tariffs, bounties, subsidies, immigration and import restrictions, navigation acts, and concessions. If we say that there was no trade without a license, we have scarcely exaggerated the economic situation of Europe in 1492 when Spain was faced with formulating a trade policy for her new possessions. And the story is not complete until it is understood that restrictions were applied as strictly *within* the area which it was sought to monopolize, as they were against outsiders. No man could trade unless he belonged to the guild, or was a member of a company holding a definite concession, or was granted a license. Being an Englishman of itself conferred no right to trade within the regions controlled by the Merchant Adventurers; that privilege was reserved to the members. Being a Castilian of itself conferred no trade rights in the newly discovered America; that privilege was reserved to those citizens of Castile licensed by the Crown.

Columbus's concession, and his early communications with his sovereigns illustrate this point. In his contract, it was assumed that the Crown had the right to dispose of the trade rights of the yet undiscovered territory. He was thinking in terms of a Crown monopoly when he said, "their Highnesses can give license and permission to a sufficient number of caravels to come here each year." [14] In 1495, the Crown decreed that discovery and trade with the new lands was open to all on condition of securing a license from the royal authorities. This is usually taken as lessening the privileges of Columbus, but the quotation above indicates that it was his own suggestion. [15] Columbus himself obtained permits and licenses for almost every act of his connected with America. [16] After the decree of 1495, a number of voyages set out for America, the Crown reserving the right to one-tenth of the space and one-tenth of the profits. No import duties were charged on goods entering Spain from these voyages.

EARLY TRADE POLICY: IMMIGRATION AND TAXATION

As a part of the control policy emigration to the new lands was also licensed. Oviedo says that until the death of Isabella only "the subjects and vassals" of Castile and León could emigrate and trade,

---

[14] *De Torres Memorandum*, cited in Thacher, *Columbus*, II, 302.
[15] Navarrete, *Colección de viages*, Vol. II, Document LXXXII.
[16] See Thacher, *Columbus*. Vol. II, and the series of documents printed there.

except with a special license, and that Ferdinand extended this privilege "to Aragonese and all his own vassals" after her death in 1504, and Charles V to all of his subjects, which included Germans, Flemish, Italians, and others, "and they go now from all his realms and from all the regions, the vassals under his monarchy." [17] In the early years of Charles V's reign, this policy aroused revolt among the Spanish subjects, and in 1523 the Cortes of Valladolid asked him to forbid foreigners to trade with the Indies. But in 1526 Charles felt strong enough to issue a decree admitting all his subjects to equal privileges. Again in 1548, the Cortes petitioned for the exclusion of foreigners from trade. [18]

Families of emigrants were sent from the Canary Islands in 1520. In 1522, the German firm of Jacob Fugger secured for the German merchants the privilege of trade in the spice of the Moluccas by way of Magellan Strait. The German Welsers, of Augsburg, were given the same privileges as Spanish traders in 1525 and allowed to establish commercial houses in Sevilla and Santo Domingo. The Welsers formed an alliance with the Ehinger firm of Constance in 1528, and received the privilege of sending over fifty German miners, of supplying four thousand slaves within four years, and of establishing a colony in Venezuela. They likewise received space in the warehouse of the Casa de Contratación at Sevilla. Ambrosius Ehinger went to Venezuela as Governor in 1528. The Fuggers received other extensive grants a few years later, and sent their agents to many parts of America. German traders and merchants continued active in the islands, Mexico, and other parts of America for a number of years, but gradually withdrew. Their settlements in Venezuela apparently did not pay and were surrendered to the Crown, leaving no permanent traces in the New World.

Encouragement of emigration was the rule. Land grants were made, and in 1499 the Crown granted a twenty-year exemption from local taxation. In 1511 emigration was permitted upon the mere registration of the name and residence, and further tax exemption was offered, but the sons and grandsons of heretics and infidels could not receive repartimientos or hold public office. Those

---

[17] Oviedo, *Historia*, Bk. III, chap. VII. Various theories have been advanced as to what section of Spain furnished most emigrants, some contending that the Basque and other northern regions supplied most, and others holding that Andalucia did. A recent study has shown that for the period from 1492 to 1592, the northern zone of Spain sent approximately 38.4 per cent, the southern 44 per cent, the intermediate zone 6.4 per cent, and the lateral zones (northwest and east) 11 per cent. Thus, Latin America was settled from every region of Spain. See, V. Aubrey Neasham, "Spain's Emigrants to the New World, 1492-1592," *H.A.H.R.*, XIX (May, 1939), 147-60.

[18] Colmeiro, *Economía política*, II, 397-99.

who accompanied Pedrarias Dávila to Panama in 1514 were allowed many privileges and exemptions. The citizens of Española urged the Crown to permit the immigration of French, Genoese, and other foreigners. In 1518, free transportation and maintenance were offered from the date of arrival in Sevilla to disembarkation in Española or Tierra Firme; and in addition to a grant of land, the settler was to receive implements, domestic animals, plants and seeds, and supplies for one year. Twenty-year exemption was granted from the *alcabala* (sales tax) and other taxes except the ecclesiastical tithe. The colonists' lands were to be hereditary and located in the most favorable places for agriculture, and the communal rights to village lands were hereditary. Medical doctors and apothecaries were to be sent. The first son of any immigrant to marry was to receive land and domestic animals on the same basis as his father. Prizes were offered for the best results in farming, amounting to 30,000 maravedís for the first twelve pounds of silk, 20,000 maravedís for the first ten pounds of cloves, ginger, or other spice, 15,000 maravedís for the first farmer to produce 1500 pounds of woad, (a plant yielding a blue dye), and 10,000 maravedís for the first hundred pounds of olive oil or rice. The same offers were made again in 1519 and 1531.[19]

Whatever might have been the results of Charles' more cosmopolitan policies, circumstances eventually were to make it impossible to follow them. In the eastern Mediterranean the Ottoman Turks had already entered Europe, captured Constantinople (1453), and were advancing steadily westward. Charles, as King of Spain and Emperor of the Germanies, was their chief opponent. In Africa, he was fighting the Mohammedans. At the same time Francis I, who had ascended the throne of France in 1515, formed an alliance with the Turks, and undertook a vigorous policy which included attacks on Spain and the Holy Roman Empire, and active encouragement of the pirates who were preying on the commerce with America. The Protestant Revolution began in 1517, and broke out into open warfare in 1522. Pirates of almost all nations were plundering Spanish commerce throughout the period. The internal situation of Spain was such that Charles had to suppress a revolt of the Communes during the years 1520-23. The wonder is that he ever attempted a cosmopolitan policy in his situation. The broader policy was modified slowly and inevitably as the attacks on Spanish-American commerce increased.

There was no satisfactory way of distinguishing the friendly

[19] Haring, *Trade and Navigation*, pp. 96-107.

foreigner from the unfriendly. Moors and Jews were considered undesirables because of their religion, and all emigrants to the New World were required to prove *limpieza de sangre* (i.e. that they and their ancestors were Christians) and to obtain a license. This rigid exclusion can be understood if we remember that Spain was almost constantly at war with the peoples she sought to exclude.

The change was not easy. Many foreigners were well established when the necessity of altering the policy became manifest, and Charles hesitated to revoke their privileges openly. Therefore, he answered an appeal of the Council of Indies asking that foreigners be excluded from trade with America by refusing publicly to forbid the trade of foreigners, but he instructed the Casa de Contratación to find reasons for excluding them when they appeared at the Casa for license. Under Philip II this was the established policy. Rigorous efforts were made to bar foreigners, and the increasing piracy of the French and English in no way convinced the Spanish Crown that its policy was erroneous.

TAXES ON COMMERCE

Taxes levied on American trade in the sixteenth century were extremely light in comparison with similar taxes of modern times. Up to 1543 practically no duties were levied on exports and imports from and to Sevilla. In America a 7½ per cent import tax (*almojarifazgo*) was levied and the proceeds applied to the benefit of the colonies. No duties were laid on goods exported from America, Spain thus deriving practically nothing from customs on American trade. But by 1543, Charles V was at war with Francis I, piracy was making inroads, and new sources of income were urgently needed. A tax of 2½ per cent was levied at Sevilla on merchandise bound for America, but at the same time the duty in America was lowered to 5 per cent. Thus American commerce paid the same tax as before, the difference being that Spain now retained a portion of the revenue. At Sevilla an almojarifazgo of 5 per cent was levied, and an *alcabala* (sales tax) of 10 per cent, making a total import duty of 15 per cent, much higher than any previous tax, but still infinitesimal in comparison with tariffs of modern nations. Goods imported into Spain from America now paid twice as much duty as goods sent from Spain to America. All except the 5 per cent levied in America went to the Crown. The alcabala was not generally collected in America until 1570.[20]

It would appear from these measures that Spain's early policy

---

[20] Hussey, "Colonial Economic Life," in Wilgus, *Colonial Hispanic America*, pp. 306-7; Haring, *Trade and Navigation*, pp. 6, 83-84.

toward her new territories was not extremely harsh, though she followed the usual economic practices of the times, and sought to secure to herself the benefits of the discoveries. Her attitude in the time of Charles V was, in fact, unusually liberal in permitting many different nationalities to come to America. Soldiers of many nations could be found among the first settlers, and most Spanish ports were open to trade with America, while the taxes levied in America were less than those of Spain, and the privileges granted American settlers were greater in many respects than those of Spaniards remaining at home. The later changes to a more restrictive policy were brought about largely by Spain's efforts to protect herself from foreign pirates and contrabandists.

PIRACY AND CONTRABAND

Piracy and contraband[21] trade were as much a part of the economic practices of Mediaeval and Modern Europe as legitimate trade. In many cases it was impossible to differentiate between the two, since there were no well-defined rules governing international relations. Trade areas and privileges conflicted, and the result was continuous war, usually undeclared, in which the ships of one power preyed on those of another. These semiofficial pirates came from all nations. England and France are to be distinguished in the fifteenth and sixteenth centuries only because of their greater success; while in the seventeenth century Holland won respect for herself in this activity. To the Christians all Mohammedans were pirates, and the Mohammedans looked upon Christian ships in the same light. Some ships carried letters of marque, but hundreds of others operated as buccaneers without government aid. The line between the two was invisible at times, and several monarchs notoriously encouraged piracy while they signed solemn treaties with "friendly" sovereigns, promising to punish their own nationals, a situation not unlike modern nonaggression treaties. The Atlantic seaboard from Great Britain to Spain was pirate-infested. Certain points which mariners used as landmarks, such as Cape St. Vincent in Portugal and the northwest Spanish coast, facilitated piracy. Brittany in France was the home of a piratical tradition that included designing ships for the "trade."

Piracy and contraband went hand and hand in these enterprises, for goods robbed from the nationals of one country were smuggled into another, or where the piracy had official sanction, divided with the sovereign.

---

[21] The works on piracy in America are numerous. See Philip Ainsworth Means, *The Spanish Main* (New York, 1935), pp. 51ff, and references cited there.

THE PROMOTION OF PIRACY: FRENCH AND ENGLISH

The discovery of America widened the opportunities for enter-prising pirates (and the monarchs who encouraged them).[22] Columbus evaded French pirates near the Canaries on his first voyage in 1492, and on his third voyage, was forced to detour to avoid a French fleet lying in wait off Cape St. Vincent.

Spain sought to protect herself from such pirates,[23] and in 1501 authorized the building of carracks to pursue them, offering a premium for those larger than one hundred and fifty tons. Ferdinand protested to Portugal in 1512 against receiving French pirates in Portuguese ports, and provided two armed ships to escort incoming merchant vessels from the Canaries.[24] But the protection of the coast of Spain was not sufficient, for the raiders had already extended their activities to American waters. In 1513, Ferdinand sent two armed vessels to America to protect ships from the French.[25] With the advent of Francis I to the French throne the situation grew worse.[26] Francis refused to acknowledge the right of the Pope to divide the world between Spain and Portugal. He was embroiled with Ferdinand over Navarre and after the accession of Charles to the Spanish throne in 1516 and to that of the Holy Roman Empire in 1519, fought a series of wars with him, the first in 1521. Whatever excuse was needed for piracy and contraband trade, was furnished by the war. [27] Thus began the long train of circumstances through which America has been affected by European affairs. Some of the American ships came through to Spain unharmed, among them the first remittance of treasure by Cortés, but all were not so fortunate.[28] This was a period of open war, and the French fleets operating against Spanish shipping may not have been pirates in the technical sense, but the effects on American commerce were the same.

The vessels sent by Cortés in 1523, under the command of Alonso

[22] Haring, *Trade and Navigation*, pp. 231-57; Arthur Percival Newton, *The European Nations in the West Indies, 1493-1688* (London, 1933), pp. 1-16. On French trade see Girard, *Commerce français à Séville et Cadix*, pp. 43-54.

[23] Roland D. Hussey, "Spanish Reaction to foreign aggression in the Caribbean to about 1680," *H.A.H.R.*, IX (August, 1929), 286-302.

[24] Date sometimes given as 1514, cf. Riva Palacio, *México*, II, 503-5.

[25] Haring, *Trade and Navigation*, pp. 67-70.

[26] Newton, *European Nations in West Indies*, pp. 47-60.

[27] Irene A. Wright, *Historia documentada de San Cristóbal de la Habana en el siglo XVI* (2 Vols., Habana, 1927), I, 5-31 and 49-53, gives an excellent picture of the terror inspired by the French in Havana, and elsewhere in the Indies, during the first years of the Conquest.

[28] On the international situation see John Tate Lanning, "Mare Clausum and the Theory of Effective Occupation" in Wilgus, *Colonial Hispanic America*, pp. 351-82.

de Avila and Antonio de Quiñones, were attacked near the Azores, and captured.[29] San Germán, Puerto Rico, was sacked and burned in 1529 by French pirates, who defeated a fleet sent against them. A French raider in 1538 seized a shipload of horses from Santo Domingo in the port of Chagres, Isthmus of Panama, and a few weeks later captured three Spanish ships off Havana. English pirates captured a cargo of sugar and hides off Santo Domingo in 1540. In the same year, San Germán was again pillaged, as was La Burburata, Venezuela, in 1541.

To protests in 1541, Francis I replied that he was as interested in making discoveries in America as other Christian rulers. He manifested his intentions in action, and during the following year, thirty-five vessels sailed from Normandy to raid American commerce and make incursions into the interior.

Cartagena, in Colombia, was attacked by three hundred Frenchmen in 1544, and plundered, the loot including 35,000 pesos in precious metals. [30] This episode was only one of many that caused the Spaniards to look upon every foreigner as an enemy. The French fleets were sometimes repulsed, but Santa María de los Remedios was sacked, its residents driven out, and the countryside looted. Cartagena and Santa Marta were forced to pay ransom in 1545 to keep from being pillaged.

So numerous were the attacks that defense measures could not keep pace with the increasing aggressiveness of the raiders. Such important towns as Cartagena, Nombre de Dios, Santa Marta, and Havana were reported in 1548 as being either without defense, or too weak to protect themselves. In 1549, the city of Santo Domingo petitioned the Emperor for means of protection. Charles V was involved in so many European complications, however, that he found it difficult to respond to the appeals of his American subjects, and pirates continued to infest the Caribbean. Santiago de Cuba was sacked and held for thirty days by the French in 1554. The following year, the Frenchman, Jacques Sore, captured the fortification of Havana, massacred his Spanish prisoners, burned the cathedral and hospital, sacked most of the town, and pillaged plantations. A few months later, another French fleet raided

---

[29] Accounts of this vary greatly. Haring, *Trade and Navigation*, p. 70, says there were three vessels, two of which were captured before arriving at the Azores, a third escaping to Santa María. When Alonso's fleet came in May to escort this ship home, two of its vessels and the Cortés ship were seized by the pirate, Jean Florin (identified by some as Giovanni de Verrazano). Another account says only that Florin captured one of the Cortés vessels near Cape San Vincent (see Riva Palacio, *México*, II, 505). Lanning, in Wilgus, *Colonial Hispanic America*, pp. 353-54, says Jean d'Ange of Dieppe captured two of the Cortés ships in 1523.

[30] Riva Palacio, *México*, II, 305-6.

Havana, repeating the looting and burning. Such attacks were a constant strain on the economic development of the settlements, which frequently had to rebuild every few years.

French raids on American commerce should theoretically have received less official help after the peace of Cateau-Cambrésis between Spain and France in 1559.[31] But this did not prevent the French from attempting settlement in America, at San Augustín, Florida, for example, in 1562-63. In 1571, a French force landed at Sisal in Yucatán, and marching inland, sacked Hunucma. About the same time an attack on Cozumel, perhaps by the same group, was repelled. Probably other raids were made, for the treaty of Vervins in 1598 stipulated their cessation.

But raids also came from other nations than the French. England, grown strong and united under Henry VII and VIII, began under Elizabeth a vigorous foreign expansion. Philip II had attempted to bring England into the Spanish sphere of influence by his marriage with Mary Tudor, but her death in 1558, and the accession of Elizabeth had reversed things. England became the foremost enemy of Spain.[32]

SLAVE TRADE AND CONTRABAND

Contraband traders appeared very early in America. French ships traded along the coast of Brazil from the beginning of the sixteenth century, bringing back the wood that gave Brazil its name. An English ship sailed to Española and Puerto Rico in 1527, and three years later William Hawkins went from Africa to Brazil. In 1560, when Philip II was on the throne, a warning was sent out that several French vessels had departed with cloth to be sold in America, and that other vessels were sailing to America to trade. A complaint from the Crown in 1563 indicates that cargoes from Portugal and other foreign nations had been landed in several places and sold with the consent of the local authorities for gold, silver, and colonial produce. Some vessels, claiming to be bound for Brazil and driven by storm into the Caribbean sold their cargo there and loaded another. Many of the harsh rules prohibiting the succor of foreign vessels resulted from this practice.

Trade and piracy were combined. Negroes captured in Africa were carried to America for sale.[33] John Hawkins reached America in 1563 with his first shipload of Negroes, trading them in spite of Spanish laws. Three years later he and Francis Drake attacked Río

[31] Haring, *Trade and Navigation*, p. 77.
[32] Newton, *European Nations in West Indies*, pp. 80-192.
[33] Newton, *European Nations in West Indies*, pp. 61-79.

de la Hacha on the mainland, but were driven off when they assaulted Vera Cruz. They continued their piratical and slaving voyages for some years thereafter, and were merely the most famous of a long line of English freebooters, many of whom have been converted into national heroes.

Foreigners profited from the American trade by the use of commission merchants, embarking merchandise in the name of a Spaniard, who received a small commission while the bulk of the profits went to the foreigner. In any case, America got the merchandise, foreign or Spanish, and paid for it. After 1592 it was unlawful for a foreigner to sell goods to a Spaniard on condition that these were to be paid for in the Indies, payment being required at some point in Spain.

Other methods were used to encroach on the Spanish monopoly. The Portuguese were accustomed to sail from Spain to the Canaries, and then to the Indies, selling their cargo and buying another which they carried directly to Portugal. The Portuguese shipmaster sometimes made a fraudulent sale of his ship to a Spaniard in the Canaries and then continued his voyage in a "Spanish" ship. These vessels could charge lower rates, partly because they did not have to pay the taxes that the Spanish ships were paying for protection against them. But regardless of the nationality of the ships, America was the center of a rich trade for which all were competing.

TRADE INSTITUTIONS OF SPAIN: THE CASA DE CONTRATACION [34]

Bearing in mind the incessant and powerful efforts of all Europe to wrest from Spain the benefits of her American discoveries, we can better understand the system through which Spain in turn attempted to keep her colonies. Spanish policy was also postulated on two prevailing economic theories which seemed eternal and sacred: Spain believed that she had a right to monopolize the trade of her colonies, and that the best way to defend her monopoly was to grant special privileges to a few men, who in protecting their own interest would protect Spain's.

In accordance with such ideas, the Crown inaugurated its system of control in 1493. Bishop Juan Rodríguez de Fonseca was charged with the preparations for the second voyage of Columbus, and thereafter matters of license came under his jurisdiction. Trade and exploration had grown too great by 1503 for Fonseca to handle affairs without a more complete organization, and the *Casa de Con-*

---

[34] Haring, *Trade and Navigation*, pp. 3-58; Bernard Moses, *The Spanish Dependencies in South America* (London, 1914), I, 240-262.

tratación came into being.[35] The first ordinances of establishment indicate that it was designed to be a business house carrying on trade with the Indies for the Crown. The Casa was to handle all merchandise and naval stores for American commerce and all imports from the Colonies.

Ferdinand and Isabella, it would seem from these provisions, intended to monopolize the trade or to take an active part in it. Either policy would have been in keeping with the practices of other monarchs of the times, since trade activities were one of the means used to finance national states. Henry VII of England participated actively in commerce, and issued elaborate laws and rules to assure himself the benefits of the rapidly expanding commerce. After the return of Vasco da Gama, Manoel I of Portugal, placed the India trade exclusively in the hands of royal agents, who equipped and chartered fleets for India and the Malabar coast. A *Casa da India* was established to carry on trade, and private individuals, sometimes Portuguese but at times Italians or Germans, were allowed to participate under strict limitations. Prices were fixed by the Crown. From 1512, the spice trade was entirely a royal monopoly, the Crown disposing of its goods to merchants in Lisbon.

The Spanish Casa de Contratación carried on a similar business for Spain for a short time and royal ships from which the Crown received the profits were sent out to America. Private ships were also allowed, however, and presently the royal ships seem to have been discontinued. The circumstances of trade between Spain and America and Portugal and India were very different, and a royal monopoly over America was not practicable.

Portugal in the East was trading with an area where the mechanics of commerce were highly developed, and where trade routes, trade practices, and the manufacturing and merchandising of goods were far better organized than in Europe itself. European nations could and did profit from this commerce merely by establishing trading posts on the coast. No conquests of India, China, and other parts of the East were necessary, and none were undertaken at this early period. The American situation was quite different. Spain rapidly occupied a large part of two vast continents where trade in the European sense was either small or nonexistent. It had to be organized, not merely seized. The vast trade that came out of

---

[35] *Gobernación espiritual y temporal*, Bk. VII (*C.D.I. Ultramar*, Vol. XXV), shows the laws regulating the *Casa* as they were about 1570. See, José de la Peña Cámara, "El Manuscrito llamado 'Gobernación Espiritual y Temporal de las Indias' y su verdadero lugar en la historia de la Recopilación," *Revista de la Historia de América*, No. 12 (August, 1941), 5-72.

America after discovery was a result of European conquest and economic development. The chief items of American export, gold, silver, sugar, hides, cochineal, logwood, and brazil, were all derived from Spanish and Portuguese enterprise.

The Crown alone could not undertake to develop such vast areas, even if it had contemplated such a policy for a time. The settlement of America and exploitation of its trade possibilities were a task for the whole nation. The system devised was one in which the State licensed, encouraged, aided, and protected its citizens, granting to certain of them monopolies and privileges in return for the expenditures and risks they undertook in the hope of profit. The function of the Casa de Contratación was to superintend the monopoly of Spain over America, and of the privileged merchants within Spain and America.

THE STRUCTURE OF THE CASA

The Casa, as first constituted, had as chief officers a treasurer, business manager, and comptroller *(contador)*; but quickly acquired other important officials. One of the earliest additions, was a "chief pilot," whose duties called for voyages of exploration, and preparation of nautical charts compiled from data which all ships were required to keep and report to the Casa; maintenance of a school for training marine officers, pilots, and cosmographers; manufacture of nautical instruments; and the licensing of officials for the marine. The school of navigation was greatly admired by the mariners of other nations, and England established one in imitation of it in 1563. The Casa also had a chronicler who recorded the history of America and scientific facts and discoveries connected with it.

A *correo mayor,* or postmaster-general, was appointed in 1514 and, although the office suffered considerable alteration from time to time, was a part of the Casa. The Casa also acquired a chapel and chaplain, and a jail and jailer. The Casa had judicial powers from the time of its creation and in 1539 these were broadened. Those who violated the regulations of the Casa or committed crimes while going to or from America were subject to its criminal jurisdiction. All civil suits affecting the revenue of the Crown, or violations of laws governing American trade were tried by the Casa, with right of appeal to the Council of Indies in particularly important cases. In 1543, civil suits involving the merchants were placed under the authority of the *consulado* (merchants' guild) of Sevilla, but the judicial functions of the Casa continued to increase to the point where a special court with two *oidores* (magistrates) was created in 1583. [36]

Such was the growth of the functions of the Casa that by the middle of the century each of the chief officials had several secretaries and assistants and was in reality the director of a bureau. The Casa was the practical equivalent of a government ministry. It also had legislative powers and was authorized to issue rules regarding trade and navigation which were in effect laws. As the Council of Indies had superior authority, the ordinances of the Casa were subject to its approval, but much of the Casa's legislation stood without revision by the Council.

Sevilla was the center of the Casa, its activities and warehouses were there, and all commerce between Spain and America was required to pass through Sevilla. Charles V, whose interests were as much German as Spanish, desired to have the northern Spanish ports participate in the American and Eastern trade. In 1522, he ordered the establishment of a Casa at Coruña in Galicia for trade with the Moluccas. However, the Moluccas were sold to Portugal in 1529. In this same year, Charles opened Coruña, Bayona, Avilés, Laredo, Bilbao, and San Sebastián, on the Atlantic coast, and Málaga and Cartagena, on the Mediterranean, to American trade. Cádiz, on the Atlantic received the same privilege. But all ships were required to return to the Guadalquivir for inspection.

Several things combined to make this liberty less useful than it might have been. Vessels sailing from these ports were to be Spanish in construction and ownership, foreign-built vessels being authorized to sail only if there was a lack of Spanish ships. Geographically, it was less easy to penetrate into the heart of Spain from the north, where the mountains closed in abruptly, than from the south, where the river valleys furnished communications. Sevilla monopolists were opposed to opening other ports. The French pirates made the ports of the Bay of Biscay hazardous, while in the Mediterranean the Turks and Moors preyed upon the commerce of Málaga and Cartagena. Some use was made of the privileges granted the northern ports, however, for as late as 1573 the Galician cities were trading with America, "according to the custom they have followed up to this time." [37] But the American trade of these ports never competed with that of Sevilla and Cádiz. [38] Philip II revoked the trade privileges of the northern ports in

---

[36] Merriman, *Spanish Empire,* III, 624-26.
[37] Quoted in Haring, *Trade and Navigation,* p. 16.
[38] Merriman, *Spanish Empire,* III, 627-29.

1573, but not those of the Mediterranean. However, Sevilla, with Cádiz as a subsidiary, enjoyed a practical monopoly.

THE JUZGADO DE INDIAS AND THE CONSULADO

Granted the monopoly, conflict arose over the selection of a port of trade. The appointment of Rodríguez de Fonseca, then Archdeacon of Sevilla, to aid Columbus in 1493 had led to the establishment of the Casa de Contratación there. But Cádiz merchants saw themselves cut off from the American trade and began a campaign against Sevilla. They gained a restricted privilege of trade with America, and in 1535 secured the establishment in Cádiz of a branch of the Casa, known as the *Juzgado de Indias* and presided over by a *juez oficial* who was to superintend the trade between Cádiz and America. His acts were subject to revision by the Casa, and he seems to have been looked upon as the representative of the Sevilla merchants. The Casa sought to impede the actions of the *juez oficial* by failing to appoint his subordinates, and after 1556 he was empowered to act alone. The struggle between the would-be monopolists was not abated by the establishment of the *Juzgado de Indias* and was to become one of the central themes of colonial history.

The creation of the *Consulado* of Sevilla in 1543 added another piece of machinery to the monopoly system. The *Consulado* was a form of merchant guild already well known in Spain, [39] where there were *consulados* in Burgos, Valencia, and other cities, and also in other countries of Europe. The functions of a consulado of this type were to protect the commerce of the city against outsiders, to maintain the monopoly of its members, and to prevent unfair trade practices by its own members. For these purposes, it had a Prior and two Consuls elected by the merchants, and its authority extended to all civil suits between its members. This body was representative of the merchants of Sevilla, just as was the Casa, and its functions were complementary. Therefore close co-operation marked their relations in contrast to the rivalry of the *Casa* with the *Juzgado de Indias* at Cádiz.

SYSTEM OF LICENSE

Spanish colonial policy, controlled by the institutions just described, gradually evolved in the sixteenth century to meet new situations as they arose. The Crown did not monopolize the trade for itself, but did reserve trade rights in certain articles for revenue

---

[39] Robert Sidney Smith, *The Spanish Guild Merchant, a History of the Consulado, 1250-1700* (Durham: Duke University Press, 1940).

or reasons of state. An early ordinance of the Casa (1504) provided that "No one shall carry to the Indies gold, silver, money, horses, mares, slaves, arms, or base gold *(guañines)* under the penalties of the royal ordinance *(premática),*" without a license, and without paying the taxes and customs prescribed. The specific list of things that could be exported freely was several times as long as those for which a license was required. [40] Nicolás de Ovando, Governor of Española (1501-1509), received similar instructions in 1504.

Prohibition of the export of bullion was in accordance with the monetary policies followed by Europe during the sixteenth century, as well as before and after, (and renewed by many nations in the twentieth century). There were various reasons for the licensing of other articles.

Since slaves had already been introduced in 1502, and earlier voyages had carried them as members of the crew, there was no intention here to prevent their introduction into America, but only to regulate the slave trade and derive a revenue from it. Slaves were exported to America under license and the Crown received a payment per head from the merchants selling them. Certain slaves could not be brought because they were of the Mohammedan or Jewish religion. In May 1526, it was forbidden to transport *ladinos* (slaves who had served one year or more) to the Indies, on the ground that they had acquired bad habits in Spain and would corrupt the obedient Negroes. In December of the same year a prohibition was laid against bringing Berber slaves to America. Slaves from the island of Gelofe were barred in 1532, because they were "arrogant, disobedient, rebellious, and incorrigible." Nor could mulatto slaves be taken to the Indies. In 1543 and 1550 the judges of the Casa in Seville were instructed that the export of Negroes from Sardinia, Mallorca, Menorca, and some parts of the Levant, where traders could obtain them at less cost than in Guinea, was forbidden, because such Negroes were Mohammedans, or had associated with Moors, "and in a new land where our Holy Catholic Faith is being planted, people of this type are not desirable." [41]

Owing to the considerable revenue derived by the Crown from the slave trade, every effort was made to prevent evasion of the tax. In 1563, it was decreed that slaves might not be used in any capacity on shipboard, and in 1572 shipowners were allowed to

[40] *D.I.I.,* XXXI, 233-37; *C.D.I. Ultramar,* V, Document 26, pp. 94-97; Haring, *Trade and Navigation,* p. 134.
[41] Quoted in Riva Palacio, *México,* II, 499-500

use slaves only if they gave security of 50,000 maravedís guaranteeing their return to Spain.

Nor does it seem that there was ever any intention to prohibit bringing horses into America. They were imported almost from the first, and the license requirement was doubtless due to the Crown's desire to reserve for itself trade in the articles which were most in demand, and which would bring the most certain profits. Similarly, the fact that the colonists had arms demonstrates that licensing of arms was not for the purpose of banning them.

Effect of Piracy on Navigation and Trade Policies

Piracy and warfare also left their marks on the trade and navigation policies. To admit foreign ships and sailors to American trade was to invite piracy and contraband. As early as 1538, a royal decree excluding foreigners from trade and navigation indicates a change of policy. Efforts were made to require all vessels to be of Spanish build or ownership, and all sailors of Spanish nationality, although many ordinances permitted foreign ships and sailors under certain conditions. [42]

Further regulations arose from attempts to prevent the raids on shipping. The early protection afforded by the armed ships sent out by Ferdinand having proved insufficient to curb the ever increasing piratical and smuggling activities, stronger measures had to be taken. These necessarily imposed restrictions on sailings and expense to pay for protection. Freedom to sail unprotected came to mean the freedom to be captured. Ships could no longer depart with the mere formality of registering; [43] they became subject to regulations for their mutual defense.

A system of flying squadrons was used as early as the beginning of the fifteenth century to patrol the area from Spain to the Azores and Canaries. After America was opened to commerce, a fleet, known as the *Armada de la carrera de Indias,* was organized in 1522; and at about this same time a special tax the *avería* was levied on the merchants in the trade for its support. The merchants at the same time proposed the establishment of a permanent fleet to patrol between Spain and the Canaries, and measures were taken to draw up regulations for the size of the fleets, wages to be paid, provisions and arms, and the taxes to be levied. From 1526, merchant vessels were required to sail in groups to and from America. The *armada de la carrera de Indias* was reorganized in 1528, and new contracts, renewed from time to time, were signed with the

---

[42] Haring, *Trade and Navigation*, pp. 258-61.
[43] Riva Palacio, *México*, II, 502-3.

merchants for its support. In the same year the Council of the Indies determined upon the construction of fortifications in the harbors and important strategic places of America. [44] But conditions were forcing the development of a better system of protection for shipping. Blasco Núñez Vela in 1537 convoyed to America a fleet of twenty-eight vessels, not counting a number of smaller lighters; and in 1542 Martín Alonso de los Ríos took over another fleet. In August, 1543, the merchants of Sevilla secured from the Crown a decree making obligatory the sailing of convoyed, yearly fleets.

Another armada was prepared in 1552 and a change of policy was attempted. All ships going to America within nine months were to sail with the armada, but after that each ship was required to be armed, and might sail alone. Two squadrons, one in Europe and the other in America, were to keep the seas clean of enemies. The American squadron was delayed in Europe to conduct Philip to his wedding with Mary Tudor, and did not reach America until 1555. In the meantime the Consulado of Sevilla secured a royal order restoring the fleets for the duration of the war with France. Single, armed ships continued to sail from time to time, but the fleet system was to prevail.

The entire convoy left Spain as a unit but divided on reaching the Caribbean, one part sailing to Vera Cruz, another to Cartagena and Nombre de Dios (after 1584 to Portobelo), with a few ships going to subsidiary ports. On the return journey the fleets gathered in Havana. This practice was not invariable, however, and many ships returned in groups of three to twelve. Between 1561 and 1566 the system was altered and two fleets left Spain.

The establishment of three principal ports in America for the reception of merchandise, Vera Cruz, Cartagena, and Nombre de Dios, came in part from geographical factors and in part from administrative problems and the ubiquitous piracy. Collection of duties and the building of ample fortifications at numerous ports were hardly possible. Vera Cruz became the designated port for all New Spain on the Atlantic side, since it was as centrally located for trade with the Mexican highlands as any other harbor, and the terrain made maintenance of more than one route of communication too expensive. The northern part of Mexico was at first undeveloped, and the southern regions were served by subsidiary sailings from Vera Cruz to coastal ports of Tabasco and Yucatán. Central America's economic development justified only a few ships,

[44] Riva Palacio, *México*, II, 505.

some of them coming from Vera Cruz and some being detached from the fleets that came to America.

Farther south, Nombre de Dios (supplanted later by Portobelo) became the main port. From here, goods were sent across the Isthmus to Panama City, and transshipped to Callao and other ports in Ecuador, Peru, and Chile. Maintenance of more than one Panama route was not feasible, but a port on the Isthmus was essential for traffic with the Pacific coast colonies. Merchandise could be transshipped to the Pacific from Mexico or the Río de la Plata, or around South America, but none of these routes was economically profitable until a later day. [45]

Northern South America was supplied by the Cartagena fleet, the selection of that port again being determined by geography and the international situation. The Caribbean islands were served by ships detached from the fleet.

In 1561 the Crown issued the order that "no ship shall sail from Cádiz or San Lúcar except in convoy under pain of loss of the ship and its cargo," and that one fleet should sail for Tierra Firme in January and another for New Spain in August of each year. Further regulations were laid down, 1564-66. One fleet was to sail for New Spain in April (after 1582 in May) taking with it the ships for Honduras and the Antilles, and another for Tierra Firme in August with the vessels for Nombre de Dios, Cartagena, Santa Marta, and other ports in northern South America.

REGULATIONS OF SHIPPING

A complete set of regulations was drawn up by the Crown through its agencies, the Council of the Indies, the Casa de Contratacion, and the Consulado of Seville for the guidance of American commerce. These concerned the condition of the ships, their tonnage, fitness and training of the crews, and other similar points.

High freight rates were a subject of constant legislation. The merchants complained that the prices demanded by the shipowners precluded profits. As the evil was supposed to result from the avarice of the owners, the Crown decreed in 1572 that the Casa should fix the rates. But there were possibly other causes that influenced freight rates. The trip to America was long and dangerous, and the great number of ships lost, through both natural risks and the operations of pirates, increased the expense. Since insurance was not yet general usage, the full loss fell on the shipowner. The merchants of the Seville monopoly also bid against each other for space in the ships, thus running up the rates. Holding

[45] Merriman, *Spanish Empire*, III, 632-35.

that a limited cargo sold at a high price was more profitable than a larger cargo sold at a lower price, they themselves encouraged limitation of the fleets, raising both rates and prices. [46]

Commerce with America was by no means confined to these Spanish ships sailing under license. Illegal entries of Spanish and foreign ships played an important role in colonial trade. The illegal ships have been called "one of the most flagrant sources of harm to the India commerce," [47] but this is true only if we are looking at it from the Spanish side. The Spaniard, Veitia Linaje, speaks of these "arribadas maliciosas," but many of the "malicious arrivals" were welcome to the people of America and must be considered a part of American commerce. The volume of such trade is naturally unknown, since no complete statistics can exist, but if we judge by complaints of the Crown and merchants, it was considerable.

* * * * * * * *

Commerce between America and Europe began with Columbus and expanded rapidly with the development of the Caribbean colonies and the opening up of Mexico and Peru. Although trade monopolies were the prevailing European practice, and regulation by the Crown through licenses the established policy, Spain's trade with the New World was not at first heavily burdened with taxes and restrictions. Charles V was especially liberal in permitting foreign merchants to trade with the Spanish colonies.

The profits to be made shortly attracted pirates and smugglers of many nations. During or between wars, Spain was compelled to defend her shipping and colonial ports from raiders by building up her fleet, patrolling the seas, and establishing convoys. Need for revenue also led to trade restrictions, and American commerce was regulated through such institutions as the Casa de Contratacíon and Consulado of Seville. The consequence was a policy much less liberal than in the early days, but the protective measures neither prevented a considerable illicit traffic with America nor stopped the growth of the licensed Spanish trade. European commerce with America increased throughout the sixteenth century.

[46] Riva Palacio, *México*, II, 498.
[47] Haring, *Trade and Navigation*, pp. 139-140.

Indian Classes, Customs and Populations

MUCH OF WHAT LATIN AMERICA is today can be traced directly to the pre-Conquest social customs and mores of the Indians and their blending with those of the invading Europeans. In the early period following the Conquest, the interaction of European and Indian elements could be seen in three important ways: (1) the formation of a stratified class society based on a fusion of Spanish and Indian models, (2) the evolution of a set of mores and customs likewise originating in those of both the conqueror and the conquered, and (3) the intermixture of Spanish and Indian populations.

CLASS SOCIETY IN THE CARIBBEAN

It might be thought that among people whose living conditions were as primitive as those of the Caribbean Indians there would be no distinction of property or class, but this was not the case. "Classes or social differences existed in Cuba among its primitive inhabitants. . . . Even if we disregard the superior government of the *caciques*, it is certain, it is entirely beyond doubt, that two characteristic classes existed: one the masses or common people, the other the privileged or higher class. . . ."¹ The Caribs, who were victimizing the Arawaks in the Caribbean at the time Columbus arrived, were distinguished by "the complete absence of a graded society and of an inherited chieftainship," but the "more cultured Arawak" had developed "stratified classes, and a highly centralized chieftainship." Even among the Caribs, however, certain families were given a "special position and accorded the title of chief." ² The relatively small Indian populations of the islands

---

¹ Nicolás Fort y Roldán *Cuba indígena* (Madrid, 1881), p. 85.
² Paul Radin, *Indians of South America* (New York: Doubleday, Doran and Company, 1942), pp. 51, 23, 25.

soon emigrated, or were killed or absorbed by the European invaders.

CLASS SOCIETY IN MEXICO

The Indians of the continent, much more numerous in some regions than in the Caribbean, and more highly developed culturally, continued to form the bulk of the population after the Conquest. This is the case particularly of portions of Mexico and of the Indians of the Andes, and it is therefore essential to understand their social organization.

Among the Aztecs, it is possible to distinguish four main social groups:[3] The ruling hierarchy was composed of the nobility, the tribal chieftains, the military aristocracy and the clergy, although these were not clearly differentiated. The military and clerical classes came usually from the nobility, but in any case, the condition of nobility was combined with the control of land the prevalent form of wealth in Aztec Mexico. The first nobility was composed of a comparatively small number of great lords, some of whom had thousands of subjects, and hundreds of lesser nobles. They held the chief offices of the government, and collected taxes, but were themselves largely exempt from all taxation except military services. An elaborate system of honors and insignia for the lower nobility was somewhat similar to the medieval European system. The merchants formed the secondary nobility, but were frequently identical with the first nobles.

Farther down in the social scale were the free peasants (*maceguales*), whose position was also based on land ownership, and the artisans whose skill had raised them to a slightly higher level. The serfs (*mayeques*)[4] and the slaves formed the base of the social pyramid. The mayeques, corresponding rather closely to medieval cotters, who were bound to the soil but owned little if anything more than a hut, worked the large estates of the nobility. At the absolute bottom were the slaves, who were bought and sold in the way so familiar in European markets. The slave class was composed of prisoners of war, condemned criminals, debtors,

---

[3] Bernardino de Sahagún, *Historia general de las cosas de Nueva España* (4th ed.; 5 vols., México: Pedro Robredo, 1938), II, 275-394. Sahagún's history written in the 16th century was first published in 1829-30. It is the most carefully prepared and detailed work on Mexico at the time of the Conquest. It is indispensable for a knowledge of social, religious, and political conditions among the Indians. Perhaps the best secondary account is by Manuel Orozco y Berra, *Historia antigua y de la conquista de México* (4 vols. and atlas, México, 1880), I, 202-26; 252-77; 362-87 and *passim*. Prescott, *Mexico*, Bk. I, chaps. II, III, V, gives a good account of Aztec society. For the modern archeological view see: Vaillant, *Aztecs*, pp. 108-138.

[4] The *mayeques* were also known as *tlalmatecas* or *tlalmaites*.

those who because of poverty renounced freedom for slavery, and children sold into slavery by their parents. Thus the Aztec state was in reality a class society held rigidly in place by property, with social distinctions no less fixed than in Europe of the old regime.

The disparity between the living standards of the masses and those of the nobility was marked. One sixteenth-century chronicler tells us: "These people live with very little food, as little perhaps as any other people in the world. Only the Lords have a great variety of viands, sauces and vegetable soups, pies and pastries of all the animals which they have, fruits, vegetables, and fish, which are in abundance. . . . They are served by two or three chief waiters and the Lords eat all they wish; and then what is left over is divided among other Lords, their vassals, who are there in order to make their court to them." [5]

THE CLASS STRUCTURE OF THE INCA EMPIRE

The Inca Empire has sometimes been presented as a society in which there were no poor and no suffering for want of material things, in which social distinctions existed but were unimportant, in which there was little, if any, private property, and in which the benefits of production were evenly distributed by a paternal government that looked to the needs of a well-cared-for people. The very limited extent to which land was socially owned has already been shown, but the whole topic of Inca society will bear closer examination.

The social structure was featured by sharply defined classes. These were: an upper nobility, the Incas or *orejones,* [6] consisting of the Sapa Inca and those of royal blood; a secondary nobility, the *curacas,* chieftains of tribes conquered by the Incas; the *purics,* landholding peasants; and the *yana-cunas,* who were landless and worked at various occupations. Father Bernabé Cobo admired the social stratification:

"In this, there was not lacking the system that all well-regulated societies *(repúblicas)* maintain of making a distinction between nobles and plebeians. The title and privilege of nobles was enjoyed in the first place by all the Incas of the royal blood, called by our Spaniards *orejones. . . .* These with a few other gentlemen comprised the order of cavaliers *(caballería). . . .* After them, the governors, captains, *caciques,* and judges of the

---

[5] The Anonymous Conqueror, *Narrative of Some Things of New Spain,* ed. and tr. Marshall H. Saville (New York: The Cortes Society, 1917), pp. 37-38.

[6] The Spaniards called them *orejones,* big ears, because of their custom of stretching the lobe of the ear, sometimes until it reached the shoulder.

Incas, with their children, enjoyed the immunities and privileges of *hidalgos,* equally with the *orejones;* all of whom were not only exempt from the taxes that the common people paid, but in addition drew perquisites *(gajes)* from their king, and were maintained with the tribute of personal service rendered them by the *mitayos* (corvée workers) and *pecheros* (tribute payers)." [7]

It is clear that the poor did exist. "No rich person," says Cieza, "could wear more decoration or ornaments than the poor, nor differentiate his clothing and dress, except the lords and curacas; for owing to their high rank, these could take advantage of ample exceptions and privileges, and the same was true of the *orejones.*" [8] The gulf that separated the upper from the lower social classes was also evident in their herds: "The common Indians were poor in livestock, of which even the curacas had hardly enough for themselves and their families; and on the other hand, the Sun and the Inca had such quantities that they were innumerable." [9]

The Inca system was definitely a class system, even if the concern for the welfare of other classes was as great as Garcilasco found it, "the inferiors studying how to serve and please their superiors, and the superiors how to favor and befriend their inferiors, from the Inca, the king, down to the lowest *llamamiche,* who is a shepherd." [10]

CONDITION OF THE MASSES IN THE INCA EMPIRE

The *yana-cunas* were at the bottom of the social pyramid. Their duties were to serve the Inca and the priesthood as domestic servants, shepherds, and farm workers. Cieza de León remarks that the Incas had their *"anaconas,* which is the name for perpetual servants, who were so numerous that they sufficed to till the royal fields, and do service in the palace." [11] Garcilaso speaks of the *yana-cuna* as an "Indian house servant." [12] From this it would appear that the *yana-cuna* was a sort of perpetual slave, who was perhaps not bought and sold in the manner of a chattel, but yet was not free to leave the service of his master.

Next above the yana-cuna in the social scale were the *purics,* small landholders within the *ayllu.* They were subject to tribute of three kinds: a portion of the products of their lands, labor, and

---

[7] Cobo, *Nuevo Mundo,* Bk. XII, chap. XXVII.
[8] Cieza, *Señorío,* chap. XIX.
[9] Garcilaso, *Comentairos,* Bk. V, chap. IX.
[10] Garcilaso, *Comentarios,* Bk. IV, chap. XIV; see also chaps. XII, XIII,
[11] Cieza, *Señorío,* chap. XVIII.
[12] Garcilaso, *Comentarios,* Part II, chap. XXVII.

military service. The work-tribute was called *"mita-cuna,"* which seems to have meant work in turns. This might be on the land, in the mines, or anywhere else the Inca cared to use them.

In theory work may have been entirely honorable with no social stigma connected with it, since the Incas and the nobles worked on the land. But Father Bernabé Cobo shows that their work was purely a gesture, and had no more to do with actual labor than our modern symbolic first spadeful dug up by mayors and presidents:

> "The lands dedicated to the gods were divided among the Sun, Lightning and the other idols, the chapels, and the communal and private *guacas* of each province and town *(pueblo)*. The portions of each god and guaca were measured off and cultivated first, before those of the Inca and the community. The pueblos gathered to cultivate them in the following manner: if the Inca himself was present, or his governor, or any other great *señor* whatever, he was the first to put his hand to the task with a *taclla,* a golden plow, which they took to the Inca for this purpose, and all the great *señores* and gentlemen who accompanied him followed suit. But the Inca soon quit work; and afterwards the other señores and important men began quitting also, and they sat down with the king to hold their banquets and festivals, which were very solemn in those days."

Following this the straw bosses and common people worked all day, the man being "rich" who had children to help, and he who had none, "poor." [13]

Each Indian was supposed to render a definite amount of service, after which he was free to return to his own home for the remainder of the year. Moreover, Garcilaso definitely states that the work done by these Indians was so heavy that many of them became sick from their excessive labors. If this is actually the way the tribute system operated, it is evident that the labors required of each man corresponded not in the least to his ability to perform them. [14]

While the houses of the nobles and the masses were similar in structure, all windowless and open to the air, there was a considerable difference in size, and even more in furnishings and equipment. The nobles had practically everything in the way of gold and silver vessels and ornaments, chairs, and the finest of woolens for clothing and bedding, whereas the masses had none of these. The misery of the masses contrasted sharply with the luxury of the

[13] Cobo, *Nuevo Mundo,* Bk. XII, chap. XXVIII.
[14] Cf. Means, *Ancient Civilizations,* pp. 301-302.

nobility. The "famous physicians" did not treat the poor "but only the sovereigns and those of noble blood, and the curacas and their relatives. The common people doctored one another according to hearsay medicine." [15] The masses were on a level with the animals:

"The common and poor people when sick were but little better off than beasts." [16]

Cobo relates that the Indians were so ignorant they could not tell a doctor where they felt pain. [17] The best that can be said for the masses of the Inca Empire reveals a state of permanent poverty:

". . . the poor, who were the common people, had a scarcity of everything, but not actual want." [18]

THE PRIVILEGED CLASSES OF THE INCA EMPIRE

The two chief privileged classes were the Incas (orejones) and the curacas, whose position was infinitely above that of the people. The Incas belonged to the imperial caste and, in theory at least, married strictly within their own caste, the numerous concubines taken from other classes apparently not counting in their minds, and the children born of such unions being considered bastards. The imperial family surrounded itself with members of the curaca class, drawn from the rulers of the conquered tribes. The curacas ruled their districts under the governors sent out by the Inca, while the children of the curacas were frequently reared at the Inca court as hostages for the obedience of their parents, and to prevent rebellion in the conquered territories. [19]

There were others who had been adopted into the royal caste and were known as honorary Incas. Special titles were reserved for those of the royal blood; [20] and the curacas, however honored otherwise, were not permitted to assume such titles.

The Sapa Inca himself occupied a position that has no comparison except to that of an oriental despot. "Everything the Incas had was spent solely on ornaments for their persons and decorations for the temples and the upkeep of their houses and palaces." [21] The Inca "sat on a seat of solid gold." All his palaces, in Cuzco

---

[15] Garcilaso, *Comentarios,* Bk. II, chap. XXIV. The last phrase is *La gente común se curaban unos a otros por lo que habían oido de medicamentos.*
[16] Garcilaso, *Comentarios,* Bk. II, chap. XXIV. The exact wording is: *La gente común y pobre se había en sus enfermedades poco menos que bestias.*
[17] Cobo, *Nuevo Mundo,* Bk. XIV, chap. X.
[18] Garcilaso, *Comentarios,* Bk. VI, chap. I.
[19] Garcilaso, *Comentarios,* Bk. VII, chap. III.
[20] Means, *Ancient Civilization,* p. 304; Cieza, *Señorío,* pp. 49-50; Cobo, *Nuevo Mundo,* Bk. XII, chaps. XXXV- XXXVI.
[21] Cieza, *Señorío,* pp. 49-50.

and along the royal roads, were furnished with silver and gold dishes and utensils. The Inca "never donned a garment for a second time," but passed his clothing on to relatives. The Inca's bedding of vicuña wool appeared so fine to the Spaniards that they carried it to Spain for the bed of King Philip II. In contrast to the scanty fare of the masses, the Inca's food was "extremely abundant." [22]

Each Inca ruler built himself an entirely new palace adorned with gold and silver. His royal household commanded a vast body of servants, some of whom were *yana-cunas,* and others were purics doing their mita turn. The latter frequently comprised entire villages which had been required to attend the Emperor from the time of their subjection. [23]

Only those of noble rank, as a rule, received instruction. It was held that "the children of the common people should not learn the sciences, which should be known only to the nobles, lest the lower classes should become proud and endanger the commonwealth." [24] Only the nobility could enter the priesthood.[25] Even in the matter of holidays, the difference between the upper and the lower classes is evident. The numerous holidays were for the nobility only, and the purics and yana-cunas did not participate in these vacations. [26]

Class structure of Indian society was not confined to the sedentary, agricultural peoples such as those of the Andes; it was characteristic of all but the most primitive. Evidences of class distinction were present not only among the Caribs and Arawaks of the islands, but among these same tribes on the South American continent, where, however, their respective positions were reversed. On the continent, the Arawaks composed an "Arawak-speaking caste of apparent overlords." [27] Even among tribes "as simple from every point of view" as the Abipones of the Chaco, there was a "definite division of the people into non-hereditary 'nobles' and 'non nobles' " [28] while the majority of the more important Indian peoples, including the Calchaqui, the Araucanians, and the Chané, had class divisions of society. [29]

---

[22] Garcilaso, *Comentarios,* Bk. VI, chap. I.

[23] Means, *Ancient Civilizations,* pp. 324-25.

[24] Garcilaso, *Comentarios,* Bk. IV, chap. XIX, quoted also in Means, *Ancient Civilizations,* p. 305; cf. Cobo, *Nuevo Mundo,* Bk. XIV, chap. VI.

[25] Means, *Ancient Civilizations,* p. 370.

[26] Means, *Ancient Civilizations,* p. 385.

[27] Radin, *Indians of South America,* p. 31.

[28] Radin, *ibid.,* p. 186.

[29] Radin, *ibid.,* pp. 192, 193, 205.

MORES AND CUSTOMS IN INDIAN SOCIETY

The tendency, beginning with many early chroniclers, has been to blame the Spaniards for corrupting the Indians. It is true that the conduct of the conquerors was by no means exemplary, and the Europeans did not always set a high standard for the new subjects of Spain and converts to Christianity. It is true also that moral judgments are relative, depending on the accepted concepts of the period and society in which they are made. To say that the native customs were better or worse before the Conquest means nothing unless there is a general agreement on moral standards—a subject on which mankind's outstanding philosophers have never agreed. The difference between what the Spaniards found and what they introduced was fundamentally a difference in ethical ideals. According to the Christian ethic introduced by the Spaniards, customs that aroused no social opprobrium among the Indians were vicious, although most of them—with the exception of cannibalism and ritual human sacrifice—were not unknown in practice in European society. To condemn certain customs as vices would tend to limit them, or at least keep them somewhat under cover; to that extent, in any case, the introduction of the ethical standard may be regarded as an advance.

But quite aside from any question of comparative ethical evaluations, a study of the customs and mores of Indian society before the Conquest is not irrelevant. Native customs were a basic element in post-Conquest society, in which they were fused with those of the Europeans. From a knowledge of the Indian mores we can determine whether certain practices were introduced by the Spaniards or whether they already existed.

CANNIBALISM, MARRIAGE, AND SEXUAL PRACTICES IN THE CARIB-
    BEAN AND MEXICO

"Cannibalism was widespread in the two Americas." [30] It seems to have had a triple nature; it was frequently connected with warfare, it was sometimes ritualistic, and it served to supply food for peoples who lacked other sources of meat. We have already given instances of it in discussing Indian warfare. Other chroniclers besides Cortés and Bernal Díaz were witnesses of cannibalism in New Spain. [31]

"All of this province of New Spain and of those other prov-

---

[30] Radin, *Indians of South America*, p. 97. See also 49-74, and especially 72-74; 87-95; 97-109.
[31] Torquemada, *Monarchia indiana*, Bk. XIV, chap. XXVI; and see evidence in Orozco y Berra, *Historia antigua de México*, I, 176-201.

inces eat human flesh, which they have in greater esteem than any other food, so much so that many times they go to war and place themselves in peril only to kill some one to eat." [32]

The Caribbean Indians' code of sexual relations required neither monogamy nor premarital chastity. Speaking of the Cuban marriage customs, López de Gómara remarks: "When they marry, another is the [wife's] first lover. Because that is the usual custom and practice. If the bridegroom is a cacique, all the caciques invited [to the wedding] try out the bride before he does. If he is a merchant, the merchants; and if a worker, the lord or some priest; and she is then held to be very desirable." [33] Plural marriages were the custom in Española and husbands and wives all slept together "like chickens." The custom was to have the sister's children inherit if a man had no son, because they considered these the "most certain" near kinsmen. [34]

Polygamy existed also in Mexico. "They have many women, like the Moors," says the Anonymous Conqueror, "but one is the principal one and the mistress, and the sons of this one inherit the property of the father." [35] There is also evidence of the practice of sodomy. The early Spaniards were greatly intrigued with small gold figures which showed men apparently in the act of committing sodomy. [36]

The social customs of Maya society did not differ greatly from those of the Aztecs. At least, the general outline was much the same, although the details might vary. [37]

CANNIBALISM, MARRIAGE, AND SEXUAL PRACTICES IN COLOMBIA

The conquerors encountered cannibalism on the South American continent, as they had in New Spain. Near Ancerma, in Colombia, Cieza found a square enclosed with bamboo stakes on the tops of which were placed "many heads of Indians they had eaten" for they were "carnivorous and fond of eating human flesh." In another case, a group of starving Spaniards ate eagerly from a kettle filled with cooked meat which they had found, believing

---

[32] Anonymous Conqueror, *Narrative of New Spain*, pp. 79-80.

[33] López de Gómara, *Historia de las Indias*, fol. XXVI, verso.

[34] *Ibid.*, fol. XVI, verso.

[35] *Narrative of New Spain*, p. 75. See also Vaillant, *Aztecs*, pp. 111-12, 118-19, who notes that polygamy and prostitution were among the Aztec customs.

[36] *D.I.I.*, XXXV, 366-70.

[37] The classical description of Maya society is Diego de Landa, *Relación de las cosas de Yucatán*, ed. Brasseur de Bourbourg (Paris, 1864); also found in *C.D.I. Ultramar*, XIII, 265-411. See also Eligio Ancona, *Historia de Yucatán* (4 vols., Mérida, 1878-81); and Daniel G. Brinton, *The Maya Chronicles* (Philadelphia, 1882).

the meat to be that of guinea pigs until they ran across a human hand in the pot. This "made them regret that they had eaten that food, since it nauseated them to see the fingers and hands. But finally the feeling vanished, and they returned well-fed to the camp from which they had gone dying of hunger." [38]

In certain instances, cannibalism had a ceremonial nature. The intended victims were placed in cages where, after being "well-fed, and when they are fat, they are taken out to the squares . . . and, on the holidays they are killed with great cruelty and eaten. I saw some of these cages or prisons in the province of Arma [Colombia]. . . . I have seen what I describe too many times." [39]

Some of the depopulation of the period just prior to and during the Conquest was attributable to cannibalism, in the opinion of this same chronicler. In the Cali region of Colombia, time and the wars with the Spaniards had destroyed a large part of the people, he writes, but "the fact that they disappeared so quickly has been due in great part, and indeed principally, to their bad custom and accursed vice, which is eating one another." [40]

Sexual customs resembled those of the Indians of New Spain. Among the Indians of Colombia the custom was to "marry off their daughters after they have lost their virginity, and they do not consider it a thing of importance to have a virgin when they get married." [41] Polygamy was the rule and marriage to close relations was not banned. But whereas the "lords can have many wives," the other Indians were confined to "one, or two, or three," depending on their wealth. "And the other Indians marry, some their daughters and sisters, and others without any order whatever; and very few find their wives virgins." [42] "They marry their nieces and some chieftains marry their sisters, as all the others do." [43]

Excessive drinking was combined with their sexual practices. Some Indians drank an arroba (about three gallons) at one sitting and "having the belly full of this drink they vomit and throw up." They sat all day at this. "And this habit of drinking is an old vice practiced generally by all the Indians that up to now have been discovered in these Indies." [43b]

[38] Cieza, *Crónica*, chap. XVI.
[39] Cieza, *Crónica*, chap. XXVI.
[40] Cieza, *Crónica*, chap. XXX.
[41] Cieza, *Crónica*, chap. XVI.
[42] *Ibid.*, chap. XIX.
[43] *Ibid.*, chaps. XXIII, XXVIII.
[43b] *Ibid.*, chap. XXIII.

CUSTOMS IN THE INCA EMPIRE

The control of their subjects' conduct by the Inca rulers appeared admirable to some of the European invaders, one of the conquerors, Mancio Sierra Lejesema, being sufficiently impressed to write: "The Incas dominated them [the Indians] so completely that there was not a single thief, vicious man, vagrant, adultress, or prostitute, nor were people of loose morals allowed among them." [44]

But this, and similar statements by Garcilaso and other chroniclers give anything but a complete picture of Indian customs in the Empire. The same chroniclers, Garcilaso for instance, supply details, perhaps not in contradiction to the existence of a well-ordered Inca police system, but certainly in contradiction to the idea of native mores presented by the passage quoted.

BURIAL CUSTOMS IN PERU

Human sacrifice was practiced as part of the funeral rites. [45] According to Cobo, in addition to the other burdensome tributes that "so sorely oppressed the poor," the Incas demanded *"niños y niñas"* "to be killed in their abominable sacrifices." Children of nine or ten, or even less, were preferred. "They killed them by strangling them with a rope, or garroting them." [46]

The funeral services seem to have appeared altogether shocking to the Christians: "And what it is said that they were accustomed to do, I do not wish to set down because they are heathenisms. And let the Christians who were in Cuzco in 1550 [47] remember what they saw done during the anniversary funeral of Paullu Inca, after they [the Indians] had become Christian, and they can imagine what it would have been during the reign of the former kings." [48]

SEXUAL CUSTOMS IN THE INCA EMPIRE

The imagination could run pretty far in this case, since the chroniclers are sufficiently graphic in their descriptions of orgies. The Indians of the Inca Empire, one chronicler states, were addicted to drinking "neither more nor less" than the other Indians, and "spend the whole day drinking the *chicha* or wine that they make from maize, having a glass in hand constantly." They were "always drinking, until becoming very drunk and having lost the power of reason, they seize any women they desire and . . . have intercourse with them." [49]

[44] Quoted in Prescott, *Peru,* Appendix IV.
[45] Cieza, *Crónica,* chaps. XII, XVI, XXII, XXXIII, LXIII, C.
[46] Cobo, *Nuevo Mundo,* Bk. XII, chap. XXXIV.
[47] Means, *Fall,* p. 116, says 1549.
[48] Cieza, *Señorío,* chap. LX.
[49] Cieza, *Crónica,* chap. XLI.

The *casas de escogidas,* or houses of chosen women, of the Inca, were an institution subject to various interpretations, in which a religious factor entered. But while the women lived in monastic retirement, it is clear they functioned as concubines of the Inca. According to Cobo, "they lived in perfect seclusion and chastity like the nuns among us," and were assembled at the age of ten or twelve as a part of the "tribute" collected by the Inca. There were two classes, *mamaconas* and *acllas.* The latter Cobo calls "seculars," but the distinction was not great. Their chastity was lifelong, and they were free of knowledge of all men "except the Inca," who "sometimes" visited them.[50] Cieza, Garcilaso and others agree on the terrible punishments inflicted on any who violated their vows. The principal house was in Cuzco, but Garcilaso describes numerous other houses scattered throughout the Empire.

"Girls of all classes entered them, the legitimate daughters of the royal blood as well as those we call bastards because of their mixed blood. There were also taken in, as a great favor and boon, daughters of the curacas, lords of vassals, as well as girls of the common people who were selected for their great beauty, because they were to be the women and concubines of the Inca . . . . In summary, all belonged to one house [or order] except that in the one in Cuzco they entered as women of the Sun and they had to be legitimate of the royal blood, and they maintained a perpetual cloister. And in the other houses of the kingdom, women of all classes entered, provided they were pretty and virgin, because they were for the Inca. From here, when the Inca asked for them, the most beautiful were taken out and carried to him to be his concubines." [51]

The houses would appear to have been more analogous to harems than to convents, since the *escogidas* were the prettiest women of the realm, gathered from all classes to serve as concubines for the Inca. Pedro Pizarro so describes them. [52]

Premarital chastity was not generally demanded. "No account of it is taken whether or no their daughters be virgins." [53]

But after marriage, chastity seems to have been required. Cieza speaks of women among the Collas "who, . . . although they may lead a loose life before they marry, are killed if, after giving themselves to their husbands they betray him by having relations with another man." [54]

---

[50] Cobo, *Nuevo Mundo,* Bk. XIII, chap. XXXVII.
[51] Garcilaso, *Comentarios,* Bk. IV, chap. IV.
[52] Pedro Pizarro, *Conquest of Peru,* I, 194-96.
[53] *Ibid.,* II, 408-10.   [54] Cieza, *Crónica,* chap. C.

A PROSTITUTE CLASS EXISTED

"It remains to say something about the public women, who were permitted by the Incas in order to avoid greater evils. They lived in the fields in miserable huts, each one to herself and not together. They were not allowed to enter the towns, so as to prevent them from associating with other women. They were called *Pampayruna*, a name which indicated the place of residence and their business, because it is composed of *pampa* which is a public square or a level field (it means both) and *runa* which in the singular means a person, man or woman, and in the plural means people . . . . Used together, if the signification is taken to be "field", pampayruna means people who live in the field, that is, for their evil trade. And if the meaning "square" is used, it means a person or woman of the square, in the sense that as the square is a public place ready to receive all that want to go to it, so are they public to all the world. In short, it means a public woman . . . . They were not called by their own names, but merely pampayruna, which is a prostitute." [55]

Polygamy was the rule for the nobility, and monogamy was enforced upon the poor. Only the chief wife of a noble was considered legally married, the others being mere concubines. The Inca might take as many women as he wished. When Huayna Capac went on a military campaign to Quito he took 2000 wives with him and left another 4000 wives home.[56] On the other hand the plebeian was required to be monogamous, and sometimes a widower would not have a new wife allotted to him for a space of two or three years. The public prostitutes, however were in all probability at the service exclusively of the plebeians, since the nobility had practically an unlimited number of wives and concubines.[57]

Noble families placed their sons in the hands of nursemaids who were usually the first mistresses. Orphans were given to widows who became their concubines, and remained so even after official marriage to another woman. During wars of conquest the nobility distributed among themselves the conquered women, or the Inca himself made such a distribution. Other concubines were given by the Inca from the *casas de escogidas* as rewards for service. Or again, a son would inherit all of the wives (except his own mother) of his father or brothers. Marriage by the Inca to his own eldest sister for the purpose of having an heir to the throne took place

---

[55] Garcilaso, *Comentarios*, Bk. IV, chap. XIV.
[56] Cieza, *Señorío*, chap. LXIII.
[57] See Means, *Ancient Civilizations*, pp. 358-66, for a discussion of marriage.

in some cases, and was perhaps customary. Members of the higher nobility were permitted to marry their paternal half-sisters.

From other evidence, it is clear that priestly pederasty was practiced in some parts of the Empire. [58]

THE POPULATION OF THE INDIES

How many people were living in America at the time of the Conquest has been a matter of dispute since the first reports of discovery. The number was placed very high by some of the earliest writers. The population of pre-Conquest America was not as large, however, nor the depopulation after the Conquest as great, as is frequently believed. The wars of conquest, enslavement, harsh treatment, and disease undoubtedly contributed to a decline in population; but much of the "Black Legend" concerning Spain in the New World has arisen from inflated estimates of the numbers of pre-Conquest peoples.

Bartolomé de las Casas estimated the population in millions. For example, he believed that the island of Cuba had at least 200,000 Indians in 1492.[59] Another estimate placed the population of Cuba at the beginning of the Conquest in 1511 at 1,000,000, and in 1517 at only 14,000 people. Fray Luís Bertrán, however, in an estimate made between 1555-69, gave Cuba 200,000 Indians. Yet in the same period (1553) López de Gómara asserted that while "Cuba was once heavily populated with Indians, today there are only Spaniards." His explanation was that "They all turned Christian. Many died of work, of hunger, and of smallpox, and many went to New Spain after Cortés conquered it. And thus, there is none of their race left." He estimated that Española "once had a million men." [60] Equally high and contradictory estimates were made for the mainland. Oviedo remarks: "in this region of Castilla de Oro [a relatively small area taking in parts of Panama and Colombia] there were two million Indians, or, they were innumerable." [61] The eighteenth-century writer, Antonio de Ulloa, estimated that "there is not in America the eighth part of the population that existed at the time of discovery," basing his statement on the assumption that America of 1492 had 120,000,000 people. Clavigero notes that Riccoli placed the total for America at 300,000,000 people. De Pauw stated that while others esti-

[58] Cieza, *Crónica*, chap. LXIV.

[59] Fort y Roldán, *Cuba indígena*, p. 63.

[60] López de Gómara, *Historia de las Indias*, fols. XXVI verso, XXVII recto, XVI recto.

[61] Oviedo, *Historia*, Bk. XXIX, chap. X.

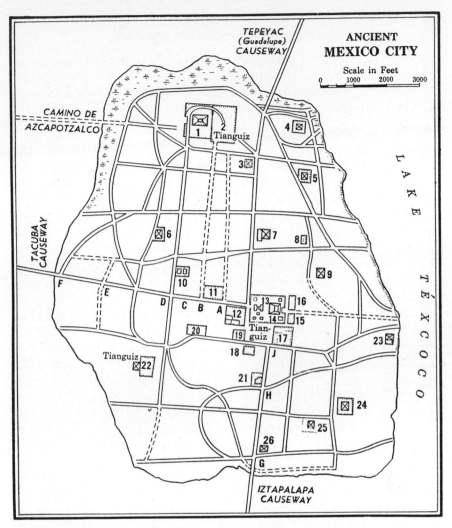

ANCIENT
MEXICO CITY

Scale in Feet
0   1000   2000   3000

1. Great Teocalli of Tlaltelolco
2. Tianguiz (Market-place)
3. Xacaculco,—Sta. Ana.
4. Tenantitech,—Conception Tequizpeca
5. Xocotillan,—San Antonio Tepito
6. Cuepopan,—Santa Maria la Redonda
7. Tezontlalamacoyan,—Sta. Caterina Martyr
8. . . . . . El Carmen
9. Atzacoalco,—San Sebastian
10. . . . . . Convento de la Conception
11. Palace of Guatemoc
12. Old Palace of Montezuma
13. Great Teocalli of Tenochtitlán
14. Teocalli of Tezcatlipoca
15. Aviary, (Casa de Aves)
16. Palace of Axayacatl
17. New Palace of Montezuma
18. Palace of Tilancalqui
19. Cuicacalli, Dance House (Casa de Danzas)
20. House of the Wild Animals (Casa de Fieras)
21. Huitzilan,—Hospital de Jesus Nazareno
22. Teocalli & Tianguiz de Moyotlan,—San Juan de la Penetencia
23. . . . . . San Lazaro
24. Avauhcalco,—St. Tomás Apóstol
25. Huitznahuac Ayauhcultitan,—San Pablo
26. Xoluco,—San Antonio Abad
A. 1st Cortadura
B. 2d Cortadura
C. 3d Cortadura
D. Tecpantzingo,—Puente de la Mariscala
E. Tolteacalli,—San Hipolito
F. Tolteacaalapan,—Puente de Alvarado
G. Xoluco,—Puente de San Antonio Abab
H. Huitzilan
J. Puente de Palacio

178a

mated the pre-Conquest population at 100,000,000 he thought 30,000,000 to 40,000,000 was about right.[62]

All these early statements are so little in agreement that it is hard to accept any of them. To illustrate the difficulties of finding the true population from early estimates, Humboldt points out that the population of the island of Otaheite [Tahiti] was estimated by Captain Cook when he disovered it at 100,000, by the missionaries at 49,000, by Captain Wilson at 16,000, and by Turnbull at 5,000. [63] In view of this uncertainty about the population of one small Pacific island in the eighteenth century, it is not strange that there is confusion in determining the population of a much greater area in the sixteenth.

A large population for Cuba and other tropical regions has been assumed on the basis of their great fertility, which could support millions of people. Yet, wherever we find large populations in tropical regions, they have developed conventionalized civilizations with at least relatively advanced agricultural and economic systems. Pre-Conquest Cubans had no such things. They farmed but little, their trade was practically nonexistent, and their villages were small and situated many miles apart. The total population in all probability was not more than a few thousand naked and halfnaked people in 1492. The same thing is true of the island of Española, Puerto Rico, and many other tropical areas.

PRE-CONQUEST MEXICAN POPULATION

The figures given for Mexican population are subject to the same doubts, and it is necessary to use other evidence for a more accurate estimate. With the exception of Sinaloa, [64] both coast lines and most of the northern part of Mexico were thinly populated. The great bulk of the people were concentrated in Vera Cruz, the Central Valley, Puebla, Morelos, Oaxaca, and Michoacán. Torquemada dwells on the great population, large cities, and fine buildings here when the Spaniards arrived. [65]

---

[62] Clavigero, *Mexico*, Dissertation VII, Section II.

[63] Humboldt, *New Spain*, I, 93-94 [*Nouvelle Espagne*, I, 321].

[64] Carl Sauer and Donald Brand, *Aztatlán* (Ibero-Americana, No. I, University of California Press, Berkeley, 1934), pp. 41-51, and Carl Sauer, *The Road to Cíbola* (Ibero-Americana, 3) pp. 1-9, give the evidence for a population equal to that of today at the time the Spaniards reached the region in 1530-1531. Professor Sauer in his *Aboriginal Population of Northwestern Mexico* (Ibero-Americana, 10, 1935), concludes that Northwestern Mexico, including parts of Nayarit, Sinaloa, and Sonora, had "almost three-fourths the number now living in that part of Mexico." (p. 32). He uses *vecino* as synonymous with family for his calculation, reckoning six to a family.

[65] Torquemada, *Monarchia indiana*, Bk. III, chap. V.

Of Mexico City he writes: "It is said of this city that when the Spaniards entered, it had 120,000 houses, and in each house three, four, and up to ten people (*vecinos*), so that, according to this count, its inhabitants (*vecinos*) numbered more than 300,000." [66] He adds, "And granted that it is true (which it is) that this city of Tenochtitlán was so populous and famous, it is so much more so now that it belongs to, and was built by the Spaniards, that there is no comparison." [67] He estimated the population at only "7,000 Spanish vecinos" and "8,000" Indians, a total of 15,000 at the time he wrote [1615] which is difficult to reconcile with other estimates and his own statements. After the rebuilding of Mexico City in 1524, Cortés wrote to the Emperor that the city already numbered 30,000 inhabitants.

There is one indication, however, that the population of Aztec Mexico City was not great. At the time of the Conquest the lakes covered a very large part of the area which is today heavily populated. The maximum area of Tenochtitlán was about three and a half square miles, as compared with the modern Federal District of 572 square miles with a population of under 2,000,000. The discrepancy is too great to permit an assumption of a large population in 1520. Modern London, for example, has only 12,000 people to the square mile. Did Tenochtitlán have more? If so, how was the population clothed and fed in a land with no wheeled vehicles and no beasts of burden? The whole of Aztec Mexico, moreover, comprised possibly not more than one-fourth or one-fifth of the area of the present Mexican nation. The Franciscans, to be sure, claim to have baptised more than 6,000,000 Indians in the region of the capital city alone between 1524 and 1540. But if the population was so extremely dense, why the fierce competition for encomiendas far beyond the number the Spaniards could give out?

The Spaniards in this early period numbered only a few hundred, and had there been so many millions, or even hundreds of thousands of Indians, to distribute there would have been no such problem. The grants made to Cortés himself indicate that the Indian population was not great. He received 22 towns with the surrounding land and 23,000 vassals, which he interpreted as 115,000 people. His grants were in Morelos, Oaxaca, Puebla Mexico, and Vera Cruz, the choicest and most densely populated parts of Mexico at that time as well as today. The area was not less than 25,000 square miles, equal to approximately one-fifth or

---

[66] *Monarchia indiana*, Bk. III, chap. XXIII.
[67] *Monarchia indiana*, Bk. III, chap. XXVI.

MUMMY, CHANCAY REGION OF PERU

GRAVE WITH BURIAL URNS, CHANCAY, PERU

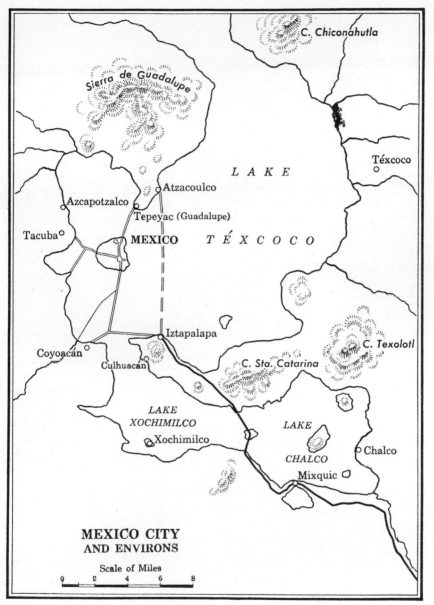

C. Chiconahutla

Sierra de Guadalupe

LAKE

Téxcoco

Atzacoulco

Azcapotzalco

Tepeyac (Guadalupe)

Tacuba

MEXICO   *TÉXCOCO*

C. Texolotl

Iztapalapa

Coyoacán

Culhuacan

C. Sta. Catarina

LAKE XOCHIMILCO

Xochimilco

LAKE CHALCO

Chalco

Mixquic

MEXICO CITY
AND ENVIRONS

Scale of Miles

0   2   4   6   8

Ancient Mexico City

180a

one-sixth of the dominions of Montezuma. Judged from this, the population of Montezuma's empire would not have reached a million people.[68] Humboldt thought that in 1800 New Spain contained more people than the same area had about 1500.

THE POPULATION OF THE INCA EMPIRE

The Inca Empire is usually considered to have comprised 8,-000,000 or 10,000,000 people. One modern authority places the population at from 16,000,000 to 32,000,000, [69] with the city of Cuzco itself having as many as 200,000 people.

This view receives support from the descriptions of the early chroniclers, almost all of whom agree that the early population was dense. Cieza repeats almost monotonously as he traverses the valleys and highlands of ancient Peru, "in former times (*antigua-mente*) this valley was heavily populated." For example, of the valley of Santa he says, "there were in former times many thousands of people, and today you cannot find 400 natives." He states that, whereas formerly the Indians built impressive irrigation projects throughout the valley and high up on the hillsides, "now, since there are so few Indians, as I have said, most of the fields are uncultivated, having become woods and brambles with such thickets that in many places it is impossible to penetrate them." In the valley of Parmonga, he reported that there was "nothing but deserted groves and wooded fields." [70]

But, at the same time, there are evidences that much of the population had disappeared before the Spanish invasion, and that it was never so heavy as first appearances indicate. It may be taken as axiomatic that vast populations will of necessity form a number of cities. And yet Cieza makes it clear that Cuzco was the only town in the whole of the Inca Empire that was of any size and importance.

"And in no part of this kingdom of Peru was there found any sort of a city of beauty (*con noble ornamento*), if it was not this city of Cuzco . . . And except for this city, the other provinces of the Indies are villages. And if there are any towns they have neither plan nor order." [71]

Nor is the evidence clear on the population trend after the Conquest. While to Cieza it seemed that there had once been many

[68] McBride, *Land Systems of Mexico*, pp. 48-49; Bernal Díaz, *Conquest of New Spain*, IV, 291-92.
[69] Means, *Ancient Civilizations*, pp. 295-96.
[70] Cieza, *Crónica*, chap. LXX.
[71] *Ibid.*, chap. XCII.

more Indians than there were fifteen years after the Conquest, judging from the remains found everywhere, he says that "even when the Spaniards discovered them and conquered them there were a great number of people," indicating that he believed some of the depopulation occurred before Spanish discovery.[72]

An undetermined degree of depopulation is revealed in an Ordinance issued by the Cabildo of Cuzco in 1543, ten years after the conquest of the city by the Spaniards. This Ordinance was concerned with preserving the *tambos* (supply and lodging stations along the Inca roads) and highways. More tambos were abandoned than occupied, because "in these said kingdoms and provinces there has been, and is a great diminution of the Indian natives." [73] Yet it is not at all certain that there were tremendous decreases after the Conquest. A careful reading of the first and second parts of Cieza de Leon's *Crónica* demonstrates that very frequently when he says "antiguamente" he really means *anciently* and not *formerly*. Many of the places of which he speaks as having large and sumptuous buildings and large populations "antiguamente" were pre-Inca ruins.[74] Hence the Spaniards cannot be held responsible for the extinction of their populations. In other places once thickly settled, only uncultivated fields with trees as big around as an ox remained, indicating that they were abandoned many years before the Spaniards entered South America.

There are other reasons to doubt the large population of ancient Peru. From the time of the first conquerors, the extremely broken and mountainous nature of the country and the vast uninhabited areas received considerable attention from Cieza and other chroniclers. The coastline was a desert absolutely barren of vegetation except for the few valleys where the rivers break through to the sea.[75] These valleys occupy only about three per cent of the entire coast line. Probably not more than one per cent of ancient Peru was habitable. The question then arises how large a population could be sustained with the available arable and pasture land.

Squier made extensive explorations in Peru in the nineteenth century and was impressed by the small area available for cultivation. He thought that previous estimates of the population were far too high and brought his estimate down to "between ten and

[72] Cieza, *Crónica,* chap. XXXIII.
[73] Garcilaso, *Comentarios,* Part II, Bk. VIII, Appendix I.
[74] Bailey W. Diffie, "A Markham Contribution to the *Leyenda Negra,*" *H.A.H.R.,* XVI (February, 1936), 96-103, and the evidence offered there.
[75] G. R. Johnson and Raye R. Platt, *Peru from the Air,* (New York: American Geographical Society, No. 12, 1930).

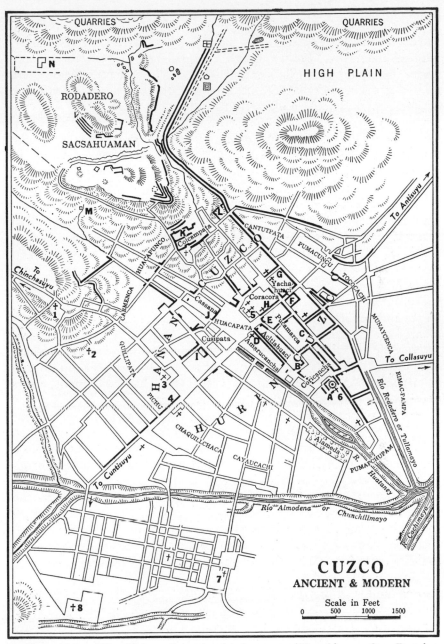

1. Santa Ana (Church); 2. Beaterio de Arcopata (Church); 3. San Francisco (Church); 4. University; 5. La Catedral; 6. Santo Domingo (Church); 7. Belén (Church); 8. Iglesia del Panteón. INCA RUINS—A. Temple of the Sun; B. Palace of Virgins of the Sun; C. Palace of Inca Tupac Yupanqui; D. Palace of Huayna Capac; E. Palace of Inca Yupanqui; F. Palace of Inca Rocca; G. Palace of Yachahuasi; H. Palace of Inca Viracocha; I. House of Garcilasso de la Vega; J. Palace of Inca Pachacutic; K. Palace of Manco Capac; L. Intahuatana, or Gnomon of the Sun; M. Pila, or Bath, of the Incas; N. Ruins of Inca building. Heavy lines indicate ancient Inca walls

twelve millions." [76] Cobo was so struck by the small amount of arable land that when he wrote his work, after more than half a century in Peru, he remarks on "the very few people who formerly inhabited it, and the still fewer it has at present, relatively to its great size and expanse." The heading he gives his chapter on this subject, "On how America was lightly populated and the causes for this," reveals his conclusions. His explanation demonstrates that because of the immense deserts where it seldom or never rained, the swamps where it never ceased raining, the jungles where the vegetation was too dense for people to live, the mountain regions that were too cold, the immense areas of bad lands composed of mountains, sand or salt flats, and finally the good land that was not settled by the Indians, the population was small. He did not, however, venture a guess at the total.[77] After reading Cobo's description of Peru's geography and travels through the country, it is difficult to believe it was ever heavily peopled.[78]

Most estimates of population are dependent on the translation of the Spanish word *vecino*. A vecino in the sixteenth century could mean either the head of a family, or a citizen with political rights within the community (the majority of the people did not enjoy political rights), or merely *one* person. On the one hand, vecino may be taken to represent an average family of five or ten, as Means does in his calculations, or the unit vecino may be multiplied by as much as twenty-five or thirty. On the other hand, it may be taken to mean only one person and it was so used at times by Garcilaso and Torquemada. Thus, the vecino is not a reliable basis of calculation. A better method is to estimate the number of people that ancient Peru could have supported with its methods of production.

The Inca Empire had an area of some 380,000 square miles,[79] comprising parts of modern Ecuador, Peru, Bolivia, Argentina, and Chile. The area within the boundaries of these nations today is several times that of ancient Peru. Modern Peru alone is one-third larger, and occupies a great deal of territory not included in the Inca Empire.

Peru has in cultivation today about 3,715,000 acres,[80] and ap-

---

[76] E. G. Squier, *Peru: Incidents of Travel and Exploration in the Land of the Incas* (Philadelphia, 1877), pp. 13-15.

[77] Cobo, *Nuevo Mundo*, Bk. XI, chap. I.

[78] Cobo, *Nuevo Mundo*, Bk. II, chaps. I-XXXI. See also N. Andrew N. Cleven, *The Political Organization of Bolivia* (Washington, D. C., 1940), pp. 3-15.

[79] Means, *Fall*, p. 4.

[80] *South American Handbook*, 1942, p. 539.

proximately 17,000,000 in pasture.[81] The maximum arable land (except that east of the Andes where the Inca Empire did not extend) with the maximum irrigation possible, and using modern engineering science, is about 4,000,000 acres. How many people could have been supported if the Incas had cultivated every foot of arable land?

On the basis of the probable consumption of corn per person,[82] the corn alone necessary for 1,000,000 people each year would have been approximately 8,660,000 bushels. With a production of 20 bushels to the acre (in the United States the average yield per acre is 23 bushels, and it was undoubtedly much less in Inca Peru), each million inhabitants would have needed 433,000 acres in corn a year. Other agricultural products besides corn, however, took up much arable land; at least three times as much land was cultivated as was used for corn. Altogether 1,300,000 acres of land would have been required to support a million people. Moreover, a great deal of land could not be cultivated every year. On an average, one year's cultivation in five was the rule, making scarcely more than 2,000,000 or 3,000,000 acres in cultivation at one time in ancient Peru. Thus, that part of ancient Peru included in modern Peru could not have had more than 1,500,000 people, assuming the maximum use of the land.

As for the parts of the Inca Empire that lay outside the present-day Peru, they consisted of the high plateau of Bolivia, which Garcilaso classed as having "few people" and being "scarcely inhabited," [83] the northwestern part of Argentina, likewise lightly populated; northern Chile, which was, and is properly a desert; and Ecuador, which could hardly have contained a greater proportion of people than Peru.

Significant also was the lack of enough Indians to give out in encomiendas. Pizarro, who of course received the largest encomienda, around Atabillos northeast of Lima, claimed 100,000 Indians.[84] Other conquistadores received only a few hundred Indians, or less, or even none.[85] The governors were hard put to find Indians to distribute, and this was one of the main causes of the civil wars from 1538-54.

Also pertinent to the question of population was its rapid redistribution after the Conquest. While early chroniclers point out

---

[81] *Foreign Commerce Year Book,* 1933.
[82] See Appendix to this chapter for a more detailed treatment of this topic.
[83] Garcilaso, *Comentarios,* Bk. IV, chap. XVII.
[84] Means, *Fall,* p. 66.
[85] Garcilaso, *Comentarios,* Part II, Bk. VI, chap. I.

the numerous deserted valleys, they also stress the establishment of dozens of Spanish towns stretching from Ecuador into Peru, Bolivia, Argentina, and Chile. Cieza, Garcilaso, and others make it clear that many of these towns were in regions in which there had been no previous population, or but little. Lima itself is an example.[86] Potosí, the great silver-mining center, soon had 100,000 people, and attained 160,000 at its maximum. Besides these, there were a large number of small settlements, inhabited by Indian populations; in fact, perhaps 90 per cent or more of the people in most of these centers were Indian. The depopulation in certain areas was largely attributable to the migrations of the resettlement.

Finally, there is the city of Cuzco itself, to which have been attributed as many as 200,000 people. The area of the city, less than one-square mile after Spanish settlement, when admittedly both its area and population increased, could scarcely have contained so many inhabitants.[87] The Jesuit historian, José de Acosta, takes the view that the Indians were not decreasing but increasing in 1590.

"What causes these lands to be inhabited, and some of them heavily populated, is the wealth of the mines that are found in them, because gold and silver control everything. In these lands, thanks to the mines, there are some very large towns of Spaniards and Indians, such as Potosí and Huancavelica in Peru and Zacatecas in New Spain. Throughout all the mountains (serranías) there is a heavy population of Indians, and today they are maintaining their numbers, and they even say that the Indians are increasing, except that the work in the mines uses up a great many; and some general epidemics, such as the Cocoliste in New Spain have killed off a great part; but in truth, judging from their dwellings, it cannot be seen that they are decreasing." [88]

Cobo records that the driving back of savages never conquered by the Incas resulted in the occupation and peopling of much good land.[89]

* * * * * * *

While the population of pre-Conquest America cannot be definitely determined, it is clear that the early figures were not only in such disagreement regarding specific localities in the same period

---

[86] See Appendix, chap. 9.
[87] See Appendix, chap. 9.
[88] Acosta, *Historia de las Indias*, Bk. III, chap. XIX.
[89] Cobo, *Nuevo Mundo*, Bk. VI, chap. I.

as to be subject to doubt, but were far too high. If we take into account all available evidence regarding geographical features, the sources of food and agricultural methods of the Indians, and the chroniclers' descriptions of the most populous centers, it is certain that even the most densely settled regions, such as Mexico and Peru, could not have supported anything like the huge numbers of people attributed to them.

Acceptance of the early estimates has given rise to a belief that the decline in native population as a result of the Conquest was much greater than it actually was. In reality, some of the apparent depopulation came from the rapid resettlement after the Conquest, when the Indians migrated to the new mining and agricultural centers opened up by the Spaniards. The Indians, far from being exterminated, continued to form the majority of the population of post-Conquest Latin America.

APPENDIX: POPULATION OF PRE-CONQUEST AMERICA

The per capita yearly consumption of corn may have been about 485 pounds, equal to 8 2/3 bushels, the amount consumed by the Mayas of modern times.[90] On the basis of the probable consumption of corn per person, the corn alone necessary for 1,000,000 people each year would have been approximately 8,660,000 bushels. The modern ear of corn is eight to twelve inches long, but the ears found in the graves of the Incas were as a rule not more than three to four inches, although modern Indians produce much longer ears, and it is possible the pre-Conquest peoples also did. What the yield per acre was cannot be known, but such small ears might not produce five bushels to the acre.

The following table shows the size and weight of various types of corn:

Size	Weight	Type	No. for one bu. (by wt.)
10 x 2¼ in.	1 lb.	Yellow Dent	70
8 x 1⅜ in.	5 oz.	Squaw	224
7 x 1½ in.	5 oz.	Squaw	224
6 x 1½ in.	4 oz.	Squaw	280
	On basis of above:		
4 x 1⅜ in.	2½ oz.	Squaw	448

[90] New York Industrial Museum Maya Exhibit, Rockefeller Center, April, 1937. In the United States the per capita consumption is about 16 bushels annually. See J. H. Kempton, "Maize—Our Heritage from the Indian," in Annual Report of the Smithsonian Institution, 1937 (Washington, D. C., 1938), pp. 387-89.

The relation of yield to the size of corn ears may be judged from the following expert opinion:

"It is difficult to give a definite figure as to the estimate of probable yield per acre of corn 3 to 4 inches in length. Small ears do not necessarily indicate a small yield per acre, because fertility and closeness of planting also affect the yield. In a number of places in Mexico and Peru, more than one crop was raised in one year. Ears much larger than 4 inches in length are grown in parts of Mexico and were probably grown in prehistoric times.

"The average yield per acre of corn in the United States is 23.0 bushels. The average length of the fair grade of modern corn is about 8 to 10 inches. On the basis of weight about 70 to 80 ears of well-matured corn would be required for one bushel." [91] But presuming a production of, say, twenty bushels to the acre, 433,000 acres in corn each year would be needed for each million inhabitants.

Corn, however, was only one item of food. There were potatoes, oca, quínoa, peppers, coca, and numerous other food products. Cotton, bamboo, and other such crops which grew in the lowlands, took up a considerable part of the arable land. There was a total of at least three times as much land in cultivation as in corn only; and Garcilaso states that only irrigated lands were used for corn. Thus, every million people needed a minimum of 1,300,000 acres of land for their support.

However, a great deal of land in the Inca Empire could not be cultivated every year. Some was cultivated only every four or five years, and some only every twenty or thirty. On an average, one year's cultivation in every five was the rule in both ancient and modern times.[92] If this is the case, hardly more than 2,000,000 or 3,000,000 acres were in cultivation at any one time. Thus, that part of ancient Peru included in modern Peru could not have had more than 1,500,000 people, assuming maximum use of the land.

Another basis can be used to calculate the possible population. Each *puric* received a *tupu* of land, equal to a *fanega y media* of Spain, or 2 4/10 acres. For each son there was an extra tupu and for each daughter one-half, making a total of 7 8/10 acres on an average for five people in a family. According to this, every million people held 1,560,000 acres. But Garcilaso says that this meant corn land and that they received other land in addition. Again we can see that with the available amount of land placed

[91] Communication from U. S. Department of Agriculture, August 18, 1939.
[92] George McCutchen McBride, *The Agrarian Indian Communities of Highland Bolivia*, American Geographic Society Research Series, No. 5 (New York, 1921), p. 7.

at the maximum of 4,000,000 acres, the population of that part of the Inca Empire within modern Peru could have been little more than 2,000,000 people, granted always the absolute maximum use of the land at all times.

These allowances are more liberal than those made by a modern botanical authority, who says that "in maize the American Indian developed a food plant capable of supporting a family of five for an entire year on the production of four acres." [93] This would necessitate 800,000 acres of corn land for a million people, and if accepted as a basis of calculation, would cut the population of ancient Peru even more than indicated above. It is significant to note that neither modern Peru nor Mexico, where corn is the staff of life, have heavy yields. Mexico, for example, produces about 6 to 7 quintals a hectare (or 10 to 11 bushels an acre), barely one-fourth per acre what Canada produces, and less than one-half of the United States' yield per acre. "Indeed, in yield per hectare of corn, Mexico ranks among the lowest in the world. Out of 45 countries for which average corn yield per hectare figures are given in the *International Yearbook of Agricultural Statistics* for the period 1923-27, Mexico ranked 39!" [94]

PRE-CONQUEST POPULATION OF LIMA

Bandelier, the archeologist, speaks of "the Rimac Valley [Lima] during the aboriginal period" and says that "agriculture was much more limited" than when he was writing from there in 1890, and before the recent important advances made in Peruvian agriculture. He makes a similar observation about the region of Pachacamac (or Irma): "The maximum number of souls that Irma can have contained was twelve thousand, and this represented, with the exception of two more insignificant clusters, the entire population of that fertile valley previous to the coming of the Spaniards." [95] Other regions, such as Trujillo Valley, were also lightly populated, as Bandelier points out.

PRE-CONQUEST POPULATION OF CUZCO

The population of the city of Cuzco has been estimated to have been as great as 200,000. The area covered by Cuzco was less than one square mile after the Spanish settlement. The Indian city, according to all testimony, contained numerous palaces, courtyards, and public squares which took up much of the space. The residences

---

[93] Kempton, *Maize*, p. 386.
[94] Eyler Simpson, *Ejido*, p. 160.
[95] Bandelier letter to Thomas Janvier, quoted in Radin, *Indians of South America*, pp. 245-47.

were of one story, or in rare cases two. Such an area is hardly capable of holding 200,000 people if the city proper is meant, and if the surrounding province is included, the relative population was extremely small. Manhattan Island, for example, one of the most densely populated areas on earth, where residences run as a rule from three to thirty or more stories in height, has only 122,000 people to the square mile.

But the most interesting fact regarding Cuzco is that it *increased* in size and population after the Conquest. Garcilaso, who is noted for his descriptions of the disasters befalling the Inca Empire because of the Spanish Conquest, makes this point very definitely. Describing the city of Cuzco as it was in 1560 in comparison to what it had been before the Conquest, he says:

"Far from this ward and toward the west there was a town of more than 300 vecinos, called Cayaucachi. It was more than 1,000 paces from the last houses of the city. This was in the year 1560; now when I am writing in 1602, it is already (as I have been told) inside the city of Cuzco, the population of which has grown so much that it has grown around Cayaucachi on all sides.

"To the west of the city, also 1,000 paces from it, there was another ward called Chaquillchaca . . . . Also, they have told me, the population of the city now reaches to Chaquillchaca . . . . To the north there was another ward called Pichu. It was also outside the city . . . . There was another ward called Quillapata which was also outside of the populated area." [96]

---

[96] Garcilaso, *Comentarios,* Bk. VII, chap. VIII.

People and Work in the
Sixteenth Century

L ATIN-AMERICAN COLONIAL SOCIETY rapidly took shape in the
sixteenth century from the elements of the old, both Indian
and Spanish. Since the Indians continued to form the bulk of the
population in many regions after the Conquest, native institutions,
customs, and mores profoundly influenced the social life of the
colonies. We have already seen how Indian systems played their
part in the seizure of the land by the Spaniards, and in the agricultural and economic development of the early years of Spanish
settlement. It is now essential to examine the social structure arising from the fusion of Spanish and Indian class societies, the labor
systems that evolved, and the composition of the population deriving from the intermixture of Indian, Spaniard, and Negro.

WANTED: AN INDIAN POLICY

The search for an Indian policy that would be both profitable
and equitable was one of the chief preoccupations of the Spanish
Crown. Given the uncharted course which the discovery of the New
World forced the Spanish monarchs to follow, the Crown's policy
was necessarily subject to quick changes, and even sudden reversals.
It was not until the end of the sixteenth century that Indian policy
was stabilized (if it can be said ever to have been stabilized), and
the intervening period was characterized by several devices for
securing the labor of the Indians. The chief of these were slavery,
the *encomienda,* the *repartimiento,* and the *congregación.* These
have been mentioned in connection with other aspects of the Spanish
colonial economy, but it is necessary here to examine them as a
part of the Indian labor system.[1] Negro slaves were introduced into

---

[1] Simpson, *Encomienda,* gives a good picture of Indian policy.

America soon after the Conquest, and also came to occupy an important position in the general labor system and the population.

Colombus foresaw in Indian slavery a source of profits, and believed the Indians would rival the Negroes brought from Guinea. His opportunity to carry out his slaving project in an entirely legal manner came in 1495, when he returned to Española, found it in revolt, and spent several months in defeating the Indians. From the war came Indian prisoners, who were infidels and, therefore, according to the concepts of the times, legitimately slaves. Several hundred of them were sent to Spain, where they were offered for sale by Juan Rodríguez de Fonseca, in charge of Indian affairs. The Crown ordered the sale suspended until an investigation could be made of the reasons for their enslavement. In the meantime, the Indians were sent to work in the galleys. The Crown's policy at this date neither approved nor disapproved Indian slavery; it was yet to be formulated.

Other cargoes of Indian slaves soon reached Spain, but for a number of years the Crown continued to waver, at times permitting their sale, and again ordering their return to Española, or their release. In 1503, regulations were finally issued which authorized slaving expeditions and provided the Crown with its share of the profits, at first a third, later a fifth. The excuse given for the enslavement of the Indians was their cannibalism; through slavery they could be converted to Christian practices. This same year saw the legalization of the encomienda system, which was justified as serving to protect the peaceful Indians from the warlike cannibals.

Henceforth for many years, a double Indian policy was to be followed. Enslavement was permissible of Indians captured in war, of cannibals and, through purchase, of those Indians who were slaves of other Indians. Friendly and peaceable natives were to be distributed in encomiendas, or were to be direct vassals of the Crown.

After the death of Isabella in 1504, Ferdinand continued to authorize and regulate Indian slavery. The Caribs of the Islands and of the north coast of South America, and Indians of other islands near Española, such as the Bahamas, might be brought to Española, but the latter were to be given wages. The demand for Indians in Española at this early date arose from the greatly increased economic tempo as a result of the Spanish settlement. Even had there been the large Indian population which many asserted existed before the Conquest (and it is unlikely such large numbers ever existed), the amount of labor performed after the Conquest was so much greater that more Indians had to be found to perform the new tasks, and to take the place of those who died under the hard working conditions.

The nearby islands supplied a part of the needed labor. The Bahamas, Florida, and the Atlantic coast as far north as the Carolinas, Yucatán, and the coast northward along the Gulf of Mexico were all discovered by slaving expeditions. When Cortés and other conquistadores entered the mainland, enslavement of the Indians was customary, those not enslaved being distributed in encomiendas, or reserved for the Crown. On the mainland a new source of slaves was found. Slavery existed among the Indians, and the Spaniards bought the slaves from their Indian masters, or seized them. These were known as *indios de rescate*. Such slaves were frequently taken in lieu of tribute, or if the tributary had no slaves, he might produce members of his own tribe or family and, forcing them to swear they were slaves, give them to the Spaniards. They were then branded and marched off to the mines or other work. This was a legal practice, frequently mentioned by Cortés, Bernal Díaz, and other early writers.

HUMANITARIANISM AND THE INDIANS

In the meantime, many protests about the treatment of the Indians were pouring into Spain, and the Crown was constantly seeking a more satisfactory policy, one that would permit the use but not the abuse of the Indians. A wish for good treatment was expressed in the instructions given to the explorers and governors sent to America, the larger part of their directives being concerned with justice for the Indians.[2] The Crown sought to protect the Indians by requiring religious instruction, a minimum wage, and kind treatment. The systematic introduction of the Negro from 1502 was in one respect a measure designed to protect the Indians. Gradually, however, in spite of legislation to the contrary, religious instruction was neglected, the working hours of the Indians increased and frequently, even where specified, no wages were paid to them.

Perhaps the first voice in defense of the Indians in America was that of the Dominican, Fray Antonio de Montesinos, in Santo Domingo in 1510. He condemned his parishioners for their oppression of the Indians, and they demanded that he recant. Instead, he announced that he would refuse the sacraments of the Church to those who did not change their way of treating the Indians.

---

[2] Merriman, *Spanish Empire*, II, 230-31.

One of the results of this sermon was a controversy in Spain itself, which led Ferdinand to publish the Laws of Burgos in 1512. The code provided maximum working hours, adequate food and shelter, and royal officials to see that the Indians were well treated. The laws were neglected and the abuses continued.

Three years later Las Casas, who had become a monk, surrendered his encomienda, and returned to Spain to become an advocate of the Indians. He presented his case to Ferdinand and later to Charles V, arousing a controversy which was to last for many years.

The encomenderos held that the conquest of "inferior" peoples by "superior" peoples was warranted. The view that the Indians were naturally inferior was extremely convenient for the European nations of the early sixteenth century. Francis I of France, for example, declared that the Indians were "savages living without the knowledge of God or the use of Reason." [3] Many argued that the Indians were slaves by nature, and Aristotle was cited as proof. Some alleged that the Indians were not rational beings, and asked whether this did not justify their enslavement. It was contended the Indian had no soul, thus stirring up a tremendous religious controversy which Charles V submitted to a council of theologians. Arguments and counterarguments were offered. Antonio de Villasante, a citizen of Española from 1493, testified that the wisest Indian did not know how to govern himself as well as the most ignorant Spaniard. He said that if the Indians were freed, they would return to their customs of dancing, nakedness, idleness, eating of snakes and spiders, drunkenness and gluttony, and that the colony would face economic ruin. [4] Lucas Vásquez de Ayllón argued that it was better for the Indians to be *hombres siervos* (servile men) than *bestias libres* (free beasts).

The reasons for the failure of the early series of social experiments, through which the Crown had tried to protect the Indians, were summarized by a Cuban bishop, who declared such an attempt "convenient to the service of neither God, the King, nor the Indians." When the whole concept of society was based upon the belief that men were naturally made by the Creator to live in either superior or inferior conditions, it was not possible to secure any great amelioration of the Indians' situation. The theological controversy as to whether they had souls, and which Charles V had

---

[3] Hanke, *First Social Experiments*, p. 5-6. The subject of the treatment of the Indians and the various theories concerning them has been thoroughly studied by Dr. Hanke.

[4] Hanke, *First Social Experiments*, p. 32.

referred to a council, was eventually carried for decision to the Papacy; and in 1537 Paul III (1534-1549) declared them to be sons of Adam and members of the human race.[5]

In 1530, the Crown, moved by the numerous reports of abuses and violations of the law, decreed the abolition of the slave traffic, and ordered the registration of all slaves. The slave trade was not to be so easily abolished. Many exceptions were made in the law, and excuses were found for enslaving more Indians.

In this same year, the Crown established the office of *Corregidor de Indios,* an official whose duty it was to protect the Indians. Indians not under encomienda, or who had reverted to the Crown when encomiendas were vacated for any reason, were under his charge. The country was divided into *corregimientos,* or administrative districts with a corregidor at the head. The idea of this office had arisen from the Crown's desire to have protectors for the Indians after the abolition of the encomiendas, a project on which it was engaged at the moment. But conditions in America, rather than theories in Spain, were ultimately to determine the fate of the Indians. The first settlers needed laborers. Hence, the encomienda persisted despite the intentions of the Crown, and the establishment of the *corregimientos* created a dual system. The abuses that arose in the office of corregidor also prevented the Indians from receiving the protection designed.

The Indians were now divided into four general groups: encomienda Indians, corregimiento Indians, slaves, and nobles (caciques or curacas), whose special status will be noted shortly. This was the situation in 1542, when the Crown decided to clear up the whole Indian situation with an exhaustive set of New Laws.

THE INDIAN AND THE NEW LAWS [6]

The New Laws were the supreme effort of the Crown to solve the Indian problem in a way that would relieve the Indians of oppression but at the same time enable the Spaniards to use them as a working class. These laws were in part the work of Las Casas, who to the end of his life, carried on a consistent campaign in favor of the Indians.[7] The Indians were declared free men, equal in all respects to other subjects of the King. All officials, whether clerical or state, and all who held encomiendas without license were to

[5] Lewis Hanke, "Pope Paul III and the American Indians," *The Harvard Theological Review,* XXX (April, 1937), 65-102; Colmeiro, *Economía política,* II, 384; Means, *Fall,* p. 269.

[6] Henry Stevens, ed. and tr. *The New Laws of the Indies* (London. 1893), a facsimile reprint and translation.

[7] Means, *Fall,* pp. 82-100.

surrender them to the Crown. Overlarge encomiendas were to be reduced in size and all were to revert to the Crown at the death of the holder, that is, they were not to be hereditary. Failure to give proper education to the Indians, or mistreatment of them, was cause for forfeiture of the encomienda. In Peru, for example, all those involved as leaders in the fight between the Pizarros and the Almagros were to lose their encomiendas.

Concerning slavery and encomiendas, it was provided: "We order and command that henceforth for no reason of war or for any other, even though it be by title of rebellion or purchase, is any Indian to be made a slave, and we wish them to be treated as vassals of the Crown of Castile, since such they are. No person may make use of any Indian, either as a *naboría or tapia* [servant or encomienda Indian], or in any other way, against his will." [8] Indians held as slaves illegally were to be set free at once, and Indians were to be used as carriers *(tamemes)* only where it could not be avoided, and only with their consent.

These laws never went fully into effect. When Tello de Sandoval, who had been appointed *juez de residencia,* or special investigating judge, arrived in New Spain and inquired as to the wisdom of the New Laws, the Dominicans, who had distinguished themselves since the time of Montesinos in Española in 1510 as protectors of the Indians, replied: ". . . great good comes to the state and his Majesty from having the Indians help the Spaniards in their commerce and on their estates, because without Indians all trade and profit cease . . . ." [9]

. The emphasis on the need of Indian labor had its effect. Viceroy Mendoza recognized the difficulty of destroying overnight a complicated labor system that had been half a century in developing, and suspended execution of the laws until the Crown could be consulted. In Peru, attempted enforcement provoked open rebellion.

The Crown, recognizing its weakness, decreed modifications that profoundly changed the original intent of the New Laws. The article Number 35 of the New Laws requiring all encomiendas to revert to the Crown on the death of the holder was repealed. By a special. cédula, wives and children of encomenderos were allowed to inherit. Indian slavery had not been prohibited by the New Laws, only illegal enslavement, and ways were found to avoid the letter of the law here as elsewhere. Nor did the use of the Indians as carriers *(tamemes)* cease; they continued to serve until beasts of

[8] Article 26, in Simpson, *Encomienda,* pp. 150-54.
[9] Quoted in Simpson, *Encomienda,* p. 170.

burden supplanted them, and where the country was too rough for mules or burros, they were used until almost the end of the colonial period.

Paternalistic legislation did not cease with the partial repeal of the New Laws, but one important question was settled. The encomienda as a system of labor was to continue.

INDIAN EMANCIPATION

The next important move of the Crown was the abolition of slavery. The early legislation on the subject of the freedom of the Indians [10] always contained enough loopholes to permit slavery under specified restrictions, which were frequently so poorly enforced as to be of little effect. Such laws were passed specifically in 1526, 1530, 1532, 1542, and 1548, to mention only some of the most important. While enslavement by no means ended with the law of 1548, a sufficient degree of enforcement was obtained (in part because the epoch of conquest was ending and fewer Indians were taken in open warfare) to use it as a point of departure. The intent of the law was to put into effect those provisions of the New Laws of 1542 (Articles 26 and 27) which prohibited enslavement in the future, and demanded the emancipation of Indians held as slaves illegally. The law of 1548, and the subsequent orders for carrying it out provoked immediate and bitter protests from the colonists. [11] Despite these protests, the Crown persisted in its intention. The titles of the slaveholders were examined, the burden of proof falling on the owner rather than on the slaves, and emancipation was put into effect. Some of the Indians were restored to their homes, some freed to go where they wished, and others were settled in villages, or *congregaciones,* in keeping with the Crown policy of gathering the Indians into settlements where they could be Christianized at the same time their labor was utilized.[12]

A number of things indicate that the emancipation had more than a little success in freeing the Indians. Apparently it served to decrease the amount of work done by the Indians, for reports to the Crown similar to the following were sent from all parts of New Spain:

"Now that the slaves have been removed and a Spaniard is prohibited by law from using a *naboría* or *tapia* against his will,

---

[10] For legislation on slavery see *Leyes de Indias,* Libro VI, Título II.

[11] See Lesley Byrd Simpson, *Studies in the Administration of the Indians in New Spain: IV. The Emancipation of the Indian Slaves and the Resettlement of the Freedmen* (Ibero-Americana: 16, Berkeley: The University of California Press, 1940).

[12] On the *congregación* see pp. 72; 198-200.

and since personal services and the use of Indian carriers have been disallowed, how can the land be cultivated, settled or increased? . . . The land is of such a nature and [the Indians] . . . are so accustomed to having their own way . . . that (if one awaited their pleasure) rather than work they would spend their lives with a torn blanket and a handful of chocolate. . . ." [13]

The evidence also demonstrates that at this period the Indians were not being forced to labor in Peru. Cieza de León noted:

"Porco was formerly extremely rich, and it still is, and it is believed that it will be so forever . . . . And it is held certain from what has been observed, that there is so much of this metal that if there were someone to search for it and extract it, they would mine but little less of it than of the iron extracted in the province of Biscay [Spain]. But because they do not mine it with Indians, and because the region is too cold for Negroes and it is very costly, seems to be the reason why this great wealth is lost." [14]

The Repartimiento

Things could not remain in this state. There was work to be done, and if the Indians would not work under one system, they had to be forced to work under another. And so the *repartimiento* was born. It was not new. We have seen Columbus distributing the Indians; and we have seen what was at first a temporary grant of Indians grow into the hereditary encomienda. All Indians were not encomienda Indians, however, nor were all non-encomienda Indians slaves. Many thousands of Indians, some authorities say half, were direct vassals of the Crown. It was these Indians for whom the *corregidores de Indios* were responsible, although the *corregidores* were as severely limited as the encomenderos by the New Laws of 1542. To these Indians were now added, thanks to emancipation, many more.

The repartimiento which sprang up to meet this situation rested at first on no secure legal footing. It was designed to force the Indian to work, and at the same time to meet the laws which declared him a free man who could not be forced to labor without compensation. As recognized by the authorities and executed by them, it was a temporary allotment of Indians granted to some individual who was deemed to be performing a work of public

---

[13] Quoted in Simpson, *Emancipation of the Slaves*, p. 11.

[14] Cieza, *Crónica,* chap. CVIII.

interest, the latter requirement being interpreted liberally enough
to include work on private estates as well as public roads, mines,
or churches. [15] Since the repartimiento in this form did not achieve
full legal standing until 1609, its discussion will be deferred until
our treatment of the Indian labor system during the seventeenth
and eighteenth centuries, but it is worth while noting that it had
roots in both the Aztec and Inca social systems, as well as in those
of other Indian peoples.

The masses of the people subject to the Aztec, Maya and Inca
rulers (as well as those subject to many other Indian chieftains)
were accustomed to various types of forced labor. Before the Conquest in Mexico, the *mayeques,* or serfs bound to the soil, were
responsible for numerous kinds of work for the lord of the lands, in
addition to the portion of their crops which they gave him. The
maceguales, or free peasants who held a share in the community
holdings, were required to work on the various public lands belonging to the chieftains and priests, or designed for the support
of certain public offices, and to pay a tribute in addition to this
labor. [16]

In Peru the obligations of the masses to the nobles were almost
numberless. [17] The very name under which the repartimiento was
known in Peru, *mita,* was of Indian origin. Under the mita, the Indians were obliged to perform a definite stint of work, or serve for
a specified period of each year at road building, tilling the fields of
the Inca and the nobles, constructing temples and palaces, mining,
or whatever was demanded of them. [18] The Spaniards found it comparatively easy to adopt the system to recruit Indians for work on
their farms, in commerce, as carriers, in the mines, or at other
types of labor. [19]

REDUCCIONES AND CONGREGACIONES

One other method used by the Spaniards to accomplish their
double purpose of Christianizing and utilizing the Indians was the
establishment of villages known as *reducciones* or *congregaciones,*
on the Spanish model, and the concentration therein of the Indians.
The use of this system in the formation of the post-Conquest land-

[15] Lesley Byrd Simpson, *Studies in the Administration of the Indians in New
Spain,* III. *The Repartimiento System of Native Labor in New Spain and Guatemala*
(Ibero-Americana: 13 Berkeley: The University of California Press, 1938).

[16] McBride, *Land Systems of Mexico,* pp. 117-22.

[17] Garcilaso, *Comentarios,* Bk. V, chap. XV.

[18] Acosta, *Historia de las Indias,* Bk. VI, chap. XV.

[19] Arthur Franklin Zimmerman, *Francisco de Toledo; Fifth Viceroy of Peru,
1569-1581* (Caldwell, Idaho: The Caxton Printers, 1938), pp. 29-30 and *passim.*

tenure system has been noted. (Chapter IV). But the Spaniards also used it for general social and economic purposes. As early as the Laws of Burgos, [20] the Crown had visualized settling the Indians in villages or towns adjacent to Spanish towns, where they could be at hand for work and religious instruction. When the mainland was reached and encomiendas granted, the encomenderos were instructed to establish the Indians in such settlements. [21] From 1546, it was resolved that "the Indians should be reduced to villages and not be allowed to live divided and separated in the mountains and wildernesses." All civil and religious officials were ordered to cooperate in this activity, which became one of the settled policies of the Crown. It was also the policy of the Crown for such villages to be ruled by Indian chieftains. [22]

In New Spain the work of forming *congregaciones* went on throughout the latter half of the sixteenth century, but the greatest progress was made under the Viceroy Count of Monterey, who resettled many towns from 1598 to 1605. [23] Indian towns were similarly established in other parts of the Spanish possessions. In Peru, the work of resettlement was carried out chiefly by Viceroy Francisco de Toledo (1569-81). [24] The towns established by Toledo were ruled by Christian Indians, elected to office under Spanish rule and subject to the higher authority of Spanish officials. [25]

In addition, there continued to exist many hamlets and villages already centuries old, but which now formed a part of an encomienda or were subjected directly to the Crown. These were governed by the representatives of the encomenderos, who might maintain in office the caciques of the Indians, or by representatives of the corregidor who was the King's appointee. There was also, as a rule, some religious representative. In many places the Indians were gathered into these villages around military posts, mines, or monasteries.

Minute instructions were provided for the settlement of the Indians in the new towns, and the provisions for their welfare were laid down, including the beds they were to sleep on (in substitution of the floor to which they were accustomed under pre-Conquest conditions), and the houses in which they lived. "It is obvious,"

---

[20] See Lesley Byrd Simpson, *Studies in the Administration of the Indians in New Spain:* I. *The Laws of Burgos of 1512;* II. *The Civil Congregation* (Ibero-Americana: 7, Berkeley: The University of California Press, 1934).

[21] See *Leyes de Indias,* Libro VI, Título III.

[22] *Relación* of Viceroy Antonio de Mendoza to his successor, in *D. I. I.,* VI, 501-03.

[23] Simpson, *Civil Congregation,* 31 ff.

[24] Zimmerman, *Francisco de Toledo,* pp. 72-73, 121-27 and *passim.*

[25] *Memorial* of Viceroy Toledo to the King, in *D. I. I.,* VI, 528-37.

says one modern historian, that the Spanish-type town was more "commodious, convenient, and salubrious" than the Indian hamlet. [26]

In order to protect the Indians, it was at first prescribed by law that the encomenderos should live among their Indians, but when this led to abuse rather than protection it was decreed that neither the encomendero nor his mestizo, mulatto, or Negro servants or slaves should live in Indian villages, which were to be governed by Indians.

PRE- AND POST-CONQUEST INDIAN CONDITIONS

There was no tremendous difference in the position of the Indians before and after the European Conquest. The masses subject to the Aztec and Inca rulers were peasants, serfs, or slaves. They remained so after the European Conquest. Many of the Indian chieftains, on the other hand, were incorporated into the Spanish system of subordinate officials. Torquemada speaks of the rulers of Mexico before the Conquest, "oppressing the poor and treating them not like rational creatures but like dumb brutes." This, he says, was done by the "chieftains and princes." [27] Cortés, in writing home, speaks of the beggars in Cholula when the Spaniards first entered.

"For, such is the multitude of people who live in these parts, that there is not a palm of land which is not cultivated, and even then there are many places in which they suffer for want of bread, and there are many poor who beg amongst the rich in the streets, and at the market places, just as the poor do in Spain, and other civilized countries." [28]

There is ample evidence also that after the Conquest not all of the Indians were treated harshly and unjustly. Bernal Díaz, whose period of observation covers the period from 1541 to 1568, makes it clear that many received some education and were taught various trades and arts. He says:

"Many sons of Chieftains know how to read and write, and to compose books of plain chant, and there are craftsmen in weaving satin and taffeta and making woolen cloth . . . sackcloth, and cotton cloths and rugs. They are carders, woolcombers, and weavers in the same manner as there are in Segovia and in Cuenca, and others are hat makers and soap makers. There

[26] Means, *Fall*, pp. 158-59.
[27] Torquemada, *Monarchia indiana*, Bk. IV, chap. CVI.
[28] Cortés' Second Letter, MacNutt translation.

are only two crafts they have not been able to undertake, although they have tried; these are to make glass, and to become druggists, but I believe them to be so intelligent that they will acquire them very well. Some of them are surgeons and herbalists. They . . . make very good guitars, and indeed they were craftsmen by nature before we came to New Spain. Now they breed cattle of all sorts, and break in oxen, and plough the land, and sow wheat, and thresh, harvest, and sell it, and make bread and biscuits, and they have planted their lands and hereditaments with all the trees and fruits which we have brought from Spain, and sell the fruit which they produce." [29]

Torquemada also speaks of the great facility of Indians in learning the mechanical arts. [30] Many others mention their technical efficiency, and modern handcraft carried over from ancient times is a good witness for the Indians. But their technical dexterity did not gain them admission into the *gremios,* or guilds, which the Spanish brought with them from the Old World as a part of their labor organization. The Indians were limited in general to work for Spaniards as apprentices or journeymen, although they were at times permitted to have their own establishments, and the living conditions of the skilled worker were doubtless considerably better than those of the common laborer.

In Peru many Indians grew moderately wealthy from their labor in the mines.

"Indians came from all the provinces to mine silver from this peak . . . For, as soon as the Spaniards took possession, they began the extraction of silver. This was the method: to the man who had a mine, the Indians who went into it [each] gave one mark a week. And if it was very rich, two marks every week. And to the *encomenderos* of Indians who had no mine, they each gave half a mark every week. [31]

"So many people were needed to mine silver that that place had the appearance of a great city . . . . And as the Indians have had no inspectors over them, nor is it possible to be alongside them when they are mining silver, since they went (as has been said) to the mountain peaks to extract it, it is believed that many have become rich and carried great quantities of silver to their own homes. And this was the reason why Indians came

---

[29] Bernal Díaz, *Conquest of New Spain,* V, 268-69.
[30] Torquemada, *Monarchia indiana,* Bk. XVII, chaps. I-III.
[31] To an encomendero with Indians but without a mine, each Indian gave ½ mark (apparently for the privilege of working). The original passage is obscure, and usually mistranslated.

from many parts of the kingdom to this mining district of Potosí to take advantage of it, since there was such a great opportunity." [32]

But not all accounts paint such a bright picture. Fray Rodrigo de Loaysa writing about 1586 dwells on the corruption of the officials and clergy, and the resultant hardships of the Indians. [33] Conditions of the *mita* Indians in Peru were beyond doubt extremely bad after the Conquest. Their sufferings are reminiscent of labor conditions in eighteenth-century European factories. They worked long hours, on scant food, and many of them died because of overwork and privation. [34] Father Motolinía, who was a defender of the encomienda system, says that the roads and environs around the mines in Mexico were so covered with cadavers and bones of the Indians who had died of hunger and fatigue that "it was hardly possible to walk except over dead men or bones, and so great were the numbers of the birds and buzzards that came to eat on the bodies of the dead that they cast a huge shadow over the sun." [35] He eloquently describes the ten "plagues" of Mexico: smallpox, the Conquest, famine, calpixques, tribute, the mines, building the city of Mexico, slavery, transport to and from the mines, and the civil wars among the Spaniards. [36] There is no doubt that the lot of the common Indian, both before and after the Conquest, was a hard one.

One of the worst abuses was that of the strawboss, or foreman, in New Spain designated by the term similar officials bore during the Aztec period, *calpixques*. The encomendero or landholder often lived away from his estate and its management was left in the hands of these subordinate officials. Many of these calpixques were Indians, frequently the very caciques who had ruled before the Conquest. Such were the abuses committed by this group that many complaints were made to the viceroy and the King. [37] The same situation prevailed in Peru where the Viceroy Francisco de Toledo found that the curacas, now subordinate to Spanish officials, mistreated their own people. [38]

The clergy formed one of the principal groups of calpixques. They came to America in such great numbers that they found

---

[32] Cieza, *Crónica*, chap. CIX.
[33] *C. D. I. España*, XCIV, 554-605.
[34] Colmeiro, *Economía política*, II, 385-86.
[35] Motolinía, *Indios de Nueva España*, I, 20-21.
[36] *Ibid.*, I, 14-21.
[37] Motolinía, *Indios de Nueva España*, I, 17.
[38] *Memorial de D. Francisco de Toledo*, C. D. I. España, XXVI, 122-59.

themselves without employment in religious work, and so hired themselves out to the encomenderos and landowners, their influence as clergymen and the respect that they received from the Indians because of the clerical garb being a particular asset in keeping the Indians submissive.

Another abuse of the Indians before the propagation of domestic animals was their use as porters. This work, of course, they had been accustomed to during many centuries before the Conquest, when no domestic beasts of burden were known to them. But after the Conquest many of the encomenderos hired their Indians out to the merchants and miners, and long trains of Indians carrying heavy burdens were customary. Whatever they earned in this way went to the encomendero. [39]

DISEASE AND DRINK

Many other things had an adverse effect on the Indians, perhaps the most important being disease. In Peru, during 1546, which was also the period of the civil wars, "there was a general epidemic throughout the whole kingdom of Peru, beginning beyond Cuzco and spreading over all the country, where people without number died." [40]

It is not clear just what this disease was. Among the maladies that attacked the Indians, smallpox, allegedly brought into Mexico in 1520, was one of the most disastrous. It continued to be a scourge down to the end of the colonial period. Measles also took a heavy toll after 1531 in Mexico. In 1545, typhus fever appeared in Mexico, killing thousands of Indians. In the province of Tlaxcala it is estimated that 150,000 Indians died; and 100,000 in Cholula, with proportionate death rates for the other parts of New Spain, although the totals are probably exaggerated. Because of the coincidence of dates, it is quite possible that typhus was the disease which struck Peru in 1546. There were many other epidemics, such as those Mexico suffered in 1564, 1570, and 1588. Some of these diseases, according to the contemporary chronicles, attacked the Indians only, and the Spaniards and mestizos were not affected. [41]

Excessive drinking had been characteristic of the Indians, before the Conquest. The Spanish contribution to this vice was not its introduction, but the commercializing of the manufacture and sale of liquors. One cleric wrote to the King from sixteenth century New Spain:

[39] Cieza, *Crónica*, chap. XXIX.
[40] Cieza, *Crónica*, chap. XXIV.
[41] Riva Palacio, *México*, II, 479.

"Let your Majesty give orders for the destruction of all the taverns in Mexico City, where many Spaniards gain their living by making the native wine and intoxicating the Indians, not without creating great commotion, obstacle, and confusion to the gospel; and let none of our people sell Castilian wine to the Indian natives, for besides their being intemperate in drinking, very noticeable evils follow. The Spaniards give them vinegar for wine, and at times half water, and they pay whatever is asked for it, even their wives and daughters." [42]

POST-CONQUEST CACIQUES AND CURACAS

We have been speaking of the masses of laboring Indians. As for the ruling classes, the chieftains who governed before the Conquest, many were killed by the Spaniards, others in their own civil wars, and still others were degraded and sank into the ranks. But not all Indians of property were dispossessed. As a class, whether the same individuals, their heirs, or others, the caciques (as they were called by the Spaniards in New Spain) and the curacas (their name in the Andean region) played an important part in colonial Spanish America, as they do indeed in many regions even today. The Spanish viceroys and governors soon found that the surest way of getting Indian obedience was to incorporate the chieftains into the governing class as subordinate rulers. Their position was recognized in the laws of the Indies.[43a] Indian towns, and even large districts, were under Indians who, while subordinate to encomenderos or corregidores, were immediately responsible. Many of them gained for themselves unenviable reputations for their severity in dealing with their own people.

In sixteenth century New Spain:

". . . many of the Caciques are rich, and possess horses, and bring good saddles with trappings, and ride abroad through the cities and towns and places where they are going for amusement, or of which they are natives, and bring Indians and pages to accompany them.[43b]

The same situation existed in many other regions. More will be said of the caciques in the later discussion of the structure of colonial government.

CONQUISTADORES AND CONQUISTADORAS

The conquerors were the top stratum of colonial society. From

---

[42] Quoted in Riva Palacio, *México*, II, 478-79.
[43a] *Leyes de Indias*, Libro VI, Título VII.
[43b] Bernal Díaz, *Conquest of New Spain*, V, 269-270.

among their ranks came the rulers, the encomenderos, the great landowners, and the élite. [44] But only a few were nobles of Spain, and not many more were wealthy. While it is true that in general Spaniards held the best political offices, the best positions in the Church, and controlled the wealth of America, only a small group was privileged. Many of the conquistadores remained poor, landless, and in debt. [45] During the very period of the Conquest in Peru and other regions, many Spaniards were so poverty-stricken that they had to take refuge in Indian villages, and beg food and clothing of the people they had just conquered. In other words, the Spaniards in America might be either the most privileged aristocrats, or the poorest proletarians. Many of them were lower in the economic and social scale than the Indians who had maintained their position as caciques and landholders after the Conquest.

Spanish colonization has been differentiated from that of the English because of the presence of women among the English. This is in part true. The Spaniards who came a century before the English, and who were exploring and conquering a hitherto absolutely unknown part of the earth, did not take their wives, sisters, and mothers along in the initial stages of the Conquest, when they would have been subjected to the vicissitudes of war and conquest. Women did appear in America, however, almost from the beginning of the first settlements. When Ovando came to Española in 1502, he brought with him, among the 2500 settlers, 73 families; and women were in Cuba within a very few years after its settlement.

Bernal Díaz cites many examples of women in New Spain. He speaks of a military engagement at Tuxtepec in which "sixty Spanish men and women from Castile" were killed. Cortés married in Cuba, and his wife came to Mexico with "her sister" as well as "many other married women," [46] and there were Spanish women with other early conquerors. [47] "Alonzo de Estrada married off his two daughters, one to Jorge de Alvarado, brother of Don Pedro de Alvarado, and the other to a gentleman named Don Luis de Guzmán." On one of Cortés' Pacific expeditions, among those who joined him were "thirty or forty married men" making a total of more than three hundred persons "including the married women." [48]

When Narváez embarked upon his conquest of Florida (1528),

---

[44] Justo Sierra, *Evolución política del pueblo mexicano*, pp. 59-105.
[45] Cieza, *Crónica*, chap. XXVI.
[46] Bernal Díaz, *Conquest of New Spain*, IV, 228, 236-37.
[47] *Ibid.*, V, 222-49.
[48] *Ibid.*, V, 125, 184.

he was accompanied by a great many women who went along with their husbands. Pedro de Alvarado brought back with him to Guatemala in 1539 "twelve noble ladies." [49] As a final example of the contribution of European women to the settlement in America, we may cite the case of Doña Isabel de Guevara who accompanied Pedro de Mendoza to Argentina in 1535, and who with other women assumed all the responsibility that the men could not because of their starvation and illness. [50]

THE NEGRO IN AMERICA

With the increasing demand for laborers in the New World, had come the introduction of the Negro. The Crown had authorized the importation of Negro slaves as early as 1501, when Nicolás de Ovando was appointed governor of Española, and when he arrived in 1502 Negroes were among his settlers. There was some hesitancy at first about introducing infidel Negroes, but the Indians were too few, and too unaccustomed to the labor which characterized the new economy of the Indies. One Negro was reckoned as worth two, four, or even more Indians at work production. The greatest early difficulty, from a purely mercenary point of view, was their costliness, for to bring them from Africa was almost prohibitive. Soon, however, the introduction of new crops in the Caribbean, such as sugar, made slaves profitable over and above their initial cost and subsequent unkeep. With the use of Negro labor, sugar could be exported with a profit.

In 1510, the Casa de Contratación was directed to send over fifty slaves, and thereafter they came in increasing quantities. In 1517, the Crown decided to ship four thousand slaves within the next eight years. The method adopted was to let out a contract, or *asiento,* to individuals or firms who would ship the Negroes to America and dispose of them at an agreed-upon maximum price. In 1528, another asiento provided for four thousand Negroes in four years, and the tempo rose thereafter. While the great importation of Negroes did not come until the economic developments of the eighteenth century, sufficient numbers came in the sixteenth century to form a substantial part of the population. They grew to be one of the early preoccupations of the Crown, and legislation on the subject was frequent. [51]

They also revolted frequently, or fled into the wilds and set up their own small governments, some of which at a later date became

---

[49] Pereyra, *América española,* V, 143, note 1.
[50] *Ibid.,* IV, 75-76.
[51] *Leyes de Indias,* Libro VII, Título V.

large and important. For the most part, however, they comprised the working class of the tropical agricultural regions. Comparatively few lived in the mountain valleys of New Spain and Peru, except those kept as house servants. [52]

THE RACIAL MIXTURES

A large part of the population of America was composed of the mixed races, resulting from the unions of European, Negro, and Indian, and their innumerable combinations.[53] In the first years the mingling went on unrestrained, and the mestizos (European crossed with Indian) increased in proportion much more rapidly than either the Europeans or Indians. They formed an intermediate population, without the status of either Spaniards or natives. Having no standing and lacking the small plots of land which remained to many of the Indians, their economic position was unenviable. When unacknowledged by their fathers, they did not inherit the social position which might have fallen to them. They also were urban rather than rural dwellers. They could not receive religious orders "not even the habit of lay priests" during the first years of the Spanish Conquest, nor hold other positions of honor. [54] Thus, socially they were inferior to the property-holding Europeans, and even in many cases to the property-holding Indians. Yet gradually, many of them worked their way up.

It should be noted, however, that not all the mestizos were the result of casual unions. The Europeans frequently married the Indian women of title to acquire their land. Others, although they lived with Indian women without benefit of clergy, recognized the children and provided for their education and maintenance. Among the famous mestizos of early times were Martín Cortés, Muñoz Camargo, Garcilasco de la Vega, Blas Valera, and Ixtlilxochitl, to mention only a few.

A great variety of names arose to denote the various degrees of mixture between European, Indian, and Negro. There were in all seventeen or more such expressions. At first glance, this looks a bit exaggerated. But since the degree of mixture frequently determined both legal and social position, these distinctions had a purpose. In general, only those of European descent could enjoy full legal

---

[52] On Negro slavery see Edward Gaylord Bourne, *Spain in America*, 1450-1580 (New York, 1904), pp. 269-81; George Scelle, *La Traite Négrière aux Indes de Castille* (2 vols., Paris, 1906), I, 22-198; José Antonio Saco, *Historia de la esclavitud de la raza africana en el Nuevo Mundo* (Barcelona, 1879).

[53] C. E. Marshall, "The Birth of the Mestizo in New Spain," *H. A. H. R.*, XIX (May, 1939), 161-84. Nicolás León, *Las castas del México colonial* (Mexico, 1924).

[54] Riva Palacio, *México*, II, 477-78.

privileges; Indians were granted exemption from the tithes and certain other obligations, but paid a head tax not assessed on the European; the Negro faced the possibility of enslavement or re-enslavement. Those nearly white might rise if they could escape the class designation. If the mestizo married a European the child was called a *castizo,* and from a castizo married with a European came an *español,* the Indian blood having been legally eliminated.

From the union of the Spaniard with the Negro came the mulatto, who might tend either to whiten or darken according to future unions. From the Negro and Indian came the *zambo;* while the crossing of the mestizos, mulattos, and zambos produced an astounding variety, for each of which there was a special name. Although they lacked the legal significance of those just enumerated, many of these names are picturesque. The *salta-atrás,* for example, was a child of negroid characteristics born of apparently white parents. Terms such as *tente-en-el-aire, no-te-entiendo, ahi-te-estás, chino, lobo,* and others expressed the infinite variety of race mixture. These romantic-sounding and often humorous names express one of the most important facts of Latin America: the mixture of Indian, Negro, and European to the point where at least a large percentage of the population is none of these, but an amalgam of all. [55]

The Negro and the mulatto tended to live in the lowlands of the West Indies, Mexico, and Central America, and on the hot tropical coast stretching both ways from the Isthmus of Panama. Those areas which had a heavy Indian population prior to the Conquest— the highlands of Mexico, Central America, and the valleys and plateaus of the Andes—continued as Indian centers with a relatively small mixture of European and Negro blood. On the other hand, large areas of America, previously only sparsely inhabited, now became centers of mining, agriculture, or cattle-raising which attracted a greater population. Among such regions were most of Mexico from the Central Valley northward, Venezuela, Colombia, Chile, and the Río de la Plata. In these the mestizo, sometimes with a slight mixture of Negro blood, was an important element. The Indians were in most cases rural dwellers, but the cities had large populations of mestizos and mulattoes. Therefore, the mestizos were gradually able to take advantage of the superior opportunities of the cities. They acquired education or learned intricate trades and arts, and tended to form a middle class.

A distinction arose between Spaniards and those of European

---

[55] Riva Palacio, *México,* II, 472; Means, *Fall,* pp. 69-70.

CEREMONIAL VASES, ANCIENT PERU

TIGER DEVOURING A MAN, ANCIENT   MOTHER MONKEY WITH BABY ON BACK,
    PERUVIAN POTTERY   ANCIENT PERUVIAN POTTERY

AZTEC CALENDAR STONE
Courtesy of the Mexican Government Travel Bureau

DETAILS OF STONE WORK, MACHU PICCHU

INCA CITY OF MACHU PICCHU, NEAR CUZCO

descent born in America. The former were called Peninsulares, Gachupines, or some other term to indicate that they came from Spain. The latter were termed *criollos,* to indicate birth in America; and legally, they were without mixture of Negro or Indian blood. On the whole, in the early sixteenth century these names had no further significance. But in time, the enmities engendered between the two groups lent these terms an economic and social significance that became of very great importance in the eighteenth century.

CIRCA 1600

By the end of the sixteenth century [56] there were two hundred chartered, and numerous unchartered, towns and mining centers where Spaniards were residents. One hundred and sixty thousand people of European descent, of whom 4,000 were encomenderos, lived in America. The Indian population was 5,000,000, counting only those under Spanish rule. There were 40,000 Negro slaves and an undetermined number of mestizos, mulattoes, zambos, and others. The economic importance of the West Indies had decreased relatively, but New Spain and Peru were thriving.

Spain had brought under control most of what is today Mexico (not counting the territory which became a part of the United States), Central America, Venezuela, Colombia, Ecuador, Peru, Chile, and Paraguay. The region of the Río de la Plata had already been colonized and Buenos Aires established, but it was not until later centuries that this area assumed much importance. There was still, however, a great problem of colonization around each of the established Spanish centers. Practically every Spanish settlement had a frontier. Many towns had been founded in the midst of a large territory not thoroughly under Spanish control and influence. In the succeeding centuries, the task was one of increasing the civilized area around already established centers. The lines of communication were tenuously held, guarded by soldiers, and traversing territory where settlements were infrequent. It was essential to populate the routes between the cities, to guarantee safe transit for commerce, to civilize the Indians, and to establish a greater number of agricultural settlements.

* * * * * * * *

It was entirely natural that the colonial society we have seen

[56] The state of America in 1574 may be judged by the report of Juan López de Velasco in his *Geografía y descripción universal de las Indias.* Analysis of this report taken from Arthur S. Aiton, "The Spanish Conquest and the Settlement of the Indies," in Wilgus, *Colonial Hispanic America,* chap. VI.

evolving in the sixteenth century was a class society, based on forced labor and slavery, with a small privileged class of hereditary landholders in control of the labor as well as the land. The elements that went to compose it—Indian and European—were both class systems. While some Indian caciques retained property as well as authority, Spanish conquerors had largely replaced the Indian rulers as the dominant class, a minority even among the Spaniards, and had received legal recognition from the Crown for the devices, such as the encomienda, that their economic requirements led them to adopt. Negro slavery had been introduced when Indian labor proved inadequate.

Although the Indians continued to be in the majority in New Spain and the Andes, the population was becoming an amalgam of all three racial stocks, Indian, European, and Negro. But the masses of people, whatever their racial origin or degree of mixed blood, toiled in poverty without prospect of bettering their status. The Crown had tried to prevent the exploitation of the Indians, but eventually the Indian policy was forged, not by humanitarian theories, but by the demands of the expanding economy for labor.

The Foundation of Latin-American Culture

MEANING OF CULTURE

CULTURE IN ITS WIDEST MEANING embraces all the activities of man. Viewing it thus, we have already laid the groundwork for this discussion in dealing with the Conquest and the economic and social foundations of Latin America. One other important element in Latin-American culture, religion, because of its peculiar importance and significance will be discussed separately. Our task at this point is to relate the fine arts and intellectual activities to the general social conditions already depicted.

But if we were to limit our concept of Latin America culture to the fine arts and intellectual history alone, we would scarcely need to go back of the Conquest in a study of the colonial period. With few exceptions, the fine arts and intellectual output of Latin America during colonial days were the reflections of European forms and conceptions. On the other hand, if we look upon culture as the full development of a people, it is important to know something of pre-Conquest times. This is increasingly evident today, when the Indian element has assumed an importance which was not recognized for several centuries. Recent trends have led to the discovery of an Indian culture that existed, though neglected, throughout the colonial period, and which has been recently expressed in the revival of arts, music, and literature with Indian inspiration. In the fields of economic, social, and political development, there has been a decided attempt during the present century to adjust all institutions so as to incorporate the Indian into the full current of national life. [1]

---

[1] For a picture of Indian culture viewed as an adjustment to environment see Edgar L. Hewett, *Ancient Andean Life* (Indianapolis and New York, 1939), and other works by the same author, notably *Ancient Life in the American Southwest* (1930), and *Ancient Life in Mexico and Central America* (1936).

PRE-CONQUEST AMERICA: LANGUAGES AND WRITING

Pre-Conquest Americans spoke a striking diversity of tongues. Within the territory embraced in New Spain alone, about twenty major linguistic stocks were known (for fourteen of which grammars and dictionaries were prepared by the Spaniards after the Conquest), divided into perhaps one hundred eighty sub-languages and dialects. [2] These, it was remarked about 1800, "far from being the dialects of the same . . . are at least as different from one another as Greek and German, or French and Polish . . . . The variety of idioms spoken by the people of the new continent,—and the languages, without the least exaggeration, number some hundreds,—offers a very striking phenomenon, particularly when compared with the few languages in Asia and Europe." [3]

What was observed of New Spain applies to every part of America. Hundreds of different dialects, so unlike one another as to be mutually unintelligible, made America a linguistic Babel for which there could be no remedy save the implantation of some common language. Only two regions produced pre-Conquest tongues with serious claims to being written languages: Central Mexico (the Nahua region) and Yucatán and adjacent Central America (the Maya region). [4]

The Mayas, who developed one of the most advanced civilizations of America up to the Conquest, had two chief centers of culture. Their first was located in Guatemala and Honduras. There, by about 613 B. C. (some authorities say later), they had already evolved a hieroglyphic. From about the beginning of our era to about 700 A. D., the "Old Empire" of the Mayas was flourishing; it consisted of some twenty-five cities, each with its own government and group of magnificent public edifices. A cultural lapse was followed by a revival which brought into existence a "New Empire" from approximately 990 to 1200 A. D. This was located in Yucatán, to which Maya civilization had shifted. From about 1200 to 1450, the Mayas were to a degree under the influence of powerful invaders, but apparently with no diminution of their cultural achievements. After 1450 the Mayas definitely declined, and by the time the Spaniards arrived, they had ceased to be a living cultural force.

---

[2] See J. Alden Mason, "The Native Languages of Middle America," in *The Maya and Their Neighbors*, Clarence L. Hay, et al., eds. (New York and London, 1940), pp. 52-87, and Frederick Johnson, "The Linguistic Map of Mexico and Central America, in *Ibid.*, pp. 88-114. The number of linguistic stocks varies according to the way in which the different Indian languages are grouped, being given as low as thirteen and as high as thirty.

[3] Humboldt, *New Spain*, I, 138 [*Nouvelle Espagne*, I, 378].

[4] See Clavigero, *Mexico*, Dissertation VI, Section IV, "On the want of letters."

Maya writing was largely hieroglyphic, with conventionalized pictographic and ideographic elements, though occasional phonetic symbols seem to have been used. [5] This writing was used mainly to record time and the events of the past upon public buildings, although there were also books of bark, skin, or maguey-leaf paper. "Analyzing . . . the progress that has been made in deciphering the Maya inscriptions, both on stone and in the codices, it is at once apparent that time in its various manifestations . . . constitutes the major content of Maya writing . . . . In so far as they have been deciphered, and we are now able to read perhaps as much as one-third of the hieroglyphs, the Maya inscriptions and codies have been found to deal exclusively with the counting of time in one way or another. . . ." [6] The Spaniards destroyed most of the Maya books, because they believed that they contained "superstition or the falsehood of the devil," but it seems likely that the lost works were concerned also with time. A few of the pre-Conquest Maya works, today called codices, still exist. [7]

Toward the end of the sixteenth century, according to a contemporary writer, the Maya writing was still in use. "The Mayas are highly praised for three things over all other people of New Spain. One is that of old they had writing, and letters with which they wrote their histories, and the ceremonies and rites of their sacrifices to their idols, and their calendar, in books . . . . These letters and writings were not understood by anybody except the priests of the idols . . . and an occasional Indian of importance. After the Conquest, some of our friars understood them and could read, and even write them. And because these books contained many idolatrous things they were almost all burned, and thus was lost the knowledge of many ancient things of that land." [8]

While it is difficult to doubt evidence of men who were on the ground, and who claimed to be able both to read and to write ancient Maya, [9] it must be pointed out that not one of the codices left to us is historical in character. "One may perhaps hazard the guess that the remaining undeciphered glyphs deal with further

[5] Compare, Daniel C. Brinton, *The Maya Chronicles* (Philadelphia, 1882), pp. 61-79, with Sylvanus Griswold Morley, "Maya Epigraphy," in Hay, et al., eds., *The Maya*, pp. 139-40; Spinden, *Ancient Civilizations of Mexico and Central America*, pp. 125-35.

[6] Morley, "Maya Epigraphy," in Hay et al., eds., *The Maya*, pp. 146-47.

[7] Brinton, *Maya Chronicles*, p. 62. Brinton reproduces and translates five early post-Conquest manuscripts and discusses ancient pre-Conquest books, post-Conquest manuscripts, grammars, and dictionaries of the Maya language.

[8] *Relación de algunas cosas que sucedieron al padre Fray Alonso Ponce (C. D. I. España*, vols. LVII-LVIII) LVIII, 392.

[9] Thomas Gann, *Maya Cities* (New York, 1928), pp. 34-35, accepts the belief that the early priests understood Maya hieroglyphics.

ceremonial matters, . . . that is to say, more and more of ritual, of liturgy, of astrology and religion, and less and less of history in the Old World sense of personal and national records." [10]

Fortunately we are not dependent entirely on the records the Mayas left us. After the Conquest, many of their traditions, myths, and legends were written in Spanish script and have come down to us. Among the most important are the *Popul Vuh* and the *Books of Chilam Balam*. [11]

The Aztecs, who had inherited much of their culture from the Toltecs, Mixtecs, and others of their kindred Nahuatl-speaking people, had a pictograph writing that has so far proved easier to decipher than the Maya, giving us a clearer picture of the Aztecs than we have of the Maya past. [12]

Aztec writing had perhaps gone farther toward developing a phonetic system without having matched the Egyptian achievement in this respect. A mid-nineteenth century French archeologist who studied both Aztec and Egyptian writing made the following comparison: "Without danger of contradiction, it may be said that what are called Mexican hieroglyphics have not the same interest as Egyptians hieroglyphics. The latter form a true and complete writing composed for the major part of phonetic signs, that is, representations of sounds, rather analogous in principle to letters. In Mexican hieroglyphics . . . *it seems to me that what chiefly predominates is the representation of objects and not of sounds*. Mexican writing is above all a painting, illustrating an action to the eyes rather than transmitting the expressions of a narration. It is clearly a less advanced stage of the art [of writing]. I even believe that the meaning of their historical books could not be understood without the aid of an interpretation transmitted by tradition. Most Aztec manuscripts offer a direct and abridged indication of a visible act. When Hernando Cortés was received in Mexico, there came with Montezuma's envoys painters who made drawings of the men, the horses, and the ships; this was their way of writing their report. I cannot comprehend how Montezuma could have understood it without an explanation." [13]

Time and modern research have confirmed this judgment. "Aztec

---

[10] Morley, "Maya Epigraphy," in Hay, et al., eds., *The Maya,* p. 149.
[11] See R. L. Roys, ed., *The Books of Chilam Balam of Chumayel* (Carnegie Institution of Washington, pub. no. 438, Washington, 1933); and Charles Etienne Brasseur de Bourbourg, ed., *Popol Vuh: Le livre sacré et les mythes de l'antiquité américaine* (Paris, 1861).
[12] See *Historia de los Mexicanos por sus pinturas,* in García Icazbalceta, ed., *Nueva C. D. Mexico,* III, 228-63; Orozco y Berra, *Historia antigua de México,* I, 388-535.
[13] J. J. Ampère, *Promenade en Amérique* (2 vols., Paris, 1855), II, 292-93.

writing was pictographic and was arriving at the stage of syllabic phonetics, which is an important part of the hieroglyphic writing of Egypt. There was no alphabet, but a picture of an animal or thing could be combined with the picture of another animal or thing to give a third meaning in terms of sound value, much like our method of rebus writing." If such a writing had its uses, it also had certain limitations. "Aztec writing offered no way of ·making general statements or expressing abstract ideas. Yet the full accounts of historical events, set down after the Conquest in Spanish or Nahuatl, indicate that oral traditions, possibly learned as a chant or saga, supplemented these ideographic records." [14] "The pictographic writing of the Aztecs was too simple to record a literature. However, the many references to oratory and the wealth of allusions and synonyms referring to the gods and goddesses give a picture of rich fantasy and poetic imagination . . . . Thus a rythmic and rich verbosity existed as a form of polite address that, given a system of writing, might have been transmuted into literature." [15]

LITERATURE OF THE INDIANS

The literature of these three most important civilized peoples of America was slight. It consisted in the main of wise sayings of their rulers, religious injunctions, and some history. [16] Among the Aztecs there was an academy which maintained educational standards and schools. Literary contests were held and prizes given for the best historical and literary contributions. Verse was the chief form of literature and the subject was usually religious or philosophical. The King of Téxcoco, Nezahualcoytl, who lived in the latter half of the fifteenth century, left a series of philosophical injunctions whose content may be judged by his saying: "The goods of this life, its glories and its riches, are but lent to us, its substance is but an illusory shadow, and the things of today shall change on the coming of the morrow. Then gather the fairest flowers from thy gardens to bind around thy brow and seize the joys of the present, ere they perish." [17]

There existed in addition a type of drama which was little more than a modified procession. Traditions of the past were preserved in popular song. Other songs of a warlike or amorous nature were common. One writer characterizes the spirit behind Aztec writ-

[14] Vaillant, *Aztecs,* pp. 206-207.
[15] Vaillant, *Aztecs,* p. 168.
[16] Sahagún, *Cosas de Nueva España,* II, 39-250.
[17] Quoted in Williams, *People and Politics of Latin America,* p. 47.

ings by saying: "They breathe a sweet and melancholy philosophy, but are full of confidence in a future life." [18]

The literature of the Incas could hardly be said to exist except orally, since they were without a system of writing. Tales of their mythological past and the achievements of their heroes all formed subject matter for this oral tradition. Memorized song and poetry were recited at their numerous festivals.

Among the Incas, as among the Aztecs, the wise sayings of the rulers formed an important part of their literature. In the following quotation we may see a mixture of various philosophies:

"When the subjects and their captains and *curacas* obey the king with good will, then the kingdom enjoys complete peace and quiet.

"Envy is a worm that gnaws and consumes the entrails of the envious.

"He who is envious and is envied, is doubly unhappy.

"He that envies another, injures himself.

"He that kills another without authority or just cause condemns himself to death.

"It is very just that he who is a thief should be put to death.

"Adulterers who sully the reputation and character of another, and who destroy the peace and happiness of others, ought to be declared thieves, and hence condemned to death without any exception whatever.

"The noble and generous man is known by the patience he shows in adversity.

"Judges who secretly receive gifts from lawyers and litigants should be considered as thieves, and punished with death as such.

"The physician or herbalist who is ignorant of the virtues of herbs, or who, knowing the uses of some, has not attained to a knowledge of all, understands little or nothing. He should work until he knows them all, the useful as well as the injurious plants, in order to deserve the name to which he pretends." [19]

An Inca drama in which masks were used, and wherein the actors represented various types of animals, was a regular part of their religious profession. The *Amautas* (scholars or wisemen) composed tragedies on the subjects of war and heroic deeds.

Melancholy seems to have been a prevailing characteristic. Inca philosophy and literature of love are strongly tinged with it. The melancholic note is still predominant in Andean music.

[18] Barros, Arana, *América*, I, 55-56.
[19] Garcilaso, *Comentarios*, Bk. VI, chap. XXVI.

INDIAN EDUCATION

Education in the Indian world as in contemporary Europe, was confined largely to members of the upper classes. For example, among the Aztecs, the clergy held a monopoly over education and learning, their instruction being limited entirely to the nobility and privileged elements of society. [20] The sons of the landlords and the chief merchants were educated for a definite position in life and their education, except when they were destined to the priesthood, had this practical end in view. In training for the priesthood, however, mathematics, astronomy, and the writing of hieroglyphics were taught. Schools for girls were maintained by monastic orders similar to the nuns of our modern churches; and the boys were educated by the priests. Rigorous religious training was a prominent feature of the educational system.

The vast majority of the people received no formal education whatever. They belonged to the classes that were supposed to remain, forever, as either slaves, landless farm workers or serfs; and they were not considered deserving of or needing formal education. If we except the practical training which such people received for the occupations they followed, we may consider them entirely outside the educational system.

Among the Incas, education was entirely in the hands of a small group of instructors, the *Amautas*. [21] The center of their teaching in Cuzco was the *Yachahuasi* or Teacher's House. Garcilaso refers to the school: "In the Indian language they call the schools Yacha-huasi, which means the house of teaching. In it lived the learned men and masters of that commonwealth, called Amautas, which means philosophers, and the *Haravecs* or poets, all of whom were much esteemed by the Incas and by all the Empire. Many students lived with them, chiefly those of the royal blood." [22]

Students were drawn entirely from the imperial caste and from the sons of the various conquered chieftains within the Inca Empire. They learned the language of the Incas, the use of the *quipu* (a counting device), the official version of Inca history, the religion of the Incas, and the scientific knowledge then available. The education was strictly patriotic and along class lines. Training for the task of administration and for military leadership was a prominent characteristic of the school. The principle behind this education was enunciated by the Inca Roca, the traditional founder of the *Yachahuasi*. "The children of the common people should not

[20] Orozco y Berra, *Historia antigua de México*, I, 227-51.
[21] Cobo, *Nuevo Mundo*, Bk XIV, chap. VI.
[22] Garcilaso, *Comentarios*, Bk. VII, chap. X. See also Bks. II-IV inclusive.

learn the sciences, which should be known only by the nobles, lest the lower classes should become proud and endanger the commonwealth. They should be taught the trades of their fathers, which are good enough for them." [23]

The influence of the schools over the intellectual training of the Inca nobility was great. From childhood, every boy and girl of the aristocracy was formed for this one position, and conditioned to believe in the vast superiority of the Incas over all other peoples and over the masses of the common people. Education was thus used to create an impenetrable barrier between the classes.

INDIAN SCIENCE

Science among the Indians was remarkably developed in some lines, although deficient in others. Among the Aztecs, there were hospitals for the wounded and the sick, and for disabled soldiers. One Spaniard testifies that the physicians "were so far better than those in Europe that they did not protract the cure in order to increase the pay." They were well versed in the medical uses of a number of plants and were skilled in some lines of surgery.

The Aztecs used (perhaps borrowed from the Mayas) a fifty-two-year calendar cycle. Its chief use was for computation of holy days, and its connection with religion is its most remarkable characteristic, aside from its purely scientific aspect. [24] They understood eclipses and something of astronomy, which partook largely of the nature of astrology. [25] Their numerical system was based upon the same standard as that of the Mayas, namely twenty. [26] Their year was eighteen months, of twenty days each, with an extra five days at the end of the year. A month had four weeks of five days each, the last day of which was a market day and holiday. La Place found this system so accurate that he believed the Aztecs must have borrowed it from Europe; but since Europe used a less accurate system up to the time of the Gregorian calendar, and as all other evidence is contrary to this, the modern archeologists have decided that the Aztec and Maya systems were two variations of one scientific development native to America. [27]

[23] Garcilaso, *Comentarios,* Bk. IV, chap. XIX.
[24] Clavigero, *Mexico, Bk. VI,* and Dissertation II. Orozco y Berra, *Historia antigua de México,* II, 5-167. Sahagún, *Cosas de Nueva España,* I, 77-254. Vaillant, *Aztecs,* pp. 187-200.
[25] Sahagún, *Cosas de Nueva España,* II, 251-74.
[26] Orozco y Berra, *Historia antigua de México,* I, 536-80.
[27] On the influence of the Mayas, see Herbert J. Spinden, "Diffusion of Maya Astronomy," in Hay, et al., eds., *The Maya* pp. 162-78, who says that "the classical learning of the early Mayas was broadcast among other nations of Mexico and Guatemala during the two or three centuries preceding the coming of the Spaniards." p. 178.

It is among the Mayas that we find some of the most remarkable scientific developments. They had learned the use of a place-numeral system. In this system numbers have both a constant value and a value according to place. In the number 111, for example, the 1 has three separate values. This was an invention made also by the Hindus and the Incas, the difference being that the Hindu and Inca systems were decimal, while the Maya was vigesimal. Particularly remarkable was the Maya calendar instituted about 580 B.C., with a date reaching back to 613 B.C. The accuracy of this calendar for practically all purposes was perfect, far exceeding that in use in Europe at the time of the discovery of America, and is not less accurate than the calendar we use today. [28]

The Andean civilizations had not made as great progress in mathematics or astronomy. The Incas had worked out a good system for measuring the land, and could make relief maps in clay, and their achievements in the building of irrigation projects and water conduits give them high rank as engineers. However, their calendar system, which was without even a hieroglyphic form of record, was more rudimentary than that of the Mayas or Aztecs. The astronomical knowledge on which their ceremonial year was based was not so extensive, and it is doubtful that they had a concept of a series of years, or cycle, such as the fifty-two-year cycle of the Aztecs. [29] They used a lunar calendar of twelve months, adjusted to the solar year by adding eleven extra days, six of which came at various times through the year. [30]

A singular invention of the Incas was the *quipu*. This was a rope from which dangled a number of strands of various colors and which, when tied into combinations of knots, served as a sort of tabulator. With this they were able to keep records of the numbers of people, llamas, or anything else for which an account was needed. It is possible that the quipu also served as a mnemonic aid to the *Amautas* (scholars) who were charged with keeping a record of the past, but if it served at all in this way, its utility was slight. Early accounts of the quipu, which considered it to be a system of writing, were more romantic than accurate. Cieza de León describes the quipu and its use:

"They had another method for knowing and calculating the amount of the provisions contributed in the provinces . . . and

[28] Brinton, *Maya Chronicles*, pp. 37-61; E. Wvllis Andrews, "Chronology and Astronomy in the Maya Area," Hay, et al., eds., *The Maya*, pp. 150-61.
[29] Philip Ainsworth Means, "The Philosophic Interrelationship between Middle American and Andean Religions," in Hay, et al., eds., *The Maya*, pp. 430-40; Prescott, *Peru*, Bk. I, chap. IV.
[30] Means, *Ancient Civilizations*, pp. 367-90.

the method was so good and subtle, that in ingenuity it exceeded the *carastes* which the Mexicans used to make their calculations and business transactions: these were the *quipus,* which are long strands of knotted cords. Those who were accountants and knew the combinations of these knots, gave account by means of them of the disbursements made, or of other things that might have happened many years before; and on these knots, they counted from one to ten, and from ten to a hundred, and from a hundred to a thousand; and in one of these strands is the count of the one, and in another of the other; in such a way, that for us it is amusing and blind computation, and for them excellent. In every provincial capital there were accountants who were called *quipucamayoc,* and by means of these knots they had the record (*cuenta y razón*) of what those who resided in the district had to pay as tribute, from silver, gold, clothing and livestock, to wood and other less significant things, and with the same *quipus* an account was rendered at the end of a year, or ten, or twenty, to whoever had charge of taking the accounts, so accurate that not a pair of sandals could be concealed." [31]

It will be observed that this statement of Cieza's credits the Incas with the discovery of a decimal system. His estimate of the utility of the *quipu* is probably exaggerated, however, in view of studies made by recent scholars. As one specialist in Peruvian history remarked: "It must be borne in mind that the *quipus,* or knotted cords, which were used to continue the records, were a clumsy and inadequate contrivance for perpetuating dates and numbers. They were, at best, only aids to memory, about on a par with Robinson Crusoe's notched calendar . . . . Even if they had a proper numerical significance (and this is by no means certain), they were in every other respect inferior to the rudest pictorial symbols of our North American Indians, and still far inferior to the painted records of the Mexicans, or the . . . writings of the aborigines of Central America." [32] In an exhaustive study, a modern scholar has demonstrated that the *quipu* was at most an aid to the memory, used somewhat like a rosary in prayer, and could not be used for calculation. [33]

The medicine of the Incas displayed a considerable knowledge of the medical uses of a number of plants as well as of surgery

[31] Cieza, *Señorío,* p. 41; Cobo, *Nuevo Mundo,* Bk. XII, chap. XXXVII.
[32] E. George Squier, *Peru, Incidents of Travel and Explorations in the Land of the Incas* (New York, 1877), pp. 571-72.
[33] L. Leland Locke, *The Ancient Quipu or Peruvian Knot Record* (New York: The American Museum of Natural History, 1923) pp. 31-32.

and trepanning. Purging and bleeding were common remedies.
They recognized a white tongue as a sign of illness, but they knew
nothing of taking the pulse or of examining urine and faeces. Their
medicines were made of single herbs, and they had no knowledge
of compounds. They used, however, a considerable number of
medicinal plants, among them tobacco and coca. [34] Coca was not
employed in the form or on the scale its derivative cocaine is used
in modern medicine. As a rule, the leaf was chewed, and its effects
gained in this way.

A detailed description of Inca medical practices given by Garcilaso reveals that some of them were very primitive, even in the
light of sixteenth-century European medicine.

"These purges and blood lettings were ordered by those most
experienced in this, particularly old women (just like the mid-
wives over here [in Spain]) and great herbalists, for very famous
ones existed in the time of the Incas who knew the virtue of
many herbs, and by tradition they taught their children; the
latter were considered doctors, not to attend everybody, but only
the kings and their kin, and the curacas and their relatives. The
common people people treated one another with what they knew
about medicaments from hearsay. Nursing children, when they
felt some indisposition—especially if there was a fever—were
washed with urine during the mornings before being swaddled,
and when they could get some of the child's urine, they gave
him some of it to drink. When at a child's birth, they cut the
umbilical cord, they left a navel string as long as a finger, which,
after it fell off, they guarded with extreme care, and gave it to
the child to suck whenever they felt that he was indisposed . . . .
Fever they recognized from the excessive heat of the body; their
cathartics and blood lettings were given before the sickness had
completely set in, rather than after it had become pronounced.
Once they had succumbed to the sickness they gave no medica-
ment; they let nature take its course, and kept their diet. They
did not discover the common use of the remedy which is called
purgadera, which is an enema, nor did they know how to apply
poultices or ointments, except for a few, and then of very common things." [35]

Garcilaso concludes his opinion of Inca medicine with the statement:

"This was the medicine that the Inca Indians of Peru ordi-

[34] Means, *Ancient Civilizations,* p. 445.
[35] Garcilaso, *Comentarios,* Bk. II, chap. XXIV.

narily knew, which consisted in using simple herbs and not compound medicines, and beyond this they did not go; in things of such great importance as health, they studied and knew very little . . ." [36]

INDIAN ARTS AND CRAFTS

In the field of arts and crafts, the magnificent architecture of the Mayas was probably the most remarkable accomplishment of the pre-Conquest Indians. Scattered from Honduras through Guatemala and into southern Mexico and Yucatán, are the ruins of dozens and perhaps even hundreds of cities of the Mayas. Some of these had been in ruins for probably more than a thousand years when the Spaniards entered America, others for the comparatively short period of fifty or a hundred years. [37] In the matter of technique and decoration, few, if any, other indigenous people matched the Mayas in the construction of temples, palaces, and public buildings.

They built with the use of the corbeled arch, also employed in ancient times by the Egyptians, Greeks, and other Old World peoples. A corbeled arch is achieved by placing two sets of opposing stones so that each stone projects beyond the one below it until the gap between is closed, or nearly so, and covered with a capstone. The cantilever principle is used to hold the outer end of the stones firm while the inner, projecting end is free and unsupported. [38]

The corbeled arch is found in the Maya area from Honduras on the south to the Tehuantepec Peninsula on the north (including Yucatán), but there are sections within this district where it does not exist. Outside this area, it is used rarely if at all, in the Mexican and Central American regions. [39]

The Mayas also used the beam and mortar type of roof. "Although of great use to the Maya, the corbeled vault had its disadvantages and in some ways was not so practical as the thatch or beam and mortar roof. It required more labor to construct, was much heavier, and, while it was more durable, it sacrificed breadth. A room that carries a corbeled vault can be made as long as desired, but the breadth is strictly limited. The widest span known is in the Mercado at Chichén Itzá [Yucatán], where the far beyond

---

[36] Garcilaso, *Comentarios,* Bk. II, chap. XXV.

[37] For a summary of the research and writings on Maya art and architecture, see H. E. D. Pollock, "Sources and Methods in the Study of Maya Architecture," in Hay, et al., eds., *The Maya,* pp. 179-201.

[38] A. Ledyard Smith, "The Corbeled Arch in the New World," in Hay, et al., eds., *The Maya,* pp. 202-21, and illustrations on 209 and 219.

[39] Smith, in *ibid.,* pp. 212-13.

average breadth of fourteen feet, eight inches (4.52m.) is attained."[40]

In Aztec, Zapotec, and Mixtec Mexico are the remains of a splendid architecture, most of which was likewise in ruins before the European discovery of America. One of the chief characteristics of this architecture was the pyramid, and many of them exist in an excellent state of preservation. Their construction is usually accredited to the Toltecs because the Aztecs considered them products of an age even at that long time long since past, but other peoples also used the pyramid structure.

The Mayas and Aztecs reached a high degree of skill in weaving and in the working of gold, silver, and copper. [41] Their pottery was of an excellent character and their sculpture and frescos had advanced to the point of a highly conventionalized art.

Certain inventions found useful in the Old World were unknown to the New World, or if known, so little used that they were not part of the cultural equipment of the native peoples. Among the most important of these were the wheel and the true arch. While examples of the true arch exist, and "the aborigines on occasion did unintentionally use the principle of the true arch, they never recognized it." [42] To build edifices of more than one story, it was necessary as a rule for each story to rest upon its own foundation, which extended from the ground. In other words, tall structures had to be built in such a manner that each story formed one step in a large staircase. Cement and stone were the common materials used in public buildings, adobe in the house of the common man.

Glazing of pottery and the use of the potter's wheel had not been discovered, nor was there skill in mixing and preparation of the clays from which the pottery was made.

Among the Andean peoples, architecture was likewise a foremost achievement.[43a] At Chan-chan in northern Peru, at Tiahuanaco in Bolivia, and at numerous other places in Ecuador, Peru, and Bolivia, there are beautiful examples of pre-Inca architecture. All these were in ruins when the Spaniards entered the Inca empire, and were as ancient to the Incas as the Inca ruins are to us. The accomplishments of the Incas in the field of architecture are remarkable for their massiveness, because they had mastered a knowledge of how to work and handle gigantic stones. Garcilaso remarks concerning Inca architecture:

[40] Smith in *ibid.*, pp. 210-211.
[41] Clavigero, *Mexico,* Dissertation VI, Sections, I-II.
[42] Smith, in Hay, et al., eds. *The Maya* p. 220.
[43a] Cobo, *Nuevo Mundo,* Bk. XIV, chap. XII.

"Their houses, temples, gardens, and baths were extremely fine, made of a hewn stone marvellously worked, the stones fitting together so well that no mortar would enter; and although it is true that they did use it, it was a red clay (which in their tongue they call *lancac allpa,* for it is a sticky clay) made into a paste, of which no trace remained between the stones. Because of this, the Spaniards say that they worked without mortar." [43b]

The corbeled arch was found in the Andean area from northern Peru to northern Argentina, an area fifteen hundred miles in length. But instead of being used in temples and palaces, it was employed mainly in the houses of the common people. Inca temples were only one story high and covered with straw. Massive pyramids and fortresses with cyclopean stone walls were also characteristic of the Andean region.[44]

In weaving cloth, working metals, making pottery, cutting semiprecious stones, and sculpture, the Incas had attained a high degree of technical proficiency.[45]

The examples left prove that throughout the civilized areas of America the Indians were accomplished artisans in practically all those trades and arts which flourished in Europe before the age of the machine.

The technical achievements of the Indian peoples have excited the admiration of many observers and elicited much praise. Dr. Herbert J. Spinden, archeologist and Curator of American Indian Art and Primitive Cultures of the Brooklyn Museum, remarks: "Artists are everywhere of the opinion that the sculptures and other products of the Mayas deserve to rank among the highest art products of the world." [46] The late Dr. George Vaillant, of the American Museum of Natural History, in speaking of Mexico, says: "Mexican craftsmanship, whatever the tribe and whatever the era, was superb in that it answered the necessities and the ideals of both the time and the people . . . . The measure of Aztec civilization cannot be gauged solely by its technical achievements. The arts and crafts transcend the products of the Old World peoples at the same mechanical level. The spirit of the Aztec people, as exemplified in their religious art, soared to the lofty heights attained by the creators of those ancient civilizations, like Egypt

---

[43b] Garcilaso, *Comentarios,* Bk. VI, chap. I.
[44] Means, *Ancient Civilizations,* pp. 524-35.
[45] Cobo, *Nuevo Mundo,* Bk. XIV, chap. II, clothing; chap. III, villages and houses; chap. IV, decorations and house furnishings; chap. XI, spinning and weaving; chap. XV, metal working and other arts.
[46] Spinden, *Ancient Civilizations of Mexico and Central America,* p. 73.

MAYA ARCHITECTURE, CHICHÉN ITZA, YUCATÁN

CROSS OF PALENQUE, CHIAPAS. FINDING CROSSES OF THIS TYPE PERSUADED THE MISSIONARIES THAT CHRISTIANITY HAD ONCE EXISTED IN AMERICA

Courtesy, Brooklyn Museum

CURACA COSTUME

Courtesy, Brooklyn Museum

MEXICO — POST-CONQUEST SCENE

and Mesopotamia, whose monuments reflect the glory of their builders' religious devotion." [47] "Not even the pyramids of Egypt present so carefully calculated a plan to dominate the individual with the sheer weight of supernatural power." [48] Many others have expressed similar appreciation of New World accomplishments in comparison with those of the Old World.

Any judgment, however, of artistic quality is, of necessity, largely subjective. There are few objective standards by which we can reach an absolute decision as to the relative merits of the Egyptian or Aztec, Aegean or Inca, Etruscan or Maya art. The author offers the following statements as his purely personal conclusions, fully realizing that they are not in accord with what is generally accepted.

It is hardly possible to say that the pottery of America was superior to that of the Aegeans, or the Greeks, or the Etruscans. To the present author, for example, the various potteries of America, as well as the work in metals, wood and stone, are not even comparable to the works produced in Europe. This is a conclusion reached after repeated examination of specimens in the museums of Berlin, Paris, London, Madrid, New York and many of the leading Latin American countries. Moreover, pre-Conquest American arts and crafts seem, on the whole, inferior to many exhibits in our modern museums representing the work of the African tribes. The author cannot see that, either in quality of materials, or in concept, or in craftsmanship, or in use of colors, the native American work was the equivalent of that found in Europe or Africa.

There are, of course, some very notable exceptions. Africa (except the ancient civilization of the Nile) produced no architecture to rival the American, nor pottery and textiles to equal those of the Incas, nor anything like the Maya scientific achievements.

One more personal observation may be made here. Skill in crafts is not always a reliable index to the degree of civilization achieved among the various American peoples. To cite only one outstanding example, there is little evidence that the island of Marajó in the mouth of the Amazon River ever attained anything more than a primitive civilization. And yet to the present writer, Marajó pottery is comparable to anything that was produced by the Incas, Mayas or the Aztecs and their kindred peoples.

Another instance of the difference in appreciation may be seen in a comparison of the Indian and the Barbarian European arts.

[47] Vaillant, *Aztecs*, p. 153-154.
[48] *Ibid.*, p. 157.

The American Indian rooms of the British Museum are located (as of 1938) adjacent to those of the Barbarian tribes of Europe (Vandals, Goths, Franks, etc.). The American Indian exhibit is one of the finest extant, and after admiring the work of the Aztecs, Mayas, Incas, and others, this writer wandered rather aimlessly into the rooms of the Barbarians, expecting to find a much cruder art. It took, however, only a few minutes to discover that the statuary, jewelry, and above all the metal work, of the Barbarians was incomparably more delicate in workmanship and concept than that of the finest examples of American Indian art. This is cited to illustrate the difficulties of determining the "value" of the arts. Historians still unblushingly label the rude invaders of Western Europe of the fourth to the eighth centuries as Barbarians, but their skill was superior in some respects to that of the American Indians, whose workmanship has so frequently been compared with that of Etruscans, Greeks, and Egyptians.

EUROPEAN BACKGROUND OF COLONIAL LATIN-AMERICAN CULTURE

Modern Latin America is a composite of native American culture and the European importations. Various European influences affected profoundly the course of American culture, and in some respects the present American culture is almost entirely European in origin.

To two continents speaking dozens of different languages and hundreds of different dialects, the Europeans brought four languages: Spanish, Portuguese, English, and French. To the vast American area which had no writing whatever in most of its extension, or a very crude writing at best, the Europeans brought the most advanced forms that the world had developed. To an America that was practically without recorded literatures, the Europeans brought the best of the literatures, and the printing press to disseminate them. Europe brought the wheel, which not only improved the making of pottery, but enabled America to utilize methods of transportation and engineering that would never have been possible otherwise. Europe brought the true arch, a more flexible architectural device than the corbeled arch. Europe brought to America the use of iron to supplement copper and bronze as a metal for crafts and trades.

These contributions that Europe made to America render it indispensable to study European culture at the time of its entrance into America. The Indians absorbed much of European culture after the Conquest. Few, if any, areas of America remained free of European influence.[49] The capacity for development already demonstrated by the Indians was sufficient to indicate that they could adopt any cultures with which they might come in contact.

That they did not assimilate more after the Conquest was in part due to the partial disappearance of the Indian élite. Learning, science, and the fine arts in pre-Conquest America as in Europe were in the hands of a small group. What was known of architecture, sculpture, astronomy, medicine, writing, and literature was limited to a few only. This small group was replaced by the conquerors and the best of the Indian heritage destroyed. The masses who remained could not preserve what they had never shared; and under Spanish rule they continued to be an oppressed class with limited opportunity for intellectual advancement.

More important, however, as a reason for the secondary position of Indian culture after the Conquest, was the superiority of European cultural techniques. The introduction of the true arch rendered Indian architecture obsolete; Arabic notation and mathematics were superior to even the best of the Maya; European writing supplanted the ideographs of the Aztecs; superior metals were adopted in the place of stone and copper; Renaissance painting and sculpture easily replaced Indian models. Thus, while it is true that the elimination of large numbers of the Indian élite was significant, more significant was the fact that those who remained quickly and gladly accepted the imported techniques. The art of the post-Conquest was mainly European in origin.

While this meant that America took almost a completely new start, indigenous cultures did survive, if not in the form of their greatest achievements, at least in folk arts and crafts. Much of America's music and many designs of modern art have come from Indian models, albeit much changed with European additions.

Spain discovered America at one of the most propitious moments for America. During some three centuries prior to 1492, Europe had enjoyed an intellectual advancement that was second to none, with the possible exception of Ancient Greece. From the middle of the twelfth century, Europe was recovering from the stagnation which Christendom had undergone after the decline of imperial Rome. Two great periods of renaissance were reaching their zenith; the one that flourished in the thirteenth century saw the best achievements of the Scholastics and the laying of the foundation stone of European science by Roger Bacon and Albertus Magnus; and the Italian renaissance brought to Europe the revival of Greek

[49] See A. L. Kroeber, "Conclusions: The Present Status of Americanistic Problems," in Hay. et al., eds., *The Maya*, pp. 460-89.

and Roman arts and letters and the simultaneous birth of European national literatures. During the sixteenth century America had the privilege of importing in a few years the culture which Europe had been centuries in developing.

Spain of the sixteenth century, whose culture Spanish America was receiving, was a more vital intellectual force than it became later.[50] Spain boasted eight universities in 1516; and by 1584 the University of Salamanca had 6,778 students. Twenty-one more universities were founded in the sixteenth century. In all of these the influence of the Church was paramount; and after the introduction of the study of Greek at Salamanca in 1508 there were no more innovations in the curriculum. The sixteenth century was a time when the Castilian language was achieving its classical expression, and from the end of the fifteenth century when Antonio de Nebrija published the first Castilian grammar, there came a series of important contributions to literature in Spanish. The poet, Garcilaso de la Vega, and the dramatist, Lope de Rueda, were the forerunners of the Golden Age in Spanish literature. From Spain, America received much of her cultural framework. Colonial Spanish America could not avoid becoming in many essential aspects a reflection of the mother country.

INTRODUCTION OF EUROPEAN CULTURE INTO AMERICA

The first intellectual influence in America was that of the Church. Spain of the sixteenth century shared with the rest of Europe a common educational characteristic: illiteracy of the masses and formal education for the upper classes only. Except for the private instruction the nobility of Europe provided its children in order to prepare them for a definite and foreordained position in life, education was very largely in the hands of the Church. This system was transferred to America. Clerical schools were started for the children of the European settlers, and for the sons of Indian caciques. Franciscan friars came to teach in New Spain soon after the Conquest. One of the most important early schools was that of Pedro de Gante, who founded a school for Indian children in 1522. This school taught (in addition to religion) reading, writing, arithmetic, music, drawing, and various trades and mechanical arts. It eventually had perhaps a thousand students. Another school for Indians, Santa Cruz de Tlaltelolco, was opened in 1536 under the direction of the Franciscans and with the help of viceroy Antonio de Mendoza. The curriculum consisted of reading, writ-

---

[50] Bernard Moses, *Spanish Colonial Literature in South America* (London and New York: *The Hispanic Society of America*, 1922), pp. 1-27.

ing, Latin grammar, rhetoric, philosophy, music, and Mexican medicine. Within a few years the students turned out from this school were themselves teaching, some of them having posts in the same school. The viceroy recommended the school to the attention of his successor, Luis de Velasco, seeing in it an efficient measure for the propagation of the religion and civilization of the Spaniards through its Indian graduates.[51]

Antonio de Mendoza also founded the school San Juan de Letrán (opened after his death), in 1553, for the innumerable fatherless mestizo children resulting from the unions of Indian women with Spaniards. It was to be supported with funds from the sale of wild cattle, likewise innumerable. The Emperor Charles V gave it his blessing and some financial support, and it remained in existence more than three centuries. There were two types of students in San Juan de Letrán. "Those who showed no aptitude for learning were taught a trade and elementary letters in the colegio itself, where they could remain up to three years; those of sufficient ability, to the number of six each year, chosen from among the most intelligent and virtuous, followed the literary course for seven years." [52]

The ayuntamiento, or city government, established a primary school for boys, and there appeared in Mexico and other places private teachers who set up schools. Some of these received small subsidies from the King. Mendoza also established a refuge and school for mestiza girls where they learned "womanly arts such as sewing and embroidery, receiving instructions at the same time in the Christian religion, and marrying when they arrived at the proper age." [53] Spanish girls were also taught at this school, which was supported in part by royal revenues.

These are merely examples of an educational impulse that was common to all of Spanish America. Monasteries, convents, city governments, and private individuals gave to Latin America of the sixteenth century an educational plant that was perhaps the equivalent of those in Europe at this time. It was, however, an age when popular education as now conceived in the more advanced nations was not even a dream. Education in the sixteenth century was of a vocational nature for most of these who went to school at all; and for a very few only it meant opportunity for intellectual pursuits.

---

[51] Viceroy Mendoza's *Instrucción*, D. I. I., VI, 488-89; Riva Palacio, *México*, II, 519; Altamira, *Historia de España*, III, 712-16; Vicente G. Quesada, *La vida intelectual en la América Española* (Buenos Aires, 1917), pp. 85-112.
[52] Quoted in Riva Palacio, *México*, II, 520.
[53] Francisco Cervantes Salazar, *Diálogos*, quoted in Riva Palacio, *México*, II, 520.

With such a system it was logical that the university and not the common school was more esteemed. A university under the aegis of the Dominican order in Santo Domingo was sanctioned by Papal Bull in 1538, although it apparently did not function at that early date. The secular university of Santiago de la Paz or Gorjón opened in 1558. Before this date Charles V had, in 1551, authorized the establishment of the Royal and Pontifical University of Mexico (opened 1553) and the University of San Marcos in Lima, Peru (opened 1571-1576), both based on the model of Salamanca.[54]

Their privileges were also similar to those of Salamanca. The teachers were usually Dominicans, Franciscans, or Jesuits, but were not invariably clerics. The curriculum, however, was dominated throughout by theology, which was not absent from any study. Neither was the internal government of the universities always smooth, since the theological disputes of the day were often reflected within the halls of the schools. The university was the intellectual center of colonial life, and while comparisons are very difficult to make, the New World institutions probably compared favorably in many respects with those of Spain. Perhaps the most notable and unique contribution made by the universities was the training of the scholars in the native languages, and the preparation of grammars and dictionaries.

Medicine benefited by the Indian as well as the European knowledge, and the numerous medicinal plants of America immediately offered a field of study. Civil and canon law were indispensable studies.[55]

Many books of historical, literary, and scientific interest were written in America during the sixteenth century, or were written in Europe about America because of the great interest provoked by the Discovery. Columbus himself initiated the literature of America with his Journal. Peter Martyr took up the thread of American history as soon as the first news of Columbus' return was known and through a series of letters and histories spread the news of America. This quick and early interest in America was sustained throughout the colonial period, and books and treatises on the phenomena of the Indies were produced in great numbers.

The reasons for this interest are obvious. A New World had been discovered, and when the discovery of America followed quickly on the African explorations, and was succeeded by the Vasco

---

[54] See John Tate Lanning, *Academic Culture in the Spanish Colonies* (London and New York-Toronto: Oxford University Press, 1940), pp. 3-33, for an authoritative study of the Spanish foundations and transplantation of the university to the colonies.

[55] Riva Palacio, *México*, II, 521-22.

da Gama voyage to India, the intellectual curiosity of Europe was stirred. It is difficult to realize today the full import of America to the European mind, or to measure the effect on those who came to America as conquerors, travelers, merchants, or priests. The inhabitants, plants, governments, social conditions, customs, and cultures of America were all new, different, incredible. They called for chroniclers, commentators, scholars; and these were not lacking. The intellectual atmosphere of Europe, which had been enriched only half a century before with the printing press, and had once again become fairly familiar with Latin and Greek learning, was further quickened by the study of the New World. Letters by the thousands crossed the seas to reveal the wonders of the new lands. Chronicles and memorials abounded. Poetic descriptions imitative of the epics of the Greeks and Romans were popular, and no book about America was complete unless it had citations to Virgil and Cicero, Pliny and Herodotus. Theological literature was not less abundant since the churchmen were suddenly faced with the task of fitting a hitherto unknown world with hitherto unknown peoples into the scheme of Christianity. They were especially embarrassed since the Church's position on various scientific points was now untenable.

One of the first tasks was the systematic study of the most important of the Indian languages, which must be learned before Christianity could be taught. Study of the native tongues became part of the curricula of the schools and universities. Numerous grammars and dictionaries were prepared. By the end of the sixteenth century there were books in ten different Indian languages in New Spain alone, not counting others already done or in preparation in every part of America where the Spaniards had penetrated. Histories of the Indians and the early years of Conquest were prepared by many.

Epic poetry was the preferred literary form. Like poetry throughout the ages, there was more bad than good; but all is valuable as a reflection of the sixteenth century. Military and other heroic exploits offered subject matter for much of this creative activity and there were few important conquerors to whom some poem was not dedicated. Judging by these poems, there was no question in the minds of the conquistadores as to the epoch-making work they were doing. Spain was conquering a New World, knew it, and sang of it.

Such poetical efforts were not left to chance but were encouraged in the literary *certamen*, or poetic contest, and by universities, schools, city governments, viceroys, and others. Prizes were offered for the best works extolling the virtues of some man or event, the poems were read aloud and eventually some were printed. The first printing press in America was installed by Viceroy Antonio de Mendoza in Mexico City in 1535-38. Peru had a press in 1584.

Drama came into being as a part of the religious processions and festivals and such was its enduring influence that one may still see Indian groups acting out events in the history of Christianity that have only the remotest, if any, connection with their own lives.

Architecture with the advantages of the arch was almost purely Spanish. But the architects could not resist the Indian influence, and in decorations and sometimes in form we may see that Inca, Maya, or Aztec concepts were incorporated. The church edifice was the foremost structure in every Spanish settlement. After this, came the public buildings and the more imposing private houses, some of which are still standing and are the show places attracting many modern tourists.

European technique in painting also entered the New World; perhaps the first artist being Rodrigo de Cifuentes who came to Mexico two years after its conquest. He painted portraits of Cortés, Doña Marina, Martín de Valencia, Nuño de Guzmán, and Viceroy Antonio de Mendoza. European sculpture likewise formed the basis of American development in this line, and art had a ready market in the thousands of statues and paintings needed for the rapidly multiplying Christian churches. [56]

* * * * * * *

By the second half of the sixteenth century colonial culture was well established on its double foundation of Indian plus European elements. The Indian contribution was submerged, apparent only in folk arts or such minor decorative motifs as had been applied to primarily Spanish structures. Underneath the European importations, the native cultures survived inconspicuously as a part of the life of the masses, despite their adoption of the European religion and whatever European education was available to them. Colonial literature, art, and educational institutions in the sixteenth century were predominantly Spanish. The story of their concrete developments is reserved for a future chapter.

[56] Riva Palacio, *México*, II, 527-34; Means, *Fall*, p. 272.

Religion and the Church

N O OTHER SINGLE INFLUENCE is so important in the history of
Latin America as the Church. Religion was an all-pervading
influence among the Indians before the Conquest, as it was among
the conquerors. No matter what aspects of Latin America life we
consider, economic, social, political, or cultural, we find the Church
occupying a chief position. It is therefore important to understand
the Indian religions, the Spanish religion before the Conquest, and
the blending of these two after the Conquest.

THE SPANISH CHURCH

Spanish religion was shaped by the history of several centuries
preceding 1492. The Moorish conquest had swept over Spain in
711, and the years immediately following. All of Spain had been
conquered by the Moors except for a small portion in the northwest, Asturias, and from there came the Christian counter offensive.
Sheltered behind the mountains, Pelayo, traditional leader of the
Asturians, organized his forces and in 718 was able to oppose the
Moors. Those who gathered around Pelayo submerged the many
differences which had existed in Visigothic Spain by uniting on one
single point, opposition and hatred of the Moors and their religion.
This immediately placed Christianity in a dominant position. There
had already emerged in Visigothic Spain a strong ecclesiastical influence in the government and this tradition facilitated the union
between the sovereign of Asturias and the Church. The churchmen
rallied their own followers around the Asturian Kings, pleading
that opposition to the Moors was a Christian duty, and threatening
ecclesiastical punishments for those who failed to follow them.
This was effective; Asturias slowly won back territory from the
Moors. But the churchmen demanded and received payment, and a
very large portion of the lands so regained became ecclesiastical
property on which were built monasteries, churches, and cathedrals.
Church influence was increased in the course of the ninth century

233

by the announcement that the tomb of Saint James the Elder, known among the Spaniards as Santiago, had been discovered in Galicia. The bishop of the district confirmed the discovery, and the King erected a church at the site, which developed into a shrine visited by thousands of people each year. From this time Santiago became the patron saint and the chief warrior of Spain, and every battle fought by the Spaniards was opened with the cry: *"Santiago y a ellos!"* Although "according to strictly historical data the coming of Santiago to Spain and his preaching are not proved,"[1] a famous Jesuit historian of Spain has well expressed the sentiment that existed: "Some grave and Learned Persons have made a doubt, whether Saint James the Apostle ever was in Spain, and consequently of the Invention of his Body. I will not undertake to discuss the point, but must confess I think the general consent of all Christendom in this behalf appears to me more convincing than all of the Arguments they can bring to oppose it."[2] Santiago definitely linked the destinies of the kingdom with Christianity.

Thus the Reconquest of Spain from the Moors became in a sense a crusade. Soldiers from all over Europe came to help, with the blessings of the Church and with the rewards of the lands reconquered. However, Christian and Moor were not invariably opposed for during the eight centuries of Moorish occupation there were frequent alliances between Christians and Moors to fight other Christians and Moors, a characteristic of all the crusades. Bohemund, one of the chief leaders of the first crusade to the Holy Land, carried a large contingent of Mohammedans in his army; and Frederic II, in the thirteenth century, had an army composed almost entirely of his Neapolitan and Sicilian Mohammedan subjects.

During the centuries of Reconquest in Spain there were long epochs in which great toleration prevailed on both sides. Mohammedans lived within the reconquered territories, and Christians were tolerated within Mohammedan areas. Many of the Christian kings, in fact, gave their Mohammedan subjects the maximum guarantees since they recognized their economic importance. Despite this there was one way men could always be distinguished one from another. They were either Mohammedans or Christians, and regardless of the alliances which were formed between them and of the numerous times they fought side by side, this distinction never died out.

[1] Ramón Menéndez Pidal, ed., *Historia de España* (Madrid: Espasa-Calpe, 1935), II, 448.

[2] Steven's *Mariana*, p. 110, quoted in Merriman, *Spanish Empire*, I, 60.

A great deal of the tolerance that existed down to the fourteenth century was gradually lost during the course of the fifteenth. The Mohammedans had been driven steadily back, and it was increasingly important for the Christian monarchs to have dependable subjects living within their territories. Every Mohammedan became an object of suspicion, and this suspicion was carried over to the Jews because of their close relations with the Mohammedans. Religion became patriotism. It had no more necessary connection with morality and ethics than modern nationalism has with good citizenship. The important thing was which side a man took when there was a division of parties. This is what divided men into Christians and non-Christians, and the Christian monarchs became increasingly intolerant of the Mohammedans within their borders because of the dangers of uprising and alliance with the Mohammedan state of Granada.

In the latter part of the fifteenth century when the active war against Granada was renewed, the allegiance of every person within the Christian territory was considered a necessity. The Sovereigns of Aragon and Castile, Ferdinand and Isabella, adopted religious unity as a political program and, as one of their measures, they brought the Inquisition to Spain. The Inquisition, it may be observed, was not originally Spanish; and it was not new, for Pope Innocent III had first used it against the Albigensians in the early thirteenth century. It became a regular institution of the Church's judicial system during the time of Pope Gregory IX (1227-41), and while it had functioned in Spain at times prior to the fifteenth century it had never been extremely active.

In Castile in the middle of the fifteenth century, John II had asked for Inquisitorial powers as a result of the measures which had forced thousands of Jews to become Christians. Since many converted Jews quite naturally retained their own religion and were Christians in name only, it was thought necessary to purge the nation of those converted for expediency's sake. Pope Sixtus IV attempted in 1474 to institute the Inquisition in Spain but Ferdinand and Isabella objected to an Inquisition under foreign control and secured from the Pope in 1478 the right to appoint and remove Inquisitors at will. This was the beginning of the "Spanish Inquisition." From this time it acted as a powerful politico-religious weapon to guarantee unity within Spain.

Religious and Political Unity

Spain lacked unity even after the union of Aragon and Castile. Towards the end of the fifteenth century many Moors and Jews within the Christian states of Spain lived in their own towns or within their own sections of the Christian towns. The *Siete Partidas* (laws) of Alfonso X (1252-84) outline in great detail the privileges and immunities of both groups. Christians were not to enter Moorish towns and quarters, which had their own officials, courts of justice, and codes of law, often written in Spanish since the Moors had largely forgotten their native language. Christians were not to force them to accept Christianity nor to oppress them in any way. Jews were excused from attending courts of justice on Saturday and enjoyed religious liberties. However, they paid special imposts in addition to all the regular taxes which fell upon the Christians; but many of the royal tax collectors were Jews. The policy of the kings of Castile was, during the time of Alfonso X and later, to maintain a strict separation between the groups. The Jews could not bathe, drink, or eat with the Christians, and sexual intercourse between Christian and non-Christian was punished with mutilation. Jews and Moors were required to wear a distinctive badge or dress, or to wear their hair in a way that marked them off from Christians. These regulations, however, were not consistently obeyed.

During the fourteenth century, policies regarding Moors and Jews changed. Usury laws which had enabled Jews and Moors to lend money were revoked and the position of the Jews in the courts became much worse. Many disasters, including the black death, were laid at the door of the Jews and thousands of them were massacred. Since conversion to Christianity was their only salvation there came into existence the converted Jew, known by the name of *conversos* or *marranos*. This was the group whose faithfulness to Christianity, and therefore to their Christian Sovereigns, was considered doubtful. Furthermore, as Christians the *conversos* had been able to prosper and to occupy high positions in the government. It was therefore easy to arouse jealousy on economic grounds.

With the renewal in the latter part of the fifteenth century of the wars against the Mohammedans of Granada, both Jews and Moors were regarded as potential enemies within the Christian lines. A tremendous anti-Jewish and anti-Moorish sentiment arose which made futile the efforts of the Crown to protect them from riots and massacres, and the massacres went unpunished. With the Reconquest of Granada in 1492, came a demand for the expulsion of the Jews. A few months after the fall of Granada a decree required all Jews to profess Christianity or to leave Aragon and Castile within four months. Some accepted Christianity, but great numbers emigrated, leaving behind them most of their property and wealth, which fell into the hands of Christians. [3]

The Moors were tolerated for eight years following the fall of Granada. Ferdinand and Isabella had promised: "It has never been, nor is it now our will that any Moor be forced to become a Christian, we hereby promise, on our word and honor, that we will not consent to any such procedure." [4] Archbishop Fernando de Talavera had followed a policy of conversion by persuasion, and there were some signs that the Moors would accept the peaceful overtures thus made to them. Ferdinand and Isabella permitted the Moors expelled from Portugal to settle in Spain. Cardinal Jiménez de Cisneros, however, attempted to hasten conversion by applying pressure. So many accepted Christianity that in one day three thousand were baptised. In some quarters, however, the policy of Jiménez was opposed on the grounds that it violated the treaty made with the Moors at the rendition of Granada. Jiménez, angered at the opposition to his plans, closed the Moorish schools and destroyed thousands of rare Moorish manuscripts. Bad matters became worse when some of the Mohammedans appealed to the Sultan of Egypt for protection, thus introducing a political aspect that converted Ferdinand and Isabella to the idea of expulsion.

Such was the state of Spanish religious feeling during the first few years after Columbus returned with the announcement that he had discovered new lands and new people. The Reconquest of Spain from the Moors had just been completed and the Jews were being expelled. Every non-Christian was regarded not merely as a religious but as a political enemy as well. It would have been little less than a marvel if the Spaniards could have abandoned their religious feeling in their treatment of the inhabitants of the New World. From the very beginning, the Indians were regarded as subjects of the Crown to be converted to Christianity as a political measure, lest they remain both religious and political enemies of the State.

The political importance of religion, recognized in the rights of patronage which the Crown exercised in the territories conquered from the Mohammedans, was to exert its influence in America. Columbus had no sooner returned than the Spanish Crown secured from Pope Alexander VI, in 1493, a Bull granting absolute control of America to the Spanish Sovereign. "We give, concede, and assign them in perpetuity to you and the Kings of Castile and of Leon,

---

[3] Merriman, *Spanish Empire*, I, 197, 202.
[4] Quoted in Braden, *Religious Conquest of Mexico*, p. 14.

your heirs and successors: and we make, constitute, and depute you and your heirs and successors, the aforesaid lords of these lands, with free, full and absolute power, authority, and jurisdiction." [5]

Eccelesiastically, "the whole region was governed by the King, and was subject to his direction, administration, or nomination, or to those who acted in his stead in virtue of the commission and delegation which they held for this purpose from the Apostolic See." [6]

While Spain was conquering America, religion was also playing a predominant part in the international politics of Europe. Charles V (1516-56), who followed Ferdinand and Isabella, was waging his wars against the Mohammedans in North Africa and in the Balkans, and against Francis I of France, allied with the Turkish sultan, and was trying simultaneously to suppress Protestantism, as a result of Luther's revolt in 1517. It was in this atmosphere of war against Jew and Moor within Spain, and against Mohammedan and Lutheran outside, that the Spaniards began their conquest and conversion of the Indians of America.

American Indian Religions

Religion among the Indians was scarcely less important than among the Spaniards. Seldom if ever in history have two more zealously religious peoples come together. To both peoples, religion meant not only the worship of a definite set of divine beings, but political control of the people as well. Spain of the sixteenth century was a semitheocracy; and the states of the Aztecs, Mayas, and Incas, not to speak of numerous minor Indian peoples, were also theocracies.

The missionary, Toribio de Motolinía wrote concerning the Aztec religion:

"The idols which the Indians had were extremely numerous and were found in many places, especially in the temples of their demons and in the patios; and prominent places like forests, large hills and ports, or in high mountains and in every convenient, pleasant resting place. Those who passed by sprinkled them with blood from their ears or tongue, or threw on a little incense; . . . others threw roses that they gathered along the way, and when they did not have anything else, they threw a bit of green grass or straw upon them . . .

Likewise they had idols near the water, chiefly near foun-

---

[5] Quoted in Bernard Moses, *South America on the Eve of Emancipation* (New York, 1908), p. 120.

[6] Solórzano Pereira, *Política indiana*, II, 122, quoted in Moses, *Eve*, p. 121.

tains they built their altars with covered steps . . . and some devotees of the water gods sacrificed themselves there . . . . Some idols had the figure of bishops with mitres and croziers . . . others had figures of men. These had a mortar on the head instead of the mitre. On them they threw wine because they were gods of wine. Some had the figures of women, some of wild beasts, lions, tigers, dogs, deer, etc. Also they had idols in the form of serpents, long and intertwined, some with the face of a woman . . .

Then also there were idols of birds like eagles, of night birds, vultures, kites, and of large handsome plumed birds. The chief was the sun, also the moon, and the stars, and the large fish and lizards of the water, even frogs and toads . . . They had for gods the fire, the water, and the earth and of these they painted images . . . . They had figures of many other things, even of butterflies, fleas and lobsters, large and well carved." [7]

One cannot read accounts of the Aztec religion without feeling that it permeated all classes from the lowliest to the highest. [8]

Among the Incas [9] the importance of religion was not less, as we may judge from Cieza's account of the joy with which both men and women accepted their own sacrifice to the Inca gods as a special blessing which enabled them to go directly to the service of these gods in another world.

"Around this temple [*Coricancha*] there were numerous small homes of the Indians who were assigned to its service, and there was an inclosure where they put the white llamas and the children and men they sacrificed.

After the temple of Coricancha, the second shrine of the Incas was the hill of *Huanacauri*, within sight of the city, and it was much frequented and honored by them. . . . And formerly there was an oracle on this hill from which the accursed devil spoke, and a great treasure was buried around it; and on some days they sacrificed men and women, who, before they were sacrificed were given to understand by the priests that they were to go to

[7] *Motolinia, Historia de los Indios de Nueva España* (Barcelona, 1914), pp. 32-33; quoted also in Braden, *Religious Conquest of Mexico*, pp. 20-21.
[8] See Clavigero, *México*, Dissertation VIII; Torquemada, *Monarchia indiana,* Bks. VI-X, discusses in great detail the religions of the Indians in the Caribbean, Mexico, and Peru; See also Orozco y Berra, *Historia antigua de México*, I, 3-251; Sahagún, *Cosas de Nueva España*, I, 13-299, II, 7-37.
[9] Among the sources of information for Peruvian religion are: *D. I. I.*, III, 5-58; and Cobo, *Nuevo Mundo*, Bk., XIII, who discusses all phases of Inca religion: fables, *guacas,* belief in future life, *Viracocha*, sun, moon, minor gods, worship of dead, temples, ceremonies, ideas of sin, festivals, clergy, and convents.

serve the God who was worshipped there. . . . The men adorned themselves brilliantly and dressed in fine woolens . . . and after having heard the sermon that the lying priests made to them, they were given a great deal of *chicha* to drink from large golden goblets, and the sacrifice was solemnized with songs which proclaimed that in order to serve their gods they offered their lives in this manner, considering it a great happiness to embrace death in life's place. And having repeatedly sung these sentiments in funeral songs they were drowned by their priests . . . and buried in the sepulchres around the oracle. And these were considered among them as consecrated saints, they [the Incas] believing without any doubt that they were in heaven serving *Huanacauri.* The women who were sacrificed also dressed richly in fine clothing of colors and feathers . . . and thus dressed, after they had drunk a great deal, they were drowned and buried, believing, they and those who killed them, that they were going to serve their devil, Huanacauri; and they had great dances and song festivals when they made sacrifices like these." [10]

The leading Indian religions at the time of the Conquest had some concept of a supreme being or creator. Among the Mexicans the supreme being received the name of Teotl. This, however, did not mean monotheism, for there were many lesser gods. The philosopher King Nezahualcoyotl expressed his belief in a supreme being in his statement: "These idols of wood and stone can neither hear, nor feel, much less could they make the heavens and the earth and men the lord of it. Some all powerful unknown god is creator of the universe on whom alone I must reply for consolation and support." [11] The Incas likewise had a creator god, Viracocha or Pachacamac.[12]

Belief in such a supreme being was confined probably to a very few. For the great masses of the subjects of Montezuma as well as of the Incas, there were a variety of gods, each having a special function. Among the Aztecs, for example, there were some thirteen principal gods and over two hundred minor gods. *Tezcatlipoca* was the invisible god of the sky, the earth and the underworld, who stirred up wars and enmities, who "alone had to do with ruling the world," and who had the power either to give or deny riches. *Quétzalcoatl* was a god who was supposed to have departed from the Aztecs some centuries before with a promise to return. He is

---

[10] Cieza, *Señorio*, chaps. XXVII, XXVIII.
[11] Quoted in Braden, *Religious Conquest of Mexico*, p. 23.
[12] Means, *Ancient Civilizations*, pp. 422-30.

AZTEC SACRIFICIAL STONE

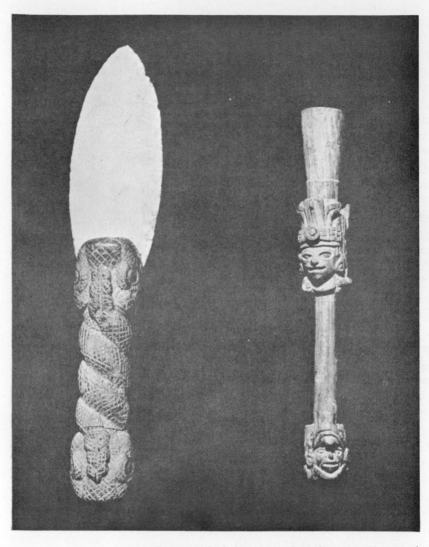

SACRIFICIAL KNIFE WITH STONE BLADE, PRE-SPANISH

represented as a great teacher, not only of the arts and sciences but also of morality. In the various stories concerning his origin he is accredited with a virgin birth. He engaged in constant warfare with Tezcatlipoca and this eventually led to his exile across the waters to the east, whence he was to return. The date he set for his return was the year *Ce Acatl,* one of the years in the 52-year Mexican calendrical cycle. The year 1519, in which Cortés appeared in the Aztec kingdom, was *Ce Acatl. Huitzilopochtli,* the god of war, was the most venerated among the Aztecs. To him was dedicated the chief temple and it was he who demanded human sacrifices in countless thousands. Originally he was supposed to have been a man whose warlike prowess gained him great honor while alive and deification when dead. It was he who led the Aztecs in battle, it was he to whom they prayed for victory, and it was to him that they ascribed their Conquests.

These were the chief gods, but there were others of great importance. *Civecoatl,* or *Cihuacoatl,* was the chief goddess. Her popular name, *Tonantzin,* meaning "our mother," caused the priest Sahagún to identify her with Eve. She was also goddess of fertility in both the animal and vegetable world. Her shrine at Tepeyac was one of the most sacred. Other gods who performed important functions were *Tonatiuh* the sun, and *Metztli* the moon. *Tláloc* was the god of paradise, *Centeotl* god of the earth and corn. The Aztecs also had gods of hunting, fishing, salt, physic, wine, flowers, mirth, and numerous other things. One of the most interesting was *Tlaculteotl* the goddess of lust to whom the Indians confessed their carnal sins. The Aztec gods and goddesses, however, did not intermarry, did not themselves sin and were regarded as holding all sin in aversion. Worship therefore was directed to appeasing the anger provoked in the gods by the sins of man.

The chief gods of the Incas, in addition to the supreme being already mentioned, were *Inti* the sun, and *Quilla* the moon. The Incas also had an infinite variety of gods of a minor character known as *huacas.* The *huacas* were gods of various tribes, regions, and places who were appealed to as the controlling powers over nature. The Incas also had household gods known as *conopas.* Among the Incas as among the Aztecs, these minor gods were represented by images made of wood, stone or other material. Small figurines representing the gods were worn as bracelets, pendants, and other jewelry.

In his description of the Chancas, Garcilaso gives a good idea of the everyday religion of the masses.

"This nation is called Chanca. They boast of having descended from a lion, and therefore they considered the lion to be a god and worshipped it; and in their great festivals, both before and after being conquered by the Inca kings, they paraded two dozen Indians in the clothing in which Hercules is pictured, covered with the skin of a lion, the head of the Indian inside the head of the lion. I saw them thus in the festival of the Most Holy Sacrament in Cuzco.

"Under this general name Chanca are included many other nations which boasted of having descended from different ancestors, some from a spring, others from a lake, and still others from a very high hillock. And each nation held its ancestor to be its god, and offered sacrifices to him." [13]

SIMILARITY OF SPANISH AND INDIAN RELIGIOUS CONCEPTS

The Spaniards found the Indian religious practices and ceremonies similar enough to their own to believe that Christianity had been preached in America and had become corrupted through the influence of the devil. The modern anthropologist recognizes that many of these practices and symbols are found among peoples of various cultures, but the sixteenth-century Spaniard regarded them as peculiar to Christianity. Therefore, when he saw Indian religious customs resembling his own he tended to exaggerate them. Among those which seemed most like Christianity were: belief in the immortality of the soul, the expected return of a Messiah, church organization, monasteries and convents, and the use of the cross, confession, baptism, and communion.

Belief that the soul was immortal, and that after human death it went to an intermediate place of judgment where it passed through a process of purification in preparation for entering paradise, was a part of the Aztec religion. There were legends of resurrection after death. Montezuma's sister allegedly died, remained in the tomb for four days, and was then resurrected. This same sister, the Princess Papan, was one of the first to embrace Christianity after the Conquest. The Aztecs believed that the world was to come to an end at the termination of one of their 52-year cycles; and special religious services were said at each of these.

They also had a definite hierarchy, with a chief priest and officials whom the Spaniards called bishops. These performed regular services in the temples and were consulted in all important matters.

[13] Garcilaso, *Comentarios,* Bk. IV, chap. XV.

Numerous other officials may be compared to the various dignitaries of a cathedral, such as the treasurer, a major sacristan, a precentor (in charge of temple music), choir boys, and a schoolmaster, as well as archdeacons, and vicars-general. Such were their powers that many historians have considered the priest more influential than the King and the nobles. "The great men even vied with one another in consecrating their children for some time to the service of the temples, while the inferior nobility employed theirs in works without, such as carrying wood, feeding and keeping up fires in the temple stoves, and other things of that kind; all considering the honor of serving in the worship of the gods as the greatest to which they could aspire." [14]

The priestly class was large and impressed the conquerors as being moral in their conduct. The early Spaniards who recorded their impressions of the Aztec religion agree that the prestige of the Aztec priest was extremely high in the community. Some attributed the chastity of the Aztec priest to the devil. Torquemada remarked: "The Indian priests of New Spain were under the same law of chastity, because the Devil wanted them to be chaste . . . not because he is clean, but in order to imitate God in some way in his purity, he required that his priests live chastely." [15]

Some Aztec priests served for a lifetime; others for a limited number of years. Women also entered the temples where they received religious instruction and served the Church, some for a year or two, and some from the ages of four or five up to sixteen or eighteen, when they were married. "Both the latter and the former [types of priestesses] lived in great purity of manners, silence, and retirement, under their superiors, without having any communication with men." "Nothing was more zealously attended to than the chastity of these virgins." [16] Many different orders of priests served the various gods; the Indian temples being as numerous as the importance of their religion might lead us to suspect. Besides the chief temples there were thousands of shrines throughout Mexico.

The hierarchy of the Incas was not unlike that of the Aztecs. At the head was the *villac-umu,* or high priest, usually a brother or uncle of the Inca, who held his position for life. From the same family came the priests for the temples throughout the Empire. Minor priests usually came from the lower nobility. The influence of the priesthood was very great, and the family from which the

---

[14] Clavigero, *Mexico,* Bk. VI, Section XIV.
[15] Quoted in Braden, *Religious Conquest of Mexico,* p. 51.
[16] Clavigero, *México,* Bk. VI, Section XVI.

chief priest came may have at times seriously threatened the power of the Inca himself. [17]

The Incas also had an institution which resembled the convent more closely than the similar institution of the Aztecs. This was the House of the Virgins of the Sun (the *casa de escogidas* previously described, chapter IX). The chief convent was in Cuzco where hundreds of women, nominally dedicated to the worship of the sun, were more immediately occupied in serving his earthly representative, the Inca. Throughout the Inca Empire were other subsidiary convents. Strict virginity was allegedly required of the chosen women and strong punishment, such as burial alive, followed the breaking of this law. [18] But we have already indicated that this rule applied, if at all, only to the house in Cuzco.

The finding of the cross in America was to the Spaniards especially significant. They did not know that crosses of various styles, far from being peculiar to Christianity, were known long before Christ. The cross was found in America in a great many places. Two of the most famous were the cross at Cozumel, considered by the Indians as a rain god, and the cross at Palenque. The robe of Quétzalcoatl carried a red and black cross, and the cross was frequently used in the Aztec writings. One of the crosses had before it a child being lifted up as if for worship. At Mitla, near Oaxaca, underground openings in the form of a cross, perhaps tombs, were hewn out of the rock.

The Indians also practiced various forms of baptism. Among the Aztecs the midwife—sometimes called a "priestess"—took the child at sunrise and baptised it from an earthen vessel of water. The Spaniards were struck by the fact that the child was baptised in its infancy, that it was named at the ceremony of baptism, and that water was used for baptism. Bishop Landa described the baptism among the Mayas and thought it peculiar to them, not knowing the Aztec custom. It was performed by a priest who sprinkled crowds of boys and girls. The Maya word for baptism meant "to be born again." Since the Indians were already accustomed to baptism before the arrival of the Spaniards they accepted eagerly the only slightly new form offered by the Spanish priests.

Confession was also a well established practice in Indian America. Among the Aztecs they confessed twice a year and did a penance to atone for their sins. Confession seems to have been made to the

---

[17] Means, *Ancient Civilizations,* p. 408.

[18] Garcilaso, *Comentarios,* Bk. IV, chaps. I-VII; Means, *Ancient Civilizations,* pp. 408-12 gives conclusive evidence that the chosen women did not remain virgins but instead were used as concubines by the Inca and by the nobility.

doctors and not to the priests. However, confession to the priests was also common, especially to the priests of the goddess of love, who imposed upon the penitent fasting or the sticking of thorns into the tongue, through the genitals, or in the ears. Penance might require four hundred thorns to be passed through the tongue. The priests guarded the secrets of those who confessed, this prerogative being recognized by the government.

Communion existed among the Indians in a form very similar to that of the Christians. The Jesuit, Acosta, attributed it to the devil. "Who will not marvel," he says, "that the devil should have taken such care to get himself worshipped and accepted by the same methods which Jesus Christ, our God, ordained and taught, and which the holy Church practices." [19] The bread used for communion among the Aztecs was made of a mixture of cornmeal with other plants to form a sort of *tamal*. They accompanied this with beating on a drum and singing, believing that the *tamales* so blessed suffered a transubstantiation and became the flesh of Tezcatlipoca. The tamales were for the children; the adults ate human flesh in this communion service.

Another communion service was held in honor of the war god Huitzilopochtli, of whom a large image was made, blessed, broken into pieces, "and, beginning with the elders, passed out as a sort of communion to the whole people, children and adults, men and women. And they received it with such reverence, fear and tears, saying that they ate the flesh and bones of God, being unworthy, that one was obliged to marvel." [20]

Aztec fasting and the observance of holy days also struck the Spaniards as being like their own practices. "They had designated days of the year for each of the devils, for whom they held festivals . . . just as we have dedicated a day in this or that month for each of the saints." [21] There were such holy days for each month of the year, of which there were eighteen, during the five days at the end of the year, and on many other occasions.

Fasting was a frequent practice of the people, and more especially of the priests. In this they "conformed to the custom of our Catholic Church, and rightly, for it is only just that those who are dedicated to divine service should be more diligent in these penitential acts than those who are not so consecrated." [22] Fasting periods were

[19] Acosta, *Historia de las Indias,* Bk. V, chap. XXIV.
[20] *Ibid.,* chap. XXIV.
[21] Gerónimo de Mendieta, *Historia eclesiástica indiana,* ed. Joaquín García Icazbalceta (Mexico, 1870), p. 97.
[22] *Ibid.,* p. 102.

of twenty, forty, or even eighty days, accompanied by acts of self-torture in which two, three, or four hundred thorns would be passed through the tongue at the end of each twenty day period. The fast was not a complete abstinence from food.

Such similarities as we have noticed here between the religion of the Spaniards and that of the Mexican Indians were present in practically every part of America. The Incas practiced a form of baptism and also had a ceremony very like confirmation. Some form of the cross was found in many places, and the number of their feast days and holy days in which their gods and minor gods were honored were not less numerous than among the Aztecs. [23]

RELIGION IN THE CONQUEST

Religion, we may conclude from the evidence just presented, was no less important to the Indians than to the Spaniards. It is not surprising, in view of the Spanish feeling in religious matters and of the importance of religion as a political force in Spain during the time of the Conquest of America, that every advantage should have been taken to make religion in the New World as much a servant of the state as it was in the Old. Columbus on his first voyage symbolized the connection between the religious and the political powers by planting the cross. On his second voyage Columbus was instructed that "the King and the Queen . . . desire nothing other than to augment the Christian religion; and to reduce many simple nations to the divine worship; . . . having more regard for the augmentation of the faith than for any other utility." [24]

Twelve friars accompanied Columbus on this second voyage and from the first were an important element in the new society. At the head was an apostolic Vicar, Fray Bernal Boyl, appointed by the Pope. When the Vicar returned a year later, the Sovereign ordered Fonseca to appoint a successor, but what was done is not known. A papal Bull in 1504 authorized the establishment of an archbishopric and two bishoprics in Española, but a dispute between Ferdinand and Julius II over rights of patronage prevented fulfilment. In 1508, the Pope provided that no Church establishment should be built in America without the consent of the Spanish Sovereigns. Two bishoprics in Española and one in Puerto Rico were established by the Pope in 1511. By 1513, the bishops or their representatives had reached the New World, and the Church organization was an accomplished fact. [25]

---

[23] Means, *Ancient Civilizations,* pp. 336-7.
[24] *The Libretto,* quoted in Thacher, *Columbus,* II, 489.
[25] Elizabeth Ward Loughran, "The First Episcopal Sees in Spanish America," *H. A. H. R.,* X (May, 1930), 167-87.

Cortés used religion as one of his most important instruments of conquest and considered himself as chosen by God to effect the Christianization of the Indians. His letters and the writings of Bernal Díaz are a constant repetition of the idea that God had selected the Spaniards [26] to bring Christianity to the New World. Many of the early missionaries looked upon things in the same way and Mendieta wrote:

"It ought to be well pondered how, without any doubt God expressly elected and took the valiant Captain, Don Hernando Cortés, as his instrument for opening the door and preparing the way for the preachers of His gospel in this New World, where the Catholic Church might be restored and compensated by the conversion of many souls for the great loss and damages which the accursed Luther was to cause at the same time within established Christianity. So what was lost on the one hand was won back on the other. . . . Thus it is not without mystery that in the same year in which Luther was born in Eisleben, in Saxony, Hernando Cortés saw the light in Medellín, a town in Spain; the former to upset the world and bring beneath the banner of Satan many of the faithful who from fathers and grandfathers and times far back had been Catholics; and the latter to bring into the fold of the Church an infinite multitude of people who for years without number had been under the dominion of Satan, immersed in vice, and blinded with idolatry." [27]

The cross was used by Cortés and by a great many other conquerors as a standard of battle. "Let us follow the cross," said Cortés, "for if we have faith in this sign we shall conquer." He preached long sermons to the Indians explaining to them the origin of Christianity and his mission of Christianization, destroyed the images in the Indian temples, and supplanted them with the cross. The Spaniards themselves could see no other reason for their great success, if we may judge by their actions and by the words of Cortés. "As our Lord has been pleased to help us, we have hope that so it may be in the future, for ever since we have penetrated into this country, in all the towns we have passed through, we have preached the holy doctrine as well as we are able, and have induced the Indians to destroy their idols." [28] Cortés was constantly urging his men forward with the encouragement: "God is our holy strength."

[26] Torquemada, *Monarchia indiana*, Bks. XV-XVI, discusses Cortés and the missionary work of the early years.
[27] Mendieta, *Historia eclesiástica indiana*, pp. 174-5. Luther, b. 1483; Cortés, b. 1485.
[28] Bernal Díaz, *Conquest of New Spain*, I. 253-54.

Religion and the Church
(*Continued*)

THE CHRISTIAN MISSIONARIES

WHILE THE CONQUEST OF MEXICO was still in progress Cortés wrote to the Emperor asking that missionaries be sent. Within a few months twelve Franciscan friars arrived.[1] They preached, destroyed the churches and images of the Indian gods, and announced to the Indians the temporal power of Charles V and the spiritual supremacy of the Pope. "We come from far distant lands . . . not to seek gold, and silver, nor any other temporal interests or benefit, but your perpetual salvation. And for this reason, beloved brethren, it is necessary . . . that you put your young children into our hands that they may first be taught, because they have nothing to do while you are very busy with the government of your subjects and with the service of our brothers the Spaniards. Also because they, being but children, will understand more easily the doctrines we teach. Afterwards they will at times aid us in teaching you and the other adults what they have learned."[2]

Backed by the influence, prestige, and force of the conquistadores, the missionaries gathered the children into doctrinal schools where they learned the rudiments of Catholic practice. Churches and other buildings with large rooms which could be used for teaching were built. The Indians, who had long been accustomed among the Aztecs, Mayas, Incas, and other peoples to work at whatever occupation was required of them by their rulers, responded readily to the demands for the construction of new buildings. If we may believe the testimony of these early missionaries—and even if

---

[1] Torquemada, *Monarchia indiana*, Bks. XX-XXI, portrays the life and works of the first missionaries.

[2] Mendieta, *Historia eclesiástica indiana*, pp. 214-15.

exaggerated, a part is certainly true—their success was phenomenal. The Indians sent delegations to request the missionaries to teach and baptise them, and if the missionaries did not come they took to the roads and came for hundreds of miles to solicit baptism, remarriage, or instruction. Some of them, perhaps even thousands, were baptized over and over again because they believed this pleased the Spaniards.[3] What the missionaries say regarding the spread of the Faith is borne out by the hundreds of churches that sprang up within a few years, scattered over the thousands of miles the Spaniards had occupied. Women teachers were brought to Mexico in 1534 to establish a school for girls, and soon orders of nuns were transplanted for this purpose. In no work were the early missionaries more zealous than in the establishment of these schools, in which the education was extremely rudimentary but the indoctrination as thorough as possible. In many schools the young Indians were trained to be *doctrineros,* or teachers of doctrine, but they were not allowed to take orders.[4]

One of the missionaries, Pedro de Gante, described their work after he had been in Mexico a great many years:

"We are distributed in nine convents, living in houses which the natives built for us, separated from each other seven, ten, and even fifty leagues . . . . Because the land is so extensive and populated with an infinite number of people, and because the friars are few for the teaching of such a multitude, we take into our houses the sons of the chief men in order to instruct them in the Catholic faith that afterwards they may teach their parents . . . . Of these I have in my charge close to five hundred or more in this city of Mexico, for it is the principal center. From this number I have chosen fifty or more of the more sagacious, and each week I teach them separately what they are to preach on the Sunday following . . . . On Sundays they go out to preach in the city, and all the territory round about for a distance of four, eight, ten, twenty, or thirty leagues, setting forth the Catholic faith, and with its teaching, preparing the people for baptism.

We go out with them, destroying idols and temples in one

---

[3] The work of the Indians in building churches is discussed in Torquemada, *Monarchia indiana,* Bk. XVII, chaps. IV-V; their faith and devotion to religion and their zeal in worship, *ibid.,* chaps. VII-IX; their "natural aptitude" for Christianity, *ibid.,* chaps. X-XIV, and Bk. XIX.

[4] For the early work of the missionaries see *Cartas de religiosos de Nueva España,* 1539-1594, in García Icazbalceta, ed. *Nueva C. D. México,* Vol. I; and other information in *ibid.* II, 1-266; *ibid.* IV and V. See also *Relación de algunas cosas que sucedieron al Padre Fray Alonso Ponce, C. D. I. España,* Vols. LVII-LVIII.

section while they are doing the same in another . . . . I, myself, by the mercy of God . . . have erected more than a hundred houses consecrated to the Lord, churches and chapels, some of them magnificent temples." [5]

The alacrity with which the Indians accepted Christianity has been a subject for amazement. To account for the ease of conversion, many different explanations are offered. Acosta quotes an Indian chief as saying:

"Do not think, father, that we accepted the law of Christ so inconsiderately as you say, for I wish to make it clear that we were already so weary and discontented with the things which the idols required of us that we had tried to leave them and find another law. And since that which you preached to us seemed to us to be without cruelty, and exactly suited to us, so just and good, we knew that it was the true law and so received it very willingly." [6]

Conversion was facilitated by a number of factors of which the Spaniards took full advantage. Favoring it were: "(1) the similarities, real or apparent, between the two forms of religion; (2) the high character of the early missionaries; (3) the support and co-operation of the government, both imperial and local; and (4) the character of the Indians." The factors that tended to hinder conversion were: "(1) the hostile or indifferent attitude of the Spanish inhabitants toward the conversion of the Indians; (2) the evil example set by the Spaniards; (3) the gross mistreatment of the Indians; (4) the lower moral character of the priests who came later; and (5) the conflict between the religious orders and, even more, that between the secular and regular clergy." [7]

ATTITUDE OF SPANISH GOVERNMENT TOWARD MISSIONARY WORK

The attitude of the Spanish government was no less important in the conversion of the Indians than the similarities of the Spanish and Indian religions and the work of the early missionaries. [8] The Bull of Alexander VI placed a moral obligation on Spain to Christianize the Indians. Charles V's letter to Cortés in 1523 commanded their immediate conversion. The Emperor further ordered the Indians to be kindly treated, the Spaniards who mistreated them punished, and expressed his belief that "more contact with

[5] Quoted in Braden, *Religious Conquest of Mexico*, pp. 172-173.
[6] Acosta, *Historia de las Indias*, Bk. V, chap. XXIII.
[7] Braden, *Religious Conquest of Mexico*, p. 180.
[8] See *Gobernación espiritual y temporal*, Bk. III, Title I, "De la conversión y doctrina de los Indios."

the Christians . . . is the best way to bring them to the knowledge of our holy faith, which is our chief desire and intention. One hundred converted in this way are worth more than one hundred thousand by any other." [9]

Although the wishes of the Crown were not carried out faithfully, no small part of the success of Christianization may be attributed to the continuous reiteration of the Crown's desires. The encomiendas and the large estates which dominated the economic life of colonial Latin America were instructed to establish chapels and monasteries, and maintain in them a corps of clerics for the indoctrination of the Indians. In 1535, the Emperor in his instructions to Viceroy Mendoza ordered: "First, before everything else, you will inform yourself as soon as you have arrived in that land and have begun to understand something about it, what provisions have been and are being made in spiritual and dynastic matters, especially in building temples for the divine worship and in the conversion and training of the native Indians." [10]

The following year, the King wrote the Viceroy to see to it that the holders of encomiendas carried out their charge of providing religious instruction for the Indians—with due care not to interfere with the hours of labor—and that Indian slaves in the mines or on the farms were also instructed in the Faith. He demanded that those who hindered the teaching of the Indians, whether Spaniards or chiefs, be punished. [11]

The fiscal policies of the Crown in regard to the Church also reflect its interest in Christianization. In 1501 a Papal Bull conceded the tithes to the King. The greater part of this income was used in religious worship, the King returning most of it to the Church, as well as providing additional funds from his own treasury.

Aside from the religious zeal which might have animated Charles V with concern for the conversion of the Indians, he was deeply impressed with the political aspects of Christianization. A Sovereign who was fighting Mohammedans on one front, and Lutherans on another, was apt to consider religious faith as synonymous with loyalty to the regime.

CHARACTER OF THE INDIANS: CONTRIBUTION TO THEIR CONVERSION

The personal qualities of the Indians were another factor in their conversion. The early missionary, Mendieta, ascribes the ease

---

[9] Quoted in Braden, *Religious Conquest of Mexico*, p. 187.
[10] *D. I. I.* XXIII, 426-43.
[11] Braden, *Religious Conquest of Mexico*, pp. 194-5; see also Cieza, *Crónica,* chap. CI.

with which they were won, to their being meek, peaceful, gentle, simple, poverty-stricken, and content with this condition, and very humble. He emphasizes their extreme docility. "The shepherd carries off a son, the cartman a daughter, a Negro the wife, a mulatto insults him, and on top of this comes another *repartimiento* which sends him to the mines, where his life ends . . . . Certainly, considering the injuries and vexations which these miserable people receive from us, I marvel that they do not flee to the mountains and wilds with the savages (*chichimecas*)." [12] He was impressed by the resignation with which they approached death, observing that they seemed little attached to the things of this world, but expectant of what a future life might offer.

The results achieved indicate that the statements concerning the ease of conversion are true. Bishop Zumárraga wrote in 1531 that the Franciscans had baptised a million and a half. He painted a glowing picture of the piety and devotion of the converts, and their zeal in taking the idols from their parents, "for which some of them have actually been killed by the parents and crowned by Christ in Glory." [13] In the middle of the seventeenth century Gil González Dávila estimated that the Franciscans and Dominicans alone had baptised ten million people.

It is not necessary to accept such patently exaggerated estimates to see what happened during the first years of the Spanish occupation. The Indians poured into the centers where Catholic missionaries had established themselves and begged for baptism. It was impossible for the priest to attend them and, it seems clear from a resolution taken by the first Church council in America in 1555, that mass baptisms were the custom, since the council provided that mass baptism should be administered only on Thursday afternoon and Sunday morning.

Confession presented a similar problem. The Indians were already accustomed to confession, and they flocked to the Spanish priests beseeching the opportunity to confess. Priests traveling on the road would be followed by throngs of Indians. Many of these were women, either pregnant or with small children, while old people on crutches hobbled to the road sides and the blind were sometimes carried fifteen or twenty leagues. The able-bodied Indians might travel as much as eighty leagues looking for a confessor. Mendieta, who wrote after 1554, saw such crowds that the friars could not make their way along the road. One priest tried to escape

---

[12] Mendieta, *Historia eclesiástica indiana*, pp. 441-42.
[13] Quoted in Braden, *Religious Conquest of Mexico*, pp. 222-23.

from the Indians by taking a boat across the lake, but they followed him in canoes, some of them jumping into the water in order to gain precedence in confession.

Administration of the eucharist was not generally given until after the Bull of Pope Paul III in 1537, ordering that the Indians be granted communion as were all other Christians. Even after this date it was sometimes refused to the Indians on the grounds that they were not capable of understanding it. Extreme unction was frequently denied by the clerics on the grounds that they were not numerous enough to administer it to all.

Marriage of the Indians furnished one of the most difficult tasks as well as one of the most puzzling ethical points faced by the priests, for polygamy was the rule in most of the Americas. Some Indians had several wives, and chieftains might have a great number. With the implantation of Christianity, monogamy was, in theory at least, instituted by the Church, and the question immediately arose as to what should be done about the surplus wives of Christian Indians. One of the procedures was to bring witnesses to determine which one of the many was to be considered a lawful wife. After this was done there arose the problem of what was to become of the wives and children for whom the Indian was not now responsible.

It is quite probable that there were more women than men or polygamy could not have been practiced. Dismissal of the supernumerary wives left them and their children homeless and unprotected, presenting as great a moral difficulty as did plural marriage. Some of the priests questioned whether there had been any marriage in America before the implantation of Christianity, and this was not decided definitely in the affirmative until the Bull of Paul III referred to above. Settling the question, however, of whether the Indians were legally married before Christianity, did not help in the least to provide a solution for the hardships involved in the shift to monogamy. We may judge that the problem was not settled in an entirely ethical manner from the accounts left to us by these same priests, which indicate that there were great numbers of homeless, wretched children roaming America shortly after the Conquest. The moral question regarding the Indians' legal marriage was, moreover, largely fictitious, since the indiscriminate unions of European men with Indian women made such discussions hypocritical.

DESTRUCTION OF IDOLS AND FOUNDING OF CHURCHES

One of the accomplishments of which the early priests were proudest was the destruction of what they termed idolatry, and the substitution of Christian worship and images. A modern Catholic historian says:

"Idolatry was destroyed among the masses, though here and there cases of it were found. Human sacrifice was completely blotted out . . . . There are those who multiply gratuitously the cases of idolatry, deducing thereby that the Indians generally continued to practice it. The most insistent in sustaining this thesis have not been able to prove the historicity of even thirty cases. Even though they were able to prove three thousand cases, scattered over three centuries and the whole of the nation, it would mean nothing. In 1538, Motolinía wrote: 'If there exist in any village an idol, it is either rotten or so forgotten or so secret that in a population of ten thousand souls, not five of them know anything about it and they hold it for what it is, that is, a stone, or as wood. Idolatry is as completely forgotten as if a hundred years had passed.' " [14]

The same results were claimed for other parts of America. Cieza de León who saw the process in South America remarks: "The ancient temples, which are generally called *guacas,* are all now demolished and profaned, and the idols smashed; and the devil, being evil, cast out of those places where because of the sins of men he was so greatly esteemed and worshipped, and the cross is now planted there. Verily, we Spaniards must give everlasting thanks to God for this." [15]

Undoubtedly one of the most important influences in this early period was the building of Christian churches on the site of Indian religious shrines. The early chronicles repeatedly show that the priests deliberately selected as a site for a Christian church the place in which the Indians were accustomed to worship. Perhaps the outstanding example of this was near Mexico City where the modern church of Guadalupe stands. On the very spot where the Indians had been accustomed to worship their mother goddess, Tonantzín, there appeared, according to the version accepted by the Church, the Virgin Mary. This appearance dated from 1531, and whatever its authenticity, for several centuries it has served to tie the new religion of the Europeans to that of the Indians.

---

[14] Mariano Cuevas, *Historia de la Iglesia en México,* II, 20, cited in Braden, *Religious Conquest of Mexico,* p. 252.

[15] Cieza, *Crónica,* chap. LVII.

When Pizarro allotted Cuzco to the various conquistadores, he gave to the Church the temple of Viracocha as a cathedral site; and many other Inca religious shrines were selected as suitable places for the establishment of Christian churches. [16]

EFFECT OF CHRISTIANITY ON NATIVE BEHAVIOR

What was the effect of the introduction of Christianity on the behavior of the Indians? This question has been hotly debated by historians from the beginning of the Conquest. Any discussion of morality is of necessity subjective. When we attempt to evaluate moral behavior in our own times, we usually take into account the prevalence of lying, cheating, stealing, physical violence, murder, drunkenness, treachery, violations of our code of sexual relations, and the degree of assiduity in the observance of the precepts and forms of our religion. Immediately after the Conquest, the conduct of the Indians was seen to combine all these censured practices with a desire to be baptized, married by Christian ceremony, and to confess their sins. They violated practically all Christian ethical precepts.

To decide whether Indian behavior improved or deteriorated after the Conquest, we should have to agree upon set standards and apply these to both the pre- and post-Conquest conditions. Numerous descriptions in the early chronicles justify the most laudatory statements concerning the Indian ethical code on the one hand, while the same chronicles furnish no less evidence of unethical conduct after the Conquest. Too often, conclusions concerning customs before and after the Conquest are reached by assuming that the Indians lived up to their own moral codes. But this line of reasoning is no more valid than if we asserted that the ten commandments and the beatitudes indicate the way we ourselves live today. It is probable that neither before nor after the Conquest was the observation of ethical standards worthy of emulation. Since, however, so many historians have quoted statements of the chroniclers concerning conditions after the Conquest to prove that the Spaniards were responsible for the introduction of immorality into the midst of an extremely moral people, the reader should be warned that only by a perusal of a few of the early chronicles is it possible to get a fair concept of pre-Conquest customs. [17]

If the Spaniards were not responsible, however, for the introduction of reprehensible conduct among the Indians we can find little

---

[16] Means, *Fall*, pp. 46, 73.
[17] On Indian customs and morals see chap. 9.

evidence that Christianity was effective in raising moral standards. The work of conversion was frequently rendered difficult by the evil example of a great many of the Spaniards. The word Christian became synonymous in the minds of many of the Indians with a being who came to kill and plunder them. "If you think this is not true," says Mendieta, "go to the Chichemecas for example and tell them the Christians are coming. At once they fly to the mountains with cries of alarm, as one who cries, 'thief, thief' or 'the enemy!' To the priests they say, 'we welcome you, but do not bring any Christians with you.' Even when they complain of one of the priests who has proved to be unworthy, they say, 'he is like a Christian.' " [17b] Another early writer says:

> "Thus among the poor Indians, when a friar happens to approach, someone says, 'Here comes a Christian,' but another who sees better says, 'No, he is a priest.' And if one asks an Indian, 'Are you a Christian?' he replies, 'No.' The Mexicans who best understand the things of God do not call the Spaniards Christians, because they see that they do not act like Christians; but they call them *Castiltecas.*" [18]

Moreover, the fair words of friars, monks, and priests frequently served only to lull the Indians into submissiveness so that they might be subjugated the more easily by the laymen.

CHURCH ORGANIZATION: THE THEOCRATIC STATE

Church organization in America was in the hands of the Crown, a close relation between church and state that was not unique in history. For example, ancient Egypt, various empires in the Tigris-Euphrates Valley, and the Roman Empire were theocratic or semitheocratic states. State control over the Church in Latin America, therefore, while not unique, was of sufficient significance to warrant our study. The origin of this relationship may be found in the conditions in Spain in the late fifteenth century, and in Europe and America at the beginning of the Conquest. In Spain, the Crown had received as a reward for its crusade against the Moslem state of Granada the control of the Church in that area. The Conquest of America was in many respects another such crusade for America represented to the Pope a vast pagan area that must be brought to the Christian faith; and the political reasons which dictated the delegation of power to the Spanish Crown in Spain, operated in America.

[17b] Quoted in Braden, *Religious Conquest of Mexico,* p. 213.

[18] Fray Rodrigo de la Cruz, quoted in Braden, *Religious Conquest of Mexico,* p. 213.

Royal control of the Church in America was delegated in a series of Papal Bulls. [19]

The Bulls of *inter caetera* and *eximae devotionis* of 1493 granted the New World to the Catholic Kings and imposed upon them the obligation of Christianizing the native. This, it was believed, transferred to the Spanish Crown exclusive jurisdiction in ecclesiastical matters in America. The Bull *eximae devotionis* granted to the Spanish Kings the powers and privileges hitherto given by other Popes to the Portuguese Crown in its new possessions. Calixtus III in 1456 having transferred "complete spiritual jurisdiction" to the Grand Master of the Order of Christ, who was later identical with the King of Portugal.

Ambiguities concerning the prerogatives of the Spanish Crown were in part clarified by later grants. For example, in 1501, in a Bull also entitled *eximae devotionis,* Alexander VI awarded to the Crown the tithes collected in America and imposed the obligation of paying all expenses of the cult. This was greater power than the Spanish Kings exercised in Spain itself, since Church revenues there were more independent of the Crown. Another Bull, *universalis ecclesiae* of 1508, was granted to clear up certain doubts which arose when Julius II in 1504 failed to concede royal ecclesiastical patronage, that is, the right to nominate clerical officials in America. In providing for bishoprics in America, Julius II had not recognized the authority granted to the Spanish Kings in previous Bulls, and Ferdinand refused to permit the establishment of the bishoprics. Ferdinand won his contentions in this case, and was strong enough to force Julius II to grant the Bull of 1508 transferring to him patronage over the Church.

From this time on, the Crown exercised this patronage continuously. Later the question came up as to the source of the Kings' patronage powers and it was debated by two schools of thought, the *canonists* and the *regalists*. The canonists propounded that patronage, being spiritual, can originate only in the Pope, while the regalists held that patronage is laical in character. The arguments raised need not concern us here; but when the Spanish colonies broke away from Spain the division of opinion on the origin of the patronage provoked bitter fights between the new nations and the Papacy, and between the partisans of each theory within the new nations.

As a practical political matter, patronage was of the utmost importance. The exercise of this right by the King meant that all

[19] For early Papal Bulls see *D. I. I.*, XXXIV, 14-110.

abbots, bishops, and archbishops, as well as all minor clerical offices, were in his power. The Pope could not seat a cleric in America who had not been previously nominated by the King. In practice the King exercised this right alone up to the time of Philip II who, in 1574, because of the tremendous administrative problem now involved, transferred to the various viceroys, presidents, governors, and captains-general the power to make nominations to minor church positions.

As a corollary to the right of appointment, a cleric could not be removed from office without the consent of the viceroy or King, nor could one resign without informing the King in full of the reasons.

All emigration of clerics to the New World was directed by the King through the Council of Indies and the Casa de Contratación. Clerics were required to go to a designated post, were not allowed to preach without a proper license, nor could they return to Spain without the consent of the King. The Crown also required all papal messages to be transmitted to the royal authorities for approval. If the message was rejected, the Pope was informed but given no explanation; if approved, the Crown granted a *pase* which permitted circulation of the Pope's message in América. The principal object was to prevent the Pope from legislating in temporal matters without the consent of the Spanish Crown; but many papal messages circulated without royal consent.

The collection of the tithes strengthened royal control of the Church, although in practice only a very small part of the tithe was retained by the Crown. One-fourth went to the bishop of the diocese in which the tithe was collected, one-fourth to the cathedral chapter. The other two-fourths were divided into nine parts of which only two were reserved by the Crown, the other seven going for church buildings, charities, and maintenance of the lower clergy. The King retained but one-ninth of the whole tithe. In addition to this the Crown made further contributions to Church expense. As a political measure, however, the right of the Crown to collect and allocate the tithes was important, since it placed the purse strings of the Church in the hands of the State. The parish priests received considerable additional income from masses, burials, marriages, and baptisms, but the amount that might be collected for these services was regulated, at least in theory, by the State.

Such matters as the fixing of ecclesiastical boundaries were also under royal control. Royal authorities legislated on controversies between ecclesiastical councils and bishops, between parish priests and bishops, or between priests and their parishioners, and on practically everything concerning the rights and prerogatives of the clergy. A permit to build a cathedral required a Bull from the Pope which could be issued only with the consent of the Spanish sovereign. The Council of Indies issued permits for the erection of other buildings. Viceroys could authorize the building of convents and monasteries until 1593 when, because of their excessive number, the King reserved such permissions to himself. Costs of building were paid by the royal treasury, the encomenderos, and the Indians in equal parts, at least in theory. In actuality, the Indians paid the whole cost in the form of manual labor: in building the church, in working for the encomenderos, and in tributes to the royal treasury.

Another feature of Church organization in America, carried over from European practice, was the clerical court. Each diocese had a church court in which cases were tried by the bishop or a subordinate official known as the provisor. Appeals could be made to the archbishop. Cases that came before the ecclesiastical court concerned marriages, tithes, patronage, benefices, legitimatizing of children, funerals, donations to the Church, legacies left to the Church, and all matters that came within the purview of pious works. If a civil case arose between two priests or if a layman brought an action against a priest, an ecclesiastical court had jurisdiction. On the contrary, an action by a priest against a layman was tried in civil courts. This privilege of the Church was called the *fuero eclesiástico*. But, since it was never possible to delimit the authority of civil and ecclesiastical courts, there were constant quarrels between the two throughout the colonial period.

The Crown exercised patronage over the religious orders, as well as over the secular clergy, and all appointments made by the heads of these orders required the approval of the Spanish authorities. The establishment or abolition of a convent required royal consent, and the viceroys of the Indies were instructed to keep a close supervision over the religious orders.

Thus the powers of the King over the Church were almost complete. Solórzano Pereira, who surveyed the development of the King's power over the Church up to the seventeenth century, held that the King enjoyed not merely the powers of patronage but also the prerogative of papal delegate. He wrote: "Your Majesty enjoys greater rights in the Indies than the right of patronage gives to the patron, because you have the position of papal delegate for the aforesaid object of conversion of the Indians." [20]

The Crown's view of its own powers may be judged from a statement found in the Laws of the Indies:

"Inasmuch as the right of ecclesiastical patronage throughout the Indies belongs to us. . . . We order and command that this right . . . always be reserved to us and our royal Crown . . . . No person, secular or ecclesiastical . . ., shall intervene in any thing pertaining to the royal patronage; . . . nor appoint anyone to a church, or benefice, or ecclesiastical office, or receive such . . . without our nomination or that of the persons to whom we by law or writ may intrust it." [21]

CHURCH ORGANIZATION: SECULAR AND REGULAR CLERGY

The organization of the Church in America[22] was divided, as in the Old World, between the *regular* clergy of monks, nuns, and friars belonging to religious orders, and the *secular* clergy of priests from the archbishopric down to the parish. The work carried on by the lower clergy was definitely divided into various types of duties. Spanish towns were ministered to by *rectores* who could give the sacraments and preach while Indian villages were under the charge of *doctrineros* whose duty was to instruct the new converts. These two classes were usually members of the secular clergy, although it was not unusual for the regulars to serve as *doctrineros*. An attempt was made to prevent quarrels between regulars and seculars by prohibiting the establishment of monasteries in towns where the *doctrineros* were members of the secular clergy.

The first bishoprics in America were those of Española and Puerto Rico, established in 1511. The bishopric of Cuba was set up in 1522. The earliest in New Spain was that of Cozumel in 1519, transferred a few years later to Tlaxcala. The diocese of Mexico City was created in 1527, and Juan de Zumárraga appointed the first bishop. In Colombia the diocese of Santa Marta was established in 1529, with Cartagena and Popayán becoming bishoprics within the next two decades. A bishopric was set up in Peru in 1534 and one in Venezuela in 1532. Others were created in important towns as rapidly as the population warranted. Under

---

[20] Quoted in Dalmacio Vélez Sarsfield, *Relaciones del estado con la iglesia,* Buenos Aires, 1919), p. 65.

[21] *Leyes de Indias,* Libro I, Título, VI, ley I.

[22] On the organization of the Church as it was about 1570 see *Gobernación espiritual y temporal,* Bk. I, in *C. D. I. Ultramar,* Vol. XX; J. Lloyd Mecham, "The Church in Colonial Hispanic America," in Wilgus, ed. *Colonial Hispanic America,* 200-39.

BISHOP JUAN ZUMÁRRAGA'S "DOCTRINA BREVE," MEXICO CITY, 1543-44

Charles V there were twenty-two bishoprics in addition to the archbishoprics of Santo Domingo, Mexico, and Lima. By the end of the sixteenth century there were five archbishoprics and twenty-seven bishoprics.

The regular clergy in America arrived before the seculars, and was responsible at the outset of the Conquest for most of the missionary work. Beginning with the twelve friars who came with Columbus on his second voyage, there were groups of monks, or friars, and later, nuns, in many if not most of the fleets. The Franciscans, Dominicans, and Augustinians were at first the most numerous and important. Later the Jesuits predominated, but also represented were the Mercedarians, Benedictines, Carmelites, and many others. These were governed by their generals in Rome but were under the control of the Crown, as previously indicated. In America each viceroyalty had a commissary general, and was divided into provinces, each of which had a provincial as head. There were many other subdivisions, among which were the frontier missions under the *presidentes,* and subsidiaries under the *procuradores.*

In converting the Indians, the religious orders were particularly active. It was they who established the first churches, schools, and hospitals, and who pushed out to the frontier territories, sometimes even ahead of the conquistadores. At the end of the sixteenth century there were some four hundred monasteries and convents, and an uncounted number of religious brotherhoods (*cofradías*). The number of monasteries, however, does not always indicate a tremendous number of clerics. For example, Nueva Galicia (in Mexico) had twenty-eight Franciscan monasteries with but fifty friars, and ten monasteries in Yucatán had only twenty monks. In general the clerics were concentrated in the towns and were not numerous in the rural districts.

THE INQUISITION IN AMERICA

Among the religious institutions implanted in the New World was the Inquisition. Although a Tribunal of the Holy Office of the Inquisition was not set up in America until 1569, ecclesiastics in the colonies were given inquisitorial powers almost as soon as settlements were established. The Inquisitor General of Spain, Cardinal Cisneros, delegated such rights to the bishops of the Indies in 1517. [23] The Franciscans who arrived soon after Cortés'

[23] Altamira, Historia de *España,* II, 463-69; Henry C. Lea, *The Inquisition in the Spanish Dependencies* (New York, 1908), pp. 191-546; José Toribio Medina, *La primitiva inquisición americana* (2 vols., Santiago de Chile, 1914), I, 1-50.

conquest of Mexico exercised inquisitorial powers as early as 1524, in accordance with the authority granted them in the will of pope Adrian VI in 1522.[24] Friar Martín de Valencia, who founded the Franciscan Order in Mexico, was invested with powers of Inquisitor when he passed through Santo Domingo in 1524, and such powers were also granted the Dominicans. During the regime of Fray Domingo de Betanzos, down to 1528, some seventeen people were convicted of blasphemy.

The Visitador Francisco Tello de Sandoval held the title of Inquisitor of New Spain, and Bishop Zumárraga was named Inquisitor of New Spain in 1535. The formal installation of his office in 1536 was accompanied by the prosecution of 131 trials, of which thirteen were of Indians and 118 of Spaniards. Up to 1600, there were 902 accusations, and six hundred convictions, with thirteen sentenced to death. The prosecutions were for such crimes as evil words, witchcraft, and bigamy; and the convictions included sixty-eight for heresy, fifty for Judaism, and forty of priests for soliciting from the confessional.

The first Archbishop of Lima, Jerónimo de Loaysa, performed *autos de fé* in Charcas, Cuzco, and Lima from 1548, in one of which a Flemish protestant, Jan Miller, was burned. Because of the care with which immigrants were selected, heretics were not numerous, though in spite of the laws some Jews and "New Christians," had come to America and these occasionally fell afoul of the inquisitors.

The Tribunal of the Holy Office of the Inquisition in America was established by Philip II in 1569; and began functioning in Lima in 1570 and in Mexico in 1571. Each court had a large number of subordinates, especially a numerous group of voluntary helpers known as "familiares." This position was sought after by those in the highest society since it lent distinction to their names and marked them off as especially zealous in the persecution of heresy.

The first auto de fé after the formal establishment of the Inquisition in Lima was the trial of a Frenchman, Mathieu Salade, in 1573. He was accused of heresy, convicted, and burned to death before an assemblage including the most distinguished Christians of Lima. In another auto de fé in 1578, before Viceroy Toledo and the oidores, six priests, a lawyer, a merchant, and other victims, sixteen in all, were paraded with ropes around their necks, some given two hundred lashes, some burned alive, and all had

---

[24] Mecham, "Colonial Church" in Wilgus, *Colonial Hispanic America*, pp. 231-35.

their property expropriated. [25] The Indians were excused from the Inquisition after about 1575 "because of their ignorance and their weak minds."

The proceedings were secret, just as in the Old World. The victim was not informed of his crime, nor who accused him, nor was he faced with witnesses. Both the victim and the witnesses were tortured if necessary to secure evidence. No one, not even the closest blood relation, was excused from giving evidence, and it was held to be the sacred duty to denounce mother or father, brother or sister. A rigorous spy system thus made it dangerous to confide "heretical thoughts" to one's most intimate relations. Anonymous accusations were received and acted upon by the Inquisition, and conviction on such information was not unusual. In fact, the citizens of the Spanish colonies were such enthusiastic supporters of the Inquisition that it was submerged with accusations and complaints of every description.

The slightest mental reservation about the divine source and supreme power of the Church was considered dangerous. Not only this, but the agents of the Church were considered as divinely guided and no one might oppose them with impunity on any matter, regardless of whether it touched religion. Accusation was practically conviction. Although the Inquisition in America burned only a small fraction of the number burned in Spain in the same period, its actions in other ways were probably more destructive. Fines, imprisonment, flogging, consignment to the galleys, and exile were the usual punishments, and with these the Inquisition stifled freedom of thought, prevented exchange of ideas upon all matters either religious, political, or social, and rigorously censored reading matter brought into or published in America. Only the failure to enforce such regulations saved the colonists from complete mental subjection to the Church. There was a market for "contraband ideas," as well as for contraband goods. The profits from contraband ideas were small, however, in comparison with those to be derived from smuggling goods, and fewer people were willing to take the risk of thinking independently or reading "heretical works."

Political as well as religious matters were within the purview of the Inquisition. The Inquisitors were Crown appointees, subject to the King alone, and in every aspect of colonial political life, other officials were required to uphold, aid, and use the Inquisition as an instrument for the maintenance of the King's authority. In

[25] Means, *Fall*, p. 131.

time, the Inquisition grew to be extremely wealthy, owing to its
right to confiscate and take for itself the property of condemned
individuals, which gave it so much power that in later centuries,
it opposed the authority of the Crown in many instances.

FOREIGN CHARACTER OF CHURCH ORGANIZATION

The Church organization throughout was a Spanish institution,
and remained Spanish rather than colonial. The history of Latin
America was enormously influenced by the fact that the Church
organization was implanted by foreigners, staffed by foreigners,
controlled from abroad, and hence could with difficulty develop as
an American institution. Control by the Crown in Spain tended
to place the great majority of offices in the hands of Spaniards
from Spain. For example, between 1493 and 1637, there were in
America some 369 bishops of whom less than one dozen were
American-born. Neither Creoles, that is, Americans born of European stock, nor mestizos, nor Indians, nor Negroes could hope to
achieve high place in the Church. Almost all colonials, in fact,
were excluded from high Church office.

During the first days of the Conquest, many Indians who entered the early schools established by the churchmen were trained
in doctrine and entrusted with the indoctrination of other Indians.
They were not, however, admitted to clerical orders, nor does it
seem that the use of Indian missionaries continued, since America
was soon well populated with clerics of Spanish origin. Much later
in the colonial period, the Indians were permitted to take orders,
but not until after the sixteenth century. [26]

The position occupied by the Indians was something like that
of lay brothers, who might remain in the monasteries, or be discharged, or leave in order to marry. They were called *donados*
but since they took no vows and were bound by no rules, they
were not *donados* in the sense that the word is now used in the
Catholic Church. The reason the Spaniards gave for excluding
the Indians, many of whom manifested a desire to enter the Church,
was that they were not capable of becoming priests and monks.
Mendieta says that he tried some of the Indians in his own monastery, but that after a year's probation they were found not fit
for a clerical service and were discharged. A council in 1539 permitted Indians to be ordained to the positions of porter, reader,
exorcist, and acolyte, but such offices did not require celibacy, and
if the holders wished to sacrifice their benefices, they were per-

---

[26] Braden, *Religious Conquest of Mexico,* p. 269.

mitted to marry. The council of 1555 definitely excluded, together with descendants of Moors, mestizos, Indians and mulattoes. The exclusion of mestizos did not endure as long as that of the Indians, and some time before 1588 mestizos were admitted to the priesthood. Negroes and mulattoes, however, seem to have been permanently barred from clerical orders, unless recognized as legally white.

Thus in effect, the Church was largely administered by Europeans. Creoles, however, were admitted to orders, and before 1542 a school was founded in Michoacán to prepare them for the priesthood. Likewise, the primary purpose of the early universities was to prepare Creoles for the Church, but they seldom achieved the higher offices. The deliberate policy was to keep control in the hands of the Spaniards, and it had much to do with the struggles over clerical matters.

Character of the Priesthood

Undoubtedly one of the most influential factors in the early religious history of America was the character of the priesthood. It would be difficult to find men who devoted themselves more unselfishly to a cause than did Pedro de Gante, Mendieta, Valencia, and others of the first clerics who came to America. A Chilean historian who is frequently critical of the Church gives a glowing tribute to the missionaries:

"They plunged deep into the virgin forests of the New World, studied the languages and customs of their uncivilized inhabitants, and endured joyfully the greatest afflictions. Many of them suffered martyrdom with resignation in order to carry out their fervent vows to extend the bounds of the Christian faith. They are to be thanked not only for having civilized a bit the customs of some of the savage Indians and conquered others, but also for furnishing extremely important information concerning the history, customs and the languages of the barbarian tribes. It is they who are the authors of the grammars and dictionaries of the American languages, and of a multitude of historical books of the greatest interest." [27]

Motolinía, one of the original twelve Franciscans who came to New Spain, glorified the work of his fellow friars and said that lazy and unworthy priests were "uncomfortable here and suffered torments until the land throws them off as dead bodies and un-

[27] Barros Arana, *América,* II, 46.

profitable." [28] He said this, however, to contrast the character of priests who arrived later with those who had come first, much to the disadvantage of later arrivals.

Cortés himself recognized the extreme importance of maintaining a clergy of high moral quality when he wrote to the King requesting him to send monks, instead of secular priests, because "if we have the bishops and other prelates, they will follow the customs, which as a punishment for our sins exist today, of disposing of the gifts of the Church and wasting them in pomp and other vices, leaving family estates for their children. . . . If they [the Indians] now saw the servants of God's Church in the power of Mammon, practicing vanities, and learned that they were ministers of God, and beheld them falling into vice, as is the case in our times in Spain, it would bring our Faith into contempt and the natives would hold it as a mockery; and this could do such mischief that I do not believe any amount of preaching would be of any avail." [29]

While Cortés may also have had other motives for wishing to restrict the clergy in America, the existence of the conditions to which he refers was well known. In Spain at this very time, and for many years before, an attempt was being made to rid the Church of a great body of corrupt practices. Queen Isabella tried to cleanse the monasteries, convents, and secular clergy of the violations of the rule of celibacy which were common. There had grown up in Spain, in spite of all laws to the contrary, a system of clerical marriage (concubinage) known as "barraganía," so strongly embedded, that it was impossible to eradicate.

Bishop Zumárraga complained that the clergy were ignorant, immoral, and corrupt. Mendoza, first viceroy, wrote to his successor in 1550: "The clergy who come to these parts are wicked and motivated by self-interest. If it were not for what His Majesty has commanded, and for baptism, the Indians would be better off without them so far as other things are concerned." Mendoza, after making this complaint, said: "This is in general, because some priests are good as individuals." [30]

Among the clerical abuses cited during the sixteenth century in the instructions each viceroy left to his successor were concubinage, theft of money, disobedience, luxurious living, and violation of Church rules. Quarrels between Spanish and Creole clergy,

---

[28] Quoted in Braden, *Religious Conquest of Mexico*, p. 215.
[29] Francis Augustus MacNutt, *Letters of Cortés*, (2 vols, New York and London: G. P. Putnam's Sons, 1908), II, 214-15.
[30] Mendoza, *Instrucción*, D. I. I., VI, 485-6.

and riots between the seculars and the regulars were frequent. The nuns, as well as the priests and monks, caused trouble. When the civil authorities sought to correct ecclesiastical abuses, the Church took refuge in its sacred privileges. Since it was impossible to prevent concubinage, it became a necessity to recognize the legal status of the children of the clergy. [31]

The bishop of Puebla complained in 1556 of the scandals created by ignorant and covetous priests who had fled from their superiors, and who in coming to America were actuated more by avarice than by love of the faith. The early council legislated against the clergy's attendance at bullfights, acting in plays, leaving clerical establishments at night in civilian clothes, and carrying guns. Oviedo, historian of the first half of the sixteenth century, cites the case of a cleric with one of the conquering expeditions who "ordered the chieftain thrown under his hammock, and took the cacique's wife into the hammock and slept with her, or better said, did not let her sleep." [32]

Viceroy Toledo, on his way to Peru in 1569, discovered that the clergy of Panama was similarly lax. After arriving in Peru, he found them inefficient, many of the parishes without priests, and the administration of the sacraments either neglected completely or performed with indifference. Most of the clergy in the outlying settlements were reported as spending their time in commerce, gambling, and making love to their mistresses. [33]

A large part of the trouble arose from the fact that the Church had become a career that many entered upon because it furnished an easier life than they could find elsewhere. During the early days, the Church received vast grants of land, and although it was theoretically illegal for churchmen to receive encomiendas, they apparently did so. It is estimated that nearly half of the land in Spain in the sixteenth century belonged to the Church, and the same system was transplanted to New Spain and other parts of America with the Conquest. The laws of the Indies provided that land could not be sold to either Church or monastery or to "any other ecclesiastical person," but nevertheless the Church continued to accumulate property. Cortés gave it important grants, and this custom was followed by practically every person of wealth. In fact, it was nearly impossible to avoid giving, since a refusal to do so would have made one liable to accusations of heresy. Because of

[31] Bourne, *Spain in America* (New York, 1904), pp. 306-07, Toledo, *Memorial,* D. I. I., VI, 516-24.
[32] Oviedo, *Historia,* Bk. XXIX, chap. X.
[33] Means, *Fall,* pp. 130-1.

the custom of providing for masses to be said for the souls of the dead, almost all people who had sufficient money left permanent endowments to the Church to pay for this service.

As early as 1556 Archbishop Montúfar of Mexico wrote: "Another matter is that some check should be put upon the extravagant costs and expenditures, personal services, and sumptuous and superfluous works which the monks build in the villages of these Indians, entirely at the cost of the latter. So far as the monasteries are concerned, some of them are so splendid in places where there are not more than two or three monks, that even in Valladolid they would be inordinately superb." [34] The Cabildo of Mexico City complained in 1578 that the property of the Dominicans and Augustinians included the greater and best part of the municipality.

The clergy added to their property by commercial enterprises and assiduous collection of fees for the performance of those Christian duties considered indispensable for salvation. The Augustinian friar Juárez de Escobar advised Philip II that the clergy should not charge for the sacraments since "besides smacking of simony, it works great injury to the Indians, since, if two *reales* is charged and the native has not that to give, he must remain without the sacrament; or requiring a *tostón* for marrying, the natives remain unmarried for lack of money; and the children die without baptism simply because the parents have not the four or five *tomines* which is charged for the rite." [35] They continued to require fees, however, down to the end of the colonial period, and after.

Even the praiseworthy missionary work of the first clerics was soon converted into a mere medium for making an easy living. Thousands of clerics who flocked to America in the early sixteenth century found themselves without charges and without means of livelihood. In this condition, they were considered particularly fortunate if they could get a royal concession to build a monastery or church, a grant of land to go with the edifice, and then gather a group of Indians from whose labor they could live practically without exertion. This explains the large number of monasteries housing a small number of clerics, since those who did not participate in the establishment of a monastery or failed to obtain a grant for themselves, remained in the position of unemployed, while their more fortunate brothers enjoyed luxury. [36]

* * * * * * * *

[34] *Relación del arzobispo de Méjico* (D. I. I., IV, 491-530), p. 519.
[35] Quoted in Braden, *Religious Conquest of Mexico*, p. 218.
[36] Riva Palacio, *México*, II, 490.

Despite all the grumbling against the clergy and complaints about their behavior, they continued to flourish throughout the colonial period. Religion had been a strong force among the Indians before the Conquest, and their priests had great power and prestige. In Spain likewise, the influence of the Church was enormous at the time of the discovery of America, and religious fervor had reached a high pitch, stimulated by the Reconquest of Spain from the Moors, the expulsion of the Jews, and the cult of Santiago. The Crown had won from the Popes a large degree of control over the Church, which it used, as it did the Spanish Inquisition, for national ends. Charged with the duty of Christianizing America, the monarchs were given greater rights of ecclesiastical patronage in the colonies than at home.

The obligation to convert the Indians had been carried out zealously by both Church and Crown. The missionaries who accompanied the conquistadores, destroying idols and native shrines, establishing churches and monasteries, and making the most of the similarities between native religious practices and those of Christianity, had easily brought the Indians under the domination of the Catholic Church. In organization, the Church remained a completely Spanish institution, but the Indian masses continued to serve the imported religion as they had served their own priesthoods. Church property increased, its influence in government grew stronger, and its hold upon the intellectual life of the colonies was all but absolute. It is doubtful whether there is an example of an institution in any country, in any epoch, whose responsibility for the type of civilization was as great as that of the colonial Catholic Church.

Foundations of Latin-American Government

SPANISH AND INDIAN ELEMENTS OF COLONIAL GOVERNMENT

THE GOVERNMENT OF COLONIAL SPANISH AMERICA was the result of three influences: the type of government existing before the Conquest; the Spanish tradition brought by the conquerors; and the merging of these two systems.

Colonial government was in a sense a projection of the Spanish system, and this 'fact is sometimes treated as the whole key to government in America. But influential as the Spanish Crown was, its policies were too frequently violated for us to accept Spanish legislation *about* America as an indication of what was happening *in* America. Conditions in America effected such profound modifications that the system must be considered as it was altered by the American environment, rather than as it was projected from Spain. In order to do this, it is necessary to understand both the Spanish and the indigenous American systems.

Both were based on an identical theory of government, that certain people are divinely ordained as the *señores naturales* or "natural rulers." This has been well stated by a modern historian.

"The concept of the *señor natural* was an integral part of the political thought of Castile in the middle ages and the renaissance, and the term occurs frequently in Castilian codes . . ."
". . . The *señor natural* is to be defined as a lord who, by inherent nature of superior qualities, goodness, and virtue, and by birth or superior station, attains power legitimately and exercises dominion over all within his lands justly and in accord with divine, natural, and human law and reason, being universally accepted, recognized, and obeyed by his vassals and subjects and acknowledged by other lords and their peoples as one who right-

fully possesses his office and rightfully wields authority within his territory . . . . The concept of the *señor natural* was applied in the Indies with reference to the dominion and position held by native rulers and lords and to the relation of these lords to the king of Castile. In its practical aspects it was employed as a means of assuring the subjection of the masses of the people through control of their already established *señores* . . . . Hence Montezuma was the *señor natural* of all within the Aztec Empire, while subject to him were lesser lords who were the *señores naturales* of the peoples of the lands over which they held sway. The Inca, likewise, was the *señor natural* of his realms . . . . The king of Castile was, in turn the *señor natural* of the native lords and of their subjects." [1]

INDIAN GOVERNMENT: KINSHIP AND TERRITORIAL

Indian government included a great variety of systems, ranging from the most primitive kinship groups to highly conventionalized territorial governments. On the one hand were the tribes whose rule was based almost entirely upon actual or supposed blood relationship. On the other hand were the Aztecs, Mayas, and Incas whose governments, while not entirely beyond the kinship concept, were based primarily upon definite territorial limits. Most of America lived under one form or another of semikinship government, where the tribe with its war chief, shamans, and council of elders was the characteristic form. These less advanced groups, however, were, as a rule, either exterminated or bottled up, so that they had only a minor influence upon the permanent governmental structure.

Such is not the case with the Aztec, Maya, and Inca civilizations. Their forms of government were sufficiently advanced and their populations sufficiently numerous to modify greatly the essence of Spanish government. A few other groups were also able to do this in a less complete way. Among these were the Pueblos of the Southwest, the Araucanians of Chile, and the Guaranís of Paraguay.

THE MAYA CITY-STATE

The Mayas lived in city-states somewhat like the classical Greek or medieval city-states. There were approximately eighteen of these at the time of the Conquest. Each had a wall or natural defense, a

[1] Robert S. Chamberlain, "The Concept of the *Señor Natural* as Revealed by Castilian Law and Administrative Documents," *H. A. H. R.*, XIX (May, 1939), 130-37.

theocratic despotism as its form of government, and governed a territory for a considerable distance around the city. Occasional alliances and confederations were formed but the essential unit of government was the individual city. Frequent wars between the cities prevented the concept of citizenship from embracing more than the locality. This, in fact, was the situation in most of America. Because of the great distances, the lack of communication, and the many naturally limited areas created by such geographical factors as mountains, rivers, lakes, swamps, and valleys, many people lived almost entirely isolated from their nearest neighbors. They thus developed local patriotisms which have profoundly affected the history of Latin America.

It is also worthy of note that the Mayan form of government was distinctly oligarchic. The Maya states were ruled by a small class of landed nobles, military leaders, and priests. The vast majority of the people, such as the artisans, serfs, and slaves, did not participate in government. [2]

AZTEC GOVERNMENT: CONFEDERATION

The Aztecs had developed a federation form of government. Three of the chief cities, Tenochtitlán, Téxcoco, and Tlacopan, after more than a century of warfare among themselves, had formed an alliance and directed their attention to the conquest of their neighbors.[3] From the time of Montezuma I, 1440-71, to the time of Montezuma II, 1502-1520, who was ruling when Cortés entered Mexico, the history of the Aztec confederation is one of constant aggression, which had brought under the domination of the three cities a strip of territory extending from the Atlantic to the Pacific at about the latitude of modern Tampico, and as far south as modern Guatemala. The conquerors established a tribute-collecting empire whose prerogatives were maintained by permanent garrisons of Aztec soldiers. [4] The confederation was extremely vigorous and entirely unscrupulous in its methods of expansion.

The Aztecs were the only major political group in America still

---

[2] Brinton, *Maya Chronicles,* pp. 25-27; Diego de Landa, *Relaciones de las cosas de Yucatán,* [1566], ed. Charles Étienne Brasseur de Bourbourg (Paris, 1864), chaps. VII-IX, XXIV, XXIX, also published in *D. I. I. Ultramar,* XIII, 265-411, and by Jean Genêt, Paris, 1928. See also an English text, *Yucatán before and after the Conquest,* tr. and ed. William Gates (Maya Society, pub. no. 20, Baltimore, 1937).

[3] See *Relación de la genealogía y linaje de los Señores que han señoriado esta tierra de la Nueva España,* in García Icazbalceta, ed. *Nueva C. D. México,* III, 263-81; Clavigero, *Mexico,* Bks. II-V, and Dissertation II, Section III; Sahagún, *Cosas de Nueva España,* II, 275-334.

[4] Zurita, *Breve y sumaria relación,* in García Icazbalceta, ed. *Nueva C. D. México,* III, 71-227; Torquemada, *Monarchia indiana,* Bk. III, chaps. VI and XVII.

STREET IN CUZCO: SPANISH COLONIAL ARCHITECTURE ON LEFT; INCA
ARCHITECTURE SURMOUNTED BY SPANISH COLONIAL ON RIGHT

developing and expanding at the time of the Conquest. Not merely were they expanding, but their government was rapidly changing from a kinship-territorial form, ruled by a group of aristocratic elders, into a one-man despotism. Montezuma II came to the throne in 1502, elected as the successor of his uncle by the council of elders, who were required by custom to select some member of the ruling family. His policy was to take the control of the state out of the hands of the landed aristocracy, and lodge it in himself. This policy, which might in the long run have made him a despot or provoked revolt, was in process when Cortés entered Mexico. [5]

Gathered around the court in Tenochtitlán was a small group of the higher nobility who held power through their land and subjects. The exact number is not known, but is sometimes stated to be 3000. Their powers extended through a wide area into other parts of Mexico. Some of these, according to the early chronicles, had as many as 100,000 subjects governed by a numerous lesser nobility. They exercised complete jurisdiction, raised taxes, and were themselves tax-exempt except for military services. The degrees of nobility existing within the Aztec confederation were distinguished by various insignia and special privileges. While it was possible for one of humble birth to achieve a distinction of this sort, an actual rise to the ranks of the nobility was improbable. The subject nobles of the Aztec confederation were required to live in the capital city and to leave hostages when absent in their own provinces. This nobility was hereditary, and the land they held could be sold only to other nobles. The system of courts within the Aztec confederation emphasized the independence of the various nobles prior to their subjugation. Each province had a supreme judge, with jurisdiction in both civil and criminal cases, who, although named by the sovereign, was entirely independent. His decisions were final and could not be reversed by the King himself. [6] The character of the Aztec confederation is described by various chroniclers who saw it in operation or at least were close enough to it in time to get an idea of the system. Its despotic nature impressed the Anonymous Conqueror:

"The Lords are so dreaded and obeyed that they are adored like gods. There was such justice among them that for the least crime or dereliction that any one committed, he was put to death or reduced to slavery. Theft and murder were severely punished,

[5] Thompson, *Mexico Before Cortés*, pp. 29-34.
[6] *Leyes que tenían los indios de la Nueva España*, García Icazbalceta, ed. *Nueva C. D. México*, III, 308-19.

and above all the entrance into another man's land, in order to steal fruits or grain. If any one entered a field and stole three or four ears of maize he became the slave of the owner of the field. If any one was guilty of treason or any other crime against the Emperor or the King he was condemned to death with all his relatives into the fourth generation." [7]

This despotism was perhaps tempered somewhat by the lower courts which were elected by the people. These courts are described as rigidly honest and as dispensing justice to all alike. The death penalty was frequently meted out to murderers even if the victim was a slave, and to robbers. Adulterers were stoned and various offenses were punished by the enslavement of the criminal. The courts may have been impartial in administering justice, but they were undoubtedly harsh.

Acosta's description of the Aztec system reveals a stratified society with a king and a ruling nobility whose main function was to superintend the tribute collection and live on the proceeds. [8] The sovereign held extensive areas of land in all the provinces, the products of which were devoted to his use, and necessary slaves or serfs for its cultivation were considered as belonging to the land. In addition many districts were required to supply workmen for the building of palaces, temples, or any other structure desired by the sovereign, and were forced to furnish the material for such structures. A portion of the produce of every district was devoted to the royal service. [9]

A rigid system of tax-collecting and a staff of tax-collectors was established. There are still in existence some of the tax-assessment maps in which the tribute of each district is indicated in the Aztec picture writing. Failure to pay taxes was punished with enslavement and the complaints of the various peoples subject to the confederation indicate that the taxes were onerous.

Montezuma ruled in oriental splendor.

"He had over two hundred chieftains in his guard . . . and when they went to speak to him they were obliged to take off their rich mantles and put on others of little worth . . . and they had to enter barefoot with their eyes lowered to the ground, and not to look up in his face. And they made him three obeisances, and said: 'Lord, my Lord, my Great Lord,' . . . and on taking leave they did not turn their backs but kept their faces toward him

[7] Anonymous Conqueror, *Narrative of New Spain*, p. 45.
[8] Acosta, *Historia de las Indias*, Bk. VI, chap. XXV.
[9] Prescott, *Mexico*, Bk. I, chap. II for further information.

with their eyes to the ground . . . . I noticed another thing, that when other great chiefs came from distant lands about disputes or business, when they reached the apartment of the Great Montezuma, they had to come barefoot and with poor mantles, and they might not enter directly into the Palace, but had to loiter about a little on one side of the Palace door, for to enter hurriedly was considered to be disrespectful." [10]

Great reverence was shown to Montezuma by his subjects even after his imprisonment by the Spaniards. "Twenty great chiefs always stayed in his company holding their ancient offices, as well as his Councillors, and he stayed there a prisoner without showing any anger at it and Ambassadors from distant lands came there with their suites, and brought him his tributes and he carried on his important business." [11]

One further point reveals the continuity between pre- and post-Conquest New Spain. "Montezuma . . . set off in his rich litter in great state and with many great Caciques in his company as was his custom, and they carried his insignia in front of him in the form of a sort of staff or rod, which was the sign that his royal person was going that way (just as they do [now] to the Viceroy of New Spain)." [12]

For the great masses of the Mexican people, the Conquest effected no considerable change in the aristocratic and despotic nature of their administration. They had not participated in the government before, and they did not participate after Spanish domination. Before, they were ruled by an hereditary Indian aristocracy; after, they were ruled by Spaniards who took the place of their old chieftains, or who utilized their old chieftains as instruments of Spanish power.

INCA GOVERNMENT: ORIGINS

Inca government had evolved into a more thoroughgoing despotism than that of the Aztecs. Through long centuries of warfare, in which the various valleys had been bound together into great confederations, the original political unit of this territory had changed from the kinship to a territorial type.

One such large confederation occupied all the northern coast of Peru, another all the southern coast, and similar confederations were formed in the mountain valleys. Recurrent warfare between the confederations was the rule. From war developed a form of

[10] Bernal Díaz, *Conquest of New Spain*, II, 60-61.
[11] Bernal Díaz, *Conquest of New Spain*, II, 96.
[12] Bernal Díaz, *Conquest of New Spain*, II, 110.

government which gradually became permament. The leader during the wars was known as a *sinchi*. He lost his position during peace times; but since peace seems to have been rare, his office became practically permanent, and around him arose a ruling aristocracy. This was the situation between the eleventh and fifteenth centuries when Inca power was gradually growing. The Incas began as one of the ayllus living in the mountains. Through confederation and conquest, they came to rule a relatively large area, perhaps 380,000 square miles, including the mountains and coastal sections of Ecuador, Peru, and Bolivia, and small portions of northwestern Argentina and northern Chile. [13]

When the Spaniards conquered the country in the sixteenth century, the ayllu, though still of great social importance, had diminished politically into a purely administrative unit known as the *pachaca*, stated by the early chroniclers to consist of 100 families. As such it was the basic unit of administration, although both below and above this there were further administrative divisions. [14]

Administrative System of Incas

The system, beginning with the *Sapa Inca*, who was the hereditary despot of the empire, extended down through four chief territorial divisions lying respectively to the north, east, south and west of the capital city of Cuzco, (each of which was divided into further provinces and subprovinces) to the lowest political division consisting of ten men.

"The Incas . . . commanded all the citizens *(vecinos)* in all the towns of their empire, large and small, to register in squads of ten, and one of them known as a decurion to have charge of the other nine. Five of these squads of ten had a superior decurion in charge of fifty. Two groups of fifty had another superior in charge of one hundred. Five groups of one hundred were subject to a decurion captain who commanded five hundred; two companies of five hundred obeyed a general who commanded a thousand, but the companies did not go beyond a thousand citizens (vecinos) each, because they said that for a commander to give a good account of himself it was enough to entrust him with a thousand men *(hombres)*." [15]

[13] Cobo, *Nuevo Mundo,* Bk. XII, chaps. I-XXII, Bk. XIV, chap. IX.

[14] Means, *Ancient Civilization,* pp. 193-97, 222-27, 284-87, 291-92.

[15] Garcilaso, *Comentarios,* Bk. II, chap. XI. It may be observed that Garcilaso here uses *vecinos* as synonymous with *hombres.* The word *vecinos* is frequently used as the equivalent of head of family, and multiplied by five, or even ten, to get the population of the empire. Such a procedure is questionable. Garcilaso uses the two words in such a way as to indicate that he is talking of administrative and military divisions, and that all men were included.

There were officials above those mentioned by Garcilaso, how-ever, in charge of 10,000 and 40,000 men. The next highest rank to the Inca was that of the four officials in charge of the four parts of the empire, each of whom was under the direct command of the Sapa Inca himself. [16] Authority was vertical. All major officials belonged to the royal family. Subordinates were selected from the chieftains of the conquered district. The minor officials in charge of ten or fifty men were chosen from among the common people.

Much of the Inca system was carried over into the colonial period.

"It has been ascertained for certain that the Sovereigns of this realm . . . had their delegates in all of the capital cities of the provinces . . . . These governors had great authority, and enough power to raise armies and mobilize soldiers if some dis-turbance or uprising should suddenly occur, or if foreigners should come from any direction to make war. And they were honored by the King and given privileges, and of these many re-mained in permanent command in their provinces when the Spaniards came. I know some of them and they are so thoroughly in possession that their children inherit what once belonged to others." [17]

---

[16] The hierarchy was allegedly as follows:

1. *Chunca-camayu-cuna-* Officials *(camayu-cuna)* in charge of ten *(chunca)* households.
2. *Pichca-chunca-camayu-cuna-* in charge of fifty *(pichca-chunca)* households.
3. *Pachaca-camayu-cuna-* in charge of one hundred *(pachaca)* households.
4. *Pichca-pachaca-camayu-cuna-* in charge of five hundred households.
5. *Huaranca-camayu-cuna-* in charge of one thousand *(huaranca)* households.
6. *Hunu-camayu-cuna-* in charge of ten thousand *(hunu)* households.
7. *Tucuiricuc-cuna-* They-who-see-all, ruling jurisdictions containing forty thou-sand households, equivalent to "province."
8. *Apu-cuna* or *Hatun-apu-cuna-* each ruling one of the four parts *(suyu-cuna)* of the empire. They composed an imperial council and resided at Court much of the time.
9. The *Sapa Inca-* the chief ruler.

Means, *Ancient Civilizations,* p. 292.

The completely symmetrical divisions of the Inca Empire seem too perfect to be believable. There is no conceivable way in which these groups could be kept at the exact figures set for them. If a group of ten men or ten families was desig-nated, either death, birth, or marriage would shortly alter the original figure. On the other hand, if there was an annual redistribution so as to keep these groups as they were originally formed, it is hard to see how the kinship idea embraced in the ayllu was maintained. Much of the difficulty disappears when the administra-tive units are held to be applicable to men who served in military or work battalions, which could be formed and reformed at the will of the administrators. To accept this is to abandon in part the kinship-ayllu interpretation. The present writer believes that the whole idea of the symmetrical organization of the Inca Empire is unfounded, and that in time closer study by competent anthropologists will dis-count much of it. It is included here not because we believe it accurate in detail, but because it indicates there was at least an hierarchial administration of the Inca Empire.

[17] Cieza, *Señorío,* chap. XX.

One of the most important features of the Inca system was the incorporation of conquered chieftains or *curacas* into the ruling hierarchy. They were given administrative functions, although required to live in the court or leave hostages to guarantee their fidelity to the Inca. [18]

Inca Government: Administration and Taxes

The function of this whole administrative system was the collection of tribute. [19] The lowest officials in the rank, the *chunca-camayu-cuna* and the *pichca-chunca-camayu-cuna*, in charge of ten and fifty men respectively, were responsible for the direction of the laborers, who were to be supplied with clothing and food as well as the tools for work and the seeds for planting. Their authority extended to flogging or stoning their charges for minor offenses, and to reporting other offenses to superior officials. The whole population was so divided as to get the maximum amount of labor from every individual. The working man, the *puric,* was between twenty-five and fifty, but below this age children were expected to help their elders in the performance of their various tasks. Above fifty a smaller amount of work was expected.

Labor was the principal tribute due the Inca. Garcilaso would have us believe this was so equitably adjusted that no one ever paid excessively and no one was ever overworked.

> "Although there were some annoyances owing to the tribute or the service to the King or the curacas, the Indians bore them with pleasure and contentment because of the small amount of the tribute and the help *(ayuda de costa)* they had, as well as because of the numerous benefits they derived from these small jobs.
>
> "The privileges and laws protecting the taxpayers, which were invariably respected to such a degree that neither the judges nor the governors, nor the captains-general, nor the Inca himself could vitiate them to the detriment of the vassals, were the following. The first and principal one was that those who were tax exempt could at no time nor for any reason whatever be obliged to pay taxes." [20]

Garcilaso lists as tax-exempt, in addition to the youths and the aged, all of royal blood, the captains-general and minor officials down to the centurions, with their families, and all curacas and their

---

[18] Cieza, *Señorío,* chap. XIV; Cobo, *Nuevo Mundo,* Bk. XII, chap. XXV.
[19] Cobo, *Nuevo Mundo,* Bk. XII, chaps. XXXII-XXXV.
[20] Garcilaso, Bk. V, chap. XV.

kindred. Minor officials not of royal blood paid no tribute during their term of office, nor did soldiers during time of war. Women were also free of tribute, as were the sick and disabled.

"The second law stated that all the other Indians except those mentioned above, were taxpayers obliged to pay tribute, unless they were priests of the temples of the Sun or the chosen virgins. The third law stated that under no circumstances was any Indian obliged to pay anything from his own property (hacienda) as tribute, but only what he paid with his labor, or with his trade, or the time that he was employed in the service of the King or his own province (república), and in this both the poor and the rich were equals, for the latter did not pay more nor the former less." 21

Garcilaso's frank admiration of this system does not hide the important fact that there was a great body of tax-free nobles, and as we have already seen from our study of the labor system, he himself admits that many plebeians fell ill from excessively hard work.

In addition to labor, the tribute consisted of every product within the entire Empire. The Inca sent out assessors who reported on the fertility of each region and the possibilities of collection, taking account of foods, metals, livestock, and other things.

When the agents of the Incas entered a province, they took note of the population of all ages and occupations, and of the gold and silver mines. They ordered a certain number of thousand miners to the mines while Indians from other provinces, or the same province, were assigned to work the miners' fields. Accountants were placed in the mines to see that the required metal was produced. Married men exclusively were used as miners so that their wives might prepare their food and drink. "This was all done with such good order that although they might be all of their lives in the mines, they did not consider it excessive labor and nobody died because he was given too much work to do." However, the same Indians did not always work in the mines, some coming in as others went out. "And if there was no metal to mine in the other provinces (tierras), in order that they should make their contribution, they were assessed taxes and levies of small things, and of women and boys, who were carried away from the village (pueblo) without any affliction whatever, because if a man had only one boy or girl this one child was not taken away from him, but if he had three or four, one was taken for the payment of the [royal] service."

21 Comentarios, Bk. V, chap. XV.

Some provinces contributed so many thousand loads of corn every year "in accordance with the number of houses in it." Still others contributed *chuño* or *quínoa,* or other crops. Some places were required to give a number of shirts *(camisetas)* corresponding with the number of inhabitants, while still others were taxed lances or slings, or other arms. Some provinces were required to send a certain number of thousand Indians to Cuzco for the public service, and some contributed coca. All things collected for war were used for the soldiers, but when there was peace these things went to the poor.

An annual inspection was made to see whether any man had been taxed too much or had failed to pay his tribute, and officials were sent to mete out justice in either case. Also from time to time the heads of the provinces appeared before the Inca to render an account, "the Incas being certain that they were not telling lies, but the truth, because if there was any double dealing the Incas punished it severely and increased the tribute." [22] Tribute also included internal tariff collected at the bridges which all were forced to cross in traveling from one province to another. [23]

MOST HIGH AND POWERFUL LORD

The position of the Inca at the head of this structure was as one separated by divine ordinance from the common run of human kind. As the representative of God on earth, no honor that could be accorded him was too great. When traveling he was carried in a magnificent gold and silver embossed litter on the shoulders of his chief nobles, and screened from the view of the people by curtains. A numerous guard preceded and followed the Inca, while the masses filled the roads crying: "Most high and powerful Lord, child of the Sun, thou alone art Lord, verily, the whole World obeys Thee." [24]

Other details strengthen the impression of the power and despotism of the Incas.

"It is worthy of note . . . how these kings governed . . . such an extensive land, in part so rough, full of mountains, snow-covered ranges and sandy plains devoid of trees and lacking in water. Great wisdom was necessary for the government of so many nations, so distinct one from another in languages, laws and religions, in order to keep them in tranquility. And so . . .

[22] Cieza, *Señorío,* chap. XVIII.
[23] Cieza, *Crónica,* chap. CIV.
[24] Cieza, *Señorío,* p. 77; see also Means, *Ancient Civilizations,* pp. 337-38.

they had appointed their delegates and governors . . . . And as
these were loyal and none of them dared rise in rebellion, and
[the Inca] had the mitimaes on his side, not one of the natives,
no matter how powerful he might be, dared try any uprising
whatever, and if he attempted it, the town where he rose up was
immediately punished, the instigators being sent prisoners to
Cuzco. And by these methods the kings were so greatly feared
that if, in traveling through the kingdom, they permitted any of
the curtains of the litter to be drawn back to permit their vassals
to see them, the vassals raised such a great shout that they caused
the birds to fall from the skies where they were flying, so that
they might be caught bare handed; and all feared the Inca so
much that they did not even speak ill of his shadow." [25]

The respect shown the Inca did not end with his death. He carried with him many victims, sacrificed to keep their sovereign company in the world to which he was going, and long after his death,
his mummified body was accorded great honor. A large number of
people were assigned to till the fields dedicated to its care. Since the
dead could not eat the produce, this went to maintain in idleness
a sizable group of the nobility who were specifically consecrated to
the service of the dead Inca.

THE INCA SYSTEM OF JUSTICE

For those who did not maintain a proper regard for the nobility,
there was a rigid system of law enforcement embracing every
possible act that could be committed by any of the Inca's subjects. [26] Garcilaso asserts that no Inca was ever known to violate
any law, but it is difficult to know what inducements there could
have been for a member of the royalty to violate the laws, or what
they could have done which would have been considered a violation,
for every material necessity was amply provided for, and the whole
ruling hierarchy could legally requisition any amount of provisions
or labor desired. The nobles were free of tax and tribute, and the
Inca furnished them with harems of such size that they could hardly have desired any more women. This was not the case for the
lesser subjects of the Inca.

Cieza remarks of Huayna Capac that: "He wished to be so
feared that the Indians would dream of him at night," and judging
from the various punishments for the infringement of his laws he

---

[25] Cieza, *Señorío,* chap. XIII.
[26] Cobo, *Nuevo Mundo,* Bk. XII, chap. XXVI.
[27] Cieza, *Señorío,* chap. LXI.

must have achieved his wishes. [27] Thieves were stoned or whipped publicly for their first crime, tormented in various ways for their second, and killed slowly and painfully for their third. Gossips, vagabonds, and all who failed to accomplish their assigned tasks were lashed, or if the crime was particularly serious, hanged head down and left to die. A distinction was made, however, between a theft committed by a deliberate criminal and one committed by a person in need of food. In the latter case the official who should have furnished the food was punished. This particular crime and punishment, however, casts some doubt upon the assertion that there were no poor and no suffering. [28]

The nobility were punished for their crimes by public exposure, which was considered serious enough. They could also be removed from office and have their privileges taken from them. The one crime which it seems the nobility could and did commit was treason, and it was against this crime that the Inca directed his most terrible punishment. The Incas had several prisons near Cuzco where traitors were tortured, or imprisoned for life. [29]

Cobo's condemnation of the despotism of the Incas is drastic:

"The yoke which these miserable Indians bore was so heavy that I do not doubt that if all the men in the world should pool their wits to invent a type of subjection and tyranny so great as that in which they lived, they could not devise anything more than the Incas had already developed . . . . And whoever may consider carefully their system of administering and maintaining their empire, will find that everything was directed toward this end, without pretense of anything else whatever. To prove this, I could very well pause to enumerate in detail all the things they ordered for the oppression of their subjects, but it is sufficient to say that the pitiable people did not have the right to possess for themselves anything whatever without the permission of the Inca or of his governors, although it might be nothing more than killing a llama or having two suits of clothing. Nor did they have the right to eat what they wished, but what the Inca would permit; nor to marry whom they wished, and even less the right to marry off their children. Nor (what is more) were they masters of their own wives and children. On the contrary, their wives were taken from them to give to others, and their children to be killed in the sacrifices." [30]

---

[28] See Garcilaso, *Comentarios,* Bk. III, chap. XIII; Bk. IV, chap. III; and Bk. VI, chap. XI.

[29] Means, *Ancient Civilizations,* p. 348.

[30] Cobo, *Nuevo Mundo,* Bk. XIII, chap. XXXV.

DECAY OF THE INCA SYSTEM

Despite all the machinery devised by the Inca for the maintenance of his empire, it had been falling apart for some years prior to the appearance of Pizarro. There are indications, indeed, that the Inca's authority over his more distant subjects was never so complete as Garcilaso would have us believe. Cieza, for example, makes the following observation on the system of justice.

"As Cuzco was the principal city in the whole of Peru, and the sovereigns resided in it the greater part of the time, they had in the same city many of the principal men of the country . . . ; and so that the roads might be secure and no assaults or robberies be committed anywhere, some of the most highly esteemed of these were appointed to punish systematically any who might be criminals. To do this, they traveled widely throughout the realm. So wise were the Incas in dispensing justice that nobody dared commit any offense or robbery. This is to be understood as meaning those who had become thieves, or raped women, or conspired against the laws. For, as regards other things, there were many provinces that waged war with one another, and the Incas could not break them from it entirely." [31]

If it was customary for the various provinces to make war on one another, it would seem that the Inca's power over them was concerned principally with their remaining faithful to him for tribute-collecting purposes. Other indications show that the Inca acted as mediator between the various provinces in their wars and boundary disputes. During the last days of Inca Huayna Capac (d. c. 1528) the end was in sight. Rebellions had broken out in various parts of the Empire.

Why the Inca Empire was falling to pieces is difficult to say, but it seems probable that revolt was always latent among the subjugated peoples. Numerous uprisings occurred in practically all periods of the Empire. The final split into contending factions was the work of the Emperor Huayna Capac in dividing the Empire between his two sons, Huáscar and Atahualpa, whose series of wars of extermination were still in progress when the Spaniards arrived. These wars had so weakened the Empire, and so broken it into factions, that Pizarro was able to utilize them to complete its downfall.

Thus the Spaniards entered the Empire at a time when it had all but destroyed itself. Their task was not one of destruction alone,

---

[31] Cieza, *Señorío,* chap. XXVI.

although no one can deny the evidence of the disastrous effects of the Conquest upon many aspects of Andean civilization. The Spaniards also acted as a unifying influence, and the Andean area was more integrated after than before the Spanish Conquest.

OTHER INDIAN GROUPS

After the Conquest, and down to the present time, a number of other Indian peoples influenced the trend of political evolution in Latin America. Particularly, hundreds of small groups of Indians, who were neither exterminated nor entirely incorporated into the colonial and modern political system, have continued to be "governmental problems" in Latin America. Owing to geographical isolation, they have maintained a sense of distinctness and separation from the rest of the nations of which they are nominally a part. They have continued to have a local patriotism, a feeling for the *patria chica* which, when combined with economic rivalry with their neighbors, offers one of the most logical explanations for political instability in certain Latin-American areas.

SPANISH BACKGROUND OF COLONIAL GOVERNMENT

Spanish political tradition was brought to America by the first conquerors in very much the form it had taken after several centuries of evolution in the Iberian Peninsula. [32] Owing to the strength of this political tradition, it must be studied from its origin. It has been pointed out that whereas it is possible to study the British Empire without going back of the Tudors, it is not possible to understand Spanish history without going back to the Moslem conquest, or even to the time of the Roman Empire. [33]

It is also necessary to note that legal theories must be distinguished from the facts of Spanish government. If Spanish government had been what it appeared in such law codes as the *Siete Partidas,* the King would have been an absolute sovereign. The terms of the laws established the hereditary character of the Castilian King, the divine origin of his power, and the numerous duties of the King to his subjects and of the subjects to the King. The prerogatives of royal power were set forth at great length; and while the privileges of the subjects were likewise delineated in detail, including many points which suggest a contract between the Sovereign and his subjects, the theory of the code would still make it appear that the King was absolute.

---

[32] Charles H. Cunningham, "The Institutional Background of Spanish-American History," *H. A. H. R.,* I (February, 1918), 24-39.
[33] Merriman, *Spanish Empire,* I, 2-3.

In reality, however, numerous "liberties" of the subjects curtailed royal authority. Lest the word liberty, as used here, be misunderstood, it must be defined.

"Spanish liberty consisted principally of the limitation of monarchical power by the legal position of the classes sharing in the sovereignty and in the government. We have already seen that these classes not only resisted the usurpations of the Crown, but that by fighting among themselves incessantly they prevented one another from taking control of the public destiny. There were, therefore, four powers that aspired to dominate within the nation's bosom: throne, nobility, municipalities, and clergy." [34]

The Components of Spanish Government: Towns

The Castilian towns were one of the first factors in the limitation of royal authority. Their importance arose from their origin. After 718, a customary way of recovering land from the Moors was by granting privileges to some group which would undertake its reconquest. These privileges frequently consisted of the right to establish a town, fortify, and maintain it, as well as to govern it and the surrounding territory. The concessions granted to the town were usually specified in a charter *(fuero)*, a form of constitution which the inhabitants of that particular district could use as a protection for their privileges. The fuero often excused the inhabitants of the town from obedience to such royal laws as were in conflict with their chartered rights. The towns holding such privileges were numerous; and while the charters might resemble one another in some respects, there was enough variation to make each town different in law from every other town.

The towns thus enjoyed a large measure of autonomy. Generally they were conceded the right of electing a *concejo* or town assembly. Those who were eligible as voters, or for election to the concejo, were the *vecinos,* or citizens consisting of the heads of families and property owners, usually taken to be synonymous, since few if any except property holders were considered citizens. Elections of municipal officials were influenced by the social standing of the candidate and by a tradition of rotation in office.

The members of the concejo, or legislative and executive group, known as *regidores,* varied in number from thirty-six to eight and were assisted in the management of the town by the alcaldes or judges, and by various minor officials. The powers of the concejos

---

[34] José Manuel Estrada, *Lecciones sobre la historia de la república Argentina* (Buenos Aires, 1898), I, 14.

included maintenance of an armed force, regulations of the standards of weights and measures, management of the municipal lands,
fixing of prices, and the building of municipal buildings. In addition they could collect taxes, maintain police forces, and perform
many other duties necessary to government. The concejo might be
called upon to decide whether or not it would wage war, and what
attitude the town should take toward royal legislation, or toward
some powerful local lord. The towns also enjoyed in theory the
right of electing representatives to the third estate of the national
Cortes, but in actuality, privilege and tradition minimized this
theoretical right.

The degree of autonomy has caused some to call the municipalities democratic. [35] Whether or not this is justified depends largely
upon our conception of democracy. Spain may have been "the most
democratic country in medieval Europe," but still fell far short of
democracy when we consider the whole population, and not merely
the privileged burghers and knights.

> "The presumptuous cities, which legislated through their
> representative to the *Cortes,* were surrounded by rural popula-
> tions whose vitality and blood served only as food for the vanity
> of others. What was the lot of the poor peasant? It was to live,
> struggle, and perish beneath the insolent despotism of the gran-
> dees. It was to live, struggle, and die sacrificed to the interests of
> the city . . . . The liberties of Spain were, therefore, artificial
> and spurious . . . . Man was nothing, personal liberty was void.
> The point of view of every vital movement was summed up in
> class, and class interests. And class interests, the guarantee
> granted by law, is not liberty; it is privilege." [36]

Components of Spanish Government: Aristocracy

The Spanish aristocrats were the second element whose rights
restricted the power of the Crown. They occupied a place in society which had come down from Visigothic times, and many of
them traced their powers and privileges farther back than the
King's. There were three general classes of nobles: the *ricos hombres,*
(grandees), the *hidalgos,* (or *infanzones*), and the *caballeros.*

The *ricos hombres* were at the top of the social scale. They
were in general exempted from direct taxation, from seizure of
their property or imprisonment for debt, from whipping or hang-
ing and, except for certain crimes, from torture. They had pre-

---

[35] Merriman, *Spanish Empire,* I, 185-90.
[36] Estrada, *Argentina,* pp. 16-17.

cedence in the granting of offices by the Crown, and they could raise an army and maintain it. They could also renounce allegiance to the King by the simple method of sending a message to that effect. An extremely important prerogative of the ricos hombres was the right in their own domain of criminal and civil jurisdiction (in all cases except high justice exercised by the King). They also had the right to levy taxes and grant *fueros,* and in a great many cases they could refuse to permit the officials of the Crown to enter their estates for collection of taxes or enforcement of the King's justice. In medieval Spain, the actual power of the higher nobility was limited only by the personal vigor of the ruling sovereign. If the King was weak, as happened many times, the nobility in practice were actually sovereign within their own estates.

The *hidalgos* had less authority, but possessed rights which raised them far above the masses of the people. The *caballeros* were still less privileged and it was possible for a commoner to achieve the title of caballero, although it did not happen frequently. The privileges of a caballero, however, were sufficient to create a gulf between him and the commoner.

According to the principles of Spanish law, the Crown did not delegate its political power with the lands it granted to the nobility. However, in practice, political power was exercised, especially by the higher nobility, within their own territories. From the middle of the thirteenth century, when the Reconquest had progressed to the point where it no longer absorbed all the energies of the nobility, they tended more and more to assert their legal or pretended privileges, and thus to divorce themselves from the King's authority. They became turbulent, almost independent, privileged by law and even more so in fact. Since the reign of Alfonso X (1252-84) they had been permitted to form *mayorazgos* (entailed estates) by which their domains were passed on intact to their heirs without diminution. This system enabled them to maintain the various privileges which they had been granted legally, or had usurped.

COMPONENTS OF SPANISH GOVERNMENT: CLERGY

Clerical privilege was the third factor limiting the Spanish sovereign's political power. The clergy occupied a predominant position in the Reconquest, as already indicated, in return for which they received extensive grants of land and numerous concessions. Among these was an exemption from regular taxes greater than that granted to nobility, since the clergy declined to pay some of the taxes which fell on the former. They held many other legal immunities, and in general occupied a special place in the community. Some clerical orders were more favored than others, and not all had an equal position before the law. Clerical privileges were very often extended to their kinsmen, servants, and dependents.

Their powers were increased by the enormous expanses of land that they held. In addition to the grants made by the kings, the nobility had given them large areas. The powers of the bishop or an abbot within his clerical estate cannot be compared to anything less than those of the King himself. These included justice, legislation, executive power, and the maintenance of an episcopal army, which was used against foreign foes at times but more generally against the nobility, the King, or other clergy. It was not unusual, and perhaps even customary, for the combined powers of a nobleman and a bishop to be held by one man. In such cases his strength was so great that he could exact from the King appointment as the King's representative in his own district, and thereby become almost absolute.

The great wealth, power, privilege, and corruption of the Spanish high clergy was a subject of constant censure and frequent discussion before the *Cortes* during the fourteenth and fifteenth centuries. The complaints, however, went unheeded. The ambition of a large part of society was to get admitted to the Church, after which they could enjoy all the privileges of the clergy without leaving their regular occupations, whether law, business, or whatever profession. Contests over appointments to ecclesiastical offices between the clergy and the King, and of these two with the Pope were a great source of trouble.

The military-clerical orders which had performed important functions during the Reconquest, and which claimed ecclesiastical privileges, were a branch of the clergy. Since the members were largely of the nobility, they combined with their clerical privileges those of the particular aristocratic rank they possessed. These Orders included not merely the Knights Templars and the Knights of St. John of Jerusalem, which were European-wide in their organization, but those of Spanish origin, *Calatrava, Santiago,* and *Alcántara,* all dating from the twelfth century. For their services in driving back the Mohammedans, they were granted lands and privileges, and acquired political rights and exemptions that made them almost an independent power within Spain. When the work of repelling the Moors was finished, their reason for existence had ceased; but because of the great power which they had obtained and which they showed no inclination to relinquish, they directed the bulk of their energies to maintaining or increasing their already excessive privileges.

COMPONENTS OF SPANISH GOVERNMENT: THRONE

The Throne was the fourth important political institution. We may well ask after reviewing the other political powers, what ground was left for the Throne to occupy. This depended in large measure upon the extent to which each successive monarch could convert his legal prerogatives into actual powers. How, for example, did the kings of Spain achieve the position held by the Hapsburgs and Bourbons?

One of the first ways in which the Crown increased its authority was through a gradual encroachment upon the municipalities. During the thirteenth and fourteenth centuries, the municipalities of Spain had organized various *hermandades*, or leagues, to defend the individual and collective privileges of the towns.[37] These leagues began to decay in the fourteenth century when municipal privileges and the internal governments of the towns were weakening, as a result of the extreme turbulence provoked by contests over public office. Sometimes the King intervened in order to reestablish harmony within the municipality; and it soon became customary to use municipal troubles as an excuse for such intervention. Another reason for royal intervention in the towns arose from the frequent struggles, and even wars, between the municipalities and the nobles, or the municipalities and the clergy. The Kings were able, little by little, to use local disturbances as an entering wedge for royal authority. Thus, the Crown of Spain gradually gained powers which had been exercised by towns, nobles, and clerics.

The royal officials used to curb the municipal authority were the *corregidores*, who, as the title indicates, were appointed as co-governors with the *regidores*. Gradually the co-operative features of the system were superseded, and the corregidores exercised power *over*, not *with*, municipal councils. By establishment of life terms for some regidores, through election or royal appointment, and by the establishment of hereditary tenure for certain municipal offices, the independence of the municipality was diminished. Sometimes town offices were sold, thus further decreasing the dignity and the independence of municipal officials.[38]

---

[37] Ulick Ralph Burke, *A History of Spain* (2 vols., London and New York, 1895), I, 293-95.

[38] Merriman, *Spanish Empire*, I, 185-90; 194-5; II, 144-50.

This was the situation of Spain, generally speaking, when Ferdinand inherited the throne of Aragon (1479) and Isabella that of Castile (1474). Spain was not unified politically, because of the existence of various kingdoms such as Castile, Aragon, and Navarre with separate political traditions; nor religiously, because of the existence of separate groups of Christians, Moors, and Jews; nor administratively, because of numerous privileged classes whose fueros, or special privileges, were so extensive as to diminish considerably central authority.

Spanish particularism and regional diversities had much to do with the lack of centralization and national unity about 1500. Not only did each class in Spanish society, particularly the nobles and clergy, enjoy designated immunities from the royal laws, and each community claim its own privileges, but some towns accepted no law and governed themselves according to custom, tradition, and their own institutions. Spain was, moreover, a land of numerous law codes, of both Visigothic and Roman derivation, which it had never been possible to unify into a single legal system.[39]

The kingdom of Castile, frequently cited by historians as the most unified, had eight different codes at the time of the discovery of America. Navarre had its general fuero and numerous other fueros that had been granted to one or another division of that kingdom. The Basque provinces had their general fuero, in addition to the separate fueros of parts of this territory such as Álava, Viscaya, and Guipúzcoa. Catalonia enjoyed a number of different fueros, ranging from the *Usatges* of 1068 to those enjoyed by towns and individuals. Aragon was not less privileged than the others and had some nine or ten different fueros in addition to those of municipalities, nobility, and Church. Valencia had its own separate fueros as did the island of Majorca. Municipal fueros were still more complicated. There were royal villages (*pueblos de realengo*), señorial villages (*de señorío*), Church villages (*de abadengo*), and within this last category, villages belonging to the military orders (*de órdenes*).

Frequently the same territory would be subject to more than one lord. In Alfaras, the Marqués of Alfaras had civil jurisdiction and the King had criminal jurisdiction. Alcolea belonged at the same time to the prior of the monastery of Junquiera in Barcelona and to the municipality of Lérida. The monastery of Monblanquet belonged to the abbot of Collet and to the King. In some places the rivalries between the owners of these districts broke out in

    [39] Merriman, *Spanish Empire*, I, 236-37.

open war; and other towns and districts would be at war with one another, as for example, Irún and Fuenterrabía. [40]

It is of no small consequence that America was discovered and Spanish government extended to America at the very moment when the decisive point had been reached in the struggle between the Crown and the privileged groups. The desire for religious unity brought expulsion of the Jews and the Moors. The personal union effected between Castile and Aragon by the marriage of Isabella and Ferdinand resulted in a cessation of the recurrent hostilities between those two kingdoms, and in a united effort which resulted in the conquest of Granada. A large degree of administrative unity was effected by reorganization within the respective realms. In Castile, the turbulent nobility were curbed by strong measures, and the great military orders became servants, and not rivals, of the Crown when Ferdinand assumed for himself the grand masterships. Reorganization of the royal councils, of the systems of administering justice, and of the Castilian Cortes, all placed more power in royal hands. Financial reorganization enabled the Crown to have greater independence in the collection of its revenues. Furthermore, Ferdinand and Isabella pursued vigorously the policy of absorbing municipal powers. An example is the city of Cáceres where, in 1477, the Queen decreed that in place of being elected annually, municipal officers were to be chosen by lot, hold office for life, and that future vacancies would be filled by royal appointment. Isabella converted the municipal *hermandades* into an instrument of royal power by organizing the *Santa Hermandad* in 1476-77. The *Santa Hermandad,* unlike the earlier municipal organizations, was essentially a *royal* police force, with both police and judicial powers. [41] As such it was transferred to New Spain in 1552. [42]

In order to secure increased centralization, the Catholic Kings extended the institution of the corregidor and increased the powers of this office. From 1480, corregidores were sent to every Castilian city. In 1500, the authority of the corregidores was fixed by a decree which remained in force throughout the sixteenth century. The coincidence of this effort to centralize administration with the conquest of the New World magnified in the minds of the sovereigns the necessity of establishing in America a government that

[40] G. Desdevises du Dezert, "Les institutions de l'Espagne," *Revue Hispanique,* LXX, 151-52; 185.
[41] Burke, *History of Spain,* II, 78-80.
[42] Lillian Estele Fisher, *Viceregal Administration in the Spanish American Colonies* (Berkeley: University of California Press, 1926), p. 173.

would be less subject to the numerous privileged classes which had characterized Spain for so many centuries.

The *visitador* was still another administrative official designed to increase royal authority. From time to time, and if possible without previous warning, the Crown would dispatch an official with the right to inspect the work being carried on by its servants. Likewise, at the end of the administration of a corregidor, or of other officials, a form of trial known as the *residencia* was held. For a specified period of time after he had relinquished his office, the official was required to live within the territory he had administered, in order that charges might be preferred against him if he had abused his power. The manner of taking this residencia was definitely prescribed by Ferdinand and Isabella and a *juez de residencia* created. [43]

These were the principal factors in the government of Spain and its status at the time of the discovery of America, although there are other matters of importance that will be discussed in connection with the establishment of Spanish institutions in the new continent.

---

[43] Merriman, *Spanish Empire*, II, 150-52.

Foundations of Latin-American Government (Continued)

TRANSFER OF GOVERNMENT TO AMERICA

THE EVOLUTION OF SPANISH GOVERNMENT in America could not follow a prearranged program. On first discovery, nothing was known of the New World, and it was not possible, even from a purely intellectual point of view, to plan in advance a complete system of administration, much less to foresee all the various conflicts in interests of which the government must become the arbiter.

The administration of America, in fact, was initiated before America was discovered. Columbus received the titles of viceroy, admiral, and captain general, and on the first establishment of government in Española, he exercised the authority implied in these titles. A *cabildo* was immediately set up in Española, as we discover from instructions to Antonio de Torres when he sailed back to Spain in 1496, and in which Columbus refers to De Torres as "Alcalde of the city of Isabella." [1] The towns of Española petitioned the Crown in 1507 to cede them the privileges enjoyed by the towns of Spain, and their petition was granted. They obtained the right to elect their own officials and powers of local legislation and administration. [2]

Other cabildos were soon established. Balboa, for example, had himself elected at Darién in 1510 as alcalde of a town of his own creation. [3] One of the first acts of Cortés after landing near Vera

---

[1] *The De Torres Memorandum,* quoted in Thacher, *Columbus,* II, 297.

[2] Charles Henry Cunningham, *The Audiencia in the Spanish Colonies as Illustrated in the Audiencia of Manila 1583-1800* (Berkeley: University of California Press, 1919), pp. 8-15.

[3] Merriman, *Spanish Empire,* II, 229.

Cruz was, as we have seen, to form a new city and create a municipal government, of which he was the head. Cortés, Balboa, and other early conquistadores who also created cabildos, did so in order to protect themselves with the privileges and immunities which were a part of the traditional power of the cabildos in Spain. Balboa had no legal basis whatever for his acts until the creation of the cabildo established his position. [4]

A marked feudal tendency was also apparent in the early colonization of America. As one writer has observed: "If the system established by the sovereigns, and provided by their laws and decrees, had been observed in the discoveries and conquests, the government of America would have been completely feudal throughout, since [the conquests] were made through conventions and contracts with the discoverers and conquerors and these became the lords of the land, being rewarded with perpetual fiefs and titles of marquis or other [titles] which the King saw fit to grant them." [5]

This is an accurate appraisal of the situation. The powers granted to Columbus, had they been continued, would have been sufficient to enable him to govern without a great deal of interference from the Crown. Even after the cancellation of the authority given Columbus, Francisco de Bobadilla, sent out in 1500 to replace Columbus, as well as Nicolás de Ovando in 1501, Diego Columbus in 1509, and Pedrarias Dávila in 1514, all had extensive powers. Subordinate officials were to take their orders directly from the governor, and he was not required to take the advice of any assistant, nor was he responsible to anyone. The first governors ruled practically as they saw fit. [6]

Although Cortés was not made ruler of Mexico, he received an encomienda and a grant of land with political jurisdiction which converted him into a powerful feudal lord, collecting taxes, maintaining an armed force, and exercising justice independently of the Crown. The early *capitulaciones* (contracts) with Pedro de Alvarado and Francisco Pizarro were not quite so inclusive perhaps, but nevertheless granted extensive authority.

Desire for Centralization

The tendency to cede such unlimited rights was not continued.

[4] The function of the cabildo is well treated by William Whatley Pierson, Jr., "Some Reflections on the Cabildo as an Institution," *H. A. H. R.,* V (November, 1922), 573-96.

[5] Alamán, *Méjico,* I, 37-38.

[6] Merriman, *Spanish Empire,* II, 228-29.

As quickly as the Crown realized the importance of America, it began a policy of transplanting those political institutions which it was utilizing for the centralization of administration in Spain. [7] It was not extraordinary that a monarch ruling over territories with such divergent forms of government and extensive privileges should desire to avoid the establishment of a similar system in his new territories. America, moreover, did not belong to Spain nor to Castile, but was a private possession of the King of Castile. In theory, the whole of America was his patrimony and might be disposed of as he saw fit. This policy, as we have seen, was expressed in an early preference for the subjects of Castile rather than of Aragon, and was to have its permanent effect in the transfer of Castilian institutions to the New World. We have seen, too, how the Crown used its ecclesiastical patronage rights for political control of the Church in America, and through the Church, of the people.

THE COUNCIL OF THE INDIES

As soon as it was realized that the New World was of great commercial importance, the *Casa de Contratación* was created to maintain the royal monopoly over trade. During the early years of the sixteenth century, the officials of the *Casa,* and others gathered around the King, administered the New World. But after the conquest of Mexico, American administration grew more complicated. The informal government was insufficient.

In 1524, on the death of Bishop Fonseca, who had for thirty years been largely in charge of American affairs, Charles V created the Council of the Indies. [8] This Council was in keeping with Spanish political tradition. Castile and Aragon, as well as other territories of the Spanish sovereign, were governed by such councils, whose members were appointed and removed by the Crown. The creation of an entirely separate council, not subject in any way to the other councils, meant that the government of America was directly subject to the Crown of Castile, and not to Castile itself. In other words, America was theoretically separate from Spain, and joined to it only by a common sovereign. In fact, it was

---

[7] Clarence H. Haring, "The Genesis of Royal Government in the Spanish Indies," *H. A. H. R.,* VII (May, 1927), 141-91; Altamira, *Historia de España,* III, 245-98.

[8] Ernesto Schäfer, *El consejo real y supremo de las Indias* (One volume to date, Sevilla, 1935), I, 1-95. Schäfer shows that the belief that the Consejo may have been founded in 1511 is erroneous, pp. 24-32; Bernard Moses, *The Spanish Dependencies in South America* (2 vols., New York, 1914), I, 230-264; Altamira, *Historia de España,* III, 317-23.

not possible to maintain any such distinction. The Crown could govern America only through the medium of Spanish subjects.

The Council of the Indies was given definite obligations and restrictions. In 1542, Charles V subjected it to a rigorous inspection (*vista*) and ordered the preparation of a definite set of rules (*ordenanzas*) which governed its actions until 1571 when, after a second and third *vista* of the Crown, new *ordenanzas* were drawn up. [9] The Council had to reside at the court, and the King could preside over its deliberations if he wished. In this capacity, it held exclusive and supreme jurisdiction in American affairs, and its powers included the whole range of government. Inasmuch as it prepared the laws governing America, it was a legislature; inasmuch as it had original jurisdiction in other matters, it was a supreme court; and inasmuch as practically all acts nominally emanating from the King for the administration of the Indies actually originated in the Council, it was an executive body.

From its creation in 1524, it was given "the same exemptions and privileges as the Council of Castile; the same power to make laws with the consent of the King; the same supreme jurisdiction in the East and West Indies, and over the natives of these regions, although they might reside in Castile, subjecting to itself the audiencia of the Contratación of Seville, and declaring it expressly prohibited to all the councils and tribunals of Spain, except the Inquisition, to take cognizance of anything concerning the Indies." [10]

In dealing with matters of America, it was considered good policy to have men well acquainted with the American situation, and the King sought to find men who had lived in the New World and had a practical knowledge of its problems. At the end of the reign of Charles V, the Council consisted of a president, a grand chancellor of the Indies, a Crown prosecutor (*fiscal*), a secretary for New Spain, another for New Castile, and eight councilors. [11] A numerous body of minor officials performed the multitudinous tasks of the Council.

It is difficult to determine how much of the policy-making power exercised by the Council originated with it, and how much with the King. In theory, the King was the chief legislator, but it is quite probable that most of the time the Council legislated and the King approved or rejected. Charles V was too preoccupied

[9] Schäfer, *El Consejo de Indias,* I, 61-70; 129-146.
[10] Alamán, *Méjico,* I, 34.
[11] Merriman, *Spanish Empire,* III, 620-23.

with world-wide activities to give the Council his consistent personal attention. Philip II, on the other hand, kept a close check on its activities, in keeping with his penchant for minute personal regulation of all matters of government, a check which the Council resented on several occasions. The most effective curb on it by Philip II came in 1556, when he transferred matters concerning the finances of the Indies to the *Consejo de Hacienda,* a central agency designed to unify the fiscal activities of Spain. This effectively limited the Council's autonomy. [12]

In any case, the Council's interpretation was most effective in the actual administration of the laws over a long period. It had the duty of carrying on correspondence with the viceroys, audiencias, adelantados, captains-general, bishops and other American officials, and also of supervising their work. It had much to do with their appointment, and provided for their trials, or *residencias,* at the end of their terms. Ecclesiastical affairs of the Indies were under its authority. The laws, decrees, and ordinances issued by it, in the name of the King, formed a separate code which was later compiled as the Laws of the Indies. The Council determined the territorial delimitations, both secular and ecclesiastical in America and was charged with the affairs of the Indians. It might also intervene in law suits which had come up before other Spanish officials, where American interests were concerned. Its judicial powers included original jurisdictions in cases concerning encomiendas of Indians, if the income from these was more than 1000 pesos. It had appellate jurisdiction in the residencias of viceroys, presidentes, corregidores, governadores, judicial officials, and other civil and military officials.

The Council of the Indies stood at the head of the Spanish colonial system almost to the end of the colonial period. We shall note later certain changes in its functions and powers.

THE AUDIENCIA

The *audiencia* was the first royal machinery to receive a definite standing in the New World. [13] Like other institutions implanted in the New World, this already had a long history in Spain, where it was a law court designed to aid the monarch in the maintenance of his authority. In America, however, it was to have much wider powers than it had ever exercised in Spain. [14] The first audiencia

---

[12] Schäfer, *El Consejo de Indias,* I, 96-129.

[13] For divisions of audiencia see *D. I. I.,* XXXIV, 5-13; Cunningham, *Audiencia,* pp. 16-18; also Charles W. Hackett, "The Delimitation of Political Jurisdictions in Spanish North America to 1535," *H. A. H. R.,* I (February, 1918), 40-69.

[14] Cunningham, *Audiencia,* pp. 18-31, shows the various powers of the audiencia.

was established in Santo Domingo in 1511, with jurisdiction over the West Indian Islands, and for a time over the adjacent mainland. Owing to the special circumstances existing in the New World, the judicial functions of the audiencia were increased by the acquisition of legislative, and even of executive functions. One of the principal purposes of the audiencia set up in Santo Domingo in 1511 was to check the power of the governor of Española. That the audiencia was acquiring political power at an early stage is indicated by the part it played in the differences that arose between Cortés and Velásquez.

The audiencia of Mexico was created by imperial decree in 1527. Panama had an audiencia from 1535,[15] which was abolished in 1542, and created again in 1563-4. The New Laws of 1542 created the audiencias of Lima and of Santiago de Guatemala. The audiencia of New Galicia, or Guadalajara, dates from 1548, and of Bogotá from 1549. New audiencias were created from time to time.

The number of *oidores* or judges in the audiencias varied. Santo Domingo seems to have begun with three and Mexico with four, but later on, these, and other audiencias, had much larger bodies of oidores, at times comprising as many as fifteen. On the other hand, Bogotá had only two oidores in 1550. Ordinarily there was also a *fiscal,* or royal prosecutor.

The audiencia had jurisdiction within a designated territory. The original audiencia of Santo Domingo exercised its power in the Caribbean, the coast of Central America and Mexico, and the coast of northern South America including all of Venezuela and a part of Colombia. Mexico's jurisdiction extended over the southern and eastern regions of the present republic (except Tabasco, Yucatán, and Chiapas) and over the gulf coast to Florida. To the north of the audiencia of Mexico lay the audiencia of New Galicia and to the south the audiencia of Guatemala, the boundaries of which extended from the Isthmus of Tehuántepec to Panama. The territories of the audiencias were not entirely stabilized until later in the colonial period, but the Viceroyalty of New Spain in the middle of the sixteenth century consisted of the four audiencias above named. The Viceroyalty of New Castile (Lima, Peru), had within its bounds the audiencias of Lima, Bogotá and Panama (after its re-creation in 1563-4).

The audiencias of Mexico and Lima were not superior in legal theory to others, but because of their position in viceregal capitals

---

[15] Sometimes given as 1538.

they exercised a greater influence. The viceroy was empowered to issue orders which the lesser audiencias were compelled to execute. The duty of the audiencia was to keep the viceroy informed of the conditions within its bounds. Each audiencia was considered as exercising sovereignty in the name of the King and under the direction of the Council of Indies. The boundaries of the audiencia were usually the same as the captaincy-general; and the presidency of the audiencia, except in the capital city of the viceroyalties, was frequently held by captains-general. On the other hand, if there were no other authority responsible, the audiencia exercised military powers.

In judicial matters, the audiencia [16] was a supreme court for all minor courts in its own district, and appeal could be made to the Council of Indies only where large sums of money (10,000 pesos or more) were involved, or in other important cases. It exercised original jurisdiction in all cases where the Crown's interests were concerned; and was given special authority in matters concerning the Indians. Also, very frequently, the audiencia was given the responsibility for investigating royal officials.

Audiencias were empowered to try viceroys, captains-general, and their own presidents, in which cases the persons under trial were required to be absent from the proceedings. [17] When *residencias* and *visitas* were held in their districts, they were authorized to review the decisions of the *visitadores* and put them into effect. From 1545 they were required to take special cognizance of the welfare of the Indians. The affairs of persons who died intestate, and of deceased persons, came into their province.

The political powers of the audiencias included the right to serve as advisers to the excutive officials of their districts. [18] Their decisions in such cases were called *acuerdos* (which also often meant "committee meetings") and when promulgated *autos acordados*. These decisions converted the audiencia into a legislative body, with powers similar, within their districts, to those of the Council of Castile in Spain.

Before the arrival of the first viceroy of Mexico in 1535, the audiencias exercised this power alone; after that time in conjunction with the viceroy. In cases where the viceroy or captain-general died, or had not yet arrived, the audiencia of Lima was empowered in 1550 to act in the place of the viceroy when this office was

[16] Cunningham, *Audiencia,* pp. 83-119.
[17] Cunningham, *Audiencia,* pp. 121-59.
[18] Cunningham, *Audiencia,* pp. 160-91.

vacant, and all other audiencias in the viceroyalty were required to obey its decisions "without excuse, difficulty or delay." In judicial matters, the audiencia was supreme, and the viceroy could not interfere with its judicial functions. In executive and administrative matters, its position depended largely upon the relative vigor of the oidores and the viceroy at any particular time. A vigorous viceroy might influence the decisions of the audiencia in the cases where he was required to consult it. On the other hand, if the oidores were stronger characters they might practically take the government of a viceroyalty or a captaincy-general into their own hands.

In order to maintain justice, a number of restrictions were placed upon the oidores. They could not be godfathers, attend weddings or burials, marry within the audiencia without special permission from the King, go into business, borrow or lend money, own property, or maintain close friendships. The circumstances of government in America served to give the audiencia as well as other officials in Spanish America greater influence than was granted to them under the law. The Council of Indies might legislate, the King might decree, and the viceroy might execute; but in the last analysis the audiencia by its advice to the viceroy, and its great judicial powers, could affect the actual administration of the laws as much as any of these officials. [19]

THE VICEROYALTY

The viceroyalty was definitely established in America in 1528, and the first viceroy, after Columbus, Antonio de Mendoza, took office in New Spain in 1535 and ruled to 1550. [20] The Viceroyalty of New Castile (Peru) at Lima was established in 1542, in the midst of the civil wars between the Pizarros and the Almagros. The first viceroy of Peru, Núñez de Vela, arrived in 1544. [21]

The viceroy was the direct representative of the King. A supreme effort was needed if the early feudal tendencies, which put great rights and privileges in the hands of the conquistadores, adelantados, and governors, were to be curbed. The actions of Cortés and Pizarro proved that strong-willed men, placed in independent

---

[19] Merriman, *Spanish Empire*, I, 229-30; II, 640-48.

[20] C. Pérez Bustamante, *Los orígenes del gobierno virreinal en las Indias españolas: Don Antonio de Mendoza* (Santiago, Spain: *Anales de la Universidad de Santiago*, Vol. III, 1928); Aiton, *Mendoza;* Lillian Estelle Fisher, *Viceregal Administration;* Zimmerman, *Toledo.*

[21] The state of New Spain at this date is revealed in the *Relación que dió Antonio de Mendoza a Luis de Velasco, D. I. I.,* VI, 484-515. For Peru of the same period, see a recapitulation of the laws as drawn up by Mendoza (by this date transferred to Peru) and the Audiencia, 1552. *D. I. I.,* VIII, 35-101.

circumstances at a long distance from the King, would necessitate powerful executives to force their obedience to the royal authority. The selection of an official to be entrusted with such powers was of great importance. Absolute loyalty to the Crown was the prime requisite. The term of office was at first made dependent on the pleasure of the King, and altered later to six years, and still later to three. But the rule was not followed strictly, and several viceroys held office for periods of from six to fourteen years.

The instructions issued to Mendoza show that he was to be to New Spain what the King himself was to Spain, and he was to be received by all his subjects with the pomp and circumstance due the monarch. [22] Bernal Díaz observed that the display with which the viceroy surrounded himself was similar to that of the court of Montezuma, perhaps intentionally. The salary was at first something over eight thousand ducats annually, plus numerous perquisites.

Mendoza's duties made him both the ecclesiastical and temporal head. He was instructed to build churches, fix the boundaries of the districts, and provide for the instruction of the Indians. He held the power of patronage in the name of the King, was required to make a tour of inspection throughout the viceroyalty, to supervise the encomiendas, seek precious metals, and report on the practicability of government ownership and operation of the mines. [23]

One of the special duties of the viceroy, as chief magistrate of the audiencia, was to see to the welfare of the Indians. Mendoza set aside one day each week to listen to and redress their grievances, and his successors followed the custom until 1573, when the great number of Indian cases coming before the audiencia led to the creation of a special Indian Court, the *Juzgado de Indios*. [24] In Peru, Indian cases were heard by the audiencia, but Viceroy Toledo designated special attorneys to look after the interests of the Indians. [25] The duties of the viceroy were set forth in a law of 1542: "The viceroys of Peru and New Spain are to be governors of the provinces under their charge, and in our name are to rule them: they are to make such gifts and grants as seem meet to

---

[22] Fisher, *Viceregal Administration*, pp. 1-26.

[23] Arthur Scott Aiton, "Real Hacienda in New Spain Under the First Viceroy," *H. A. H. R.*, VI (November, 1926), 232-45.

[24] Simpson, *Many Mexicos*, pp. 57, 120-21, 124-26; Simpson, *Repartimiento System*, pp. 22-24 in *Studies in the administration of the Indians in New Spain* (Berkeley, 1934-1940); Fisher, *Viceregal Administration*, pp. 172-73.

[25] Zimmerman, *Toledo*, 187-90.

them, and to fill such offices of government and justice as are customary, and not forbidden by our laws and ordinances; and the subsidiary audiencias, judges, and justices, and all our subjects and vassals are to recognize and obey them as rulers, and permit them freely to exercise their offices; and give them, and cause to be given them all the aid they desire and need." [26]

In actual practice the viceroy was less powerful [27] than this statement indicates since he was controlled by the Crown, and compelled by local circumstances to restrict his theoretical powers in accordance with existing conditions. He was empowered to execute all royal laws, and the audiencia was prohibited from interfering with him in this duty, but the requirements to consult the audiencia operated to curb his authority. When the audiencia acted as a court of law his only function was to sign the decisions they made. [28]

CAPTAINS-GENERAL AND PRESIDENTS: VISITAS AND RESIDENCIAS

The captain-general possessed both military and civil powers resembling, within the territory governed, those of the viceroy. He was president of the audiencia in his district, charged with the execution of royal law, and empowered to communicate directly with the King in all matters. But he was dependent upon the viceroyalty for various specified powers.

Certain districts, which corresponded to the captaincy-general in other details, were designated as *presidencias* because their administrative heads exercised civil jurisdiction only. Military jurisdiction in these districts, was placed under a separate official.

Still another office, with which we are already familiar because of its history in Spain, was that of the *corregidor*. [29] Under the code of the corregidores, which took effect in 1500 and remained in force throughout the sixteenth century, the duties of the corregidor were outined. In Spain, he took his oath of office before the Council of Castile, in America before other officials. In Spain, he was not to impose illegal taxes, take sides in factional fights in his *corregimiento*, buy property or build a house unless specifically per-

---

[26] *Leyes de Indias*, Libro III, Titulo III, ley V, quoted in Merriman, *Spanish Empire*, III, 652-53; see Fisher, *Viceregal Administration*, for an account of the civil administration of the viceroys (pp. 51-93); economic powers (pp. 94-130); relations with the audiencia (pp. 131-181); ecclesiastical powers (pp. 182-233); educational and charitable functions (pp. 234-50); military powers (pp. 251-303); relations with the people: Whites, Castes, Indians, and Negroes (pp. 304-42); and a list of the viceroys with their dates of administration (pp. 343-47).

[27] Fisher, *Viceregal Administration*, pp. 26-34.

[28] Fisher, *Viceregal Administration*, pp. 34-39; 44-50.

[29] C. E. Castañeda, "The Corregidor in Spanish Colonial Administration," *H. A. H. R.*, IX (November, 1929), 446-70.

mitted to do so, nor was he allowed to select his assistants from within his district or to farm out the powers granted to him. His duties required him to prevent ecclesiastical and feudal jurisdictions from infringing upon those of the Crown, to see that no fortified houses or castles were built, and to prevent the imposition of new taxes by subordinate and local authorities. He also supervised local finances, collaborated with the regidores, and sought methods to increase the wealth of his district. In Spain he was charged with supervising the relations between Christians and Moors, and with superintending local customs dues, and the executive and police authority within his district. He was the royal answer to centuries of Spanish individualism, and the office was implanted in America with the object of securing the King's control there. [30]

The duties of the corregidor in America included promotion of agriculture and other sources of wealth in his district, construction of public buildings, regulation of weights and measures, collection of taxes, and the collection of the Indian tribute. He was required to promote trade with the Indians and to act as their protector from the Spaniards. He presided at the meetings of the cabildos, although he had no vote except in the case of a tie. If his corregimiento was large, he might appoint an administrative assistant. He was charged with the administration of the public labor required of the Indians in the mines, on the roads, or elsewhere. America knew two classes of corregidores: the *corregidores de españoles,* who lived in the Spanish towns, presided over the cabildos and received their appointments from the Crown; and the *corregidores de Indios,* who lived in the Indian towns, also presided over the cabildos, and were appointed by the viceroy. Among other officials in America were the *alcaldes mayores,* who governed a subdivision of the audiencia and whose functions were the same as those of the corregidores.

A notable feature of administration was the numerous special courts. These included the tribunals of the *gremios* (corporations or guilds of tradesmen who enjoyed special *fueros*), ecclesiastical courts, military tribunals, and later on in the colonial period, others which will be discussed.

Finally, in America as in Spain, the Crown sought to keep a strong rein upon its officials through the medium of the *visita* and the *residencia.* At any moment any official, from the viceroy down, might be checked upon by a *visitador.* This official was usually empowered to inspect the financial records of the viceroy, captain-gen-

---

[30] Merriman, *Spanish Empire,* I, 195-96; II, 147-50.

eral, or other official, and to listen to complaints from all of his subjects. Every official, including the viceroy, was also required to submit to a *residencia* at the end of his term of office. [31]

CENTRALISM VERSUS LOCALISM

Implantation of royal authority in America was not accomplished by the mere process of setting up the machinery. More than fifty years passed after the discovery of America before royal government achieved the form just described. In that same period, the Crown had followed policies which resulted in building up privileged forces determined to resist the encroachments of the King's officials. These forces were notably the early governors, cabildos, and the encomenderos, who held a large part of the inhabitants and land of America, and exercised powers that were in many ways feudal. With the Spanish tradition implanted among peoples whose form of government was similar in many respects, the encomenderos were inclined to use their power to the full.

In 1542 the Emperor, heeding the pleas of those who for humanitarian reasons opposed the encomienda, but also anxious to curb the powers which the encomenderos were assuming, promulgated the New Laws. As we have seen, they not only called for the termination of Indian slavery, but for the surrender of many encomiendas and imposed restrictions on those remaining; the attempt of the Viceroy of Peru to put them into effect led to the uprisings previously described. When Viceroy Marquis of Cañete arrived in Peru in 1556, he found the country still in a state of incipient rebellion, and he reported in February of the following year that he had executed more than eight hundred of the sympathizers of the recent revolt. Many others were sent into exile.

Although Viceroy Mendoza of New Spain had avoided possible revolt by judiciously postponing the execution of the New Laws in his territory until he could obtain a modification, an unsuccessful rebellion broke out there in 1566, led by Martín Cortés. Thus failed the Crown's attempt to destroy overnight a form of feudalism to which it had heretofore given a legal basis; the New Laws had to be amended before they could be enforced.

These circumstances are indicative of a situation that affected profoundly the actual government of America, as contrasted with the theoretical. Just as it was not found practicable to enforce the revocation of the encomiendas until the eighteenth century, so it was not found practicable in many other cases to carry out the

---

[31] Cunningham, *Audiencia,* pp. 121-58; Fisher, *Viceregal Administration,* pp. 34-39; 44-51.

Courtesy of the Mexican Government Travel Bureau

COURT OF GOVERNMENT PALACE, MEXICO

King's decrees to the letter of the law. Hence the real ruling powers in America were often the local governments rather than the monarchy in Spain. [32]

LOCAL GOVERNMENT IN THE SPANISH COLONIES: THE CABILDO

Several factors contributed to the development of local government in the Spanish colonies. Among the most important were the traditions of local rule in Spain, carried to America and reinvigorated by their new environment; the large economic and political powers of the encomenderos; the authority that remained to the Indian nobility; the arbitrary powers assumed by the King's own officials; and finally, what was probably the essence of all these, the great distance of America from the seat of central Government in Spain, and the immense distances and topographical diversity within America, which *de facto* created literally hundreds of local communities largely cut off from their neighbors.

The *cabildo,* already mentioned as having a long history in Spain and as being transplanted to America with the first conquistadores, was a primary factor in local government. Cabildos, or town governments, sprang up in almost every place that a few Spaniards settled. Their officials were the same in general as in their Castilian counterpart: municipal *regidores* and *alcaldes,* chosen in various ways. In some of the first municipalities, they were appointed by conquistadores; but the custom in most was election by *vecinos* (property-holding citizens) of the community. In time, some offices became hereditary and some officials were appointed by the Crown.

The cabildo represented local property interests, and in matters of great importance a *cabildo abierto,* that is a meeting of all the property holders of the community, might be held. The cabildo's duties were numerous. Among the most important were levying local taxes, providing for municipal buildings and public works, and in general, all matters which affected the community.

It was frequently in conflict with the King's laws and the King's officials. Such conflicts might take the form of an open break; but the cabildo's main strength arose from the fact that it could subtly misinterpret the intent of the royal laws. This rendered it one of the most important institutions of government in America, and during the course of the centuries, it produced a profound change in the laws emanating from Spain. The power of the cabildo was usually stronger in direct relation to its distance from a viceregal capital

---

[32] For the New Laws and the rebellions in Peru see Means, *Fall,* pp. 84-85; 100-101; 151-153.

or a captaincy-general. Outlying cabildos readily became centers of localistic sentiment.

One attribute, however, which the Castilian municipalities had developed to a high degree, the right of sending representatives to joint town assemblies, was destined to be cut short in Amrica. Through their right of representation in the Cortes of Castile, and of gathering in intermunicipal assemblies, to which they sent delegates, the Spanish municipalities had great collective strength. In this tradition, the American municipalities began an embryo representational system. The *procuradores* of the various cities of Española held a Cortes as early as 1518, in which they discussed matters of interest to all and gave instructions to the governor to see to the general welfare. Without waiting for action from Spain after the settlement of Cuba, annual meetings of this type were held in Santiago. New Spain and New Castile (Peru) were likewise the scenes of intermunicipal assemblies. There were perhaps as many as forty such meetings during the sixteenth century in all the colonies.[33]

It was not the intention of the Emperor, however, to permit such an institution to grow. Charles V had hardly come to the throne when he was faced by the rebellion of the *comuneros* in Spain. The cities, he found, were among the strongest opponents of his absolutist tendencies, despite the royal controls devised by Ferdinand and Isabella. His method of curbing them was to recognize the legality of such meetings and to grant Mexico City in New Spain and Cuzco in Peru the honor of being designated cities with "first vote," an honor held by Burgos in Spain, but to permit meetings only on the orders of the Crown. The Crown never gave such orders. The failure of this form of municipal activity to develop in America deprived the cities of the collective strength they might have had, and created a false impression that the cabildo in America decayed after this time. The records of the cabildos, however, show that they were an extremely active factor in government. [34]

Where municipalities, or other institutions of local character sprang up in the early days, they were forced frequently to make rapid adjustments to new situations, which often had permanent effects on the legal structure. This was particularly true of the *Real de Minas,* or mining camp. It was not always possible for the settlers around new mines to await "instructions" from Spain. They took matters in their own hands, made local laws, and set

[33] Altamira, *Historia de España,* III, 312-17.
[34] Barros Arana, *América,* II, p. 40.

up temporary institutions. Much of what they did was incorporated into the royal laws. [35]

LOCAL GOVERNMENT: ENCOMIENDA AND CACICAZGO

The encomienda and the cacicazgo were also significant forms of local government. In addition to the powers granted by the Crown, the encomenderos gradually assumed others. They and the conquistadores (largely the same people) slipped into the places occupied by the Indian rulers before the Conquest. Cortés, during and after the conquest of Mexico, found himself arbitrating and deciding the questions which would normally have been brought before Montezuma. In these cases, Cortés arbitrarily deprived some of the old caciques of the places they had occupied and appointed others in their stead. [36]

In this and other ways the Spanish rule was blended with that of the Indians. As an example of the methods used to accomplish this, we may cite one of the speeches of Cortés, in context similar to those he made to practically all of the Indians with whom he came in contact.

"As soon as the caciques of the four most important pueblos were assembled, Cortés spoke to them through Doña Marina and told them things touching our holy faith, and that we were all vassals of a great Emperor named Don Carlos of Austria, who had many great lords as his vassals and had sent us to these parts . . . [We] came in order that they should give their fealty to so great a King and Lord as he had told them we possessed, and pay tribute by service from what they might possess, as all of us vassals did, and he told them many other things which Doña Marina knew well how to express, and that those who would not come and submit themselves to the rule of his Majesty he would punish." [37]

This method of subjecting the Indians was combined with a system in which many of the Indian caciques continued to hold their positions, but as subordinates of the Spaniards. This occurred among the Tlaxcalan Indians of Mexico,[38] as well as among the former nobles of Téxcoco, [39] and numerous other Indians, including the various grades of chieftains in the Andes. [40]

---

[35] J. Lloyd Mecham, "The Real de Minas, as a Political Institution," *H. A. H. R.,* VII (February, 1927), 45-83.

[36] Bernal Díaz, *Conquest of New Spain,* IV, 267.

[37] Bernal Díaz, *Conquest of New Spain,* V, 60-61.

[38] Muñoz Camargo, *Tlaxcala,* pp. 78-9.

[39] Juan Bautista Pomar, *Relación de Téxcoco,* García Icazbalceta, ed. *Nueva C. D. México,* III, 1-70.

[40] Means, *Fall,* pp. 128-30, and *passim.*

There are many instances of the continuation in power of the
Indian chieftain after the Conquest, or of the inheritance of this
power' by Spaniards who intermarried with Indian women of the
nobility. In either case the encomenderos were able to exercise great
authority over the Indians. With their legal rights enhanced by in-
heriting the prestige of former Indian chieftains, the encomenderos
were in a position to make the royal laws applying to the Indians
whatever they decided they were to be. Actual government di-
verged even more from legal theory when the encomendero exercised his authority through the medium of a steward or majordomo.
This official was extralegal and responsible only to the encomendero,
who was inclined to overlook abuses if the revenues which he produced from the encomienda were sufficient. The failure to curb the
encomenderos effectively by the New Laws increased their powers.

The encomenderos stood in a middle position in government.
Above them were the royal officials, and below them the native chieftains. The Indian nobility was specifically recognized in the laws,
and was maintained in its privileges so long as it was obedient to its
Spanish superiors. Indian chiefs were not allowed to call themselves
"señores", but otherwise they held considerable authority, through
law and custom, over the Indians. The type of government prevailing before the Conquest was studied, and the essentials of the Indian political system adopted as the Spanish machinery for dealing
with the immediate and local government of the Indians.[41]

LOCAL GOVERNMENT: THE INDIAN VILLAGE

The Indian village provided still another form of the local government. [42] During the sixteenth century as we have seen, many
Indians were gathered together under Church or royal supervision
in settlements known variously as *reducciones, congregaciones,* or
pueblos de Indios. Bernal Díaz has described their administration:

"I will speak of the laws which we have shown them how to
guard and execute, and how every year they are to choose the
Alcaldes ordinarios and Regidores, Notaries, Alguacils, Fiscals
and Mayordomos, and have their municipal houses (Cabildos)
where they meet two days in the week, and they place door-
keepers in them, and give judgments and order debts to be paid
which are owed by one to another. For some criminal acts they
flog and chastise, and if it is for a death or something atrocious
they remit [the case] to the Governors . . . . According to what

[41] Means, *Fall,* pp. 153-65; Zimmerman, *Toledo,* pp. 215-21 and *passim.*
[42] On organization 'of Indian towns, see G. Desdevises du Dezert, "Les Institutions de l'Espagne," *Revue Hispanique,* LXX (1927), 227.

people who know very well have told me, in Tlaxcala, Texcoco, Cholula, Oaxaca, and Tepeaca and in other great cities, when the Indians hold Court (Cabildo), Macebearers with gilt maces precede those who are Governors and Alcaldes (the same as the Viceroys of New Spain take with them), and justice is done with as much propriety and authority as among ourselves, and they appreciate and desire to know much of the laws of the kingdom." [43]

He was probably referring here not merely to the royal laws on this point but also to the decree of Viceroy Mendoza requiring the alcaldes of the *pueblos de Indios* to be selected from among the Indians themselves.

Viceroy Toledo of Peru elaborated this into a complete system of Indian government. He issued instructions for the gathering of the Indians (from the various small villages in which they lived) into special towns, laid out according to definite plans. Such communities were distinct from those settlements on the encomiendas, which were governed by the encomendero through Indian chieftains. The officials of the Indian village were Christian Indians elected by rules provided for them by the Spaniards, and pre-Conquest institutions were utilized, with such Spanish additions as it was thought fit to make. The Indian hierarchy was left in control wherever possible, under Spanish supervision. This hierarchy was usually hereditary, but Spanish officials were empowered at times to choose the officers of the Indian towns. The instructions which Toledo issued for the laying out of Indian towns indicate the continuance of the Indian nobility and its use in government.

"You will lay out the house of the principal cacique in such a way as to make it more spacious and give it a somewhat greater air of authority than the houses of private Indians. First, there shall be a court and a living room large enough to permit the cacique to assemble there the principal Indians, and the Indians of the repartimiento, whenever he has to discuss with them matters concerning the public welfare and the government of the repartimiento." [44]

Indian towns of the colonial period contained much larger populations than the hamlets of pre-Conquest times. Viceroy Toledo gathered fifty-two hamlets into one such town, Sipe-Sipe. This town

---

[43] Bernal Díaz, *Conquest of New Spain*, V, 269-270.

[44] *Libro de la visita general del Virrey Don Francisco de Toledo, 1570-1575,* ed. by Carlos A. Romero, *Revista Histórica* VII (Lima, Peru, 1924, pp. 113-216), p. 164; Means, *Fall,* p. 156. See also Zimmerman, *Toledo,* pp. 121-27, and *passim.*

had four Indian caciques who paid no tribute, who received their
food and all necessary services from the inhabitants, and who ruled
under the supervision of Spanish officials. In addition to these
Indian towns established by the Spaniards, a large portion of the
Indians (it is not possible to determine what percentage) continued to live in their ancient villages, likewise under the immediate
rule of their own chieftains. The officials who linked the Indian
with the Spanish system were the corregidores and the alcaldes
mayores, appointed as protectors of the Indians. It was their responsibility to promote the economic welfare, and to guard the
Indians against the abuses of the Spaniards. In some cases they
undoubtedly did this; in others they used their positions to enrich
themselves, becoming in fact the chief oppressors of their charges.

Thus the Spanish officials were not the only ones guilty of
mistreating the Indians after the Conquest. The Indian caciques
themselves abused the power with which they were entrusted by
the Spaniards. In 1557 Damián de la Bandera wrote that the principal cause of the increase of the caciques' tyranny over their subjects was that while during Inca rule they exercised but slight
power over their Indians, with the arrival of the Spaniards, they
arrogated to themselves all the power which formerly belonged to
the Inca, each cacique giving himself "in his own dungpile" the
authority formerly held by the Inca in the whole realm. [45]

Not all of the early chroniclers are in agreement as to the wholly
bad effect upon the Indians of the introduction of Spanish government. Cieza, as harsh a critic of his fellow conquistadores as we
can find, indicates that by the middle of the sixteenth century the
government was rendering a fair degree of justice.

"Therefore, His Majesty learning of the injuries that the
Indians suffered, having been advised of this and of the measures
necessary for his own and for God's service, and for the good
government of those parts, has seen fit to appoint viceroys and
audiencias with presidents and oidores, with which it seems that
the Indians have revived and the ills they suffered ceased. This
is so true that no Spaniard, however high his rank, dares do
them any harm. Because, in addition to the bishops, religious,
clergy, and friars which His Majesty continually provides, very
ample for teaching the Indians the doctrine of the holy faith
and the administration of the sacred sacraments, there are
learned men in the audiencias, very great Christians, who casti-
gate those who mistreat or do any violence to the Indians, or

---

[45] Means, *Fall,* p. 129.

commit any excesses whatever. Thus today, there is no one who dares offend them, and in the greater part of those realms they are the masters of their own goods and persons, like the Spaniards themselves, and every town (*pueblo*) is assessed a moderate amount which it must pay as tribute. I remember that when I was in the province of Jauja a few years ago the Indians told me with great contentment and happiness: 'these are happy, good times, similar to those of Inca Tupac Yupanqui' . . . . Certainly, all of us who are Christians should rejoice and give thanks for this to our Lord God, that in such vast areas and lands, so far from our Spain and all Europe, there should be such justice and such good government." [46]

THEORY VERSUS FACT IN AMERICAN GOVERNMENT

Despite all efforts of the Crown to remedy abuses and centralize colonial government, a great divergence persisted between the intent of the laws and their execution. The thousands of miles separating Spain and America might well mean at least a year between the time the King could receive notice of an abuse and the time he could legislate against it. With the tendency to delay, to send back for further instructions, or to execute the laws in an evasive manner, their effect was sometimes vitiated completely and seldom carried out in spirit.

Royal laws were further weakened by many conflicting authorities in America. Frequently it was not clear who had jurisdiction in a specified case. Their arguments and contests filled the royal courts with thousands of cases, and sometimes reached the point of armed conflict. The quarrels between the viceroy (or captain-general) and the audiencia, or even the efforts of a viceroy to control the corregidores, produced such disputes. The civil authorities and the Church authorities were also in disagreement and armed violence between the two was rather frequent. Furthermore, the efforts of the King to make the American government effective were thwarted by his own numerous appointments; and he succeeded in establishing a bureaucracy of thousands of scriveners whose interests did not reach beyond the transcription of the royal laws and edicts in double or triple ledgers.

Added to this confusion of administration, there was open corruption. Alcaldes mayores, and corregidores found that they could enrich themselves by using their offices for trade with the Indians. Viceroys were not free from corruption in all cases, although they

---

[46] Cieza, *Crónica,* chap. I.

were customarily less venial. The system of the *visita* and the *residencia* was not always effective, since the judges themselves might be suborned.

Finally, there was no real public opinion to enforce good government. The Indians forming the bulk of the population were, on the whole, powerless to help themselves. The Negroes were slaves and had no voice whatever. Most of the mestizos were without political privilege. Government was in the hands of a minority which had got its position either through privilege or heredity. Property was a requirement for citizenship and the possession of an office was frequently regarded as an opportunity to turn public funds into private pockets. [47]

---

[47] The best source of information for government when it had achieved its fundamental organization is *Gobernación espiritual y temporal, C. D. I. Ultramar,* Vols. XX-XXV, where every phase is treated in detail.

The Evolution of Colonial
Latin America to 1810

Expansion and Agricultural Development to 1810

I<small>T HAS BEEN SHOWN</small> how the Conquest of America by the Spaniards resulted in the merging of Spanish and Indian elements into a new civilization. We shall now trace the evolution of this civilization from the sixteenth century, when it was fairly well established, to the beginning of the nineteenth century, when the Wars of Independence resulted in the creation of new nations.

The original settlements in the Caribbean Islands, Mexico, and Peru, which we have seen growing in size and economic importance during the sixteenth century, continued to expand, making effective the occupation of the conquered territories and opening up the frontiers around them. At the same time, entirely new areas of colonization, such as the north of Mexico, Chile, and the Río de la Plata, some of which were eventually to equal or surpass the older colonies, were being explored and settled. Latin-American history is too frequently reduced to conquest by Spain, succeeded by stagnation and decay under Spanish rule, and then by resurgence into independence. Stagnation came to certain regions at times, of course, but the colonial period as a whole was one of progress and development, with the tempo greatly accelerated during the last fifty or sixty years of the colonial era. Our treatment of sixteenth-century colonial history was concerned chiefly with the first settlements. From this time on, however, the younger colonies begin to play an increasingly important role, and now warrant attention. [1]

---

[1] The state of colonization in the late sixteenth century is well described in Antonio de Herrera, *Descripción de las Islas y Tierra Firme del Mar Océano* (2nd ed., Madrid, 1725-26). A description of the towns of the Indies in the early seventeenth century can be found in *D. I. I.*, IX, 58-503.

ECUADOR

The territory that is today Ecuador was during the colonial period embraced in the Audiencia of Quito. The number of settlements in this region increased steadily, and by the eighteenth century, the corregimiento of Quito had twenty-eight pueblos. In these were produced maize, barley, and wheat in the temperate valleys, while in the hotter altitudes there were "very beautiful and extensive areas of sugar cane" with *trapiches,* or sugar mills for the manufacture of sugar, molasses, and *aguardiente* (rum from molasses). Livestock raising was general throughout. Ecuador shared with other parts of the Andes the attribute, which never fails to attract the traveler, of simultaneous sowing, cultivating, and harvesting, since "crops are gathered throughout the year without distinction of seasons."

The pueblos of the region of Chimbo had developed an active trade in their produce. There were mule trains of 1500 to 2000 mules, carrying food products and textiles made from Ecuador's wool and cotton from the interior to the ports, whence they returned with the wines and aguardientes (brandy from grapes) of Peru, and with the rice, fish, and salt of Guayaquil.[2] From Ecuador was exported the cacao which remained one of its staple products down to the twentieth century. In the valley of the Guayas River, tobacco, cotton, sugar cane, bananas, coconuts, yuca, and peanuts were grown; around Esmeraldas there was produced an excellent grade of cacao which competed with that of Guayaquil.

PERU

Peruvian agriculture was still concentrated, as during the Indian period and in the early days of the Conquest, in some thirty river valleys along the coast and in a few valleys of the mountains, owing to the scarcity of good farm land. Although, even to the present time, there can be found Indian communities in which the staple crops are the same as those before the Conquest, wheat and various other European grains were grown.

Wine was produced in sufficient quantities for export to the other colonies. The statement is frequently made that the planting of grapes, as well as of olives, was prohibited. While it is difficult to interpret all the various measures of Spanish colonial policy, it would seem that the ban was never meant to be absolute, but merely to limit such privilege to those holding royal license, and to protect

[2] Pereyra, *América española,* VI, 187-201; Federico González Suárez, *Historia general de la república del Ecuador* (7 vols., Quito, 1890-1901), vol. II, chap. XI, vol. III, chap. X; vol. IV, chap. VIII; vol. V, chaps. X-XI.

them from competition. [3] The colonial system was one of privilege and licensing. The *right* to trade did not exist; only the *privilege* where granted by the Crown.

Philip II gave instructions to his viceroy, Francisco de Toledo, to prevent additional planting of grapes, but Toledo did nothing effective about this. Toward the end of the sixteenth century, and at various other intervals, it was proposed, principally by the wine producers of Spain, that Peru should not be allowed to make wine. In order to restrict Peruvian production, it was forbidden in 1614 and 1615 to export wine or olives from Peru to Guatemala or Panama, since these regions could be supplied from Spain. From 1595, a tax of two per cent was levied on Peruvian wine, and in 1609 the use of *mitayos* (*mita* Indians) in its production was prohibited. Nevertheless, after these dates both wine and olive production increased in importance. Arequipa, in southern Peru, grew to be a famous center of the manufacture of *aguardiente* (brandy). [4]

Very frequently the efforts of the government were directed not toward the restriction, but the promotion of certain agricultural products. Wheat production, for example, was early developed to the point where Peru supplied not merely her own market but produced a surplus which was at times exported to Panama and Guayaquil. [5]

Lima is described by an eighteenth century Peruvian writer in terms which indicate a prosperous agriculture. The natural fertility of the soil was augmented by numerous irrigation ditches and the valley in which the city lies was "filled with fields of all kinds of grain, plantations of sugar cane, garden plots, and olive groves, and in an area of more than ten leagues, stretching from the shores of Callao to the slopes of the Sierra, there was a large number of farmhouses and haciendas scattered through the valley. The harvests of wheat and barley were very copious before the earthquake of 1687, which caused the sterility of that land for the cultivation of cereals during a period of forty years. Then the residents of Lima and its environs resorted to Chile, a province rich in grains, wines, and liquors, and did a very active trade in sugar, syrup, and tobacco, in exchange for wheat, nuts, almonds, cordovans, fats, and ship rigging [jarcias] between the ports of Callao and Valparaiso." [6]

[3] Colmeiro, *Economía política*, II, 393-94.
[4] Haring, *Trade and Navigation*, pp. 125-26.
[5] Moses, *Eve*, pp. 307-9.
[6] Colmeiro, *Economía política*, II, 392-93, citing Bravo de Lagunas, *Voto consultivo*, an eighteenth century Peruvian writer.

The eighteenth-century writer, Feyjoó, complained that the once flourishing and fertile valleys of Chicama, Chimu, Viru, and Chao were all but deserted and very badly cultivated,[7] but it is hard to believe this in view of the many other descriptions of the numerous products of Peru. An interesting aspect of Feyjoó's report is its evidence that, in the middle of the eighteenth century, the crops alleged to have been destroyed by the Crown's restrictive policies were still prospering. Feyjoó describes olive groves and vineyards, as well as maize, wheat, rice, other grains, beans, cotton, alfalfa, and vegetables.

In Peru, as well as in all parts of the Andes, earthquakes were one of the chief menaces to agriculture. The earthquake of 1687 destroyed the fertility of the soil for many years. Prior to this time, Peru had exported wheat, but was afterwards obliged to import it, principally from Chile. By 1722, the fertility of Peruvian soil had been restored. During the epoch in which the soil was sterile, taxes were reduced upon Peruvian wheat farmers and the production was encouraged by requiring merchants to handle an equal proportion of Peruvian and Chilean wheat. Later, dealers had to dispose of all their Peruvian wheat before they could sell Chilean wheat, and in 1815 a tax of one peso a fanega was still collected on Chilean wheat. Viceroy O'Higgins required the farmers of western and central Peru to plant a part of their farms in wheat.

One of the great difficulties faced by Peruvian agriculture was the lack of an external market. The products of Peru were largely identical with those of Mexico and the Caribbean. Cuban sugar, for example, could be sold in Spain at a profit of a half peso on each quintal, and that of Martinique at an even better profit. Peruvian sugar, however, because of the great shipping costs incurred, could not compete with the Caribbean product and, when shipped to Spain, was sold at a loss. Peru's effort to sell her cotton in Europe met with the same results. This explains to a great extent why Peruvian exports continued throughout the colonial period to be gold and silver rather than agricultural products. [8]

Earthquakes, too, continued to be a serious menace, with severe shocks in 1725 and 1746. The quake of 1746 demolished a large part of Lima and a tidal wave almost completely destroyed Callao, the port of Lima, carrying ships anchored there up into the town. [9] In 1759 there was still another earthquake, about which Feyjoó

---

[7] Cited in Means, *Fall*, pp. 195-207.
[8] Moses, *Eve*, pp. 307-9. Perhaps earthquakes lowered water level.
[9] Moses, *Eve*, p. 7.

says that after it many food crops could not be produced, but that some vegetation, sugar cane, and grass continued to grow.

CHILE: CONQUEST AND SETTLEMENT

Chile developed into one of the chief agricultural regions of South America, coming in time to outweigh in importance some of the earlier settlements. The conquest of Chile was in a sense the continuation of the conquest of Peru.

Pizarro's companion, Almagro, made the first attempt to conquer Chile from 1535 to 1537.[10] Almagro's effort sheds light not only upon the political situation in the Inca Empire at this time, but also upon the general condition of the country from Cuzco southward to Chile. Almagro left Cuzco in 1535 with about 550 Spaniards and perhaps 15,000 Indians, led by Paullu Tupac, one of the Inca royal family, and the Villac Umu, or high priest of the Sun. In other words, Almagro's expedition was officially sanctioned by the Inca dynasty. In theory, he should have been able to march unmolested, amply supplied with food, along the Inca highways to the boundaries of the Empire, which Garcilaso and other chroniclers placed at the Maule River south of Santiago.

His expedition was delayed several months so that he might harvest a maize crop with which to provision himself. This indicates that the Inca food-supply system, with numerous store houses along the roads for feeding troops, was wanting in this section of the Empire. Almagro's route lay southward from Cuzco to Lake Titicaca, through Bolivia and the province of Tucumán in modern Argentina, and then across the Andes, in order to reach Chile south of the worst desert areas which extend for several hundred miles along the coast. The hardships of this journey have been dilated upon as a means of adding to the glory of Almagro and his companions, but they demonstrate that Almagro did not have the magnificent and broad highways frequently shown on maps, over which to travel. He had to make his way through all but inaccessible mountains, and the journey required months.

Orgóñez, who set out a few months later to join Almagro with supplies and reinforcements, leaving Cuzco in October or November of 1535 (spring of the year in the southern hemisphere), took seven or eight months to cover the distance to Chile and suffered terrible hardships on the way. Herrera says that when they put up their tents at night the cold was such that "the majority of the

---

[10] For details of the Almagro expedition to Chile see Oviedo, *Historia*, Bk. XLVII, chaps. I-V; Herrera, *Hechos castellanos*, Decade V, Bk. VII, chap. IX; Bk. X, chaps. I-III; Decade VI, Bk. II, chaps. I-IV.

Indians and Negroes died, and those who escaped were left blind
or with their fingers frozen off." Orgóñez himself had his fingers
frozen and his nails dropped off "as if he had been burned with
St. Anthony's fire." The expedition had to abandon twenty-six
horses, and with them were lost all their saddles and equipment. [11]

After almost two years of privation, in which Almagro's men
suffered the plagues of hunger, thirst, cold, and warfare, they
were able to make their way back to Peru across the desert of
northern Chile where they found no road and only occasional
water holes, silted up from long disuse.

The definite settlement of Chile came with the expedition of
Valdivia who left Cuzco in midsummer, January, 1540, with 150
men and about 1000 Indian allies.[12] He carried with him domestic
animals, the seeds of various plants, fruit trees, and all of the instruments necessary for farming. The fruit trees were necessary,
for as Oviedo remarked: "It is a strange thing that in eight
hundred leagues of road (from Cuzco to the Strait, they say)
there is not a tree bearing fruit which can be eaten." [13]

Valdivia founded the city of Santiago in February, 1541, and
a cabildo was formed the next month. His object in its formation
was the same as that of Cortés in Mexico or Balboa in Panama.
Valdivia did not have an uncontestable contract for the conquest
and settlement of Chile, and the cabildo gave him legal standing.
Settlement only began the troubles of this new colony. Owing to
the hardships encountered by the expedition, they had lost all their
domestic animals except "two sows and a boar, a hen and a
rooster." These animals became special charges of Inés Suárez,
the Spanish mistress of Valdivia, and two years later they began
to reproduce. Corn and wheat were sown. "We all dug, plowed
and sowed, being at all times armed and with our horses saddled,"
wrote Valdivia.

The new population suffered from that eternal plague of the
conquerors of America, hunger, and was also without sufficient
clothing. Some had no shirts and wore leather breeches. Some had
one woolen shirt which they had got from the Indians and in

---

[11] Herrera, *Hechos castellanos*, Decade V, Bk. X, chap. III-V. These chapters
contain descriptions of the bad roads and the difficulties of getting food.

[12] For details of the Valdivia expedition see: *D. I. I.*, IV, 5-84; Herrera, *Hechos
castellanos*, Decade VII, Bk. I, chaps. IV-VII; Bk. IX, chaps. II-III; Decade VIII,
Bk. VII, chaps. IV-XI Cf. R. B. Cunninghame Graham, *Pedro de Valdivia, Conqueror of Chile* (London, 1926), containing a biography and the five letters Valdivia
sent to Charles V; and *Cartas de Pedro de Valdivia*, ed. José Toribio Medina
(Sevilla, 1929), with letters to Charles V, Francisco Pizarro, and others, in facsimile
and in print.

[13] Oviedo, *Historia*, Bk. XLVII, chap. IV.

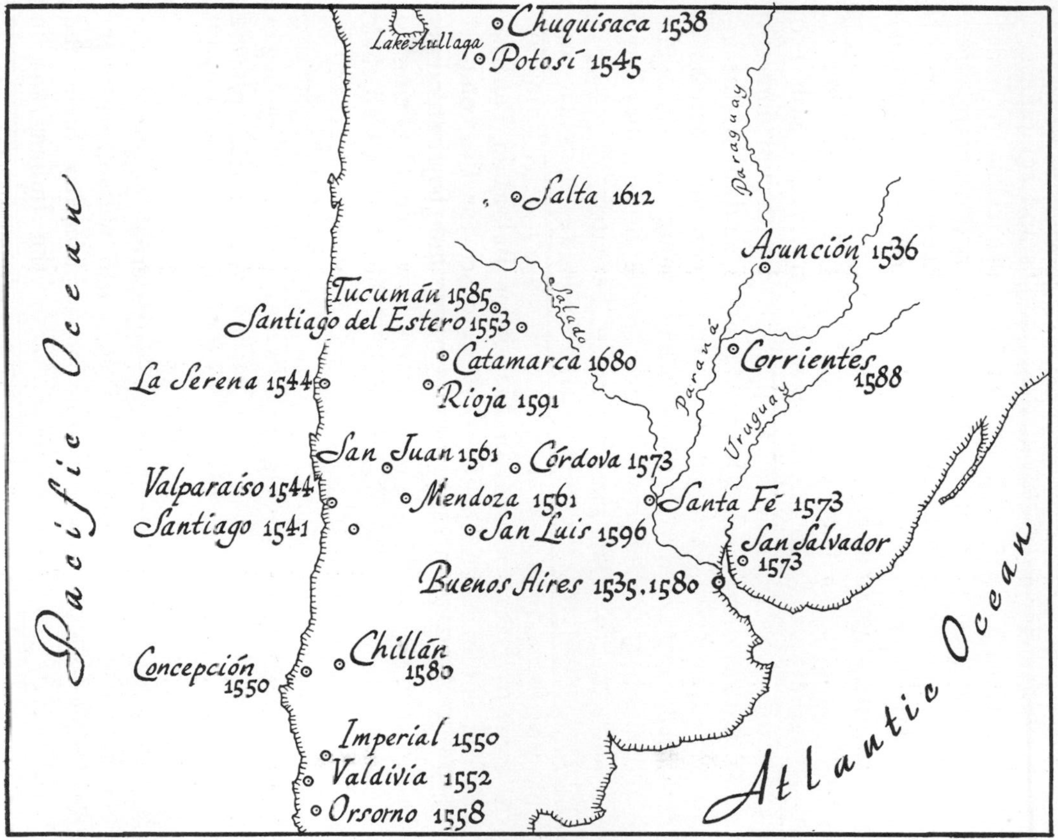
Chuquisaca 1538
Lake Aullaga
Potosí 1545
Paraguay
Salta 1612
Asunción 1536
Salado
Tucumán 1585
Santiago del Estero 1553
Paraná
Catamarca 1680
Corrientes 1588
La Serena 1544
Rioja 1591
Uruguay
San Juan 1561
Córdova 1573
Valparaiso 1544
Mendoza 1561
Santa Fé 1573
Santiago 1541
San Luis 1596
San Salvador 1573
Buenos Aires 1535, 1580
Pacific Ocean
Atlantic Ocean
Concepción 1550
Chillán 1580
Imperial 1550
Valdivia 1552
Orsorno 1558

Adapted from A. Curtis Wilgus, *Latin America in Maps*

order not to wear this out they stripped while they were digging and plowing. "And thus we were in rags and the Indians called us *cupais,* which was the name of their devils."

In spite of the privations suffered at Santiago, Valdivia was forced by the flight of the Indians southward to make further conquests. This he did, hemming in the Indians between two settlements in order to conquer them and distribute them in encomiendas. The small native population is indicated by the difficulty of finding Indians to divide. The settlers, many of whom had come to Chile because they had been left without encomiendas in Peru, were now in the same predicament in Chile, and threatened trouble for Valdivia. He made a distribution in January, 1544, that was "an illusory creation of sixty encomenderos without encomiendas." Valdivia himself said: "To induce them to go in good spirits, I gave them Indians that had never been born so as to conceal from them that they were embarking on new hardships." Four Spaniards disputed the possession of one Indian chieftain and Bartolomé Flores, one of the settlers, wrote: "The present *repartimientos* have so few Indians that the majority are of a hundred, fifty, or even thirty." [14] Valdivia could allot to himself only 1500, and to his mistress only 500, in comparison with the 100,000 claimed by Pizarro in Peru and the 123,000 by Cortés in Mexico.

CHILE: AGRICULTURAL DEVELOPMENT

Small amounts of gold and silver were found, but Chile was destined to remain almost to the end of its colonial period without the stimulation which these metals brought to other colonies. Cows, horses, burros, hogs, sheep, and goats, together with agricultural products, were its wealth. Soon glowing descriptions of Chile were sent home, telling stories of ears of corn "half a vara in length." [15] The first ten cows and ten bulls were brought to Chile in 1548. There were four flour mills by 1553 and wine was being made by 1555. The first olive trees were introduced in 1561. [16] A soldier who served in Chile in the early seventeenth century wrote:

---

[14] Quoted in Pereyra, *América española,* VIII, 50-53; see also Diego Barros Arana, *Historia general de Chile* (2nd ed., Santiago, 1930-), Vol. I, Part II, chap. VI, paragraph 7.

[15] Herrera, *Hechos castellanos,* Decade VII, Bk. I, chaps. IV-VII; Bk. IX, chaps. II-III; Barros Arana, *Chile,* Vol. I, Part II, chap. IX; George McCutchen McBride, *Chile Land and Society* (American Geographical Society Research series, No. 19, New York, 1936), pp. 15-34.

[16] Pereyra, *América española,* VIII, 88.

"That kingdom is so fertile that the ewes and goats give birth to two, three, and more young. Every type of livestock of our own Spain abounds . . ., representing the principal source of wealth of our Spaniards, who use only the tallow, suet, and hides, from which they make cordovans, a few dressed sheep skins, and leather for soles. These make up the chief exports carried by sea to the City of Kings [Lima] five hundred leagues distant by sea. And all the carcasses are usually burned, which might appear to be a great loss if compared with how it is valued and what it is worth in Spain . . . ." [17]

From Chile's disasters we learn something of the progress being made. An earthquake in May 1647, the effects of which were felt from Cuzco in Peru to Valdivia in Chile and across the mountains in Argentina, devastated a large part of the country. The regions between the Choapa and the Maule, one of the most fertile in the country, suffered most. There was not a single building that escaped without some damage. Streams dried up and a tidal wave reached to the foothills of the mountains. The ships in the harbors were destroyed and with them cargoes valued at 250,000 pesos. This sum, even if it combined the total imports and exports of Chile for an entire year, would indicate a fairly active commerce in a country whose wealth was almost exclusively in agriculture and livestock. Flood followed immediately upon this earthquake and all crops were lost, the soil sterilized, the wine cellars inundated, and 60,000 head of cattle perished in the regions of Colchagua and 40,000 head in other parts of Chile. [18]

During the course of the eighteenth century, Chile continued to suffer from earthquakes. There were shocks in 1724 and 1730, the latter destroying 80,000 *fanegas* of wheat ready for export from Valparaiso. In many other parts of the country, damage was so severe that mills, churches, convents, public buildings, and farmhouses had to be rebuilt. [19]

Such disasters were not able to stop entirely Chile's economic development. The country was still "a pasture of half a million square kilometers." Livestock was so numerous that a cow sold for two pesos and a horse for three. Chile developed an export business in hides and tallow, as well as in dried fruits, olives, wines, and various forest products. Chile benefited from the mis-

---

[17] Alonso González de Nájera, *Desengaño y reparo de la guerra de Chile,* C. D. I. *España,* XLVIII, 53.

[18] Pereyra, *América española,* VIII, 110.

[19] Barros Arana, *Chile,* VI, 71-83.

fortunes of Peru, when the earthquake of 1687 forced that country to live on Chilean wheat. The French traveler Frézier, who visited Chile in 1712, describes the relatively bustling activities of Chile's wheat export business:

"During the eight months we stayed at Valparaiso, thirty ships sailed from there laden with corn [wheat], the burden of each of which may be reduced to 6,000 hanegas, or 3,000 Mule Burden, which is enough to feed 60,000 men a year. Notwithstanding that Great Exportation, it is very cheap . . . . Unless a man be acquainted with the nature of the soil, which generally yields 60 to 80 for one, he cannot comprehend how so desert a country, where no tilled Lands are to be seen, but only in some Vales at ten Leagues Distance from each other, can furnish so much Corn, besides what is requisite for the maintenance of the Inhabitants." [20]

Frézier speaks with special admiration of the valleys of Coquimbo, from which enough wheat was drawn to load four or five vessels of four hundred tons each for the Lima market. [21]

La Concepción was also a center of wheat export, sending out annually eight or ten vessels of four or five hundred tons each. But the most important activity of Concepción was in livestock, and this city exported great quantities of meat, hides, and tallow. Tallow was used industrially and the lard for cooking. Peru imported Chilean hides. Fruit trees had so multiplied in Chile that, in contrast to the absolute dearth of them described by Oviedo, they were now growing wild. Apple trees formed "extensive and almost impenetrable forests," some of which were eighteen or twenty miles in length. [22]

The settlement of new towns indicated a growth of population and a need for expansion in the eighteenth century. General José Manso de Velasco (1740-45), the governor who was later Viceroy of Peru, established numerous villages. Domingo Ortiz de Rozas (1745-55), following the example of Manso, founded others.

Royal legislation had its effect on Chilean economic life. The monopolistic economic ideas prevailing throughout America and Europe during the colonial period were applied to various agri-

[20] Amadée François Frézier, *A Voyage to the South Sea and along the Coasts of Chile and Peru in the Years 1712, 1713 and 1714*, ed., Jonah Bowyer (London, 1717) pp. 116-17.

[21] *Ibid.*, p. 133.

[22] P. Felipe Gómez de Viduarre, *Historia geográfica natural y civil del reino de Chile*, in *Colección de historiadores de Chile*, Diego Barros Arana, J. T. Medina and others, eds. (48 vols., Santiago, 1861-), XIV, 161 ff.

cultural products. In 1634 Philip IV monopolized the sale of pepper and other articles in Peru, and in the same year tobacco was monopolized in Spain itself. Similar policies were applied from time to time in various American colonies. Ferdinand VI authorized the viceroy of Peru to apply the tobacco monopoly to his viceroyalty. Tobacco was a crop produced in practically all of the colonies and this measure aroused strong opposition from both the growers and the merchants, especially when it was applied in the Andean areas of Peru in 1752 and in Chile in 1753, at a time when they were still suffering from the earthquake of 1746. Chile was not so greatly affected by this measure as other areas since much of her tobacco was imported from Peru, but the cabildo of Santiago and the merchants guild protested ineffectually to the Crown. The planting or sale of tobacco in Chile, and of course in other colonies, was restricted to those to whom the King had granted a monopoly. [23]

Natural forces, however, rather than the restrictive measures applying to some of Chile's crops, prevented a greater development of Chilean agriculture. Fertile soil and the almost unlimited grass land produced far in excess of the amounts needed by the Chilean people, if production had been more equitably distributed. The natural outlet for Chile's excess would have been through export, to Peru and other areas on the Pacific coast. Beyond this Chilean produce had no market. The export of food products to Europe, except in very limited quantities, and this not until late in the eighteenth century, was economically impossible. Other colonies produced more or less the same things or were too far away to offer a market. Chile at the end of the eighteenth century was living in comparative poverty in the midst of an almost unlimited abundance of food. Most farm products were cheap.

Fresh fruits were so abundant as to have scarcely any value, and were not usually sold, except in the cities of Santiago and Valparaiso. Each family had its own orchard with fruit to give away. Even in Santiago fruit prices were low, a hundred apples selling for half a real during the winter season. Yet the daily wage of but one to two reales was insufficient to permit the landless classes to live well.

Livestock was numerous but no special care was taken to improve the breeds, their very abundance making the development of better stock seem unnecessary. Grazing was confined largely to natural pastures and there was little irrigation outside of vine-

---

[23] Barros Arana, *Chile*, VI, 207-9.

yards, fields, orchards, and alfalfa. Goats were produced principally in the north, cattle in the central part, sheep between the Maule and Bio-Bio, and hogs farther south, particularly in Chiloé. This distribution was largely attributable to climate and topography.

The cattle industry of central Chile was responsible for a variety of enterprises. Cheese was manufactured in a limited way for domestic use and export to Peru, but the slaughter of cattle during the summer and fall for tallow, suet, and skins was still the most important branch of the industry. Until the end of the seventeenth century, tallow exported to Peru was the principal Chilean article of commerce. With the introduction of the salting process and the making of jerky (charqui)[24] in the eighteenth century the meat became valuable, while the growth of the tanning industry increased the value of the hides. Consequently, although cattle continued to be less important than wheat, the price of a cow or ox reached eight to ten pesos, some four or five times that of a century earlier. Sheep were worth only half a peso each or a little more, and were esteemed only for the meat. The wool was worth so little that in some places sheep were sheared only once in two years. Goat and sheep skins with the fleece attached were used for various purposes, or were tanned to make leather of poor quality for shoes.

Statistics are lacking for a careful appraisal of the value of Chilean agriculture. During the last fifty years of the colonial period, the value of rural property, at least around Santiago and some other cities, more than doubled; and the yield of an hacienda was calculated at about five or six per cent of the capital invested. The tithe may be used as a rough index of agricultural wealth. It brought in about two hundred thousand pesos, but owing to various means of avoiding full payment, this figure should be raised fifty per cent or more, making it possible to estimate the total agricultural produce of Chile at from three to four million pesos a year at the end of the colonial period. [25]

Río De La Plata: Early Expeditions

Colonization in the region of the Río de la Plata and the western part of Argentina developed more slowly. [26] In 1516, Juan

[24] The process of preparing jerked beef is interestingly described by an English traveler who saw it early in the nineteenth century. See Basil Hall, *Extracts from a Journal Written on the Coasts of Chile, Peru, and Mexico in the Years 1820, 1821, 1822.* (3rd ed., 2 vols., Edinburgh, 1824), I, 166-71.

[25] Barros Arana, *Chile,* VII, 396-402.

[26] F. A. Kirkpatrick, *The Spanish Conquistadores* (London, 1934), pp. 328-44; Levene, ed., *Nación Argentina,* II, 553-610; III, 179-330.

Díaz de Solís reached this region, but was killed (and eaten along with several of his companions) by the Indians,[27] the survivors of his expedition being forced to leave and take refuge on Santa Catalina Island off the coast of southern Brazil. Ten years later, Sebastián Cabot came to La Plata, where on the banks of the Paraná River he established the colony of Sancti Spiritus, which, like the earlier one, was destroyed by the Indians. The next effort was made by one of the most powerful colonizing expeditions ever sent out. A settlement was made at Buenos Aires in 1536.

Pedro de Mendoza, bearing the title of adelantado, brought approximately fourteen ships and 2,500 colonists, with food, seed, livestock, and implements.[28] Ulrich Schmidt, a German who accompanied Mendoza, states that "We also brought from Hispania on board the fourteen ships seventy-two horses and mares." He relates that the first landfall was made among the Charrúas, Indians "who have nothing to eat but fish and meat." Mendoza made a settlement across the river from the first landfall, and called it Buenos Aires. This was the original, but unsuccessful settlement of the city.

Soon fighting with the Indians, and the ever-present accompaniment of American exploration, hunger, reduced the colony to desperation. According to Schmidt: "So great was the suffering and ravages of hunger that there were not enough rats, nor mice, nor snakes, nor other reptiles (sabandijas); everything had to be eaten, even shoes and leather." Three Spaniards stole and ate a horse, for which they were hanged. "They had scarcely been executed when, the same night, other Spaniards cut off their thighs and pieces of flesh from the bodies, and took these pieces home and ate them." Conditions became even worse after this. [29]

The reasons for the difficulties of the Spaniards in the Plata basin are not hard to discover. Domestic animals for food were nonexistent, and the Indians around the mouth of the river were not agricultural. Schmidt speaks of the Indians "sharing with us

[27] Some historians deny that Solís and his fellow colonists were eaten by the Indians on the grounds that the Indians around the Estuary were not cannibals. Professor Charles E. Chapman, Colonial Hispanic Amercia, p. 64, note 1, accepts this viewpoint and bases his authority on Rómulo B. Carbia, Manual de la Historia Argentina, I, 259; cf. Levene, ed., Nación Argentina, II, 567, for evidence of cannibalism.

[28] See Levene, ed., Nación Argentina, Vol. IV, Sección I, Part I, chaps. III-IV.

[29] Ulrich Schmidt, Voyage of Ulrich Schmidt to the Rivers La Plata and Paraguai, ed. Luis L. Dominguez (London: The Hakluyt Society, 1st Ser., No. 81, 1891) pp. 6-15. Schmidt, called by the Spanish-language historians "Schmidel," left one of the most valuable early accounts, first published in German in 1567; cf. a recent translation into Spanish by Edmundo Wernicke, Derrotero y viaje a España y las Indias (Santa Fé, Argentina, 1938), pp. 42-49.

what little they had, and we did the same by them," but getting food was a constant problem. [30]

PARAGU

Mendoza left the settlement in charge of Domingo de Irala and Juan de Ayolas and set out for Spain, dying en route. The colony was moved to Paraguay in 1537, and the town of Asunción was established. Moving the settlement upstream a thousand miles placed the Spaniards in contact with the Guaraní Indians, who were at least agricultural, even if cannibalistic. The Guaranís are described as "assiduous farmers, disciplined warriors, and cannibals by ineradicable custom." [31] They cultivated maize, manioc, sweet potatoes, and peanuts, habitually went nude, and made long expeditions against their enemies. Schmidt mentions that "when these said Guaranís make war on their enemies, whoever is captured, man or woman, young or old, or children, they fatten them as we do swine [in Germany]." [32] But if the Guaranís looked upon the Spaniards as a new meat supply, they were also able to furnish the Spanish with food from the abundance of their crops. The Paraguay settlement managed to exist as much because of this one factor, probably, as any other.

Domingo de Irala, at the time he definitely became governor (1549-57) took the action customary upon the establishment of every new colony; he distributed the Indians in encomienda. Ruy Díaz de Guzmán relates that when Irala received confirmation of his powers from the King, he had a census made of the Indians for this purpose:

"When the census had been taken it was found that there were 27,000 warrior Indians from the boundaries of the said city of Asunción fifty leagues northward and an equal distance toward the east and south to the Paraná River, because those farther down to the west and in other neighboring regions, being of different nations, very barbaric and unconquerable, could not be counted and distributed at the time . . . . And thus a repartimiento of these Indians was made among 400 encomenderos [by the Governor] with no small sympathy for them on account of the great and excessive labors and suffering they had endured, which he had seen them undergo in that country, and seeing how slight was that distribution to compensate them for such meritorious service, and to the injury of the natives, who being

[30] Schmidt, *Derrotero*, pp. 63, 64-65, and *passim*.
[31] Pereyra, *América española*, IV, 75.
[32] Schmidt, *Derrotero*, p. 70.

few would be worked very hard, since there were many encomiendas of thirty and forty Indians." [33]

A similar distribution was made a short time later, in 1557,
when near the city of Ciudad Real, "forty thousand hearths" were
given to sixty citizens "each hearth being understood as an Indian
and his wife and children, although it always corresponded to many
more." These encomenderos were fortunate as compared to others.
"They lived for some years in peace and quiet and very well served
and respected by all the Indians of that province and so well supplied with the products of that land, as well as wine, sugar, cotton,
wax and linen that is made in the looms, that they were held to be
the richest of that province." [34]

No other event was more important in the early history of Paraguay than the introduction of the first cattle; and the manner in
which they were brought shows the perseverance of the Spanish
colonists. The men who accompanied these cattle, landing on the
Atlantic coast, "marched overland to the Paraná . . . There they
embarked in rafts and canoes furnished by the Indians, and following the waters of the Paraná until they struck the River Paraguay,
reached Asunción early in 1555 . . . They carried seven cows and
a bull, which were the first bovine cattle [ganado vacuno] seen in
Paraguay and the Río de la Plata." [35]

ARGENTINA

In the meantime colonization had begun in the region that is
today northwest Argentina.[36] Juan Núñez de Prado coming southward from Potosí in Bolivia made a settlement at Barco in 1550
which was later moved to Santiago del Estero in 1553-54. Two
currents of population flowed into western and northwestern Ar-

---

[33] Ruy Díaz de Guzmán, Historia argentina del descubrimiento, población y conquista de las provincias del Río de la Plata [1612], Bk. III, chap. I, in Pedro de Ángelis, ed., Colección de obras y documentos relativos a la historia antigua y moderna de las provincias del Río de la Plata (6 vols., Buenos Aires, 1836-37), I, 1-156.

[34] Díaz de Guzmán, Historia argentina, Bk. III, chap. III.

[35] Félix de Azara, Descripción e historia del Paraguay y del Río de la Plata (2 vols., Madrid, 1847), II, 144-45.

[36] Fr. Reginaldo de Lizárraga, Descripción Colonial, (2nd ed., in Biblioteca Argentina, vols. XIII and XIV, director Ricardo Rojas, Buenos Aires, 1928). Fray Lizárraga (1545-1615) was born either in Spain or Lima and traveled in Peru, Chile, and Río de la Plata. His book is a description of the territories he covered, with some attempt at depicting pre-Conquest as well as colonial affairs. It is an ex-cellent companion piece to Cieza and covers some of the same ground. It is very good for accounts of early Spanish governments and the Church during the first century of colonization, describing the cities and convents minutely, as well as incidents of each governor's and viceroy's reign; Levene, ed., Nación Argentina, III, 331-539.

gentia. Valdivia claimed western Argentina as coming within the grant which he had received. As a result of his claim, a Chilean expedition settled Mendoza in 1561-62, San Juan in 1562, and San Luis in 1594-96. But northwestern Argentina was settled largely from Peru.

Shortly after the middle of the sixteenth century, one of the *oidores* of Charcas, Matienzo, became an advocate of a line of settlements which would reach across Argentina to connect the mouth of the Río de la Plata with Peru. Santiago del Estero had already been settled, and around it had sprung up a number of smaller towns, some of which were later abandoned or refounded. Partly as a result of the program Matienzo advocated, and partly for other reasons, further settlements were made. Tucumán was founded in 1565, Córdoba in 1573, Salta in 1582, Rioja in 1591, and Jujuí in 1593.

The successful settlement of these towns can be attributed largely to the food supplies available from the already established colonies of Peru and Chile. Before the introduction of livestock, the vast plains of Argentina had offered little upon which the Spaniards could live. When Juan Ortiz de Zárate was named governor of Paraguay in 1567 his *capitulación* required him to take, in addition to four or five hundred men, four thousand cows and four thousand sheep from his estate in Charcas. These numbers are an index to the rapid increase in livestock within one generation after the settlement of Peru. The transfer of these animals fell to the lot of Juan de Garay.

In 1573 the citizens of Asunción had made a settlement down river from Asunción at Santa Fé. Now Garay was delegated to make another attempt to establish a port at the mouth of the river. He left Asunción with sixty men, five hundred cows, and one thousand horses, and so supplied was able to refound the city of Buenos Aires in June 1580. The advantages of the port of Buenos Aires had been pointed out by Matienzo in 1566. "The voyage to Spain is very short and good, because after the mouth of the river no land is seen until reaching the Terceras, islands belonging to the King of Portugal, or, if it is desired, until San Lúcar, which is a reason why the silver and things that might be sent from here should be safe from corsairs; if the ships do not sail near land they are safe, as corsairs do not cruise around on the high seas to rob, but rather keep near the ports." [37]

---

[37] *Carta a S. M. del Licenciado Matienzo, Oidor de Charcas,* in *La Audiencia de Charcas, Colección de publicaciones históricas de la Biblioteca del Congreso*

The cattle introduced into the Río de la Plata basin multiplied rapidly, and became the principal source of wealth for the next three centuries. Father Cobo, writing early in the seventeenth century, compares the livestock of Española and that of the Plata. Of the horses he says: "In Española where I traveled, I saw in the fields and valleys great herds of them take fright and flee like wild animals when they saw human beings. But they are in much greater numbers in the provinces of Paraguay and Tucumán. They [the settlers] go out hunting these wild horses and capture a few colts to break them, as if they were wild boars or other wild beasts." [38] Félix de Azara, who was in this region in the eighteenth century, calculated that by 1780 there were forty-eight million head of livestock between parallels 27 and 41 in territory extending forty-two thousand square leagues (378,000 square miles), and that after this date they were killed off so rapidly that they were reduced to six and a half millions. [39] The estimates of Azara are almost certainly an exaggeration, but there was a decrease because the great demand for hides and tallow that developed in the eighteenth century led to precipitate killing to supply the new market.

The Irishman, Thomas Falkner, who spent many years in Argentina, from 1732 to 1768, wrote in 1774:

"The great commerce of this country is that of cattle . . . . On my first arrival in this country, not a year passed, but from five to eight ships set sail from Buenos Ayres laden chiefly with hides. Immense slaughters were made, without more gain than the fat, suet, and hides; the flesh being left to rot . . . . Hundreds of thousands [were slain annually]." [40]

URUGUAY

Across the river from Buenos Aires, colonization was made difficult by the same factors that impeded the Spaniards in Argentina: warlike Indians and little food. Irala, one of the founders of Asunción, sent Juan Romero to make a settlement on the San Juan River in 1552, but the continued hostility of the Indians and

Argentino (Madrid, 1918), I, 177 and *passim*. See also Matienzo, *Gobierno del Peru*, pp. 181-89.

[38] Cobo, *Nuevo Mundo,* II, 353-56.

[39] Félix de Azara, *Memorias sobre el estado rural del Río de la Plata en 1801* (Madrid, 1847), cited in Pereyra, *América española,* IV, 115.

[40] Thomas Falkner, *A Description of Patagonia and the Adjoining Parts of South America* (Hereford, 1774, facsimile reprint by Arthur E. S. Neumann, Chicago, 1935), p. 38. The French traveler, Bougainville, who visited the region in 1766-67, gives excellent descriptions of the country. See Louis Antoine de Bougainville, *A Voyage Around the World* (London, 1772), Part I, chaps. I, II, V, VII, VIII.

the lack of food caused its abandonment within two years. In 1603, Hernando Arias de Saavedra attempted an establishment in Uruguay, but the warlike Charrúas exterminated practically the entire expedition. The missionaries succeeded in making a settlement at Santo Domingo de Soriano, in 1624, but the persistent forays of the Charrúas made colonization all but impossible. As late as 1657 Acarete du Biscay wrote: "The country on the North side of the River de la Plata is of great extent and inhabited by none but savages, called Charrúas." [41]

A century and a half after the discovery of America, when Paraguay and Argentina already had flourishing settlements, Uruguay was still almost without European inhabitants. Cattle were the first real settlers. It is not clear when or by whom the first cattle were introduced into Uruguay and the adjoining Brazilian state of Rio Grande do Sul. What is most probable is that a few strays from the herds of Mendoza and Garay gradually filled every valley and available bit of pasture in a territory that was extremely propitious for their development. Great herds running wild and thriving on the abundant grasslands attracted hunters who came from the Portuguese settlements of the north and from the Spanish settlements farther west to kill the cattle for their hides and tallow. Parties of forty or fifty hunters made expeditions lasting for months, during which they crossed the territory from end to end and gave names to the streams and natural features.

The inexhaustible supply of food afforded by these herds made it possible for Europeans to establish themselves. The Portuguese founded Colonia del Sacramento in 1680 and began a series of border wars which were not to be concluded until the nineteenth century. The Spanish established Montevideo in 1724-26 and divided the land among the settlers.[42] In 1730, the Italian cleric, Cattaneo, who was engaged in founding one of the Jesuit missions farther up the river, said that one cattle ranch would occupy approximately thirty-six miles and would have 30,000 head of cattle. Diego de Alvear in the eighteenth century describes estancias with as many as "twenty, thirty and forty thousand head and even up to eighty and one hundred thousand" head of cows, sheep, mules and horses. [43]

---

[41] *A Relation of Mons. Acarete du Biscay's Voyage Up the River de la Plate, and from thence by Land to Peru, and his Observations on it,* p. 8, in *Voyages and Discoveries in South America* (S. Buckley, London, 1698).

[42] Levene, ed., *Nación Argentina,* III, 541-91.

[43] Cited in Pablo Blanco Acevedo, *El gobierno colonial en el Uruguay y los orígenes de la nacinalidad* (Montevideo, 1929), pp. 63-65.

The rapid development of the livestock industry in Río de la Plata begins about the middle of the eighteenth century. Europe, and especially England, was on the threshold of the industrial revolution. Markets for materials of various kinds increased at a rate not previously conceivable, and America, which had always furnished certain products to Europe, now found itself in a position to sell immensely greater quantities. Better ships and fewer restrictions on European commerce also favored the development of American agricultural and livestock industries, giving the ports of the Plata an opportunity to trade directly with Europe. Montevideo became for a time the chief port of the region. Juan Francisco Aguirre, a contemporary observer, wrote in 1782 that its inhabitants were surprised at "the rapidity with which the city had sprung up."

The number of hides exported was enormous. A convoy of twenty-five ships sailed on March 5, 1781, with a cargo of 432,000 cow hides. A few years later, in 1787, the exports reached 321,000 for only a part of the year. In addition to the authorized commerce, clandestine exports through Brazilian ports reached such proportions that about 1790 the Spanish dealers could buy hides in Lisbon cheaper than from the Spanish colonies of the Plata.

The latter part of the eighteenth century saw the introduction of *saladeros,* slaughter-houses where meat was salted so that it could be preserved for several months. The Minister José de Gálvez instructed the Governor of Buenos Aires in 1776 to "hear the secular *cabildo* and the *vecinos* and *hacendados* on this matter [and] . . . advise concerning the ways and means" best suited to the development of the industry. [44] Now it was possible to use the entire carcass and profits were greatly increased. The first *saladero* in Uruguay was built in the province of Colonia by Francisco de Medina and had a capacity of eight thousand quintals a year. It was soon followed by similar establishments, and the export of salt meat from Montevideo reached 138,075 quintals between 1785 and 1793.

During these years, vacant lots in the city were piled high with hides awaiting export. Aguirre asserts that in 1782 no fewer than a million and a half hides were ready for shipment, which at the current price of two pesos each represented a considerable sum for so small a city. Other animal products, such as hoofs and horns

---

[44] José Nicolás Matienzo and Luis M. Torres, eds., *Documentos para la historia del Virreinato del Río de la Plata* (3 vols., Buenos Aires, 1912-13), III, 34.

of cattle, and horsehair and hides, brought in still more wealth. This prosperity created, of course, a class of rich *estancieros* with ranches occupying thousands or even hundreds of thousands of acres of land (some took in from 575 to 3,600 square miles) with herds whose value might be numbered into the millions of pesos.

While agriculture as distinguished from stockraising was not an important source of wealth for the Plata, it was sufficiently developed to make many foods too abundant and cheap to be of much commercial value. Meat and bread were available at very low prices, and vegetables and fruits were plentiful. Fruits grown around Montevideo were exported to Buenos Aires. Wheat in excess of the demand was produced near Montevideo, and merchant vessels calling there sometimes took it as cargo, but Buenos Aires imported wheat flour in the late eighteenth century, even from the United States.

In spite of this abundance of food, it was necessary for the cabildo to legislate against execssively high prices. Meat was supplied in the city by concessionaires, or by public auctions in which the maximum price for the consumer was set. Bread prices were also regulated by supervising the weight of the loaf and the price of the wheat. At a slightly later epoch a monopoly was established by some of the millers, and to counteract its effect an *alhóndiga* (public market) was created to stabilize prices. [45] The cabildos also regulated other prices, fixing them every four months, and providing severe punishments for infringements of the regulations. For example, in a meeting on May 16, 1804, prices were fixed on bread, wine, aguardiente, anise, vinegar, syrup, oil, chickpeas, rice, sugar, *yerba mate,* soap and other articles. [46] While price fixing might have prevented abuses in the cases of products brought in from outside, or products that were scarce, the policy of granting monopolies to a few individuals to supply Montevideo and other towns with food found in abundance must certainly have caused higher prices to be charged. [47]

Simultaneously with the increased prosperity of the livestock industry in the latter half of the eighteenth century and the growth

[45] Municipal legislation of prices was frequent. See *Bandos* on this subject in Matienzo and Torres, *Doc. Hist. Río Plata,* Vol. I, documents Nos. 12, 15, 19, 26, 27, 28-31 and *passim,* and Vols. II and III, *passim.*

[46] Blanco Acevedo, *Uruguay colonial,* pp. 197-203.

[47] The prices in the late colonial period are listed in an interesting inventory, *Noticia circunstanciada de la industria y comercio del virreynato del Río de la Plata, con interesantes datos sobre su agricultura, artes . . . precios corrientes de mercaderias y frutas, fletes terrestres y maritimas con expresion de provincias y partidos,* Matienzo and Torres, *Doc. Hist. Río Plata,* III, 13-29.

of Montevideo, came the settlement of numerous towns. A listing of the new towns will mean little to the reader who is not well versed in the geography of the region, but a summary will indicate the rapid development that was taking place in the colony. In 1760 the only towns of consequence were Montevideo, Santo Domingo de Soriano, Colonia, and Maldonado. After this date there were established San Carlos (1763-1800), Paysandú (1772), Guadalupe or Canelones (1774), Florida (1779-1809), Mercedes (1781), Santa Lucía (1781), San José (1783), Minas (1783), Pando (1787), Rocha (1793), Melo (1795), and Rosario (1810). The significance of these settlements is not their rapid growth,[48] for most of them remained small, but as evidence of the general movement of expansion that touched not merely Uruguay and Argentina, but Chile, northern New Spain, and other parts of Latin America during the last years of Spanish rule.

VENEZUELA AND COLOMBIA

This same expansion was occurring around the Caribbean and Central America. To the settlements which had been made by Rodrigo Bastidas at Santa Marta (1525),[49] Pedro de Heredia at Cartagena (1533) and Jiménez de Quesada at Bogotá (1538),[50] further towns were gradually added in what is today Colombia.[51] Early colonization in Venezuela, as we have seen, began with the Welsers. After the middle of the century, when their concession had reverted to the Crown, settlements were made at Caracas (1567), which became the seat of the government in 1576, and at other places along the coast, in the interior and up the Orinoco.[52]

The economic problems of the territories lying around the Gulf of Mexico and the Caribbean differed considerably from those in the Plata region. Here man learned that the productivity of the soil and abundant rain might be an enemy as well as a friend. The soil was sometimes leached of its fertility by the tropical downpours, but in much of the rain belt the rains were not excessive for the plants native to the tropics. They grew lavishly,

[48] Blanco Acevedo, *Uruguay colonial,* pp. 66-67.
[49] *D. I. I.,* II, 362-467.
[50] Herrera, *Hechos Castellanos,* Decade V, Bk. III, chaps. XIII-XIV; Bk. IV, chaps. XI-XII; Bk. V, chaps. I-III; Bk. VII, chaps. XIV-XV; Decade VI, Bk. I, chaps. I-II; Bk. III, chap. XVI; Bk. V, chap. V; Bk. VII, chap. III; Decade VIII, Bk. III, chaps. V-XI.
[51] Henao and Arrubla, *Colombia,* pp. 173-76; 190-94; 206-07; 220-23.
[52] Rafael María Baralt, *Resumen de la historia de Venezuela desde el descubrimiento de su territorio por los castellanos en el siglo XV hasta el año de 1797* (2nd ed., Burgos and Paris, 1939), pp. 118-306; Herrera, *Hechos Castellanos,* Decade V, Bk. II, chaps. II-IV; Decade VIII, Bk. II, chaps. XVIII-XIX; Bk. VIII, chap. II.

MATÉ CUP, EIGHTEENTH CENTURY

COLONIAL AQUEDUCT, MICHOACAN, MEXICO

GAUCHOS

HACIENDA DE LA CAPILLA, PUEBLA

the produce of a small area furnished a low standard livelihood for many people. In traveling through these tropical regions, Humboldt observed that the quantities produced on small cultivated areas enabled relatively dense populations to live in a district that seemed almost uninhabited.

"We might be surprised at the small extent of these cultivated spots, if we did not recollect that an acre planted with plantains produces near twenty times as much food as the same space sown with cereals. In Europe our nourishing grains, wheat, barley and rye cover vast spaces of ground; and in general the arable lands touch each other wherever the inhabitants live upon cereals. It is not the same under the torrid zone . . . . An immense population finds abundant nourishment on a narrow space, covered with plantains, cassava, yams, and maize. The isolated situation of the huts scattered through the forest indicates to the traveler the fecundity of nature, and often a small spot of cultivated land suffices for . . . several families." [53]

The natural fertility of the soil and heavy rainfall, however, did not relieve the farmers in many parts of these tropical lands from the necessity of irrigating, since the rain sometimes fell irregularly. In Venezuela, Humboldt noticed that "Persian wheels, pumps worked by mules, and other hydraulic but imperfect machines" had been erected for irrigation purposes, "because, notwithstanding its apparent sterility, the soil is extremely productive wherever humidity is joined to the heat of the climate." [54]

Much of the land lying within the tropical belt was influenced by the fall of the mean temperature with the rise in elevation, permitting the growth of temperate climate crops. A large part of the Caribbean, Central America, and Mexico benefits from a climate more temperate than elsewhere in the equatorial belt. In parts of Venezuela, Cuba and other tropical regions wheat may be grown at elevations as low as 1500 feet, although its quality is inferior to that of colder regions, or to that grown at higher elevations in the tropical belt. [55] In spite of the fact that some regions of Venezuela raised a surplus of wheat and sold several thousand quintals of flour annually, most of the flour used had

---

[53] Alexander de Humboldt and Aime Bonpland, *Personal Narrative of Travels to the Equinoctial Regions of the New Continent* . . . *1799-1804* (Vols. I and II, 3rd ed.; Vols. III-IV, 2nd ed.; Vols. V-VII, 1st ed., London, 1822-1829), III, 13-14. The second French edition, Paris, 1816-1831, is cited as *Voyage* [*Voyage,* III, 16-17].

[54] *Travels,* II, 209-10 [*Voyage,* II, 264-65].

[55] For products of colonial Venezuela see Baralt, *Venezuela hasta 1797,* pp. 363-85 and 471-82.

to come from Spain or the United States during the last years of the colonial period. [56]

Cotton was one of the chief crops of the far north coast of South America by the end of the eighteenth century, as a result of the stimulus given its production by the invention of the cotton gin and the industrial revolution, and it was less subject to fluctuations than cacao, formerly so important. The annual exports of the captaincy-general of Venezuela reached as high as 22,000 quintals, equal to half the exports of the Caribbean area. Apparently this area was well launched on an expansion of cotton growing, but competition from other regions soon cut short the expected increases. Of the 61,380,000 pounds used in England in 1805, 31,000,000 came from the United States, 10,000,000 from Brazil, and 10,000,000 from the West Indies. In the United States the exports increased from 1,200,000 pounds in 1797 to 83,000,000 in 1815, leaving the Caribbean far behind.

Tobacco production after 1777 was confined to the districts authorized by the "farm," or monopoly. [57] All but a few areas were forbidden to grow tobacco, and while the value of the crop was about 600,000 pesos annually, almost half of this was consumed in the expenses of administering the "farm" and Venezuelans were compelled to smuggle tobacco from Brazil for their own use. [58]

In the interior of Venezuela (extending into Colombia) lie the great plains of the Orinoco, known as the Llanos. The chief resource of the region during the colonial period was its livestock, the first cattle having been introduced in 1548 by Cristóbal Rodríguez. In the early nineteenth century, Depons reckoned the cattle at 1,200,000, the horses at 180,000 and the mules at 90,000,[59] but Humboldt thought there were more. Some ranchers branded as many as 14,000 calves annually and sold five or six thousand. The total value of the produce amounted to approximately a million pesos.[60] The Llanos were far from ideal for cattle raising. A rainy season which inundates the plains is followed by prolonged drought, which burns up the grass and cracks the earth.

[56] Humboldt, *Travels*, IV, 105-113, [*Voyage*, V, 126-134].
[57] Baralt, *Venezuela hasta 1797*, pp. 368-374.
[58] Humboldt, *Travels*, I, 57; IV, 165-66; VI, 368.
[59] F. Depons, *A Voyage to the Eastern Part of Terra Firma* (3 Vols., tr. An American Gentleman [Washington Irving], New York, 1806), I; p. X; II, 136-259.
[60] This may be compared with Azara's estimate of 12,000,000 cows and 3,000,000 horses in the Pampas with an annual export of 800,000 hides. Azara, *Voyage au Paraguay*, I, 30. The large herds of cattle of America in the colonial period are less impressive when compared with European cattle of the same period. France had 6,000,000 cattle and the Austrian realm, 13,400,000 in a much smaller area.

"The savannahs in this basin are covered with twelve or four-teen feet of water; and present, at the period of rains, the aspect of a great lake. The farms and villages placed on a sort of shoals, scarcely rises two or three feet above the surface of the water . . . . In the rainy season the horses, that wander in the savannah, and have not reached the rising grounds of the Llanos, perish by hundreds." [61]

Cacao was for a long period one of the staple crops of the Caribbean area. It was probably brought into northern South America from Guatemala. Caracas was the principal area of production until the end of the eighteenth century, when the plantations began to give way to cotton, coffee, sugar, and other crops, while Cumaná and New Barcelona expanded their cacao plantings. Venezuela adjacent to Trinidad (New Andalucía), increased greatly in prosperity and population after the English captured Trinidad in 1797. Cotton, coffee, and sugar cane were all grown in larger quantities. [62]

The fruit of the cacao cannot be kept easily in damp climates for more than a year, and since the crop could not be stored, the cacao plantations were sometimes deprived of their market when Spain was at war. Cacao had other disadvantages, such as the long period (eight to ten years) needed to bring the tree to maturity, the great fluctuations in the yield due to climatic changes, and the susceptibility to attack by insects, birds, animals, and disease, but it also had virtues which made it the leading crop of Venezuela. A smaller number of slaves was needed for its production than for sugar, Europe was developing a growing taste for it, its commercial value was high for its weight, and it was greatly prized for its nutritive qualities.

The export of cacao apparently began in the early seventeenth century and was augmented by Dutch smuggling, particularly after the Dutch seized Curaçao in 1634, but few figures on production are available before the eighteenth century,[63] when legal exports from Venezuela were roughly as follows:

[61] Humboldt, *Travels*, IV, 393-94 [*Voyage*, VI, 166-167]. For the Llanos see Humboldt, *Travels* Bk. VI, chap. XVII and Bk. IX, chap. XXV.

[62] Humboldt, *Travels*, III, 190-97; Depons, *Voyage*, II, 145-62.

[63] Hussey, *Caracas Company*, pp. 52-53.

Average annually to	1730	30,000 fanegas
" " "	1730-48	47,000 "
For	1763	80,659 "
	1789	103,655 "
	1792	100,592 "
	1794	111,133 "
	1796	75,538 "
	1797	70,832 " 64

Contraband in undetermined quantities must be added to this. The annual produce of the cacao crop in Venezuela from 1800 to 1806 was about 193,000 fanegas annually, or 21,230,000 pounds. Of this total, 145,000 fanegas were exported to Europe, either through Spain or by contraband. The value of the total crop varied with price fluctuations but may have been as much as 5,000,000 pesos in the best years. There were 16,000,000 trees in 1814, and Venezuela with Ecuador could supply all Europe. Total European consumption at this time was estimated by Humboldt at 27,600,000 French francs, two thirds of which came from Venezuela.

A better idea of the comparative value of cacao and the three other chief colonial products may be gained by considering that in the second decade of the nineteenth century Europe made the following importations:

	Million lbs.	Francs		Francs
Cacao	23	at 120	a hundred wt.	27,600,000
Tea	32	at 4	a pound wt.	128,000,000
Coffee	140	at 114	a hundred wt.	159,600,000
Sugar	450	at 54	a hundred wt.	243,000,000
			Total	558,200,000

Of these products tea alone was not produced in America in great quantities. 65

Coffee planting in South America began rather late, reaching the Caribbean shores of South America as an important product only after the Haitian revolution in 1789. Coffee was preferred over

64 Humboldt, *Travels*, IV, 230-39 [*Voyage*, V, 290-295]. The fanega was approximately 110 pounds. The statistics vary considerably. See Depons, *Voyage*, II, 267-70, 346 ff. Humboldt's figures are based on the customs records of Venezuela and Spain. A recent study by Hussey, *Caracas Company*, pp. 56-58, 86-87, 101-103, 233-34, and 305-18, gives figures that sometimes agree with Humboldt's but are generally lower.

65 The total imports of England amounted to an average of 1,200,000,000 francs annually from 1805 to 1810. Humboldt, *Travels*, IV, 242-43 [*Voyage*, V, 296].

cacao by many growers because it could be kept for long periods of time, and hence was not so subject to trade difficulties occasioned by war. Haiti exported about 76,000,000 pounds in 1780, but only 36,000,000 in 1812. [66] At this same time the production in neighboring regions was as follows:

	Pounds
Jamaica	26,500,000
Cuba	20,000,000
Venezuela	5,000,000

The total American export amounted to some 100,000,000 pounds, valued at 15,000,000 pesos, at fourteen pesos per quintal.

Indigo was another of the crops important to the Caribbean area, and the chief producing regions were Venezuela, Guatemala, and Mexico. During prosperous times the indigo of Venezuela rivaled in value that of Guatemala, reaching perhaps a million pounds in comparison with 1,200,000 to 1,500,000 for Guatemala, and being valued at 1,250,000 pesos. At the end of the colonial period, however, cacao and coffee were more important than indigo. According to official figures, the annual average export of indigo from La Guaira alone rose from 20,300 pounds in 1784, to 898,353 pounds in 1794, and 737,966 pounds in 1796. [67] The contraband trade increased the amount shown in the official figures by at least one-fourth or one-fifth.

Indigo also illustrates the immense productivity of small areas of land. The largest crops were produced on a total area of only four or five square leagues (a maximum of forty-five square miles). The Aragua valley, for example, had a population of some two thousand people to the square league, almost equal to the most populous sections of France at the beginning of the nineteenth century, and was supported by the four chief crops, cacao, coffee, indigo, and cotton.

The indigo production of America met serious competition from Asia after 1786. At that date the East India Company marketed not more than 250,000 pounds in London, but by 1810 their imports had risen to 5,500,000 pounds.

---

[66] French pounds, 105 of which equal 112 English pounds.
[67] Humboldt, *Travels*, IV, 118-121 [*Voyage*, V, 144-46].

Expansion and Agricultural Development (Continued)

MEXICO AND CENTRAL AMERICA

THE EARLY SPANISH COLONIES in Mexico and Central America had to subdue a wild frontier before they could be secure in the regions already occupied or expand into new territories. The Indians north of Mexico's Central Valley were, for the most part, nomadic and extremely warlike. [1]

As Humboldt has observed: "Toward the beginning of the sixteenth century, the Santiago river separated the agricultural nations of Mexico and Michoacán from the barbarous and nomadic hordes called Otomites and Chichimecs. These savages frequently pushed their incursions as far as Tula, a town situated near the northern bank of the valley of Tenochtitlán. They occupied the plains of Zelaya and Salamanca, which we today admire for their fine cultivation, and the multitude of farms scattered over their surface." [2] These words reveal both the hazards faced by the Spaniards and their success in overcoming them.

NEW SPAIN: TERRITORIAL EXPANSION

Nuño de Guzmán established Nueva Galicia along the coast, northwest of Mexico City, in 1530-31. Alvar Núñez Cabeza de Vaca reached Mexico in 1536 from the north, after eight years of wandering in Texas and northern Mexico. In 1539 a Franciscan, Marcos de Niza, who was sent out to investigate, reported that he

---

[1] Regarding the north of Mexico see *Historia de Nuevo León con noticias sobre Coahuila, Tejas, y Nuevo México por el Capitán Alonso de León, un autor anónimo y el general Fernando Sánchez de Zamora* in Genaro García, ed., *Documentos inéditos o muy raros para la historia de México* (36 vols., México, 1905-11), Vol. XXV. The conditions of the Indians at the time of the Conquest is described in pp. 31-71; the land and its products, pp. 79-89; cf. Vito Alessio Robles, *Coahuila y Texas en la época colonial* (México, 1938).
[2] *New Spain*, I, 11-12 [*Nouvelle Espagne*, I, 218].

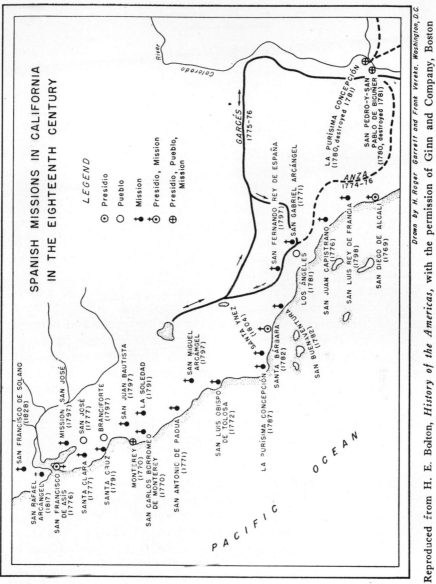

SPANISH MISSIONS IN CALIFORNIA
IN THE EIGHTEENTH CENTURY

LEGEND

⊙ Presidio
○ Pueblo
✝ Mission
⊙✝ Presidio, Mission
⊕ Presidio, Pueblo, Mission

SAN RAFAEL ARCÁNGEL (1817)
SAN FRANCISCO DE SOLANO (1828)
SAN FRANCISCO DE ASÍS (1776)
MISSION SAN JOSÉ (1797)
SANTA CLARA (1777)
SAN JOSÉ (1777)
SANTA CRUZ (1791)
BRANCIFORTE (1797)
MONTEREY (1770)
SAN CARLOS BORROMEO DE MONTEREY (1770)
SAN JUAN BAUTISTA (1797)
LA SOLEDAD (1791)
SAN ANTONIO DE PADUA (1771)
SAN MIGUEL ARCÁNGEL (1797)
SAN LUIS OBISPO DE TOLOSA (1772)
LA PURÍSIMA CONCEPCIÓN (1787)
SANTA YNEZ (1804)
SANTA BÁRBARA (1782)
SAN BUENAVENTURA (1782)
LOS ÁNGELES (1781)
SAN FERNANDO REY DE ESPAÑA (1797)
SAN GABRIEL ARCÁNGEL (1771)
SAN JUAN CAPISTRANO (1776)
SAN LUIS REY DE FRANCIA (1798)
SAN DIEGO DE ALCALÁ (1769)
LA PURÍSIMA CONCEPCIÓN (1780, destroyed 1781)
SAN PEDRO-Y-SAN PABLO DE BICUÑER (1780, destroyed 1781)

GARCÉS 1775-76
ANZA 1774-76

Colorado River

PACIFIC OCEAN

Drawn by H. Roger Garrett and Frank Vereka. Washington, D.C.

Reproduced from H. E. Bolton, *History of the Americas*, with the permission of Ginn and Company, Boston

"saw" one of the seven marvelous cities reported by Cabeza de Vaca. Acting upon this report, Cortés organized an expedition which reached the twenty-ninth degree north along the coast of Baja California, and Francisco Vásquez de Coronado explored parts of Arizona, New Mexico, Texas, Oklahoma, and Kansas from 1540 to 1542. In 1542-43, Rodríguez Cabrillo and his successor, Ferrelo, coasted as far north as Oregon. The mine of Zacatecas was opened up in 1548, stimulating further exploration and settlement, in the process of which Nueva Vizcaya, north of Nueva Galicia, was founded by Francisco de Ibarra, 1554 to 1562.[3] Farther east the province of Nuevo León, extending from north central Mexico to the Gulf of Mexico, was founded by Luis de Carbajal in the years following 1579.[4] Other northern explorations led to the founding of New Mexico by Juan de Oñate at the end of the century.

Throughout the seventeenth century, Spanish colonization advanced always with the opposition of the hard-fighting, nomadic Indians. The State and the Church worked hand in hand in these new advances, the State establishing *presidios* or military garrisons with which a missionary was frequently associated. By the end of the century, Mexico extended as far north as the southern borders of California and was fairly well occupied, although there were still large groups of unconquered Indians within the nominally settled areas.

The occupation of California was largely the work of the eighteenth century, but the long preparatory process which took place during the two previous centuries was indispensable. Sebastián Vizcaíno, who explored the coast to Cape Mendocino north of San Francisco (1602-03) in an attempt to find an adequate harbor for ships en route to the Philippines, Isidro Atondo [or, Otondo] y Antillón, who carried Father Kino with him (1683), Francisco de Itamarra (1694), and Father Juan María de Salvatierra (1697)[5] were forerunners of Spanish penetration into California. The Jesuits established missions in Lower California,[6] and in

[3] J. Lloyd Mecham, *Francisco de Ibarra and Nueva Vizcaya* (Durham, North Carolina: Duke University Press, 1927).

[4] *Historia de Nuevo León, Coahuila, Tejas, Nuevo México*, in Garcia and Pereya, eds., *Documentos Historia México*, XXV, 73-79; 89-142; 148-394; cf. Vito Alessio Robles, *Francisco de Urdiñola y el norte de Nueva España* (Mexico, 1931).

[5] Riva Palacio, *México*, II, 662-63; Manuel Orozco y Berra, *Apuntes para la historia de la geografía en México* (Mexico, 1881), chaps. II-III; Herbert E. Bolton, *Rim of Christendom: A Biography of Eusebio Francisco Kino, Pacific Coast Pioneer* (New York, 1936), pp. 75-75, 87-90 and 100 ff.

[6] Constantino Bayle, *Historia de los descubrimientos y colonización de los padres de la Compañia de Jesús en la Baja California* (Madrid, 1933); Peveril

Arizona, under the leadership of Salvatierra and Kino respectively. But progress stopped for a time here.

It was only when the increasing danger of Russian and English penetration [7] became evident, that the Spaniards acted. Gaspar de Portolá was sent out in 1769, and reached San Diego where both a mission and a *presidio* were set up. The expedition discovered San Francisco Bay the same year and founded Monterey (*presidio* and mission) in 1770. San Francisco was established in 1776, almost at the moment that the liberty bell was ringing out the news that the English colonists were in revolt against the mother country. England was in retreat, and Spain was to hold her colonies for another fifty years. [8]

At the end of the colonial period the kingdom of New Spain lay approximately between the sixteenth and thirty-eighth parallels, and embraced not only what is Mexico today, but Texas and the southwestern part of the United States as well as Florida and the southeastern United States. [9] The captaincy-general of Guatemala extended to the borders of Panama. The occupation of this large territory extending from Panama to Oregon was not a result of military conquest alone, but also of livestock raising, agriculture, and mining, which combined to supply the resources indispensable to missionary and soldier. [10]

The hunger for gold and silver, as we have seen, was a powerful force for expansion and, beginning with the discovery of silver at Zacatecas and Guanajuato, the mines furnished the basis for new colonization. The wealth from the mines enchanced the value of agriculture and livestock, which at the end of the colonial period produced greater riches than minerals.

Humboldt, who made extensive observations upon the relative conditions of mining and agriculture and the effect of mining upon agriculture, remarked:

"Those who know the interior of the Spanish colonies only

Meigs, 3rd., *The Dominican Mission Frontier of Lower California* (Berkeley: University of California Press, 1935).

[7] The discovery of the Bering Strait (1725-30) caused the Russians to begin to trade freely in the Pacific and to push toward Oregon. The end of the Seven Years' War left the English free to penetrate westward from Canada and the Ohio Valley.

[8] Herbert E. Bolton, *The Spanish Borderlands* (New Haven: Yale University Press, 1921), chaps. VII and X.

[9] Herbert Ingram Priestley, *José de Gálvez: Visitor-General of New Spain* (Berkeley. University of California Press, 1916), pp. 46-50; Orozco y Berra, *Historia de la geografía en México*, chaps. IX-XXIII.

[10] Harry Bernstein, "Spanish Influence in the United States: Economic Aspects," *H.A.H.R.*, XVIII (February, 1938), 43-65.

from the vague and uncertain notices hitherto published will have some difficulty in believing that the principal sources of the Mexican riches are by no means the mines, but an agriculture which has been progressing noticeably since the end of the last century . . . . It cannot be doubted that under improved social institutions the countries which most abound with mineral productions will be as well if not better cultivated than those in which no such productions are to be found." [11]

He adds: "The working of the mines, far from being unfavorable to agriculture, has favored cultivation in the most uninhabited regions." [12] This conclusion is confirmed by the Mexican historian Alamán, whose life covered the first half of the nineteenth century and who, therefore, saw both the end of the colonial period and the beginning of the Mexican nation; "The enormous sums that poured out of the mines were spread out for many leagues around, stimulating agriculture and industry by reason of the consumption of the products of both one and the other which came from the working, and drainage of the mines, and the processing of the metals." [13]

NEW SPAIN: AGRICULTURAL PRODUCTS

Agriculture in New Spain from the sixteenth through the eighteenth centuries did not vary its products to any great extent. Corn (maize) continued to be the chief grain produced in practically every community, and theoretically there should have been a superabundance of it. But while New Spain produced more than enough maize in most years, the grain had to be transported over roads that made equitable distribution difficult and raised the price above what could be afforded by the urban poor. The same was true of wheat, which became more important with the increase of the Spanish and mestizo population though never displacing corn in the diet of the Mexicans. It seemed for a time in the eighteenth century that New Spain might become a great exporter of wheat but transportation difficulties and other considerations caused her to lose her trade to the United States, which gained the wheat markets of Cuba, Venezuela and other Spanish colonics.

Although corn and wheat were the principal grains New Spain raised many other agricultural products. The Irish potato, a native

---

[11] Humboldt, *New Spain*, II, 404-06 [*Nouvelle Espagne*, III, 8-10]. Where not otherwise specified the discussion of agriculture in Mexico is based on Humboldt, *New Spain*, Vol. II, chap. IX, 399-531 and Vol. III, chap. X, 1-103.

[12] *New Spain*, IV, 280 [*Nouvelle Espagne*, V, 85].

[13] Alamán, *Méjico*, I, 101.

American crop, was produced in New Spain in colonial times and was important because of the great amount of food that could be obtained from a small area. [14]

The banana was the standard food product of the tropics and its productivity does much to explain why tropical regions could (and still can) maintain their populations when only a fraction of their total available ground is in cultivation. In the eighteenth century one hundred square meters of ground (about 1/40 of an acre) with thirty to forty banana plants produced in a year about 4,400 pounds of bananas, as compared with about thirty-three pounds of wheat and ninety-nine pounds of potatoes, or forty-four times as much as potatoes and one hundred and thirty-three times as much as wheat. [15]

The agave or maguey plant, whose numerous products, especially pulque, had become highly commercialized, occupied extensive areas in the highlands. The agave resists drought, earthquake, and general climatological conditions better than wheat, corn, and other plants. It thrives in very poor and arid soil where nothing else can be grown. One plant valued at about five pesos would produce in the most barren soil one hundred and fifty bottles of liquid in five months, and this could be sold for approximately twenty pesos. It was, therefore, much favored by farmers. The Indians and mestizos drank pulque as a regular ration and the Europeans also became addicted to it, either in its simple fermented state or in its refined state as *tequila*. Many clergymen preached against the use of pulque, and one archbishop, Mateo Sagade Bugueiro (term of office 1655-62), excommunicated the merchants who sold it. The Crown prohibited its use. But the people were accustomed to drinking pulque, the Crown needed the revenues the pulque tax yielded, and the farmers suffered great losses during the intervals of prohibition. In the long run, the drinking of pulque persisted and the cultivation of the agave plant continued to be an important branch of agriculture. [16] In 1793 in three cities alone, Mexico, Toluca, and Puebla, the Crown derived from it a revenue of 817,739 pesos.

Sugar production began in Mexico almost simultaneously with the Conquest, and exportation to Peru had begun by 1553. Much of the sugar was grown in the moderately cool upland valleys rather than along the tropical coast line, because of difficulties

---

[14] Humboldt estimated that nine people could be fed on potatoes produced from an acre and a quarter of ground. *New Spain*, II, 496-98 [*Nouvelle Espagne*, III, 125].

[15] Humboldt, *New Spain*, II, 426-27 [*Nouvelle Espagne*, III, 35-36].

[16] Riva Palacio, *México*, II, 674.

of transport from the tropic coast to tableland. The exports from the port of Vera Cruz at the beginning of the nineteenth century amounted to a half million arrobas, worth about three pesos of the arroba, or one and one-half million pesos.

In the vicinity of Puebla there were haciendas of cane yielding from twenty to thirty thousand arrobas annually. This compared very favorably with the yield in Cuba, where only one plantation produced as much as 40,000 arrobas and not above eight plantations averaged more than 35,000 arrobas, at the same date. Another difference between sugar farms in Cuba and in Mexico was that in Mexico almost all the labor was done by free Indians, whereas in Cuba the work was done by Negro slaves.

In the comparably fertile parts of Mexico and Cuba, in 1800 the annual yield was some 1,400 kilograms of sugar per hectare, and in Santo Domingo, it was 1,550 kilograms. Irrigated ground yielded from 2,100 to 2,800 kilograms of raw sugar per hectare. With the arroba valued at three pesos, a hectare of irrigated cane land at Vera Cruz yielded from ten to twelve times as much income as wheat, but the great expense of milling and of slave labor reduced the profit from sugar relatively. Most of the sugar produced in New Spain about 1800 was consumed within the country, the total consumption amounting to approximately sixteen million kilograms. The consumption per capita of sugar in America was very much greater than in Europe during the same period, that of Cuba being some fifteen times as much as that of France. New Spain exported only one-eighth as much as Cuba at this time.

At the end of the eighteenth century a notable increase in the production of sugar occurred in Mexico, Louisiana, Venezuela, Dutch Guiana, and Brazil. In Haiti alone of the chief sugar producing regions of the world was there a decline of production at this time, as a result of the continued civil wars arising from the French Revolution. While American sugar increased rapidly it was forced to meet the competition of sugar from the East Indies. After a sea passage of 12,000 miles or more, sugar from India sold in New York for less than sugar from Jamaica, only 1,400 miles from New York. The difference in cost of production was entirely in favor of the East. The yield per hectare in India in 1800 was about double that of the West Indies [17] and the cost of labor was about one-third that of Cuba. The sugar yield in the East was one pound of sugar for each six pounds of cane juice, while on the island of Jamaica eight pounds of cane juice were

---

[17] Some 4,650 kilograms per hectare.

required to yield one pound of sugar. The cost of production in India was about one-third the market price in Havana.

These factors, rather than lack of enterprise on the part of the colonial Spanish Americans, were responsible for the small amount of land in cultivation in comparison with the enormous acreage available. What America could produce did not depend so much upon the theoretical potential production capacity as upon what could be done with the produce. Once the local market was supplied, additional profits in sugar could come only from exports, which were limited by the relatively small per capita consumption of Europe at the end of the eighteenth century and the competition of other markets.

Cotton cultivation in New Spain had also made progress. In 1791 the export was six times that of the United States. The consumption of cotton increased enormously after 1793 when Whitney's cotton gin made it possible to supply cotton for the new power machinery derived from applying Watt's steam engine to the textile inventions of Kay, Hargreaves, Arkwright, Cartwright, and Crompton. Exports from the United States, counting both exports from domestic production and foreign cotton passing through American ports, increased 377 times in twelve years. The cotton of New Spain did not increase at this rate, probably because the cost of production appears to have been greater, making competition with the United States impossible. The cost of transportation alone doubled the price.

Coffee and cacao were produced in New Spain in insignificant quantities, being imported from Venezuela, New Granada, and Quito. Vanilla, on the other hand, was almost exclusively produced in New Spain, and Europe did not receive vanilla from any other source. Its cultivation, however, was not highly developed. The Indians gathered it from the forest and brought it into the towns where the merchants acted as middlemen in exporting it.

This is the manner in which a great deal of colonial agriculture and commerce was carried on in the eighteenth century. A few merchants known as *habilitadores* advanced money to *cosecheros,* who produced or gathered the crop. The latter were obliged to sell their crop to the merchants or middlemen by whom they were financed. Humboldt says that the *habilitadores* drew " almost the whole profit of this branch of Mexican industry . . . . The purchasers far from paying the Indians in ready money, supply them in barter and at a very high price, with brandy, cacao, wine, and more especially with cotton cloth, manufactured at Puebla. In this barter consists part of the profits of these monopolists." [18]

Tobacco was one of the important crops and was a monopoly of the Crown.[19] The tobacco monopoly or "farm" (the *estanco real de tabaco*) was established in 1764 and after that date a special permit was required for planting tobacco, all of which had to be sold at the price fixed by the government monopoly. Except in the section around Orizaba, Córdoba, and Vera Cruz, tobacco cultivation was prohibited. Officials entitled *guardias de tabaco* were designated to travel through the country, uprooting all tobacco plants found outside of those licensed districts. Prior to the monopoly the area around Guadalajara was noted for its tobacco. The tobacco production of New Spain, and consequently the revenues derived from it by the Crown, were much larger than those of Peru. In America consumption per capita was so much greater than in Europe that New Spain did not raise enough tobacco for its own needs and had to import from Cuba.

Indigo was not produced in large quantities in New Spain, which received its supplies from the abundant productions of Venezuela and Guatemala.

Livestock furnished New Spain with a source of wealth and a means of extending civilization that was entirely unknown in pre-Conquest times. The multiplication of domestic animals made it possible to expand northward to the borders of Oregon. From this time, the development of the industry in New Spain, like that in the rest of America, depended more upon the effective demand of the European market than upon the production possibilities of America. The former was limited, whereas the latter was practically without bounds. Humboldt observed:

"The horses of the northern provinces and, particularly those of New Mexico, are as celebrated for excellent qualities as the horses of Chile; both descend, as it is pretended, from the Arab race; and they wander wild in herds, in the Savannahs of the *Provincias Internas*. The exportation of these horses to Natchez and New Orleans, becomes every year of greater importance. Many Mexican families possess in their *Hatos de Ganado,* from thirty to forty thousand head of horses and oxen. The mules would be still more numerous if so many of them did not perish on the highways from the excessive fatigues of journeys of several months. It is reckoned that the commerce of Vera Cruz

[18] Humboldt, *New Spain*, III, 34-35 [*Nouvelle Espagne*, III, 207-09].
[19] Priestley, *Gálvez*, pp. 135-171; Fisher, *Viceregal Administration*, p. 104.

alone, employs annually nearly 70,000 mules. More than 5,000 are employed as an object of luxury in the carriages of the city of Mexico." [20]

Sheep and goats attained a similar importance and the killing and preparation of hogs, especially the making of *chorizo* (sausage) and the smoking of hams, became an industry of importance which had its center in the city of Toluca.

Beeswax was a valuable article for use in making candles for church worship. "An enormous quantity [was] consumed in the festivals of the Church, both in the capital and in the chapels of the smallest Indian villages." Wax was produced in Yucatán but New Spain was forced to import a considerable quantity from Cuba.

Cochineal, a dye derived from a small insect which breeds on the *nopal* (cactus) plant, was in demand in Europe. Oaxaca was one of the most celebrated centers of production.[21] Some plantations had from fifty to sixty thousand cactus plants but most of the cochineal was gathered in small *nopal* farms, or nopaleries, belonging to the Indians. The export from Oaxaca at the beginning of the nineteenth century averaged thirty-two thousand arrobas annually, a quantity exceeded only in the very best years of the preceding 45-year period. The exports from Vera Cruz were as follows:

1802 46,964 arrobas valued at 3,368,557 pesos
1803 29,610 arrobas valued at 2,238,673 pesos

Wine and olive oil were both produced in New Spain but never achieved the status of leading industries. In theory their production was prohibited. Humboldt predicted that the removal of restrictions would result in great increases, and that "the maguey plantations would be gradually succeeded by vineyards." [22] This prediction was not fulfilled.

Here, as in Peru, it is doubtful that the prohibitions were ever strictly enforced, and more likely that natural conditions limited the amount of wine and olive oil. At various times, the viceroys were required to prevent the enlarging of vineyards or the replacement of overaged vines. Olive orchards were permitted only if their products were destined to some one of the charitable works maintained by the Church. Such instructions had been issued as early as the sixteenth century, but since they were repeated in 1774 it seems probable that they had not been observed.

[20] Humboldt, *New Spain*, III, 49-50 [*Nouvelle Espagne*, III, 226-27].
[21] Alamán, *Méjico*, I, Appendix, Doc. 8.
[22] Humboldt, *New Spain*, II, 529-30 [*Nouvelle Espagne*, III, 165-167].

Moreover, these restrictions apparently were intended merely to prevent production without a license in accordance with the system of privilege. For example, in New Spain in 1796, there was a "prohibition" against the manufacture of *aguardientes,* yet "a tax of six pesos a barrel" was levied upon the manufactured product. Alamán remarks: "The vineyards had increased considerably in various places, especially in Parras, and the King approved the permit given to plant new vineyards in the province of Guanajuato, whose intendant encouraged this type of industry, which also increased in the province of San Luis Potosí; and orchards of olives had been planted within sight of the capital in the Morales hacienda, and not merely did the viceroy Iturrigaray approve but he actually encouraged it." [23]

The laws held only against the masses of the people who could not cultivate certain plants except for home consumption. Viceroy Branciforte granted licenses in 1796 to José Joaquín Márquez, Fernando Movellán, and Ignacio de Celis for the planting of vineyards. The assessor general of New Spain argued that the prohibitions were annulled and had been disregarded for many years, citing numerous examples to prove that the law no longer existed. [24] The privileges were sought by many, and much of the dissatisfaction of the later colonial period came from rivalries so created. The Creoles looked upon every Spaniard who obtained such a privilege as a usurper and an intruder.

Alamán cited his own experience to show that neither vineyards nor olive groves prospered after the prohibitions were removed, because the climate was not propitious for them. "I myself have made the costly experiment of what I set down here." [25] Other new products that were not restricted, but were, on the contrary, promoted, failed nonetheless; Alamán gives as examples flax and hemp for which skilled workers were sent from Spain, yet which did not succeed. Viceroy Revilla Gigedo II tried in vain to revive the silk-raising industry in the last years of the eighteenth century.

New Spain: Value of Agricultural Products at End of Colonial Period

Agricultural production was increasing rapidly at the end of the colonial period. An index of this is the tithe which was collected on most agricultural products. In six dioceses of New Spain the tithes rose from thirteen million pesos during the period from

[23] Alamán, *Méjico,* I, 103-105.
[24] Alamán, *Méjico,* I, 104-105, notes 29 and 30.
[25] Alamán, *Méjico,* I, 105, note 33.

1771-79, to eighteen million during the period from 1780-89, an increase of thirty per cent.[26]

The relative value of minerals and agricultural produce is also interesting. The wealth of Chile, the Río de la Plata colonies, much of Venezuela and Colombia, and the Islands of the West Indies was almost entirely in agriculture and livestock. If anywhere in the Spanish colonies the mineral wealth exceeded the agricultural, it should have been in New Spain. That this was not true, however, even in New Spain, offers evidence that while minerals were a valuable stimulant to agriculture, they did not exceed it in value. Humboldt discovered "the interesting fact that the value of the gold and silver of the Mexican mines is less, by almost a fourth, than the value of the territorial [agricultural] produce." [27]

Alamán, using the tithes as a basis for calculation, and taking into account that the Indians were exempted from paying tithes (with certain exceptions),[28] that many articles did not pay a full ten per cent (sugar paid only four and syrups almost nothing), and that others such as cochineal were entirely free from tithes, calculated the annual income from agriculture at thirty million pesos, as compared with twenty-three to twenty-five million pesos in metals.[29]

CUBA AND THE WEST INDIES

Cuba and the other West Indian Islands were predominantly agricultural in their wealth, and their principal problems were those affecting other tropical regions. A productive potentiality far in excess of market demands meant that only a comparatively small percentage of the arable ground was utilized. Frequent hurricanes were another handicap. As early as the time of Columbus, hurricanes devastated one or more of the islands; and while they followed no definite cycle, there were few years in which hurricanes did not damage some portion of the West Indies or the neighboring mainland. From 1770 to 1795 for example, there were seventeen hurricanes in the West Indies region.[30]

West Indian agriculture was in large part industrialized by 1800. There, the word agriculture did not "offer to the imagination the

[26] Humboldt, *New Spain*, III, 96 [*Nouvelle Espagne*, III, 383].
[27] Humboldt, *New Spain*, III, 97-98 [*Nouvelle Espagne*, III, 285-286].
[28] Woodrow W. Borah, "The Collection of Tithes in the Bishopric of Oaxaca during the Sixteenth Century," *H.A.H.R.*, XXI (August, 1941), 386-409.
[29] Alamán, *Méjico*, I, 103.
[30] The discussion of agriculture in the West Indies is based, unless otherwise indicated, on Humboldt, *Travels*, vol. VII, compared with the edition issued by Fernando Ortiz, *Ensayo político sobre la isla de Cuba* (2 vols., Havana, 1930).

idea of harvests which [served] for nourishment of man, but of ground which [produced] objects of commercial exchange, and raw materials for manufacturing industry," as well as "plains carefully planted with sugar-cane and coffee; . . . watered with the sweat of African slaves!" [31]

Although sugar cane production in the West Indies began very early, livestock raising and the export of skins and hides was a more important branch of rural wealth from the sixteenth to the beginning of the eighteenth century. Tobacco was grown and bees were kept for honey and wax. In the eighteenth century, cane and coffee came into prominence. All these products were intended for export, but Cuba and the other West Indian Islands produced dozens of kinds of vegetables for local consumption. Exports made considerable progress during the eighteenth century, and the export of tobacco, coffee, sugar, and wax from Cuba at the beginning of the nineteenth century had an annual value of approximately fourteen million pesos.

CUBA: SUGAR

The following table shows the average annual export of sugar from the port of Havana from 1760 to 1824.

1760-1763	13,000	cases
1770-1778	50,000	"
1786-1791	85,014	"
1791-1796	120,374	"
1796-1801	159,841	"
1801-1806	156,510	"
1806-1810	186,672	"
1811-1814	206,481	"
1815-1820	215,593	"
1820-1824	245,329	" [32]

During sixty-four years, the annual average sugar export from Havana increased about eighteen times. In the last eight years of this period, the average annual export was 235,000 cases from Havana alone, with an additional 70,000 cases shipped from other ports, and an extra twenty-five per cent of contraband, bringing the total export to 380,000 cases (approximately seventy million kilograms). This does not take into account the consumption of sugar in Cuba itself, which amounted to approximately 298,000 arrobas, or 18,600 cases in 1794 for Havana, and for the whole

[31] Humboldt, *New Spain*, II, 403 [*Nouvelle Espagne*, II, 6-7].
[32] Humboldt, *Travels*, VII, 163-64.

island 730,000 arrobas, or 45,600 cases. By 1825, the total annual consumption in the island was 88,000 cases, and the total average annual production at least 440,000 cases, equivalent to 81,000,000 kilograms. During the same period, the average annual sugar export from Jamaica to Great Britain and Ireland was approximately 81,000,000 kilograms, equivalent to the total production of the island of Cuba.

Figuring 1330 kilos of sugar to the hectare, 60,872 hectares in Cuba, which was only ½ per cent of Cuba's area and equal to about one-ninth of an average sized department of France, was sufficient to supply the entire 440,000 cases which the island produced about 1825. To produce the sixty million kilograms of sugar consumed by the thirty million people of France in 1825, only thirty thousand hectares in any one of the tropical regions we are considering had to be cultivated. In the temperate climates, by contrast, approximately four times as much ground had to be planted in beets to produce sugar for the same number of people. This illustrates again how small an area was required in tropical lands to produce large amounts of food stuffs. Since the beginning of the eighteenth century, the increase in the production in the West Indies had been phenomenal and yet in such islands as Cuba the arable land was scarcely touched.

In the midst of a period in which the production of sugar had increased consistently for more than a century, and was to continue to do so, there appeared in 1812 a book entitled *Sobre la decadencia del ramo de azúcar (On the Decline of Sugar)*. Too frequently judgments have been formed about the progress of colonial agricultural production from some such work, which had little or no validity, being based upon the history of a particular district, or written at a time when there had been one or two bad crop years.

Towards the end of the eighteenth century, improvements in the sugar manufacturing process were made. Mules replaced oxen in the *trapiches,* thereby speeding up the rate of grinding. Water mills, used as early as the sixteenth century, were either increased in number or reintroduced and, finally, steam engines made their appearance. At the end of the first quarter of the nineteenth century, there were at least twenty-five of these in use in Cuba. The number of Cuban sugar factories (*ingenios*) increased from 473 in 1775 to 780 in 1817. Furthermore the improvements in them were such that the best *ingenio* in 1775 produced only about a quarter as much as a second class *ingenio* in 1817.

The increased capitalization of the sugar industry was one of the most important trends, although it has been noted that sugar growing required large capital from the beginning. The expense of installing a new *ingenio* led many farmers to secure the capital needed by appealing to the merchants. The legal rate of interest was five per cent, but through various devices it was considerably increased.

"The most common loans are an advance of capital to the hacendado who furnishes every quintal of coffee at two pesos and every arroba of sugar at two *reales de plata* below the current price at the period of harvest. Thus a harvest of a thousand cases of sugar is sold in advance (or *refacción*) at a loss of four thousand pesos. The amount of business and the scarcity of money are so great at the Havannah, that the government itself is often compelled to borrow at ten per cent, and private persons give twelve or sixteen. The enormous profits of the slave trade, which amount sometimes at the island of Cuba in a single voyage to one hundred and one hundred and twenty-five per cent, have contributed much to the rise of interest, several speculators having borrowed at eighteen and twenty per cent for the purpose of that vile and execrable commerce." [33]

CUBA: OTHER AGRICULTURAL PRODUCTS

There were great increases in coffee production in Cuba by the end of the eighteenth century. Coffee exports rose from 50,000 arrobas in 1804 to 895,924 in 1823, and 661,674 in 1824.[34] These figures were lower than the actual exports because of the contraband trade. The value of coffee exported from Havana in 1815 was in excess of 3,445,000 pesos. In the average year Cuba exported about 14,000,000 kilograms of coffee and from 1818-1824 Cuba exported more than Java, which in 1823 exported 11,628,000 kilograms, or Arabia, which exported seven to eight million kilograms.

Tobacco also increased in value as a crop during the eighteenth century, the mean annual production from 1748 to 1753 being 75,000 arrobas. From 1794 to 1803, the increased attention given to coffee and sugar resulted in a drop of fifty per cent in tobacco production, but between 1822 and 1825 the mean annual production was between three and four hundred thousand arrobas.

Beeswax production became increasingly important after 1772.

[33] Humboldt, *Travels*, VII, 198-200 [*Voyage*, XI, 409-11].
[34] Humboldt, *Travels*, VII, 209-10 [*Voyage*, XII, 7-8].

The export principally to New Spain, from 1774 to 1779 was 2,700 arrobas annually and increased to 42,700 arrobas by 1803.

The following table, based upon tithes collected, shows the progress of agriculture in Cuba from 1789 to 1804.

1789-1792	792,386 pesos
1793-1796	1,044,005 "
1797-1800	1,595,340 "
1801-1804	1,864,464 "

The total agricultural exports of Havana and other ports of Cuba during the first years of the nineteenth century (about 14,000,000 pesos a year) were half of the exports of New Spain, including New Spain's precious metals, which averaged 24,500,000 pesos from 1800 to 1810. This is quite a different picture from that usually given of a colonial wealth almost exclusively mineral.

THE SYSTEM OF LAND TENURE

The system of land tenure evolved along the lines laid down in the first half century of conquest. *Encomiendas,* which were not originally intended to be outright grants of land but which frequently amounted to that, persisted, new *encomiendas* being granted from time to time. The Indians held lands in subordinate tenure. Church estates became more extensive, and there was also a class of small farmers whose holdings, based upon the grants of *caballerías* and *peonías,* were not large enough to be considered *haciendas* and who, therefore, comprised a middle class among the land owners. *Encomiendas,* at first granted for the life of the holder, were successively extended to two, three, four, five and more generations so as to become in effect permanent. They were located principally in those sections with the heaviest sedentary Indian population, and throughout the colonial period most of the *encomiendas* continued to be in those parts of Mexico, Central America, and Peru where the Indians had established stable forms of agriculture.

Simultaneously with the grant of *encomiendas,* many separate grants of land were made to the conquistadores or to individuals whom the King wished to reward for services rendered him. Throughout the colonial period, lands were granted from the *realengos,* or crown lands, or were sold or auctioned off under various schemes. Frequently it was found that the lands so granted already belonged to the Indians, or at least in part encroached upon their lands. In an attempt to guarantee honesty in the sale of land at public auction, the Crown in 1616 issued decrees to the effect

that no Indian lands could be sold. "In spite of the great precautions of the monarchs," says one author, "property, unevenly
divided in the sixteenth century, was more unevenly divided in
the seventeenth." [35]

Titles to land were granted by the *composiciones,* to which we
have already referred. By the end of the sixteenth century, it was
found that some people were holding a great deal of land in excess
of their grants, while other lands were occupied by people who had
received no grants whatever. In 1571 the King issued a royal
cédula, ordering restoration to the Crown of "all lands held by
whatsoever person . . . without just and legitimate title," but
permitting, "principally in order to favor my vassals," the existing
owners to receive title by means of the *composición.* Due care was
ordered that all lands reserved for communal uses should be respected, and that the Indians should be assigned "whatever they
need for cultivation and livestock." All other lands might be
granted through payment of a reasonable and just price. The
King permitted the cession by a *composición* of lands which had
never been occupied, "reserving always those . . . that it might
be found convenient to settle anew, and for the Indians those
that they needed and lacked for their crops and livestock."

Many *composiciones* of this type were made in the succeeding
centuries, but the lands of the Indians were not respected as
stipulated by the royal cédulas. Furthermore, the areas granted in
the *composiciones* frequently, or perhaps usually, were exceeded
to such an extent that a grant of twenty *caballerías* would be
stretched perhaps into as many as fifty.[36] These *composiciones* helped
to establish the hold of the European upon the land.

The *encomiendas* were abolished during the course of the eighteenth century, beginning with a royal order of 1720, but this
measure affected the personal status of the Indian under the law
much more than it did the land-tenure system. Although the abolition of the *encomiendas* met strong opposition from the holders,
it did not compare to the resistance offered in the sixteenth century
when the conquistadores were fighting for the possession of both
the land and the Indians. By the eighteenth century, land was
held by separate titles upon which no attack was being made,
and the labor of the Indians was easily obtained through a wage
system which bound the Indian to his master as effectively as had
the *encomienda.*

[35] Riva Palacio, *México,* II, 671-73; McBride, *Land Systems of Mexico,* pp. 50-54.
[36] Riva Palacio, *México,* II, 700-01; McBride, *Land Systems of Mexico,* pp. 56, 61.

The original order of 1720 did not include the *encomiendas* in Yucatán and Tabasco, and by various processes of delay other territories put off the abolition until the reigns of Charles III and IV at the end of the eighteenth century. The abolition of the *encomiendas* was extended to Yucatán and Tabasco in 1785. But the tendency toward concentration of land in a few hands was unchanged, remaining consistent throughout the century. Viceroy Revilla Gigedo II in his instructions to his successor dwells on the evils of land concentration.[37]

The abolition of the *encomienda* system in Chile was put into effect by Ambrosio O'Higgins, captain-general, in 1789, when it was more feasible than it had been earlier. In the entire bishopric of Santiago, which extended as far as Caucanes south of the river Maule in Chile, there were in the middle of the eighteenth century only fifty-three *encomiendas,* comprising a total of 963 adult Indians. The number had decreased for several reasons, but one of the most important was that in Chile the Indians had almost completely fused with the Europeans, forming a thorough mixture of mestizos who were not bound by the *encomienda.* The largest *encomiendas* had from 90 to 120 Indians, while some had but three or six.

Many of the *encomenderos* threatened to expel from the land the Indians they could no longer use as serfs, but O'Higgins ordered them to leave the Indians on the land and to distribute small plots which the Indians were to be allowed to cultivate for themselves. The King approved this order in 1791 and the *encomiendas* were incorporated in the crown patrimony. The land system thereby took a slightly different form, since the Indians were now established in *asientos de Indios,* where they cultivated their plots of ground, while working for wages upon the adjoining *haciendas.* They were also required to pay a municipal tax to the *pueblos* to which they were attached. These asientos evolved gradually into villages in the national period.

Many Indians remained on *haciendas,* forming with the mestizos the working class known as *inquilinos,* which had appeared as a gradual modification of the *encomienda* in the eighteenth century. Under this system, the *hacienda* sought inhabitants and workers by granting them certain rights which guaranteed their subsistence. The *inquilino* was free in theory to change his residence and his job, but gradually, as in other parts of America, this liberty was

[37] Count Revilla Gigedo, *Instrucción reservada que el Conde de Revilla Gigedo dió a su svresor* [1794] (México, 1831), pars. 406-408; 1279-1280; McBride, *Land Systems of Mexico,* pp. 60-64.

lost by the accumulation of a debt to the *hacienda,* the law preventing the *inquilino* from leaving the *hacienda* to which he was
indebted.

O'Higgins was extremely enthusiastic about the abolition of the
encomiendas, and pictured to the King a great surge of individual
initiative in response to the freedom the Indians had been given.
"The natives," he wrote to the King on August 13, 1789, "have
warmly taken to their industrial operations, and manifest a desire
to make their liberty useful and profitable, applying themselves to
agriculture and mining with the painstaking care inspired in them
by the idea of working for themselves and having their work result to their own profit." [38]

But they profited little. "The poor Indians, freed from the repartimientos, but ignorant, miserable, and discouraged, were not in a
good position to make use of the liberty granted them. They could
not suddenly change in months, or even years, the habits and ideas
resulting from the state in which they had lived; much less acquire
the feeling of order, regularity and foresight which would have
been necessary to make their work productive. The Araucanians,
as far as they were concerned, were still farther from appreciating
the advantages resulting from that reform, which in their invincible distrust they could not consider sincere, and which, moreover,
did not interest them in the least, since they preferred, above all,
the independent and savage life to which they were accustomed." [39]

At the end of the eighteenth century, the great estates owned by
a very few continued to be the salient feature of the land tenure
system. Throughout the colonies, the small and medium sized
farms (*peonías* and *caballerías*) never formed a large part of the
total agricultural areas. Some of these grew into much larger
estates, but others remained more or less the same size as the
original grant. In Mexico these small and medium sized holdings
were known as ranchos, but each colony of Spanish America had
its own name for this particular type of farm. In certain frontier
sections, such as northern Mexico or southern Chile, the proportion of these holdings tended to be much larger. In Mexico at the
end of the colonial period there were approximately 6,884 *ranchos.* [40]

CHURCH HOLDINGS

A large portion of the land of America at the end of the colonial

---

[38] Barros Arana, *Chile,* VII, 38; Domingo Amunátegui Solar, *Las encomiendas
de indíjenas en Chile* (Santiago de Chile, 1909-10), II, 227-66.
[39] Barros Arana, *Chile,* VII, 38.
[40] McBride, *Land Systems of Mexico,* pp. 88-91.

period was concentrated in the hands of the Church. Lucas Alamán, historian of Mexico during the first half of the nineteenth century, and a man who distinguished himself in his zeal for the protection of the Church, estimated that in Mexico it controlled at least half the real wealth of the country. [41] Humboldt gave the following estimate of the capital invested by convents, chapters, religious societies, and hospitals in land in Mexico:

		Pesos
Archbishopric of Mexico	....	9,000,000
Bishopric of Puebla	....	6,500,000
Bishopric of Valladolid (very accurate valuation)		4,500,000
Bishopric of Guadalaxara	....	3,000,000
Bishoprics of Durango, Monterey and Sonora	..	1,000,000
Bishoprics of Oaxaca and Merida	....	2,000,000
Obras Pías of the regular Clergy	....	2,500,000
Endowments of Churches and Communities of Monks and Nuns	....	16,000,000
		44,500,000 [42]

When the Jesuit properties were confiscated in 1767, they comprised some of the largest and most productive estates in America. In Mexico, for example, there were offered for sale to the public 128 estates which had formerly belonged to the Jesuits. [43] There is little indication, however, that these estates were broken up so as to effect a more equitable distribution of the land. When in 1804 the State ordered the liquidation of Church properties in America, the cleric, Abad y Quiepo, made a calculation of the Church wealth as compared with the total liquid capital of New Spain. [44] For the total productive capital of New Spain, he arrived at the figure of 59,000,000 pesos, taking into consideration that during the previous twenty years the population of New Spain had increased by one-fifth, the annual income by one-third, and the income of the Crown by one-half. Thus the wealth of the Church in 1804 was estimated at three-fourths of the productive capital, and there was not enough accumulated currency in the colony to pay the 44,500,-000 pesos demanded by the Crown without the bankruptcy of a large number of land-owners.

[41] Alamán, Méjico, I, 67.
[42] "Extracted from an official paper (Representación de los vecinos de Valladolid al Excelentísimo Señor Virrey en fecha del 24 Octubre del año 1805," as given in Humboldt, New Spain, III, 99, [Nouvelle Espagne, III, 287].
[43] McBride, Land Systems of Mexico, p. 62.
[44] Escrito presentado a Don Manuel Sisto Espinoso, cited in José María Luis Mora, Obras Sueltas (2 Vols., Paris, 1837), I, 100-118.

In other parts of America, the Church properties likewise formed a large proportion of the total landed wealth. In Chile, "The Jesuits alone . . . came into possession of close to sixty rural properties, some of which were more extensive than some of the departments into which the republic is divided today." [45]

LAND-HOLDING TOWNS

The land-holding towns with their collective property, whether of purely Indian origin or whether established after the Conquest, continued to be important. It has already been observed that it was part of Spanish colonial policy to form towns in which were gathered and settled the emancipated Indians, Indians under the King's encomienda, others held in encomienda by individuals, and nomadic Indians or those scattered in small hamlets. This movement became particularly marked in New Spain and Peru during the last half of the sixteenth century, and perhaps hundreds of such settlements were made.

There were three main types: towns settled by the direct order of the King or viceroy, known usually as a *congrega, congregación,* or *reducción;* towns formed around missions or monasteries, known also as a *reducción* or *misión;* and towns that grew up around military posts (*presidios*). The terms were not exclusive, however, and one settlement might partake of all three kinds. All served a triple purpose: settlement of land, mobilization of a labor force, and conversion of the Indians to Christianity. [46]

Although the nominal purpose of the missionary *congregación* was the salvation of the Indians' soul, it served in effect to give the clergy control over the land and the authority to make the Indians work it. Mechanical trades were taught; weavers, carpenters, masons, and blacksmiths were trained. Each individual had to learn some trade, but "the common trade which all had to know and be expert in was agriculture. So that the tilling of the fields had to be common to all." [47] In the "civil congregations," the Indian village was under civil authorities (directly under its own *caciques* or *curacas*), rather than the clergy, but the general economic features of the two were similar. They formed the essence of the Spanish system of land-labor control.

As the frontiers of Latin America expanded into areas previously inhabited by nomadic Indians, the land-holding town was one of the chief forms of land tenure. Along the frontiers, land would be

[45] Barros Arana, *Chile,* VII, 390-91.
[46] Toledo, *Memorial, D. I. I.,* VI, 519-37; Simpson, *Civil Congregation,* pp. 29-129.
[47] Teja Zabre, Alfonso, Guide to the History of Mexico (Mexico, 1935), p. 153.

taken up either by a mission or a *presidio* and this in many cases eventually evolved into a town with a definite organization and a distribution of the land to the *vecinos*. Many of these had much larger areas than the early sixteenth century towns, and their *ejidos* frequently comprised as much as four square leagues, where one square league was more usual in the early sixteenth century. The size of the common lands and of the individual allotments, however, depended more upon the fertility of the soil and of the available water than upon any fixed custom. In such cattle-raising regions as northern Mexico, Texas, New Mexico, and California, or southern Chile and Argentina, the town holdings would be extremely large since most of the land would be pasture. Thus we find towns with areas of from 86,400 acres to more than 200,000 acres. [48]

Throughout the colonial period the hacienda, the rancho, and the land-holding towns were in competition. Sometimes a town would encroach on the lands of the hacienda. The laws of the Indies permitted the settlement of free towns wherever the requisite number of people existed, and at times this right was exercised on property belonging to individuals. The foundation of new towns in Chile led the hacienda owners to protest vigorously to the King:

"We cannot adequately express, Your Majesty, the perturbation of the whole kingdom because of the multiplication of towns. Not only has the land selected for a settlement been lost, but also that next to it. The haciendas have no considerable products except livestock, the tallow and hides from which are marketed in Lima and Peru . . . . When anyone of these haciendas is chosen for a town, it makes it impossible to sustain and raise livestock in the midst of a community which, for lack of other means, has to avail itself of the livestock in order to subsist. The neighboring haciendas likewise suffer, because the right of transit over the roads facilitates theft . . . . All the haciendas lack servants, and thus we are all reduced to the same wretchedness, since those who formerly accepted some form of work on the haciendas have become settlers, preferring to live on their own lands rather than on the lands of others . . . ." [49]

More frequently the hacienda encroached upon the lands of the adjoining Indian or Spanish pueblo, or absorbed the ranchos in its neighborhood. This tendency did not result so much from the

[48] McBride, *Land Systems of Mexico*, pp. 103-31.
[49] Cited in Pereyra, *América española*, VIII, 136-37. Also in Barros Arana, *Chile*, VI, 183.

real need of the hacienda for more land in general, but rather from its need or desire for a particular piece of land. An especially fertile strip, or one affording an outlet to good communications, or above all, one with access to water, would be seized by an hacienda whenever a pretext could be found. If the land could not be bought outright, it would be acquired by a ruse.

Many of the land-holding towns eventually were absorbed into some large hacienda, and either lost their holdings entirely or lost effective control of them. In the other land-holding towns, a few of the vecinos who had acquired lands from the families of the original grantees absorbed all the town property. The common property of the town might still exist in theory but actually be controlled by a small percentage of the town's inhabitants, while the masses of the people were precluded by law and circumstances from owning any property whatever. The encroachment of the hacienda upon the Indian pueblos had in many cases reduced the holdings of the Indians to little if anything more than a subsistence. The occupants of the land-holding town frequently had to depend upon work on the hacienda as a means of livelihood.

Juan and Ulloa observed of Ecuador and Peru about the middle of the eighteenth century that "avarice has gradually curtailed them [Indian lands] to such a degree that the tracts which remain to them are circumscribed within narrow limits, and the greater part has been wrested from them altogether. Some Indians have been despoiled of their lands by violence; others, because the owners of the neighboring estates have compelled them to sell at any price they may choose to give; and others because they have been induced to surrender them under false pretenses." [50]

The Indians tried to defend their rights by litigation and this further impoverished them. Some authors have sought to make it appear that repeated lawsuits were one of the idiosyncrasies of the Indians, but it is more likely that the Indians, who had tried desperately to prevent seizure of their property by the conquistadores and failed appealed to the courts as a last resort against the encroachments of the European settlers.

INCREASE IN PROPERTY CONCENTRATION

In the long run, the concentration of property became progressively intensified during the later colonial period. In this, New Spain and America in general were following a line of development closely patterned on that of Spain itself. Father Mariana, historian

[50] Cited in Moses, *Eve*, p. 185.

of Spain in the seventeenth century, called attention to the accumulation of property in a few hands and demanded state action to prevent it and to require more efficient cultivation. Pedro de Valencia in the late sixteenth century directed a memorandum to Philip II in which he said: "It is necessary to furnish land to everybody who needs it, and on the other hand nobody should be allowed to hold more than he himself can cultivate."

In the mid-seventeenth century, Francisco Martínez de Mata advanced the idea that "labor was the fundamental origin of the value of all things, and all riches," and carried his idea to the point of demanding a leveling of all fortunes. For this doctrine he was prosecuted by the authorities in Sevilla about 1660. [51]

Theories about the evils of property concentration went hand in hand with a still greater concentration of that property in Spain, which it is important to keep in mind since Spain was legislating for America. From the time of the expulsion of the Moriscos in 1610 and the seizure of their holdings by the Christian landlords, if we may judge from the constant complaints to the Crown, the concentration of property increased progressively. Moreover, with the large properties went extensive privileges. An example was the Mesta, or guild of livestock breeders of Spain, whose privileges hindered the development of agriculture and prevented the small proprietor from using his own land. Stock was driven from place to place for pasturage, frequently overrunning the crops of the small farmer. The laws of the sixteenth and seventeenth centuries took special care to protect this already powerful group. "Cattle runs" through the fields were permitted and farmers were forbidden to sell pastures without selling the livestock with them, prevented from renting pastures if they had no livestock, and from plowing up pastures; they were even obliged to return to pasturage any which had been plowed. Those who were owners of no animals or of a single yoke of oxen were discriminated against, [52] and the common pastures and the *propios* of the land-holding towns became in effect the property of the nobles whose privileges were guaranteed by the Council of the Mesta. This was a system in which the have-nots were effectively guaranteed permanence in their condition.

The situation in America was similar. The livestock of the vast plains of Argentina had grown to incredible numbers. Horses, cattle, and other stock existed in a wild state, having no owners and no brands, though the cabildos sought to regulate the conditions under which they could be killed.

---

[51] Carrión, *Latifundios*, pp. 2-5.   [52] *Ibid.*, pp. 294-95.

Living in the midst of these millions of animals were a few thousand people who looked upon themselves as the owners of the herds. They held no title, but they and their ancestors had lived on the land for several generations. They had hunted and killed the wild cattle freely. In the eighteenth century, however, there had come about a "new order of things under which the lands were claimed as private property, and the herds had individual owners," and this situation "had been brought about by the decrees of persons, who, from the viewpoint of the dweller on the plains, had no right to either. Why should the favoritism of a governor deprive them of their ancient privilege of wandering or settling at will? As the generations passed and the blood of the white man flowed in the veins of the proletariat of the plains, their views remained practically unchanged." [53]

This was true of all parts of the Plata region. "Back of Buenos Aires were spread out the vast and fertile plains of Argentina, occupied by a few land-holders and the multitude of a homeless proletariat. In 1744, for 186 proprietors there were 5,897 dependents." [54] The large fortunes and estates of Argentina, which existed at the end of the colonial period and which have grown in size since that time, were not the product of the initiative or the labor of the owners. They were created by legal privileges; the owners produced nothing, paid nothing for their lands and herds, and their heaviest labor was wheedling the monarch into giving them a grant of land and livestock.

In Chile at the end of the colonial period [55] the land situation was similar. The original immense grants with vague boundaries had been somewhat subdivided. In the middle of the seventeenth century, the Jesuit historian, Alonso de Ovalle, remarked that "the lands and possession which are today [about 1650] divided among ten families, formerly belonged to one." The extremely large and indefinite early grants, the titles of which had been legalized through *composiciones,* had made the subsequent competition for land by later settlers intensive. According to Ovalle:

"The lands . . . which could be bought, as the saying goes, for a song [a *huevo*] in those times, have at present risen so

---

[53] Moses, *Eve,* pp. 96. On this point see "Bando del Teniente del Rey don Diego de Salas, Agosto 25 de 1775," in Matienzo and Torres, *Doc. Hist. Rio Plata,* I, 25-29; 239-41.

[54] Bernard Moses, *Spain's Declining Power in South America, 1730-1806* (Berkeley: University of California Press, 1919), p. 253.

[55] George McCutchen McBride, *Chile,* pp. 61-122; Helen Douglas-Irvine, "The Landholding System of Colonial Chile," *H. A. H. R.,* VIII (November, 1928), 449-95, shows the relation of the Indian land system to that of the Spaniards.

much in price that an estancia, however modest it may be, cannot be found for less than thousands in cash [*dineros*], and such is the hunger and greediness for land that there is almost no other kind of suit before the royal audiencia except over rights and possession of lands, because the early settlers, upon taking possession of a corner of a valley to which they had title, thought that the whole was theirs; and as those who arrived later also tried to establish themselves, they took new titles and new properties, which has been the cause of many law suits." [56]

Subdivision of the land progressed but little after this, however, for several reasons. The Church had already accumulated large areas, the livestock ranches required lands extensive enough to permit driving the herds from place to place so that they might have access to the best grass, and the wealthy families began to entail their estates. [57]

In Peru, Venezuela, Cuba, and New Spain, wealth was likewise unevenly distributed, although there were no fortunes in Peru comparable to some of those in New Spain. Humboldt noted that in Venezuela and Cuba "agriculture has founded more considerable fortunes than has been accumulated by the working of mines in Peru. At Lima an annual revenue of [3,333 pounds sterling] is very uncommon . . . But in New Spain there are individuals who possess no mines whose revenue amounts to [41,670 pounds sterling]." [58] Of New Spain, he says: "A small number of powerful families who live on the central table-land possess the greatest part of the shores of the intendancies of Vera Cruz and San Luis Potosí. No agrarian law forces these rich proprietors to sell their *mayorazgos* [entailed estates], if they persist in refusing to bring the immense territories which belong to them under cultivation. They harass their farmers, and turn them away at pleasure." [59]

In 1810, at the end of the colonial period, New Spain had some 3,749 haciendas of which the greatest number were in the central valley, and 1,195 *estancias de ganado* [cattle ranches], the large majority of which were in Yucatán, making a total of 4,944 great estates or latifundios. [60]

Cuba's landowning system varied only in detail from those de-

[56] *Histórica Relación del Reino de Chile y de las Misiones y Ministerios que exercita en el la Compañía de Jesús*, in *Colección de Historiadores de Chile*, Vols. XII-XIII, Bk V, chap. V.
[57] McBride, *Chile*, pp. 61-122.
[58] *New Spain*, I, 223-24 [*Nouvelle Espagne*, II, 25].
[59] *New Spain*, II, 256 [*Nouvelle Espagne*, II, 342].
[60] McBride, *Land System of Mexico*, pp. 62-64.

scribed. The essential factor was ownership by a minority and work by slaves. [61]

* * * * * * * *

The end of the colonial period found agriculture the chief source of wealth in Spanish America, the value of farm products and livestock exceeding that of the minerals, even in New Spain. The entire period had been one of expansion, the original colonies pushing beyond their early frontiers, and entirely new regions, such as Chile and the Río de la Plata, being opened up to settlement and exploitation. In the older colonies, agriculture continued to progress; in the newer ones, it became established and rapidly advanced. The real riches of all were in such products as sugar, cattle, cacao, and coffee.

But this wealth throughout the colonies was in the hands of a few owners of large estates who controlled all the best agricultural land. Encomiendas had been abolished in the eighteenth century, but the same proprietors held title to the land. The great estates had gradually encroached on the lands of the small holders and of the landholding towns. The vast majority of the people found themselves dispossessed; the laws guaranteeing the possessions of those who had property, and barring the landless from acquiring property.

[61] Duvan C. Corbitt, "Mercedes and Realengos: A Survey of Public land Systems in Cuba," *H. A. H. R.*, XIX (August, 1039), 262-85.

Mining: Development and Influence in the Later Colonial Period

HARRY BERNSTEIN AND BAILEY W. DIFFIE

THE FOUNDATIONS OF SPANISH AMERICAN mining during the sixteenth century have been discussed in an earlier chapter with the chief contributions of the epoch of the Conquest, the discovery of principal mining sites, and the invention of the *patio* process of separating silver and gold from their ores, by amalgamation with mercury or quicksilver. There were several refinements and improvements of this process during succeeding centuries, enabling the science of mining to advance in Spanish America. The Spanish were good enough technicians to develop their methods and contributed an outstanding book on mining, written by Alvaro Alonso Barba, which was translated several times into German. [1]

The first American mines to yield large amounts of silver were, as we have seen, those of Potosí in Upper Peru (modern Bolivia), and the Mexican mines at Zacatecas, Guanajuato, and San Luis Potosí. Roughly speaking, two-thirds of the mineral production from 1531 to 1660 came from continental South America, and about one-third from New Spain. This period marks the end of an era, for after 1660 the relative positions began to change rapidly, and New Spain took the lead (Table VI).

THE MINES OF PERU

Potosí was the most famous of silver-yielding mines in the Andes region, but its greatest prosperity was over before the middle of the seventeenth century. The first eleven years of its silver produc-

---

[1] Originally published in 1640, it went into the four separate German editions in 1676, 1726, 1739, and 1749. It gained wide circulation under its title *Arte de los Metales*. Pereyra, *Obra*, p. 236.

TABLE VI

Percentages of Imports into Spain by Producing Regions

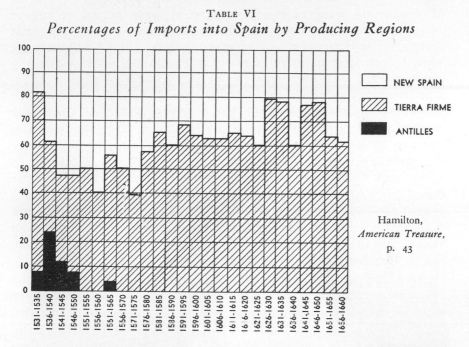

Hamilton,
American Treasure,
p. 43

tion are not included in the official tables of *quintos* paid to royal agents, but the total output for this period, 1545-1555, was probably less than 43,000,000 pesos.[2] Official statistics show that 788,258,512 pesos of eight reales were produced from 1556 to 1789.[3]

The era of the greatest production came between 1579 and 1635, when the yield sometimes reached 7,000,000 pesos a year. During this period, the mines were a veritable fountain of seemingly inexhaustible wealth. There were one hundred and forty *ingenios* for smelting the ore at Potosí in 1601. The mines supported eighty mine owners, two hundred eighty majordomos, and two hundred merchants from Spain who dealt in wholesale wares. The native labor supply consisted of thirteen thousand Indians of the *repartimiento general*, or impressed labor, and forty thousand Indians known as *aventureros*, or day laborers, who were paid at the rate of eight reales and who "stole as much more." [4] After the peak

---

[2] Clarence H. Haring, "Ledgers of the Royal Treasurers in Spanish America in the Sixteenth Century," *H. A. H. R.,* II (May, 1919), 173-187.

[3] This is equivalent to 92,736,294 marks of silver at eight and one-half pesos to the mark, and would represent 60,864,358 troy pounds. Humboldt, *New Spain,* III, 170-172; 356-360 [*Nouvelle Espagne,* III, 377-78; IV, 174-78].

[4] Felipe Fernández de Santillán, *Relaciones del estado de algunas cosas de la Villa Imperial de Potosí y cerro rico de ella. C.D.I. España,* LII, 451-453.

of production was reached in the twenty-year period ending in
1635, the output at Potosí gradually declined, until a slight rise
took place in the twenty-year period before 1789. The average
annual duty paid in to the Crown at Potosí fell from 1,217,010
pesos between 1605 and 1624, to 346,449 pesos from 1696 to 1715.
The trend was generally downward thereafter until a low of 83,410
pesos was registered for 1736. From 1737, production again rose
gradually and rather consistently to attain an average for the years
1770 to 1789 of 346,454 pesos. [5]

Other mines of importance in Peru were Pasco, discovered in
1630, and Gualgayoc, Guamachuco, and Conchuco, which were
mined after 1771. Pasco was producing about 2,000,000 pesos a
year at the end of the eighteenth century, and the other mines more
than half a million.[6] The total minted at Lima increased from an
annual average under four million pesos, 1754-1772, to more than
five million from 1797 to 1801, as follows:

1754-1772	3,628,659 pesos
1773-1791	4,496,570 ”
1792-1794	5,875,189 ”
1797-1801	5,206,530 ” [7]

The progression of gold production in Peru (not including Bolivia) indicates a steady increase through the centuries from settlement to independence, as follows:

Gold Mined in Peru

1530-1600	average annual production in ounces				11,000
1601-1700	”	”	”	”	”	16,000
1701-1800	”	”	”	”	”	17,000
1801-1810	”	”	”	”	”	25,000 [8]

Bolivia's production of silver after the discovery of Potosí in
1545 reached more than half the world output. It was not until
after 1661 that Peru proper began to produce more silver than
Bolivia, but in turn lost first place in American production to
Mexico after 1680.

[5] Compiled from Humboldt, *New Spain*, III, 356-359 [*Nouvelle Espagne*, IV, 174-77].

[6] Humboldt, *New Spain*, III, 341-347 [*Nouvelle Espagne*, IV, 154-165].

[7] This represents gold and silver coinage. See José Hipólito Unánue, *Guia Política, eclesiástica y militar del Virreinato del Perú* (Lima, 1793-1796), pp. 40 (1793), 39 (1794), 38 (1795); see also Humboldt, *New Spain*, III, 336-38 [*Nouvelle Espagne*, IV, 152-54].

[8] Bain and Read, *Ores and Industry*, pp. 280-82, 302.

MINERAL PRODUCE OF CHILE

Chilean production of metals in the colonial period did not compare in value with that of Peru and Bolivia, but nevertheless the mining industry was important enough to influence Chile's economy. By the end of the eighteenth century, her mining activities were expanding.

A mint was established in Santiago de Chile in 1749 and began to function early in 1750, coining both gold and silver. The earliest money coined was imperfect and circulated only in the territory of Chile, but these eighteenth century coins continued in circulation until the middle of the nineteenth century. The benefits rendered by the mint were noticeable from the start. The lack of specie, which had been felt before, was remedied, and Chilean commerce was carried on with the new currency. Silver and gold mining received a stimulus since miners now had a market for their precious metal without having to send it to Peru. Before introduction of the mint, the approximate annual *quinto* was 9,300 pesos; shortly after establishment it became 25,500 pesos, and in 1771 attained 30,749 pesos.

The increase of population, trade, and wealth of Chile was due in large part to the advantages of the mint and mining. A royal *cédula* of Charles III, in 1775, noted that after the Chilean mint was established there was "a considerable increase in the royal revenues from *alcabalas* and *almojarifazgos*. From the time of the conquest of that realm and the imposition of these taxes, [revenue from them] never exceeded 70,050 pesos in any single year up to 1748, and today with increased mining and consequent increase in consumption and commerce, it reaches 115,000 annually, the quantity for which they were farmed in 1772." [9]

Many contemporary statements recognize Chilean mining as one of the main factors in the economic progress of that province. A communication of the Minister of the Indies in 1788 expressed the belief that mining aided other fields of production, although the same dispatch shows that there existed a curious and erroneous idea that mining was decadent at the very time when it was daily growing more important. "It is well known," the Minister said, "that the mining industry, even in the decadent state in which it is now found, is the only support that maintains the commerce of this realm, because its [Chile's] other activities are insufficient to cover the items of its sugar and Paraguayan tea imports, the exchange

---

[9] Quoted in Barros Arana, *Chile*, VI, 193-95.

with Spain absorbing all the produce of the mines. For this special reason I conceive it to be wise to give attention to mining, and to assist and promote it in every possible manner, in addition to the ways that are customary in other provinces." [10]

In this same year (1788) the *Ordenanza de Minería*, earlier introduced into New Spain and Peru, encouraged mining in Chile. There were "more than three hundred gold mines" being worked there at the end of the eighteenth century. The total production of Chilean mines, as indicated in official figures, was steady from 1789 to 1808, the combined amounts of gold and silver coinage being approximately 850,000 to 1,000,000 pesos a year. The statistics probably do not represent the complete amount since much gold and silver escaped taxation because of contraband trade along the Pacific ocean [11] and across the mountains to Río de la Plata. "It may be calculated that silver production in Chilean mines was more than double the quantities upon which taxes were paid." [12] Humboldt estimated that Chile produced about 1,700,000 annually of gold and silver at the end of the eighteenth century. [13] Important as Chile's gold and silver were to that colony, production was small compared with that of New Spain. All the Chilean output, even according to Humboldt's estimate, would scarcely have approached in a year the silver mined in New Spain in one month.

Silver was used in Chile in many ways, as it was in the other Spanish American colonies. A reduced list of its commercial applications would include church ornaments, dishes, combs and other toilet articles, braziers, candelabra, and adornments for saints' images and church altars. Any man who did not have riding equipment of silver ornamented bridle, saddle, and silver spurs was considered of slight social significance. George Vancouver observed in 1795 that "what still more attracted our notice . . . to our surprise, [was that] the very few utensils they possessed for their most common domestic purpose were chiefly made of silver." [14] This in the midst of the utmost general poverty.

Chile also produced relatively important amounts of copper. The chronicler Carvallo stated that at the end of the eighteenth century "there [were] more than a thousand copper mines at work in Chile and more than three hundred plants for smelting and

[10] Quoted in Barros Arana, *Chile*, VI, 492-93.
[11] Barros Arana, *Chile*, VII, 423.
[12] Barros Arana, *Chile*, VII, 414-15.
[13] Humboldt, *New Spain*, III, 352 [*Nouvelle Espagne*, IV, 170-71].
[14] George Vancouver, *A Voyage of Discovery to the North Pacific Ocean and Round the World* (3 vols. and atlas, London, 1798), III, 414.

manufacturing." Chile exported copper to Peru and Spain after 1600, but the amount was limited by bad roads, the few ships available, and the great cost of transportation. Copper in bars was exported to the extent of 6000 to 13,000 quintals a year, at prices ranging from five to eight and one-half pesos per quintal. During the later part of the colonial period there was an increase, but statistics are lacking because much of it went out as contraband in North American and English vessels. Within Chile, copper was used for cannon, bells, wire, pots, vats, and buckets. Numerous copper articles for domestic and industrial use were exported to Peru and Buenos Aires. [15]

MINERAL PRODUCTION IN NEW GRANADA

New Granada was one of the leading mineral producing regions of the Spanish colonies, and of the world, although little is heard of it in comparison with Bolivia, Peru, and Mexico. The failure of New Granada (principally modern Colombia) to achieve fame is strange in view of the fact that the gold which popular fancy attributes to Spanish America, and which gave birth to the El Dorado legends, came from New Granada rather than from the other colonies, which were mainly silver producers.

The chief mining sites of New Granada were west of the main cordillera in the provinces of Antioquia and Choco, in the Cauca Valley, and near the Pacific coast around Barbacoas. Toward the end of the colonial period the Choco region produced annually about 10,800 gold marks, or more than half the total for New Granada, while Barbacoas and the upper Cauca Valley (in the region of Popayán) produced about 4,600 marks, or nearly one-fourth the total.

Almost all, if not all, the gold came from placer deposits, and much of it was mined with slave labor. That there was considerable progress in the later eighteenth century is indicated by the increase in the number of workers. In the province of Antioquia, where fewer than fifteen hundred were employed in 1770, the number had risen to almost five thousand in 1778. Choco had slightly more than three thousand at the same date, while the Cauca Valley had more than eight thousand shortly after 1800.

One of the main obstacles to greater production was the high cost, largely due to the almost inaccessible nature of some of the mining regions. One description speaks of "the province of Antio-

[15] Barros Arana, *Chile*, VII, 415-16. Chilean gold production, from 1541 to 1810, has been figured at 7,400,000 ounces; silver at 8,500,000 ounces; and copper at 83,000 tons. Bain and Read, *Ores and Industry*, pp. 210-11.

TABLE VII

Colombia—Estimate of Gold Produced 1493-1800

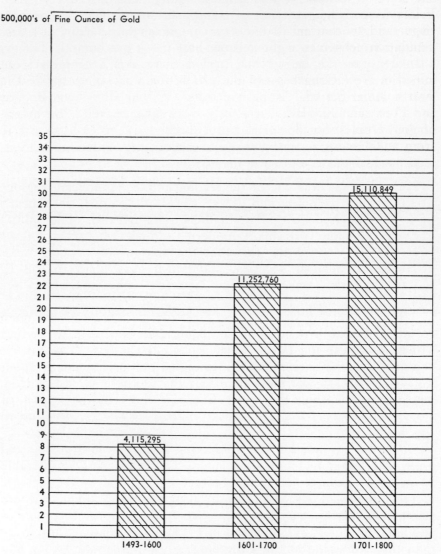

Bain and Read, *Ores and Industry,* p. 49

quia, into which one cannot enter except on foot or on the back of
a man," while in the province of Choco: "The richest country in
gold is that in which scarcity is continually felt. Inhabited by unfortunate African slaves, or Indians who groan under the despotism
of the Corregidores of Zitara, Novita or Taddo, the province of

Choco remains what it was three centuries ago, a thick forest without trace of cultivation, without pasturage, and without roads." Prices were exorbitant owing to "the enormous difficulty of carriage, and to that miserable state of things in which the whole population consumes without producing." [16]

In spite of the handicaps, significant quantities of gold were mined in New Granada, and the production was rising during the later colonial period. Mints had been established in both Bogotá and Popayán. The latter mint coined a maximum of 5,800 marks of gold from 1770-1883, and 6,830 marks equal to 928,934 pesos, from 1788 to 1794. The coinage of Bogotá was under seven thousand marks from 1782 to 1789, and climbed to an average of 8,573 marks, equal to 1,165,980 pesos, from 1789 to 1795. The over-all production had risen from about thirteen thousand gold marks in 1778 to above twenty thousand gold marks on the eve of the Wars of Independence. This was greater than the production of Brazil, which had led the world for a century after the discovery of the mines in 1694, and was approximately half of the total gold production of all Spanish America. New Granada's mining activities had shown a steady progress, in fact, throughout the colonial period, the rate of production in the eighteenth century being about 3½ times that of the sixteenth. (Table VII)

MINES OF MEXICO

New Spain was the leading producer of precious metals in America from the end of the seventeenth century. Its chief mines continued to be those discovered in the sixteenth century, to which others were added from time to time. In the last half of the eighteenth century new mines were found and opened in New Spain, as elsewhere in America. The most important fact about mineral production in New Spain for over three centuries was its progressive increase in volume.

The Mexican mint coined between its establishment in the sixteenth century [17] and the early years of the nineteenth century approximately 2,028 millions of pesos. This was about two-fifths of the entire output of America to that time. Of this sum, about 675 millions of pesos were produced before 1690, and 1,353 millions from 1690 to 1803, giving an average of more than four millions of pesos per annum for the first period and more than twelve millions for the second. In other words, the average annual pro-

---

[16] Humboldt, *New Spain,* III, 379-88 [*Nouvelle Espagne,* IV, 200-211].
[17] Arthur S. Aiton and Benjamin Wheeler, "The First American Mint," *H. A. H. R.,* XI (May, 1931), 198-215.

duction in the latter part of the colonial period was three times that in the first. Expressed in another way, the average annual coinage of metal in Mexico City was fifteen times greater in about 1800 than it had been in the period from 1537-1548, as the following table indicates:

Approximate Annual Coinage of Mexico, 1537-1803

Years	Pesos
1537-1548	1,500,000
1549-1558	2,300,000
1559-1600	3,000,000
1601-1650	3,500,000
1651-1689	4,000,000
1690-1729	6,000,000
1730-1769	10,000,000
1770-1799	20,000,000
1800-1808	24,500,000 [18]

The years of maximum production were 1796, when 25,644,000 pesos were minted in Mexico City, and 1805 when the total was 27,165,888 pesos.[19]

There were many rich mines in Mexico, distributed in a number of different intendancies, that were producing considerable quantities of metal at the beginning of the nineteenth century. In order of their volume of production they were:

Guanajuato	Intendancy of	Guanajuato
Catorce	" "	San Luis Potosí
Zacatecas	" "	Zacatecas
Real del Monte	" "	Mexico
Bolaños	" "	Guadalajara
Guarisamey	" "	Durango
Sombrerete	" "	Zacatecas
Tasco	" "	Mexico
Batopilas	" "	Durango
Zimapan	" "	Mexico
Fresnillo	" "	Zacatecas
Ramos	" "	San Luis Potosí
Parral	" "	Durango

Most of these mines produced a small amount of metal, the

[18] Table compiled from Riva Palacio, *México*, II, 686, and Humboldt, *New Spain*, III, 289-94 [*Nouvelle Espagne*, IV, 95-104].

[19] Humboldt, *New Spain*, IV, 369 [*Nouvelle Espagne*, V, 187].

greater part coming from the provinces of Guanajuato, San Luis Potosí, and Zacatecas which supplied more than half of New Spain's metals.[20] The amount produced at Guanajuato was superior in volume to that of any other American mine, even though Potosí in Peru had greater fame. Whereas average annual production of Potosí was about two and one-half millions during the eighteenth century, that of Guanajuato was approximately 4,727,000 pesos in a thirty-eight year period, from 1766 to 1803. At the beginning of the nineteenth century, the Guanajuato mines were still yielding more than one-fourth of all Mexican silver output, and one-sixth of all American silver.

Produce of Guanajuato 1766-1803

Years	Total Production Pesos	Average Annual Output Pesos
1766-1775	30,320,503	3,032,050
1776-1785	46,692,863	4,669,286
1786-1795	48,682,662	4,868,266
1796-1803	39,306,117	4,913,265 [21]

The Valenciana mine in Mexico had first been worked in the sixteenth century, abandoned, and reopened in 1760. From 1771 to 1804, production averaged almost 3,000,000 pesos annually. It employed about 3,100 "men, women and children." Some years were so productive that profits for the owners amounted to more than a million pesos. Silver mines in the Freiberg district of Germany earned profits that came only to one-twelfth of those of Valenciana.[22]

The Purísima mines in the Catorce district yielded a net profit of around 200,000 pesos annually after 1778, and in 1796 produced 1,200,000 pesos, with a working cost of only 80,000 pesos. In 1762, one Pedro Tereros reopened the Biscaina Vein and drew a

---

[20] Humboldt, New Spain, III, 118; 137-39 [Nouvelle Espagne, III, 312; 111, 336-37].

[21] Humboldt, New Spain, 111, 175-76 [Nouvelle Espagne, III, 379-82].

[22] Humboldt, New Spain, III, 193-201 [Nouvelle Espagne, III, 406 ff.]. The Valenciana accounts from 1794 to 1802 were itemized as follows:

Total produce of sales of minerals .... 13,835,380 pesos
Cost of Production .... 8,046,063 pesos
───────────
Net profits to shareholders .... 5,789,317 pesos

Over the nine year period this indicated an annual net profit of some 640,000 pesos for the shareholders. The shares of this mine were so divided that the Count of Valencia (who was one of the original owners by the name of Obregón) owned 10 shares, the Otero family (another original owner) held 12, and the Santana family owned 2, of a total of 28 shares.

profit of more than five million pesos (£1,041,750) by 1774; he was granted the title of Conde de Regla.[23]

Throughout the colonial period, the idea existed that American mines were so rich that minerals came in almost pure form. The truth is quite the contrary. American ores were poorer on the whole than European ores, and the amount of metal produced in the New World resulted rather from vast deposits than from rich ores. The Director of Mines of Mexico, Fausto de Elhuyar, familiar with German and Spanish production, found that a quintal of Mexican ore which contained some 16,000 ounces, yielded only three to four ounces of silver. José Garcés y Eguia, who studied the Zacatecas mines, stated that "the great mass of Mexican ores is so poor, that the three millions of marcs of silver produced annually by the kingdom in good years are extracted from ten millions of quintals of mineral, partly smelted and partly amalgamated." This gives a production of two and two-fifths ounces of metal per quintal of ore.[24] In comparison, the yield of the famous *Obergebirge* mines in Germany was as much as ten and fifteen ounces from each quintal. The great volume of silver ore compensated for its quality, although costs of production and machinery were higher in Mexico than in Europe.

MERCURY AND MINING

Mercury production affords one of the best indices of the trend of silver and gold mining, since there was a direct connection between amounts of mercury used by gold and silver miners and the total of precious metals that were being extracted. The crown itself used the consumption figures for mercury as a check in determining the quantity of gold and silver output.[25] A considerable amount of mercury came to the New World from the mines of Almadén in Spain, but after 1570 the Peruvian mines at Huancavelica produced much of the quicksilver used in Spanish America. Between 1570 and 1807, more than 1,096,000 quintals of mercury were mined from Huancavelica, as indicated in the following table:

Huancavelica Mercury Production in Approximately
Thirty-Year Periods, 1570-1807:

Years	Quintals
1570-1601	177,787
1601-1630	126,623

[23] Humboldt, *New Spain*, III, 212-18 [*Nouvelle Espagne*, IV, 4 ff.].
[24] Quoted by Humboldt, *New Spain*, III, 162-75 [*Nouvelle Espagne*, III, 364 ff.].
[25] Whitaker, *Huancavelica*, pp. 6-7.

1630-1660	165,499
1660-1689	140,920
1689-1718	107,538
1718-1748	130,518
1748-1778	154,386
1778-1807	93,063

1,096,334 [26]

Huancavelica produced from four to six thousand quintals of mercury each year. The best years were between 1586 and 1589, when annual output averaged 10,500 quintals. A standard was fixed at the end of the seventeenth century by a contract between the viceroy (for the government) and the *gremio de mineros* (miner owners guild). The agreement lasted from 1683 to 1744, and called for an annual production by the miners of 6,820 quintals of mercury. This quantity amounted to fifteen per cent more than Peru's needs of 6,000 quintals, and more than the average annual production for the ten years immediately preceding the signing of the contract. The level agreed upon was difficult to attain, and almost impossible to maintain, because of administrative difficulties, wars, earthquakes, and the profits sought by the government on one hand, and the mining guild's monopoly on the other.

From 1689 to 1701, average production dropped from the high of a century before to 4,544 quintals; it went down further to 3,000 quintals from 1701 to 1728, but rose again to almost 5,000 under the influence of reforms in mining policy from 1729 to 1758. As management reforms continued, production mounted to 6,300 quintals from 1759 to 1768. The peak years of eighteenth-century mercury production in Peru were 1763 and 1768, when the output was 9,824 and 12,492 quintals respectively. Thereafter, mercury production in Peru went into a decline which continued to the end of the colonial period and into the present time. Mercury yields fell to 1,619 quintals in 1788. There was a brief spurt to 6,112 in 1800, but afterwards the downward trend was resumed.[27]

[26] "Razon del Azogue entrado en estos reales almacenes desde septiembre del año en que empezó a trabajarse de cuenta del real erario, la real mina de Huancavelica, hasta el de 1790." [Supplemented by the chart: "Estado de lo que produjo desde 1791 hasta 1813."] Manuel de Mendiburu, *Diccionario histórico-biográfico del Perú formado y redactado por Manuel de Mendiburu.* (2nd ed., 11 vols., Lima, 1931-35), VI, appendix 5.

[27] Mendiburu, *Diccionario,* VI, appendix 5; Whitaker, *Huancavelica,* pp. 12-18 and *passim.*

The failure of Huancavelica to supply the needs of the Potosí and other silver mines of Peru did not mean the shut-down of the mines. What Huancavelica did not produce had to be brought from Almadén in Spain, by way of Panama and Lima in the sixteenth and seventeenth centuries, and through Buenos Aires after the middle of the eighteenth century. Naval wars added to the cost of transportation imposed by long distances, yet the Crown found that the cost of Almadén mercury to the Potosí miners was lower than the price maintained by the Huancavelica contract. At the same time, the quantity of Spanish-produced mercury reaching Peru was apparently less than Peruvian needs, with the result that New Spain, almost always supplied from Almadén, began to exceed Peruvian production during the eighteenth century.[28]

The amount of precious metals produced also depended upon the price and quality of the mercury which was available. New Spain at the beginning of the nineteenth century used annually some 16,000 quintals of quicksilver, while all of Spanish America required 25,000 quintals. The price of quicksilver varied greatly and there was a close relationship between the quantity used and the market price, as the following table shows:

Mercury Consumption, 1762-1782

Period	Price of Mercury (per quintal) pesos	Total Mercury Consumed quintals
1762-1766	82	35,750
1767-1771	62	42,000
1772-1777	62	53,000
1778-1782	41	59,000

During the Viceroyalty of Luis Velasco II, in 1590, the price of quicksilver per quintal was 187. pesos. The price was fixed in 1750 at 82 pesos by the Crown which monopolized its sale, and between 1767 and 1776, its price was 62 pesos the quintal. In 1777, the price of Almadén (Spain) mercury was set at 41 pesos and 2 reales, and German mercury at 63 pesos. The higher price of Germany's mercury caused mine owners to avoid buying it whenever possible.[29]

This situation in turn led to favoritism in the distribution of mercury by the Crown officials. As one contemporary writer remarked:

---

[28] Humboldt, *New Spain*, III, 314-15 [*Nouvelle Espagne*, IV, 126-27].
[29] Humboldt, *New Spain*, III, 281-86 [*Nouvelle Espagne*, II, 87-90].

"The impartial distribution of mercury (*el repartimiento del azogue*) is of the greatest consequence for the prosperity of the mines of New Spain. So long as this branch of commerce shall not be free, the distribution should be entrusted to the *Tribunal de Minería* which alone is able to judge of the number of quintals indispensably necessary to the amalgamation works of the different districts. Unfortunately, however, the viceroys and those persons who are about them, are jealous of the right of administering this branch of the royal revenue themselves. They know very well that to distribute mercury, and especially that of Almadén, which is one third cheaper than that of Idria, is to concede a favour; and in the colonies as everywhere else it is profitable to favour the richest and most powerful individuals. The result of this is that the poorest miners, those of Tasco, Temascaltepec or Copala, cannot procure mercury when the great works of Guanajuato and Real del Monte have it in abundance." [30]

TOTAL GOLD AND SILVER PRODUCTION

At the end of the colonial period, New Spain was producing more than half the total value of the gold and silver mined in America, with Peru and the Viceroyalty of Río de la Plata (mainly Bolivia) in second and third places, far behind. Brazil occupied fourth place, her production being almost exclusively gold, as disclosed in the following table:

Annual Production by Political Divisions at the Beginning of the Nineteenth Century

Political Divisions	Gold		Silver		Value in silver pesos
	Marks of Castille	Kilo-grams	Marks of Castille	Kilo-grams	
Viceroyalty of New Spain	7,000	1,609	2,338,220	537,512	23,000,000
Viceroyalty of Peru	3,400	782	611,090	140,478	6,240,000
Captaincy General of Chile	12,212	2,807	29,700	6,827	2,060,000
Viceroyalty of Río de la Plata	2,200	506	481,830	110,764	4,850,000
Viceroyalty of New Granada	20,505	4,713	....	......	2,990,000
Brazil	29,900	6,873	....	......	4,360,000
Total	75,217	17,291	3,460,840	795,581	43,500,000 [31]

Taking the colonial period as a whole, however, South America produced more than New Spain. Approximately two-fifths (or

[30] Humboldt, *New Spain*, III, 284 [*Nouvelle Espagne*, IV, 90-91].

[31] The silver was valued at 9.4 pesos to the mark, and gold at 145.82 to the mark. Humboldt, *New Spain*, III, 394. Production given here is same as European imports in table below, although some gold and silver remained in America.

slightly less) of the precious metals between 1492 and 1803 may be attributed to New Spain, while the Viceroyalty of Peru produced more than two-fifths and Brazil nearly a fifth. The remaining fraction was produced principally in the gold washings of Colombia. The regional origins, and the respective amounts produced during the colonial period by the principal divisions of Latin America were as follows:

Regional Sources of American Metal Production, 1492-1803

	Pesos	Pesos
New Spain	2,028,000,000	
Peru and Buenos Aires	2,410,200,000	
New Granada	275,000,000	
Chile	138,000,000	
Spanish Colonies		4,851,200,000
Portuguese Colonies		855,500,000
Total		5,706,700,000 [32]

What is more remarkable is the production of Latin America in comparison with that of other parts of the world in this epoch of three centuries. By about 1800, approximately ninety per cent of the world's gold and silver was being produced in Latin America, as follows:

Annual Produce of the Gold and Silver Mines of Europe, Northern Asia and America

	Gold		Silver		Value of Gold and silver in francs
	Marks of France	Kilo-grams	Marks of France	Kilo-grams	
Europe	5,300	1,297	215,200	52,670	16,171,888
N. Asia	2,203	538	88,700	21,709	6,677,333
America	70,647	17,291	3,250,547	795,581	236,353,667
Total	78,147	19,126	3,554,447	869,960	259,202,888 [33]

The effect of American precious metals was all the greater because of the progressive increase throughout the three centuries. Fluctuations occurred, naturally, and the output of some of the mines dwindled in the later period, but what was lost in one place was made up in another, and an ever swelling stream of metal poured into world economic channels. An illustration of this may be seen in the following table, which shows the approximate annual imports from America into Europe of gold and silver from the discovery of America to 1803:

[32] Humboldt, *New Spain*, III, 420 [*Nouvelle Espagne,* IV, 244].
[33] Humboldt, *New Spain*, III, 420 [*Nouvelle Espagne,* IV, 244].

European Imports of American Precious Metals, 1492-1803

Period	Pesos (per annum)	Remarks
1492-1500	250,000	From West Indies
1500-1545	3,000,000	Period of "Spoils" and early Spanish mining
1545-1600	11,000,000	Spanish discovery and development of Potosí (Bo_livia), Zacatecas, and Guanajuato (Mexico)
1600-1700	16,000,000	Potosí (Bolivia) declines, mines of New Spain increase; discovery of Yauricocha (Peru) and placers of Barbacoas and Choco (Colombia).
1700-1750	22,500,000	Brazil gold production at height, new Mexican mines and new veins at old sites (Biscaina, Batopilas, Sombrerete).
1750-1803	35,300,000	Tasco, Valenciana, Catorce (Mexico), and Gualgayoc (Peru)
About 1803	43,500,000	Spanish and Portuguese colonies [34]

IMPROVEMENTS IN MINING SCIENCE

The application of scientific technique to mining underwent considerable improvement in Latin America towards the end of the eighteenth century. The Crown, interested in mining revenues and the economic prosperity of its possessions, encouraged the scientific study of minerals, and went so far as to employ European mining engineers to go to America in order to direct and advise mine operators on improvement of methods.

Latin America had developed its own interest in mining engineering and studies. In Mexico, producers grouped together to organize the School of Mines under the direction of Fausto de Elhuyar. The School was located in the capital, Mexico City, and was to become one of the foremost institutions of mining science in the western hemisphere. Instruction was offered, and laboratories and libraries were maintained. The School of Mines served as the intellectual and research center for the mining experts who were sent to Mexico.

Elhuyar was among the most prominent of these. An internationally known mining authority and the discoverer of tungsten, he had been commissioned by the Crown to apply to Mexican mining the newly discovered amalgamation process of separating silver from the ores, which had been invented by the Austrian, Born. Elhuyar was named Director-General of Mexican Mines, and also appointed superior to Baron von Nordenflicht, head of the group which went to the Peruvian and Bolivian mines. Elhuyar and Nordenflicht left Spain for their respective destinations in 1788.[35]

When Humboldt reached Mexico, it was Elhuyar and his equally

---

[34] Humboldt, *New Spain*, III, 433-34 [*Nouvelle Espagne*, IV, 259].

[35] Arturo Arnaix y Freg, "D. Fausto de Elhuyar y Zubice," *Revista de Historia de América*, No. 6 (Mexico, 1939), pp. 75-96.

famous instructor at the School of Mines, Andrés del Río, who guided the Prussian scientist to the mines of Mexico. "Baron von Humboldt worked in the laboratories of the School of Mines, seeking the chemical composition of unusual mineral species. Don Fausto, won over by the encyclopedic knowledge of Humboldt, invited him to give a course . . . in the School. His lectures were printed by the Mining Tribunal, and Humboldt dedicated the work to his Mexican students." [36]

It was Elhuyar's "Reflections on the working of the mines and Refining Operations in the Real de Guanajuato," issued in 1789, which first indicated his estimate of Mexican mining methods and science. His studied opinion was that Mexican metallurgy was adequate to the type of ore found in New Spain:

> "This appears most clearly in his discussion of the relative merits of the established *patio* process of amalgamation and the new Born process, the introduction of which was one of the main purposes of his mission. After a close study of this problem at Guanajuato, he concluded that each of these processes had certain advantages over the other; that the Born process was superior for high grade ore, which was rare at Guanajuato, but of more doubtful value for low grade ore, which was abundant there, and that the problem required further study in the other mines of Mexico." [37]

Elhuyar remained in Mexico throughout the colonial period, returning to Spain after the revolution to become Director-General of the Spanish mines. It should be noted that his New Spain mission was only part of his services: he engaged the experts for the mission to Upper Peru, and advised his brother who went to New Granada in a similar capacity.

The work of Baron Nordenflicht in Peru was assisted by trained metallurgical experts, whose purpose was also to investigate the suitability of the Born process of amalgamation to the ores of the Andean region. Although, in general, the Bolivian ores were not as high grade as the European ores, to which the new process could be applied most readily, Nordenflicht did introduce reforms into the Potosí region before 1793. [38]

[36] *Ibid.,* pp. 84-85.

[37] Arthur Preston Whitaker, "More about Fausto de Elhuyar," *Revista de Historia de América,* No. 10 (December, 1940), 125-130.

[38] *Mercurio Peruano de Historia, Literatura y Noticias Públicas que da a Luz la Sociedad Académica de Amantes de Lima,* y en su nombre Jacinto Calera y Moreira (Lima, 1791-1795), volume VII, January-April, 1793, numbers 216, 217.

MINING AND ECONOMIC PROGRESS.

The effects of mineral production upon general economic growth, which have been described in Chapter VI, were just as marked in the later colonial period. As average production rose during the colonial era, purchasing power, both domestic and foreign, also rose progressively. During the eighteenth century especially, the Latin American colonies afforded an enlarged market for manufactures from an expanding Europe. The Spanish and Portuguese settlements were more than ever the "El Dorado" of European drama. Much, though by no means all, of Latin American wealth was owed, indirectly even more than directly, to gold and silver production in the colonies. It is not difficult to agree with the Mexican writer who pointed out that "every one of the principal mining sites was a center of prosperity for the country and a source of great revenue for the Treasury."[39]

Mining undoubtedly was the magnet which attracted settlers either to work the mines, or to profit by selling, purchasing, or transporting necessaries and foodstuffs for the miners. In eighteenth century Mexico the effect of opening a new mine was to repeat the process of settlement which characterized Latin American economy. When, in 1749, the Bolaños mine was discovered, the then Viceroy, Conde de Revilla Gigedo, informed his successor of the extent to which agriculture and manufactures served the miners and supported economic life:

"What happened everywhere mines were discovered also occurred at this mine: crowds of people came from all over the kingdom, and in a short while a large town was established. Since the land here is fertile, watered by great rivers, near mountains and woods, which will support herds and agriculture, it [the settlement] promises stability."[40]

To a corregidor sent to Bolaños in 1755 Viceroy Revilla Gigedo pointed out the link between the mining, agricultural, and manufacturing interests:

"You will take care to clear all roads leading to and away from the town and maintain roads to neighboring communities in order to facilitate transport of commodities. You will take into account the project formed by several Bolaños citizens to open a more direct and shorter road to Mexico City, in order

[39] Alamán *Méjico,* I, 99.
[40] "Informe del Conde Revilla Gigedo sobre el Real de Minas de Bolañas," in *Instrucciones que los Virreyes de Nueva España dejaron a sus Sucesores* (Mexico, 1867) p. 54.

to bring silver to the Mint. Because if this should be successful, commerce would be greatly eased, and would be beneficial to the inhabitants there." [41]

The mining industry of Upper Peru gave equally great stimulus to widespread trade in agricultural and manufactured products. During the eighteenth century, Potosí was the center of much economic activity that radiated to Arequipa and Arica on the Pacific, Salta, Jujuy, and Tucumán in Northwestern Argentina, and to Cuzco and Lima in Peru proper. Jujuy was the principal source of supply for Potosí miners who were consumers of meat, candle-tallow, and grease-fat. Thousands of mules were sold to Potosí miners by Tucumán and Buenos Aires ranchers. The trade with Córdoba, Argentina, for mules and cattle amounted to nearly 600,000 pesos annually, and most of it went by way of Salta into Upper Peru and sometimes into Cuzco. Inhabitants of Tucumán manufactured carts from *Quebracho* wood, and the mule trade engaged the energies of hundreds of contractors, drivers, and buyers, who traveled from Arequipa, bringing Huancavelica mercury to Potosí. The mule trains returned with the silver from the mines.

Potosí and other mining towns in Upper Peru consumed goods and foods from the sea, the Argentine grasslands and hills, and from the Bolivian valleys. Oruro, like Potosí, was supplied from the fertile Cochabamba valley. "Sugar, wine and liquors, olives, raisins, almonds come from a great distance and are sold at moderate prices because the great demand has stimulated supply, and hence a low price for most of the year." [42]

Peruvian cities grew wealthy or poor as their regional products were affected by the prosperity or poverty of the mines. By no means was all Peruvian production marked for export through Lima. The town of Chucuito, situated on the Bolivia-Buenos Aires road, acquired great commercial importance for supplying not European but rather domestic products. Cuzco sold hand worked textiles to Potosí, and the southern Peruvian port of Arica rose to a position of first-rank importance because of the volume and value of its trade with the Andes mines. The introduction of the fairs of

---

[41] *Ibid.,* p. 54.

[42] Calixto Bustamante Carlos Inca [Concolorcorvo], *El Lazarillo de ciegos caminantes desde Buenos Aires hasta Lima con sus itinerarios según la mas puntual observación, con algunas noticias útiles a los nuevos comerciantes que tratan en mulas; y otras históricas.* [First printed, Gijón, 1773]. *Biblioteca de la Junta de Historia y Numismatica Americana,* (Buenos Aires, 1908), IV, p. 179. New ed. in *Biblioteca de cultura peruana,* vol. 6, Paris, 1938.

Ayacucho in south Peru, helped to give greater solidity to this regional commerce, which rested upon the mining interest.[43]

*   *   *   *   *   *   *   *

The swift increase in mining production in the eighteenth century, the improvement in technique through the work of the scientists sent by the Crown, the commercial reforms of the eighteenth century, and the rapid development of agriculture were all parts of one whole which added up to substantial economic growth for the colonies during the last century before independence. The influence of mining on this progress was notable. The location and purchasing power of the mines had supplied the original impetus for the entire economy. At the end of the colonial era, while mining was still prosperous, agriculture, manufacturing, and trade were lusty enough to have a significance of their own as independent sources of wealth and strength for Latin America.

[43] Emilio Romero, *Historia económica y financiera del Perú: antiguo Perú y virreinato* (Lima, 1937), pp. 202-205.

Evolution of Manufacturing
and Trade

By Harry Bernstein and Bailey W. Diffie

W HAT LATIN AMERICA MANUFACTURED, bought, and sold revolved largely around her agriculture, ranching, and mining.
Most of what was used by the common man, the vast majority
working on the land or in the mines, was made in America; and
most, though not all, goods which came from abroad were within
the purchasing power only of the well-to-do who owned the greater
part of the land and the mineral wealth.

Spain's Policy on Colonial Manufactures

Latin America's economic evolution during the three centuries
of her colonial life was necessarily a part of the larger world
economic development usually described under the names of the
Commercial Revolution and the Industrial Revolution. To these
revolutions Latin America made an important contribution, but
her own development was at the same time largely conditioned by
the pace of events beyond her own control. Thus it was that the
acceleration of world demand (mainly European) for Latin American products increased purchasing power, gave birth to new industries or stimulated the old, promoted expansion and increase
of the population, and caused Latin America to experience a
quickened economic life during the last century of the Colonial
period.

Within this world framework, Spain was forced to mold her own
economy, albeit constantly working under conditions that could
not be entirely of her own choosing. Her colonies were perforce
a composite of what Spain would have them be and what outside
conditions made them. The true picture of colonial economic life

cannot be drawn from Spain's designs; for that, it is necessary to sketch in the extralegal and illegal economic activity.

But it should not be inferred that Spain's restrictions on her colonies were unusually repressive for the times. True, colonial commerce was conducted under the monopoly ideas characterizing commerce for many centuries, but domestic manufactures were less hampered by restrictions in the Spanish colonies than in those of the French and English. In other words, the monopolistic tendency was not so pronounced in manufactures as in trade. Among the many possible reasons for this, we may single out the fact that, while manufacturing was done in small establishments by men of modest means (Latin America like Europe being still in the handcraft stage until the event of power machinery late in the eighteenth century), trade was carried on by wealthy merchants who could persuade the government that its best interest was coincident with their own.

Spain's colonial policy regarding manufactures varied, however, from time to time. Frequently, the Crown demonstrated a tendency to promote manufactures instead of placing them under handicaps, although this characterized the earlier colonial era, rather than the later. During the eighteenth century, some Spanish economists advocated policies which would have prevented American manufacture of all goods produced in Spain, or capable of production in the mother country. Among these items were woolens, linen, silk, iron, steel, copper, tin-plate, brass, and all types of hardware. Peninsular writers complained that otherwise production of the Indies eliminated the demand for Spanish imports. Mexico, they said, produced enough materials to satisfy the needs of its Indian and middle price consumers. Other Spanish writers disagreed, and proposed the encouragement of manufacture everywhere in the Empire, since that would bring benefits for the whole. Increase of production would augment Spanish and Spanish-American population, and widen the market for all goods.[1] Some Spanish economists held that Spain's policy compared very favorably with that of other nations:

"Critics of our colonial system may say what they will, there is something, even a great deal worthy of praise in the policy of Spain towards its colonies. While England drove the mechanical arts from its possessions, we had manufactories of coarse cloth in the vice-royalties of Mexico and Peru, silk looms in Puebla

---

[1] Colmeiro, *Economía política,* II, 395-396, citing Campillo, Ward, Ulloa, and Mora y Jaroba.

in New Spain, sugar centrals in Española and other places; agave and cotton were processed, and above all flax and hemp in Chile where our South Sea fleet was equipped with ships' stores and sails." [2]

This should not be taken to mean, however, that Spanish commercial and manufacturing laws did not reflect a mercantilist spirit. Spain was forced to pursue a double objective with regard to her American colonies: 1) to permit the Indies to manufacture, and 2) to try to confine their trade to Spanish merchants in the Peninsula. For instance, the textile industry in America was allowed to prosper. Although new *obrajes* were forbidden after 1774 (apparently, the ban of 1598 had little effect), the number of factories continued to increase, and their cloth production was considered to be of rather high quality. Many towns in America drew their revenues from the weaving of cottons and woolens. The Viceroy of Mexico, Count Revilla Gigedo II, however, warned the home government and his successor in 1794 against too great an extension of manufacturing in New Spain:

"One should not lose sight of the fact that this is a colony which should be dependent on the Spanish motherland, and compensate her with some returns for the benefits it receives from her protection. Thus great skill is necessary to interweave this dependency so that it will make interests mutual and reciprocal, which would cease to be the case the minute the manufactures and products of Europe were not needed here." [3]

The Spanish policy on the whole was restraint, without elimination, of colonial manufacturers. Undoubtedly, America was a "hewer of wood and drawer of water" to Spain, but there was still considerable room for domestic manufacture of cotton, woolen, and leather goods, metal wares, and other consumer goods, as well as for industries such as shipbuilding. The dualism of Spanish tolerance and restriction can be seen from a review of the attitude of the Crown toward colonial manufacturing.

During the sixteenth century, a royal decree of 1548 had authorized the inhabitants of Puebla to produce silk without restrictions. As we have seen, the silk industry in Mexico became a thriving one in the early colonial period, and there was an exportable surplus of woolen cloths as well. The Crown's order in 1565 that "In the Indies the laws and ordinances of this kingdom of Castile

---

[2] Colmeiro, *Economía política,* II, 396-97.
[3] *Instrucción,* par. 364.

shall be observed in the manufacturing of cloth," [4] would seem to indicate that textile producers in America were on the same legal plane as Spaniards.

Laws regulating manufacture which applied to America did not originate precisely from a political-economic theory that Spain should confine colonial activity to Peninsular benefit. They were shaped by the pressure of various economic groups, whose interests sometimes conflicted. Mercantile and manufacturing interests both petitioned the Crown, seeking advantages for one at the expense of the other. At the same time, the Crown attempted to avoid colonial and Spanish competition within like categories of production. For example, in 1569, Philip II instructed Francisco de Toledo, then leaving for Peru as Viceroy, to close down all textile mills producing a quality of goods similar to those manufactured in Spain. Toledo found that the demand for textiles in Peru was much larger than the amount Spain could supply, and he therefore did not carry out his orders. Instead, in 1577, he published *ordenanzas* (ordinances) regulating manufacture and Indian labor conditions. Manufacturers were permitted to produce as much cloth as they desired, and of any quality. In 1596, Viceroy Luis de Velasco again found it impractical to enforce decrees similar to those received by Toledo. Factories in operation were allowed to continue, but could not be expanded, nor new ones introduced without royal consent.

One unique factor in the Toledo-Velasco legislation for Peru was the long-lived policy which exempted factories run by Indian caciques from these restrictive ordinances. Although Toledo introduced humane principles in the treatment of Indian workers, there was little in Spanish policy which curbed the extraordinary domination by the caciques of their own people. It might be said that the segregation of the Indian community from the Spaniards in America delivered the workers into the hands of their own employers, and favored Indian factories over those owned by Spaniards. In 1601, the Crown prohibited Peruvians from employing Indians in any type of workshop—a policy which tended to raise wages in Spanish factories, and was therefore opposed until modified.

Generally speaking, it is obvious that the difference was great between royal orders and compliance, but there has been much disagreement as to the influence of Spanish law upon American economy. It has been contended that Spanish restrictions effectually stifled colonial economic development, but also that evasions were

---

[4] Quoted in Haring, *Trade and Navigation,* pp. 126-127.

so frequent as to nullify the intent and effect of the legal restrictions. The production and commerce which existed in the colonies were sufficient to demonstrate that the policy of Spain did not succeed in suppressing domestic enterprise. But on the other hand, while strict enforcement of the legal provisions would have curtailed manufactures and trade more than they actually did, the growth of American economy cannot be attributed entirely to illegal activity.

As a matter of fact, much Spanish legislation which has been interpreted as prohibitory, did not have that intent. The home government, acting on the theory that the Crown should promote, license, and authorize economic activity, and constantly besieged by conflicting economic interests in Spain for favors, adopted the policy of closely superintending all economic action. Thus the Crown took for granted the right to license many types of production, and licensed them for production and merchandising in the colonies. Had domestic manufactures not been permitted, the majority of the people of Spanish America would have been without necessities, since they could not afford to buy goods of European origin.

MANUFACTURES AND DOMESTIC TRADE: THE WEST COAST

Basic manufactured articles, supplying the fundamental needs of food, shelter, and clothing, were made almost everywhere in Latin America, as we have already seen, and many regions produced specialities. Ecuador was an important producer of textiles, with factories at Riobamba and La Tacunga, where woolens, baize, coarse frieze, and cotton were woven. Textiles were also made at Ambato. In the middle of the eighteenth century, Juan and Ulloa remarked: "In former years, the woolen manufactory was confined to the province of Quito; but it has recently been introduced into other districts, although articles manufactured in provinces south of Quito are nothing but coarse cloths of very ordinary texture." [5]

The textile industry in Quito declined or was moved to other centers, however, during the eighteenth century partly on account of foreign competition, but also because of a commercial interest in encouraging imports into the region. Don José Garrido León, head of the Quito *Audiencia,* tried to introduce a policy which would restore the cloth factories to their earlier prosperity. He suggested a 25 per cent reduction in the volume of cheaper foreign imports coming on the register ships around Cape Horn, and a

---

[5] Quoted in Moses, *Eve,* 180; Pereyra, *América española,* VI, 187-201.

doubling of their duty. The vested interests of the Lima *Consulado* took issue with this proposal of the Quito president, stating that the former demand for cheap Ecuadorean cloths had given way to appreciation of finer European cloths, due to larger importation. [6].

In Peru, there were many looms for weaving cotton in Cajamarca, and the Indians continued their handcrafts. Lima listed among the occupations of its inhabitants, in the first half of the seventeenth century, tailoring, shoemaking, carpentry, silversmithing, and other crafts. [7] But Lima derived its principal wealth from the land or from imports and exports, not from manufactures. A few shops and merchants dominated its trade, which was largely in luxury goods imported from all parts of the world.

Chile was the center of important tanning, leather, textile, and metal-working industries. Tanning and leather work was carried on around Santiago, but principally in the south on the Maule River, where the great abundance of *lingue* afforded excellent material for tanning the skins of goats and cattle into cordovans and shoe soles. A considerable proportion of the hides was sold in Peru and Buenos Aires, the rest being made into shoes and other leather goods for Chileans.

Textiles were manufactured throughout Chile, but mainly for home use. Methods were primitive since crude looms were employed. Yet, in the province of Chillán, some four hundred miles south of Santiago, one hundred thousand *varas* of colored cloth were produced and sold to Chilean merchants, who disposed of it in the capital city. The Indians participated in this type of manufacture, which was characterized by the Domestic System, in which the principal profits were earned by merchant-entrepreneurs. This system depended for its success on restricted competition from the outside, and suffered from foreign rivalry in the late eighteenth century. On the whole, Chile's manufacture existed as rudimentary handcrafts, probably similar to those in other parts of America, or even of Europe, except where workmen were more highly skilled. [8]

In colonial Chile, as in other parts of America laws regulated the craft guilds. No workman could participate in production and exercise his craft without being a member of the guild. After 1789, Charles IV greatly modified the guild system, giving workmen in the textile factories the right to change, invent, or imitate new pro-

---

[6] Ricardo Cappa, *Estudios críticos acerca de la dominación española en América,* (7 vols., Madrid, 1889-1891), VII, 198.

[7] Means, *Fall,* 240-241.

[8] Barros Arana, *Chile,* VII, 404.

cesses as they wished without adhering to previous restrictions. The Crown also decreed that any workman might operate a textile mill. A later ordinance provided that it was not necessary to belong to craft guilds, and some of these, such as the twisters and spinners of silk, were abolished. [9]

Production in Chile, as in other parts of America, was hindered by problems of transportation, communication, and distribution. In the north there was a thousand miles of desert and in the east the Andes, both of which challenged the best efforts of man. Land travel was so difficult that the chief trade was seaborne. Chilean commerce with Peru was carried on in ships owned by Callao shippers, who were at the same time purchasers of Chilean products. They exercised a sort of monopoly due to the handicap of transportation, and together with the warehousemen, controlled Chilean Pacific trade. The sea trip between Chile and Peru required about one month each way, and constant naval warfare increased its hazards, and added high freight rates to the price of goods. [10] Yet, in spite of monopolies, a small external market, and the difficulties of communication and transport, Chile had made considerable commercial and manufacturing progress by the end of the colonial period. There was an active overland trade with Buenos Aires. Chile-Argentine trade amounted to about one-half million pesos a year, compared to Chile-Peruvian trade which reached two million pesos a year at the end of the colonial period. For most of the eighteenth century, much of what is now western Argentine (Mendoza and Cuyo), were Chilean provinces linked to the Pacific by a trans-Andean road. Many Chilean exports were manufactures, including soap, tanned skins, wrought copper, steamboilers, copper buckets, and large copper tanks used for butchering and vintage. Chilean imports included Paraguayan mate and woolen rugs or blankets. There was also a middleman trade in Negroes, who were sent on to Peru from Buenos Aires.

MANUFACTURES AND DOMESTIC TRADE: RIO DE LA PLATA

Río de la Plata industry and trade were based largely on the vast livestock herds, but included forest and farm products, while the importation of foreign goods stimulated some industries. The settlement of Buenos Aires after 1580 helped to give Paraguay

[9] Barros Arana, *Chile,* VII, 404-410.

[10] Humboldt, *New Spain,* IV, 15-16. Cf. "Relación por método alfabético comprehensivo do los géneros, frutos y efectos nacionales y extrangeros de Europa, Asia, Peru, Ultramarinos y del Reyno de Nueva España de frecuente entrada y consumo en Mexico," printed July 3, 1792, in *Papeles varios sobre administración, aduanas, aranceles* . . . (6 vols., Madrid, 1730-1823), II, No. 6

and western Argentina an Atlantic outlet for their products, and also to furnish them with a center for receiving goods from the outside. There was a rivalry between Córdoba, the center of western Argentine trade, and Buenos Aires, the hub of Río de la Plata trade. Córdoba, in 1716, was still the site of the customs house for goods going overland to Peru, and claimed that Buenos Aires was given undue preference by being allowed to trade with Potosí without having to pay the duty levied on merchandise passing through Córdoba. [11]

Buenos Aires gradually won recognition from the Crown as a logical point for trade in southern South America, in spite of opposition from the Sevilla-Panama-Lima monopoly. The location of Buenos Aires at the mouth of the Río de la Plata had a profound effect upon colonial and modern Argentine history. The river was an important means of communication and trade, tapping the drainage basin and watershed of southern Brazil, Uruguay, Paraguay, western Brazil, and Bolivia. In 1602, the Crown granted Buenos Aires authority to trade with Brazil, Guinea, and "adjacent islands," but not with other parts of the Indies or overseas and only in certain enumerated products. This permission, first given for six years, was extended three years, and reissued at other times. It was limited to vessels of a hundred tons, which might stop and buy in Brazil when en route to Sevilla. [12]

By 1610, there were some two hundred ships a year in the Portugal-Brazil-Río de la Plata trade. Buenos Aires had become an important contraband center by 1622. Goods moved overland to Chile, western Argentina, Upper Peru and Potosí, and even to Lima. [13] Trade between the Río de la Plata and Peru was fairly active, although statistics are lacking. Many mules, so essential to overland transport, were bred and marketed in the Plata region. The line of communication ran northwest from Buenos Aires to Lima by way of Córdoba, Santiago del Estero, Tucumán, Salta, Jujuy, Oruro, La Paz, Cuzco, and Huancavelica. [14]

Paraguay exported woods, tobacco, and mate, used throughout South America as tea, and imported wrought iron, metal tools, textiles, musical instruments, images, and weapons. There was also an overland trade from Paraguay to Mendoza and Chile, by way

---

[11] Roberto Levillier, *Antecedentes de la política económica en el Río de la Plata* (2 vols., Buenos Aires, 1915), I, 360-361.

[12] José Gutiérrez de Rubalcava, *Tratado histórico, político, y legal del comercio de las Indias Occidentales* (Cadiz, 1750), pp. 111-115; D. I. I., XVIII, 323-328.

[13] Gutiérrez de Rubalcava, *Comercio de las Indias*, pp. 209-227.

[14] Concolorcorvo, *Lazarillo de ciegos caminantes*, pp. 57, 99; Pereyra, *América española*, IV, 116-118; Moses, *Eve*, 326-327.

of Santa Fé on the Paraná River. Uruguay, then an administrative province of the Viceroyalty of La Plata, was an economic competitor of Argentine ranchers and merchants. The great development of livestock in this region, and the trade of Montevideo in hides, salt meat, and tallow have already been noted. Montevideo became a commercial center, distributing goods to the whole river region, as well as to western Argentina.

Throughout the Río de la Plata region, considerable internal trade existed in wines, hides, textile fabrics, mate, and mules. Córdoba, Salta, and Jujuy became jobbing centers for overland commerce, while Tucumán produced wagons and carts. There was, however, a setback in the internal trade as it became economically cheaper during the eighteenth century for Buenos Aires and Montevideo to receive goods by water rather than overland from western Argentina. Mendoza wines could not compete with foreign wines; Corrientes, Córdoba, and Catamarca textile production declined; and Tucumán rice cost more in Buenos Aires than did Brazilian. [15] This cost differential provoked disputes between the interior cities (Córdoba, Santa Fé, Tucumán) and Buenos Aires. Their fear of Buenos Aires was deep-seated, and destined to furnish the Plata region with its most troublesome politico-economic problem of the nineteenth century, during and after the Independence struggle.

MANUFACTURES AND DOMESTIC TRADE: THE CARIBBEAN AND
    NEW SPAIN

In the Caribbean area, in addition to agricultural products and the numerous handcrafts practiced in all the colonies, and which contributed to industry and commerce, there was an active trade in salt meat (*tasajo*) shipped from Venezuela to Cuba as food for large numbers of Negro slaves. Salt works were in operation in Venezuela during the sixteenth century, and possibly even before, although Indians used comparatively little salt. In 1799, the annual consumption of salt in two Venezuelan provinces, Cumaná and Nueva Barcelona, amounted to some four million pounds, or sixty pounds per capita, in comparison to an annual individual average in France of twelve or fourteen pounds. This gives an index to the amount of salt meat cured in Venezuela. [16]

Cuba carried on a flourishing trade, not only with Venezuela, but with Campeche and Buenos Aires.

A number of cities of New Spain prospered from the manufac-

---

[15] Pereyra, *América española*, IV, 211-212.
[16] Humboldt, *Travels*, II, 248-254 [*Voyage*, II, 321-326]

ture and processing of *géneros de la tierra,* which included various types of textiles from cottons or woolens, and other articles made of domestic raw materials. On the whole, production was of low quality, and finer goods were imported for the upper classes from France, England, Germany, and China. [17] The once-active silk industry had now almost completely decayed, as it could no longer compete with imported products.

Guadalajara manufactured cotton and woolen cloth. Before 1765, this region had sent its raw products to Puebla, Querétaro and San Miguel el Grande to be processed there. Factories in Guadalajara, Lagos, and other towns of that province wove cottons and woolens, made soap, and tanned hides. The oldest cloth establishments in Mexico were in Téxcoco. Saltillo was a manufacturing metropolis for the northern area.

Most weaving was not done in large factories or establishments, but on numerous small looms scattered through such towns as Puebla, Cholula, Huexochingo, and Tlaxcala. Puebla gave employment to about 1,200 weavers of cotton cloth. The printing of calicoes, both those manufactured in Mexico and those imported from the East, was another important industrial occupation of Puebla. For almost the entire colonial period, the town of Puebla was one of the centers of manufacturing prosperity. Both in Puebla and Querétaro, the ownership and operation of the textile factories was in the hands of mestizos and Indians. There were two different types of cloth works, the larger of which were called *obrajes,* and the smaller, *trapiches.* [18]

The city of Puebla was long noted for its manufacture of hats, many of which were exported by way of Acapulco to Peru. The city was also foremost as a center of chinaware, although at the beginning of the nineteenth century production had declined because of the competition of European ware which could be brought in at a low price. In 1793 there were 46 factories in Puebla which produced *delftware,* but by 1802 there were only 16, and but two which manufactured glass. This decline was so far from being the result of a restrictive policy laid down by Spain, that the falling off of production followed the reforms of the eighteenth century.

Some of the products which were manufactured in New Spain came under a royal monopoly. Among the most important of these was tobacco. The tobacco factories were located chiefly in Querétaro and Mexico City. Paper for cigarettes and cigar wrappings

---

[17] *Papeles varios,* II, no. 7.

[18] Humboldt, *New Spain,* III, 460-463 [Nouvelle Espagne, IV, 290-294].

was not produced in Mexico but came from Spain, and continuous production was sometimes affected by the lack of supply, especially during wars. Royal monopoly extended to manufacture of powder for firearms, munitions and mining. Illegal manufacture of powder on the far-flung ranches and haciendas was considerable. [19]

An important agricultural product useful to manufacturing was the maguey plant. It served as a rope fiber, in the construction of native huts, and especially for the alcoholic beverage, *pulque*. The plant was processed for these different purposes largely within the present state of Hidalgo. The fiber was made into ropes and cables for the mines, especially the nearby Pachuca mine. It was also in great demand for straps and tie-ropes in transport. [20]

Pulque from the maguey plant brought large revenues to the Crown and hacendados. From 1781 to 1790 the royal revenue in pesos from the imposts on pulque amounted to 8,734,088, the highest average since the reforms of José de Gálvez in New Spain. [21] The Conde de Regla, a Mexican mining magnate, who had speculated in the seized lands of the Jesuits of New Spain, devoted his estates to the production and sale of pulque. Large scale producers also owned chains of taverns and pulque stations where the drink was sold. [22]

At the end of the eighteenth century the value of all manufactures of New Spain was estimated at seven or eight million pesos annually, as compared with a mineral value of approximately 25,000,000 pesos, and an agricultural production of 30,000,000 pesos. [23] While these figures for manufacturing are probably at the minimum, it is fairly certain that in colonial Mexico, factory production had less importance than cattle raising, agriculture, commerce, and mining. Although wars and maritime isolation gave impetus to the production of Mexican minerals and textiles, peace time eliminated some of the incentive, and renewed imports of many manufactures from Spain and Europe.

New Spain's interior trade consisted of the distribution of manufactures imported through the two chief ports of Vera Cruz and Acapulco, in addition to the inland exchange of domestic articles between the different provinces of Mexico. Moreover, there was an importation of the products of other colonies, such as Peru,

[19] Humboldt, *New Spain*, III, 63-470 [*Nouvelle Espagne*, IV, 294-300] Lillian Estelle Fisher, *The Background of the Revolution for Mexican Independence* (Boston, 1934), 171.
[20] Miguel Othón de Mendizábal, "La Evolución agropecuaria en el Valle del Mezquital" *Investigación económica*, I (México, 1941), No. 2, p. 165.
[21] Mendizábal, *ibid*, chart, p. 182.
[22] Mendizábal, *ibid*, 188-189.
[23] Humboldt, *New Spain*, III, 460 [*Nouvelle Espagne*, IV, 290].

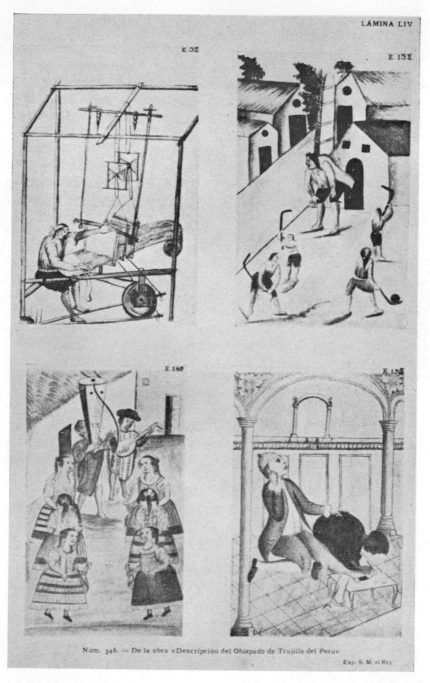

Núm. 346. — De la obra «Descripción del Obispado de Trujillo del Perú»

Exp. S. M. el Rey

Courtesy of the Hispanic Society of America

FROM THE BOOK "DESCRIPCIÓN DEL OBISPADO DE TRUJILLO DEL PERÚ"

COLONIAL SILVER WORK, MEXICO, 18TH CENTURY

GILDED BED, PERU

Ecuador, Guatemala, and the Caribbean. Some of these goods were distributed within New Spain, and others passed in transit on the way to Europe. Of particular importance was the internal commerce stimulated by the production of the Mexican mines, the influence of which upon the trade of New Spain was vital. [24] Agricultural and manufactured materials were sent throughout the Viceroyalty, even to Santa Fé in New Mexico, then a province of New Spain. There was a regular wagon train between New Mexico, Sonora, and Chihuahua.

Ship Building

Spanish America was forced to rely in large part upon sea rather than land routes for distribution of goods, especially along the Pacific Coast. Consequently, ship building became an essential industry, particularly at Panama and Guayaquil. From the time of Balboa, caravels and brigantines were constructed along the Pacific shore, for the most part at the port of Panama. During the sixteenth century, ships of from 60 to 175 tons were built there annually. In the first century and a half of Spanish American settlement, ships were built at Havana, and their artillery was cast at local foundries in Cuba. In 1638, a royal cédula (decree) granted to shipbuilders of Havana, Campeche, Puerto Rico, Jamaica, and Santo Domingo all the privileges granted to Spanish yards. Ten years later, similar privileges were extended to all America. [25]

One of the largest and most important shipyards in Spanish America was located at Guayaquil, in Eucador. Units of the Spanish Pacific fleet were constructed in the Guayaquil yards, which could produce vessels capable of carrying sixty cannon. [26] Spanish American officials in a position to know, considered the wealth derived from the Guayaquil yards as equal in importance to that from Oruro, Potosí, Huancavelica, and other mines. Dionisio de Alcedo, an outstanding servant of the Crown in that part of America, in the early part of the eighteenth century called the Guayaquil shipyard "better than any in America, and superior to the most famous in Europe, because of its location on the coast, and the nearness of mountains with woods that are durable." [27]

The shipping industry stimulated allied occupations. Manta

---

[24] Humboldt, *New Spain*, IV, 12-14 [*Nouvelle Espagne*, IV, 342-345].

[25] Haring, *Trade and Navigation*, pp. 266-268.

[26] Cappa, *Dominación española*, VI, 170.

[27] Dionisio de Alcedo y Herrera, *Compendio Histórico de la provincia, partidos, ciudades, astilleros, ríos y puerto de Guayaquil en las costas de la Mar del Sur* (Madrid, 1741), chap. IV "De la Descripción de los Astilleros," 18-26. Alcedo was one time President of the Quito Audiencia, and Captain-General of that district.

manufactured ship supplies, and ship chandlery developed as trade along the Ecuadorean coast. Pitch and tar came from Guatemala; a large supply was held by merchants in Guayaquil warehouses, while henequen fiber for ship ropes came from Chile. Punta Elena was another advantageous site for shipbuilding, but was too attractive to illicit traders.

At Buenos Aires a shipbuilding industry sprang up to supply vessels needed in her river traffic. All kinds of boats were built, ranging from the *barco,* which could accommodate about 15,000 arrobas of goods, to the smaller *piraguas, canoas,* and *balsas.*[28] The *balsa* and *piragua* were modeled upon Indian river vessels, which held cargo and men, and could hold sail, being well adapted to river navigation.[29]

STATUS OF DOMESTIC MANUFACTURES AND TRADE IN GENERAL

It may safely be said that geographical and physical conditions in Latin America had more influence upon the development of manufactures than the policy of the Spanish home government. Certain natural disadvantages of terrain, communication and distance affected the supply of goods coming from abroad, or from the rest of America. Widespread distribution of manufactured products depends on access to markets, and low-cost transport. For the most part, these conditions were unfavorable. The majority of New Spain's population, for example, lived in the central valleys of the interior plateau, which had to be climbed from the Pacific or Caribbean direction. The cost of transport from Acapulco and Vera Cruz handicapped importers, and favored internal duplication of products by manufacture in Mexico.

The tablelands of Colombia were in the interior of the country, and a journey of several days up the Magdalena or Cauca Valleys was necessary to reach the populated cities. To transport goods to the highlands of Central America, or the interior of Venezuela, Ecuador, Peru, or Argentina required an arduous, risky, overland trip, the cost of which frequently drove the price of imports above that of the local manufacturer. Maritime, coastal transport on the Pacific was affected by the contrary direction of the winds and currents along the west coast.

Thus, while the home government at times legislated against certain colonial manufactures, and the Spanish merchants sought to influence colonial legislation to suit their own ends, the important

[28] Pereyra, *América española,* IV, 121-125.
[29] Georg Friederici, *Die Schiffahrt der Indianer.* Studien und Forschungen zur Menschen-und Völkerkunde (Stuttgart, 1907), pp. 16-26.

fact remains that domestic manufacturing inevitably supplied the majority of the people with most of their everyday necessities.

INTERNATIONAL TRADE: PACIFIC OCEAN

American foreign trade flowed from three major sources: The Philippines, and the Orient, Spain and Europe in general.

Trade between the Pacific Coast of America and the Far East began in the latter half of the sixteenth century. There was much opposition to this commerce since it aroused the fears of the Sevilla monopolists, and competed with the silk industry in Spain. The privileges of Spanish monopolists secured them protection, and restrictive legislation was passed in 1587 to prevent trade in Chinese silks and cloths between Mexico and Peru. At about the same time, direct trade between the Philippines and South America was also forbidden.

There were important international problems connected with the development of Spanish Far Eastern commercial policy. From the beginning, Spanish discoverers, navigators, and merchants were concerned with eliminating Portuguese competition in the trade with China. Manila became a center of great commercial activity. Peru, after 1591, was allowed to import Oriental goods only by way of New Spain, and was eliminated as a direct trader with the East, as were Panama and Guatemala in 1593 and 1595, so that Mexican and Manila merchants shared between them the great profits of commerce with the Orient. The merchants after 1593 were permitted to employ two ships a year, not to exceed three hundred tons each in capacity in the Manila trade. They could import 250,000 pesos of Oriental goods into New Spain and return to the Philippines with 500,000 silver pesos.

During the first quarter of the seventeenth century, an attempt was made to develop trade between the Spanish at Manila and Acapulco, and the Japanese. Peaceful methods were agreed on, and a commercial mission left Japan for Mexico and Spain. Both the Japanese policy of isolation and the opposition of the Sevilla merchants rendered these efforts useless, with the result that the participation of Japan in the Mexico-Manila trade of the Pacific declined after a flurry of interest and activity. [30]

The town of Acapulco was the clearing center for New Spain's Oriental trade. [31] It was south of Mexico City some three hundred

---

[30] Zelia Nuttall, "The Earliest Historical Relations between Mexico and Japan. From Original Documents preserved in Spain and Japan," *University of California Publications in American Archaeology and Ethnology,* IV, (April, 1906), 4-6.

[31] Vito Alessio Robles, *Acapulco en la historia y la leyenda* (Mexico City, 1932), p. 37.

and twenty-five miles by mule train. Its harbor was excellent, and the town entertained hundreds of merchants when the world-renowned fairs were held on the arrival of the Manila galleons. [32]

The amount of trade consistently exceeded that allowed by law. By about the beginning of the seventeenth century, New Spain shipped more than two million pesos a year to be exchanged for Oriental goods. Some of these imports into New Spain were reshipped to Peru in spite of the natural and legal difficulties. Reexport to Peru brought into Mexico such large amounts of Peruvian silver that at the end of the seventeenth century there were more Peruvian than Mexican pesos in circulation in New Spain. In 1697, for example, two Peruvian ships brought more than two million pesos to Mexico.

The extent of contraband was the chief preoccupation of the authorities. Among the efforts to stop it was the establishment of a customs house in Acapulco in 1646. Even the fulminating power of the Church was directed against smuggling: in November 1657 the archbishop Sagade Bugueiro, who "tried to remedy everything by means of excommunications," published a major excommunication against the contrabandists of silk. [33]

Appeals for authorization of a larger amount of legal trade persisted, and in 1734 the amount was raised to 500,000 pesos, and a million pesos for the return journey. [34] Commerce increased in spite of all laws, and in some years as many as five galleons unloaded cargo for the Fair at Acapulco. In 1784 the prohibitions and restrictions were repealed, and in 1785 the Crown sponsored the creation of the Royal Philippines Company, a Spanish monopoly, capitalized at 8,000,000 pesos divided into 32,000 shares of stock held by the Peninsular monopolists. [35]

Trade was so great that it brought into China the use of the Spanish silver dollar, which was the basis of Chinese currency down to the middle of the nineteenth century, when it was replaced by the Mexican dollar. [35a] By the end of the eighteenth century the tonnage of the galleon to Manila had been increased from 800 to between 1,200 and 1,500 tons. When the California way-stations were established, the return journey was reduced from five or six

---

[32] The laws regarding the Philippine trade are given in N. A. N. Cleven, *Readings in Hispanic American History* (Boston, 1927), pp. 287-330.

[33] Riva Palacio, *México*, II, 676.

[34] Haring, *Trade and Navigation*, pp. 144-149.

[35] Alessio Robles, *Acapulco*, p. 89; William Lytle Schurz, "Mexico, Peru, and the Manila Galleon," *H.A.H.R.*, I (November, 1918), 389-402, and Schurz, *The Manila Galleon* (New York: E. P. Dutton, 1939).

[35a] Anita Bradley, *Trans-Pacific Relations of Latin America* (New York: Institute of Pacific Relations, 1942), p. 5.

months time, to three or four, and the vessels were more seaworthy. Cargoes consisted of printed calicoes, muslins, raw silks, coarse cotton shirts, China-silk stockings, spices, jewelry from Manila or Canton, and aromatic oils. Return cargo was composed of iron and silver, New Spain cochineal, Guayaquil cacao, wine, oil, and Spanish wool. [36]

TRADE WITH SPAIN

Most of Latin America's trade with Europe continued to be conducted through Spain by means of the convoy system, although there was an ever larger number of *registros,* or ships which were granted special permission to sail without convoy. [37] The number of ships returning from America was usually smaller than those inbound, since return cargoes were of much greater value for their bulk, requiring less space. There is no full account of all the vessels in the various fleets but those returning from Nombre de Dios from 1585 to 1603, numbered between 32 and 94.

The number of ships in seventeenth-century fleets was less than in the sixteenth, probably because an increase in ship capacity permitted fewer ships to carry more goods. Tonnage is frequently mentioned as one hundred tons or even less during the sixteenth century, whereas vessels of two and three hundred tons or more were customary in the seventeenth; and in 1628, a royal decree forbade construction of vessels over five hundred and fifty tons for the American trade, because such ships were too large for the harbors. Total convoy tonnage of the Indies fleets trading between America and Spain in the seventeenth century was about ten thousand tons per convoy with approximately two-thirds going to New Spain. [38]

The condition of the fleet trade may be judged from the following figures: there were fifteen *flotas* sent out to Vera Cruz from 1565 to 1600; sixty-six *flotas,* from 1601 to 1699, of which forty-four *flotas,* or sixty-six percent of the total, sailed during the first half of that century, and twenty *flotas* from 1706 to 1776, a period of frequent international war and privateering. [39]

The *registro* ships supplemented the convoys and account in part for the smaller number of convoys in the eighteenth century. In 1642, a decree granted to any Spanish vessels the right to sail for America without license from the Council of the Indies provided

---

[36] Humboldt, *New Spain,* IV, 70-81 [*Nouvelle Espagne,* IV, 404-416].

[37] Trade regulations as they were about 1570 are revealed in "Gobernación temporal y espiritual," Bk. VII, in *C.D.I. Ultramar,* vol. XXV.

[38] Haring, *Trade and Navigation,* p. 212; Cappa, *Dominación española,* VII, 78; Means, *Fall,* 225.

[39] Miguel Lerdo de Tejada, *Comercio exterior de México desde la conquista hasta hoy* (Mexico, 1853), appendix I.

they sailed in groups or with the regular convoy fleet. They had
also to pay a tax on tonnage. The ports of destination indicate a
considerable activity in the Caribbean outside of Vera Cruz, Portobelo, and Cartagena. *Registros* entered Havana, Honduras, Campeche, La Guaira, and Gibraltar on Lake Maracaibo, where they
paid a tonnage tax of two silver ducats. Ships bound for Margarita,
Nueva Córdoba, Santa Marta, Cumaná, and Río de la Hacha paid
one and one-half silver ducats. Ships to Española and Puerto Rico
paid one silver ducat, and for some minor ports, they paid no tonnage tax whatever. The continuance of these register ships is indicated by the taxes collected. We also learn from the increase in
taxes that other ports were among those to which ships might sail.
The list includes, aside from those already mentioned, and for
which the taxes were raised, Trinidad, Tabasco, and Buenos Aires.
These vessels, known as *registros sueltos,* must not be overlooked
in considering the total tonnage of American trade during the seventeenth and eighteenth centuries. [40] Many ships came to America
without payment of license, or discharged cargo in ports to which
they were not assigned. [41]

One of the best indications of the value of American trade and
its distribution may be seen in a contract between Spanish merchants
and the Crown in 1660, concerning the funding of the *avería* tax.
This tax formed the basis of collection of moneys with which to
organize and build the Royal Spanish Navy to protect Indies trade.
The tax had previously been collected on a percentage basis, or was
farmed out. [42] In 1660, however, a royal decree permitted importation of gold and silver from America without a declaration at the
Casa de Contratación, and exempted Indies products from customs,
avería, and other import duties. In exchange, American firms engaged in trade were to subsidize the royal treasury as follows:

Merchants of Peru	350,000	ducats
" " New Spain	200,000	"
" " New Granada	50,000	"
" " Cartagena	40,000	"
Royal Exchequer	150,000	"
TOTAL	790,000	"

Although revised in 1667 to throw a proportionate share of responsibility upon the Andalusian merchants, the table adequately

[40] Haring, *Trade and Navigation,* p. 87.
[41] *C. D. I. Ultramar,* XII, 17-18.
[42] Haring, *Trade and Navigation,* 78-80.

shows the importance of American trade, and the larger share held by the merchants of Peru at this time. [43]

ILLEGAL FOREIGN TRADE WITH AMERICA

The complete picture of trade with America must take in foreign shipping as well as Spanish fleets and register ships. Trade by English, Portuguese, French, and Dutch ships was always an important factor in the commerce of America.

THE DUTCH

The Dutch entered the Indies trade during the last half of the sixteenth century, while fighting for independence from Spain. When Philip II became king of Portugal as well as of Spain in 1580, the Dutch centered their attacks upon both Spanish and Portuguese possessions. They established direct trade with the East Indies (several important islands fell to them) and at the same time began an active commerce with the Spanish-American colonies in the Caribbean. [44] Before 1600, the Dutch had penetrated the Spanish Main. In 1605, an armada of fourteen Spanish vessels attacked and burnt nineteen Dutch ships which were loading salt. The number of the Dutch vessels indicates the scale of their trading and raiding efforts, since the regular Spanish fleets which put in at Cartagena, Portobelo, and Vera Cruz were sometimes not much larger. The Dutch introduced cargoes of Negroes and textiles, purchasing gold, silver, pearls, and salt in exchange. Their trade in cocoa and tobacco amounted virutally to a monopoly up to the time of the incorporation of the Caracas Company in the eighteenth century. The colonists paid for Dutch purchases with hides, indigo, coffee, and sugar, (about 3/5) and gold and silver (about 2/5). [45]

The Dutch West India Company was established in 1621, to perform for American trade the same profitable service which the Dutch East India Company was effecting for the Far East. With the support of the Dutch government and capital, great fleets of war and merchant ships entered the New World, setting up Dutch rule in Brazil and the Caribbean offshore islands. After 1625, the Dutch came as colonizers. The island of Curaçao came into Dutch possession in 1634, giving them a center from which trading ships went out to various Spanish Caribbean colonies, and Dutch armadas sailed to attack Spanish fleets. Profit from raids was sometimes larger than profit from trade; in 1628 the Dutch commander, Piet

---

[43] Haring, *Trade and Navigation*, 80-82.
[44] Irene A. Wright, "The Dutch and Cuba," *H.A.H.R.*, IV (November, 1921), 597-634.
[45] Haring, *Trade and Navigation*, 118-119; Moses, *Eve*, 315.

Heyn, captured thirty Spanish merchant vessels, seizing goods and bullion to the extent of fifteen million Dutch guilders, and enabling the Dutch West India Company to pay a dividend of fifty per cent.[46]

THE ENGLISH

The English, who came as traders and privateers in the sixteenth century, established themselves in the West Indies during the seventeenth century.[47] The preliminary activity of Raleigh and Gilbert developed into organized settlement by joint-stock enterprises, occupying the islands leading to the strategic Bahama channel, and establishing English rule on the mainland of North America, particularly in Virginia.[48]

The British conquest of Jamaica in 1655 gave them an outpost of great importance and commercial value, from which they could dominate the flow of trade into the Spanish Main and the neighboring logwood country of Campeche, Yucatán, and Honduras. Jamaica became the starting point of numerous trading and contraband expeditions. At the same time, sugar plantations were flourishing on the island, and during the eighteenth century Jamaica sugar production rivaled that of Brazil and other sections of America.[49]

From the mid-seventeenth century, England's imperial position in America was second only to Spain's. After the restoration of the Stuarts to the British throne in 1660, peace was established between England and Spain. The treaty signed at Madrid in 1670, called, "A Treaty for Composing of the Differences, Restraining the Depredations and Establishing Peace in America between the Crowns of Great Britain and Spain," merely postponed settlement of the question of trade with America. The Spanish refused to legalize British trade with the Indies, although the treaty did confirm English title to Jamaica. The establishment of English factors, agents, and traders was permitted in Spain, where they could ship goods through the Andalusian monopolists of Sevilla-Cádiz. On the other hand, the British persisted in trade demands, constantly seeking commercial concessions or instructing governors in America to persuade or force Spanish-American local authorities to sanction trade.

The Treaty of Madrid in 1670 was supposed to have outlawed

[46] Haring, *Trade and Navigation*, 234-239.
[47] Juan Pérez de la Riva, "Inglaterra y Cuba en la primera mitad del Siglo XVII," *Revista Bimestre Cubana*, XXXVI (July-October, 1935), 50.
[48] Irene A. Wright, "Spanish Policy toward Virginia, 1606-1612," *American Historical Review*, XXV (1920), 448-479.
[49] Haring, *Trade and Navigation*, 244-248.

piracy and contraband, but there is little doubt that contraband trade with Spanish-America continued to grow rather than decline, and that the increased commerce with foreigners was beneficial to the colonies. The type of semipiratical trade is well illustrated in the life of William Dampier, an Englishman who spent many years in America. In 1675, he sailed from England to Campeche where he engaged in log cutting. He was back in America in 1679, and participated in an attack on Panama, 1680-1681, "because there are much Goods brought that way from Panama; especially when the Armado lyeth at Portabell." [50] The whole of Dampier's *Voyages* in America is a running commentary of privateering, piracy, attacks on Spanish-American towns, plunder, burning, and pillage, narrated in a matter-of-fact tone that indicates how normal such aggression was to the age.[51]

THE FRENCH

The French were no mean rivals of Britain in the international textile trade, the race for colonies, the competition for trade with the Indies and for political and commercial influence in the Iberian peninsula. British predominance in Portugal was based on treaties of the fourteenth and seventeenth centuries, and the Methuen Treaty of 1703 which gave British merchants unusual opportunity for trade with Brazil. The purpose of French merchants was to employ royal inflence in Spain to acquire parallel influence in Spanish America.

French colonies in America were as strategically located in the Caribbean and Gulf, close to Spanish settlements, as was possible. Joint stock companies were organized in France to populate French colonies and derive great profit from contraband trade with America. Shortly after England seized Jamaica, the French, through their West India Company, took possession of the western end of the island of Española. The French (and others) justified their conquest of Spanish colonies by alleging that the settlements were languishing because of trade restrictions, and that the invaders were bringing prosperity to abandoned lands.[52] Another French-owned island, Tortuga, became, like Jamaica, a center of piracy up to the end of the seventeenth century.[53] The French interest in Indies trade was intense and was supported by the

---

[50] William Dampier, *Dampier's Voyages*, John Masefield, ed., (2 vols., London, 1906), I, 57
[51] *Ibid.*, I, 1-291.
[52] Pierre François Xavier de Charlevoix, *L'Isle Espagnole ou de St. Domingue* (2 vols., Paris, 1730), I, 480-482.
[53] Charlevoix, *L'Isle Espagnole*, II, 77-359.

merchants of St. Malo, Nantes, La Rochelle, and Bordeaux, and the textile producers of Rouen, Lyons and Cambrai, who were in competition with the English.

During the reign of Louis XIV, French squadrons stood off the Andalusian coast to protect French ships, forcing the Spanish to submit to French contraband. The French Ambassador at Madrid received the following instructions in 1679:

"And as regarding the execution of all the points contained in the present instructions, His Majesty is convinced that aside from reasons of justice, equity, and conformance with treaties, it is necessary that the Spaniards understand that he has the means to uphold his rights by the exercise of his power, if they do not want to do it. His Majesty desires that the said Marquis of Villars be informed that he will always have at sea strong squadrons of vessels along the shores of his own kingdom and of Spain, and even in the islands of America and the Gulf of Mexico, which will often appear either at the port of Cádiz at the departure or the return of the fleets, or along their route when they set out from the ports of America, in order that His Majesty may take whatever measures he shall deem necessary for the good of his service." [54]

The French commercial interest in Spanish-American trade had serious political repercussions in Europe, plunging rival powers into the War of the Spanish Succession. English fears of French trade expansion into the Indies were considerably justified, even before the Bourbons ascended the Spanish throne. In 1680, Louis XIV sent a French admiral to America to visit Santo Domingo and Cartagena to obtain useful information for French trade promotion in the Caribbean. French joint-stock companies colonized Cayenne, attempted to settle within the jurisdiction of Brazil, and tried to occupy the Straits of Magellan. French influence within Spain was a powerful aid in expanding French commercial relations with America.

The alarm in Spain during this epoch was clearly felt by Andalusian merchants and Spanish economic writers. The concern is indicated in a memorial, *Mano de Relox,* presented by the Marqués de Varinas to Charles II of Spain in 1687, in which he predicts the "ruin of America" by contraband traders.[55] It was

---

[54] Erich Wilhelm Dahlgren, *Les Relations commerciales et maritimes entre la France et les côtes de l'Océan Pacifique* (Paris, 1909), I, 83, quoted in French in Haring, *Trade and Navigation,* pp. 114-15.

[55] *D.I.I. Ultramar,* XII, 327-386.

under these conditions and at this time, that the Nouvelle Compagnie was formed to systematize the French trade. Expeditions were sent out by this company from 1698 to 1701, and from 1701 to 1703, with the object of securing trade and perhaps colonies. At this particular moment also the dynastic change from Hapsburgs to Bourbons occurred in Spain (1700), giving a new orientation to Spanish politics.

The results were felt immediately. In January, 1701, the new Spanish king, Philip V, issued a cédula granting French ships the right to provision in colonial ports. They were forbidden to trade, but this was more an invitation to carry on commerce than a prohibition. During the thirteen years of war which followed, the French took full advantage of the situation to push their trade. Spanish historians have noted with irony that Philip V was actively protecting French merchants trading with the Spanish colonies in violation of treaties which Philip had signed with France. Frenchmen traded directly with the Spanish colonies, as well as indirectly through Spain. French merchants entered Spain and consuls were appointed to protect French interests.[56]

French goods entered Spanish America on a large scale, and French linens competed with English and even Spanish textiles and silks. An extensive South Sea trade grew up with Lima and Valparaiso, and thence with Canton in China. Not a few Frenchmen took up residence in Chile,[57] while one exporter, who had shipped 500,000 livres of Breton and Norman cloths by way of the New Spain *flota,* demanded the protection of the regime of Louis XIV, for it was, "of the greatest importance to support this commerce, not only because it disposes of our manufactures and brings in money, but it accustoms Spain and its Indies to the use of our cloths . . ."[58] Tours and Lyons silks, velours, and serges were widely used in colonial Lima, Mexico City, and Bogotá. Local merchants along the Pacific Coast made high profits from the French commerce, luxury goods sank to the price levels of the modest purse, the monopolists of Sevilla-Cádiz-Lima lost their trade, the Spanish government lost its revenue, and the galleons to and from Panama could not sail. But in any case the people of Peru,

---

[56] Albert Girard, *Le Commerce français à Seville et Cadiz au temps des Habsbourg* (Paris, 1932), pp. 538ff, 563, 567, 574-575; Barros Arana, *Chile,* V, 454, 504-505.

[57] Frézier, *Voyage, passim.* The New York Historical Society possesses the manuscript log and account book of a French merchant trading to Spanish America, dated from March 25, 1713, to August 27, 1715. An appendix to the log gives current prices of French goods in Tenerife, Buenos Aires, Concepción, Valparaiso, and Lima.

[58] Dahlgren, *op. cit.,* I, 79.

Chile, and Ecuador were getting more goods, and more cheaply than before.[59]

BRITISH AND FRENCH COMPETITION

The English were also taking advantage of the War of Spanish Succession. William Dampier, to whom we have already referred, conducted a trading expedition to Peru, 1703-1704, and Woodes Rogers another, 1708-1711, to take only samples of English activity. In addition, the Jamaica contraband trade with the Spanish American colonies grew to large proportions, bringing prosperity to shippers, merchants, and producers. During the years after the Treaty of Utrecht in 1713, contraband trade in logwood with Honduras, Campeche, and Central America brought great profits both to Englishmen and North Americans. Toward the middle of the eighteenth century, British illegal trade with Spanish America was estimated by a Frenchman at 1,500,000,000 livres tournois.[60]

The greater knowledge of America from these trading expeditions, and the intensified economic activity in Europe at this same time led to two of the most gigantic and concerted efforts to make a profit out of the Spanish-American colonies. These were the English South Sea Company and the French Mississippi Company.

In 1711, the Earl of Oxford, lord treasurer of England, secured the passage of a bill by Parliament establishing a company to take over the English national debt. In addition, it was to have exclusive rights to trade with all Spanish territories from the Orinoco River to Tierra del Fuego on the Atlantic side, and with the entire Pacific coast of North and South America. Portuguese and Dutch territories were exempted, but all those "which are reputed to belong to the Crown of Spain," were included. At the end of the War of Spanish-Succession, Philip V granted to Queen Anne, which meant to the Company, the right to import 4800 Negroes annually into America for a period of thirty years, and also to take one 500-ton ship of merchandise each year.[61]

It must be recalled that Europe was just entering the economic stage in which industrial and commercial values were represented by stocks. Joint-stock companies had been in existence in England

---

[59] Sebastián Lorente, *Historia del Perú bajo los Borbones, 1700-1821,* (Lima, 1871), pp. 6-14.
[60] G. M. Butel-Dumont, *Histoire et commerce des Antilles Anglois. Où l'on trouve l'Etat actuel de leur population et quelques détails sur le commerce de contrabande des Anglois avec les Espagnols dans le Nouveau Monde* (Paris, 1748), p. 93.
[61] Arthur S. Aiton, "The Asiento Treaty as reflected in the Papers of Lord Shelburne," *H.A.H.R.,* VIII (May, 1928), 167-177; William Thomas Morgan "The South Sea Company and the Canadian Expedition in the Reign of Queen Anne," *H.A.H.R.,* VIII (May, 1928), 143-166.

for much more than a century, but their development to the point where the average investor utilized them as a means of saving was only being reached. Stories of the fabulous wealth of America and of the enormous profits to be got from the American trade caused hundreds, and perhaps thousands of people to invest their money. That Spain would not freely consent to the company's operations, that the price of the stocks was based upon theoretical future earnings rather than the company's performance, and that there was not business enough to bring the expected profits were essential facts ignored by the investors, or of which they were ignorant. The stocks priced at 76 in 1711 rose to 1100 in 1720. No profits had been realized, the inevitable reaction came, and England was introduced to her first great stock market crash. The failure of the South Sea Company carried numerous other businesses to the wall with it. Thousands of people who had dreamed of riches woke up in a debtor's prison.[62]

At the same time France had organized a company to trade with the Gulf and Mississippi region and solve France's pressing economic problems. This scheme was originated by John Law, a Scotsman who in 1716 opened in France a bank which was placed under the protection of the Regent, the Duc d'Orléans, and which was accorded in 1718 the status of a Royal Bank. In 1719, the price of the shares had reached eighty times the value of all the specie in France. Fleets were sent out to Peru in 1719 and 1720. The system, like that in England, collapsed in 1720, throwing France into an economic crisis.

Despite these spectacular failures of French and British efforts to exploit Spanish-American trade, foreign contraband traffic did not abate in the Spanish possessions. The scope and intensity of the illicit trade was graphically revealed in 1761, when Captain Dionisio Alcedo y Herrera, a famous soldier and civil servant of the Spanish Crown in Quito and Panama, concluded his geographical description of the smuggling region.[63] The King and Council of the Indies then learned that the contraband area included nearly 2300 miles of Caribbean coastline, and that foreign contraband and the South Sea Company factors after the Treaty of Utrecht had driven Spanish-American merchants and agents of

---

[62] Means, *Fall,* pp. 236-39.

[63] "*Descripción de las extensivas situaciones y distancias de las costas de la América Meridional por la vanda del norte y del modo de hacer en ellas el contrabando los tratantes de las colonias de las naciones estrangeras . . . .*" A copy exists in the Rich Collection of the New York Public Library, item No. 99 in the manuscript volume called: "Spain. Documents relating to Spanish Affairs in the Latter Part of the 17th and Beginning of the 18th century."

the guilds-monopolies out of the region. There was a grave de-
cline, consequently, in royal revenue from the customs houses at
Maracay, Santa Marta, Portobelo, Panama, Campeche, and
Havana.

Most of the mainland rivers flowing into the Spanish Main
were "frequented by colonial [English] merchants who do an
active business with the Provinces of Comayagua, Nicaragua and
Guatemala." South of Cape Gracias a Dios lay the Bahía del
Almirante, inhabited largely by *zambos* (Negro-Indian), whose
chieftains the English stirred up against Spain while carrying on
trade with them.[64] Below Almirante Bay, smugglers put in at the
mouths of the Cocle and Chagres rivers. Alcedo described the
Chagres mouth, northwest of Limón Bay, as

"a free port for all trading ships from all the foreign-owned
islands, and in the last war (1739-1748) the English sent regular fleets here from Jamaica reinforced by companies of contrabandists and they settled here until they were ousted." [64b]

THE PORTUGUESE

The Caribbean and Pacific were not the only areas of contraband
trade with America. Portuguese trade during this period was conducted on a regular and prosperous basis and the Portuguese
settlements in Brazil took advantage of their favorable situation
to organize illicit commerce along the Río de la Plata. During the
earlier part of the seventeenth century, ships sailed to America
annually from Oporto or Lisbon, carrying silk, woolens, and other
textiles obtained from French, Flemish and English producers.
After Brazilian stops, they went to the Río de la Plata, whence
the goods were carried overland into Paraguay, western Argentina,
Chile, and into Peru as far as Lima. Peruvian merchants maintained commercial agents in Brazil as well as in Sevilla.[65]

The Río de la Plata trade route increased in importance during
the seventeenth century, with the growth of the livestock industry on the plains of Uruguay and Argentina and the development
of Argentine cities. The Portuguese, who had pushed westward
toward Paraguay, and southward toward Uruguay, were in a good

---

[64] Here also Spain later carried on the same tactics against the English, employing Jeremiah Terry, an American of Virginian birth, as a counter to the Jamaicans
and British. *Colección de libros y documentos referentes a la historia de América*
(Madrid, 1908), VIII "Relaciones históricas geográficas de la América Central";
also Vera Brown Holmes, "La Expedición del aventurero Norte-Americano Jeremiah
Terry a Nicaragua en el siglo XVIII," in *Segundo congreso internacional de historia
de América* (5 vols., Buenos Aires, 1938), IV, 531-540.
[64b] Alcedo, *Loc. cit.*
[65] Haring, *Trade and Navigation*, pp. 117-118.

geographical position to supply the needs of the Spanish colonists and to buy their products. So long as Spain and Portugal were under one monarch (1580-1640), this trade had an outward appearance of legality, but after 1640 it became distinctly contraband and Portuguese advances were strongly opposed by the Spanish. At the same time, British commercial treaties with Portugal allowed import of British goods into Brazil, whence they went to La Plata, giving Britain a stake in the contraband activity in this part of the South Atlantic.

In 1680, moreover, the establishment of a Portuguese settlement on the Río de la Plata opened up a new illegal trade center that was destined to be the hub of a large commerce, as well as the focus of Spanish-Portuguese rivalry. On January 1, 1680, Portugal settled Colonia del Sacramento on the river above where Montevideo now stands. A town was laid out, lots and agricultural lands distributed, crops planted, and preparations made for a permanent settlement. The alarm in the Spanish colonies was immediate, and it did not diminish when Buenos Aires discovered that the trade of Colonia was diminishing its customs duties, and that contraband goods were being bought by Buenos Aires merchants without payment of any tax to the city. The trade of Peru and Chile also, along with their silver, began to flow increasingly through Colonia. The Cabildo of Buenos Aires petitioned the King in 1699 for permission to undertake the conquest of Colonia. Diego Altamirano, procurador of the Jesuits in Paraguay, informed the authorities that the Portuguese sold their dry goods cheaper than those sold by Castilian merchant ships, and twice as cheaply as those coming by way of Lima. Under such conditions, it was predicted, "All the inhabitants of the provinces of Río de la Plata, Paraguay, and Tucumán would buy from the Portuguese, and it is believed certain that those of Cuyo, Chile, and even of Chicas, Potosí and Charcas would do the same." [66]

The citizens of Buenos Aires were alternately indignant over the Portuguese occupation of Colonia, and grateful for the opportunity afforded to buy and sell merchandise. The governors of Buenos Aires frequently pointed out to the Council of the Indies the disadvantages of Portuguese Colonia to the revenues and interests of the Crown. The Treaty of Utrecht had granted recognition to Portuguese title in this region, and the governor of Buenos Aires, García Roo, protested that Colonia's existence might put an end entirely to Buenos Aires and other Spanish-American

---

[66] Quoted in Blanço Acevedo, *Uruguay colonial,* pp. 37-38.

towns, which would be unable to sell their wool, charcoal, woods, and cattle.

Colonia became the center from which Buenos Aires and Montevideo were supplied by Portuguese ships with European goods, and also a center from which large shipments of Uruguayan hides were sent out. After its destruction by the Spanish in 1777, following several frontier wars with Portuguese Brazil, its place was taken by the Spanish towns of Maldonado and Montevideo.

OTHER CLANDESTINE TRADE METHODS

In addition to contraband trade and piracy, there were pseudolegal ways in which English, French, and Dutch merchants could send and receive Indies cargoes. In some cases Spanish and non-Spanish commercial houses formed partnerships, or Spanish merchants bought their goods directly from European manufacturers. Frequently Spanish merchants acted as commission houses for foreigners in American trade, and in yet other instances Peninsular mercantile firms were mere fronts for foreign firms, receiving a small portion of the profits as their share. It might be said that the Indies trade about 1700 profited the rest of Europe more than Spain, since Spain was the bridge across which goods passed, and gold and silver recrossed on the way to France, Germany, Italy, Holland, Flanders, and England.[67]

What percentage of Spanish-American trade was in the hands of Spain or of non-Spanish commercial powers is impossible to determine with accuracy because of the clandestine nature of much of it. Seventeenth century authors were inclined to estimate the foreign portion as five-sixths of the total. The galleons arriving at Cádiz in 1682 brought a cargo valued at 22,809,000 pesos, of which thirteen millions were consigned to foreign merchant accounts: two and one-half million each for France and England, three and one-half million for Holland, and four and one-half million for Genoa.[68]

SPANISH-AMERICAN TRADE WITH THE UNITED STATES

Eighteenth-century foreign trade was accompanied by a prolonged series of wars which further menaced and interrupted Spain's maritime communications with her American colonies. The older contraband commerce of the French, English, Dutch, and

---

[67] Ferrer del Río, *Historia del Reinado de Carlos III,* chap. I, cited in Riva Palacio, *México,* II, 678; Jean O. McLachlan, *Trade and Peace with Old Spain, 1667-1750: A Study of the Influence of Commerce on Anglo-Spanish Diplomacy in the First Half of the Eighteenth Century* (Cambridge, 1940), pp. 120-121; Haring, *Trade and Navigation,* pp. 20, 111-113.

[68] Haring, *Trade and Navigation,* pp. 114-115.

Portuguese continued as aggression harassed Spanish defenses. The entire scope of British interest in the Caribbean was involved in the attacks on Cartagena,[69] which offered a gateway to the Pacific both by way of Panama, and the Atrato Valley.

Throughout the eighteenth century, and especially after 1783, French and English contraband commerce found a new rival in the United States. Despite British commercial and governmental restrictions on one hand, and Spanish resistance on the other, colonial and independent North America developed a growing trade with Latin America. It was contraband, the logwood trade, privateering, and slave traffic which first attracted colonial North American shipping into Spanish Caribbean waters.

As early as 1662, "the English from the North Continent of America began to cut the logwood trees on the Coast of Yucatán and the Bay of Campeachy where they made a Settlement." [70] In times of war, North American trade and naval activity shifted to privateering against the Spanish. Quick profit from prizes filled North American counting-house coffers as long as war lasted, and supplemented the efforts of England against Spain. New Englanders displaced Spaniards in the logwood industry, and influenced the price of the commodity in European markets.[71]

North Americans also engaged in the slave traffic, which led to an extension of commodity trade with the Caribbean lands. Before the American Revolution, North Americans traded with Honduras, Montecristi, Tortuga, and occasionally with Puerto Rico. Trade with this Spanish area aroused the hostility of Jamaicans and British home mercantilists, but persisted nevertheless. Probably the clearest, summary statement of United States' interest at this time may be found in the attempt to obtain legal authority for inter-American colonial trade. The Governor of New York Province wrote to Lord Pitt in 1760 in support of a treaty with Spain which would allow North Americans to trade directly with the Spanish colonies:

"It seems evident to me that could a mutual intercourse in Trade be obtained between the British and Spanish Colonies, it must be highly advantageous to Great Britain. Or could a Treaty be made with the King of Spain by which the Inhabitants of the Spanish Colonies were permitted to purchase provisions in the Northern Colonies, and the inhabitants of the British

[69] James Alexander Robertson, "The English Attack on Cartagena in 1741 and plans for an Attack on Panama," *H.A.H.R.*, II (February, 1919), 62-71.
[70] David Macpherson, *Annals of Commerce* (4 vols., London, 1805), II, 504.
[71] *Ibid.*, III, 429; Butel-Dumont, *op. cit.*, p. 110.

Colonies to sell Provisions in the Spanish Colonies it would greatly advance the Trade and Riches of Great Britain and cannot in any case be detrimental to it." [72]

The interest of North American merchants in Spanish America continued to grow during the latter part of the eighteenth century. In 1800, United States trade with the whole Spanish Empire was divided as follows:

Exports to Spain[73]

Tenerife and Canaries	$4,743,678
Campeche, Honduras	303,630
Philippines	291,717
"Spanish West Indies"	14,112
Floridas, Louisiana	8,270,400
"Other Spanish American Lands"	2,035,789
Northwest Coast	1,280
"South Sea"	946,153
TOTAL	$16,606,759

During the 1780's, Americans entered the South Pacific trade and followed French contrabandists into Chile, carrying democratic propaganda with their wares.[74]

The wars of the Napoleonic era gave both Britain and the United States an additional opportunity to penetrate Spanish-American markets, the former as mistress of the seas, and the latter as a neutral nation. French commercial interest was damaged by this competition, and Great Britain took over a large part of the textile market in America.[75] The demand for goods in Latin America, resulting from the inability of Spain to communicate with her colonies, led to royal permission for vessels of neutral nations to supply America. The result was the quick appearance of North American ships in Chilean ports.[76] They engaged in whaling and carried on a trade in commodities which grew into a stable commerce.

"Most of the English and Anglo-American vessels which enter the Great Ocean [Pacific] have the double view of carrying on the cachalot (sperm whale) fishing, and an illicit com-

[72] Colden to Pitt, October 27, 1760, December 27, 1760 in Colden Letters, *Bancroft Transcripts*, New York Public Library.

[73] *Gazette of the United States and Daily Advertiser*, Philadelphia, February 27, 1801. For trade with the Floridas and Louisiana, Arthur P. Whitaker, "The Commerce of Louisiana and the Floridas at the end of the Eighteenth Century," *H.A.H.R.*, VIII (May, 1928), 190-203.

[74] Barros Arana, *Chile*, VII, 39-45.

[75] Dorothy Burne Goebel, "British Trade to the Spanish Colonies, 1798-1823," *American Historical Review*, XLIII (January, 1938), 288-320; Vera Lee Brown, "Anglo-Spanish Relations in America in the closing Years of the Colonial Era," *H.A.H.R.*, V (August, 1922), 323-483.

[76] Barros Arana, *Chile*, VII, 300-304.

merce with the Spanish colonies. They double Cape Horn after attempting to leave contraband goods at the mouth of the river Plata, or at the *presidio* on the Falkland Islands. They begin south of Concepción, Chile. After remaining . . . a month and carrying on a contraband trade with the island of Chiloé, the fishing vessels generally coast Chile and Peru . . . (then) continue . . . northwards to beyond Cape Corrientes on the Mexican coast of the Intendancy of Guadalajara." [77]

North Americans also established direct trade bonds with important Spanish American merchants in Buenos Aires and Montevideo. North American cargoes and imports were very large, and were distributed from Buenos Aires by mule-train into the interior as far as Peru and Chile.[78] Forty-three United States ships were in the Río de la Plata in 1801-1802, while others were on the West Coast of Latin America.[79]

In order to protect this trade from the uncertainties of Spanish policy—which might at any time revoke the advantages of neutrals —Americans urged that consuls be sent to Spanish America, in spite of Spanish refusal to accept credentials.[80]

While Spain periodically rescinded its neutral decrees, and in the face of war emergency had to restore them, Latin-American merchants were profiting from neutral trade permission. North Americans were helping to dispose of colonial products which otherwise would have been unsold. Both in Argentina and Peru, economic writers put the case for the Spanish-American point of view. The Peruvian, Dr. Hipólito Unánue, arguing for abrogation of Spanish mercantilism in the face of international war and blockade, wrote:

"It is therefore evident that our articles of export are worth little to England and we must find another destination for them: that is the United States whose flag has free entry into all ports of continental Europe, even into those of France, Holland, and Italy. Recognizing this as truth, what is there to do but take the responsibility assumed by the Governor of Havana in

[77] Humboldt, *New Spain*, III, 87-88 [*Nouvelle Espagne*, III, 272-274].

[78] *Documentos para la historia de Argentina* (20 vols., Buenos Aires, 1913-1936), VII, "Comercio de Indias."

[79] C. L. Chandler, "United States Merchant Ships in the Río de la Plata, as shown by early newspapers," *H.A.H.R.*, II (February, 1919), 26-54; also C. L. Chandler, "River Plate Voyages, 1798-1800," *American Historical Review*, XXIII (July, 1918), 816-24.

[80] Roy F. Nichols, "Trade Relations and the Establishment of the United States Consulates in Spanish America, 1779 to 1809," *H.A.H.R.*, XIII (August, 1933), 289-313.

1808: to permit our boats to leave Callao and take our immense surplus of products to the United States . . . . We know that in 1803 copper and tin paid no tariff in the United States, no doubt because they lacked those minerals. It is very possible that in the crowded ports of Boston, New York, Philadelphia, Baltimore, and Charleston one could place cargoes of Peruvian products without a change in prices." [81]

On the whole, by the end of the colonial period, the United States had become an important factor in Latin-American commerical economy.[82] In the early nineteenth century, United States relations with Mexico led to an increase in American shipping, to the point where British consuls in Vera Cruz were genuinely concerned about loss of "the greater part of the carrying trade of this country." [83]

* * * * *

The course of wars, maritime-commercial rivalries, and the decline of Spain's navy, led to an extensive contraband trade with Spanish America by France, England, Holland, and Portugal. Naval warfare opened avenues to northern and southern Latin America, while illicit trade, privateering, and smuggling diverted Spanish commerce with her own colonies into the hands of foreign merchants. The contraband trade, however, while a loss to Spain, was a benefit to the colonies and their expanding economy.

Cut off from Europe by the series of wars near the end of the colonial period, the Spanish colonies and the former British colonies developed a profitable commerce. A century and a quarter had elapsed since Anglo-French-Spanish rivalries had sought to exploit for themselves the markets, resources, and bullion of Latin America. Yet neither English, French, nor Spanish mercantilism could hold the New World. Before 1810, the United States, last on the scene, became influential in the foreign trade of Latin America. Yankee skippers furnished an outlet for the stocks of Argentine hides, Cuban sugar, and even Brazilian products, and mutual interests enlarged as inter-American trade came into being.

[81] *Peruano Extraordinario,* Lima, April 13, 1813.

[82] Harry Bernstein, *Origins of Inter-American Interest: 1700-1810, with Special Reference to the Relations of New York, New England and Pennsylvania with Latin America* (Philadelphia: University of Pennsylvania Press, 1945).

[83] *British Consular Reports:* "Mexico (Vera Cruz)." Charles Mackenzie to George Canning, July, 1824, p. 314.

Trade Policy and Reform to 1810

By Harry Bernstein and Bailey W. Diffie

Spain's Monopoly System

Long before many of the events which we have recorded, it had become clear that Spain's trade policies needed adjustment; and such an adjustment began a full century before the wars which brought independence to Latin America. It should not be presumed, however, that the modifications made in the Spanish Commercial system were designed to give foreign nations a larger share of the American trade. The objective was precisely the opposite; it was to overhaul the system in such a way as to prevent contraband and recover the lion's share for Spain herself. The mother country did not question for one minute her right to promote and defend her own commerce, however bitter the disputes within the ranks of her statesmen and economists about the best methods of accomplishing this. We have already pointed out that the contemporary policies of rival nations were hardly more liberal in this respect, though differing somewhat in detail. We may distinguish two principal theories about methods of acquiring national wealth followed by Spain, and other nations as well. Neither system contemplated resigning trade to rivals. The first was the monopoly theory; the second, presently to be taken up, admitted all Spanish subjects on an almost equal basis to trade privileges.

The theory of the monopoly system seemed sound to its advocates and beneficiaries. Assuming its basic principle that the colonies belonged to the Crown, the deduction was logical that the Crown was duty bound to promote and protect their commerce. This could best be accomplished, it was generally believed, by entrusting trade to privileged groups, who, because of the benefits derived would defend the interests of the Crown and the colonies against interlopers, thus working to the advantage of the entire nation.

This economic theory produced a double monopoly system: the monopoly of Spain against all foreign nations; and the monopoly of the licensed Spanish class against all Spaniards not admitted to the privilege of trading with the Indies. Merchants in America quite as strongly as those in Spain, upheld the monopoly system, for the merchant monopolists in the Indies were likewise concerned with retaining control over imports and exports. The Spanish commercial system should not be regarded merely as a policy discriminating against America for the benefit of Spain, but rather as favoring a privileged, preferred class in both Spain and America. We find in America, especially in Lima and Mexico City, merchant guilds and organizations that strongly advocated the system, even though merchants of the Indies occasionally clashed with their Sevilla-Cádiz confreres. Spanish-American monopolists sought relief from the restraints of the Peninsular monopolists, but in turn pressed constantly for their privileges in America against non-organized merchants, retailers, and manufacturers. They never advocated free trade.[1]

We have seen that Spain had her difficulties in keeping other nations out of her colonies, and was by no means entirely successful. We have now to see how the monopoly of the privileged few was slowly broken, although the process was not complete even when the Latin-American nations gained independence. The instruments through which the monopoly was maintained, the Casa de Contratación, the Consulado, the convoy system, the privileged ports, (Sevilla-Cádiz in Spain; Cartagena, Portobelo, and Vera Cruz in America), already described, were altered as time moved on.

DIFFICULTIES OF MAINTAINING THE MONOPOLY

Under the monopoly system, merchants shipped only the amounts of goods that could be exchanged for a sufficient quantity of bullion and other American products to yield a high profit—sometimes as much as three or four hundred per cent, or more. The assumption was that the Indies had only a definite purchasing capacity, and that a better profit could be made by exchanging a limited amount of goods at the maximum price. This was strictly in accord with contemporary mercantilist notions. Apparently no

---

[1] Haring, *Trade and Navigation*, pp. 136-137.

consideration was given to supplying America's actual needs. Obviously, such a system could be effective where the monopoly was maintained successfully, and no contraband or foreign trade drained off bullion or stole the market from the Sevilla-Mexico City-Lima Consulados. Since this was the perpetual menace to the vested interest of the merchants, great efforts were made to protect the monopoly.[2]

Maintenance of the monopoly was at all times difficult. Not only did foreign nations break in on Spanish trade with America through the contraband and illegal trade already noted; Spain was unable to prevent foreigners from settling in her colonies. Close immigration restrictions (discussed earlier) were designed to help Spain keep her hold on the Indies, and maintain the commercial ascendancy of Sevilla and Cádiz. There were frequent edicts against illegal entrance into the Indies from the beginning, and further decrees to that end were issued in 1739, 1758, 1778, and 1785. The government had long since been forced to legalize the position of immigrants to America, and at various times authorized payment of a fine *(composición)* for the privilege of trading in America.[3]

Another respect in which the monopoly system failed to carry out its purpose was with regard to foreign sailors in foreign ships.[4] Ships had to be hired from the Italians, French, and Dutch, and fleets were taken over with their entire crews. This provided the Crown with a source of taxation as well as the opportunity to encourage the development of a Spanish marine, and in 1681 a special tax of three ducats a ton was levied on foreign ships in the Indies trade.[5]

COUNTER-MEASURES AGAINST FOREIGN ENCROACHMENT

Faced with the unremitting foreign encroachments, Spain entered desperately into competition for the trade of her own colonies. As soon as the War of the Spanish Succession was ended in 1713, she took measures to restore her commerce with America. Crown agencies were constantly preoccupied with the increasing menace of contraband trade and the need to curtail it.[6] It was during this

---

[2] Haring, *Trade and Navigation,* pp. 89-91.

[3] Haring, *Trade and Navigation,* pp. 103-111; Laudelino Moreno, "Los extranjeros y el ejercicio del comercio de Indias," *Anales de la Sociedad de Geografía e Historia de Guatemala,* XIV (June, 1938), 441-454.

[4] Paul S. Taylor, "Spanish Seamen in the New World during the Colonial Period," *H. A. H. R.,* V (November, 1922), 631-661.

[5] Haring, *Trade and Navigation,* p. 88.

[6] John Campbell, *A Compleat History of Spanish America . . . with a Particular Detail of the Commerce with Old Spain by the Galeones, Flota etc.   As*

period that the Spanish overseas commercial center was shifted from Sevilla to Cádiz, to which the Casa de Contratación was transferred in 1717-18. A trade act of 1720 envisioned the restoration of Spain's commerce with her colonies by regulating the sailing of the fleets according to schedule, supervising those permitted to trade, assigning freights and rates of shipment along uniform lines when cargoes were shipped to Vera Cruz, Cartagena, or Portobelo, or when the *registros* went to Santa Marta, or other ports.[7]

Yet Spain was in no effective position to bar foreign merchants, especially the French, and in 1722, a royal order permitted foreign consignment and delivery of goods into Spanish territory, "because of the present impossibility of carrying out the laws that prohibit it."[8] Repeated regulations stressed the warnings of the Council of the Indies, and authorized surveys to prevent the "slightest illegality." The Casa de Contratación exerted all its efforts to supervise the Andalusian coasts, and through the Crown demanded thorough control of the Caribbean and Spanish Main to curb illegal entry. But those waters lay too exposed to traders and privateers. Continuous war, before and after 1700, had weakened the Spanish Navy for convoy purposes, and made it useless as a coast guard to prevent illicit trade, contraband, and privateering.

When it became evident that the existing system could not protect Spain's colonies from foreign rivals, a number of changes were made. The earliest of these did not disturb radically the older Sevilla-Cádiz monopoly system, but sought rather to organize commerce so as to cut into the foreign contraband where it was particularly vigorous, in the Caribbean. The first device used to accomplish this was the monopoly trading company, already tried by England, Holland and France, and by Spain herself.[9] The monopoly company was intended to sustain the old system under the newly-arrived Bourbons, and was tested before the liberalizing legislation of the mid-century.

also of the Contraband Trade with the English, Dutch, French, Danes and Portugueze (London, 1742), pp. 301-303; Bernard Moses, *South America on the Eve of Emancipation* (New York, 1908), pp. 321-322; Vera Lee Brown, "Contraband Trade: A Factor in the Decline of Spain's Empire in America," *H. A. H. R.,* VIII (May, 1928), 178-189.

[7] Gutiérrez de Rubalcava, *Comercio de las Indias,* pp. 266-280.

[8] Rafael Antúñez y Acevedo, *Memorias historicas sobre la legislación y gobierno del comercio de los Españoles con sus colonias de las Indias Occidentales* (Madrid, 1797), p. 273.

[9] Roland D. Hussey, "The Antecedents of the Spanish Monopolistic Overseas Trading Companies (1624-1728)," *H. A. H. R.,* IX (February, 1929), 1-30.

The first was the Honduras Company, organized in 1714, which was followed by the Guipúzcoa (Caracas) Company in 1728. The Havana Company was created in 1740, and a Santo Domingo Company in 1757. The Royal Maritime Company was authorized later in the century to exploit fisheries, especially in the South Atlantic. The Patagonian coast and the Falklands were frequented largely by English, North American, and Spanish whalers toward the end of the colonial period, and the Royal Maritime Company was given monopoly rights over whaling and salt in this region.[10] The Caracas Company began paying dividends in 1735, issuing 20 per cent that year and in 1737-39, and paying 25 per cent in 1751. In 1752 a stock dividend of 100 per cent was voted, and thereafter, from 1754 to 1784, some 28 annual dividends of 5 per cent were issued, with 10 per cent extra, half of which was paid in 1777 and half in 1778.[11]

THE ERA OF ECONOMIC REFORM

The closed economic system could not be maintained forever, and changes were introduced throughout the eighteenth century. One of the most important modifications came in the improvement of the communications system with the Indies.

THE POSTAL SYSTEM

A formal postal system to the Indies had been inaugurated in 1514 when the Crown granted the office of *Correo Mayor de las Indias* (Postmaster General), to Lorenzo Galíndez de Carvajal and his heirs.[12] The Carvajal concession was nullified in 1768, although the Crown compensated the former owners. Even before this time a Postmaster General had been appointed for the provinces of the Río de la Plata. This position had fallen to the Basavilbaso family, and mail was delivered by a chain of stations from Buenos Aires to Lima.[13]

During the seventeenth century, maritime mail was sent direct from Seville under the jurisdiction of the consulado, in two boats which were required to go each year to New Spain. Two vessels

---

[10] *Documentos para la historia del Virreinato del Río de la Plata* (5 vols., Buenos Aires, 1913), III, 92-121. The document, dated 1786, refers to many Americans who had violated the monopoly by coming to the Argentine South Atlantic coast to hunt whale.

[11] Hussey, *The Caracas Company,* appendix 4.

[12] Means, *Fall,* pp. 226-228, in dealing with the Carvajal concession, suggests that there was a separate Peruvian department, operated by direct descendants of the Carvajal family, down to 1768 when the King merged the Postal System with the agencies of the Crown.

[13] Concolorcorvo, *Lazarillo de ciegos caminantes,* pp. 44 and *passim.*

also were sent to Tierra Firme. This procedure was progressively modified until 1764, when monthly sailings of packet boats were allowed from Coruña to Havana, and sailings to Buenos Aires authorized at slightly longer intervals. By the middle of the eighteenth century, an intercolonial postal system linked Paraguay, Buenos Aires, and Chile with Lima, Bogotá, New Spain, and the Northwest, as well as bringing the Indies in closer communication with Spain.[14]

LIBERALIZATION OF TRADE RESTRICTIONS

The first reforms in the direction of removing trade restrictions were limited to the Caribbean area and a few Spanish ports. The decree of October 16, 1765, allowed trade with Cuba, Santo Domingo, Puerto Rico, Margarita, and Trinidad, by Spanish merchants in Cádiz, Sevilla, Alicante, Cartagena, Málaga, Barcelona, Santander, Coruña, and Jijón. All that was needed was a license from the customs officials, and sailings could be made at any date, with any class of cargo. Former duties were abolished and replaced by a 6 per cent tax. Ships carrying merchandise from the Caribbean could return to any one of these Spanish ports and sell their cargoes, paying duty in the port of landing. By other decrees of March 23, 1768, and July 5, 1770, these concessions were extended to Louisiana, Yucatán, and Campeche.[15]

Spanish trade and revenues increased rapidly in the areas affected. The Count of Campomanes, an adherent of Spanish reform and head of the Council of Castile, wrote in 1775 that "the island of Cuba brings in more to Spain at the present, since the new regulations established for its commerce, than did all the possessions in Italy, Flanders and Burgundy." [16] Both Campomanes, who was in a political position to influence the Crown, and Bernardo Ward, a prominent Spanish economist of the day, contributed to the course of economic reform by charging the Seville-Cádiz monopoly with the decay of Spanish foreign trade. Bernardo Ward put the case clearly in his analysis of the need for liberalizing Spanish trade rules:

> "If Spain's enemies, envious of our having such a jewel [the Indies] could not take it away by force, they could hit on no better device than to continue a system that has produced these effects." [17]

[14] Haring, *Trade and Navigation*, p. 230; Barros Arana, *Chile*, VI, 359-363.
[15] Barros Arana, *Chile*, VI, 406.
[16] Campomanes, quoted in Barras Arana, *Chile*, VI, 406-407.
[17] Bernardo Ward, *Proyecto económico*, (2nd ed., Madrid, 1762), pp. 229, 251,

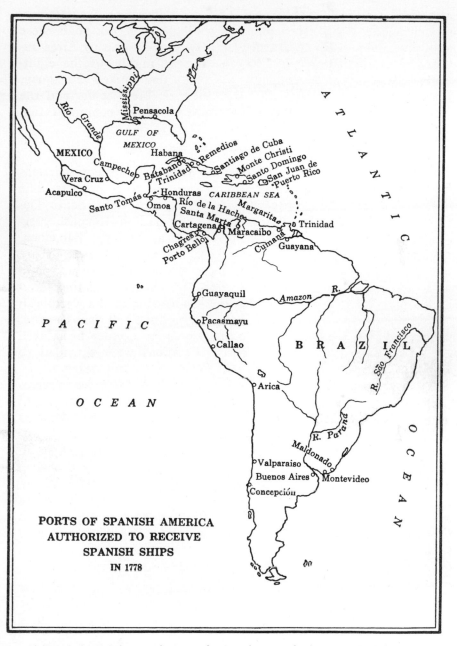

PORTS OF SPANISH AMERICA
AUTHORIZED TO RECEIVE
SPANISH SHIPS
IN 1778

Adopted from *History of the Latin-American Nations* by W. S. Robertson

Among the general reforms of the reign of Charles III were those which broadened the rights of the colonies to trade among themselves. Intercolonial commerce became a part of imperial trade interest, as monopoly in Spain could not maintain its exclusive character.

The reform measure of January 20, 1774, authorized trade between colonies of Spain in America, abolishing "the prohibition which has existed in the four kingdoms of Peru, New Spain, New Granada, and Guatemala of reciprocal trade by way of the South Sea [Pacific Ocean] of their respective products, crops, goods and to permit . . . all the natives and inhabitants to engage freely in these activities" regardless of all laws to the contrary. This did not include all the provinces in America, and the colonies permitted to trade with each other could deal only in their own products, but the decree moved one step further in the direction of American liberty of economic action. [18] Provinces not included in the reform acts were still subject to the system of fleets and register ships which could sail from Cádiz only. In 1777, the Río de la Plata was authorized to trade with Spain proper, and directly with the other Spanish colonies in America. This meant that the Platine region was now placed on a par with the provinces of Peru, New Spain, Guatemala, and New Granada.

The Act of February 1778, *"Comercio Libre de España a Indias,"* generally known as the Free Trade Act, granted to Buenos Aires, Chile, and Peru the right to trade with most of the chief Spanish ports. The words of the decree express the real purpose of this important measure: "Considering that only a free and protected commerce between European and American Spaniards can restore agriculture, industry, and population of my dominions to their former vigor, I determined to open up the trade of the Indies to various ports." Since the object was to secure the Indies trade for Spain, the act stressed that foreigners were to be excluded strictly and that ships engaged in trade must be of Spanish construction or bought within two years of the decree, be the property of Spaniards, officered by Spanish citizens, and manned by crews two-thirds of whom were Spaniards. A supplementary act of October, 1778, extended this law to New Granada and Guatemala.

---

and 278, for his arguments for freer trade throughout the Spanish Empire. Ward, Campomanes, Ulloa, and other reformers felt that change and the abolition of monopoly would eliminate contraband, increase royal income, and not least, rebuild the Royal Navy and Spanish shipping.

[18] Barros Arana, *Chile,* VI, 407-408.

Some twenty-four American ports were opened to freer trade with Spain through the 1778 legislation.

To develop Spanish industry and Spanish American trade, a ten-year exemption from duties was granted to textiles of wool, cotton, and hemp, and to hats, glassware, and other products of Spanish manufacture. Tariffs were raised on certain products, such as wood, in order to build a merchant marine from colonial woods, while colonial hides and flour also received preference. [19] Certain products of American origin were entirely exempted from customs or export duties, and other tariffs were lowered. Spanish-American sugar was exempt except for a drawback duty of four reales an arroba by an amendment of 1785. A decree of 1800 added another four reales to the duty on sugar in order to finance a paper money issue of the Crown and consolidate interest. Guayaquil, Caracas, Maracaibo, and other Spanish-American cocoa was also subject to a drawback payment if it was being reshipped through Spain to European markets. Otherwise the following products of colonial origin were admitted free to Spain: coffee, quinine, salted meat, leather and tanned skins, Campeche logwood, mate, and Michoacán rice. Alpaca and guanaco wool paid a duty. [20]

These tariff reforms were part of the uniform overhauling of Spanish economic policy during the eighteenth century. In the Peninsula, tariffs were lowered, monopolies adjusted, privileges abolished, and export taxes revised. [21]

While Cádiz opposed these reforms because of the many years of its unquestioned monopoly, it should not be thought that the appearance of new trading cities in the Peninsula or in America displaced its ascendancy. Its long establishment as a trading center, the number of commercial houses, factors, agents, and consuls in that city, and the number of ships in its excellent harbor, all continued to make it the commercial leader of Spain over its Peninsular competitors.

THE NEW TRADE POLICY AND RÍO DE LA PLATA

The results of the liberalized trade policy were important to Spanish-American cities and their merchants. The ports of Montevideo and Buenos Aires were among those for whom new commercial freedom proved most effective. As long as they were sub-

---

[19] *Papeles varios*, II, No. 6. A decree of 1783 supplemented that of 1778 by providing tariff protection for colonial woods.

[20] *Papeles varios*, II, *passim*.

[21] G. Desdevises du Dezert, "Les Institutions de l'Espagne au XVIIIe siècle," *Revue Hispanique*, LXX (1925), 287-289.

ject to Lima politically and commercially, and to the Sevilla-Cádiz monopoly, their economic growth was hampered. After 1776, the Río de la Plata provinces (and the territory that is modern Bolivia) were separated from Peru and placed under a new Viceroyalty of La Plata. Trade to and from the interior mining and agricultural country now flowed through Buenos Aires by way of overland routes or along the Paraná-Plata river system and its tributaries. [22] Products were shipped to Cádiz, Barcelona, Málaga and other Spanish ports, as well as to Havana and to various American ports on the Atlantic and Pacific coasts. [23]

Montevideo also enjoyed new trade benefits which aided commercial progress. Warfare forced Spain to permit her colonies to trade with neutrals, and Montevideo was permitted to be the port of destination for goods shipped directly from Hamburg, Germany. This permission, moreover, serves as an example of the system of privilege which continued to exist. Trade with Hamburg was not general, but limited to the company of Brentano, Vobara, and Urbieta of Hamburg, with factors in Montevideo, who were allowed to import four hundred tons of general cargo into Montevideo, and return to Hamburg or any neutral port of North Europe with American products. The firm of Joaquín Fernández da Silva of Oporto, Portugal, could bring into Montevideo five hundred tons of general cargo and return to Europe with American produce. Other concessions provided for trade in neutral ships. A royal license allowed the merchants, Joaquín Mariá de Ferrer, Antonio Tastet y Compañía, "to ship for themselves or in the name of the neutral commercial houses that they may designate, from foreign ports, under neutral flag to Montevideo the ships that they wish, with products, goods and effects of whatever kind, without any exception and bring back gold, silver, crops and produce of the country (Montevideo) to any ports convenient to them." [24]

Much of the history of the Río de la Plata region during the late colonial period and the early years of the nineteenth century revolved around the rival commercial and political position of Montevideo and Buenos Aires. The commercial growth of Montevideo began after 1750, with the arrival of register ships which gave the port direct contact with Europe. Montevideo, also a stopping point

[22] *Documentos Historia de Argentina,* VII, "Comercio de Indias-Consulado, Comercio de Indias y de Extrangeros, 1791-1808." For the continental trade of Buenos Aires merchants and their wide interests see *Acuerdos del Extinguido Cabildo de Buenos Aires,* series III, 1796-1800, II, *passim.*
[23] Moses, *Eve,* pp. 45-46.
[24] Reales Ordenes Reservadas of October 31, 1805, and February 18, 1806, quoted in Blanco Acevedo, *Uruguay colonial,* pp. 248-249.

for Pacific-bound vessels, became a jobbing, transshipping and re-
fitting center. Livestock formed the chief wealth of Uruguay, however, and millions of cattle were killed and hides and salted meats
were prepared in the *faenas* or cattle centers of the interior. The
exploitation of this form of wealth took on a regular organization,
and individuals and companies were actively engaged. [25]

The growth of the port was aided by a series of administrative
acts. These (December 7, 1770) regulated mail ships which were
to sail six times a year between Montevideo and Coruña; and provided (November 16, 1776) that all ships coming from Callao put
in at Montevideo, en route to Spain, in order to receive orders;
and (November 26, 1776) that all ships going from Spain to the
Pacific Coast make Montevideo, to be inspected by the governor
there.

Montevideo was also aided by the superiority of its port over
that of Buenos Aires, which was built on the flats and lacked harbors. Juan Francisco de Aguirre, a surveyor-engineer employed by
the Crown in that region during the later eighteenth century, referred to Montevideo as "almost the only port in the Río de la
Plata, key to the immense provinces of this region and master of
the riches of these plains: cattle."

Diego de Alvear, who entered the region as a member of the
commission surveying the Brazilian-La Plata boundary, also com-
mented on the importance of Montevideo:

"The population and commerce of Montevideo have made
noticeable progress since the establishment of the Coruña mail
service . . . . But the recent rapid progress is due to the Regla-
mento de Libre Comercio of 1778. This is Montevideo's hap-
piest era, giving it daily greater growth and new energy. Its
vacant lots are filling up overnight with fine houses with box windows and obelisks. The farms, and cottages of the fertile Mig-
uelete Valley are multiplying incredibly, and Uruguay's colonists
arrive unceasingly on ships reaching these shores . . . . The
port [of Montevideo] alone, the only one in all the Río de la
Plata that can admit large vessels, gives it all the advantages we
have just mentioned, making it the first port of contact for the
Vice-royalties of Buenos Aires and Lima . . . ." [26]

A customs house was set up in the port in 1779 to receive the
registro vessels' cargoes, which were loaded on lighters and sent

[25] Blanco Acevedo, *Uruguay colonial*, p. 197.
[26] Quoted in *ibid.*, pp. 215-216, note 9.

CARVED WOODEN BOX, ECUADOR

to Buenos Aires across the Plata estuary. Montevideo's site favored and encouraged contraband in the South Atlantic, although many Spanish officials were located in the town, charged with inspection of all vessels making port there. [27] Montevideo was made the sole port of entry for slaves in 1791, and was the distributing point for inland slave trade to the provinces of La Plata, Chile, and Peru. Spanish monopolies such as the Maritime Company, Philippines Company, as well as individual Spanish traders, maintained factors and trading stations in Montevideo.

In the last half of the eighteenth century, Montevideo's prosperity induced the rise of a middle, commercial class of moderately wealthy citizens. Observers estimated fortunes of more than one hundred thousand pesos. [28] These fortunes do not compare, perhaps, with the property of Mexicans and Cubans, but they indicate the already considerable prosperity of the livestock industry which down to the present time is the source of Uruguayan wealth.

The fact that both Buenos Aires and Montevideo were supported by largely identical economic interests, led to keen commercial rivalries throughout this region, since outlying districts and towns along the Paraná-Plata river system were affected. During the early years of the nineteenth century, Buenos Aires overtook many of the advantages formerly enjoyed by Montevideo. [29]

The free trade acts had definitely tied a large hinterland to Buenos Aires as the port of outlet, and was therefore a considerable factor in the economic development of the city. Foreign trade was also of especially vital significance, since—more than Lima, Santiago, or Mexico City—Buenos Aires lived and developed from the products which flowed through its port bound for the interior provinces, or came from them to a foreign market. The *consulado* of Buenos Aires was created in 1794 in recognition of the port's growing importance and at the same time as a move to bind its merchants more closely to the trade of Spain. [30]

By this time, the commerce of Buenos Aires had grown rapidly, and its exports in 1796 amounted to 5,000,000 pesos. The number of ships entering the port of Buenos Aires increased from 35 in

---

[27] The *Comandante de Resguardo* had complete charge of everything dealing with the free commerce to America. The Montevideo *resguardo* was modeled after that of Cádiz, whose function was to protect the royal financial stake in trade. *Papeles varios*, I, 1.

[28] Francisco de Aguirre, cited in Blanco Acevedo, *Uruguay colonial*, pp. 68; 196-202.

[29] Woodbine Parish, *Buenos Aires and the Provinces of the Río de la Plata* (2nd ed. London, 1852), *passim*.

[30] Pereyra, *América española*, IV, 207-209.

the years between 1772 and 1776, to 62 in 1792, and to 77 in 1796, and the average annual value of the city's commerce was 7,212,000 pesos. [31]

The basis for the trade of Buenos Aires was still the cattle industry, but the nature of the industry had changed. By the beginning of the eighteenth century, the famous *vaquerías* had grown up. But the wild cattle had been killed to such an extent that by 1778 they were disappearing. As they became more rare and valuable, the cattle were claimed and branded as private property and great cattle ranches began to appear. [32] The rate of increase in hide shipments after 1778 is indicated by the following estimates:

Hides shipped in 1778   150,000
Hides shipped in 1780   800,000
Hides shipped in 1783 . . . .   1,400,000 [33]

The free trade decree was in part responsible, but other factors enter into consideration.

Hides were not the only source of wealth from cattle in the late eighteenth century. The new business made possible by the discovery of the process of drying and salting meat was stimulated when Viceroy Loreto improved the port facilities of Buenos Aires and opened up the Salinas Grandes salt mines, lowering the price of salt by two-thirds. The customs figures of Buenos Aires show the economic improvement. Collections were 287,107 pesos in 1779, fell during the war with England, and then rose to 368,967 in 1783. [34] After 1783, the number of hides shipped continued to be great, the total of legal shipments from 1779 to 1795 amounting to almost 13,000,000 hides.

The lowering of the price of salt from fifteen pesos to five pesos a fanega, and royal permission in 1794 to ship to Asia and Africa, proved to be of great advantage. Coopers had to be brought from Europe to make the barrels in which the meat was shipped. By 1802 there were not enough ships to carry the salt meat. The *Telégrafo Mercantil,* earliest Argentine newspaper, in its issue of September 3, 1802, estimated that 389 ships manned by 7,789 men were necessary to ship 1,800,000 quintals of salt meat, and 72,000 quintals of tallow and mineral products. The result was further noticeable in the increase of provincial commerce with Buenos Aires as the flow of goods from the interior to the seacoast

[31] R. A. Humphreys, ed., *British Consular Reports on the Trade and Politics of Latin America, 1824-1826* (London: Royal Historical Society, 1940), note 29.
[32] Levene, ed., *Nación Argentina,* IV, Sección I, 367-70.
[33] Pereyra, *América española,* IV, 209-210.
[34] Levene, ed. *Nación Argentina,* IV, sección I, 191.

town swelled. This trend is illustrated by the following figures based upon customs collections in Buenos Aires on products entering that city from the inland regions of the Viceroyalty:

	Pesos
1773	2,502
1776	2,266
1778	7,416
1779	13,078
1780	20,428
1785	31,329
1790	28,136
1795	32,974
1800	46,390 [35]

PERU

Naturally, the growing trade of Montevideo and Buenos Aires meant a shift in the center of commerce from Peru, on the Pacific, to the area closer to Europe on the Atlantic. Peru was therefore, the region most likely to lose by the reforms and their commercial consequences. With ships trading directly with ports once subject to the Lima consulado and its monopoly, Peru's trade with Spain and its position as the wholesale distributor for South America was affected adversely. There were other disadvantages for Peru. Peruvian exports were largely mineral, and her agricultural products could not compete with those of the Caribbean.

Peruvian commerce, like that of the entire west coast, suffered also from transport difficulties. It took from three to five months to sail to the port of Callao around the Horn, while the cost of transporting freight by land across the Isthmus was still too high. The Isthmus route, described as all but impassable in 1569, when Viceroy Francisco de Toledo had to pass over it, was called by a traveler in 1640 a "terrible road, the worst I have seen in all my travels." [36]

Overland routes from the west coast in any direction were few, and even the best traveled were poor. There was one road across the Andes, from Aconcagua to Mendoza (now in Argentina), widened sufficiently to accommodate trains of pack mules and provided with brick shelters to house travelers. Carriage travel was still so rare in late colonial Chile that a trip from Santiago to Concepción in 1792 was considered something of an adventure. No carriage road was built from Valparaiso, the port, to Santiago, the capital, until 1795. [37]

---

[35] Levene, ed., *Nación Argentina*, IV, sección I, 419.

[36] Quoted in Haring, *Trade and Navigation*, p. 183; see also Roland Dennis Hussey, "Spanish Colonial Trails in Panama," *Revista de Historia de América*, No. 6, (August, 1939), 47-74; for the internal roads of Venezuela and their tremendous difficulties, Humboldt, *Travels*, III, 164; IV, 74-75.

[37] Barros Arana, *Chile*, VII, 435-437.

Because of the drawbacks of the Panama route, west coast merchants at the first opportunity began to send Guayaquil cacao, Peruvian quinine, and Chilean copper southward into the Atlantic by way of Cape Horn. This route had other than navigational and climatic hazards, for it was frequently blocked during the late eighteenth century by the war vessels of the English and other nations. At such times of international hostility, Pacific coast products were shipped north to Acapulco in New Spain, transported overland, and taken to Vera Cruz. [38] The Acapulco-Mexico City-Vera Cruz road carried annually metals, agricultural and manufacturing products worth approximately, 65,000,000 pesos, (13,334,400 sterling) even though the Vera Cruz road was nothing but "a narrow, crooked path, and the most difficult, in all America, with the exception of that by which the goods of Europe are transported from Honda to Santa Fé de Bogotá, and from Guayaquil to Quito." [39]

From an early date, shortly after the opening of the Philippines, goods had been shipped from Acapulco to Peru, and the Peruvians sent back Peruvian gold and silver coins. War and Sevilla pressure curtailed this trade before the eighteenth century, but during that century the Pacific route became increasingly used, in spite of natural handicaps, for West Coast intercolonial commerce. This route of commerce northward had many defects:

"The distance and the extreme difficulty of the navigation from Acapulco to Lima are the greatest obstacles to trade between the inhabitants of Peru and Mexico. From Callao to Guayaquil is easily navigated in the space of six or eight days; and from Guayaquil to Acapulco requires three, four and five weeks; but the passage from the northern to the southern hemisphere, from the coast of Mexico to the coast of Quito and Peru is a continual struggle against winds and currents. The distance from Guayaquil to Callao is only 210 marine leagues, yet very often the time required for this short passage from north to south is double that from Acapulco to Manila by a course of more than 2800 marine leagues; and it also frequently happens, that more weeks are necessary to go from Guayaquil to Callao than days from Callao to Guayaquil." [40]

There was one way to avoid the dangers of winds and currents, wars and piracy: that was the development of overland, internal trade between Upper Peru, Chile, and Buenos Aires (or Monte-

[38] Humboldt, *New Spain*, I, 36-37 [*Nouvelle Espagne*, II, 248-250].
[39] Humboldt, *New Spain*, IV, 3 [*Nouvelle Espagne*, III, 332].
[40] Humboldt, *New Spain*, IV, 63-64 [*Nouvelle Espagne*, IV, 395-96].

video). Coastal trade between Chile and Peru was not greatly vexed by the interruptions of privateers and since Chile no longer had to depend upon Peruvian transit of European goods, a trade arose in the products of each province. The port of Talcahuano in Chile was shipping approximately 2400 tons annually, largely to Peru. In 1785, sixteen vessels with cargoes worth some twenty-four millions of dollars, made the port of Callao.

The trade of Peru with other sections of Spanish America was still considerable after the reform of 1778. By 1780 there were some thirty-two vessels in the service of the shippers of Callao, ranging from a tonnage of 1800 tons to the small packet, *San Antonio,* of one hundred and twenty-three tons. Obviously, commerce and the capacity of American shipping had come a long way since Spain had to limit ships to six hundred tons because of the restricted port facilities. A vessel of 1800 tons was equivalent in merchandise capacity to some of the entire fleets of the sixteenth century. The total tonnage of all thirty-two Callao vessels was 16,375 tons. They carried products from Peru to Chile and return, or up the coast to Guayaquil and Panama, and further to Guatemala and Acapulco.

The trade of Peru with other colonies at this time was more than four million, five hundred thousand pesos, which was distributed by sea and land to American markets, as follows: [41]

Exports to Buenos Aires ....$	2,034,980
Imports from Buenos Aires ....$	864,790
FAVORABLE BALANCE ....$	1,170,190
Exports to Chile ....$	458,317
Imports from Chile ....$	629,800
UNFAVORABLE BALANCE ....$	171,483
Exports to Chiloé ....$	30,000
Imports from Chiloé ....$	51,200
UNFAVORABLE BALANCE ....$	21,200
Exports to Guatemala ....$	28,350
Imports from Guatemala ....$	124,500
UNFAVORABLE BALANCE ....$	96,150
Exports to Santa Fé ....$	128,295
Imports from Santa Fé ....$	284,460
UNFAVORABLE BALANCE ....$	156,165
TOTAL OF EXPORTS ....$	2,679,942
TOTAL OF IMPORTS ....$	1,954,750
BALANCE IN FAVOR OF LIMA, TOTAL $	725,192

Peru continued to be the leading commercial province on the

---

[41] Joseph Skinner, *The Present State of Peru* (London, 1805), pp. 95-101.

West Coast, as it maintained a large volume of trade with Cádiz. In 1792, the port of Callao imported 4,656,484 pesos of goods from Cádiz, and exported 9,240,951 pesos. [42] Imports to Callao from Cádiz in 1794 were 3,633,240 pesos, and exports declined to 5,546,474.

CHILE

In Pacific Coast trade the province of Chile came to figure importantly through its commerce with Buenos Aires, with Spain by way of the Horn and with Peru. The export-import trade of Chile rose from half a million pesos around 1700 to about four million pesos during the late years of the colonial period. Chilean isolation from Spanish supply was clearly marked during the frequent war periods of those latter years. [43] One consequence was the increase of trade between Chile and Buenos Aires, which contributed greatly to the importance of the latter port. [44]

The commerce of Chile and Peru had undergone considerable change after the free trade legislation. Peru no longer sent quantities of European goods to Chile, and the main trade between Chile and Peru was in colonial produce. Chile continued to export wheat to Peru, in addition to other agricultural products, minerals, and some manufactured goods. Peru shipped some 800,000 arrobas of sugar annually to Chile, as well as cotton and woolen textiles, salt, indigo from Central America, rice, cacao, and tobacco. Chilean wheat exported to Peru brought in about 300,000 pesos a year, while other exports included wine, ships stores, fish and dried fruits, jerked meat, hides, and various other agricultural items, for a total value of about 700,000 pesos annually. Towards the end of the eighteenth century the balance of trade was almost always in favor of Chile. After the free trade laws, European imports through Lima declined. [45]

Twenty years after the reform of 1778, Manuel de Salas, secretary of the Santiago consulado, praised the reign of Charles III as one that "will be looked upon as the epoch of the re-establishment of the merchant marine, and agriculture, and of the promotion of the industry of Spain, and advancement of her overseas possessions, which by this act [Trade Act of 1778], were freed of the oppression of monopoly and of onerous taxes." The trade of Chile at this

[42] José Hipólito Unanue, *Guía Política, eclesiástica y militar del virreynato del Perú* (4 vols., Lima, 1793-1796), I, 20.

[43] Barros Arana, *Chile,* VII, 424.

[44] Samuel Hull Wilcocke, *History of the Viceroyalty of Buenos Aires* (London, 1807), chap. XII.

[45] Barros Arana, *Chile,* VII, 426-427.

time amounted to "almost three millions of pesos counting its commerce with the metropolis, Buenos Aires, the provinces of the Río de la Plata, the adjacent islands, and Peru. [46]

There were some thirty or forty rich Spanish merchants of Santiago and Concepción who controlled this steady and profitable commerce, fixing prices and the flow of goods into the retail markets. The director of the Customs House of Santiago wrote in 1800: "For four years the present war with England has condemned us to an appalling scarcity of all the goods and products of Europe. In all this time, not one register ship has arrived from the mother country, and meanwhile the needy groan under the greed of the merchants." [47]

NEW GRANADA

While the colonies along the Pacific Coast and the Río de la Plata were exploiting their minerals, hides, wheat, and salted meats, the colonies of the Caribbean region, and Mexico, were experiencing a rapid development in such things as cotton, sugar, indigo, cochineal, cacao, coffee, tobacco, and other products of the tropics.

The colonies of the northern part of South America enjoyed a notable expansion at the end of the colonial period in spite of the foreign wars in which Spain was engaged. Wars in Europe seemed to stimulate, rather than interrupt, illegal trade. It was observed around 1800 that "everything at Puerto-Cabello seemed to announce the increase of population and industry. Among the most active branches of fraudulent intercourse are those with the islands of Curaçao and Jamaica." [48] Towards the end of the eighteenth and the beginning of the nineteenth centuries, Spanish viceregal officials were dismayed at the continued contraband trade that went on even while trade with Spain was practically cut off. The Viceroy of New Granada in 1803 reported to his successor that "since the declaration of war, and since I have come to this kingdom, I have been a witness to the almost absolute interruption of commerce between this kingdom and the mother country and its supplanting in part by contraband." [49]

La Guaira in Venezuela was one of the principal ports of this region, and the harbor for the city of Caracas, which is near the

[46] Barros Arana, *Chile*, VI, 411.
[47] José de Manso, cited in Barros Arana, *Chile*, VII, 446.
[48] Humboldt, *Travels*, IV, 209-211 [*Voyage*, V, 256-257].
[49] "Relación del estado del Nuevo Reino de Granada presentada por el Excmo. Sr. Virrey Don Pedro Mendinueta a su sucesor año de 1803," in José Antonio García y García, ed., *Relaciones de los Virreyes del Nuevo Reino de Granada* Nueva York, 1869), p. 497.

coast but 3,000 feet up in the mountains. Its annual legal trade varied from two to six million pesos or more, depending on war conditions. Principal exports of La Guaira were indigo, cotton, cacao, coffee, hides, tobacco, and copper. Of these products Spain took by far the larger part, with the exception of hides, which were shipped chiefly to the islands of the West Indies. In 1792, for example, Spain took ninety-eight and one-half per cent of the indigo, eighty-five per cent of the cotton, more than ninety-six per cent of the coffee, all of the cacao, but only about twenty per cent of the hides. This was the case up to about 1797, when Spain's war with England wiped out commerce with Spain, and drove Spanish merchantmen off the Middle Atlantic route to America, leaving foreign nations and American colonies to absorb Venezuelan exports. Spanish imports sank to about twenty per cent of the total. Other Venezuelan ports sharing in trade were Angostura, Maracaibo, Puerto Cabello, and some smaller ports. Total exports on the eve of the Wars of Independence amounted to about six million pesos. [50]

The commerce of the whole Viceroyalty of New Granada was much greater. The political jurisdiction of the Viceroyalty covered much of the area later included in the state created by Bolívar under the name of Great Colombia. It embraced a vast territory, and the ports of Guayaquil, Panama, Portobelo, Cartagena, and Maracaibo, in addition to the already cited Venezuelan towns. "Even amidst the shackles of the colonial system," wrote Humboldt, "the value of the exports of the products of agriculture, and of the gold washings amount to 11 or 12 millions of Pesos . . . ." [51] The region sent 30,000 mules annually to the Caribbean islands, [52] although many of these probably came from the captaincy-general of Venezuela.

The foremost port of New Granada faced the Caribbean and was located in the shelter of the harbor and fortress of Cartagena. During the seventeenth century Cartagena was an opulent place, since it was a port of call for the monopolistic fleets, and the site of commercial fairs. Its exclusive trade position was ruptured by the *asiento* arrangement and the appearance of British factors of the South Sea Company in that region. The annual ship allowed that Company provided the opportunity for a great deal of competitive selling, which weakened the position of the merchant monopolists of Lima, Sevilla-Cádiz and their merchant factors in

[50] Humboldt, *Travels*, VI, 223-226 [*Voyage*, IX, 304-308].
[51] *Ibid.*, VI, 219 [*Voyage*, IX, 297].
[52] Altamira, *Historia de España*, IV, 289-299.

New Granada (Cartagena and Portobelo). The port of Santa Marta was the avenue for commercial exports from the interior, since Cartagena was about forty miles from the Magdalena River which offered the best access to Bogotá and the interior. [53]

Colombia's commerce abroad was largely a Caribbean trade with the British colonies, especially at Jamaica. Difficulties of interior communication up the Cauca, Magdalena, and Atrato rivers which run north to south, retarded internal trade between the coastal and highland provinces, despite the commercial activity of the Pacific and Caribbean ports.

NEW SPAIN

New Spain was easily the economic leader of Spanish America in almost every line of production and volume of trade at the end of the colonial period. The mineral output was far above that of other colonies, and in most agricultural and livestock industries Mexican production was almost equivalent or superior to the rest of America. During the later years of the colonial period, New Spain added a few products to her normal exports. Among these were sugar, which had been exported for a time in the sixteenth century but scarcely thereafter until 1775. Sugar exports reached 120,000 quintals at the beginning of the nineteenth century. [54] Her shipping grew with the increase in trade that developed toward the end of the century, partly based upon the general expansion under way and partly owing to the reforms. In the twelve years from 1784 to 1795, 1142 vessels entered Vera Cruz, compared with 164 vessels in the earlier dozen-year period from 1728 to 1739, or five times as many in the latter years. [55]

The figures for the year 1802 indicate the extent of Vera Cruz trade with other parts of America, as well as with Spain. The total value of trade in pesos (imports and exports) between Spain and Vera Cruz in 1802 amounted to 54,275,078 pesos, compared with a value of 6,188,877 for the commerce between the other colonies and Vera Cruz. There was a total of 558 vessels which engaged in this trade, of which 143 came from Latin-American ports and 148 from Spain, while 112 sailed for Spain and 153 for other Latin-American ports. [56] The commerce of the port in the early years of the nineteenth century was greatly affected by the wars in

[53] *British Consular Reports,* Edward Watts to George Canning, Colombia (Cartagena), 260.

[54] Humboldt, *New Spain,* I, 236-237 [*Nouvelle Espagne,* II, 39-40].

[55] Lerdo de Tejada, *Comercio exterior,* Appendix, No. 12.

[56] Humboldt, *New Spain,* IV, 39 [*Nouvelle Espagne,* IV, 371].

which Spain was engaged. From 1802 to 1805, the years 1802, 1803, and most of 1804, were years of peace and trade boomed, but with war renewed between England and Spain in December of 1804, legal trade declined and contraband increased. The total reaching perhaps as much as six or seven millions of pesos annually. [57]

Evidence of the great increase in New Spain's production and commerce may be seen by the rise of royal revenue produced by taxation upon minerals, agriculture, and trade. Between the beginning and ending of the eighteenth century the annual public revenue of New Spain had increased more than six times, as follows:

Increase in the Public Revenues of New Spain

1712	3,068,400 pesos
1763-67 annual average	6,169,964 "
1780-84 annual average	18,176,479 "
1802	20,200,000 " [58]

In addition to their direct effects on foreign and intercolonial commerce, the reforms affected New Spain's economy in other respects:

"The results of this change were very important not only because of the abundance of goods and the low prices produced by it; but because with the monopoly and the high profits made from little labor by the monopolists having now been made impossible, the *flotistas*, who were those engaged in the fleet business, withdrew and put their capital into agriculture and mining, giving a great impulse to these, especially to mining. As a result, a greater number of people devoted themselves to trade instead of the few with large capital as formerly. Since it was necessary for them to work hard to get along, numerous small fortunes came into being everywhere. The towns advanced greatly because the small fortunes were distributed among all of them." [59]

The growth of a small middle class was a most noticeable factor during the later years of the eighteenth century.

CUBA

Cuba before the end of the eighteenth century was already showing signs of the agricultural wealth that was to enrich it at a later

[57] Humboldt estimated that it reached four or five millions annually in times of peace, and six or seven during wartime. *New Spain*, IV, 94-96, 367. The secretary of the Vera Cruz consulado concluded that annual contraband from 1796 to 1820 must have been from 12 to 15 million pesos. Lerdo de Tejada, *Comercio exterior*, Appendix, Nos. 14-19; also Humboldt, *Travels*, VI 229-231 [*Voyage*, IX, 312-315].

[58] Humboldt, *New Spain*, IV, 207-208 [*Nouvelle Espagne*, V, 4-5].

[59] Alamán, *Méjico*, I, 112-113.

period. Its products were tropical, the principal items in the export trade being sugar, tobacco, coffee, wax, and skins. Cuba naturally produced a wide variety of tropical fruits and vegetables which were consumed locally, but were not in demand in the international market. The importance of Cuba as a commercial center arose not only from the eighteenth-century demand for its products, but also from its location. Havana was ideally situated for trade with the other parts of the Caribbean, with the Gulf and Atlantic ports of the United States, and with European nations. Its products could find a market more easily than those from almost any other part of tropical America.

Cuban tobacco was appreciated at an early date, but there are statistics for its production and export only after 1748. Production attained about 250,000 arrobas yearly from 1789 to 1794. The competition of other products caused a temporary decline after the latter date, but the total crop is thought to have reached between three and four hundred thousand arrobas from 1822 to 1825. In spite of the fact that Cuba was an ardent consumer of its own tobacco, a surplus was left to ship to Spain, Panama, Peru, Mexico, and Buenos Aires. In the best crop years, Spain received from Cuba as much as 128,000 arrobas of tobacco, valued at more than five million pesos. [60]

Beeswax, as we have already seen (chapter XVII), became a leading export commodity. Of the 42,700 arrobas, exported in 1803, New Spain received 25,000 arrobas. Havana alone shipped an average of 22,000 arrobas from 1815-18, dropping to an average of about 16,000 arrobas from 1819-25. [61]

Coffee became a prominent export crop after the French Revolution in Haiti, when a considerable number of Haitian planters fled to Cuba. There were some 60 coffee plantations in Cuba in 1800, and their number rose to 779 in 1817. Exports from Havana amounted to 320,000 arrobas in 1809, and 918,263 arrobas in 1815. Coffee is a crop that varies greatly from year to year, and the exports of Havana reached a low of 370,229 arrobas in 1816 and a high of 895,924 in 1823, the average from 1817 to 1824 being about 700,000 arrobas a year. Humboldt gives the total Cuban export from 1818-1824 as averaging:

[60] Humboldt, Travels, VII, 214-20 [Voyage, XII, 13-20].
[61] Humboldt, Travels, VII, 220-21 [Voyage, XII, 20-21].

At Havana   694,000 arrobas, registered
At Matanzas, Trinidad, Santiago   220,000 arrobas, registered
From all ports   304,000 contraband
                                                    ———————
Total export   1,218,000 arrobas

This was a greater export than Java in 1820, and almost double
that of Jamaica in 1823. [62]

Sugar began to assume in the mid-eighteenth century that importance that it was to have in the twentieth in Cuba. From 1760
exports steadily rose. While Havana was the chief port for export,
sugar was also shipped from Matanzas, Santiago, and other ports,
and a considerable amount was smuggled out. It is probable that
the total of legal and illegal exports reached 380,000 cases, equal
to about 70,000,000 kilograms of sugar yearly for the best period
up to 1825. [63]

The total increases in exports of coffee, tobacco, wax, and sugar,
as well as other products exported in smaller quantities, had brought
Cuba to the position of the foremost shipper of agricultural products in the Spanish dominions, and second only to New Spain in
total exports. By the end of the first quarter of the nineteenth century, the harbor of Havana was receiving from 1000 to 1200
ships annually with a tonnage of 150,000 to 170,000 tons capacity.
These figures are to be compared with New York's 299,617 tons
and Boston's 143,420 tons in 1816. The value of Havana's exports in 1823 was probably fifteen million pesos, and perhaps even
greater. For the island as a whole, the exports perhaps rose to
20 or 22 million pesos, and the imports to perhaps 22 to 24 million
pesos. The United States took half of the tonnage and one-third
of the value of the exports. [64]

Whereas during the colonial period, the deficit in Cuba's treasury had been met from a Mexican subsidy, this was no longer required at the end of the colonial period. "The increase of internal
wealth has little by little rendered unnecessary the pecuniary succor which Cuba used to draw from the Mexican treasury. Of all
the Spanish possessions, that island has most prospered; the port
of Havana has risen, since the troubles of Saint Domingue, to the
rank of one of the first places of the commercial world." [65]

---

[62] Humboldt, *Travels*, VII, 209-14 [*Voyage*, XII, 7-13].
[63] Humboldt, *Travels*, VII, 163-168 [*Voyage*, XI, 366-373]. See chapter XVII
of the present work for extensive treatment of Cuba's sugar industry and exports.
[64] Humboldt, *Travels*, VII, 221-248 [*Voyage*, XII, 21-27].
[65] Humboldt, *Travels*, VII, 5-6 [*Voyage*, XI, 181-182].

POSITION OF SPANISH AMERICAN TRADE AS A WHOLE

The trade reform acts, the increase of population in Europe and America, the commercial and industrial progress of Europe in the eighteenth century, the improvement of shipping and ports, and the increased production of American mines and agriculture, which led to greater American buying power, were all definite and clear reasons for a pronounced commercial expansion and prosperity in Spanish America towards the turn of the eighteenth century. It is evident that the commercial reforms of the Spanish home government were not altogether responsible for the trade expansion in America, since it had got under way before the first reforms. Indeed, a good case could be made out for the argument that the Crown introduced reforms in order to benefit from the increased commerce of America and to enlarge Spain's share of her colonial trade.

For a well-rounded conception of the trade position of Spanish America at the end of the colonial period, there remain two important considerations: the total colonial trade and the relative position of Spanish-American trade in world affairs. The statistics offered here must be looked upon as only approximate, but even so they are of sufficient value to warrant presentation.

The following figures, taken from the works of Humboldt, show the imports and exports of the principal political divisions in the first years of the nineteenth century:

Importation and Exportation of the Spanish Colonies of the New Continent

Political Divisions	Importation from Europe and Asia including contraband	Exportation from Colonies	
		Value of Agricultural Produce	Value of Gold and Silver
Cuba and Puerto Rico	11,000,000	9,000,000	....
New Spain and Guatamala	22,000,000	9,000,000	22,500,000
Viceroyalty of New Granada	5,700,000	2,000,000	3,000,000
Venezuela	5,500,000	4,000,000	....
Peru and Chile	11,500,000	4,000,000	8,000,000
Rio de la Plata	5,500,000	2,000,000	5,000,000
Total in pesos	61,200,000	30,000,000	38,500,000 [66]

A point to observe is that the agricultural and mineral exports nearly balance, indicating that the agricultural production of Spanish America was considerably greater in value than the mineral output, since most of the minerals were exported while only a small part of the agricultural produce was sent abroad. Still another fact of importance is that the buying capacity was largely

---

[66] Humboldt, *New Spain*, IV, 127-28 [*Nouvelle Espagne*, IV, 472-73].

concentrated in the Gulf and Caribbean areas. Mexico and Cuba together accounted for more than half of the foreign purchases, while the addition of New Granada and Venezuela brings the foreign imports of the northern area to more than three-fourths of the total for Spanish America. The total foreign purchases, including legal and illegal trade, amounted to 61,200,000 pesos.

What of Spanish America's relative position in world trade? It has been observed that throughout three centuries the nations of Europe competed with fire and sword for Spanish-American commerce. That the trade they sought to capture was worth the expenditure in men and materials from the financial viewpoint is demonstrated by the statistics. The United States exported in 1791 goods to the value of about $19,000,000, and increased this to about $71,957,144 by 1802. At an equivalent date, the exports of Spanish America were about 69,000,000 pesos, or approximately the same, since the dollar and peso around 1800 were similar in value. English commerce also gives a standard by which to measure the relative importance of Spanish-American trade. The exports of England in 1790 were:

		Pesos
To France	....	5,700,000
Portugal	....	7,600,000
Germany	....	12,400,000

The imports from America of the single port of Cádiz in 1802 (more than 81,800,000 pesos) were equivalent to the total [67] imports of England in 1790 (18 millions sterling).

These figures indicate that the commerce of Spanish America was one of the most lucrative in the world. It is not surprising that it tempted many European nations, whose merchants dreamed of the riches they could gain if they had a larger proportion of American trade. The colonies on their part grew aware of their own importance, and found even the liberalized trade laws too restrictive for their expanding economy. The commerce of the New World had created an enriched class of Creole and Spanish merchants whose patriotism was measured by their profits. This was a factor that was soon to weigh heavily, and to be perhaps a decisive influence in bringing about independence.

[67] Humboldt, *New Spain*, IV, pp. 117-131 [*Nouvelle Espagne,* IV, 459-476]. The discrepancy between the 69,000,000 pesos exports of America and the 81,800,000 imports of Cádiz can perhaps be accounted for by the enhanced value of the goods in Spain; perhaps by shipments made in 1801 and arriving in 1802.

Social Evolution to 1810—
Populations

PEOPLE OF LATIN AMERICA

THE POPULATION OF SPANISH AMERICA, as a result of the territorial and economic expansion of the colonial period, was considerably greater at the beginning of the nineteenth century than it had been in the sixteenth, and its composition was naturally not the same. An understanding of society at the end of the colonial era requires an examination of the peoples who constituted it—their numbers, racial composition, and geographic distribution —and a comparison with the populations both of other sections of America and of other parts of the world at the same date.

The three principal groups which formed the population of Latin America—the Indian, the European, and the Negro—were mingling, as we have seen, immediately after the Conquest, and producing the mestizo, the mulatto, the zambo, and numerous variations. Gradually these groups took on characteristics, in addition to those of color and race mixture, which established their relative position in, and contribution to colonial society. These differences were not merely of social classes. Distinctions in the make-up of the populations of the various colonies were to influence history, the peoples of some being more thoroughly amalgamated racially than those in other regions. For instance, in Chile, Paraguay, certain parts of Colombia, Venezuela, and northern Mexico the Indians and Europeans were so fused that the great majority of the people were mestizos. Other sections developed important population groups not found elsewhere. On the plains of Argentina and Uruguay and in the vast river valleys of the Orinoco, as well as in northern Mexico the gauchos, llaneros and vaqueros (all plainsmen and cowboys), exerted tremendous influence in the development of these regions.

441

THE MESTIZO: CHILE

Chile was one of the regions in which the most thorough mixture of the races occurred. By the end of the seventeenth century the populated section of Chile, reaching from the desert of Atacama in the north to the river Bio-Bio in the south, was inhabited by about 100,000 people, of whom the majority were mestizos. The Indians lived to the south of this region: they had practically ceased to exist as a distinct social unit within the territory outlined. The only language now spoken there was Spanish, and in the Creole population the European blood was more or less mixed.

"But in addition to the fact that it was not difficult to prove that in certain families of the same upper social classes there was some mixture of other blood, the lower classes (*bajo pueblo*) of the colony, the rural inhabitants as well as the city dwellers, formed a single race in which the fusion of Spaniards and Indians had slowly operated to such an extent that it would have been difficult to find the latter in their pure form." [1]

RÍO DE LA PLATA: GAUCHO AND VAQUERO

On the plains of Argentina and Uruguay had developed the *vaquero* and the *gaucho*. The gaucho might be Indian, or European, or Negro (or all three). His social environment, however, had made him distinct from any one of his progenitors.[2] In part he sprang from the Indians of Argentina and Uruguay, who were in the main nomadic and untamable savages not easily assimilated or dominated. The Charrúas of Uruguay and the Pampas of Argentina resembled in their traits the indomitable Comanches and Apaches of the southwestern United States. The introduction of cattle gave them an abundant food supply, and the horse furnished a means of transport they were quick to utilize. Vast regions of La Plata, reaching practically to the outskirts of Buenos Aires and Montevideo were dominated by the Indians.

An eighteenth century traveler, Félix de Azara, described the Charrúas, whose occupation was largely war, and whose skill rendered them hard to conquer: "Better horsemen than the Spaniards, more resistant, without the inconvenience of having to carry food and equipment nor the necessity of having to stop for rivers, gulches, lakes, and swamps, the Charrúas were in a very advantageous condition in fighting and checkmating the conquering armies [of Spaniards]." [3] These characteristics, common to

[1] Barros Arana, *Chile*, VII, 454-56.
[2] Juan Carlos Davalos, *Los Gauchos* (Buenos Aires, 1928) *passim.*
[3] Quoted in Blanco Acevedo, *Uruguay colonial*, pp. 6-7.

other plains Indians, led to constant warfare throughout the centuries and it was estimated that the wars with the Charrúas caused more bloodshed than the conquest of the Aztec and Inca Empires.

But it was from these wars and from the Indians, mixed with the Europeans, that there developed the gaucho. From the beginning of the eighteenth century began the gradual transformation which brought the gaucho into being.

"Distant from the centers of civilization, in constant conflict with the Spaniards, with the Portuguese, with the Jesuit Missions, their tents and haunts were the refuge of contrabandists and deserters who, joined with the Indian women, produced a new type: the *gaucho*." "A heterogeneous mixture of aborigines and Spanish deserters, irregular troops, Creoles born in the country itself, Brazilians and Portuguese, the conditions of the gauchos, wandering life in the immense plains . . . stamped him a product typical of this environment, with the precise and indelible characteristic by which he has become known to posterity." [4]

Bougainville, the French explorer, refers to the gauchos in 1767:

"A set of robbers united into a body, a few years ago, on the north side of the river, and may become more dangerous to the Spaniards than they are at present, if efficacious measures are not taken to destroy them. Some malefactors escaped from the hands of justice, retired to the north of the Maldonados; some deserters joined them; their numbers increased insensibly; they took wives from among the Indians; and founded a race of men who live upon robberies. They make inroads, and carry off the cattle in the Spanish possessions, which they conduct to the boundaries of the Brasils, where they barter it with the Paulistas, against arms and clothes. Unhappy are the travelers that fall into their hands. They are now, it is said, upwards of six hundred in number, have left their first habitation, and are retired much further to the north-west." [5]

This picture is doubtless a bit harsh and unfair, but it is probably a more accurate view of the initial stages of the gauchos than that offered by some modern romanticized versions.

With the formation of the large cattle estancias and the more

---

[4] Blanco Acevedo, *Uruguay colonial*, pp. 16-17 and 186.
[5] Bougainville, *Voyage*, pp. 25-26.

established and regular order of the late eighteenth century, the gaucho was gradually incorporated into the general population. He was no longer free to roam the vast plains and hunt wild animals, for the plains had been assigned to definite owners and the animals were branded. The gaucho now became a part of the great cattle ranches of Argentina and Uruguay. "All the ranches," says a document of 1790, "are full of gauchos. Their pay is so much for each hide cut off or skinned, stretched and stacked, the price being two or three reales according to whether the agreement was to use the horses of the employer or the gaucho's own, the distance, the dangers, or whether the pay was in money or clothing." [6]

Not all of the rural population of these regions, however, can be properly classed with the gauchos. The *vaquero* was, like the gaucho, a cattleman, but a legal element of society, whereas the gaucho was largely an outlaw and cattle rustler. The distinction between them was not always closely maintained, since they were both plainsmen and cowboys. The tendency was for the two to merge into one as conditions forced the gaucho to become law abiding. But the name *gaucho* came to be the one by which the plainsmen were known. [7]

The farmers who lived in the cultivated river valleys of the Río de la Plata were distinct from the cowmen in their characteristics. The *campesinos,* or farmers, were different in clothes, habits, and thought. Their attitude toward society in general was as unlike the gauchos' as that of the American farmers of the east and south was unlike the cowpunchers' of the western plains.

Paraguay was characterized by the development of a mestizo society in which the Indian and European elements were almost completely fused, neither persisting in large numbers in an unmixed form. The isolation of Paraguay, the relatively few women of European blood who came in the early years of the Conquest of this colony, and the ready adoption by the Europeans of the Indian system of polygamy created a single people. All claimed to be European, although ethnically this was pure fiction. "As the Spaniards brought very few women from Europe and they needed many, they seized the Indian women as concubines. By this means the number of Indians diminished considerably, being transformed

---

[6] Quoted in Blanco Acevedo, *Uruguay colonial*, p. 192.

[7] For an excellent treatment of the gaucho see Madaline W. Nichols, "The Historic Gaucho," *H.A.H.R.*, XXI (August, 1941), 417-24; Nichols, *The Gaucho; Cattle Hunter, Cavalryman, Ideal of Romance* (Durham: Duke University Press, 1942).

into Spaniards because the King declared the resulting mestizos to be Spaniards." [8]

MESTIZOS IN NEW SPAIN

New Spain, too, developed a large number of mestizos, notably in the cities and in the vast region reaching from the Central Valley of Mexico to the present-day southwestern United States. Most of the region north of Mexico City was thinly settled before the Conquest, and northward expeditions had carried the Indian and the Spaniard into this territory together. A considerable fusion resulted; and the typical inhabitant of northern New Spain in the eighteenth century was a mestizo. [9]

Had the mixtures of Indians and Europeans continued throughout the colonial period at the rate characteristic of the first half century after discovery, the entire population would have been fused into one by 1810. But natural conditions decreed otherwise. The *mestiza* was more attractive to the European than the *india,* and when the supply increased, mestizas became the concubines and wives of the white men. A report issued by the cabildo of Mexico City in 1770 states that there was little mixture of Spanish men and Indian women at that time, because the Indian women "are ugly and dirty." The report adds: "There was a great deal of mixture at the beginning of the Conquest, but it soon disappeared." [10]

THE INDIAN AREAS

In Mexico, Central America, parts of Colombia, Venezuela, and the Andes, where the Indians had been most thickly settled before the Conquest, they continued to be the basis of the population. The proportion of mestizos probably increased slowly and the number of Negroes and whites grew in certain areas; but in the regions mentioned, the Indian was in the majority, and in other places he was practically as numerous as the mestizo.

The mixture of the races tended to increase, although at a slower pace, with the growth of towns, the immigration of more Europeans settling in new districts, and the constant traveling back and forth which commerce, livestock raising, and mining, entailed. In Mexico City, for example, the *traza,* or line which

---

[8] Félix de Azara, *Histoire physique, économique et politique du Paraguay* (Paris, 1860-64), I, 252.

[9] Sierra, *Evolución política de México,* Bk. II, chaps. V and VI; T. Esquivel Obregón, "Factors in the Historical Evolution of Mexico," *H.A.H.R.,* II (May, 1919), 135-72.

[10] Quoted in Terán, *El Nacimiento de la América española* (Tucuman, Argentina; 1927), p. 245.

separated the Indian from the European city, had practically disappeared by the end of the seventeenth century. The Europeans
had built their houses in the Indian quarters and mestizos of
property had been able to free themselves from subjection to the
restrictions imposed upon the Indians. The serving quarters in
wealthy households were inhabited principally by Indian workers.
All these things had erased the distinction between Indian and
European wards in Mexico City, and to a greater or lesser extent
in practically all the towns of America.[11]

POPULATION TRENDS

During the course of the seventeenth and eighteenth centuries
the population of Latin America expanded in two ways, num-
erically and geographically. Especially during the last century of
the colonial period the number of people increased greatly, and
the new regions settled were numerous. The fact that impressed
the eighteenth century writers, however, was that vast regions
were almost uninhabited, or were very thinly populated. Still laboring under the impression that pre-Conquest America had a population of hundreds of millions, an erroneous idea which has been
brought down to our own day, [12] many Spanish and foreign writers
lamented Latin America's unpopulated condition. As late as the
mid-nineteenth century the noted Spanish political economist,
Manuel Colmeiro could say:

"The population of the Indies diminished with such rapidity
that [Spanish] America, at the end of two centuries appeared
to be little less than a desert. Mexico and Peru, two great empires in the hands of the natives were, in spite of being regions
very highly favored by nature, almost uncultivated and uninhabited in the middle of the eighteenth century. In such an extensive area as that which our overseas dominions had, scarcely
15,000,000 subjects obeyed the sovereign, not counting the
Spaniards." [13]

Such ideas arose from various misconceptions. The natural advantages for a heavy population were not as great as these authors
imagined; nor the population relatively so small as they pictured
it, since the idea of a great decline was postulated on an allegedly
enormous pre-Conquest population which never existed. The eighteenth-century authors not only thought that the native population

---

[11] Riva Palacio, *Mexico*, II, 665-7.
[12] See Chapter 9.
[13] Colmeiro, *Economía política*, II, 387.

of America had been much larger than it was, but they were also obsessed with the idea that the population was declining. Campillo remarked that "it seems an incredible fact that since there crossed over to the Indies an innumerable quantity of Spaniards in addition to the nations already settled there, [Spanish America] should be today almost uninhabited." [14]

FACTORS RETARDING POPULATION

By the end of the eighteenth century, however, the increase was so evident that few could doubt, and we find a tendency to predict future Latin American populations at figures they have never reached. One author thought that by 1913 Mexico would have "one hundred and twelve millions of inhabitants" and the United States "one hundred and forty millions." [15]

Such predictions were not based on valid data, as Humboldt saw. He remarked:

"I admit, that the United States will contain more than eighty millions of inhabitants a hundred years hence, allowing a progressive change in the period of doubling from twenty-five to thirty-five and forty years; but, nothwithstanding the elements of prosperity to be found in equinoxial America, notwithstanding the wisdom, which I am willing to attribute simultaneously to the new republican governments formed on the south and on the north of the equator, I doubt whether the increase of the population in Venezuela, Spanish Guiana, New Granada, and Mexico, can be in general so rapid as in the United States. The latter, situated entirely in the temperate zone, destitute of high chains of mountains offer an immense extent of country of easy cultivation . . . The most enterprising and robust planters cannot advance in the mountainous districts of Mérida, Antioquia, and los Pastos, in the llanos of Venezuela and Guaviare, in the forests of Río Magdalena, the Orinoco, and the province of las Esmeraldas, west of Quito, as they have extended their agricultural conquests in the woody plains on the west of the Alleghenies, from the sources of the Ohio, the Tennessee, and the Alabama, as far as the bank of the Missouri and the Arkansas. In calling to mind the account of my voyage on the Orinoco, we may appreciate the obstacles which the force of nature opposes to the efforts of man in burning and humid climates. In Mexico, large extents of soil are destitute of springs; rains seldom fall,

[14] Quoted in *ibid, loc cit.*
[15] Robinson's *Memoirs on the Mexican Revolution*, II, 315, cited in Humboldt, *Travels*, VI, 121 [*Voyage*, IX, 148-149].

and the want of navigable rivers impedes communication. As the ancient native population is agricultural, and had been so long before the arrival of the Spaniards, the lands of more easy access and cultivation already have their proprietors. Fertile countries of vast extent, at the disposition of the first occupier, or ready to be sold in lots for the profit of the state, are much less common than is imagined in Europe." [16]

These same factors and others retarded the growth of the population throughout the colonial period and explain to a great degree why the increase was not as rapid in some places as in others. The writers who spoke of the emptiness of America were confronted with evidence that seemed, to them, conclusive. America was so vast that a very large number of people could be absorbed without having much visible effect upon the empty spaces. Even to the present time, the traveler who traverses Latin America for long distances will gather the impression of emptiness. How much deeper must this impression have been at a time when there was not one-seventh of the present population! There were, and are, many cogent reasons for the small population that has always characterized Latin America.

Disease must be reckoned as one of the most important influences in keeping the population down. Thousands were easy victims of tropical diseases of various sorts—malaria, other fevers, and intestinal parasites—which shortened their lives. The incredibly low living standard of the great masses rendered them easy victims of the diseases which were spread by the lack of sanitation. Undernourishment, or even starvation, was the rule. But when these "normal" causes of death failed to work fast enough, epidemics were ever ready to take away the population.

Smallpox was introduced to America, supposedly, in 1520, and took its regular toll of victims. Motolinía asserted that the first epidemic of smallpox carried off half of Mexico's population. We may be sure that this is a considerable exaggeration and still admit that the effects of smallpox on a population which had no immunity or means of combating it must have been devastating. As rapidly as each generation grew up, the disease was able to convert itself into an epidemic. The system of combating smallpox and other diseases by holding religious processions guaranteed that everybody in the community would be exposed. It would be impossible to cite all of the epidemics, so frequently was some part of America the victim. But we may note that in the years

---

[16] Humboldt, *Travels*, VI, pp. 121-24 [*Voyage*, IX, 149-52].

1763 and 1779 Mexico suffered epidemics, about nine thousand people or almost one-tenth of the people of Mexico City dying in the latter year.

Matlazahuatl, a disease known before the Conquest, frequently attacked the Indian population, killing thousands. In the years 1545, 1576, 1736, 1737, 1761 and 1762 Mexico suffered attacks. This malady was confined to the highlands and attacked Indians principally, while at the same time Yellow Fever made the coastal regions almost uninhabitable. Various diseases, which the doctors of the time could not treat, killed other thousands. The epidemic of 1759 for example invaded the highlands from Ecuador to Bolivia.

Father Torquemada, historian of Mexico, asserted that some 800,000 Indians died in the Matlazahuatl epidemic of 1545 and 2,000,000 in another epidemic of 1576, but the only fact we feel safe in accepting here is that there was a high mortality during these plagues. It is evident that no count, even an approximate one, could have been made. Still another epidemic of Matlazahuatl raged in 1736.[17]

GROWTH OF POPULATION: LA PLATA

If, in the absence of accurate figures, uncertainty is understandable as to the relative pre- and post-Conquest populations in the regions most densely inhabited before the Spaniards came, there can be none with regard to areas such as the Río de la Plata; these were only sparsely occupied, if at all, before the European settlements.

Buenos Aires, destined eventually to become the chief city of Latin America, had grown slowly at first because it had neither agriculture nor commerce to feed it. During the eighteenth century this situation changed. The great cattle development and the increase of commerce had started the city on its rise. In 1744 the city had about 10,000 people and the surrounding country some 6,000. By 1770 this had doubled. The census of viceroy Vertiz in 1778 showed 24,754 in the city and 12,925 in the country around. By the beginning of the nineteenth century the population of Buenos Aires was about 40,000 or perhaps more.[18] In the viceroyalty of Río de la Plata a partial count of the population about 1820 found:

---

[17] Humboldt, *New Spain*, I, 111-137 [*Nouvelle Espagne*, I, 346-366].
[18] Pereyra, *América española*, IV, 237; Levene, ed. *Nación Argentina*, IV, Sección I, 516-19.

	non-Indians	Indians	total
In the Audiencia of Buenos Aires	655,000	155,000	810,000
In the Audiencia of Charcas			
Intendency of Charcas	92,000	154,000	246,000
Intendency of Potosí	85,000	230,000	315,000
Intendency of La Paz	169,000	231,000	400,000
Intendency of Cochabamba	164,000	371,000	535,000
Santa Cruz, Moxos and Chiquitos	......	......	220,000
[19] Totals	1,165,000	1,141,000	2,526,000

The growth of the city of Montevideo is indicated in the following figures:

At foundation 1726	35
1757	1667 in 170 houses
1778	4270 in 920 houses
1820	7000 [20]

POPULATION: CHILE

Population in Chile showed a perceptible increase throughout the seventeenth and eighteenth centuries. In 1630 the population of Chile was 8,000 of European extraction, not counting the Indians. The mestizo population increased rapidly. As pictured in 1630 by Bishop Salcedo of Santiago: "The Indian women . . . do not marry because the young ones live in sin with mestizos and Spaniards . . . by whom they have many children, so that today there are more mestizos in this kingdom than Spaniards." [21]

The total population of Chile was estimated in:

1700 at	80,000
1740 "	120,000
1778 "	259,646
1808 "	500,000 [22]

Thus, the population of Chile more than quintupled during the eighteenth century.

Another means of measuring the increase of the population approximately is by the increase in taxes collected. They were:

1684	44,000 pesos
1700-50	100,000 "
1775	500,000 "
1789	592,178 " [23]

---

[19] Humboldt, *Travels*, VI, 363-65 [*Voyage*, XI, 86-88].

[20] Blanco Acevedo, *Uruguay colonial*, pp. 177-78; Humboldt, *Travels*, VI, 366 [*Voyage*, XI, 88].

[21] Quoted in Pereyra, *América española*, VIII, 106.

[22] Moses, *Eve*, p. 218; Barros Arana, *Chile*, VI, 153-54; VII, 336-39.

[23] Pereyra, *América española*, VIII, 162. Figures by Humboldt are much larger. He gives 980,000 in 1813 and 1,200,000 for 1823. *Travels*, VI, 138 [*Voyage*, IX, 175].

POPULATION: PERU

Peru offers more difficulties than any other region, perhaps, for one who seeks to determine the size of the population. Beginning with the sixteenth-century records of populations reaching into many millions we quickly come to a series of descriptions of the rapid destruction of the people. But such accounts differ among themselves. Some asserted early in the sixteenth century that the Indians had been killed off, while others gave large figures for the population and predicted the disappearance of the Indians. It is not difficult to draw the conclusion from some early chroniclers that the Indians of Peru had been all but destroyed by the middle of the sixteenth century. On the other hand, some estimates of the population are very large after this date. There are sufficient grounds for scepticism regarding all these population figures.

"A striking example may serve to show us how circumspect we ought to be in yielding implicit faith in the numbers found in the old descriptions of America. It has recently been printed, [*Relación de la ciudad de Truxillo por el Doctor Feyjoó*, 1763, p. 29.] that in the enumeration of the inhabitants of Peru, made by the Archbishop of Lima, Fray Geronimo de Loaysa, in 1551, were found 8,285,000 Indians. This is a painful fact for those who knew that in 1793, on a very exact enumeration ordered by Gil de Taboada y Lemos, the viceroy, the Indians of the present Peru (since the separation of Chile and Buenos Ayres) did not exceed 600,000 individuals. Here we might be tempted to believe that 7,600,000 Indians had disappeared from the face of the globe. Luckily, however, the assertion of the Peruvian author is entirely false; for on the most careful investigation of the archives of Lima by Father Cisneros, it has been discovered that the existence of eight millions in 1551 rests on no historical document. M. Feyjoó, the author of the statistical account of Truxillo, has even since declared that this bold assertion was merely founded on a supposititious calculation from the enumeration of so many ruined towns since the epoch of the Conquest. These ruins appeared to him demonstrative of an immense population in Peru at a remote period. It frequently happens, however, that the examination of an erroneous opinion leads to some important truth. Father Cisneros, on rummaging in the archives of the sixteenth century, discovered that the viceroy Toledo, very justly regarded as the Spanish legislator of Peru, reckoned in 1575, in the examination of the kingdom which he made in person from Túmbez to Chuquisagua (which is nearly the present extent of Peru), only about a million and a half of Indians." [24]

It may be observed that this later figure of one and a half million of Indians would correspond closely to the estimates which the present author considers most logical for the whole of the Inca Empire, about two million people.[25]

The total population of the Viceroyalty of Lima in 1793, after the Viceroyalty of the Río de la Plata was separated, was placed at one million. Humboldt estimated the population in 1800 at approximately 1,200,000 without Chile or Quito, and at 1,400,000 in 1823.[26]

The increase of population is indicated by the city of Lima itself, which had in:

1700	30,000
1764	54,000
1810	87,000

Lima in 1810 was about a mile long from east to west, and contained about 3641 houses.[27]

POPULATION: ECUADOR, COLOMBIA, VENEZUELA

The area which forms the three northern countries of South America today, Ecuador, Colombia, and Venezuela, had a population of 2,643,000 to 2,900,000 in 1820, according to official figures. Slightly different figures show that the region had a total and relative population as follows:

Area in marine leagues		Comparative area	Population	Relative pop. per. sq. league
New Granada (with Quito)	58,250	almost 4 Spains	2,000,000	34
Venezuela	33,700	more than 2 Spains ..	785,000	23
New Granada and Venezuela	91,950	six Spains	2,785,000	30 [28]

POPULATION: NEW SPAIN

No official census was taken in New Spain prior to 1793, hence all previous figures are based on estimates. Many of these, especially for the pre-Conquest period, are greatly at variance with one another.[29]

---

[24] Humboldt, *New Spain*, I, 92-93 [*Nouvelle Espagne*, I, 319-320].

[25] See Chapter 9.

[26] Humboldt, *Travels*, VI, 137-142 [*Voyage*, IX, 174-183].

[27] Moses, *Eve*, 4-6.

[28] Humboldt, *Travels*, VI, 137; 191-92. [*Voyage*, IX, 172-173; 257-258].

[29] See Chapter 9.

Post-Conquest figures begin with the estimate made by Cortés himself of 30,000 people for Mexico City in 1524. Fray Alonso Ponce estimated the population at 3,000 *vecinos españoles* at the end of the sixteenth century, not counting mestizos, Indians, and Negroes. [30] Mexico City about 1650 had eight thousand inhabitants of Spanish origin, not counting the mestizos, Negroes, Indians, and others. [31]

The total population of Mexico City was found to be 112,926 by the census of 1793, but Humboldt considered this estimate too low and set the figure at 137,000 for the early years of the nineteenth century. [32] Mexico City contained more people at the beginning of the nineteenth century than any city of Great Britain or France except London, Dublin, or Paris and more than New York, Philadelphia, Boston, or Baltimore. It was, in almost every respect, the leading city of the Western Hemisphere. [33]

For all of Mexico the census of 1793-1794 showed:

Names of the intendancies and governments in which the enumeration was completed in 1793.	Population Of the intendancies and governments	Of the capitals
Mexico	1,162,886	112,926
Puebla	566,443	52,717
Tlaxcala	59,177	3,357
Oaxaca	411,366	19,069
Valladolid	289,314	17,093
Guanaxuato	397,924	32,098
San Luis Potosi	242,280	8,571
Zacatecas	118,027	25,495
Durango	122,866	11,027
Sonora	93,396	
Nuevo Mexico	30,953	
The two Californias	12,666	
Yucatan	358,261	28,392
Total population of New Spain deduced from the enumeration of 1793	3,865,559	
In a report to the King, Count de Revilla Gigedo estimated the intendancy of Guadalaxara at 485,000		
Intendency of Vera Cruz 120,000		
Province of Cohahuila 13,000		
	618,000	
Approximate result of the enumeration in 1793.	4,483,559 inhabitants [34]	

Since the figures given in this table were considered too low at the time, because of the difficulties of taking an accurate census, the total population was estimated at a minimum of 5,200,000 people. [35]

---

[30] *C. D. I. España*, LVII, 174.
[31] Riva Palacio, *Mexico*, II, 665.
[32] Humboldt, *New Spain*, II, 82 [*Nouvelle Espagne*, II, 173].
[33] *Ibid.*, 87-90 [*Nouvelle Espagne*, II, 177-181].
[34] Humboldt, *New Spain*, I, 97 [*Nouvelle Espagne*, I, 325].
[35] *Ibid.*, 98-99 [*Nouvelle Espagne*, I, 326-327].

The population did not remain stationary, however, and there is ample evidence of rapid increase in the later years of the colonial period. Births exceeded deaths by about 150,000 "in years without famine, epidemical small pox, or matlazahautl." Since there were no bad epidemics between 1793 and 1810, it is probable that the population was considerably augmented.

Other data also indicate increase, notably the relation between food production and population. In colonial Mexico there was an excellent index to food production in the tithe levied by the Church. As one late colonial observer remarked:

"The only true sign of a real and permanent increase of population is an increase in the means of subsistence. This increase, this augmentation of the produce of agriculture, is evident in Mexico; and appears to indicate a much more rapid progress of population than has been supposed. . . . In a Catholic country, the ecclesiastical tenths are as it were, the thermometer by which we may judge of the state of agriculture; and these tenths . . . have doubled in less than 24 years." [36]

These considerations led Humboldt to place the population at 5,800,000 in 1803 and 6,500,000 in 1808, but both figures were estimates and not to be thought of as exactly accurate.

POPULATION: THE WEST INDIES

The West Indies had also undergone a rapid increase in population in the eighteenth and nineteenth centuries, largely because the demand for tropical products had stimulated immigration of both free and slave peoples. Cuba, the largest of the Spanish colonies in the West Indies, more than quadrupled its population in fifty years, as the following figures indicate:

Population of Cuba: 1775-1825

1775	170,862
1791	272,140
1817	630,000
1825	715,000

Havana was one of the leading cities of the New World. Its population doubled between 1791-1810, reaching 96,000 at the latter date. By 1825 its population was three times that of 1791, being about 130,000. New York in the same period had about 140,000 people, a few thousand more than Havana and about the same number as Lyons, France. Mexico City with 170,000 people was the largest city in the Western Hemisphere with New

[36] Humboldt. *New Spain*, I, 109-110 [*Nouvelle Espagne*, I, 341-342].

York, Philadelphia, Havana, Rio de Janeiro, and Baia following in that order, all with more than 100,000 each.

The Spanish islands were the most populous of the West Indies, as the following figures indicate:

POPULATION OF THE WEST INDIES: 1823

	Total Population	Slaves
English West Indies	766,500	626,800
Haiti, French and Spanish	820,000	
Spanish Islands		
Cuba	715,000	256,000
Puerto Rico	225,000	25,000
French Islands	219,000	178,000
Dutch, Danish and Swedish	84,500	61,300 [87]

RACIAL DISTRIBUTION OF POPULATION

While the races in Spanish America were tending to merge, with the number of mixed bloods constantly growing, the racial distribution in the different colonies varied considerably, one stock predominating in one section, and another elsewhere.

In Chile and Paraguay, as we have seen, the population was most largely mestizo. In Peru, to a somewhat lesser extent, the mestizos were an important element. The million people estimated for the Viceroyalty of Lima, in 1793 included 600,000 Indians, 240,000 mestizos, and 40,000 slaves. Lima's population of 87,000 in 1810 had only 29,000 whites, the rest being Indians, Negroes, and mixed bloods.[88]

In the Viceroyalty of the Río de la Plata in 1820, according to Humboldt's figures previously cited, the division between Indians and non-Indians was fairly equal, the total population of 2,526,000 comprising 1,141,000 Indians and 1,165,000 non-Indians, large numbers of whom are probably of mixed blood rather than white.

Although the Indians predominated in New Spain, the mestizos were numerous. The population of Mexico City, estimated by Humboldt at 137,000 for the early years of the nineteenth century, was divided as follows:

> 2,500 white Europeans
> 65,000 white Creoles
> 33,000 Indians
> 26,500 mestizos
> 10,000 mulattoes

These figures show 69,500 "men of colour" and 67,500 whites, but are not to be taken too literally. Many men of some color

---

[87] Humboldt, *Travels*, VI, 820-27 [*Voyage* XI, 145-154].
[88] Moses, *Eve*, pp. 4-6.

classed themselves as white, and "a great number of the mestizos are almost as white as the Europeans and Spanish creoles." [39]

The approximate distribution of the population of New Spain by groups was as follows in 1803:

Racial Distribution of population of New Spain 1803

Indians		2,500,000	or about 42.9%
Whites or Creoles	1,025,000		
Spaniards: Europeans	70,000	1,095,000	18.8%
Negroes		6,100	0.1%
Mixed (Indian, White, Negro)		2,231,000	38.2%
[40] Total		5,832,100	100%

Within New Spain the geographical distribution of the peoples varied greatly. The Indian population lived, generally speaking, to the south of Mexico City, and the mixed peoples to the north. To illustrate, the distribution in four intendancies according to the 1793 census was:

	Total population	European descent
Guanajuato (northwest of Mexico City)	398,000	103,000
Valladolid (northwest of Mexico City)	290,000	80,000
Puebla (southeast of Mexico City)	638,000	63,000
Oaxaca (southeast of Mexico City)	411,000	26,000

These four intendancies contained some 272,000 descendants of Europeans in a total population of 1,737,000. Of each 100 inhabitants there were in:

Valladolid	27 descendants of Europeans
Guanajato	25 descendants of Europeans
Puebla	9 descendants of Europeans
Oaxaca	6 descendants of Europeans

The percentage of Europeans in New Spain may be compared

---

[39] Humboldt, *New Spain*, II, 81-82 [*Nouvelle Espagne*, II, 173].

[40] These figures are adjusted from Humboldt's statistics. In his *New Spain*, II, 356 [*Nouvelle Espagne*, II, 449] he gives the mixed population as 1,231,000, but in other places (*New Spain* I, 243; *Nouvelle Espagne*, II, 48) he speaks of their amounting to almost 2,400,000 and the figures of population have been adjusted accordingly. However, in still another place (*Travels* VI., 129; *Voyage*, IX, 160) Humboldt placed the Indian population at 3,250,000 in a total of approximately 6,500,000, making the Indians half the population. This latter calculation is more nearly in agreement with Fernando Navarro y Noriega, who reckoned the population of New Spain in 1800 as 6,122,000 distributed as follows:

Europeans and American Spaniards	1,097,928
Indians	3,676,281
Mixed Races	1,338,706
Secular ecclesiastics	4,229
Regular clergy	3,112
Nuns	2,098
Total	6,122,354

Humboldt, *Travels*, VI, 130. [*Voyage*, IX, 161-62].

with that in some of the West Indies, where the Negro population was heavy. In 1788 Haiti had:

Total	Whites	Free Negroes	Slaves	Whites per 100	Negroes
520,000	40,000	28,000	452,000	8	92

Jamaica had 10 whites and 90 Negroes for each 100 people in 1787. Thus the two islands had a larger percentage of white population than the southern intendancies of New Spain.[41] Cuba in 1804, however, had per 100 people:

Whites (creole and European), 54; Free Negroes, 21; Negro Slaves, 25. In the United States, the whites amounted to 83 per cent of the whole; in Cuba 54; New Spain (without the *provincias internas*)16; Peru, 12; Jamaica, 10.[42]

The population of Guatemala, which included all present-day Central America, was about 1,600,000 of whom about 55 per cent were Indians and 25 per cent or more mixed.

A comparison of the proportion of Negroes in the populations of the tropical regions, where Negroes were most numerous, shows that the West Indies had 83 per cent Negroes, free and slave; Brazil 76 per cent, and the United States 19 per cent.[43]

America as a whole, including the United States, had a total of 6,433,000 Negroes of whom:

5,047,000 were slaves, equal to 79 per cent
1,386,000 were free, equal to 21 per cent

Haiti alone had 870,000 free Negroes, amounting to about sixty per cent of the total in America.

The Indians were still extremely numerous, the predominantly Indian countries being Mexico, Guatemala, Ecuador, Peru and Bolivia, with heavy Indian population living also in parts of Colombia, Venezuela, northwestern Argentina, and Brazil. The Indians represented forty-five per cent of the total population of Spanish America, but only twenty-five per cent of the population of all America (including the United States) as indicated in the following table:

Distribution of the Races of America 1823-25

Whites	13,471,000 or 38.6 per cent
Indians	8,610,000 or 24.6 per cent
Negroes	6,433,000 or 18.4 per cent
Mixed	6,428,000 or 18.4 per cent

An interesting fact connected with race distribution is that Span-

[41] Humboldt, *New Spain*, I, 206-208 [*Nouvelle Espagne*, II, 4-7].
[42] Humboldt, *New Spain*, I, 208-9 [*Nouvelle Espagne*, II, 7-8].
[43] Humboldt, *Travels*, VII, 101-102, [*Voyage*, XI, 292-93].

ish America had but little more than twelve per cent of the total number of Negroes in America while Brazil had about thirty-five per cent of the total and the United States almost as many. Spanish America was predominantly white and Indian (and their mixtures) with only four per cent of the people being Negro.

In Spanish America, as distinct from America as a whole, which we were treating in the figures above, the racial distribution of population about 1823 was:

Indians	7,530,000	44.5 per cent
Mixed	5,328,000	31.5 per cent
Whites	3,276,000	19.4 per cent
Negro	776,000	4.6 per cent[44]

RELATIVE POPULATION OF AMERICA

Having examined the absolute populations of the various regions of America, it will be interesting to make some comparisons of the relative populations. Vast regions of America were all but unpopulated at the beginning of the nineteenth century; others had concentrated settlements. The two intendancies of Mexico and Puebla in New Spain contained, in 1823, a total population of 2,800,000,[45] approximately equal to that of the whole of Colombia, but in area they were no larger than the single province of Caracas. The two Mexican intendancies whose density of population came nearest Caracas, but still exceeded it, were Zacatecas and Guadlajara occupying the seventh and eighth positions among the intendancies of New Spain.

Of great significance is a comparison of the relative density of population in Latin America and other parts of the world. The minimum density of Europe as compared with the maximum of America, shows:

The Minimum of Europe Per square league		The Maximum of America Per square league	
Russia (four least populated regions)		United States	
Archangel	10	Massachusetts	900
Olonez	42	Massachusetts, Rhode Island	
Vologda and Astrakhan	52	and Connecticut	840
Finland	106	Latin America	
Cuenca (Spain's least peopled part)	311	Intendancy of Puebla (Mexico)	540
Duchy of Lunebourg	550	Intendancy of Mexico	460
Upper Alps (France's least)	758	Caracas (Venezuela) excluding	
Departments of Creuse, Var and Aude		the Llanos or interior plains	208
(thinly peopled parts of France)	1300	Central part of Intendancies of	
		Mexico and Puebla	1300

The most densely populated parts of America approached the

[44] Humboldt, *Travels*, VI, 832-45[*Voyage*, XI, 160-175]. Both the numbers and the percentages are approximate.

[45] *Ibid.*, VI, 196-97 [*Voyage*, IX, 262-264].

density of the Spanish provinces of Navarre, Galicia, and Asturias. The maximum density of America fell considerably short of the mean density of France which had 1778 people to the square league.[46] America as a whole had a relative population of only 29 to the square league, Spanish America only 45, South America but 21, and Brazil only 15, whereas the Russian Empire had 87, The Chinese Empire 377 and Europe 639, Spain and Portugal 805, India 925, China proper 1172, Germany 1432, France 1778 and the British Islands 2120.[47]

Thus we see that of the great land bodies, America was the least populated (possibly excluding Siberia), and that only by selecting a small part of the most populous part of New Spain, (Mexico and Puebla), can we find a density equal to that of three of the least populated parts of France.

---

[46] With the exception of certain confined areas and islands, "for instance on the coast of Brazil, in the valley of Mexico, on the table lands of Sante Fé de Bogotá and Cuzco; or finally, in the small West India islands (Barbadoes, Martinique, and St. Thomas), of which the relative population is from 3000 to 4700 inhabitants to the square league, and consequently equal to the most fertile parts of Holland, France and Lombardy." Humboldt, *Travels* VI, 194-95 [*Voyage,* IX, 261-262].

[47] A population of 1300 to a square league is 109 to a square mile of 69.2 miles to a degree. Humboldt, *Travels,* VI, 195-96; 336-341.

22

Social Evolution to 1810— Class Structure

E VERYWHERE IN THE COLONIES, regardless of the racial composition of the population, the class divisions were fundamental. Many of these were based on racial distinctions, real or fancied, certain stocks or mixtures tending to occupy a certain place in society.

The Negroes, on the whole, remained in slavery, but a small percentage became freed men. The Indians constituted the majority of the laboring masses in those regions where they had been most numerous prior to the Conquest. The mestizos, to some extent, took on the attributes of a middle class. People of European origin gradually divided into Creoles (those of European stock born in America) and *Peninsulares* (those born in Spain), terms which acquired an economic, political, and social significance that was very influential upon the evolution of colonial society. A proletariat drawn from all types, including Creoles, Europeans, Negroes, Indians, and their mixtures, developed by the end of the eighteenth century. There was also a middle class largely composed of those of European extraction, but which drew its members from all groups.

POSITION OF THE INDIANS

Since the persistence of the Indian population is a basic factor in Latin-American history, the conditions under which the Indians lived, and the degree to which their status changed, are of primary importance. The successive stages of forced labor through which the Indians passed from the time of the Conquest to the end of the colonial period may be classified under three heads: The early stage was that of slavery, the *indios herrados,* or the Indians who were branded like cattle; the second stage was that of the

460

indios encomendados, which came simultaneously, but gradually supplanted chattel slavery, and endured until late in the eighteenth century, with perhaps a half, or even more of the Indians living under it; the third was the *mandamiento, mita,* or *repartimiento,* through which the Indian fell victim to a system under which certain people acquired a right to command his labor.

Many forms of forced labor were demanded of the Indians. In Mexico City, thousands of Indians were used during the seventeenth and eighteenth centuries in the digging of the *desagüe,* or great canal, designed to drain the Valley of Mexico and prevent the inundation of the city. Sometimes whole villages were brought to this work; at times the villages served in turns. The extremely hard labor, the dangers of the work, and the epidemics resulting from the poor sanitary conditions under which they labored were cited by contemporaries as the reason for the death of thousands of Indians:

"The Indians entertain the most bitter hatred against the desagüe of Huehuetoca. A hydraulical operation is looked upon by them in the light of a public calamity, not only because a great number of individuals have perished by unfortunate accidents . . . but especially because they were compelled to labour to the neglect of their own domestic affairs, so that they fell into the greatest indigence . . . . Many thousands of Indian labourers have been almost constantly occupied in the desagüe for two centuries; and it may be considered as a principal cause of the poverty of the Indians in the valley of Mexico. The great humidity to which they were exposed in the trench of Nochistongo gave rise to the most fatal maladies among them. It has been only a very few years ago that the Indians were cruelly bound with ropes, and forced to work like galley slaves, even when sick, till they expired on the spot." [1]

It is extremely difficult to get at the truth regarding the social conditions of the masses of the Indians. The laws of the Indies required just treatment for them, and at times were effective. On the other hand, the descriptions of the wretched living conditions of the Indians are too numerous to ignore. Towards the end of the sixteenth century the working conditions in the mines under the *mita* and *repartimiento* system were undoubtedly much improved by the rigorous enforcement of the laws. But in this same period the system of the *congregaciones,* established in Mexico and other parts of America, led to the revolt of the Indians, who during the

---

[1] Humboldt, *New Spain,* II, 168-70 [*Nouvelle Espagne,* 247-249].

late sixteenth and seventeenth centuries all but wiped out European control in certain parts of America.[2]

INDIAN CONDITIONS: THEORY VS. FACT

Indian policy in practice was never consistent, varying with time, place, and the character of the various Indian peoples. The attitude towards the Indians changed considerably within a few years after the Conquest. Along with the cruelty of the conquistadores, should be chronicled the attention given to the education of the Indian. Before the establishment in Mexico of a single institution for the education of the Europeans, the colegio of Santa Cruz was founded for the Indian nobility.

But the first impulse to accept the Indians on a more or less equal footing was soon altered.[3] With the competition of numerous individuals for the few available places, the conquering peoples reserved to themselves positions of privilege and profit, and the common Indians were relegated to the working class. This in spite of the laws which in theory rendered them immune from abuses and excessive work and taxes.

"To protect them in their innocence from the frauds of the Spaniards, they were granted, as were the churches, the privileges of minors. They were not subject to military service, nor to the payment of tithes and taxes, except a small personal tax which they paid once a year, a portion of which was dedicated to the maintenance of hospitals dedicated to their assistance, and from which the Tlaxcalans, caciques, women, invalids, and aged were exempt . . . . They had lawyers obligated by the law to defend them free of charge; the King's prosecutors were their protectors ex-officio; they were not included in the authority of the Inquisition, and in ecclesiastical matters they had numerous and very important privileges. They lived in villages separated from the Spaniards, governed by themselves, forming municipalities which were called republics, and they preserved their languages and native costumes . . . . All this made the Indians an entirely separate nation; they considered as foreigners all who did not form one of them; and, as they were harassed by all of the other classes in spite of their privileges, they looked upon all of them with an equal degree of hate and suspicion."[4]

There had also been created in New Spain in 1573 a spe-

[2] Riva Palacio, *Mexico*, II, 535-36; 585; 663-69.
[3] Alamán, *Méjico*, I, 26-7.
[4] Alamán, *Méjico*, I, 22-5.

cial court *(Juzgado de Indios)*, as we have already indicated, for their protection. The viceroy was the ex-officio protector of the Indians, but his work in legal cases was done through the *Juzgado de Indios,* and the viceroy merely signed the decisions. The cases decided by this tribunal might be of considerable importance, and the Indians could bring before it Creoles and Spaniards. The Indian villages brought their accusations against the corregidores and subdelegados before this same court.[5] The *Juzgado* undoubtedly checked some of the mistreatment of the Indians, since its decisions consistently favored them, but it should be understood that the abuses were mitigated, not abolished.

Under the system known in New Spain as the *repartimiento* and in Peru as the *mita,* which followed the abolition of legal Indian slavery (with exceptions shortly to be noted), the Indians were distributed to private individuals to work on specified tasks for fixed periods of time. The Indians were assembled each week (or at other stated intervals), on Sunday usually, and assigned to tasks for the coming week. Nominally, each Indian was to serve only once in four weeks (a time period that also varied), and was to be paid. A *real* a day was frequently set as the pay, though this too differed in various regions and epochs.

At first arising extralegally from the Spaniard's desire for workers and the Indian's inheritance of a similar custom from pre-Conquest times, the system was in due course recognized and regulated by law, one of the most important such enactments being the Ordinances of 1609. Numerous provisions of these Ordinances sought to protect the Indians against abuse, and evoked the principle that the Indians could be used only for the public good and not for private profit. In practice, however, it was difficult to draw a sharp line between the two, but the main occupations at which the Indians were supposed to labor were public works, mining, transportation, manufacturing, building churches and convents, and agriculture. Subsequent legislation sought to strengthen and clarify the act of 1609.[6]

But whatever his theoretical protection, the lot of the Indian in Latin America at the end of the colonial period was not happy. And if the "civilized" Indians lived hard, those just being brought under Spanish control were infinitely worse off, whether in New Spain, Venezuela, or Chile. They were enslaved, contrary to the

[5] G. Desdevises du Dezert, "Les Institutions de L'Espagne", *Revue Hispanique,* LXX, 159.
[6] For the standard treatment see Simpson, *Repartimiento System,* already cited, and his *Many Mexicos,* pp. 103-31.

spirit of the law. In South America, the monks raided peaceable native settlements for Indians to add to the missions' labor force, justifying their enslavement on the ground that these Indians were savage, since they had not learned, like the mission Indians, to make the sign of the cross. The mission Indians themselves, anxious to have the captives to work for them, incited and participated in such excursions. In Mexico, the prisoners taken in frontier warfare with the Apaches and other warlike tribes, had a worse fate. Too intractable to be converted into laborers, they were incarcerated or deported to Vera Cruz or Cuba, where the tropical climate soon killed off these natives of the highlands.[7]

The conditions of the masses of the Indians were more a product of the class division of society, however, than of racial distinctions. Within the Indian ranks there persisted the same class distinctions which characterized pre-Conquest Indian society. The noble Indians occupied a privileged position in the social and political hierarchy and participated in the systematic mistreatment of the masses.

The condition of the Indians in Mexico at the end of the colonial period, however, was probably better than in the sixteenth and seventeenth centuries.

"In the eighteenth their situation assumed progressively a better appearance. The families of the *conquistadores* are partly extinguished; and the *encomiendas,* considered as fiefs, were not redistributed. The viceroys, and especially the *audiencias,* watched over the interest of the Indians; and their liberty, and, in some provinces, their ease of circumstances even, have been gradually augmenting . . . . The establishment of intendancies, during the ministry of the Count de Gálvez, was a memorable epoch for Indian prosperity. The minute vexations to which the cultivator was incessantly exposed from subaltern Spanish and Indian magistracy, have singularly diminished under the active superintendance of the intendants; and the Indians begin to enjoy advantages which laws, gentle and humane in general, afforded them, but of which they were deprived in ages of barbarity and oppression." [8]

It should not be inferred from the statement, however, that they lived well. A final judgment on the Indians of New Spain could be that: "The Mexican Indians . . . *en masse,* offer a picture of extreme misery." [9]

---

[7] Humboldt, *New Spain,* I, 237-9 [*Nouvelle Espagne,* II, 40-42].
[8] Humboldt, *New Spain,* I, 183-84 [*Nouvelle Espagne,* I, 426-428].
[9] Humboldt, *New Spain,* I, 185-86 [*Nouvelle Espagne,* I, 429].

INDIAN CONDITIONS: VENEZUELA AND COLOMBIA

Nor were the Indians (and other propertyless people) of Venezuela and Colombia better off. The northern coast of South America was long an area to which slave hunters resorted, and the treatment of the Indians could be compared only to the cruelties meted out to the Negroes of Africa. "The motives of this insatiable avarice seemed to be ennobled by the pretence of an enthusiastic zeal for religion" and the churchmen moved in and established missions on the coast and in the interior along the Orinoco.[10] But the benefits to the Indians, unless we hold that an increase in numbers is progress, were small, in view of the use the missions made of Indian labor. Nor were conditions good near the viceregal capital, Santa Fé de Bogotá. The viceroys left touching descriptions of the poverty and disease in their reports of 1789 and 1796.[11]

TREATMENT OF INDIANS IN THE ANDES

In the Andes the Indians also suffered, as we can see from a long series of reports which begin in the sixteenth century and extend to the end of the eighteenth. The corregidores, in theory the protectors of the Indians, became in fact their oppressors. Within a quarter of a century after the corregidores were first installed in the viceroyalty of Lima, complaints of their treatment of the Indians became frequent.

In 1586 Friar Rodrigo de Loaysa wrote that the "miserable Indians . . . are being finished and consumed with the greatest speed." [12] The corregidores, he said, were interested in making money out of the Indians and were thereby in conflict with the parish priests, who also wished to exploit them. The corregidores committed more crimes, Loaysa reported, than the encomenderos had. Viceroy Marquis of Cañete attempted in 1594 to correct certain abuses. Among these were: the custom of forcing those under eighteen or over fifty to work, although in theory exempted; the overworking of the Indians so that they had no time left to take care of their own properties; and the mistreatment of the Indians by the mestizos, mulattoes, Negroes, and zambos who were permitted to enter the Indian towns, contrary to the law.[13] In the seventeenth century an attempt was made to ameliorate

---

[10] Humboldt, *Travels*, III, 2-5 [*Voyage*, III, 3-5].

[11] See *Relaciones de Mando*, in *Biblioteca de historia nacional* (Bogotá, 1910), VIII, 236-49, 291-99, 322-31.

[12] Quoted in Means, *Fall*, I, 179-80.

[13] Means, *Fall*, 180-181.

conditions by taking some of the authority from the corregidores and entrusting it to the *alcaldes ordinarios*. But they too exploited the Indians. It was customary to give short measure, charge high prices, take an excessive share of the irrigation water leaving the Indians without, and sell the food products which the Indians had not been able to produce for themselves at extremely high prices in the market.

Diego de Luna, in a report to the King in 1630, related that the *mita* system would probably lead to the extermination of the Indians, since the number of Indians remaining for work in the mines of Huancavelica was but one third of those set aside by Viceroy Toledo a little more than a half century before. Viceroy Mancera (1639-48) reported that "the worst enemies of these poor Indians are the greed of their Corregidores and the cupidity of their priests and caciques (chiefs), who are all intent upon growing rich by the sweat of the Indians," and who all engaged in selling wine and other liquors to the Indians, contrary to the law. Manuel Ribeiro Teixera de Morais, who wrote about 1635 and who served as corregidor of the Indian town of Paucarcolla, listed the abuses as overwork, exploitation of the weavers and spinners who were forced to labor night and day and without sufficient time for their crops or other necessary work, and the collection of tribute twice or more in each year with the aid of the caciques. Furthermore, he said, the corregidores either robbed the Indians of their farm produce or paid for it with bad wine.[14] More than half a century later, in 1692, Lorenzo de las Llamosas cited the friction between the corregidores and the parish priests over the collection of tribute from the Indians, the priests complaining that they did not receive their share. A remedy had been sought for this in 1684 or 1685 by permitting priests to collect directly from the caciques.

So frequent had been the complaints that the government attempted a drastic remedy in 1720, abolishing the mita, but enforcement proved difficult. Repeated royal orders indicate that the abuses and the mita continued.[15]

A quarter of a century later came still more harrowing accounts. In the 1740's Jorge Juan and Antonio de Ulloa were sent to Peru with a scientific expedition, and instructed by the King to make a secret report on the conditions of the Indies.[16] This they

---

[14] Means, *Fall*, 181-86.

[15] Lorente, *Perú bajo los Borbones*, pp. 33-38, 57-60, 86-88; Fisher, *Viceregal Administration*, p. 317.

[16] Jorge Juan and Antonio de Ulloa, *Noticias secretas de América* (London,

did, revealing much about the condition of the Indians in the middle of the eighteenth century.

INDIANS ON THE ESTATES

Indians on the estates were required to work 300 days in the year, for which they received a maximum annual salary of eighteen pesos. The tribute of eight pesos was deducted by the estate owner, leaving the Indian an annual income of ten pesos. But this too was exacted from him,

". . . so that the unhappy Indian, after working three hundred days a year, besides cultivating a garden of vegetables in the remaining sixty-five, having received only a cloak of coarse cloth (*capisavo*) and six *fanegas* of corn, becomes indebted to his master . . . on account of the labor he has to perform the following year. . . ."

". . . at the close of the year, his debts exceed his earnings, while he has neither handled money nor got in his possession any articles of value whatever. His master claims the right of his person, obliges him to continue in his service until the debt is paid; and as payment can never be made by the poor Indian, he becomes a slave for life; and, in defiance of all natural and national law, children are required to pay, by their personal services, the unavoidable debts of their parents." [17]

When the price of corn and other products rose because of a short crop, the wages of the Indian remained the same. The estate owner would be induced by the high prices to sell all his crop, leaving the Indian to shift for his food as best he could.

THE OBRAJES

The sufferings of the Indians on the plantations, cattle ranches, and sheep farms, were less, however, than in the obrajes, or workshops.

"The labor of the *obraje*, or factory, begins before the day

---

1826). This work has been the subject of bitter controversy since it was discovered in Madrid and published by Barry in 1826. Some have alleged it to be a forgery, and others, while admitting its authenticity, have contended that it did not present a true picture. Both these contentions have been successfully refuted. See: Arthur P. Whitaker, "Antonio de Ulloa," *H.A.H.R.*, XV (May, 1935), 155-94; *Ibid.*, "Jorge Juan and Antonio de Ulloa's Prologue to their Secret Report of 1749 on Peru," *H.A.H.R.*, XVIII (November, 1938), 507-13; Lewis Hanke, "*Dos Palabras on Antonio de Ulloa* and the *Noticias Secretas*," *H.A.H.R.*, XVI (November, 1936), 479-514.

[17] Juan and Ulloa, *Noticias secretas*, pp. 268-270, quoted in Moses, *Eve*, pp. 178-180. This translation is from Moses, with some revision. Moses frequently abbreviates his translations but repeated checking has revealed no case where he distorted the meaning and spirit of the original.

dawns, at which time every Indian takes his place in the room where the weaving is in progress and the tasks of the day are distributed as may be expedient; and when this process is concluded, the owner of the house closes the door, and leaves them immured as in a prison. At midday the door is opened for the women to go in with their scanty allowance of food, which is soon partaken, and they are again locked in. When the darkness of the night no longer permits them to work, the owner goes round to gather up the stints; those who have not been able to finish, in spite of apologies or reasonings, are punished with indescribable cruelty; and those unfeeling men, as if transformed into cruel executioners, inflict upon the wretched Indians lashes by hundreds, for they use no other method of counting; and to complete the punishment, they remand them again to the workshop, and although the whole building is a prisonhouse, a portion of it is expressly reserved for the shackles and stocks, where they are punished with greater indignity than could be practised towards the most delinquent slaves." [18]

All delinquencies in meeting their work quota were charged to their accounts. Each year found the Indians deeper in debt. Their food was composed of semi-rotten corn and barley, and putrid meat. As a result of overwork and undernourishment "the greater part of these die in the very factories with their tasks in their hands." [19] Indians who failed to pay their tribute were forced to work in the obrajes as punishment, to which they were sentenced for the most minor offenses. Juan and Ulloa reported: "We frequently meet Indians on the highway, tied by the hair to the tail of a horse, on which a mestizo is mounted, who is conveying them to the workshops, and perhaps for the trivial offence of having evaded the tyranny of the overseer, from fear of punishment." [20] To justify this system of compulsory labor, it was alleged that the Indians would not work unless forced, but Juan and Ulloa found that the Indians when paid for their labor worked willingly, and that the free Indians cultivated their fields "without being compelled by force, and without using compulsion towards those who labor for them." [21]

In plantations and factories there was usually an overseer, an assistant overseer, and a foreman. The latter acted as a taskmaster

[18] Juan and Ulloa, *Noticias secretas*, p. 276, quoted in Moses, *Eve*, p. 180-181.
[19] Juan and Ulloa, *Noticias secretas*, 277-8, quoted in Moses, *Eve*, p. 182.
[20] Quoted in Moses, *Eve*, p. 182.
[21] Quoted in *ibid.*, p. 183.

and was frequently himself an Indian who whipped the Indians severely for minor offenses.

EXTORTION BY THE CLERGY

The priests called themselves the protectors of the Indians but a great number of them were actually oppressors. Numerous fees were collected from the Indians on the occasions of Saints' days, four and a half pesos for high mass,

". . . and an equal amount for the sermon, which consists in merely repeating a few words in praise of the saint"; "to this is to be added the customary offering which the overseers are compelled to make to the curate on every saint's festival, which consists of two or three dozen hens, as many chickens, guinea-pigs, eggs, sheep, and a hog if they happen to have any; so that when the saint's day arrives, the curate sweeps off all that the Indian has been able to collect in money during the whole year, and also all the fowls and animals which his wife and children have reared in their huts, so that his family are left almost destitute of food, and are reduced to wild herbs and to the grains which they cultivate in their small gardens. The Indian who has not been able to rear a sufficient number of animals for the customary offering is bound of necessity to purchase them, and should he not have the money, as is usually the case, he is to take it upon pledge, or hire it for the time required, in order to obtain it and pay it without delay. As soon as the sermon of the day is concluded, the curate reads a paper on which he has inscribed the names of those who are to be masters of ceremonies for the festival of the following year, and if any one does not accept it of his free will, he is forced to give his consent by dint of blows; and when his day comes, there is no apology that can exonerate him from having the money ready; for, until it is all collected and delivered to the curate, mass is not said, the sermon is not preached, and the whole service is deferred until three or four in the afternoon, if necessary, to allow time to collect the amount, as we have had occasion to observe repeatedly." [22]

Indian boys and girls were required to come every day for religious instruction, and to bring with them fuel for the priest's house and hay for the cattle and horses. All this sounds extortionate enough, but Juan and Ulloa found that the monks and their

---

[22] Juan and Ulloa, pp. 335-337, quoted in Moses, *Eve*, pp. 186-187.

mistresses were more oppressive than the priests. Concerning the mistresses of the monks, Juan and Ulloa say:

"This woman, who is known as such, and without exciting surprise, because it is everywhere so common, takes under her charge all the Indian women and children, and converting the whole village into a manufactory, she assigns to some tasks in spinning wool or cotton, and to others pieces for weaving; and to the aged, and to those who are incapable of performing this service, she gives hens, and imposes on them the obligation of delivering to her, within a definite time, ten or twelve chickens for each one; it being their duty to feed them at their own expense and, if the fowls should die, to replace them with others; and by these means no one is exempted from contributing something to the revenue of the curate." [23]

But the Indians did not always submit peacefully to this oppression.

"Unable to endure the hardships, and longing to escape from bondage, many of them have risen in rebellion, and found their way to unconquered districts, there to continue in the barbarous practices of their idolatrous neighbors; and in view of the foregoing, what conclusions are they to form from the scandalous lives of their parish priests, especially when we reflect that the Indian is very simple *(tan rústica)*, and is taught more by example than by precept?" [24]

CONTINUATION OF ABUSES AND INDIAN REVOLTS

Conditions around Lima are disclosed in a report made about 1750. Children were bought and sold, robbed from their parents, or seduced away by the priests. The Indians attempted a revolt in 1748, but their plans were revealed in the confessional and reported to the authorities before they could make effective resistance. Corregidores and clergymen participated in mulcting the Indians, and protests were in vain. A nineteenth century Peruvian historian has pointed out that the clergy multiplied the religious holidays and ceremonies to collect more from the Indians, and that the sacraments were administered for fees. Marriages were enforced for the same purpose, sometimes on those already married; and the funeral ceremonies absorbed what should have been the inheritance of the survivors. "And when nothing else remained, they demanded the young children of the deceased, who were given

---

[23] Juan and Ulloa, *Noticias secretas,* p. 340, quoted in Moses, *Eve,* pp. 188-89.
[24] *Noticias secretas,* p. 343, quoted in Moses, *Eve,* p. 189.

or sold under the name of *cholitos*. . . . After the burial there came the honors of the recent dead, at the end of nine days; those of a fresh cadaver, at the end of six months; those of a seasoned cadaver, after one year; and the general honors of the dead, perpetually, all accompanied by forceful exactions." [25] Twenty years after the investigation by Juan and Ulloa, the city of Cuzco in 1768 issued another report which showed that conditions had not improved.[26] A few years later, 1775-76 the Indians were pictured as being in virtual slavery to the corregidores; and there were several Indian rebellions. The frequent uprisings were cruelly suppressed throughout the Indies in the final years before the wars of independence.[27]

DEBT SLAVERY

The abuses of the Indians took other forms also, only one more of which will be mentioned here: debt slavery. As has been stated, various legislation during the course of the eighteenth century released the Indian, at least in part, from the *encomienda, mita,* and *repartimiento*. But just as the emancipation of the Indian slaves and the partial enforcement of the New Laws in the sixteenth century caused the Spaniards to find in the *repartimiento* a system by which they could continue to exact labor service, the legislation against the repartimiento and the mita led to debt slavery as still another form of forced labor.

This practice arose before repartimientos were abolished and was used in combination with it, complaints about debt slavery coming as early as 1634. It can be seen clearly from the observations of Juan and Ulloa, as well as others, that the Indian labor system was in the transitional stage during the eighteenth century. When the Indian could no longer be forced legally to do repartimiento labor, he was driven into debt by the great gulf separating his needs from his purchasing power. Once in debt, he almost never was able to pay, and consequently was compelled year after year to continue payments through his labor on a debt that grew larger as he worked. Such debts became hereditary. The law upheld the creditor's contract for liquidation of the debt by labor, and the

---

[25] Lorente, *Perú bajo los Borbones,* pp. 135-38. This was a few years after the time of Juan and Ulloa and during the reign of Viceroy Manuel Amat, 1761-76. One priest buried a corpse head down, saying it could not go to heaven, until he was paid 500 pesos.

[26] Moses, *Eve,* p. 194.

[27] Philip Ainsworth Means, "The Rebellion of Tupac-Amaru II, 1780-1781," *H.A.H.R.,* II (February, 1919), 1-25.

Indian was caught in a net from which there was little chance to escape.[28]

CONDITIONS OF THE NEGRO SLAVES

Negro slavery in the Spanish America colonies was confined principally to the tropical lowlands, especially the coastlines from Peru to Panama and those of Mexico, Central America, and northern South America. By 1522 the slaves were numerous enough in Española to revolt, but without success.[29] Other revolts came in the following years, and in 1550 the slaves rose in Venezuela, only to fail as usual.[30]

Heartrending descriptions of their conditions could be cited by the dozens, but a few will suffice to show how they fared in both the French and Spanish colonies. Writing in the eighteenth century, Charlevoix, the French Jesuit historian, remarked concerning the Negroes of Haiti:

"I end by speaking of the Negroes, today the great majority of the inhabitants of that colony. Nothing is more deplorable than the condition of these people. It seems that they are the most abject of men and the refuse of nature. Exiled from their country, and deprived of that blessing of which all other nations are most jealous, liberty, they are reduced almost to the condition of pack animals. . . . Their work is almost continual, their sleep exceedingly short, salary nil, and twenty blows of the whip for the least mistake." [31]

The situation in the Spanish colonies of the same epoch was no different. In a slave market in Venezuela in 1800:

"The persons who came to purchase examined the teeth of these slaves, to judge of their age and health, forcing open their mouths as we do those of horses in a market. This degrading custom dates from Africa, as is proved by the faithful picture, which, in one of his dramatic pieces Cervantes, released from his long captivity among the Moors, has drawn of the sale of the Christian slaves at Algiers. It is distressing to think that even at this day there exist European colonists in the West Indies, who mark their slaves with a hot iron, to know them again if they escape." [32]

---

[28] Chester Lloyd Jones, *Guatemala: Past and Present* (Minneapolis, 1940), pp. 139-40; Simpson, *Repartimiento System*, pp. 93-116. Jones, *Guatemala*, pp. 113-67 has a good discussion of Indian Labor.

[29] Charlevoix, *L'Isle Espagnole*, I, 423-24.

[30] Herrera, *Hechos castellanos*, Dec. VIII, Bk. VI, chap. XII.

[31] Charlevoix, *L'Isle Espagnole*, II, 596-97.

[32] Humboldt, *Travels*, II, 245-47 *Voyage*, II, 312, who quotes also La Buryère, *Caractères*, ch. XI (ed. 1765, p. 300).

Negro slavery, however, was not only accepted as an economic necessity; it was defended by the Church as being compatible with Christian ethics. When the Jesuits were expelled from America in 1767 a large part of their property consisted of slaves. In Chile for example, where Negroes were few, the Jesuits owned some 1200 slaves. The total number of Negroes and mulattoes in Chile was about 10,000 or 12,000, of which less than half were slaves. The Jesuits must have owned at least one-fifth of the total slaves of Chile. [33] At the mission of Catarro in Venezuela, Baron Humboldt was regaled by one of the missionaries on "the necessity of the slave trade, on the innate wickedness of the blacks, and the benefit they derived from their state of slavery among the Christians." [34]

There was also a difference between the laws and the actual treatment of the blacks.

"The mildness of the Spanish legislation compared with the Black Code of the greater part of other nations that have possessions in either India, cannot be denied. But such is the state of the Negroes, dispersed in places scarcely begun to be cultivated, that justice, far from efficaciously protecting them during their lives, cannot even punish acts of barbarity, that have caused their death. If an inquiry be attempted, the death of the slave is attributed to the bad state of his health, to the influence of a warm and humid climate, to the wounds which he has received, but which, it is asserted, were neither deep nor dangerous. The civil authority is powerless with respect to whatever constitutes domestic slavery; and nothing is more illusory than the effect so much vaunted of these laws, which prescribe the form of the whip, and the number of lashes which it is permitted to give at a time." [35]

Spanish America did not have as many slaves at the beginning of the nineteenth century however, as Anglo-America, the number being smaller than in the single state of Virginia.

In the importation of slaves into America, the number of men considerably exceeded the women. This was rationalized on religious grounds, but since we know that women sold for about one-third less than men, while the cost of capture and transportation was the same, we are justified in believing that it was the economic rather than the religious motive which prevented the

[33] Barros Arana, *Chile,* VII, 479-80.
[34] Humboldt, *Travels,* III, 179 [*Voyage,* III, 224].
[35] Humboldt, *Travels,* III, 179-80 [*Voyage,* III, 224-225].

introduction of the Negro women. Negro men were forced to be celibate, also on the grounds of morality. "The Jesuits and the Bethlemites monks only had renounced that fatal prejudice, and encouraged negresses in their plantations." This observation regarding Cuba reveals not only that the Church there, as elsewhere, customarily owned slaves, but also why it was necessary to import so many thousands of slaves, and why they multiplied so slowly.[36] The Negroes seem to have been everywhere regarded in about the same way a man would regard his work stock. The number who died each year varied considerably "according to the kind of culture, the humanity of the masters and overseers, and the number of negresses who can take care of the sick. There are plantations in which fifteen to eighteen per cent perish annually. I have heard it coolly discussed, whether it were better for the proprietor not to fatigue the slaves to excess by labor, and consequently to replace them less frequently, or to draw all the advantage possible from them in a few years, and replace them oftener by the acquisition of *bozale negroes*." [37]

Emancipation was legally possible, and not infrequent in the Spanish colonies. The means were several. A slave might be freed as a religious act on the part of his master or, under the economic system of the late colonial period, the owner might rent out his slaves and give them a portion of whatever sums they earned. With money thus gained a slave could sometimes save enough to buy his freedom. The opportunity to earn enough to buy freedom was, however, not common. The statement that "a slave, who by his industry has procured a little money, may compel his master to give him his liberty on paying the moderate sum of 1500 or 2000 *livres*" indicates an ease of manumission that did not exist. The sum cited was equal to three or four hundred pesos, an amount far in excess of the earning capacity of any but an occasional skilled workman. Spanish legislation provided means of emancipation which, when compared with English and French laws, seemed easy, but though emancipation was possible, it was not likely. The total number of free Negroes at the end of the colonial period was probably not in excess of ten per cent of the Negro population.

Even while the Negro was gaining freedom from chattel slavery, other methods were being devised to keep him in an economic subjection scarcely less binding. Semi-serfdom and debt slavery had already made their appearance before 1800 and their importance grew *pari passu* with the legal emancipation of the Negro.

[36] Humboldt, *Travels*, VII, 142 [*Voyage*, XI, 340-341].
[37] Humboldt, *Travels*, VII, 152-153 [*Voyage*, XI, 353-355].

Condition of Free Labor

The condition of the laboring classes in colonial Latin-America was only indirectly related to their legal position. That a Negro was a chattel slave, or the Indian subject to the encomienda and the mita, did not mean that his economic position was relatively any worse than that of a considerable proportion of the population who were classed as freemen, but who were free only in a relative sense. The class system hedged them about with numerous restrictions, recognized by law. But they were considered free men, and while studying their economic condition, we should keep in mind that they were so classified.

From the first days of the Conquest a class of free, propertyless individuals existed. This group became more numerous during the course of the colonial period with the increase of mestizos, zambos, mulattoes, and Europeans who were not fortunate enough to own property. Since the system of land control prevented the majority of the people from owning any land whatever and also concentrated in a few hands the commercial and mineral wealth, it became inevitable that a proletariat should form. This propertyless class was drawn from all of the racial groups represented in America and tended to increase both relatively and absolutely with the development of some of the more important urban centers in later colonial times.

The proletariat of America had been created by the gradual separation of the peasantry from the soil by other occupations. Mining was one of the first of these. The development of commerce, necessitating large numbers of workers for transportation, was another, and various types of manufacturing, especially textiles, still another. In the obrajes or cloth factories, for example, the Indian worked under the mita system or perhaps, in the beginning, as a voluntary wage earner who was gradually converted into a debt slave. The conditions in the obrajes were so bad that remedies were sought in just labor laws. Similar legislation attempted to relieve the conditions of the mine worker. The relative ineffectiveness of such legislation has already been indicated by the reports of Juan and Ulloa, and others.

Similarly ineffectual was the royal cédula of 1602 in which Philip III established a free labor market for the Indians who worked in domestic service, farming, and mining. It was intended to replace the system of repartimientos. The viceroy of New Spain in carrying out the decree ordered all Indian workers to gather in certain designated places each Sunday so that the employers might hire them at good wages and a judge was appointed to preside over this labor market. The whole system immediately became subject to abuses. The judge demanded a bribe of all the Indians who received a job, and a group of middle men sprang up who "began to speculate in the labor of the Indians, contracting to draw a large number, the more the better, away from the public square in order, by reason of the scarcity of workers, to rent out those whom they had drawn off at a wage greater than that which they paid them, the speculators keeping the difference." [38] These abuses led to the repeal of the legislation and the reestablishment of the repartimientos.

The position of the skilled and semiskilled worker was controlled by the craft guild which everywhere existed on the usual European models. Guild masters received apprentices for a definite payment and trained them in certain skilled crafts. At the end of his apprenticeship, the worker could, in theory, become a master; but admission to mastership depended largely upon the economic ability of the individual to set up an establishment of his own and the willingness of the other masters to admit him to the guild. As a matter of fact, most of the apprentices were never permitted to become masters, nor could any man practice one of these trades without the consent of the guilds. This system prevented most of the proletarian workers from making the advancement which their talents might have secured for them under freer conditions.[39]

The forced labor in the mines had been abolished in the last half of the eighteenth century in New Spain, and Baron Humboldt considered labor as "free", saying "Nowhere does the lower people enjoy in greater security the fruit of their labours than in the mines of Mexico; no law forces the Indian to choose his species of labour, or to prefer one mine to another; and when he is displeased with the proprietor of the mine, he may offer his services to another master, who may pay perhaps more regularly." [40] This "freedom" of the workers was particularly emphasized for purposes of comparison with the concepts of "free" and "regulated" labor in Europe of the time. The influence of Adam Smith upon writers was very strong and they usually felt constrained to adopt or combat Smith's ideas. Humboldt's own words, however, show that his concept of labor was legalistic; he failed to realize that the economic situation of a man might be as bad when he was legally free as when legally a slave.

[38] Riva Palacio, *México*, II, 536.
[39] Riva Palacio, *México*, II, 680.
[40] *New Spain*, I, 124 [*Nouvelle Espagne*, I, 360].

Descriptions of the conditions of the American workers indicate that their economic status was hardly less unfortunate than that of the European proletariat of the same time. Humboldt and others make a point of insisting that the American worker was no worse off than his European contemporary, but in so doing they reveal that both were in a deplorable state of economic degradation.

LABOR IN NEW SPAIN

The viceroy of New Spain, Linares, in his instructions to his successor in 1716, wrote concerning the propertyless classes of Mexico:

"They awake at the break of day not knowing what they are to eat during the day because what they earned the previous day has been dropped in the gambling house or the house of the girl friend the night before. Not wishing to work, they raise the cry that God does not leave anyone in want, and this is because, reciprocally, those who at the time have a place with a master, . . . for the sake of charity feed those they can. With a cup of chocolate and a few tortillas they are satisfied (*les es bastante*) . . . . When they commit some crime they risk nothing in moving from one place to another except the fatigue of the trip, because all of the wordly goods that they have they carry with them in the form of their own cunning, and even the beds are found ready wherever they end up. In Mexico City it is sufficient to move from one section to another to be well hidden." [41]

The instructions of another viceroy, Revilla Gigedo II to his successor in 1794 likewise throw light on the abject state of the propertyless masses. Of the Indians, he said that they alone of all the classes did not seek to improve their conditions "because these in themselves prevent them from aspiring to reach better conditions." [42] His observations on the maldistribution of wealth and the causes of the extreme poverty among Europeans as well as Indians are illuminating:

"The former system of government and commerce, which very greatly resembled one another, prevented the equal division of property. The merchants, the *alcaldes mayores,* some few fortunate miners, and thrifty ecclesiastics were able to accumulate a considerable fortune, while at the same time the rest of the population of these dominions did not rise above an extreme

[41] Quoted in Alamán, *Méjico,* I, 28-29.
[42] Revilla Gigedo, *Instrucción,* par. 150.

poverty, extending for the great part to almost the whole of its individuals. . . ." [43]

Many were so poverty-stricken that they had few clothes or none whatever.

"The poor, both the healthy and the sick, use the same furniture and clothes, and many have nothing except what they have on their backs in both sickness and health. . . ." [44]

"No small contribution to the epidemics which this city suffered was made, doubtless, by the dirtiness and filth in which people almost universally lived, both in the interior of their houses and in the streets, which were really just so many filthy dung heaps, not excepting the street in front of the palace, in which there were a multitude of shacks or huts (barracas o jacales) constituting a shantytown erected without plan, everyone building his own according to his own idea, and housing day and night countless persons of both sexes who committed excesses of various kinds, since it was impossible to supervise what went on in that disorderly and jumbled district." [45]

Revilla Gigedo noticed certain improvements in his time, especially in the "personal cleanliness of the lowest class of the plebe," who went about

"almost entirely naked, the greater part of the people of this class being content with wrapping themselves in a blanket or sheet which served them as clothing and bed, and for all purposes for which it was needed. To correct this slovenliness (abandono) which required attention, in March 1790 I ordered the directorate of the tobacco monopoly and the superintendent of the mint to take measures to see that all of the workers in these establishments should be dressed, deducting a part of their daily wage for this purpose.[46] . . . The naked were prohibited from attending public functions, entering the public walks, and attending the cathedral on important holy days, by means of which, with other similar orders such as that only those workers who were dressed should be allowed to work on public works, nakedness has been largely eliminated in the greater part of this capital, and it is stated that in imitation the same thing has been done in other cities of this kingdom, which was normal

---

[43] Revilla Gigedo, *Instrucción,* par. 146.
[44] Revilla Gigedo, *Instrucción,* par. 229.
[45] Revilla Gigedo, *Instrucción,* par. 244.
[46] Revilla Cigedo, *Instrucción,* par. 247-249.

and almost obligatory since all the other cities follow the example of this capital." [47]

Labor in Uruguay and Chile*

There is at least one example, in Uruguay, of workers having succeeded in improving their own conditions.

Towards the end of the colonial period complaints were voiced against labor organizations, and the consequent high prices of labor. In April, 1809, the *síndico* of the cabildo of Montevideo alleged that the Negro workers of that city "have been able to hit upon a certain plan by which their labors have come to be of incalculable price." For one day's work in the warehouse they asked as much as two pesos or twenty reales. "And they not only ask this amount, but it is necessary to give it. All are in agreement on that price." Anyone who violated it exposed himself to drastic punishment, and, "not one Negro can be found to enter into a contract because all of them refuse to dedicate themselves to a fixed job . . . . Whoever works in a warehouse on a daily basis, or by the week or the month, can count on six to eight reales a day at the most; but working at what they call *changadas,* that is to say, unloading a lot of goods or doing a specific job, two pesos or twenty reales a day may be easily earned." [48]

In Chile, the state of the working classes could scarcely have been worse. The cabildo of Santiago offered as one of its arguments for the building of an irrigation system that by this measure "people useful to the republic would be made out of the numerous idle and vagabonds of this city, who, having nothing to do and no work, take up all the vices and dedicate themselves to thievery, murder, and highway robbery." [49] This class in Chile, largely composed of mestizos, was given the name of "rotos" as a term of opprobrium. [50] Their condition was in sharp contrast to the wealth which their labor produced.

"Nothing is commoner [said Manuel de Salas who observed conditions at the beginning of the nineteenth century] than to see in the identical fields that have just produced abundant crops the very same hands that have gathered them held out to beg bread, and this perhaps in the selfsame spot in which the *fanega* of wheat was just sold at a miserably low price . . . . Daily one may see in the streets and squares robust workmen offering their

[47] Revilla Gigedo, *Instrucción,* par. 251.
[48] Quoted in Blanco Acevedo, *Uruguay colonial,* pp. 204-205.
[49] Quoted in Barros Arana, *Chile,* VII, 246.
[50] Barros Arana, *Chile,* VII, 474-5.

underpaid labor in exchange for goods which are frequently useless and marked at very high prices. They are seen at the break
of day at the doors of the farmhouses begging work, and their
proprietors in the sad situation of having to send them away. I
am a continual spectator of this same thing in the public works
of the capital, where they present themselves in miserable swarms
to ask for work, begging to be taken on, with the result that in
order not to increase their misery by refusing them, or at least
to do it with decency, I offered them as a wage in the winter one
real a day, and the children a half, the lowest wage [for private
work] being a real and a half, which rises by degrees in other
work to double this. As many people are employed this way as
the funds permit, there never having failed to be an excess of
workers . . . Nobody will say that any task or work has been
stopped for lack of hands. Scarcely is a job announced when
hundreds apply. The wheat harvests, which require numerous
workers at one time, are carried out without delay in spite of
abundant crops. The vintage, which requires more workers than
in Spain because the wine is treated in a different way, is finished
in a few days with men only working. The mines, which offer
very hard labor, have an excess of laborers; from which it appears that it is not sloth that predominates, it is the lack of work
which forces them to be idle. Some have no work during the
greater part of the year in the slack season, and others find no
work during the greater part of their lives." [51]

To complete this picture he adds: "This lack of objectives in
which to employ the time makes more common the dismal use of
ways to stifle thought, to lift the weight of a gloomy and melancholy existence, by using those beverages with which the unfor-
tunates, in order to escape from their afflictions, seem to seek a
method of shortening life. Thus broken . . . their lives are shortened to such an extent that the one who has escaped the dangers
attending such a state of abandonment rarely reaches old age, and
thus there is not a country in the world where there are fewer old
people." [52]

The English explorer Vancouver corroborates Salas' testimony.
He was in Chile in the late eighteenth century, and traveled from
Valparaiso to Santiago through some of the most fertile parts of
the country. He expressed great surprise at the barrenness of the
area he traversed, and "the few miserable inhabitants [who] lived

[51] Quoted in Barros Arana, *Chile,* VII, 475-476.
[52] Barros Arana, *Chile,* VII, 476-77.

in wretched little hovels, or huts, made principally of mud." But, "the inside of the dwelling more forcibly displayed the poverty of its inhabitants than had been exhibited by its external appearance . . . . Yet it was not without some decorations of a religious nature." The people, he observed, lived in "indolence and superstition" and were "marked with a greater degree of uncleanliness and those characteristics that distinguish the very lowest order of society than I had ever before witnessed amongst any people who had ever had the advantage of living amongst those connected with the civilized world." [53]

Position of the Upper Classes

In contrast to the Indians, Negro slaves, and the proletariat of various racial compositions, a small part of the population held a position which set it off economically and socially from the masses. [54] The nominal dividing line was the distinction between those of European and those of Indian or Negro origin. Nevertheless, many with Indian and Negro ancestry held places among the elite. The persistence throughout the colonial period of an Indian aristocracy which co-operated with the European conquerors in governing the Indian masses has been noted. Moreover, the distinction between whites, Indians, and Negroes was to a certain degree fictitious. The mestizos of Paraguay, for example, were recognized by law as being white, and entirely of European origin, and the same was true of the mestizos of Chile. In Peru, most of those who occupied the upper rungs of society claimed to be of unmixed European ancestry, but actually had a large proportion of Indian, and sometimes Negro, blood.

The process known as "whitening" was very common; and it was customary for people who had acquired a sufficient amount of money to purchase a certificate of purity of blood which attested that they were entirely of European origin. In New Spain about 1800, declarations that they were white were obtained from the audiencia even "by very swarthy mulattoes." If the skin of the petitioner was too dark for such a statement to be credible, he might receive the more equivocal verdict, "that such or such individuals may consider themselves as whites (*que se tengan por blancos*)." [55] The terms Indian, Negro, and European were by no means synonymous with proletariat or peasant, slave and aristocrat.

[53] Vancouver, *Voyage*, Bk. VI, chap. V.

[54] The legal position of the Spaniards is described in *Gobernación espiritual y temporal*, Bk. IV.

[55] Humboldt, *New Spain*, I, 246-47 [*Nouvelle Espagne*, II, 52].

The gradations between the various classes were based in the first place upon property, and in the second upon legal privileges which had been granted to those who had property, or who were descendants of the original conquerors.

"The few remaining descendants of the *conquistadores,* and others who inherited a distinguished origin from ancestors who were famous in Spain, with the high-ranking employees and the wealthy who had obtained a title or a decoration, or obtained some municipal office in perpetuity, composed a nobility which was not set off from the rest of the Spanish caste except by wealth, and who, when this was lost, dropped again into the ordinary ranks (*a caer en la clase común*). They still retained, nevertheless, in their decadence certain prerogatives, since it was necessary to belong to this class to be admitted to the clergy, the judicial career, and the militia. Because this class, to which was added everybody who acquired a fortune since they all pretended to be Spanish and nobles, was distinguished from the rest of the population by its clothing. Those people composing it being more or less well dressed, whereas the people generally speaking were not, it was known as decent persons (*gente decente*), and this, rather than birth, was the distinguishing characteristic by which it was recognized."[56]

At the end of the seventeenth century, there were already some eleven titles of marquis, eleven of count, and one of marshal in New Spain alone,[57] many more in other parts of America, and additional titles were created and sold during the course of the eighteenth century. Titles and decorations were sought avidly by those who had grown rich in commerce or mining. The titles carried with them the establishment of an entail, although there were many other entails without titles of nobility.[58]

The opulence of the wealthy Europeans and Creoles was such as to separate them entirely from the proletariat, and their legal privileges, combined with money, created a dividing line which, although it could be and was crossed sometimes, was usually permanent. From the sixteenth and seventeenth centuries onward, there are numerous descriptions of the fine houses and luxurious clothing of the wealthy in contrast to the complete nakedness and homelessness of a very large part of the population. "The traditions relate how it was a customary thing for the rich to lay down

---

[56] Alamán, *Méjico,* I, 15-16.
[57] Riva Palacio, *México,* II, 694.
[58] Alamán, *Méjico,* I, 16-17.

a path of silver bars from their houses to the nearby parish church or at least from the vestibule to the alcove, for those who carried the capitalist's baby for baptism. All of the wealthy families used dishes of silver for table service. Furniture of this metal was common, and fabulous the quantity of bouquets, candlesticks, candelabra, lamps and other objects dedicated to worship in the churches." [59]

Many observers were struck with the contrasts of wealth and poverty.

"Mexico is the country of inequality. Nowhere does there exist such a fearful difference in the distribution of fortune, civilization, cultivation of the soil, and population. The architecture of the public and private edifices, the finery of the ladies, the tone of society, all announce a refinement with which the nakedness, ignorance, and vulgarity of the lower people form the most striking contrast. This immense inequality of fortune does not only exist among the cast of whites (Europeans or Creoles), it is even discoverable among the Indians." [60]

The picture given of New Spain could, with small variations, serve for all Latin America. Peruvian creole aristocracy, which from the ethnological viewpoint had a considerable degree of Indian blood, owned the bulk of the wealth of the country, and through means of entailed estates and other legal devices maintained itself as the dominant social group. In Lima alone, not including other parts of the viceroyalty such as Quito, La Plata, and Chile, there were countless entailed estates, a duke, two viscounts, forty-four counts, and some fifty-eight marquises. [61]

In Chile, most of the land was owned by a small group of people who, because of the social position derived from their land and titles, occupied the most influential position in society. [62] Their estates gave them practically all of the income from the agriculture of Chile and each family on its estate was the supreme economic and political power to which were subjected the Indians, slaves, and free proletariat.

Colonial Uruguay and Argentina differed little from the other colonies in this respect, and the privileged, landed families there as elsewhere held the supreme power in the local community. Their

---

[59] Riva Palacio, *México*, II, 724-25.

[60] Humboldt, *New Spain*, I, 184-185 [*Nouvelle Espagne*, I, 428-429].

[61] Means, *Fall*, pp. 208-11. Javier Prado, *Estado social del Perú durante la dominación española*, C.L.D. Perú (3rd Ser., Lima, 1941), pp. 124-85, gives an excellent picture of Peruvian social conditions during the colonial period.

[62] Barros Arana, *Chile*, VII, chap. XXVI.

authority in the colony as a whole was naturally subordinate to that of the King's officials, whom they envied, and whose powers they sought to diminish either by direct or subtle means; or else they themselves sought appointment to one of the higher offices. [63] These higher offices were largely held by those born in Spain, a fact of importance which will be discussed later.

LEGAL PRIVILEGES OF THE UPPER CLASSES

The upper social classes had been marked off long before the end of the colonial period, and the law guaranteed the preservation of their superior position.

"The Spanish class [including those born in America as well as those born in Spain] was thus the predominant class in New Spain, and this was not owing to its numbers but to its influence and power; and since the smaller number cannot prevail over the greater in political institutions except through the privileges which it enjoys, the laws had as their principal object the maintenance of the preponderance of this class. It possessed almost the whole of the wealth of the country; in it was whatever learning was extant; it alone secured the public offices, and could have arms; and it alone enjoyed political and civil rights." [64]

Special privileges were accorded by the various *fueros* or charters. The nobility, those holding decorations from the Crown, the military, the clergy, the mine-owners, the merchants, and the Indian caciques were so honored and protected. [65]

The merchants had special privileges through the *consulados*. These, because of the jurisdiction they enjoyed in certain matters of commerce, exercised legal functions in affairs affecting general welfare, but which had been conceded to them in accordance with the prevailing concepts of special privileges. [66]

Various special provisions were designed to promote mining and secure the position of the mine owners. They were declared nobles; they could not be imprisoned for debt nor could their dependents be so imprisoned, both having the right of remaining on their estates or on their mining properties during arrest; they had many other privileges before the law and they and their children and descendants were given preference in public offices, military positions, and church dignities. Mining offered one of the best oppor-

---

[63] Blanco Acevedo, *Uruguay colonial,* pp. 97-100.
[64] Alamán, *Méjico,* I, 20.
[65] Desdevises du Dezert, "Les Institutions de l'Espagne," *Revue Hispanique,* LXX, 186.
[66] Alamán, *Méjico,* I, 57-60.

tunities to rise above the masses, for once elevated into the mine-owning class, the lucky individual found that he was set apart not merely by his riches but by legal privileges as well. [67]

THE PRIVILEGES OF THE CLERGY AND MILITARY

The most privileged group in many respects, with the possible exception of the nobility, was the clergy, whose rights antedating the conquest of America had been transplanted from Spain. During the course of the eighteenth century, however, there was some diminution of the clerical privileges owing to the royal policy of centralizing authority, but still enough remained to set the clergy off from the mass of common men.

Tax exemptions of innumerable kinds also divided the clergy from the laymen, and the State fought a difficult but gradually winning battle to subject the churchmen to the taxes paid by others. [68] Lawsuits between the clergy and the State over payment of taxes were frequent, the Jesuits for example contending that their *fueros* exempted them from payment of the tithes. Other clergy also resisted payment of tithes, including the nuns, who insisted that their *fueros* granted them exemption. The high fees charged by the churchmen for administering the sacraments, combined with their own exemptions from taxes, readily enabled them to acquire riches in addition to the wealth from the great land-holdings of the clergy. Thus they had an economic prestige and power in keeping with the authority their privileges gave them in political as well as spiritual matters. [69]

The Church had not been able, however, to maintain all its pretensions, and the rising resistance of the people had enabled the government to transfer much of the Church's former jurisdiction to the civil courts. In a famous memorial presented to the Crown at the end of the eighteenth century, Bishop Abad y Quiepo reminded the Sovereign that his authority rested on two privileged classes, the nobility and the clergy, and that the restrictions placed on the clergy were alienating the affections of this essential group. [70]

---

[67] Alamán, *Méjico*, I, 97-99.

[68] Altamira, *Historia de España*, IV, 236-40.

[69] Lillian Estelle Fisher, *The Background of the Revolution for Mexican Independence* (Boston: The Christopher Publishing House, 1934), pp. 224-25, and documents cited there.

[70] Manuel Abad y Quiepo, "Representación sobre la inmunidad personal del clero," December 11, 1799, cited in José María Luis Mora, *Obras Sueltas*, (2 vols., Paris, 1837, I, 3-54; cf. Lillian Estelle Fisher, *The Background of the Revolution for Mexican Independence*, pp. 244-27; Alamán, *Méjico*, I, 68-70. The observations of Abad y Quiepo on the social conditions of the late colonial period are among the most valuable documents on the period. See Lillian Estelle Fisher, "Manuel Abad y Quiepo, Bishop of Michoacán," *H. A. H. R.*, XV (November, 1935), pp. 425-47.

The military had been a privileged group in Spain before the conquest of America and had brought their privileges with them. During the eighteenth century, however, there was a notable extension of the powers of the military class. This had arisen when the Bourbon kings had transferred several regiments of regular troops to America, and when provincial militia had been organized. In order to give the military in America the same prestige as that in Spain, the jurisdiction of the military and its *fueros* were expanded. Membership in the provincial militia was coveted by all and the Creoles paid fancy prices for commissions as officers, but the majority of the chief officers in Mexico were Europeans. In America as a whole, however, the militia was one of the principal outlets for Creole ambition. The privileges of the officer class were such that Viceroy Revilla Gigedo II complained of the evils and recommended their reduction. [71]

It is clear from what has been said that no "rights of citizenship" existed in the laws, nor was there any concept of legal equality. All society was divided into two major classes: the upper, enjoying privileges not given to the masses of the people, but itself divided into several categories with each having its own special position; and the majority of the people, likewise divided into several groups, each suffering its own peculiar disabilities. Equality before the law was both a treasonable and heretical idea. As long as this concept prevailed in the colonies, the "classes" could not fall, nor the "masses" rise.

RIVALRY OF CREOLES AND SPANIARDS

The further division of the population of European descent into European-born and American-born, important from the second half of the sixteenth century, was increasingly significant during the seventeenth and eighteenth centuries. The population of European descent did not, however, form a class universally higher in the social scale than the Indians and Negroes. The proletariat drew a large proportion of members from those of European origin.

The distinction between the European born and the American born, did not necessarily have to take on the bitterness that characterized it. But from the sixteenth century, their relations were marked by quarrels. [72] The European born were called *Godos, Gachupines, Chapetones,* and other names, all of which were regarded as insulting, as was the term *Peninsulares.* The Marquis of Mancera, Viceroy of New Spain, wrote to his successor in 1673:

[71]Alamán, *Méjico,* I, 77-82; Revilla Gigedo, *Instrucción,* pars. 98, 117-119.
[72]Alcides Argüedes, *Historia de Bolivia; la fundación de la república* (Madrid, 1920), pp. 25-28, gives an excellent brief picture of Creole vs. Spaniard.

"There has been indicated in the proper place the little unity which customarily exists between the subjects born in the Indies and those who come from Spain. From this deep-rooted habit, which has now come to be considered natural, neither the most austere sackcloth (*sayal*) nor the remotest cloister is free because there resounds on all sides, if not the echoes of enmity (which should never be supposed to exist between persons professing virtue and religion), those of discord, the Creoles claiming for the great part not to be inferior to those of Europe, and these latter scorning equality." [73]

This rivalry, whether it was within the monasteries, or among the general population, seems to have been based on economic inequality. The ambitious and pushing qualities of some of the new Spanish immigrants invited the hatred of the Creoles; and when a penniless immigrant succeeded in acquiring wealth, or even a small competence, the envy of the Creoles was aroused. When the newly-rich immigrant purchased a decoration, membership in one of the Orders, or a title, the hatred grew. Wealth also enabled the immigrant to marry into the "best" families, thereby cutting out the Creole sons, who perhaps had less to offer financially. This type of rivalry is perhaps common to all societies and operates in all countries where immigrants make a place for themselves, as in the United States of today, but in a society where status was regulated by privileges, and where class feeling was based on the real economic advantage of belonging to the privileged class, envy became rancorous hatred.

The Creoles, furthermore, regarded themselves as superior culturally.

"The literary education which they were sometimes given, the airs of gentlemen that they assumed [living] in idleness and abundance, made them look with disdain on the Europeans, who appeared to them to be avaricious and greedy because they were economical and industrious; and they held them to be inferior to themselves because the [Europeans] were engaged in trading and professions which were considered unworthy of the class to which, with the practice of these trades, their fathers had raised them." [74]

According to the law, the Europeans and Creoles were equals, but actually,

---

[73] Quoted in Riva Palacio, *México*, II, 669.
[74] Alamán, *Méjico*, I, 10-11.

"The Europeans held, as was said before, almost all the high offices . . . . The Creoles obtained such offices rarely . . . and although they held all the subaltern places which were in much greater number, this encouraged their ambition to occupy the higher offices also, rather than satisfied them . . . . In 1808 all the bishops of New Spain except one, the greater part of the canonships, and many of the fattest (*pingües*) curacies were in the control of the Europeans. They were in the majority also in the monasteries, and to avoid the frequent disturbances caused by the rivalry resulting from birthplace, some religious orders made alternate selection a matter of law, European prelates being named in one election and Creoles in another. But a distinction having been introduced between the Europeans who had come in orders and those who had taken orders in America, in whose favor a third election was established, there came about two elections of two Europeans for one of Creoles." [75]

Only four of 170 viceroys prior to 1813 were born in America, and this because their fathers happened to be government employees in America. Three of these were viceroys of Mexico; Luis de Velasco II, (1590-1595) son of the viceroy of the same name; Juan de Ocuña, Marquis of Casafuerte, born in Lima, who served as viceroy from 1722 to 1734; and the Count of Revilla Gigedo (1789-1794), born in Havana while his father was captain-general. Of 602 captains-general and presidentes, fourteen were born in America. At the Cortes of Cádiz in 1812, the deputy Alcocer pointed out that all the high offices of New Spain except the bishopric of Puebla and the directorship of the lottery were in the hands of Europeans. There were a few *oidores* and canons who were Americans. Of the 706 bishops in America prior to 1812, 105 were Creoles, although most of these served in minor dioceses. [76]

One aspect of the eighteenth century situation that merits special consideration is the fact that fewer offices were open to Americans than earlier, the tendency being to limit the number of Creoles in office at the very time their consciousness of being Americans was growing. This naturally increased the tension between the two parties.

The same feelings between the two classes were manifested in other parts of America. A memorial directed to Philip V in the first half of the eighteenth century pointed out the dangers of such feeling:

---

[75] Alamán, *Méjico,* I, 12-14.
[76] Alamán, *Méjico,* I, 12-13, notes 6 and 7.

"As the natives of those, your Majesty's dominions, are equally deserving of filling the principal offices of their own country, it appears reasonable that they should not be divested of all management in their own homes. I am fully persuaded, that in those countries there are many discontented persons, not because they are under the control of Spain; but because they are cast down, and tyrannized by the very persons, who are sent over to exercise the duties of the judicature. Let Your Majesty give these offices to subjects of that country, and by this means disturbances will be avoided." [77]

But the granting of offices to the Creoles did not suffice in all cases to satisfy them, nor to decrease their hatred of the Spaniards. In Chile, for instance, there were a number of high officials who were Creoles, among them two oidores, the superintendent of the mint, the chief of the customs of Santiago, and the brigadier general in command of the Bio-Bio post. Chile had furnished bishops to Nicaragua, Trujillo, Tucumán, Cartagena, Panama, Santa Fé de Bogotá, Santa Cruz de la Sierra, Huamanga, and two archbishops to Charcas. Seven of the nine bishops of Santiago for a hundred years prior to 1808 were Creoles, and six of the eight bishops of Concepción in the same period. [78]

THE RISE OF A MIDDLE CLASS

Toward the end of the colonial period a middle class began to play a more important role in Latin American affairs, although it by no means assumed a preponderant place in society. It drew its members from all races, European, Indian, and Negro, but was predominantly of the first. Economically, its members were merchants and professional men, although here again the preferred positions were occupied by the Spaniards from the Peninsula or the Creoles from among the privileged families. Since this middle class was to play an important part in the events which led to the independence of Latin America, it is well to explain its origin and position.

Trade and commerce, as previously explained, were a monopoly of a few firms located in Sevilla and Cádiz, and in the chief cities of the New World. They were not able, however, to keep absolutely all trade in their own hands. Two types of commerce escaped them: contraband and retailing. Contraband was partly in the hands of foreigners and partly conducted by Latin Americans,

[77] *Memorial* of Malchor Macanaz, quoted in Moses, *Eve*, pp. 103-104.
[78] Pereyra, *América española*, VIII, 209-10.

who built up interests in conflict with those of the Spanish monopolists, and of the government supporting the latter. While not a numerous element in the Latin-American population, the native merchants were in a position to make their influence felt. Many of the retailers were also Creoles. Economically and socially they were considerably above the masses, while deprived of the commercial concessions enjoyed by the monopolists and the social preferment granted to the upper-class Creoles. Some of them, in the chief cities, were relatively important figures in the community. They had sufficient wealth, education, and cohesion to be conscious of their economic superiority to the masses and their social inferiority to the upper classes.

Intercolonial commercial rivalries also enhanced the importance of the middle class, and sprung in part from the interests represented by the local merchants of the various colonies. Santiago de Chile, Buenos Aires, Montevideo, the interior cities of the Plata region, and numerous other towns had begun to feel more and more the restrictions of the three-port system, the operations of which had confined legal entry of goods largely (though by no means completely) through Vera Cruz, Panama, and Cartagena. When the reforms of the latter half of the eighteenth century lifted many of the former commercial restrictions, a great impetus was given to the commercial growth of other cities. Thus, Santiago and Valparaiso chafed at the remaining ties which bound them to Lima; the interior cities of the Plata resented the Spanish monopoly, as well as the growing importance of Buenos Aires; Montevideo and Buenos Aires were strong rivals; Caracas and other nearby towns were eager to throw off the remaining restrictions on their freedom; and the trade centers of north Mexico were equally envious of the preferred positions occupied by Vera Cruz and Mexico City.

In every respect, a growing middle class was made more conscious of its disabilities (and its powers) by the gradual removal of some of these. When the eventual separation came between Spain and her colonies, the middle class was to take a vigorous and, in many cases, a decisive part.

* * * * * * *

The class divisions were as sharp at the end of the colonial period as they had been in the early days. There had been certain modifications in the class structure, new labor systems replacing older ones, new elements such as the rising middle class, and some curtailing of the original feudal privileges of the nobles and clergy.

FIEL

Copia de otra que deſi hizo, ydeſu mano pintó la R. M. Juana Ynés de la Cruz Fenix dela America, Glorioſo deſempeño deſu Sexo, Honrra dela Nacion deeſte Nuevo Mundo, y aſſumento delas admiraciones, y eloctos deel Antiguo. Nació eldia 12. de Nov. deel año de 1651. àlas onſe dela noche. Recivió el Sagrado Habito deel Maximo D.S.S. Geronimo enlu Convento deſta Ciudad de Mexico de edad de 17. años. Y murió Domingo 17 de Abril deel año de 1695...

Courtesy of the Philadelphia Museum of Art, Philadelphia

SOR JUANA INÉS DE LA CRUZ, SELF-PORTRAIT

La Señora Dª Juana María Romero Nació el día 23 de Junio del año de 1760. se desposó con el Sr D. José Manuel García ...
... del ... el día 28 de Oct. de 77 y se Retrató en México a 1º de Nbre de 94 ... haviendo tenido 2 partos y 5 malos partos siendo el vivo en México el ... de ...

PORTRAIT OF DOÑA JUANA MARÍA ROMERO

But the distance between the small peak of the social pyramid and the great masses at its base was still enormous.

The Negroes were still mostly slaves. Despite the abolition of the *encomienda,* the Indian masses were held in subjection by the *repartimiento* or *mita* that succeeded it, and by a new system of debt slavery. Free labor was equally degraded, living for the most part in abject poverty. On the other hand, the few at the top, chiefly Spanish-born and Creoles, had wealth and legal privileges to guarantee their position and authority.

The Development of Education and the Diffusion of Culture

THE CULTURE OF COLONIAL SPANISH AMERICA was, as we have already seen, primarily European.[1] The Indian foundation remained largely submerged throughout the colonial period, although there were contributions from both Indian and Negro elements.

The predominance of Spain's influence brought both advantages and disadvantages. Since the Conquest came at the moment when Spain was entering the most glorious century of her literary and artistic development, her American colonies received the full benefit of the mother country's cultural flowering. But the distinct and unmistakable limitations which the events of the sixteenth century placed on Spanish culture were also felt by Spanish America. Particularly, the fear of Protestantism, which haunted the Spanish rulers, prevented Spain from participating more fully in the intellectual expansion of Western Europe from the sixteenth to the nineteenth century. The emphasis on religious orthodoxy led to the belief that learning was dangerous for the masses and should be confined to a select few. Illiteracy in turn, combined with the prevailing supernatural view of life, encouraged metaphysical speculation at the expense of scientific studies, causing Spain to fall behind in the scientific developments which characterize our modern world.

A wide opportunity was open, however, for Spanish artistic expression. In imaginative novels, poetry, drama, descriptive narrative, and historical chronicles, Spanish literature is second to none. The impact of the New World on the discoverers and settlers in America inspired some of the finest chronicles and natural histories written anywhere. In the realm of fine arts too, the Spanish Ameri-

---

[1] See chapter 11. Portuguese America is discussed separately; see chapters 28-33.

cans were free to follow the European models or to develop their own, and the colonial period produced worthy painters, sculptors, and architects.

EDUCATION FOR THE FEW

This is not to say that the restrictions on the intellectual freedom failed to affect the cultural evolution of Spanish America. The numerous handicaps, natural and man-made, left their imprint. In the field of constructive political and economic thought especially, both Spain and Spanish America were confined to the narrow bounds permitted by a society which insisted upon religious and political orthodoxy. But until recently almost everybody, including the Spaniards and Spanish Americans themselves, has taken too pessimistic a view of the cultural contributions of Spain and her colonies. Spanish American scholars have been the first to condemn the mother country as deliberately keeping her possessions in ignorance, a natural conclusion in view of the widespread illiteracy in the Spanish colonies.

Illiteracy was general and customary to the end of the colonial period, as it was in most of the world at that time. The statement of a modern North American historian that "Hispanic America was certainly as much as ninety per cent illiterate at the beginning of the independence era" [2] gives a much more favorable impression than the statements of many Latin Americans. The noted Argentine sociologist and historian, José Ingenieros, writes: "The great mass of the populations subordinated to the colonial sovereignty— much more than 99 per cent—remained in complete illiteracy. Only in the urban centers, where populations of semi-European origin congregated, could their descendants attend schools erected in the style of and similar to those of the mother country, although inferior in quality." [3]

[2] Charles Edward Chapman, *Republican Hispanic America: A History* (New York, 1937), p. 114.

[3] José Ingenieros, *La evolución de las ideas argentinas,* in *Obras completas* (Buenos Aires, 1937), XIII, 50. This picture of the mass illiteracy of the Spanish colonies is supported by the bulk of primary and secondary evidence. A modern school of historians, notably in Argentina, is attempting, however, to prove that colonial culture was on a higher level than that of today. They date the alleged decadence of the Spanish colonies (and Argentina in particular, it would seem) from the expulsion of the Jesuits in 1767. One of the leaders of this school of thought is the Right Reverend Father Guillermo Furlong Cardiff, a member of the Argentine Academia Nacional de la Historia, who asserts: "The real and exact truth is that primary instruction from the first days of the Conquest to the May Revolution [1810] was universal, wise and methodical, such as there has not been among us in later times." Guillermo Furlong Cardiff, "Las bibliotecas coloniales en el Río de la Plata," *Boletín de la Academia Nacional de la Historia,* XIII (Buenos Aires, 1940), 120 [hereafter *BAN* Hist.]. This is rather strange in view of the fact that Argentina today has reduced illiteracy to below twenty per cent as

The educational situation of the Spanish colonies was the result of policy, not neglect. The vast majority were prevented from receiving formal instruction by the structure of the society that encompassed them. Colonial society was a class society. In Europe at the time, as well as in Latin America, it was axiomatic that people are by nature born "unequal" and that divisions were the product of a divine plan. The logical conclusion was that only a few, in America mainly the Spaniards and Creoles, were fit subjects for education. It was considered dangerous to give the masses learning that might lead to their economic and social emancipation. In their existing condition, they were valuable slaves and peons, while education might well lead to discontent, and discontent to revolution. The ignorance of the masses was accompanied by poverty, filth, squalor, and disease, which would have made their schooling a gigantic social task, even if the sincerest of rulers had attempted it. But such a task was not attempted during the colonial period; and has been attempted by only a few Latin-American countries even to the present time.

Another factor which served to place a brake on the cultural evolution of Latin America was the subservience to the supernatural, which was not confined to the uneducated but characterized the whole of society. Every normal manifestation of nature was considered an act of God, directed purposefully to reward mankind for its virtues or punish it for its sins—which must have been great indeed, judged from the earthquakes, floods, tornadoes, and volcanic eruptions ascribed to God's anger. Those who held such physical phenomena to be the result of natural causes were condemned in sermons which contributed to the fear and panic provoked by the disasters, as in the Peruvian earthquake of 1746,[4] and on innumerable other occasions throughout the colonial period, although some scientists like Sigüenza y Góngora held differently. The churchmen of Peru alleged that the Cuzco earthquake in 1707 was a punishment of God because certain Indians, mestizos, and slaves were "worshipping the Devil," and therefore the clergy proceeded to chastise further these innocent victims. The belief that all knowledge not sponsored by the Church was dangerous to the soul strengthened the clergy's hold on education.

---

compared with perhaps 99 per cent in 1810, and has several excellent universities and technical schools which stand at the head of one of the best educational systems in the Western Hemisphere. But Father Cardiff's view probably arises from his special sense of values. His writings indicate that he regards ecclesiastical culture as the *summum bonum,* and contrary to a secular democratic culture which places the welfare of the individual above other considerations.

[4] Lorente, *Perú bajo los Borbones,* pp. 18; 31-33; 89-97.

The Church exercised a near monopoly over education from the first days of colonization. Both in pre-Conquest America among the Indians and in Spain from which the conquerors had come, the priesthoods had dominated education. When Christianity was introduced into the New World, Church control over education was natural.

Primary and secondary schools were maintained by the religious orders, missions, convents, and town parishes; and a few private teachers, usually clerics, were available for those who had money enough. *Colegios* (which were primary or secondary schools, not colleges) were established in practically all towns of size, and those in the wealthier centers were numerous. The quantity of schools and numbers of students increased during the course of the colonial period, but up to its end, elementary and secondary education was limited to the upper classes, although the work of indoctrination covered with a thin veil of Christianity a much larger number of people. Whereas in the first years the establishment of a single school, with five hundred to a thousand students, such as that of Pedro de Gante in Mexico in 1523, was rightfully looked upon as a great event, it should have been merely a start. Mexico needed at least a thousand such schools, but never got them.

Later, especially towards the end of the eighteenth century, more initiative in education was assumed by the government authorities. Many of the cabildos established secondary schools and supported them with tax funds. The teachers were still predominantly clerics, however, and the curriculum adjusted to the children of the upper classes. The Crown also decreed aid to education from time to time, and provided funds for it, but always within the narrow limits of the social ideas of the times. The laws passed requiring the establishment of schools for instructing the Indians in Spanish may have had some effect, but it is difficult to determine to what extent these were carried out.[5]

The Negroes, the great majority slaves, although composing four per cent of the population of Spanish America and nineteen per cent of all America (North and South), were almost outside the currents of formal education. They and other "low born" were not permitted to go to the schools with the children of the upper social elements.

The *Telégrafo Mercantil* of Buenos Aires remarked on June 27, 1801, that "All of us who inhabit this part of the globe know how great is the multitude and variety of races or castes in America

---

[5] Riva Palacio, *México*, II, 735.

held to be and judged base and low, either by law or through custom, or abuse. Such are the Negroes, zambos, mulattoes, mestizos, quarteroons, puchuelos, etc. . . . Debased by their condition or birth, they are not admitted to the public primary schools so that they may not associate with nor rub up against the children of Spaniards." [6]

The Indians, who comprised forty-five per cent of the population of Spanish America (and eighty or ninety per cent of such areas as Bolivia, Peru, Ecuador, and Guatemala), were almost as completely deprived of educational opportunity, although they received more indoctrination. Pedro de Gante's and other early schools were intended for the children of the Indian nobles, not for the great majority. The graduates were apparently eager scholars and able. But what could they do? There were not jobs enough in government or church for the thousands who were coming from Spain. Were the Indians, from whom the country was conquered, to be educated to fill places that might be occupied by Spaniards, or, a little later, by Creoles? Events proved that this was not to be the case. The various mixtures, such as mestizos, mulattoes and zambos, totaling thirty-two per cent of the Spanish-American population, were little if any better off as a whole, although individuals among them had considerably more opportunity to rise into the ranks of the privileged. This left instruction as a near monopoly of the whites, who comprised but one-fifth of the entire population.[7]

It would be erroneous in the extreme, however, to think of the whites as an educated class. Most of them were as far removed from educational opportunity as the rest of the population. The instructional facilities of colonial Argentina have been described by one of its foremost historians as follows:

"The general education was limited to the schools of reading and arithmetic which each convent was required by its statutes to maintain. In Córdoba there were six of these schools, and in Buenos Aires four. The attendance was confined to the children of the well-dressed families,[8] who attended with more or less regularity. The rest remained in complete ignorance. But the women, even those of the highest class, received not even elementary instruction. It was considered an immorality for them

---

[6] Quoted in Levene, ed., *Nación Argentina*, vol. IV, sección I, pp. 515-16, note 2.

[7] These figures on population percentages are taken from Humboldt, *Travels*, VI, 832-39 [*Voyage*, XI, 160-72].

[8] The word used is *familias visibles*, or families fit to be seen, indicating that the rest of the population was not in that condition.

to know how to read, and even a greater disgrace to know how to write, 'two things which served only to tempt them to sin and enabled them to evade the vigilance of their parents.' At the beginning of our century [nineteenth] there were still very few married women who could read even a single page." [9]

In Buenos Aires, with forty thousand people, the only four schools had about seven hundred students in 1773.[10]

In Santiago de Chile, with a population of about 30,000 at the end of the colonial period, only about five hundred children were in regular attendance in the various primary and secondary schools.[11] When the English explorer, Vancouver, visited Chile in 1795 he noticed that few of the women of the upper classes could even write their own names. The situation in Peru was as bad, general education being unknown, while the school facilities in New Granada and Venezuela were equally limited.[12]

In New Spain, which stood out above the other colonies as a center of culture, the masses were equally ignorant, since this region gained its distinction from the superior achievements of its intellectual élite, rather than from wide-spread public instruction.[13]

But despite the ignorance and superstition of the great majority of the people, there still was room for an educational system compatible with the type of society that existed in the Spanish colonies, a society characterized by a landed and merchant aristocracy, a divine-right concept of government, and an ecclesiastical culture. An educational system was needed to perform four chief functions: to give the aristocrats a schooling that would brighten the lustre of their titles, principally in the classics but without neglect of religion; to produce men with the indispensable knowledge for conducting the government, as well as lawyers and notaries expert in civil and canon law for protecting the interests of both the aristocracy and clergy; to supply the Church, which was carrying on an enormous work of indoctrination, with a large body of ecclesiastics; and to train painters, sculptors, and architects for the building and ornamentation of the Houses of God.

---

[9] Vicente F. López, *Historia de Argentina*, I, 243, quoted in Ingenieros, *Ideas argentinas*, in *Obras completas*, XIII, 49.

[10] Altamira, *Historia de España*, IV, 340.

[11] Barros Arana, *Chile*, Vol. VII, chap. XXVII, note 2.

[12] Javier Prado, *Estado social del Perú durante la dominación española*, in C. L. D. *Perú* (3rd Ser., Lima, 1941), I, 144-45; *Relación de mando del Virrey Antonio Caballero y Góngora*, 1789, in *Biblioteca de Historia nacional* [Colombia], VIII, 236-55; *Relación del Virrey José de Espeleta*, 1796, in *ibid.*, 322-39; Henao y Arrubla, *Colombia*, pp. 294-99; Depons, *Voyage to the Spanish Main*, I, 112-20.

[13] Alamán, *Méjico*, I, 17-22.

Universities

University education occupied a relatively more important place in the colonies than primary and secondary instruction. [14] This arose naturally from its chief functions, to prepare officials for government service and ecclesiastics for the Church. Beginning with the universities in Santo Domingo, Lima,[15] and Mexico City, the number gradually increased until there were about twenty-five (ten major and fifteen minor) before the end of the colonial period. Some of the universities were founded by the Church, some by the Crown, but all were under theological influence. In the seventeenth century, the University of Mexico offered thirteen courses, of which six were on theology, four on law (largely ecclesiastical also), two on medicine and one on Indian languages, while Sigüenza y Góngora held the chair of mathematics later in the century. By the end of the colonial period perhaps ten more courses were added.[16] When the University of San Felipe opened classes in Santiago de Chile in 1758, its curriculum was also chiefly theological; but there was a chair of medicine held by Doctor Domingo Nevin, a Frenchman by birth, "and the only physician in Santiago at that time." A chair of mathematics was added a little later in 1758 on the express recommendation of the King.[17] San Marcos in Lima had fifteen professorships in 1796.[18] Serving as vocational schools for the clergy, the universities had a considerable task which they seem to have performed well. Perhaps 150,000 degrees, the vast majority in theology, were granted to students of the colonial universities during the more than three centuries of the colonial period. It is very doubtful, indeed, whether most of the institutions called universities were actually more than theological seminaries.[19]

---

[14] Lucas Ayarragaray, "Las universidades coloniales," *Revista de derecho, historia y letras,* XIX (Buenos Aires, August, 1904), 245-61; Lanning, *Academic Culture,* pp. 3-33.

[15] Carlos Concha, "The Oldest University in South America," *H.A.H.R.,* IX (February, 1929), 107-115.

[16] Riva Palacio, *México,* II, 735; Arthur L. Campa, "The Churchmen and the Indian Languages of New Spain," *H. A. H. R.,* XI (November, 1931), 542-50.

[17] Barros Arana, *Chile,* VI, 217-18.

[18] *Memorias de los Virreyes que han gobernado el Perú* (6 vols., Lima, 1859), VI, 55. Other universities were founded in Córdoba, Argentina, 1614-22; Guatemala, 1678; Quito, Ecuador (San Gregorio, 1586; Santo Tomás, 1594); Chuquisaca (Sucre), Bolivia, 1624; Huamanga, Peru, 1680-85; Cuzco, 1628, and a second university, 1692; Bogotá, Colombia, the Thomistic University, 1594, 1655; Mérida, Yucatán, 1624; Guadalajara, Mexico, 1791; Panama, about 1749; León, Nicaragua, 1815; Mérida, Venezuela, 1807; Caracas, Venezuela, 1721-22; Havana, Cuba, 1728. The dates assigned for the different universities vary, according to whether the date of the founding decree, the inauguration, or the actual opening is given.

[19] For a more detailed account of the curriculum of the university, and a more favorable view of the content of education, see Arthur S. Aiton, "The Spanish

The universities of the New World were modeled on Salamanca, the leading university in Spain, and credits were exchangeable between the chief institutions of America and Spain. The restrictions surrounding entrance into the university, such as purity of blood, legitimacy, and religion, while not strictly enforced, limited them almost exclusively to the few of the upper ranks of society. The exceptions to this rule were generally boys who showed aptitude for clerical studies, for many of whom (as well as for some others) scholarships were provided. The requirement that instruction be given in Latin limited the eligible students still further.

The teaching staffs were usually clerics, among whom Jesuits, Franciscans, and Dominicans predominated. During the sixteenth and seventeenth centuries, the Jesuits were reputed more progressive in their methods than the other orders, but if this was the case they did not maintain their record into the eighteenth century. The content of their teaching, their attitude toward the new sciences and the inventory of the books in their libraries would indicate that the reputation they had gained in the past was weighing heavily on eighteenth-century America's hopes for the future. There is little documentary justification for the view that the expulsion of the Jesuits in 1767 was a blow to progressive education.

It is doubtful that an education dominated by an intellectual monopoly would be progressive under any circumstances, but it proved to be an impossibility where the monopoly claimed divine sanction, as did the Church. The search for truth can hardly be built on the assumption that all truth has been revealed and entrusted to one institution. The incentive to investigate further is not only lacking, but the threat of punishment for intellectual curiosity is ever present.[20] Fortunately the monopoly could never be made absolute.

Some of the deleterious effects of the clerical influence have been noted by a modern authority in his description of San Marcos in Lima.

Thought, according to Philip Ainsworth Means, had to conform to the Church's doctrines, and there were confusing doctrines at war with one another. The University suffered from the squabbles of the monastic schools and, in 1636, the University was reduced to filling its classrooms by permitting the rival religious groups to establish chairs for teaching one or another brand of theology, on

Conquest and Settlement of the Indies," in Wilgus, ed., *Colonial Hispanic America*, pp. 158-61; and Lanning, *Academic Culture*, pp. 34-58.
    [20] Means, *Fall*, pp. 270-71. See also Riva Palacio, *México*, II, 843-44.

condition that they bring their students to the university. As a result, says Means, the University became a theological seminary, frequently disturbed by monkish brawls. [21]

The universities did offer courses in the arts, law, and medicine, but the arts course were largely Latin and rhetoric, logic as applied to dogma, metaphysics, physics, and mathematics. The mathematics courses in both Lima and Santiago de Chile were at times suspended because there were no students. Law was also very largely concerned with theology, and medicine was "little appreciated." [22] The University of San Marcos about 1740 is said by a Peruvian historian to have been "without any serious study whatever." [23]

A picture of the University of San Felipe in Santiago, Chile, is equally depressing:

"The unequal distribution of the chairs in the various branches of science, the limited knowledge of the professors, the scope and direction of the teaching, and even the ritual adopted for the examinations and other public acts of the university, were a reflection of the type of organization then existing in Spain and her colonies, and reveal a deplorable backwardness." [24]

The instruction received even by the most privileged evoked harsh criticism from some of the contemporaries of the late colonial period. Lucas Alamán, who saw the last days of Spanish rule in Mexico, remarked on the generally low state of culture there:

"It cannot be said that the Spanish element, including in this classification both those born in Spain and in America, was the educated class; but whatever enlightenment existed in the country belonged exclusively to it. . . . Nevertheless, this instruction was limited almost entirely to legal and ecclesiastical studies, and confined to Mexico City and the seats of the bishoprics where there were *colegios*." [25]

Of Chile, Barros Arana observed:

"It would not be proper to say that the Creoles comprised the educated class of the colony, given the fact that in the midst of the general ignorance that prevailed, no class merited the term educated; but it can be said that what little learning existed in the colony was confined almost exclusively to this class." [26]

---

[21] Means, *Fall,* pp. 269-70.
[22] Alamán, *Méjico,* I, 19.
[23] Lorente, *Perú bajo los Borbones,* p. 69.
[24] Barros Arana, *Chile,* VI, 218.
[25] Alamán, *Méjico,* I, 17.
[26] Barros Arana, *Chile,* VII, 471.

García del Río, another writer of the later colonial period, corroborates this with regard to other colonies, saying, "We learned to wrangle rather than reason . . . An impenetrable veil shut us off from foreign languages, chemistry, natural history, and the history of society. A black cloud separated us from knowledge of our own country, of our planet, of the general mechanics of the universe. We had not the slightest idea of the relations between men in society, or of societies among themselves." [27]

The archbishop-viceroy of Nueva Granada in 1789, in recommending educational reforms, suggested that it would be a good thing "to substitute the useful exact sciences in the place of those merely speculative studies in which up to the present, unfortunately, time has been lost. For in a country full of products to be utilized, with mountains to conquer, roads to be opened and swamps and marshes to be drained, it is certain that what is needed most is individuals who know how to understand and observe natural phenomena, use calculus, the compass and the rule, rather than those who are interested in discussing what is reason, the Primary Substance, and its form." [28] Deán Gregorio Funes, who took over the rectorship of the University of Córdoba late in the colonial period also condemned the metaphysical character of the instruction in drastic terms,[29] as did others who had experiences with universities in other parts of colonial America.[30]

This gloomy survey of the universities and general education is not a full view of the colonial scene, however. The conditions about 1740 represented the dark that comes before the dawn. In the last half of the eighteenth century, the educational tempo of the colonies was quickened by the introduction of new types of schools. Particularly important was the shift of some schools from religious to secular control, which improved instruction and rendered it more responsive to the needs of the students. This was a timid but important step in the direction of delivering the people from the intellectual blight of systematized superstition.

Considerable reform occurred within the universities after 1750, and will be discussed presently, but the most important new intellectual currents of the last years of the colonial period formed outside the university halls.

---

[27] Quoted in Javier Prado, *Estado social del Perú,* pp. 145-46.
[28] Quoted in Henao and Arrubla, *Colombia,* p. 295. The recommendations of the viceroy for educational reforms were not carried into effect.
[29] Ingenieros, *Ideas argentinas,* in *Obras completas,* XIII, 63-70.
[30] See Barros Arana, *Chile,* VII, chap. XXVII, par. 3.

RESTRICTIONS ON BOOKS: THE LAWS

What was the intellectual horizon of the Spanish colonies outside the schools? Obviously it varied considerably from the sixteenth to the eighteenth centuries and from place to place in the colonies. But no task is more difficult than to find its true dimensions. By many Latin Americans it has been placed at "zero," their judgments being based on the state of education and the Spanish policy toward printing and the circulation of books.

In view of the fact that Charles V forbade the importation and printing, sale, or possession in the colonies of books "that treated of profane and fabulous matters, and of imaginary histories," one of Chile's most distinguished historians asserts that the Spanish Americans "might read neither poetry nor novels, nor any other work designed for pleasure or diversion. According to the literal text of this law, which was not repealed, the colonists would not have been able to enjoy Don Quixote or the comedies of Calderón and Lope de Vega." [31] An Argentine scholar, whose works have long been considered classics of Latin-American intellectual history, came to the conclusion "that such a prohibition was equivalent to depriving Americans of all reading matter, since all neither could nor wished to read religious and juridical works. [32]

Latin-American scholars who made such deductions during the nineteenth century, and more recently, founded them on the laws enacted for the Indies. The legal measures have been accepted as determining the intellectual climate in the Spanish colonies. Such was not entirely the case, however; the laws regulating intellectual matters were perhaps as generally disregarded as those pertaining to economics or political subjects. But the legislation did express the spirit of the times and the intent of government and church, and hence was significant.

Spain's laws on intellectual matters for her colonies are contained in a series of acts beginning as early as 1531 (or earlier) and continuing to the eve of Latin American emancipation. That the early laws were regarded as in force to the end is indicated by their inclusion in the *Recopilación de las Leyes de Indias* issued in 1682 and the *Novísima Recopilación* issued in 1805.[33]

The earliest law of which we have a copy is that of 1531. This reads:

---

[31] Miguel Luis Amunátegui, *Los precursores de la independencia de Chile* (2nd ed., 3 vols., Santiago de Chile, 1909-10), I, 238.

[32] Vicente G. Quesada, *La vida intelectual en la América española*, pp. 60-61.

[33] See *Leyes de Indias,* Libro I, Título XXIV; and *Novísima Recopilación,* Libro VII, Título XVI.

"I have been informed that many fictional and irreligious books in Romance [the vernacular], such as Amadís and others of this sort, go to the Indies, and since this is bad practice for the Indians and something which it is not well for them to be concerned with or to read, I command you, therefore, from this time henceforth neither to permit nor allow any person at all to take any book whatever of fictional and irreligious matters there, but only those relating to the Christian religion and morality with which the above mentioned Indians and other inhabitants of the Indies may concern themselves and practice the art of reading, because nothing to the contrary is to be allowed." [34]

The instruction given to Viceroy Mendoza when he came out in 1535 repeated the injunction that "no books in Romance [the vernacular] of irreligious and fictional subjects should be carried to [the Indies]." In 1543 the order was repeated to the Casa de Contratación, the Audiencia of Peru, and probably to the other officials in America as well.

More than a century later an abbreviated form of this royal decree was included in the *Recopilación de leyes de Indias* in 1682, showing that it was nominally in force at that date. It provided:

"There shall not be permitted in the Indies books of irreligious and fictional character. Because to carry to the Indies books in the vernacular [Spanish] that treat of irreligious and fictional material and imaginative histories will bring numerous troubles: we command our viceroys, audiencias, and governors not to permit them to be printed, sold, possessed, or carried to their districts, and that they see that no Spaniard or Indian read them." [35]

Evidence that the Crown intended these laws to be respected is found in a statute of 1550 which commanded the Casa de Contratación to see that the "permitted books" be "listed in detail one by one, with a declaration of the material they contain, and they shall not be registered by lots." Legislation in 1556 and 1560 forbade the printing, sale, or possession of any book concerning the Indies without the permission of the Council of the Indies, and during the reign of Philip IV still another statute provided

[34] The texts of the laws cited here are in José Torre Revello, *El libro, la imprenta y el periodismo en América* (Buenos Aires, 1940), pp. 37-137 and appendices nos. 1, 2, 3, 4, 20, 55, 78, 79, 82, 83; see also, Irving A. Leonard, *Romances of Chivalry in the Spanish Indies* (Berkeley: University of California Press, 1933), pp. 219-23.

[35] *Leyes de Indias,* Libro I, Título XXIV, ley iv.

that no printed book treating matters of the Indies should be carried to the Indies without the license of the Council.[36]

Similar decrees, reminders, and orders for enforcement continued throughout the colonial period.[37] In 1741 the Crown ordered its officials not to permit the circulation of books treating American matters unless they had the license of the Council of the Indies even when licensed by both the Crown and the Council of Castile, and this was repeated the next year in a decree directed to New Spain. In 1750 a royal cédula prohibited the publication of any *papel* without license, while other cédulas from time to time directed the seizure of this or that work.[38]

CIRCULATION OF BOOKS IN THE COLONIES

Had these laws been fully observed, it is possible that Spanish America would have had nothing to read but legal and religious works. But whatever the laws intended, and it may be that changes in the meaning of certain words of the Spanish language have led to a misinterpretation of the sixteenth-century import of this legislation, they very evidently did not prevent the legal entrance of works of fiction and "imaginative histories." It has been amply demonstrated that from 1583, and in all probability from a much earlier date, chivalric romances, picaresque novels, poetry, comedies, fables, and other types of "literature of entertainment," including works of the Latin and Greek pagan authors, came into the colonies.[39]

The colonists were apparently addicted to reading the chivalric romances and picaresque novels popular in Spain of that day, and which corresponded somewhat to the Nick Carter thrillers of the early part of this century or to contemporary detective fiction. They were familiar with such picaresque novels as *Lazarillo de Tormes* and *Guzmán de Alfarache,* and such novels of chivalry as *Amadís de Gaula,* the *Crónica de don Florisel de Niquea* and the *Espejo de Príncipes y Cavalleros,* as were the people of Spain itself, and it is probable that the entire first edition of *Don Quixote* was sent to the Indies.[40] The great dramatists, Lope de Vega,

---

[36] *Ibid.,* Libro I, Título XXIV, leyes i, ii and v.

[37] Torre Revello, *El libro,* appendix 20 and appendix 55; *Leyes de Indias,* Libro I, Título XXIV, ley xv.

[38] Torre Revello, *El Libro,* appendices 78, 79, 83, 91.

[39] On this point see the works of Leonard and Torre Revello, cited above, where a number of inventories of books brought to America, with the license of both secular and religious authorities, are reproduced. See also Irving A. Leonard, "Best Sellers of the Lima Book Trade, 1583," *H.A.H.R.,* XXII (February, 1942), 5-33, where a book order from Lima is reproduced.

[40] Irving A. Leonard, "*Don Quixote* and the Book Trade in Lima, 1606," *Hispanic Review,* VIII (October, 1940), 285-304; "Guzmán de Alfarache in the Lima Book Trade, 1613, *ibid.,* XI (July, 1943), 210-220.

Pérez de Montalbán, Lope de Rueda, Tirso de Molina, and Calderón de la Barca were also read in America, as were Garcilaso de la Vega and other poets.[41]

The discovery that the Spanish colonies openly received and read the very types of fiction which the laws prohibited has led to an abrupt reaction in the attitude of many historians. Where it was once customary to denounce Spain for keeping her colonies in intellectual bondage, there is now a school which contends that since the laws were not enforced, the colonies were not restrained at all. This school of thought is well represented by the Reverend Father Guillermo Furlong Cardiff of the Argentine Academy of History. Relying on his own researches and those of others he asserts:

"Señor Torre Revello . . . has shown in erudite pages . . . how much the presumed prohibition against introducing books into América has been exaggerated, and how great, how limitless, how free was the trade in books during the whole of the extensive period we call colonial . . . . [Spain manifested] a growing enthusiasm for the philosophical and natural sciences which were to have in Spain an astonishing and unequaled development . . . . Neither in Spain nor in its overseas possessions was there ever any obstacle to the circulation of any books except those written by Lutheran theologians, those that were obscene, without literary merit whatever, and those that treated necromancy and witchcraft . . . . And it is to be noted that neither in the mother country nor in the colonies was there a law of absolute exclusion, even for books of that triple and wretched type. They were not given a general passport, but there were all the necessary concessions to the general culture. The men of learning and science, and the spiritual guides obtained full license for all types of reading, even the most heretical and dangerous. Not even the *Ethics* of Spinoza, and even less the works of Bacon, Descartes, and Gassendi, for example, met with barriers or obstacles. And thus it is explicable that the works of those philosophers, as well as their popularizers, were even current in the Río de la Plata . . .

"There were no odious restrictions in the Peninsula nor in the American colonies; and there was in the mother country, and by force of irradiation in the colonies also, a resplendence of culture that it is impossible to ignore in view of the concrete

[41] Irving A. Leonard, "Notes on Lope de Vega's Works in the Spanish Indies," *Hispanic Review*, VI (October, 1938), 277-93.

facts offered to us by history . . . ." ". . . a culture so intense that it would perhaps not be too much to assert that proportionately it was not inferior to that we possess today." [42]

The assertion that the culture of colonial Argentina was equal to that of today is the antithesis of the statement previously cited from the Argentine historian Quesada, who concluded that the Argentines were virtually deprived of reading matter during the colonial period.

WHAT SPAIN AND THE COLONIES READ

Where lies the truth concerning the circulation of books in America? Although the masses of the people were illiterate and could scarcely have created a demand for books, thousands of books were imported or printed in the Indies. The question is, what were they? We may divide them into two main classes: books destined for the professions, and fiction. Professional books existed in proportion to the numbers of the professional groups, and including books published in the colonies and brought in from abroad were perhaps about as follows: (1) Religious books, for the thousands of ecclesiastics, among which were devotionals and prayer books; (2) school books, which may have existed in even larger number than religious books, but which were less important volume for volume and were largely dictionaries, grammars, and Latin texts with religious content; (3) law books, for the courts and attorneys, and works on medicine, surgery, mineralogy, and other professions; (4) limited numbers of books on secular philosophy, history, and the classical pagan literatures. Fiction included dramas, novels, poetry, and short tales and stories. That the books imported into and produced in the colonies were in the main religious in character seems almost certain.[43]

Evidence of the situation in the colonies is to be found in the libraries. From a very early date, not later than 1517 when Las Casas brought books to America, the formation of libraries began. Many of the conquistadores brought books with them, and there were not a few learned men numbered among these from the first years of occupation. Numerous private libraries were formed, some of which contained thousands of volumes, but the most important collections were those in the monasteries and churches. These were largely composed of orthodox religious books, but a small num-

---

[42] Furlong Cardiff, "Bibliotecas coloniales," in *BAN Hist.*, XIII, 116-19, 128-29.
[43] Professor Irving A. Leonard of the University of Michigan, in a note to the author, says that about 70 to 75% were religious.

ber of prohibited works found their way into them for reasons which will be presently discussed.

Despite the legal restrictions, there is considerable evidence that there was no actual discrimination against the colonies with regard to the circulation of books. The real situation in all probability was indicated by the modern Argentine historian, Torre Revello, in his statement that ". . . the colonists of [Spanish] America read whatever they wished that was permitted to the peninsular subjects of the monarchs of Spain." [44]

CENSORSHIP OF BOOKS IN SPAIN

The point is, what was permissible reading in Spain? In 1502, Ferdinand and Isabella issued legislation providing that no book should be printed, imported, or offered for sale without prior examination and license. Both religious and state officials were designated to enforce the law; and penalties for infringement were severe.[45] Considerably before this, in 1479, Pope Sixtus IV had delegated powers of censorship to the University of Cologne in Germany, and when Alexander VI in 1501 instructed the bishops of Germany to keep a strict watch on the press, the model for later legislation by both church and state was established.

The Lutheran revolt accentuated the desire of the churchmen to prevent the circulation of heretical works. Rome called on Spain in 1521 to curb Lutheran writings and took it for granted that this was the function of the Inquisition. By various acts of 1525, 1530, and 1531, the Inquisition asserted its powers of censorship, and continued to exercise such authority until the end of its existence. It condemned books and other printed matter, seized prohibited books and punished authors, possessors, and sellers. It also assumed the right to grant licenses for publication after 1527, a power that it shared with judges and bishops who had previously received such authority. In 1536, the Inquisition ordered that no book should be printed without a preliminary license from the Holy Office, but after 1550 it seldom exercised this power, confining its functions to stopping the books before publication and leaving to the Crown the issuing of licenses. A law of 1554 provided that the Royal Council would issue licenses after examina-

---

[44] Torre Revello, El libro, pp. 243-44.

[45] The discussion of censorship in Spain is based on Henry Charles Lea, A History of the Inquisition of Spain (4 vols., New York, 1906-1907), III, 480-549, except where otherwise indicated. For a Roman Catholic view of the Inquisition see Francis Borgia Steck, "Some Recent Trends and Findings in the History of the Spanish Colonial Empire in America," in The Catholic Historical Review, XXVIII (April, 1942), 29-42.

tion, but even books so issued could be condemned by the Inquisition, and were.

This soon led to the creation of a large staff of examiners, called *calificadores,* and once a book was condemned, the fact was widely publicized by posting notices in public places and on the doors of all churches. The consequence was the formation of a long list of prohibited works, and eventually an Index of Prohibited Books *(Index Librorum Prohibitorum).* The practice rose simultaneously in England (under Henry VIII) and the Netherlands (under Charles V) in 1526. The earliest Spanish list dates from 1540, but was for the use of the Inquisition only. A public list was first issued in 1546 by the University of Louvain (in Spanish dominions), and reissued in Spain the next year. Obviously such a list had to be revised periodically and new issues of the Index came out from time to time. In the meantime Rome was issuing its own Index, at least from 1557 and 1559. Also in 1559 the first Spanish Index directed at indigenous works was issued. From this epoch dates the vigorous searches through book shops and libraries of Spain, examiners and revisors visiting the libraries of universities, monasteries, private individuals, and book sellers.

The Crown vigorously co-operated with the Inquisition in this work. A law of 1558 cited the Lutheran scare of the previous year in Spain, and decreed the death penalty and confiscation of property for keeping a book condemned by the Inquisition. Such books were to be publicly burned, and the Index was to be printed and exposed by all booksellers so that everybody might see it. The death penalty was also provided for importing books in Romance without a license, even from Aragon into Castile. All books throughout the kingdom were to be inspected and if deemed suspicious held until the Royal Council could pass on them. This for books already in print.

A rigid censorship was provided for forthcoming publications. Death and confiscation were the lot of everyone who should give out for printing a book that did not have the license of the Royal Council, and the same penalty was decreed for those who owned or exhibited a manuscript on religion not previously licensed. This law was not repealed until the Revolution forced reform on Spain in 1810. Pope Paul IV strengthened this statute when in 1559 he required all confessors to inquire of their penitents whether they owned or knew of the existence of such works and to denounce the culprits.

Thus the Inquisition, the Crown, and the Papacy were joined in the effort to confine Spanish reading to approved matter. The attempt continued throughout the whole of the Spanish colonial period in America, and was applicable in America. The prosecutions for printing, possessing, circulating, or selling prohibited books in America and in Spain were identical. The epochs of the severest enforcement were also the same: the sixteenth century for "Lutheranism", the mid-seventeenth against the Portuguese and the "Jew", and the period after 1776 against American and French revolutionary literatures which were penetrating Spanish lands.

An important feature of the censorship system was the granting of licenses to read and possess prohibited books. This was necessary since somebody had to be authorized to read and refute heretical and seditious writings. The necessity was recognized as early as 1536 by Pope Paul III in the bull *Caena Domini,* but perhaps antedates that document. Thereafter, such licenses were granted from time to time by the Papacy and the Spanish Inquisition, and on occasion by other high dignitaries. In periods of stress it was also usual for licenses to be withdrawn when it was felt the privilege was being abused or too many licenses had been granted. The system was based on the hierarchical concept of knowledge: that some have special faculties for comprehending what must remain forever unknown to the masses, a concept which formed the basis for the educational system and the intellectual atmosphere of Spain and her colonies, but which was not limited to them, being common to many regimes which considered themselves to have supernatural approval.

CENSORSHIP OF SPEECH AND THOUGHT

Censorship of reading matter was not the only way in which Spain sought to control thought. One of the most important functions of state and church was the censorship of Speech. It was the duty of the ecclesiastical officials, especially of the Inquisition,[46] to suppress heretical and seditious utterances. Thoughtless or deliberately unorthodox expressions might lead to charges of "Propositions," i.e., statements of a suspicious character. Toward the end of its existence, the principal activity of the Inquisition was handling cases of "Propositions." Some of the most distinguished men of Spain and her colonies were prosecuted for holding ideas not strictly in accordance with those of the authorities.

Among the propositions most dangerous to the individual were

---

[46] Lea, *Spanish Inquisition,* IV, 138-78.

those that threatened the divine-right concept of monarchy, or church. In such cases, the guilty party might be prosecuted by either ecclesiastical or state authorities. During the eighteenth century, the Inquisition was useful to the Crown in this work, though strictly political matters were not a part of its function in the early days under Ferdinand and Isabella.[47] With the rise of eighteenth-century Philosophism, or Naturalism, as it was called in Spain, and the anticlerical and anti-divine-right implications of the new philosophy based on natural law, both secular and ecclesiastical authorities were hard pressed to compete with the new politico-religious heresies. The difficulty was all the greater because many of the foremost Spanish statesmen, Aranda, Floridablanca, Jovellanos, Campomanes, Roda, and others were strongly influenced by the new currents of thought. Not even they were exempt from the laws, however, and several of them either fell from grace, or were imprisoned, or both.[48]

In this epoch there was the curious contradiction of a government encouraging the regeneration of Spain with one hand, while sternly repressing the regenerators on the other. Philip V, for example, warmly commended the Inquisition in 1724. At this time, the Inquisition was actively prosecuting numerous individuals for heretical and political activity,[49] including the historian Belando; his history of the reign of Philip V was approved by and dedicated to Philip, but the author was prosecuted for writing it. Such statesmen as Jovellanos and Olavide spent years in prison after even longer years of service to the state.[50]

Thus the intellectual development of Spain was confined by two cardinal obligations: loyalty to the Church and the Monarchy. The effects of such a policy left a deep mark on Spanish thought, and on the colonies as well. For generations the Spaniard was required to guard his tongue, be careful of what he wrote, and trust not even his nearest friend and kin. The impression created by the policy is epitomized in a popular saying: *Con el Rey y la Inquisición, Chitón!* (About the King and the Inquisition, Hush!) [51]

BOOKS, THOUGHTS, AND CENSORSHIP IN THE COLONIES

Briefly stated, the system as applied to Latin America was as follows: books that went to America had already been censored

---

[47] *Ibid.*, IV, 248-83.
[48] *Ibid.*, IV, 307-15.
[49] Between 1721-1728 sixty-four *autos* were held, 962 trials, and 151 persons were relaxed in person and effigy. Relaxation meant turning the culprit over to the secular authorities for strangulation, burning or both. *Ibid.*, IV, 386.
[50] *Ibid.*, IV, 385-471.   [51] *Ibid.*, IV, 515.

and licensed by the ecclesiastical and secular authorities of Spain, and subjected to special examination and purging by the Inquisition. If then acceptable, they were submitted to the Council of Indies for examination and licensing. At Sevilla or Cádiz they were examined before embarkation, and again when they reached port in America the authorities examined them. After arrival, they were still subject to search and seizure, and penalties for having prohibited books were severe, including confiscation of property, fines, imprisonment, and death.[52]

Books that treated colonial matters could not be published or circulated without a special license, and from fear of this provision, many works were submitted for examination that had nothing to do with America. On the other hand, books were published and circulated without license of the Council of Indies even when they contained material about the colonies. The gauntlet which books ran after reaching America included that of the Inquisitorial Courts in Mexico City, Lima, and Cartagena, and books not prohibited were sometimes confiscated, "because the Inquisition abused its privileges." [53] A book might circulate for a time and then be banned, leaving all possessors of books in a permanent state of uncertainty. Sometimes a license to print was denied temporarily, sometimes permanently. Not a few of the most famous and authoritative works on America were not printed until the nineteenth and twentieth centuries, some have not yet been printed, and some of whose existence we have notice, have not been found.

Nevertheless, prohibited books reached the colonies. They were found in the possession of individuals and in the libraries of religious orders, although not in great numbers.[54] It has already been pointed out that the presence of such books has caused some scholars to conclude that their circulation was not prohibited. As a matter of fact, while an enumeration of forbidden books found in the colonies (not counting the works of fiction which were not banned in Spain, and apparently not in the colonies) may give the impression that they were numerous, they were comparatively few. Most libraries contained an overwhelming majority of religious books, while the balance was made up mainly of works on law, history, or classics not on the prohibited list.[55] That more

---

[52] On these points see Torre Revello, *El libro*, chaps. II, III, VI and *passim;* Leonard, *Romances of Chivalry*, pp. 28-35. Leonard holds that these inspections were routine and largely ineffective.

[53] Torre Revello, *El libro*, p. 62. Leonard believes that only occasionally was this a real hazard to the books.

[54] Torre Revello, *El libro*, pp. 117-126.

[55] This conclusion is warranted from checking the lists given by Torre Revello,

fiction circulated, however, than library inventories indicate, is entirely probable. Such works were quickly destroyed by more frequent reading than was accorded to law or religion; and in times of paper shortage were likely to be the first used for scrap.

A misleading impression of liberality is created also by overlooking certain important circumstances connected with the presence of forbidden works: many of them were found in libraries of commissioners of the Inquisition, whose duty it was to confiscate them; or they were in the possession of individuals who held a license to read prohibited books (an infinitesimal percentage of the total population); or they were discovered by the Inquisition and held as a part of the evidence on which their possessors were prosecuted. Such is the case, for example, of the famous architect, Melchor Pérez de Soto, who was arrested in Mexico City by the Inquisition in 1655, and in whose library were found forbidden works.

That prohibited books did arrive in the Indies, however, and that they circulated and influenced the course of colonial history, is equally certain. But the circulation of prohibited books was the unusual thing, not the customary. This is clear from the long record of the secular and ecclesiastical authorities in hunting them down, and particularly of the Inquisition in prosecuting people for "Propositions" and the possession of heretical books. As an outstanding authority on this subject has said: ". . . it was, in the last analysis, difficult for any [Latin] American whatever to read any book whatever that was prohibited by the Holy Office." [56]

The work of censoring books had begun, in fact, before the Inquisition was formally established in 1569. The audiencia and bishop of Lima were both ordered in 1556 to seize prohibited books of which an Index was included with the order, and to send them to the Inquisition in Spain. All ships were to be met and searched. The Inquisitor General of Spain directed the archbishop of Mexico in 1561 to visit all book stores and libraries of the country, including those of the monasteries, university, and individuals, and to seize all books appearing in the Index prepared at Valladolid, Spain, in 1559. He was to see that nobody should read these "nor others of which there might be a suspicion of error or which it is not well to read." [57] The books seized were to be burned and the owner prosecuted.[58]

Leonard, and Furlong Cardiff, all cited above, although these authors, especially Furlong Cardiff, reach broader conclusions.

[56] José Toribio Medina, *Historia de la Inquisición en México* (Santiago de Chile, 1905), p. 415.

[57] José Toribio Medina, *La primitiva inquisición americana* (2 vols., Santiago de Chile, 1914), I, 60.

[58] *Ibid.*, I, 51-66.

Similar activities were taking place in Peru, Chile, and the Río de la Plata, and prosecutions for the possession of forbidden books or the holding of "Propositions," among the most dangerous being those that might lead to the accusation of "Judaism," acted as a damper on independent thought and free speech.[59]

Nor did the Inquisition limit itself to seizing the books listed in the Index of Spain or Rome. It had, or usurped, the power to seize any books or persons it deemed dangerous. The Argentine historian, Torre Revello, who believes that the circulation of books was freer than we have indicated above, has published lists of works seized by the Inquisition "in which may be seen a series of books whose retention was not justified. Only the abuses and omnipotent prerogatives of this tribunal [the Inquisition] explain the inspection and sequestration of books which were in no way numbered among the prohibited. In the same list are registered other hunted works which circulated in our continent in spite of all obstacles and denunciations." [60] The Mexican author, Francisco Fernández del Castillo, in his *Libros y libreros en el siglo XVI*[61] found the same situation in colonial New Spain. The possession of books might become a source of danger even to the man of letters, while to the unlettered who could not know its contents a book was practically taboo.

The intellectual atmosphere created by this system was by no stretch of the imagination liberal and free; yet oppressive as it was, some types of intellectual activity managed to flourish. Despite restrictions on education, and the taboos of censorship, colonial Spanish America made cultural contributions of her own.

---

[59] For numerous details and examples see José Toribio Medina, *El tribunal del Santo Oficio de la inquisición en las provincias del Plata* (Santiago de Chile, 1900), chap. VII and *passim*; ...., *Historia del tribunal del Santo Oficio de la inquisición en Chile* (2 vols., Santiago de Chile, 1890), II, chaps. III, IV, IX, XVI and *passim*; ......, *Historia del tribunal del Santo Oficio de la inquisición de Lima* (2 vols., Santiago de Chile, 1887), I, chap. XVI; II, chaps. XVII, XVIII, XXII and *passim*; ...., *Historia del tribunal del Santo Oficio de la inquisición de Cartagena de las Indias* (Santiago de Chile, 1899), pp. 358-93 and *passim*; see also Henry Charles Lea, *The Inquisition in the Spanish Dependencies* chaps. VI-VIII.

[60] Torre Revello, *El libro*, p. 104, note 1.

[61] In *Publicaciones del Archivo General de la Nación*, vol. VI (Mexico, 1914) [hereafter *AGN Mexico*].

Cultural Contributions of the
Spanish Colonies

WITH ALL THE HANDICAPS to the diffusion of learning, Spanish America was not a cultural desert during the colonial period. Within the confines of absolute fidelity to the Church and the theory of divine-right, there was room for literary activity and intellectual exercise; and outside these confines, a larger field of activity was open in studies that were not deemed to impinge on the prerogatives of the established institutions.

Maintaining orthodox religious and political beliefs implied not merely rejection of heresy and treason; it meant answering them. The exegesis required to reject or incorporate the whole body of human learning could not but produce a vast religio-philosophical literature, as it did both in Spain and in her colonies, as well as in Europe. The literature produced was, of course, Roman Catholic in spirit and content, and this must not be forgotten if we are to understand the Spanish colonial culture. Nor did acceptance of the theory of divine-right preclude political speculation. Quite the contrary, judging by the vast legal literature produced in the Spanish-speaking world.

Studies outside the religious field were pursued with considerable vigor. The description of the New World was one of the foremost tasks for men of learning, leading to important studies in geography, the history and languages of the Indians, travel accounts, chronicles of conquest and settlement, observations on the flora and fauna of the New World, medicine, and no small amount of scientific observation that was quite permissible within the framework of Catholic orthodoxy.

In the field of the fine arts, the Church was the chief mobilizer of the wealth expended on painting, sculpture, and architecture, and many excellent examples were produced. While creative literature was not comparable to that of the mother country, the colonies produced drama as well as epic and lyric poetry in great quantity (and some of excellent quality). In the realm of imaginative literature such as the novel the colonies were singularly deficient, but this is perhaps attributable to the fact that the wonders of the New World dwarfed the imagination, and what might have become a novel of adventure became instead a factual chronicle of conquest.

SCHOLARSHIP IN AMERICA: EARLY HISTORIANS AND TRAVELERS

Thus, in spite of the restrictions, opportunity was open to those who could make their interests conform to the prescribed pattern. If we accept the productions in this field for their positive contributions, rather than looking at what they might have been under freer circumstances, we find a large number of works worthy of study.[1]

The immediate interest excited in the Old World by the discovery of the New let loose a flood of letters and memoirs from the explorers. Columbus and his companions became the first historians of the New World, their reports being a valuable source of information. Much of the literature about America was not produced by Americans, of course, but no attempt will be made here to draw a thin line between Americans and Europeans. Our interest is directed toward those who contributed to knowledge of America.

Among these, the first after Columbus himself was Pietro Martire d'Anghiera, or Peter Martyr (c. 1455-1526). Peter Martyr was an Italian professor of Latin who came to Spain in 1487, teaching for a time at Salamanca University and serving in the Spanish diplomatic service. His most important achievement, however, was the record he left of the first reports from America. His insatiable curiosity about the New World impelled him to write hundreds of letters in which he demonstrated rare powers of observation. Of these, 812 are gathered together in his *Opus epistolarum*. His most direct contribution to the history of America was his *Decades de orbe novo,* the first three decades of which were published in 1516 and the complete work in 1530. This was the earliest work on the discovery that can be ranked as a history. Peter Martyr accepted as truth many things we regard as fables,

---

[1] Bernard Moses, *Spanish Colonial Literature in South America* (New York and London, 1922).

but this makes him all the more valuable as a mirror of what the world of that time believed about the newly-discovered lands. His work was translated into English as early as 1555, and is available in an excellent annotated translation by F. A. MacNutt, published in New York in 1912.

There were many other early accounts by those who were participating in the Conquest, some of which were published while more remained in manuscript for years, or even centuries. The five letters of Cortés, available in English, give an excellent picture of his exploits and of the condition of Mexico at the time. The first biographer of Cortés was Francisco López de Gómara, whose *Historia de las indias y conquista de México* appeared in Zaragoza in 1552-53. López de Gómara served for a time as chaplain and secretary to Cortés in Spain, but he was never in America. His praise of Cortés, which made the Conquest seem a one-man job, together with other alleged inaccuracies, excited the criticism of his contemporaries.

The circulation of his history was forbidden soon after publication, but this did not prevent its reaching the hands of Bernal Díaz del Castillo (1492-1584), who was with Cortés during the Conquest. Bernal Díaz was incensed by the neglect of his companions, and wrote his *Historia verdadera de la conquista de la Nueva España* about 1568, partly in reply to López de Gómara and partly to eulogize his fellow conquerors. His work remained in manuscript for many years, but was issued in 1632 by the Mercedarian Friars in Madrid, in a corrupted form. The Mercedarians suppressed the parts that did not please them and inserted falsified information of interest to their Order. The work circulated in this inaccurate version until Genaro García the Mexican historian issued an authentic edition (1904-05) from a photographic copy of the original manuscript, which is in the Guatemala National Library. It is from this edition that Alfred Percival Maudslay made his translation in five volumes for the Hakluyt Society, London, 1908-16. Bernal Díaz's history is one of the best sources of information for the conquest of Mexico and conditions at the time of the Conquest, although the "honest and simple chronicler" himself was not above inserting things that sometimes belie his reputation.[2]

Bernal Díaz came to America when a mere boy and had participated in two previous expeditions to the shores of Mexico before

---

[2] See Ramón Iglesia, "Two Articles on the Same Topic, etc.," *H.A.H.R.*, XX (November, 1940), 517-50.

he joined Cortés. He served throughout the conquest of Mexico and received an encomienda south of Vera Cruz, but gave it up to go to Guatemala with Cortés. He settled down there and was a respected member of the community until his death in 1584. He was not a man of much education, nor did he achieve high rank among the conquistadores. His history is not a piece of finished writing, but the story of a man in the ranks who had great capacity for remembering details. It is incomparable, and perhaps this is its greatest value, as a reflection of the Spanish mind in the sixteenth century. One of the most impressive things about Bernal Díaz was his belief that God had sent the Spaniards to convert the Indians to the true religion. The modern poet, Archibald MacLeish, based his epic poem, *Conquistador,* on Bernal Díaz's history.

A historian in a broader sense of the word was Gonzalo Fernández [or Hernández] de Oviedo (1478-1557), first official Chronicler of the Indies. Fernández de Oviedo came to America in 1514 with the expedition of Pedrarias de Avila as *veedor.* He later made six or seven trips to America, serving as governor of the province of Cartagena, alcalde of the fort of Santo Domingo, and in other positions of responsibility. He kept careful notes on all he saw, and collected vast information on every phase of the New World. His first work was a brief *Sumario* of the natural and general history of America, published in Toledo in 1526. The work for which he is justly famous, however, was first published in part in Sevilla in 1535 and entitled *Historia general y natural de las Indias.* This consisted of nineteen books, and a twentieth was added at Valladolid in 1557. Only in 1851-55 was there another edition, when fifty books were published in four volumes.

The value of this work lies in its extent and in its quality. It is a full account of the initial years of the Spanish occupation of the Caribbean islands and the coastline of South and Central America, and includes the early history of the Conquest. The author's powers of observation and his knowledge of the stuff of which history is made give his work a high rank. Where Bernal Díaz should be read for the picture of a single action, Fernández de Oviedo paints on a broad canvas the whole historical scene of the first half of the sixteenth century.

The best known of the sixteenth-century historians is perhaps Bartolomé de las Casas (1474-1566), but he is celebrated for his missionary activity rather than for his histories. He should be ranked, nevertheless, as one of the foremost historians of his age.

His first-hand knowledge of the early years of the Conquest equals that of Fernández de Oviedo. He came first to America in Ovando's expedition in 1502, landing in Española where he held an encomienda for a time. Horrified at the treatment the Indians were receiving, and impressed by the passionate sermons of the Dominicans against the cruelty, he surrendered his encomienda and became a lay cleric. He returned to Spain in 1515 to appeal for aid for the Indians and was instrumental in having new legislation drawn up and a commission of Jeronimite Friars sent to effect reforms. He lived and traveled for many years in America, joining the Dominicans; and in addition to attempting a colony in Cumaná, he was made bishop of Chiapas in Mexico.

Discouraged by the failure to enforce the New Laws in 1542, he returned to Spain where he published his *Brevísima relación de la destrucción de las Indias,* in 1552. This won world fame and was extensively translated, because it added much fuel to the fire with which rival nations were attempting to drive Spain from her new possessions. It is less a history, however, than a lawyer's brief in defense of his clients. Las Casas exaggerated the plight of the Indians and the cruelty of the Spaniards in order to gain sympathy for the former.

His two historical works are much more important, but unfortunately they were not published until recent times and have failed to attract the attention they deserve. The *Historia de las Indias* was published in six volumes in Madrid in 1875-79. It treats the early years of the Conquest and relates events of which Las Casas was an eye-witness or contemporary. Aside from long passages concerned with theological points of small interest to the modern reader, the *Historia* is valuable source material for the early period. His *Historia apologética de las Indias* is a complementary work. It did not appear in a complete edition until 1909.[3]

A chronicler whose work is indispensable for a knowledge of South America (Colombia to Bolivia) at the time of the Conquest is Pedro de Cieza de León. Cieza came to America as a boy of thirteen in 1532 and remained until 1550. He participated in the conquests of Colombia, Ecuador, Peru, and Bolivia, and held an encomienda until the time of his return to Spain. He took full advantage of his opportunities for gathering knowledge about America. He kept a diary of his experiences, incorporating the fruits of his insatiable curiosity into a series of accounts of the New World.

---

[3] Altamira, *Historia de España,* II, 435-38; III, 233-38.

His *Crónica del Perú* (Sevilla, 1553) is a valley by valley and mountain by mountain account of the territory from Colombia to Bolivia, depicting the geography, the peoples and their customs, the war between Indian tribes, and the Spanish invasion. So detailed are Cieza's descriptions that they would serve as an excellent guide book for anyone who wished to repeat his travels. Added to his acute powers of observation is a transparent honesty that has survived the test of time even better than that of Bernal Díaz. His aim was accuracy, with none of the partianship that marks other accounts. The second part of his chronicle, *Señorío de los Incas,* was not published until 1880. This is a detailed description of the society of the Inca Empire and its social structure. Other parts of his chronicle deal with the civil wars between the Spaniards in Peru. For those who wish to understand Inca society, Cieza's works are indispensable and should be the first read.

The historian who has long held the highest rank among those writing about the Incas is Garcilaso de la Vega, El Inca. Garcilaso was born in Peru in 1539, his father being one of the Spanish conquistadores and his mother a princess of the Inca royal family. Garcilaso may thus be considered as the national historian of the Incas. He left Peru for Spain in 1560 when a boy of twenty, and his *Comentarios reales de los Incas* did not appear until 1609 (second part, 1617). But his memories were keen and he had the advantage of several chronicles prepared on the ground by Spaniards who had lived in Peru, as well as the lost chronicle of Blas Valera, a fellow mestizo, and he corresponded with people in Peru.

Garcilaso's version of the traditions of the Incas is probably as accurate as any we have. The many deficiencies result more from the scanty knowledge the Incas had of their own past than from Garcilaso's personal faults as an historian. But it must be taken into consideration by the modern reader that Garcilaso was frankly an apologist for the Incas. He was extremely conscious of his Inca ancestry. To him the Inca realm was perfect, his own "Paradise Lost." Yet not everything he set down in praise of the Incas can be considered to their credit in the light of the concepts of modern civilization. It is possible to form a very unfavorable opinion of the Inca Empire, using only Garcilaso as evidence. From his work emerges a picture of the misery of the masses that is doubly damaging to the Incas since he was presenting their society as ideal. His *Comentarios* are an implied rebuke to the Spaniards, but he has been accused, it would seem unjustly, of being too subservient to those who destroyed his fatherland.

The reader should also bear in mind that Garcilaso, ever conscious of his royal Inca blood, makes a distinction between *los Incas* and *los Indios,* the former being the nobility, the latter the plebeians. Many of the apparent contradictions in his writings become clear when his use of these terms is properly understood. Garcilaso and Cieza are the best chroniclers of the Indian civilization, both being considered rather favorable to the Incas, but there are numerous other useful early accounts.

A work regarded as the antithesis of Garcilaso's is the *Historia indica* of Pedro Sarmiento de Gamboa. This is the second part of a history perhaps never completed. Sarmiento de Gamboa was commissioned by Viceroy Francisco de Toledo to make a summary of the numerous reports on Peru prepared at the latter's command when he came in 1569. One of the objectives was to prove that the Incas were usurpers, and that therefore the Spanish conquest was justified. In view of the glorification of aggression that characterized the Incas, this would not seem to have been a difficult task, at least in so far as Inca usurpations were concerned. Sarmiento de Gamboa's work did not appear in print until 1906, when the German scholar Richard Pietschmann published it as *Geschichte des Inkareiches.* It was translated somewhat inaccurately the next year by Sir Clements R. Markham, [4] and branded as a libel on Inca civilization. As a matter of fact, the basic elements of Inca society as presented by Sarmiento de Gamboa are not vastly different from those of Inca Garcilaso de la Vega.

The *Historia natural y moral de las Indias* (Sevilla, 1590) of José de Acosta is another of the numerous excellent works produced in part in colonial Spanish America. Acosta was a Jesuit who spent the seventeen years from 1570 to 1587 traveling in areas as widely separated as Peru and Mexico. His observations on agriculture, the land systems, and the political and social institutions of the Indians are among the most valuable. He is equally useful for the transplanting of European plants and animals to America, the development of mining in the New World by the Spaniards, the colonial institutions, and the Indian and colonial religions as seen through the eyes of a sixteenth-century churchman. One cannot read Acosta without being greatly impressed by the concrete evidence of Spanish contributions to America.

Even more detailed was the *Historia general de las cosas de Nueva España* by Bernardo Sahagún (d. 1590), written in Mexico

---

[4] See Harry Bernstein and Bailey W. Diffie, "Sir Clements R. Markham as a Translator," *H.A.H.R.,* XVII (November, 1937), 546-57.

in the last half of the sixteenth century, but not published until 1829-30. Sahagún had an intimate knowledge of the Indians from long years of contact with them and wrote in Aztec and Spanish. His history is filled with the small details of Indian things missed by most writers. Few works are so valuable to the anthropologists, ethnologists, and archeologists as that of Sahagún. An English translation entitled *A History of Ancient Mexico* was begun by Fanny Bandelier in 1932.

The history of the region now comprised in Venezuela and Colombia was written by several men who have achieved less fame than the chroniclers of Mexico and Peru, but who are probably not inferior as historians. Pedro de Aguado prepared two manuscripts on this region at the end of the sixteenth century. One, entitled *Historia de Santa Marta y nuevo reino de Granada,* was first published in a complete edition of two volumes by Jerónimo Becker in Madrid in 1916-17. Another, *Historia de Venezuela,* was also edited by Becker in Madrid in 1918-19.

Juan de Castellanos has the distinction of having written the longest poem in the Spanish language, 150,000 lines, but it is more properly history than poetry. The first part was published in Madrid in 1589 under the title *Elegías de varones ilustres de Indias.* Castellanos dedicated his life to compiling the biographies of the conquerors and recording them in verse. The second and third parts were published in 1850 and the fourth part, under the title *Historia del nuevo reino de Granada,* in 1886.

Two seventeenth century works which are valuable for the early history are the *Historia general de las conquistas del nuevo reyno de Granada* by Lucas Fernández de Piedrahita, published in Antwerp in 1688, and the *Primera parte de las noticias historiales de las conquistas de Tierra Firme en las Indias Occidentales* by Pedro Simón, published in 1627. Piedrahita's work was supposedly based on manuscripts left by the conqueror Gonzalo Jiménez de Quesada, although the authorship of these is disputed.

With a few exceptions, the men discussed above rank as chroniclers rather than as historians. At the beginning of the seventeenth century there was published in Madrid a work that is more properly history, although its author, Antonio Herrera y Tordesillas, was officially the Chronicler of the Indies. Herrera's *Historia general de los hechos de los castellanos en las islas y Tierra Firme del Mar Océano,* published from 1601 to 1615 in 4 volumes (8 decades), covered the period to 1555 and was one of the first attempts to write a comprehensive work on the New World. Much of it was based on manuscripts such as Las Casas, that remained unpublished for two centuries after the appearance of Herrera's work, and much was taken from other documentary sources to which Herrera had access because he was working at the direct command of the monarch. Not until the end of the nineteenth century, when many hitherto unedited manuscripts were published, were there histories available of the value of Herrera's.

An excellent work of this character, published only in 1890-95, is the *Historia del Nuevo Mundo* by Bernabé Cobo, written in Peru from 1642 to 1653. He went there when only a boy, later became a Jesuit, and spent many years traveling and studying. His discussion of the plants and animals, native and European, is the best known to this writer, and the parts of his work dealing with the social and political structure of the Inca Empire are excellent.

Juan de Torquemada's *Monarquia Indiana,* published in Madrid in 1613, dealt largely with the pre-Conquest history of the Indians of Mexico. It has been ranked since its publication as one of the best sources of information, filling for Mexico the same mission as Garcilaso for Peru, although Torquemada never achieved Garcilaso's fame, and he was guilty of giving his history a slant favorable to his friends and unfavorable to his enemies.

Central America does not boast the innumerable chroniclers who wrote of Peru and Mexico, but two works worthy of notice are Antonio de Remesal's *Historia de la provincia de San Vicente de Chyapa y Guatemala* published in Madrid in 1619, and Francisco Antonio de Fuentes y Guzmán's *Historia de Guatemala,* written toward the end of the seventeenth century but not printed until 1882-83. Remesal's history took on special importance because of its publication at the time it was written.

Chilean history of the seventeenth century is represented by Alonso de Ovalle, whose *Histórica relación del reino de Chile* was published in Rome in 1646, and Diego de Rosales, whose *Historia general del reyno de Chile,* written in the second half of the seventeenth century, did not appear until 1878. Both of these works treat at length the struggles between the Araucanians and the Spanish conquerors. Ovalle's history is also an index to the superstitious mentality of the times, since the author, a Jesuit, represented the cream of colonial intellectuals.

LATER HISTORIES

Seventeenth-century historians failed to achieve the renown of those of the sixteenth century, and this was even more true of the eighteenth century writers. The reason is not hard to find. The

Courtesy of the Museum of Modern Art, New York

PORTRAIT OF D. MANUEL TOLSA, BY RAFAEL XIMENO

Courtesy of the Mexican Government Travel Bureau

DOOR IN YEPOSTLÁN. NOTE TILE AND DETAIL WORK

earlier historians were pioneers, the conquistadores themselves, or the priests and friars who first established the Church in America. Their accounts related hitherto unknown facts about newly-discovered lands. Each history was a novelty, a vicarious participation in the work of conquering and Christianizing what seemed to be fabulous kingdoms. The sixteenth century historians had the advantage of describing new lands, strange men, unknown plants and animals, with the fascination that the "lost world" has had for our own.

But as the seventeenth and eighteenth centuries approached, there were few new men, plants, and animals to be described, no new and fabulous kingdoms were being conquered, and the wars with the Indians had become routine military actions. It was too late to fascinate with tales of the marvelous, and a little early for the scientific studies of modern times. The historians were confined to recapitulating earlier histories or chronicling the more prosaic aspects of colonies that were well established.

This is not to say that America had lost its glamor in the eighteenth century; the glamor was there, but it attracted mainly the interest of foreigners, especially the English and French who saw in the commerce of America the "El Dorado" that was so eagerly sought at an earlier date by Sir Walter Raleigh and others. Their interest may be likened to that shown by North Americans in the twentieth century. But their historical accounts can hardly be considered as a part of Latin-American literature, valuable as they are for the bibliography of Latin-American studies. While the line between Latin-American literature and literature *about* Latin America has been kept purposely vague, it would be going too far afield to include the works of Raynal, Robertson, Humboldt, and many others. Those interested are referred to the bibliography at the end of this book.

Works about America by Latin Americans and Spaniards were produced in the eighteenth century, however, and many of them are extremely valuable. The *Diccionario geográfico-histórico de las Indias Occidentales o América* by Antonio de Alcedo, published in Madrid from 1786-89 is one of the most useful sources of information about the colonies shortly before independence. The English translation (1812-15) is even more useful than the original.

Antonio de Ulloa, Spanish scientist, produced another of the generally valuable studies in 1772 in his *Noticias americanas*. Ulloa was a member of a scientific expedition that went to Ecuador and Peru in the seventeen-thirties. He spent several years there and collected a vast amount of information, only a part of which appears in the work cited. Another part was written in conjunction with Jorge Juan y Santacilia as the *Relación histórica del viaje a la América meridional hecho de orden de Su Majestad*, published in Madrid in 1748, and translated into English as *A Voyage to South America*.

The most remarkable contribution of these two men, however, is the *Noticias secretas de América*, a secret report on the state of the colonies prepared at the command of the King, which was not published until 1826 in London. It is such a devastating denunciation of the colonial system, and portrays such a horrible picture of conditions in Peru and Ecuador, that several Spanish and Latin-American authors have sought to label it as spurious. The authenticity of the work is beyond question, however, and several other accounts contemporary with it corroborate its testimony.

José Antonio Villaseñor published a work entitled *Teatro americano* in Mexico in 1746-48 that is one of the richest sources of information on social and economic conditions. The Italian Jesuit, Francisco Javier Clavijero (or Clavigero), who may be considered an American because of his long residence, published his *Storia antica del Messico* in 1780-81. It was translated into English a few years later. Although it abounds in information about the Indians and their archeology, it has enjoyed a reputation greater than its merits. Clavijero also wrote a history of California, published in 1789. Both Villaseñor and Clavijero drew on the unpublished researches of Sigüenza y Góngora, a Creole scholar, for parts of their material. Another history of California was that of Miguel Venegas, *Noticia de la California*, issued in three volumes in Madrid in 1757.

The history of Venezuela by José de Oviedo y Baños Sotomayor, entitled *Historia de la conquista y población de la provincia de Venezuela*, the first part of which was published in 1723 although the complete edition in five volumes did not appear until 1885, is one of the chief works of the century. There were several other works on Venezuela and northern South America in the eighteenth century that merit the attention of those interested in historical literature. The history of Ecuador was written by Juan de Velasco in 1789 but remained unpublished for some years. After several incomplete editions, it appeared in three volumes at Quito, 1841-44. The late colonial history of Peru is represented by the important *Guía política, eclesiástica y militar del Virreynato del Perú*, issued in Lima from 1793 to 1797, by José Hipólito Unánue.

For the Plata region the *Descripción corográfica* of the Gran Chaco by Pedro Lozano, appearing in Córdoba, Argentina, in 1733, and the *Historia de la conquista del Paraguay, Río de la Plata y Tucumán* in 5 volumes by the same author, published in 1873-75, are among the most useful but not by any means the only accounts. Two foreign missionaries who lived many years in southern South America, Thomas Falkner and Martin Dobritshofer, both published interesting and valuable accounts of the people among whom they lived. Still another writer, Félix de Azara, accompanied the commission sent to America to delimit the boundaries of Spanish and Portuguese America as provided in the treaties of 1777-78. Azara was a man of learning and used his extensive travels as the basis for voluminous studies of the Plata basin. His work was published in various forms at various times but the two most useful titles are the *Voyages dans l'Amerique méridionale, depuis 1781 jusqu 'en 1801,* published in Paris in 1809, and his *Descripción e historia del Paraguay y del Río de la Plata,* published in 1847. Azara's personal observations are good, but where he embarks on history he must be used with caution.

INTEREST IN INDIAN LANGUAGES

It was evident from the first day of contact that the Europeans must either learn the Indian languages or teach the Indians their own if there was to be any degree of understanding. Both processes went side by side, but because the number of Europeans was much smaller, the first tendency was for them to learn the Indian languages. To this the Church and the State made important contributions, the former in order to convert the Indians and the latter in order to govern them.

The Church's contribution was the greater since, owing to its practical monopoly of all learning, there were few scholars who were not clerics. It set out immediately to study the Indian languages. None of these was in a written form, if we except the inadequate pictographs among the Mayas, Aztecs, and a few other tribes. The languages had to be learned, analyzed, transcribed, and grammars and dictionaries had to be prepared for the missionaries. All this was done in a remarkably short time.

Interest in language structure, dictionaries, and grammars was characteristic of the period. The sixteenth century was the time of the definite formation of many of the European languages. Spain, having contributed the grammar of Antonio de Nebrija in 1492, caught the spirit of systematizing her own language, and transmitted this to the New World.

Books were printed in ten Indian languages in Mexico alone, including Mexican, Otomí, Tarascan, Mixtec, Chuchón, Huastec, Zapotec, and Maya, before the end of the sixteenth century.[5]

Quechua was taught in Lima and books circulated in that tongue; and in the Jesuit missions of Paraguay-Uruguay one of the first tasks was the preparation of grammars and dictionaries of Guaraní and other Indian languages. One of the favorite publications in Indian languages was the sermon, and the priest who could not compose his own had only to possess a book of sermons in the tongue of the people to whom he was preaching.[6]

LAW AND LEGAL LITERATURE

Colonial law derived from both Indian and Spanish sources, as we have already observed in the discussion of government. But the process of blending and applying Spanish legal concepts to America required the assistance of many legal theorists and commentators. Such were not lacking either in the colonies or in Spain. Las Casas himself may be considered in this light, and his distinguished contemporary, Francisco Vitoria, was engaged for many years in examining the validity of the Spanish title to the New World from the ethical point of view. The question of Spain's moral and legal justification was debated heatedly from the time of Columbus for more than a century, but, as the reader may have suspected, even the most pious jurists vindicated her claims. Nor did the scholars of other nations find greater difficulty in vindicating the conquests their sovereigns were making.[7]

Although the conquistadores went about their work and the government implanted its institutions with but little regard for fine legal theories, the legal specialists did important work. America presented a vast new problem that had to be resolved in the light of both Roman and Canon law, and in the evolution of colonial law the opinions of the jurists and the decisions of the courts wielded an influence that could be traced only in a voluminous study. Legal theories played their part from the formulation to the final execution of a law and the lawyers were powerful factors at every stage.[8]

---

[5] Cecil Knight Jones, "The Transmission and Diffusion of Culture in the Spanish American Colonies," in Wilgus, ed., *Colonial Hispanic America*, p. 293.

[6] Riva Palacio, *México*, II, 736.

[7] Luis Alberto Sánchez, *Breve historia de la literatura americana* (Santiago, Chile, 1937), pp. 50, 64, 120; Marie R. Madden, "The European Background," in Wilgus, *Colonial Hispanic America*, chap. V. This chapter is especially recommended for those who want an interpretation of the Spanish mind in its approach to the colonial problem.

[8] Altamira, *Historia de España*, III, 555-562.

The Laws of Burgos of 1512 were the first code applying to the New World. The New Laws promulgated by Charles V in 1542 in order to regularize the position of the Indians under the Spanish administration, were published in Alcalá in 1543 but the revolts of the encomenderos, as we have seen, prevented full enforcement. More legislation was accumulating daily, of course, and the Viceroy of New Spain, Luis de Velasco, ordered the compilation of the laws of his kingdom, the result being the *Provisiones, cédulas, e instrucciones de Su Majestad,* published by Vasco de Puga in Mexico in 1563. A few years later the president of the Council of the Indies, Juan de Ovando, prepared a compilation of the laws pertaining to America. This work was in seven books, and although it served a valuable purpose, only a part of book two was published, in 1571. Philip II had prepared in 1573 the *Ordenanzas de nuevos descubrimientos y poblaciones,* as a sort of summary of the colonizing experience of almost a century.

The most systematic attempt to compile, codify, and simplify the multiple laws was made by the Viceroy Francisco de Toledo, who arrived in Peru in 1569. He set about immediately to organize the viceroyalty, traveling extensively and carrying with him a large retinue of learned men of various disciplines. Among his helpers were Polo de Ondegardo, Juan de Matienzo, and Sarmiento de Gamboa. The fruit of this work was the *Ordenanzas* of Toledo, bearing on every aspect of colonial government.

Aside from their work with Toledo, both Ondegardo and Matienzo prepared valuable commentaries on the laws of the Indies. Alonso de Zurita likewise made an attempt at codification, and Diego de Encinas, of the Council of the Indies, published a *Cedulario* which came down to 1596. Rodrigo de Aguiar y Acuña, oidor of the Council of Indies, with the aid of Antonio de León Pinelo and Diego de Zorilla, prepared a *Sumario* of the laws of the Indies, which was published in 1628.

The most important commentator on the laws of the Indies, however, was Juan de Solórzano Pereira. Solórzano was a student and professor in the University of Salamanca, and later an oidor of the Audiencia of Lima, and member of the Council of Indies. He prepared additions to the *Cedulario* of Encinas, and then published his *De indiarum jure* in two volumes, 1629-39. This work he expanded greatly and published as *Política indiana* in 1648, the most complete study of the laws of the Indies issued anywhere. It served Spanish colonial law much as Blackstone's *Commentaries* have English law, and like that work is still used as an authority for many cases whose legal roots reach back into the colonial period.

The culminating event of the legal history of the seventeenth century was the issuing of the *Recopilación de las leyes de Indias,* in 1681. This comprised nine books, with 6377 laws classified under 218 main subjects (*títulos*). Each statute was numbered and preceded by a short summary and the name and date of the monarch who promulgated it. The contents of the *Recopilación,* as divided into books, were as follows: I. Ecclesiastical legislation, including matters pertaining to education; II. and III. Administrative law, judicial organization, and private, military, and naval law; IV. Discoveries, settlement of towns, town government, public works, mines, fisheries, and factories; V. Attributes, powers, and jurisdictions of the royal officials and other colonial officers; VI. Social legislation, especially the treatment of the Indians, hours of work, wages, and other such matters; VII. Legislation of social character, regulating marriage, separation, gaming, vagabondage, slavery, and penitentiaries; VIII. Public finance; and IX. Commercial and maritime law. It is necessary to go back to the Romans to find a previous comparable codification of laws; the only thing lacking to make colonial legislation nearly ideal was its faithful execution.

The *Recopilación,* like all legal codes, was prepared to serve as a summary of past legislation and as a point of departure for further laws. In a sense it marks the end of an epoch, since the change from the Hapsburg to the Bourbon kings was only a few years away. The advent of the Bourbons was destined to coincide with great changes in the colonies, in part because of the introduction of new monarchial concepts, but more largely because the eighteenth was to be the century of great economic development and scientific enlightenment. Such an epoch demanded adjustments, and Spanish colonial law of the eighteenth century passed through an almost incessant series of alterations. Tomás de Salazar prepared a commentary that perished before publication in the earthquake of Lima, 1746. Rezabal y Ugarte compiled more than two thousand royal orders subsequent to 1680, but this work too was lost. Juan del Corral Calvo de la Torre began a commentary on the *Recopilación* which was planned to include all later legislation, but only three volumes, reaching book four of the *Recopilación* were published. The only known copy of this is in the Harvard University Library.

An example of the legal commentaries of the eighteenth century is the work of Francisco Javier de Gamboa, *Comentarios a las Ordenanzas de minería,* published in Madrid in 1761. Fruit of the same influences were the commentaries on Spanish economic and government institutions, mainly by Spaniards and not Latin Americans, in the eighteenth century. Several men, contemporaries of Adam Smith in England, dedicated themselves to seeking the truth of economic laws. Jerónimo de Ustáriz wrote *Teoría práctica de comercio y de marina* in 1724. While not a legal study of ·the nature of Solorzano's, its significance for the legislation of Spain was great. Bernardo Ulloa's *Restablecimiento de las fábricas, tráfico y comercio marítimo de España* (1740), and Bernardo Ward's *Proyecto económico* (1779), along with José del Campillo's *Nuevo sistema económico de gobierno para América* (written in 1748 and published in 1789) were powerful influences in the changes that American legal and political institutions were undergoing.[9]

POETRY

Latin American poetry followed closely the footsteps of the first conquistadores in the newly discovered lands; and dramatic presentations were not far behind. Aside from ballads and poetry of folklore type, for which the peoples of Latin speech seem to have an inexhaustible genius, formal poetry soon gained a recognized place. The folklore sprang from the experiences of the Conquest; formal poetry was a conscious imitation of Italian and classical models. Both were in a large measure adaptations of forms and themes known to the Spaniards before the discovery.

Much of the first popular poetry of America is lost, and while it is not possible to be sure of its literary merit, the loss is undoubtedly unfortunate. It was poetry of action, of the Conquest, of spontaneous reactions to the new things of a new environment. The conquistadores quickly adapted to the Conquest of America the models inspired by the long years of the Reconquest. The traces left are sufficient to evoke regret that there is not more of the early poetry extant.

But if the conquistadores did not record in writing the everyday doggerel that gave relief from the hard realities of constant campaigning, they did leave a vast body of consciously-formed verse. The epic was a conventional medium but the lyric was never far

[9] On American legal, political, and economic literature see: Jorge Basadre, *Historia del derecho peruano* (Lima, Peru, 1937), pp. 219-331; Altamira, *Historia de España,* III, 328-340; IV, 258-299; 312-17; 365-70; Sánchez, *Literatura Americana, passim.*

under the surface. For the epic the models were Tasso, Ariosto, or Dante; and Virgil and Homer had their imitators. But there were literary forms other than the epic, and Boccacio and Ovid were not without their counterparts. Imitation amounted frequently to outright plagiarism, with the verse but slightly adapted to its new environment. Nevertheless, a vast body of poetry was produced, some worthy of high rank.

The epic poem that has achieved the greatest renown was *La Araucana* of Alonso de Ercilla y Zúñiga, dealing with the conquest of Chile. Much of it was written on the field of battle and its vigor arises from that fact. Its model is Ariosto, but Ercilla was superior to slavish imitation, and his poem has a ring of authenticity rarely achieved by most of his contemporaries and followers. There is a chivalric quality in the poem also, Ercilla choosing for his heroes the Indian chieftains of the Araucanians. The first part of the poem was published in 1569, the second in 1578, and the third in 1589, with subsequent continuations by others.

In 1591 Pedro de Oña, a Chilean creole, published his *El Arauco domado,* dwelling more on the Spanish side of the wars with the Araucanians. His work also treats of many other subjects, such as the adventures of the pirates along the Pacific, fauna and flora which were Chilean only in his verses, and imaginary visits of the Greek gods to Chile. He has been called by Torres-Rioseco "perhaps the greatest epic poet born in the New World." [9b] His epic is admired for its special scheme of rhyming verses in the octaves, and its lyricism. [9b] The Araucanian wars also inspired other poets whose works are usually regarded as inferior.

A poem illustrative of the tendency of the times was *Bernardo o la victoria de Roncesvalles* (1624) by Bernardo de Balbuena. This poem makes Bernardo, a Spaniard, the hero of the famous battle, and brings in America by having the hero come to the New World. This type of historical imagination was not unusual, and has good antecedents in the works of Homer and Virgil. Bernardo de Balbuena's *La Grandeza mexicana* (1604) is of more significance, however, for Latin-American literature. It gives a lengthy description of the capital city and illustrates the patriotic theme.

A work of a very different sort was written by Diego de Ojeda of the Dominican order. His *La Cristiada* (1611) had for its subject the passion of Jesus, and was full of "grandiloquent imprecations and metallurgical comparisons." The poem is character-

[9b] Arturo Torres Rioseco, *The Epic of Latin America Literature* (New York-London-Toronto: Oxford University Press, 1942), p. 21.

ized as "vigorous" by one of the foremost modern critics.[10] It is considered the best sacred epic in the Spanish language and likened to Milton's "Paradise Lost." In the world in which we live, where modern poetry is less frequently inspired by religious themes, such poems have little appeal. But at that time, religion was the chief preoccupation of the vast majority of the people, and it was but natural that there should be a large body of religious poetry. It was a significant and integral part of colonial culture.

The first poetry of Peru was concerned with the battlefield. An example is the *Nueva obra y breve . . . sobre la muerte del Adelantado Don Diego de Almagro,* a stirring and virile work by an adherent of Almagro, breathing the fire of the battlefield. [11]

An example of what may be termed the "catch-all" poem is the *Miscelánea austral,* written by Diego de Avalos y Figueroa composed in the form of a dialogue and published in Lima in 1602. It treats such heterogeneous subjects as love, music, Inca architecture, Peruvian bird-life, interpretation of dreams, and the origin of finger rings. The descriptions of these incongruous matters are often beautiful.

A poet who gained fame by a single poem was Amarilis, who sent her *Amarilis a Belardo* to the famous Spanish dramatist Lope de Vega to express her admiration for him. Lope responded with *Belardo a Amarilis,* both poems being published in 1621. Of the many epic poems dealing with events in the history of Peru, one of the best is *Armas antárticas,* written early in the seventeenth century by Juan de Miramontes Zuázola, which has considerable vigor. Its theme is the history of Peru, touching the Incas, conquistadores, and events of colonial life.

Until near the middle of the seventeenth century, the poetry of America had been influenced largely by the Italian models, or their Spanish counterparts. About this time, a new Spanish influence crept in, Gongorism. Luis de Argote y Góngora (1561-1627) was a Spanish poet who used an involved and metaphorical style, the object being to give every word and phrase a double meaning, or to wrap the real meaning in words that ostensibly meant something different. While Gongorism never obtained the great following in America that it did in Spain, its influence could be felt from about 1630.[12]

---

[10] Sánchez, *Literatura americana,* p. 79; Torres-Rioseco, *Latin American Literature,* p. 22.

[11] Means, *Fall,* pp. 272-281.

[12] Sánchez, *Literatura americana,* p. 90, holds that there were very few gongoristic poets in America.

The little poetry worth citing after this time was not gongoristic in character, notably that of Juan del Valle y Caviedes, who lived in the last half of the seventeenth century, and led a riotous, unconventional, and varied life. His literary antecedents were Francisco Gómez de Quevedo, the Spanish satirical writer, and the picaresque novels, but as he was uneducated his poetry reflects the bitterness of his own existence rather than adherence to a literary school. He satrized the upper levels of society in blunt and sometimes "low" language, his critical spirit reacting sharply to the artificiality and pomposity of the literary affectation universally cultivated. Suffering from a protracted, and at that time incurable, disease, he made the medical men a special target. He was bitter, hating, witty, vitriolic, and scurrilous, but brilliant and characterized by robust humor. He has been called a "low-lifer, a drunkard, and all kinds of a reprobate," but credited with writing poetry more vital and more readable "(adults only!)" than all the other Peruvian poets put together. [13] His poems are gathered together in a volume entitled *Diente del parnaso y poesías diversas*. [14] At times Caviedes showed gongoristic tendencies, but these tendencies were so rare as to be negligible and he may be considered the archtype of antigongorist.

Few have praise for the poetry of the last half of the seventeenth century and the beginning of the eighteenth century in Peru. In spite of official patronage by the viceroys, among them the Marquis of Castell-dos-Rius (1709-1710) who established an "Academy" in Lima, and perhaps because of the official gongorism adopted as the model by the group around the viceroy, the poetry was of low quality. Two figures of this group are usually ranked above their contemporaries, Luis Antonio de Oviedo Herrera y Rueda, Count of la Granja, and Pedro de Peralta Barnuevo. Granja's *La vida de Santa Rosa de Santa María* is classified among the religious poems, but brings in numerous historical incidents. Other works by this author, also religious in nature, are considered inferior. Pedro de Peralta Barnuevo won fame for his encyclopedic activities. If we were to judge by the contents of his library (not always a reliable index), he could read several languages. He was strongly influenced by Gongorism, as his many poetic works indicate. His best-known poem, *Lima Fundada,* was published in 1732 and is described as being "abominable as poetry and unreliable as history," but is notable for the erudition which it revealed.[15]

[13] Means, *Fall,* pp. 278-79.
[14] Sánchez, *Literatura americana,* p. 104.
[15] Means, *Fall,* pp. 280-281.

Recently Peralta has been singled out as the *"primer afrancesado"* because of the French influence visible in his writings. While much of his literary production has been labeled dull and heavy, his dramatic works are interesting and significant. Notable among these are his skits, satiric or *costumbrista* in character. [16]

A poet who represents a new spirit toward the end of the colonial period was Pablo de Olavide y Jáuregui. He attained high honors early in life, went to Spain where he became an encyclopedist and suffered several years of imprisonment for his pro-French ideas, but managed to flee to France. Sánchez calls him the "first atheist —or better, atheistic spirit—and the first 'encylopedist' of America." Late in life he was converted and wrote his *Evangelio en triunfo* and other religious poems.

The poetry of New Spain followed the same influences as that of other parts of America. Antonio de Saavedra Guzmán published *El peregrino indiano* (1599), an epic poem dealing with the conquest of Mexico, and there were innumerable descriptive, historical, and religious poems which are the exact counterparts of those already cited. The two poets who gained the widest acclaim were Carlos de Sigüenza y Góngora, and Sor Juana Inés de la Cruz. Sigüenza published *La primavera indiana,* on the subject of the Virgin of Guadalupe, and other religious and historical poems.

Inés de la Cruz was a nun who had retired to the convent after gaining distinction early in life for erudition and beauty. She gathered a large library and devoted her time to literary work, writing poetry, letters, and religious dramas. Many of her poems are profane in character considering her religious vocation, frequently dealing with human love. Their renown won for her the designation of the tenth muse. Participation in a theological dispute subsequently moved the bishop of Puebla to bring pressure on her to sell her library and abandon her literary career. Her death occurred soon after. Her *Poesías sagradas y profanas* reached six editions before 1700. Her style was touched by gongorism, especially in her *Sueños* and *Neptuno alegórico.* The part of her work perhaps most appreciated today are the poems of love, called by the Spanish critic, Menéndez y Pelayo, "the gentlest and most delicate that have come from the pen of a woman." [17] Her three-act play, *Los Empeños de una Casa* (A Household Plagued by

---

[16] See Irving A. Leonard, ed., *Pedro de Peralta Barnuevo, obras dramáticas con un apéndice de poemas inéditos* (Santiago de Chile, 1937) and other writings on Peralta by Leonard, cited in Lewis Hanke, ed., *Handbook of Latin American Studies* (Cambridge, Mass., 1936 and 1937).

[17] Sánchez, *Literatura americana,* p. 94; Riva Palacio, *México,* II, 742-744.

Love) is a comedy of intrigue with a complicated love plot, abounding in "extraordinarily lovely lyric verse." [18]

DRAMA

Drama in America was of liturgical and didactic origin. It has already been noted that in this, as in so many points, the customs of the Indians and Spaniards were similar. The religious ceremonies of all peoples are dramatic in their nature, and it is only a step from the religious service *per se* to a dramatic presentation with religious significance.

Among peoples who cannot read, or who are allowed to learn their religious codes only indirectly, it is necessary to teach by visual means. Thus it was the early custom to act out the stories of the Bible, of lives of saints, or of other events of religious significance. When the Spaniards came to America their own religious dramas began to supplant those of the Indians. The process was never completed, much of the ceremonies remaining an amalgamation of Spanish and Indian practices. Throughout hundreds of towns and villages, it soon became commonplace to see Indians dramatizing religious experiences not their own, with a strong infiltration of original Indian custom.

The chief religious festivals, such as Easter, Corpus Christi, and Christmas, were observed, of course, but they were only the beginning of a vaster body of religious folklore. Every town and village had its own religious patron, or patrons, and each its variation on the central theme. Hundreds of saints' days were observed. Some of the themes which have come down to modern times are incongruous. Indians who never heard of a Moor in any other connection still engage solemnly and vigorously in mock battles in which the Moors are driven out, from where it is not exactly clear. But the ceremony was a part of Spanish folklore and came over to the Indians with other parts of Spanish culture.

The first missionaries used the *auto,* or allegorical and religious play, as a means of catechizing the Indians. As early as 1538 in New Spain, and perhaps earlier, we hear of four *autos* being given, as well as a play, *Adán y Eva,* in which by means of simple verses burdened with much repetition of the same phrases to make them intelligible, the Indians were taught that God suffered because Eve ate of the forbidden fruit. It may not be possible to determine

[18] See James C. Bardin, "A Song from Sor Juana," *Bulletin of the Pan American Union,* April, 1942, pp. 195-198. See also a study written a generation after her death, Juan José de Eguiara y Eguren, *Sor Juana Inés de la Cruz,* in *Biblioteca Histórica Mexicana,* vol. II (Mexico, 1936). The best recent study is in the *prólogo* of E. Abreu Gómez to *Sor Juana Inés de la Cruz. Poesías* (Mexico, 1940).

what moral or ethical effect was achieved by such plays, but it can be seen that the Indians adopted them as an integral part of their cultural pattern. The *auto* was an educational institution, and it likewise served to stimulate the will to war when the occasion arose.

Juan de Torquemada used the *auto* in the Mexican tongue, producing the plays on Sundays. Characteristic of such works is the *Adoración de los reyes,* one of the most popular themes for the artist of every medium. Perhaps the most notable among the dramatists of Mexico was Fernando González de Eslava whose *Coloquios espirituales,* written and performed in Mexico City, were remarkable for their natural dialogue, simple plot, and comic touches.

Bishop Zumárraga tried to prohibit the drama because it could not be kept strictly in the bounds prescribed by religion, and the same effort was made in Peru, but to no avail. The play was the most spectacular relief from reality in an environment and in an age that afforded few amusements; and it could not be suppressed.

From religious to secular drama was a short step, and one that had been taken long before by Greeks and Mediaeval Christians. The secular drama became at times *very* secular, and it is hardly surprising that the Church objected. Mexico had its *Casa de Comedias* in the sixteenth century, and a theatre in the palace in the seventeenth. Peru had its *Casas de Corrales* in the last decade of the sixteenth century. The second church council in America, held in Peru, prohibited comedies on religious themes, and in 1598 an attempt was made to carry out Philip II's order to abolish comedies entirely. But this failed and in 1600 the theatre reopened. A coliseum was inaugurated in Peru about 1600, and several of the viceroys, notably Esquilache, encouraged the theatre. In the eighteenth century Viceroy Amat of Peru was a patron of the theatre, and under his patronage the actress, "La Pericholi," became famous. Mexico developed several dramatists who enjoyed great favor, among them González de Eslava, already mentioned, Miguel Zumaya, and Francisco Soria. Zumaya's *El Rodrigo,* and Soria's *La Mágica mexicana* were among the most popular plays.

The one dramatist who gained world renown was Juan Ruiz de Alarcón (1581-1639). Alarcón was born in Mexico, but went to Spain where his talent for the theatre developed. His work reflects very little of his Mexican background, however, and he is a

Spanish rather than a Spanish-American literary figure.[19] Among his most famous plays are *La verdad sospechosa,* and *Las paredes oyen.*[20]

MUSIC

Music evolved in the colonial period from three separate influences: Indian, European, and Negro.[21] It is difficult to determine the exact contribution of each of these. From the Indian came the melancholy strains still heard in much Latin-American music. The Negro contributions have grown stronger with time, and today form the essence of Latin-American music of the Caribbean area, especially of the lighter type so popular in the United States. But the Europeans undoubtedly had the greatest technical influence, their musical development being far in advance of that of either Indian or Negro.

Indian music was relatively poor in musical instruments, monotonous in theme. It did not, however, fail to affect colonial music. Not only did Indian music comprise the bulk of that heard by many millions of Indians, but Indian instruments and motifs crept into religious songs. Even today one may attend religious services in many parts of Latin America where the Indian elements are evident.

The Europeans brought with them the music of the Renaissance and the growing body of musical instruments that have so greatly enriched our musical life since the sixteenth century. The religious music, long based on Gregorian chants and broadened in the sixteenth century by Palestrina and other composers, was vastly superior in concept and execution to anything the Indians had known. The same was true of secular music. A large importation of European musical instruments into the colonies was noticeable, especially during the eighteenth century, and music for worship or pleasure was an important part of colonial life. The guitar became an almost indispensable adjunct to courtship, the harp and the clavichord were considered the proper medium for female musical expression, and the important cities had bands and orchestras. The piano became more common in the eighteenth century, as did the opera. It is doubtful, however, that musical performance

---

[19] For contrasting viewpoints: Sánchez holds that Alarcón retained the flavor of Mexican life, while Leonard holds not. Sánchez, *Literatura americana,* p. 107; Leonard, communication to the author.

[20] Sánchez, *Literatura americana,* 107-111; Riva Palacio, *México,* II, 745-47.

[21] Alberto V. Munz, "The Tonal System of Indian Music," *Inter-America,* V (April, 1922), 257-65; J. Álvarez, "Orígenes de la música argentina," *Revista de Derecho, historia y letras,* XXXII (Buenos Aires, January, 1909), 26-67; on Andean music see Raoul and Marie d'Harcourt, *La musique des Incas et ses survivances* (2 vols., Paris, 1925).

was on a high level, except for church music in the larger cathedrals.

Negro influence became increasingly strong during the colonial period, and especially so in the last half of the eighteenth century when the importation of slaves was so great. The marimba band is the best known of their instrumental contributions, and the European members of colonial society did not long remain aloof from the powerful, primitive strains of Negro percussion music. This influence made its way eventually into traditional European music, and the poetry that was to flourish in the national period.

ARCHITECTURE, SCULPTURE, AND PAINTING

Colonial architecture was essentially of European origin, as already noted, in spite of a few Indian contributions. When viewed from the standpoint of both artistic and utilitarian values, European architecture was superior to the native American. Despite the skill displayed in Inca stone work, Mayan palaces, or Toltec pyramids, the Indians had not solved the essential problem of architecture: the construction of edifices with sufficient interior space and light for use as dwellings or public meeting places. The Europeans had not only solved this problem before America was discovered; they had created numerous forms of public and private buildings of great beauty. It is not strange, therefore, that colonial architecture was a projection of already known European models. It was equally natural that the Renaissance style should predominate among Spanish colonial architects.

In domestic architecture, the chief contribution of the Europeans was the home built around a patio, or court. This style had been found appropriate for the Mediterranean heat and, except where applied unthinkingly to conditions that were not the same, was suitable to most parts of Latin America.[22]

The decoration of the houses depended on the resources of the builder, but most ornamentation was in the interior, the houses being built flush with the street so that the entire family life could go on out of sight of the passerby. Tiles were extensively used for exterior and interior decoration, and the walls were built of adobe, or of the stone afforded by the community. Wood construction was rare except in a few of the forest sections.

Churches and public buildings were the principal architectural

---

[22] Houses of one story built around a court are convenient and suitable for family life, and the inventors are to be congratulated. But the modern application of the same style to apartment houses of several stories, as seen today in Latin America, strikes one as being the invention of a madman. The patio throws dozens of strangers together in such a way that none has privacy, and the well formed by the patio creates a din that precludes sleep, rest, or pleasant thought.

forms aside from the private dwelling. The commercial building (except for public markets) and the apartment house were unknown. While Spanish Renaissance was the basic style, some variations were known in America. The thousands of churches and mission chapels were built from a standard model, with each community making its own slight deviations, more ornamental than structural. In the larger cities there were dozens of churches and the cathedrals of Mexico City, Lima, and other important cities are majestic. The Renaissance style in Spain gave way before the Baroque in the seventeenth century and the Churrigueresque in the eighteenth; colonial architecture tended to follow the Spanish changes.

Sculpture was almost entirely religious in nature. Statues of Christ, Mary, and hundreds of saints were used. to decorate the churches; and no home, however humble, was complete without its niches for religious images, before which a candle customarily burned. A large market was thus created for the output of the sculptor. Bone, stone, and wood were his materials. Most of the work was crude, but it satisfied the artistic tastes of the masses, and it came within their purchasing power. However, there were a few artists of considerable merit. Wood carving of great beauty was produced, one type of wood (*palo santo*) being known especially for its suitability.

In Quito the Indian sculptor, Manuel Chile (known as Caspicara), executed the *Assumption of the Virgin,* which gained for him European fame. Mexico at the end of the eighteenth century was the center of a school of sculpture fostered by Manuel Tolsa, a Spaniard, whose work is ranked with the best of his age. One of his pupils, Mariano Perusquia, executed some very fine wood carvings decorated with gold and silver leaf. Of Tolsa's own work, the equestrian statue of Charles IV, which still stands in Mexico City, is perhaps the finest example.

Both churches and private homes were filled with religious pictures. Painting in the colonial period began with the early pictures made by the missionaries to illustrate the doctrines of the Church. Such works were crude in the extreme, but, like the *auto,* proved of great utilitarian value in indoctrination. Two years after the conquest of Mexico, Rodrigo de Cifuentes, born in 1493 and a student of Bartolomé de Meza at the age of ten arrived, and began his work. His early portraits of Cortés and other contemporaries have been mentioned, and he also painted large numbers of religious pictures.

Toward the end of the sixteenth century, Alonso Vázquez arrived from Spain, and Andrés de Concha was working at the same time. Also at the end of the sixteenth, but principally in the seventeenth century, Baltasar de Echave *el Viejo* began to decorate the churches with his paintings. Luis Juárez, Mexican-born and the first of four painters to bear the same name, was a contemporary of Echave *el Viejo* and of the same school. José Juárez, second of the name, worked between 1642 and 1698. Sebastián de Arteaga, notary of the Inquisition, was a contemporary who painted little, but gained for himself a reputation for vigor and coloring not hitherto known in Mexico. From about 1665, Baltasar de Echave, son of the elder painter, and Manuel Echave of the same family were active. The bold strokes and carelessly finished work of the younger Echave contrasted with the care his father dedicated to detail.

Near the end of the seventeenth century, Juan Herrera, known in Mexico as *El Divino,* and Diego de Becerra, Nicolás and Juan Rodríguez Juárez, nephews of José Juárez, were painting. Nicolás Rodríguez Juárez founded the school of Mexican painting that flourished in the eighteenth century and he achieved such fame that he was called the *Apeles Mexicano.* Two of the most celebrated Mexican painters of the century were José María Ibarra and Miguel Cabrera. In Quito, Miguel de Santiago, who had been to Spain where he met Velásquez, established a school of painting, principally devoted to religious works. He also painted portraits of good quality.

The fine arts were promoted with great zeal during the last years of the colonial period, and large sums of money were devoted to the founding of schools and academies and the teaching of painting, sculpture, architecture, and design. All of the colonies shared to a certain extent in this, but New Spain, the richest, led the way. Humboldt's enthusiasm is worth citing:

"The revenues of the Academy of Fine Arts at Mexico amount to 123,000 francs, of which the government gives 60,000, the guild of Mexican miners nearly 25,000, the *consulado,* or merchants guild of the capital, more than 15,000. It is impossible to deny the influence of this establishment on the taste of the nation. This influence is particularly visible in the symmetry of the buildings, in the perfection with which the hewing of stone is conducted, and in the ornaments of the capitals and stucco reliefs . . . . Instruction is communicated gratis at the Academy of Fine Arts. It is not confined alone to the drawing of landscapes and figures; they have had the good sense to employ other means for intensifying the national industry. The academy labors successfully to introduce among the artisans a taste for elegance and beautiful forms. Large rooms well lighted by Argand's lamps contain every evening some hundreds of young people, of whom some draw from relief or living models, while others copy drawings of furniture, chandeliers, or other ornaments in bronze. In this assemblage (and this is very remarkable in the midst of a country where the prejudices of the nobility against the castes are so inveterate) rank, color, and race are mingled together: we see the Indian and the Mestizo sitting beside the white, and the son of a poor artisan in competition with the children of the great lords of the country." [23]

SCIENCE

The early interest in the natural history of the New World and its inhabitants made the work of such men as Acosta and Cobo as much a part of the history of science in America as of the general history. But there were other, more specialized, scientific studies.

Medicine could draw from both European and Indian sources, and while both were still burdened with a body of superstition and misinformation that seems appalling today, the medicine and medical men of America made useful contributions in the field. Cristóbal Méndez published *Del ejercicio y de sus provechos* in Jaén in 1553; Pedrarias de Benavides the *Secretos de cirugía* in Valladolid in 1567, and Dr. Bravo *Opera medicinalia* in 1570. Alonso López de Hinojoso's *Suma y recopilación de cirugía*, and Augustín Farfán's *Tratado de medicina* were both valuable.

While these works cannot be considered strictly American in every case, their inspiration was drawn in part from the scientific curiosity and material provided by the New World. Nicholás Monardes wrote a work directly inspired by the discoveries, as disclosed by its title, *Primera y segunda y tercera partes de la historia medicinal de las cosas que se traen de nuestras Indias Occidentales que sirven de medicina*. A first and incomplete edition came out in 1565 and complete editions in 1574 and 1580. It was translated into many languages. Francisco Hernández, who was sent to Mexico by Philip II to study medicinal plants, published *De antiquitatibus Novae Hispaniae* dealing with pre-Conquest medicine, and *Cuatro libros de la naturaleza y virtudes de las plantas y animales de uso medicinal en la Nueva España*, in 1615.

---

[23] *New Spain*, I, 213-14 [*Nouvelle Espagne*, II, 13-15]; Riva Palacio, *México*, II, 531-34, 746-50.

Enrico Martínez, engineer and cosmographer in New Spain, prepared a plan for draining the Valley of Mexico early in the seventeenth century, and also published a work dealing with natural history and astronomy, the *Repertorio de los tiempos y historia natural desta Nueva España*, in 1606. Martínez also wrote works on agriculture and other scientific subjects.

The most distinguished scholar in New Spain during the seventeenth century was Carlos de Sigüenza y Góngora (1645-1700), who was primarily a mathematician and astronomer, but is also ranked as an historian, poet, antiquarian, philosopher, and critic. His activity was greatest in the last quarter of the century. A just evaluation of his position as a scientist is difficult. His writings contain fewer titles concerned with science than with other matters, but his *Libro astronómico* has considerable significance. As the champion of scientific attitudes in an almost wholly unscientific environment he is worthy of honor. It has been suggested that in a comparison with his contemporary, the New England savant, Cotton Mather, he does not come off second best, [24] although Mather made notable scientific contributions which were published by the Royal Academy in England.

Peru also produced a scholar of encyclopedic talents, Pedro de Peralta Barnuevo Rocha y Benavides (1663-1743), whose active period was the first half of the eighteenth century. Like Sigüenza y Góngora he wrote in numerous fields, including poetry, drama, history, navigation, engineering, astronomy, and metallurgy, and held the chair of mathematics in the University of Lima. He should perhaps be judged more by the influence he wielded in his time, rather than for the merit or originality of his scientific achievements. A partial inventory of his library shows that it was composed largely of works on scientific subjects, in French.[25]

If Sigüenza y Góngora, of Mexico, and Peralta, of Peru, were not typical of their age, and if the major portion of their contributions was not scientific in character, they were at least harbingers of a trend already visible: the gradual secularization of colonial society. A new scientific spirit and new philosophies were to modify the culture of the colonies in their last years of Spanish rule.

---

[24] See Irving A. Leonard. *Don Carlos de Sigüenza y Góngora, a Mexican Savant of the Seventeenth Century* (Berkeley, 1929) ; Riva Palacio, *México*, II, 738-41.
[25] Irving A. Leonard, "Los libros en el inventario de bienes de Don Pedro de Peralta de Barnuevo," *Boletín Bibliográfico de la Biblioteca Central de la Universidad de San Marcos* (Lima, 1941), nos. 1-4; see also Leonard's "Don Pedro de Peralta Barnuevo," *Revista Histórica*, X (Lima, 1936), No. I, pp. 44-71.

25

New Currents and Growth of the Scientific Spirit

DEVELOPMENT OF SECULAR THOUGHT: NEW INFLUENCES FROM
    ABROAD

THE EIGHTEENTH CENTURY SAW an appreciable change in the scientific outlook and accomplishments of the New World. Secular culture was not to triumph completely over the prevailing supernaturalism in Spanish America (as it has not, indeed, down to the present moment), but it was to produce significant modifications, many of which help to explain the later movement for independence. The origin of the new trend is to be found partly in the growth which Latin America itself had experienced, and partly in influences from abroad.

The world at large was rapidly accepting the physical and mathematical discoveries of Copernicus, Bacon, Galileo, Kepler, Descartes, and Newton. European scientific circles were astir and popularization had set in through the application of Newtonian physics to every branch of learning, including religion. The eighteenth century also saw the rise of experimental science and the adaptation of the inductive method to natural history and chemistry. Some of this scientific ferment began to reach the New World in spite of the censorship. Moreover, the policies of the Bourbons placed America in closer contact with Europe, loosened the hold of the Church to some extent, and led to the expulsion of the Jesuits. This latter event, in spite of the great reputation the Jesuits enjoyed as teachers and scholars, was both a contribution to and a sign of the more liberal atmosphere necessary for scholarship.

Suggestive beginnings of the new spirit are visible from the first part of the century, but it was not until the last quarter that the most significant achievements came. Of prime importance were

542

a series of scientific expeditions to America, some of which were financed by the Crown, including those of Juan and Ulloa with Godin, Bouguer and La Condamine, who had spent several years in Ecuador and Peru (1735); Ruiz, Pavón and Dombey (1777); Mutis (1782); Sessé and Mociño (1787) and Neé and Pineda (1789), to mention only a few. Finally, the expedition of Humboldt and Bonpland, from 1799 to 1804, was the highlight of scientific investigation in America.[1]

Such expeditions of Europe's leading scientists had an appreciable influence on many men of the colonies. They had a chance to see for the first time, and actually to study and work with, men who were masters of the new sciences. At the same time, there was a parallel travel of Latin Americans to Europe. Some attended the universities of Spain, some pursued independent studies, and some merely traveled; but in Spain (and in other parts of Europe) they found a different intellectual atmosphere.

True, Spain herself was not beyond persecuting her own leading intellectuals when they skirted too close to lèse-majesté or anticlericalism, and neither was France. Nonetheless, the Enlightenment had many followers in both countries. Spain was increasingly influenced by the French thought of the eighteenth century, and during the last half of the century it was a commonplace saying among Spanish intellectuals that: "He who has not spat in Paris is uneducated." However zealously the partisans of metaphysics persecuted the followers of the new science, and we have seen that "Propositions" furnished one of the main activities of the Inquisition in this epoch, the persecutors were not entirely successful. And what was true of Spain, was true of her overseas possessions.

Other reasons, too, may be found for the increasing secularization. The economic activities of the colonies were growing rapidly during this century. Spain was doing more business with her own territories, and either indirectly through Spanish merchants or directly through contraband, foreigners had a large participation. In some cases their agents lived in America, and where contraband touched, contact with foreigners accompanied it and could not leave the colonials unaffected. It mattered not that the average foreign merchant trading with the colonies was neither a scientist nor a propagandist of prohibited ideas; this limited intercourse was enough to bring new influences.

---

[1] Altamira, *Historia de España,* IV, 330-33; 348-61; Levene, ed., *Nación Argentina,* Vol. IV, sección I, pp. 545-86.

INFLUENCE OF AMERICAN AND FRENCH REVOLUTIONS

This was particularly true after the American and French Revolutions. American merchants from the Atlantic seaboard and Gulf coasts had long conducted trade with the Spanish American ports, but with the independence of the United States this traffic increased tremendously. The United States merchants were to the Spanish colonies an open demonstration of how their own commerce might grow with more freedom, and there was no small amount of deliberate pro-independence propaganda conducted by United States merchants and seamen.

It was natural that the two Americas, English- and Spanish-speaking, should have some communication. As early as 1699, Cotton Mather studied Spanish in order to write a tract on Christianity for distribution in Latin America, because, he said, "the way of our communication with the *Spanish Indies* opens more and more." Judge Samuel Sewall, friend of Cotton Mather, hoped to see New Spain become the New Jerusalem and advised printing of the "Spanish Bible" to "bombard" Mexico and other places. Latin Americans, however, were scarcely to be influenced by New England Puritanism, which was little suited to seduce them from their own brand of Christianity.

The United States was to affect Latin America mainly through material and intellectual channels. Benjamin Franklin became a well-known figure and many of his works were translated into Spanish. Alexander Garden, the South Carolina botanist, was also known to Latin Americans, as were the transactions of the American Philosophical Society. The publications of Dr. Benjamin Smith Barton, of Philadelphia, on goitre were translated and printed in the *Gazeta de Guatemala* in 1801, and 1802. The same periodical quoted Drs. Barton, Rush, and Coxe of Philadelphia on the new discovery, vaccination. In Colombia, Francisco Caldas published scientific notes from the United States in his *Semanario de la Nueva Granada,* and sought correspondence with American scientists. These are but a sample of the contacts between North and South America, and while their influence should not be overestimated, they had a discernible effect.[2]

The French Revolution increased greatly the infiltration of ideas from abroad. Since the French influence in Spain had been strong,

---

[2] On United States-Latin American contacts to 1810 see Harry Bernstein, "Some Inter-American Aspects of the Enlightenment," in Arthur P. Whitaker, ed., *Latin America and the Enlightenment,* (New York, 1942), pp. 53-69; and Bernstein, *United States and Latin America, 1700-1810,* which shows not only the amount of commerce, but the influence emanating from the United States after 1700.

and since the drama of the French Revolution appealed strongly to the Latin Americans, the currents of new thought penetrated into the Spanish colonies in spite of all efforts to stop them. Travelers, both Europeans and American, brought the new ideas.

NEW FORBIDDEN BOOKS

But more important than the travelers, perhaps, were the books.[3] More and totally different forbidden books found their way into Spanish America in the eighteenth century than earlier, and their influence was to be much greater. Evidence of books on the new philosophy in the colonies comes from several sources.

One of the most important libraries of the colonial period was that of Juan Bautista Maciel, a prominent cleric of Buenos Aires who died in 1787. The inventory of his library revealed more than a thousand volumes, including books in Greek, Latin, Italian, Portuguese, and French, among which were works by Bayle, Voltaire, Bossuet, Massillon, Fléchier and Fénelon. A considerable number of the volumes were on the Index.[4] The presence of such books in America is evidence that somebody wanted to introduce them into the colonies, which is significant; but it is equally significant that they were found in Maciel's possession. He was a *comisario* of the Inquisition and, therefore, provided with a license to read prohibited works and sequester them. That Maciel had such books proves only that they had perhaps been confiscated and held by him as *comisario,* rather than that he himself was a follower of the new philosophy.[5]

When Bishop Azamor of Buenos Aires died in 1796 the inventory of his books made by the comisario of the Inquisition of Lima revealed "an entire shelf of prohibited books." Among them were works of Milton, Voltaire, Rousseau, Josephus, Robertson (History of America), Montesquieu, Bayle, and Filangieri. Far from manifesting indifference to these books, the Inquisition ordered them sent to Lima, which was done. In the ordinary course of events they would have been burned or sent on to Spain, where they would have been burned unless they rotted away in the worm-infested vaults of the Inquisition there.[6]

---

[3] See Whitaker, ed., *Latin America and the Enlightenment,* for essays by Professors Whitaker, Roland D. Hussey, Harry Bernstein, John Tate Lanning, Arthur Scott Aiton, and Alexander D. Marchant, which place more emphasis on the Influence of the Enlightenment and less on the restrictive force of the Church and the State than the present writer.

[4] Torre Revello, "Bibliotecas e imprentas en la América colonial," *BAN Hist.,* XIV, 218.

[5] Medina, *Inquisición del Plata,* p. 254.

[6] *Ibid.,* pp. 255-56.

Forbidden books were also found in other colonies, and songs of French origin and inspiration helped propagate the new spirit. The Viceroy of Mexico, Branciforte, complained in 1794 that his predecessor, the famous Viceroy Revilla Gigedo II, had been too complacent about the French influence and the circulation of French literature in spite of the efforts of the Holy Office. The same type of evasion of the laws seems to have beset other Spanish governors.[7]

When the Viceroy Jáuregui reached Peru in 1781 he was greeted, as was customary, with great ceremony and a "welcoming address" known as an *elogio,* delivered in this case by José Baquíjano y Carillo and printed the same year. Baquíjano revealed knowledge of authors prohibited by the Inquisition and the Crown, among them Marmontel, Montesquieu, Linguet, Raynal, Machiavelli, Legros, and the contributors to the French Encyclopedia. For this audacity the author was reprimanded by the viceroy, forced to recant, and his work was sequestered and sent to Spain. That the court viewed this incident with no slight alarm is indicated by the strict orders that soon were sent out to sequester and burn prohibited books.[8]

EDUCATIONAL INSTITUTIONS AND THE NATURAL PHILOSOPHERS

Inevitably the entrance of such books and the propagation of new ideas by word of mouth, produced changes in the system of education, though much less in the old established institutions than in new schools. What the net result was on the small amount of primary and secondary instruction known to the colonies is difficult to say. It was in the universities that the science of Copernicus, Descartes, and Newton aroused alarm, and eventually forced a partial revision of their teaching.

As training schools for the clergy, the universities were the centers of a deductive learning based on the "authority" of Aristotle, the Bible, Thomas Aquinas, and a few subsidiary masters. Of inductive, rational, or experimental science there was little. In this the Latin American universities were not very far behind their European and North American counterparts. The most important differences were that in Europe more institutions founded on the secular rather than the metaphysical principle had come into being, and that in the United States, where secularism

---

[7] See Ricardo R. Caillet-Bois, "La América española y la revolución francesa," *BAN Hist.,* XIII, 159-216. On burning of prohibited books see Torre Revello, *El libro,* p. 113.

[8] Torre Revello, *El libro,* pp. 113-117.

had made great strides, the existence of numerous religious sects had weakened the metaphysical aspects of religion.

Thus it proved more difficult for the natural philosophy of the eighteenth century to penetrate the cloisters of the Latin American universities. The circulation of the blood, demonstrated by William Harvey in 1628 was not recognized in Peru until 1723 although long since accepted in Spain. Against the scholasticism of the Church it was difficult for even such able naturalists as Cosme Bueno (1711-1798) and José Eusebio de Llano Zapata (about 1720-1790), both of whom went to nature rather than to "authorities" for their facts, to make any real headway." [9]

The difficulty of getting the ideas of Copernicus and Newton recognized in the New World is illustrated by the case of Mutis, who gave lectures on the Copernican system in Bogotá in 1773. For this he was accused of heresy by the *Universidad Tomística* which offered to prove by the Scriptures, St. Augustine, and St. Thomas Aquinas that the Copernican theory was contrary to Catholicism and prohibited by the Inquisition. The viceroy stated that "in order that there may be no teaching that could induce the least doubt," the matter should be examined. This was done and the comisario of the Inquisition in Bogotá referred the case to the Inquisition in Cartagena.[10] The *fiscal,* or prosecutor, stated that Mutis was perhaps the only man in Latin America to uphold Copernicus.[11]

But the period between 1773 and 1810 brought changes in this respect, and in any case, the lack of advocates of Copernicanism did not indicate that there were no men in America who knew of its existence. Through certain eclectic philosophers who were acceptable reading in the Spanish-speaking world, some intimation of the new sciences was introduced. Fray Benito Jerónimo Feijóo (1675-1764) was among the most outstanding, his *Teatro crítico universal* (1726-39) and *Cartas eruditas y curiosas* (1742-60), although "a complete expression of the uncultured condition of the country [Spain], notable even among the people who con-

---

[9] Means, *Fall,* p. 272; Jose Torre Revello, "Noticia sobre José Eusebio de Llano Zapata, historiador peruano del siglo XVIII" *Revista de Historia de América,* No. 13 (December, 1941), 5-39.

[10] For the proceedings in this case see Medina, *Inquisición de Cartagena,* pp. 380-86.

[11] The Copernican theories and other modern scientific ideas were allegedly taught in Ecuador in 1736, see Lanning, *Academic Culture,* p. 65, but if so they were apparently taught by members of the La Condamine expedition and there is little evidence to show that they exerted any influence, and much to demonstrate that Ecuador continued in the Scholastic tradition to the end of the colonial period, and even later.

stituted the upper classes," [12] served as an introduction to the new sciences in both Spain and the colonies.

Two currents of divergent thought stemming from the Natural Philosophers could be perceived in the Indies. One, based on Descartes, was compatible with traditional scholasticism; the other, inspired by the eighteenth century encyclopedists, was antagonistic. Cartesianism became the thought of the conservative forces, encyclopedism "of the liberal spirits, adjusted to the surging rhythm of the Revolution." [13]

That Cartesianism should have been acceptable to the academicians of colonial Spanish America is not difficult to understand. Descartes' system was based on a Creator. "I plainly see," he remarks, "that the certainty and truth of all knowledge depends only upon the knowledge of the true God, so much so that before I knew Him, I could know nothing perfectly about any other thing." [14] Thus God was not an incidental, but the vital element in his system of thought. Descartes drew a precise dividing line between those attributes of man which were divine and those which were material. And here again his thought was orthodox, in keeping with the distinction made by medieval philosophers between the corporeal and incorporeal mind (animus). [15] The *soul* was thus exempted from the material world as conceived by Descartes and other proponents of a mechanical universe.

Cartesianism made its way into the academic circles of Spanish America and brought about a reconsideration of the traditional scholastic philosophy. Metaphysics was by no means abandoned, but the theses presented in the universities indicate that Cartesian rather than Aristotelian metaphysics was increasing in popularity. [16]

To have gone farther and accepted the full implications of the mechanical interpretation of nature would have been too much to expect of the scholastics. If it had been accepted that soul was matter, and subject to the same universal mechanistic laws, no scope would have been open for free will, and hence no reason would have existed for an institution (the Church) whose func-

---

[12] Altamira, *Historia de España,* IV, 312.

[13] Ingenieros, *Ideas argentinas,* in *Obras completas,* XIII, 92-102.

[14] Quoted in Hyman Stock, *The Method of Descartes in the Natural Sciences* (Jamaica, N. Y., 1931), p. 11. Where no other citations are given this discussion is based on Dr. Stock's authoritative work.

[15] T. V. Smith and Marjorie Grene, *From Descartes to Kant* (Chicago, 1940), p. 56.

[16] On this point see the recent interesting and provocative work of Professor John Tate Lanning of Duke University, *Academic Culture,* pp. 61-89, based on a study of colonial university theses. Dr. Lanning concludes there was a wider acceptance of mechanistic concepts in colonial Latin America than is indicated here.

tion was the salvation of the soul. After the rise of Newtonian physics, the scholastics were faced with three essential aspects of eighteenth century thought: "The interest in analyzing scientific method and knowledge in general, the problem of relating mechanical to mental phenomena in the world and in man, and the attempts to deduce phenomena other than those of physics from simple and universal laws." [17] But the scholastics especially avoided the application of Newtonism to religion, psychology, economics, and society, and the philosophers who did so (Voltaire, Locke, Diderot, Montesquieu, Rousseau) were anathematized. Toward the end of the colonial period, the Spanish-American scholastics permitted Cartesian metaphysics to apply the principle of "Methodic doubt" to the Pagan Aristotle, but not to the Christian Thomas Aquinas. To the end, their foremost thought was defense of the Christian cosmos.

It was left for the second current of thought stemming from the Cartesian-Newtonian science, and which was more interested in its mathematical and experimental implications, to accept the main tenets of a mechanistic philosophy. This current had its followers in the colonies, and toward 1800 they were increasing, but they existed mainly outside the academic halls and were combated by the academicians who still had the authority of the State and the Church behind them.

NEW SCHOOLS AND DEVELOPMENT OF SCIENCE

The changing spirit of the late colonial epoch was visible in several fields of intellectual and artistic activity. Among the most significant were: the establishment of new schools; greater attention to scientific mining; an intensified interest in natural phenomena, based in part on the scientific achievements of Europe; the development of the critical spirit, directed toward outworn institutions of which the Spanish regime was an expression; and the appearance of newspapers and literary reviews to provide vehicles for criticism.

New schools were to play a leading part in the evolutionary process. With the expulsion of the Jesuits in 1767, their properties were confiscated and their schools reorganized. While the Jesuits' successors were far from exemplars of modernity, they adopted studies that were at least a nod in the direction of modern education. Their libraries, too, found shelf room for books which departed from the theological pattern as much as the Inquisition would allow or, fortunately, a little more in many cases.

---

[17] Smith and Grene, *From Descartes to Kant*, p. 50.

Other schools of a still more secular kind were founded. A favorite type was the school specializing in mathematics, drawing, and music; and the new physics, chemistry, and natural history were also finding a place in the curriculum. Important in this trend were the many scientific expeditions, of which that of José Celestino Mutis is one of the most outstanding and influential in the field of natural history. A Spanish scientist who had taught in Bogotá, he was commissioned by the viceroy, Archbishop Antonio de Caballero de Góngora, to organize a "botanical expedition." He spent many years gathering and classifying the plants for his *Flora de Bogotá,* which he left unfinished. His work was carried on by a student, Francisco José Caldas, who had more than five thousand plants in his herbarium before he lost his life in the Wars of Independence. Humboldt and Bonpland had the highest praise for the work of Mutis and Caldas.

Cultural progress, however, was by no means evenly distributed. Humboldt was struck by the contrast between the "very superior" civilization of New Spain and the "scanty culture" of the parts of South America he had visited previously (Venezuela, Colombia, Ecuador, and the Peruvian coast.)[18] New Spain was the leader of the intellectual life of Spanish America. Three of its promient scientists of the new school were Joaquín Velásquez Cárdenas y León, José Antonio Alzate, and Antonio León Gama. Velásquez had an observatory in Santa Ana, California, and made worthwhile contributions there. Alzate was chosen a corresponding member of the Academy of Science in Paris. The organization of the School of Medicine in 1768, the Botanical Garden in 1788, and the School of Mines in 1791 were all manifestations of the growth of a new scientific spirit in Mexico. [19]

The Botanical Garden in Mexico was under the direction of Vicente Cervantes, and while he never achieved the fame of Mutis, he introduced the new botanical methods into New Spain. Humboldt was impressed with the chemical and physical laboratories of the School of Mines, which had not only the finest foreign instruments, "but also models executed in the capital itself, with the greatest precision." He noted that the "best mineralogical work in the Spanish language, the Manual of Oryctognosy, by M. del Río," was printed in Mexico, as was the first Spanish translation of Lavoisier's *Elements of Chemistry.* The ardor for the exact sciences in New Spain was "much greater than that with which they

---

[18] *New Spain,* I, 1, 9. [*Nouvelle Espagne,* I, 203-4; 214].
[19] Riva Palacio, *México,* II, 892-95; Altamira, *Historia de España,* IV, 339-48; Alamán, *Méjico,* I, 116.

dedicate themselves to the study of languages and ancient literature." [20]

Humboldt is perhaps the best authority on the state of science in America at the end of the colonial period. What he says reveals a great eagerness there to learn; wherever he went he attracted crowds who gathered to watch his work. He also found a vast gulf between the knowledge in the urban centers and the provinces, and a tendency on the part of the Creoles to exaggerate their scientific achievements.[21]

The inhabitants of the provinces were inclined to overestimate the importance of Spain, believing it still held the dominant position in Europe occupied during the sixteenth century, but the opposite opinion prevailed among the urban dwellers. Whereas to the provincials the Peninsula appeared "the very center of European civilization," the "Americans of the capital" held Spain in a low esteem, "and they flatter themselves with the idea that the intellectual cultivation has made more rapid progress in the colonies than in the Peninsula." [22]

This self-appreciation was perhaps slightly higher than the facts warranted but it created an atmosphere favorable to scientific achievement. The age when popular superstition and official repression prevented the systematic development of the sciences was disappearing, even if it did not pass entirely.

INTELLECTUAL TENDENCIES OF THE LATE COLONIAL PERIOD

The developments in science were reflected in other intellectual tendencies of the later colonial period. Among the more important of these was the interest in utilitarian knowledge fostered by clubs and societies organized to promote the progress of the colonies. These sprang up almost simultaneously throughout Spanish America, and had their origin in many cases in the informal but regular meetings of groups of friends in the café. The latter, which owed its being to the happy companionship of coffee and sugar, became much more than a place to enjoy the newly-popularized drink; it was the center for those who wished to discuss subjects of every kind. Formal meetings might, and did, arouse the suspicions of the authorities, but it was difficult to interfere with the café, which was primarily a commercial establishment. In time each café became so categorized that its clientele was drawn from one stratum of society only, and its patrons found themselves exchanging ideas

---

[20] *New Spain*, I, 216-17 [*Nouvelle Espagne*, II, 17-18].
[21] Humboldt, *Travels*, II, 239-40 [*Voyage*, II, 304-05].
[22] Humboldt, *New Spain*, I, 210-11 [*Nouvelle Espagne*, II, 9-10].

with men of similar economic class and social standing. So firmly was this characteristic implanted that it has persisted down to the present time in Latin America, Spain, and Portugal.

The scientific and literary circles and clubs were born of the same conditions that converted the cafe into a social institution. The desire to promote the arts and sciences found in these clubs the vehicle for expression. In Spain during the last half of the eighteenth century such organizations began to appear and only a short time was necessary to bring them to America. The *Asociación Filarmónica* was formed in Lima in 1787 and transformed into *Los Amantes del País* in 1790. In Havana, there were formed the *Real Sociedad Económica de la Habana,* and the *Sociedad Patriótica de Investigaciones,* while Mexico had a secret society called the *Guadalupes.* About 1808, the priest Navarrete organized *La Arcadia Mexicana.* Río de la Plata had its *Sociedad Patriótica y Literaria,* and Colombia its *Tertulia Eutrapélica.*[23] Such societies were signs of changing times, of changing mentalities.

Whether cause or effect, the expulsion of the Jesuits in 1767 is a point of departure in this new age. It affected America not only by removing their weight from the American intellectual scene, but also by turning the Jesuits into bitter critics and attackers of the Spanish regime from their places of refuge. Pablo Vizcardo, exiled from Peru, wrote a *Carta a los españoles americanos* (1799), printed also in Philadelphia, in which he defended the thesis of independence. And many other writings by exiled Jesuits, even when they did not come out boldly for independence, tended to exalt the spirit of the Creoles and increase the contempt for the mother country.

Under such influences, there was formed a group of Creole writers who differed greatly from their forerunners. The scientists among them have been discussed but there were others who wielded a wider influence through their literary activity. Francisco José de Caldas (1771-1816), previously mentioned for his valuable contributions to science, was also an author of social influence. His *Estado de la geografía del virreinato con relación a la economía y el comercio,* and *La influencia del clima sobre los seres humanos* had social content as well as scientific value. He was a collaborator of the *Semanario de Nueva Granada,* one of the many new reviews that was springing up. The Spanish authorities recognized his contribution to the new revolutionary ideas by having him executed during the temporary reaction in New Granada in 1816.

---

[23] Sánchez, *Literatura americana,* pp. 136-39.

In Ecuador, Francisco Xavier Espejo (1747-96) distinguished himself for his satires on society. He assailed the customs of his times in his *El nuevo Luciano* (1779), *Reflexiones sobre la viruela y la hygiene en Quito,* and other works. Espejo was bold enough to point out the errors of his times in America, after the style of the contemporary encyclopedists of Europe.

Argentina produced Manuel José de Lavardén (1754-1811), "great renovator of Argentine and American literature." His famous *Oda al Paraná* (1801) came at the right moment to give poetic expression to a nascent nationalism. Much earlier he had written a drama, *Siripo* (1789), the theme of which was the union of the Indians and Spaniards into one people.[24] Many others could be named, because there was hardly an important city that did not have its representative of the "new philosophy." .

Toward the end of the century came a new flowering of the "popular" literature that characterized the early conquistadores; and for the same reason. There were new things to recount. The revolt of Tupac Amaru, the expulsion of the Jesuits, the numerous revolts in Colombia, and many other incidents furnished fuel for rhymes, fables, satirical dialogues, all drawn from the immediate life of the colonies. Many of these lampoon the government, the clerics, or the officials. Some are filled with compassion for the sufferings of Indians and slaves.

Enter the Newspaper

Symptomatic of the new spirit in the Spanish colonies, and contributory to its spread, was the development of the newspaper. Accustomed as we are to a report on the latest world happenings along with our breakfast, it is difficult to realize that for centuries people throughout the world lived without news except that furnished by the occasional traveler. This was true of Europe as well as of the Indies. The colonies seldom knew what was happening in Europe in general or in Spain. And they knew even less of what was occurring in the other parts of America. Prior to the eighteenth century, the only published news were the laws and orders posted on public buildings and churches by the civil and ecclesiastical authorities, and *hojas volantes,* or fly-sheets on the arrival of fleets or mail ships from Europe. One such *volante* was produced about 1540 to record the destruction of Antigua, Guatemala and the death of Alvarado's wife. They seem to have been printed regularly on the arrival of fleets in the seventeenth century, and probably in the sixteenth. As early as 1594, for example, an *hoja volante*

---

[24] Levene, ed., *Nación argentina,* vol. IV, sección II, pp. 117-21.

was printed in Lima to announce the capture of an English ship. And during the seventeenth century, similar special announcements or bits of news were circulated via *hojas volantes;* but the newspaper proper did not come until the eighteenth century. [24b]

The increase in the number of printing presses was the indispensable prerequisite for the birth of the Latin-American newspaper. To the two initial presses, Mexico City about 1535-38 and Lima 1584, many more were added. By 1808 there were probably not fewer than twenty-five presses in various parts of Latin America, New Spain having ten with others in Havana, Caracas, Bogotá, Quito, Buenos Aires, and perhaps a dozen other places, although some of these were small and inefficient.[25] The newspaper was established to bring to the colonies not only news in the conventional sense, but to furnish a medium for essays, poetry, satires, suggestions for improvements and discussions of the latest economic, political, and scientific ideas. No other development expresses quite so well the transition from metaphysics to utilitarianism as the appearance of the newspaper.

The first newspaper of the Spanish colonies was the *Gaceta de México y noticias de Nueva España,* which appeared in 1722, and of which six issues were published. In 1728 a second paper, entitled *Gaceta de México,* was started by Juan Francisco Sahagún y Arévalo Ladrón de Guevara. With some interruption this continued to 1742, changing its name during the period, and reaching number 157 before ceasing publication. In the meantime, the *Gazeta de Goathemala* appeared in that country in 1729 and continued to 1731.

In its first issue the *Gaceta de México* in 1722 expressed its purpose, saying that a newspaper "is not lacking in utility, since in addition to the usual motives, Gazettes by furnishing a true account of what occurs in these extensive regions, will aid the historians in preparing their chronicles." In keeping with this aim, the *Gaceta* printed news from all New Spain, including regions as far apart as California and Vera Cruz. It included notices on the output of the mines, arrivals of the Manila Galleon, imports and exports, arrival of the English factors of the *asiento* in Vera Cruz, trade with other colonies and news from London, Madrid,

---

[24b] Irving A. Leonard, The *Mercurio Volante* of Don Carlos de Sigüenza y Góngora (Los Angeles: The Quivira Society, 1932).

[25] Torre Revello, *El libro,* pp. 138-59. See also Virgilio Rodríguez Betela, "Laws Relative to the Printing Press in Colonial America," *Inter-America,* IX (April, 1926), 307-16; Manuel Sánchez, "The Origin of the Printing Press in Venezuela," *Inter-America,* VIII (December, 1924), 149-51; Torre Revello, "Bibliotecas e imprentas en la América colonial" *BAN Hist.* XIV, 209-228 and bibliography cited there.

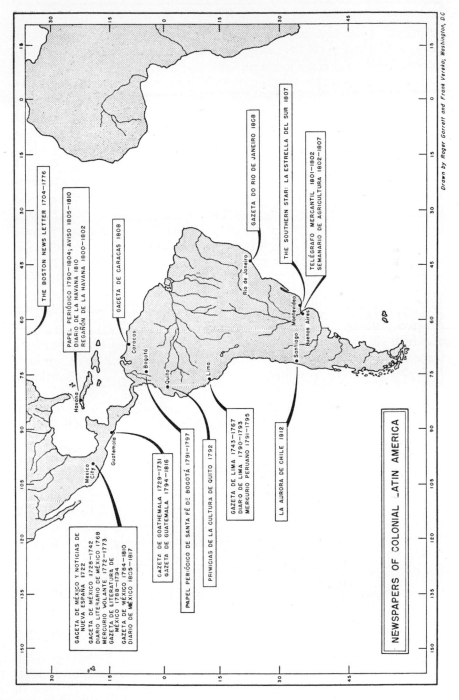

NEWSPAPERS OF COLONIAL LATIN AMERICA

THE BOSTON NEWS LETTER 1704-1776

PAPEL PERIÓDICO 1790-1804; AVISO 1805-1810
DIARIO DE LA HAVANA 1810
REGAÑÓN DE LA HAVANA 1800-1802

GACETA DE CARACAS 1808

GAZETA DO RIO DE JANEIRO 1808

THE SOUTHERN STAR: LA ESTRELLA DEL SUR 1807

TELÉGRAFO MERCANTIL 1801-1802
SEMANARIO DE AGRICULTURA 1802-1807

GAZETA DE GOATHEMALA 1729-1731
GAZETA DE GUATEMALA 1794-1816

PAPEL PERIÓDICO DE SANTA FÉ DE BOGOTÁ 1791-1797

PRIMICIAS DE LA CULTURA DE QUITO 1792

GAZETA DE LIMA 1743-1767
DIARO DE LIMA 1790-1793
MERCURIO PERUANO 1791-1795

LA AURORA DE CHILE 1812

GACETA DE MÉXICO Y NOTICIAS DE
NUEVA ESPAÑA 1722
GACETA DE MÉXICO 1728-1742
DIARIO LITERARIO DE MÉXICO 1768
MERCURIO VOLANTE 1772-1773
GAZETA DE LITERATURA DE
MÉXICO 1788-1794
GAZETA DE MÉXICO 1784-1810
DIARIO DE MÉXICO 1805-1817

Havana

México City

Guatemala

Caracas

Bogotá

Quito

Lima

Río de Janeiro

Montevideo
Buenos Aires

Santiago

Drawn by Roger Garrett and Frank Vereka, Washington, D.C.

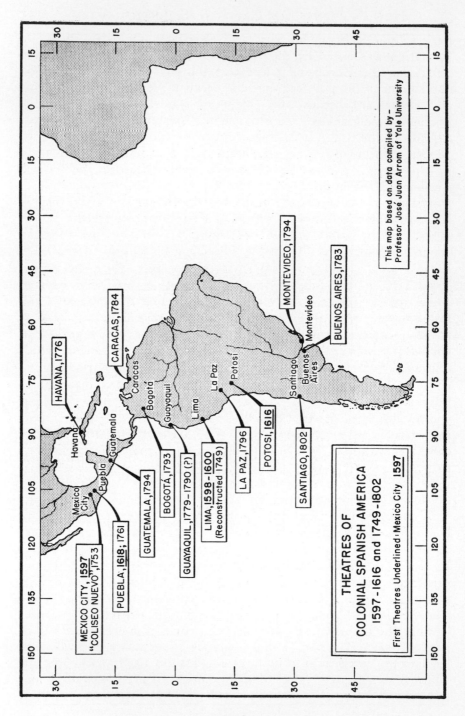

THEATRES OF
COLONIAL SPANISH AMERICA
1597-1616 and 1749-1802

First Theatres Underlined: Mexico City 1597

This map based on data compiled by –
Professor José Juan Arrom of Yale University

HAVANA, 1776

CARACAS, 1784

MONTEVIDEO, 1794

BUENOS AIRES, 1783

MEXICO CITY, 1597
"COLISEO NUEVO", 1753

PUEBLA, 1618; 1761

GUATEMALA, 1794

BOGOTÁ, 1793

GUAYAQUIL, 1779-1790 (?)

LIMA, 1598-1600
(Reconstructed 1749)

LA PAZ, 1796

POTOSÍ, 1616

SANTIAGO, 1802

Havana

Guatemala

Mexico
City

Puebla

Caracas

Bogotá

Guayaquil

Lima

La Paz

Potosí

Santiago

Buenos
Aires

Montevideo

Paris, Rome, Lisbon, Manila, and elsewhere. One gap in its information was noted by the *Gaceta* in its Number 6, of 1722, in comparing the European journals of the day with itself: "We do not comment on political matters because we enjoy a peaceable government and because the maxims of state are governed by the irrefutable judgment of our sovereign." An item of special interest appears in the July, 1729 issue: notice of the expected arrival of 787 cases of books. Also significant was the publication in 1729 of the titles of the prize essays presented before the French Academy of Science.

These early efforts were the harbingers of a more active period later. Among the foremost in time and importance were the papers established by José Antonio de Alzate y Ramírez, the Mexican scientist eulogized by Humboldt. He began his *Diario Literario de México* in 1768, but after eight issues appeared it was suppressed by the government. Four years later, in 1772, he published *Asuntos varios sobre ciencias y artes,* its title expressing the interest manifested in new types of learning. The appearance in this same year of José Ignacio Bartolache's *Mercurio volante con noticias importantes y curiosas sobre varios asuntos de física y medicina,* which continued to 1773, emphasized the trend toward utilitarian knowledge represented by the newspapers. Alzate resumed his publications in 1787 with *Observaciones sobre la física, historia natural y artes útiles,* of which twelve numbers appeared. The next year he began his more famous monthly *Gazeta de literatura de México,* consisting of eight, twelve, or sixteen pages, and which continued to 1794.

We are now well into the epoch of newspapers. A bare enumeration of those that appeared after 1790 would require a catalogue. Only the most important and illustrative of the new tendencies can be noticed. A notable example is the *Gazeta de México, compendio de noticias de Nueva España,* started in 1784 by Manuel Antonio Valdés. This paper rounded out twenty-six years of continuous existence, achieving the fame of being the longest-lived colonial periodical. Its appearance was noted by Viceroy Matías Gálvez whose report to the court indicates the official attitude. He wrote: "I hold the *Gazeta* to be very useful, provided it confines itself to noncontroversial news *(noticias indiferentes)*: ship arrivals and departures, cargoes of ships and reports on natural phenomena, elections of prelates and of alcaldes, notices of accessions of canons and other events of importance which occur in such a vast country

. . . and since furthermore it is important to furnish innocent information about things in which the public takes great interest, it seemed to me that this enterprise was very beneficial and should be given efficacious support." [26] Restricting the newspapers to what could be regarded as "innocent information" was not always possible. Indeed, it was precisely the desire to know things regarded as dangerous or useless by the State and the Church that inspired the editors of this new literature to take the risks involved.

A good example of the motivation for, and the dangers of, publishing a newspaper is the *Diario de México,* which first appeared in 1805 with Jacobo de Villaurrutia as director and Carlos María Bustamante as editor. Viceroy Iturrigaray permitted its publication, but subjected it to a severe censorship which he himself frequently exercised. This caused numerous delays in publication, and many articles were suppressed altogether. Bustamante describes the tribulations of the paper:

"The archbishop did not fail to cause us trouble, complaining of some poems which sounded bad to his excessively chaste ears. This prelate would have wanted us to publish only hymns and Christmas carols, and consequently he prohibited the nuns from reading the paper. In spite of this, we continued steadfastly; and thanks to our efforts we made it clear that this colony, regardless of the inquisitorial and governmental obstacles, had in its midst poets, orators, statesmen (*políticos*), historians, and men versed in every kind of science who had educated themselves and were abreast of the times; and we opened up the stage so that there might be revealed on it the *Tagles, Navarretes, Lacunzas, Barqueras, Barzábales,* and others, men of talent who would have merited acceptance and respect in cultured Europe." [27]

In spite of censorship and other difficulties, this first Mexican daily continued publication until 1817.

A *Gazeta* of Guatemala had meantime reappeared in 1794. The editor was Ignacio Beteta and one of its most famous contributors Simón Bergaño y Villegas. The latter was called to appear before the Inquisition several times because of his articles, and the paper suffered from severe attacks for its adherence to the new ideas, but it continued until 1816. The editors of the *Gazeta* defended themselves before the Inquisition by saying that their ideas could be taught openly in the United States and that the books prohibited

[26] Quoted in Torre Revello, *El libro,* p. 165.
[27] Quoted in Torre Revello, *El libro,* p. 166.

in Guatemala were circulated freely and advertised widely in that country "where there is true equality and entire liberty." [28]

Lima was the scene of some of the most important publications. Volantes, handbills, and pamphlets appeared during the seventeenth and early eighteenth centuries, but the first regular periodical was the *Gazeta de Lima* which was published bi-monthly from 1743 to 1767, with some interruptions. The more significant papers came later. In 1790 a daily, the first in Spanish America, the *Diario de Lima curioso, erudito, económico y comercial,* appeared and continued to 1793. The editor was Jaime Bausate y Mesa, who had arrived from Spain only five months before he started his paper.

More famous was the *Mercurio peruano de historia, literatura y noticias públicas,* published by the literary and scientific club, the *Sociedad Amantes del País.* Issued every three days, the *Mercurio* began publication in 1791 and continued to 1795. Its contents were significant, including articles on Peruvian commerce and mining with tables of statistics (vol. I); an article on the cultural progress of Peru, and a history of San Marcos University (vol. II); "The physical geography of Peru" (vol. III); "Principles of physical chemistry to aid in the study of the natural history of Peru" (vol. VI); and many others of similar nature. In giving a history of the *Sociedad de Amantes de Lima,* the *Mercurio* points out that the fields of study had been divided so that the following subjects were considered:

1. Antiquities, medicine, legislation, weaving, hydraulics, agriculture, etc. of the Incas.
2. Modern civil history: Lima, the viceroyalty, audiencia, etc.
3. Geography of Peru
4. Church history
5. Peruvian literature

---

[28] José Felipe Flores to Padre Liendo y Goicoechea from Philadelphia, December 4, 1797, published in *Gazeta,* p. 352, quoted in R. A. Salazar, *Historia del desenvolvimiento intelectual en Guatemala,* I, 86. That the books customarily banned in the Spanish colonies were circulated freely in the English colonies is indicated by the wide advertising they received. From the establishment of *The Boston News Letter* in 1704, book advertisements were a prominent feature, the latest works of English, French and other writers including Hobbes, Locke, Newton, Voltaire, Montesquieu being in great demand. Before 1700, such books were available in public and circulating libraries. As the eighteenth century progressed the multiplication of newspapers, the freedom of the press, the increase in private and public libraries and the attention given to education created an atmosphere of intellectual freedom which Latin America did not attain until the nineteenth century, if then. See James Truslow Adams, *Provincial Society, 1690-1763* (New York, 1928), pp. 113-38; 258-92; 302-09; see also Sidney I. Pomerantz, *New York: An American City 1783-1803* (New York, 1938), pp. 432-59.

6. Politics
7. Moral education
8. Commerce and agriculture
9. Physics, chemistry, mineralogy, botany, anatomy, medicine, and other scientific subjects. (vol. X).

The Viceroy Gil y Taboada both approved of the *Mercurio* and saw that censorship kept it within bounds. "Ever since the medium of the press has made easier the communication of ideas between men, the newspaper has been recognizd as one of the best, most expeditious and certain ways of promoting them [ideas], always provided that a prudent ruler keep them within the strict limits prescribed by religion and the law of the State." [29] The limits visualized by the Viceroy were narrower than those of the editors of the *Mercurio,* and eventually it was not possible to contain the successors of the *Mercurio* within them. [30]

Havana had two papers for a time as early as 1764-1766, and another in 1782, but the most important was the *Papel periódico.* It began publication in 1790 and was taken over by the *Sociedad patriótica* in 1793 and issued weekly until 1804, reappearing in 1805 as the *Aviso,* and changing its name to the *Diario de la Havana* in 1810. Still another paper, the *Regañón de la Havana,* published by Buenaventura P. Ferrer, was issued from 1800 to 1802. Toribio Medina calls it the best of all the colonial newspapers.

Bogotá's first important newspaper was the *Papel periódico de Santa Fé de Bogotá,* published by the *Tertulia Eutropélica* under the editorshop of Manuel del Socorro Rodríguez from 1791 to 1797. Among its chief editors was Francisco Xavier Eugenio Santa Cruz y Espejo, of Quito, who was a doctor of medicine, and part Indian of humble parents. His literary activities brought official displeasure and "cruel persecutions, confiscation of his papers and books, and painful imprisonments." [31] Accused in 1788 of writing a satirical work, *El Retrato de Golilla,* he was imprisoned and prosecuted. At a hearing before the viceroy in Bogotá, he was absolved and permitted to return to Quito, He obtained a post as librarian of the public library, which had opened in 1792, but he was regarded with suspicion by the authorities. In 1791, he helped to organize the *Sociedad Patriótica de Amigos del País de Quito* and a newspaper it published for a time in 1792,

[29] *Relación, Memorias de Virreyes, Perú,* VI, 92-95.
[30] Other papers in Lima were the *Semanario crítico* 1791, a moralistic journal; the *Gaceta de Lima,* 1793-95 and 1798-1804; and the *Minerva Peruana* 1805-10.
[31] Torre Revello, *El libro,* pp. 183-86.

the *Primicias de la cultura de Quito.* The attacks of Espejo's enemies soon brought it to an end. Three years later, in 1795, he was arrested and imprisoned for nine months, being released only to die in 1796 from the effects of his imprisonment.

It was with much difficulty that newspapers were started in the Río de la Plata, the viceroy having refused a license as late as 1796, but finally there appeared two papers reflecting the rise of the utilitarian spirit. In 1801, the *Telégrafo Mercantil, Rural, Político-Económico e Historiógrafo del Río de la Plata* began publication after finally securing a license. Its title indicates its wide range of interest, and the editor, Francisco Antonio Cabello y Mesa, declared in his prospectus that he intended to treat the same economic, literary, and scientific subjects that characterized the papers of Lima where he had resided, and, according to his own statement, had published a newspaper. In his tenth issue, he pointed out the usefulness of newspapers: "You know that people do not learn these things from volumes, but from the public press, not from Academies but in Cafes and Taverns, because the artisan, woman, child, and idler cannot read a book." And in Number 18, the Editor stated: "Learned men agree that Academies and daily papers have had the chief influence in the restoration of culture, and today constitute a considerable part of European literature" an example he wanted America to follow.[32] When a little more than a year old, the *Telégrafo* was suppressed by the viceroy for publishing material displeasing to the authorities.[33]

As the *Telégrafo* was dying, the *Semanario de Agricultura, Industria y Comercio* was born in 1802. Few papers were so truly the proponents of the useful arts as the *Semanario.* In Numbers 4-5 in 1802, it stated: "Our America, even if it is cultivating the belles-lettres, and if its illustrious writers have so often refuted the calumnies of De Pauw,[34] in the southern sections still continues to preserve in the very heart of its large cities the prejudice of looking scornfully down upon the master workmen of the trades and arts. That industrious citizen, who is everywhere esteemed as one of the most useful members of the body politic, who supplies our needs, aids our comfort, . . . is an object of contempt to the upper classes, and even to the middle classes of people." But, he adds: "Buenos Aires is by all means the city where there is the

---

[32] The *Telégrafo Mercantil* is reproduced in the *Biblioteca de la Junta de Historia y Numismática,* vols. VI-VII (Buenos Aires, 1914-15). Hereafter *Biblioteca JHN.*

[33] Torre Revello, *El libro,* pp. 186-96.

[34] De Pauw had propounded the thesis that the Creole was inferior to the European.

least tendency in this direction; where the artisan is usually inter-
woven with the middle classes; and where they therefore share
the same distinction, which is admitted nowhere else in the cities
of America."

The *Semanario* continued to carry on its utilitarian mission by
urging the formation of an Agricultural Society in Argentina on
the model of that started by Arthur Young in England, by publishing Franklin's essay on taxes and his Economic Project, and by
advocating free as opposed to slave labor. In the March 25, 1806,
issue appeared an article entitled, "On the Arts and Trades in
America as the Exclusive Patrimony of Freemen," and in April,
1806, it condemned slave labor in the workshops, and the slave
trade.[35] By sticking firmly to its utilitarian purposes, this periodical
was able to continue to 1807, with an interruption caused by the
English invasion of 1806. When the English occupied Montevideo
in 1807, a newspaper in two languages, *The Southern Star, La
Estrella del Sur,* was published for a short time.[36]

But great as the progress in publishing had been during the
later colonial years, the Spanish Colonies had not caught up with
what was going on elsewhere. Baron Humboldt noticed the difference when he went from Latin America to the United States:

> "When we remember that in the United States of North
> America newspapers are published in small towns not exceeding
> three thousand inhabitants, it is surprising to learn that Caracas,
> with a population of forty or fifty thousand souls, had no print-
> ing house before 1806; for we cannot give this name to the
> presses which served only from year to year to print a few pages
> of calendar, or the pastoral letter of a bishop. The number of
> those who feel the want of reading is not very considerable,
> even in the Spanish colonies most advanced in civiliza-
> tion . . ."[37]

After 1808, periodicals multiplied rapidly. The outburst at
that time revealed the tremendous stored-up intellectual energy
that only awaited relief from a regime which at best tolerated
newspapers under strong censorship. In spite of the fact that some
viceroys had permitted, commended, and even partially financed
several of the newspapers, the official atmosphere was distinctly
not calculated to encourage them. The men establishing the papers
of colonial Spanish America were beset by financial difficulties,

---

[35] *Biblioteca JHN, vol.* VIII-IX (Buenos Aires, 1928).
[36] Torre Revello, *El libro,* pp. 196-205.
[37] Humboldt, *Travels,* III, 478-79 [*Voyage,* IV, 213-14].

worked under severe censorship, and at times were persecuted by the officials. That they persisted is greatly to their credit. They deserve choice seats in the Valhalla of newspapermen.

THEY SHALL NOT PASS: FORBIDDEN BOOKS AND THOUGHTS

Though the newspapers had arisen as advocates of a utilitarian concept of society, and though the books and ideas of the Enlightenment entered the colonies in sufficient force to make their important contribution to the coming movement for independence, the Church and the State were still dominated by tradition to the end of the colonial period.

The Inquisition actively prosecuted forbidden books and their readers from 1775 to 1820, the period of the American and French revolutions, and as one of the victims stated in 1794, such works circulated "in spite of the vigilance of the Inquisition." [38] It was dangerous in fact to be a Frenchman in the Spanish colonies after 1789.[39] Censorship was exercised by both civil and ecclesiastical officials until November 10, 1810, when the Cortes of Cádiz granted liberty of the press.[40] Even after this decree became temporarily effective in America in 1812, it contained restrictions that made the "liberty of the press" a far different thing from the freedom we associate with it.

In 1769 the Inquisition in Mexico denounced the reading of heretical works such as those of Voltaire, blaming the presence of soldiers and foreigners for their existence, but none of the prohibited books, except Milton's *Paradise Lost* in Spanish, were found. That such books came in, however, is indicated by the fact that in 1768 one of the employees of the Inquisition had sold forbidden books to the value of 850 pesos to a cloth manufacturer who wanted them to "stiffen" his cloth. About the same time some of the works of Voltaire were found in the possession of Manuel de Linares, who had brought them from Spain but denied having read them, while eight others were found in the possession of Captain Miguel Pacheco who admitted having read *La Henriade*. In 1775 a copy of Raynal's work was found and on this occasion an order was sent out, July 31, 1776, by the Council of the Inquisition for all special reading licenses to be sent to Spain. In 1783 Manuel Carlos Bustillo was arrested in San Luis Potosí for having a copy of the *Encyclopédie,* and the next year Tomás Franco was required to give up Marmontel's *Les Incas.*

[38] Caillet-Bois, "La América Española y la revolución francesa," *BAN Hist.,* XIII, 161-69 and *passim.*
[39] Medina, *Inquisición en México,* p. 369.
[40] Torre Revello, *El libro,* p. 51.

More drastic measures came after the French Revolution. In 1790 the Council issued an edict prohibiting a multitude of books published in France. A supplementary list of twenty-five titles was issued in 1797, divided into two classes: "prohibited even for those who hold licenses" and "prohibited *in toto.*" Volney's *Les Ruines, ou Méditations sur les révolutions des empires* (1792) was "absolutely" prohibited because it "exceeded in impiousness" the works of Hobbes, Spinoza, Rousseau, and Voltaire. The next year, 1798, still another list included works of Montesquieu, Chesterfield, Volney, and Condorcet.

The search for forbidden works was intensified after this, and continued into the first years of the nineteenth century.[41] Two edicts, of June 17 and 23, 1801, banned more than eighty titles, mainly French and Italian. On December 17, 1803, the Inquisition prohibited a book entitled *Contrato social y Bororquia o la Víctima de la Inquisición* in language which achieved the maximum in vituperation. At the same time it stated: "We also renew the prohibition, even for those who have licenses to read prohibited books," of Rousseau's *Social Contract*, "prohibited in Rome by the decree of June 16, 1766, and included in the general prohibition which the Inquisition of Spain published in 1764 of all the works of this deistic and revolutionary philosopher."

In connection with this edict, the Inquisition made a statement which reveals that the banning of a book cannot be taken as evidence that it was actually circulating in America. Of the *Contrato social y Bororquia* and a 1799 translation of Rousseau's *Social Contract* the edict stated: "And although up to the present we have no notice that copies of these works have reached our district . . . we have judged it to be our major obligation to publish at the earliest moment this edict, prohibiting as we prohibit, *in toto*, even for those who hold licenses for reading prohibited books, the aforesaid two books." The penalty for possessing or failing to inform on anyone who possessed these works was excommunication and five hundred ducats fine.[42] In June 1804 the Inquisition again prohibited numerous books, almost all of them French. These edicts were published in the *Gazeta de México*, along with notices of the penalties meted out for infractions.

But the express banning of books that were not known to be circulating in America is the most significant feature of the pro-

[41] Medina, *Inquisición en Mexico*, p. 445; the above information is taken from pp. 433-45.

[42] Medina, *Inquisición en México*, pp. 446-48 and *passim* gives the text of this and other edicts.

nouncements of the Inquisition in Mexico. Until concrete evidence is found that such books reached America and were read, the soundest assumption is that the suppression was largely effective. The comparatively few examples of prohibited books known to have been circulating are sufficient only to mark them off as the exceptions, not the rule.

The spirit of the colonial regime is indicated by the events which accompanied the first abolition of the Inquisition. The decree of abolition, published in Mexico on June 8, 1813, was received by the public with undisguised glee. The *alcalde* of the Inquisitorial jails sent a vivid description of the public hatred of the Inquisition to the Council in Spain. But doing away with the Inquisition did not mean freedom of speech, press, or reading, as the people soon learned. The archbishop stepped into the breach and on June 10, two days later, published a pastoral letter requiring all persons to report cases of heresy, to turn over to him all prohibited books (unless they held a license to read them), and to denounce those who held such books. Nor did this first abolition of the Inquisition endure. Ferdinand VII was restored in 1814 and among his first acts was to reinstate the Holy Office. The revived Inquisition was given the authority to determine the method of "censoring and prohibiting books."

The Inquisition in Mexico lost no time in making clear its position with regard to dangerous thoughts and books. January 21, 1815, it published an edict which asserted:

". . . we require and order . . . that if any person or persons living, present or absent, or dead, have said or done anything against our Holy Catholic Faith and against what is ordered and established by the Sacred Scriptures and the evangelical law, resuscitating the old heresies or adopting the idiocies of the modern infidels *(libertinos)* Voltaire, Rousseau, and their disciples and followers, reading or keeping in their possession the books of these, or any other [authors] of those prohibited in the *expurgatorios* and former edicts, or even if they are not prohibited, if said books or any other printed matter or manuscript contain doctrines of an heretical or suspicious sense, false, erroneous, or contrary to the purity and honesty of custom . . . we impose and pronounce on you and on each of you the said penalty of major excommunication . . ." [43]

Throughout the colonies in the last colonial years, in New

---

[43] Quoted in Medina, *Inquisición en México*, pp. 466-69 where other information of like tenor may be found.

Granada, Peru, and La Plata, the Inquisition and other ecclesiastical and civil officials were fighting against the epoch of liberalism.[44] That they represented the dominant mentality of the Spanish-speaking countries will become clear when we see the strength of the conservative forces during the Wars of Independence and in the new nations of Latin America.

An outstanding example of this conservatism is offered by the dean of the Cathedral of Mexico City, José Mariano Beristain de Souza, whose reputation as the foremost bibliographer of the colonial period was firmly established with the publication of his *Biblioteca hispano-americana setentrional* (1816-21). His dedication is "To Ferdinand VII, Catholic King."

The "Prologue" of Beristain's work attacks with bitter vituperation the detractors of Spanish-American colonial culture. His is one of the most vehement defenses the Spanish motherland found during the years of revolution. The title of his Prologue is: "Eulogistic essay on the liberality of Spain in its American possessions, to serve as a prologue to the Biblioteca hispano-americana setentrional." Because this prologue is the epitome of the conservative position, the following extracts are quoted in order that the reader may feel the intellectual climate of the last days of the colonial period:

"In effect, wise and sensible statesmen, sincere and just philosophers, in view of the catalogue which I present you of four thousand literati who have written in New Spain, who have published their ideas on all subjects with the most ample and generous liberty of the press; in view of the many universities, seminaries, primary schools, and academies, doctors of theology and learned men which I here present to you; decide and pronounce sentence: whether a government is tyrannical that has erected and endowed so many liberal establishments, subsidized so many men of letters, rewarded and honored so many bishops, canons, doctors of theology, teachers, and erudite men . . . [You Americans should not seek to make yourselves independent of] a great and generous nation to which you owe your blood, your language, your education, arts and sciences, prosperity, and abundance, which you enjoyed until your ingratitude, pride, and ambition precipitated you into misery from which you will not easily escape except through repentance. Such fruits, such bitter fruits, have been produced perhaps by an excess of love, complacence, and freedom on the part of the government of

[44] The works of Medina, already cited, contain abundant evidence of this.

Spain, in having permitted the introduction into America of newspapers *(papeles públicos)* which have turned the formerly well-screwed on heads of my fellow countrymen. [This bibliography cannot include voluminous works like those produced in Europe because of] the great scarcity of paper and printing presses, the only cause of the scarcity of books and literary productions. Because another reason cited by Beausobre in his *Introducción al estudio de la política y comercio,* to wit: 'in the dominions of Spain a work is examined up to six times before it is published,' is a downright lie . . . . But the truth is that in Spanish America, just as in the mother country, two licenses are required for publication, that of the ecclesiastical ordinary and that of the government, and members of the regular clergy must have that of their superior prelate in addition. What obstacles are these? Only those indispensable to see that nobody dare write against religion, against the State, or against decency and good customs, or against the honor and decorum of their institutions. [The writings of Americans have been religious because it would have been] not only impertinent but execrable in the first literary men of these provinces to set themselves to write of Roman antiquities, of Collections of [Church] Councils, of mathematics, or other similar materials when the principal problem was to establish religion . . . .

"I well know that for the finicky palates of the erudite of this century of irreligion, libertinism, and materialism, except for a dozen items of this bibliography, all the rest will be but straw fit only for the flames as monuments to the fanaticism and superstition of the *devout* and of Aristotelian friars."

In a footnote, Beristain apostrophizes the men who started the revolt and sat in the Mexican Congress of 1815: "Ingrates! Perfidious men! Impostors! Would to God that Spain had not given you so much freedom nor permitted you the liberty to read these poisonous books, whose venom you vomit today against heaven and against your benefactress mother." [45]

The point of view and emotional intensity of Beristain's "Prologue" were characteristic of the intellectual atmosphere of the late colonial period. Secularization and the scientific attitude had made considerable progress, and "methodic doubt" had aroused

[45] José Mariano Beristain de Souza, *Biblioteca hispano-americana setentrional* (Vols. I, II, and III, second edition, Amecameca, Mexico, 1883); vol. IV José Toribio Medina, ed., Santiago de Chile, 1897; *Adiciones y correcciones,* José Fernando Ramírez, ed., México, 1898). [First edition of I, II, and III, México, 1816-21], I. prólogo, pp. viii-xvi.

the forces of conservatism to the need of vigorous defense; but secularism had not won, supernaturalism was not vanquished. The colonial period closed in the midst of an unfinished struggle between the forces of tradition, the divine-right State and Church, and those of the future, a government based on social contract and secularism. That the traditional forces were strong is indicated by the history of nineteenth-century Latin America, much of which revolved around the conflict between the two camps.

How Latin America won its independence, led by the men who read Rousseau and founded *Sociedades Económicas,* who rejected metaphysics and started newspapers, is a story that must be told later. But when the Wars of Independence were over, and the smoke of battle cleared away, it was the conservatives who held the positions of authority in most of the Latin-American nations.

Development of the Church
to 1810

IMPORTANCE AND INFLUENCE OF THE CHURCH

R ELIGIOUS AND CHURCH INFLUENCE DEVELOPED to a point
that made it easily the most powerful social force in Latin-
American history. The chief factors contributing to the authority
of the Church were: its strong organization, penetrating every part
of Latin America and working in every institution; its influence
over the State; the work of the Inquisition in controlling the political activity and the mental development of the people; the pioneering and educational activities of the religious orders; the intellectual monopoly of the clergy; the property holdings and
economic power of the Church; and its influence on private and
public morals.[1]

We may note at the outset that the position of the Church was
strong throughout the colonial period, with only a minor loss of
prestige at the end. In Chile, for example:

"The devotion of the masses of the people remained un-
alterable, and was revealed by the numerous Church festivals,
frequent processions, and the common belief in the stories of
miracles and apparitions, born (hija) of ignorance and superstition, rather than of an intelligent and sincere faith. Nevertheless, given the considerable growth of the population, the
number of ecclesiastics was much less than in other times . . . .
This diminution was owing in part to the precautions ordered
by the King against forced entry into the Church, because formerly it had been a frequent practice for many heads of families,
whether impelled by a circumspect religious zeal or the desire

[1] G. Desdevises du Dezert, "L'Eglise espagnole des Indes à la fin du XVIIIe
siècle," *Revue Hispanique*, XXXIX (February, 1917), 112-294.

to come into possession of quitrents and benefices, to compel their sons to take religious orders. But the diminution was due principally to the economic development of the colony, whose commerce and agriculture gave employment to many people who formerly would have sought a living in the convents, embracing for this reason the ecclesiastical career." [2]

The Church influence was felt also in realms that today we would consider purely secular. For example, early in the eighteenth century the question was posed of moving the city of Concepción de Chile to a better location, and the government ordered its removal; but the bishop, Toro Zambrano, opposed it and threatened ecclesiastical punishment, thereby keeping the city where it was until his death in 1760. His successor, Ángel de Espiñeira, who became bishop in 1764, was a partisan of the removal, however, and Guill y Gonzaga, the governor, ordered the city changed to the new site. Such incidents were not isolated, but a part of the warp and woof of Spanish colonial society.[3]

One of the staunchest of Catholics, leader of the clerical party in Mexico as well as a historian, says of clerical prestige:

"The influence of the clergy was great for three reasons: respect for religion, remembrance of its great benefactions, and its abundant riches. The people, scantily instructed in the basis of religion, made worship consist largely of ceremonial pomp; and the lack of any other diversions was provided by the religious functions, which, especially during Holy Week, represented in repeated processions the most revered mysteries of the redemption. All the religious festivals of the Church, in theory entirely spiritual, became profane (vanidad), there being an abundance of fireworks, dances, skits (loas), bull fights, cock fights, and even prohibited diversions such as cards and others, in order to celebrate at great cost the solemnities of the patron saints of the towns, into which the Indians poured the greater part of the fruits of their labors . . . . The Indians retained for the regular clergy the respect that the first missionaries had won through their justified reputation for protecting the natives against oppression, defending them against the violence of the conquistadores, and because they were their masters, not only in religion, but also in the trades necessary for earning a living. This respect, which reached fanatical devotion, had nothing dangerous in it so long as it was given to men worth of venera-

[2] Barros Arana, *Chile*, VII, 382-84.
[3] Barros Arana, *Chile*, VI, 251.

tion because of their virtues; and the government, to which they were very faithful and obedient, found in these exemplary ecclesiastics its strongest support; but it might come to be most [dangerous] if, the customs of the clergy being corrupted, this body should for personal advantage wish to abuse its influence . . .." [4]

In Uruguay, in an epoch when much of Europe was breaking away from its firm Church attachments—Montevideo, for example, was a town founded and developed during the eighteenth century —the attachment to religion was also powerful.

"Montevideo, without having experienced the exaggerations of public worship common in other cities of America, did not escape its influence. The cabildo, which deliberates upon and manages the business of the city, affirms as a sacramental formula incorporated into its deliberations that 'its members have united to discuss matters concerning the better service of God and the public good,' just as the laws and decrees that govern the society constantly inculcate religious sentiments. It is the priests who teach the children their first letters, as it is they who are the depositaries of knowledge and learning. Religion constantly plays a part in the daily happenings, and the Church is resorted to in signs of rejoicing, in thanks for fortunate events, as well as in requests for health or wealth or success, for rain if there is a drought or for the cessation of rain if there is too much water." [5]

CHURCH ORGANIZATION: ROYAL CONTROL

In its basic organization and nature of its personnel, the later Church varied hardly at all from its early establishment. The most noticeable change was the increase in numbers and variety of the regular clergy and the setting up of new bishoprics and parishes. By the end of the colonial period the organization from archbishop down to parish priest was thoroughly established. Some of the earlier restrictions against Indians, mestizos, mulattoes, and Creoles had relaxed, and a considerable number of priests, monks, and nuns were drawn from these classes. Frequently, however, this relaxation resulted from the individual's having obtained a certificate of white ancestry, rather than to official removal of the barriers. To the end of the colonial period, the Church remained

---

[4] Alamán, *Méjico*, I, 64-66.
[5] Blanco Acevedo, *Uruguay colonial*, pp. 96-97.

largely a foreign institution with the vast majority of its high officials drawn from Spain.

The Church as a career also tended to become slightly less attractive in the later colonial period. There was not the same economic necessity for making religion a profession as in the early days. The establishment of the militia rendered an army career possible, and the growth of commerce and industry afforded opportunities for a livelihood.[6]

The control of the Church in America remained legally in the hands of the Crown by right of the papal concessions made early in the sixteenth century.[7] Earlier laws on this score were confirmed by a royal decree of September 5 of 1803. This right of patronage was expanded to include the religious orders, and embraced "the whole of the ecclesiastical or spiritual authority," as stated in a cédula providing that "any provincial and visitador, prior or guardian or other prelate nominated and chosen in the realm of the Indies must, before being permitted to exercise his office, give notice to our viceroy, president, audiencia, or governor who may be in charge of the chief government of the said province, showing him the writ of appointment so that he [the nominee] may receive the protection and aid necessary for the management (uso) and exercise of his office."

Attempts of the Pope to exercise this authority were successfully resisted in the eighteenth century. Royal patronage further extended to the constitutions or charters of the religious orders, the laws authorizing the Council of Indies to "see and examine so that we may approve and order observed whatever ordinances, constitutions, or other statutes are made by the prelates, chapters, cabildos, and convents of the religious." [8] In conformity with this right, the Council of Indies prevented changes already made in the constitutions of the religious orders from going into effect. Likewise, as was expressly stated as late as 1792, the universities, colegios, and seminaries were subject to royal patronage, which included the granting of fellowships to students as well as appointments to professorships.

Whether or not the Crown assumed wider powers over patronage in America than were specifically granted in any concordat with the Papacy, the right of the Crown was never questioned by the Pope. This is clear from various restatements of the royal

---

[6] Barros Arana, *América* II, 44; Depons, *Voyage to the Spanish Main,* II, 116-18 [French ed. II, 145-47].
[7] Vélez Sarsfield, *Relaciones del estado con la iglesia,* chap. III.
[8] Vélez Sarsfield, *Relaciones del estado con la iglesia,* pp. 77-78.

authority, such as a communication to the Archbishop of Mexico in 1593, a reservation made in the Concordat with the Papacy in 1793, and finally, in the *Novísima Recopilación* of the laws in 1805 in which it was stated that "in accordance with the Bull of Pope Julius II executed in Rome the 28th of July of 1508" the Sovereigns "Ferdinand and Doña Juana" were named the "exclusive and joint patrons" *(únicos e insolidum)* of the Indies with the right of making all ecclesiastical appointments of whatever class.

The right of patronage was inalienable under all circumstances whatsoever. The King did not lose it through its customary (and of course, illegal) exercise by others. Cases of ecclesiastical appointments without the King's consent occurred, but they were vigorously combated and annulled. An exception was made for religious institutions such as chapels, churches, and monasteries founded and constructed with private funds. In such cases the patronage could be exercised by the person who endowed the institution. On all other cathedrals and seminaries the royal arms were placed to accentuate the Crown authority.[9]

The royal authority was also extended to include all disputes between the clerics concerning benefices, the limits of bishoprics, etc., with jurisdiction being invested in the civil instead of the ecclesiastical courts, although the persons concerned belonged in the ecclesiastical jurisdiction *(fuero)*.[10] In theory at least, all cases touching the Crown's patronage rights had to come before royal courts.[11]

This inclusive power of the Crown was recognized again and again in treatises written by American clerics, and passed by the Inquisition; that such rights could be publicly acknowledged in books bearing the imprimatur of the highest clerical officials is proof that the Pope acquiesced in the powers claimed by the Crown of Spain. For example, the clerical writer Juan de Silva, in his *Advertencia para el gobierno de los Indios,* addressed himself to the King, citing his authority; and Araciel, a member of the Council of Indies, formulated the same concept of the royal power in ecclesiastical matters.[12]

Viceroy Revilla Gigedo stressed the royal patronage as one of the chief powers of the King, and of the viceroy who acted in his stead. Mediation between the religious orders, and the settlement

---

[9] Vélez Sarsfield, *Relaciones del estado con la iglesia*, pp. 78-83.
[10] *Ibid.*, pp. 60-61.
[11] Moses, *Eve*, p. 126.
[12] Vélez, Sarsfield, *Relaciones del estado con la iglesia*, pp. 62-66.

of factional fights within the monasteries was also an important function of the viceroy, Revilla Gigedo citing several instances where his intervention was necessary to prevent brawls between the monks and their respective partisans.[13]

CONFLICTS BETWEEN CHURCH AND STATE

The exercise of the patronage could not, however, prevent the conflict of civil and religious authorities. Both wielded their powers in the name of the King, and there was theoretical delimitation of their jurisdictions, but actual delimitation was never achieved. To the final days of the colonies (and into the national period) the civil and religious authorities fought bitterly.

Conflicts of Church and state were among the most disrupting factors in colonial society. The barest cataloguing of the instances in which the authorities of the two institutions fought one another (sometimes with actual bloodshed) would require a large volume.[14]

The invisible line dividing the Church's privileges from the State's authority was exposed in the endless disputes at court over civil and ecclesiastical jurisdiction. Ecclesiastical tribunals were, however, but one of the several types of privileged legal bodies representing class interests. The special courts for commerce (consulados) and for mining (tribunal de minería), and the military courts, further augmented jurisdictional rivalries. The most frequent clashes, however, were between the ecclesiastical and civil courts, prolonged and involved lawsuits often arising from the consequent legal complications.[15] The existence of two "absolute" authorities side by side, both claiming "divine right" of

---

[13] Revilla Gigedo, *Instrucción,* paras. 25-43.

[14] For examples see: Lorente, *Perú bajo los Borbones,* pp. 26-27; and 49-55 where Lorente compares the disturbances which accompanied elections in the monasteries and convents with the political squabbles common in nineteenth-century Peru. The Inquisition, he says, was the worst of all. Cf. Francis Merriman Stanger, "Church and State in Peru," *H.A.H.R.,* VII (November, 1927), 410-37. The various *Relaciones* left by viceroys and captains-general contain innumerable examples. See the *Relación* of José de Solís, 1760, in the *Relaciones de Mando* published in the *Biblioteca de historia nacional* (Bogotá, 1910), vol. VIII, and other *Relaciones* in the same volume by other viceroys, particularly José de Espeleta, 1796, pp. 291-99. The classical defense of the Church in New Granada is by José Manuel Groot, *Historia eclesiástica y civil de Nueva Granada* (3 vols., Bogotá, 1869-70), particularly I, 185, but the whole work is a demonstration that the history of the Church in Latin America was a constant quarrel between the religious orders, and between church and state. Still another example of this situation is found in Pierre François-Xavier de Charlevoix, *Histoire du Paraguay* (3 vols., Paris, 1756), Bks. IV, X-XII, XVIII-XIX. The conditions in colonial Chile may be seen in Barros Arana, *Chile,* vol. IV, part IV, chap. II, paragraph IX; chap. III, par. I; chap. VII, par. IV-VI; vol. V, chap. XVI, par. VII; chap. XXIII, par. VII.

[15] Barros Arana, *Chile,* VII, 356-57.

control over the same subjects, was not compatible with orderly government or speedy justice.[16]

Still another way in which the Church exercised its power was through the maintenance of the "right of asylum" offered to criminals who could flee to a church for sanctuary thus avoiding arrest by the civil officers. This type of ecclesiastical interference with public authority was common in the Middle Ages, and came to America with the establishment of the Church. At times the Church not only harbored criminals but forcibly removed them from the custody of the civil authorities, who were powerless to resist because of the supposed sacredness of the clerics. Charles III attempted reforms in this as in so many other fields. He secured a Bull, *Ea Semper,* from Pope Clement XIV in 1772, which restricted, but did not abolish the Church's right of asylum. The bull limited the number of crimes for which the Church could grant refuge, and the number of churches in which the criminals might be harbored. This did not prove a final solution, for there were constant bickerings between the civil and clerical powers over the application of the new regulations. Charles III attempted to remedy this situation by a decree in 1787, requiring the clerical authorities to release to the civil officials the criminals they were harboring, but only provisionally and with the guarantee that neither capital nor corporal punishment would be administered. But the suit which followed such a procedure was submitted to a Church court with power to decide whether the crime in question was one permitting asylum. This in turn led to further interminable disputes between clerical and civil authorities.[17]

But harboring criminals was only one of the many causes for dispute. The Church was almost continuously in conflict with the audiencias of the colonies. It would be difficult to conceive of a more litigious civilization than that of the Spanish possessions, and it is quite probable that the greater part of all lawsuits arose over matters in which the Church disputed the jurisdiction of the State.[18]

Rivalry between two conflicting powers was not confined to judicial disputes, but was carried into every realm of authority. It became customary to designate the archbishop as successor to

---

[16] See Revilla Gigedo, *Instrucción,* pars. 92-94.

[17] Depons, *Voyage to the Spanish Main,* II, 121-35, [Fr. II, 152-69]; Barros Arana, *Chile,* VI, 399-400; VII 509-511. Cf. Elizabeth Howard West, "The Right of Asylum in New Mexico in the Seventeenth and Eighteenth Centuries," *H.A.H.R.,* VIII (August, 1928), 357-91.

[18] Desdevises du Dezert, in *Revue Hispanique* LXX, 182.

the viceroy in case of the latter's death, disability, or removal. "Each archbishop hoped to occupy the seat of government of New Spain, even if only *ad interim,* should the viceroy fall into disgrace and not finish his term of office, and every archbishop in this case could count on the support not only of his friends and partisans, but of the enemies of the viceroy, as well as of all those who had not been able to prosper under the viceroy." [19] The same situation prevailed in other colonies and led to constant bickerings, accusations, and plots against the viceroy, creating a system that was to serve as a basis for the "palace revolts" of the national period. Factionalism thrived in the court and among the populace, and usually the viceroy lost out. Frequently the King recalled both the viceroy and the archbishop, but such actions indicated more than[20] anything else that the Crown dared not leave the archbishop in the colonies where he could extend his authority.

During the course of the eighteenth century, a series of state acts had attempted to limit clerical power. Philip V reclaimed for the throne powers that had fallen into clerical hands during the time of the incompetent Charles II, "the bewitched." Ferdinand VI, in the concordat of 1753, had confirmed the reclaimed powers, and Charles III had continued the work of curbing the Church. Among his most important measures were a series of acts designed to reaffirm the royal patronage in ecclesiastical matters: the pragmatic known as *regium exequatur* required Papal Bulls to have the sanction of the Council of Castile before transmission to the clergy; civil protection for minor clergy against their superiors; the necessity of royal assent to clerical appointments, the suppression of the ecclesiastical *fuero* in cases of sedition and public disturbances; and limitations of the powers of the Inquisition.[21]

The gap between legislation and execution was great, however, and not destined to be closed during the colonial period. The State still had to contend with many privileges accorded the Church at earlier dates. The Franciscans, for example, "armed with the Papal Bulls and royal cédulas which had granted them such extensive prerogatives and powers, considered themselves independent of [state] jurisdiction and dared to usurp the powers of the alcaldes and corregidores, administering justice and ordering corporal punishments such as imprisonment and whipping." [22]

[19] Riva Palacio, *México,* II, 664.

[20] *Ibid.,* II, 710-11.

[21] See Modesto Lafuente, *Historia de España,* Bk. VII, chap. XXI for a discussion of this subject; Barros Arana, *Chile,* VII, chap. XXIV, pars. 7-9.

[22] Riva Palacio, *México,* II, 709.

Charles III also removed some of the privileges of tax exemption, such as freedom from tariffs, which had permitted the clerical merchants to compete tax free with other merchants, but he did not put a complete stop to this abuse. [23]

Church and state problems were by no means resolved at the end of the colonial period; they remained one of the unfortunate inheritances of the free nations.

THE INQUISITION [24]

The Inquisition, as we have already seen, became one of the most important colonial religio-political instruments and was as effective in America as in Spain. The simpler problems it faced in America, rather than any lack of development and zeal, enabled it to pursue a less drastic course there.[25]

Within its general purpose of assuring fidelity to the Crown and the Church, the Inquisition included the prosecution and punishment of heretics, Jews, Moriscos, clerics who were remiss in their duties, sorcerers and witches, Protestants, "Lutherans," sailors of Portuguese, English, Dutch, and other foreign nationalities found in America, bigamists, perjurers, blasphemers; and it censored all books printed in or *imported* into the colonies. This list of functions includes some hardly conceivable in modern times, and others that present-day events are again presenting as crimes. The prosecution of "sorcerers and witches" was not unknown, at some period, in other parts of the world of which we have knowledge. The English colonies executed "witches" and the belief in witches is still held in some parts of Europe. "Heresy" in colonial America was a crime comparable to "treason," and the extreme limits to which such an accusation could be carried are beyond definition. Perhaps we can derive some conception of what "heresy" meant by observing the twentieth century German Nazi persecution of Liberals, "Communists and Jews," the Italian Fascist treatment of "dissenters," or the Russian purges of "Trotskyites." "Crime" in the colonies included not merely the commission of an open offense against the Church or the State, but failure to accept the doctrines of either with absolute devotion. Thus, "not to be a Catholic" was a "crime", for which one could be accused, tried, and punished. Further, everyone in the community was under constant necessity to prove his fidelity.[26]

---

[23] Barros Arana, *Chile*, VI, 330.

[24] This discussion is based on the same authorities as cited in the previous chapters on Culture—Henry Charles Lea, José Toribio Medina, and others.

[25] Depons, *Voyage to the Spanish Main*, II, 74-84 [French ed. II, 92-105].

[26] Depons, *Voyage to the Spanish Main*, II, 74-75; (French ed. II, 92-93).

The prerogatives of the Tribunal of the Inquisition were immense. It was free from accounting to any other power, and its decisions could not be appealed or repealed. Its censorship of literature continued with vigor to the end of the colonial period, even when some of the other functions of the Inquisition were less rigorously carried out. Any book, pamphlet, or paper containing anything contrary to the dogmas of the Church, or questioning the divine right of the Sovereigns, was prohibited. Any matter considered derogatory to the laws was equally condemned. In an age when the people had no participation in making the laws, it was doubly assured that they could not protest or reject those made by their "divinely" appointed rulers. Any matters considered obscene were also banned. By 1790 the Inquisition's list of prohibited works contained some 5,420 authors and many anonymous works besides. Among those forbidden were Robinson Crusoe, the works of Boileau (the French poet, 1636-1711) and many others that would seem entirely inoffensive. Books could be banned for what they did not contain, as well as for including prohibited material, since the theory was that every book must serve the purpose of exalting the Church or the State. House to house searches were made to discover such literature, and the Inquisition encouraged secret denunciations.

"Heretics" were frequently persecuted. For example, a Dutch vessel was captured in Chile in 1725 and some of the sailors who had been made prisoners were disembarked in Coquimbo for hospitalization. This brought a strong protest from the cabildo of La Serena on the grounds of the great danger of contagion, not from the infirmity of the Dutch sailors—which was, after all, a punishment sent by God—but from the "heresy" of which the Dutch were guilty; and lest the inhabitants of this city through association with foreigners, should lose their proper horror of them. The governor of Chile (Cano de Aponte) ordered the prisoners carried to Lima, where the presence of the Inquisition lessened the dangers of heresy.[27]

The numbers prosecuted by the Inquisitions were not great in comparison with the total population, but this is in part explained by the exemption of the Indians, who formed in many sections almost the whole of the population. From the establishment of the Inquisition in Mexico City in 1571 to the end of the century, there were some 879 cases, and in the course of the seventeenth century the total number of cases was 1402. During the colonial period

---

[27] Barros Arana, *Chile*, VI, 30.

some 41 persons were burned at the stake in Mexico City, and 59 in Lima.

A large number of the cases were directed against the Jews and the "Judaizers." [28] There were also cases against "Lutherans and Calvinists" and even more against the "English pirates" who had been made prisoners. "Torture was commonly applied to the Jews and Judaizers in order to force them to denounce their coreligionists, among whom were always those closest to the accused, such as the wife, brothers, and nearest relations." The Protestants, on the other hand, were seldom tortured since they usually made an open declaration of what they knew of their own religion, of who taught them and who their families were, these being usually out of reach of the Inquisition. The common procedure with Protestants was to convert them, since they were generally willing to profess Catholicism in order to escape punishment. The first cases offered difficulties in catechism as the accused could not speak Spanish, but the Inquisitor General devised a catechism in English which he sent to Mexico. Its title was: Short Abridgement to Christian Doctrine. [29]

That the cases coming before the Inquisition were relatively few would seem to indicate that there was little resistance to the dogmas of the Church and the laws of the Crown, rather than tolerance on the part of the Inquisitors. Even toward the last half of the eighteenth century, when the Inquisition had certainly lost some of its powers, it still was vigorous enough to defy attack. Many of the boldest anticlerical writers dared not include the Inquisition in their denunciations. Campomanes, who attacked the nobility and the clergy, never ventured to write a word against the Inquisition. [30] The vast and illiterate majority had no thought of questioning the dogmas and the laws; the few who did were suppressed. The official Church policy was to limit education to those chosen by it, liberty to those who conformed, ideas to those it approved; and the Inquisition was its principal instrument for carrying out this policy.

RELIGIOUS ORDERS AND MISSIONS

Missionaries carried on throughout the colonial period the intensive work of converting the Indians begun during the first days of the Conquest. A full account of their activities offers materials for a voluminous report, around which could be woven the history

---

[28] Riva Palacio, *México*, II, 711.
[29] *Ibid.*, 712.
[30] Desdevises du Dezert, *Revue Hispanique*, L, 45.

of all Latin America. Behind the missionaries was the Crown, which desired to have frontier regions explored, conquered, and settled. Where zeal for Christianizing was lacking, the pressure from the Crown and the Church, plus the fact that many clerics had no other field open to them, was sufficient to keep the work of the missionaries going. They pioneered on every frontier from northern New Spain to southern Chile, across the Andes to the headwaters of the Amazon, and up the Paraná to the interior of Paraguay, Argentina, and Brazil.

Their technique of colonization was almost everywhere the same, since its plan was devised and ordered by one central authority. A few missionaries, usually accompanied by troops for protection, entered a region not previously Christianized. A settlement was made, and the Indians were induced to establish themselves in the mission, by peaceful means if possible, or by force if necessary. The soldiers remained to establish a *presidio*. In theory the mission was the first stage of a continuous frontier to be pushed forward every ten years, the missionaries leaving their settlements to civil officials and repeating the process further on. In practice this was not uniformly possible. Frequently at the end of ten years, the life of the mission itself was still in question, or it had already been wiped out by Indian wars, and in no two parts of America were the conditions identical. In some cases, the missionaries tried to settle in regions which, even down to modern times, have proved economically useless. Also at times the missionaries pushed on without the soldiers and those who lost their lives in such enterprises were numbered in the hundreds. Before the end of the sixteenth century, however, the mission had definitely been adopted as an agency of further colonization.[31]

The missionaries were sent into what is today northern Mexico (Sinaloa, Coahuila, Chihuahua, Sonora, Lower California) and into the southwestern and southern parts of the United States (California, Arizona, New Mexico, Texas, Louisiana, and the southeastern states then called Florida). In the latter region the work was difficult because the Indians were hostile, and because during the eighteenth century the English were crowding further and further south into the Spanish-held regions. Texas was reached in 1716 and about twenty missions were founded during the next thirty years, but most were not permanent. New Mexico had some twenty-five missions by 1744 and these held perhaps 12,000 Indians.

[31] Herbert E. Bolton, "The Mission as a Frontier Institution in the Spanish American Colonies," *American Historical Review*, XXIII (October, 1917), 42-61.

From 1746, missionary work was carried on in the region now embraced in northeastern Mexico and the part of Texas up to the Nueces river, then called Nuevo Santander, the missions numbering twenty-four in 1756. These missions to Texas and regions eastward were direct answers by Spain to the attempts of France to extend the Louisiana colonies begun early in the century.[32]

In the region northwest of Mexico City, missionaries had been active, of course, from the beginning of the Conquest, and colonies were founded as far north as Sinaloa; but the arrival of the Jesuits in 1591 marked the extension of the missionary technique in the region. By the last quarter of the next century (1678) the region of Sinaloa had been brought under mission influence; some twenty-eight missions with seventy-two *pueblos de visita* (villages visited by itinerant missionaries) with some 40,000 Indians, had been established. Near the end of the seventeenth century the Jesuit, Eusebio Kino, with the mission of Dolores (1687) in north Sonora, initiated a new series of missions that was to be extended into Arizona and California. At the same time another Jesuit, Juan María Salvatierra, established similar posts in Lower California. After 1767, the Jesuit missions were taken over by the Franciscans who, under the leadership of Miguel José Serra (known as Junípero Serra), Lasuén, and Garcés continued to establish others, founding the last one at Sonoma, north of San Francisco, California, in 1823.[33]

In the south of Mexico and in Central America the efforts of the Franciscans, Dominicans, and Jesuits did not so much extend Spanish authority to new territories as achieve more effective occupancy of territories nominally under control of the Spaniards. On the frontier of northern Guatemala and Mexico a century of effort was necessary before the Itzas were brought to accept missions at the end of the seventeenth century.[34] There were seven villages in 1767. In the other Central American countries the missionaries had carried their work from the mountain valleys (where the Indians had more easily submitted) to the lowlands where the Indians were more difficult to domesticate.

The missionaries were equally instrumental in South America in leading the way into the less accessible regions where vast

[32] J. Fred Rippy, *Historical Evolution of Hispanic America* (New York, 1932, and later editions), pp. 83-88; 101-106.

[33] Riva Palacio, *México*, II, 707-709; Charles E. Chapman, *A History of California* (New York, 1930), pp. 192-205; Chapman, *Colonial Hispanic America*, pp. 96-107.

[34] Francisco de Elzora y Rada, *A Narrative of the Conquest of the Province of the Ytzas*, Philip Ainsworth Means, ed. and tr. (Paris, 1930).

unoccupied areas existed between the Spanish establishments. There were areas as large as Texas in which settlement was impossible because of the opposition of the Indians, or because the economic needs of the colonies (and the European demands for their products) had not been sufficient to make the occupation of these territories necessary. The missionaries went into regions where Spaniards were not interested in accepting encomiendas. They demanded a smaller initial outlay for pioneering and were satisfied with a smaller financial return from the lands occupied.

Missionary activities in the Rìo de la Plata basin began with the Franciscans and Jesuits. The Franciscans established themselves along the Uruguay River among the *Chanaes* Indians, where they founded the missions of Santo Domingo de Soriano (1624), and later Viboras and Espinillo. Jesuit missionary activity was the most important, however, in the basin of the Río de la Plata. The settlement of the Plata had proved very difficult, and in 1600 there was still much left to be done, especially along the rivers between Buenos Aires and Asunción. Communications were impeded by the hostility of the Indians. Along the Uruguay and the Paraná was also a large unoccupied area; and north of Asunción settlements could be made that would, in theory, facilitate communication with Peru.

This was the situation in 1608 when Philip III authorized the Jesuits to establish missions among the Guaraní Indians. The first was established in 1609-10 in Paraguay at San Ignacio Guazú. By 1652 the Jesuits had founded "forty-eight towns, all of infidel and barbarous Indians," but all but twenty-two had been destroyed.[35] The most active period of settlement was between 1620 and 1640. The problem of the Jesuits was to induce the Indians, many of whom were warlike, to establish themselves in definite localities under the tutelage of the missionaries. The methods were in part persuasion, but once in the mission the Indians were not permitted to leave. In the beginning the Jesuits established themselves a little haphazardly, seeking the localities where the Indians were already settled. This practice had to be abandoned because of the raids of mamelucos hunting slaves to sell to the Portuguese planters of Brazil.

The Jesuit missions occupied land north and west of the Paraná in modern Paraguay, east of the Paraná in Brazil, between the Paraná and Uruguay rivers in Argentina, and south and east of the Uruguay in Brazil, thus stretching across three boundaries.

---

[35] Levene, ed., *Nación Argentina,* III, 595-622.

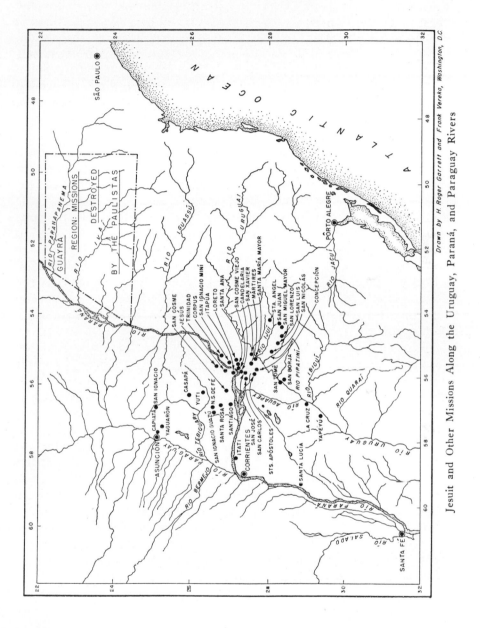

Jesuit and Other Missions Along the Uruguay, Paraná, and Paraguay Rivers

Drawn by H. Roger Garrett and Frank Vereta, Washington, DC

Map labels:

ATLANTIC OCEAN

SÃO PAULO

PORTO ALEGRE

RIO PARANAPANEMA
GUAYRÁ
REGION: MISSIONS
DESTROYED
BY THE PAULISTAS

RIO IVAÍ

RIO PARANÁ

RIO IGUASSÚ

RIO IGUAÇÚ

RIO URUGUAY

RIO JACUÍ

RIO PARANÁ

SAN COSME
JESÚS
TRINIDAD
CORPUS
SAN IGNACIO MINÍ
ITAPÚA
LORETO
SANTA ANA
SAN COSME VIEJO
CANDELARIA
SAN LORENZO
SAN XAVIER
MÁRTIRES
SANTA MARÍA MAYOR
STA. ANGEL
SAN JUAN
SAN MIGUEL MAYOR
SAN LORENZO
SAN LUIS
SAN NICOLÁS
CONCEPCIÓN

SAN TOMÉ
SAN BORJA
RIO PIPATINÍ
RIO IBICUÍ
RIO IJUÍ

ASUNCIÓN
CAPIATÁ
SAN IGNACIO
YAGUARÓN
CASAPÁ
YUTÍ
N.S. DE FÉ
SAN IGNACIO GUAZÚ
SANTA ROSA
SANTIAGO
ITATÍ
RIO TEBICUARY
RIO PARAGUAY
RIO BERMEJO

CORRIENTES
SAN JOSÉ
SAN CARLOS
STS. APÓSTOLES
LA CRUZ
YAPEYÚ
SANTA LUCÍA
RIO AGUAPEY
RIO QUARAÍ
RIO URUGUAY

RIO PARANÁ
RIO SALADO
SANTA FÉ

These were not the only Jesuit missions in the valley. The map drawn in 1750 to illustrate the boundary between Spanish and Portuguese territory shows their settlements north of Asunción along the Paraguay; and still farther north, now across the divide and in the valley of the Mamoré (eastern Bolivia).

The organization of the Jesuit Missions has been frequently described, with judgments of the results ranging from the effusive praise of the Jesuit historian, Charlevoix, to the much less flattering opinion of Félix de Azara, but with substantial agreement as to the form.[36] The capital of the Paraná-Uruguay missions was at Candelaria on the Paraná where the Father Superior lived. Each mission had two Jesuits charged respectively with its spiritual and material functions. Each village also had a *corregidor* (or *Jefe político*) and *alcaldes* and *regidores,* forming the cabildo as in Spanish villages, elected from among the Indians. The cabildo was, however, selected in effect by the Jesuits themselves, and all cases were decided by the Jesuits without appeal to civil authorities.

In the southern part of Chile the Jesuits penetrated the territory of the Araucanians and, although they suffered frequent martyrdoms, succeeded in establishing eight villages by 1767. In Peru, east of the Andes along the Marañon, the Jesuit planted other settlements, the number of families in their missions being some 15,000 by 1653; but the resistance of the Indians and the conflicts with the Portuguese reduced the number of Indians to 15,000 individuals (instead of as many families), by 1767. Other missions were founded in Ecuador to the east of the Andes along the headwaters of the Amazon among the Quijos and Maynas.[37] Missions, principally Franciscan, Jesuit, and Capuchin, were also established along the Orinoco and several of its confluents.

The difficulties of settlement in these regions, and the progress of the missions, with their good and bad points, were all observed by Alexander von Humboldt at the end of the colonial period:

"The religious orders have founded their establishments between the domain of the planters, and the territory of the free Indians. The Missions may be considered as intermediary states. They have encroached on the liberty of the natives no doubt; but they have almost everywhere been advantageous to the increase of population, which is incompatible with the unquiet life

---

[36] The classical history of the Jesuits in the Plata is Charlevoix, *Histoire du Paraguay,* written from the Jesuit viewpoint; cf. Ludovico Antonio Muratori, *A Relation of the Missions of Paraguay,* (London, 1759), an English translation of an earlier Italian work; and Félix de Azara, *Descripción del Paraguay,* chap. XIII.

[37] Pereyra, *América española,* VI, 195-98.

of the independent Indians. As the Missionaries advance toward the forests, and gain on the natives, the white planters in their turn seek to invade from the opposite side the territory of the Missions. In this protracted struggle, the secular arm continually tends to withdraw the reduced Indians from the monastic hierarchy, and after an unequal struggle, the missionaries gradually give way to curates. The whites, and the castes of mixed blood, favoured by the corregidors, establish themselves among the Indians. The Missions become Spanish villages, and the natives lose even the memory of their natural idiom. Such is the progress of civilization from the coasts toward the interior; a slow progress, shackled by the passions of man, but sure, and uniform." [38]

The missions were important in introducing organized agriculture and villages into what had hitherto been jungle. Where once were only wild tribes:

"The road leads through plantations of sugar, indigo, cotton, and coffee. The regularity, which we observed in the construction of the villages, reminded us, that they all owe their origin to monks and missions. The streets are straight and parallel; they cross each other at right angles; and the church is erected in the great square, situated in the center. The church . . . is a sumptuous edifice, but overloaded with architectural ornaments." [39]

Humboldt did not find, however, that the missions exercised a very civilizing influence over the Indians. He noted the cruelty of the *entradas* (conquests for religious motives) in which men, women, and children were brutally killed or imprisoned in the name of religion, and he found that many of the missionaries sold merchandise to the Indians at extortionate prices. Two weeks' work, for instance, was required to pay the price demanded by the missionaries of the Orinoco basin for enough coloring for an Indian to paint his body, as important to the Indian in establishing his social position as clothing is to us. The missionaries also isolated the Indians, took their produce as religious offerings and sold it, returning to the Indian little to compensate him for the loss of his freedom. [40]

---

[38] *Travels,* III, 214-15 [*Voyage,* III, 268-69].
[39] Humboldt, *Travels,* IV, 113-14 [*Voyage,* V, 137].
[40] Humboldt, *Travels,* III, 218-22; IV, 512-43; VI, 4-10, 37-39, [*Voyage,* III, 272-76; VI, 316-57; IX, 5-10; 45-47]; Depons, *Voyage to the Spanish Main,* II, 98-116 [Fr. ed. II, 123-145].

THE JESUITS

The Jesuits, owing to the extent and number of their missions, their schools, and their influence on the intellectual life of the colonies, represent the Church at its most effective usefulness. As missionaries they were among the most daring, as educators among the most assiduous, and as organizers the most efficient. Several factors favored their development. Expressly founded to combat the heresies of the Protestant Revolution, their organization was modeled on that of the Spanish army in the days of its ascendancy; their aim was to convert or reconvert through the medium of education; they had a centralized society whose world-wide activities were directed from one center; and they adopted a collectivistic economy that made the resources of one belong to all.

Not the least of the virtues of the Jesuits was the freedom of their convents from the factionalism and brawls that so often disturbed the other religious communities. Whereas many of the Orders elected their own superiors, the Jesuit leaders were appointed by the General in Rome. This was particularly important in America where many conflicting currents made the periodical elections a source of constant friction. The internal discipline of the Jesuits was much stricter than in most of the other Orders and they were more nearly free of scandals arising from sexual irregularity. They gained thereby a reputation for morality that was based too largely on chastity and ignored the broader aspects of ethical conduct.

Their educational institutions in the colonies, generally enjoyed greater reputation than those of their rivals, and among their members were some of the leading scholars of the age, the most famous teachers, and the most eloquent preachers. Their libraries were reputed the finest.

On the other hand, they never endowed the colonies with an extensive and intensive educational system. Their schools, like those of the other orders, housed a tiny portion of the total number of children, chiefly those who could pay for their education. Their libraries were composed mainly of works on theology, scholastic philosophy, the writings of church fathers, treatises on the ethics of the confessional, ecclesiastical legislation, lives of saints, accounts of miracles, and other matters of no practical value to the masses of the people. Most of these works were in Latin, and therefore available to only a small élite. The few works in their libraries on classical antiquity, history, geography, and science were usually outdated, and in the eighteenth century books of the new learning seldom found their way into Jesuit libraries.

Where they exerted a tremendous influence on the colonies was in their strict observance of the forms of religion. They were the most indefatigable preachers, not only in their own missions and monasteries, but in the convents of the nuns, in the churches, and in the jails. They had created numerous religious societies (*cofradías*). They held frequent religious celebrations, and processions organized with great pomp to impress the masses, who found in these activities one of the chief forms of diversion.

Most powerful in influencing the community was their wealth. They had devised ways of inducing legacies and grants for their order that were characteristic of their efficiency. They honored with the name of "founder" those who endowed a new convent or school, and "benefactor" those who made contributions to the same ends. For each of these they had two grades of spiritual benefits, the funerals, masses, and other honors being more or less pretentious according to the amount of the donation. But they were not dependent on private gifts alone. They received grants from the municipalities and from the governors of the various colonies. With the establishment of a new town they were usually ceded one side of the public square and extensive farm lands. Also, because of their powerful financial position, they were frequently in a position to buy up cheaply rural and urban property that was forced on the market by bankruptcy.

Slaves were among the most valuable possesions of the Jesuits. A close inventory would probably reveal that they owned thousands. That their treatment of the slaves was in keeping with the customs of the times is indicated by the stocks, chains, and other instruments of punishment found on their plantations at the time of their expulsion.

Their efficiency was displayed in the management of great fortunes. Unlike many of the other orders, each Jesuit congregation owned and managed its own properties, although it was required to make extensive donations to the central organization. The produce from their plantations and urban properties, which was actually the product of the work of slaves or mission Indians, was sold in local markets or exported to increase the Order's revenues. To avoid dependence on ordinary commercial channels, they established their own warehouses and stores, and certain of their members accompanied the goods to market. The complaints of rival merchants and the scandals produced by this commercialism caused Viceroy Amat of Peru to issue an order that the Jesuit merchants from Chile and Quito residing in Lima should return to their own

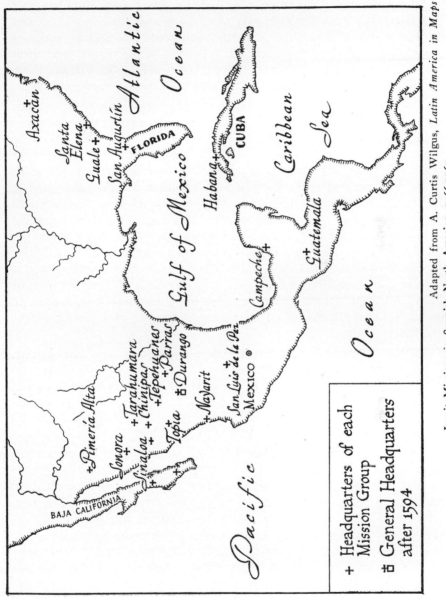

Axacan +

Santa Elena +
Guale +
San Augustin +

FLORIDA

Atlantic Ocean

CUBA

Habana +

Caribbean Sea

Guatemala +

Campeche +

Gulf of Mexico

Pimería Alta +

Sonora +
Tarahumara +
Sinaloa +
Chínipas +
Tepehuanes +
Topia +
Parras +
Nayarit +
☩ Durango
San Luis de la Paz +
Mexico ⊙

BAJA CALIFORNIA

Pacific Ocean

+ Headquarters of each
Mission Group
☩ General Headquarters
after 1594

Adapted from A. Curtis Wilgus, *Latin America in Maps*

Jesuit Missions in Spanish North America, 1566-1767

provinces because they were engaged in "the sordid exercise of commerce or trade which they carry on openly in the public squares, streets and markets, to the astonishment of the laity, and in the stores in their own convents, visiting at all hours, in order to make collections, taverns, public houses, and dives of the lowest sort whose business is of the most indecent." [41]

Other types of business they engaged in included rope making, pottery, textiles, tanneries, and ship building. They may also be accredited with the invention of the *tienda de raya,* or company store, of such dubious fame in modern times. On their plantations they had stores in which their workmen and local population traded.

And there were other sources of revenue. They collected fees for the various types of religious services rendered to individuals or the State. Missionary work in country districts was paid for by the bishops; frontier missions were supported by the Crown; the children who attended their schools paid fees; and the King paid the tuition of the Indian children in some of their schools. Whenever they suffered destruction of property because of Indian wars or other reasons, they appealed to the authorities and the Crown to recompense them, on the grounds that they were rendering a public service. Not the least among their resources was the privilege of tax exemption, which enabled them to compete with the secular merchants and other plantation owners on extremely favorable grounds.

They also established a form of collectivism, in which the members of the Order, but no others, participated. On entering the order each member surrendered his personal property and was never allowed to own anything for himself. All of their economic strength was thus centered. This fact also contributed, no doubt, to their reputation for morality. In many of the other orders and among the secular priests there was no prohibition against private property, and it was not unusual to see a priest or monk carrying on private trade, accumulating a fortune, and passing on his property to his relatives, among whom might be numbered his children.

When measured purely as an economic and commercial organization the Society of Jesus commands admiration. They were the nearest thing in their age to modern chain stores and efficient manufacturers. Their membership was drawn from all nations, and among those who arrived in America were a considerable number who introduced arts and crafts or improved processes, hitherto unknown. Their agricultural methods, and their skill in irrigation,

---

[41] Quoted in Barros Arana, *Chile,* VI, 274.

were models for the times. They enjoyed the same advantages as a great modern corporation in centralized administration, command of large capital, and even the ability to avoid taxation by using the ultimate legal technicality devised by the highest-priced lawyers. In sum, the Jesuits had acquired a position and standing in the Spanish colonies (and the world in general) that made them a state within other states, and their power transcended national boundaries. This was the character of the entire church organization, of course, but the efficiency of the Jesuits made them outstanding. Had they not aspired to even greater power they would not have been human, and had they not employed for the purpose the allegedly divine character of their mission they would have been angels.

EXPULSION OF THE JESUITS

It was inevitable sooner or later that such a mighty organization should come into head-on conflict with the State. The secular princes (and the Pope himself) believed that Jesuit ambitions included the elimination of all other powers. This may or may not have been true, but it was the motivation on which the monarchs of Europe acted. They were inspired, too, by the eighteenth-century ideas of liberalism, and the desire to tighten the strings of their own authority. The Marquis of Pombal had expelled the Jesuits from Portugal in 1759-60; Louis XV had done the same in France in 1764. Charles III of Spain followed suit in 1767.

In the Spanish colonies the expulsion was greeted with mixed feelings. Some of the other orders scarcely concealed their pleasure; and some, particularly the nuns, were griefstricken. The Carmelite nuns of Santiago, Chile, for example, placed the image of their patroness, Santa Teresa, on the altar, covered her with a black shawl, and refused to hear either mass, music, or sermon, threatening never to worship Santa Teresa again if the Jesuits were not restored. But the expulsion was carried out without serious opposition and with extraordinary speed and efficiency.

When the excitement and furor of the Jesuit expulsion had died down, and inventory could be taken, it was discovered that their accomplishments were not as solid as supposed. The Indians in their missions soon fell back into a barbarism from which, in truth, they had never been raised. [42] The missions of Paraguay disappeared, as did those of other regions. Some were taken over by

---

[42] See Moses, *Eve* p. 73, quoting Paredes, *La Provincia de Inquisivi*, pp. 75, 76: "The Indian neophyte under the Jesuits 'was a perpetual ward, restrained from the enjoyment of all civil liberties, without training for the transaction of business

other orders, only to reveal that the alleged great number of converted Indians did not exist, or that they knew but little more of
Christianity than the unconverted Indians. The Franciscans who
took over the missions of Chile reported that the Indians "were
as little enlightened, as destitute of instruction and of even the
fundamental truths of Christianity, and as settled in the gross ignorance of their errors, superstitions, and barbarous customs, as the
other nations of savages who never saw a missionary." [43]

THE CHURCH AND RELIGIOUS INSTRUCTION

The Church, as we have seen, controlled instruction, and had
what amounted to an intellectual, as well as a religious, monopoly.
Some people in the colonies escaped more or less the direct domination by the Church, but nobody (except perhaps those Indians who
never came under Spanish rule) ever escaped from the society which
the Church, more than any other institution, created. Education
was the instrument with which the Church fashioned the minds of
those destined to govern and to occupy the upper ranks of colonial
society. Those coming from Spain had already been educated by
the Church (if they received any formal instruction), and those
born in America were equally subjected to its influence. We have
already observed the defects of the Church's instruction from the
point of view of general education. From the religious viewpoint,
it was more successful, but this did not mean that the great masses
received any profound understanding of Christian doctrines.

The Clergy had complete charge of the Indians' mental training, and had nominally Christianized millions who were formerly
heathens. The *Leyes de Indias* had imposed on the Church a very
specific duty in this regard. How the duty was fulfilled in Peru in
the middle of the eighteenth century, is revealed by Juan and Ulloa.
On Sundays, when the Indians were instructed in Christian doctrine,

"All the Indians, male and female, great and small, are to
present themselves, and, gathering in the cemetery or square in
front of the church, they sit upon the ground, arranged according to age and sex, and the catechising of doctrine commences

---

on his own account, even for maintaining social relations with his fellows. He was
always a child and a semi-savage, so that when the Jesuits were expelled and he
found himself subject to the new government of violent corregidors and corrupt
parish priests, he scorned the liberty that was offered to him and to which he was
not accustomed and returned to the wilds'."

[43] Fray Miguel de Ascasubi, *Informe cronólogico de las misiones del reino de
Chile* [1789], quoted in Barros Arana, *Chile,* VI, 333-34; on the Jesuits, see Barros
Arana, *ibid,* VI, 266-334 and VII, 381-82; Means, *Fall,* 175, 201-02; Cleven, *op. cit.;*
Nos. 44 and 45; Blanco Acevedo, 156-58 and *passim;* François Rousseau, "The
Expulsion of the Jesuits in Spain; Steps of Charles III for their Secularization," *Revue
Historique,* LXXV (Paris, 1904), 113ff.

in the following manner: Each curate employs a blind Indian, whose duty is to repeat the *doctrine* to the rest. The blind Indian is stationed in the center of them all and, with a kind of recitative, which is neither singing nor prayer, he repeats the collects or offices, word for word, and the audience responds in the form of dialogue. The doctrine is sometimes rehearsed in the language of the Inca (which is that of the Indians), and sometimes in Spanish, which is not intelligible to any of them. This saying of prayers lasts somewhat more than half an hour, and it comprises all the religious instruction which is given to the Indians—a method from which they derive so little benefit that old men of seventy know no more than the little Indian boys of the age of six, and neither these nor those have any further instruction than parrots would obtain if they were so taught. . . . . As the whole instruction is confined rather to the tone of the recitative than to the sense of the words it is only by singing that they are able to rehearse detached portions; for, when they are questioned upon any distinct point, they cannot join two words together." [44]

The evidence of those who visited Mexico, or lived there in the last days of the colonial period, is similar. Humboldt observed:

"The natives know nothing of religion but the exterior forms of worship. Fond of whatever is connected with a prescribed order of ceremonies, they find in the Christian religion particular enjoyments . . . . Everywhere the Christian rites have assumed the nuances of the country where they have been transplanted . . . in the province of Pasto, on the ridge of the Cordillera of the Andes, I have seen Indians masked, and adorned with small tinkling bells, perform savage dances round the altar, while a monk of St. Francis elevated the host. [45]

Viceroy Revilla Gigedo II, in his report to his successor, also comments on the lack of religious understanding among the Indians of Mexico:

"What is regrettable is that such great expenditure, such labors and zeal, and so many wise measures. taken at all times for this purpose, have not produced the desired result, and the Indians are still very ignorant and uncultured in religious matters." [46]

This was 275 years after the Conquest, and its theoretical Christianization of Mexico.

---

[44] Juan and Ulloa, *Noticias secretas*, pp. 351-52, quoted in Moses, *Eve*, pp. 190-91.
[45] *New Spain*, I, 167-68 [*Nouvelle Espagne*, I, 411-12].
[46] Revilla Gigedo, *Instrucción*, par. 27.

In Chile, religious instruction was likewise superficial. Bishop Francisco de Borja Marán made a trip of inspection into the Indian territory in 1787, stopping at Arauco where he was led to expect that he would find the Indians well informed on Christian doctrine.

"The governing chieftain, his chieftains, subordinates, young men, and many women arrived with gifts to kiss the hand of his illustrious highness . . . . After receiving them, he started to examine them in the Christian doctrine in order to confer the sacrament of confirmation, and finding them ignorant of the barest principles, he refused them this spiritual aid . . . It is very strange that in the hundred and fifty years that have been employed in educating these people it has not been possible to teach them the catechism, and that they continue to practice their barbarous rites." [47]

The bishop found the same state of affairs in all the places he visited in southern Chile. The central cities had an abundance of clerics who lived in comparative idleness, but in northern Chile Copiapó had only one parish. The governor, Marques de Áviles (1796-98), wrote that many of the inhabitants "live such a brute-like life that they know only by name that there is a God. They are without a priest or a civil judge since, as they live in the parish of Copiapó, a priest commissioned by the curate goes among them only once a year at Easter time, and fleeing from the poverty and discomfort of that uncultured and sterile territory, he stays only twelve or fifteen days, the little instruction that he can impart to the inhabitants in such a short time being lost during the rest of the year." [48] This cleric collected from each inhabitant an *arroba* of dried eel which he sold for four to five pesos an arroba, thus making a good thing out of his fortnight of martyrdom.

It might be expected that the concept of Christianity among the Spaniards and Creoles would be of a much higher order, but this too was nearer superstition than reason. The Chilean chronicler José Pérez García, writing in 1804, asserted:

"We have for our illnesses and drouths two unique remedies which never fail. For epidemics, we have the *salus infirmorum* of our mother the Virgin of Mercedes who, when carried through the streets always, as is asked in her *novena*, 'purifies the infected air.' And when the rains fail we have our Virgin of Rosario

---

[47] *Diario del Viaje del obispo Marán en 1787,* quoted in Barros Arana, *Chile,* VII, 378.

[48] Quoted in *ibid.,* VII, 237.

who, as is said in her *novena,* never fails to bring rain when she appears in the street, for which she has acquired the name, significant of our confidence but improper for Her Majesty, of *La Aguatera* [the water girl]." [49]

Accompanying this faith in the images of saints was a cynical avoidance of Church services. Throughout the Indies, attendance was required at stated services and the communicant was given a certificate of attendance. Afterward the priest would go from house to house collecting the certificates, and those who could not produce them were subject to various ecclesiastical punishments. But there were a number of ways of avoiding the requirement, the easiest being to buy a certificate from the sacristan, or other persons who had taken communion several times in order to get the certificates. Depons observed the system in Venezuela: "The old women confess many times during Easter, and receive a receipt for each confession. They keep one for themselves and sell the others. The ordinary price is one peso, but it rises as the time to exhibit the certificate approaches." [50]

If the monopoly of mental training exercised by the Church had not succeeded in instilling any profound feeling for the essence of the Christian teaching, it had implanted a well-rooted respect for the authority of the Church, and few dared oppose it until the end of the eighteenth century. Even at that time the numbers who failed to observe its forms were extremely small.

THE WEALTH OF THE CHURCH

The wealth of the Church in America increased its otherwise great influence and, conversely, its influence increased its property. This wealth had been accumulated in spite of the Crown's intentions to prevent the Church from enriching itself as it had in Spain, and Europe generally. Philip III complained to the viceroy of Peru in 1620, less than a century after the founding of Lima, that the convents covered more ground than all of the rest of Lima. "Secular persons" had come to be "mere administrators of estates possessed by the Church" [51] and the monasteries held such large areas in Lima and other cities that "there are but few who do not pay rent to the Church, either for their houses or farms." [52]

---

[49] Cited in *ibid.,* VII, 383, note 62.

[50] Depons, *Voyage à la Terre Ferme,* I, 176 [Eng. ed. I, 104]; Barros Arana, *Chile,* VII, 387, note 65.

[51] Oliveira, *La política económica de la Metrópoli,* pp. 27-28, cited by Moses, *Eve,* p. 14.

[52] *A True and Particular Relation of the Dreadful Earthquake,* pp. 279-280, cited by Moses, *Eve,* p. 14.

When Humboldt visited New Spain he found provinces in which the Church controlled as much as eighty per cent of the land. Concerning the province of Puebla in Mexico, Humboldt states that "the greatest obstacle to the public prosperity arises from four-fifths of the whole property (*fincas*) belonging to mortmain proprietors; that is to say, to communities of monks, to chapters, religious brotherhoods, and hospitals." [53] "The wealth of the clergy," Alamán said of the Church in Mexico, "did not consist so much of the estates that it possessed, although these were numerous, especially the urban properties of the principal cities like Mexico City, Puebla, and others, as of capital invested in quitrent mortgages on the property of individuals; and the business of granting of mortgages and collecting interest made of every chaplaincy and religious brotherhood a sort of bank. The total property of the secular and regular clergy in estates and in loans of this type was certainly not less than half of the total value of the real estate of the country." [54]

In 1644 the cabildo of Mexico City petitioned Philip IV not to permit the foundation of more convents and monasteries, the nuns especially being too numerous and their servants more numerous still. The Cabildo complained of the thousands of clerics working at no useful occupation and of the great number of estates owned by the clergy, stating that unless the clergy was restricted, it would have everything. The estimate of 44,500,000 pesos for the wealth in 1805 of the clergy in México, made by Bishop Abad y Quiepo was considered too low by Alamán, who concluded that "evidently it is much greater, not only from what is known from the tax-lists on direct taxes drawn in recent years, but because of the fact that there is hardly an estate that is not mortgaged, many for the greater part of their value and others for more than their value." [55]

The tithes collected in New Spain, in addition to the revenues from estates and mortgages, amounted to more than 1,800,000 pesos annually at the end of the colonial period. In many cases the collection of the tithes was farmed out for a fixed sum, leading to oppressive measures by the tithe-farmers in order to increase the collections. The figure cited is what the Church got, not the greater amount actually collected.

There were many other types of church taxes which formed a part of its wealth. A law of 1532 decreed that new churches

[53] *New Spain*, II, 199 [*Nouvelle Espagne*, II, 277].
[54] Alamán, *Méjico*, I, 66-67.
[55] *Ibid.*, I, 68, note 46.

should be built by the royal treasury, the encomenderos of the district, and the Indians, each contributing a third of the cost. The Church paid into the royal treasury the taxes called *anatas,* which were a portion of the first year's revenue of the dioceses, parishes and other ecclesiastical units, a small part of the tithes, and other taxes known as *novenos, vacantes,* and *excusados.* Another tax collected in the name of religion, and from which the Church received benefits, was the *bula de la Santa Cruzada.* This was originally a papal indulgence for those who went to Jerusalem, but those who could not go were permitted to buy the indulgence. In America it became a religious duty to buy this *bula* every year or two, as proof of being a good Catholic. [56] The *derechos parroquiales* were fees for marriage, baptism, and burial, differing in various parts of America. In New Spain at the time of Humboldt's visit the Indians paid for baptism about two pesos, for marriage four pesos, and for burial four pesos. There was also levied on them a "voluntary" contribution of about five or six pesos a year known as *Cargos de cofradías, Responsos y Misas para sacar ánimas.* [57]

The main source of church wealth was the legacy which came from every individual who died. This custom had grown so fixed that it was impossible to avoid it. A French cleric, Father Labat, who traveled in Spain in the eighteenth century, observed: "According to the custom of this country a man would run the risk of exciting suspicions about his faith, and of being considered at the very least a Morisco or New Christian, if he did not leave a minimum of one-third of his property to the Church." That the situation in America was the same is attested by numerous writers. Depons, who lived for several years in Venezuela, noted that: "A will that did not provide some legacy for the convents was considered an irreligious act that left many doubts about the salvation of the soul that committed this error. . . . The mania for annuities accompanied that for donations to the convents. Whoever had property and failed on dying to leave a part of it subject to an annuity left a stain on his memory. Nothing more was needed to make quitrents abound. Hence, where is the property in the province of Caracas unburdened with one or many annuities? These acts, it is true, are now (1804) becoming much rarer and less important." [58]

---

[56] Riva Palacio, *México,* II, 695-703; Depons, *Voyage to the Spanish Main,* III, 31-41 [French ed. III, 34-46].

[57] Humboldt, *New Spain,* I, 186-187 [*Nouvelle Espagne,* I, 431-32]; Desdevises du Dezert, "Les Institutions de L'Espagne," *Revue Hispanique,* LXX (1927), 270-75.

[58] Depons, *Voyage à la Terre Ferme,* II, 149, [Eng. II, 119] .

Along with the great wealth of the Church there went an inequality of distribution that paralleled the general maldistribution of property. Concerning Chile, one writer comments: "If these considerable riches, the real estate possessed by the religious orders, the quitrents made over to the convents and the churches, and the produce of the tithe, had been distributed in an equitable fashion, the faith would have enjoyed a notable splendor throughout Chile, and all ecclesiastics would have led an easy life, stranger to all want. But this distribution was the most irregular imaginable. The religious orders put great stress on maintaining a certain brilliancy about their convents and churches in Santiago, Concepción, and some of the new cities, but those of the other towns and in some country districts were of the most modest construction, and usually of a shocking poverty." There was a like difference in the position of the upper and lower clergy, the higher clergy of Chile living a life of "abundance and opulence" while the lower "were subjected to a situation close to misery." [59] Such conditions were the rule. In Mexico Humboldt noted: "This inequality of fortune, is still more conspicuous among the clergy, of whom a large number suffer extreme poverty while others possess revenues which surpass those of many of the sovereign princes of Germany" ". . . in the diocese of an archbishop whose income amounts to 650,000 francs [25,085 pounds sterling a year], there are clergymen of Indian villages whose yearly income does not exceed five or six hundred francs." [60]

THE CONDUCT OF THE CLERGY

Aside from the great wealth amassed by the Church and its consequent power, the clergymen themselves, as the moral and intellectual mentors of the community, exerted an influence out of proportion to their numbers. This influence was so much the greater as the clergy were the representatives of God, and claimed to be divinely appointed to their places at the head of society. The moral codes they professed were drawn from Divine sources of which they were the sole interpreters. Therefore, their ethics and conduct should have been superior to those of other men, and they should have served (with the exceptions due to occasional human frailty) as models for others. We should be able to assume that the majority maintained the vows of poverty they professed, lived chastely, were animated by the human charity demanded by

[59] Barros Arana, *Chile*, VII, 374-75.
[60] Humboldt, *New Spain*, I, 229-32 [*Nouvelle Espagne*, II, 31-34].

the Bible, and, in short, so conducted themselves as to merit the respect they demanded of the community.

Only a brief examination is necessary, nevertheless, to find that the clergy in America fell short of this ideal. The assertion that the clergy in early sixteenth-century America were highly moral, and that the signs of decay later noted were the result of the conditions under which they lived in America, is largely erroneous. In the sixteenth century, the shortcomings of the clergy were the subject of bitter comment. For instance, the following charges were made in the last half of the sixteenth century by López de Aguirre.

"But the corruption of morals among the monks is so great in this land, that it is necessary to chastise them severely. There is not an ecclesiastic here, who does not think himself higher than the governor of a province. I beg of thee, great King, not to believe what the monks tell thee down yonder in Spain. They are always talking of the sacrifices they make, as well as of the hard and bitter life they are forced to lead in America; while they occupy the richest lands, and the Indians hunt and fish for them every day. If they shed tears before thy throne, it is that thou mayest send them hither to govern the provinces. Dost thou know what sort of life they lead here? Given up to luxury, acquiring possessions, selling the sacraments, being at once ambitious, insolent, and gluttons; such is the life they lead in America. The faith of the Indians suffers by such bad examples. If thou dost not change all this, O King of Spain, thy government will not be stable!" [61]

Aguirre's charge was made by a man whose whole manner of life was a complete negation of the Christianity he so fervently professed, but in this he was not conspicuously worse than the majority of his contemporaries, who found Christian reasons for doing the very things that their religion condemned.

Numerous other complaints against clerical corruption made in the early part of the sixteenth century have already been cited.[62] Humboldt gives the following story to illustrate the cynical attitude toward the clergy about 1800:

"The 16th of April, towards evening, we received tiding that in less than six hours our boat had passed the rapids . . . .
'Your boat will not be wrecked because you carry no merchan-

---

[61] Letter of López de Aguirre to Philip II, quoted in Humboldt, *Travels,* IV, 258-59 [*Voyage,* V, 313-16].
[62] See Chapter 13.

dise, and travel with the monks of the *Raudales,*' was said to us sneeringly by a little brown man, whom we recognized by his accent to be a Catalan, at the encampment of Pararuma . . . . 'The frail vessels,' he added, 'are those of the Catalans, when, provided with a license from the Governor of Guayana, and not with a permission from the president of the missions, they endeavour to trade beyond Atures and Maypures. After having caused our boats to be wrecked in the Raudales, which are the key of the missions of the Upper Oronoco, the Cassiquiare, and the Río Negro, they make the Indians of Atures reconduct us to Carichana, and oblige us to relinquish our mercantile speculations'." [63]

As previously noted, the Church condoned (and practiced) slavery and the slave trade on the grounds that it was better to enslave a man's body and save his soul than to leave him free and a heathen. Nor did clerical ethics scorn commerce which was frequently in contradiction to the laws and to the requirements of the Church. While the clergy made a considerable contribution to the economic development of the colonies, they were engaging in forms of trade which brought them down to the level of ordinary commercial competition, and they used their immunities to carry on tax-free trade, both regular and contraband. Merchants in Chile and elsewhere protested against the clergy's custom of bringing slaves and other goods from Argentina without paying taxes and selling them in Chile or Peru. The clergy also, as we have seen, made material profit from spiritual exercises, often robbing the very Indians whom they claimed to protect.

In 1802, at the induction of a new captain-general in Chile the welcoming speech cited the evils of the colony which, it was hoped, would be remedied; one of these was the clerical custom of cornering the fish market. Taking advantage of the Church requirement of fasting on holy days, the friars of Santiago sent their agents out to buy up all the available fish before it reached public markets. They then sold it at the doors of the convents, forcing the people (who were required on pain of ecclesiastical punishment to abstain from all meat except fish on the days specified by the Church) to pay prices much higher than those paid on other days. The abuse had long existed. Although Captain-General O'Higgins tried to stop it, it continued to the end of the colonial period. [64]

Colonial history is also full of examples of community disturb-

[63] Humboldt, *Travels*, V, 72-74 [*Voyage*, VII, 89-91]
[64] Barros Arana, *Chile*, VII, 258.

ances caused by the clergy. Among the chief causes of disruption
were the quarrels between the civil and the clerical authorities,
the rivalries among the various orders, the conflicts of these orders
with the secular clergy, and the factionalism within the monasteries
themselves. Armed attacks of one faction on another are on record, and they frequently reached the streets, involving laymen.
The convents of nuns were no more free of disturbances than
the monasteries. Complaints against the nuns included the charge
that they provoked quarrels through factionalism, did not observe
the rules of cloister laid down by their orders, and permitted unauthorized persons to enter the convents. [65]

If neglect of duty and addiction to worldly affairs had been
confined to a few clerics, or a few communities, it would have been
serious enough; but throughout the colonial period, and in all
parts of the colonies, the complaints against the clergy were numerous. Such charges were made by Chroniclers, many of whom
were clergymen themselves, and who were personal witnesses of
the corruption they condemned.[66]

One of the most arresting descriptions of clerical licentiousness
in the Viceroyalty of Peru in the eighteenth century is that of
Juan and Ulloa. If their evidence were not sustained by many other
writers it would be hard to accept, so inconceivably degraded are
the scenes they depict. But Juan and Ulloa are borne out by others,
and the following picture cannot be considered exceptional for the
Spanish colonies as a whole.

"The parish priests are extremely vicious in their habits;
but . . . disgraceful as the consequences are known to be, they
never reach such a degree of scandal as do those of the monks;
for the latter, from the first step they take, and even without
leaving the monasteries, pursue a course of conduct so notorious
and shameful that it becomes offensive in the extreme, and fills
the mind with horror.

"Concubinage is so general that the practice of it is esteemed
a point of honor; and when a stranger arrives and continues
his residence there for some time without having adopted the
customs of the country, his continence is attributed not to a
principle of virtue, but to the passion of avarice, as it is generally supposed that he lives so in order to save money.

"In large cities, the greater part of the monks live in private
houses, for the convents furnish an asylum to those only who

⁶⁵ Riva Palacio, *México*, II, 709-24,
⁶⁶ Means, *Fall*, 178-181, 198-201.

cannot keep house, or to the choristers, novitiates, and such like, who live there from choice. The same is true of the small cities, villages, and hamlets. The doors of the monasteries are kept open, and the monks live in their cells, accompanied by their women, and lead in every respect the life of married persons.

"The fandangos or balls are usually devised by the members of the religious orders, or more properly by those who call themselves religious, although, in fact, they are far from being so; for it is they who pay the expenses, who attend in company with their concubines, and who get up the fray in their own houses. Simultaneously with the dance, the immoderate use of ardent spirits begins, and the entertainment is gradually converted into acts of impropriety so unseemly and lewd, that it would be presumption even to speak of them, and a want of delicacy to stain the narrative with such a record of obscenities . . . ." [67]

Some authors attribute the "good blood" of the Spanish colonies to the system of concubinage that united the "best families" and the clergy. "It is a fact worthy of mention" says Paredes, "that in the provinces (cantones) it is rare to find a rich or white family that is not descended from some clergyman. The reputation for wealth enjoyed by the curate was such during colonial days and during the first years of the republic that the women of distinguished families did not scorn to belong to them and to live openly in concubinage (en mancebia pública) with clergymen. And in addition to this, the clergymen who went to the provinces were pleasure-loving and licentious, quick to take advantage of the favorable environment, leaving numerous descendants in the various localities in which they were stationed." [68]

The French explorer, La Pérouse, described the monks of Chile as "the most dissolute of men" and said "nobody, better than these same religious, gave our young men more exact information about the places with which the clergymen should not have been acquainted except to prohibit entrance into them." Quoting this, Barros Arana adds that "other witnesses are even more severe in their condemnation." [69]

CONCLUSION

The consensus of the charges against the Church may be stated as follows. The Church, on the basis of its claim to divine origin,

---

[67] Juan and Ulloa, *Noticias secretas*, p. 497, quoted in Moses, *Eve*, pp. 116-17
[68] Quoted in Moses, *Eve*, 73-74, note 1, in Spanish.
[69] Barros Arana, *Chile*, VII, 385.

sought to monopolize the moral and educational leadership of the
community, but failed to live up to the high standards such a
claim made incumbent upon it. The clergy customarily neglected
their duty, and used the spiritual powers of their calling for material ends at the expense of their charges. They enriched themselves through threats of ecclesiastical punishment, and profited
from flagrant injustice in the distribution of property. Individual
clergymen frequently employed their religious powers and privileges to build up personal fortunes. As individuals and collectively,
they took advantage of their tax exemption to compete unfairly
with lay craftsmen and merchants. In theory the protectors of the
natives, they often co-operated with civil officials in fleecing the
Indians of the little they had. Controlling all educational facilities,
they permitted only a small minority to receive any education whatever, and taught these the grossest forms of superstition, while
the clergy themselves remained ignorant, incapable, and unenlight-
ened. Thousands of them were idle in the cities, although in the
rural districts millions of people received neither intellectual nor
religious guidance, since no other agency but the Church was allowed to take up the task. The clergy engaged in constant quarrels
with the civil authorities, using their ecclesiastical rights to gain
purely temporal victories, and were also a disturbing element in
community life because of their incessant internal fights. Purport-
ing to set the moral standards, they frequently lived licentious
lives. As the only competent authorities for sanctifying marriage,
they condemned most children to be born illegitimate by setting
the marriage fees so high that the majority could not pay.

There is no case that does not have two sides. If all or most of
the above charges have a foundation in fact, it is equally true
that there are many points on which the Church can be defended.
Even if the divine origin of the Church were granted, it makes no
claims to have achieved perfection. Its monopoly on moral and
educational leadership was exercised largely by forfeit, there being
no other institution of the time to assume such responsibilities.
Neglect of duty was a human frailty of which laymen as well as
churchmen were guilty. Society has not yet solved the problem of
proper distribution of worldly goods, and it would be unjust to
lay too much stress on this point. If it is true that clergymen often
participated in the exploitation of the Indians, it is equally true
that many individual clerics distinguished themselves as defenders
of the native people. It may be granted also that the intellectual
training afforded by the Church was inadequate, but who would

have assumed this responsibility if the Church had not? The personal morals of the clergy were a reflection of the general morality of the time, and it could hardly be expected that the clergymen would be able to resist all the temptations placed in their way.

These are all extenuating circumstances that must be considered in making a final judgment, should the student be constrained to make one. If emphasis has been placed here on the shortcomings of the Church, it is largely in order to present an antidote to many works which have feared to deal with so delicate a matter. There is no subject harder to treat fairly. It is necessary to approach the question of the Church either from inside that institution or outside it, and in either case there are opposing viewpoints so far apart that reconciliation is impossible.

Government in Evolution

DURING THE COLONIAL PERIOD, Spanish-American government underwent considerable modification. The functions of the basic institutions, the Crown, the Council of Indies, the Casa de Contratacion, the viceroy and other royal officials, and the local government, were defined and delimited; and toward the end of the eighteenth century, alterations were made in response to the forces that were changing the world at that time.

THE CROWN

The Crown, claiming to rule by divine right, occupied an exalted position. Its claims had grown, rather than diminished, under the Bourbons, and the colonists in general did not question them.

> "The injustices and the abuses of the metropolitan government were not ascribed to the King but to his ministers and councillors, and to the administrators of those countries who had not seen to it that the truth reached the Throne. The veneration and love of the Creoles for the monarch did not extend, nevertheless, to the metropolis from which they were far removed, and which, in spite of the marvels that were told concerning the luxury and riches of the court, they supposed had sunk into a frightful and irremediable poverty." [1]

The King still stood completely above the criticisms of his subjects. The Viceroy of Peru, Gil de Taboada y Lemos, in 1796 stated: "The monarchs are the sacred substitutes of God himself for the earthly government of his peoples, and, exercising the power and the majesty *(grandeza)* which they receive from his divine hands, have as the authors of the civil codes and the guard-

---

[1] Barros Arana, *Chile,* VII, 472-73.

ians of the ecclesiastical laws, the double obligation to see that both the one and the other are observed in all purity." [2]

In accordance with the concept of absolutism nourished by both the Austrian and Bourbon houses, the Spanish administration sought to establish a uniform set of laws for Spain's vast dominions. As Philip II expressed it: "The kingdoms of Castile and of the Indies belong to the same crown; the laws and the system of government should be as nearly alike and identical as possible; likewise, the members of our Council should attempt in the laws and ordinances that they prepare for those states, to harmonize the form and method of their government with the style and methods which prevail and govern our realms of Castile and Leon, at least to the extent that the diversity of races and the differences of geography will permit." [3]

This may be taken as exemplifying the spirit in which Spain sought to govern America. Spanish administration no doubt attempted sometimes to legislate too minutely, and to force America to conform too exactly to the Spanish mold, for it was not always possible to agree just how far geographical and racial differences should be taken into account, nor to maintain the concept that America belonged to the Spanish Crown but not to Spain. While this theory might be tenable during the first years of the Conquest, it gradually became a myth. The Crown governed through the medium of its Spanish subjects, and the latter grew to look upon the American provinces as possessions of Spain, of the Spaniards themselves; and the position of the American provinces came to be that of colonies, governed by and for the benefit of Spain.

COUNCIL OF INDIES

The Council of Indies continued to administer the New World, and grew in authority as the chief legislative, executive, and judicial body for America until the eighteenth century, when its prerogatives were gradually lessened. At the height of its powers, it consisted of two chambers of government and one of justice. The first chamber of government had eleven members in 1804, and administered the colonies located in North America; the second, also composed of eleven members, was charged with the affairs of

---

[2] Gil de Taboada, *Relación*, in *Colección de memorias de los Virreyes que han gobernado el Perú*, ed. Manuel Anastasio Fuentes (6 vols., Lima, 1859-60), VI, 10; cf. Moses, *Eve*, p. 219. The best picture of the veneration of the King known to this writer is in Miguel Luis Amunátegui, *Los precursores de la independencia de Chile* (2nd ed., 3 vols., Santiago, 1909-1910), I, 31-46.

[3] Quoted in Desdevises du Dezert, "Institutions de l'Espagne," *Revue Hispanique*, LXX, 118-19.

South America. The chamber of justice had seven councillors besides various judges for special matters. There were in addition
numerous other officials, including four accountants, a treasurer,
two solicitors-general, a chronicler, a cosmographer, a professor of
mathematics, and many others with their respective assistants.
Most of the high officials had served in America. The members
were further divided into councillors of the Robe who were graduates in law, and councillors of Cape and Sword who were not
lawyers.[4]

Although by the end of the eighteenth century, the power of the
Council had been somewhat diminished, the organization was by
no means defunct. Direct royal intervention had, in a measure,
supplanted, but not extinguished its functions. The ministers increasingly acted through "royal orders," instead of through the
Council, but in judicial matters the latter often successfully resisted
arbitrary government rulings. [5]

Legislation over the head of the Council was one more step in
the succession taken by the Crown to draw power into its own
hands. Beginning in the Middle Ages, as already pointed out, the
Crown took for itself powers formerly held by the nobles, the
Church orders, or the municipalities. At the same time, the ancient
Cortes, representative of the propertied and privileged classes, were
gradually supplanted by the Councils of Castile, Aragon, Flanders,
Italy, or such special councils as those of the Mesta or the Inquisition. The Council of the Indies represented this power in America,
the Crown having quite early stifled the attempt to start the representational system exemplified in the meetings between the towns.
The measures designed to supplant the Council of Indies were still
another move in the direction of absolutism.

Casa De Contratación

The Casa de Contratación developed and extended the powers
of economic control granted to it in the sixteenth century, forming
a complementary body to the Council. "If it is said that the Council
of Indies stood for the king in political matters, and the India
House in economic affairs, the significance of the latter body is not
thereby fully presented. The activity of the India House is contrasted with that of the Council of the Indies by its larger executive
functions, its more immediate participation in the practical work of
administration, and by acting as the agent of the Spanish king in

---

[4] Desdevises du Dezert, *ibid.*, see Schäfer, *op. cit.*, for an account of the Council
to 1700; Moses, *The Spanish Dependencies,* I, 230-34.

[5] Alamán, *Méjico,* I, 36.

maintaining and carrying out the laws relating to the Indies. Its jurisdiction was without special territorial limits; it covered all matters embraced in the ordinances and reached all persons who contravened these ordinances. All cases arising from theft or any other crime committed on the voyage to, or returning from, the Indies—in fact, all cases under the laws of the Indies—fell within its exclusive province." [6]

By degrees, as points of dispute arose between the Casa and other judicial or administrative units of Spain, the Casa won a larger degree of power and respect. It was charged with fitting out the great Armada of 1588, and its officials won a position of independence from all other institutions except the Council of Indies. By the decisions of the Crown the officials of the Casa found that "their power increased; their credit rose; they appointed officers of fleets and civil magistrates; they granted passes to ships; and in importance and dignity they stood next to the royal councillors. They enjoyed the same privileges and immunities as the judges of the chancery and of the other courts." [7] From 1655, the Casa gained full judicial powers over its own members to the exclusion of all other courts, and had the authority to inflict any punishment.

During the first eighty years of its life the Casa was composed of only one chamber. However, in 1583, a chamber of justice was created to try all criminal cases except those not involving the prerogatives of the King, which might be tried in other courts at the will of the litigants. In 1546, a *fiscal* (solicitor) was appointed to act as "the king's mouth in causes wherein he is concerned, a check upon those that manage the revenues, a spy upon those who embezzle it, an informer against those that defraud it, an agent to improve it, and lastly a two-edged sword in a civil and criminal capacity to defend the patrimony of the Crown." [8]

The duties of provisioning, inspecting, and licensing the fleets and armadas of the Indies continued to be the responsibility of the Casa and grew constantly more complex. The returning fleets were examined to determine whether they had complied with all the laws, whether all of the crew had returned, whether any crimes had been committed, and whether the crew had been properly paid by the masters. In case the crew had not been paid, a three-day period was granted after which the ship master was arrested and extra pay given to the crews. Immediately upon the arrival of a fleet from America a full report was made to the Council of Indies and

[6] Moses, *The Spanish Dependencies*, I, 235-236.
[7] Moses, *The Spanish Dependencies*, I, 237.
[8] Quoted by Moses, *The Spanish Dependencies*, I, 240-41.

LATIN AMERICAN CIVILIZATION

the King. So numerous were the activities of the Casa that fourteen sets of books were kept.

The methods of the merchants in trade were in accord with the policies of the Casa de Contratación, and at times they encroached on the authority of the royal officials. Before the end of the sixteenth century, it became customary for government officials to accept the valuations of merchants without inspecting shipments, examining cargo, or checking the accuracy of certificates of lading. There were some efforts made to prevent this, but the opposition of both the Casa de Contratación and the merchants prevailed with the Crown. An important motive in resisting examination was the desire to keep the nature and amounts of shipments secret. Owing to the monopoly of quicksilver used in mining, the Casa also managed this commerce.

The year 1625 marks a turning point in the history of the Casa. Until then the officials were royal appointees and merit was considered in choosing them but, in 1625, the Count-Duke of Olivares, favorite and prime minister of Philip IV, was named as one of the commissioners of the Casa and given the office of chief *alguacil* in perpetual and hereditary right. The office of chief *alcalde* was created and similarly bestowed on the Count of Castrillo. Both of these posts included perquisites and appointive powers previously exercised by the Council of Indies. This hereditary system was certainly not calculated to increase the efficiency of the Casa. Perhaps other considerations besides merit had entered into the appointment of officials previously, but in certain offices favoritism now became the primary consideration.

The Casa was moved to Cádiz in 1717-1718 because of the greater convenience of this harbor and, though shorn of many powers, maintained an important position until 1790 when it was abolished. Its influence as an instrument of state was probably greater than that of the Council of Indies, because of its more intimate contact with America, its handling of detail, and the many political aspects of the powers granted to it. [9]

THE VICEROY

The viceroy, named by the King for a limited period, occupied the top of the governmental structure in America. He was invested with extensive powers, as has already been made clear in the treatment of his position during the sixteenth century. The quality of the men who served as viceroys varied considerably, but usually reflected fairly accurately the state of government in Spain itself,

---

[9] Moses, *The Spanish Dependencies,* I, 240-62.

Some inducement to good administration was offered by the custom of promoting the viceroy of New Spain to the post in Lima if he had served well, or of choosing ex-viceroys for high posts in the Council of Indies or the Casa.[10] As the viceroy in Lima enjoyed a higher salary and was considered superior in category, the chances of receiving this post acted as a stimulant to honesty.

By the end of the eighteenth century, the viceroys had lost some of the power granted them at the beginning of the sixteenth, but this loss could be easily exaggerated. It came largely through the complications of government machinery making it impossible for one man to assume all the duties originally assigned the viceroy. As the problems of government grew with the expansion of the Spanish rule in America, new agencies were created, or new powers given to old agencies, thus diminishing the prerogatives which had made the viceroy more powerful in America than the King himself in Spain, since the traditions and institutions binding the King had not yet evolved to the point where they restrained the viceroy to the same extent. That the viceroy still had great freedom of action in the late colonial period is clear from the following:

"In the epoch we here discuss, the power of the viceroys was modified by prudent advice arising from the intervention of other officials in various branches of governmental action, the viceroys retaining nevertheless all the splendor and pomp of the supreme authority . . . ." "But though all these restrictions had the very laudable object of limiting and reducing within the limits of the law a power that bordered on the royal, the distance and the very extent of this authority frequently rendered illusory these precautions. One viceroy of Mexico [Linares] . . . said regarding this: 'If he who comes to govern [this kingdom] does not remind himself frequently that the most rigorous residencia is that one to which the viceroy will be subjected in his personal trial by the divine majesty, he can be more sovereign than the great Turk because he will not plan any iniquity without there being someone to make it easy for him, nor perform any tyrannical act which will not meet with acquiescence.' The court contributed to these abuses by dispensing with the residencia at times. These dispensations did not always fall on those least free of responsibility, [but] . . . on the contrary, the most honest were treated with severity. Thus, in the last years [of the colony] it had been observed with horror that while the noted viceroy, the Count of Revilla Gigedo, was subjected to all of the molestations of a

---

[10] Riva Palacio, *México*, II, 665.

rigorous trial . . ., his successor, the Marquis of Branciforte, who was certainly not the most immaculate of those who had held the office, was excused from the residencia, King Charles IV, or rather his favorite, Godoy, the brother-in-law of the man thus favored, declaring himself satisfied with his [Branciforte's] integrity and good services." [11]

Viceroy Revilla Gigedo II gives an excellent picture of the powers of the viceroy shortly before independence, in the *instrucción* which he left to his successor.

"The expressions which may be read in the second law of the Title dealing with viceroys and presidents in the Recopilación de Indias confer the highest honors and give the maximum concept of the position of the viceroys. The provision is there made that in all the matters, cases, and affairs that arise they may do whatever they may see fit, and whatever seems best, and whatever His Majesty himself could do, of whatever nature or character, in the provinces under their government, provided it not be specifically prohibited." [Furthermore] "all bodies and persons are ordered to obey and respect the viceroys and their orders without excuse or interpretation and without consulting His Majesty, as if they were signed by his royal hand. And His Majesty promises, finally, on his royal word of honor, that whatever the viceroys may do in his name, and by his power and prerogatives, will be held as settled, stable, and valid forever." [12]

This last provision indicates that the limits on the viceroy's prerogatives in many cases were scarcely discernible. However complete the laws, and we have stressed the effort to make them all-inclusive, they could not possibly foresee every circumstance, leaving ample room for the viceroy to take any action "not specifically prohibited." There were many things, moreover, which preserved for the viceroy prerogatives and powers apparently denied to him by the laws.

"A governor who chooses to renounce all delicacy of sentiment, and considers himself as having come to America for the purpose of enriching his family, finds means for accomplishing his end, by favouring the richest individuals of the country in the appointments to public offices, in the distribution of the mercury, and in privileges granted in time of war to carry on free trade with the colonies of neutral powers. For some years past, the ministry

[11] Alamán, *Méjico*, I, 41-43.
[12] Revilla Gigedo, *Instrucción*, pars. 5-9.

of Madrid has deemed it to be to its interest to make appointments even to the smallest situations in the Colonies. However,
the recommendation of the viceroy is still of great importance
to the person who solicits, especially if the object solicited be a
military charge, or a title of nobility (título de Castilla), which
the Spanish Americans are in general much more eager for than
the European Spaniards. A viceroy, it is true, has no right to
make any commercial regulations, but he may interpret the
orders of the court; he may open a port to neutrals, by informing
the King of the urgent circumstances which have determined
him to have recourse to that step; he may protest against a re-
iterated order, and accumulate memoirs and informes; and if he
is rich, adroit, and supported in America by a courageous assessor, and at Madrid by powerful friends, he may govern arbitrarily without fearing the residencia. . . ." [13]

THE AUDIENCIA

The audiencia's authority continued to develop, pari passu, with
the decline of the viceroy's, although the relative powers of viceroy
and audiencia depended to a great extent on the personal strength
of one or the other at any given time. The powers of the audiencia
were nominally judicial, but the advisory functions granted by the
laws were transformed into checks on the viceroy and the captains-
general (or civil governors as the case might be), and its option
in enforcing the laws or administrative acts of the executive officers
developed into a form of judicial review similar to that of the
United States Supreme Court. The audiencias had authority over
their respective districts ressembling that of the Council of Indies,
over the whole of the New World.

The prestige of the audiencias was augmented by the reputation
for integrity the judges usually enjoyed. Owing to the honor in
which they were held, as well as the lucrative special commissions
given them to administer or inspect certain branches of the government, posts in the audiencia were much sought after. There were
established lists of promotion from offices in lesser audiencias to
those of higher rank. [14]

On account of the long service of the judges, in comparison with
the viceroy, their continuity in office, and the natural tendency of
all governmental bodies to arrogate to themselves as much power
as possible, joined with the large authority specifically given it by

---

[13] Humboldt, New Spain, IV, 232-33 [Nouvelle Espagne, V, 29-31]
[14] Alamán, Méjico, I, 44-45.

the laws, the audiencia tended to exercise very great and frequently increasing powers to the very end of the colonial period. [15]

PRIVILEGED COURTS

In addition to the audiencias, colonial government embraced many other types of courts, the most important being those of the Church and the *consulados*. Some of these have been discussed. [16] Others merit further discussion.

The Council of War, created in the reign of Charles V, was reformed by Philip V in 1706 and 1743 and reorganized by Charles III in 1773. This council converted the military of Spain into a privileged corps second only to the clergy, and its power and independence had a considerable influence on the development of Spain and hence also on colonial Latin America. The members of the Council of War were the King, the minister of war, and the chief military men. It had final jurisdiction in criminal and civil cases over all individuals brought before the military courts of Spain. The scope of its authority was much wider than that of contemporary military courts and included numerous cases that would today be tried by civil magistrates. The military were almost immune from prosecution by civil authorities; and civilians who came into conflict with the military were in many cases tried by military judges. The Council of War was constantly in conflict with the other tribunals, especially with the Council of Castille. [17]

In America likewise, the military courts formed one of the many privileged bodies which were free from civil jurisdiction in numerous cases. All these special courts disputed jurisdiction not only with the civil and criminal courts of the Crown, but with one another.

Señoríos, or feudal domains, with their courts, had been created early in the colonial period. New Spain had two, the Señorío of Cortés (Marquisate of the Valley of Oaxaca), and the Duchy of Atlixco. Judicial officials were named by the holder of the Señorío, and had authority to judge cases in the first instance, the more serious cases being appealable to the criminal court of the audiencia.

The consulados, which had been established in Mexico City (1593-94), Lima (1613), Vera Cruz, and other cities, to represent the merchants, were able to maintain their own privileges through their charters and courts, which heard and decided orally suits involving a thousand pesos or less. Where larger amounts were in-

---

[15] Blanco Acevedo, *Uruguay colonial*, pp. 135-38.

[16] See pp. 572-73.

[17] Desdevises du Dezert, "Institutions de l'Espagne," *Revue Hispanique*, LXX, 126-28.

volved, trial was held before a tribunal composed of the dean of the audiencia and two representatives of the parties with right of appeal to the Council of the Indies. Some consulados were governed by the charters previously granted to those in Spain, Mexico City's being modeled after Burgos, and that of Vera Cruz after Bilbao. During the eighteenth century, consulados were set up elsewhere in Spanish America to handle the growing trade of Cuba, Chile, and the Plata region. The most prominent of the later consulados was Buenos Aires, created in 1794. Deputies were authorized to sit in Montevideo, although a completely separate consulado was not set up for Uruguay until 1812.[18] The primary object of the consulado in judicial affairs was to decide cases between the merchants, but its prerogatives were intentionally such that it could defend the special interests of the merchants as a class, in accordance with the theories of government by privilege.

The *Cuerpo de Minería,* or mine owners, also formed a privileged group, constituted in 1774, and empowered to try many cases which were considered to concern them alone. Disputes were decided by special courts formed by the mine owners, with right of appeal to the central tribunal at Mexico City, and, ultimately to the *tribunal de alzadas,* of the audiencia.[19]

THE RESIDENCIA AND THE VISITA

The residencia, which had been established very early in America to assess the work of outgoing officials, was in theory a careful check on their honesty and efficiency. There can be little doubt that it was frequently effective. In other instances, however, the residencia was an instrument of dishonest officials to persecute honest ones, as in the case of the Count of Revilla Gigedo, or could be turned into a farce by bribery and favoritism as it was by Godoy and Viceroy Branciforte.

Officials dreaded the residencia, nevertheless, partly because it could serve to check up on them, and partly because it could serve as a vehicle by which their enemies could persecute them. Viceroy Revilla Gigedo, before the rigorous residencia to which he was subjected, condemned the system: "The residencias have been considered as a means of avoiding abuses in the administration of justice, and restraining the judges, but the truth of the matter is that experience demonstrates how little is gained by this method, more onerous in general for the faithful servants of the King, whom it

---

[18] Blanco Acevedo, *Uruguay colonial,* pp. 141-46; Haring, *Trade and Navigation,* p. 45, note 2.

[19] Alamán, *Méjico,* I, 57-62.

obliges to bear an expense they can ill afford, . . . and who are prevented from continuing in the King's service." [20]

A trial of royal officials did not always await the end of their term, since it was the custom of the Crown to send *visitadores* to inspect the affairs of a viceroy, captain-general, or other official at irregular intervals. The success of such a representative, from the royal viewpoint, depended on his honesty and the secrecy with which he could be dispatched. Some *visitadores* were subject to pressure and effected few reforms; others, notably José de Gálvez in the eighteenth century, were men of such character and ability that they promoted important changes in both the structure and the spirit of colonial government.

THE LAW CODES OF THE INDIES

With the discovery of America, and the rapid succession of new legislation that had to be promulgated for its government, there soon came into being such a multiplicity of laws that administrators, courts, and attorneys were frequently at a loss to find what law applied to the situation under consideration. A number of codifications, some partial and others outstripped by the accumulation of new laws, were made before the monumental *Recopilación de las Leyes de Indias* in 1681, embracing all phases of colonial legislation. [21] From publication, the Leyes de Indias became standard code. Its republication during the nineteenth century indicates that it was still in use in those parts of the colonies that had not been lost to Spain during the wars of independence; and a very large degree of colonial law passed into the national period of Latin-American history, "surviving the revolution and being incorporated into national legislation." [22]

The code itself provided that where the Laws of the Indies did not apply, there should be recourse to the Laws of Toro, thus expressing the desire of the Crown for administrative unity. At the same time, the Leyes de Indias also recognized the pre-Conquest laws and customs of the Indians, providing that the laws of the Indians remained in force if not in conflict with the Catholic religion or the Laws of the Indies. Indian customs had, in fact, a great influence on the development of colonial law, and were frequently cited by Solórzano Pereira and other prominent jurists. [23]

Numerous additional laws were enacted after 1681 of course,

---

[20] Revilla Gigedo, *Instrucción*, par. 140.
[21] See Chapter 24.
[22] Blanco Acevedo, *Uruguay colonial*, p. 150.
[23] Ricardo Levene, "El derecho consuetudinario y la doctrina de los juristas en la formación del derecho indiano," *H.A.H.R.*. III (February, 1920), 144-51.

and these formed a supplement to the legislation in force in America. During the last half of the eighteenth century, the tenor of the laws changed considerably, and Charles III considered a new codification, but this was not carried through and the Leyes de Indias remained in effect. [24] In 1805, on the eve of independence, a recodification was started, but not completed.

LOCAL GOVERNMENT: THE CABILDO

Government in America was only in part a matter of laws projected from Madrid, as we have already seen. The development of the powers of local institutions, and the dilution of the laws when applied to local situations in America, so modified the imperial administration as to be of equal, if not superior, influence. To study the government of colonial Latin America through legislation enacted in Spain, without taking into consideration the modifications effected by local governments in America, would be the equivalent of reading the American constitution of 1787 to find out how the United States was governed during the twentieth century. The two most important representatives of local government in Spanish America were the cabildo and the encomendero, representing urban and rural government respectively.

The cabildo, implanted by the first conquistadores, played a vigorous part in the early colonial period. The installation of royal officials with superior powers at a slightly later date has led to the interpretation of the cabildo's history in America as a "rise and decline," predicated on the assumption that the cabildo in Medieval Spain was a democratic institution which decayed with the rise of despotism. It has been previously pointed out that town government in the Middle Ages, characteristic of the whole of Western Europe and not of Spain alone, was autonomous but not democratic. [25] When local autonomy gave place before the superimposition of the national government, there was a substitution of central authority exercised by hereditary and privileged classes for local authority exercised by privileged (and in most cases) hereditary classes. Some confusion has arisen also from the use of the word *"república"* in referring to the town administrations, but this term was also used by the monarchs at times, and in the Spanish and Latin forms meant no more than "public affairs."

The cabildo as planted in America was only slightly democratic, if at all, and its development was not democratic. Since its functions

---

[24] Desdevises du Dezert, "Institutions de l'Espagne," *Revue Hispanique,* LXX, 116-19.

[25] See Chapter 14.

of local administration were so largely of an economic nature, the cabildo was from the first in the hands of men of property, and continued to be so during the whole of the colonial period. To speak of the cabildo as "decaying" is merely to acknowledge the development of national states that took place in the transition from medieval to modern times.

The cabildo did not have identical functions in all parts of America, and each cabildo varied in some respects from the others, its development being affected by its location. Cabildos under the eye of the viceroy in Lima or Mexico City naturally had less freedom of action than those farther from central authority. Others, like those in Montevideo, western Argentina, and Chile, became the centers of very definite localistic feeling which was not directed against Spain so much as against some of the neighboring colonies. However, certain minimum functions were common to all the cabildos.

Montevideo may be taken as a cabildo whose general functions were those of practically every other in America in the eighteenth century, while at the same time it developed certain local characteristics. The cabildo of Montevideo was formed in 1730, four years after the founding of the city, and its functions defined in accordance with the Laws of the Indies. Early activity was not intense, owing to the smallness of the population and unimportance of the town at the time. At first, the meetings were infrequent, and the acts mention many absences because the members "were on their estates or riding the range."

The first members were named by the governor of Río de la Plata, whose seat was in Buenos Aires, and who also appointed the military governor. The powers of the cabildo and the military governor were theoretically distinct, the former representing the political and administrative interests of the city and its surrounding territory, and the latter the military authority for the city's defense. There should have been no reason for conflict, but in practice both desired to exceed their theoretical powers. Past history, tradition, and custom in Spain made the cabildo the superior administration. The military commander lacked legal political authority, but as head of the local garrison, he was responsible for internal order, and was permitted to attend the meetings of the cabildo. Although he was not supposed to act in any but a military capacity, the commander was in constant struggle with the cabildo. Each municipality had its own type of jurisdictional strife, but in a situation like Montevideo's, circumstances inclined the balance in the cabildo's favor. The tradition behind it, its continuity, and the fact that it was made up of local men, in touch with the everyday life of the community, gave the cabildo more weight than an outsider, appointed by the governor in Buenos Aires and removable at his will.

An elaborate system of rules attempted to guarantee honest elections, but the community at large had nothing to do with the selection of members for the cabildo. The successors to the originally appointed members were named or "elected" by the outgoing office-holders, under a system that resembles the "closed vestry" of early Virginia history. The term of office was for one year. The members were required to be householders, "and notorious poverty was a cause for disqualification." [26]

Certain restrictions and obligations were placed on members of the cabildo. During their terms, they could not sell or trade for themselves, or own a store, or follow "base occupations" (oficios viles). They were forbidden to absent themselves from the city jurisdiction without the consent of the cabildo and the governor. They were required to meet once a week, a rule that was modified to once a month in the ordenanzas, and to whenever they had business in practice. Discussions and votes were secret, and the cabildo could demand the appearance of any resident of the city jurisdiction for questioning, such individuals being required to answer but having no voice beyond replying to the questions asked them.

The varied duties of the officials reveal that the cabildo exercised an extensive power within its jurisdiction. Among the matters under its supervision were urban sanitation and health, street paving and lighting, regulation and supervision of the city meat supply, stores, food shops, bakeries, and places selling spirituous liquors. The cabildo passed laws governing all these establishments or revised those already in effect. Questions concerning the beautification of the city, the construction of public buildings, hospitals, churches, convents, charitable institutions, and cemeteries all fell under its authority, as did matters concerning schools and instruction, the pase and promulgation of Papal Bulls, mail service, and weights and measures. It was responsible for policing the surrounding territory to prevent cattle running and illicit slaughter, and it supervised wood cutting and the forests, hunting and fishing, and matters regarding the farm lands surrounding the city. It regulated all public festivals, the bull fights and theatre, and "ordered religious services or prayers in the churches to seek the aid of or ward off nature's phenomena in the public interest." Jails and care of the prisoners

---

[26] Blanco Acevedo, Uruguay colonial, pp. 109-110.

were under its control. Its police powers enabled it to regulate the carrying of arms, vagrancy, meetings and music in the cafés, billiard halls, and brothels, tangos and the dances of the Negroes, as well as to enforce the curfew. The cabildo could also exact fines for violation of its ordinances or, in criminal cases, impose a prison sentence, calling on the militia and regular troops for the enforcement of these ordinances.

Other powers included assessing municipal taxes. The taxes on the slaughter houses and the revenue from the *"propios"* (lands belonging to the municipality) were its first chief income. The sale and leases of the public lands, and the prices of their crops and produce were all under cabildo management. Presently, imposts on articles of "luxury or folly," bars, cafés, billiard halls, warehouses, and business generally were added, with income from the auctioning of various public services such as lighting, and of concessions for supplying the city with food. Still another tax was levied from time to time, usually in periods of stress, on the citizens in proportion to their ability to pay. It was frequently called a "voluntary contribution," but the term was a mere euphemism. [27]

The cabildo, as representative of the municipality, also had the right of appealing to officials such as the captains-general or viceroy, or directly to the Council of Indies—the latter course being more usual perhaps since conflicts were so frequent with the King's officials. This right of appeal was of no small importance. Whereas the royal officials were supposedly impartial as between the various localities, in practice the captains-general and the viceroys, as well as others, were apt to view the interest of the whole through the eyes of the community in which they were established. Numerous lawsuits between towns sprang up in the Council of Indies. Montevideo conducted many suits against Buenos Aires, arising largely out of the commercial rivalry of the two ports, and in accordance with its rights under the Laws of the Indies, appointed attorneys to reside in the Court and watch over its interests. [28]

The development of colonial rivalry and the adjustment of the cabildo to its particular local situation must be considered among the most important aspects of the institution. Many cabildos tended to develop functions beyond those visualized by the law. True, the cabildos, unlike the medieval communes, exercised no control over foreign affairs, were liable to taxation by a higher power, and were subject to the police powers of the national government. But in the

[27] Blanco Acevedo, *Uruguay colonial*, pp. 117-19.
[28] *Ibid.*, 122-23.

innumerable details of local government, only a portion of which have been mentioned, the cabildo remained important. It was the power closest to the life of the people and probably the only institution of government that was daily visible to the majority. The extent to which people felt Spanish rule was in large measure dependent on the interpretations and enforcement of Spanish legislation by the cabildo. [29]

The powers of cabildos ranged from the limited functions of those in the towns directly under the viceroys, to near absolutism in some of the small towns far removed from the eyes of the royal officials. An example of the latter may be found in Oruro, Bolivia (which was under the viceroyalty of Lima until 1776 and thereafter under Buenos Aires), where two brothers, Juan de Dios and Jacinto Rodríguez, installed themselves for a time as local dictators. The exact reverse occurred in New Spain, where an attempt was made in the *Provincias Internas* to give to the Captain of militia and his lieutenants the rights of alcalde and lifetime regidores in each town. This experiment was of short duration, however, since it violated the whole basis of cabildo tradition. [30]

It was the audiencia which, more directly than the viceroyalty, curbed the cabildo. A strong audiencia meant a weak cabildo in the same locality. Mexico City is a case in point. During the early days of the independence movements the audiencia informed the cabildo that its powers were limited to keeping the beggars in their places. The plans made by the cabildo for the calling of a national assembly were paralyzed by the audiencia.

On the other hand, at about the same time in Buenos Aires, the audiencia "disappeared like a phantom" before the cabildo which there was much older and stronger in traditions. [31] Asunción offers another example of the strong cabildo. Very largely isolated by its geographical position, Asunción from its first establishment developed considerable independence from the central authority. Located in the midst of a continent, the cabildo of Asunción was able to exercise power over extensive adjoining regions where it had no rival, and to defy central authority for many years. In the Río de la Plata region in general, where authority was far away, cabildos were vigorous.

---

[29] For an example of the varied functions of the cabildo see: *Acuerdos del extinguido cabildo de Buenos Aires* (1st, 2nd and 3rd series in *Archivo general de la nación*, Buenos Aires, 1925). Similar records are available for Santiago, Chile, Lima, Peru, and many other cities.

[30] Desdevises du Dezert, "Institutions de l'Espagne," *Revue Hispanique*, LXX, 226.

[31] Pereyra, *América española*, IV, 224-25.

One practice springing out of the privileged character of cabildo organization was the sale of public offices. This existed in various forms as late as the nineteenth century in Europe, and has much deeper roots. Its origin springs largely from the Middle Ages when the royal power began slowly to supersede the local. The Kings, wishing to curb but not crush their noble subjects, sought to take from them much of the power they exerted while at the same time leaving them enough privilege to guarantee loyalty. The process was slow and often bloody, but in the long run the new system prevailed. When the rise of the national state gradually substituted the king's authority for that of the feudal nobility (and the towns) the *quid pro quo* was the nobility's right to continue to exercise much the same powers as before, but in the name of the King. Such powers often became hereditary. Judgeships, for example, were inherited, bequeathed, bought, and sold in the same manner as memberships on the stock exchanges today. Such practice was not considered unethical. Likewise, officerships in the army, and many other public posts, were inherited, bequeathed, bought, and sold in the French Army until the Revolution, and in England well into the nineteenth century.

These offices formed a part of the private property of individuals in their day, just as a seat on the stock exchange or ownership of an apartment house or industrial plant constitutes private property in our own day; and anyone who proposed taking such offices from their owners was no more popular (probably less so) than those who now propose the abolition of private property rights. If we accept the theory that confiscation of such positions was justifiable for the public good, we could make out an equally strong case for modern expropriation, since the seats on the stock exchange, the ownership of real estate, or the directorships of large corporations are certainly more intimately related to the welfare of thousands of people than were minor public offices in the Spanish colonial cabildo. Nor can a sharp distinction be made here between private and public property, since the thought of that time accepted such offices as just as much a man's property as his house. Whatever the merits or demerits of the system and its effect on government, it rested on a tradition far older than our modern concept of private property.

The municipal regimes of Spain were acquainted with the hereditary and salable character of public office. The consistent drive made by Ferdinand and Isabella, Charles V, and their successors against the independence of the towns led to the creation of a great body of perpetual and hereditary regidores, many of whom were perpetual regidores in more than one town. Godoy, favorite of Charles IV, was perpetual regidor of Madrid, Burgos, Guadalajara, Segovia, Santiago, Sevilla, Xérez de la Frontera, Ecija, Cádiz, Ronda, Málaga, Murcia, Valencia, Gerona, Manresa, and Nava del Rey in Spain, and Asunción in Paraguay. In many Spanish towns known as *ciudades de estatuto* the nobility alone were permitted to hold municipal office.[32]

Many of these offices were inherited by minors and women, raising the question of who should exercise power when the office of regidor fell to an infant of, say, six months. From the age of eighteen, a boy could take his place as regidor, but women had to be represented by a man, chosen by the executors if the holder was under twenty-five, or by the woman herself if she was twenty-five or over. Many regidores did not reside in the towns where they held office; they might be officers in the army or navy, or holders of some other government position, or simply privileged characters who had bought or inherited their offices. They seldom attended the meetings of the cabildos of which they were members.[33] The alcaldes, in contrast to the regidores, were not hereditary, and were named in various ways. They might be elected by the cabildo, nominated by the King or his officers, or on the feudal estates by the lord of the domain, or in the Church's territories by the bishop or other ecclesiastical official.

The creation of perpetual regidores became a common practice in the colonies as early as the sixteenth century, and continued. Pizarro was permitted to appoint three, and the purchasing of the *regiduría perpetua* by the first families of each community was usual.[34] As early as November 3, 1581 the King had permitted the regidores to name their immediate successors, in return for a payment to the Crown of one-third of the value of the office, but a new law of December 14, 1606 granted this in perpetuity, for another payment of one-third the office's value. Such offices as alguacil-mayor, membership in the regidors, alférez-mayor, and fiel-ejecutor were auctioned like produce in the public markets. The new officer, however, had to be approved by the Council of Indies.[35] The price varied with the size of the town and the im-

---

[32] Desdevises du Dezert, "Institutions de l'Espagne," *Revue Hispanique*, LXX, 205.

[33] *Ibid.*, pp. 203-6.

[34] Herbert Ingram Priestley, "Spanish Colonial Municipalities," *California Law Review* (September, 1919), 397-416.

[35] Desdevises du Dezert, "Institutions de l'Espagne," *Revue Hispanique*, LXX, 225.

portance of the office. It was influenced also, no doubt, by the state of the market at the time. In Buenos Aires, regidorships auctioned in 1644 brought from 850 to 1,250 pesos, and the office of alcalde de la hermandad sold for 1,300 pesos in 1671. Minor offices, such as *alguacil mayor* and *escribano* (clerk, or notary) might be farmed out, the incumbent reimbursing himself from the fees collected. [36]

An extralegal function of the cabildo was to consult the chief citizens of the municipality through a *cabildo abierto,* or "open meeting." This was done, as a rule, at times when matters of unusual importance faced the community, although it seems that there were also meetings of the *cabildo abierto* when the matters before it were not unusual. To the open meetings were called the most important citizens, not the whole population. On the eve of independence the cabildo abierto was destined to play a crucial part in the organization of the revolution.

The cabildo, we may conclude from the evidence offered, was a form of "local" government far from "democratic," its very concept being contrary to democracy; it had no longer the independent attributes inherent in the free cities of the Middle Ages, but it still exercised powers over a wide range of municipal affairs which were usually of such a nature as to bring it in direct contact with the whole of the population. Finally, the cabildo retained sufficient vigor in many places to play an essential part during the wars of independence, and in the early national period.

LOCAL GOVERNMENT: ENCOMIENDA, CACICAZGO, AND HACIENDA

While the cabildo was the chief instrument of local urban government (and of much of the surrounding countryside), the rural areas were under various other types of local rule. The most important of these were the encomienda and hacienda, the cacicazgo, the corregimiento, various church missions, and the slave owners.

The encomienda, in its initial stages the right to collect a tribute from the Indians, had evolved during the two centuries ending in 1720, to a point where the legal rights of the encomendero over the Indians were very great.[37] This was especially true when an encomienda embraced an entire village or district.[38] The encomendero actually assumed much of the power exercised in pre-Conquest times by the caciques. Sometimes such authority was exercised directly, sometimes through an appointed agent, and fre-

---

[36] Priestley, "Spanish Colonial Municipalities," *California Law Review,* pp. 402-3.
[37] *Leyes de Indias,* Libro VI, Títulos VIII and IX.
[38] Barros Arana, *Chile,* VII, 500-503; Means, *Fall,* pp. 151-52.

quently through the Indian chieftains, who by law were permitted to inherit their ancient offices.[39]

The cacicazgo was, in fact, one of the most important features of colonial government since, as we have already seen, a considerable number of the caciques (or curacas, the terms varied with the languages of the Indians) continued to hold their positions. Caciques were subordinate to several types of Spanish superior officials. The encomendero was one of these. Another was the owner of an estate, an *hacendado,* who might or might not hold an encomienda.

Both the encomienda and hacienda existed· from the early days of the Conquest, but with the nominal abolition of the encomienda in 1720 the legal power of the encomendero over the Indian came to an end. Much of the actual control of the encomendero had always been exercised extralegally or illegally, however, and through ownership of the land on which the Indians lived he was still their master. They could not easily move away, found little advantage in trying to change masters, and were accustomed by centuries of subservience to accept the domination of an overlord. The same thing was true of many of the free Negroes and the mestizos who lived on the numerous large estates. And since the hacendado frequently combined legal authority, such as that held by an alcalde, regidor, or other minor official, with his *de facto* power, he was a major factor in local government.

It would be difficult, in fact, to exaggerate the importance of the encomendero and hacendado in matters of government in colonial times, and they lost little if any of it during the first century after the independence of the Latin-American nations. The "master and man" relationship, placing in the hands of a few men almost the whole political authority, was for long one of the most important factors in the evolution of the Latin-American nations. This was especially true of the countries with the great Indian populations—Bolivia, Peru, Ecuador, Guatemala, and Mexico—but scarcely less so elsewhere because of other factors that influenced local colonial government.[40]

LOCAL GOVERNMENT: THE CORREGIMIENTO

The corregimiento was the division of government destined to carry out the royal laws in local areas. The whole of America was divided into several hundred corregimientos ruled by corregidores,

---

[39] *Leyes de Indias,* Libro VI, Título VII.

[40] McBride, *Chile,* pp. 3-14, 171-94; Domingo Amunátegui Solar, *Historia social de Chile* (Santiago, Chile, 1932), pp. 121-43.

or by alcaldes mayores.[41] The functions of these officials in Spain and their transfer to America have been described.[42] While primarily the King's representatives, invested with supervisory and judicial powers, they became in colonial times of much greater importance than would be deduced from a reading of those sections of the *Leyes de Indias* describing their prerogatives.[43] Of the two classes of *corregidores* appointed in America, the *corregidores de Indios* especially, governing territories peopled principally with Indians, acquired significant extralegal functions. But it would be incorrect to assume that the *corregidores de Españoles* were without influence on local government.

While the corregidores were nominally judicial officials, their powers grew far beyond this. The King used them as his right arm in both Spanish and colonial government and their administrative authority was great. Being so numerous and sometimes at immense distances from the seat of the audiencia or viceroyalty, the corregidores were hard to watch. They could so alter the royal laws, or ignore them, that they were in effect legislating. They were also in a position to devise their own codes and enforce them, almost free from interference.[44]

They were invested with actual legislative powers, however, through their right to pass ordinances dealing with local administration, in co-operation with the cabildo. They were empowered to make so many decisions in economic matters that they were almost economic dictators, and in this lay their opportunities for exploitation. The injunction to look after the general welfare of their subjects enabled the corregidores to assume many prerogatives not specified in the laws. The command to see that the bread supply was ample throughout the corregimiento, and to regulate the price or forbid export in case of shortage led to forced distribution at prices profitable to the corregidores. Similar powers to regulate meat and other goods sold in the public markets, and to test wine and oil, brought further abuses.

The most common abuse by the corregidores in economic matters was the *repartimiento,* or right to distribute goods throughout the corregimiento, which should be carefully distinguished from the labor system also known as *repartimiento.*[45] This distribution was the initial act of the corregidor on taking office. While making

[41] C. E. Castañeda, "The Corregidor in Spanish Colonial Administration," *H.A.H.R., IX* (November, 1929), pp. 446-70.
[42] See Chapters 14 and 15.
[43] *Leyes de Indias,* Libro V, Título II.
[44] Means, *Fall,* pp. 178-81.
[45] See Chapter 22.

the required visit to all parts of his district, he took with him livestock, food, and other goods, which he required the Indians to buy on time at prices yielding a handsome profit. Only his conscience and the law of diminishing returns regulated the amount he made the Indians buy. Silk stockings were forced on Indians who had no shoes, and razors on men who had no beards. The corregidor then furnished the caciques of the towns with a list of the things distributed and the prices, saddling these native leaders with the responsibility of collecting and remitting the payment. Indians unable to pay for the goods were compelled to work off their debts. In this way the caciques, whom we have seen co-operating with the encomenderos and hacendados in mulcting the Indians, became the immediate instrument of local government in the areas where the Indians were subject directly to the King rather than to an encomendero.

The corregidores were subject to the residencia and the visita, which, however, were not sufficiently effective to curb them. They had frequently paid for their appointments, sometimes a large sum if the corregimiento was rich, and they looked on this payment as an investment which they intended to recover, with ample interest. To this end they systematically devised schemes for bettering business. The Crown and Council of Indies might legislate, and the viceroys and audiencias issue orders, but it was difficult to force the corregidores to obey.

LOCAL GOVERNMENT: PARISH, MONASTERY, AND MISSION

Many other elements of local control left a deep imprint on the character of colonial government. Owing to the large size of the church parishes and the great distances of many of these from the diocesan sees, it was customary for the parish priest to exert a strong influence in his jurisdiction. Frequently this was done in conjunction with (or in opposition to) the encomenderos, hacendados, and corregidores; and the line of demarcation between the authority of the one and the other was not always clear. But, in any case, the parish priest was so closely associated with his people that he could interpret their needs far more accurately than a monarch who was thousands of miles away in space and a year away in time. The parish priests did not always use their powers for the benefit of their charges, as was made clear in discussing social conditions and the position of the Church.

The monastery and the convent were also parts of the local government. In the towns and cities their influence might not be felt so strongly among the people; but rural monasteries were very influential institutions. Living in and around them were numerous Indians, mestizos, and other people. The monks carried great weight in shaping their attitude toward government. In addition, the monastery could sometimes control, or at least modify, the law enforcement within the region of its jurisdiction. It could appeal to higher officials, collaborate with (or oppose) the encomendero or corregidor, send secret reports on the conduct of the officials, and do other things that helped determine the character of local government. Many monasteries became the centers around which localistic feeling formed.

More influential still were the missions, which were frontier, or at least, rural, institutions. Far removed from direct control of royal officials, largely independent in fact from their own Order, and empowered by law with extensive prerogatives, the missions were in many places governmental units all but complete within themselves. The Indians under their charge knew little or nothing of Spanish administration except as they received it through the medium of the monks. While in general the missions were governed nominally by a cacique and an Indian cabildo, these were but a legal fiction to cover the mission's absolutism. Interference from the outside was not welcome, although in regions where the Indians were particularly warlike (Chile and northern New Spain) a *presidio,* or fortress, was a part of the governing establishment.

LOCAL GOVERNMENT: THE SLAVE OWNER

One other form of local rule must be mentioned—the slave owner. Although slavery was not a separate unit of government, like a cabildo or a mission, it was frequently the only form of rule known to millions of people. In the West Indian Islands, along the coast of the Caribbean and on the Pacific coast as far south as southern Peru, slaves formed a large proportion of the population, with masters all but supreme over them. By the end of the colonial period there existed more than a million and a half Negroes in the Spanish and French colonies and more in Brazil and the United States, whose attitude toward government was influenced almost entirely by their being slaves. The owners held a large measure of legal authority; and exercised even more than they were granted.

It is in the local governments that one must look for the true picture of Spanish colonial administration. It is here, in the cabildo, encomienda, hacienda, corregimiento, cacicazgo, mission, and plantation, rather than in the *Leyes de Indias,* that one can find an understanding of the colonial system that sired the modern states.[46]

[46] Barros Arana, *Chile,* VII, 500-503; Means, *Fall,* pp. 151-52; 178-81.

THE COLONIAL SYSTEM IN EVOLUTION: NEW VICEROYALTIES AND CAPTAINCIES-GENERAL

Nothing could be more erroneous than to think that Spain's system of colonial administration was static. Especially during the century preceding independence, Spain's policy evolved rapidly to meet the needs of a changing world. That the system did not alter rapidly enough to maintain the political unity of mother country and colonies is hardly strange. The eighteenth century saw the beginning of the industrial revolution, the application of the science of Descartes and Newton to political and social thought and, for the Spanish colonies, the realization that Newton plus evolution spelled independence.

The success or failure of the Spanish policy should not, therefore, be measured, as it so often has been in the past, by the fact that her colonies eventually revolted and set themselves free. So did the English colonies, and so have many other colonies at many other epochs in history. It would be easy to make a case for the slogan "Spain gave birth to nations" and show that the Spanish policy enabled her possessions to build up that degree of vigor necessary for independent existence. But this would be pushing the pendulum of historical fashion a little too far back. Spain certainly did not follow a calculated policy of preparing her colonies for independence. But neither did she close her eyes to all suggestions of reform.

The first major reform of the eighteenth century was the creation of a new viceroyalty, New Granada, carved out of the northern part of Peru in 1717 (temporarily abolished in 1724 and recreated in 1739-1740). This reform was a recognition of the growing importance of the area today formed by Panama, Colombia, Venezuela, and Ecuador. It was always something of an anomaly that the King's will could be known on the north coast of South America only after traversing the Isthmus of Panama, sailing down the Pacific coast to Lima and then making its way back over seas and across mountains. On the other hand, the northern colonies had never had the importance of Peru and Bolivia. They produced less, were less known to the mother country, and perhaps warranted less attention. The events of the eighteenth century changed this situation. The world was in the midst of a series of six major (and several minor) dynastic colonial wars which began with the War of the Palatinate in 1689 and ended (only temporarily) with the surrender of Napolcon in 1815. The second of these was the War of Spanish Succession (1700 to

1713) which accompanied the ascension of the Bourbon Philip V
to the Spanish throne. These events thoroughly demonstrated that
Spain must be prepared to defend her colonies and their commerce.
A growing trade in sugar and other tropical products, and a corresponding increase in the importance of the aforementioned trade
in the Caribbean, made a tightening of the governmental reins
imperative. The attempt to dispense with the new viceroyalty in
1724 proved unwise and after its re-establishment, when the out-
break of the War of Jenkins' Ear in 1739 had revealed the continued danger to the Spanish colonies, it remained a permanent
part of the administrative structure to the end of the colonial
period.

Other similar rearrangements were made to bring about greater
efficiency and to satisfy the demands of the colonists for a more
adequate system. Venezuela was established as a separate captaincy-
general in 1731 and separated from the jurisdiction of the audiencia
of Santo Domingo. After 1740 it was a part of the viceroyalty of
New Granada; but owing to the need for better government, and
the inconsistency of having royal legislation transmitted first to
Bogotá, many days away by sea, up the Magdalena river and high
in· the Andes, only to return by the same route, Venezuela was
constituted a separate captaincy-general in 1777. Cuba became a
separate captaincy-general in 1777 also, and during the century,
Guatemala grew less dependent on New Spain while Puerto Rico
obtained separate administrative status. Louisiana was a captaincy-
general from 1763 to 1800, when it was ceded to France.

In the meantime, events of significance led to a change in New
Spain. The expansion into northern Mexico, Texas, New Mexico,
Arizona, and California had been steady since the seventeenth
century. By 1776, Spain held an area in the United States reaching
from Florida to San Francisco. Increasing population, growing
economic interests, and the need of giving the colonists better
protection determined the separation of a large part of this area
from New Spain. The newly-erected administrative unit, established in 1776, was a Commandancy-General of the Interior Provinces (Provincias Internas) and embraced Durango, Sonora, Coahuila, Texas, and New Mexico. Later the Provincias Internas
were divided into the Western Interior Provinces embracing
Sonora, Durango, New Mexico and California, and the Eastern
Interior Provinces, embracing Coahuila, Texas, Nuevo Santander
(Tamaulipas in Mexico) and Nuevo León in Mexico.

Far to the south in Río de la Plata geographic and economic

POLITICAL ORGANIZATION
OF
LATIN AMERICA
IN 1784

Scale of Miles
0   500   1000   1500

Adapted from *The People and Politics of Latin America* by M. W. Williams

624*a*

realities likewise dictated administrative reorganization. The plains of Uruguay and Argentine, once without economic resources for sustaining a heavy population, were now teeming with vast herds of cattle, horses, and sheep. Montevideo and Buenos Aires were rapidly developing into cities, and wished to have a political structure in keeping with their economic weight. From the first days of settlement the region was governed by Lima, always an awkward arrangement but partly justified in an age when long sea hauls without intermediate stops were unprofitable, and when Spain, hard pressed on all sides by her international rivals, found it simpler to direct her trade through Panama and Lima, with Río de la Plata receiving goods overland from Lima. The system once established, vested interests delayed change beyond the date when economic and political wisdom would have advised it.

But by 1776 the situation could not be ignored. Portugal was pushing persistently toward the Plata. The viceroyalty of Río de la Plata was created, the first viceroy, Pedro de Cevallos, taking office in 1777. The creation of the viceroyalty was accompanied by the defeat of Portugal and the establishment of the boundaries between the Spanish and Portuguese colonies in the treaty of 1777. The new viceroyalty included territory that is to-day Bolivia (with an arm reaching down to the Pacific in northern Chile), Paraguay, Uruguay, and Argentina. As a part of the general reform of the time Chile was made a captaincy-general in 1778 with virtual independence from Peru. The main lines of the political boundaries of the future Latin-American nations had been established.[47]

CENTRALIZATION OF GOVERNMENT: THE INTENDANCIES

Simultaneously other changes were made in the administration of the Spanish colonies, both at home and in America. A gradual transformation of the administration in Spain began early in the reign of Philip V. Ministers directly responsible to the Crown began to take over much of the administrative work of the various councils, including the Council of Indies. From 1717, when Philip V established the *secretarías de despacho* (Secretariats) the administrative powers of the Council waned; and much of its legislative power passed into the hands of the King, who dispatched his royal orders directly through his ministers of war, commerce, navigation, and treasury, ignoring the Council. Ferdinand VI continued this tendency, and Charles III assumed still more authority at the expense of the Council, although the latter was not definitely

---

[47] Levene, *Nación Argentina,* IV, sección I, 27-332.

abolished until 1854.[48] Toward the end of the colonial period it was the Minister of Indies, rather than the Council, who weighed most in government. In commercial matters also the older institutions gave way to the new, and in 1790 the Casa de Contratación was abolished, its marine functions being given to an Intendant of Marine Affairs.

The latter was a part of the general establishment of the intendancy system in Spain and America. Intendants were officials with wide judicial, administrative, and financial powers, directly subject to the King. They were of two classes, financial and military. The system appeared early in French administration and under Henry IV and Louis XIII (whose minister was Richelieu) France was divided into thirty-three intendancies with the object of curbing the powers of the nobles. France also established the system in her American colonies. Spain borrowed the system from France with the Bourbon Philip V who introduced it in 1718, with the same objectives as the French monarchs—that is, increasing the authority of the Crown over the nobles and augmenting the royal revenue. In 1749 Ferdinand VI overhauled the governmental structure and drew up a new set of ordinances for the intendants.

The results obtained in Spain encouraged the Crown to apply the system to America.[49] This too came partly through direct French inspiration. In 1761-62 the French and Spanish Bourbons had bound themselves together in the Family Compact.[50] The Compact did not save them from defeat at the hands of England in the Seven Years War, however, and they were both anxious for recovery. This idea was uppermost in the mind of the French and no doubt strongly motivated the Spanish also when, a year after the end of the war, they consulted together concerning the best methods for strengthening the Spanish colonies. They discussed, in the words of the French envoys in the negotiations with Spain "matters relative to the future security of the Spanish Indies and the augumentation of His Catholic Majesty's revenues in America, and lastly the restoration of the navy." [51] Under the inspiration of the plans thus formulated, José de Gálvez was dispatched to

---

[48] The Council of Indies was abolished in 1812, re-established in 1814, abolished in 1820, re-established in 1823, abolished in 1824, and re-established again in 1851 only to be definitively abolished in 1854.

[49] Desdevises du Dezert, "Institutions de l'Espagne," *Revue Hispanique,* LXX, 152-69; Blanco Acevedo, *Uruguay Colonial,* pp. 139-65.

[50] Arthur S. Aiton, "A Neglected Intrigue of the Family Compact," *H.A.H.R.,* XI (August, 1931), 386-93.

[51] Quoted in Arthur S. Aiton, "Spanish Colonial Reorganization under the Family Compact," *H. A. H. R.,* XII (August, 1932), 269-80.

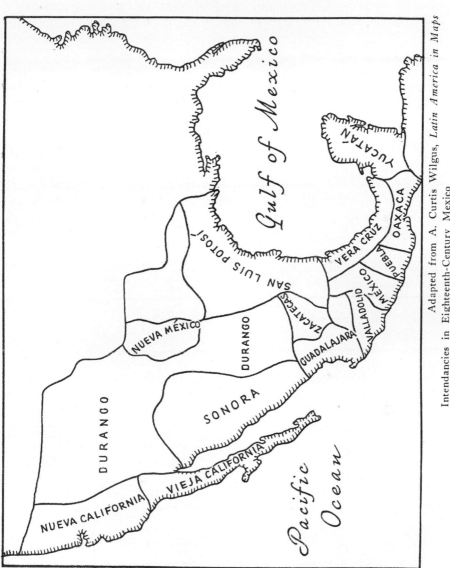

Intendancies in Eighteenth-Century Mexico

Adapted from A. Curtis Wilgus, *Latin America in Maps*

626a

New Spain to study on the ground the possibilities of economic and administrative reforms and to take measures for remedying conditions there.

Spain did not wait for Gálvez's report to start the desired reforms. In 1764 the intendant system was introduced in Cuba and modeled on the Spanish ordinance of 1749. The intendant was charged with matters of revenue and war; modifications of his powers were decreed in 1765 and again in 1767 to meet deficiencies found in the first ordinance. The experience of Cuba suggested the further extension of the system. José de Gálvez and the viceroy of New Spain, Carlos Francisco de Croix (1766-71) drew up a plan for its installation in New Spain in 1768 which the King approved in 1769, though he delayed the full adoption. Intendants had already been installed in 1768, in northern Mexico (Sonora and Sinaloa). Louisiana was made an intendancy in 1775.

The intendants, who were to be few in number, were to supplant the numerous corregidores and alcaldes mayores, and certain other minor officials. Abuses in tax collection, mistreatment of the Indians, distribution of goods to the Indians under the repartimiento system, and other evils that characterized the colonies and lowered the revenues of the Crown, were to be corrected by the intendants.

Venezuela was made an intendancy in 1777, and the system extended in part to Río de la Plata in the same year, a definitive ordinance for the intendants of that region being promulgated in 1782. Gálvez, now Minister of the Indies, drew up certain amendments in 1778 which served as the basis for the system as introduced into La Plata, Peru, New Spain, Chile, and other colonies between 1782 and 1790, when the system was applied to all parts of America. Other divisions were made subsequently, and new intendancies created—Puerto Rico coming as late as 1811. Mexico was divided into twelve intendancies, with a superintendent, Peru and La Plata into eight each, while smaller areas, such as Guatemala and Cuba, formed a single intendancy. These units were divided into districts called *partidos,* governed by subdelegates receiving no fees.

Intendants must be Spanish-born subjects; Creoles and mestizos were not trusted with so much of the King's authority. The intendant-general's responsibility in financial matters was directly to the Crown, not to the viceroy. The intendants were subject to the viceroy in judicial, administrative, and religious functions, and were to respect his military prerogatives. But the financial powers were broadly interpreted, and actually gave those officials wide judicial and administrative functions previously held by the corregidores, governors, captains-general, and viceroys. The intendants replaced the former governors in justice and civil administration, but cases could be appealed from their courts to the audiencia. In general, wide powers were given them to promote the economic and political welfare of the colonies.[52]

The result was a noticeable betterment of conditions. Much of the increased revenues of the latter eighteenth century has been attributed to the new system, although it is more accurate to say that the revenues increased because of the greater prosperity of the Spanish colonies during the century before independence. The centralizing effect of the intendants was seen clearly in the municipal governments where they superseded the corregidores. They were instituted too late, however, to destroy the considerable strength of the cabildos in many parts of the Spanish colonial realm.

It is clear that government, like other aspects of Latin-American life, was changing rapidly on the eve of independence. What might have happened is in the realm of speculation. Independence intervened to cut short the evolution of Spain's colonial system.[53]

* * * * *

The Spanish provinces, however, closed their final colonial years with a swiftly improving agricultural and commercial economy, which had expanded steadily in the older colonies and grown to flourishing proportions in the younger ones. Farming and ranching were the principal sources of wealth, but mining was prosperous, and still served as a stimulus to the whole economy. Manufacturing and trade were progressing. The Spanish-American commerce of Europe was among the most lucrative in the world. A middle class was arising, and demanding to share the powers and prestige barred to it by the feudal privileges of the landowning aristocracy and clergy. The Creole merchants, enriched by the profitable trade, were to be a decisive force for independence.

As the colonial era ended, Latin America was in the midst of a vigorous intellectual and artistic development, fertilized by the new scientific ideas and mechanistic philosophies of eighteenth-century Europe. Reactionary elements were still strong enough to

[52] Lillian Estelle Fisher, "The Intendant System in Spanish America," *H. A. H. R.*, VIII (February, 1928), 3-13; Levene, ed., *Nación Argentina,* IV, Part I, 191-242.
[53] Altamira, *Historia de España,* IV, 194-204; Desdevises du Dezert, "Institutions de l'Espagne," *Revue Hispanique,* LXX, 152-54, 168-69; Means, *Fall,* pp. 189-90; Barros Arana, *Chile,* VI, 402-403; VII, 357-58; Blanco Acevedo, *Uruguay colonial,* pp. 139-41, 165.

survive the wars of emancipation, but the Spanish colonies, far from being withered fruit without strength to cling longer to a dying tree, were energetic offspring of the Spanish trunk, ready to take an independent place in the world.

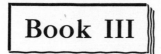

Book III

Colonial Brazil

Brazil in Formation

DISCOVERY

WHEN CABRAL SIGHTED BRAZIL IN 1500, he could little imagine the immensity of the land.[1] He believed it an island and called it Santa Cruz. From the point where he first landed in the present state of Espírito Santo, the section of the coast later to be embraced in Brazil stretched almost fifteen hundred miles to the south and more than two thousand miles to the north; and included territory from about five degrees north of the equator to almost thirty-four degrees south. To the west, the natural geographical features of the continent were to push the Brazilian boundaries to the Andes, in defiance of the Papal Bulls of 1493 and the treaty of Tordesillas of 1494. Brazil was indeed an empire. Cabral had discovered for Portugal a territory that was in time to yield far more than distant and legendary India, to which Cabral was sailing when he made his first Brazilian landing.

He stopped for a few days on the Brazilian coast and sent two men ashore with merchandise to make contact with the natives, but he was soon to discover that Brazil was far different from the India that Vasco da Gama had discovered. The men did not come back, and after seven days Cabral landed a small force to search for them. After all the members of this force but one had returned to the ships, the remaining man was surrounded by apparently friendly women, one of whom clubbed him on the head from behind. They then dragged him off, cut him up, and ate him in plain view of the Portugese, signaling that the first two men had

---

[1] The date is given as April 22 (Old Style) or May 3 (New Style). For this initial period of Brazilian discovery see J. Capistrano de Abreu, *O Descobrimento do Brasil* (Rio de Janeiro: Sociedade Capistrano de Abreu, 1929), pp. 139-188; ———, *Capítulos de história colonial* (3rd ed., Rio de Janeiro: Sociedade Capistrano de Abreu, 1934), pp. 22-23.

[2] Robert Southey, *History of Brazil* (3 vols., London, 1810-1819), I, 14-16.

met the same fate.[2] It is hardly strange, in view of this, that Cabral failed to grasp the importance of his discovery. He took formal possession in the name of the King, however, and proceeded to India, sending one ship back to Portugal with the news. He also left ashore two *degredados* or exiled criminals, who managed to survive and later served as interpreters between the Portugese and Indians.

Cabral's discovery unveiled the mass of raw material from which Brazil was to be fashioned. He never returned to Brazil; others were destined to mold and form the empire to be, a process by no means complete today.[3]

The report sent back by Brazil's first chronicler Pero Vaz de Caminha, official scrivener of the trading post that was to be established in India, was favorable but not overenthusiastic. Brazil he saw as a fine country bursting with fertility, but "it seems to me," he said, "that the best fruit that can be gathered in it will be the salvation of its people, and this should be the principal seed that Your Highness should sow there." [4]

The people whose salvation was proposed by Pero Vaz de Caminha were, of course, the Indians.[5] Their civilization more

---

[3] Fidelino de Figueiredo, "The Geographical Discoveries and Conquest of the Portuguese," *H.A.H.R.*, VI (February-August, 1926), 47-70; Carlos Malheiro Dias, ed., *História da colonização portuguesa do Brasil,* (3 vols., Oporto, 1921-1926), (Hereafter *HCP*), is the product of the collaboration of several authors and the most extensive treatment of sixteenth century Brazil and the background of its discovery. See particularly Jaime Cortesão, "A expedicão de Cabral," II, 1-39; H. Lopes de Mendonça, "De Restêlo a Vera Cruz," II, 43-71, with a discussion of the Cabral expedition from the time it left Portugal to its arrival in Brazil; and Carlos Malheiro Dias, "A Semana de Vera Cruz," II, 75-169, treating the Cabral expedition after it reached Brazil; Duarte Leite, "A exploração do litoral do Brasil na cartografia da primeira década do século XVI," II, 393-440; C. Malheiro Dias, "Introdução," to Vol. III, pp. i-lxiii; and C. Malheiro Dias, "A metrópole e suas conquistas nos reinados de D. João III, D. Sebastião e Cardeal D. Henrique," III, 1-47.

[4] The letter of Vaz de Caminha is published in *HCP*, II, 86-99, and its importance is discussed by Capistrano de Abreu, *Descobrimento do Brasil,* pp. 289-307. The priority of Brazil's discovery has been the subject of considerable controversy. The claim that Vespucci saw Brazil before Cabral did is doubtful, but still open to investigation. On the other hand Diego de Lepe, Vicente Yañez Pinzón, and Duarte Pacheco Pereira all probably preceded Cabral. For discussion of claims and counterclaims of discovery see Southey, *History of Brazil,* I, 6, who credits Pinzón with the discovery of the Amazon and Brazilian coastline in 1499-1500; and Capistrano de Abreu, *Descobrimento,* pp. 47-62, 216-240. The opposed viewpoints are best represented by Duarte Leite's "Os Falsos Precursores de Alvares Cabral," *HCP*, I, 107-225, and Luciano Pereira da Silva's "Duarte Pacheco Pereira, Precursor de Cabral," *HCP*, I, 231-262.

[5] On the Brazilian Indians see Capistrano de Abreu, *Descobrimento,* pp. 240-254; and for a more extended account, J. F. de Almeida Prado, *Primeiros povoadores do Brasil 1500-1530* (2nd ed., São Paulo, 1939), pp. 133-235. Two early accounts that portray the Indians as they were seen by sixteenth century chroniclers are Fernão Cardim, *Tratados da terra e gente do Brasil* (2nd ed., São Paulo, 1939), pp. 131-246, written in the late sixteenth century; and Frei Vicente do Salvador, *História do Brasil,* (3rd ed., São Paulo, 1918), pp. 51-69. Frei Vicente's work was finished in 1627 but not published until 1886-87 in an incomplete edition. The second edition,

closely approximated that of the Caribbean islands than that of
the highlands of Mexico and Peru. There were no Indian empires
of the Aztec and Inca type; no cities comparable to Tenochtitlán
and Cuzco; no architecture of stone and mortar; no well-established
sedentary groups. Brazil's Indians were largely food gatherers,
who subsisted by hunting, fishing, and cannibalism, with other
groups who combined some agriculture with hunting and fishing.
Not all the Indians were cannibals, but Vespucci's story of the
Indians who expressed astonishment that the Portuguese killed men
"and did not eat them" is typical of a common situation.[6]

All told, there were hundreds of groups with as many languages
and dialects, too complicated and numerous to mention here. For
the practical problems of the sixteenth-century colonizers, the
Indians fell in two main divisions: the Tupí-Guaraní linguistic
family which lived along the coast from Venezuela to southern
Brazil, spreading back into Paraguay, and speaking the *"lingua
geral"* whose various dialects were closely related, "like Portuguese
and Spanish;" and the Tapuias of the interior (or *sertão*), who
were the enemies of the Tupís, and spoke the *"linguas travadas"*
or "mingled languages." This latter classification included a large
number of groups eternally at war with one another, and with the
Tupís of the coast. But the coast-dwelling Tupí groups were not
friendly with one another merely because of their related speech.
They carried on interminable civil conflicts, a fact as useful in
aiding the Portuguese to occupy Brazil as the civil wars among the
Indians of the Caribbean, Mexico, and Peru had been to the
Spaniards. By alliances first with one Indian group and then with
another the Portuguese were able to conquer.[7]

SETTLEMENT

Portugal was well prepared for the responsibilities of the new
discovery.[8] More than a century of exploration and expansion had

---

1889 and the third, cited here, are themselves not complete, indicating that the
original manuscript has yet to be found.
     [6] Southey, *Brazil*, I. 17; Radin, *Indians of South America*, pp. 49-164.
     [7] Lemos Brito, *Pontos de partida para a história econômica do Brasil* (2nd ed.,
São Paulo, 1939), pp. 163-182.
     [8] On Portuguese preparation for colonial development see above, ch. 3.   An
excellent picture of Portuguese expansion and colonization up to the time of the
Brazilian discovery is given by Malheiro Dias in *IICP*, I, pp. i-cxxxi.   Other
chapters in the same work that contain essential information are Julio Dantas, "A
Era Manuelina," I, 3-25, containing a discussion of Portugal from 1495 to 1521;
and Luciano Pereira da Silva, "A Arte de Navegar dos Portugueses," *HCP*, I,
29-104, demonstrating the contributions of Portugal to the science of navigation.
Useful information can also be had from one of the modern classics of Portuguese
economic history, J. Lucio de Azevedo's *Épocas de Portugal Econômico* (Lisbon,
1929).   The appropriate chapters here are those dealing with "A Monarquia

evolved the two methods of colonial appropriation found most useful: the *latifundio*, or great landed estate; and the *feitoria*, or trading post. The former had served to develop the Cape Verde, Azores, and Equatorial islands off Africa; the *feitorias* had been used to tap the resources of the interior of Africa, and were to be applied to the East. Brazil was found suited to both systems.

In 1501 a new expedition of three vessels was sent out to examine more closely Cabral's newly-discovered lands.[9] One of the officials of the enterprise, in what capacity is not certain, was Américo Vespucci, who had perhaps touched on the northern coast of Brazil with the Alonzo de Ojeda expedition of 1499-1500. Vespucci had a flair for publicity, and his letters and other writings won him a position in the minds of his readers that he was far from occupying in fact. The expedition spent almost a year along the coast of Brazil, sailing far south from the region of present-day Natal, and returning to Portugal in September 1502.

In confirmation of what Cabral had already seen, the second expedition reported nothing but naked Indians (some of them cannibals), parrots, cañafistula (cassia fistula), and "brazil" wood. The latter was the most important, and appeared in quantities that seemed inexhaustible. The importance of dye wood could scarcely be overestimated in a Europe whose expanding textile industry was hard pressed to find new sources of coloring. Brazil might have no silver and gold, though hope never died and both metals were eventually discovered, but for the time being brazil and other valuable woods were to take their place.

Portugal was not free to give her full attention to Brazil. The second expedition, outward bound to America, had crossed the home-coming Cabral, who brought glowing reports from India and large profits. The contrast between the wealth and opulence of the East, with its great trade marts, its highly desirable spices, its temples and palaces, its glittering jewels and sumptuous textiles, and Brazil, with its total lack of these, was striking. In the East were easy sources of wealth, obtainable in well-organized markets. Brazil offered a more limited return, with vastly more effort and

---

Agraria," pp. 11-56, showing the formation of the type of agricultural administration that was transplanted to Brazil; "Jornada de Africa," pp. 59-87, discussing Portuguese exploration of the African coast; and "O Primeiro Ciclo de Oro," pp. 173-220, in which the importance of African minerals is treated. See also J. F. de Almeida Prado, *Pernambuco e as capitanias do norte do Brasil, 1530-1630* (4 vols., São Paulo, 1939-1942), I, 5-21.

[9] See the *Revista do Instituto Histórico e Geográphico Brasileiro* (Rio de Janeiro), vol. 47 (1873), pp. 55-63. (Hereafter *Revista IHGB*); Malheiro Dias, "A Expedição de 1501," *HCP*, II, 173-222; Almeida Prado, *Primeiros povoadores*, pp. 27-56, with a long list of the first expeditions.

greater dangers. Almost two centuries were to pass before the situation would be altered.[10]

But Portugal had definitely won the centuries-old race for establishing lucrative contact with the East. The Italian cities, long the leaders, were gradually to be displaced; Holland and England were to be a century catching up; Spain was busy conquering vast regions of North and South America. Portugal was thus definitely in the lead in the East. She had her African (and now her Brazilian) *feitorias* as stopping and supply stations; she had her long sea-going experience; and she called to her service the leading mariners and cosmographers of the times. There can be little wonder that Portugal gave preference to the "performance of India over the promise of Brazil." [11]

But Brazil was not neglected. It received as much attention from the Portuguese Crown as its economic worth merited. In 1503 a third expedition of six vessels under the command of Gonçalo Coelho with Vespucci as captain of one of the ships was sent out.[12] It reached Brazil about half way between present-day Rio de Janeiro and Baía, and spent five months exploring the coast, penetrating more than a hundred miles inland through forests, mountains, and hostile Indians to confirm the previous view that Brazil offered little that justified neglecting the more profitable East. At this early date the principal items of trade were parrots, monkeys, and brazil wood. Two of the ships were loaded with dye wood off Cabo Frio (the cape northeast of Rio), and the expedition returned to Portugal. Before leaving, however, a *feitoria* was established at Cabo Frio, the first in Brazil.

From this time a steady but small stream of Portuguese came to the new land. Some were *degredados,* a class of criminals whose crimes might be of a very minor nature judged by modern standards. Many were guilty only of political or religious dissent. These *degredados,* who frequently managed to survive even among the cannibals, were a valuable advance guard of Brazilian colonization.[13] Brazil wood may not have compared in value with spices from the East, but it was sufficiently important to warrant exploitation and soon gave its name to the whole territory, replacing the original "Holy Cross" bestowed by Cabral.

Also characteristic of Brazilian economy at an early epoch was

---

[10] Lemos Brito, *História econômica do Brasil,* pp. 1-45.
[11] Pedro Calmon, *História da civilização brasileira* (3rd ed., São Paulo, 1937), p. 19.
[12] Malheiro Dias, "A expedicao de 1503," *HCP,* II, 285-314, gives an account of the founding of the first *feitoria.*
[13] Calmon, *Civilização brasileira,* pp. 15-19; Southey, *Brazil,* I, 20-23.

its reliance on domestic agriculture. The distance from Portugal
was too great to permit shipment of quantities of food. The ships
could scarcely carry sufficient food for their crews and passengers,
and if Brazil was to survive, a local supply must be found. The
Indians in part helped solve the problem, but the Portuguese contributions to Brazilian agriculture marked the difference between
success and failure in colonization. In this Brazil differed little
from the Spanish colonies of the Caribbean.

One of the first decisive acts of the Portuguese government in
Brazilian affairs made a contribution to both the brazil-wood industry and agriculture. As a result of the reports from the three
exploratory voyages, the Portuguese Crown decided to develop
the country through a concession for brazil wood cutting granted
to Fernão de Noronha (or Loronha) in 1503 for three years.
Noronha was a Jewish nobleman and merchant of wealth. His
concession paved the way for many Jews, who just at this epoch
were suffering persecution and being driven from Portugal, to
emigrate to Brazil. The double significance of this for Brazil has
been indicated by Calmon, one of her modern historians.

"Events transpired to force the Jews to emigrate, scourged
by a ferocious persecution (1503). Their mercantile instinct
divined the natural riches of the New World. Here they would
have tranquility and security. The Holy Office would not bother
them. To the Orient went the warriors; to Brazil the peaceable
New Christians. Fernão de Noronha, contracting for the trade
in brazil wood in 1503, foreshadowed this Jewish colonization.
He was a Jew, like the majority of the settlers of Pernambuco
and Baía in the first century. To their great mobility, to their
facility of adaptation and the simplicity of their lives, these immigrants joined the virtue of patience. When others thought of
nothing but gold mines and the profits of oriental drugs, they
cultivated the earth, marveling at the similarity of its vegetation to that of San Tomé, giving a purely agricultural aspect to
the conquest of Brazil, and determining its destiny." [14]

[14] Calmon, *Civilização brasileira,* p. 20. On the plants and animals introduced
into Brazil by the Portuguese see *Revista IHGB,* Vol. 19 (1856). The most important source of information about the agriculture of sixteenth-century Brazil is
Gabriel Soares de Souza, *Tratado Descriptivo do Brasil em 1587,* first published in
1825 in Lisbon in an incomplete version. The standard edition is that edited by
Francisco Adolpho de Varnhagen in Rio de Janeiro, in 1851. References here
are to the third edition, São Paulo, 1938. Soares was the owner of a sugar mill in
Baía from 1570 to 1584. His work was dedicated to the King and designed to
stimulate interest in Brazil. It contains a minute description of the land, plants,
and people and bears favorable comparison with José Acosta's *Historia,* and
Bernabé Cobo's *Nuevo Mundo,* having the additional advantage of containing a

THE BRAZIL WOOD TRADE

But if the development of agriculture made the settlement of Brazil certain, it was the cutting of dye woods that made Brazil immediately profitable.[15] Noronha's contract was several times renewed, and later he had partners in the business, indicating there were profits to share. The main region for dye woods extended from Cabo São Roque (near Natal) to Cabo Frio (north of Rio). The concessionaire undertook to send three ships annually to Brazil, explore and fortify three hundred leagues of coastline, and pay one-fifth of the value of the wood to the Crown. In return he received a monopoly, and the King agreed to suppress the dye wood trade of the East. The cargo of the ship "Bretóa" in 1511 may be considered typical; it contained five thousand *toros* (logs of 20 to 30 kilogrammes each) of wood, a few Indian slaves, and numerous parrots and monkeys. The monopolists soon found that the strong rivalry of the French prevented them from protecting Brazil according to contract, and the Crown assumed the responsibility of defense.

The profits to Noronha and the Crown were considerable, although difficult to translate into modern values. Noronha paid an annual sum of four thousand *cruzados,* equivalent today to about one thousand *contos* Brazilian money, or $50,000.[16] As an indication of the probable profits, it may be noted that a ship of 120 tons, which could be built for the modern equivalent of 1500 contos ($75,000) had a capacity for wood valued at 1000 contos ($50,000). The same ship, however, could bring a cargo of spices from India seven times as valuable.

The brazil wood trade was carried on from trading posts along the coast, and had to be developed by the Portuguese (and other Europeans). The Indians had made no great use of the wood before the discovery. In contrast with the thriving trade of the East with which the Portuguese had merely to make contact, the brazil wood industry meant the establishment of posts, development of agriculture for food, barter with the Indians for food or labor, enslavement of Indians or Negroes, the training of these to cut and prepare the wood, and the transportation of the wood to the coast for loading. This involved a large expense before

travel account similar to Cieza's *Crónica.* On agricultural matters, native and transplanted plants, and animals in Brazil, see pp. 174-360; see also Lemos Brito, *História econômica do Brasil,* pp. 47-64; F. C. Hoehne, *Botanica e agricultura no Brasil no seculo XVI* (São Paulo, 1937); Cardim, *Terra e gente do Brasil,* pp. 31-130.

[15] Bernardino José de Souza, *O pau-brasil na história nacional* (Sao Paulo, 1940).

[16] The *conto* today is equivalent to approximately fifty dollars, but it is probable that the relative value of that time was even greater than these sums indicate.

there were any returns whatever. But the Portuguese found it profitable; and the French, who had no rival colonies in the East, found the dye woods extremely valuable for their textile industry.[17]

France was much more heavily populated than Portugal and had a vigorous trade dating from the Middle Ages. She therefore had a vital reason for breaking into the Portuguese trade area. This was the time of Charles VIII and Louis XII of France, who were vigorously pushing claims in Italy and elsewhere, and they were succeeded by Francis I, whose imperial ambitions brought him into conflict with Germany, Spain, Portugal, and the Papacy. Francis I was determined not to recognize the right of the Pope to divide the world between his enemies, leaving France outside.

The French showed no intention at first of founding colonies in Brazil. They were content with trading posts from which the dye woods and other products could be shipped. The Frenchmen came in such numbers that the Indians learned to distinguish them from the Portuguese, calling them the "blond beards," in contrast with the "black beards," who were the Portuguese. Their vessels sailed from Honfleur, Dieppe, Saint Malo, and other ports. While the merchants of France were trading, the King of France was sending out privateers who preyed on the Portuguese ships. Portugal protested, and almost constant negotiations went on between the courts, but the French did not desist.

French (and Spanish) activity along the Brazilian coast was not long in forcing the Portuguese government to take strong action. An expedition under Christóvão Jacques in 1516 destroyed a French fleet and captured its cargo. France claimed damages amounting to the modern equivalent of about seven million dollars (136,000 *contos*). Such a claim was undoubtedly greatly exaggerated, but indicates something of the value both nations placed on the trade.[18] Jacques established a feitoria in Pernambuco and his settlement prospered. Agriculture was started and sugar produced in 1521. Brazilian historians sometimes call this the first sugar of the New World, but as we have seen the Spaniards were producing sugar in the West Indies before this date.

The value of the dye wood production to Portugal seems to have increased rather steadily thereafter. In the time of Noronha, the crown revenue was probably the equivalent of 1,000 modern

[17] Roberto C. Simonsen, *História econômica do Brasil* (2 vols., São Paulo, 1937), I, 83-91; see also, Antonio Baião, "O Comercio do pau brasil," in *HCP*, II, 317-47.
[18] On French see *Revista IHGB*, vol. 81 (1890); António Baião and Malheiro Dias, "A expedição de Christóvam Jacques," *HCP*, III, 59-91; Capistrano de Abreu, *Descobrimento*, pp. 11-28.

Brazilian contos a year, rising to 3,600 at the end of the century, 4,800 in 1602, 5,500 in 1640 and 7,000 in 1823.[19]

The feitoria established by Jacques was destroyed by the French in 1530, bringing Portugal up against the fact that her Brazilian territory must be more effectively occupied or abandoned to foreign competitors.[20] It is difficult to say how many feitorias were in existence in 1530. The period since discovery was so brief, Portugal was so preoccupied with her quickly-got riches from India, and the years after 1530 were so much more productive, that it is customary to pass over the first thirty years as the period of "neglect." It is certainly incorrect to say that "Brazil was left open like a common," as Southey does, and more true to the facts to state as Southey also does, that "individuals meantime being left to themselves settled in the harbors and islands along the coast; and little towns and villages were growing up." [21] The early years were a formative period. They may be compared with Spain's first quarter century in the Caribbean. To expect that Portugal should visualize overnight that the "Island of the Holy Cross" would become the "continent of Brazil" is unreasonable. The first thirty years were the period of gestation, of essential but unpublicized activity.

THE CAPTAINCIES

The year 1530 was one of decision and action in Brazilian history. João III, the Portuguese monarch, resolved to take a firm hold and drive out his foreign competitors. Martim Afonso de Souza [22] was dispatched with two ships of the line and three smaller vessels to survey the coast, drive out the French, make new settlements, set up an administrative system for the feitorias, and report on the program best adapted to the colonization of Brazil. He captured three French vessels in Pernambuco, sent an expedition to lay claim to the region along the northern coast, and sailed southward. A settlement was made in Baia, and a fort established in Rio de Janeiro where he stayed two months, exploring the surrounding territory.

Farther south in Cananéa (in present-day Paraná) he remained for a time, and sent an expedition of eighty men inland with an "interpreter," Francisco de Chaves, who had apparently been around Cananéa for some time and had learned the language of

[19] Simonsen, *História econômica do Brasil,* I, 89-102.
[20] Calmon, *Civilização brasileira,* pp. 20-23.
[21] Southey, *Brazil,* I, 32.
[22] See Jordão de Freitas, "A expedição de Martim Afonso de Souza," *HCP,* III, 97-164.

the Indians. Chaves promised to return with four hundred Indian slaves loaded with precious metals, but nothing was ever heard of the expedition again. It was probably destroyed by disease and Indian attacks. This was not the first experience of the Portuguese with the hostility of nature and of the natives of the interior, nor was it to be the last. But it was the most impressive manifestation up to that time of the difficulties that lay ahead in the conquest of the forests and their inhabitants.[23]

From Cananéa, Martim Afonso went south as far as Chui, where shipwreck turned him back, while his brother, Pero Lopes, went on.[24] North of Cananéa, in the present state of São Paulo, he established the colony of São Vicente, destined to become Portugal's "door of entry" into the interior of southern Brazil, as were Baía, Pernambuco, São Luiz de Maranhão, and the Amazon to the interior farther north.

João III had resolved before the return of Martim Afonso to Portugal in 1533 to project the system of *capitanias* into Brazil. They had served well in the Azores and Madeiras and were to serve equally well in Brazil. The object was to circumvent foreign rivals, supplement the feitorias, and give substance to the shadow of Portuguese claims. A capitania, briefly described, was a grant of a large body of land to an individual who was endowed with ample economic and political privileges. A modern authority has likened them to "the Proprietary Colonies granted by England to court favorites—Maryland, Carolina, New Jersey, Pennsylvania, and New York after its conquest from the Dutch," differing "solely in that the North American proprietor was limited by the provision that he must make laws 'by and with the consent of the freemen.' " [25]

The feudal character of the captaincies may be detected at once, but they were not merely nor entirely so. The large political powers undoubtedly savored of medieval principalities, but they also had a strong element of the blossoming sixteenth-century capitalism. The nature of Portugal's own political and economic development up to that time made this inevitably true. To be a successful proprietor of a captaincy—a *donatário,* as they were known in Portuguese—it was necessary to bring settlers to populate Brazil, introduce agriculture and stimulate commerce, finance the whole scheme until it became self-sustaining, and organize a supply of

[23] Calmon, *Civilização brasileira,* pp. 22-23.
[24] One of the early and most important documents of Brazilian history is the diary of Pero Lopes. See J. Capistrano de Abreu, *Ensaios e estudos,* (second series, Rio de Janeiro: Sociedade Capistrano de Abreu, 1932), pp. 351-70; *Revista IHGB,* vol. 24 (1861), pp. 3-111.
[25] Roy Nash, *The Conquest of Brazil* (New York, 1926), p. 89.

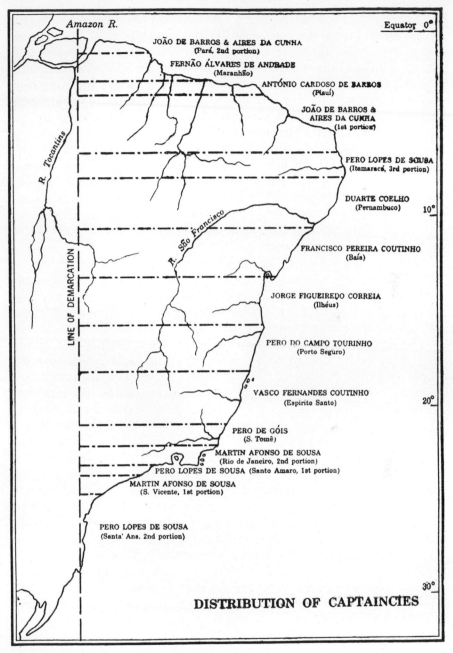

Amazon R.

Equator 0°

JOÃO DE BARROS & AIRES DA CUNHA
(Pará, 2nd portion)

FERNÃO ÁLVARES DE ANDRADE
(Maranhão)

ANTÓNIO CARDOSO DE BARROS
(Piauí)

JOÃO DE BARROS &
AIRES DA CUNHA
(1st portion)

PERO LOPES DE SOUSA
(Itamaracá, 3rd portion)

DUARTE COELHO
(Pernambuco)

10°

R. Tocantins

R. São Francisco

FRANCISCO PEREIRA COUTINHO
(Baía)

JORGE FIGUEIREDO CORREIA
(Ilhéus)

LINE OF DEMARCATION

PERO DO CAMPO TOURINHO
(Porto Seguro)

VASCO FERNANDES COUTINHO
(Espírito Santo)

20°

PERO DE GÓIS
(S. Tomé)

MARTIN AFONSO DE SOUSA
(Rio de Janeiro, 2nd portion)

PERO LOPES DE SOUSA (Santo Amaro, 1st portion)

MARTIN AFONSO DE SOUSA
(S. Vicente, 1st portion)

PERO LOPES DE SOUSA
(Santa' Ana, 2nd portion)

30°

DISTRIBUTION OF CAPTAINCIES

Adapted from Carlos Malheiro Dias, ed., *História de colonização portuguesa do Brasil.*
(Oporto, 1921-1926)

642a

labor. All of this added up to a gigantic and sometimes impossible task.

Labor was one of the most difficult of these problems. But historical traditions had already provided a ready answer to labor shortages—slavery. Tiny Portugal with her small population could not furnish sufficient workers to open up both the East and Brazil. She herself had long since resorted to Africa to supply the gap between the demand and supply of labor. Many of her large estates, especially in southern Portugal, were worked by slave labor, while the peasants on other estates could be spared in relatively small quantities for the new and gigantic task. What was more natural than the transfer to Brazil of the whole concept of labor as known on her own soil? There was scarcely a question of what type of labor would be used, only of how to get it. Africa supplied one answer. The Indians of Brazil were to supply another. But both types of labor were costly and added greatly to the expense of colonization.

The financial outlay was enormous in the terms of the time, and it was hoped someday to regain the principal and earn profits. The donatary, like any other investor, wanted returns. Some of the donataries never came to Brazil; others had partners, or borrowed large sums, further enhancing the capitalistic nature of their enterprises.[26] In short, the function of the donatary was to mobilize production, which is much the function of capital in modern society.

The captaincies were granted by the King, acting in a double capacity: temporal and spiritual, since besides his authority as the monarch, he had that of permanent Grand Master of the Order of Christ. The donations were perpetual and hereditary, with the obligation on the part of the donatary to fulfil the terms of the grant and enjoy its privileges, unless removed for treason or other high crimes. The privileges of the donataries were numerous.[27]

They were given the right to be known as captain or governor, and to control a territory fifty leagues or more along the sea.

---

[26] The controversy over the nature of the captaincies has engaged the attention of many historians of Brazil in recent times. Paulo Merêa, in "A Solução tradicional da colonização do Brasil," *HCP*, III, 165-188, stresses the historical origins of the captaincies; Malheiro Dias in "O Regimen feudal das donatárias," *HCP*, III, 219-71, discusses each captaincy separately, accentuating the aristocratic tendencies; Pedro Azevedo in "Os primeiros donatários," *HCP*, III, 191-216, also discusses the donataries one by one; cf. on captaincies and early colonization *Primeiro Congresso de Historia do Brasil* (1914), vols. I and II, for articles by various authors with different viewpoints; in Vicente do Salvador, *História do Brasil*, pp. 70-134, there is an account of the captaincies a century after their initiation.

[27] Francisco Adolpho de Varnhagen, *História geral do Brasil* (2 vols., Madrid-Rio de Janeiro, 1854-1857), I, 72-83.

Ten leagues of territory along the coast were granted as personal property, provided this area was divided into four or five non-contiguous strips, on which they paid only the tithe and no other taxes. They received the rights to enslave Indians for their estates and ships; to sell a specified number of slaves in Portugal each year free of the sales tax, the number varying with each captaincy; and to control river traffic within their captaincies. They were empowered to bestow *sesmarias*, or land grants in accordance with the laws of Portugal, the grantees to be exempt from all taxes except the tithe. The donataries were authorized to collect one-tenth of the *quinto* on metals and precious stones, and to retithe, or collect one-tenth of the tithe. They were awarded a monopoly of water mills and all other mills whatever, collecting a tax from those established with the license of the donatary; and allowed one-twentieth of all fish caught and one-twentieth of all brazil wood sold in Portugal from the captaincy (revoked in 1557).

They were given the authority to found towns, grant them charters, and name the officials; to appoint notaries, officials of far more prestige than the title suggests to North American readers; to appoint the mayors and military commanders of towns, exacting the customary oath of fealty; to censor the town election lists of *homens-bons*, or worthy men, with rights of suffrage; and to approve or disapprove the elections so held. They were granted jurisdiction in criminal cases, including the power to impose the death penalty without appeal for *peões* (plebeians), slaves, and Indians, and sentences up to ten years exile and a heavy fine for gentry; jurisdiction without appeal in civil cases in which a sum under one hundred milreis was involved; and jurisdiction as a court of appeal within the captaincy.

The donataries were also endowed with important exemptions from the King's authority. The sovereign promised never to send his *corregidores* into the captaincies; nor to permit the donatary to be suspended or sentenced without a personal hearing by the King.

An integral part of the system was the *foral*, or charter, which fixed the obligation of the donatary toward the Crown and the colonists. Each captaincy received such a *foral*, setting forth the privileges of the donatary and the rights of the landowners, as well as the prerogatives of the King. The latter were limited to collections of customs duties, monopoly of drugs and spices, the *quinto* of metals and precious stones, and the tithe. The King could also appoint *môrdomos*, or treasury officials, to see to his interests.

The *foros,* or privileges, of the colonists were: to hold *sesmarias* (land grants) without paying any taxes except the tithe; assurance that the donatary would not grant lands to his kinsmen nor expand his own lands at the expense of the colonists; permanent exemption from the *sisa* (excise taxes), salt and soap taxes, or any other taxes not specified in the *foral;* freedom from taxes on all exports to any Portuguese territory, except the usual *sisa* at the time of sale, and from import taxes on goods from Portugal, unless the merchants were "foreign," when the tithe would be paid; free commerce between the captaincies and a monopoly of the trade with the Indians.

The captaincies were declared, in accordance with Portuguese feudal usage, places of asylum (*couto e homisio*) where no one could be prosecuted for previous crimes. This was to have serious consequencies for the administration of justice in Brazil, as may be readily seen. Roman Catholic foreigners were not forbidden to come as settlers, and foreign ships could trade between Brazil and Portugal on the payment of a ten per cent tax. Of far-reaching importance, and perhaps the most significant aspect of the whole system, was the recognition in the law of distinct social classes. These were four: the donatary, *fidalgos* (gentry); *peões* (plebeians), and Indians.

With the exception of the articles monopolized by the Crown, the donataries, as well as the settlers, could send any type of goods to the markets of the kingdom of Portugal, or even to foreign markets, without paying any tax except the *sisa.* Ships coming from Portugal paid no tax in Brazil if they had already paid the Portuguese export customs; and Portuguese ships loading in Brazil for foreign ports paid the tithe to the Crown, but they paid nothing if sailing to Portugal or its possessions. Foreign vessels paid the tithe when sailing for Portugal in addition to the customs there. No vessel could be cleared from the captaincy without the consent of the donatary. No tariffs or taxes were levied between the captaincies.

COLONIZATION BY THE DONATARIES

The majority of the donataries made an effort to colonize their lands, only the donatary of Ceará failing to provide for exploration of his grant. But this was never an easy task, and in some cases centuries were required for effective settlement. The difficulties were many. The areas were enormous; much of the land in the terms of the time was of small economic value; much of it was all but inaccessible because of jungle, mountains, or desert; but little of it had a good climate, and almost all was occupied by warlike Indians. Finally, the rivalry of foreign nations led to the destruction of many nascent settlements. Sudden and easy success was not to be expected. The early problem was summed up by Duarte Coelho's statement to the King that, "We are obliged to conquer by inches the lands Your Majesty granted us by leagues."

But in spite of all difficulties, the captaincy system was destined to give Portugal victory over her rivals for Brazil. "Everything was sacrificed to the great undertaking—lives and goods. In braving the wilds, territorial and human, the blood of Portugal flowed without measure (*sem peso em medida*)." [28]

Many of the donataries and settlers embarked on their Brazilian adventure in the spirit of true colonization: they came to the New World to live. Several donataries sold or mortgaged all their property in Portugal or India. The colonists (*colonos*) likewise left everything in Portugal to find a new home. The difference between success or failure meant the difference between life and death.

The original donataries were twelve in number, with their properties divided into fifteen grants. To Martim Afonso, João III gave one hundred leagues along the coast around São Vicente (São Paulo State of today) and to his brother Pero Lopes, fifty leagues, two portions of which joined the grants of Martim Afonso and the other lay in the region of present-day Pernambuco. São Vicente became an early center of sugar production and cattle raising. The captaincy, which brought its supply of livestock from overseas, furnished cattle to other parts of Brazil, although these probably were also stocked with direct imports.[29]

Pernambuco was granted to Duarte Coelho. It attained a greater immediate success than most of the other captaincies, and became one of the most prosperous sections of Brazil. All the grants of land, except that of Martim Afonso, were for fifty leagues, although this was not always in one continuous strip of coast.

Baía went to Francisco Pereira Coutinho. Baía is one of the most beautiful bays and finest harbors in the world. It had other characteristics which were to make settlement difficult, however, and rapid success unattainable. The coast and bay region was the site of incessant Indian wars. The Tapuias, a warlike group, had been driven out by the Tupinaes who were in turn forced to give

[28] Quoted in Simonsen, *História econômica do Brasil*, I, 130-31, note 4.

[29] Southey, *Brazil*, I, 35, holds that the first cattle and sugar cane were in São Vicente. For other information on this see Lemos Brito, *História econômica do Brasil*, pp. 439-58; cf. Alfredo Ellis Junior, *A evolução da econômia paulista e suas causas* (São Paulo, 1938); and Washington Luis, *Capitania de São Paulo* (São Paulo, 1938).

Adapted from A. Curtis Wilgus, *Latin America in Maps*
Some Settlements in Brazil

646a

way to the Tupinambas, both of the former tribes retiring to the interior. When the Portuguese landed they were therefore faced with a "defense in depth" of hostile tribes. Portuguese success might have been impossible if the Indians had not engaged in civil wars, and "carried on hostilities by land and water, and all parties devoured their prisoners." [30]

Sugar and other European crops were introduced and the first basis for a colony established. The colonists were greatly aided by a Portuguese, known by his Indian name Caramurú, who had been wrecked near Baía in 1510 and had come to be a "king" among the Indians, marrying several Indian women. His influence was great and his family numerous, becoming the nucleus for many of the "best families of Baía." Caramurú's continued help through the next quarter century was to be influential in eventual success, although he was unable to assure the immediate prosperity of the colony. The settlers were forced, after seven years of war, to flee to Ilhéus. Here intervened, however, a factor that was to benefit the colonists many times; the Indians missed the articles formerly bought from the Portuguese and so invited them to return. Some of the Portugeuse were slain by hostile savages when they landed at the wrong place while returning, but Caramurú and those with him survived until they were reinforced by others, and finally by the establishment of a stronger colony at Baía in 1549. In the meantime the colony was not financially profitable. Coutinho expended his entire fortune, and he and his family were reduced to poverty.

Espírito Santo fell to Vasco Fernandes Coutinho. Cane was planted, sugar mills established, and the Indians driven back. But the early settlement did not thrive, and it was many years before the colony attained stability. Porto Seguro was colonized by Pedro do Campo Tourinho, who sold his entire possessions in Portugal and embarked with his family and a large body of colonists for Brazil. [31] Other settlements were made with varying degrees of success.

It is difficult to find a yardstick with which to measure the relative achievement of the early captaincies. Some were undoubtedly prosperous from the viewpoint of both finance and colonization. Others were financial failures, but resulted in permanent colonies. Enormous sums of money were spent. If the success was not always apparent, the blame was due as much to the immensity of the task, amounting to an impossibility in some cases, as to the incapacity of the grantees. A greater concentration of effort might have

---

[30] Southey, *Brazil*, I, 42.
[31] Southey, *Brazil*, I, 30-31, 39, 41-44.

led to fewer failures, but it would have left long stretches of coastline undefended and unoccupied except by Portugal's rivals. In
1548, there were already sixteen settlements exporting brazil wood,
sugar, cotton, tobacco, and other products. Some of these posts
were fortified, and some had yards where river boats were constructed and ocean-going vessels repaired. [32]

Brazil in 1548 was definitely established, but only along the
coastline. Geography, climate, and the aboriginal inhabitants made
the penetration of the interior difficult. In the south, along the São
Paulo and Paraná coast, the mountains crowded the sea; in Espírito
Santo the jungle presented a wall; the interior of Pernambuco and
Ceará was a desert; and along the northern coast up to the Amazon,
sandy beaches were the rule. From the Amazon south, on the coast
and inland, there were hostile Indians, and it must have seemed to
the settlers that there was an enemy behind every bush.

Nor was there great economic incentive to push inland. Ample
supplies of dye wood were obtainable within a hundred miles of the
sea. Abundant crops of sugar, tobacco, and food could be grown
on a fraction of the available coastlands. There was neither necessity nor profit in piercing the mountains and jungles. All that could
be expected of Brazil during the first century could be won from the
littoral; both common sense and economic interest limited the area
of colonization. Later the Paulistas fanned out from their mountain plateau to give Portugal a claim to southern Brazil, and in-
trepid explorers and missionaries pushed the boundaries to the
Andes. But for the moment the principal problem was to tie the
scattered coastal settlements securely together and protect them
from their foreign enemies.

THE CAPTAINCY-GENERAL

Brazil was now ready for another decisive step in her history.
Pernambuco and São Vicente were relatively prosperous, and some
of the other captaincies had survived even where they had not
prospered. But the whole lacked cohesion, and in 1549 João III
determined to create the Captaincy-General as a central government to supply the needed unity. [33] The innovation was destined
to have considerable success, although it was impossible to accomplish overnight by fiat what nature had rendered so difficult. Brazil
was too extensive, and the obstacles to internal communications too
many. The measure of the task faced by sixteenth-century Brazil
is to be found in the efforts that twentieth-century Brazil is still

---

[32] Simonsen, *História econômica do Brasil*, I, 124-32.
[33] See Pedro Azevedo, "A Instituição do Governo Geral," *HCP*, III, 327-83.

making to achieve unity. But the creation of the Captaincy-General was a move in the direction that eventually prevented Brazil from breaking into several nations, as did the Spanish-speaking colonies, where, however, the obstacles to unity were even greater.

The first captain-general was Tomé de Souza and Baía was picked for the site of the capital. [34] There in 1549, Tomé de Souza laid out his capital near the location of the previous Portuguese settlements and instituted the full apparatus of Portuguese colonial government, including a municipality, Jesuit missions, churches, fort, soldiers, settlers, court, government houses, customs house, and land grants.

The expedition of Tomé de Souza consisted of six vessels, carrying "three hundred and twenty persons in the King's pay, four hundred *degredados,* or banished men, and colonists who make up the whole number a thousand." When the fleet reached Baía it was met by Caramurú who was able to assure a welcome for the Portuguese and to initiate trade between them and the Indians. The six Jesuits accompanying the expedition were the first in Brazil, thus beginning the Jesuit activity which has exerted a profound influence on Brazil even to the present day.

The new colony achieved prosperity from the start. Its location was excellent and the experience gained by its earlier settlers useful. Tomé de Souza lost no time in getting the colony established, and four months after arrival more than a hundred houses had been built and sugar plantations laid out. The numerous inlets of the bay with their islands and peninsulas were to furnish ideal soil and transportation for the sugar and tobacco industries that rapidly sprang up.

The colony was reinforced by a second expedition that came out the next year. Still "another fleet came out the third year, on board of which the Queen sent out many female orphans of noble family, who had been educated in the Convent of Orphans; they were to be given in marriage to the officers, and portioned with Negroes, kine, and brood mares from the royal property. Orphan boys also came out to be educated by the Jesuits; and ships followed every year with like supplies." [35]

THE EVOLUTION OF AGRICULTURE

With the setting-up of the Captaincy-General, Brazil acquired its adult economic characteristics. All of the principal crops, cacao,

---

[34] Gabriel Soares, *Brasil em 1587,* pp. 125-74. Vicente do Salvador, in his *História do Brasil,* pp. 135-623 gives a chronological account of the period to 1627.
[35] Southey, *Brazil,* I, 213-16.

cotton, corn, tobacco, and cane, were well-established by 1549, although some of them did not achieve great importance at this early epoch. Livestock of many types was also being raised in several regions. Sugar cane was destined to be the leading crop during the colonial period. Portugal had a long cane-growing history before Brazil was discovered, especially in her island possessions. By the time of Brazilian discovery the Atlantic islands of Portugal were producing more sugar than the market warranted; the price fell disastrously and King Manoel attempted in 1498 to limit the export of the Madeira Islands to 120,000 *arrobas* (1,500 tons) annually. Europe was even then in the midst of greater commercial expansion, however, and it is not surprising that sugar cane should have been planted in Brazil where shortly after 1520 it figured among the products of Pernambuco. As early as 1526 Brazilian sugar was listed among the imports of Portugal.

The real sugar production of Brazil did not come, however, until the Captaincies of São Vicente, Pernambuco and Baía were well established. Cane was planted and mills constructed also in the captaincies of Ilhéus (south of Baía) where Lucas Giraldes built eight mills, and his colonos others; and in Porto Seguro and Espírito Santo, both still farther south, between Baía and Rio de Janeiro. São Vicente was more prosperous as a center of the cane industry. Afonso de Souza, Pero Lopes de Souza, and Pero Lopes da Silveira associated themselves with Flemings and Germans in this industry. The Erasmus Schetz family of Antwerp was enriched and ennobled from the profits it made in Brazilian sugar. From about the middle of the sixteenth to the middle of the seventeenth century, Brazil was the world's leading sugar exporter. The Portuguese Crown encouraged the industry. When Tomé de Souza came out in 1549 he was granted a ten-year tax exemption on sugar. Later the owners of sugar mills received titles of nobility and their mills were freed from debt seizure. Subsequently a twenty per cent tax was imposed on Brazil to prevent the destruction of the Madeira industry.

Private initiative, as well as government promotion, contributed to the growth of the cane industry. The expenses of establishing a mill were such that it was frequently necessary for several men to combine. The colonists associated themselves with Portuguese merchants who supplied the capital for building the mills, and marketed the finished product in Europe. Settlers who could not build their own mills grew cane which was ground for them by others on a percentage basis. Many of them were enabled in this way to acquire sufficient capital to build for themselves. In other cases, the government promoted the building of mills, as for instance in Baía, where the governer established a cane-grinding mill for planters who did not have their own.

Brazil's cane industry was on a much grander scale than the previous Portuguese industry in the islands. Where formerly small hand mills and slight production had been the rule, the industry in Brazil was characterized by the "big-business" methods of the times. Circumstances made it so. Brazil was far from Europe, the shipping men could not afford to haul short cargoes, European investors were waiting for profits, and the Crown could not support feeble colonies. Likewise, the expense of sending out colonists, clearing land, driving back the Indians, defending the colony from foreign rivals, and buying slaves and equipment ran into the sixteenth-century equivalent of millions. To make them pay, it was necessary to establish mills with several times the capacity of those in the Atlantic islands. Single mills customarily had three thousand arrobas annual capacity, and there were many with ten.[36]

The sugar industry soon created a prosperous colonial aristocracy. The land was fertile, Indian labor plentiful at first, with Negro labor to make up the deficiency, and the market steady. Three chief centers soon took the lead in production. In São Vicente, which represented the southern extreme of sixteenth-century Portuguese colonization, sugar was the main early wealth. Farther north in Baía, the industry thrived. And most prosperous of all in this period was Pernambuco. All of them were characterized by a rich aristocracy occupying a position infinitely above an Indian and Negro slave class from which it derived its wealth. Brazil of today still bears the distinct social characteristics branded on it by its early economy. [37]

---

[36] For a good description of the early industry see Gabriel Soares, *Brasil em 1587*, pp. 1-174.

[37] The sugar industry has properly been the subject of study by many Portuguese and Brazilian authors. See Azevedo's chapter "O império do açúcar," in his *Épocas de Portugal econômico* (Lisbon, 1929), pp. 223-298, for a study of sugar from its appearance in the island possessions of Portugal to the end of the colonial period in Brazil. In addition to Gabriel Soares cited above, see André João Antonil (João Antonio Andreoni), *Cultura e opulencia do Brasil por sus drogas e minas* (Lisbon, 1711), edited by Affonso de E. Taunay, São Paulo, 1923, pp. 67-179. Antonil's book, first published in 1711, was quickly suppressed by the Crown on the grounds that it would serve foreigners as a guide to Brazil's riches, and only a few copies survived. It is one of the essential documents for early eighteenth-century Brazil. Antonil had lived there for many years. There are today six known copies of the first edition, none of them in the United States.

29

Foreign Rivalry
and Portuguese Expansion

FRENCH AND ENGLISH INTERVENTION IN BRAZIL

I F THE PRODUCTS OF BRAZIL excited foreign cupidity at the outset when brazil wood alone afforded attractive profits, competition was intensified with the growth of the sugar and tobacco plantations. The French were persistent rivals of the Portuguese and the early efforts to drive the French out were never entirely successful. The adoption of the system of captaincies and the institution of the Captaincy-General were in part inspired by the need of counteracting the French. [1] They nevertheless continued to carry on trade with the Indians and to carry brazil wood back to Europe. Nor did they neglect piracy. Along the coast between Rio de Janeiro and Baía, and north of Pernambuco, they found ample territories where the Portuguese had not effectively settled. In these regions, allied with the Indians, they established trading posts in spite of all efforts to dislodge them.

The religious schism in France was to produce a more determined colonizing effort on the part of the French. In 1555, Nicholas Durand de Villegagnon, a friend of the Huguenot leader, Admiral Gaspar de Coligny, and a distinguished military figure in his own right, conceived the idea of establishing "Antarctic France" in Brazil. He obtained the support of Coligny and a little financial aid from King Henry II of France. An expedition of two ships, with about six hundred people, Protestants and Catholics, landed in the bay of Rio de Janeiro in 1555, and settled on an island that still bears the name of Villegagnon. [2] A reinforcement of three

[1] On the French in Brazil see *Revista IHGB*, vol. 130 (1914), pp. 191-217; Capistrano de Abreu, *História colonial*, pp. 61-81.
[2] For two accounts written by members of the Villegagnon expedition see André Thévet, *Les Singularités de la France antarctique* (Paris, 1558); and Jean de Léry, *Histoire d'un voyage fait en la terre du Brésil* (La Rochelle, 1578).

ships was sent out later, but the colony did not prosper. Religious dissension broke out and Villegagnon returned home in 1559.

In the meantime, Mem de Sá had been appointed governor-general of Brazil and had reached Baía in 1557.[3] Led by a French traitor, Jean de Cointa, who was later rewarded for his services to the Portuguese by being prosecuted by the Inquisition in Lisbon, and with reinforcements from Portugal, Mem de Sá drove the French out of their settlement in 1560. This was merely the beginning of the campaign. The French had fled from Villegagnon's island to the mainland, whence, in company with Tamoyo Indians, they carried on constant harrying attacks against the Portuguese.

Seven years later Mem de Sá returned to the attack. Assisted by the Jesuits, Nóbrega and Anchieta,[4] who recruited the Indians for service in the Portuguese forces, he succeeded in expelling the French definitely. A Portuguese town, São Sebastian do Rio de Janeiro, was founded in 1567, and grew into the present city of Rio.[5] The Jesuits were given a site for building, and provision was made for supporting a company of fifty fathers. The city was constructed and fortified largely by Indians under Jesuit control.

The French left Rio and sailed north, where they captured the town of Recife in Pernambuco. They were not strong enough to hold it, however, and were driven out. But this did not end French participation in Brazilian development. Many French continued to trade around the Rio Real, and more than half a century was to elapse before they were finally expelled from this and other points farther north on the Brazilian coast from Pernambuco to French Guiana.[6]

The English were also interested in Brazil, though to a far less extent than the French. Possibly the first English trader in Brazil was William Hawkins, father of John Hawkins, who made two expeditions to Brazil, the first in 1530 and the second in 1532. By 1540 a considerable trade had sprung up, carried on by "substantial and wealthy merchants of Southampton" according to Hakluyt. An English merchant is said to have founded a fort and trading post in Baía in 1542. Still later another English merchant established himself in Santos and carried on an active trade in sugar and other products, but the advent of Spanish rule over Brazil brought

[3] "Documentos relativos a Mem de Sá, Governador Geral do Brasil," in *Anais da Biblioteca Nacional de Rio de Janeiro*, xxvii (1905), 127-280 (hereafter *Anais BNRio*).

[4] Anibal Mattos, *Joseph de Anchieta* (Belo Horizonte, Brazil: Biblioteca Minera de Cultura, 1935), pp. 233-41.

[5] Pedro Calmon, *História do Brasil* (Rio de Janeiro, 1940), I, 259-287.

[6] Southey, *Brazil*, I, 300-302, 314-15.

this to a close. Cavendish, however, attacked and burned Santos in 1591; and the Englishman Lancaster and the Fleming Vanner assailed and pillaged Recife. The English were also active along the coast north of Recife, in the region of the Amazon, and although they were never successful as colonizers in Brazil, they managed to retain British Guiana.[7]

SPANISH DOMINATION

In the meantime the Spaniards were establishing themselves on every side. Pinzón, De Lepe, Ojeda, and possibly other early explorers had touched on territory that time was to make Brazilian. Brazil figured in the map of Juan de la Cosa, finished in October, 1500.[8] De Solís had sailed along the coast in his expedition to the Río de la Plata in 1515-16, Magellan in 1519, and Sebastian Cabot in 1526. Mendoza had led his large and well-equipped expedition to the first (unsuccessful) founding of Buenos Aires in 1535, and an offshoot of this voyage had established Asunción in 1537. When Orellana sailed down the Amazon river in 1541, giving Spain claim by discovery to lands granted her by the Treaty of Tordesillas, it appeared that Portugal's sphere of activity was being limited in every direction. [9]

Portugal was eventually to make good her claims to territories sought by the Spanish but it was to come about under conditions that made it appear that Portugal had lost her own independence. When the King of Portugal, Sebastian, was killed in a war against the Moors in Africa in 1578, there were several claimants to the throne, among them Philip II of Spain. By bribing some of the nobles of Portugal, and defeating the others in battle, he was able to have himself declared sovereign. Portugal did not become free from Spain until 1640. [10]

Philip had gained a prize worth having. In addition to the possessions of Portugal in the East, Brazil was beginning to furnish no small revenue. As disclosed by one of the early chroniclers, Pero Magalhães Gandavo, [11] Brazil had made very considerable

---

[7] Manoel Bomfim, *O Brasil* (nova edição, São Paulo, 1940), pp. 25-27; Southey, *Brazil*, I, 352-54.

[8] Capistrano de Abreu, *História colonial*, p. 28.

[9] For the history of the boundary relations of Brazil see, Simonsen, *História econômica*, II, 152-157; Capistrano, *História colonial*, pp. 196-213; *Documentos sobre o tratado de 1750, Anais BNRio*, LII and LIII (1930 and 1931).

[10] Henrique Handelmann, *História do Brasil* (eds. and trs. Lucia Furquim Lahmeyer, Bertholdo Klinger, and Basilio de Magalhães, *Revista IHGB*, Rio de Janeiro, 1931), pp. 137-168; Lucio José dos Santos, *O dominio espanhol no Brasil*.

[11] Pero de Magalhães de Gandavo, *The Histories of Brazil*, ed. and tr. John B. Stetson (2 vols., New York: The Cortes Society, 1922), *passim*. Both the *História* and the *Tratado* are given in this work.

progress before 1570. By that date, there were eight well-established captaincies, with sixty sugar mills producing an average of three thousand arrobas each annually. There were about 3,440 *vizinhos*, who with their families made a population of approximately 17,000 Europeans, not counting Indians and Negro slaves. The total "civilized" population was probably thirty thousand people, engaged in cutting brazil wood, cultivating cotton, sugar, and food crops. [12]

During the first years of the Spanish occupation, it was estimated that there lived around the bay of Baía two thousand whites, and enough Indians and Negroes to allow the raising of an army of five hundred horse and two thousand foot soldiers. Baía had more than fourteen hundred boats, of which about a hundred were capable of carrying artillery. Every man had a boat or a canoe and no sugar mill had less than four. The city and bay region had sixty-two churches and three monasteries for its population of two thousand whites plus slaves. The annual export of sugar from Baía was about 120,000 arrobas in addition to large quantities consumed locally. Cattle were abundant enough to be a menace to growing crops. Butter, milk, and cheese were plentiful. Horses were numerous, some people having as many as forty or fifty brood mares, and there were also many sheep and goats. Oranges and lemons had been introduced and were plentiful; the early Brazilians had already invented a proverb that expressed the idea that "an orange a day keeps the doctor away." Dates, cacao, pomegranates, melons, grapes, tea, coffee, and other crops were grown. Ginger thrived, four thousand arrobas being cured in 1573, but the government had prohibited it in the interest of the Eastern product.

But the settlers had early discovered that periodical invasions of ants, which stripped crops to the stalk, made agriculture a difficult trade. In some part of Brazil down to the present, the people have surrendered to the ant and make no effort to grow the more susceptible types of vegetables. This little insect comes near deserving the name given him by the first settlers, the "King of Brazil." Many other insect pests also hampered agriculture.

Baía had more than a hundred citizens whose incomes were from three to five thousand cruzados annually, and whose fortunes were from twenty to sixty thousand cruzados. The modern equivalent would probably have to be calculated in hundreds of thousands. Their dress indicated their prosperity. Women of rank would wear nothing but silk, and the men, breeches of satin damask. Gold

---

[12] Simonsen, *História econômica*, I, 134-35.

jewelry and gold table services were the rule among the rich. Fine wines were imported from Madeira, Portugal, and the Canaries.

Pernambuco was likewise flourishing. It had faced tremendous difficulties with the Indians, who held it besieged for many years, and a five-year war (1560-1565), led by the Donatary himself, had been necessary to free it of menace. But in the end the Indians had been driven into the interior. By the 1580's there were fifty sugar works, and the Donatary received ten thousand cruzados annually from taxes on sugar and fishing. The tenths on the sugar works were farmed out for nineteen thousand cruzados a year. Some fifty-five ships a year on the average were loaded with sugar and brazil wood, and the brazil wood concession yielded the Crown twenty thousand cruzados annually. The total population was about that of Baía, and three thousand soldiers could be brought into the field. Above a hundred colonists had incomes of from one to five thousand cruzados, and a few eight and ten thousand a year, the modern equivalent of which would be hundreds of thousands of dollars in purchasing power. Fortunes of great size were made in a single lifetime.

In the south of Brazil, São Vicente, near modern Santos, grew wheat and barley, but the settlers preferred the bread made from maize and manioc. The colony was thriving. Marmalade was exported to the other colonies, grapes grew well, and wine was a chief crop. The prosperity of the sugar industry in São Vicente has already been mentioned. In the mountains, São Paulo was also producing grapes; and small amounts of gold and silver were panned around São Paulo and nearby Santo Amaro. The other captaincies were generally in a less prosperous condition, but rested on firm foundations of colonization. [13]

The population of Brazil approximately twenty years after the estimates given for 1570 amounted to about 57,000 "civilized," of whom 25,000 were whites, 18,000 Indians and 14,000 Negro slaves. [14]

A considerable capital investment, measured in the relative values of the times, was involved in Brazil. When ships, armaments, warehouses, and other expenses of shipping are calculated, this one factor alone was not small. In the colonies large sums were represented by cleared lands, farming instruments, sugar mills, livestock, growing crops, slaves, and other forms of property. A modern Brazilian economist has estimated the totals as follows:

---

[13] Southey, *Brazil*, I, 317-36; Gabriel Soares, *Brasil em 1587*, pp. 1-210.

[14] João Pandiá Calógeras, *Formação histórica do Brasil* (3rd ed., São Paulo, 1938), p. 33. See also an English translation of this work by Percy Alvin Martin.

Capital invested in captaincies	283,200	contos
Capital invested in shipping	121,600	”
Value of merchandise	52,392	”
Total	457,192	”

The net return on this capital is estimated at about fifteen per cent. Translated into dollars, this amounts to only twenty-two million, but the relative values and purchasing power were very much larger. Also, the amount of goods consumed in Brazil should be added for a conception of the total capital and production. Moreover, once the goods had arrived in Europe, their value was enhanced. The value of Brazilian exports, however, was probably not more than one-tenth those of the Spanish colonies in the same epoch. [15]

This was the land Philip II inherited along with other Portuguese possessions in 1580. Spanish domination affected the internal life of Brazil to only a slight degree. The Spanish interfered but little in the affairs of Portugal, and hence of Brazil, and domestic matters went much as before. But in one respect the life of Brazil was profoundly touched. Much of the trade of Brazil and Portugal had been with the merchants of the Netherlands. These merchants now found themselves cut off in part from their former markets for they were not allowed to trade in Lisbon and Porto. With little hesitation, they overcame this temporary setback by sending their ships directly to India and the East Indies. They took over Java; soon they took over most of the Eastern possessions of Portugal.

In Brazil there were other effects. The Paulistas took advantage of the new political tie to penetrate the regions that belonged to Spain by the Treaty of Tordesillas; and the hitherto illegal trade with the Spanish colonies took on a legal aspect and increased greatly with the founding of Buenos Aires by the Spaniards in 1580. At the same time, the ships from the Netherlands came directly to Brazil until 1603, when the King gave orders for them to be treated as enemy vessels.

THE DUTCH OCCUPATION

The Dutch were not to be so lightly put off, and took action in Brazil as they had in the East. In 1604, the Dutch commander, Paul van Ceulen, attacked Baía. And in 1621, the Dutch West India Company was formed to take over the New World colonies

---

[15] Simonsen, *História econômica*, I, 134-42.

of Portugal as the East India Company had done in the East. [16]
The Dutch captured Baía in 1624, taking the city without much
effort. While they were there, a dozen Portuguese ships sailed into
the harbor before learning of the change of sovereignty, and were
seized. This first attempt was not entirely successful, however, as
the Dutch were soon driven from Baía. In 1627 they captured
Baía again, only to lose it a second time. The following year they
seized the Spanish treasure fleet, and with a part of the proceeds
fitted out an expedition that successfully assaulted Pernambuco in
1630. Eventually they occupied territory from south of Pernambuco on the São Francisco River to the Maranhão far to the north,
but this cost them years of hard fighting.

The warfare caused extensive destruction and convinced the
Dutch that they must conquer the country thoroughly in order to
reap the full profits of their venture. In 1637, they sent out Count
Maurice of Nassau, one of the most distinguished men of Holland,
and one of the ablest. Up to the time of his governorship, the West
India Company had spent some fifty-five million florins, and had
taken captive 540 enemy vessels. These and other ventures had
yielded them thirty millions of florins in prize money, two hundred
millions from the Spaniards, and almost fifteen millions in merchandise from Africa.

To compensate for the ravages of war, Nassau ordered Olinda
rebuilt, formed the tradesmen into companies, established schools,
and carried on missionary work to convert the Indians to the Dutch
Reformed religion. One of the main tasks was to start the sugar
mills to grinding again, and these he sold at auction. The value the
industry then had is indicated by the price of sale, twenty to a hundred thousand florins for each mill, the company receiving more
than two million florins in the auction.

The Portuguese were encouraged to return by the liberal terms
offered them. They were to have full liberty of conscience, their
churches were to be kept up by the State (but no Visitor was to
come from Baía and no new monks were to enter the province as
long as there were a sufficient number for the ceremonies), they
were to be subject to the same taxes as the Netherlanders, their
property was to be restored, and they were to be allowed to wear
swords.

---

[16] On the Dutch in Brazil see Hermann Wätjen, *O dominio colonial hollandez
no Brasil,* ed. and tr. Pedro Celso Uchoa Cavalcanti (São Paulo, 1938); "Memorias
históricas e militares relativas a guerra hollandeza, 1630-1757," *Anais BNRio,* XX
(1898), 119-234; Lemos Brito, *História econômica do Brasil;* pp. 65-71; Capistrano
de Abreu, *História colonial,* pp. 82-109; Handelmann, *Brasil,* pp. 169-260.

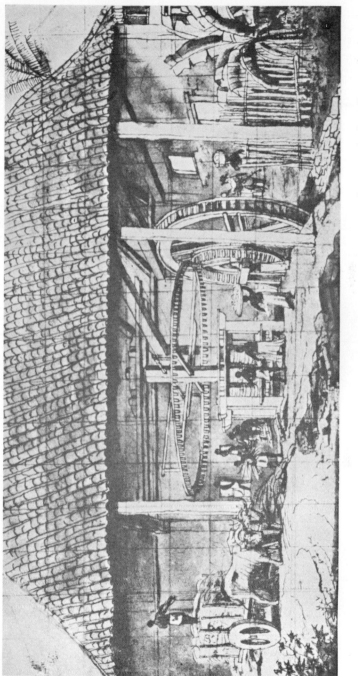

SUGAR-MILL IN BRAZIL, BY FRANS POST, DUTCH

PATRABVNT NOMEN ILLI

(Fidelitas, fortitudo et liberalitas patrarunt nomen illi)

JOÃO FERNANDES VIEIRA

(CASTRIOTO LUSITANO)

Copied from the original in The John Carter Brown Library

In 1640, Nassau signed a peace treaty with the Portuguese viceroy in Baía. The next year, word came that the Portuguese had revolted from Spain and restored their own monarch to the throne in the person of João IV. Shortly afterwards, the news came that the Portuguese had recognized the Dutch ownership of the Brazilian colonies. It seemed that the Dutch West India Company had definitely established itself in Brazil.

The company had prospered. [17] Its profits were never less than twenty-five per cent from 1626 to 1639. Sugar exports had increased from a maximum of 21,000 boxes in 1610, before Dutch occupation, to 33,000 in 1639, and this during constant war. Up to 1645 there was a rising tide of prosperity. Through Dutch occupation, Brazil was tied directly to the most profitable markets of Europe, and had every advantage over her rival producers of tropical products. Holland was at that time the leading commercial nation of the world, far outstripping Portugal, Spain, France, or England.

But if Portugal was content with Dutch possession of a part of Brazil, many Brazilians were not. A large number of the leading families of Pernambuco and other captaincies had fled from the Dutch, and their sugar plantations and mills had been confiscated. A rebellion against the Dutch in Maranhão in 1641 had spread everywhere by 1645 and Holland was faced with a compact of rebellion signed by the Brazilian planters led by João Fernandes Vieira. The clergy joined in the revolt against the heretical Dutch.

The Dutch were not as well prepared to face the rebellion as it might appear after fifteen years of occupation. They had never been sufficiently strong in Pernambuco, for example, to gather their supplies from the surrounding country, and many things had to be brought from abroad. They had also exhausted themselves with their comprehensive expeditions of conquest to all parts of the world. They had spent large sums in trying to extend their dominion south of Sergipe and north of Maranhão in Brazil; they had conquered a part of Angola to further their slave trade; they had depleted their manpower by their activities in the East; they had sent expeditions to North America, the Caribbean, Chile and Peru.

The latter enterprises had been provisioned in Pernambuco and had made inroads on the supplies and treasury of that colony. To save money, the Company ceased to send supplies to Brazil on the theory that it was self-sufficient. Nassau had gone home in the meantime, and the council of government which succeeded him

---

[17] Wätjen, *O dominio hollandez no Brasil,* pp. 494-525, shows Dutch exports from Brazil.

called on its debtors for payment, so that it in turn might pay the military and civil officials. Merchants in Holland called on their agents for remittances at the same time. The credit system of the colony was upset, money went to four per cent a month, and the borrowers went bankrupt. Many estates were sold for debt, confiscated, and the Negroes sold. Smallpox hit the settlers. Floods washed away the crops ruining many planters.

The war of the Brazilians for independence from the Dutch was complicated by the unwillingness of the Portuguese to give them full aid. Portugal had recognized Dutch rights in the treaty of 1641 as a means of getting Holland's support against Spain in her own fight for independence. Many were of the opinion that it was better not to antagonize the Dutch, who were natural allies against Spain, which had not yet fully recognized the independence of Holland. One of the chief figures on the Portuguese political stage at this time was the Jesuit, Antonio Vieira, who opposed aiding the Brazilians. He advised surrendering Brazil until a more favorable time for its recovery. His arguments were set forth in 1648 in one of the most famous documents in Portuguese history, *O Papel Forte*. In what seemed to be a spirit of utter realism he remarked:

"It is we who sell Pernambuco; we sell it for interests of greater magnitude, and shall reclaim it whenever fortune favours us; all that is now said against the conduct of the Dutch will be good in its proper season . . . . But now Brazil is at their mercy. We could perhaps be able to fit out one armament; Holland can afford to lose many. The West India Company may be poor; the East India one is rich, and will deprive us of all we have in India . . . . Castille makes a dishonorable peace with Holland, ... France suffers injuries from Holland rather than expose herself to war at once with Holland and Castille . . . and we think to resist them both! Where are our men? upon every alarm in Alentejo it is necessary to take students from the university, tradesmen from their shops, labourers from the plough! Where is our money? the expenses and losses which already have been incurred amount to five millions! Sixty ships have been captured during the present year. The last armament might have undeceived us; to raise seamen we were obliged to wait for the Rio de Janeiro fleet; to raise troops we took them from the frontiers; to provide artillery we stript the fortresses; to make up thirteen ships we left Portugal without one! Eight years have elapsed since our emancipation, and the frontiers are not yet fortified, nor is Lisbon yet put in that state of defence which we all agree is necessary; and why? . . . because the means are wanting. Compare our resources with those of the enemy! In Holland they have fourteen thousand vessels; in Portugal we have not an hundred and fifty. In India they have more than an hundred ships of war, of from twenty-four to fifty guns; we have not one. In Brazil they have more than sixty ships, some of great force; we have seven, if indeed we have them still. They are free from the power of Spain; we have the whole power of Spain to contend with. They have no enemy in Europe; We have no friend . . . . Finally, the Dutch have their industry, their diligence, their desire of gain, their unanimity, and their love of the common weal; we have our disunion, our envy, our presumption, our negligence, and our perpetual attention to individual interests . . . . It is better to deserve miracles than to expect them; but to rely upon them, even when we deserve them, is tempting God." [18]

The Brazilians, however, were not in a humor to listen to promises of freedom in better days. The war dragged on with mutual devastation, and the Dutch, pictured by Vieira as almost invincible, were slowly losing. Their commitments in many parts of the world were too great to permit full attention to Brazil. Then fell the blow which was to end the Dutch maritime supremacy. England passed the Navigation Acts in 1651 and war between the two nations followed (1652-54). At the same moment Louis XIV was becoming an uncomfortable neighbor. Holland had to leave the hard-pressed West India Company to fend for itself. The hostilities between England and Holland gave Portugal a new ally. England and Portugal signed a treaty of peace and commerce in 1642, and a few years later the friendship between Portugal and England, which dated from the epoch when John of Gaunt fought for Portugal in the fourteenth century, was cemented more firmly with the marriage of a Portuguese princess, Catherine of Braganza, to Charles II, who had been placed on the English throne in 1660.[19]

Holland withdrew from Brazil in 1654, ending the episode of Dutch Brazil. The Dutch transferred their sugar industry to the West Indies leaving Brazil free, but without an adequate market for her sugar.[20]

---

[18] Quoted in Southey, *Brazil*, II, 224-26.

[19] Southey, *Brazil*, II, 231-49.

[20] For a bibliography of Dutch Brazil see "Catálogo da Exposição Nassoviana," *Anais BNRio*, LI (1929), 1-133.

BRAZIL'S WESTWARD HO!

While Brazil was governed by the Spaniards and was engaged in the expulsion of the Dutch, she was also growing. Gradually the limits of settlement had been pushed far beyond the imaginary line of Tordesillas. The Brazilians themselves scarcely realized what had taken place. They were too busy with the preoccupations of daily life, trade, piracy, and foreign invaders to think much of the vast hinterland of mountain, jungle, and hostile Indians.

At the end of the sixteenth century, after more than seventy-five years of colonizing, Pero de Magalhães de Gandavo could write that "there are no inland settlements of Portuguese because the Indians will not permit them, and also because it is necessary to be near the sea to receive aid from and trade with the homeland." [21] In 1618, one of the characters in the *Diálogos das Grandezas* inquired: "How is it we find that in all the time the Portuguese have lived in this Brazil they have not penetrated the interior to settle even ten leagues inland, being satisfied to do nothing but cultivate sugar beside the sea?" [22]

But still a few years later, in 1627, Frei Vicente do Salvador, in his famous *História do Brasil,* remarked: "Of the extent of Brazil inland I say nothing, since up to the present there has been no one to explore it because of the failure of the Portuguese, who, although they are great conquerors of lands, do not take advantage of them, but are content to scrape along the seaside like crabs." [23] He also complained of the lack of Portuguese enterprise with regard to mining in Brazil, "because, for all that this land is alongside Peru, there being nothing but an imaginary and invisible line between them, and the Castillians there having discovered so many and such rich mines, here they do not take even one step in that direction. And when they go into the interior it is to hunt wild Indians and bring them by force and fraud in order to work them and to sell them." [24]

If there was much truth in these statements, there was also exaggeration. Although on the óne hand Brazil was far from being "alongside Peru," the penetration of the Brazilian interior had progressed more than Frei Vicente realized. Civilization

[21] Pero de Magalhães de Gandavo, *Tratado da Terra,* p. 26, cited in Calmon, *Civilização brasileira,* p. 75.

[22] *Diálogos das Grandezas do Brasil,* Capistrano de Abreu and Rodolpho García, eds. (Rio de Janeiro: Academia Brasileira, 1930), p. 28. This work is one of the most important early chronicles. It is written in the form of a dialogue with one of the characters, Alviano, serving as the Watson for the other, Brandonio, who in a superior Sherlock Holmes fashion explains the "Grandezas" of Brazil.

[23] Vicente do Salvador, *História do Brasil,* p. 19.

[24] *Ibid.,* pp. 19, 23.

moved into the interior with the cow, th horse, the hog, the dog, and the domestic fowl. Within half a :nt:ry of discovery, the Indians had adopted the dogs and the chick..s they had received from the Portuguese,[25] and where these do :estic animals went, the European soon followed.

Geography, which had placed many obstacles, also offered numerous aids, the river being of the greatest assistance. In the north, the Amazon and the Paraíba gave access to the interior; in the northwest, Pernambuco furnished a jumping-off place; a little farther south the São Francisco river and Baía were points of departure; while still farther south São Paulo became the center from which Brazil expanded. The slaver, the gold prospector, and the missionary all made contributions to Brazil's frontier movement.[26]

The introduction of domestic animals supplied a deficiency that Brazil suffered along with the rest of the New World. Cattle and hogs, and perhaps other animals, were introduced into Brazil with the settlement of São Vicente by Afonso de Souza in 1532, or possibly earlier, though additions were made from time to time by imports from Portugal and the Cape Verde Islands, notably in 1549 when the Captaincy General was established at Baía. "The cattle, after 1560, spread o· r the savannas of the Northeast [Baía and Pernambuco] with marvellous rapidity and vitality." [27]

Cattle were a necessary adjunct to the sugar industry, in addition to their value as a meat supply for the colonists and Indians.[28] Soon each plantation became the nucleus of a great herd of cattle used to cultivate the cane, haul it from the field, grind it, and transport the finished product to the ship for embarkation. But cattle were not retained within these relatively narrow limits.

---

[25] Southey, *Brazil*, I, 241.

[26] The classical work on Brazil's frontier movement is Basilio de Magalhaes, *Expansão geográphica do Brasil colonial* (2nd ed., São Paulo, 1935); see also *Revista IHGB*, vol. 30 (1867), pp. 193-240. The expansion of Baía is treated by Urbino Vianna, *Bandeiras e sertanistas bahianas* (São Paulo, 1937); and Handelmann, *Brasil*, pp. 423-62. The expansion of Pernambuco is treated by Handelmann, *Brasil*, pp. 345-421; the important place of the Jesuits and other religious orders in the growth of Brazil is treated in Serafim Leite, *História da Companhia de Jesus no Brasil* (2 vols., Lisbon and Rio de Janeiro, 1938); and Frei Antonio de Santa Maria Jaboatão, *Chronica dos frades menores da Província de Santo Antonio do Brasil* (2nd ed., 2 vols., Rio de Janeiro, 1858-59).

[27] Calmon, *Civilização brasileira*, p. 48.

[28] It is quite probable that the introduction of livestock into America increased the Indian population greatly. Before the discovery they had very little meat to eat, except wild animals and one another. After discovery, they ate all kinds of domestic animals, including the horse. It seems only logical that population should have increased with the food supply. The author is of the opinion that there are probably more Indians living in Brazil today than at the time Cabral first landed.

Pasture lands, hitherto but little used by a few wild animals, afforded grazing for millions of domestic stock. Cattle multiplied so rapidly that they became a menace to growing crops, and, as in Mexico, had to be shunted off to the interior. Before the end of the sixteenth century, the rich rancher had made his appearance.

Between 1590 and 1600 Sergipe, the region between Rio Real and the Rio São Francisco, became a center of cattle raising. Frei Vicente mentions that Christovão de Barros conquered the area, "divided up the captives and the land . . . established a large cattle ranch, and others following his example did the same, and they so multiplied because of the excellence of the pastures that Baía and Pernambuco supplied themselves from there with oxen for their sugar mills and butcher shops." [29] From here the herds ranged back through the hinterland along the São Francisco river for hundreds of miles. So great were the herds of the interior that the coast dwellers kept only the oxen needed for agriculture, supplying themselves for other purposes from the inland ranches. The São Francisco, giving access as it did to the heart of Baía and Minas Gerais, had so many ranches that it was known as the "River of Corrals." [30] The "vaqueiros" drove back the Indians, grazed their cattle farther and farther into the interior, and established communication with the upper São Francisco river which runs in a northerly direction, parallel with the coast but about four hundred miles inland. In 1711, Antonil noted that in the interior of Baía "there are today more than five hundred corrals, on this side of the São Francisco alone . . . . Along the other bank, on the Pernambuco side, I am certain there must be more . . . . And although the corrals of Baía may be numerous, those of Pernambuco are much more numerous . . . . Along the Iguassú river alone there are today more than thirty thousand cattle. Those of Baía pass half a million for certain, and those of Pernambuco must be more than eight hundred thousand in number . . . . Although the hinterland of Baía is so enormous, almost all of it belongs to two principal families of that city, the Torre family and that of the late Commander (Mestre de Campo) Antonio Guedes de Brito. For the Torre family has two hundred and sixty leagues [approximately 780 miles] upstream along the São Francesco, on the right hand, going south; and along the river to the north they have eighty leagues [240 miles]. The heirs of Commander Antonio

---

[29] Vicente de Salvador, História do Brasil, p. 336.

[30] Leite, Companhia de Jesus, I, 439-450; Basilio de Magalhães Expansão geographica, pp. 172-83; Agenor Agusto de Miranda, O Rio São Francisco (São Paulo, 1936).

BRAZIL
SHOWING REGIONS OF
LIVE STOCK RAISING

Scale of Miles

0   200   400   600

Prevailing Winds

VENEZUELA

COLOMBIA

BR.   DU.   FR.
GUIANA

Manáos

R. Amazonas

Belém   São Luiz

Fortaleza

Solimões

R.

R. Madeira

Tapajós

Xingú

R. Araguaia

R. Tocantins

Natal

Recife

PERU

B R A Z I L

R. São Francisco

Mato
Grosso

oCuiabá

Goiaz

São Salvador

BOLIVIA

Corumbá

Belo
oHorizonte

Paraguay

R.

Paraná

(São Paulo

Rio de Janeiro

PARAGUAY

Asunción

R.

Curitiba

Florianopolis

R. Paraná

C H I L E

R. Paraná

R. Uruguay

Porto Alegre

ARGENTINA

URUGUAY

Buenos Aires   Montevideo

LEGEND

Boundary of Brazil

State Boundaries

Principal Live-stock Regions

Indian Missions

Adapted from *História econômica do Brasil* by R. C. Simonsen

664a

Guedes possess, from Chapéos Hill to the source of the Rio das Velhas, a hundred and sixty leagues [480 miles]." [31]

Before this, by the time the Dutch were expelled in the middle of the seventeenth century, the interior of Brazil from Maranhão south to Baía had been colonized along its main routes of communication.[32] The effective line of occupation has never gone much further, because of the difficulty of breaching the jungle (or whatever terrain covers the unexplored interior), and the slight economic urge for doing so. Except along the river banks there are still few people.

In the meantime, Rio de Janeiro was growing slowly, although Antonil speaks of it as "that part of Brazil that has the least livestock," and was achieving the prominence that was to make it the capital city of Brazil before the end of the colonial period.[33] The territories we have been discussing are those that expanded first, chronologically speaking; it was only natural for the lands back of Baía and Pernambuco to be ahead of those far to the south or north.

THE AMAZON AND THE NORTH

The Amazon valley occupies almost one-third of South America, and two-thirds of Brazil. The story of its occupation is an epic within itself. Most of it (if not all) lies west of the Line of Demarcation, and Spain tried to occupy it by crossing the Andes; but the Portuguese had the advantage of being near the mouth of the river. In the long run it proved easier to ascend the Amazon than to cross over the fifteen thousand foot passes that separate it from the Pacific. Portugal did not find its occupation simple, however, and the first efforts of the donataries to settle along the northern coast of Brazil from Rio Grande do Norte to Pará were a failure. This region and the Amazon remained a sort of no-man's land during most of the sixteenth century.

The distances within the Amazon valley were enormous; it was all but impossible to penetrate the jungles on its banks; the Indians were frequently hostile; and the lack of proper food, coupled with tropical diseases, killed off would-be settlers. To these disadvantages must be added the lack of economic incentive for braving its perils. The valiant searchers for "El Dorado" found this out, though most never lived to tell their stories. The Pizarro-Orellana expedition of 1539-41 discovered the river while in search of the

[31] Antonil, *Cultura e opulencia do Brasil*, Part IV, chap. I.

[32] Handelmann, *Brasil*, pp. 265-344.

[33] Handelmann, *Brasil*, pp. 463-539; Leite, *Companhia de Jesus*, I, 361-436.

"Land of Cinnamon," but apart from the glory of discovery profited nothing. Orellana reached Spain and came back with another expedition to colonize, but was wrecked at the mouth of the river by the *Pororoca*, the violent waves caused by the meeting of the Amazon with the incoming tide. The expedition of Pedro de Ursua-Lope de Aguirre in 1559-61, coming from the Andean side, repeated the adventures of Orellana in an even more tragic fashion. It gained notoriety because of the well advertised iniquities of Aguirre, but did little beyond confirming the unimportance of the valley for exploitation at that time. Other expeditions set out from Colombia and Venezuela, but they found neither "El Dorado," nor much else of immediate value. The time had not come when the products of the Amazon were to build a glittering city in the midst of the jungle.

While the Spaniards were making these attempts in the Amazon, that territory and the north coast of Brazil were receiving little organized attention from the Portuguese. The first efforts of Aires da Cunha, João de Barros, Fernão Alvares de Andrade, and Antonio Cardoso de Barros, the donataries of the northern captaincies, to settle in these regions had failed.

But if the Portuguese were not in a position to utilize this region, others were. It has already been noted that the English, French, and Dutch merchants established trading posts. They bought amber, dye woods, and other articles from the Indians, and also conducted their piracy from these posts. Eventually, however, the Portuguese asserted their claims, and from 1583 to 1656 took the steps which made this part of America, from Pernambuco to Pará, Portuguese in fact as it was in theory according to the Treaty of Tordesillas.

An expedition led by Diogo Flores Valdez by sea, and overland by Fructuoso Barboza, established the village of Fillipéa on the Paraíba River in 1583. This village was destroyed by the Indians, but the Portuguese in turn went back several times to demolish French settlements. The fort of Tres Reis Magos, near present-day Natal in Rio Grande do Norte, was founded in 1598 by an expedition under Manoel de Mascarenhas.[34] In the meantime, the French had established themselves at São Luiz de Maranhão, from which they were driven in 1613-15. After the occupation of São Luiz by the Portuguese, Francisco Castello Branco founded the fort of Presepe, in 1616, near where stands modern Belêm, Pará. The

[34] *Revista IHGB*, vol. 129 (1914), pp. 9-40; Capistrano de Abreu, *História colonial*, pp. 122-139.

Travel in Brazil, by Wagener, Dutch, 17th century

problem now was to populate the region. In 1618, three hundred settlers from the Azores were sent to Maranhão; but they did not prosper. Lacking other occupations, and perhaps in some cases attracted to the region with this in view, the settlers turned to hunting Indians to be sold as slaves to the more prosperous colonies.

Because of the trade winds which blew in a northwesterly direction between this north coast and Pernambuco, navigation was so difficult that the Portuguese government decided in 1621 to establish the State of Maranhão, separate from Brazil and including the land from Cabo São Roque to the Amazon. The men who had distinguished themselves in the Conquest were given captaincies. This was the situation when the Dutch invaded Brazil. By 1641 the Dutch had taken Ceará and Maranhão, and were not finally driven out until 1654.

Up to this time the region had not prospered. As late as 1685, São Luiz had only a thousand heads of families and Belêm less than five hundred. Living conditions were extremely hard, and the barest description gives an impression of painful poverty. The north coast suffered also from bad governors; and disputes between the Jesuits and the citizens over the Indians bred factionalism, civil war, seditions, and constant appeals to the home government. Horses, mules, or donkeys were lacking to facilitate communications.[35] Slave trade, a little cotton, and a few products gathered from the forest were the only economic activities. The drugs and forest products were destined, together with cotton, and rice, to be the mainstay of Maranhão economic life in the eighteenth century.

The settlement of the north coast placed the Portuguese within striking distance of the Amazon. The arrival from across the Andes of two Spanish Franciscans in Belêm in 1637 was a warning that the time had come to act. The governor of Maranhão sent Pedro Teixeira upriver to Peru, and on his return Teixeira took possession of the entire valley in the name of the King of Portugal. The Brazilians were at last taking legal measures to claim what nature had destined them to have. From this time on, Belêm, Cametá, and Gurupá became the centers from which expeditions went up the Amazon and its confluents in search of precious metals, Indians, and spices. Of gold and silver they found none; but the Indians and spices proved to be of value, especially cacao, vanilla, cinnamon, and aromatic resins. After the explorer and trader had prepared the way, the Jesuits, Franciscans, and other missionaries

[35] Southey, *Brazil*, II, 449-50; 469-70.

established numerous *aldeas,* or villages, among the Indians, giving greater stability to the colonizing effort.

But regardless of the small economic return from Maranhão and the Amazon, there was one decisive result of Portuguese activity. The French, English, and Dutch were finally driven out, retiring to the Guianas and the Caribbean.[36]

EXPANSION FROM SÃO PAULO

Just as the population filtered back from Baía and Pernambuco to occupy the valleys of the São Francisco and Paraíba, the north coast, and the Amazon, there came from São Paulo far to the south, a similar and perhaps more significant expansion.[37] The natural features of the region made it so.[38]

Afonso de Souza had established the village of Piratininga in the mountains rising abruptly three thousand feet above his settlement at São Vicente. This sharp escarpment shuts the plateau off from the coast much more effectually than from the interior. The roads up the mountain remained among the most difficult in the world until a modern cog-wheel railway was built. It was thus very hard for the plateau inhabitants to establish trade with the sea in competition with São Vicente and Santos. But if the colony had this disadvantage, it had compensations. "The city was by its situation almost cut off from intercourse with other towns: it had little or no communication with Portugal, no trade for want of outlets; but it had every advantage of soil and climate."[39]

The original settlement of Piratininga was soon shifted a few miles away to a site where the Jesuits had established the mission of São Paulo. This became the chief settlement. By the time Tomé de Souza arrived, the village had grown to such an extent that he gave it the dignity of a town.

The Portuguese had been greatly aided by the earlier settlement of João Ramalho, who had allied himself with the Goyanazes Indians, taking one or more girls as his wife, wives, or concubines. Ramalho's exact marital status seems to be a matter of debate, since he was once congratulated by the famous Jesuit, Nóbrega,

---

[36] Basilio de Magalhães, *Espansão geográphica,* pp. 184-95; Lemos Brito, *História econômica do Brasil,* pp. 73-76; Simonsen, *História econômica do Brasil,* II, 108-17.

[37] Affonso de E. Taunay's *História geral das bandeiras paulistas* (6 vols., São Paulo, 1924-30) is the standard history of the expansionist movement of São Paulo. Cf. Carvalho Franco, *Bandeiras e bandeirantes de São Paulo* (São Paulo, 1940); Alfredo Ellis Junior, *O bandeirismo paulista* (3rd ed., São Paulo, 1938); Handelmann, *Brasil,* pp. 541-650; Capistrano de Abreu, *História colonial,* pp. 110-17.

[38] Basilio de Magalhães, *Expansão geográphica,* pp. 70-171.

[39] Southey, *Brazil,* II, 304.

for his monogamy, but in any case he left a large progeny. The far from monogamous practices of the other Portuguese aided in producing the numerous *mamelucos,* or mixed bloods, which characterized the early population of São Paulo. São Paulo became the seat of the city government in 1560, when this was moved from the original settlement known officially as Santo André; and in 1581 became the capital of the captaincy.

São Paulo did not participate in the early agricultural prosperity, nor did the brazil wood extend so far south. São Vicente had its sugar mills, marmalade export, and trade; but the plateau settlers enjoyed only an equality of poverty. Without sugar and brazil wood, some other source of wealth was imperative. It was soon found in the Indian. Slaves were needed and the Paulistas became inveterate hunters of men.

Whereas geographical features had denied São Paulo easy access to the sea, they had facilitated travel to the interior. The water divide is scarcely a hundred miles from the sea, and São Paulo stands near the divide. Numerous rivers converge on the region. To the north they lead into Minas Gerais; to the west into Goiaz and Mato Grosso; to the south and west into Santa Catarina, Rio Grande do Sul and the Paraná river. Topography did much to make the Paulistas the pioneers of a frontier movement.

Long before the end of the sixteenth century the mamelucos had started on slave-hunting expeditions. It was comparatively easy for a band of them to ally themselves with a group of neighboring Indians to hunt down the enemies of the latter. Moral justification, where the morality of the trade was questioned, was found in the plea that the Indians were cannibals; by capturing them, the Paulistas were preventing them from eating one another and at the same time were saving their souls. This sophistry served its purpose for slavers, whether their victims were copper-colored or black.

The international difficulties in which Portugal found herself gave the Paulistas further opportunity for pursuing their lucrative occupation. The normal supply of African slaves was prevented from reaching Brazil by a series of circumstances, among them the Spanish domination, 1580-1640; the period of Dutch intervention, 1624-1654; and the Portuguese war of independence from Spain, 1640-1661. Furthermore, the Dutch also occupied a large part of the Portuguese slave coast in Africa during their stay in Brazil, making it difficult for Portuguese Brazil to receive laborers for her sugar plantations. It has already been noted that the slave trade was one of the chief industries of the colonists on the north coast of Brazil and the Amazon in the early days. Both São Paulo and the northern regions were responding to the same demand from central Brazil—slaves for the plantations.

With the African slaves cut off and the coastal Indians exterminated or driven inland, the hunt for slaves went ever further into the interior. Some of the coastal tribes migrated as far as six hundred miles in their efforts to escape the slavers. And whatever the moral aspects of this trade, it was one of the prime motives for the push of European settlements into the heart of the continent. The other was gold. To the certain profits of slave hunting were joined the prospective riches of mines. Every expedition pursued a double objective. If no gold or silver was found, and little was until 1694, the captured Indians paid the expense of the *bandeira*. And the expenses were not great, for the expedition lived mainly off the country, eating pine nuts, game, fish, and a sort of bread made from the palm which they called *farinha de guerra,* or war bread. In the tropical regions manioc was used for bread, and *farinha de guerra* was made from it.

The Paulistas' slave hunting and expansion took on a patriotic aspect in the seventeenth century. It was their destiny to make good Portugal's claims to what is now southern Brazil. The Line of Demarcation between Portuguese and Spanish territory was vague, as previously pointed out. The maps of the region were inaccurate, and the claims of each party, boundless. As the Paulistas pushed southward and westward, they came into contact with the Spanish driving eastward from Paraguay where the latter had had a settlement since 1537. The vanguard of the Spanish movement was the Jesuit missions, which were being established, beginning early in the seventeenth century, along the Paranapanema river and the surrounding territory. If permitted to advance, they might reach the sea, cutting off territory which Brazil claimed as far as 44 degrees south. Here the Portuguese Jesuits were presented with a delicate problem. They might inveigh against the Paulista slave hunters, but to do so was to side against their own nation.[40] The matter was all the more complicated before 1640 by the fact that Spain and Portugal were under one monarch.

The Spanish Jesuit missions, in the meantime, proved to be a boon to the slave hunters, for the missions furnished the bandeir-

---

[40] For the Jesuit viewpoint on Paulista expansion and slavery, see Leite, *Companhia de Jesus,* I, 251-358; II, 2-110; 194-235; Anibal Mattos, *Joseph de Anchieta,* cited.

antes with their most accessible supply of slaves. The period of greatest growth of the Spanish missions corresponded exactly with the scarcity of Negro slaves and the great demand for Indians. By 1629, there were some twenty-one Jesuit missions in the region of the upper Paraná and its confluents the Paranapanema and Ivahy. This was the year of the first attack on the missions. An expedition of nine hundred Paulistas with two thousand Indian allies, under the command of Antonio Raposo, fell on the missions and captured more than 2,500 Indians, of whom some 1,500 reached São Paulo to be sold into slavery. The Jesuits protested in vain in São Paulo, Rio de Janeiro, and Baía. There was neither the disposition nor the force to stop the bandeiras.

The system of the missions made slaving an easy and safe profession. Previously, it had been necessary to hunt the Indians and fight; now they had merely to be gathered in. The mission Indians themselves became suspicious of the whole mission scheme, believing that the Jesuits had assembled them to make capture convenient. While this belief was unjustified, the Indians recognized something that the Jesuits never seemed to see, that the net effect of collecting the Indians in missions, *reducciones,* and *aldeas* was to make them easy prey. The Portuguese Jesuits also aided unwittingly in facilitating the enslavement of the Indians.

"The Jesuits, still pursuing the system which Nóbrega and Anchieta had begun, when they no longer found employment for their zeal upon the coast, sought out the natives in their recesses; these journeys sometimes were the work of from six to eighteen months. The character which they had obtained frequently induced the savages to listen to them, and follow them to the coast. The slave-hunters took advantage of this, disguised themselves like Jesuits and by this worst species of sacrilege frequently decoyed the natives." [41]

In the long run, only the "unreduced" Indians survived in numbers by fleeing far into the interior.

The raids of the Paulistas continued and the Spanish Jesuits were compelled to move their charges southward, thousands of Indians dying or being captured on the way. The ten years following 1629 were among the cruelest in Latin American history, and must have ressembled somewhat the displacement and massacre of hordes of peoples in modern war. But it was also a decisive period. The Paulistas drove the Spanish Jesuits and Indians

---

[41] Southey, *Brazil,* II, 305.

steadily south and west, beyond the 30th parallel to the south, and beyond the Paraná river to the west. Their campaigns added thousands of square miles to the Portuguese possessions by effective occupation. Skillful negotiation and distortion of the maps were to make the claim legal a century and a half later.[42]

An attempt to free the slaves by excommunicating the owners was made by Urban VIII in 1640, but when the Bull was published in Rio, Santos, and São Paulo, the people rose in revolt against it. In São Paulo the Jesuits were expelled temporarily by the rebellion, and the Bull was suspended. When the news reached São Paulo in 1641 that João IV had ascended the Portuguese throne and severed Portugal from Spain, a party of the Paulistas attempted to set up an independent kingdom. Their revolt collapsed quickly when their chosen leader, Amador Bueno, refused the throne.[43]

Although the Paulistas were severely defeated in 1642 by the Spanish Jesuits and their charges, who had now been armed, slave expeditions continued and the frontier of Brazil tended to become fixed at the outer limits of the bandeiras. Spain had lost a vast area lying on her side of the Line of Demarcation, and the road had been opened for further Portuguese expansion westward in the eighteenth century.

Cattle and horses were also important in the growth of southern Brazil. It is not known how early the first livestock reached the rolling grasslands of Paraná and the plains of Rio Grande do Sul, but they were a considerable factor from the seventeenth century. Rio Grande do Sul became the home of vast herds in the eighteenth century, as did Uruguay. The boundary between the Portuguese and Spanish part was indistinct, the people mixed, and the final delimitation delayed until 1828.[44]

Trade likewise played its part in Brazilian southern expansion. As early as 1580, the trade with Buenos Aires had begun. Buenos Aires was, in fact, merely a midway point for commerce that extended from Pernambuco to Lima, Peru. For a time during the period of Spanish domination, this trade was legal, although it was closely regulated in theory. After 1640, there were efforts to curb it in the interest of the Sevilla monopoly. Portugal, on the

[42] *Ibid.*, II, 315-24.

[43] *Ibid.*, II, 325-30.

[44] Dante de Laytano, *História da república rio grandense, 1835-1845* (Porto Alegre, 1936), pp. 13-22. Basilio de Magalhães, *Expansão geográphica*, pp. 247-57. Extensive material on Santa Catarina, Paraná and Rio Grande do Sul may be found in the *Revista IHGB,* volumes 36, 38, 54, 56, 58 and 59.

other hand, was anxious to use Brazil as a wedge into Spanish colonial trade. Behind Portugal stood France, England, and other nations who were sending their goods through Portugal. Portugal took the decisive step in 1680 of establishing a colony, Colonia do Sacramento, in what is today Uruguay. Colonia was many times the center of bitter fighting. In 1724-26, the Spaniards founded Montevideo as a counterweight, and finally, on July 4, 1777, the Spaniards occupied Colonia and destroyed the fortifications. Thus, the tide of bandeiras, livestock, and trade that had carried the Portuguese banner so far over into the Spanish territory failed to reach the mouth of the Río de la Plata, the goal of its ambition.[45]

---

[45] On Colonia do Sacramento see Capistrano de Abreu, *Ensaios e estudos,* (third series, Rio de Janeiro, 1938), pp. 55-105.

Mining, Manufacturing, and Trade

THE KINGDOM OF METALS

TWO CENTURIES PASSED AFTER THE DISCOVERY of Brazil without the finding of appreciable quantities of precious metals, but this was not because the Portuguese were less assiduous in seeking gold than were the Spanish, French, Dutch, and English. Brazil was full of tales of rivers of gold and mountains of emeralds. More than one map was drafted to show that "El Dorado" lay within its boundaries. Never a band of bandeirantes that did not search for mineral wealth, and there were many that set forth with that expressed purpose. Many were the false reports that came of rich finds, and still more numerous the small placers that were at first reported as inexhaustible.[1]

NEED FOR A NEW ECONOMIC IMPETUS

The prospector for minerals served a useful purpose, aside from the importance of the final strike, by helping to open up territories to the west, just as did the cattle rancher of Baía, the spice hunter of the Amazon, or the Indian slaver of the south. Brazil could hardly have overcome the obstacles of nature and the natives without some greater stimulus than coastal agriculture. It was the mines, once discovered, that made the conquest of the interior certain, swift, and permanent.

It was 1695 before the first important strike was announced, in

---

[1] The standard work on the mines of Brazil is João Pandiá Calógeras, *As minas do Brasil e sua legislação* (3 vols., Rio de Janeiro, 1904-05); for what was known of mines up to 1587 see Gabriel Soares, *Brasil em 1587*, pp. 428-33. See also Lemos Brito, *História econômica do Brasil*, pp. 101-14, 135-62; Basilio de Magalhães, *Expansão geográphica*, pp. 70-171; Azevedo, *Épocas de Portugal econômico*, pp. 301-95; Capistrano de Abreu, *Caminhos antigos e povoamento do Brasil* (Rio de Janeiro: Sociedade de Capistrano de Abreu, 1930), pp. 145-86.

the region of Taubaté in Minas Gerais. The strike came at a fortunate moment for Brazil. The economic life of the country badly needed a new impetus, and minerals served the purpose. The failure to find precious metals in quantity until so late had resulted in a chronic shortage of a medium of exchange. Barter and payment in kind were customary practices. This had its weaknesses, however, for foreign commerce. The sailing of the fleets was almost invariably followed by a money shortage; nor could the Brazilians get sufficient coinage for purchases abroad. In 1692, shortly before the discovery of the mines, Vieira advised the King to coin a provincial money of "such intrinsic value that nobody will profit by carrying it out of this state."

In accordance with this advice, a mint for turning out "provincial money" was set up in Baía in 1694, but the discovery of the mines the next year relieved the situation greatly. A mint was opened in Rio in 1703 and another in Baía in 1715, although it was still against the law for provincial money to circulate in Portugal or for Portuguese money to be used in Brazil. This law, and the fact that so large a part of the mineral produce was exported, prevented Brazil from receiving the full benefit of the mines. But in return for the mineral exports Brazil received the products which she did not and could not manufacture. The life of the colony was enriched. Copper money was also coined in Brazil; and Spanish pesos circulated at a value in excess of their cost. Paper money did not appear in Brazil until 1803.[2]

But lack of currency was only one of the economic ills of Brazil in 1695. The sugar industry, once the economic backbone of the coastal colonies, had suffered a decline during the last half of the seventeenth century. The reasons for this were many. The Brazilian crop had always been tied closely to the non-Portuguese European markets. Portugal, which could not consume the large amounts produced in its possessions, had been mainly a jobbing center for distributing Brazilian sugar to other nations. Several things happened almost simultaneously to upset this system. When the Dutch were expelled from Brazil in 1654, they took their sugar market with them, transferring their production and buying to the West Indies where they had established colonies. At this very moment, 1654-55, the English were in the process of occupying Jamaica, which they converted into a center of sugar production and contraband trade. The English colonies in North America also cut in on Brazil. The French too were now active in the Caribbean, and

[2] Calmon, *Civilização brasileira*, pp. 109-12; Southey, *Brazil*, III, 22-23.

Haiti rapidly became the most important sugar exporter of the world until near the end of the eighteenth century.

The West Indies had additional advantages over Brazil, principally in shorter and less costly transportation. Haiti, Jamaica, and other centers produced large crops on small areas and had a short haul to port, from which the ships had to sail only about half as far as the voyage from Brazil to reach European markets. And what was true of sugar was equally true of other crops. The Caribbean countries produced many of Brazil's chief commodities: tobacco, cacao, hides, cotton, indigo. The Spanish colonies, the Dutch, French and English, all had an active trade in these products. The English Navigation Acts (1651 and later) hurt Brazil and thus its economic problem in the later seventeenth century was not one of production, but of markets. It was suffering from an old tropical complaint, inadequate market for materials that can be produced in abundance on a small area. A lack of outlets for its products, as a result of international competition, was at the base of the Brazilian economic difficulties.

The decline was not drastic or immediate. It extended over half a century. The fleet from Baía in 1688, for example, was the largest to that date. But when it reached Lisbon it was faced with a "glut in the Lisbon market, and prices fell so much that in the ensuing year many *Engenhos* (sugar mills) stopped." The depression also cut the opposite way. Restriction on the Brazil-Buenos Aires trade caused goods valued at hundreds of thousands of cruzados to be left on the hands of the merchants of Colonia and Rio de Janeiro. Vieira's description of Brazil at the end of the seventeenth century indicates how pressing the situation had grown to be:

> "Thus all is not merely going to ruin, but well nigh ruined; . . . this Brazil, which is all that we have, we shall have no longer than till any one chuses to take it; and I no longer grieve that the kingdom should be without heirs, for if we had them, there would be nothing to inherit. . . . In this emergency, prudent men advise us to wear cotton, eat mandioc, and take to bows and arrows for lack of other arms, so that we shall shortly relapse into the savage state, and become Brazilians instead of Portugueze."[3]

It was when Brazil was in this condition that the mines came to the rescue.

[3] Quoted in Southey, *Brazil*, III, 19-34; cf. Simonsen, *História econômica do Brasil*, I, 146-74; II, 222. The usual interpretation is that the discovery of the mines produced the decline in agricultural exports. On this point compare Simonsen, II, 222, chart, with Southey, III, 64-65.

The discovery of gold (and later, in 1728, diamonds) gave Brazil a market within her own territory for agricultural products which could no longer be sold abroad, opened up opportunity for many Brazilians whose economic affairs were languishing along the coast, established new centers of population in the interior to give substance to the pioneer work of the bandeirantes and ranchers, and attracted thousands of new immigrants to populate the country.

The Gold of Minas Gerais

The Paulistas had discovered the mines,[4] but they lay westward from Baía and southward from Pernambuco. The inland valleys furnished access to Minas Gerais (the name given after discovery) and Brazilians from everywhere came there. The mines were one of the most powerful forces in making Brazilians of the inhabitants of Brazil. They gave greater cohesion to a land whose scattered population up to that time seemed like so many islands in a vast ocean. Minas Gerais became the meeting ground for every class and condition of men. Antonil wrote in 1711:

"The insatiable thirst for gold stimulated so many people to leave their own homes and to brave the rough roads, such as those to the mines, that it will be difficult to give an accurate account of the number of people who are now there . . . . It is said that thirty thousand souls are busy, some in seeking, some in directing the search in gold-bearing streams, others in business, buying and selling not only what is necessary to maintain life but luxuries also, more than in the sea ports.

"Every year great numbers of Portuguese and foreigners come in the fleets, bound for the mines. From the cities, villages, inlets, and hinterland of Brazil there go whites, browns, blacks, and many Indians who are in the service of the Paulistas. The mixture is of every kind and condition of persons; men and women; young and old; poor and rich; nobles and plebeians; laymen, priests, and monks of various orders, many of whom do not have either convent or chapter in Brazil."[5]

Commerce flourished. The roads from Minas were full of caravans carrying gold to the coast, and even larger caravans traveled to Minas with foodstuffs, goods, tobacco, liquors, and immigrants.

For further information on mining see "Informação sobre as minas do Brasil" *Anais BNRio,* LVII (1935), 155-86; Domingos Vandelli, "Sobre as minas de ouro do Brasil," *Anais BNRio,* XX (1898), 266-78; *ibid.,* "Sobre os diamantes do Brasil," *Anais BNRio,* XX (1898), 279-82.

[5] Antonil, *Cultura e opulencia,* p. 213.

The favorite route of entry was through the São Francisco valley, but all the inland waterways converging on Minas Gerais were used.[6]

The mines engendered, among other things, civil war. The Paulistas, as the discoverers, considered the mines their own. But the "foreigners" who were pouring in outnumbered the Paulistas many times, and took over valuable mining properties. War broke out in 1709,[7] and the Paulistas were temporarily successful. Soon, however, the weight of numbers turned the tide in favor of the outsiders, or *emboabas*, who had the support of the government. A new Captaincy-General of São Paulo and Minas Gerais was created in 1710, and the Paulistas were defeated in a final battle in 1711. They were consoled for this defeat by having their town elevated to the status of a "city" in 1712. They also consoled themselves by pushing further west and opening up new mines in Mato Grosso and Goiaz.

THE MINES OF MATO GROSSO AND GOIAZ

The mines of Cuiabá (Mato Grosso), which were settled about 1721, are eight hundred miles in a direct line from São Paulo, and the country between was completely wild, without a single civilized settlement, when the Cuiabá deposits were opened. The exploration and colonization of Cuiabá is a tribute to the enterprise and persistence born of the urge for gold.

The mines of Cuiabá were expanding rapidly when others were discovered in Goiaz in 1726, the third important gold-producing region found in Brazil. This gold strike is connected with a romantic, cruel, and, let us hope, untrue legend. According to the tale, as early as 1670 an old Paulista, who went by the revealing nickname of *Anhanguera* (The Old Devil), encountered on one of the tributaries of the Rio Araguaya some Indian women who wore gold nuggets in their ears. To dramatize his find, he cut off the women's ears and took them back for exhibition with the nuggets. Nothing practical came of this until 1726, when the governor of São Paulo sent the son of "The Old Devil" to locate the gold-bearing stream, which he did. Whether the story is true or not, the gold was there.[8] The sums produced in Goiaz soon rivaled those of Cuiabá. Active trade sprang up, as along the routes to Minas, but prices were extremely high. As the settlers poured in, some

---

[6] The best contemporary description of the mines is Antonil, *Cultura e opulencia,* pp. 205-61; cf. *Revista IHGB,* vol. VII (1848), pp. 53-64.

[7] Southey, *Brazil,* III, 73-85.

[8] Nash, *Conquest of Brazil,* pp. 132-33.

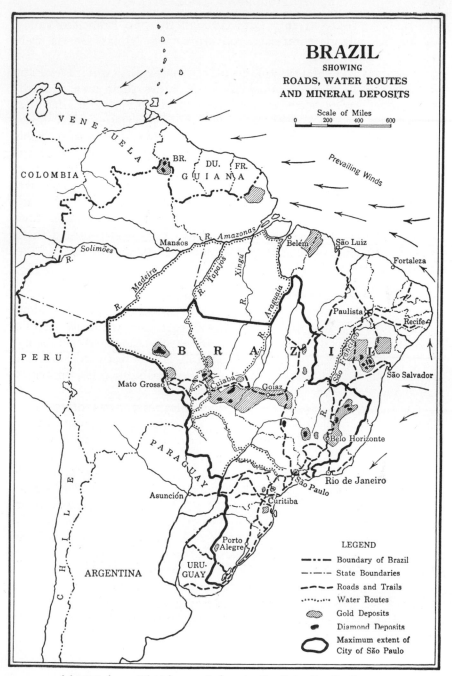

BRAZIL
SHOWING
ROADS, WATER ROUTES
AND MINERAL DEPOSITS

Scale of Miles

0   200   400   600

Prevailing Winds

VENEZUELA

COLOMBIA

BR. DU. FR.
G U I A N A

R. Amazonas

Manáos   Belém   São Luiz

R. Solimões   Fortaleza

R. Madeira

R. Tapajós

R. Xingú

R. Araguaia

Paulista

Recife

PERU

B   R   A   Z   I   L

R. São Francisco

São Salvador

Mato Grosso   Cuiabá
                    Goiaz

Belo Horizonte

PARAGUAY

Rio de Janeiro

Asunción   São Paulo
                  Curitiba

C H I L E

Porto
Alegre

ARGENTINA   URU-
             GUAY

LEGEND

— ·· — ·· — Boundary of Brazil
— · — · —   State Boundaries
— — — —   Roads and Trails
············ Water Routes
             Gold Deposits
•   Diamond Deposits
             Maximum extent of
             City of São Paulo

Adapted from *História econômica do Brasil* by R. C. Simonsen

678a

began to farm and raise livestock, giving the area the economic life it was to conserve after the mines were almost exhausted.

Gold was discovered in 1734 along the river Sarare—so plentiful that it lay on top of the ground. The region was all but inaccessible, food was scarce, and the price of supplies brought in was so great that it absorbed the profits of mining. Nevertheless, the rush went on. All suffered, some dying of hunger. But the prospectors could not be frightened by horror tales, and those who were not successful in Minas Gerais or Cuiabá rushed in, along with others from São Paulo or Portugal. The situation was relieved by a road from Cuiabá to Goiaz, where cattle existed in abundance. The region began to flourish and the miners soon were buying the finest silk that was known in Brazil.[9] Goiaz was also growing. Ten years after discovery, it was made a *comarca* (provincial or county seat), 1737, and twelve years after this it became a captaincy.[10]

Before the middle of the century it was found that merchandise could be brought to Mato Grosso more easily from Belém, Pará, than from Rio de Janeiro or São Paulo, and with less danger. The best route was by the Madeira-Guaporé rivers, capable of floating boats of two thousand arrobas from Belém to Vila Bela, today Mato Grosso. Alternate routes were by the Xingú or Tapajóz. These inland routes, plus the discovery of salt on the river Jauru, made it possible to expand the raising of cattle and support a larger population.[11]

Minas Gerais had grown to where it merited elevation to a captaincy and was detached from São Paulo in 1720. The nomadic population become stationary and towns sprang up, Villa Rica having a hundred thousand inhabitants. Other towns arose around the mines, attracting numerous settlers. Farming was a necessity to supply the large non-agricultural population, and Minas laid the basis of an economic activity that was to outlast the mines. The slave trade flourished. Many families gained great wealth, and some attained nobility. Minas Gerais became the most populous captaincy and is today the most populous state of Brazil.

TOTAL PRODUCE

The total value of the minerals produced is difficult to determine.

---

[9] Southey, *Brazil*, III, 307-10; Joseph Barboza de Sá, "Relação das povoações do Cuyabá e Mato Grosso de seos principios thé os prezentes tempos," *Anais BNRio*, XXIII (1901), 5-58; Basilio de Magalhães, *Expansão geográphica*, pp. 196-212.

[10] Basilio de Magalhães, *Expansão geográphica*, pp. 212-21.

[11] Southey, *Brazil*, II, 359-61. The bandeira of Francisco de Mello Palheta on the Madeira in 1722-23, as related by one of its members, is given in Capistrano de Abreu, *Caminhos antigos*, pp. 193-216; cf. Simonsen, *História econômica do Brasil*, II, 144-46.

The amounts went up until about 1760 and then declined rapidly. The government tried to collect its fifth directly, but found the contraband excessive. It then tried to get its share by accepting a fixed sum from the miners, but this was not entirely successful. It also tried to levy a head tax on the slaves used in the mines. None of the methods was ever satisfactory, however, and much of the gold continued to escape official taxation. Calculations vary somewhat, and the rise and fall of production is more indicative than totals. Calógeras estimated the totals from 1700 to 1801 at 65,500 arrobas, or 983,000 kilograms, as follows:

	Minas Gerais	Goiaz and Mato Grosso	Sao Paulo and Baía-Ceará
1700-1725	7,500 arrobas		
1727-1735	6,500 "		
1736-1751	12,000 "		
1752-1787	18,000 "		
1788-1801	3,500 "		
1720-1801	....	13,000 arrobas	5,000 arrobas [12]

From these figures we can deduce an annual average production for Minas Gerais as follows:

    1700-1725 a period of 26 years, average annual production 288 arrobas
    1726-1735 a period of 10 years, average annual production 650 arrobas
    1736-1751 a period of 16 years, average annual production 750 arrobas
    1752-1787 a period of 36 years, average annual production 500 arrobas
    1788-1801 a period of 14 years, average annual production 250 arrobas

The period of greatest production was probably between 1740 and 1760.[13]

The value of diamond production was also considerable. In the hundred years following the first discovery in Minas Gerais in 1728, the total production was probably three million carats. This was a considerable stimulus to the economic life of the country.[14]

Thus the discovery of gold and diamonds in Minas Gerais, Mato Grosso, and Goiaz gave the impetus to the most important of Brazil's westward movements. The United States was to have a similar movement a century and a half later; but there were essential differences in conditions, leading to profound divergences in the way the two regions developed. Where California had an outlet to the sea, and where the United States held the strategic mouth of the Mississippi, affording the abundant products of that river basin an outlet, the inhabitants of the interior of Brazil found themselves shut in. To the west they had only more jungle and the Andes mountains; to the south, the Río de la Plata, through which

    [12] Calógeras, Formação histórica, p. 54.
    [13] Simonsen, História econômica do Brasil, II, 93-96, summarizes various calculations of the value of Brazilian minerals.
    [14] Calógeras, Formação histórica, 55-57.

their products could most easily flow, was held by Argentina, Paraguay, and Uruguay. For all that Brazil trespassed on Spain's side of the Line of Demarcation, its encroachment fell short of what was needed. The interior states of Brazil are still prisoners, in an economic sense.

COLONIAL MANUFACTURING

Brazilian colonial economy had four principal characteristics: it was agricultural; commerce depended directly on the market Europe afforded for Brazil's agricultural and mineral produce; the mines supplied the medium of exchange and the inspiration for expansion; and the bulk of what was used in the colony was manufactured there in a simple handcraft industry.

That Brazil should have manufactured most of what it used was inherent in its basic situation and the nature of its agriculture centered in nearly self-sufficient *fazendas* and missions. The imports fell into the class of luxury or near-luxury goods, which the exports of the fazendas enabled their owners to buy from Europe. It was no part of fazenda economy, however, to use foreign goods as their main supply. On the contrary, the object of the fazenda (or mission) was to satisfy most of its own needs. There could be found artisans for all the fundamental crafts that go into making tools for clearing land, planting and gathering crops, and processing these crops for home use or export. Axes, saws, carts, plows, harness, saddles, and many other like tools were of Brazilian manufacture in the main. And the same was true of the houses in which people lived, most of the furniture, and all but the luxury clothing. The purchasing power of the masses of the people was too low, their effective economic demands too few, to permit of any other solution. And although it is true that Brazilian imports were relatively large, and that they prevented greater expansion of domestic manufactures, it must be borne in mind that they supplied mainly the wants of an upper ten per cent of the population.

The economic policies of the home government in Portugal discouraged the development of Brazilian manufacturing on a large scale, including that which would have sprung up naturally in the face of European competition. In this, Portugal was following the general colonial policy common to many European nations of that time, and even of today. Some important industrial activity developed, however, with the support of Portugal in some cases and against its oposition in others. One of the best examples of an approved industry was shipbuilding. Portugal was a maritime nation, and Brazil had large supplies and wide varieties of shipbuilding timber and other materials. From early in the sixteenth century, the building of coastwise vessels was a flourishing business; and long before the end of the century ocean-going ships were in production. It is well to remember, also, that sugar was an industrial as well as an agricultural occupation.

In the eighteenth century, gold and silver smithing became an important handcraft. This was a flourishing century for Brazil. Her mines and her agriculture were the source of a considerable number of large fortunes and thousands of ample incomes. The possessors of such incomes provided a market for jewelry and innumerable household ornaments of gold and silver, as well as for fine furniture and cabinet work. There is evidence also of the importance of these and other manufactories in the repressive legislation of the eighteenth century. Gold and silver smithing was prohibited as a measure for cutting down contraband trade in these metals, and to encourage the Portuguese craftsmen, among the finest in the world up to the present time. [15] In 1785 Queen María ordered the destruction of all industries and factories of Brazil in order to throw more workers into the sugar industry particularly, and agriculture in general, and in order to create a bigger market for Portuguese exports to Brazil. [16] This was late in the colonial period, however, and while the immediate adverse effects on Brazil were noticeable, such measures also helped augment the discontent with Portuguese rule that could be observed in the late colonial years.

BRAZILIAN COLONIAL COMMERCE

If the bulk of Brazilian manufacture depended very largely on the meagre consumer demand of a population with a rather low living standard, commerce on the other hand was largely dependent on European demand for Brazilian products, which, as we have seen, came mainly from pasture, field, and forest until the eighteenth century, when precious metals and diamonds were added. In the course of the eighteenth century, particularly in the last years, the accelerated demand of Europe was reflected in an increasing commercial tempo in Brazil. But while it was the expanding markets of Europe which gave Brazil a chance to develop, it was the definite limitations of these markets which determined that Brazil's growth would be stopped at a point permitting only a restricted use of the

[15] See *Revista IHGB,* vol. 25 (1862), p. 451; Lemos Brito, *História econômica do Brasil,* pp. 183-218.

[16] Simonsen *História econômica do Brasil,* II, 214; *Revista IHGB,* vol. 10 (1848), pp. 213-40.

total potential economic power of the country, an essential economic fact still true of Brazil.

Portugal's policy toward Brazil was never as comprehensive as Spain's toward her American possessions. The early policy of Portugal was to monopolize the brazil wood trade, and this was continued throughout the colonial period; but much other commerce was permitted to individuals. In São Vicente, for example, the famous Schetz family of Flanders was permitted to produce and export sugar. At other times the Crown exercised a monopoly over whale hunting, diamonds, salt, and the sale of Brazilian tobacco in Portugal.

A consistently liberal policy was not possible, however, given the constant attacks of the French, English, and Dutch on Portuguese shipping. Nor was free trade consonant with the economic ideas of the times, if, indeed, it has ever been practiced by any nation for more than a very brief period. The first restrictions came partly as a defense against foreigners, and partly as a result of the Spanish domination, when the Spanish system was partially applied to Brazil. Spain being at war with the Dutch, one of the first prohibitions was against Brazilian commerce with them. Later, all trade with foreigners was limited to that which flowed through Portugal itself.

When the revolt of 1640 came and Portugal regained its independence from Spain, it was necessary to find friends among Spain's enemies. Portugal opened the ports of the kingdom to foreign commerce in January, 1641, and signed treaties of peace, commerce, and alliance with France, Holland, and England. In 1642, England demanded, and got a treaty more favorable than the one granted Holland in 1640. Cromwell, following out those commercial policies which earned him the title of the "bourgeois king," insisted on a still more favorable treaty in 1654. English merchants established in Portugal could trade with Brazil and other Portuguese colonies, and four English families were admitted to Rio, Baía, and Pernambuco. English merchants paid a twenty-three per cent duty, and were granted first place in furnishing vessels that Portugal sought outside the country. With the restoration of the Stuarts to the English throne, this treaty was reaffirmed, and the marriage of Charles II to Catherine of Braganza brought still further advantages to the English, including dowry payment of which Brazil paid more than 20,000 cruzados annually for more than ten years. [17]

[17] Clyde L. Grose, "The Anglo-Portuguese Marriage of 1662," *H.A.H.R.*, X (August, 1930), 313-52.

The prohibition against commerce with foreign nations unless through Portugal was repeated in 1666, the only exceptions being direct trade with the colonies of Spain in the Río de la Plata region, and for Spanish vessels which needed to provision en route to the Plata River. Commerce between Brazil and this region, contraband or legal, began by the year 1580, and continued to be of importance ·during the whole colonial period. Commerce with frontier regions was usually prohibited, however, as was the case with the Spanish colonies of the upper Amazon, and the French and Dutch in Guiana.

One of the most important treaties affecting the trade of Portugal was that of Methuen in 1703. This gave Portuguese wines a preferred market in Britain, and at the same time granted British woolen manufactures preferred treatment in Portugal, and hence Brazil. The Portuguese-Brazilian imports of manufactures were thereby tied closely to Britain by this treaty, and many Portuguese and Brazilian economists have held that the Treaty of Methuen contributed to the decline of manufactures in some cases and their failure to increase in others. [18]

Briefly stated, it may be said that while Brazil was the importer of large amounts of foreign goods, and while she shipped great quantities abroad, her commerce was legally restricted to that channeled through Portugal. The policy of limiting Brazilian foreign commerce (in the main) to that conducted through Portugal continued to the end, and one of the first acts of João VI, when he moved his court to Brazil in 1808, was to open Brazilian ports to the ships of friendly nations. Brazil's economic independence came in 1808, but political independence was delayed to 1822.

COMMERCE: MONOPOLY COMPANIES

The commercial policy of Portugal passed through various phases. Trade with India, for example, was carried on by a state monopoly which conducted all but a limited amount of the commerce. On the other hand, Portugal was content to see the major part of the products of her Eastern commerce distributed by other nations. Lisbon became the center to which the other nations of Europe

---

[18] On English influence in Portugal-Brazil see Alan K. Manchester, *British Pre-eminence in Brazil—Its Rise and Decline* (Chapel Hill, 1933), pp. 1-53. Azevedo, *op. cit.*, pp. 399-477, in his chapter "No signo de Methuen," discusses the commercial development of Portugal and Brazil from the time of the Treaty of Methuen in 1703. Brazil benefited from the treaty, and Portugal probably did also, is Azevedo's contention, though most Portuguese and Brazilian authors like to believe that the commercial treaty with England stifled Portuguese and Brazilian commerce and industry. See Luis Amaral, *História geral da agricultura brasileira* (3 vols. São Paulo, 1939-40), I, 109-70, on the physical conditions affecting the economic life of Brazil.

resorted for their spices and Eastern imports. Holland was among the chief of these, growing rich from the distribution of Portugal's colonial products. With the almost simultaneous independence of Holland from Spain and the captivity of Portugal, Spain prohibited the Dutch-Portuguese trade in an attempt to ruin Holland commercially. The Dutch met this threat at first by indulging in clandestine trade, and then by direct attack on Spain's and Portugal's colonies. One result has already been seen, the attempt of Holland to wrest a portion of Brazil from Portugal in the same way that she conquered the Portuguese possessions in the East. France and England also attacked the Portuguese possessions in order to get their share of the colonies and commerce. It was in this period (the seventeenth century) that English corsairs raided Brazilian ports, and the French installed themselves in Maranhão, after being driven out of Rio and other parts of Brazil.

The agent of attack in most of these cases was the monopoly company. England's Muscovy Company, African Company, and later East India Company were followed by Holland's Dutch East India Company (1602) and Dutch West India Company (1621). It was the latter which was granted the privilege and task of conquering Brazil, and whose Brazilian venture was discussed above. The success of these companies and the dividends they paid encouraged Portugal to adopt the system. As early as 1587, Philip II of Spain (First of Portugal) thought of creating a monopoly company for the Portuguese colonies. Philip III of Spain (Second of Portugal) entrusted Jorge de Mascarenhas with the task of forming a company composed of Portuguese and Spaniards for the same task, but nothing came of it.

The first definitely established Portuguese monopoly company came in 1649, after Portugal had gained its independence from Spain. João IV, at the suggestion of the famous Jesuit, Antonio Vieira, organized the Companhia do Brasil. This company was obligated to maintain a fleet of thirty-six war vessels to convoy the merchant fleets to and from Portugal and Brazil, and to aid the government in defending Portugal, Angola, and Brazil. In return the company was granted a monopoly over the wine, oil, codfish, and flour trade of Brazil, and a little later over the brazil wood industry as well. The Brazilians were forbidden to manufacture certain distilled liquors from sugar. The company was given a twenty-year concession, and its members granted special privileges and immunities to induce them to invest. Jews convicted by the Inquisition were required to invest in the company in lieu of having their property confiscated. The company was allowed to charge ten per cent of the value of cargo for its convoy service, and so great were its privileges that it had sovereign powers in conflict with those of the Crown. It successfully sent out its first fleet in 1649, and eighty ships sailed on the return from Brazil.

Its position, however, was changed by law from time to time. In 1654 commercial vessels were allowed to sail independently of the fleet from any Portuguese port except Lisbon, and to carry any goods not monopolized. The number of war vessels to be maintained was reduced to ten in 1658, and some of the monopoly rights of the company withdrawn. In 1663 the company was converted into a *Junta do Comercio* with powers to fix freight rates, regulate the fleets, fiscalize the brazil-wood industry, and supervise other commercial matters. Vessels carrying more than twenty-one guns were allowed to sail independently of the regular fleets. The same complaints from the colonists that had provoked modifications in the company's powers led to further reforms in 1672, and to still another reorganization in 1694, in which the Crown appropriated the company and indemnified the stockholders with five per cent bonds payable from the revenues of the tobacco monopoly. It was then administered by the government until it was abolished in 1720-21. [19]

The second monopoly company in Brazil was the Companhia do Maranhão, organized in 1678-79, when a group of merchants contracted to supply five hundred Negroes a year to Maranhão and Pará in order to remedy the scarcity of labor resulting from the diminution of the Indians on the one hand, and the almost complete monopolization of those who remained by the religious orders on the other. The company later had a twenty-year monopoly of the commerce of the region and sent at least one ship each year from both Maranhão and Pará to Portugal. This contract led to the revolt of the colonists under Beckmann in 1684, and the company was abolished the same year.

The third company formed for Brazilian commerce came from the general reorganization under Pombal in the last half of the eighteenth century. [20] This was the Companhia Geral do Grão Pará e Maranhão, organized in 1755. Its capital, 1,200,000 cruzados, would be equivalent to many millions today. It was

---

[19] Simonsen, *História econômica do Brasil*, II, 181-86; Southey, *Brazil*, II, 228-32, III, 548-49; and for the protests against the company see *Revista IHGB*, vol. 25 (1862), pp. 459-64.

[20] Antonio de Sousa Pedroso Carnaxide, *O Brasil na administração pombalina* (São Paulo, 1940) pp. 71-82.

granted a monopoly over the imports and exports of Maranhão and Pará, but could not engage in retail trade. This company brought about the only important economic expansion north Brazil knew during the colonial period. It stimulated the cultivation of rice and cotton, and introduced capital and labor, both of which had always been lacking. It was abolished in 1778-79.

The Companhia de Pernambuco e Paraíba was organized in 1759 with a capital of two million cruzados, and in 1761 the State was authorized to grant it extensive loans. Given the large capital, state support, and the wealth of the regions involved, this company should have been the most successful of all, but its apparent strength proved to be its weaknesses. The loan granted by the State was an indication of the difficulty of raising capital. The wealth of Pernambuco meant that there were already prosperous landed and commercial interests, with which the company came into conflict. The company was abolished in 1778-79. [21]

These companies supplanted to some extent the British merchants of Lisbon who, under treaties of 1642 and later dates, had long held many advantages in the Brazilian trade. The strict letter of the treaties was no longer observed, but the commercial effects were still in force, since "Brazil was supplied, almost exclusively, with English manufactures through Portuguese merchants of the capital, to whom the members of the British Factory gave two or three years credit." [22] The latter statement shows how business was conducted at that time. The long-term credit resulted both from competition among the English merchants and from the long time needed for transmission of goods to Brazil, their sale, and the return of the money to Portugal, since the fleets made but one voyage a year. Thus the trade was carried on in large part in English goods and with English capital. When the companies were formed they were in a better position to regulate the conditions of trade in the interest of the Portuguese, though not necessarily of the Brazilians. The English merchants protested to their own government, asking that the clause of the treaty which gave them the privilege of direct trade to Brazil be invoked, but the English government was unwilling to interfere to this extent with Portugal's colonial policies.

What the net effect was of the policy of founding companies has been a subject of bitter controversy among the historians, as it was among the people directly involved in the eighteenth century. The Portuguese merchants expressed their attitude by having a Te Deum

[21] Simonsen, *História econômica do Brasil*, II, 186-89.
[22] Southey, *Brazil*, III, 550.

sung when news of the companies' abolition reached them. But that the companies had considerably benefited Brazil's northern coast can hardly be doubted. The stimulation of the production of rice, cotton and other products gave this region a larger share of economic return than it had ever enjoyed before. [23]

COMMERCE: CONVOYS

Toward the end of the sixteenth century Portugal was forced to adopt the convoy system to protect her commerce from foreign competitors. A law of 1571 granted preference to Portuguese ships in colonial trade and required these to be armed and travel in convoys. It is probable that the convoys were customary from that time on. In the early seventeenth century there are evidences of convoys, that of 1611-12 having seventy-four vessels not counting the warships. The system of convoys was revised in 1644 and a special tax placed on the convoyed cargoes to pay the expenses incurred. Vessels of two hundred tons or more were eligible to receive pay as convoys, and the flagship had to be of six hundred tons and carry thirty pieces of artillery. The times for the departures of the ships from both Portugal and Brazil were set at fixed periods in order to take advantage of the weather, but the sailing time varied during the centuries. The fleet outward bound to Brazil in 1709 consisted of ninety-seven merchant ships and eight men of war. At best, the system of convoys caused long delays in shipping and Pombal replaced it in 1765 with a patrol system. There was a temporary re-establishment in 1797 to 1801, but thereafter it was abolished. [24]

COMMERCE BETWEEN BRAZIL AND PORTUGAL

Commerce between Brazil and Portugal depended in part upon the demand in Portugal for Brazilian wares, but in much greater part on the general world market and international conditions. In the first years of discovery the products of Brazil were limited, brazil wood being by far the most important. After the middle of the sixteenth century, however, the market for other products, especially sugar, began to grow rapidly, and up to the middle of the seventeenth century Brazil swiftly expanded her agricultural exports. From the beginning of this century, Brazil loomed larger and larger in Portuguese eyes because of the loss of the colonies in the East.

A revealing glimpse of Brazilian commerce at the end of the

[23] Southey, *Brazil*, III, 550-53; 655-56.
[24] Simonsen, *História econômica do Brasil*, II, 190-92.

seventeenth century is afforded by William Dampier, the noted English explorer, merchant, adventurer, and buccaneer. He reached Baía in March 1699, and his ship was received with great friendliness, being conducted into safe anchorage by a Portuguese vessel. Shipping filled the harbor, and Dampier was enthusiastic:

> "A great many Merchants always reside at Bahia; for 'tis a Place of great Trade: I found here above 30 great Ships from Europe, with 2 of the King of Portugal's Ships of War for their Convoy; beside 2 Ships that traded to Africa, either to Angola, Gamba or other Place on the Coast of Guinea; and Abundance of small Craft that only run to and fro on this Coast, carrying Commodities from one Port of Brazil to another." [25]

Dampier described the merchants of Baía of this time as very rich and numerous, the majority being Portuguese, with an Englishman, a Dane, and one or two Frenchmen. His was, he was informed, the first English ship to enter the port in twelve years, all merchants being required to trade in Portuguese ships, "none of any other [nation] being admitted to trade hither."

The chief exports he listed as sugar, tobacco, hides, woods, tallow, whale oil, and other miscellaneous products—a list that need not surprise us. Sugar he found better than that of the English colonies, since it was refined or "clay'd," giving what was known in the market as "Brazil Sugar" a fine reputation. The greatest difficulty, he found at that time, was that too many ships had arrived for the amount of sugar and other goods to be exported, and some had to lie over for another year to await cargo. [26]

Before Dampier's visit, however, and beginning in the middle of the seventeenth century, a decline in trade had set in, sharp until 1670, slight from then to 1690, when there was a gradual rise until 1710, followed by a sharp rise which held to about 1760. [27] The cause for the decline during the last half of the seventeenth century was the partial loss of European markets owing to the accumulation of circumstances already noted. The rise during the eighteenth century paralleled the epoch of production from the mines. Gold and diamonds rescued Brazil from economic decay and stimulated her agriculture, the rise in sugar production continuing upward with the exports of precious metals and stones, and again declining when these fell off after 1760.

The latter eighteenth century and the early nineteenth were far

[25] Dampier, *Voyage*, II, 381.
[26] *Ibid.*, II, 382-400.
[27] Simonsen, *História econômica do Brasil*, II, 192-93 and 222.

from being a period of economic decline, however, even if the absence of quantities of gold kept the total trade down. Agricultural products were exported in increasing quantities, and the years before 1808 saw the total value of agricultural exports alone climb near the former combined value of gold, diamonds and agricultural products. About 1777, more than half of the value of Portugal's international trade was in Brazilian products. As disclosed in Portugal's export balance of 1777, made up mainly of Brazilian products, the principal of these were, in decreasing order of importance: sugar, 800 contos; hides and tobacco, 540 contos each; cacao, 300 contos; cotton, 270 contos; and brazil wood, 114 contos. It is interesting that at this epoch coffee exports amounted to only a little more than two contos. The agricultural exports of Brazil tripled in the last quarter of the eighteenth century, Rio exporting about one-third of the total, and the ports from Baía northward about two-thirds. In the later colonial days Brazil furnished about eighty per cent of Portugal's colonial imports.

The last half century of Brazil's colonial history saw the climax of the economic competition between north and south Brazil. North Brazil, mainly Baía and Pernambuco, was the colonial leader. Gold and diamonds brought Rio forward, and at the end of the colonial period the three ports were about on a level, one exporting about the same as the others with almost yearly changes of leadership. Rio was destined to push ahead of both in the national period and to give place eventually to Santos, an unimportant port during the colonial period.

A measure of the increasing value of Brazil to the motherland is seen in tax figures. In 1607 Brazil contributed only about four per cent of these; in 1718, her share had risen to about thirty per cent; and thereafter the proportion increased.

THE CHIEF BRAZILIAN EXPORTS

We have already seen that sugar was the chief export crop of Brazil. Tobacco first became of importance in Brazilian production in the middle of the seventeenth century when the Dutch occupation gave it a wide outlet. The custom of using tobacco in Europe, and the fondness of the Negroes for it in Africa, led to the increased demand. During the eighteenth century it was one of the chief crops, with Baía being the main area of production. It had a particular economic significance because it could be grown on small farms, whereas sugar was a crop requiring production on a large scale. Thus, tobacco became a small man's product while sugar was the big man's crop. The State, moreover, found tobacco one of its

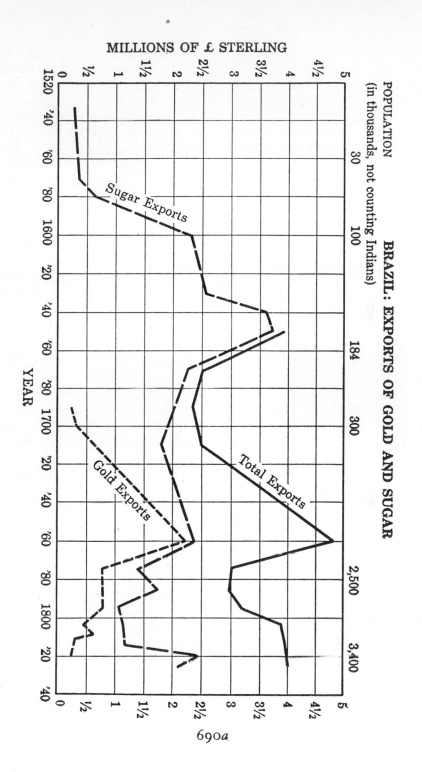

MILLIONS OF £ STERLING

POPULATION
(in thousands, not counting Indians)

BRAZIL: EXPORTS OF GOLD AND SUGAR

Sugar Exports

Total Exports

Gold Exports

YEAR

690a

best sources of revenue, and the tobacco monopoly brought more into the treasury than the fifth on minerals. The tobacco industry of Brazil had to compete with the rival European colonies. England had Virginia, and the French, Spanish, and Dutch their Caribbean possessions. In spite of this rivalry, tobacco was fifth (equal to cotton) in value among the produce of Brazil during the colonial period, being surpassed only by sugar, minerals, hides, and brazil wood, in that order.

Cotton was native to Brazil and used by the Indians. During the first two centuries of the colonial period it was produced mainly for domestic consumption. In the last half of the eighteenth century, however, it became a leading crop. The Industrial Revolution in Europe stimulated the demand as the art of spinning and weaving steadily improved. England especially offered a good market, and the close relations of England and Portugal gave colonial Brazil an advantage. After 1770, cotton increased rapidly. The later colonial prosperity of Maranhão and Pará was almost entirely due to cotton. Maranhão's exports were four times greater about 1800 than in 1771, and by 1818 had quadrupled again. In 1796 cotton represented 20 per cent of Brazil's exports, and in 1805, 28 per cent. In this latter year it surpassed sugar in value among the exports of Pernambuco. Thereafter United States cotton rapidly pushed ahead of Brazilian.

Brazil wood and skins occupied a place in the total Brazilian colonial exports immediately after minerals, though much smaller in value. Brazil wood provided the original commerce, but hides waited the development of the cattle industry, and increased in importance during the eighteenth century. In 1796, the hides exported were valued at more than twenty-five times all woods combined, and were about one-third the value of the cotton. By 1806, hides had increased about three times in value and were more than 60 per cent of the value of cotton, which had increased in value over 1796 by about 75 per cent. In 1796, exports of hides were worth but little more than tobacco, but were four times more valuable in 1806.

Brazil produced many essential crops that did not figure heavily in the export balances. Manioc, for example, was the staple food, used where European nations used grains such as wheat, oats, barley, and rye. Rice and chocolate were used domestically and also exported. Their value during the whole of the colonial period was about one-third that of tobacco and cotton, but only about one per cent that of sugar. Coffee was growing rapidly at the end of the colonial period. Vanilla, cloves, cinnamon, pepper, indigo, and numerous forest products of minor value made up the remainder of Brazil's export balances. It is interesting to observe, however, that the total value of sugar exports for the whole colonial period was more than double that of all other products combined, including gold and diamonds.[28]

---

[28] Simonsen *História econômica do Brasil,* II, 192-229, 204-222; Amaral, *Agricultura,* II, 185-193, 319-352, 361-369; Antonil, *Cultura e opulencia,* 181-204; J. F. Normano, *Brazil: A Study of Economic Types* (Chapel Hill, 1935), pp. 18-56.

31

Society and Culture

WHILE BRAZIL WAS DEVELOPING ECONOMICALLY and expanding geographically, its social and political institutions were taking shape. Fundamental elements in this process were (1) the formation of the Brazilian people, (2) the stratification of society, (3) the development of Brazilian culture, (4) the organization of the Church, and (5) the evolution of the institutions of government.

FORMATION OF THE BRAZILIAN PEOPLE: THE INDIAN

The Brazilian people of today are composed of the three major races of the earth—Mongolians, Negroes, and Caucasians—and the mixtures of these three. The story of the three races and their respective contributions to Brazil are an essential part of Brazilian history.

The Indians were discussed in recording the events of the discovery, but their influence on the development of Brazil warrants further attention. Even though fated to disappear in large numbers, the Indians' importance was great for a century and a half. The natives[1] of the coast, being partly agricultural and speaking the "lingua geral," were an aid as well as a hindrance in the Conquest. While they not infrequently made war on the white invader, they also made friends in other cases. Friendly Indians formed a nucleus of soldiers whom the white man employed against hostile tribes. They furnished a supply of laborers, and assisted the white man in capturing others to work for him. From them the European learned the geography of the country more quickly, and many of the skills necessary for survival. Not only were the Portuguese, French, and others taught the uses of manioc by the Indian; they also took from him the arts of growing and preparing tobacco,

[1] Almeida Prado, *Primeiros povoadores*, pp. 133-210; Almeida Prado, *Pernambuco e as capitanias do Norte*, I, 104-146.

693

maize, potatoes, and many other tropical plants. From the Indian came the technique of constructing from bamboo and straw the type of house needed in the tropics, and the hammock for sleeping, a type of bed still used in many parts of Brazil today.[2] The use of cotton armor, and how to dry and smoke meat without salt were derived from the Indian, as was the system of clearing fields by cutting down and burning the vegetation in preparation for planting. Indian, too, was the custom of moving on from exhausted fields to newly-cleared lands, a custom that served well enough for thinly settled peoples but left much devastated territory for the greater populations that followed. In some instances the Europeans had only to take over the Indian fields and crops as soon as they arrived.[3]

The spirit of "let the women do the work" might also have come from the Indians, to judge from their customs, although there was much of this in both the Portuguese and Negro immigrants. To a priest who reprimanded the Indians for permitting the women to work in the fields, the Indian replied:

"Father, you do not understand our custom, and that is the reason why you do not like it. Women know how to bring forth, which is a thing that we do not know. When they sow and plant, the stalk of maize produces two and three heads, the root of mandioc two or three basketfuls, and everything multiplies in like manner from their hands. Why? . . . because women know how to bring forth, and to make seeds and roots bring forth also." [4]

Women also did the spinning and weaving, where any was done, made the pottery, and attended to all household affairs. As the Indian houses in much of Brazil were of bamboo and straw, which rotted quickly, there was much moving about. It fell to the women to carry the hammocks, pots, mortars, and all household articles while the husband went burdened only with his weapons. Frei Vicente notes that this was customary even on the war path. "The principal men," he observed, "take their wives with them, and these carry the flour and the hammocks, while the men carry nothing more than their arms." [5] There may have been sound reasons for this system at one stage of social development, but it was con-

---

[2] Gilberto Freyre, *Casa-Grande e Senzala* (3rd ed., Rio de Janeiro, 1938), pp. 57-128.

[3] Calmon, *Civilização brasileira*, pp. 32-35, 37-41.

[4] Quoted in Southey, *Brazil*, I, 243.

[5] Vicente do Salvador, *História do Brasil*, p. 65.

PORTRAIT OF A NEGRO SERVANT IN BRAZIL, BY ALBERT VAN DEN ECKHOUT, DUTCH, CIRCA 1640

tinued into the colonial period, when the man carried not so much
as his own weapons and the women were still doing the work.

In still another field the pre-Conquest customs of the Indians
could be seen in operation during the colonial period; this was in
sexual matters. Frequently the Indians are pictured as having maintained a strict code of sexual relations, but if we measure them by
our own standards of monogamy and chastity (leaving aside the
question of violations of our code in practice), their standards
were far from exacting. In fact, it is hard to see how they could
have violated them. Customs differed somewhat among the numerous tribes, but the description Gabriel Soares gives of the Tupinambás around Baía is probably not far distant from the practices of
the majority of the others.

"The true wife among the Tupinambás is the first one a man
had, and they have no other marriage ceremony than the father
giving his daughter to his son-in-law, and when they have had
relations they are married. The principal Indians have more
than one wife, and he who has the most wives is the most honored
and esteemed, but all obey the first wife . . . . When they are
still very young they have relations with women, and old women
because the old women who are disdained by the men seduce
the young boys, making eyes at them and giving them presents
. . . . And these people are so lustful that they seldom respect
sisters and aunts . . . and even their own daughters, and they
are not content with one woman but have many . . . . They
are very fond of committing sodomy, which is not considered a
disgrace among them . . . .

"The females take the males very young, especially those who
live among the Portuguese. The men of the Tupinambás are
not jealous and even when they find another with their wives,
they kill no one on this account; the most they do is spank the
woman for it. And the women who love their husbands well, in
order to please them, look for young girls with whom the husbands may divert themselves . . . ." [6]

What Gabriel Soares relates is confirmed by other early chroniclers
such as Frei Vicente do Salvador,[7] Fernão Cardim,[8] and Pero de
Magalhães Gandavo.[9]

While the Indian played an important part in the formation of

[6] Gabriel Soares, *Brasil em 1587*, pp. 367-68; 372-74.
[7] *História do Brasil*, pp. 57-59.
[8] *Terra e gente do Brasil*, pp. 145-46.
[9] *História*, chap. X, in Stetson, ed. and tr., *The Histories of Brazil*.

Colonial Brazil, whether for better or for worse, he also received much from the European. De Léry cites at least one instance of Indian gratitude for benefits the European had brought, when Tupinambá hosts told their European guests: "You have brought many good things for us of which we were in want. Our forefathers left us nothing good; whatever they left us we have thrown away, because the things which you bring are so much better. How much better is our condition than theirs'! now our plantations are larger! now the children do not cry when they are sheared!" [10] The Europeans had brought them scissors.

THE NEGRO

The Negro was destined to exert a more profound influence on Brazil than the Indian, both ethnically and economically.[11] When Brazil was first discovered the Indians were thought to offer a new source of slaves, and Indian slavery persisted there until the latter part of the eighteenth century. But the Indian was not physiologically and psychologically adequate for the hard work demanded by European settlers. The selling price of the Indian soon dropped to about one-fifth that of the Negro, indicating his slight worth as a workman. Slowly at first, and then rapidly in the seventeenth century, the Negro took the place of the Indian. African slavery, an old institution in the Old World, became the newest thing in the New World.[12]

Portugal was well embarked on the Negro slave trade long before the discovery of Brazil. It needed only a chance for profit in order to orient the Negro slave trade to Brazil. Sugar was the main factor in promoting the traffic, for the setting up and running of a sugar mill demanded fifty to a hundred workmen, or at times many more. These had to be accustomed to the tropical sun, be physically fit to bear the sun-up to sun-down workday, and have some experience as workers. The Indians had none of these qualifications. Their contribution to Brazil's early colonial history was important, but it failed at the point where the European went beyond subsistence farming, and embarked on large-scale, complicated planting designed to furnish Europe with quantities of food products and European capitalists with fat profits.

---

[10] Quoted in Southey, *Brazil,* I, 246-7.

[11] Nina Rodriguez, *Os Africanos no Brasil* (2nd ed., São Paulo, 1937); Evaristo de Moraes, *A escravidão africana no Brasil* (São Paulo, 1933), pp. 11-27; Almeida Prado, *Pernambuco e as capitanias do Norte,* I, 246-307; Gilberto Freyre, *Casa Grande,* pp. 197-340; Lemos Brito, *História econômica do Brasil,* pp. 393-430.

[12] Donald Pierson, "The Negro in Bahia, Brazil," *American Sociological Review,* IV (August, 1938), 524-33.

The Negro was the logical answer to the labor problem. The supply seemed limitless. The slave trade was well organized among the Negroes themselves, where a master and man economy already existed. The Negro was an experienced shepherd and cattle raiser; his knowledge of scientific breeding in 1500 being very probably superior to that of the European. The Negro of many parts of Africa knew how to farm. The manual skills of the Negroes were highly developed; Negro workmanship in iron already had a long history in Africa before America was discovered.

The importation of Negroes into Brazil was not, therefore, merely the bringing in of poor, defenseless, and mistreated savages. The social ostracism suffered by the Negro in the United States, and his absence in modern times from most of those occupations now considered skilled, a result in part of his social position, have blinded us to the true contribution he made at an earlier epoch. If the Negro had been merely the inferior type he is often assumed to be, he would not have been so attractive to plantation owners. He was enslaved because he was capable of producing a profit to the European colonists and capitalists. His position has been well described by a modern student of Brazil:

"In the two centuries when sugar was king, the Negro shared the burdens of cultivation with the Indian. When gold came to dominate the economic life of Brazil, the Negro assumed the entire load. Every panful of earth from which the gold was washed, every clod of *cascalho* from which the diamonds were gleaned, and all the millions of tons that yielded nothing at all, were moved by Negroes carrying upon their stalwart heads the loads their masters were too stupid to move in wheelbarrows. Negroes carried upon their well muscled backs the full weight of the Portuguese Empire in the eighteenth century as they alone carried the weight of the Brazilian Empire for the first half of the nineteenth century . . . .

"It is obvious that the Negro possessed capabilities of the highest value to Brazil. Besides his fine physique and the pigmentation which enables him to labor happily under a broiling sun, his knowledge of cattle was such that he probably taught the Portuguese more of the herdsmen's tricks than he learned from them. And his skill in handling metals was revealed in every smithy of the whole mining region from Minas to Mato Grosso, a trade that was wholly foreign to the Indian's previous experience. Reason enough for the other Brazilians liking the curly-haired black lads who brought them all their gold. And because they liked them, a plot of ground on the outskirts of the gold diggings was always set aside where Negroes of a Sunday could go and wash out the dust with which one day they might buy their freedom." [13]

The entire coast of Africa was dotted with round-up centers where the Negroes were gathered in preparation for export. For the European trader this traffic was fairly simple. In most cases they did not have to hunt the Negroes down and capture them, but had only to buy them from Negro dealers. Some had been enslaved in intertribal wars among the Negroes; others because of crimes and debts. The selling price in Africa was small, consisting frequently of a type of shell found along the Brazilian coast and valued as money in Africa. Frei Vicente, writing in 1627 of the captaincy of Porto Seguro, remarks that there was "along the Rio Caravelas a great deal of *zimbo,* the money of Angola, a sort of tiny sea shell of which they carry pipes full and bring in return for them ships full of Negroes." [14] Tobacco from Baía and other products were also traded for slaves.

The voyage across the ocean was as frightful as man's inhumanity could make it. The Negroes were packed sardine-like into the hold of the ships, where as many as half customarily died before the end of the trip.[15] Once in Brazil the Negroes were sold at fancy prices by the "piece," one young buck Negro counting as a piece, while it might require three older or younger Negroes to count for two "pieces."

There was little if any opposition to Negro slavery, and it had the active support of the clergy. The Jesuits especially advocated Negro slavery and supported it as a means of inducing the planters to leave the Indians to clerical domination. The rate of import of Negroes into Brazil climbed with economic prosperity. In the sugar industry thousands were used, while others raised tobacco, cotton, cacao, livestock, or other crops. When the mines were opened other thousands were sent to the interior.

Millions were brought from Africa during the centuries of the colonial period. They came at such a rate, in fact, that they could not be assimilated. Their principal centers were from Santos north to Pernambuco, with the greatest concentration in Baía. Vieira, in the seventeenth century, estimated that there were twenty-five thousand Negroes in the city of Baía alone who re-

---

[13] Nash, *The Conquest of Brazil,* pp. 156-57.
[14] Vincente do Salvador, *História do Brasil,* p. 99.
[15] Nash, *Conquest of Brazil,* pp. 155-56.

ceived instruction in the Angolan language, and that the number outside the city was much greater. Baía in 1700 probably had ten times as many Negroes as Virginia. The French traveler Frézier estimated that Baía had twenty Negroes to one white man. Many Negroes fled from their masters and made homes for themselves in the interior. In the case of Palmares in the interior of Pernambuco, these escaped slaves became a menace to other settlements, and were destroyed in an extensive military campaign late in the seventeenth century.[16]

Brazil was spoken of as a "New Guinea" in the seventeenth century, since the Negroes often kept their customs, religious beliefs, and even political rivalries. Within their condition as slaves they had their own "kings," and in some cases their revolts against the whites failed because the factions among them could not agree upon a leader. Their contribution to Brazilian ethnography and society grew in importance to the end of the colonial period.

THE COMING OF THE WHITE MAN

We have described the dominated peoples; now let us look at the dominant one. This third ethnic component of Brazilian population was the European, principally the Portuguese in the colonial period. Racially, the white man was destined to make a greater contribution than the Indian during the colonial period, but less than the Negro.

The types of Portuguese who came to Brazil represented every condition of man in Portugal itself. It has been pointed out that the first contact of white men brought principally sailors. Traders soon followed. A subsequent immigration brought the donataries and the true colonists. It is this last element that deserves most attention. The donataries themselves were among the nobles of Portugal, and a considerable portion of them came with their families to settle in the New World. They brought their concepts of social relations, and to a large extent transplanted these to Brazil. The colonists to whom they granted lands in large amounts were drawn from among lesser nobles, gentlemen, and the retainers of their Portuguese estates. They also had a following of servants, soldiers, and artisans.

Not the least important fact about the early colonization, and throughout the colonial period, was the predominance of men. The first ships, Portuguese and French, were necessarily on military and commercial missions, and had no women aboard. After long

---

[16] Southey, *Brazil*, III, 23-29; Chapman. *Colonial Hispanic America*, pp. 82-84.

weeks or months at sea, they made port in Brazil. The Indians
frequently flocked to the shore to see them, and among these many
young women who must have looked attractive in a land "everywhere populated by people who go naked." [17] Not all the Indian
women received the sailors in the manner of the one who dined
on a number of Cabral's crew, nor were most of the women in a
position to resist the advances of the Portuguese. It is undeniable
from the record of racial mixture that the customary reception of
the European men by the Indian women was well described by
Gilberto Freyre, who says that the native women welcomed the
Europeans.

Early race mixture was wholesale. A typical case was Diogo
Alvares, known to the Indians as *"Caramurú,"* who had settled
among the Indians near Baía about 1510, married a chieftain's
daughter, and had a large mameluke family. Tracing one's ancestry back to Caramurú in Brazil is the equivalent of being a
descendant of Pocahontas in the United States. João Ramalho in
São Vicente also became the head of a famous mameluke family.
The sexual customs of most of the Indians, as previously pointed
out, assured the vigorous Portuguese a splendid co-operation.

Marriage, or concubinage, with the conquerors was attractive
to the Indian women. It elevated them above their former position,
and gave their children a higher station than if born of Indian
fathers. This second generation was of valuable assistance in
colonization. The mameluke men made excellent soldiers and leaders in the bandeiras already described. The mameluke women were
more attractive mates to the Europeans than their mothers had
been and furnished a good supply of wives.

Before the middle of the sixteenth century, the new "Brazilians"
were a prominent part of the population and in some regions they
may have predominated. In São Paulo, for instance, we hear of
them in many capacities. They may not have been the gentlest and
most cultured souls on earth, but they had the qualities necessary
if Brazil was to be successfully colonized: bravery, energy, strength.
It would perhaps be difficult to exaggerate their importance in
Brazil's colonial life.

The Negro and white mixture also became a prominent feature
of Brazilian life, particularly toward the end of the sixteenth
century. Conditions in Brazil were again responsible. It was an
environment composed almost exclusively of men, who lived under
stress that may be compared to war. They were not imbued with

---

[17] Cited from a Jesuit letter in Calmon, *Civilização brasileira*, p. 42.

the puritanical concept of sex in the first place, and in the second the conditions of their lives probably accentuated their virility, as does war. Nor was there any restraint on their desires. The women were their property and could not resist even if inclined to do so, of which there is little evidence. Many Negresses, in fact, were tall, slender, light colored, lithe, and sensuous. Their attractions are not difficult to understand. Many of them became the wives in common law of the most prominent and wealthy men and their descendants were numerous.

The tendency toward race mixture was accentuated by the failure to bring a sufficient number of Portuguese women. True, some of the early settlers had their families, and in 1549 Tomé de Souza brought a number of orphan girls, but the quantities were never sufficient. In the following years, and even late in the eighteenth century, we hear of girls being brought, some of them exiled because of prostitution in Portugal, but the ratio of men and women was never equal. And as if this were not enough, hundreds of those who did come went into convents or returned to Portugal to become nuns, for the prestige of a family was in a measure determined by the number of daughters in convents. Brazil had too few women without exporting them. In the eighteenth century the Marquis of Pombal saw the harmfulness of this policy to the growth of the European population, and forbade parents to send their children to Portugal to the convents, without a permission from the King. At the same time he moved entire families to be settled in Brazil, perhaps about twenty thousand people in all, the first large addition of whites which included women since the sixteenth century.[18]

Still another practice which must have had some effect on the rate of race mixture was the extreme jealousy of the Brazilian husband, particularly of the upper social classes. The vengeance of the husband was directed not against the guilty man alone but against his own wife who was sometimes killed for unfaithfulness, and "it was a point of honor for a husband to stab his wife once convinced of her infidelity." [19]

This long period of racial mingling had a profound effect on the attitude of the Brazilian people toward differences in race. While it would be highly inaccurate to say that they are not conscious of "color," they are probably the least inclined of any people on earth to make color an essential distinction. The terms Indian, Negro,

---

[18] Southey, *Brazil*, III, 586-92.
[19] Cited in Calmon, *História social do Brasil* (2nd ed., 3 vols., São Paulo, 1937-1940), I. 137-40.

and white by no means signify what they do in the United States. Before the end of the colonial period these terms had come to mean what they should in the strict racial sense. A Negro was an African, not a mulatto; an Indian was a full blood, not a mameluke. And all men who were not definitely Negro or Indian might be classified as white. For example, a census report of São Paulo in 1811 and 1813 listed the peoples as "Whites, Negroes, and Mulattoes." An English traveler in 1869 remarked: "Here all men, especially free men who are not black, are white; and often a man is officially white, but naturally almost a Negro. This is directly opposed to the system of the United States, where all men who are not unmixed white are black." [20]

CLASS STRUCTURE OF COLONIAL SOCIETY

In spite of the lack of bitter race prejudices, the population was sharply divided by social distinctions, founded in part on differences in wealth. Roughly speaking, the population may be divided into the wealthy land owners and the landless. Among the landowners there were further distinctions based on titles of nobility, while the landless included the vast majority of the people. At the very lowest level of the social scale were the slaves, (Negroes and Indians), although they enjoyed greater security than the free proletariat which was drawn from Negroes, Indians, and whites, and the various mixtures.[21]

The whole tone of colonial society was set by the perpetuation in Brazil of the latifundio system of Portugal. It has been noted that the first donataries were granted realms fifty leagues in extent along the sea and reaching back to the Line of Demarcation. In turn the settlers were granted *sesmarias,* large areas of one to three leagues square. Some owners had several such areas and some had dozens. The amount granted was generally greater in the interior where cattle raising was the main occupation, but in any case the estates were very large. The most extreme cases have been cited, where two families owned most of the land in the interior of Baía along the São Francisco river, but there were similar instances in every part of Brazil.

At the center of this large area was the *Casa Grande,* or "Great House," which served as the home of the owner. Along the coast where sugar was king, the most important feature of the estate was the sugar mill. "A typical large mill *(engenho)* would have

[20] Sir Richard Burton, cited in Nash, *Conquest of Brazil,* p. 143, note 3.
[21] Alan K. Manchester, "The Rise of the Brazilian Aristocracy," *H.A.H.R.,* XI (May, 1931), 145-68.

seven or eight square miles of land, part pasture, part woodland, the rest under cane; from fifty to one hundred effective Negro slaves; and about as many of both horses and oxen. Each constituted an independent, patriarchal community; self-supporting, containing in the village about the manor house, blacksmiths, carpenters, and what other artificers such works require." [22] The custom was to grant *sesmarias* of three leagues square and leave a distance of one league ungranted between seismarias, "to prevent overcrowding." At the end of the colonial period the pastoral section of Rio Grande do Sul had but 539 landholders, their estates having from 18,000 to 90,000 acres. [23]

More than property separated the classes. The gentry considered that they had been ordained by God to rule. A landowner presided over his estate like a petty king, and many of his powers were in fact those of a monarch. His family, servants, artisans, and slaves were by law subservient to him, and in fact he exercised the right of life and death. If his authority was limited somewhat in the cities and near the coast by the presence of the King's officials, this was not true of the interior. Brazil abounded in great estate owners who were bound by no laws they themselves did not choose to obey.

Those below the gentry had many obligations but few rights. In fact, Brazil of colonial times was founded on a legal and social theory that invested "classes" with privileges but did not recognize "individual" rights. The landowners, clergy, military, officials, nobility, and merchants had privileges granted to the class to which they belonged. The artisans, slaves, and proletariat suffered the disabilities of not belonging to a class participating in such privileges.

What instruction and education existed, and this was extremely sketchy and confined to a small number of schools maintained by the clergy, was a privilege of the classes able to pay fees for their children. It was the conscious policy of colonial society to confine instruction to a very few. Brazil was not unique, of course, in this concept of education, but the system of land tenure, which excluded the majority from ownership in a society almost exclusively agricultural, guaranteed that the number who enjoyed the opportunity of education would be confined to the absolute minimum.

The social system of Brazil is a partial explanation of why Brazil did not make the advances her natural riches would have

[22] Nash, *Conquest of Brazil*, p. 125.
[23] *Ibid.*, pp. 144-45.

permitted. The landowning class did not develop great ambition. A living, comparatively easy, could be gained with slight labor. The "gentlemen" performed no physical labor; and for the "ladies," exertion was even more inconceivable. This proportion of the population demanded the best the country could produce, but took no active share in improving either their own condition or that of their fellow men. At the other end of the social scale was the great majority who had no interest in any scheme of betterment because they knew they could not benefit by it. It was of no interest to the slaves to work harder, save, improve. They gained nothing, except that a few slaves bought their freedom. It was useless on the whole to study, learn, or invent. Men advanced through pull, not push. What was important was to have influence, not energy. These things left their mark on Brazil.

DIFFUSION OF LEARNING AND CULTURE

Any consideration of the cultural aspects of Brazilian life must depart from two bases: the general social conditions of the colonial period, and the predominant position of the Church.

It should be borne in mind that there were two basic social classes; those who had, and those who had not. Those who had comprised a small fraction of the people, perhaps not above ten per cent, and with exceptions too few to count, the educated people came from this upper economic class. Sugar, tobacco, cacao, cattle, and gold were the sources of wealth. The society of the time was predominantly rural, the cities being scarcely more than exalted villages until the end of the eighteenth century. Owing to the large size of the estates, some of them veritable kingdoms, people lived far apart. The life around the *Casa Grande,* or home of the proprietor, was pleasant but scarcely conducive to mental or artistic development. No great learning was essential to the maintenance of the family position—the laws of primogeniture and entail took care of that—and hence the incentive to rigorous intellectual training was lacking for the privileged orders. It was customary, in fact, for many of the upper economic classes to look with disdain on mere intellectual activity, or to regard it as worthy only of monks. This attitude was not unknown by any means in the United States, but in this latter case there were counterbalancing influences that Brazil lacked.

No less a factor than the want of incentive for learning in colonial Brazil was the position of the Church. It is almost literally true that there was no organized educational or cultural activity outside the Church. This has enabled some to contend that without the Church there would have been no schools, but the point is not so easily proved. If it is true that the churchmen predominated as teachers, it is also true that they took care to see that their monopoly was not violated. On the one hand they were the sole teaching body; on the other they failed miserably to produce an educational plant that was remotely adequate to the needs of society.

The reasons for this failure are again to be sought in the general structure of society, and the theory on which it was based, both of which were embraced and supported by the clergy. Brazil was a *master* and *man* society. The existence of the large, patriarchal, and semifeudal estates was in itself a guarantee that the majority of the people must live in subservience to these estates in order to survive. They could own no land and conduct no business. This type of society, inherited from Portugal, had the express blessing of the Church. Granted a belief in this social structure, it was logical that few if any advocated culture for the masses. And there was almost unanimous agreement that education for the masses of the people was dangerous to society, and to the souls of the people.

First in numerical importance among the masses were the slaves, Indian and Negro. It can be said that there was never any thought of affording education to these as a whole, and the exceptions to this rule hardly justify citation. Nor were the freedmen, and the freemen of various degrees of racial mixture, in much better condition. They received some vocational training in an informal manner, but little beyond this. The result was that the mulattoes and mamelukes formed a generally propertyless and discontented element. They despised the Indians and Negroes, and were in turn despised by the landowning gentry. It lent an ironical touch that the latter were in many cases the fathers of the mixed bloods. To rise meant that one had to be recognized by his father, or to receive acknowledgment as a "white." This supplied one of the chief ambitions of mulatto or mameluke in Brazil, just as it did in the Spanish colonies.

Positions of trust and preferment in church and civil government were reserved for the upper social elements. From this arose the bitter resentment of the mixed peoples, and their reputation as trouble makers and malcontents, the traces of which can be seen plainly in modern Brazil. The mixed bloods were legally free, but economically blocked. Their color, intelligence, energy, and ambitions placed better conditions within their hopes, but the monopoly of the propertied classes held them down. It availed them nothing, or at the most little, to prepare themselves for a position in life which they were not permitted to assume. The few who overcame their disabilities were of small aid to the majority, who continued (and to a certain extent still continue) in the same social position.

In such an atmosphere, it is little surprising that mass education was outside the pale. The point has been made that comparable ideas prevailed in the English colonies of North America at the same epoch. Particularly, the statement of Governor Berkeley of Virginia has been cited to demonstrate the similarity of ideas held by the governing classes in both colonial societies.

"I thank God there are no free schools nor printing, and I hope we shall not have any these hundred years, for learning has brought disobedience and heresy and sects into the world and printing has divulged [them] and libels against the best government. God keep us from both." [23b]

Berkeley, however, represented a reactionary regime against which rebellion soon broke out. That he and his kind would have stifled intellectuals development if they could have, few can doubt. But he did not represent the feeling that prevailed in the English colonies. And that is precisely where the English and Portuguese situations came to differ. For various reasons, such as the existence of small landowners, the relatively easy emancipation of the indentured servants, and the possibility of migrating westward, the situation in the English colonies changed, but changes in the Portuguese colonies came more slowly. If the United States had continued under control of a landed gentry, it is within the possibilities that the educational concepts would have remained unaltered.

MONASTIC SCHOOLS

Within the structure of the society outlined, the monks set up their schools. The early establishments of the Jesuits, called *colegios* significantly enough rather than monasteries, labored valiantly to give an education to their Indian charges. Reading, writing, and the catechism, plus vocational training, were the curriculum. Their institutions multiplied rapidly, and were set up in almost every available center: Baía, Espírito Santo, Pernambuco, Rio de Janeiro, São Paulo. The Jesuit aldeas were also educational centers where some literary, but principally vocational training was given.

[23b] Quoted in *ibid*, p. 128.

The Jesuit schools began, naturally, with the primary grades, although they were never considered as being an objective *per se*. They were intended basically as a testing ground for those who were to advance to the secondary school and the university. It was the secondary school that held the chief attention of the Jesuits, destined, as Pedro Calmon says, to prepare "an educated and cultured religious élite who would carry out the mystical and social objectives of Saint Ignatius [Loyola]." The secondary schools also taught the children of the upper classes, on a fee basis, and took some of them in as members. For the latter there were advanced seminaries of training, or they were sent to Coimbra, Portugal, where the university was under Jesuit control from 1555. The latter fact probably explains why there was never an institution of higher education in Brazil during the colonial period. A university under any auspices other than Jesuit would have been unacceptable to them, and they could carry on their work well enough through the University of Coimbra.

At the time of their expulsion in 1759, they had nine colegios, three independent seminaries, and two others attached to colegios, thirty-six missions, twenty-five residences, and five other "houses" in Brazil. On expulsion, these and their properties were auctioned off and passed into other hands. The educational establishments passed to other orders, to the secular clergy and to the civil government, the latter a radical departure in Brazilian history.

There is little agreement about the effects on education of the Jesuit expulsion and the evidence is conflicting. Frequently the post-Jesuit period is presented as one of educational decadence. It is easy to cite testimony of those who lamented the educational decay of the colony. Change there certainly was. Where the Jesuits had concentrated on the subjects considered by them necessary for their own purposes, there was a diversity of voices to take their place. Pombal, who had expelled the Jesuits, directed the establishment of primary schools and schools where languages, rhetoric, Greek, Hebrew, Latin, and mathematics were taught. The teachers were paid by the *câmaras* (city councils). Among the most frequent complaints were that good teachers would not go to the country districts, nor come from Portugal.[24]

The other side of the picture is that the intellectual achievements of Brazil under the Jesuits are easily and customarily exaggerated. Their educational system was hardly one that prepared the student for the solution of the problems of this life, and the Jesuits them-

---

[24] Pedro Calmon, *História social*, I, 117-36; Leite, *Companhia de Jesus*, I, 47-104.

selves made no such claim for it. But after their expulsion the changes were hardly revolutionary in character, although, at the same time, the colony's intellectual life was to make some of its most important contributions. Minas Gerais, where Jesuit influence was small, furnished some of the chief literary figures in the last half of the eighteenth century, as well as much of the intellectual basis on which independence rested. This will become evident when literature is discussed.

BRAZILIAN LITERATURE: CHRONICLES, LETTERS, AND SERMONS

The first literature of Brazil was literature *about* Brazil. It was the literature of description, the chronicle of the discoverer and the conqueror. Its tone was eulogistic, awestruck, wondrous. Brazil was enormous, its land of astounding fertility, its people strange, its promise infinite. Naturally enough, the early theme of Brazilian literature was exaltation of the country, depiction in exaggerated terms. Few authors have escaped this feeling, a sort of enchantment, a fact that may be verified by picking up the latest travel book about Brazil, whoever its author may be.

Brazilian literature started the day Cabral made his discovery. With Cabral was Pero Vaz de Caminha, official scrivener of the trading post later established in India. Pero Vaz wrote home, his letter being the first description of the land and its people. Americo Vespucci included Brazil in the famous letters destined to give America its name.

The next important contribution was a "Gazette" written in German from Madeira in 1515, extolling the commercial possibilities. A few years later, Francisco Antonio Pigafetta, who accompanied Magellan on the first circumnavigation of the globe, recorded the days spent along the coast, and gave a short list of words of the Tupí tongue. More complete was the *Diario de Navegação* of Pero Lopes de Souza, the brother of Martim Afonso de Souza. Pero Lopes explored the coastline from the region of Pernambuco to the Río de la Plata, and his diary was the first comprehensive effort to describe the country.

These were soon followed by other chronicles of exploration which, though sometimes written by others than Portuguese, were as much a part of the literature of Brazil as any at a time when it was not yet clear whether the territory would be Portuguese, French, Spanish, or English. Among the most important was the "Voyage" of Hans Staden, a German who spent many years along the coast, and whose work, first published in 1556, is entertaining and useful. Two other accounts were written by men who participated in Villegagnon's attempt to colonize Rio de Janeiro: André Thévet published *Singularités de la France Antarctique* in 1558; Jean de Léry wrote his *Histoire d'un voyage fait en la terre du Brésil* in 1563 and published it in 1578.

In the meantime the most characteristic form of Brazilian literature in the colonial period—the letters and sermons of the Jesuits —made its appearance. There were thousands of letters written by hundreds of men. It will be possible to mention only a few. Manoel da Nóbrega arrived in Baía in 1549 and his letters began soon after. They comprise an excellent description of the country, its new and old inhabitants, and the moral and religious conditions of his times. João de Aspilcueta Navarro is less known than Nóbrega, but his letters and hymns were among the most important early contributions to Brazilian literary culture, while his study of Tupí earned for him the title of "the first who rendered into the Brazilian language some of the sermons and dialogues of our Holy Faith."

Most famous of the early Jesuit writers was José de Anchieta. He came to Brazil in 1553, and was immediately made headmaster of the new Jesuit Colegio in São Paulo, where he and his companions taught "first letters" and Latin to the children of Indian chieftains. He quickly learned the Tupí language, wrote religious poems in Tupí to instruct the Indians in matters of the Faith, and prepared the first grammar of Tupí. Among his other literary compositions were dramas to illustrate the Christian religion to his charges. His letters have an outstanding place in the early Portuguese literature from the New World.

During the last quarter of the century three of the most important contributions to Brazilian history and literature were written. Pero de Magalhães de Gandavo prepared two works on Brazil: *Tratado da terra do Brazil,* written about 1570, but not published until 1826, and *Historia da Provincia Santa Cruz,* published in 1576. Both works were translated and published by the Cortés Society in 1922. Fernão Cardim, a Jesuit, wrote several short accounts of Brazil which were gathered together as *Tratado da terra e gente do Brazil,* in 1925. Perhaps of greater value than the works of either of these was the *Tratado descriptivo do Brasil en 1587* by Gabriel Soares de Souza, a planter of Baía. The first part of his account is a minute description of the coast line of Brazil, with its people, physical characteristics, and plant life. The second part is the finest early description of the plants and animals of Brazil, the people, and the conditions at the time he wrote.

During the course of the seventeenth century, as well as during the eighteenth, there were numerous travel accounts and descriptions of Brazil written by Frenchmen, Englishmen, Germans, and others. These form a part of the literature about Brazil, but there is not the same justification for enumerating them as for those of the first years of discovery. They form, more properly speaking, a part of the bibliography.

Early in the seventeenth century some of the most important contributions were made to Brazilian descriptive and historical literature. The *Diálogos das grandezas do Brasil,* written in 1618, was first published in the nineteenth century. The authorship has been attributed to a number of people, among them Bento Teixeira. The work consists of dialogues between Alviano, who asks numerous questions about Brazil, and Brandonio, who knows all the answers. A more informative work, *História do Brasil,* was written by Frei Vicente do Salvador in 1627. Frei Vicente was the first native-born historian of Brazil, and his work is one of first rank in Brazilian historiography. Unfortunately, it was not published until the nineteenth century, but since that time it has been indispensable for the student of Brazilian history. Another author whose historical works are necessary for the student of Brazilian affairs is the Jesuit, Simão de Vasconcellos. Among his most important publications were: *Chronica da Companhia de Jesus do Estado do Brasil* (1663), and *Vida do Veneravel Padre José de Anchieta* (1672). He published numerous works in addition to these.

The most commanding figure of the seventeenth century, and one of the most important literary personages, was the Jesuit, Antonio de Vieira. Vieira was born in Portugal in 1608 and came to Brazil in 1614. Thereafter most of his life was concerned with Brazilian affairs. His pugnacious personality and devotion to the cause of his Order earned for him high rank among the statesmen of his day. Much of his career is discussed in treating Jesuit and Indian affairs. His literary position is measured less by works of a formal character published in his lifetime than by the collections of his letters, memoirs, sermons, and other works, numbering many volumes. Critics of Portuguese prose rank Vieira second to no one, and the force of his sermons is obvious to the most confirmed unbeliever.

LATER HISTORICAL WRITINGS

It must have become apparent that the literature of Brazil to this point has been principally history, chronicle, sermon, and letters.

Imaginative literature was not characteristic of Brazil during the first two centuries of colonial life. With the eighteenth century, the literary contributions of Brazil increased in quantity and improved in quality, but during the first half of the century largely maintained their factual character. Among the first works of the period was *Cultura e opulencia do Brasil,* published in Lisbon in 1711 and immediately suppressed by the Crown. Only six known copies of the first edition now exist. The author signed himself André João Antonil, a pseudonym since identified as that of João Antonio Andreoni, an Italian Jesuit resident in Baia. Few chronicles are more entertaining or instructive.

Several years later, in 1728, Nuno Marques Pereira published his *Compendio narrativo do pergrino da America.* This work passed through many editions and was one of the most popular on Brazil. It is principally a treatise on morals, and rather boring to the modern reader, but its historical information is important. A complete edition (the first) was published in Rio in 1939. Sebastião da Rocha Pitta's *História da America Portuguesa,* covering the years from 1500 to 1724 was issued in 1730. Rocha Pitta long enjoyed the reputation of being Brazil's first historian, both chronologically and qualitatively. While his work is still excellent and essential, the later publication of the works of Frei Vicente do Salvador, who was born in Brazil, and of other authors who, though born in Portugal, wrote of Brazil, has lessened the relative importance of Rocha Pitta. Another historical work of interest is the *Novo orbe seraphico brasilico,* an account of the religious orders in Brazil, by Antonio de Santa Maria Jaboatão, first published in part in 1761 and in a complete edition in 1858-59. Jaboatão wrote numerous other works. Pedro Taques de Almeida Paes Leme, of São Paulo, was one of the most active of all Brazilian historians. His many volumes, of which a number are lost, give him high rank. The most important are his *História da capitania de São Vicente,* and *Informação sobre as minas de São Paulo,* both historical, and *Nobiliarchia Paulistana,* a valuable genealogical work. Still another book on São Vicente was written by Frei Gaspar da Madre de Deus, who also wrote numerous other volumes on colonial Brazil.

These are only a few of the historians of Brazil whose works are necessary for study of the colonial period. Many of these works are not yet published.

IMAGINATIVE LITERATURE

The dearth of imaginative literature in the early colonial period has already been noted. Perhaps the explanation is partly to be found in the fact that nature challenged the spirit of the writers with its marvels, leaving little to literary invention. Perhaps the explanation lies in the more prosaic fact that the general culture of Brazil was low, producing few poets and still fewer writers of other forms of fiction.

At the start of the seventeenth century a short poem, *Prosopopéa*, by Bento Teixeira, had appeared in praise of Jorge de Albuquerque Coelho, governor of Pernambuco. This brief epic was based on the model set by Camões in *Os Lusíadas* in 1572. Its importance rests in part on its own merits, and in part on the belief that Teixeira was the first poet born in Brazil, although some authorities hold that his birthplace was Oporto, Portugal. The most distinguished Brazilian-born poet in the seventeenth century, however, was Gregorio de Mattos Guerra, 1633-1696. Mattos was educated in Portugal and returned to Brazil, where he held several ecclesiastical positions. His life was not in conformity with the clerical rules, in either word or deed. He was exiled to Angola, but later returned to Brazil. His works were mainly satirical poetry in which he lampooned colonial society. His fame was great and his poems were widely circulated in manuscript form. His popular songs, known as *modinhas,* were frequently imitated. Much of his work was copied from other poets, however, and publication in modern times has not added to his stature as a poet.

During the course of the eighteenth century Brazil was subject to important literary influences which gave her types of literature not previously produced in important quantities: principally romantic poetry in both epic and lyric forms, though all forms of literature appeared. The first suggestion of this was perhaps the work of Manoel Botelho de Oliveira, of Baía, who spent a portion of his life in Portugal. Among his writing were *Musica de Parnasso,* Lisbon, 1705, and a poem, *A Ilha da Maré,* notable for its accentuated nationalistic character.

A near contemporary was Antonio José da Silva, born in Rio de Janeiro in 1705 and burned by the Inquisition in Lisbon in 1739, on charges of being a "New Christian." His work was poetry and comedies of a satirical character, very popular in Lisbon where he lived, and which reflected his Brazilian background as well as the influence of Europe of his time.

More famous, and more representative of the nationalistic trend, were several men who wrote in the last half of the eighteenth century. José Basilio da Gama, born in Minas Gerais in 1740, began his education in Rio and continued it in Portugal and Italy. For a time he was accused of "Jesuitism" after the expulsion of that order, because he was a student in the Jesuit colegio of Rio. Later he became a friend of Pombal and gained a reputation for being "anti-Jesuit." His chief literary work, the epic poem *Uraguay*, was concerned with the events arising from the Treaty of 1750 delimiting the boundaries of Spain and Portugal. The Jesuits opposed the treaty, were accused of inciting the Indians to rebellion and a rapid military campaign was conducted against them by Spain and Portugal. This was one of the chief events in the series which brought about their expulsion from Portugal and its possessions in 1759. The tone of Basilio da Gama's poem was anticlerical and political and, while it has intrinsic value as poetry, its fame has been enhanced by the anticlerical historians of Brazilian literature. It shares the trait which characterizes so much Brazilian poetry, praise of nature. No great originality can be claimed for it, however, since it was based on classical Portuguese lines, and in places is dangerously close to borrowing from Petrarch. The poem has always been a favorite of the Brazilian people because of its "beautiful verses, fluid and tuneful," and has passed through many editions.

A contemporary epic was *Caramurú*, by José de Santa Rita Durão, 1781, its protagonist being the famous pioneer of Baía whose close friendship with the Indians was so important in the success of the early colonization there. Santa Rita Durão was born in Minas Gerais in 1722 but went to Portugal as a boy and became an Augustinian friar, dying in Portugal in 1784. His well known poem is nationalistic in theme, and shares the favors of Brazilians with Basilio da Gama's *Uraguay*.

A work of a different sort was that of Thomaz Antonio Gonzaga. Gonzaga was born in Portugal in 1744 of a Brazilian father, and spent only twelve years of his life in Brazil. While in Brazil, however, he fell in love with Maria Joaquina Dorothea de Seixas, who was to inspire his greatest poem, *Marilia de Dirceu*. The name "Dirceu" came from the eighteenth century fashion of romanticizing the past, the same influence that created the "noble red man" in Europe, and provoked a desire to get back to "nature," which was conceived as perfect and pure. One branch of this tendency became the "Arcadian" with which Americans are familiar. Gonzaga had chosen as his "Arcadian" name Dirceu, when he was engaged to marry Maria, the "Marilia" of the poem. Before their marriage, however, Gonzaga was accused of complicity in the Tiradentes conspiracy of 1789 and exiled to Mozambique, where he died in 1807. *Marilia de Dirceu* was published in Lisbon in 1792, the year after Gonzaga's exile. It is a poem of chaste love, compared by the Brazilians to Petrarch's poems to Laura. Its popularity has carried it through at least thirty-five editions, and perhaps more.

THE ACADEMIES AND NEW CURRENTS IN THE EIGHTEENTH CENTURY

Contemporary with the writers we have been discussing was a movement for the formation of "academies" in Brazil. The academies were probably a result of, as well as a contribution to, the literature of the time. The first was perhaps the *Academia Brasilica dos Esquecidos* (Brazilian Academy of the Forgotten) organized by Viceroy Vasco Fernandes Cesar de Menezes in 1724, and which held eighteen meetings during 1724-25. Its members were interested in natural, military, political, and ecclesiastical history, as well as literature. The members adopted pseudonyms, the distinguished historian, Rocha Pitta, being "Vago" (The Restless One), while others were called "Cloudy," "Busy," "Unhappy," and "Obsequious." The preoccupations of the academy members varied greatly. Rocha Pitta, "The Restless One," read a paper that seemed little in keeping with his historical work: "Who demonstrated the greater love, Clytie for the Sun or Endymion for the Moon?" while "Cloudy" who was Caetano de Brito e Figueiredo, a judge of the high court of Baía, contributed a paper that would have been in keeping with Rocha Pitta's own field, as indicated by its title: "Memoranda concerning the past history of the Luso-American colony."

The *Academia dos Felizes* was organized in Rio de Janeiro in 1736, and continued intermittently until 1740. Another similar organization, *Academia dos Selectos,* was organized in Rio de Janeiro in 1751 or 1752. Its works were published as *Júbilos da America* in Lisbon in 1754. Better known was the *Academia Brasilica dos Renascidos* (Brazilian Academy of the Reborn), founded in Baía in 1759. It had forty members and as many as 115 associates. The Marquis of Pombal was the patron, but the academy dissolved, after holding fourteen meetings in 1759-60, when Pombal ordered the arrest of the president. Still another academy was the *Arcadia Ultramarina,* organized perhaps as early as 1768, whose membership list included many of the outstanding literary figures of colonial Brazil. Among them were José Basilio da Gama, Manoel Ignacio da Silva Alvaranga, Santa Rita Durão, Thomaz Antonio Gonzaga, and many others. A different type of academy was the *Academia Scientifica do Rio de Janeiro*, 1771-72, the members of which interested themselves in the science of Brazil and Europe. The *Sociedade Literaria do Rio de Janeiro*, 1786, was devoted to scientific and political affairs. The latter concern brought the dissolution of the society and the arrest of some of its members. [25]

Brazil was influenced profoundly by the revolutionary events of the last years of the eighteenth century, first the American Revolution and then the French. There sprang up a vogue of "Americanism" which brought the thought of American statesmen to Brazil, albeit to a limited extent. More profound perhaps was the influence which Brazilians received at the University of Coimbra in Portugal —one of the results of there being no university in Brazil. Brazilians from every part found Coimbra a common meeting ground, a more fertile field of nationalism perhaps than any in Brazil itself. While it would not be correct to think of Coimbra as a hothouse of revolutionary ideas, it is true that Brazilians came into closer contact with the ideas animating Europe and America than if they had remained at home. The later academies in Brazil all had numerous men whose ideas stemmed from their European residence.

Not until the end of the colonial period did Brazil overcome her major literary handicap, the lack of a printing press. An attempt had been made in 1747 to found a press in Rio de Janeiro, but it was immediately suppressed. There may have been a press for a time in the Dutch Brazil, but this is not certain. The first press definitely to operate came in 1808, after the Portuguese court had moved to Rio de Janeiro during the Napoleonic invasion of Portugal. Its activity is more properly a part of the history of Brazil as an independent nation.

ARTS AND ARCHITECTURE

The evolution of Brazil's arts was also conditioned by her social structure. It is well to bear in mind that the immensity of the country gave even the most gigantic efforts the appearance of feebleness. Only those who have traversed the country thoroughly can visualize the problem in road construction and bridge building that faced the

[25] On Brazilian Literature see: Arthur Motta, *História da litteratura brasileira* (2 vols., São Paulo, 1930); Francisco Sotero dos Reis, *Curso de litteratura portugueza e brasileira* (5 vols., Maranhão, 1866-73); Jorge O. e Almeida Abreau, *História da literatura nacional* (Rio de Jeneiro, 1930); Afranio Peixoto, *Noções de história da literatura brasileira* (Rio de Janeiro-São Paulo, 1931); Sylvio Romero, *História da litteratura brasileira* (2nd. ed., 2 vols., Rio de Janeiro, 1902-1903); Alexander Marchant, "Aspects of the Enlightenment in Brazil," in Whitaker, ed., *Latin America and the Enlightenment*, pp. 95-118.

settlers. Furthermore, not until the eighteenth century was there great necessity for penetrating the interior with public works.

Brazil's civic structures remained grossly inadequate even to the end of the colonial period. Where billions were needed, Brazil had not even thousands to spend. Public works that could not be paid for with the restricted incomes of the municipalities were undertaken at the expense of wealthy individuals or of the Crown. The captains-general or governors of captaincies usually undertook public works, while the municipal câmaras confined themselves to police duties. Because of the lack of wealth in part, and largely because Brazil had not yet developed the type of civilization in which extensive public works are characteristic, there were few bridges, aqueducts, or notable public buildings (except in Baía and Pernambuco) during the first two centuries of occupation. The municipalities begged off because of their lack of funds, and the officials of the Crown devoted most of their funds to military establishments. As late as 1690, Vieira remarked in Baía that there were no bridges in the country owing to the "natural inertia of the climate." [26]

The eighteenth century brought notable improvements, however; in the civic face of Brazil. No small share of this is to be attributed to the urbanization taking place in this century. With the increase of population, the greater stability of the various colonies, the growth of commerce, and perhaps most important, the discovery of the mines, Brazil began to assume an appearance hitherto unknown. Up to the eighteenth century, many of the chief cities were really little more than villages. That Brazil's was a rural civilization cannot be too often stressed. From the *fazenda* (the large estate), and the *engenho* (the sugar mill), Brazil took the tone of her civilization. Wealthy as many of the fazendeiros were, they had not the means to undertake the type of large public structures that came to be fairly common after the later seventeenth century. Brazil in this respect was considerably behind the Spanish colonies, where splendid public edifices date from the sixteenth century, some of them rising out of the midst of the Conquest.

But once the wealth was present and accumulated in a few places, Brazil, too, began her epoch of building. To this both State and Church made their contribution, particularly the latter. Whereas the church of the Ajuda in Baía had a straw roof until 1572, magnificent and elaborately adorned convents and churches were common during the eighteenth century. Baía has perhaps the finest examples, but Rio de Janeiro, Pernambuco, Pará, São Paulo, and

[26] Calmon, *Civilização brasileira*, p. 122.

Minas Gerais abound in religious structures that are a delight to believer and unbeliever alike.

Brazil had little colonial art that can be considered native Brazilian. While some of the Indians produced interesting basketry, featherwork, and carving, none of them had developed an art that invited imitation on a large scale. The principal exception to this rule would be the pottery of the Indians who lived on Marajó Island, at the mouth of the Amazon. Thus it came about that Brazilian art was drawn mainly from Europe, with Indian and Negro mixtures, the latter probably being stronger than the Indian. The wood carving of Baía, for example, shows pronounced Negro influence, and much of it was probably wrought by Negroes. The stone sculpture of Minas Gerais, on the other hand, was more European in spirit.

Two principal types of colonial churches were built. One had a very simple exterior, white walls faced with gray stone. The inside was as elaborate, however, as the resources of the country permitted it to be. The other was built on three sides much like the first type, but its façade was characterized by an exceedingly elaborate baroque style. Interiors were often gold flake, some of the churches of Baía and Rio de Janeiro presenting an almost completely gold finish. To supply the elaborate sculpture and painting demanded by the churches, artists appeared. A school of painting sprang up in Baía and another in Rio de Janeiro. The work of the artists was mainly religious scenes for the churches and portraits of the famous and the wealthy citizens.

The most distinguished name in Brazilian fine arts is that of Francisco Antonio Lisboa, known as the "Aleijadinho" (The Little Cripple), whose contributions to the architecture of Minas Gerais were numerous. His style was essentially baroque, but he added elements of his own to give colonial Brazil some of the most attractive and beautiful churches of this type. The break between colonial and modern Brazilian arts came in 1816, when the court brought a school of French artists, among whom were Taunay, Lebreton, and Debret, to teach and work in Brazil.

32

The Church in Brazil

Organization of the Church

THE DEFINITE ORGANIZATION OF THE CHURCH in Brazil followed shortly on the establishment of the Captaincy-General in 1549. There had been members of the secular clergy in Brazil before this time, of course, but no Brazilian hierarchy. This lack was filled in 1550 when the King, while strengthening the colony at Baía with new settlers and supplies, petitioned the Pope to create a bishopric for Brazil. Up to this time Brazil had belonged to the diocese of Funchal in the Azores islands. The Pope acceded to the request and the first bishop, Pero Fernandes Sardinha, reached Baía in October of 1551. The Bull creating the new bishopric was promulgated in 1552, giving Baía control of the religious organization for all Brazil.[1]

Almost simultaneously, in 1551, the kings of Portugal were made permanent Grand Masters of the Order of Christ, a significant accretion of the royal powers over the Church. The office carried with it rights of patronage over all territories conquered from the infidel, in accordance with a Bull of Leo X of January 1514. Hitherto the monarchs of Portugal had enjoyed this patronage only when holding the grand mastership temporarily. Now they held it in perpetuity, and hence they were more powerful in church matters in Brazil than the Pope himself, and all Bulls and other papal documents were customarily transmitted through the Portuguese government.

Gradually, as the population of Brazil increased and the area of territory effectively occupied expanded, the Church administration grew more extensive. In 1572, the government of Brazil was divided into a northern and southern branch. The civil division thus made was abandoned in 1577, but not so the ecclesiastical.

---

[1] Moreira de Azevedo, "O primeiro bispo do Brasil," *Anais BNRio*, XXIII (1901), 59-70.

The southern captaincies were separated from the diocese of Baía and entrusted to an administrator independent of the bishop. Not until the next century, however, were more bishoprics created. In 1576, the governor general of Brazil was given authority to make the nominations for clerical positions in Brazil, of course greatly enhancing his powers.[2]

The latter part of the seventeenth century saw the creation of new dioceses. There were several reasons why this was expedient. The population had naturally increased, necessitating a larger number of officials, and likewise the amount of territory to be administered was greater. Whereas in 1550 Brazil was no more than a few scattered settlements between Pernambuco and São Paulo, it now reached to the Amazon River and a considerable distance inland, owing to the activities of the expeditions that went out from São Paulo, Baía, and Pernambuco. The Papacy therefore resolved to provide better for the spiritual work of Brazil by strengthening the church organization. Innocent XI issued Bulls in 1676-77 for the creation of bishoprics in Rio de Janeiro and Pernambuco, both suffragan to Lisbon. This action helped improve the relations of Portugal and the Papacy, which had been strained since 1649 because of disputes which arose during Portugal's war of independence from Spain and Brazil's fight against the Dutch.

Only a few years after these new dioceses were created, Brazil began the period of her greatest geographical expansion. The missionary orders pushed up the Amazon to the Andes during the seventeenth and eighteenth centuries, and the discovery of the mines lured the Portuguese and Brazilians to the very heart of the continent. The existing dioceses were insufficient, and therefore five new prelacies were created before the middle of the eighteenth century. The first new bishopric was Pará, established in 1720 with authority over the vast region of the Amazon, and, like Maranhão, suffragan to Lisbon. The reason for making these two dioceses dependent on Lisbon was the same that had previously impelled the court to make their economic and political affairs subject directly to Lisbon: the ocean currents and winds rendered communication easier with Portugal than with Brazil from Pernambuco southward. The archbishopric of Lisbon was designated a patriarchy from 1716. The honors accorded the bishops at this time indicate the prominent position they held in the community. The people were required to kneel when the bishop passed, the

---

[2] Varnhagen, *História geral*, I, 208-9, 277-78.

governor had to grant him the seat of honor and give him the treatment of "Illustrious," and he received the same military honors as the governor himself.

Slightly later the vast expansion in the mining regions brought about the erection of two additional bishoprics and two prelacies. The bishoprics were São Paulo and Marianna (Minas-Gerais), and the prelacies were Goiaz and Mato Grosso. No prelates were named for the latter two, however, during the eighteenth century.[3]

THE REGULAR CLERGY: THE JESUITS

The aims of the Church in Brazil were the same as in the Spanish colonies—to secure salvation for the Christians colonizing the new lands, and for the heathens inhabiting them. In this mission the secular clergy were aided by the regular clergy. The most important of the orders in Brazil were the Jesuits, Franciscans, Mercedarians, Benedictines, Capuchins, and Carmelites, and several convents of nuns.

The Jesuits were the first monks to arrive in Brazil, coming out with Tomé de Souza in 1549. The Benedictines, Capuchins, and Carmelites came out shortly after 1580, and the first convents of nuns were not established until the next century.

The Jesuits became the most important of the regular orders, in part because of the leading place they took in educational and religious work, in part because of their defense of the Indians, and in part because of their numerous contentions with the colonists and the government. Because of their importance, their history is worth following in some detail. This may give the reader an exaggerated impression of their place in the colony, and minimize the work of the other orders, but a detailed account of all the religious orders would complicate rather than clarify the essential points in Brazilian history.

When Tomé de Souza reached Baía in 1549, the six Jesuits he brought with him were under the leadership of Manoel da Nóbrega.[4] Four years later the new governor and general, Duarte da Costa, brought seven more Jesuits, among whom was José de Anchieta. Nóbrega and Anchieta were to become the two most prominent Jesuits of the sixteenth century in Brazil, as was Antonio de Vieira in the seventeenth. At the time of the arrival of the second group, Brazil was designated a separate province with Nóbrega and Luis de Gram as joint provincials. Other groups ar-

[3] Varnhagen, História geral, II, 70-72, 156-57.
[4] Serafim Leite, Companhia de Jesus, I, 17-104.

rived from time to time, and as soon as they came they were sent to the various captaincies.

One of the most important early establishments was near Piratininga, where Nóbrega and two others in 1553 founded a colegio for Portuguese and mameluco children. Anchieta, with thirteen Jesuits, came as a schoolmaster. So famous became this institution, São Paulo, that it gave its name to the town and province. The work the Jesuits were carrying on is well illustrated by a letter which Anchieta wrote in August, 1554, to Ignatius Loyola.[5]

"Here we are sometimes more than twenty of us in a little hut of wicker work and mud, roofed with straw, fourteen paces long and ten wide. This is the school, this is the infirmary, dormitory, refectory, kitchen, and store-room, yet we covet not the more spacious dwellings which our brethren inhabit in other parts, for our Lord Jesus Christ was in a straiter place when it was his pleasure to be born among beasts in a manger; and in a far straiter when he deigned to die for us upon the Cross . . . . I serve as physician and barber, physicking and bleeding the Indians, and some of them have recovered under my hands when their life was not expected, because others had died of the same diseases. Besides these employments, I have learnt another trade which necessity has taught me, that is, to make *alpergatas;* I am now a good workman at this and have made many for the brethren, for it is not possible to travel with leathern shoes among these wilds."[6]

Anchieta's work was even greater than he indicated. While he was teaching his charges Latin, he learned their language, Tupí, for which he prepared a grammar and dictionary. For each of the students he wrote down the lesson of the day, there being no books. From the secular songs of the Portuguese he fashioned hymns in Latin, Portuguese, and the Indian tongue. Likewise he prepared interrogatories for confessors on all occasions, and catechisms for the Indians.

The Jesuit settlements multiplied rapidly. Missionaries were quickly sent to Ilhéus, Porto Seguro, Espírito Santo, São Vicente, Rio de Janeiro, Sergipe, Pernambuco, Paraíba, Rio Grande do Norte, and in time, to other places south of São Paulo and along the north coast and the Amazon River. Before the end of the

[5] On Anchieta and early Jesuit activity see Pedro Rodrigues, "Vida do Padre José de Anchieta." *Anais BNRio*, XIX (1897), 1-49, XXIX (1907), 181-288. Vol. XIX of the *Anais BNRio* also contains letters and other material relating to the Jesuits and their educational work; cf. Leite, *Companhia de Jesus*, I, 269-314.

[6] Quoted in Southey, *Brazil*, I, 263-65.

governorship of Mem de Sá in 1572, the Jesuits had at least ten missions in the region of Baía alone, some of which had five thousand neophytes. The Indians were baptized by the thousands, a work in which the bishop often participated. Another work was the marriage of the Indians by Church ceremonies, involving frequently the choice of *one* of the Indian's wives from among several. The schools maintained often had three hundred *piasinhos* (little red skins) or more, who were taught the cathechism, reading, and writing. The missions were nominally under the control of the Indians themselves with their own "mayor," but in fact the latter merely carried out the orders of the Jesuits, who set him up as a dignified official, dressed in a special manner to impress the Indians. The Jesuits, while teaching the Indians, studied the Tupí language, as did Anchieta in São Paulo, to aid them in their work. They referred to Tupí as Greek, and found it far more practical.[7]

In converting the Indians, the Jesuits used simple but effective methods. They appeared always as the defenders of the Indians against the colonists, an attitude enabling them to gain the confidence necessary to success. The Indians were taught songs, trained in playing musical instruments, and allowed to march in processions wearing special dress. This appealed to old and young alike. Presents were also given to the children. So successful were the Jesuits that they made friends with some of the tribes, persuading them to become allies of the Portuguese and to lay down their arms, or use them against other Indians. This sometimes led to the enslavement of the Indians, as we have seen. That they were serving as instruments in the enslavement and extermination of the Indians the Jesuits failed to see, or if they did, considered it merely incidental and a necessary evil in their great work of saving souls.

Two tasks that the Jesuits and other orders set themselves were not easy: persuading the Indians to abandon polygamy and cannibalism. Some of the Indians ate human flesh ceremonially and some used it as a regular food. But in neither case were they willing to give up the practice. The Jesuits wrote glowing reports of their success, but there is ample room to doubt whether cannibalism did not last as long as the Indians. Conversion to monogamy was equally difficult. It was known neither legally nor as an ethical standard among the pre-Conquest Indians, and while the Portuguese practiced legal monogamy, they were promiscuous among the Indians, as were practically all men who came into

---

[7] Varnhagen, *História geral*, I, 243-44.

contact with the primitive peoples. It was hard to make the Indians see the virtue of monogamy in the face of the universally contrary practice of the Portuguese laymen, and even of many clergy.

The attempt to wipe out cannibalism was apt to arouse the anger of the Indians. In some cases the Jesuits baptised the Indians who were to be eaten, but when the cannibals decided that this ruined the taste of the meat, they had to desist. They then tried to baptise secretly so that the Indians would not know of it. At other times the Indians decided that the Jesuits, and especially their practice of baptising, caused epidemics of colds, catarrah, and other diseases, and wanted to quit the missions. The Indians thus ascribed to water a magic power, but in a sense contrary to that of the Jesuits. Some Indians also believed that the Jesuits killed people by baptism, this belief arising from the sacraments of infant baptism and extreme unction. Thus the Jesuits found that their practices at times appealed to the Indians, and at other times repelled them.

It was customary for the missionaries to persuade the Indians to build a church, and then to teach them the cathechism, preach to them in their own language, and hold services that would attract them. This was not difficult among a simple people who had few amusements. In doing this they copied and improved upon the ceremonies of the *Payes,* the Indians' medicine men. The Jesuit services were so appealing to the children that they sometimes ran away from their parents to live in the missions.

The net religious and moral effort of missionary activity is very difficult to determine, although there is no doubt that the bad example set by other members of the community made their task harder. The contention is sometimes advanced that the almost universal deviation from Christian precepts in the conduct of Indians and Portuguese before 1550 was due to the lack of priests in Brazil. But as a matter of fact, there were priests in America before the Jesuits came; and there was no discernible improvement after this date. The facts would seem to be that religion to both Indians and Portugese was a formal matter, having little to do with ethical conduct.

At times the Jesuits were beset with moral questions concerning their charges. One, monogamy for the Indians, has been mentioned. A still more delicate question was what to do with the Indian concubines of the Portuguese men. If the Indian women were taken from the men and returned to their people, they would probably continue the same customs and at the same time lose their souls.

If allowed to live with the Portuguese men, both lived in sin, but
they were available for salvation. While the missionaries debated
this perplexing point, the Portuguese peopled Brazil with a large
mameluco and mulatto population. Nóbrega and his companions
refused the sacraments to those holding Indians as concubines or
slaves, and claimed good results, but nevertheless both polygamy
and slavery remained a constant source of worry throughout the
colonial period.[8]

The Jesuits and Conditions of the Indians

The interest of the Jesuits in the Indians had begun even before
the Society of Jesus was officially sanctioned by the papacy as a religious order. They boasted that they were instrumental in persuading Paul III to recognize the Indians as human beings in 1537.
Thus they arrived in America as defenders of the natives, and in
their own view never compromised with Indian slavery. The
colonists, on the other hand, because of their need for slaves, resented Jesuit intervention. The lines of battle were clearly drawn
from the minute the Jesuits landed in Baía in 1549. The Jesuit
attitude on slavery in general, however, was not one of uncom-
promising opposition. While objecting to Indian servitude, they
approved African slavery. It has been seen that in Spanish America
the Jesuits owned slaves. In Brazil, as one modern historian states,
"The Jesuits skillfully transferred from the Indian to the Negro
the preference of the planters on the coast. They stimulated, encouraged, and promoted the importation of African slaves, by
which they liberated the Brasis [Indians], in the meantime destroyed or driven back by numerous wars that neither the fathers
with their kindness nor even the governors like Mem de Sá, such
great friends of theirs, could prevent."[9]

The introduction of the Negro did not entirely remove the
menace to the Indians. There was almost no interval in the struggle
between the pro- and anti-slavery forces. This struggle, with victory temporarily with one side and then the other, caused the
Indian policy of Portugal to vary swiftly from time to time, and
even place to place. Some Indians lived constantly at peace with
the Portuguese, some were at war most of the time; some worked
for wages, some were enslaved.[10] Sometimes efforts were made to

[8] Southey, *Brazil*, I, 252-58.
[9] Calmon, *Civilização brasileira*, p. 127.
[10] Handelmann, *Brasil*, pp. 126-32. Alexander Marchant in his interesting and
provocative work, *From Barter to Slavery: The Economic Relations of Portuguese
and Indians in the Settlement of Brazil, 1500-1580* (Baltimore: The Johns Hopkins
Press, 1942), sustains the thesis that the first relations of the Portuguese with the

distinguish carefully between those who could and could not be enslaved; at other times slavery was prohibited entirely. In the meantime, the Indians were either killed off or absorbed, but so much of the history of colonial Brazil concerns this struggle over the Indians that its story must be told.

Although the leaders of the antislavery forces from the time of Nóbrega and Anchieta, the Portuguese Jesuits too often demonstrated that they would permit slavery provided they could control it. They owned Indian as well as Negro slaves. The early settlers considered their opposition to slavery insincere, and accused them of saying in effect, "You leave the Indian alone, so that I may use him for my own ends." Nor were the Jesuits always advocates of gentle treatment for the Indians, nor opposed to the use of violence in their subjugation. Nóbrega, writing in 1559, remarked:

"And if the Indians are left in liberty to do as they please, nothing can be done with them since they are a brutish people, as we have seen from our experience with them during the long time we have been dealing with them with much labor, without accomplishing anything but the salvation of a few innocent souls that we have sent to heaven." [11]

After one of the numerous battles with the Indians the Jesuit Ruy Pereira rejoiced that the governor Mem de Sá had at last ceased to follow a "pseudo-philanthropic" policy with the Indians, noting that "this conversion of the governor was greatly aided by his realizing that without instilling fear nothing could be done." Anchieta himself wrote a short time later that it had been decided to make war on the enemy Indians "so that they may live in peace and quiet, and at the same time begin to open up a way to preach the gospels to the enemy as well as our own Indians, who, we have learned, are more easily converted by fear than by love." [12]

Presented in this light, Indian matters seem to have been reduced to the question of who should control the Indians and with what methods. The colonists believed they had the right to take Indians captured in battle as workers in order to compensate themselves for loss of life and property. The donataries from the beginning took the Indians prisoners, either keeping them as slaves or distributing

---

Indians were through barter and that as the economic life of the colony grew more complex the Portuguese turned to slavery. While this thesis is correct in part, it should be remembered that even the first Portuguese enslaved Indians, that they bought Indian slaves from Indians who practiced a system of slavery, and that there was a mixed system of barter with free Indians and slavery long after 1580.

[11] Letter of Nóbrega, 1559, cited in Varnhagen História geral, I, 179.

[12] Quoted in Varnhagen, História geral, I, 179.

them to their colonists. Abuses arose, and a better system was sought, one that would permit the Indians more freedom. This was what the Jesuits advocated, but "more by word than by example, for they did not begin by liberating those who were under their control," as Varnhagen remarked. The colonists saw a threat to their very existence and to Portuguese possession of Brazil, especially when workers began to be scarce. The Portuguese court, with little knowledge of the Indians, leaned toward absolute freedom. The Jesuits in the meantime had formed the Indians into missions or aldeas, and the colonists pointed out that, while the Indians of the missions were protected from outside dangers, they were in effect serfs since they worked not merely around the colegios but also on the so-called "Indian lands," which were nothing more nor less than the estates and sugar mills of the Jesuits.

In view of the conflicting evidence, the King, aided by the Mesa da Consciencia, a religious body of Portugal, created in 1532 and to which the Indian affairs were entrusted, sought to find a solution that would please both sides. The Crown experimented with entrusting children to "godfathers" who were to educate them and permitting Indians over twenty years of age to sell themselves into slavery. The abuses committed under this system caused the court to order the governor, Mem da Sá, to see that the Indians were well treated, and to consult with the other officials and the Jesuits as to how they could be protected. The rules drawn up in consequence gave effective control of the Indians to the Jesuits.

King Sebastian in 1570 declared that no Indian should be enslaved unless in open warfare carried on at the express command of the court, or from among the cannibalistic Indians. The Indians who worked for the Portuguese were to be considered as free men and not slaves, by another law of the epoch. The complaints that followed the statute of 1570 led to modifications in 1574 that destroyed the principal protective features of the earlier measure. When Philip II (First of Portugal) came to the throne, he affirmed previous legislation providing that only those taken in warfare should be slaves. Philip III (Second of Portugal) decreed that the Indians should not be considered slaves in any case, in two laws of 1605 and 1609. This was met with the usual protest and compromise. It was decreed that they should be taken in "just wars" for a period of ten years and settled in aldeas protected by "colonists of exemplary life." Such legislation did not prevent the bandeirantes from making their slaving expeditions, but did encourage Negro slavery, since the colonists were not periodically worried

Copied from the original in The John Carter Brown Library

SEVENTEENTH-CENTURY SHIP

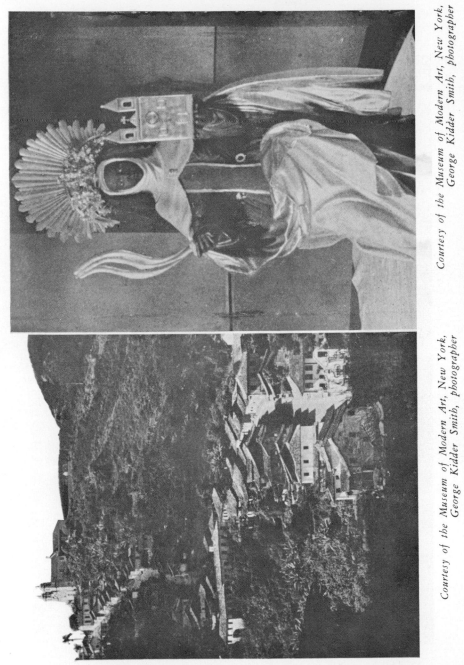

SANTA IFIGENIA, MINAS GERAIS, 1785

SANTA IFIGENIA CHURCH, MINAS GERAIS, 1785

about the legal titles to them, whereas their Indians might be taken away at almost any time. [13]

These shifts in policy were accompanied with recriminations among the Jesuits, colonists, and civil officials. In 1610 the governor complained of the "bad disposition of these Fathers and the slight pretexts with which they complained about the governors in the past, how little truth they speak in everything, not doing anything but making complaints and obscuring the truth." The next year he wrote to the King complaining that the Jesuits were the cause of all the troubles and disputes, adding:

"In order that the Fathers of the Company may understand that they are subordinate to Your Majesty, it is necessary for you to reprimand them, because they absorb so much of Your Majesty's treasury that in this state alone . . . Your Majesty loses in the manner of payment [in sugar at a price above the market] more than one-third, and what they profit from the Indians is worth more than anything else . . . . Your Majesty should inform yourself of these things and others, and remedy them by taking the aldeas from the Jesuits . . . and if the Fathers wish to teach the Indians to be Christians, there will always be the opportunity for them to do so." [14]

In the midst of allegations by the Jesuits that the colonists were exterminating the Indians, and of counterclaims by the colonists that the Jesuits were enriching themselves by unfair competition in selling goods produced with the labor of the Indians, the colonists in 1611 asked that they be allowed to contract the Indians for work, and the governor consented. When the Indians failed to live up to the contract, they were brought to court where the Jesuits, from whose aldeas they came, protected them. This added to the incentive for the Paulistas to go on bandeiras. They could escape contracting for the Jesuits' Indians by capturing their own.

The era of the bandeiras, whose greatest activity followed in the next few decades, brought attacks on the Jesuit missions in the Spanish possessions, as we have seen. Some of the Spanish Jesuits who came to protest these attacks were in Rio de Janeiro in 1640 when the Bull of Urban VIII (issued 1639) was published, forbidding the capture, enslavement, or sale of the Indians. The people rose in revolt, and broke down the gates of the Jesuit college in Rio; they were prevented from killing the Spanish Jesuits only

---

[13] Varnhagen, *História geral*, I, 257-60; Southey, *Brazil*, II, 452-54; Lemos Brito, *História econômica do Brasil*, pp. 269-92; Calmon, *Civilização brasileira*, pp. 127-28.

[14] Varnhagen, *História geral*, I, 321-24 bis.

by the intervention of the governor. In Santos they attacked the vicar general who was trying to post the Bull, and prevented its enforcement. There were disturbances in other places also, the worst being in São Paulo where the Jesuits were expelled, and the unsuccessful attempt made to set up an independent state with Amador Bueno as king. The bill of complaints sent to the King of Portugal by the câmara of São Paulo accused the Jesuits of almost everything, but the substance of the quarrel was that there were two different authorities trying to govern in the same territory.

São Paulo finally came to a settlement with the Jesuits in 1655 and permitted their return, but not until they promised not to interfere in Indian affairs. Up to this time, São Paulo had refused to make peace with the Jesuits in spite of an *alvará* (royal writ) of October 3, 1643, ordering them to restore to the Jesuits their properties, and an offer of amnesty, in 1647, if they obeyed. [15] The intervening period was one of much disturbance. Clergy and populace were in constant conflict. As Varnhagen remarks: "The ecclesiastical administrators and their substitutes, always aided by the Jesuits, arrogated to themselves temporal powers to such an extent in their capacity of agents of the Inquisition, Papal Bulls and vice-collectors of the Pope, that the people were in a constant state of hostility with them, and all of them came to a bad end, some apparently poisoned." [16] The extent of trouble between the clergy and the people is indicated by a royal order of 1646 to the *ouvidores* (judges) of Rio de Janeiro. This forbade the bishop to arrest laymen, an indication that up to this time it had been done.

The Câmara of São Paulo tried to settle its disputes with the Jesuits in 1676 by signing an agreement with them to the effect that they would not try to influence the court to free the Indians, but the policy was not successful. At about the same time, the Câmara of Rio de Janeiro was involved in a quarrel with the Jesuits, arising partly from the perennial Indian question and partly from the charge that the Jesuits held a monopoly of the best lands and shipbuilding wood. The rector of the Jesuits appealed to the ecclesiastical administrator of the diocese for support, and this official anathematized the Câmara and excommunicated its members. When an appeal was made to the court the Jesuits were upheld. [17]

Maranhão and Pará in the north were also the scene of a protracted struggle between the colonists and the Jesuits over Indian slavery and other matters. After the recovery of the region from

[15] Varnhagen, *História geral,* I, 406-14; II, 40-41; Nash, *Brazil,* pp. 100-105.
[16] Varnhagen, *História geral,* I, 405.
[17] *Ibid.,* II, 73.

the Dutch, it was divided into two captaincies in 1652, and the governors who were sent out had orders to free the Indians. When they attempted to enforce the King's edict a rebellion broke out. The governor agreed to suspend enforcement—he probably could not do otherwise—until a commission could be sent to Portugal to take up the matter with the court. This was the beginning of a fight that lasted until the expulsion of the Jesuits by the Marquis of Pombal during the reign of José I of Portugal, in 1759.

At this juncture, in 1653, the Jesuit, Antonio Vieira, arrived with a royal order permitting him to take whatever action he saw fit in regard to the Indians. His report to the monarch pictured deplorable conditions. He reported that heathen and Christian lived alike, without cathechism or sacraments. The people were divided between those who enslaved and tyrannized, and those who approved of both practices. The inhabitants of Pará and Maranhão, according to Vieira, heathen and Christian, were "on the road to Hell."

The state of the Indians was wretched. In spite of all laws, the aldea Indians of Maranhão and Pará were worse off than slaves. Their labor was under the directon of the capitão-mor who used and abused them at will, forcing them to work at anything he liked. Many were so badly treated that they voluntarily took up residence among the enslaved Indians, whose owners at least desired to preserve their property. The aldea Indians were rapidly dying off. One of the chief abuses was that of the "cord" Indians—those captured by their Indian enemies and tied to a "cord" to prevent escape while they were being fattened for eating. The law provided that when such Indians were captured by the Portuguese they might be enslaved and the capitães-mores (captains) never seemed to find any other type of Indians when they went on slaving expeditions. Apparently every Indian in the Amazon valley was tied to a stake. When brought to the city by the slaves, the latter swore before the judges, who connived with them, that the Indians were legally captured. [18]

During Lent in 1653, Vieira preached a sermon on the Indians that has become the most famous simultaneous condemnation and condonation of slavery in Brazilian history:

"Do ye know, Christians, do ye know, nobles and people of Maranhão, what is the fast which God requires of you this Lent? It is that ye loosen the bands of injustice, and that you set those free whom you hold captives, and whom you oppress. These are the sins of Maranhão; these are what God commands me to

---

[18] Varnhagen, *História geral*, II, 40-41; 46-50; Southey, *Brazil*, II, 454-71.

announce: 'Shew my people their transgression!' Christians, God commands me to undeceive you, and I undeceive you on the part of God! You are all in mortal sin! You are all living and dying in a state of condemnation, and you are all going straight to Hell' . . . . Every man who holds another unjustly in servitude, being able to release him, is certainly in a state of condemnation. All men, almost all men in Maranháo, hold others unjustly in servitude: all, therefore, or almost all, are in a state of condemnation . . . . My brethren, if there be any who doubt upon this matter, here are the Laws, here the Lawyers, . . . let the question be asked. You have three orders of Religioners in the State, and among them so many subjects of such virtue and such learning: ask them . . . examine the matter . . . inform yourselves. But Religioners are not necessary: go to Turkey, go to Hell . . . for there can be neither Turk so beturked in Turkey, nor Devil so bedeviled in Hell, as to affirm that a free man may be a slave . . . . But you will say to me, this people, this republic, this state cannot be supported without Indians. Who is to bring us a pitcher of water or a bundle of wood? Who is to plant our mandioc? Must our wives do it? Must our children do it? In the first place, as you will presently see, these are not the straits in which I would place you: but if necessity and conscious require it, then I reply, yes! And I repeat it, yes! You and your wives and your children ought to do it! We ought to support ourselves with our own hands; for better is it to be supported by the sweat of one's own brow than by another's blood. O ye riches of Maranhão! What if these mantles and cloaks were to be wrung? They would drop blood!" [19]

The sermon would have been more impressive to the colonists if the Jesuits had been more inclined to take the advice. But the Jesuits made liberal use of the aldea Indians, being willing enough to support themselves by the sweat of others' brows, and even by others' blood. So much righteous indignation over the Indians seemed out of place in an Order which owned Negro slaves. The upshot was that the colonists reached the easy decision that if they were to go to Hell they would go well attended by slaves.

And Vieira himself was not above suggesting a method by which slavery of the Indians might be continued, under regulations in which the religious orders would assist in the slave hunting expeditions. A plan was adopted which called for freedom under certain conditions, and the examination of the Indians was begun. Not long

---

[19] Southey, *Brazil*, II, 477-79.

afterwards, Vieira and the governor fell into disagreement on the use of some of the Indians, Vieira wanting them for an expedition, and the governor wanting them to work on his own tobacco plantations. Vieira then went to Pará where he and the governor disagreed over an expedition to "civilize" the Poquiz Indians.[20]

Vieira now advocated that the Indians should not be under the authority of the civil administration, but under the religious authorities exclusively, as in the other parts of Brazil. A *Procurador Geral* of the Indians would govern them and make an annual census and distribution of the Indians to the colonists for a work period of four months a year. One religious Order alone, Vieira did not want to suggest which, should have charge of the Indians and be allowed to use them only in work around the convents. In the meantime a new royal edict arrived in June 1654 permitting slavery under conditions which were supposed to protect the Indians. Vieira went to Portugal, protested against this, and obtained its revocation. In its place the Jesuits were given a monopoly over the Indians.[21]

Regulations were issued in 1655 aimed at protecting the Indians, and giving Vieira extensive powers, but it was difficult to stamp out slavery piecemeal in a society that recognized it as a legal and moral institution. When in 1661 the colonists complained to Vieira that the restrictions imposed on Indian slavery had reduced them to want, he replied that in the previous six years more than three thousand Indians had been brought down from the Amazon and other interior regions, and that of these more than eighteen hundred were slaves. He promised them that a mission was going out soon by way of the Tocantins river, and that since it was reported that there were many slaves along the Araguaia, the mission would follow the Araguaia route in order to take the slaves. The colonists found this no answer to their fundamental complaint, the power of the Jesuits, and rebellion soon broke out. Secular clergy and the other religious orders joined with the colonists and expelled the Jesuits from Maranhão in 1661.[22] Their control over the Indians was sharply curtailed in 1663, but they were allowed to return to Maranhão in 1665.

The Jesuits played an important role in 1684, during the revolt of Beckmann, and thereafter. Their authority over the Indians was restored. The status of the Indian slavery question is indicated by

---

[20] Southey, *Brazil*, II, 479-86.

[21] Southey, *Brazil*, II, 486-96. On Jesuits in Maranhão see João Felippe Betendorf, *Chronica da missão dos Padres da Companhia de Jesus no Estado do Maranhão, Revista IHGB*, vol. 119 (1909), written circa 1700.

[22] Southey, *Brazil*, II, 500-33; Amaral, *Agricultura*, I, 305-18.

a Bull of 1741 which prohibited Indian enslavement by either clergy or laymen. But the culmination of Jesuit troubles came during the reign of José I, whose minister of state was the Marquis of Pombal. In 1750, Spain and Portugal had drawn up a treaty to settle their centuries-old dispute over the exact location of the Line of Demarcation. Revolts among the Indians broke out, and it was evident they were inspired by the Jesuits who opposed the new treaty. Pombal now took the Indian aldeas from the Jesuits, and when they attempted to have him removed as minister, expelled them from the Portuguese realms in 1759. [23]

REGULAR CLERGY: OTHER ORDERS

In the meantime, other orders had long since established themselves in Brazil. The Benedictines reached Baía in 1584, where the governor reported that they were prospering and recommended to the King that he make them a grant of land. Shortly after this they founded an abbey in Rio de Janeiro. In the long run, they had seven abbeys and several presidencies in Brazil. Both the Capuchins and the Carmelites reached Brazil before 1589. The Capuchins seem to have done well, perhaps even better than the Benedictines. They at first formed a single province, but later divided into two, one in Baía, the original settlement of the Order, and the other in Rio de Janeiro. The Carmelite Observantines arrived at about the same time as the Capuchins, settling first in Olinda and Santos, later dividing the country into two provinces, one for the north of Brazil and the other for the south. Other orders of Carmelites also came to Brazil. Soon the number of convents was becoming so great that complaints arose, and the Crown intervened to fix conditions for their establishment. In 1609, and again in 1624, there was royal legislation on this subject. It was provided that further convents could be established only with the permission of, and under the conditions laid down by the Crown. [24] The Franciscans, for example, were forbidden to increase the number of their establishments in 1723. Italian Capuchins, French Capuchins, the Congregation of the Oratory, barefoot Augustinians, and other Orders played a great or lesser part in the life of Brazil.

The first convents of nuns were founded in the last quarter of the seventeenth century. Prior to this time as early as 1603, the Câmaras of both Baía and Pernambuco had petitioned the court to permit the establishment of such orders, but the court had responded

---

[23] Southey, *Brazil*, II, 2-3; 364-74; 511-47; Varnhagen, *História geral*, II, 63-65; 197-204.

[24] Varnhagen, *História geral*, I, 293 and footnotes.

in the negative, alleging the small population of Brazil. New petitions from Baía and Rio resulted in the first convent in Baía for
four Franciscan nuns, and in Rio a retreat for a mother and her
three daughters. In the middle of the eighteenth century there were
six convents of nuns who had taken vows, as well as others in minor
orders. Among the six were the nuns of Santa Clara in Baía; Santa
Thereza (barefoot Carmelites) in Rio de Janeiro; two Franciscan
convents in Rio de Janeiro; and two of the Ursulines in Baía.

How many different orders eventually came to Brazil, and the
total number of establishments founded by them is difficult to determine. Some of their houses were primarily urban establishments,
engaged in charitable and educational work. Others were primarily
rural, designed for the salvation of the Indians. By the time the
Jesuits were expelled in 1759, there were in northern Brazil
alone, not counting the rest of the country, some sixty Indian aldeas.
Five belonged to the Mercedarians, twelve to the Carmelites, fifteen
to the Capuchins, and twenty-eight to the Jesuits. The total for all
Brazil was naturally somewhat larger. [25]

It has been noted that there were bitter complaints and struggles
against the Jesuits throughout the colonial period. In like manner,
there were accusations of immorality and slackness in duty against
other clergymen. The clergy were charged with failure to carry out
the work for which they were destined, and over which they held a
monopoly, but it is not possible to determine to what extent many
of the accusations were justified. Success in saving souls and incul-
cating moral precepts cannot be accurately measured. It is certain,
however, that on a quantitative basis the educational plant built by
the Church in colonial Brazil left about nine-tenths of the people
without educational opportunity.

On matters of specific moral corruption the charges are more
definite. Nóbrega had hardly reached Brazil before he petitioned
the King to send a bishop, or at least a vicar-general to punish and
correct the clergy who were living in concubinage in all the captaincies, their practice in this resembling those of the laymen. It
was reported that in Pernambuco the clergy customarily led sinful
and scandalous lives. The bishop was appointed, as noted, in 1551.
When he arrived, he took note of the corruption but did little about
it, writing to the King: "In the beginning, there are many more
things to ignore than to punish, more so in a new country." [26]

---

[25] Southey, *Brazil,* III, 511-16; Varnhagen, *História geral,* II, 206, says there
were nineteen Jesuit, fifteen Capuchin, twelve Carmelite, and five Mercedarian aldeas
in the Amazon region alone.

[26] Varnhagen, *História geral,* II, 209; 204-06.

One reason at least for the lack of strict adherence to vows lay in the manner of recruiting many of the clergymen. A career in the Church was one of the vocations for the well-to-do, and younger sons were sent into the Church whether they showed a particular liking for it or not. As stated by one of Brazil's modern historians, the first son inherited and managed the estates, the second was sent to the university in Portugal, and

> "The third son entered the Church. He professed at fifteen. His pious mother made a friar of him. There was not a numerous family without its friar, an advocate at the feet of God. . . . The unmarried daughters, if they had a dowry, also entered convents. The high walls of the convent sheltered the soul, assuring its Christian purity. The call would come later with the ecclesiastical dress, tonsure, and the vow. What was important was to penetrate the shadows of the convent, forever. The girls never came out. On the other hand, the boys always came out." [27]

This picture of the friars spending their time outside their monasteries is confirmed by a bishop of 1777, who speaks of their having "a life and customs little in conformity with their vows," and "living more in the houses of kinsmen and friends, or around the engenhos [sugar mills] than in their convents." [28] Much of this arose from the fact that the Church was a monopoly of the wealthy classes, who used it in large part to their own ends. To be socially acceptable, one had to support the Church. Prominent families did so in many ways, of which making their sons and daughters friars, or priests, and nuns, was one. The case is cited of a man who sent six daughters with dowries of six thousand cruzados each to convents in Portugal. Thus Brazil was deprived of both capital and women. In 1632, Portugal already had 338 monasteries and 111 convents, not counting the institutions where boys and girls were removed from normal life, even when not full-fledged monks or nuns. Brazil did not have so many in proportion, but in Baía alone there were seven convents for women by 1755, and eleven for men. The bishop remarked that "in this part of the world, men are religious (*religiosos*) because they occasionally wear the clerical vestments, for if they did not wear them there would be no distinction whatever between them and the father of a family." [29]

The entry of the nuns into the convents at the age of eight or nine served in many cases to develop a spirit that was very little

---

[27] Calmon, *História social*, I, 85-86.
[28] Quoted in Calmon, *ibid.*, p. 76.
[29] Quoted in Calmon, *ibid.*, 86-89.

religious. In theory they were withdrawn from the world to serve God, but in fact the atmosphere around some of the monasteries in Portugal and Brazil resembled that of a girls' dormitory with a lenient matron. The nuns, being generally of the moneyed classes, had numerous servants, sometimes four or more for every nun. These served as note carriers to young men outside the convents and "scandals" resulted. The serenades, poetry of love, and court-ships at grilled windows differed little from those indulged in by young ladies who had not "forsaken" the world. These customs may have "inspired belles lettres and created the music and litera-ture of the serenade," as one author remarks, but they were con-trary to the vows taken by the nuns. Bishops and governors in-veighed against these things in vain.

In the convent of the *Desterro* (Exile) in Baía the traveler, La Barbinais, witnessed a theatrical representation in 1717 in which the nuns appeared in public and "posed in ways inappropriate to the place and to themselves." The same convent was richly deco-rated with scenes of a "worldly" nature. In this convent, there were seventy-five nuns with four hundred slaves, the nuns leading the lives of noble ladies. In 1764, the prelate Manuel de Santa Inez in Baía wrote:

> "Although there are some nuns who lead a good life in this convent, yet because of the nonobservance of the laws appro-priate to the state and profession, which is the rule, the said con-vent is the scandal of the city, in spite of which many people encourage and protect it either out of kinship or friendship, licit or illicit." [30]

On one occasion when a young girl was entering the monastery of Soledade the ceremony resembled a debutante party. "The ships in the harbor drew up in a semicircle and fired a salute. In front of the convent bands played all day, and there was an auction of souvenirs. At night there was a really magnificent exhibition of fireworks." [31]

The evidence concerning clerical neglect of duty and corruption could be multiplied a thousand fold. Whatever its virtues, it is clear that the Church in Brazil fell far short of the aims it professed.

THE INQUISITION IN BRAZIL

The doctrinal purity of Brazil was subject to the Inquisition of Portugal. Although Manoel I (1495-1521) had sought to establish

---

[30] Quoted in Calmon, *ibid.,* I, 90.
[31] Quoted in Calmon, *ibid.,* I, 93.

the Holy Office in his dominions, it was not until the time of his successor, João III (1521-1557), in 1531, that the first Bull authorizing an Inquisitor General was issued by the Papacy. There was still considerable hesitancy on the part of the Papacy after this, however, with inquisitorial powers being several times granted and withdrawn before their definitive establishment by a Bull of Paul III in 1547. In the meantime, however, the Inquisition had been functioning in Portugal, and its authority reached out to Brazil even before it was definitely established in Portugal. .No separate tribunal was ever set up for Brazil. Its authority was granted to bishops and other agents, and the accused were sent to Portugal for trial.

Brazil's first inquisitorial case was that of Pero do Campo Tourinho, the Donatary of Porto Seguro. He was denounced in Lisbon in 1543 on the charge of calling himself pope and king, and forcing his subjects to work on Sunday. In 1546, at a moment when the Inquisition was temporarily suspended by Paul III, Campo Tourinho was seized by several priests and monks who had constituted themselves judges (under what authority is not clear), and was sent in irons to Portugal where as late as 1550 he was still under trial. A contemporary of the occurrence reported that the affair was provoked by Friar André do Campo, son of the accused, who wished to succeed his father as Donatary, "which he did."

From this time forward, cases were fairly frequent. Next in fame, if not in time, was that of the Frenchman Jean de Cointa, who aided the Portuguese in driving the French out of Rio de Janeiro and was later tried by the Inquisition for heresy. Another Frenchman was burned at the stake for heresy in Baía in 1573. Shortly after this, in 1579, the power of the Inquisition in Brazil was strengthened by Henrique (1578-1580), who was king, cardinal, and Inquisitor General of Portugal, when he despatched a special commission to the bishop of Brazil and the Jesuits in 1579. This was not a formal installation of the Inquisition, however, merely a delegation of powers. In 1585, Anchieta could write:

"No Inquisitorial court has been established here up to the present since the bishops exercise this right by commission, appeal to the Holy Office of Portugal being permitted, and thus an heretical Frenchman has already been burned in Baía." [32]

Soon after this came an extension of the work of the Inquisition

---

[32] Quoted in J. Capistrano de Abreu, *Primeira visitação do Santo Ofício as partes do Brasil . . . 1591-92* (Rio de Janeiro: Sociedade Capistrano de Abreu, 1935), Preface, p. IV, which gives a summary of the Inquisition in Brazil.

in Brazil which, though not a formal installation of the Holy
Office there, brought its powers closer to the Brazilians. It will be
recalled that Philip II of Spain had come to the Portuguese throne
in 1580. Soon afterwards, he named his uncle, Archduke Albert
of Austria, Viceroy of Portugal, and shortly thereafter the same
individual was made Inquisitor General of Portugal by the Pope in
1586. In this capacity he ordered the first *Visitação,* or Visitation,
of Brazil by the Inquisition. The Visitador, Heitor Furtado de
Mendoça, arrived in Brazil in 1591, and the records show that
trials were still being held as late as 1595, and perhaps later. The
denunciations and confessions were those familiar to every student
of the Inquisition. The first confession was that of João Serrao,
who asked to be pardoned for representing himself as an "Old
Christian" when he was in fact a "New Christian." The days
were over when Portugal permitted New Christians to find refuge
in the New World, and when the decrees against the Jews were
enforced with reluctance and tolerance. The Inquisition in Brazil
would indeed have been busy if it had ferreted out and prosecuted
all those descended from the Jewish colonists of the first period
of Brazilian settlement, since it will be recalled that they had come
over in large numbers.

Among the other cases before the Visitador, the most common
were for sexual perversion, witchcraft, blasphemy, heresy, breaking the commandments of the Church, and reading forbidden
books. An interesting case was that of Ana Rõiz, accused of being
a New Christian, who confessed that seven or eight years before
she had been seriously ill and "became delirious and was told that
she raved, but did not remember whether at this time she said
anything offensive to God." Others remembered, and told.[33]

A second Visitation was held in 1618, but the details are not so
well known. What is clear is that the authority of the Inquisition
was felt in Brazil with some regularity from this time forward.
Some of the accused in the second Visitation were among those
tried a quarter of a century before, including Ana Rõiz, who was
burned at the stake.

Although there is no record of a Visitation of Brazil after 1618,
the work of the Inquisition went on. What was lost by not having
a Tribunal on the ground was gained by the ardor with which
the Familiars of the Inquisition denounced all whose acts, words,
or thoughts could make them prospective cases for the Holy
Office. The position of Familiar was coveted. To be eligible one

[33] Capistrano de Abreu, *Primeira visitação,* pp. XVII, and 135-38.

had to have a clear certificate of pure ancestry *(limpeza de sangue)* showing neither heretical nor Jewish forbears—a possession of no small value in a society where Christian orthodoxy was a prerequisite of social position and preferment. In addition, the Familiars were granted numerous privileges, among them exemptions from some forms of taxes, the right to bear arms, and extension of these favors to the family of the Familiar.

The number accused by the Inquisition probably increased during the eighteenth century. There were years when as many as a hundred and sixty persons were arrested. When the Marquis of Pombal came to power, he diminished the powers of the Inquisition considerably, but after his time it regained its authority. The abolition of the Inquisition came in 1821, after the revolution of 1820 in Portugal had led to the calling of a Cortes of liberal characteristics.[84]

---

[84] On the Inquisition in Brazil see also Varnhagen, *História geral,* I, 87-88, II, 179-83, 244-45; Capistrano de Abreu, *Ensaios e estudos* (2nd ser. Rio de Janeiro, 1932), pp. 243-95, 305-22; *Anais BN Rio,* XLIX (1927), 75-198.

Colonial Brazilian Government

COLONIAL GOVERNMENT DEVELOPED GRADUALLY. Portugal never devised a system that compared in organization with Spain's Council of Indies, although a number of bodies concerned with Brazilian affairs were created.

Nor did the native Indian contributions to government compare with those in Mexico and Peru. On the other hand, it would be incorrect to assume that the Indians had no influence whatever on the evolution of political institutions. And finally, it must be remembered that the importation of Negroes in great numbers to Brazil could not but have some influence on the development on Brazil's administration.

The first form of government devised for Brazil by Portugal was the concession given to Fernão de Noronha in 1503. While this concession was primarily for the exploitation of Brazil's economic products, it necessarily carried with it sufficient political powers for the control of the regions conceded. Successive expeditions for exploring and trading carried powers similar to those customarily given to ship captains and concessionaires in those times.

THE CAPTAINCIES

Decisive governmental organization began, however, with the institution of the captaincy system in 1534. The powers granted to the Donatários were much like those held by the feudal nobles of Portugal, but at the same time they included, as we have seen, ample economic prerogatives which resembled those of the rising capitalism. The system was therefore a mixture of the passing and coming ages.[1] This is not surprising. The settlement of the Azores

---

[1] Varnhagen, *História geral*, I, 72-83; Max Fleiuss, *História administrativa do Brasil* (2nd ed., São Paulo, 1925), pp. 1-13. See Chapter 28 above for the provisions and nature of the grants.

and other territories of Portugal had been accomplished successfully with a mixed system. The change of dynasties in Portugal
as far back as 1383-85 had been brought about by the rising
merchant class, but had resulted in a governmental compromise
that recognized the still great powers of the landed nobility. When
Brazil was discovered, the evolution from one form of government to the other was as yet incomplete (if, indeed, it is complete
today).

Brazil was ideal territory for the dual system. It was an immense land with immediately available commercial wealth in the
form of brazil wood and other products, but it was also evident
that Brazil offered fertile soil for colonization. The commercial
products demanded the encouragement of the capitalists; the
colonization prospects suggested the necessity of investing powerful concessionaries with the privileges that would attract them to
the new land. The captaincy system was the result. It was a re-
versal in many ways of the trend of Portuguese history, but so
were the first steps of colonization by Spain, England, and other
powers.

All powers and privileges not specifically granted by the donations and charters (doações e foraes) were reserved to the Crown
and covered by the general laws of the kingdom. These laws,
known as the Leis Manuelinas or Ordenações Manuelinas after
Manoel I (1495-1521), were in force until superseded by the Leis
Filippinas (so named after Philip III of Spain) at the beginning
of the seventeenth century. The latter code formed the basis of
Brazilian law when the national period began in 1822.

But the Crown had granted so many privileges and exemptions
from its own supervision to the Captaincies that it actually had
little authority over them.

"In this way the Crown ceded, to the donataries' benefit, the
majority of its sovereign powers and reserved little but a limited
protectorate over the new Brazilian captaincies, with very
limited powers, in return for a few taxes including the tithe,
from which the Crown itself paid the expenses of religious
worship and the retithe to the donataries. We can almost say
that Portugal recognized the independence of Brazil before
colonizing it." [2]

CENTRALIZATION OF THE GOVERNMENT

The rights given the donataries were too extensive to be con-

[2] Varnhagen, História geral, I, 73-74.

sistent with the growing powers of the monarch, and were the source of considerable administrative difficulty. It was for this reason, among others, that in 1549 the government of Brazil was revised and centralized. Several things in fact made this desirable. Portugal had been unable to stop the foreign traders and pirates who were growing constantly more dangerous to Portuguese possession of Brazil. The great financial burden of establishing and maintaining a captaincy had prevented most of the captaincies from performing the colonizing mission for which they had been formed. The colonists had protested against many abuses, and the Crown had not derived the revenues it expected. All of these complaints and others impelled Portugal to reform the government.

The Captaincy-General was established to carry out the reforms, with Tomé de Souza as the first Captain-General. To him was delegated a portion of the powers of the King, with a consequent lessening of the political authority of the captaincies. The capital city was set up at Baía, the Crown buying back this concession from its owner. The functions of the Captaincy-General were: to centralize administration so that the various captaincies would participate in common defense, whereas before each had depended on its own strength; to curb the abuses of power by the captains; to arbitrate between the colonists and the donataries; and to act as the King's fiscal agent.

Administrative centralization was accompanied by both judicial and fiscal unity, and the appointment of an *ouvidor geral* (justice) and a *provedor mor* (treasurer). Coast defense was centralized under a *capitão mor*. The new Governor-General, Tomé de Souza, was a man of long experience in government in Portugal and India. The *ouvidor geral* was Pero Borges, a *desembargador,* or high judge, who had been corregidor in Algarve, Portugal. His authority superseded that of the donataries in many cases and was exercised independently of the Governor-General. The *provedor mor* controlled the customs houses, collected taxes, accounted for the royal income, and supervised the subordinate *provedores* distributed throughout the captaincies. Colonists were forbidden to travel from one captaincy to another overland, in order better to control maritime commerce. The *provedor mor* also had judicial powers pertaining to his function which were independent of the other law courts. In this way the various high officials were all made directly responsible to the Crown, and acted as a check on one another.

The donataries were made responsible for defense of their

own territories and all were required to equip themselves with a specified list of arms, and to co-operate with the Governor-General for common defense. Every *senhor de engenho* estate or mill owner) was also required to arm for defense according to specifications laid down by the Crown.

The establishment of the bishopric of Brazil and the powers invested in the Jesuits sent out with Tomé de Souza were also important contributions to governmental authority.[3]

The years from 1549 to 1572 were busy ones for Tomé de Souza and his successors, especially for Mem de Sá (1557-72), because of the necessity of organizing the government and keeping out the foreign competitors. The most persistent of these were the French, who made an especially determined effort to settle at Rio de Janeiro in 1555 and were not finally driven out until 1567.[4]

Owing to the difficulties encountered in protecting the colony, the Crown decided to divide the territory into two administrative districts. This was done in 1572, Baía remaining as the capital of the territory from Porto Seguro north, and Rio de Janeiro becoming the center of the Captaincy-General to the south. This arrangement proved to be temporary. In 1578 the unity of administration was restored with Baía still the capital city of Brazil. Ecclesiastical division continued after this date, however, as previously noted, with Rio de Janeiro as the seat of an administrator independent of the bishop of Baía. In the meantime, 1576, the Crown had granted to the Governor-General the right to make nominations for clerical vacancies in Brazil.[5]

THE SPANISH ERA

Brazil was at this time on the eve of a change of sovereignty. The era of "Spanish Captivity" for Portugal, and hence for Brazil, was but a short time ahead. When Sebastian, the King of Portugal, was killed in Africa in 1578, the throne was occupied temporarily by Cardinal Henrique while the several claimants pushed their respective titles. Philip II of Spain had a good legal title as son of the Portuguese princess, Isabel, wife of the Emperor, Charles V. But Philip had more effective weapons than blood. He was close at hand, and he had the finest army and (as everybody thought at the time) navy in Europe. In 1580 his pretensions were recognized and he became Philip I of Portugal.

---

[3] Varnhagen, *História geral*, I, 193-96; Calmon, *História do Brasil*, I, 204-30; Handelmann, *Brasil*, pp. 93-103; Fleiuss, *História administrativa do Brazil*, pp. 13-45.

[4] Calmon, *História do Brasil*, I, 230-316; Handelmann, *Brasil*, pp. 113-26.

[5] Varnhagen, *História geral*, I, 277-78.

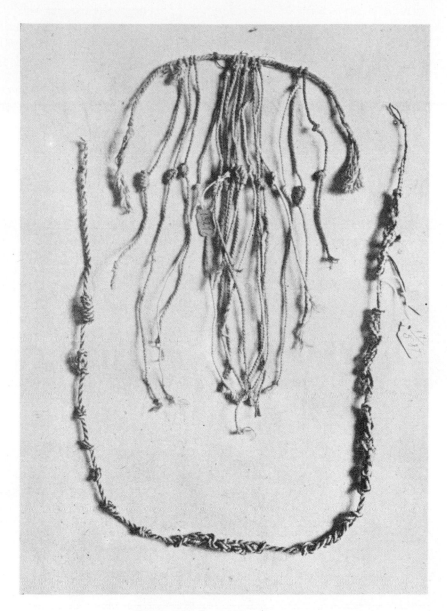

QUIPU, THE INCA COUNTING DEVICE

CHURCH IN CHOLULA, MEXICO. NOTE THE WALLS BUILT FOR FORTIFICATION

The change in dynasty wrought only slight alterations in the administration of Portugal and Brazil. True, the laws of Manoel were superseded in part by the *Leis Filippinas,* but the new code was little more than a revision of the older one designed to smoothe out its major inconsistencies. Philip was content to rule Portugal through Portuguese laws and with Portuguese officials. Portugal was an independent kingdom still, with a new dynasty that by coincidence also ruled Spain. Brazil was to benefit greatly from the eighty years of Spanish rule in one important way: she spread out into territory that was legally Spanish through the Treaty of Tordesillas. In the meantime Brazil continued to be Portuguese, governed by Portuguese who enjoyed a monopoly of her commerce. "Brazil was therefore absolutely indifferent to the dynastic question. It seemed the same to her whether the monarch were of this or that branch of the royal family, or whether he lived in Lisbon or Madrid." Brazil, in fact, could expect to derive benefit from the protection of the strongest monarch of Europe. But this changed with the defeat of the Spanish Armada in 1588, after which Brazil was as much exposed to foreign attack as previously. [6]

The most significant act of the Spanish period was the creation of the *Conselho da India* in 1604, with functions similar to those of the Council of Indies which governed the Spanish-American possessions. This Council prepared the laws for Brazil and supervised its administration, with which it dealt directly. At its inception, it also had judicial functions but these were transferred soon to the *Relaçáo da Baía,* a high court created in Baía in 1608, and to the *Casa de Supplicação* and the *Desembargo do Paço,* two other courts with specialized judicial functions.

The Conselho was granted considerable power. No vessel could sail from Portugal to Brazil without its permission, nor were the orders of any authority or tribunal, including those of the *Conselho da Fazenda* (treasury) and the *Mesa da Consciencia* (ecclesiastical tribunal), effective in Brazil unless transmitted through the *Conselho da India.*[7]

The establishment of the Relação da Baía in 1608 was an important act that had been long contemplated. The first decree for its establishment dated from 1588, but was deferred until after the Conselho da India had been set up and had taken action. The new court regularized many judicial matters but also slowed up justice greatly, since many cases that had been previously decided

[6] Varnhagen, *História geral,* I, 279-80.
[7] Varnhagen, *História geral,* I, 313-15; Handelmann, *Brasil,* pp. 137-39; 154-55.

by the governors and local judges now went to the Relação. It also brought to Brazil a host of lawyers, scriveners, and court satellites who were unpopular with the people. Many complaints were made that Brazil had a surplus of "lettered" persons who consumed a large part of the revenues and instigated legal differences which benefited nobody but themselves. The first Relação existed for only sixteen years and was then abolished for a quarter of a century.

Simultaneously with the creation of the Relação in Baía, the Court made a new division of the administration of Brazil. Espírito Santo, Rio de Janeiro and São Vicente were placed under a separate Governor and Captain-General in 1608, an *ouvidor* was appointed for the new unit, and a superintendency of mines was created for the South. The administrative division was again abandoned after a short trial, in 1612, but the *ouvidor* continued.

An administrative division that was to endure came after the French were driven out of the northern regions of Brazil in 1613-16. Two new captaincies, Grão Pará and Maranhão, were first created; and then in 1621 Pará, Ceará, and Maranhão were formed into a new state, separate from Brazil. From this period, Portugal thought of Brazil as one colony and Maranhão, as the new state was most frequently called, as another.[8]

DUTCH OCCUPATION AND RESTORATION OF PORTUGUESE INDEPENDENCE

This action had just been taken when the Dutch intervened in Brazil, 1624, and remained until 1654. It was natural that there should be a considerable disruption owing to Dutch occupation of a large part of the country, their territory at its maximum extending from the São Francisco river almost to the Amazon. During the Dutch epoch, Portugal started her war of independence from Spain, 1640, and with the accession of the new line of kings, the Braganzas, administrative changes were made. The first viceroy was named in 1640, but a century passed before Brazil was officially designated a viceroyalty. In 1642 the Conselho da India was abolished and a new council, the Conselho Ultramarino, created. The functions of the two were similar, the reorganization being specifically aimed at promoting the economic and spiritual welfare of Brazil.[9] Shortly afterwards, in 1646, the political status of Brazil was to be elevated by its designation as the Principality

---

[8] Varnhagen, *História geral*, I, 319-22; 332-35; Handelmann, *Brasil*, pp. 166-68; 265-344.

[9] Varnhagen, *História geral*, I, 418-19; Handelmann, *Brasil*, pp. 169-218.

of Brazil, the heir to the throne of Portugal being known hence-forth as the Prince of Brazil.[10]

The Relação da Baía was re-established in 1652, after having been abolished in 1626. This abolition was in part due to the Dutch intervention and Portugal's financial stringency, only two desem-bargadores having been left to carry on the work. Restoration in 1652 was one of the by-products of Portuguese independence and the defeat of the Dutch. The Câmara of Baía, the governor, and the chief citizens appealed for re-establishment so as to avoid the expense of carrying their cases to the courts in Portugal.[11]

After the recovery of the northern captaincies from the Dutch they were divided into two states in 1652, Maranhão and Pará, the governors of each having the title of *capitães mores*. [12] When Governor Roque da Costa Barreto came in 1678, he brought a new *regimento,* or instrument of government, to supplant that given to Tomé de Souza in 1548. The terms dealt mainly with technical administrative problems, but the purpose of the new laws was to tighten the administration and give more authority to the central authority in Baía.[13]

ADMINISTRATIVE CHANGES IN THE LATE COLONIAL PERIOD

Early in the eighteenth century, the expansion provoked by the opening up of the mines necessitated further administrative changes. São Paulo had grown in importance and was made a captaincy, 1709. In 1720 Minas Gerais was detached from São Paulo and made a separate Captaincy-General. A few years later the still further increase of the interior population around the mines brought new territorial divisions. Goiaz was designated a *comarca* in 1736, and a captaincy in 1744. Cuiabá (Mato Grosso) was made a captaincy in 1748. In the same epoch, Brazil had been extending southward. Santa Catarina, which had been previously governed by a capitão mor, was given a governor in 1739; and Rio Grande do Sul, previously governed by a military commandant only, in 1760. Far to the north, Piauí was separated from Maranhão and made a captaincy in 1750. [14]

A new colonial administration was established in Portugal in 1736 with the creation of the ministry of *Marinha e Ultramar* (Marine and Overseas). Its functions were largely those of the Council up to this date. The administration was rather complicated

---

[10] Varnhagen, *História geral,* II, 2-3.
[11] Varnhagen, *História geral,* I, 354; II, 44-46; Handelmann, *Brasil,* pp. 423-24.
[12] Varnhagen, *História geral,* II, 40-41.
[13] Varnhagen, *História geral,* II, 74-79.
[14] Varnhagen, *História geral,* II, 155-56, and appendices.

by this time, and in 1739 an effort was made to lessen the number of military positions. No city was to have more than one capitão mor, who was to serve for life instead of triennially as before. [15]

From this period on, a large number of reforms were made in colonial government, especially after the influence of the Marquis of Pombal was felt. A new Relação was created in Rio in 1751 with functions like those of Baía, and powers extending over the thirteen southern *comarcas,* including Minas Gerais and Cuiabá. Simultaneously a move was started to buy back all the captaincies from their owners, compensation being given in the form of quit-rents or lands. The dates of purchase were usually 1753-54, although the exact time is not known in some cases. A reform of great importance was the integration of all the laws affecting Brazil in one code in 1754-57. It consisted of thirty-nine volumes.

In 1750 Portugal and Spain signed a treaty for the settlement of the boundary dispute that had existed since the Line of Demarcation was laid down in 1493, and ineffectually "settled" by the Treaty of Tordesillas in 1494. The new demarcation as agreed on by Spain and Portugal was not acceptable to the Jesuits and the Indians under their charge, and war broke out. Neither side was satisfied, and the 1750 settlement had to be reconsidered, a new treaty being drawn up in 1777.

As a result of the boundary dispute, Brazil took on the appearance of a military garrison. Many new troops were brought from Portugal, and colonial regiments were organized in Brazil. It was in the same epoch that the militia was assuming unaccustomed importance in the Spanish colonies. In Brazil almost every town had its capitáo mor, a Brazilian in many or perhaps most cases, who was promoted from the auxiliary forces to troops of the first line, much as is done to reserve or national-guard officers in the United States in critical times. But this had an important political effect. The Brazilians who were so promoted gained new importance and prestige, not to speak of the actual power they could wield (and later did wield) at critical moments. Through the militia, many colonials achieved prestige and power which mere wealth and family had not given them, although it should be observed that it was the members of the wealthy and distinguished families who received the military commissions. [16]

A judicial reform of importance in the late colonial period was the creation of the *Juntas de Justiça* in 1765. These courts had

[15] Varnhagen, *História geral,* II, 178-79.
[16] Varnhagen, *História geral,* II, 239-40.

existed in Maranhão and Pará previously, but were now extended to all Brazil. Wherever there was an *ouvidor*, two other judges were appointed to sit with him. This court could grant relief (stays or injunctions) in petitions against the decisions of ecclesiastical courts without waiting for a decision from the Relação or the Desembargador do Paço. The effect of this was to increase the civil over the clerical power, and avoid prolonged and painful appeal to courts hundreds of miles away.[17]

The economic balance in Brazil had gradually shifted southward with the opening up of the interior. This was signalized administratively in 1763 by the shift of the viceregal capital from Baía to Rio de Janeiro.[18]

LOCAL GOVERNMENT: THE CAMARA

The discussion has been confined so far to the institutions decreed by Portugal. There was another very important side to colonial government in Brazil, however, just as there was in the Spanish colonies. What Lisbon decreed was one thing; what actually happened was frequently quite another.

Colonial Brazil was divided, not only into captaincies, but into various types of city governments. Their size, prestige, and importance varied greatly. The town of São Paulo, for example, had at one time jurisdiction over an area larger than the present state of that name. The governing body in these cities was the *senado da câmara*, or city council, equivalent in many respects to the *cabildo* in the Spanish colonies. The number of its members varied greatly, and its powers were in inverse ratio to the strength of the royal officials, but even in the most important coast cities, the *senado* was an institution of great influence.

Some of the câmara's members were lifetime, hereditary officials, and some were elected by an extremely limited suffrage, but all were chosen from the leaders of the community. This meant that they were the chief merchants, fazendeiros, and professional men, whose personal interests were those most frequently the subject of legislation, both local and royal. Shipping laws, taxes, customs duties, public improvements, army and marine, and many other matters were of direct concern to them. In many local affairs they had extensive powers; but in most matters their influence lay in their practical monopoly of the power to make their voices heard in Lisbon. They kept their legal representatives at the Court,

[17] Varnhagen, *História geral*, II, 240-43.

[18] Handelmann, *Brasil*, pp. 425-46; 463-46; Fleiuss, *História administrativa do Brasil*, pp. 46-96.

and the history of Brazil is full of the suits and petitions of the câmaras.

While far from being a democratic body, since the Indians, slaves, and most of the mulattoes and whites could not vote, the câmara was the nearest thing to a representative body in Brazil. It represented extremely narrow interests, it is true, but indirectly this redounded to the benefit of Brazil. The câmara was the nucleus around which a spirit of Brazilianism sprang up. The farther the câmara was from the coast and the royal authorities, the greater its *de facto* powers. And in Brazil the vast areas made it relatively common to be far from central government. The existence of large estates was an encouragement to local semiautonomy, manifested sometimes through the câmara, and sometimes independent of every authority.

The câmara began to play a part in the first years, before Portugal had formed a government for Brazil. Calmon remarks:

> "The [city] council of the first [sixteenth] century—a Portuguese version of Greek democracy—was the faithful government of the people by the people. The scant population, small villages, well-defined interests, the danger from the Indians, the natural hierarchy, made the council respected and strong in Brazil, as it had been in the Peninsula before the monarchical centralization." [19]

We may disagree with the classification as "democratic," but the force of the câmaras cannot be denied. In literally hundreds of cases, they took matters into their own hands and faced the royal officials with a *fait accompli*. Perhaps the most notable example was the expulsion of the Jesuits from São Paulo and Maranhão by the câmaras.

As the riches of Brazil grew and the size of its cities increased, the powers of the municipalities also developed. Rio, Baía, Recife, and other towns gained "exemptions" and privileges similar in character to those enjoyed by medieval Portuguese cities though never so great.

Many local matters were almost entirely in the hands of the câmara, frequently with the co-operation of the Church. Such were public works and churches, hospitals and monasteries. Control of artisans and the formation of the codes under which silversmiths, cobblers, tailors, and others worked, and public health, street cleaning, police, and control of markets were among the affairs under their jurisdiction.

---

[19] Calmon, *História social*, I, 240-45.

THE CAPITÃO MOR

But the câmara was only one form of local government. Another arose from the powers given to or assumed by the *capitão mor*. These officials were the administrative and military assistants to the governors of the captaincies and municipalities. Varnhagen observes that "The fame which these officials achieved, or rather the ideas of terror and arbitrariness which we still associate with the name *capitão mor,* is such that it is necessary to explain their functions and powers at various periods."

At the start of colonization, a capitão mor was no more than a commander of a squadron at sea or the head of a political unit on land. The powers of such officials were specifically stated in their *regimentos,* or instructions. When the captaincy was instituted each donatary was made capitão mor of his territory, originating therewith the term "captaincy." The same policy was followed at later epochs. When the Crown colonized Rio de Janeiro, Sergipe, Paraíba, Rio Grande do Norte, Ceará, Maranhão, Pará, Santa Catarina, and Rio Grande do Sul on its own account, rather than through donataries, it named capitães mores to govern some of them, giving them three-year appointments and regulating their powers through a *regimento* from the Crown or the governor. Such regimentos outline their financial, judicial, and administrative authority, and also stated the limitations placed on them. The viceroy forbade them to grant sesmarias, for example, in 1663.

The extensive powers of the capitães mores, however, could not be curbed by legal fiat. Even had there been no officials with the King's authority to maintain order, conditions would have produced them. As has been consistently pointed out for all Latin America, vast distances separated the King from his subjects and they habitually undertook to solve problems beyond his effective range of action. Had the citizens as a body been an educated and civic-minded class, this independence of royal authority would have meant self-government as it did in the English colonies in many cases. But there was no widespread culture, no general spirit of self-reliance among the Brazilian masses. The whole system trained them to be governed, not to govern themselves. And when local absolutism arose, the people were conditioned to accept it. This gave the capitães mores their power, which they did not hesitate to use, as the following picture of their activities indicates:

". . . Charged with economic powers and the enforcement
of the laws, judges without appeal in the recruitment [of the
local militia], with authority to imprison deserters, malefactors

and vagrants, the [capitães mores] became the terror of the people by their oppression and abuse. They intervened capriciously in court trials, ordering them continued or dismissed; they intervened in ecclesiastical affairs, forcing some to marry and preventing others who ran to them for protection from having to do so; they intervened, in fact, in everything, arresting, convicting, committing an excess of evils . . . . They did whatever they wished without fear of consequences or responsibility to the laws and the government.

"They were the only rulers of the localities . . . . Nobody dared complain of their violence, because, . . . neither the ouvidor nor the governor would listen to the complainant. When on his trip of inspection, the ouvidor lodged in the house of the capitão mor, enjoying his hospitality, accepting his favors, and listening to absolutely nobody else . . . .

"From this the capitão mor derived greater power and new incentives for exercising his local despotism. There being no remedy for his abuses, everybody submitted and some sought to curry favor with the omnipotent authority, and if they succeeded they too did what they pleased." [20]

The term capitão mor was gradually extended to officials with other powers. Such were the *mestres do campo,* or *coroneis,* who had the power to choose the auxiliars, or militiamen, and were similar to the commanders of national guard units. Laws of 1570 and 1574 stipulated the method of electing these officials, but were little applicable to Brazil until a much later epoch when, as previously stated, the rivalry with Spain led to the formation of many units of militiamen in Brazil. Prior to this there were only a few capitães and no capitães mores elected by towns. When the militia was formed, the position became of great honor and importance and was coveted by the most powerful men of the community. This led to strong rivalry among the chief families. Things became so bad that a reform was attempted in 1709, because the elections had taken place "with fraud and violence, from which crimes, expenses, and the discredit of whole families result, provoking feuds which pass down from father to son . . . the majority of the councils [câmaras] being divided into factions, with great injury to justice." [21] But the evils were never eliminated.

In the interior the *capitães do mato,* subordinates of the capitães

---

[20] Quoted in A. Tavares de Lyra, *Organisação política e administrativa do Brasil* (São Paulo, 1941), pp. 34-35.
[21] *Ibid.*

mores, had authority over escaped Negroes and Indians. In the later colonial period capitães móres without authority were named to honor promient men and allow them to wear medals and showy uniforms.

The great increase of the powers of the capitães mores came in 1764, however, when in order to expedite recruiting, they were empowered to impress men for the army without appeal to a higher court. This gave them practically unlimited authority. According to the record, they more frequently abused than used this authority. After their original military powers were lessened, they remained the political bosses of their districts.[22]

Their authority was based more on their standing in their communities than on the powers granted by the King. In other words, the office merely enhanced the privileges conferred by the social and economic position of the holder. Land was the basis of this position. On the *fazenda,* or large estate, the owner was frequently little less than an absolute monarch. Two families, as previously pointed out, owned the vast interior of Baía. Other estates covered less territory but were greater in value, especially those in the sugar-growing regions. Legal and social position alone gave such estate owners vast powers over their slaves and servants, and they assumed still greater authority over anyone in their districts. Their personal entourage formed a small army that they used to control the community; and when named capitão mor such men could and did use the militia under their command to increase their personal powers. The time and distance that separated them from Lisbon, or even from Baía or Rio de Janeiro, was such as to make them all but exempt from royal control. They exercised an autonomy that remained effective to the end of the colonial period, and persisted as the basis of Brazil's actual political system into the twentieth century.

"Brazil was governed in fact not by the King in Lisbon, nor by the Governor-General in Baía, but by the municipal câmaras in the cities and towns, by the capitães mores where they existed, and by the heads of families in their scarcely populated and vast zones of influence." [23]

THE ALDEAS AND MISSIONS

Still another form of local government should receive attention. The religious orders held several thousand Indians in their aldeas and missions. Much legislation on Indian affairs came out

---

[22] Varnhagen, *História geral,* II, 79-80.
[23] Calmon, *História social,* I, 240.

of Lisbon, and a considerable amount of it was effective, but the missionaries had too much prestige for such statutes to remove the Indians permanently from their control. After the Jesuits were expelled in 1759, their aldeas were given to other orders. The government in these aldeas was neither democratic nor constitutional. The only guarantee the Indians had was the mercy of the missionaries. Rules were made by the missionaries and could be changed by them at any moment. The use of a "mayor" as the figurehead of government gave the Indians neither authority nor training in self-government, less even than they had enjoyed before the Conquest. Thus the complete picture of local government was: câmara, capitão mor, fazendeiro, and missionary, all having great prestige to the end of the colonial period, and later.

INDEPENDENCE OVER THE HORIZON

The year 1808 was one of crisis in the history of Brazil and Portugal. More than three hundred years had passed since discovery and settlement. Portugal's hold on Brazil was at first uncertain and tenuous. It was more than a century after discovery before it became clear whether Brazil was to be Portuguese or French, and then it would have taken a rash prophet to say that Portugal was destined to hold her Brazilian possessions and enlarge them. Scarcely had the bold challenge of France died away, and the French sailed from São Luiz, when the Dutch jeopardized Portugal's hold on Brazil, in 1624.

But Brazil was not merely Portuguese by this time, she had become Brazilian. Not the Portuguese, but the Brazilians drove out the Dutch; and by this date Brazil extended from the Amazon southward to near the Río de la Plata, and for a considerable distance into the interior. With the progressing years of the seventeenth century came further penetration of the interior and, in 1695, the discovery of gold. Quickly Brazil expanded into hitherto unpenetrated regions, and took possession of a vast territory lying on the Spanish side of the Line of Demarcation. In the long run, she was to occupy almost half South America. The population was three or four millions before the end of the colonial period, with the principal centers being Pernambuco, Baía, Minas Gerais, Rio de Janeiro, and São Paulo. Baía was one of the five largest cities in the New World. The one-time loosely knit "islands of population" were bound together by coastwise shipping; and trails, even if not roads, placed the inhabitants in contact with the seaboard. Owing to the localism which we have described, however, the process of integration was far from complete. Brazil's institutions of government, while being oligarchic rather than democratic in nature, were sufficiently matured to give her the most stable government in Latin America during the nineteenth century. Relatively speaking, Brazil manifested many signs of a maturing nation. Her institutions and her culture were drawn from the Portuguese, the Negro, the Indian, and many varied influences; but by 1808 Brazil had become Brazil.

Brazil's coming of age was signalized by a dramatic event: the Portuguese Court landed in Rio de Janeiro. Europe was in the throes of the Napoleonic wars. Portugal was invaded. The armies of Napoleon arrived at Lisbon in time to see the sails of the Portuguese fleet bearing away the King and his court to Brazil. Time had reversed the positions of the two countries. Following out the inexorable laws of nature, the offspring now sheltered the parent. Brazil was adult. Events of the years before 1808 had increasingly given proof of this. But the hour of her recognition by other nations was not yet. The Portuguese monarch remained in Brazil until 1821, when circumstances permitted him to return home. But his son stayed behind, and when Portugal sought again to renew the relationship of metropolis and colony, Brazil proclaimed and maintained her independence. This, however, is a long and interesting story that must be kept for later telling.

Kings of Spain

Ferdinand and Isabella, king and queen (Fernando and Isabel)	1479-1504
Ferdinand and Philip I (Fernando and Felipe I)	1504-1506
Ferdinand and Charles I (Fernando and Carlos I)	1506-1516
Charles I (Holy Roman Emperor as Charles V) (Carlos I)	1516-1556
Philip II (Felipe II)	1556-1598
Philip III (Felipe III)	1598-1621
Philip IV (Felipe IV)	1621-1665
Charles II (Carlos II)	1665-1700
Philip V (Felipe V)	1700-1746
Ferdinand VI (Fernando VI)	1746-1759
Charles III (Carlos III)	1759-1788
Charles IV (Carlos IV)	1788-1808
Joseph Bonaparte	1808-1813
Ferdinand VII (Fernando VII)	1813-1833
Isabella II (Isabel II)	1833-1868

Kings of Portugal

Emmanuel I (Manoel I)	1495-1521
John III (João III)	1521-1557
Sebastian (Sebastião)	1557-1578
Henry (Henrique)	1578-1580
Philip I (II of Spain) (Felipe I)	1580-1598
Philip II (III of Spain) (Felipe II)	1598-1621
Philip III (IV of Spain) (Felipe III)	1621-1640
John IV (João IV)	1640-1656
Alfonso VI	1656-1667
Peter II (Pedro II)	1667-1706
John V (João V)	1706-1750
Joseph I (José I)	1750-1777
Maria I, and Peter III (Maria I and Pedro III)	1777-1786
Maria I	1786-1816
John VI (João VI)	1816-1826
Peter IV (Pedro IV)	1826
(Peter I, Emperor of Brazil (Pedro I of Brazil	1826-1831)

A Brief Bibliography:

See footnotes for more complete references

Bibliographical Works:

Altamira y Crevea, Rafael, Historia de España y de la civilización española. 4a. edición, corregida y aumentada. 4 v. Barcelona, 1928-1930.

Blake, Augusto Victorino Alves Sacramento, Diccionário Bibliográphico Brazileiro. 7 v. Rio de Janeiro, 1883-1902.

Brunet, Jacques Charles, Manuel du libraire et de l'amateur de livres. 5 ed. originale. 6 v. in 12. Paris, 1860-65.

California, University of, Spain and Spanish America in the libraries of the University of California. 2 v. Berkeley, 1928-30.

Chapman, Charles E., Colonial Hispanic America: a history. Contains valuable bibliographical information. New York: The Macmillan Co., 1933.

García Icazbalceta, Joaquín, Bibliografía Mexicana del Siglo XVI. México, D. F., 1886.

Goldberg, Isaac, Studies in Spanish American Literature. New York: Brentano's, 1920.

..............., Brazilian Literature. New York, Alfred A. Knopf, 1922.

Goldsmith, Peter H., A brief bibliography of books in English, Spanish, and Portuguese relating to the republics commonly called Latin-America, with comments. New York, 1915.

Grismer, Raymond L., A reference index to twelve thousand Spanish American authors; a guide to the literature of Spanish America. New York, Wilson, 1939. (Inter-American bibliographical and library association publications. ser. III, vol. 1).

............., A new bibliography of the literatures of Spain and Spanish America, including many studies on anthropology, archaeology, art, economics, education, geography, history, law, music, philosophy and other subjects. 2 v. Minneapolis, Minn.: Perine Book Co., 1941.

Gruening, E., Mexico and its heritage. New York: Appleton-Century Co., 1928.

Handbook of Latin American studies, a guide to the material published from 1935. Cambridge, Mass.: Harvard University Press, 1937-41.

Harrisse, Henry, Bibliotheca americana vetustissima. A description of works relating to America published between the years 1492 and 1551. New York, 1866. Additions. Paris, 1872.

Hilton, Ronald, ed. Handbook of Hispanic source materials and research organizations in the United States. Toronto, Can.: The University of Toronto Press, 1942.

Jones, C. K., Hispanic-American bibliographies. Baltimore, 1922.

León, Nicolás, Bibliografía mexicana del siglo XVIII. Sección primera. 5 v. Mexico, 1902-08.

Means, Philip A., Ancient Civilizations of the Andes. New York: Scribner's Sons, 1931.

..............., Fall of the Inca Empire and the Spanish rule in Peru, 1530-1780. New York: Scribner's Sons, 1932.

..............., The Spanish Main, focus of envy, 1492-1700. New York: Scribner's Sons, 1935.

Medina, José Toribio, Biblioteca hispano-americana, 1493-1810. 7 v. Santiago, Chile, 1898-1907.

..............., Biblioteca hispano-chilena, 1523-1817. 3 v. Santiago, Chile, 1897-99.

Moses, Bernard, Spanish-colonial literature in South America. New York, Hispanic Society of America, 1922.

Palau y Dulcet, Antonio, Manual del Librero Hispano-Americano. 7 v. Barcelona, 1923-27.

Pedreira, Antonio S., Bibliografía Puertorriqueña, 1493-1930. Madrid, 1932.

Sabin, Joseph, Bibliotheca Americana. A dictionary of books relating to America, from its discovery to the present time. Begun by Joseph Sabin, continued by Wilberforce Eames, and completed by R. W. G. Vail for the Bibliographical Society of America. 29 v. New York, 1868-1936.

Sánchez Alonso, B., Fuentes de la historia española e hispanoamericana. 2 v. Madrid, 1927.

Silva, Innocencio Francisco da, Dicionário bibliográfico português. Estudos de Innocencio Francisco da Silva, aplicaveis a Portugal e ao Brasil. 22 v. Lisboa, 1858-1923.

Vindel, Francisco, Manual gráfico-descriptivo del bibliófilo hispanoamericano, 1475-1850. 11 v. in 12. Madrid, 1930-31.

Wilgus, Alva Curtis, Histories and historians of Hispanic America. New York, H. W. Wilson, 1942.

..............., ed., Colonial Hispanic America. The George Washington University Press, Washington, D. C., 1936. Extensive footnotes and a separate bibliographical section by A. Curtis Wilgus, Appendices A to I.

GEOGRAPHY:

Huntington, Ellsworth, Civilization and climate. 2d ed. with a new introduction. New Haven: Yale University Press, 1922.

James, Preston E., Latin America: a human geography. New York: Lothrop, 1942.

GENERAL STUDIES:

Cleven, N. Andrew N., ed. Readings in Hispanic American history. Boston: Ginn and Company, 1927.

Kirkpatrick, Frederick A., Latin America, a brief history. New York: The Macmillan Company, 1939.

Moses, Bernard, The establishment of Spanish rule in America. 2 v. New York: Putnam's, 1898.

.............., South America on the eve of emancipation. New York: Putnam's, 1908.

.............., The Spanish dependencies in South America. 2 v. New York: Harpers, 1914.

.............., Spain's declining power in South America, 1720-1806. Berkeley: University of California Press, 1919.

Munro, Dana G., The Latin American republics, a history. New York: D. Appleton-Century Co., 1942.

Navarro y Lamarca, Carlos, Compendio de la historia general de América. Prólogo de D. Eduardo de Hinojosa. 2 v. Buenos Aires, 1910-1913.

Pereyra, Carlos, Historia de le América española. 8 v. Madrid, 1920-26.

Rippy, J. Fred, Historical evolution of Hispanic America. 2d ed. New York: F. S. Crofts & Co., 1942.

Robertson, William Spence, History of the Latin-American nations. 3d ed. rev. and enl. New York: Appleton-Century, 1933.

Wilgus, Alva Curtis, The development of Hispanic America. New York: Farrar & Rinehart, 1941.

.............., ed. Colonial Hispanic America. Washington: George Washington University Press, 1936.

Williams, Mary W., The people and politics of Latin America. New ed. Boston: Ginn & Co., 1938.

GENERAL STUDIES: *Alphabetical by countries.*

Kirkpatrick, Frederick A., A history of the Argentine republic. Cambridge, [Eng.]: The University Press, 1931.

Levene, Ricardo, A history of Argentina. Translated and edited by W. Spence Robertson. Chapel Hill: University of North Carolina Press, 1937.

.............., ed., Historia de la nación argentina.   12 v.
Buenos Aires, (1935———).

Argüedes, Alcides, Historia general de Bolivia.   La Paz, 1922.

.............., Pueblo enfermo.   3d ed. Santiago de Chile,
1937.

Cleven, N. Andrew N., The political organization of Bolivia.
Washington, D. C.: Carnegie Institution of Washington,
1940.

Armitage, John, History of Brazil, 1808-31.   2 v. London, 1836.
Continues Robert Southey's "History of Brazil."

Calógeras, João Pandiá, A history of Brazil.   Translated and
edited by Percy Alvin Martin.   Chapel Hill: University of
North Carolina Press, 1939.

Oliveira Lima, Manoel de, Dom João VI do Brasil.   2 v. Rio de
Janeiro, 1908.

Ribeiro, João, História do Brasil.   Rio de Janeiro, 1929.

Southey, Robert, History of Brazil.   3 v. London, 1810-19.

Varnhagen, Francisco Adolpho de.   História geral do Brasil.
Madrid, 1854-57.

Bancroft, Hubert Howe, History of Central America.   3 v. San
Francisco History Company, 1886-87.

Fernández Guardia, Ricardo, Historia de Costa Rica: El descubrimiento y la conquista.   San José de Costa Rica, 1905.

Jones, Chester Lloyd, Guatemala, past and present. Minneapolis:
The University of Minnesota Press, 1940.

Munro, Dana Gardner, The five republics of Central America.
New York: Oxford University Press, 1918.

Barros Arana, Diego, Historia general de Chile.   16 v. Santiago,
1884-1902 (Second edition 1930-).

Galdames, Luis, A history of Chile, translated and edited by Isaac
Joslin Cox.   Chapel Hill: The University of North Carolina
Press, 1941.

Henao, J. M., and *Arrubla, G.,* History of Colombia, translated
and edited by J. Fred Rippy. Chapel Hill: The University of
North Carolina Press, 1938.

Portell Vilá, H.   Historia de Cuba en sus relaciones con los Estados
Unidos y España.   Habana, Cuba, 1938-40.

Welles, Sumner, Naboth's Vineyard: The Dominican Republic,
1844-1924.   2 v.   New York: Payson & Clarke Ltd., 1928.

Leger, J. N., Haiti: Her history and her detractors.   New York:
Neale Publishing Company, 1907.

Alamán, Lucas, Disertaciones sobre la historia de la república

Mexicana desde la época de la conquista. 3 v. Mexico, 1844-49.

.............., Historia de Méjico. 5 v. Mexico, 1849-52.

Bancroft, Hubert Howe, History of California, 1542-1890. 7 v. San Francisco History Company, 1884-90.

.............., History of Mexico. 6 v. San Francisco, 1883-88.

Cavo, Andrés, Los tres siglos de Méjico durante el gobierno español hasta la entrada del ejército trigarante. Méjico, 1852.

Clavijero, Francisco Javier, History of Mexico, translated from Italian by Charles Cullen. 2d edition. London, 1807.

Mora, José Maria Luis, Obras sueltas de José Maria Luis Mora, 2 v. Paris, 1847.

Orozco y Berra, Manuel, Historia antigua y de la conquista de Méjico. 4 v. Mexico, 1880.

Priestley, Herbert Ingram, The Mexican nation, a history. New York: The Macmillan Company, 1930.

Riva Palacio, Vicente, ed., México a través de los siglos. 5 v. Barcelona, 1888-9.

Simpson, L. B., Many Mexicos. New York: G. P. Putnam's Sons, 1941.

Baez, Cecilio, Historia del Paraguay. Asunción, 1919.

Wiesse, C., Historia del Perú y de la civilización peruana. Lima: E. Rosay, 1914.

PRE-CONQUEST:

Bandelier, Adolph Francis, On the distribution and tenure of land, and the customs with respect to inheritance, among the ancient Mexicans. Cambridge, 1877.

.............., On the social organization and mode of government of the ancient Mexicans. Cambridge, 1879.

Durán, Diego, Historia de los Indios de Nueva España. 2 v. Mexico, 1867-80.

Kingsborough, Lord, Antiquities of Mexico. 7 v. London, 1831.

Prescott, William Hickling, History of the conquest of Mexico. New and revised edition. Edited by John Foster Kirk. 3 v. Philadelphia: J. B. Lippincott & Co., 1879.

Sahagún, Bernardino de, Historia general de las cosas de Nueva España. 5 v. Mexico, 1938.

Spinden, H. J., Ancient civilizations of Mexico and Central America. 2d and revised edition. New York: American Museum of Natural History, 1922.

Thompson, John Eric, Mexico before Cortez. New York: C. Scribner's Sons, 1933.

Vaillant, George Clapp, The Aztecs of Mexico. Garden City, New York: Doubleday, Doran & Co., 1941.

Zurita, Alonso de, Breve y sumaria relación de los señores . . . de la Nueva España. Mexico, 1891.

Ancona, Eligio, Historia de Yucatán. 4 v. Barcelona, 1889.

Blom, Frans, Tribes and temples. A record of the expedition to middle America conducted by the Tulane University of Louisana in 1925. 2 v. New Orleans, 1926.

Gann, Thomas Francis, Glories of the Maya. New York, Charles Scribner's Sons, 1931.

Landa, Diego de, Relación de las cosas de Yucatán. A translation edited with notes by Alfred M. Tozzer. Cambridge: Peabody Museum of America, Archaeology and Ethnology, 1941.

Morley, Sylvanus Griswold, An introduction to the study of the Maya hierogylphics. Washington, 1915.

Squier, Ephraim George, Nicaragua, its people scenery, monuments, and the proposed inter-oceanic canal. 2 v. New York: Appleton-Century, 1852.

Bandelier, Adolph Francis, The gilded man (El Dorado) and other pictures of the Spanish occupancy of America. New York, 1893.

Karsten, R., The civilization of the South American Indians, with special reference to magic and religion. New York: Knopf, 1926.

Means, Philip A., Ancient civilizations of the Andes. New York: Scribner's Sons, 1931.

Muñoz-Camargo, Diego, Historia de Tlaxcala. Mexico, 1892.

Prescott, William Hickling, History of the conquest of Peru. Various editions. New York: Harper Brothers, 1847.

Squier, E. G. Peru: Incidents of travel and exploration in the land of the Incas. New York, 1877.

SPAIN AND PORTUGAL

Armstrong, Edward, The Emperor Charles V. 2 v. London, 1902.

Bouchier, Edmund Spenser, Spain under the Roman Empire. Oxford, 1914.

Chapman, Charles E., History of Spain. New York: The Macmillan Company, 1927.

Cheyney, Edward Potts, European Background of American history (1300-1600). New York: Harper, 1904.

Ferrer del Río, Antonio, Historia del reinado de Carlos III. 4 v. Madrid, 1856.

La Fuente, Modesto, Historia general de España. 27 v. Barcelona, 1922-30.

Lea, Henry Charles, The Moriscos of Spain. Their conversion and expulsion. Philadelphia: Lea Brothers and Co., 1901.

Merriman, Roger Bigelow, The Rise of the Spanish Empire in the Old World and in the New. 4 v. New York: The Macmillan Co., 1918-1934.

Oliveira Martins, Joaquim Pedro, The Golden Age of Prince Henry the Navigator. Translated by J. J. Abraham and W. E. Reynolds. New York: Dutton and Co., 1914.

. . . . , A history of Iberian Civilization. Translated by Aubrey F. G. Bell. London, 1930.

Prescott, William H., History of the reign of Ferdinand and Isabella the Catholic. 3 v. New York: Harper and Brothers, 1851.

Scott, Samuel Parson, History of the Moorish Empire in Europe. 3 v. Philadelphia: J. B. Lippincott Company, 1904.

Stephens, H. M., Story of Portugal. New York, 1891.

Exploration and Colonization

Beazley, C. Raymond, Prince Henry the Navigator. New York: Putnam's, 1897.

Bolton, Herbert, and *Marshall, T. M.,* The colonization of North America. New York: The Macmillan Company, 1920.

Bolton, H. E., Outposts of Empire. New York: Alfred A. Knopf, 1931.

. . . . , The Spanish border lands. New Haven: Yale University Press, 1921.

Bourne, Edward Gaylord, Spain in America, 1450-1580. New York: Harper's 1904.

Chapman, Charles E., The founding of Spanish California, the Northwestward Expansion of New Spain, 1687-1783. New York: The Macmillan Company, 1916.

Cunninghame Graham, R. B., The Conquest of New Granada. Boston: Houghton Mifflin Company, 1922.

. . . . , The Conquest of the River Plate. Garden City: Doubleday Doran and Company, 1924.

. . . . , Pedro de Valdivia. London, 1926.

Díaz del Castillo, Bernal, True history of the Conquest of New Spain, 5 v. London, 1908-16.

Keller, Albert Galloway, Colonization: A Study of the Founding of New Societies. Boston: Ginn and Company, 1908.

MacNutt, Francis Augustus, Bartolomé de Las Casas. New York: Putnam's, 1909.

. . . ., Fernando Cortés and the Conquest of Mexico. New York: Putnam's, 1909.

Madariaga, Salvador de, Hernan Cortés, Conqueror of Mexico. New York: The Macmillan Company, 1941.

Means, Philip A., History of the Spanish conquest of Yucatán and of the Itzas. Cambridge: Peabody Museum of Harvard University, 1917.

. . . ., The Spanish Main, focus of envy, 1492-1700. New York: Scribner's Sons, 1935.

Morison, Samuel Eliot, Admiral of the Ocean Sea: A life of Christopher Columbus. 2 v. Boston: Little, Brown and Company, 1942.

Prescott, William Hickling, History of the conquest of Mexico. New and revised edition. Edited by John Foster Kirk. 3 v. Philadelphia: J. B. Lippincott & Co., 1879.

. . . ., History of the Conquest of Peru. Various editions. 1843.

Prestage, Edgar, The Portuguese Pioneers. London, 1933.

Priestley, Herbert I., The Coming of the White Man, 1492-1848. New York: The Macmillan Company, 1929.

Richman, Irving Berdine, Spanish Conquerors. New Haven: Yale University Press, 1921.

Sedgwick, Henry Dwight, Cortés the conqueror. Indianapolis: Bobbs-Merrill Company, 1926.

Thacher, John Boyd, Christopher Columbus. 3 v. New York: Putnam's, 1903-04.

ECONOMIC AND SOCIAL CONDITIONS

Brown, V. E., Contraband trade: a factor in the decline of Spain's Empire in America. Hispanic-American Historical Review. Durham: Duke University Press, 1926.

Cappa, Ricardo, Estudios críticos acerca de la dominación española en América. 7 v. Madrid, 1889.

Gage, Thomas, A new survey of the West Indies. New York: McBride, 1929.

Haring, Clarence H., Buccaneers in the West Indies in the 17th century. New York: E. P. Dutton, 1910.

. . . ., Trade and Navigation between Spain and the Indies. Cambridge: Harvard University Press, 1918.

Humboldt, Alexander von, Political Essay on the Kingdom of New Spain. Translated and edited by John Black. 4 v. London, 1811.

Hussey, Roland Dennis, The Caracas Company, 1728-84. Cambridge: Harvard University Press, 1934.

Juan y Santacilia, Jorge, and *A. de Ulloa,* Voyage to South America. London, 1807.

Klein, J., The Mesta, Cambridge:Harvard University Press, 1920.

McBride, George M., Chile: Land and Society. New York: American Geographical Society, 1936.

..............., The Land Systems of Mexico. New York: American Geographical Society, 1923.

Means, Philip A., Fall of the Inca Empire. New York: Scribner's, 1932.

Saco, José Antonio, Historia de la esclavitud de la raza Africana en el Nuevo Mundo. Barcelona, 1879.

Simpson, Eyler N., The Ejido: Mexico's way out. Chapel Hill: The University of North Carolina Press, 1937.

Simpson, Lesley B., The Encomienda in New Spain; Forced Native Labor in the Spanish colonies, 1492-1550. Berkeley: University of California, 1929.

..............., The repartimiento system of native labor in New Spain and Guatemala. Ibero-americana No. 13, Berkeley, 1938.

Villaseñor y Sánchez, J. A., Teatro Americano. 2 v. Mexico, 1746.

Whitaker, Arthur P., The Huancavelica mercury mine. Cambridge: Harvard University Press, 1941.

Intellectual History and Fine Arts

Coester, Alfred, The Literary History of Spanish America. New York: The Macmillan Company, 1928.

Caso, Alfonso, and others, Twenty Centuries of Mexican Art. New York, 1940.

Fernández de Lizardi, J. J., El Periquillo Sarniento. 2 v. Mexico, 1816.

Flores, Francisco A., Historia de la medicina en Mexico. 3 v. Mexico, 1886.

Lanning, J. T., Academic Culture in the Spanish colonies. New York: Oxford University Press, 1940.

Moses, Bernard, The intellectual background of the revolution in South America, 1810-1824. New York: Hispanic Society of America, 1926.

Quesada, Vicente G., La vida intelectual en la América española durante los siglos XVI, XVII, y XVIII. Buenos Aires, 1910.

THE CHURCH

Ayarragaray, Lucas, La Iglesia en América y la dominación española. Buenos Aires, 1920.

Braden, Charles S., Religious Aspects of the Conquest of Mexico. Durham: Duke University Press, 1930.

Castañeda, C. E. Our Catholic heritage in Texas, 1519-1936. 4 v., Austin, 1936-1939.

Lea, Henry C., History of the Inquisition of Spain. 4 v. New York: Macmillan, 1906-1907.

.............., The Inquisition in the Spanish Dependencies. New York: Macmillan, 1908.

Mecham, John Lloyd, Church and State in Latin America. Chapel Hill: The University of North Carolina Press, 1932.

Medina, José T., Historia del tribunal del santo oficio de la inquisición en México. Santiago de Chile, 1905, and many other works on the same subject by this author.

Vélez-Sarsfield, Dalmacio, Derecho público eclesiástico, relaciones del estado con la iglesia en la antigua América española. Buenos-Aires, 1889.

COLONIAL ADMINISTRATION:

Aiton, Arthur Scott, Antonio de Mendoza, First Viceroy of New Spain. Durham: Duke University Press, 1927.

Carranca y Trujillo, Raul, La evolución política de Iberoamérica. Madrid, Editorial América, 1925.

Cunningham, C. A., The Audiencia in the Spanish Colonies. Berkeley: University of California, 1919.

Fisher, Lillian E., The Intendant System in Spanish America. Berkeley: University of California, 1929.

.............., Viceregal administration in the Spanish-American Colonies. Berkeley: University of California Press, 1926.

Means, Philip A., Fall of the Inca Empire and the Spanish Rule in Peru, 1530-1780. New York: Scribners' Sons, 1932.

.............., The Spanish Main, focus of envy, 1492-1700, New York: Scribners' Sons, 1935.

Priestley, Herbert Ingram, José de Galvez, Visitor-General of New Spain, 1765-1771. Berkeley, 1916.

Smith, Donald Eugene, The Victory of New Spain. Berkeley: University of California Press, 1913.

Index

A

Abad y Quiepo, Manuel: 485; estimates wealth of the clergy, 591; "Representación sobre la inmunidad personal del clero," 485, note

Abipones (Chaco Indians), 171

Abreau, Jorge O. e Almeida, *Historia da literatura nacional*, 715, note

Abreu, *see* Capistrano de Abreu

Abreu Gómez, E., *Prólogo a Sor Juana Inés de la Cruz, Poesías*, 534, note

Absolutism, *see* Government

Academies, in Brazil and Portugal, 714-15

Acapulco: 71; shipping from, 430; trade center for New Spain, 399-400

Acllas, 176

Acosta, José de: 520; *Historia natural y moral de las Indias*, 21, note; lists plants of America, 83; on the Aztec system of government, 274; on barter among the Indians, 132; on the land system of the Incas, 21, 75-76, 77; on lowlands of Mexico, 86; on numerous cattle in the Caribbean, 94; on reasons for Indian conversion, 250; on tribute rights of the Inca, 78; on the wealth of Potosí, 116

Acuerdos, 299

Acuerdos del extinguido cabildo de Buenos Aires, 615, note

Adams, James Truslow, *Provincial Society*, 1690-1763, 557, note

Adán y Eva, religious play, 534

Adelantado, Bartolomé de Columbus, 60

"Adelantado of the South Sea," title given Balboa, 42

Administrative system: of the Incas, 276-78; of the Aztecs, 274

Adoración de los reyes, 535

Adrian VI, 262

Africa, 30, 31, 56

African Company, 685

Agave, *see* maguey

Agricultural development to 1810, *see* Chapters 16 and 17

Agricultural Society of Argentina, 560

Agriculture: Andean Indian, 87-92; basis of Conquest, 37-39; Crown policy on, 102-103; developed by mining, 112-13, 115; in Brazil, 638, 675-77; evolution, 649-51: plants and animals, 638, note; progress of, 654-57; in the Caribbean, 92-94; in Central America, 84-85, 340; in Chile, 321-25; in Colombia, 98, 334-39; in Ecuador, 99-100, 316; in Jamaica, 92; in New Spain, 84-85, 340, 343-50; in Panama, 98; in Peru, 99-100, 316-17; in Río de la Plata, 333; in South America, 98-102; in Venezuela, 334-39; pre-Conquest, 83-84; progress according to Acosta, 100-101; progress of Indian, 5-6; summary, 465; values of Brazilian exports, 690-92

Agua de hierro process of mining, 111

Aguado, Pedro de, 521

Aguilar, interpreter for Cortés, 43

Aguirre, Juan Francisco de, report on Montevideo, 426

Aguirre, Lope de, 594, note; 666

Aigues-Mortes, 31

Aiton, Arthur S.: 545, note; *Antonio de Mendoza, First Viceroy of New Spain*, 72, note; "The Asiento Treaty as Reflected in the Papers of Lord Shelbourne," 408, note; "A Neglected Intrigue of the Family Compact," 626, note; "Real Hacienda in New Spain under the First Viceroy," 301, note; "Spanish Colonial Reorganization under the Family Compact," 626, note; "The Spanish Conquest and the Settlement of the Indies," 209, note; "The Spanish Conquest and Settlement of the Indies," 498

Aiton, Arthur S. and Wheeler, Benjamin, "The First American Mint," 373, note

Alamán, Lucas: *Historia de Méjico*, 67, note; on olive and wine restrictions, 349; on tithes, 350; on the viceroy, 605-606

Alarcón, Juan Ruiz de, Mexican dramatist, 535-36

Álava, 290

Albertus Magnus, 227

Albigensians, 235

Albuquerque Coelho, Jorge de, 712

Alcabala, 149, 150

Alcaldes: 72, 305, 617; Indian, 309; *alcaldes mayores*, 310

Alcántara (Military order of), 59, 288

Alcedo, Antonio de, 523

Alcedo y Herrera, Dionisio de: *Compendio Histórico de la provincial . . . de Guayaquil,* 397; *Descripción de . . . la América meridional,* 409; on smuggling, 409

Alcolea, 290

Aldeas, influence in local government, 751-52

Alcijadinho (Francisco Antonio) Lisboa, 717

Alexander VI, Pope: 36; Bull for Christianizing the Indians, 250; cedes control of America to Spain, 237-38; censors German press, 507

Alfaras, Marqués de, 290

Alférez-mayor, 617

Alfonso (*or* Afonso) V, of Portugal, 32

Alfonso X, laws on Jews and Moors, 236

Alguacil-mayor, 617

Alhóndiga, 333

Alliance of Tenochtitlán, Téxcoco and Tlacopan, 15

Allí-te-estás, 208

Almagro, Diego de: expedition to Chile, 54, 319, 320; expedition to Peru, 50, 51, 53

Almeida Paes Leme, Pedro Taques de: *História da capitania do São Vicente,* and *Nobiliarchia Paulistana,* and *Informação sobre as minas de São Paulo,* 761

Almeida Prado, J. F. de: *Pernambuco e as capitanias do norte do Brasil, 1530-1630,* 636, note; *Primeiros Povoadores do Brasil, 1500-1530,* 634, note

Almojarifazgo, 150

Alonso de los Ríos, Martín, 162

Altamira, Rafael, *Historia de España,* 34, note

Alvarado, Pedro de: 74, 294, in Mexico, 46-48, 67; in Guatamala, 4, 206; *An Account of Conquest of Guatemala in 1524,* 74, note

Alvares, Diogo, *see* Caramurú, 700

Álvarez, J., "Orígenes de la música argentina," 536, note

Alvear, Diego de: on *estancias* in Uruguay, 331; on Montevideo, 426

Alzate y Ramírez, José Antonio de, journalist and scientist, 550, 555

Amadís de Gaula, 504

Amantes del País, Los, 552

Amaral, Luis, *História geral da agricultura brasileira,* 684, note

Amarilis a Belardo, Peruvian poem, 531

Amat, Viceroy: 584-85; patron of the theatre, 535

Amautas, 216, 217

Amazon: inland water routes, 679; missions along, 581

America: 28, 45, 55, 56, 59, 60, 92; areas controlled by Spain, 209; books about, 230; discovery, 230; European interest in, 230-31; ecclesiastical position of, 237-38; European culture in, 228-32; food in, 38; in 1600, 209; interchange of ideas between North and South, 544; invaded from Asia, 12-13, 26; languages and writing of pre-Conquest, 212-15; Spanish ownership of, 57-58

American Philosophical Society, 544

American Revolution, 544-45

American trade, European rivalry for, 146

Ampère, J. J., *Promenade en Amérique,* 214, note

Amunátegui, Miguel Luis, *Los precursores de la independencia de Chile,* 502, note

Amunátegui Solar, Domingo; *Las encomiendas de indíjenas en Chile,* 357, note; *Historia social de Chile,* 619, note

Anais da Biblioteca Nacional de Rio de Janeiro, 653, note

Anatas, form of taxes, 572

Ancerma (Colombia), 173

Anchieta, José de (*or* Joseph): 709, 720-21; assist in expelling the French from Rio, 653; on the Indians, 725; on the Inquisition, 736; on work of the Jesuits, 721

Ancona, Eligio, *Historia de Yucatán,* 173, note

Andagoya, Pascual de, 53

Andalusian, 58

Andean irrigation system, 87-92

Andes: 13, 18, 26, 83, 84, 86-87; compared to Mexican mountains, 87; trade in the, 132; treatment of the Indians, 465-67; unproductive areas, 18

Andrews, E. Wyllis, "Chronology and Astronomy in the Maya Area," 219, note

Ángeles, Pedro de, ed., *Colección de obras*

y documentos relativos a . . . Rio de la Plata, 328, note

Angolan language, 699

Angostura, 434

Anhanguera, 678

Animals, domestic: imported, 92; 95-96; importance in the Conquest; lack of in America, 18; lack of pack, 136-37; post-conquest, 137

Anonymous Conqueror, *Narrative of Some Things of New Spain,* 167, note

Antarctic, 87

Antioquia, mining in, 371

Antonil, André João (João Antonio Andreoni), *Cultura e Opulencia do Brasil por sus drogas e minas,* 651, note; 711; on expansion of Brazil, 664; on gold fields in Brazil, 677

Antúñez y Acevedo, Rafael, *Memorias históricas sobre la legislación y gobierno del comercio de los Españoles con sus colonias de las Indias Occidentales,* 420, note

Antwerp, 31

Apeles Mexicano, see Nicolás Rodríguez Juárez

Aponte, Cano de, governor of Chile, 576

Aposento (warehouse), 91

Apostolic See, 238

Apurimac River, 134

Aquinas, Thomas, 549

Aragon: 32; *fueros* of, 290

Aragua Valley:
    indigo production in, 339

Araguaya River: gold discovery, 678

Aranda, Count of, 510

Araucanians: 171, 271; Jesuit missions among the, 581

Arawaks, wars with the Caribs, 35

Arcadia Mexicana, club, 552

Archbishoprics of Lima, Mexico and Santo Domingo, 261

Archbishops, Crown distrust of, 573-74

Architecture: 515; in Brazil, 716-17; Indian, 222-24; mixture of Spanish and Indian, 232, 537-38

Arciniegas, Germán, *The Knight of El Dorado,* 74, note

Arequipa: 88, 116, 384; bell foundries at, 127

Argentina: 13, 18, 26, 83, 328-330; culture of colonial, 506; Inquisition, 513; principal cities, 329; wealthy classes, 483-84

Argüedes, Alcides, *Historia de Bolivia,* 486, note

Arias de Saavedra, Hernando, attempts settlement in Uruguay, 331

Arica, 116, 384

Aristocracy: *see also* class society; Spanish, 286-87

Aristotle, philosophy in American education, 548-49

Arma, 74

Armada de la carrera de Indias, 161-62

Armas antárticas, historical poem, 531

Arms, 144

Arnaix y Freg, Arturo, "D. Fausto de Elhuyar y Zubice," 381, note

Art, European origin of post-Conquest, 227

Arte mayor de seda, silk syndicate, 125

Arte para criar seda en la Nueva España, 125

Arts and architecture, influence of Brazilian social structure on, 716-17

Arts and crafts, Indian, 222-26

Arts, Fine: Academy of, 539; development of, *see* Chapter 24; Humboldt on, 539-40

Ascasubi, Fray Miguel de, *Informe cronológico de las misiones del reino de Chile,* 587, note

Asia, Central, 29

Asiento, 206

Asociación Filarmónica, in Lima, 552

Aspilcueta Navarro, João de, 709

Assumption of the Virgin, sculpture by Caspicara, 538

Astronomy, Aztec, 218

Asturias, stronghold of Christianity, 233

Asunción, founded, 329

Asuntos varios sobre ciencias y artes, 555

Asylum, right of, 573

Atahualpa: ransom, 107; wars with Huáscar, 23-25, 53-54, 283

Atlantic, exploration, 30, 32

Atondo (*or* Otondo) y Antillón, 341

Atrato Valley, 413

Atrisco, Duke of, 67

Audiencia de Charcas, Colección de publicaciones históricas . . ., 329, note

Audiencia: origin and functions of, 297-300, 607-608; in Española, 63; Church conflicts with, 573

Augustinians, property owners in Mexico City, 268

Auto, religious play form, 534-35

Autos acordados, 299

Autos de fé, in Cuzco, 262

Ávalos y Figueroa, Diego de, Peruvian poet, 531

Ávila, Alonso de, 152-53

Áviles, Marqués de, on the religious ignorance of the Indians, 589

Aviso, of Havana, 558

Ayacucho, fairs at, 384-85

Ayarragaray, Lucas, "Las universidades coloniales," 498, note

Ayllu lands, 75-78, 276

Ayolas, Juan de, 327

Ayuntamiento, 239

Azamor, Bishop, owned prohibited books, 545

Azara, Félix de: *Descripción e historia del Paraguay y del Río de la Plata*, 328; *Histoire Physique, économique et politique du Paraguay*, 445, note; *Memorias sobre el estado rural del Río de la Plata en 1801*, 330, note; on the Charrúas, 442; on Jesuit missions, 581; writings of, 525

Azevedo, J. Lucio de, *Épocas de Portugal econômico*, 635, note

Azevedo, Moreira de, "O primeiro bispo do Brazil," 718, note

Azevedo, Pedro: "A Instituição do Governo Geral," 648, note; "Os primeiros Donatarios," 643, note

Azores, 30, 31, 36

Aztecs: 44, 46, 56, 82, 91; class system, 69; compared with Brazilian Indians, 635; Confederacy, 70-71; culture, 214; empire, 15, 26; gods, 240-41; government, 272-75; medicine, 218; land system, 65-68; religion, 238-39, 242, 244-46; social groups, 166; treasure, 107; writing, 214-15

B

Baía: 647, 649-51, 663-65; commerce, 689; Dutch occupation, 657-58; population and progress, 655-56

Baião, Antonio, and Dias, Malheiro, "A Expedição de Christóvam Jacques," 640, note

Baião, Antonio, "O Comercio do pau brasil," 640, note

Bain, H. F., and Read, Thomas T., *Ores and Industry in South America*, 117, note

Baja California: 100, expedition of Cortés to, 341

Balboa, Vasco Núñez de: arrest and beheading, 42, 53; discovers Pacific Ocean, 42; plans expedition to Peru, 50; sets up *cabildo* at Darién, 293-94; shipbuilding by, 128

Balbuena, Bernardo de, poet, 530

Baldíos, 72, 74

Ballesteros, Antonio, *Historia de España y su influencia en la historia universal*, 60, note

Balsa, 398

Baltic, 29

Bananas, in New Spain, 344

Bandeiras, 669-73

Bandelier, A. F., on agriculture of the Rimac Valley, 188

Bandera, Damián de la, describes tyranny of Indian caciques, 310

Baptism, Indian, 244

Baquíjano y Carillo, José, 546

Baralt, Rafael María, *Resumen de la historia de Venezuela*, 334, note

Barba, Álvaro Alonso, *Artes de los Metales*, 366

Barbaro, Giosafat, 29

Barbosa, Fructuoso, 666

Barboza de Sá, Joseph, "Relação das povoações do Cuyabá e Mato Grosso," 679, note

Barco, 398

Bardin, James C., "A Song from Sor Juana," 534

Barnuevo Rocha y Benavides, Pedro de Peralta, Peruvian encyclopedist, 541

Barros, João de, 666

Barros Arana, Diego: *Compendio de historia de América*, 15, note; *Historia jeneral de Chile*, 321, note; on early missionaries, 265

Barter, 132

Bartolache, José Ignacio, journalist, 555

Barton, Dr. Benjamin Smith, scientific writings of, 544

Basadre, Jorge, *Historia del derecho peruano*, 529, note

Basavilbaso family, held postal monopoly, 421

Bastidas, Rodrigo, 50

Baudin, Louis, *L'Empire socialiste des Inka*, 75, note

Bayle, Constantino, *Historia . . . de la Compañía de Jesús en la Baja California*, 341, note

Beans, 83, 84

Becerra, Diego de, painter, 539

Becker, Jerónimo, 521

Beckmann, Manoel, 686, 731-32

Beeswax: in Cuba, 353-54, 437; in New Spain, 348

Belalcázar, Sebastián de, 51

Belardo a Amarilis, poem of Lope de Vega, 531

Benavides, Pedrarias de, medical writings of, 540

Benedictines, in Brazil, 720, 732

Benzoni, Girolamo, *La historia del Mondo Nuovo,* 36

Bergaño y Villegas, Simón, 556

Beristain de Souza, José Mariano, *Biblioteca hispano-americana setentrional,* 546-66

Bernardo o la victoria de Roncesvalles, 530

Bernstein, Harry: "Spanish Influence in the United States," 342, note; *Origins of Inter-American Interest, 1700-1812,* 416, note; "Some Inter-American Aspects of the Enlightenment," 544, note; and Diffie, B. W., "Sir Clements R. Markham as a translator," 520, note

Betanzos, Domingo de, Fray, 262

Betendorf, João Felippe, *Chronica da missão dos Padres da Companhia de Jesus,* 731, note

Beteta, Ignacio, 556

Biblioteca hispano-americana setentrional, 564

Biblioteca de historia nacional (Colombia), 497

Bio-Bio, 325

Biscaina mining vein, 375-76

Bishoprics: in the colonies, 260; in Española and Puerto Rico, 246

Black Code, 473

Black Legend, 178

Black Sea, 29

Blanco, Tomás, *Prontuario histórico de Puerto Rico,* 39, note

Blanco Acevedo, Pablo, *El gobierno colonial en el Uruguay,* 331, note

Bobadilla, Francisco de, 294

Bogotá: 87, 117, 334, 435; audiencia in, 298; founded, 51

Bohemund, Crusade leader, 234

Bohio, 35

Bolaños, mine at, 383

Bolivia: 13, 83, 98, 117; mining in, 368

Bolsa de comercio, in Flanders, 31

Bolton, Herbert E.: "The Mission as a Frontier Institution," 578, note; *Rim*

of Christendom, 341, note; *The Spanish Borderlands,* 342, note

Bomfim, Manoel, *O Brasil,* 654

Bonpland, Aimé, accompanied Humboldt, 543

Book of Privileges, 60

Books: censorship (in the colonies), 510-13; (in Spain), 507-509; circulation in Spain and the colonies, 504-507; on colonial matters, 511; histories, 514-25; Index of forbidden, 508, 512; on law, 526-29; prohibited, 509, 511-12, 545-46; 561-66; restrictions on, 502-504; written in and about America, 230

Books of Chilam Balam, 214

Borah, Woodrow W.: "The Collection of Tithes," 350, note; *Silk-raising in colonial Mexico,* 124, note

Borges, Pero, 741

Borja Marán, Bishop Francisco de, 589

Born process of amalgamation, 381, 382

Botanical Gardens, in Mexico, 550

Botelho de Oliveira, Manoel, *Musica de Parnasso,* and *A Ilha da Maré,* 712

Bougainville, Louis Antoine de: *Voyage,* 330, note; on the *gauchos,* 443

Bourgeoisie, Portuguese, 30

Bourne, Edward G., *Spain in America, 1450-1580,* 207, note

Boyl, Fray Bernal, 246

Bozale Negroes, 474

Braden, C. S., *Religious Aspects of the Conquest of Mexico,* 34, note

Bradley, Anita, *Trans-Pacific Relations of Latin America,* 400

Branciforte, Viceroy of Mexico, condemns French influence, 546

Brasseur de Bourbourg, Charles Etienne, *Popol Vuh,* 214

Bravo, Dr., *Opera medicinalia,* 540

Brazil: 13, 18, 26, 55, 83; arts and architecture, 715-17; aristocracy, 651; British goods in, 411; *capitão mor,* 745-46, 749-52; captaincies, and captaincies general, 641-49, 739-40; chronicles, 708-10; the Church, *see* Chapter 32; Clergy, 720-24, 732-35; commerce, 682-92; culture, *see* Chapter 31; discovery, 633-35; early agriculture, 638; education, 704-708; eve of independence, 752-53; expansion, 662-81; expansion in the Amazon and the North, 665-68; expansion in Baía and Pernambuco, 663-65; expansion in Maranhão, 666-67; expansion in Rio Grande do Sul, 672; expansion in Rio de Janeiro, 665; expansion in São Paulo, 668-77; expansion in Sergipe, 664; expulsion of the Dutch, 659-62; gold production, 373; government, *see* Chapter 33, (centralized), 740-42, (Dutch occupation), 744-45, (local), 747-52; historical writing, 708-11; immigration of white men to, 699-702; Indians compared to Caribbean, Mexican and Andean, 634-35; Jews in, 638; law courts, 743-44; learning and letters, 704-17; literary and scientific academies, 714-15; literature, influence of French and American Revolutions on, 715; militia, 746; people, 693-702; poverty compared to the wealth of India, 636-37; Principality, 744-45; printing press, 715; products, 690-92; progress, 654-57; route for Portuguese contraband, 410, 411; settlement, 635-41, 647-48; 663; the Spanish Era, 742-44; as treated in this work, 10-11; trade with England, 405; Viceroyalty, 744; wealth in the 16th century, 256-57

Brazil wood: 636; commerce, 639-41; contraband, 154; exports, 690-99; French trade, 640

Brazilian Indians: characteristics, 634-35, 693-96; languages, 635; position of women, 694-95; sexual customs, 695; society and economy, 635; work of missionaries, 720-24

Brentano, Vobara and Urbieta, Hamburg firm in Montevideo, 425

Bretóa, 639

Brevísima relación de la destrucción de las Indias, 518

Bridges, Inca, 134

Brinton, Daniel C., *The Maya Chronicles,* 173, note

Bristol, 32

British Consular Reports, 416, note

Brito de Figueiredo, Caetano de. *See* Figueiredo, Caetano de Brito

Bronze, 118-19

Brown, Vera Lee: "Anglo-Spanish Relations," 414, note; "Contraband trade," 420, note

Bueno, Amador, 672, 728

Buenos Aires: authorized to trade with Brazil, 393; *consulado,* 609; customs collections, 429; feared by inland trade centers, 394; Free Trade Acts, 427; freedom of the port, 424, 425; growth, 449; hides shipped (table), 428; port limitations, 426; Portuguese contraband, 411-12; provincial trade, 428-29; rivalry with Montevideo, 425-26, 427; schools, 497; settlement, 326; trade expansion, 427-28; trade with Chile, 432; trade with Potosí, 384; trade with the United States, 415; versa Sevilla-Panama-Lima trade monopoly, 392

Building: authorization for, 258-59; Indian, 120

Bull, Papal: authorizing establishment of an archbishopric in Española, 246; *caena domini,* 509; conceding tithes to the King, 251; *Ea Semper,* 573

Burgos, Laws of, 63, 193, 199

Burial customs in Peru: 175; human sacrifice, 281

Burke, Ulick Ralph, *A History of Spain,* 34, note

Bustamante, Calixto Carlos Inca (Concolorcorvo), *El lazarillo de ciegos caminantes,* 384

Bustamante, Carlos María, 556

Bustamante, C. Pérez, *Los Orígenes del gobierno virreinal,* 300

Bustillo, Manuel Carlos, arrested for reading *Encyclopédie,* 561

Butel-Dumont, G. M., *Histoire et commerce des Antilles Anglois,* 408

Byzantine Empire, 29

C

Caballerías: 67, 72; position of the, 287

Cabello Balboa, Miguel, *Historia del Perú bajo . . . los Incas,* 18, note

Cabello y Mesa, Francisco Antonio, on newspapers, 559

Cabeza de Vaca, Álvar Núñez, reaches Mexico, 340

Cabildo, the: 63, 72, 611-18; American contrasted with Spanish, 306; character of, 611-12; conflicts with Crown authorities, 305-306; conflicts with military governors, 212-13; curbed by the *audiencia,* 615; duties, 305, 612, 614-15; in America, 303; in Asunción, 615; in Darién, 293; in Española, 293; in Indian villages, 308-309; in local government, 305-307; in Montevideo, 612-13; in Río de la

Plata, 615; in Vera Cruz, 293-94; powers, 613-15; sale of public offices, 616-18

Cabildos abiertos, 305, 618

Cabo Frio, feitoria, 637

Cabo São Roque, 639

Cabot, John, voyages, 32

Cabot, Sebastián: explores Brazilian coast, 654; founds Sancti Spiritus, 326; in Río de la Plata, 50

Cabral, Pedro Alvares, discovers Brazil, 633-36

Cabrera, Amador de, 111

Cabrera, Miguel, 539

Cabrillo, Juan Rodríguez, 341

Cacamatzin, Cacique of Téxcoco, 46

Cacao: 83, 144; annual crop in Venezuela, 1800-1806, 338; disadvantages as a crop, 337; exports from Brazil, 690-92; exports from Venezuela, 337; in the Caribbean, 337; in Ecuador, 316, 346; in New Spain, 346; smuggled by the Dutch, 337-38

Cacicazgo, 68, 307-308, 619

Cacique, 61, 167; Indian under Spanish rule, 310; post-conquest, 204

Cactus, 83, 85

Cádiz: 163; Cortes of, 561

Caena Domini, 509

Café, importance of the, 551-52

Caillet-Bois, Ricardo R., "La América española y la revolución francesa," 546, note

Cajamarca, land grants in, 79

Calatrava, Military Order of, 59, 288

Calchaqui, 171

Caldas, Francisco José, published scientific material in Colombia, 544, 550, 552

Calderón de la Barca, 505

Calendar: Aztec, 218; Inca, 219; Mayan, 218, 219

Cali (Colombia), 98; commerce with Buenaventura, 137; founded, 51

Calificadores, 508

California, occupation of, 341

Callao, 163

Calmon, Pedro: História do Brasil, 653, note; História da civilização brasileira, 637, note; História social do Brasil, 701, note

Calógeras, João Pandiá: As minas do Brasil e sua legislação, 674, note; Formação histórica do Brasil, 656, note

Calpixques, 202

Calpulli, defined, 69

Câmara: in Brazil, 747; schools of the, 707

Caminha, Pero Vaz de, letter on discovery of Brazil, 634-35, 708

Camões, Os Lusíadas, 712

Campa, Arthur L., "The Churchmen and the Indian Languages of New Spain," 498, note

Campbell, John, A Compleat History of Spanish America, 419, note

Campeche (Campeachey), 144, 413

Campesinos, 444

Campillo, José del: on population, 447; writings of, 529

Campo, André do, 736

Campo Tourinho, Pedro do, 647, 736

Campomanes, Count Pedro Rodríguez de: 59-60, 510; feared the Inquisition, 577; on Cuban prosperity in 1775, 422

Canada, 85

Canals, irrigation, Inca, 79

Cananéa, 641-42

Cañaris, 25

Canary Islands: 74, 143; colonized by Spain, 32; given to Spain, 36; repartimientos, 59

Cannibalism: ceremonial, 174; in Brazil, 633-35; in the Caribbean and Mexico, 44, 172-73; in Colombia, 173-74; reported by Columbus, 36; victims fattened for, 173; feared by Caribbean Indians, 35

Canoa, 398

Canonists, 257

Cañafistula (cassia fistula), 636

Candelaria, capital of the Paraguay-Uruguay missions, 581

Cañete, Viceroy Marquis of: puts down revolt in Peru, 304; tries to correct abuse of the Indians, 465

Cape Blanco, 30

Cape Bojador, 30

Cape of Good Hope, 30

Cape Horn, shipping via, 429

Cape Verde Islands: 36; occupied by Portuguese, 30

Capellán, Juan, improved patio process, 111

Capistrano de Abreu, João: Caminhos antigos e povoamento do Brasil, 674, note; Capítulos da história colonial, 633, note; O descobrimento do Brasil,

633, note; *Ensaios e estudos,* 642, 673, 738; *Primeira visitação do Santo Oficio as partes do Brasil, 1591-92,* 252

Capitães do mato, 750-51

Capital investments in Brazil, 687

Capitania, see Captaincies

Capitão mor, 745, 746, 749-52

Capitulación, 110, 294

Cappa, Ricardo, *Estudios críticos acerca de la dominación española en América,* 391, note

Captaincies: in Brazil, 641-48, 739-40, 744, 745, 747; reclaimed by the Crown, 746

Captains-general: 302-304, 623-25; in Brazil, 648-49, 741-42

Capuchins, in Brazil, 720, 732-33

Caracas, 334

Caracas Company, 403, 421

Caramurú (Diogo Alvares), 647, 649, 700, 713

Caranques, revolt of the, 23

Carastes, 220

Carbajal, Luis de, 341

Carbia, Rómulo D., *Manual de la historia argentina,* 326

Cardiff, Father Guillermo Furlong, on restrictions on books, 505-506

Cardim, Fernão, *Tratado da terra e gente do Brasil,* 634, note; 709

Caribbean: 17, 26, 35, 38, 56, 74, 83, 98, 144, 163; agriculture, 39, 41, 92-94; buying capacity, 439-40; class society, 165-66; cannibalism, marriage and sexual practices, 172-73; cattle, 94; colonization, 35-37; conquest, 5; supply base for the conquistadores, 39; trade policy liberalized, 422; trade in Habana, 437-38; trade in New Granada, 434

Caribs: class distinctions, 165; wars with the Arawaks, 35-36; 165

Carlos V, *see* Charles V

Carmelites, in Brazil, 720, 732-33

Carnaxide, Antonio de Sousa Pedroso, *O Brasil na administração Pombalina,* 686, note

Carney, James J., "Early Spanish Imperialism," 57, note

Carrión, Pascual, *Los latifundios en España,* 58, note

Carta a S. M. del Licenciado Matienzo, 329, note

Cartagena: 51, 80, 144, 162, 334; British

attack on, 413; importance of, 434-35; plundered by the French, 153

Cartas de religiosos de Nueva España, 1539-94, 249, note

Cartas eruditas y curiosas, 547; *Cartas a los españoles americanos,* 552

Cartesian philosophy in America, 548

Carvalho Franco, Francisco de Assis, *Bandeiras e bandeirantes de São Paulo,* 668, note

Carvalho e Mello, Sebastião de, *see* Pombal, Marquis of

Casa da Guiné, established in Lagos, 31

Casa da India, 31, 156

Casa de Comedias, Mexican theatre, 535

Casa de Contratación: 102, 145, 155, 206, 402, 419, 420, 602-604; abolished (1790), 626; and the Council of Indies, 602-603; as a governing force, 295; duties, 603-604; established, 1503, 155; hereditary offices, 604; location of branches, 158; purposes, 156; regulations on "permitted books," 503-504; structure, 157-59

Casa de Corrales, Peruvian theatre, 535

Casa de Supplicação, 743

Casa dos Escravos, Lisbon slave market, 31

Casa Grande, 702, 704

Casas de escogidas, 176, 177, 244

Cascara, 84

Caspian Sea, map of, 29

Caspicara, *see* Manuel Chile

Cassava (Mandioc *or* manioc), 83, 93, 144

Castañeda, C. E., "The Corregidor in Spanish Colonial Administration," 302, note

Castellanos, Juan de, 521

Castell-dos-Rius, Marquis of, established Lima "Academy," 531

Castello Branco, Francisco, 666

Castile: 57, 93; at the Conquest, 290; Council of, 574; Inquisition, 235; nobility curbed, 291; towns limit royal authority, 285-86

Castilian, first grammar of, 228

Castilian institutions in America, 295

Castilians, 58

Castilla del Oro, 42

Castizo, 208

Castrillo, Count of, 604

Castro, Gabriel de, 111

"Catálogo da Exposição Nassoviana," 661, note

Catalonia, *fueros* of, 290

Catarro, mission of, 473

Cateau-Cambrésis, Peace of, 154

Catherine of Braganza, 661

Catholicism, similarity to Indian religions, 242-46

Cattle, herds in Española, 93, 94

Cauca Valley, explored, 51

Cavendish, Thomas, attacks Brazil, 654

Caviedes, Juan del Valle y, poet, 532

Cayaucachi, 189

Ce Acatl, Aztec year, 241

Cedulario, published by the Council, 527

Cédulas, granting *encomiendas,* 63

Celis, Ignacio de, 349

Cempoala, chief of, 43

Cempoalans: curbed by Cortés, 44; battle of Cholula, 45

Censorship: in Mexico, 562-63; of books, 507-509, 561-66; Church, 507; Crown, 507-508; of ideas, 561-66; of newspapers, 556; of speech and thought in the colonies, 510-13; in Spain, 509, 510

Centeotl, Aztec god, 241

Central America: 13, 26, 50, 56, 65, 74, 83, 86, 117, 144, 522; Conquest, 48-49; discovered, 41; Indian agriculture, 84; missionaries, 579; Negro slaves, 472

Central Valley of Mexico, 47, 85

Centralism versus localism, 304-305

Centralization: desire for, 294-95; growth of, 625-28

Centralized government, 304-305

Certamen, 231

Cervantes, Vicente, Mexican botanist, 550

Ceulen, Paul van, 657

Ceuta, 30

Cevallos, Pedro de, Viceroy, 625

Chachapuyas, 23

Chagres Bay, 410

Chagres River: 144, 153; transport via, 145

Chalchihuites (precious stones), 121

Chamberlain, Robert S., "The Concept of the *Señor Natural,*" 270-71, note

Chanaes Indians, 580

Chancas, 22, 241-42

Chan-Chan (Peru), pre-Inca architecture at, 223

Chandler, C. L.: "River Plate Voyages, 1798-1800," 415, note; "United States Merchant Ships in the Río de la Plata," 415, note

Chané, 171

Chapman, Charles E.: *A History of California,* 579, note; *Republican Hispanic America,* 493, note

Chaquillchaca, 189

Charlemagne, 28

Charles II, of England, 661

Charles VIII, of France, 640

Charles III, of Spain: 611; attempts to curb Church power, 573-75; expels Jesuits from Spain, 586; trade reforms, 423, 432

Charles IV, of Spain, statue of, 538

Charles V, of Spain: 43, 742; and the Council of Indies, 296-97; attitude toward trade, 148-49; benefactor of schools, 229; censorship under, 508; letter to Cortés, 250-51; opposes the *encomienda,* 63-64; policy toward foreigners in America, 150-51; restricts importation of books, 502; wars of, 34, 238

Charlevoix, Pierre François Xavier de, Jesuit historian: *Histoire du Paraguay,* 572, note; *L'Isle Espagnole,* 405, note; on condition of Negroes in Haiti, 472

Charqui, 325

Charrúas, 331, 442

Chaves, Francisco de, 641-42

Chemistry, Lavoisier's *Elements,* translated into Spanish, 550

Cheyney, E. P., *European Background of American History,* 32, note

Chiapas, 49

Chiapenecs, 49

Chichén Itzá (Yucatán), *Mercado* at, 222

Chichimecs, 14, 340

Chile: 13, 18, 21, 55, 83, 86, 98, 118, 134, 163; agriculture, 321-25; the Church, 567-68, 595; conquest and settlement, 54-55, 319-21; *consulado,* 609; Creole officials, 489; education, 500; expansion, 323; furniture manufacturing, 127; guilds, 391-92; "Heresy," 576; Inquisition, 463; Jesuit missions, 581; labor, 463, 479-81; leather industry, 391; livestock, 321, 322; manufacturing difficulties, 392; the Mestizo, 442, 479, 481; mining, 116-19, 321, 369-71; the Negro and mulatto, 373; poetry, 530-31; population, 442, 450; Portuguese contraband trade, 411; property, maldistribution of, 593; racial distribution, 455; religious instruction, 589-90; slaves, 595; struggle for land and resources, 26; tax collections 1700-1808, table, 450; trade, 411, 414-15, 432-33; Valdivia's settlements, 320-21; woolen mills, 391

Chile, Manuel, Indian sculptor, 538

Chiloé, 325

Chimbo, agriculture near, 316

China, 29

Chino, 208

Choco, mining in, 371-73

Chocolate: as a drink, 85; *see also* cacao

Cholitos, 471

Cholula: 46, 71; battle of, 45; beggars in, 200

Christian I, of Denmark, 32

Christianity: difficulties of fitting the discovery into the scheme of, 231; effect on Indian behavior, 255-56

Christianization policy of Cortés, 42

Christians, 32-33, 236

Chronicles: Brazilian, 708-10; of the New World, 230-31, 515-25

Chucuito, commercial importance of, 384

Chunca-Camayu-cuna, 278

Church, The: (*see also* Inquisition); Chapters, 12, 13, 26; a foreign institution, 9; asylum given criminals, 573; attempts to suppress the drama, 535; death duties collected, 592; importance and influence of, 567-69; in America, 9, 82, 269; in Brazil, *see* Chapter 32; in Chile, 567-68; in Spain, 233-35; intellectual influence, 228-29; power, Crown attempts to limit, 574-75; privileges, 485-86; religious instruction, 587-90; in the Reconquest, 33; role in Fine Arts, 514-15; tithes and taxes collected, 391-92; to 1810, see Chapter 26; upholds slavery, 473; wealth, 590-93

Church architecture, 537-38

Church control: of censorship, 507-509; of education, 494-95; of thought, 499-500; of universities, 499

Church courts, conflicts with civil, 572-73

Church lands: 73, 357-59, 364, 590; in Chile, 359; in Mexico (table), 359; in Spain, 233; Jesuit holdings confiscated, 358

Church monopoly of commerce, 595

Church offices, held by Spaniards, 264

Church organization: 256-60; foreign

character, 264-65; in America, 246; royal control of, 569-72

Church personnel, largely Spanish, 569-70

Church seminaries, 597-99

Church-State controversies, 568, 572-75

Church-State relations in Spain, extended to America, 256-57

Churches: built, 248, 254; replaced Indian shrines, 255

Cid, national hero of Spain, 32

Cieza de León, Pedro; *La Crónica del Perú, primera parte,* 17, note; 518-19; *segunda parte,* 519; on the Andean region, 86-87, 90; on colonial government in Peru, 277; on the difficulties of conquering certain regions, 52-53; on emancipation of Indians in Peru, 197; on *encomiendas* in Peru, 79-80; on Inca religion, 239-90; on the Inca road system, 134; on the power of Huayna Capac, 281-82; on Inca system of justice, 283; on the savagery of the Indians, 74-75; on Spanish agriculture in Panama and Colombia, 98; on Spanish justice in America, 310-11; on warfare of the Indians, 17, 25

Cifuentes, Rodrigo de, first American artist, 232, 538

Cihuacoatl (*or* Tonantzin), 241

Cingapacinga, enemies of the Cempoalans, 44

Cisneros, Cardinal, 261

Cities, scarcity of, in the Inca Empire, 181

City-State, the Maya, 271-72

Ciudad Real, 328

Cívecoatl, 241

Civil war: among the Incas, 283; among Indians of Brazil, 635; in America and Europe in 1492, 35; between Christians after the Reconquest, 34; in Peru, 80-81

Class conflict in Portugal, 31

Class, rise of a middle, 427, 489-90

Class society: in the Caribbean, 165-66; in the Inca Empire, 167-71; in Mexico, 166-67; in Peru under the Spaniards, 82; Indian continued by the Spanish, 227

Class structure: see Chapter 22; 171, 490-91

Class warfare, in Mexico, 16-17

Classes: Aztec, 69; hope of the lower to rise in America, 38; Indian, *see*

Chapter 9; legal privileges of the upper, 484-85; participation in the Reconquest, 33-34; privileged, among the Incas, 170-72

Clavigero (*or* Clavijero), Francisco Javier: 524; *History of Mexico*, 14, note

Clement XIV, Pope, 573

Clergy, The: 58; abuse of the Indians, 469-70; abuses of, 266-67; acknowledged Crown authority over patronage, 571; *calpixques* from among, 202-203; candidates for, decline, 570; corruption of, 593-99; courts of, 259; Creoles and Indians, 569-70; education of, 546; emigrate to America, 258; engage in commerce, 268, 595; in Brazil, 733-35; in Chile, 593; in Panama, 267; in Peru, 267; in Spain, 266, 287-89; power and prestige of, 568-69, 574-75; privileges of, 485-86; schools of, 228; secular and regular, 260-61; slaves owned by, 473; teachers from, 499; versus civil authority, 572-75

Cleven, N. Andrew N., *The Political Organization of Bolivia*, 183, note; *Readings in Hispanic American History*, 400, note

Clothing: 143; Andean Indian, 122; Mexican Indian, 120, 121

Clubs, scientific and literary, 552

Coahuila, 100

Cobo, Father Bernabé, 522; compares livestock of Española and Río de la Plata, 330; describes Inca despotism, 282; *Historia del Nuevo Mundo*, 20, note; on the geography of Peru, 182-83; on the Inca land system, 169

Coca, 84, 133

Cochineal, 95, 144, 348

Codices, Maya books, 213-14

Coelho, *see* Albuquerque, Jorge de

Coelho, Gonçalo, Voyage to Brazil, 637

Coffee: in Brazil, 690-92; in Cuba, 353, 437; in Haiti, 338-39; in New Spain, 346; in Venezuela, 339, 346

Coimbra, University of, 707, 715

Coinage, in Brazil, 675

Cointa, Jean, 653, 736

Colden Letters, *Bancroft transcripts*, 414, note

Colección de documentos inéditos . . . de las antiguas posesiones españolas de Ultramar, 60, note

Colección de documentos inéditos relativos al descubrimiento, conquista y organización . . . de Indias, 63, note

Colección de documentos para la historia de España, 75, note

Colección de documentos para la historia de México, 66, note

Colección de libros y documentos referentes a . . . América, 410, note

Colección de memorias de los virreyes que han governado el Perú, 601, note

Colegios, in Brazil, 706-708

Coligny, Gaspar de, 652

Collas, 176

Colmeiro, Manuel: evaluates the Conquest, 55-56; *Historia de la economía política en España*, 56, note; on population in America, 446

Cologne, University of, censors books, 507

Colombia: 13, 17, 42, 51, 53, 56, 74, 83, 334-39, 550; agriculture 98; cannibalism, marriage, and sexual practices, 173-74; conquest, 50-53; fertility and rainfall, 334-35; gold production, 116-17 (table), 372; history, 521; Indian conditions, 465; irrigation, 335; population, 452, 457; scientific publications, 544; temperature variations, 335-36; trade, 435; transport of goods, 398

Coloni, later known as serfs, 33

Colonia del Sacramento, 334, 411, 411-12

Colonia do Sacramento (*or* del Sacramento), 673

Colonists: induced to come to America, 58; types of, 41

Colonos, 646

Coloquios espirituales, drama, 535

Columbus, Bartolomé, 60

Columbus, Christopher: 41, 56, 60, 92; finds war in America, 26; first voyage, 35; friars brought by, 246; gold and spices sought, 142; Indian policy, 60, 142; introduces animals, 37, 92; *Journal* of, 35, note, 230; on gold and silver found, 104-105; title to discovered lands claimed for Spain, 36, 57-58; trade concessions to, 147; urges immigration to America, 58

Columbus, Diego, 294

Comentarios a las Ordenanzas de minería, 529

Comentarios reales de los Incas, 519

Comercio Libre de España a Indias, 423-24

Commerce: *see* trade; contraband

Commercial rivalries, intercolonial, 490

Commission merchants, 155

Commonlands, Aztec, 69

Communion, Indians granted Catholic, 253

Companhia do Brasil, 685-86

Companhia do Maranhão, 686

Companhia de Pernambuco e Paraíba, 687

Companhia Geral do Grão Pará e Maranhão, 686-87

Composiciones, land grants by, 355

Comuneros, in Spain, 306

Concepción (Chile): agriculture and livestock at, 323; dispute over location of, 568

Concha, Andrés de, 539

Concha, Carlos, "The Oldest University in South America," 498, note

Conchuco, mines at, 368

Concubinage, among the clergy, in Peru, 596-97

Confederation, Aztec, 272-75

Confession: Indian insistence on, 252-53; in Indian religions, 244-45

Congrega or Congregación, 72, 190, 196, 197-200, 308, 359, 461

Conquest, The: 61, 70, 73; *see* Chapters 2 and 3; a business venture, 40; continued throughout the colonial period, 10; definition of, 5, 45; effect on the masses, 275; elements involved in, 35; essence of, 55-56; purposes of the Spanish and Portuguese in, 6; religion in, 246-47; unified portions of America more readily subjugated, 52

Conquistador, the: described by Pereyra, 39; in colonial society, 204-206; varied economic status of, 204-205

Consejo, powers of the, 285-86

Conselho da India, 743-44

Conselho Ultramarino, 744

Consulados (merchants' guilds): 157, 159; control over trade, 609; jurisdiction of, 572; purpose of, 609; in Mexico City, Lima and Vera Cruz, 608-609; Sevilla-Mexico-Lima, 419

Contador, 157

Conto, value of, 639 note

Contraband: 151-54, 161, 387, 400, 416, 419, 440, 489-90; Alcedo y Herrera

on, 409-10; causes decline in Spanish trade, 409-10; favored by site of Montevideo, 427; Dutch, 403-404; English, 404-405, 408; French, 405-408; in cocoa, textiles and tobacco, 403; in New Granada, 433; methods, 412; Portuguese, 410-12; slave trade, 154-55, 403; Spanish opposition to, 406-407; spurred by European wars, 433

Contrato social y Bororquia, forbidden, 562

Convents: in Brazil, 732-35; Inca, 244; *see Casas de escogidas*

Conversion of the Indians: Acosta's explanation, 250; facilitated by their character, 251-53

Conversos, 236

Convoys: to Brazil, 688; used against pirates, 161-62

Copernicus, 547

Copper: 118-19; mining in Chile, 370-71; money, in Brazil, 675

Coquimbo, agriculture of, 323

Corbeled arch: use by the Incas, 224; use by the Mayas, 222

Corbett, Duvan C., "Mercedes and Realengos . . . in Cuba," 365, note

Córdoba (Argentina): founded, 329; livestock trade with Potosí, 384; University of, 501

Coricancha, Temple of, 239-40

Corn, yield related to population, 186-87

Coroneis, 750

Corregidor, The: 310; abuses by, 620-21; curbs on, 621; duties, 302-303, 620; *de españoles,* 303; *de Indios,* 194, 197, 303; in Brazil, 644; in Spain and America, compared, 302-303; powers, 289, 291

Corregimiento, 194, 197, 619-21

Correo mayor, 157, 421

Corte-Real, João Vaz, 32

Cortés, Hernando: 5, 26, 55, 63, 64, 67, 73, 74, 92; aided by the Tlaxcalans, 43; arbitrates Indian conflicts, 47; arrests Montezuma's tax-gatherers, 44; authority of, 294; buys from Spain, 143; defeats Narváez, 46; describes march to Central America, 49; describes Tenochtitlán, 70-71; destroys his fleet, 42; encomienda of, 66; fights Indians at Cholula, 45-46; *Five Letters,* 64, note; founds Vera Cruz, 42; frees the Chiapaneca slaves, 49; instructed on *encomiendas*, 64; introduces sugar into Mexico, 41; introduces silk into Mexico, 124; on beggars in Cholula, 200; on the *encomienda* in Mexico, 64; on markets in Mexico, 130; on the role of the cross, 247; position on clerical morality, 266; preaches Catholicism, 44; rebuilds Tenochtitlán, 71; retakes Tenochtitlán, 47, 53; ships attacked near Azores, 153; wife of, 205

Cortés, Marín, claims he introduced silk into Mexico, 124

Cortés, Martín, revolt of, 304

Cortes, the Spanish, 286

Cortesão, Jaime, "A expedicão de Cabral," 634, note

Coruña, *casa* established at, 158

Corzo y Lleca, Juan and Carlos, 111

Cosa, Juan de la, makes map of Brazil, 654

Cotton: 83, 84, 95; Brazilian exports, 690-92; culture in Jamaica, 92-93; in Cape Verde Islands, 31; Indian manufacture of, 120, 121, 122

Cotton textiles: in Ecuador, 316; in New Spain, 346; in Peru, 318; in Venezuela and the Caribbean, 336

Council of Indies: 295-97, 300, 401, 409, 411, 527; authority over the Church, 570; duties of, 297; licensing of books by, 504; made America subject to the Crown, 295-96; membership, 296; organization, 601-602; policy-making powers of, 296-97; powers withdrawn, 625

Council of War, 608

Courts: Aztec, 273; conflicts between Church and civil, 572-73; of justice, 303; Indian, 309; privileged, 608-609

Cozumel, Cross at, 244

Crafts: in the Andes, 121-23; in Mexico, 120-21; Indian, 120-24; summary, 141

Credit, granted Portugal and Brazil by English merchants, 687

Creoles: admitted to Church Orders, 265; as archbishops, 489; limited number in office, 488; position in society, 482-83; rivalry with Spaniards, 486-89

Criminals, harbored by the Church, 573

Criollos, 209; *see also* Creoles

Croix, Carlos Francisco de, Viceroy, 627

Crónica de don Florisel de Niquea, 504

Crónica del Perú, 519

Cross: banner of the Spaniards in the Conquest, 57; in Indian religion, 244

Crown, the: 60, 64, 81, 289-92, 600-601; attempts to curb Church land-holding, 73; attempts to limit Church power, 574-75; desires to convert the Indians, 251; encroaches on town authority, 289; granted jurisdiction over ecclesiastical matters in America, 257; legislation over Council of Indies, 602; restricts books, 503-504; retains title to land in America, 72; rewards conquistadores with land and Indians, 63; shares spoils of Reconquest with Church, 33; use of the Inquisition, 510

Crusades, stimulated trade in Europe, 29

Cruz, *see* Sor Juana

Cuatro libros de la naturaleza . . . en la Nueva España, 540

Cuauhtémoc, Aztec chieftain, 47

Cuba: 17, 39, 63, 92, 118; agriculture, 350-53, 437-38; *consulados*, 609; *encomiendas*, 63; importance of location, 437; Negro slaves, 353, 474; population, 179, 454, 457; settlement, 41, 50; tobacco trade, 437; trade policy and reform, 436-38

Cuernavaca, 71

Cuerpo de Minería, 609

Cuevas, Mariano, *Historia de la Iglesia en México*, 254, note

Cuiabá, mines of, 678

Culture: anthropological interpretations of, 8-9; contribution of the Spanish colonies to, *see* Chapter 24; diffusion of, *see* Chapters 11 and 23; diversity in various colonies, 550; European background, 226-28; evolution, 10; in Brazil, *see* Chapter 31; in colonial Argentina, 505-506; Indian, Aztec, Mixtec and Toltec, 214; introduction of European into America, 228-32; meaning, 211; mingling of Indian and European, 227; relation of Brazilian class society to, 704-708

Cumaná, settled, 50

Cunha, Aires da, 666

Cunningham, Charles Henry: *The Audiencia in the Spanish Colonies*, 293, note; "The Institutional Background of Spanish American History," 284, note

Curacas: 18, 167; lands of the, 77-78; position in the ruling hierarchy, 278; post-Conquest, 204

Curriculum of Indian schools, 228-29

Customhouse: at Montevideo, 426-27; at Santiago, 433

Customs: Indian, *see* Chapter 9

Customs receipts, an index to trade, 145

Cuzco: 17, 19, 23, 24, 25, 87; designated "first vote" city, 306; education, 217; hub of the road system, 133; Ordinance issued by the *cabildo*, 182; population, 185; pre-Conquest population, 188-89; road to Quito, 135; soldiers mutiny, 81; trade with Potosí, 384

D

Dahlgren, Erick Wilhelm, *Les relations commerciales et maritimes entre la France et les côtes de l'Océan Pacifique*, 406, note

Dairy products, in Chile, 325

Dampier, William: *Dampier's Voyages*, 405; on commerce of Brazil, 689

Dantas, Julio, "*A era manuelina*," 635, note

Darién, 42

Dávalos, Juan Carlos, *Los gauchos*, 442

Dávila, Pedrarias, *see* Pedrarias

Death duties, collected by the Church, 592

De antiquitatibus Novae Hispaniae, work on pre-Conquest medicine, 540

Debt: aristocracy exempted from imprisonment for, 484; slavery of the Indians for, 471-72

Decades de orbe novo, 515

Decimal system, Inca, 220

Degredados, 634, 637, 649

De indiarum jure, 527

Del ejercicio y de sus provechos, medical work, 540

Delgadillo, Diego, silk culture in Mexico, 124

Depons, F.: *A voyage to the eastern part of Terra Firma*, 336, note; on compulsory attendance at mass in Venezuela, 590; on death duties to the Church, 592

Depósito (Inca grain storage center), 91

Desagüe (of Huehuetoca), 461

Descripción corográfica, 525

Descripción e historia del Paraguay y del Río de la Plata, 525

Desdevises du Dezert: "Les institutions de l'Espagne," 291, note; "L'Église espagnole des Indes à la fin du xviiie siècle, 567, note

Desembargador, 741

Desembargo do Paço, 743

Diálogos das Grandezas do Brasil, 662, note; 710

Diamonds, discovery in Brazil, 680

Diario de la Havana, 558

Diario de Lima, 557

Diario de México, 556

Diario literario de México, 555

Diario de navegação, by Pero Lopes de Souza, 708

Diario del Viaje del obispo Marán en 1787, 589

Dias, Malheiro, *see* Malheiro Dias, Carlos

Díaz, Bartholomew, 30

Díaz, Dionís, 30

Díaz del Castillo, Bernal: *A True History of the Conquest of New Spain*, 328, note; on administration of Indian settlements, 308-309; on arbitration of Indian disputes, 47; on the battle of Cholula, 45; on cannibalism in Tlaxcala, 44-45; on Cortés' journey to Central America, 49; on the court of Montezuma, 274-75; on desire of the conquistadores for land and Indians, 64; *Historia de la Nueva España*, 516-17; on Indiana slave trade, 131; on traders' stations in Mexico, 128-29; on treatment of the Indians, 200; on women in New Spain, 205

Díaz de Guzmán, Ruy: *Historia argentina*, 328, note; describes census of Guaraní Indians, 327-28

Díaz de Solís, Juan, expedition to Argentina, 50, 325-26

Diccionario geográfico-histórico de las Indias Occidentales o América, 523

Diente del parnaso y poesías diversas, 532

Diffie, B. W.: "Estimates of Potosí Mineral Production," 115, note; "A Markham Contribution to the *Leyenda Negra*," 182, note

Dios, Juan de, dictator of Oruro, 615

Diplomacy, in Cortés' conquest of Mexico, 43

Disease, effect on population, 448-49

Distance from Europe, difficulties of, 38

Doações, 740

Dobritshofer, Martin, writings of, 525
Doctrineros, 249, 260
Documentos para la historia de Argentina, 415, note
Documentos para la historia del virreinato del Río de la Plata, 421, note
Documentos inéditos o muy raros para la historia de México, 340, note
Documentos referentes al virreinato del Perú, 81, note
"Documentos relativos a Mem de Sá," 653
Documentos sobre o tratado de 1750, 654, note
Dominicans: policy of, in Indian affairs, 195; property of, in Mexico City, 268
Donatário, see Donatary
Donatary, 642-48, 741-42
Don Quixote, 502, 504
Douglas-Irvine, Helen, "The Landholding System of Colonial Chile," 363, note
Drake, Francis, attacks Río de la Hacha and Vera Cruz, 154-55
Drama: 534-36; Aztec, 215-16; Inca, 216; in Mexico and Peru, 535-36; religious origin of, 232; use of religious, 534-35; secular, 535-36
Drunkenness, among the Indians, 174, 203-204
Duarte Coelho, 646
Dulcert, map of Caspian sea, 29
Dutch: prey on Spanish vessels and colonies, 403-404; in Brazil, 657-62, 744-45; trade with America, 403
Dutch East India Company, 658, 685
Dutch sailors refused hospitalization as "heretics," 576
Duties (customs): at Buenos Aires, 429; reform of, 422, 424
Dyes, Inca, 122
Dye wood, Brazilian, 636, 639-41

E

Eannes, Gil, passed Cape Bojador, 30
Earthquakes: A True and Particular Relation of the Dreadful Earthquake, 590, note; Church interpretation of, 494; in the Andean region, 318-19, 324; in Chile, 322
East, European knowledge of the, 29
East India Company, 685
Ecclesiastical boundaries, fixed by the Crown, 258-59
Echave, Baltasar de (el Viejo), painter, 539

Echave, Baltasar de, son of the foregoing, 539
Economic activity, effect on secularism, 543
Economic conditions, in Brazil, 674-77
Economic factors in the Reconquest, 32
Economic progress and mining, 383-85
Economic reform: 421-40; contribution of Campomanes and Bernardo Ward to, 422; reciprocal trade between colonies, 423
Economy: Brazilian commerce, 682-92; characteristics of Brazilian, 681; Latin-American, land factor in, 82
Ecuador: 13, 21, 83, 98, 128, 163, 550; agriculture and livestock, 99-100, 316; criticism, 553; development, 316; missions, 581; population, 452, 457; scientific expeditions, 543; sugar mills, 316; tanning, 127; textile industry, 390; woolen industry at Quito, 390-91
Education: changes in, 546-49; Church control of, 495, 704-708; Crown aid to, 495; development of, see Chapter 23; for the few, 493-95; functions of, 497; hierarchical concept of, 509; improvement after 1750, 501; in Brazil, 703-708; in Chile, 500; in Mexico, 500; Inca, a barrier between classes, 218; Indian, 217-18; Jesuit schools, 583; limitations of, 496-97; missionaries, 248-50; policy of, 494; religious, 228-29; science in, 549-51; university, 498-501
Eguiara y Eguren, Juan José de, Sor Juana Inés de la Cruz, 534, note
Egypt, Sultan of, appealed to by the Moors, 237
Ehinger firm, alliance with the Welsers, 148
Ejido, 72, 360
El Arauco domado, epic poem of Chile, 530
El Dorado, 665-66, 674
Elegías de varones ilustres de Indias, 521
Elhuyar, Fausto, mining authority, 381-382
Ellis Junior, Alfredo: A evolução da econômia paulista, 646, note; O bandeirismo paulista, 668, note
El peregrino indiano, epic poem, 533
El Retrato de Golilla, satire, 558
El Rodrigo, drama, 535
Elzora y Rada, Francisco de, Narrative

of the Conquest of the Province of the Itzas, 579, note

Emancipation: of Indians, 196-97; of slaves, 474

Emboabas, 678

Emigrants, point of origin in Spain, 148, note

Emigration from Europe encouraged, 148-49

Empresario, 40-41, 72

Encinas, Diego de, 527

Encomenderos, see encomienda

Encomienda, 58, 190, 193, 271, 425, 618-19; abolished, 355; authority over the Indians, 65, 308; contrary to Crown monopoly, 67; definition, 59; chapels established by, 251; efforts to reform, 63, 304; encroachment on towns, 360-61; granted military orders, 59; in America, 59-63; in Chile, 356-57; in Peru, 79-80; in Yucatán and Tabasco, 356; in local government, 307-308; legalized, 191; persistence of, 354; resistance of the Indians to, 74; size an index to population, 184; tribute rights of, 618; under the New Laws, 80-81, 195, 304

Encyclopédie, forbidden, 561

England: allied with Portugal, 30; enmity toward Spain, 154; contraband trade of, 408, 412; French competition with, 408-10; interest in Brazil, 652-54, 683; Navigation Acts of, 66; trade with America, 404-405, 411; treaty with Spain, 404-405

English, the: occupy the Bahamas and Jamaica, 404; rights of, in Portugal and Brazil, 687

English South Sea Company, 408, 409

Enlightenment, The: 543; fought by the Inquisition, 561-66

Ercilla y Zúñiga, Alfonso de, epic poet, 530

Español, 208

Española: 17, 35, 39, 60, 62; *audiencia* authorizes branding slaves, 63-64; bishoprics, 246; *cabildo* set up by Columbus, 293; cattle, 93, 94; distribution of Indians, 62; population in 1502, 40; slave revolts, 472; towns settled, 41

Espejo, Francisco Xavier, satires of, 553; journalist, 558-59

Espejo de Príncipes y Cavalleros, 504

Espineira, Angel de, Bishop, 568

Espírito Santo: 647; Cabral's discovery of, 633

Esquilache, Viceroy, patron of the drama, 535

Estancias, formation of, in Río de la Plata, 443-44

Estates, *see estancias, encomienda, hacienda, latifundios, ranchos*

Estrada, Alonzo de, marries his daughters in America, 205

Estrada, José Manuel, *Lecciones sobre la historia de la república Argentina,* 285, note

Ethiopia, 32

Europe: 45, 55, 86; contributions to American life, 226-27; culture introduced into America, 228-32; influence on secular thought, 542-46; plants and animals brought to America, 5

European background of Latin-American culture, 226-28

Europeans: 52, 56, 441; enter America, *see* Chapter 3; held high offices, 488; in New Spain, position of, 481-84, 486-87

Evangelio en triunfo, religious poem, 533

Exchange, monetary, 400

Excusados, form of taxes, 592

Expansion of Latin-America to 1810, *see* Chapters 16 and 17

Exploration, Portuguese, 30

Export facilities from Pacific Coast to Spain, 145

Exports: agricultural and mineral compared, 439-40; Brazilian, value of, 690-92; from America to Spain and Peru, 95; to the Indies, 143

Extremadura, 58

F

Falkner, Thomas: *A Description of Patagonia,* 330, note; on Argentina cattle, 330; writings of, 525

Familiars of the Inquisition, 737-38

Farfán, Augustín, medical writings of, 540

Farm and ranch, *see* Chapter 5

Farming among Andean Indians, 87-92

Fasting, Aztec belief in, 245-46

Feather work, 121

Feathers, trade in, 31, 95

Federmann, Nikolaus, representative of the Welsers in Colombia, 51

Feijóo, Fray Benito Jerónimo, writings of, 547-48

Feitoria, in Portuguese Africa and Brazil, 636-37, 640-41

Ferdinand, dispute with Pope Julius 11, 246-57

Ferdinand and Isabella: 510; Columbus statement of land claims, 57-58; curb municipal authority, 291; state policy, 235; union of Castile and Aragon under, 291

Ferdinand VI, reformed the intendancy system, 626

Fernandes Coutinho, Vasco, 647

Fernandes Sardinha, Pero, 718

Fernandes da Silva, Joaquín, Portuguese firm in Montevideo, 425

Fernández de Lugo, Pedro, 51

Fernández de Oviedo, see Oviedo

Fernández de Piedrahita, Lucas, 521

Fernández de Santillán, Felipe, Relaciones . . . de Potosí, 367, note

Fernández de Velasco, Pedro, improved patio process, 111

Fernández del Castillo, Francisco, on books in New Spain, 513

Fernão I, of Portugal, 30

Ferrelo, reaches Oregon, 341

Ferrer, Buenaventura P., publisher of the Regañón, 558

Ferrer, Joaquín María de, merchant, 425

Ferrer del Río, Historia del Reinado de Carlos III, 412, note

Fertilizer: scarce in Mexico, 84; used by Andean Indians, 87-92

Feudal system, in America, 294

Feudalism, political function in Europe, 28

Fidalgos, 645

Fiel-ejecutor, 617

Figueiredo, Caetano de Brito, 714

Figueredo, Fidelino de, "The Geographical Discoveries . . . of the Portuguese," 634, note

Fillipéa, settled, 666

Financial crises in Europe, 409

Fine arts, summary, 541

Fish trade, Church monopoly of, 595

Fisher, Lillian E.: The Background of the Revolution for Mexican Independence, 396, note; "Manuel Abad y Quiepo, Bishop of Michoacán," 485, note; Viceregal Administration in the Spanish American Colonies, 291,

note; "The Intendant System in Spanish America," 628, note

Fishing, 83

Flanders, merchandise sent from Liston, 31

Fleets, sail from Spain at fixed dates, 163

Fleiuss, Max, História Administrativa do Brasil, 739, note

Flora de Bogotá, 550

Florida, 50

Florida (Uruguay), 334

Floridablanca, Count of, 510

Flour, 93, 143

Fonseca, Bishop, 295

Food: chronic lack of, 6, 20, note, 38, 51; in Brazil, 691-92; processed, 127

Foraes, 740

Foral, 644-45

Foreign Commerce Year Book, 184, note

Foreigners in the colonies, 149-50

Foros, 645

Fort y Roldán, Nicholás, Cuba indígena, 165, note

Foundations of Latin-American Culture, see Chapter 11

Fox, John S., The Beginnings of Spanish Mining in America, 105, note

France, 28

Francis I: alliance with the Turks, 149; declares the Indians "inferior," 193; preys on Spanish ships and colonies, 153; war with Charles V, 238

Franciscans: 228, 248; defy State authority, 574-75; in Northern Brazil, 667; in Río de la Plata, 580

Franco, Tomás, 561

Franklin, Benjamin, 544

Frederic II, Mohammedan army of, 234

Free Trade Act: 423-24; effect in Buenos Aires, 427; effect in Chile, 432

Freight rates, regulation of, 163-64

Freitas, Jordão de, "A expedição de Martim Afonso de Souza," 641, note

French, the: attack Yucatán, 154; colonize in America, 405; in Brazil, 640-41, 652-53, 666; rival British in America, 406, 408-10; sell goods in America, 407-408

French Mississippi Company, 408-409

French Revolution: 544-45; influence condemned, 546, 562

French stock companies, 406

French trade: 405, 407-408; hurt by Napoleonic Wars, 414

French West India Company, 405

Freyre, Gilberto, *Casa-Grande e Senzala*, 694, note
Frezier, Amadée François: *A Voyage to the South Sea*, 323, note; describes Chilean wheat exports in 1712, 323
Friederici, Georg, *Die Schiffahrt der Indianer*, 398, note
Fruit: 99, 100; production in Chile, 324; in Río de la Plata, 333
Fuentes y Guzmán, Francisco Antonio de, 522
Fuero eclesiástico, 259
Fueros in Spain, 285, 290
Fugger, Jacob, secured trade privileges in spices, 148
Fundo legal, 73
Funes, Deán Gregorio, 501
Furlong Cardiff, Guillermo, "Las bibliotecas coloniales en el Río de la Plata," 493, note
Furniture making, 126-127

G
Gaceta de México y noticias de Nueva España, 554-55
Gage, Thomas, *A New Survey of the West Indies*, 137, note
Gajes, 168
Galíndez de Carvajal, Lorenzo, Postmaster General, 421
Gálvez, José de: Minister of Indies, 627; promotes meat industry in Argentina and Uruguay, 332; studies reforms in New Spain, 626-27; *visitador*, 610
Gálvez, Viceroy Matías, on newspapers, 555-56
Gama, José Basilio da, *Uraguay*, 712-13
Gama, Vasco da: 156, 637; voyage to India, 31, 230-31
Gamboa, Francisco Javier de, legal writings of, 528-29
Gamboa, Sarmiento de: 527; *Historia Índica*, 24, note
Gann, Thomas, *Maya Cities*, 213, note
Gante, Pedro de: on the work of the missionaries, 249-50; school of, 228, 495, 496
Garay, Francisco de, governor of Jamaica, 92
Garay, Juan de, resettled Buenos Aires, 329
Garcés, Enrique, 111
Garcés, Francisco, Franciscan missionary, 579
García, Genaro, ed., *Documentos inéditos ... para la historia de México*, 340, note
García y García, José Antonio, *Relaciones de los Virreyes del Nuevo Reino de Granada*, 433, note
García del Río, quoted in Javier Pardo, *Estado social del Perú*, 501, note
Garcilaso de la Vega, El Inca: *Los comentarios reales de los Incas*, 20, note; 242, 505, 519-20; attributes inventions of preceding civilizations to the Incas, 87; on class consciousness among the Incas, 88; on *guano* deposits, 88-89; on the Inca administrative system, 276; on Inca architecture, 223-24; on Inca education, 217; on Inca granaries, 91; on the Inca irrigation system, 88; on Inca medical practices, 221-22; on the Inca tribute system, 79, 278, 279; on the land system and the masses, 76; on the landless class in Peru, 81; on the lands of the Curacas, 78; on the lands of the Incas, 77; on the lands of the *Mitimaes*, 20-21; on the population of Cuzco, 189
Garden, Alexander, Botanist, 544
Garlic, 93
Gaucho, 442, 443, 444
Gazeta de Goathemala, 554
Gazeta de Guatemala, 556-57
Gazeta de Lima, 557
Gazeta de literatura de México, 555
Gazeta de México, compendio de noticias de Nueva España, 555
Gazette, in Brazil, 708
Gazette of the United States and Daily Advertiser, 414, note
Genoese colony in Lisbon, 14th century, 30-31
Geography: as treated in this book, 3; influence of, 85-87
Germany, 28, 34
Gil y Taboada, Viceroy, encouraged the *Mercurio*, 558
Giraldes, Lucas, 650
Girard, Albert, *Le Commerce francais à Séville et Cadix au temps des Habsbourgs*, 146, note
Giron, Hernández, rebellion of, 81
Glass manufacture, 127
Gobernación espiritual y temporal de las Indias, 61
Goebel, Dorothy Burne, "British Trade to the Spanish Colonies," 414, note

Goiaz, captaincy of: 679; mines of, 678-79

Goitre, Dr. Barton's work on, translated, 544

Gold: 31; economic influence of, 675; from mining and plunder, compared, 107; in the Antilles, 1501-1519, table, 106; in Brazil, 674, 679-81; in Chile, 369, 370; in Española 106; in Minas Gerais, 677-78; in New Granada, 371-73; in Peru, 368; in the Sarare River, 679; minted at Bogotá, 373; Spanish interest in, overemphasized, 6, 92; total production, 117-18, 379-83

Gold and silver: annual production of Europe, Northern Asia, and America, 380; crafts in Mexico, 121; in Chile, 321; in Chile and Colombia, 116-17; production, 1533-1560, table, 114; sent to Spain, table, 108, 118

Golden Age of Spanish literature, 228

Goldsmithing, 127

Gómez de Quevedo, Francisco, Spanish satirist, 531

Gómez de Viduarre, P. Felipe, Historia geográfica . . . de Chile, 323, note

Gonçálvez, Antonio, Portuguese explorer, 30

Góngora, Luis de Argote y, father of Gongorism, 531-32

Gonzaga, Thomaz Antonio, Marilia de Dirceu, 713-14

González Dávila, Gil, conquest of Central America, 48, 74; estimates number of Indians baptised in the 17th century, 252

González de Eslava, Fernando, dramatist, 535

González de Nájera, Alonso, Desengaño y reparo de la guerra de Chile, 322, note

González Suárez, Federico, Historia general . . . del Ecuador, 316, note

Government in Brazil: see Chapter 33; the captaincy-general, 741-42; centralization, 740-42; changes, 745-47; concession to Fernão de Noronha, 739; in Portugal, 739-40

Government in Spanish America: see Chapters 14, 15, and 27; Aztec, 272-75; the cabildo, 305-307; the cacicazgo and encomienda, 307-308; centralization, 625-28; colonial system, 294-95, 623-25; difficulties resulting from distance from Spain, 311;

fusion of Indian and Spanish, 9-10, 270-71; Inca, 271, 275-80; Indian villages, 308-11; in Spain, powers of the aristocracy, 286-87; in the Spanish colonies, actual versus theoretical, 270, 304-305, 311-12; local, Mayan, 271-72, 611-12; pre-Conquest 293; Real de Minas, 306-307; Spanish in America, 293-94

Graham, R. B. Cunningham, Pedro de Valdivia, 320, note

Gram, Luis de, 720

Granada, 34, 236-37

Granary, Inca system, 91

Greece, culture of, 227

Greenland, 32

Gregory IX, Inquisition under, 235

Gremios, 303

Grijalva, Juan de, 42

Groot, José Manuel, Historia eclesiástica y civil de Nueva Granada, 572, note

Grose, Clyde L., "The Anglo-Portuguese Marriage of 1662," 683, note

Guadalquivir, 158

Guadalupe: church, 254-55; virgin, 533

Guadalupes, Mexican Secret Society, 552

Guaira (La), 433-34

Gualgayoc, mining in, 368

Guamachuco, mines at, 368

Guanaco, 145

Guanajuato, mine: 71, 112, 117; table of production (1766-1803), 375

Guano, 88-89

Guañines, 160

Guaraní Indians: 13, 271, 327-28, 635; Jesuit missions among, 580

Guatemala: 13, 14; audiencia, 298; captaincy-general, 342; center of Maya culture, 212; conquest of, 48; Gazeta de, 544, 556-57; history, 522; missionaries, 579

Guayaquil: 53; ships built at, 397; trade in cacao, 316

Guayas River, 316

Guedes de Brito, Commander Antonio de, 664

Guevara, Doña Isabel de, 206

Guía política, eclesiástica y militar . . . del Perú, 524

Guianas, The, 13, 144

Guichot, Joaquín, Historia de Andalucía, 58, note

Guilds: Indians not admitted to, 201; merchant in America, 418; powers of, 147

Guill y Gonzaga, governor of Concepción, 568

Guinea, 36

Guipúzcoa, 290

Guipúzcoa (Caracas) Company, 421

Gutiérrez de Rubalcava, José, *Tratado . . . de las Indias Occidentales,* 393, note

Guzmán de Alfarache, 504

H

Hacienda: in Chile, 356-57; legal powers of the, 619

Hackett, C. W., "The Delimitation of Political Jurisdictions in Spanish North America to 1535," 297, note

Haiti, 118; condition of the Negroes in, 472

Hall, Basil, *Extracts from a Journal,* 325, note

Hamilton, Earl J., *American Treasure,* 106, note

Handelmann, Henrique, *História do Brasil,* 654, note

Handicrafts, introduced by the Spaniards, 6

Hanke, Lewis: "Pope Paul III and the American Indians," 194, note; *Handbook of Latin American Studies,* 533, note; *The First Social Experiments in America,* 12, note; "Dos Palabras on Antonio de Ulloa and the Noticias Secretas," 467, note

Hanseatic League, 147

Haravecs, 217

d'Harcourt, Raoul and Marie, *La musique des Incas et ses survivances,* 536, note

Haring, Clarence H.: *Trade and Navigation between Spain and the Indies,* 103, note; "American Gold and Silver," 107, note; "Ledgers of the Royal Treasurers," 367, note; "The Genesis of Royal Government," 295, note

Hat manufacturing in New Spain, 126

Hatos de Ganado, 347

Havana: 128; captured by Jacques Sore, 153-4; Company, 421; newspapers, 558; population, 454; settled, 41

Hawaii, population estimates of, 179

Hawkins, John, 154

Hawkins, William, in Brazil, 154, 653

Hawks, Henry, 126

Henao, J. M. and Arrubla, G., *Historia de Colombia,* 51, note

Henriade, La, forbidden, 561

Henrique, Cardinal, 736, 742

Henry VIII, of England, censorship under, 508

Henry II, of France, 652

Henry the Navigator, 29-31

Herbs, Inca knowledge of, 221-22

Herds of the Inca and the Huacas, 77

Heredades, defined, 69

Heredia, Pedro de, acquires gold in Colombia, 116

Heresy, 575, 576

Hermandades: 289; as instruments of royal power, 291

Hernández, Francisco, sent to Mexico to study medicinal plants, 540

Hernández de Córdova, Francisco, 42, 48, 49

Hernández de Oviedo, Gonzalo, *see* Oviedo

Herrera, Juan *(El Divino),* painter, 539

Herrera y Tordesillas, Antonio de: 521-22; *Descripción de las Islas y Tierra Firme del Mar Océano,* 57, note; *Historia general de los hechos de los castellanos,* 61, note; on the origin of encomiendas in America, 60-61

Hewett, E. L.: *Ancient Life in Mexico and Central America,* 211, note; *Ancient Life in the American Southwest,* 211, note; *Ancient Andean Life,* 211, note

Heyn, Piet, 404

Hidalgos: 85, 168; rights of, 287

Hides: Brazilian exports, 690-92; exports from the Caribbean to Spain, 94; horses killed for, 40; in Chile, 322, 323, 325, 432; in Río de la Plata, 332-33; shipments from Buenos Aires, 428

Hierarchy: in the Aztec religion, 242-43; in the Inca religion, 243-44

Historia apologética de las Indias, 518

Historia de Guatemala, 522

Historia de la conquista del Paraguay, Río de la Plata y Tucumán, 525

Historia de la conquista y población de la provincia de Venezuela, 524

Historia de la provincia de San Vicente de Chyapa y Guatemala, 522

Historia de las Indias y conquista de México, 516

Historia de los Mexicanos por sus pinturas, 214
Historia de Nuevo León, 340
Historia de Santa Marta y nuevo reino de Granada, 521
Historia de Venezuela, 521
Historia del Nuevo Mundo, 522
Historia general de las conquistas del nuevo reyno de Granada, 521
Historia general de las cosas de Nueva España, 520
Historia general de los hechos de los castellanos en las islas y Tierra Firme del Mar Océano, 521-22
Historia general del reyno de Chile, 522
Historia general y natural de las Indias, 517
Historia índica, 520
Historia medicinal de las cosas que se traen de nuestras Indias Occidentales que sirven de medicina, 540
Historia natural y moral de las Indias, 520
Historia verdadera de la conquista de la Nueva España, 516
Historians: early, 515-22; contrasted with later, 522-23
Histórica Relación del reino de Chile, 364, note, 522
History of Latin America, theme of, 4
Hoehne, F. C., *Botanica e agricultura no Brasil no seculo XVI*, 639, note
Hoja volante, 553-54
Holland, trade rivalry with the Portuguese, 684-85
Holmes, Vera B., "La Expedición del aventurero Norte-Americano Jeremiah Terry a Nicaragua en el siglo XVIII," 410, note
Holy Days: Aztec, 245-46; Inca, 171
Homens-hons, 644
Honduras: 42, center of Maya culture, 212
Honduras Company, 421
Horses: licensing of import, 161; place in the Conquest, 39
House of the Virgins of the Sun, 244
Houses, Inca, 169-70
Huacas: herds of the, 77; Inca gods, 241
Huanacauri, shrine of, 239-40
Huancavelica (Peru), mercury mines in, 111, 377-78, 384
Huancavillcas, reconquered by the Incas, 23
Huánuco, products of, 99

Huarochiri mountains, 134
Huáscar: 23, 53-54; wars of, 283
Huayna Capac: 22-23; builds road to Quito, 135; despotism of, 281-82
Huguenots, in Brazil, 652
Huitzilopochtli: Aztec god of war, 241; communion service in honor of, 245; sacrifices to, 15
Human sacrifice: in Mexico, 15; in Peru, 175, 281
Humanitarianism and the Indians, 192-94
Humboldt, Alexander de: *Essai politique*, 107, note; *New Spain*, 107, note; *Travels*, 335, note; and Bonpland, Aimé, expedition of, 543; and El-huyar, 381-82; contrasts journalism in North and South America, 560; on the barbarous Indians of Mexico, 340; on the Caribbean region, 335, 337; on Church lands in Mexico, 358; on the condition of Negroes, 473; on cynicism toward the clergy in 1800, 594-95; on financing of commerce in New Spain, 346-47; on Fine Arts, 539-40; on fortunes in Venezuela and Cuba, 364; on "free" labor, 476; on Indian labor in Mexico, 461; on Indian treasure, 107-108; on lack of animals in America, 136-37; on livestock in New Spain, 347; on mercury distribution, 379; on the missions, 581-82; on ownership of land, 591; on population, 447-48, 451-52, 454, 455-56; on the relation of mining and agriculture, 342; on religious instruction in Mexico, 588; on science in New Spain, 550-51; on shipping routes, 430; on slaves in Cuba, 474; on sugar in Cuba, 353; on the viceroy, 606-607; works in the School of Mines in Mexico, 382
Humboldt Current, 87
Humphreys, R. A., ed., *British Consular Reports*, 428, note
Hunting, 83
Hurtado de Mendoza, Andrés, Viceroy of Peru, redistributes *encomiendas*, 81
Hussey, Roland D.: "The Antecedents of the Spanish Monopolistic Overseas Trading Companies (1624-1728)," 420, note; "Colonial Economic Life," 106, note; *The Caracas Company, 1728-1774*, 142, note; *Latin America and the Enlightenment*, 545, note; "Spanish Colonial Trails in Panama."

429, note; "Spanish Reaction to Foreign Aggression in the Caribbean to about 1680," 152, note; "Text of the **Laws of Burgos (1512-1513)** concerning the Treatment of the Indians," 63, note

I

Ibarra, Francisco de, founds Nueva Vizcaya, 341

Ibarra, José María, 539

Ica, sugar production in, 99

Icaza, Francisco A. de, *Conquistadores y pobladores de Nueva España*, 65, note

Idols, Indian, destroyed, 249-50, 254-55

Iglesia, Ramón, "Two Articles on the Same Topic," 516, note

Ilhéus, 647

Illiteracy in America, 228, 493-97

Immigration, 147-150

Imports, restricted by high prices of European goods, 123

Inca, The: 280-81; lands of, 77-78; power of, 175, 281; representative of God on earth, 280

Inca Empire: 26, 44, 53, 88; building of, 17-19; character, 53-54; decay, 283-84; extent, 21-22; rebellions in, 283; territorial divisions, 18

Inca Roca, 217-18

Inca Sinchi Roca, 19

Incas: *see* Atahualpa, Garcilaso de la Vega, Huáscar, Huayna Capac, Manco Capac

Incas, The: administrative system, 19, 275-78; agriculture, 91-92; architecture, 223-24; attitude toward virginity, 176; baptism, 246; calendar, 219; civil wars, 18, 22-26; civilization, 87; compared with Brazilian Indians, 635; condition of the masses, 168-70; confederations, 275-76; convents, 244; cross in religion, 246; decimal system, 220; despotism, 21-22, 175, 275; duties of the *mitimaes*, 20-21; education, 217-18; food system, 319; gods, 241; granary system, 21, 91; holy days, 246; irrigation system, 219; justice, 281-83; lack of a literature, 216; land measurements, 219; land system, 75-78, 168-69; markets, 133; medicine, 220-21; oppression of others, 17; priesthood, 243-44; privileged classes, 170-72; prostitute class, 177-

78; *Quipu*, counting system, 219-20; relief maps, 219; religion, 239-46; taxation system, 278-80; transplanting of populations, 22; tribute, 78-79, 168-69; treasure, 107; Virgins of the Sun, 244

Independence, Wars of, 315

Indian towns: instructions for laying-out, 309; laws governing, 72-73, 308-11; population of, 309-10; Sipe-Sipe, 309 10

Indians: 52, 53, 441; abuse of, 192-93, 202, 310, 469-70, 471; agriculture, 84-85; Andean, 87-92, 465; aptitude at trades, 200-201; aristocracy, 68-69, 227; arts and crafts, 222-26; baptism, 249, 252; behavior affected by Christianity, 255-56; branding of, 460; Brazilian, 634-35; 693-96; 720-24; *see* Brazilian Indians; cannibalism, 172-74; census of the Guaranís, 327-28; character, 251-53, 462, 477; Charrúas, 331; civilized by missionaries, 582; classes, customs, and populations, *see* Chapter 9; colonial government of, 270-71; condition of the masses, 200-203; 464-65, 467; conflicts with the missionaries, 580; conversion, 48, 237, 250, 252-253; courts, 462-63; Crown policy (Spanish), 61, 190-92, 197; (Portuguese), 726-27; culture, 2, 3, 7, 8; disease and drunkenness, 7, 174, 175, 203-204; distribution in encomiendas, 60, 62, 64, 74-75; education, 217-18, 249, 496; emancipation, 196-97; enslavement, 463-64, 471-72, 669-73; *gaucho* and *vaquero*, 442; government, 271, 284, 309; groups, division into, 194; Guaranís, 13, 271, 327, 635; histories, 231; in Chile, 357; in Colombia, 465; in Mexico, 340, 445-46, 464; in New Spain, 453, 456, 464; in Venezuela, 465; in land-holding towns, 359; incest and polygamy among, 173-77; Jesuit efforts to control, 724-32; Jesuit expulsion, effect of, 586-87; *Juzgado de Indios,* 301; knowledge of precious metals, 104-106; land system, Mexican, 68-71; languages, books in, study and teaching of, 425-26, 231, 526; lay brothers in the Church, 264-65; literature, 215-16; music, 536; Nahuas, 13, 14, 16; *New Laws,* 194-96; of estates and *obrajes,*

467-69; origin, 12-13; population, 442-45, 457; position in society, 460-62; principal groups listed, 13; prosperity of certain, 201-202, 395; prostitution among, 177-78; religions, 238-46, 587-90; revolts against the Spaniards, 46, 470-71; science, 218-222; segregation, 389; sex practices, 7-8, 172, 173-74; society, defects of, 7, 13-14; theoretical inferiority of, 193; used as porters, 203; used to dig Mexican canal, 461; Vieira's attitude toward, 729-32

Indies: Laws of the, 527, 610-11; Council of, see Council of Indies; Minister of, 626

Indigo: 144; competition with Asian, 339; exports from Venezuela and Guatemala, 339, 347

Indios: encomendados, 461; herrados, 460; de rescate, 192

Influencia del clima sobre los seres humanos, 552

"Informação sobre as minas do Brasil," 677, note

Ingenio (sugar mill), 353, 354

Ingenieros, José, La evolución de las ideas argentinas, 493, note

Innocent III, Pope, Inquisition of, 235

Inquilinos, in Chile, 356-57

Inquisition, The: against editors in Guatemala, 556-57; against heretics, 510; against Jews, 577, 685-86; against liberalism, 563-66; against Protestants, 577; censorship by, 507, 508; condemns Copernican theory, 547; Familiars of, 737-38; In America, 261-64; in Bogotá and Cartagena, 547; in Brazil, 735-38; in Mexico, 562-63; in Mexico City, Lima and Cartagena, 511; origin in Spain, 235; people persecuted by, 575; prohibitions on books, 545, 561-63, 576; Tribunal of, 576; under Gregory IX and Innocent III, 235

Inquisitorial powers in America, 261-62

Instrucciones que los Virreyes de Nueva España dejaron, 383, note

Intellectual development of Spain, 510

Intellectual tendencies of the colonial period, 551-53

Intellectuals persecuted, 543, 547

Intendancies, 625-28

Intendants, functions and selection of, 627-28

Intercolonial trade, 126, 140-41, 143, 144, 392

Inti, Inca god of the sun, 241

Intolerance bred by the Reconquest, 34

Irala, Domingo de: 327; of Asunción, 330; takes census of the Indians, 327-28

Iron foundries, 127

Irrigation: Inca, 87-92; in Mexico, 84

Isabel, founded, 37

Isabella: see Ferdinand and Isabella

Isthmus route, 429

Italian influence on American poetry, 531

Italian Renaissance, 227-28

Itamarra, Francisco de, 341

Itzas, 579

Ivory, trade in, 31

J

Jaboatão, Frei Antonio de Santa Maria, Chronica dos frades menores da Provincia de Santo Antonio do Brasil, 663, note

Jacques, Christóvão, 640

Jamaica: agriculture, 92-93; center of pirate trade, 404, 405; encomiendas, 63; English occupation, 404, 675; opposes North American trade with the Caribbean, 413; sugar, 41, 675

Jaramilla, Juan, 67

Jáurequi, Viceroy, 546

Jeronimite Friars, 63

Jesuit missions, 341, 579, 580-81

Jesuits: 580-81, 583-86, 667, 670-73, 720-24, 742; attitude toward the Indians, 724-32; expulsion, 499, 549, 552, 553, 586-87, 728-29, 732; fanaticism, 584

Jewelry, Aztec and Mayan, 120-121

Jews: despoiled by Christians, 34; emigration to America, 150, 638; expulsion, 236-37; forced to invest in the Companhia do Brasil, 685; persecution, 235-36, 577

Jicalango, 144

Jiménez de Cisneros, Cardinal, conversion of the Moors, 237

Jiménez de Quesada, Gonzalo, 51, 74, 521

João I of Portugal, 30

João III, 642, 648, 736

João IV: 659; forms Companhia do Brasil, 685-86

João VI, transfers court to Brazil, 684

John II of Castile, 235

Johnson, Frederick, "The Linguistic Map

of Mexico and Central America,"
212, note
Johnson, G. R., and Platt, R. R., *Peru from the Air*, 87, note
Joint-stock companies in Europe, 408-09
Jones, Cecil Knight, "The Transmission and Diffusion of Culture in the Spanish American Colonies," 526, note
Jones, Chester Lloyd, *Guatemala: Past and Present*, 49, note
Journal of Columbus, 35, note
Journalism: in America, 553-61; censorship of, 556-57; Humboldt's estimate of, 560
Jovellanos, 510
Juan y Santacilia Jorge, 466-67, 470-71, 475, 524
Juan, Jorge, and Ulloa, Antonio de, *Noticias secretas de América*, 466, note; expedition to America, 543; on Indian lands in Ecuador and Peru, 361; on religious instruction of the Indians, 587-88; *Voyage to South America*, 524
Juárez, José and Luis, Mexican painters, 539
Júbilos da América, 714
"Judaism," accusations of, 512
Jujuy (or Jujuí), 329, 384
Junquiera, 290
Junta do Comercio, 686
Juntas de Justiça, 746
Justice, Inca system of, 281-83
Juzgado de Indios, 159, 301, 462-65

K

Kempton, J. H., "Maize—Our Heritage from the Indian," 186, note
King of Spain, 72-73, 600-601, see also Crown
Kino, Father Eusebio, Jesuit missionary, 341, 342, 578
Kinship government, 271
Kirkpatrick, F. A.: "Repartimiento-Encomienda," 61, note; *The Spanish Conquistadores*, 325, note
Klein, Julius, *The Mesta*, 59, note
Knights of St. John of Jerusalem, 288
Knights Templars, 288
Kroeber, A. L., "Conclusions: The Present Status of Americanistic Problems," 227, note

L

Labor: condition of free, 475-77; forced, in mines, 476; pre-Conquest, 198; in America and Europe, compared, 477; in Brazil, Indian, 693-96; Negro, 696-99; in the Spanish Colonies, 477-81; Inca system of, 169, 279; scarcity of, 191-92; skilled, 476
La Burburata, 153
La Condamine Charles-Marie de, expedition of, 543
La Cristiada, religious poem, 530-31
Lafuente, Modesto, *Historia general de España*, 34, note
La Gasca, Pedro de, 81
Lagos Company, 31
La Grandeza Mexicana, 530
Laguna de Términos, 144
Lagunas, Bravo de, *Voto consultivo*, 317, note
La Navidad, 36, 37
Lancac allpa, 224
Land: allotment of, 64, 72, 73-74; Church, 73, 267-68, 357-59; concentration, in the Spanish colonies, 361-65; control in Mexico, 63-71; grants to encourage emigration, 148-49
Landholding towns, 71-73, 359, 360-61
Land ownership: among the Incas, 75, 78; struggle for, see Chapters 2, 3, and 4
Land system: Aztec and Spanish, 65-68; Inca, 75-78; colonial in Peru, 79-82; Spanish and Indian, 57; origins, Indian, 68-71, Spanish, 58-59; tenure, by towns, 359-61; uncultivated in Mexico, 96-98
Landa, Diego de: *Relación de las cosas de Yucatán*, 173, note; on Maya baptism, 244
Languages: European, 226; Indian, 212-15, 231, 525-26
Lanning, John Tate: *Academic Culture in the Spanish Colonies*, 230, note; "Colonial International Relations," 36, note; Mare Clausum and the Theory of Effective Occupation," 36, note; in *Latin America and the Enlightenment*, 545, note
La Paz, 87
La Pérouse, Jean François de, on the degeneracy of the clergy, 597
La primavera indiana, poem, 533

Las Casas, Bartolomé de: 63, 506, 517-18; *Historia de las Indias*, 35, note
Las Casas, Francisco, 48-49, 193
Las paredes oyen, drama of Alarcón, 536
Lasuén, Fermín Francisco de, 579
Latifundio, 59; in Portugal and Brazil, 636, 702-703
Latin America and the Enlightenment, 544, note
Latin American Culture: *see* Chapters 11, 23, 24, 25; European Background of, 226-28
Latin American government: *see* Chapters 14, 15, 27, and 33
Latin American history, plan of approach used, 4
Lavardén, Manuel José de, Argentine literary figure, 553
La Verdad sospechosa, drama of Alarcón, 536
La vida de Santa Rosa, 532
Law: commentaries on, 527-29; literature of, 526-29
Law, John, 409
Laws: governing Indian towns, 72-73; of Brazil, 740, 743-44; of Burgos, 527; of Toro, 610; on books, 502-505; Spanish, written and in practice, 284-85; *see New Laws*
Laws of the Indies, *see Leyes de Indias;* on Crown authority over Church matters, 260; Solórzano Pereira's commentaries on, 527
Lawsuits between towns, 614
Laytano, Dante de, *História da república rio grandense, 1835-1845*, 672, note
Lazarillo de Tormes, 504
Lea, Henry Charles: *History of the Inquisition of Spain*, 507, note; *The Inquisition in the Spanish Dependencies*, 261, note
Lead, 119
Learning and letters: in Brazil, 704-710; in Spanish America, *see* Chapters 23, 24, and 25
Leis Filippinas, 740, 743
Leis Manuelinas, 740
Leite, Duarte: "A exploração do litoral do Brasil na cartografia da primeira decada do século XVI," 634, note; "Os Falsos Precursores de Alvares Cabral," 634, note
Leite, Serafim, *História da Companhia de Jesus no Brasil*, 663, note
Lemos Brito, José Gabriel de, *Pontos de partida para a história económica do Brasil*, 635, note
Leo X, 718
León, Nicolás, *Las castas del México colonial*, 207, note
León, Ponce de, 41, 50
León Gama, Antonio, scientist, 550
León Pinelo, Rodrigo de, *Sumario*, 527
Leonard, Irving A.: "Best Sellers of the Lima Book Trade, 1583," 504, note; *Don Carlos de Sigüenza y Góngora*, 541, note; "Don Pedro de Peralta Barnuevo," 541, note; "Don Quixote and the Book Trade in Lima, 1606," 504, note; "Guzmán de Alfarache in the Lima Book Trade," 504, note; "Los libros en el inventario de bienes de Don Pedro de Peralta de Barnuevo", 541, note; *The Mercurio Volante of Don Carlos de Sigüenza y Góngora*, 554, note; "Notes on Lope de Vega's Works in the Spanish Indies," 505, note; *Pedro de Peralta Barnuevo*, 533, note; *Romances of Chivalry in the Spanish Indies*, 503, note
Lepe, Diego de, explores Brazilian coast, 654
Lerdo de Tejada, Miguel, *Comercio exterior de México*, 401, note
Léry, Jean de, *Histoire d'un voyage fait en la terre du Brésil*, 652, note; 709
Letters of Marque, 151
Levene, Ricardo: "El derecho consuetudinario, 610, note; *Historia de la nación Argentina*, 32, note
Levillier, Roberto, *Antecedentes de la política económica en el Río de la Plata*, 393, note
Leyes de Indias, 526-29, 587, 610-11
Leyes que tenían los indios de la Nueva España, 273, note
Liberalism, fought by the Inquisition, 563-66
Liberty, Spanish conception of, 285-86
Libraries, formation of, 506-507
Libro astronómico, work of Sigüenza, 541
Libro de la visita general del Virrey Don Francisco de Toledo, 1570-75, 309, note
Libros y libreros en el siglo XVI, 513
Licensing system for the colonies, 159-161
Lima: abuse of the Indians around, 470-71; Academy of, 532; Audiencia in, 298; Cathedral of, 538; Church

ownership of land in, 590; founding of, 80; Inquisition at, 262-63, 511, 513, 576; orchards near, 99; population, 452, 455; pre-Conquest, 188; prosperity of, 317; publications in, 557; road from, 134; University at, 230, 498

Lima Fundada, poem, 532

Limpieza de sangre, 150

Linares, Manuel de, tried by the Inquisition, 561

Linares, Viceroy, on the proletariat in Mexico, 477

Line of Demarcation, 746

Linen, 144

Lingua geral, language of the Tupi-Guaraní Indians, 635

Linguas travadas, languages of the Brazilian Indians, 635

Linguistic differences in America, 212

Lisboa, Francisco Antonio (Aleijadinho), 717

Lisbon, 15th century trade center, 30

Literacy in the Spanish colonies, 493-97

Literature: in Brazil, 708-715; dramatic, in the Spanish colonies, 534-36; effect of the Discovery on, 492-93; European, 226; Indian, 215-216; in Spain and the colonies, Chapters 11, 23, 24, 25; legal, 526-29; poetic, 529-34; popular, 553; scientific, 540-41

Livestock: 43, 672-73; in Argentina, 329, 330, 392; in Brazil, 663-65; in Chile, 321-22, 324-25; in Ecuador, 99-100; in Paraguay, 99-100; in New Spain, 347-48; in Uruguay, 331, 332, 394; in Venezuela, 336; multiplication of, 95-96; number estimates, 330; ownership of, 362-63

Lizárraga, Fr. Reginaldo de, *Descripción colonial,* 328, note

Llama, wool from the, 84, 145

Llamamiche, 168

Llamosas, Lorenzo de las, 466

Llanos, livestock in the, 336

Loaysa, Jerónimo, Archbishop, Inquisitor, 262

Loaysa, Fray Rodrigo de: on the conditions of *mita* Indians in Peru, 202; on Indians in the Andes, 465

Lobo, 208

Local government: 304-305; the cabildo in, 305-307; in Brazil, 747-52

Locke, L. Leland, *The Ancient Quipu or Peruvian Knot Record,* 220, note

Logwood, contraband trade in, 408, 413

Loosley, Allyn C., "The Puerto Bello Fairs," 144, note

Lope de Rueda, 505

Lope de Vega, Felix, 504, 531

Lopes de Mendonça, H., "De Restêlo a Vera Cruz," 634, note

Lopes da Silveira, Pero, 650

López, Vicente F., *Historia de Argentina,* 497, note

López de Gómara: Francisco, historian of Cortés, 516; *Historia de las Indias,* 17, note; *Conquista de México,* 95, note, 516; quoted on gold found in America, 107

López de Hinojoso, Alonso, medical writings of, 540

López de Velasco, *Geografía y descripción universal de las Indias,* 82, note

Lorente, Sebastián, *Historia del Perú bajo los Borbones, 1700-1821,* 408, note

Los Empeños de una Casa, comedy, 534

Loughran, Elizabeth Ward, "The First Episcopal Sees in Spanish America," 246, note

Louis XII, of France, 640

Louis XIV, of France, 661; and American trade, 406

Lozano, Pedro, *Descripción corográfica,* 525

Lugo, Pedro Fernándes de, 51, 74

Luna, Diego de, reports on the *mita* system, 466

Luque, Hernando de, 53

Lutheran revolt, effect on censorship, 507

M

Maceguales, defined, 69, 166, 198

Maciel, Juan Bautista, prohibited books of, 545

MacNutt, F. A., *Letters of Cortés,* 266, note

Macpherson, David, *Annals of Commerce,* 413, note

McBride, G. M.: *The Agrarian Indian Communities of Highland Bolivia,* 76, note; *Chile, Land and Society,* 321, note; *The Land Systems of Mexico,* 66, note

McLachlan, Jean O., *Trade and Peace with Old Spain: 1667,* 412, note

Madariaga, Salvador, *Christopher Columbus,* 35, note

Madden, Marie R., "The European Background," 526, note

Madeira Islands, 30, 36, 650

Madre de Deus, Frei Gaspar da, 711

Madrid, Treaty of (1670), 404-405

Magalhães, Basilio de, *Expansão geográphica do Brasil colonial,* 663, note

Magalhães Gandavo, Pero de, 662; cited on progress of Brazil, 654-57; *The Histories of Brazil,* **654, note, 709;** *Tratado da Terra do Brasil,* and *Historia da Provincia Santa Cruz,* **709**

Magdalena River, 51

Magellan, Ferdinand: circumnavigates the globe, 50; touches Brazil, 654

Maguey (agave): 83, 84, 96; its cultivation and uses, 85; in New Spain, 344; products of, 96, 396

Mail, maritime concessions, 421-22

Maize: 83, 96; cultures in America, 84; in New Spain, 343

Majorca: 59, *fueros* of, 290

Malabo, 51

Malaysia, 29

Maldonado (Uruguay), 334

Malheiro Dias, Carlos: "A expedição de 1501," 636, note: "A expedição de 1503," 637, note; *História da colonização portuguesa do Brasil,* 634, note; "A metrópole e suas conquistas nos reinados de D. João III, D. Sebastião e Cardeal D. Henrique," 634, note; "O Regimen feudal das donatárias," 643, note

Mamaconas, 176

Mamelucos: 669, 700; slave hunters, 580

Mancera, Viceroy: on Indian conditions, 466; on the rivalry of Creoles and Spaniards, 486-87

Manchester, Alan K.: *British Pre-Eminence in Brazil and Its Rise and Decline,* 684, note; "The Rise of the Brazilian Aristocracy," 702, note

Manco Capac, founds Cuzco, 17

Mandamiento, 461

Manila, trade center, 399

Manioc (*or* mandioc, *or* cassava), 83, 85

Mano de Relox, 406

Manoel I, of Portugal, 650, 735, 740

Manso de Velasco, José, settles towns in Chile, 323

Manufacturing: evolution of, *see* Chapter 19; in Brazil, 681-82; in the Caribbean, 394-97; in Chile, 391-92; in Ecuador, 390-91; in New Spain, 124-27, 396; in Peru, 391; Indians forbidden employment in, 389; licensing of, 390; on the west coast, 390-92; restrictions on, 387; Spanish policy on colonial, 386-390; status of domestic, 398-99; stimulated by high European prices, 123; and Trade, *see* Chapter 7

Maracaibo, 434

Maranhão: Companhia do, 686; emigrants from the Azores settle in, 669; separated from Brazil, 667; struggles between colonists and Indians, 728-32

Marchant, Alexander: "Aspects of the Enlightenment in Brazil," 545, note, 715, note; *From Barter to Slavery,* 724, note

María, Queen, policy toward Brazilian manufacturing, 682

Mariana, Father, Juan, on concentration of property in Spain, 361-62

Marignoli, Juan de, 29

Marimba music, 537

Marina, Doña, interpreter for Cortés, 43, 307

Marinha e Ultramar, ministry of, 745

Market days, fixed, 139-40

Markets: lack of, 318, 324; in Mexico, 129-30

Marques Pereira, Nuno, *Compendio narrativo do peregrino da America,* 711

Márquez, José Joaquín, 349

Marranos, 236

Marriage: between Moors and Christians, 32; customs in the Caribbean, Colombia, and Mexico, 172-74; Indians and Church, 253

Marshall, C. E., "The Birth of the Mestizo in New Spain," 207, note

Martin, Percy Alvin, Translation of João Pandiá Calógeras, *Formação histórica do Brasil,* 656, note

Martinez, Enrico, plans drainage of Mexican Valley, 541

Martínez de Mata, Francisco, on labor as a basis of wealth, 362

Martins Homem, Alvaro, 32

Martyr, Peter: 230, 515-16; *Decades de orbe novo;* and *Opus epistolarum,* 515

Mascarenhas, Jorge de, effort to form a **monopoly company, 685**

Mason, J. Alden, "The Native Languages of Middle America," 212, note

Masonry: in Mexico, 121; in the Andes, **122**

Masses: condition among the Incas, 76, 168-70; in Spain, 32-33; living standards of the Aztec, 167

Matalcingo, Cacique of, 46

Mather, Cotton, 544

Matienzo, Juan de: 527; advocates settlements in Argentina, 329; *Gobierno del Perú*, 81, note

Matienzo, José Nicolás, and Torres, Luis M., eds. *Documentos para la historia del Virreinato del Río de la Plata*, 332, note

Matlazahuatl, pre-Conquest disease, 449

Mato Grosso, mines of, 678

Mattos, Anibal, *Joseph de Anchieta*, 653, note

Mattos Guerra, Gregorio de, *Modinhas*, 712

Maule River, 319, 325

Maya and Their Neighbors, The, 212, note

Maya: architecture, 222-23; baptism, 244; books, 213; city-states, 271-272; culture, 212; government, 272; writing, 213-14

Mayeques, 69, 166, 198

Maynas, missions among the, 581

Mayorazgo, 68

Means, Philip Ainsworth: *Ancient Civilizations of the Andes*, 18, note; *Fall of the Inca Empire*, 79, note; "The Philosophic Interrelationship between Middle American and Andean Religions," 219, note; "The Rebellion of Tupac-Amarú II, 1780-1781," 471, note; *The Spanish Main*, 151, note

Measles, 203

Meat: in Río de la Plata, 333; salted: Caribbean trade, 394; shipments from Buenos Aires, 428; from Chile, 325, 432; from Montevideo, 332

Mecham, J. Lloyd: "The Church in Colonial Hispanic America," 260, note; *Francisco de Ibarra and Nueva Vizcaya*, 341; "The *Real de Minas*," 307, note

Medicine: 540-41; Aztec, 218; benefited by the Discovery, 230; Inca, 220-21; of pre-Conquest America, 84

Medina, Bartolomé de, *patio* process introduced by, 110-111

Medina, Francisco de, built slaughterhouse in Uruguay, 332

Medina, J. Toribio: *Cartas de Valdivia*, 320, note; *Historia del tribunal del*

Santo Oficio de la ınquisición en Chile, 513, note; *Historia del tribunal del Santo Oficio de la Inquisición de Cartagena de las Indias*, 513, note; *Historia del tribunal del Santo Oficio de la Inquisición de Lima*, 513, note; *Historia de la Inquisición en México*, 512, note; *La primitiva Inquisición americana*, 261, note; *El tribunal del Santo Oficio de la Inquisición en la provincias del plata*, 513, note

Mediterranean: 30, 31, 55; dominated by Italian towns, 29, 146

Meigs, Peveril, 3rd, *The Dominican Mission Frontier of Lower California*, 341-42, note

Melo (Uruguay), 334

Melons, 83, 100

Memorial de D. Francisco de Toledo, Virrey del Perú a Felipe II, 75, note; 199, note

"Memorias históricas e militares relativas a Guerra hollandeza," 658, note

Memorias de los Virreyes que han gobernado el Perú, 498, note

Méndez, Cristóbal, medical writings of, 540

Mendiburu, Manuel de, *Diccionario histórico-biográfico del Perú*, 377, note

Mendieta, Gerónimo de: *Historia eclesiástica indiana*, 245, note; ascribes Indian conversion to their character, 251-52; on role of the Catholic Church in America, 247

Mendizábal, Miguel Othón de, "La evolución agropecuaria en el Valle del Mezquital," 396, note

Mendoza, Viceroy Antonio de: *Relación . . .* to his successor, 199, note; first viceroy of New Spain, 72, 95, 228; founds school of San Juan de Letrán, 229; installs printing press, 232; instructed on books, 503; instructed on the conversion of the Indians, 251

Mendoza: settled, 329; wine of, 394

Menéndez Pidal, Ramón, *Historia de España*, 234, note

Menezes, Viceroy Vasco Fernandes Cesar de, 714

Merced a Hernán Cortés de tierras inmediatas a México, 66, note

Mercedarians, in Brazil, 720, 732-33

Mercedes (Uruguay), 334

Merchant adventurers, 147

Merchants; dealings with the *Casa,* 604; importance of native, 490

Mercurio Peruano de Historia, Literatura y Noticias Públicas: 382, note; contents, 557-58

Mercurio volante con noticias importantes y curiosas, 555

Mercury: consumption (1762-82), table, 378; distribution, 379; from Almadén, 376; from Huancavelica, table, 376-77; importance to mining, 111; price of, 378

Merêa, Paulo, "A Solução tradicional da colonização do Brasil," 643, note

Merriman, Roger B.: *Rise of the Spanish Empire in the Old World and in the New,* 33, note; quoted on the Reconquest, 33

Mesa da consciencia, 726, 743

Mesta, guild of livestock breeders, 362

Mestizos: areas inhabited by, 208; in Chile, 442; in New Spain, 445, 453; position in the community, 207; in Paraguay, 444-45; list of prominent, 207; terms for describing, 207-209

Mestres do campo, 750

Metal crafts: in the Andes, 122; Aztec and Mayan, 223

Metals, precious: 379-83; annual produce of Europe, Northern Asia and America, 380; European imports from America, table, 381; regional sources of, 1492-1803, table, 380

Methuen, Treaty of, 684

Metztli, Aztec moon god, 241

Mexico: agriculture, areas cultivated, 83, 96, 445; expansion, 340-41; Indian, 84-85; *Audiencia* in, 298; cannibalism, marriage and sexual practices, 172-73; civil wars, 43; conquest by the Indians, 13-17, 42-43; conquest and colonization, Spanish, 41-49, 50; education, 500; inequality, 483; Inquisition, 262; land system, 63-71; Manila trade with, 399; mines, 111-113, 373-76; money coined, 1537-1803, table, 374; School of Mines, 381; missionaries, 578-79; Negro slaves, 472; newspapers, 554-56; population by intendancies, table, 453; prestige of the clergy, 568-69; products, 96-98; pre-Conquest population, 179-81; private schools, 229;

quicksilver, 111; racial distribution, 456, 457; religious instruction, 588; Royal and Pontifical University of, 230; scientific development, 550-51; "ten plagues" of, according to Motolinía, 202; tithes, 464; trade inside, 129-31; United States trade with, 416

Mexico City: *cabildo* protests numerous clergy, 591; cathedral, 538; "first vote" city, 306; Inquisition, 576-77; mission, 579; population, 180, 453, 455; printing press installed, 232; tobacco factories, 395

Mexico, Gulf of, 50

Meza, Bartolomé de, master painter, 538

Michoacán: not subject to the Aztecs, 47; mines in, 112; school for Creole priests, 265

Military: abuses and privileges of, 485-86

Military Orders: 58, Spanish, 288-89; curbed by the Crown, 291; *repartimientos* of, 59

Militia, Brazilian, 746

Miller, Jan, burned at Cuzco, 262

Mills: flour, 144; woolen, 390-91, 394

Minas Gerais: captaincy, 679; captaincy-general, 745; civil war in the gold fields, 678; gold discovered, 677-78

Mineral production: in 16th century Mexico, 113; value compared with agriculture, 350; total, *see* Chapters 6, 18

Mines: 674-81; effect on economic progress, 109, 342-43, 383-85; important, *see* Antioquia, Barbacoas, Biscaina, Bolaños, Choco, Conchuco, Gualgayoc, Guamachuco, Guanajuato, Huancavelica, Oruro, Pasco, Potosí, Purísima, Real del Monte, San Luis Potosí, Valenciana, Zacatecas; in Mato Grosso and Goiaz, 678-79; in Mexico, 105, 111-13, 373-76; in Minas Gerais, 677-78; in New Granada, 371-73; in Peru, 105-106; laws governing, 110; School of Mines, in Mexico, 381; source of wealth to some Indians, 201-202; summary, 385

Mining in America: *see* Chapters 6 and 18; governed by the *Cuerpo de Minería,* 609; Inca system, 279; privileges of the aristocracy, 484; technique, 110-11, 381-83

Mint: in Baía, 675; in Bogotá, 373; in Lima, 368; in Mexico, 373-74; in

Popayán, 373; in Rio de Janeiro, 675; in Santiago, 369

Miramontes Zuázola, Juan de, 531

Miranda, Agenor Agusto de, *O Rio São Francisco*, 664, note

Miscelánea austral, 531

Missions *(misiones)*: 359, 720-24; in local Brazilian government, 751-52; in Paraguay, 670-77

Missionaries: 248-50; 577-83; *see also* Jesuits, Dominicans, Franciscans, Benedictines, etc.; areas covered by, 578-79; attitude of the Spanish Crown toward, 250-51; in agriculture, 582; in commerce, 585-86; in northern Brazil, 667-68; in the Spanish colonies, 578-81; technique of colonization, 578, 580; work of, 247, 249-50

Mita: 198, 461, 463, 466, 471, 475; Indians, bad condition of, 202

Mita-cuna, 169

Mitayos, 168

Mitimaes, or *mitmaccuna,* Inca system of government, 20

Mitla, cruciform caverns at, 244

Mixtec architecture, 223

Mohammedans: 38; considered pirates by Christians, 151; Neapolitan and Sicilian, 234; trade with Sicily and Spain, 28; wars with Charles V, 238; with Visigothic Christians, 32

Monardes, Nicholás, medical historian, 540

Monarquia Indiana, 522

Monasteries and convents, 261, 621-22

Monblanquet monastery, 290

Money, shortage in Brazil, 675

Monks, mistresses of the, 469-470

Monopolies, 139-40

Monopoly: Sevilla-Cádiz-Lima, 407, 420, 434; companies, Brazilian, 684-88; English, Dutch, and French, 685; Spanish, 420-21; Spanish system, 417-19

Monte Corvino, John de, Bishop of Peking, 29

Monterey, 342

Monterey, Viceroy Count of, settles towns, 199

Montes, 72

Montes Claros, Marqués de, Viceroy, 144, note

Montesa (Military Order), 59

Montesinos, Fray Antonio de, 192-93

Montesinos, Fernando de, *Memorias antiguas historiales y políticas del Perú,* 19, note

Montevideo: commercial growth of, 450, 425-26; *consulado,* 609; customshouse, 426-27; founded, 331; freedom of the port, 424-25; Negro workers, 479; new trade benefits, 425; port of entry for slaves, 427; religious influence in, 569; rise of commercial middle class, 427; rivalry with Buenos Aires, 425-26, 427; shipping and livestock trade, 394, 425-26

Montezuma I, 272

Montezuma II: 15, 42, 45, 47; aggression of, 272; court, 274-75; enemies and rivals, 43-44, 46; imprisonment and death, 46, 275; policy, 273

Montúfar, Archbishop of Mexico, on the extravagance of the clergy, 268

Moors: 34, 56, 67, 233-35; conflicts with Christians, 30, 32-33; conversion, 237; enslavement, 59; expulsion, 237; fourteenth century policy toward, 236; immigration to America, 150; intermarriage with Christians, 237

Mora, José María Luis, *Obras sueltas,* 358, note

Moraes, Evaristo de, *A escravidão africana no Brasil,* 696, note

Mordomo, 644

Morelia, 85

Morelos, 66, 71

Moreno, Laudelino, "Los extranjeros y el ejercicio del comercio de Indias," 419, note

Morgan, William Thomas, "The South Sea Company and the Canadian Expedition in the Reign of Queen Anne," 408, note

Morison, Samuel E., *Admiral of the Ocean Sea: A Life of Christopher Columbus,* 35, note

Morley, Sylvanus Griswold, "Maya Epigraphy," 213, note

Moses, Bernard: *Spain's Declining Power in South America, 1730-1806,* 363, note; *Spanish Colonial Literature in South America,* 228, note; *The Spanish Dependencies in South America,* 295, note; *South America on the Eve of Emancipation,* 238, note

Motolinía, Toribio de: describes hardships of the Indians in Mexico, 202; describes the work of Franciscan friars, 265-66; *Historia de los Indios de Nueva España*, 125, note; on the Aztec religion, 238-39; on destruction of idols, 254; on the silk industry in New Spain, 125

Motta, Arthur, *História da litteratura brasileira*, 715, note

Movellán, Fernando, 349

Mulatto, 208

Muñoz Camargo, Diego: 16th century chronicler, 14-15; describes the Indian land system in Mexico, 68; *Historia de Tlaxcala*, 15, note

Munz, Alberto V., "The Tonal System of Indian Music," 536, note

Muratori, Ludovico Antonio, *A Relation of the Missions of Paraguay*, 581, note

Muscovy Company, 685

Music in America: Andean, 216; Indian, 536, 537; Negro, 536; religious, 536-37

Musical instruments, 536

Mutis, José Celestino: accused of heresy, 547; expedition, 543; influence on study of natural history, 550

N

Naboría, 196

Napoleonic wars, effect on trade, 414

Narváez, Pánfilo de: explores Florida, 50; sent to arrest Cortés, 46; takes women to Florida, 205-206

Nash, Roy: *The Conquest of Brazil*, 642, note; on the Negro in Brazil, 697-98

Nassau, Maurice Count of, Dutch governor of Brazil, 658-59

Natal, 636

Naturalism, 510

Navarre: contested between Ferdinand and Francis I, 152; privileges of, 290

Navarrete, Martín Fernández de, *Colección de los viages y descubrimentos que hicieron por mar los españoles desde fines del siglo XV*, 35, note

Navigation Acts, 676

Navy, Royal Spanish, 402

Nazca, sugar production in, 99

Neasham, V. Aubrey, "Spain's Emigrants to the New World, 1492-1592," 148, note

Nebrija, Antonio de: 228; Castilian grammar, 525

Neé and Pineda, expedition of, 543

Negro: areas inhabited by the, 208; contribution to Brazil, 697-98; definition of, 702; the, in America, 206-207; in Brazil, 696-99; worker, compared with the Indian, 206

Negroes: conditions of slaves, 102-103, 472-75; cost of, 206; distribution of, 457; English rights to trade in, 408; excluded from education, 495-96; *gaucho* and *vaquero*, 442; importance to sugar cane production, 41; in the Andes, 445; in Brazil, 669-70; in the Cape Verde Islands, 31; in Central America, 445; in Colombia, 445; in New Spain, 453, 455-56; in Venezuela, 445; in the West Indies, 456-57; introduced to protect the Indians, 192; proportion of the population, 206; revolts of, 206-7, 472; social position of, 460

Neptuno alegórico, 533

Nevin, Dr. Domingo, 498

New Castle, viceroyalty of, 298

"New Christians": in America, 262; in Brazil, 638

New Granada: 39; contraband, 433; educational reforms, 501; effect of trade policy on, 433-35; exports, value of, 434; gold production, table, 372; mineral production, 371-73; prosperity of, 443; viceroyalty of, 623-24

New Laws, The: 194-96, 298, 471, 518; abolishing the *encomiendas* in Peru, 80-81; actually increased the powers of the encomenderos, 308; in New Spain, 304; modified by the Crown, 195-96; modified under La Gasca, 81; revolt against, in Peru, 304

New Mexico: 47; missions in, 578

New Spain: 55, 57, 163; administrative changes, 624; agriculture, 343-50; archbishops became viceroys, 574; areas cultivated, 96; aristocracy, 483, 484; at the end of the colonial period, 342; the *auto*, 534-35; *caciques*, 204; Church lands, 591; commercial methods, 346-47; exports, 435; Indian areas, 445-46; intellectual leader among the colonies, 550-51; labor, 463, 477-79; livestock, 347; *mestizos*, 445; mining, 366-67, 373; poetry of, 533-34; population, 452-54, 458; poverty, 478; racial distribution, 455, 456; restrictions on books, 504, 513; revenues, tables of, 436; revolt against the New Laws, 304; schools, 497; territorial expansion, 340-43; tithes, 591; trade, 398-400; trade policy and reform, 435-36; trade with Peru and Ecuador, 396-97; value of manufacturing, 396; viceroyalty, 298; whites, 481

New York, advocates trade treaty with Spain, 413-14

Newspapers: *see also* journalism; censorship of, 556; first Argentine, 428; in America, 553-61

Newton, Arthur Percival, *The European Nations in the West Indies, 1493-1688,* 152, note

Newtonism, 549

Nezahualcoytl: King of Téxcoco, 215; religious belief of, 240

Nicaragua: 13, 48-49; shipbuilding in, 128

Nichols, Madaline W.: *The Gaucho: Cattle Hunter, Cavalryman, Ideal of Romance,* 444, note; "The Historic Gaucho," 444, note

Nichols, Roy F., "Trade Relations and the Establishment of the United States Consulate in Spanish America, 1779 to 1809," 415, note

Nicuesa, Diego de, granted Veragua, 42

Nina Rodríguez, Raymundo, *Os Africanos no Brasil,* 696, note

Niño, Andrés, 48

Niza, Marcos de, explorations of, 340-41

Nobility, 58, 483

Nóbrega, Manoel: 668-69, 709, 720-21; aids in expulsion of the French from Rio de Janeiro, 653; on the Indians, 725

Noche Triste (La), 46

Nombre de Dios, 162, 163

Nordenflicht, Baron von: and the Born process, 382; reforms made at Potosí by, 382; visits Peruvian mines, 381, 382

Normano, J. F., *Brazil: A Study of Economic Types,* 692, note

Noronha, Fernão de, granted concession for brazil wood, 638-41

Norsemen, established trading colonies, 28

North America, 83

No-te-entiendo, 208

Noticia circunstanciada de la industria y comercio del virreynato del Río de la Plata, 333, note

Noticia de la California, 524

Noticias americanas, 523

Noticias secretas de América, 524

Nouvelle Compagnie, 407

Novenos, form of taxes, 592

Novísima Recopilación (1805), 502, 570

Novita, *Corregidores* of, 372

Nueva Colección de documentos para la historia de México, 14, note

Nueva Galicia: 261; established by Nuño de Guzmán, 340

Nueva Granada, *see* New Granada

Nueva obra . . . sobre la muerte del Adelantado Don Diego de Almagro, poem, 531

Nueva Vizcaya, founded, 341

Nuevo León, founded, 341

Nuevo Luciano, El, 553

Nuevo Sistema económico de gobierno para América, 529

Numerical system: Aztec and Maya, 218-19; Inca and Hindu systems compared to Maya, 219

Nuns: complaints against the, 596; in Brazil, 732-35

Núñez de Prado, Juan, settles Barco, 328

Núñez de Vela, Vicero Blasco, abolishes the *encomiendas,* 80-81; convoys fleet to America, 162; executed, 81

Nuts, 83

Nuttall, Zelia, "The Earliest Historical Relations between Mexico and Japan," 399, note

O

Oaxaca, 66, 71, 112, 144

Obrajes: 127, 388, 395, 467-69; conditions in the, 475

Obregón, T. Esquivel, "Factors in the Historical Evolution of Mexico," 445, note

Observaciones sobre la física, 555

Ocuña, Juan de, Marquis of Casafuerte, 488

Oda al Paraná, Argentina poem, 553

O'Higgins, Ambrosio, Viceroy, 318

Oidores: 93; restrictions on, 300

Oil: 93, 143; trade in, 31

Ojeda, Alonso de: land grant to, 41-42; in Brazil, 636, 654

Ojeda, Diego de, religious poet, 530-31

Olavide y Jáuregui, Pablo de, poet, 510, 533

Olid, Cristóbal de, expedition of, 47-48

Olinda, Dutch occupation of, 658

Olivares, Count-Duke of, 604

Olive growing: in Chile, 321; in New

Spain, 348-49; in Peru, 101, 316, 317, 348; prohibitions on, 317, 348-49

Oliveira, Manoel Botelho de, *see* Botelho

Ollas, 89

Ondegardo, Polo de, 527

Oña, Pedro de, Chilean poet, 530

Oñate, Juan de, 341

Oporto, trade center, 30

Opus epistolarum, 515

Ordenações Manuelinas, 740

Ordenanza de Minería, effect on mining in Chile, 370

Ordenanzas, defined, 296

Ordenanzas de Minas de Guamanga, 110, note

Ordenanzas de nuevos descubrimientos y poblaciones, 527

Ordenanzas de Toledo, 110, note

Order of Christ, 718

Orejones, Inca nobles, 20, 167

Orellana, Francisco de, 665-66

Ores, American compared to European, 376

Orgóñez, expedition to Chile, 319-20

Orígen de los Mexicanos, 14, note

Orinoco, missions along the, 581

Orizaba, 71

Orozco y Berra, Manuel: *Apuntes para la historia de la geografía en México,* 341, note; *Historia antigua y de la conquista de México,* 166, note

Ortiz, Fernando, 350, note

Ortiz, Fray Tomás, sent to protect the Indians, 51

Ortiz de Rozas, Domingo, settles in Chile, 323

Ortiz de Zárate, Juan, governor of Paraguay, 329

Oruro, mines at 384

Oryctognosy, Manual of, printed in Mexico, 550

Othón de Mendizábal, Miguel, "La Evolución agropecuaria en el Valle del Mezquital," 396, note

Ouvidor geral, 741

Ovalle, Alonso de, 522

Ovando, Juan de, compiles the laws, 527

Ovando, Nicolás de: Governor of Española, 40, 160, 294; brought women to Española, 205; instructed on silk culture in America, 124; instructed to treat the Indians as vassals, 61-62; introduces Negroes into Española, 206; protests grants of Indians to people in Spain, 63

Oviedo y Baños Sotomayor, José de, 524

Oviedo y Valdés, Gonzalo Hernández de: 401, 517; *Historia general de las Indias,* 40, note; on horses in America, 39; on immigration to America, 147-48; on the immorality of the clergy, 267; on investment necessary to become a sugar producer, 94; on poor colonists, 101

Oviedo Herrera y Rueda, Luis Antonio, Count of La Granja, poet, 532

Oxford, Earl of, forms trading company, 408

P

Pachaca, 276

Pachacamac or Viracocha, Inca god, 240

Pacheco, Captain Miguel, tried on prohibited book charge, 561

Pachuca, 71, 112

Pacific Coast: 83, 86, 87; settlements, 49

Pacific Ocean: 413; as a trade route, 138; discovered by Balboa, 42; international trade via the, 399-401

Painting: 515, 538-40; European technique of introduced into America, 232

Palenque, The cross at, 244

Palestrina, religious composer, 536

Palmares, 699

Palo de tinto, 144

Pampas, 442

Panama: 17, 48-49, 53, 98, 163; agriculture, 98; importance of trade, 144-45, 413; Negro slaves in, 472; ships built at, 397

Panama City, development, according to Cieza, 144-45

Pando (Uruguay), 334

Papacy: attempts to contest Crown authority in America, 570; censorship by the, 507-509; Concordat of 1793, 571

Papal Bulls: of Alexander VI, 36; circulation in America controlled by the Crown, 258; subject to Council approval, 574

Papan, Princess, 242

Papel forte, 660-61

Papel periódico: of Havana, 558; of Bogotá, 558

Papeles varios sobre administración, aduanas, aranceles . . . 392, note

Paper from agave, 121

Paper money, in Brazil, 675

Paradise Lost, Milton's, forbidden, 561

Paraguay: 26, 327-28; exports and imports of, 393-94; Guaraní Indians, 327-28; introduction of cattle, 328; mestizo society, 444, 455, 481; Portuguese contraband trade, 410-11; trade routes, 393-94

Paraná, 672

Paraná River, Missions along the, 580

Paredes, La Provincia de Inquisivi, 586, note

Pariacaca mountains, 134

Paris, Academy of Science, 550

Parish, the, in local government, 621

Parish, Woodbine, *Buenos Aires and the Provinces of the Río de la Plata,* 427, note

Parras, 100

Parrots, 636

Pasco, mining at, 368

Patio process of mining, 110-111, 366

Patronage: Crown control of, 570-71; importance of, 257-58

Pátzcuaro, 85

Paul III, Pope: Bull regarding prohibited books, 509; declares the Indians human, 194

Paulistas, 669-73, 678

Paullu Inca, 175

Paullu Tupac, accompanied Almagro to Chile, 319

Payes, 723

Paysandú, 334

Pecheros, 168

Peddlers in Mexico, 131

Pedrarias Dávila: 42, 53, 66, 74, 149, 294; founds Panama, 48; governor of Nicaragua, dies, 49

Pegolotti, Francisco Balducci, 29

Peixoto, Afranio, *Noções de história da literatura brasileira,* 715, note

Peking, Catholic bishop of, 29

Pelayo, leader of the Asturians, 233

Peninsula, The, 39

Peninsulares, 209

Peña Cámara, José de la, "El Manuscrito llamado 'Gobernación Espiritual y Temporal de las Indias,'" 156, note

Peões, 644-45

Peonías, 67, 72

People of Latin America, *see* Chapter 21

Peralta Barnuevo, Pedro de, poet and encyclopedist, 532

Pereira, Ruy, attitude toward the Indians, 725

Pereira, Duarte Coelho, *see* Duarte Coelho

Pereira Coutinho, Francisco, 646

Pereira da Silva, Luciano: "A Arte de Navegar dos Portugueses," 635, note; "Duarte Pacheco Pereira, Precursor de Cabral," 634, note

Pereira de Souza, Washington Luis, *see* Washington Luis

Pereyra, Carlos: *Historia de la América española,* 49, note; *La obra de España en América,* 39, note; on animals in the Conquest, 39

Pérez Bustamante, C., *Los orígenes del gobierno virreinal en las Indias españolas,* 300, note

Pérez de Montalbán, 505

Pérez de la Riva, Juan, "Inglaterra y Cuba en la primera mitad del Siglo XVII," 404, note

Pérez García, José, on religious instruction in Chile, 589-90

"Pericholi," La, Peruvian actress, 535

Pernambuco: captured by the French, 653; progress of, 656

Persia, 28, 29

Peru: 17, 18, 26, 38, 42, 49, 51, 52, 55, 57, 78, 83, 86, 98, 144, 165; agriculture, 99-100, 316, 317; areas suitable for cultivation 182-84; burial customs, 175; civil wars among the Spaniards in, 80-81; colonial land system, 79-82; conquest of, 53-55; development, 316-19; disadvantage of trade reforms, 429; drama, 535; earthquakes, 318-19; *encomenderos* threatened, 195; expeditions to, 50; French thought condemned, 546; industries in Lima, 391; livestock, 89-100; mercury, 111; mining, 113-16, 366-69, 384; missions, 581; Negro slaves, 472; Philip II orders textile mills closed, 389; poetry of, 531-33; population, 181-89, 451-52, 457; Portuguese contraband trade with, 411; printing press, 232; revolts against the *New Laws,* 304; scientific expeditions, 543; Spanish class society, 82, 481; textile industry, 391; Toledo-Velasco legislation, 389; trade, 429-32; vineyards, 100-101

Peruano Extraordinario, 416, note

Perusquia, Mariano, sculptor, 538

Peruvian silver in Mexico, 400

Philip II (First of Portugal): 657, 742; and the Council of Indies, 297; closes textile mills in Peru, 389; ideas of government, 601; Indian legislation in Brazil, 726; intolerance toward foreigners in the colonies, 150; orders compilation of the laws, 527; revokes trade privileges of northern ports, 158-59; sets up the Inquisition in America, 262

Philip III: 740; authorizes the Jesuits to e s t a b l i s h missions among the Guaraní, 580; establishes free labor market for Indians, 475-76; Indian legislation in Brazil, 726; objects to Church monopoly of the land in Lima, 590

Philip IV: 604; monopoly on pepper, 324; restrictions on books, 503-504

Philip V: attempts to limit clerical power, 574; commends the Inquisition, 510; reforms of, 625, 626

Philosophism, 510

Philosophy, natural, 547-49

Pichca-chunca-camayu-cuna, 278

Pichu, 189

Pierson, Donald, "The Negro in Bahía Brazil," 696, note

Pierson, W. W., Jr., "Some Reflections on the Cabildo as an Institution," 294, note

Pietschmann, Richard, Geschichte des inkareiches, 24, note

Pigs, 93

Pineda, Alonzo de, 50

Pining, Didrik, 32

Pinzón, Vicente Yáñez, explores the Brazilian coast, 654

Piracy: 151-54; see contraband; effect of, on navigation and trade policies, 149, 161-63; French and English, 152-54; in European waters, 158; off Cape St. Vincent and Brittany, 151

Piragua, 398

Piratininga, 668, 721

Pirua, 91

Piura, 79

Pizarro, Francisco: 5, 25, 26, 42, 44, 51, 55, 55, 66-67, 294; astonished by result of civil wars, 25; encomienda of, 79; expedition to Peru, 50, 53; policy in the Inca civil war, 54

Pizarro, Gonzalo, instigates rebellion against the New Laws, 80-81

Pizarro, Pedro, Relation of the Discovery and Conquest of the Kingdoms of Peru, 17, note

Pizarro-Orellana, expedition along the Amazon, 665-66

Placer mining, 105

Plano Carpini, John de, 29

Plants of pre-Conquest America, 83-84

Plunder of the Indians, 106-108

Poesías sagradas y profanas, 533

Poetry: 515, 529-34; Chilean, 530-31; epic, popular in America, 231; of the Conquest, 529-30; of New Spain, 533-34; Peruvian, 531-33

Pogo, Alexander, La Conquista del Perú, 134, note

Política indiana, 527-28

Pollock, H. E. D., "Sources and Methods in the Study of Maya Architecture," 222, note

Polo, Marco, Nicolo and Matteo, 29

Polygamy: in Colombia, 174; in the Inca Empire, 176-77; in Mexico, 173; problem among the Indians 253

Pomar Juan Bautista, Relación de Téxcoco, 307, note

Pombal, Marquis of: 714; expels the Jesuits from Portugal, 586, 732

Pomerantz, Sidney I., New York: An American City, 1783-1803, 557, note

Popayán (Colombia), 51, 98

Pope, arbiter in territorial claims, 36

Popul Vuh, 214

Population: according to various writers, 178-79; density of, 13, 548-59; effect of geographical conditions in Peru, 182-83; effect of mining on, 185; estimates based on land given each Indian, 187-88; estimates based on size of encomiendas, 184 factors retarding, 447-49; Indian, see Chapter 9; Indian, in Argentina and Uruguay, 442-43; of Argentina, 184, 449-50; of Bolivia, 184; of Brazil, 655-56; of Buenos Aires, 449; of Chile, 442, 450; of Cuba, 454; of Ecuador, 184; of Ecuador, Colombia, and Venezuela, 452; of Española, 40; of Europe and America, 459; of Havana, 454, 455; of the Indies, 178-189; of Lima, 452; of Mexico City, 453, 454; of Montevideo, 450; of New Spain, 452-54; of Peru,

181-89, 451-52; of the West Indies, 454-55; pre-Conquest, 8, 179-89; racial elements of, 455-58; redistribution of, 184-85; relation to maize production, 186-87; relative, 458-59; trends, 181-82, 185, 446-47; to 1810, see Chapter 21

Porco, effect of Indian emancipation on the mining at, 197

Pordenone, Odorico de, 29

Pororoco, 666

Porto Santo, 30

Porto Seguro, 647

Portolá, Gaspar de, 342

Portugal: 28, 56, 58; the Braganzas, 744; class conflicts, 31; commerce with Brazil, 688-92; contraband trade with the Spanish colonies, 154; government, 739-40; independence from Spain, 683; laws, 740, 743-44; Moors expelled from, 237; political and economic growth of, 29-32; trade, 31, 410-12; treaties of commerce with, 683-84

Portuguese: in Santa Marta, 51; occupy Cape Verde Islands, 30; settle Colonia del Sacramento, 411

Portuguese ships, masquerade as Spanish, 155

Portuguese-Spanish rivalry, 411

Pósito, 91

Postal system: 421-22; in Río de la Plata, 421

Potatoes: 83, 99; in New Spain, 343-44

Potosí: 144, 366-67; economic activity, 384; opening of mines, 114; production of silver, 1556-1560, table, 115

Pottery: Aztec and Mayan, 121, 223; Inca, 122

Poverty: among the Incas, according to Cieza, 168; in America, 101-102

Prado, Javier, *Estado social del Perú durante la dominación española*, 483, note

Precious metals: 674-81; Indian knowledge of, 104-106

Premática, 160

Prescott, William H.: *History . . . of Mexico*, 14, note; *History . . . of Peru*, 22, note; on military despotism of the Incas, 22

Presepe, settled, 666

Presidencias: 261; defined, 302-304

Presidio, the, 359-60, 622

Press, liberty of the, 561

Prester, John, 30, 32

Price fixing: attempted by the Crown, 123; by Cortés, 94; in Río de la Plata, 333

Prices: rise after the Conquest, 123; high in America, 144

Priesthood: Aztec, 69, 243; character of, 265-68; education for the Indian, 217; Inca, 243-44

Priestley, Herbert I: *The Mexican Nation*, 14, note; "Spanish Colonial Municipalities," 617, note; *José de Gálvez*, 342, note

Primera parte de las noticias . . . de Tierra Firme, 521

Príncipe Island, 30, 31

Printing press: first installed, 232; in Brazil, 715; increase in number, 554

Privateering, *see* Contraband

Privilege in Spain, 286

Privileges: of the clergy and military, 485-86; of the upper classes, 484-85

Prizes: for agriculture in Española, 149; for poems, 232

Procuradores, 261, 306

Products, European demand for Latin-American, 386

Prohibited books, 545-46, 556-57; *see also*, Books, prohibited

Proletariat: 475; of European origin, 486; in New Spain, 477

"Prologue" of Beristain, quoted, 564-65

Property, maldistribution of, 593

Propios, 72

"Propositions," 509-10, 512, 513

Prostitution among the Incas, 177-78

Protestant Revolution, effect on Spain, 34

Protestants: 45; attitude of the Inquisition toward, 577; fought by Charles V, 34

Provedor mor, 741

Provincial money, in Brazil, 675

Provincias Internas, 347, 615, 624

Provisiones, cédulas e instrucciones de Su Majestad, 527

Proyecto económico, 529

Public office, sale of, 616-18

Publicaciones del Archivo General de la Nación, 513, note

Puebla: 66, 71, 85; Bishop of, reproves the priests, 267; important manufacturing center, 395

Pueblo Indians, 271

Pueblos: de abadengo (Church villages), 290; *de Indios*, 308, 309; *de órdenes*,

290; *de realengo* (royal villages), 290

Puerto Cabello, 434

Puerto Rico: 17, 39, 128; bishopric of, 246; conquest by Ponce de León, 41; sugar cane in, 41

Puga, Vasco de, laws, 527

Puná, conquered by Huayna Capac, 23

Punishment under Inca law, 282

Punta Elena, shipbuilding at, 398

Puric, 132, 167, 278

Purísima, mines of, 375

Puritanism, in New England, 544

Pyramids, Toltec, 223

Q

Quechua, taught in Lima, 526

Querétaro, textile industry at, 395

Quesada, Vicente G.: *La vida intelectual en la América Española*, 229, note; on prohibitions of books, 502, 506

Quétzalcoatl, Aztec god, 240-41, 244

Quicksilver, *see* Mercury

Quijos, missions among the, 581

Quilla, Inca god of the moon, 241

Quillapata, 189

Quinine (cinchona), 84

Quínoa, 99

Quiñones, Antonio de, 153

Quinto: 110; in Brazil, 644

Quipu, described by Cieza, 219-20

Quipucamayoc, 220

Quito: 23, 24, 87, 134; audiencia of, 316; Belalcázar appointed governor of, 51

R

Race: attitude of the Brazilians toward, 701-702; second to land in importance during the Reconquest, 33

Racial distribution of population: 455-58; tables, 457, 458

Racial mixtures, 207-209, 693-702

Radin, Paul, *Indians of South America*, 165, note

Rainfall: 86-87; in the Caribbean, 334; effect on livestock, 336-37; in Mexico, 96-97; in Peru, 86

Raleigh, Sir Walter, opens the way for English trade, 404

Ramalhó, João, 668, 700

Ranching in the Caribbean, 92-94

Ranchos: competition with land-holding towns, 360; in Mexico, 357

Raposo, Antonio, 671

Rattio, Hector R., 32, note

Raynal, Guillaume, 523

Real de minas: 110; government of, 306-307

Real del Monte, mines at, 379

Real Sociedad Económica de la Habana, 552

Reales Órdenes Reservadas, 425, note

Realengos, grants made from the, 354-55

Rebellion against the New Law, 80-81

Reconquest: 56, 66, 67; class wars during the, 32-33; importance of the, 234; role of religion in the, 33

Recopilación de las Leyes de Indias, 502, 503, 528, 610

Recuas (pack trains), 137

Reducciones, 198-200, 308, 359

Reflexiones sobre la viruela y la hygiene en Quito, 553

Reforms, Economic: effect on Chile, 432; effect on New Spain, 436; effect on Peru, 429; effect on trade, 439-40; era of, 421-40

Regal, Alberto, *Los caminos del Inca*, 135, note

Regañón de la Havana, called best colonial newspaper, 558

Regidores, 72, 285, 305, 617

Regimento, 745

Registros, 401-402

Regular clergy, in Brazil, 720-24

Regulations of shipping, 163-64

Relação da Baía, 743, 745

Relação, of Rio, 746

Relación histórica del viaje a la América meridional hecho de orden de Su Majestad, 524

Relación del arzobispo de Méjico, 268, note

Relación del estado del Nuevo Reino de Granada, 433, note

Relación de la genealogía y linaje de los Señores . . . de la Nueva España, 272, note

Relación hecha por el señor Andrés de Tapia, sobre la conquista de México, 95, note

Relación of José de Solís, 1760, 572, note

Relación de mando del Virrey Antonio Caballero y Góngora, 1789, 497, note

Relación del Virrey José de Espleta, 1796, 497, note

Relación que dió Antonio de Mendoza a Luis de Velasco, 300, note

Relación por método alfabético, 392, note

Relación verdadera de algunas cosas . . . que sucedieron al Padre Fray Alonso

Ponce en Nueva España, 83, note, 213, note

Relation of Mons. Acarete du Biscay's Voyage up the River de la Plata, 331, note

Religion: and the Church, *see* Chapters 12, 13, 26; Aztec, 238-39; Inca, 239-40; in the Conquest, 246-47; in international politics, 238; in Spain, 33-34; instruction of the Indians in, 469-70, 587-90; political role in Spanish and Indian societies, 9; similarity of Spanish and Indian, 242-46; Spanish attitudes carried to America, 237

Religious Orders: 577-83; *see also* Jesuits, Franciscans, Benedictines, etc.; government of, 261; under Crown control, 259

Religious unity: program of Ferdinand and Isabella, 235-38

Religious wars in France, 45

Remesal, Antonio de, 522

Renaissance in Europe, 227-28

Reparaz, Gonzalo de (Hijo), *La época de . . . descubrimientos españoles y portugueses,* 29, note

Repartimiento in America: 59-63, 190, 197-98, 461, 463, 471; abuse by the *corregidores,* 620-21; granted military orders, 59; in Mexico, size of, 66-67; rooted in Aztec and Inca social systems, 198

Repertorio de los tiempos y historia natural desta Nueva España, 541

Representaciones de los vecinos de Valladolid, 358, note

Representative government in America, 306

Residencia: 292, 302-304, 312, 609-10; advantages and disadvantages, 609-10; *juez de,* 292

Restablecimiento de las fábricas, tráfico y comercio marítimo de España, 529

Revilla Gigedo, Conde, Viceroy of New Spain: "Informe . . . sobre el Real de Minas de Bolaños," 383, note, 384

Revilla Gigedo II: son of the preceding, 488; adherent of French ideas, 546; *Instrucción reservada,* 356, note; on maldistribution of wealth in Mexico, 477; on mining as a spur to economic progress, 383; on powers of the viceroy, 606; on religious instruction in Mexico, 588; stresses royal

patronage, 571-72; tries to revive the silk industry, 126; warns against colonial manufacturing, 388

Revista do Instituto . . . Brasileiro, 636, note

Revolutions, French and American, influence of, 544-45, 562

Rezabal y Ugarte, compiled royal orders, 528

Ribeiro Teixera de Morais, Manuel, 466

Rice: 95; in Tucumán, 394

Ricos hombres, authority and privileges of, 286-87

Rio de Janeiro: French settlement, 652; Portuguese settlement, 653

Río de la Plata: 163, 325-27, 442-45; administrative changes, 624-25; *consulados,* 609; development of livestock, 332-33; difficulties of settling, 326-27; expeditions of Cabot, 326, of Díaz de Solís, 50, of Mendoza, 326; *gaucho* and *vaquero,* 442-45; missionaries, 580; newspapers, 559-60; New Trade Policy, 424-29; population, table, 450, growth, 449-50, Indian, 442-43; Portuguese contraband, 410-11; postal concessions, 421; racial distribution, 455; settled, 55; trade and manufacture, 392-94; trade restrictions, 423; viceroyalty, 425, 452, 625

Rio Grande do Sul, 331, 672

Rioja, settled, 329

Rippy, J. Fred, *Historical Evolution of Hispanic America,* 579, note

Riva Palacio, Vicente, ed., *México a través de los siglos,* 71, note

River of Corrals, 664

Rivers: of the Andes, used for irrigation, 90; Mexican, direction of, 97

Roads: absence of, in Mexico, Central America and northern South America, 136; in Chile, 429; in Mexico, 138-39, 430; of the Incas, 133-35; pre-Conquest, 7, 135

Robbery among the Indians, 130

Robertson, James Alexander, *The English Attack on Cartagena in 1741,* 413, note

Robertson, William, *The History of America,* 19, note

Robinson, *Memoirs on the Mexican Revolution,* 447, note

Robles, Vito Alessio: *Acapulco en la historia y la leyenda,* 399, note; *Fran-*

cisco de Urdiñola y el norte de Nueva España, 431, note; Coahuila y Texas en la época colonial, 340, note

Rocha (Uruguay), 334

Rocha Pitta, Sebastião, História da América Portuguesa, 711, 714

Rodrígues, Pedro, "Vida do Padre José de Anchieta," 721, note

Rodríguez Betela, Virgilio, Laws Relative to the Printing Press in Colonial America, 554, note

Rodríguez, Jacinto, co-dictator of Oruro, 615

Rodríguez de Campomanes, see Campomanes

Rodríguez de Fonseca, Bishop Juan: established the casa de contratación, 155, 159; prepared second voyage of Columbus, 155; sold Indian slaves in Spain, 191

Rodríguez Juárez, Nicolás and Juan, painters, 539

Rõiz, Ana, prosecuted by the Inquisition, 737

Rome, economy of, replaced by fuedal estates, 28

Romero, Emilio, Historia económica y financiera del Perú, 135, note

Romero, Juan, makes settlement on San Juan River, 330-31

Romero, Sylvio, História da litteratura brasileira, 715, note

Roof, Maya types of, 222-23

Rosales, Diego de, 522

Rosario, 334

Rousseau, François, "The Expulsion of the Jesuits in Spain," 587, note

Rousseau, Jean Jacques, reading forbidden, 562

Royal control of Church organization, 569-72

Royal Maritime Company, 421

Royal resistance to papal authority, 570

Royalists, 257

Royalties on mining, 110

Roys, R. L., ed., The Books of Chilam Balam of Chumayel, 214, note

Rueda, Lope de, dramatist, 228

Ruisbrock [Rubruquis], William de, 29

Ruiz, Pavón, and Dombey, expedition of, 543

S

Sá, Mem de, governor-general of Brazil, 653, 742

Saavedra Guzmán, Antonio de, poet, 533

Saco, José Antonio, Historia de la esclavitud de la raza africana en el Nuevo Mundo, 207, note

Saddlery, 127

Sagres, 30

Sahagún, Bernardino de: 520-21; Historia general de las cosas de Nueva España, 166, note

Sahagún y Arévalo Ladron de Guevara, Juan Francisco, 553

Salade, Mathieu, tried by the Inquisition, 262

Saladeros, 332

Salamanca: 340; University of, 228, 230, 499

Salas, Manuel de: on poverty in Chile, 479-80; praise of Charles III, 432

Salazar, R. A. Historia del desenvolvimiento intelectual en Guatemala, 557, note

Salazar, Tomás de, law commentary of, 528

Salt: price decrease affects the meat industry, 428; trade in Venezuela, 394

Salta-atrás, 208

Salta settled, 329

Salvatierra, Father Juan María de, 341, 342

San Carlos (Uruguay), 334

San Diego, mission at, 342

San Felipe, University of, 498, 500

San Francisco, 342

San Germán, sacked by pirates, 153

San Ignacio Guazú, mission of, 580

San José (Uruguay), 334

San Juan (Argentina) settled, 329

San Juan de Letrán, school for mestizos, 229

San Lúcar, 163

San Luis (Argentina), settled, 329

San Luis Potosí: 71, 117; importance of mining at, 375

San Marcos, University of: 230, 498, 499; in 1740, 500

San Miguel (Peru) founded, 79

Sánchez, Luis Alberto, Breve historia de la literatura americana, 526, note

Sánchez, Manuel, "The Origin of the Printing Press in Venezuela," 554, note

Sancho, Pedro, *Relación para Su Majestad,* 108, note

Sancti Spiritus, 326

Sanctuary, *see* Asylum

Sandoval, Gonzalo de, exploration of, 47-48

Santa Ana (California), 550

Santa Catalina, 326

Santa Cruz, name given Brazil by Cabral, 633

Santa Cruz de Tlaltelolco, school for the Indians, 228

Santa Fé (Argentina), 329

Santa Hermandad, powers of the, 291

Santa Inez, Manuel de, on the customs of the nuns, 735

Santa Lucía (Uruguay), 334

Santa María de los Remedios, sacked, 153

Santa Marta; forced to pay ransom, 153; settled (1525), 50

Santa Rita Durão, José de, *Caramurú,* 713

Santiago: 233-34, 288; patron saint of Spain, 234; (Military Order of), 159

Santiago, Miguel de, painter, 539

Santiago de Chile: schools in, 497; University at, 498

Santiago de Cuba, governed by Cortés, 42

Santiago del Estero, settled, 328

Santiago de la Paz (Gorjón), established, 230

Santo Domingo: 128, 153; the Audiencia in, 297-98; founded (1496), 37, 41; mining city, 106; petitions for protection from pirates, 153; University, 230, 498

Santo Domingo Company, 421

Santo Domingo de Soriano: mission of, 580; settlement at, 331

Santo Tomás, 100

Santo Tomé, 30, 31

Santos, Lucio José dos, *O dominio espanhol no Brasil,* 654, note

São Francisco River, 658, 664

São Luiz de Maranhão, settled by the French, 666

São Paulo: 646; agriculture and trade of, 669; captaincy-general of, 678

São Vicente: 646, 650, 669; progress of, 656

Sapa Inca, 167, 170-71

Sarare River, gold discovered, 679

Sarmiento de Gamboa, Pedro, 520

Sarsaparilla, 84

Sauer, Carl: *Aboriginal Population of Northwestern Mexico,* 179; note; *The Road to Cíbola,* 179, note; and Donald Brand, *Aztatlán,* 179, note

Scandinavians, 32

Scelle, George, *La traite négrière aux Indes de Castille,* 207, note

Schäfer, Ernesto, *El consejo real y supremo de las Indias,* 295, note

Schetz, Erasmus, 650

Schmidt, Ulrich, *Voyage . . . to the River La Plata and Paraguai,* 326, note

Scholarship: early historians and travelers, 515-22; (scope of, 514-15)

Scholastics, 227, 548-49

School of Medicine, in Mexico, 550

School of Mines, in Mexico, 550

Schools: Church, 495; established by missionaries, 228, 248-50, 341, 579, 580-81, 667; in Brazil, 720-24; in the Spanish colonies, 497; influence on the Inca nobility, 218; maintained by Brazilian câmaras, 707; monastic, in Brazil, 706-708

Schurz, William Lytle: The Manila Galleon, 400, note; "Mexico, Peru and The Manila Galleon," 400, note

Science: 540-41; development of, 549-51; Indian, 218-22

Scientific expeditions to America, 542-43

Scientific spirit: *see* Chapter 25; growth in Europe, 242-43; influence on education, 546; summary, 565-66

Sculpture: 515, 538; European, formed basis for American, 232; religious, 538; school of Tolsa, 538

Sebastian, King of Portugal: 654, 742; Indian legislation under, 726

Secretariats, 625

Secretos de Cirugía, medical work, 540

Secular Thought: development of, 542-44; in the schools, 549-51; progress summarized, 565-66

Semanario de Agricultura, Industria y Comercio, 558-59

Semanario de Nueva Granada, 544, 552

Senado da Câmara, 747-49

Señores naturales, 270-71

Señorío: 69, 290; *de los Incas,* 519; courts of the, 608

Sergio de Sousa, Antonio, *História de Portugal,* 30, note

Sermons, in Brazil, 709

Serra (Junípero), Miguel José, Franciscan missionary, 579
Sertão, the hinterland of Brazil, 635
Sesmaria, 644
Sessé and Mociño, 543
Settlements, dates of important, 50
Sevilla, center of the Casa, 158
Sewall, Judge Samuel, on New Spain, 544
Sexual customs: in Brazil, 700-702; among Caribbean and Mexican Indians, 172-73; in Colombia, 173-74; in the Inca Empire, 175-76, 177
Shipbuilding: at Buenos Aires, 398; rise of, 127-28; stimulated industry, 397-98; types of boats, 398
Shipping: from Acapulco, 430; from Buenos Aires, 427-28; from Cuba, 437-38; growth in New Spain, 435; regulations, 163-64; rights given Montevideo firms, 425; tonnage, 431; via Cape Horn, 429
Ship-rigging, manufacture of, 127
Ships: illegal entries of, 164; jurisdiction of the Casa over, 603-604; patrol between Spain and the Canaries, 161
Shrines, in Mexico, 243
Sicily, 28
Sierra Lejesema, Mancio, 175
Siete Partidas, the, 236, 284
Sigüenza y Góngora, Carlos de, scholar of New Spain, 498, 524, 533, 541
Silk: 144; American industry contrasted with Spanish, 125-26; decline of, 126; encouraged by Zumárraga and Mendoza, 124-25; guilds in Mexico City and Puebla, 125; in Mexico, 388-89, 395; in the colonies, 98, 349; Oriental, enters New Spain, 126
Silva, Antonio José da, 712
Silver: 95; in Mexico and Peru, 107; mines, important, 366; mining (in Bolivia), 368; (in Chile), 369-71; (in Peru), 367-68; minted (at Lima), 368; (at Santiago), 369; total mined, 117-18, 379-83
Silver and gold, annual production in Europe, North Asia and America, table, 380
Simón, Pedro, 521
Simonsen, Roberto C., História econômica do Brasil, 640, note
Simony, charged by Juárez de Escobar, 268
Simpson, Eyler N., The Ejido: Mexico's Way Out, 97, note

Simpson, Lesley Byrd: Many Mexicos, 72, note; The Encomienda in New Spain, 61, note; Studies in the Administration of the Indians in New Spain, 63, note; 137, note
Sinchi, a war chief, 18, 19
Sipe-Sipe, town in Peru, 309-10
Siripo, Argentina drama, 553
Sixtus IV, Pope: delegates censorship powers, 507; seeks to institute the Inquisition in Spain, 235
Skinner, Joseph, The Present State of Peru, 431, note
Slavery: for debt, 471-72; defended by the Church, 473
Slaves: chattel, 474-75; Church ownership of, 595; Columbus' policy on, 191; discrimination against certain, 160; emancipation of, 474; importance to the Cuban sugar industry, 353; importance to sugar in the New World, 41; in Brazil, 669-73; in Cuba, 474; Indian, 191-92, 195, 196, 724-32; Jesuit position on, 698; Montevideo sole port of entry for, 427; Negro, 190-191, 473-74 (in Brazil), 696-99; Negro compared with Indian in Brazil, 696; places of origin, 160; position of owners in local government, 622; Portuguese trade in, 31; taxes on, 160-61; trade in, Crown policy, 191-92, 194; trade, contraband, 154-55; trade in Indian, 131-32; under the New Laws, 195
Smallpox, among the Indians, 203, 448-49
Smith, Adam, influence in America, 476-77
Smith, A. Ledyard, "The Corbeled Arch in the New World," 222, note
Smith, Robert Sidney, The Spanish Guild Merchant, 159, note
Smith, T. V., and Grene, Majorie, From Descartes to Kant, 548, note
Smuggling, see contraband
Soares de Souza, Gabriel: Tratado descriptivo do Brasil em 1587, 638, note, 709; on sexual customs of the Brazilian Indians, 695
Social concepts regarding the Indian, 193-94
Social evolution to 1810, see Chapters 21 and 22
Social groups among the Incas, 167
Sociedad Amantes del País, in Lima, 557
Sociedad patriótica, in Havana, 558

Sociedad patriótica de Amigos del País de Quito, 558

Sociedad patriótica de Investigaciones, 552

Sociedad patriótica y literaria, in Río de la Plata, 552

Societies, secret, 552

Society: Spanish-American, *see* Chapters 10, 21 and 22; Brazilian, 633-35, 638, 651, 677, 702-704 and Chapter 31; colonial class, in Peru, 82; contribution of the white man in Brazil, 688-702; structure of, 16th century, 190

Socorro Rodríguez, Manuel del, editor, 558

Soil, fertility in Española, 37

Solís, Juan Días de, explores Brazilian coast, 654

Solórzano Pereira, Juan de: jurist, 610; *De indiarum jure,* 527; on the laws of the Indies, 527-28; on royal control of the Church, 259; *Política Indiana,* 238, note

Sor Juana Inés de la Cruz, religious poet, 533-34

Sore, Jacques, captures Havana, 153

Soria, Francisco, Mexican dramatist, 535

Sotero dos Reis, Francisco, *Curso de literatura portugueza e brasileira,* 715, note

Soto, Hernando de, 53

Soul, immortality of the, 242

South America: 86, 117, 163; agriculture, 98-102; Conquest, 49-55; crafts, 127; discovered by Columbus, 41; geography, 18; missionaries, 579-80

South American Handbook, 1942, 183

South Sea Company, 434-35

Southern Star, The, bilingual newspaper of Montevideo, 560

Southey, Robert, *History of Brazil,* 633, note

Souza, Bernardino José de, *O pau-brasil na história nacional,* 639, note

Souza, Gabriel Soares de, *see* Soares, Gabriel

Souza, Martim Afonso de, 641

Souza, Pero Lopes de, *Diario de navegação,* 642, 646

Souza, Tomé de, 649-50, 741-42, 745

Souza Vianna, Urbino de, *Bandeiras e sertanistas bahianas,* 663, note

Spain: 28, 55, 56, 58; at the Conquest, 290-91; attitude of the government toward missionaries, 250-51; censorship in, 507, 510; clergy in, 287-89; colonial estimates of intellectual advance in, 551; conflicting legal systems in, 290; contributions to colonial government, 270-71, 284-85; The Crown, 289-92; cultural contributions of, 493; cultural level at the Conquest, 228; economic, political, and religious development of, 32-35; government in, 285-92; imports of gold and silver into, table, 118; Inquisition in, 235; kingdoms of, 290; land system transferred to colonial government, 58-59; literature in, 1500, 228; mercantilism condemned, 415-16; monopoly system, 417-18; occupies the Canaries, 32; policy in America, estimated, 623; policy on colonial manufactures, 386-90; reading in, 506-507; religious groups in, 290; representative sent to Ethiopia, 32; rivalry with Portugal, 146; sectionalism in, 290; trade with America, 201-203; trade with the Mohammedans, 28; universities of, 228; War of Spanish Succession, 419

Spaniards: 51, 56; act as commission merchants for foreign firms, 412; assume ownership of America, 57-58; blamed for destroying the Inca system of agriculture, 91-92; domination of Brazil by, 654-57; extent of colonization in Mexico, 341; explore the Atlantic, 32; explore the Brazilian coast, 654; form aristocracy in America, 286-87; fight one another as bitterly as the Indians, 48; in the Amazon, 665-66; liberty as understood by, 285; not primarily interested in gold, 92; outstripped Indians in productive capacity, 40; principal landholders in new towns, 71; rivalry of Creoles and, 486-89; war among themselves for Peru, 54

Spanish Captivity, the, 742-44

Spanish colonies, cultural contribution of the, *see* Chapter 24

Spanish-Indian land system, 82

panish towns: 71, 285-86; transplanted to America, 72

Spanish trade: percentage in America, 412; policy, 146-47

Spanish-American trade: compared with

English, 440; importance of, 439-40; imports and exports, table, 439; with the United States, 412-16

Speech, censorship of: in the colonies, 510-13; in Spain, 509-10

Spinden, Herbert J.: *Ancient Civilizations of Mexico and Central America*, 12, note; "Diffusion of Maya Astronomy," 218, note; on Mayan sculpture, 224

Squier, E. G., *Peru . . . Land of the Incas,* 220, note

Staden, Hans, *Voyage,* 708

Stancone, Percivale, 29

Stanger, Francis Merriman, "Church and State in Peru," 572, note

Starvation, delayed settlement of the mainland, 38

State, Church conflicts with the, 572-75

Steck, Francis Borgia, "Some Recent Trends and Findings in the History of the Spanish Colonial Empire in America," 507, note

Stevens, Henry, ed.: *The New Laws of the Indies,* 194, note

Stock, Hyman, *The Method of Descartes in the Natural Sciences,* 548, note

Stone cutting, Inca, 134

Storia antica del Messico, 524

Straw weaving in Mexico, 120

Students, Inca, 217

Suárez, Inés, mistress of Valdivia, 320

Sueños, poems, 533

Sugar: 93, 144; competition of American and East Indian, 345-46; consumption in America and Europe, 345; exported to Spain, 94-95; from corn, 85, 121; in Brazil, 345, 647, 650-51, 675, 689-92; in the Caribbean, 624, 675; in Cuba, 318, 345, 350 53; in Dutch Guiana, Haiti, and Venezuela, 345; in Ecuador, 316; in Española, 41; in Jamaica, 345-46; in Mexico, 344-45; in Peru, 101, 318, 344; in Santo Domingo, 345; investments represented by mills, 93-94; monopoly in Madeira, 31; rivalry of English, French, Dutch, and Portuguese, 675-76

Suma y recopilación de cirugia, medical work, 540

Sumario, 517

Sun: Lands of the (Inca), 77 78; Virgins of the, 244

Supernatural, the, as a factor in culture, 494-95

Surgery, Aztec knowledge of, 218

Syllacio—Coma letter, 36, note

T

Tabasco (Mexico), 128, 144, 162

Taboada, Gil de, *Relación,* 601, note

Taddo, *Corregidores* of, 372

Talavera, Archbishop Fernando, policy toward the Moors, 237

Tamemes, 195-96

Tapuias, Indians of Brazil, 635, 646

Tarapacá, 88

Tariffs, *see* Duties

Tasco, 112

Tastet y Compañía, Antonio, shipping right given, 425

Taunay, Affonso de E., *História geral das bandeiras paulistas,* 669, note

Tavares de Lyra, Augusto, *Organisação política e administrativa do Brasil,* 750, note

Tax exemption: 485; Aztec, 273; Inca, 278-79

Taxes: on commerce, 139, 147-51; municipal, 614; in Spain, 287

Taylor, Paul S., "Spanish Seamen in the New World during the Colonial Period," 419, note

Teatro americano, 524

Teatro crítico universal, 547

Tecpan, 69-70

Tecpantlaca, Aztec workers, 70

Tehuántepec Isthmus: 47-48

Teive, Diego de, 31

Teixeira, Bento, *Prosopopéa,* 712

Teja Zabre, Alfonso, *Guide to the History of Mexico,* 359, note

Telégrafo Mercantil, Argentine newspaper, 428, 559

Tello de Sandoval, Francisco, 195, 262

Temperature, variations in the tropical belt, 335-36

Temples: Aztec, children dedicated to, 243; Indian, destroyed, 249-50

Tenochtitlán: 15; described by Cortes, 70-71; government, 272-73; in the Aztec Confederacy, 70; taken by Cortés, 46-47

Tente-en-el-aire, 208

Teoría práctica de comercio y de marina, 529

Teotl, 240

Terán, Juan Bautista, *El nacimiento de la América española,* 445, note

Tereros, Pedro, reopens Biscaina Vein, 375-76
Terraces, in the Andes, 78-79, 87-92
Terrazgueros, 68
Territorial delimitations, 297
Territorial government, 271
Tertulia Eutropélica, 552, 558
Texas: 51; missions in, 578, 579
Téxcoco: 15; in the Aztec alliances, 272
Textiles: in New Spain, 124, 394-95; in South America, 127
Tezcatlipoca, Aztec god, 240
Thacher, John B., *Christopher Columbus,* 35, note
Theatre, *see* drama
Theocratic State, in America, 256-60
Theological literature in America, 231
Theology, in American universities, 230
Thévet, André, *Les singularités de la France antarctique,* 709, note
Thirty Years War in Germany, 45
Thompson, J. Eric, *Mexico before Cortés,* 12, note
Thought: censorship of, 509-10, 561-66; Church control of, 499-500; in Spain and the colonies, 510-13
Throne, The Spanish: 289-92; *see also* Crown
Tiahuanaco (Bolivia) pre-Inca ruins at, 223
Tierra del Fuego, 408
Tierra-Firme, 92, 163
Tierras: calientes, 86; *frías,* 86
Tile, 127
Tin, 118
Tirso de Molina, 505
Tithes: in America, 482; in Cuba, 354; in New Spain, 349-50, 591; paid to *encomiendas,* 67; strengthened royal control of the Church, 258
Tlacopan, in Aztec Alliances, 70, 272
Tlaculteotl, Aztec goddess, 241
Tlalmaites, 70, 166, note
Tláloc, Aztec god, 241
Tlaxcala, 44
Tlaxcalans: 16-17; aid Cortés, 43, 44, 46
Tobacco: 84, 144; Brazilian exports, 690-92; in Cuba, 353, 437; in New Spain, 347; monopoly, 324, 336, 347; smuggled from Brazil, 336
Toledo, Viceroy Francisco de: codifies the law, 527; on Indian land system, 75; works for resettlement in Peru, 199

Toledo-Velasco legislation on manufacturing, 389
Tolsa, Manuel, school of sculpture of, 538
Toltec, meaning of, 14
Toluca, mines in, 112
Toluca Valley, 85
Tomatoes, 83
Tonantzín (Cívecoatl), Aztec goddess, 241
Tonatiuh, Aztec sun god, 241
Tonnage: comparison of, 401; in Manila-Mexico trade, 400-401; tax on, 402
Tools, manufacture of, 122
Tordesillas, Treaty of, 633, 654, 657, 672-73, 746
Toro Zambrano, Bishop, 568
Torquemada, Juan de: 522; *Los veinte i un libros rituales i monarchia indiana,* 12, note; on Aztec priests, 243; on pre-Conquest oppression of the Indians, 200; on technical efficiency of the Indians, 201; used the *auto,* 535
Torre family, 664
Torre Revello, José: "Bibliotecas e imprentas en la América colonial," 545, note; *El libro, la imprenta y el periodismo en América,* 503, note; "Noticia sobre José Eusebio de Llano Zapata, historiador peruano del siglo XVIII," 547, note; on prohibition of books, 505, 513
Torres, Antonio de: *alcalde* of Española, 293; *Memorandum* of, 38, note
Torres Rioseco, Arturo, *The Epic of Latin American Literature,* 530, note
Tortuga: center of pirate trade, 405; North American trade with, 413
Town, the Spanish: in America, 72; authority curbed by Ferdinand and Isabella, 291; autonomy of, 285-86; offices sold, 289
Towns: built by the Spaniards in Mexico, 71; wars between, 290-91
Trade: 6-7, 141, 316, 489; African, 31; Aztec, 130-31; Byzantine, 29; Charles V's policies, 148-49; Chile-Argentina, 392; Church monopolies, 595; coastal, 421; *see* contraband; convoy system, 401, 688; diamonds and gold in Brazil, 689; domestic on the West Coast, 390-92; early, 143-44; effect of population on, 398; evolution, *see* Chapter 19; foreigners engaging in, 689; from Panama

south, 144-45; general status of, 398-99; illegal, see contraband; in the Andes, 132, 133-35; in Brazil, 405, 676-77, 679, 682-92; in Buenos Aires, 393, 427-29; in the Caribbean, 128-29, 394-97; in Chile, 323-24, 392, 432; in Colombia, 435; in Cuba, 436-38; in Europe prior to 1500, 28-29; in Mexico, 138-39; in New Granada, 433-35; in New Spain, 396-97, 398, 400, 435-36; in the Pacific, 399-401; in Paraguay, 393-94; in Peru, 384, 429-32; in Río de la Plata, 332, 392-94, 424-29; in neutral ships, 425; internal, tax free, 139; Institutions, Spanish, 155-59; intercolonial, 126, 140-41, 143, 144, 392; international, 142-164, 399-401; methods, 18th century, 346-47; mining a stimulus to, 115-16, 397; Mohammedan, with Spain, 28; monopoly companies in Brazil, 684-88; monopolies, 324, 333, 336, 387; pirate attacks on, 149, 151; policy, Spanish, see Chapter 20, pp. 146-47, 151; Portuguese, 31, 410-12, 688-92; Portuguese policy in Brazil, 682-92; post-Conquest expansion, prohibitions to colonies, 159-60; pre-Conquest, 128-29, 137-39; prospects in America, 142-43; regulations, 139-40; restrictions, 126, 316, 317, 318, 323-24, 332, 333, 336, 399, 419-21, 422-24; Spanish American, 439-40; taxation of, 150-51; treaty favored between England and Spain, 413-14; Treaty of Madrid, 404-405; United States exports to Spain, table, 414; United States, with the Spanish Colonies, 412-16; value of, table, 402; value of English contraband, 408; with the East and America, contrasted, 156-57; with Portugal, 688-92; with Spain, 143, 401-403

Trade routes: from Acapulco, 430; overland, 429, 430-31; via Cape Horn, 430; from Panama, 143; to Buenos Aires, 393; by water, 393

Trades, Inca youth instructed in, 122

Transhipment of goods in America, 162-63

Transport: land and sea, 398; in Mexico and Central America, 138

Transportation: across Panama, 145; difficulties of, 137-38

Trapiche de caballo, 93

Tratado de medicina, 540

Travelers, early, 515-22

Traza, 445

Treasure: of Cuzco, value of, 108; found in Colombia by Heredia, 51

Treaties: Portuguese with France, Holland and England, 683-84; of Alcaçovas, 36; between England and Spain, 413-14; of Madrid, 404-405; of Methuen, 684; of Utrecht, 408, 411; see Tordesillas

Trepanning, Inca, 220-21

Tres Reis Magos, settled, 666

Tribunal of the Holy Office of the Inquisition, 262

Tribunal de minería, 572

Tribute, in the Inca system: 78-79, 278; bridge tolls, 280; paid by labor and produce, 79-80, 280

Tristán, Nuño, reached Cape Blanco, 30

Trujillo, Spanish estates of, 99

Tucumán: founded, 329; mule trade with Potosí, 384

Tudela, Benjamín de, 29

Tudor, Mary, 154, 162

Tula, 67, 340

Túmbez, Cieza describes devastation of, 25

Tumipampa, devastated by Atahualpa, 25

Tungsten, discovered by Elhuyar, 381

Tupac Amarú, revolt of, 553

Tupí-Guaraní, Indians, 635

Tupinaes, 646

Tupinambas, 647

Turkestan, 29

Turks: entry into Europe, 149; fought by Charles V, 34

Typhus, epidemic in Mexico, 203

U

Ulloa, Antonio de, 466-67, 470-71, 475, 523-24

Ulloa, Bernardo, writings of, 529

Unánue, José Hipólito: 524; Guía política, eclesiástica y militar del Virreinato del Perú, 368, note; opposed to Spanish mercantilism, 415-16

United States: 86; trade with the Spanish colonies, 412-16; see also Trade, United States

Unity, religious and political, 235-38

Universidad Tomística, 547

Universities: 498-502; affected by Cartesian and Copernican philosophy,

546, 548; compared with European, 546-49; curriculum of, 498, 500; modeled on Salamanca, 499; in America, 230

Urban VIII, 672

Urbino Vianna, *see* Souza Vianna

Ursua, Pedro de, 666

Uruguay: 18, 26, 83, 330-34; cattle first settlers in, 331; labor, 479-81; position of the Church, 569; settlement of towns, 333-34; the wealthy classes, 483-84

Uruguay River, Franciscan missions along the, 580

Usatges, 290

Ustáriz, Jeronimo de, legal writings of, 529

Usury, forbidden, 236

Utrecht, Treaty of, 408, 409, 411

V

Vacantes, form of taxes, 592

Vaccination, treatises on, 544

Vaillant, G. C.: *Aztec of Mexico*, 12, note; on Aztec arts and crafts, 224-25

Valdés, Manuel Antonio, journalist, 555

Valdez, Diogo ̃Flores, 666

Valdivia, Pedro de: claims western Argentina, 329; conquers Chile, 54; makes settlement at Santiago, 320-21

Valencia, *fueros* of, 290

Valencia, Mártin de, Friar, 262

Valencia, Pedro de, on the evil of land concentration, 362

Valenciana, mines at, 375

Valladolid, Cortes of, seeks to restrict exports to America, 123

Vancouver, George: *A Voyage of Discovery*, 370; on poverty in Chile, 480-81; on literacy in Chile, 497

Vandelli, Domingos: "Sobre os diamantes do Brazil," 677, note; "Sobre as minas de ouro do Brasil," 677, note

Vanilla: 83; in New Spain, 346

Vaquero, 442, 444

Varnhagen, Francisco Adolpho de: *História geral do Brasil*, 643; on government, 740; quotes governor on churchmen, 727, 733

Vasconcellos, Simão de, *Chronica da Companhia de Jesus do Estado do Brazil*, and *Vida do Veneravel Padre José de Anchieta*, 710

Vásquez de Ayllón, Lucas: argues against free Indians, 193; discovers Maryland, 50; tries silk-raising in the Caribbean, 124

Vásquez de Coronado, Francisco, explorations of, 341

Vaz de Caminha, *see* Caminha

Vázquez, Alonso, painter, 539

Vecino, 183, 285

Veítia Linaje, quoted on "malicious arrivals," 164

Velasco, Juan de, 524

Velasco, Luis de, 229

Velasco, Luis de, II, 488

Velásquez, Diego, governor of Cuba, 42, 46

Velásquez Cárdenas y Léon, Joaquín, scientist, 550

Vélez Sarsfield, Dalmacio, *Relaciones del estado con la Iglesia*, 260, note

Velhas, River of, 665

Velosa, Gonzalo de, brought sugar experts to Española, 93

Venegas, Miguel, 524

Venezuela: 13, 51, 56, 83, 98, 118, 128, 144, 334-39, 550; agriculture, 335-39; captaincy-general, 624; conquest, 49-50; fertility of the soil, 334-35; first settlement at Cumaná, 50; history, 521, 524; importance of the cacao crop, 337-38; Indian labor, 463, 465; irrigation, 335; land grant to the Welsers, 50, 51; livestock, 336-37; Negro slave revolts, 472; population, 452, 457, 458; rainfall, 334, 336; slave markets, 472; temperature variations, 335-336

Venice: right to the Adriatic, 36, 146; sugar trade with Portugal, 31

Venta de la Cruz, 145

Vera Cruz: 43, 46, 63, 71; designated a port for receiving merchandise, 162; discovered, 42; trade with the colonies and Spain, 435

Veragua, granted to Nicuesa, 40

Verse, Aztec, 215

Vespucci, Américo, role in the discovery of Brazil, 635-36

Viboras, mission of, 580

Vicente do Salvador, Frei: 662; *História do Brasil*, 634, note; 710

Viceroy: 604-607; Bernal Díaz describes the display of the, 301; class of society from which selected, 488; duties toward the Indians, 301; of Lima, superiority of, 605; of New

Spain, 301; of Peru, 301-302; position coveted by the archbishops, 573-74; powers and duties of the, 300-302, 605-7; remuneration of the, 301; term of office of the, 301

Viceroy Toledo, system of Indian government of, 309

Viceroyalty: 300-302; of Brazil, 744; of New Castile, 298, 300, 301; of New Granada, reasons for creation, 623-24; of New Spain, 298, 300, 301; of La Plata created, 425, 625

Vicuña, 145

Vieira, Antonio de: advice on provincial money, 675; attitude on the Dutch occupation of Brazil, 660-61; Indian policy of, 729-32; literary position of, 710; O Papel Forte, 660-61; on the economic state of Brazil, 676; suggests the formation of a monopoly company, 685

Villac Umu, accompanied Almagro to Chile, 319

Villasante, Antonio de, theory of Indian inferiority, 193

Villaseñor, José Antonio, 524

Villaseñor y Cervantes, Juan de, encomienda of, 67

Villaurrutia, Jacobo de, 556

Villegagnon, Nicholas Durand de, 652-53

Vinegar, 93, 144

Vineland, trade of, 28

Viracocha, or Pachacamac, Inca god, 240

Virginity, Inca attitude toward, 176

Virgins, in the Aztec religion, 243; in the Inca religion, 176, 177, 244

Viscaya, 290

Visigothic Spain, 233

Visita: defined, 296, 312, 610; powers of, 302-304

Visitação: first Visitation of the Inquisition to Brazil, 737; second Visitation, 737

Visitador, designed to increase royal authority, 292

Vitorio, Pascual de, 29

Vivaldi, Benedetto, 29

Vizcaino, Sebastián, explored the Pacific coast, 341

Vizcardo, Pablo, Jesuit writer, 552

Volney's works prohibited, 562

Voltaire, reading of, forbidden, 561

Voyages dans l'Amérique méridionale, depuis 1781 jusqu'en 1801, 525

W

War: Council of, see Council of War; of the Palatinate, 623; of Spanish Succession, 406, 408, 623-24

Ward, Bernardo, Proyecto económico, 422, note; writings of, 529

Washington, Luis, Capitania de São Paulo, 646, note

Water rights, Aztec, 69

Water trade routes, 136

Wätjen, Hermann, O dominio colonial hollandez no Brasil, 658, note

Wealth: concentration of, in the Spanish colonies, 361-65; maldistribution of, in Mexico, 477; monopolized by the upper classes, 482, 483; social position promoted by, 487

Weapons, Indian, 120, 121

Weaving: Aztec, Maya, and Inca, 223-24; in Mexico and the Andes, 121-22

Welsers, The, 50, 148, 334

Wernicke, Edmundo, ed., Derrotero y viaje a España y las Indias, 326, note

West, Elizabeth Howard, "The Right of Asylum in New Mexico in the Seventeenth and Eighteenth Centuries," 573, note

West Indies: 13, 57, 117; agriculture and livestock, 350-54; and system, 65-68; population, 454-55; sugar industry, 351, 675-76

Wheat: 95, 143; tax, in Peru, 318; in Chile, 322-23; in New Spain, 343; in Río de la Plata, 333; in Venezuela, 335-36

Wheel, unknown in America, 121, 223

Whitaker, Arthur P.: "The Commerce of Louisiana and the Floridas at the End of the Eighteenth Century," 414, note; The Huancavelica Mercury Mine, 111; "Jorge Juan and Antonio Ulloa's Prologue to their Secret Report of 1749 on Peru," 467, note; "More about Fausto de Elhuyar," 382, note; Latin America and the Enlightenment, 544, note

Wilcocke, Samuel H., History of the Viceroyalty of Buenos Aires, 432, note

Wilgus, A. Curtis, Colonial Hispanic America, 94, note

Williams, M. W., The People and Politics of Latin America, 49, note

Wine: 93, 100, 143; Portuguese, 31; in

Peru, 316-17; in Chile, 322; in New Spain, 348, 349

Woad, 149

Women in America: European, 205-206; Inca, skilled in crafts, 122; position among Brazilian Indians, 694-95; position in the Aztec church, 243; shortage of in colonial Brazil, 700-701; teachers in Mexico, 249; in the Conquest, 41

Wool and woolen cloth: in Chile, 325; in Ecuador, 316; in New Spain, 126; *llama*, weaving of, 122; trade between Peru and Spain, 145

Woolen mills, in the Spanish Colonies, 390-91, 394

Wright, Irene A.: "The Dutch and Cuba," 403, note; *The Early History of Cuba, 1492-1586*, 120, note; *Historia documentada de San Cristóbal de la Habana en el siglo XVI*, 152, note; "Spanish Policy toward Virginia, 1606-1612," 404, note

Writing of pre-Conquest America: 212-15; Aztec, 214-15; Maya, 213-14

Y

Yachahuasi, 217

Yana-cunas, 167, 168

Yáñez Pinzón, Vicente, 41, 62

Yellow fever, epidemic in America, 449

Yucatán, 13, 84, 144, 162; center of Maya culture, 212; discovery, 42

Z

Zaachila, 71

Zacatecas, 71, 112, 117; mining in, 111, 341; mineral production, 375

Zambo, 208

Zapotec architecture, 223

Zapotecs, 48

Zárate, Augustín de, 134, note

Zavala, Silvio R., *La encomienda indiana*, 61, note

Zelaya,, 340

Zimbo, 698

Zimmerman, Arthur F., *Francisco de Toledo: Fifth Viceroy of Peru, 1569*, 198, note

Zinc, 119

Zitara, Corregidores of, 372

Zorilla, Diego de, *Sumario*, 527

Zultepec, 112

Zumárraga, Juan de, Bishop: 260, 262; describes Indian baptism, 252; encouraged the silk industry, 124-125; tries to prohibit the drama, 535

Zumaya, Miguel, Mexican dramatist, 535

Zurita, Alonso de: 527; *Breve y sumaria relación de los señores y maneras y diferencias que había de ellos en· la Nueva España*, 69, note; on Aztec land system, 70